BRITISH HIT SINGLES

PAUL GAMBACCINI • JONATHAN RICE • TIM RICE

9th EDITION

GUINNESS PUBLISHING

Editorial Assistant: Tony Brown

ACKNOWLEDGEMENTS

The three authors would like to thank Alan Jones, Graham Walker, John English, Anne Fowey, Jason Hunter and Scott Whittock for their contributions to this edition.

Special thanks, too, to Eileen Heinink and Jan Rice. We also want to thank *New Musical Express* and *CIN* for their charts, Redferns, LFI, Popperfoto and Pictorial Press for their photographs, and the many record company press offices for their patient help.

Published in Great Britain by Guinness Publishing Ltd., 33 London Road, Enfield, Middlesex.

Distributed in the United States by Billboard Books, an imprint of Watson-Guptill Publications, a division of BPI Communications, Inc., 1515 Broadway, New York, NY 10036.

Printed and bound in Great Britain by The Bath Press.

'Guinness' is a registered trade mark of Guinness Publishing Ltd.

The right of Paul Gambaccini, Tim Rice and Jonathan Rice to be identified as Authors of this Work has been asserted in accordance with the Copyright, Designs & Patents Act 1989.

EDITOR: David Roberts
DEPUTY EDITOR: Paola Simoneschi
PAGE MAKE-UP AND TYPESETTING: Ace Filmsetting Ltd, Alex Reid, Stewart Newport and Sallie Collins
DESIGN: Moore Lowenhoff

A catalogue record for this book is available from The British Library.
ISBN 0–85112–526–3

All statistics and
information cover the
period 14 November
1952 to 1992, and are
as follows:

CONTENTS

1

ALPHABETICALLY BY ARTIST:

4261chart acts listed alphabetically with chronological title list showing date disc first hit the chart, title, label, catalogue number, highest position reached and number of weeks on chart. Top Ten placings and number ones are highlighted.

2

ALPHABETICALLY BY TITLE:

17 296 hits listed alphabetically by title, with artists' names and year of initial chart entry. Different versions of the same song and different songs with the same title are indicated.

3

FACTS AND FEATS:

All you need to know and more about the record charts record breakers including
● Most Weeks On Chart
● Most Top Ten Hits
● Longest Gap Between Chart Hits
● Top Twenty Acts Of All Time
● Chart 'Geography'
● A League Of Football Hits
● Least Successful Chart Acts
● The Number One Hits

e are in the future, and we do not recognize it. The singles chart that readers of this book have long loved is now a stranger to us. Changes that more accurately reflect tastes in popular music are now inevitable.

During the years 1991–92 records flew in and out of the top 75 at a record pace. 888 discs appeared in the chart in 1991, followed by 1,032 in 1992. Both figures were new all-time highs. The explanation for this phenomenon requires reference to both record buyers and record companies.

It is no secret that the answer to the question 'Who are the Beatles and Stones of the early 90s?' is 'Sega and Nintendo'. These, of course, are not musical acts at all, but manufacturers of computer games. Statistics in 1992 showed an approximately 5–3 lead in expenditure in favour of the games which, of course, were much more

have been convinced, since Michael Jackson's *Thriller*, that singles are more valuable as publicity for albums than as commercial properties in their own right. Labels release song after song from the same album to keep what they see as free radio and TV plugs going. With the exception of the first single from an album, usually released a month in advance to encourage interest in the project, there is no time when a major artist's single cannot already be found on an album. One reason the three long-running number one hits mentioned did so well was that they appeared on soundtrack albums, not regular releases by the artists themselves, and hence did not have their sales diluted as much as could otherwise have been the case.

For this financial reason, which has nothing to do with music itself, the singles market has been virtually left to acts who are too new, too poor or

INTRODUCTION

expensive per unit than music discs. Sonic the Hedgehog made more money than Simply Red, and the Super Mario Brothers outgrossed Simple Minds. The 80s children, now grown to the age where their predecessors made popular music, show little interest in doing so, at least in producing material with conventional song structure and strong attention to lyrics and melody.

Previous generations, however, are still desperate to *buy* strong songs. When one comes along it utterly dominates the field to an extent that top tunes did not during the rock era of the mid-50s through to the mid-80s. Bryan Adams enjoyed 16 consecutive weeks at number one in Britain in 1991 with 'Everything I Do (I Do It For You)', the longest straight run at number one ever and the second highest cumulative total. The following year, Boyz II Men tallied 13 weeks in succession in America with 'End of the Road', overtaking Elvis Presley's 11-week double-sided 1956 winner 'Don't Be Cruel/Hound Dog' to tie Patti Page's 1950–51 marathon 'Tennessee Waltz'. At the end of 1992, Whitney Houston settled in for long runs on both sides of the Atlantic with 'I Will Always Love You'. She finally faded after 10 weeks at number one in the UK and 14 in the US having bested Boyz II Men.

Audiences want these mass appeal records, but they too rarely get them. One reason is that major artists only release singles these days when they have albums to promote. Record companies

large number of unfamiliar names in any week's chart. These fresh faces either have not yet made albums or have not yet established a broad audience base.

Furthermore, recent young talent has not been interested in making mass appeal music, but has worked in fragmented fashion. Not since the 1940s, if ever, has popular music been divided into so many mutually hostile constituencies with so few transcendent stars. The lion will lay down with the lamb before ravers buy the same music as metalheads and rappers attend country concerts.

One change in recording habits has led to an alteration in our book, too. During the last few years it has become fashionable for artists to release singles with featured vocalists who are not ordinarily part of the act. Other singers have been frequent duettists with a variety of partners. The consequence for us is that not only the list of hit titles but the number of different acts has swelled dramatically and, in some cases, farcically. For example, Aretha Franklin, who began in our first edition on her own, later entered as part of 'Aretha Franklin and George Benson', followed by 'Eurythmics and Aretha Franklin', 'Aretha Franklin and George Michael' and then, in her *annus duetus*, 'Aretha Franklin and Elton John' *and* 'Aretha Franklin and Whitney Houston'. We have now decided, quite sensibly we hope, that Aretha Franklin is in fact only one artist. All her hits are listed under her own name. Asterisks next to titles credited to someone other than merely

Aretha Franklin indicate a full billing is listed in a footnote. One asterisk is used for the first chronologically different billing, two asterisks for the second different credit, and so forth until five asterisks denote 'Aretha Franklin and Whitney Houston'. Of course, all these duets are also credited to the relevant partners, too, so 'I Knew You Were Waiting For Me' also turns up on George Michael's list, with how many asterisks you will discover when you look to see under how many different billings he has charted. Don't worry if you can only recall the name of a featured vocalist, say Angie Brown, rather than the full artist credit. If you look up the singer's name, you will be referred to the act which employed her.

The phenomenon of rave is what is most likely to force a change in the way the chart is compiled. This would be the first significant alteration since the record sales chart was introduced in 1952 and gradually replaced the sheet-music list. Thousands of club deejays buy dance singles to play in clubs, giving these records entry into the low regions of the best-sellers. But rave is an environment music – that is, a sound intended to be heard in a particular location. It does not transmit well on radio and alienates, rather than appeals to, listeners outside its core audience. Even worse, the dance audience, which is the cutting edge of popular music, pays more attention to current work than the wider public. It tires of material quickly and soon moves on to new sounds.

Material not only unloved but actually disliked by a significant percentage of the popular music audience thus occupies a large portion of the singles chart, with rapid turnover. This is a disaster for both radio, which either must program records that encourage its listeners to tune out or else devise alternative playlists, and for the record companies, who cannot get discs to develop over time and build into big sellers.

In the last couple of years, these music firms have probably been their own, and certainly the chart's, worst enemies. Since the cores of the fragmented audiences referred to above are easily reached through identifiable clubs, shops and publications, fans of an act have been prepared for the precise date of their favourite's new release. The result is a high chart entry that cannot be bettered and probably not even sustained in the following fortnight, resulting in a rapid descent down and off the chart. Whereas singles used to climb for weeks and possibly months, many now enter high and then suffer precipitous falls. Titles that opened at number one and then quickly tumbled are easily identified in the list of chart toppers in part three of this book. One might think that some artists would be embarrassed at having reached number one through target marketing, only to immediately go into free fall. If so, they have yet to speak out.

By the end of 1992 it was apparent the situation was desperate. In an address to the Radio Academy, John Peel attacked the music business for being less interested in cultivating new talent than finding novel ways of selling old material. Certainly the introduction of both DCC and the Mini CD in the depth of recession was unsustainable given market conditions, and at least one of the new forms seemed doomed to fail. Record companies countered that they would encourage young music makers if they were in fact there, but new talent seemed thin on the UK ground.

It seemed beneficial for many parties in the music business if the British singles chart was altered to resemble its American counterpart. This may even have been done by the time you buy this book (and if you have got this far without a purchase, Shirley and Company have a song title for you). The *Billboard* Hot 100 is compiled with roughly the same weight given to sales and airplay. Since commercial radio stations will by their nature tend to play records large audiences will like, hence attracting advertisers, familiar names sustain chart runs at the expense of unknowns. Mainstream music has the edge over minority forms. If the UK list changes to accommodate an airplay factor during the next couple of years, the rate of turnover will decrease and singles will presumably show growth over periods of time longer than seven days. The main impediment to introducing the airplay factor earlier has been that attempts to influence the chart previously directed exclusively at shops might now be targeted at broadcasters. Radio and records alike will have to convince the public that the introduction of the airplay factor has not also opened the door to new opportunities for corruption.

In our role as The Watcher in all of this, we can only say that there have been golden ages and flat periods in popular music before. The longer the view one takes, the less one is alarmed if a particular stretch of time yields fewer classic pieces than another. A new musical day always dawns. We can certainly say that the high sales of our last edition of *The Guinness Book of British Hit Singles* prove that the public still holds popular music close to its heart. In recent years the industry has not employed the methods it once used to measure the appeal of songs, including sheet music sales and jukebox plays, but the decline in the use of these forms of measurement has not meant that interest in music charts has waned. Incorporation of an airplay factor will only mean that the way success is tabulated has changed again.

If the sales chart does go, we would be remiss not to give it a fond farewell. It has dominated the way we measure music for four decades, and that's far longer than Bryan Adams, Boyz II Men and Whitney Houston combined.

In compiling this book, we have used the charts published by the *New Musical Express* from the date of their first chart, which was the first UK record sales chart, for the week ending 14 November 1952. We continue to use the *NME* chart, as the longest established and most complete chart available, until the appearance of the first UK Top 50 in what was then called the *Record Retailer* (now *Music Week*), on 10 March 1960.

THE CHARTS

It is possible to argue that the *Record Retailer* chart in the first few years of its existence was not the most widely accepted chart, and we often receive angry letters from people wondering why, for example 'Please Please Me' by the Beatles or 'Are You Sure' by the Allisons are not listed as number ones, because they were on other charts. However, the *Record Retailer* was always the fullest chart, and it was always the one compiled and supported by the industry, and was certainly no less accurate than any other available chart. By the mid-60s, it was accepted as the national chart of record, something which no other chart since the earliest days of the *NME* chart could claim.

The size of the chart has varied over the years:

14 NOV 52	First ever chart, a 'Top 12' containing 15 hits!
1 OCT 54	Chart becomes a Top 20
30 DEC 55	Top 25 published, for this week only
13 APR 56	Chart becomes a Top 30
26 FEB 60	Last *NME* Top 30 used by *British Hit Singles*
10 MAR 60	*Record Retailer* chart inaugurated. This is a publication date, the chart date being week ending 5 March
3 JAN 63	Top 50 now independently audited
13 FEB 69	Top 50 now 'compiled for Record Retailer and the BBC by British Market Research Bureau'
6 FEB 71	Top 40 only, for 7 weeks as postal strikes limit the collection of chart sales information
27 MAR 71	Top 50 resumes
6 JAN 73	Top 30 only, for one week
22 DEC 73	Top 30 only, for one week
6 MAY 78	Top 75 begins
8 JAN 83	Chart compilation taken over by Gallup. By the end of 1992, the charts were the copyright of Chart Information Network Co. Ltd (CIN), and 'compiled by Gallup for Music Week, BBC and BARD. Produced in conjunction with the BPI and BARD, based on a minimum sample of 500 record outlets, incorporating 7", 12", cassettes and CD singles'

Occasionally a week went by with no chart being compiled (this often happened at Christmas in the early years of the chart). In these cases, the previous week's chart has been used again. If ever a chart was compiled but not published, this chart has been found and used in the compilation of *The Guinness Book of British Hit Singles*.

(Everything that was done) was done by Bryan Adams. So it seemed in 1991, when the talk of the year was the incredible achievement of the Canadian rocker's love ballad from *Robin Hood: Prince of Thieves*, '(Everything I Do) I Do It For You'. This worldwide smash topped the British chart for 16 weeks, overtaking the previous record for a consecutive run at number one by a full five weeks. Frankie Laine retained the distinction for most total weeks at number one, 'I Believe' having accumulated 18 weeks in

1991

three separate stays in 1953, but because this disc came from the days before rock and roll few commentators even bothered to mention it.

Ironically, Slim Whitman, whose 11-week queen 'Rose Marie' reigned for 26 years, slipped from second to fourth in the all-time most weeks at number one total when 'Bohemian Rhapsody' by Queen added to its original nine-week run upon re-release in December. The 1975 classic was re-released after the death of lead singer Freddie Mercury as part of a double A-side with the valedictory 'These Are the Days of Our Lives', with proceeds going to the Terrence Higgins Trust to fight AIDS. It entered the chart at number one and sold enough in the final three weeks of the year to be the second best seller of 1991, behind '(Everything I Do) I Do It For You'. Continued success in early 1992 gave 'Bohemian Rhapsody' five more weeks at number one for a grand total of 14, third behind the Laine and Adams classics. The posthumous achievement also gave Queen the distinction of being the only act to have two number ones during the calendar year 1991, 'Innuendo' having been a one-week wonder in January. Additionally, 'Bohemian Rhapsody' was the first single to reach number one in two different chart runs.

Compared with Bryan Adams and Queen the rest of the runners this year seriously underachieved. The only act with more than one single in the top thirty of the year was KLF, who accounted for 10% of this select group with a number one and a brace of number twos. The artist with the most weeks on the chart during the year was another acronymic outfit, R.E.M. However, the American quartet led the list with the lowest total in chart history, a mere 36 weeks, and they accumulated this figure without managing to ever reach the top five. British newcomer Kenny Thomas shadowed the Georgians with 35 weeks, achieved by four different hits, one of which peaked at number four.

The only performer besides Bryan Adams to appear in the top ten of the Most Weeks on Chart list *and* have a number one was Cher. Her version of Betty Everett's 'The Shoop Shoop Song (It's In His Kiss)' was the third best-selling single of the year. Cher was far and away the leading female star of 1991. Madonna was between albums this year and had to be content with a new hit from her *Immaculate Collection* compilation, 'Rescue Me', and a re-mix of her 1985 success 'Crazy For You'. By reaching number two, this song from the film *Vision Quest* became the highest-charting re-mix of all-time.

Proof that the best-selling discs are not always the ones that get to number one was provided by two of the year's top ten. 'I'm Too Sexy' by Right Said Fred finished at four for the year, even though it was held at number two in the weekly charts by '(Everything I Do) I Do It For You'. 'Insanity' by Oceanic wound up at nine for 1991 though it never climbed above three in seven-day sales figures.

A crisis in contemporary songwriting was illustrated by the fact that four of the year's eight favourite discs were of old material. 'Bohemian Rhapsody' was of course a re-issue, but it was still noteworthy that 'The Shoop Shoop Song' was first a hit for Betty Everett in 1964 in the US and 1968 in the UK, 'Dizzy' was a number one for Tommy Roe on both sides of the Atlantic in 1969, and 'Any Dream Will Do' originated from the late 1960s musical *Joseph And His Amazing Technicolour Dreamcoat*. One old song that came back stronger than ever was 'Don't Let The Sun Go Down on Me', which soared to number one in a live duet by George Michael and original artist Elton John. This hit went on to also top the American chart, a double only achieved in the calendar year 1991 by '(Everything I Do) I Do It For You' and Michael Jackson's 'Black And White'.

With 'Do The Bartman', the Simpsons became the first non-humans to top the chart since Spitting Image in 1986. Clash crashed off the list of Most Hits Without a Top Ten Hit, which they once led, by scoring a number one with a re-issue used in a jeans commercial, 'Should I Stay Or Should I Go'. Diana Ross extended her total of most consecutive years on chart by a still active artist to 21, 27 if one counted her service in the Supremes.

FREDDIE MERCURY tells Paul Gambaccini about Queen's forthcoming single 'Flash' at the 1980 House of Commons launch of *The Guinness Book of Hits of the 70s*.

Nobody rules, OK? 1992 was the most anarchic year in chart history. No artist had more than one of the 30 best-selling singles of the year, and only three record labels had at least two. The ten artists who spent the most weeks on chart had between them the lowest cumulative total of any year ever.

1992

SHAKESPEARS SISTER had the longest run at number one in 1992.

For the first time, over 1000 singles entered the chart during a year – 1,032 hits scooted in and out of the top 75 so quickly that any disc with a run of more than ten weeks was a living oldie. This rapid turnover and the fragmentation of the market were the big stories of the 1992. Independent labels had never had it so good, with small outfits like Network, Tug and One Little Indian competing successfully with established indies like Mute and PWL companies. The majors could only watch in horror as the singles scene passed completely from their control. Even the two big outfits who had multiple major hits, Arista and Motown, had started life as independents.

Arista was the label of the year, achieving the two best-selling singles. Whitney Houston's 'I Will Always Love You' was the only single of the year to sell a million. The song was written by

Dolly Parton, who first took it to number one in the country chart in 1974 and did so again in 1982 in a rendition for the movie *The Best Little Whorehouse In Texas*. Houston's version was for her film *The Bodyguard*. 'I Will Always Love You' eventually passed 'The Power Of Love' by Jennifer Rush to become the best-selling single ever by a female artist. Until the Houston release it had that appeared the number one of 1992 would be 'Rhythm Is A Dancer' by Snap, also on Arista. The company also had another of the year's top 30, 'It's My Life' by Dr. Alban.

The other firm in the news was Motown. Berry Gordy's historic label of the 60s and 70s had been sold and became virtually dormant in recent times. This year it enjoyed two of the biggest hits, 'End Of The Road' by Boyz II Men and 'I Love Your Smile' by Shanice. Lionel Richie also reached the top ten and 'My Girl' by

the Temptations got to number two as a re-issue on a licensing deal with Epic, who released the soundtrack to the film of the same name.

Capitol had two important successes, 'Would I Lie To You' by Charles and Eddie and 'Hazard' by Richard Marx. Both PWL International and PWL Continental had major hits, but otherwise the most important chart action came from scattered sources. Young artists were making and selling records at grass roots level, particularly in the area of dance music. Developments in technology had made it possible to record inexpensively at home, and discs could also be distributed and sold, particularly to target audiences in select locations, without the assistance of major companies. This was, depending on one's perspective, either liberating for art or threatening to business. The lack of interest in developing lasting artists' careers that was a part of this process was another aspect of the great change in the role popular music plays in society.

Michael Jackson, one of the few remaining transcendent stars, spent the most weeks on chart in 1992 with a scant 38, the lowest winning total of all-time bar the previous year's 36. Even so, none of his work was new, all of it being mined from his 1991 album *Dangerous*. Shakespears Sister followed Jackson with 32 weeks on chart, mainly thanks to 'Stay'. This hit had the longest number one run of the year, eight weeks. To indicate further how no act was dominating the singles market, none of the ten artists in this year's Most Weeks on Chart table repeated from 1991.

Queen did achieve a record that will be difficult to beat when 'Bohemian Rhapsody/These Are The Days Of Our Lives' began its run at number one, running over from 1991. 'Bohemian Rhapsody' had now been number one in four different calendar years. The song 'Do They Know It's Christmas' could say the same, but it achieved the feat in two different versions.

Due to the paucity of mass-appeal hits, discs that did get to number one tended to stay there. 1992 was the first year since 1971 without a number one that only lasted one week in the top position.

ALPHABETICALLY BY ARTIST

In this first section of *The Guinness Book of British Hit Singles*, we list every record that has hit the UK singles chart from 14 November 1952 to the final chart of 1992. The information is presented alphabetically by artist, and then chronologically for each artist. Each hit single is catalogued with the following information: *date disc first hit the chart, title of hit, label and catalogue number, highest position the hit reached on the chart, the total number of weeks it spent on the chart.*

Records which were not hits are not listed. A record is a hit if it appears in the charts, even for just one week at number 75, the lowest position listed.

It should be noted that the date given for the entry of a disc into the chart is the week ending date, which is the way the

The fourth career number one by WHITNEY HOUSTON was the best-selling single of 1992, 'I Will Always Love You'.

charts have historically been dated. In other words, Abba's 'Waterloo' entered the chart in the week ending 20 April 1974, which means that their first day of chart action was actually 14 April 1974.

Number one records are highlighted with a star, other top ten records by a dot. A dagger indicates hits still on the chart at the end of 1992, as follows:

★ **NUMBER ONE SINGLE** ● **TOP TEN SINGLE**

† **SINGLE STILL ON CHART AT 31 DECEMBER 1992**

For the purposes of this book, a record is considered a re-issue if it hits the chart for a second time with a new catalogue number. Otherwise, the reappearance of any record is considered a mere re-entry.

In this edition, for the first time, we have credited hits in combination with other chart acts to both artists' lists. So, for example, you will find George Michael and Elton John's number one hit 'Don't Let The Sun Go Down On Me' listed twice, once under Elton John and once under George Michael. There is no separate entry for them as a duo, and the weeks that record spent on the chart are credited to both singers. An asterisk or asterisks after the catalogue number of any hit will indicate that the credit on the record label is not just that of the artist in whose list of hits the asterisks appear. At the foot of each act's list there is an explanation of the details of each of these alternative label credits.

Describing a recording act in one sentence is often fraught with danger, but we have attempted to do so above each act's list of hits. Although we are aware that many of the 'vocalists' thus described also play an instrument, we have only mentioned this fact where the artist's instrumental skills were an important factor in their chart success.

Once more we have calculated the total weeks spent on the chart by every single act, and this total appears at the top right of each act's entry. Alert readers will note that some acts (e.g. Elvis Presley and Cliff Richard) have a weeks on chart grand total that is slightly less than the figure obtained by adding up the weeks totals of each of their hit titles. This is because in the early days of the charts (the *NME* charts of 1952 to 1960) both sides of the same record were sometimes listed simultaneously in different positions (e.g. Elvis Presley's 'Party' and 'Got A Lot O' Livin' To Do'). In these instances the two sides score only one week towards the act's total, not two.

Catalogue numbers are generally those of the 7-inch version of the single, but where there is a good reason for using an alternative (if, for example, the record was not issued on a 7-inch single), then the best-selling alternative format catalogue number is used.

ABBA *Sweden/Norway, male/female vocal/instrumental group* 253 wks

20 Apr 74 ★	WATERLOO *Epic EPC 2240*	1	9 wks
13 Jul 74	RING RING *Epic EPC 2452*	32	5 wks
12 Jul 75 ●	I DO I DO I DO I DO I DO *Epic EPC 3229*	38	6 wks
20 Sep 75 ●	S. O. S. *Epic EPC 3576*	6	10 wks
13 Dec 75 ★	MAMMA MIA *Epic EPC 3790*	1	14 wks
27 Mar 76 ★	FERNANDO *Epic EPC 4036*	1	15 wks
21 Aug 76 ●	DANCING QUEEN *Epic EPC 4499*	1	15 wks
20 Nov 76 ●	MONEY MONEY MONEY *Epic EPC 4713*	3	12 wks
26 Feb 77 ★	KNOWING ME KNOWING YOU *Epic EPC 4955*	1	13 wks
22 Oct 77 ★	THE NAME OF THE GAME *Epic EPC 5750*	1	12 wks
4 Feb 78 ★	TAKE A CHANCE ON ME *Epic EPC 5950*	1	10 wks
16 Sep 78 ●	SUMMER NIGHT CITY *Epic EPC 6595*	5	9 wks
3 Feb 79 ●	CHIQUITITA *Epic EPC 7030*	2	9 wks
5 May 79 ●	DOES YOUR MOTHER KNOW *Epic EPC 7316*	4	9 wks
14 Jul 79 ●	ANGELEYES/VOULEZ-VOUS *Epic EPC 7499*	3	11 wks
20 Oct 79 ●	GIMME GIMME GIMME (A MAN AFTER MIDNIGHT) *Epic EPC 7914*	3	12 wks
15 Dec 79 ●	I HAVE A DREAM *Epic EPC 8088*	2	10 wks
2 Aug 80 ★	THE WINNER TAKES IT ALL *Epic EPC 8835*	1	10 wks
15 Nov 80 ★	SUPER TROUPER *Epic EPC 9089*	1	12 wks
18 Jul 81 ●	LAY ALL YOUR LOVE ON ME *Epic EPC A 1314*	7	7 wks
12 Dec 81 ●	ONE OF US *Epic EPC A 1740*	3	10 wks
20 Feb 82	HEAD OVER HEELS *Epic EPC A 2037*	25	7 wks
23 Oct 82	THE DAY BEFORE YOU CAME *Epic EPC A 2847*	32	6 wks
11 Dec 82	UNDER ATTACK *Epic EPC A 2971*	26	8 wks
12 Nov 83	THANK YOU FOR THE MUSIC *CBS A 3894*	33	6 wks
5 Sep 92	DANCING QUEEN (re-issue) *Polydor PO 231*	16	5 wks

ABBACADABRA *UK, male/female, vocal/instrumental group* 1 wk

5 Sep 92	DANCING QUEEN *PWL International PWL 246*	57	1 wk

Russ ABBOT *UK, male vocalist* 22 wks

6 Feb 82	A DAY IN THE LIFE OF VINCE PRINCE *EMI 5249*	61	1 wk
20 Feb 82	A DAY IN THE LIFE OF VINCE PRINCE (re-entry) *EMI 5249*	75	1 wk
29 Dec 84 ●	ATMOSPHERE *Spirit FIRE 4*	7	13 wks
13 Jul 85	ALL NIGHT HOLIDAY *Spirit FIRE 6*	20	7 wks

Gregory ABBOTT *US, male vocalist* 13 wks

22 Nov 86 ●	SHAKE YOU DOWN *CBS A 7326*	6	13 wks

ABC *UK, male vocal/instrumental duo* 92 wks

31 Oct 81	TEARS ARE NOT ENOUGH *Neutron NT 101*	19	8 wks
20 Feb 82 ●	POISON ARROW *Neutron NT 102*	6	11 wks
15 May 82 ●	THE LOOK OF LOVE *Neutron NT 103*	4	11 wks
4 Sep 82 ●	ALL OF MY HEART *Neutron NT 104*	5	8 wks
15 Jan 83	THE LOOK OF LOVE (re-entry) *Neutron NT 103*	71	1 wk
5 Nov 83	THAT WAS THEN BUT THIS IS NOW *Neutron NT 105*	18	4 wks
21 Jan 84	S.O.S. *Neutron NT 106*	39	4 wks
10 Nov 84	HOW TO BE A MILLIONAIRE *Neutron NT 107*	49	4 wks
6 Apr 85	BE NEAR ME *Neutron NT 108*	26	4 wks
15 Jun 85	VANITY KILLS *Neutron NT 109*	70	1 wk
18 Jan 86	OCEAN BLUE *Neutron NT 110*	51	3 wks
6 Jun 87	WHEN SMOKEY SINGS *Neutron NT 111*	11	10 wks
5 Sep 87	THE NIGHT YOU MURDERED LOVE *Neutron NT 112*	31	8 wks
28 Nov 87	KING WITHOUT A CROWN *Neutron NT 113*	44	3 wks
27 May 89	ONE BETTER WORLD *Neutron NT 114*	32	4 wks
23 Sep 89	THE REAL THING *Neutron NT 115*	68	1 wk
14 Apr 90	THE LOOK OF LOVE (re-mix) *Neutron NT 116*	68	1 wk
27 Jul 91	LOVE CONQUERS ALL *Parlophone R 6292*	47	2 wks
11 Jan 92	SAY IT *Parlophone R 6298*	42	3 wks

The act were a UK, male vocal/instrumental group for first six hits, and a UK/US, male/female vocal/instrumental group for the next four.

Paula ABDUL *US, female vocalist* 64 wks

4 Mar 89 ●	STRAIGHT UP *Siren SRN 111*	3	13 wks
3 Jun 89	FOREVER YOUR GIRL *Siren SRN 112*	24	6 wks
19 Aug 89	KNOCKED OUT *Siren SRN 92*	45	3 wks
2 Dec 89	(IT'S JUST) THE WAY THAT YOU LOVE ME *Siren SRN 101*	74	1 wk
7 Apr 90 ●	OPPOSITES ATTRACT *Siren SRN 124* *	2	13 wks
21 Jul 90	KNOCKED OUT (re-mix) *Virgin America VUS 23*	21	5 wks
29 Sep 90	COLD HEARTED *Virgin America VUS 27*	46	3 wks
22 Jun 91 ●	RUSH RUSH *Virgin America VUS 38*	6	11 wks
31 Aug 91	THE PROMISE OF A NEW DAY *Virgin America VUS 44*	52	2 wks
18 Jan 92	VIBEOLOGY *Virgin America VUS 53*	19	6 wks
8 Aug 92	WILL YOU MARRY ME *Virgin America VUS 58*	73	1 wk

* Paula Abdul with the Wild Pair

Colonel ABRAMS *US, male vocalist* 35 wks

17 Aug 85 ●	TRAPPED *MCA MCA 997*	3	23 wks
7 Dec 85	THE TRUTH *MCA MCA 1022*	53	3 wks
8 Feb 86	I'M NOT GONNA LET YOU (GET THE BEST OF ME) *MCA MCA 1031*	24	7 wks
15 Aug 87	HOW SOON WE FORGET *MCA MCA 1179*	75	2 wks

AC/DC *Australia/UK, male vocal/instrumental group* 118 wks

10 Jun 78	ROCK 'N' ROLL DAMNATION *Atlantic K 11142*	24	9 wks
1 Sep 79	HIGHWAY TO HELL *Atlantic K 11321*	56	4 wks
2 Feb 80	TOUCH TOO MUCH *Atlantic K 11435*	29	9 wks
28 Jun 80	DIRTY DEEDS DONE DIRT CHEAP *Atlantic HM 2*	47	3 wks
28 Jun 80	HIGH VOLTAGE (LIVE VERSION) *Atlantic HM 1*	48	3 wks
28 Jun 80	IT'S A LONG WAY TO THE TOP (IF YOU WANNA ROCK 'N' ROLL) *Atlantic HM 3*	55	3 wks
28 Jun 80	WHOLE LOTTA ROSIE *Atlantic HM 4*	36	8 wks
13 Sep 80	YOU SHOOK ME ALL NIGHT LONG *Atlantic K 11600*	38	6 wks
29 Nov 80	ROCK 'N' ROLL AIN'T NOISE POLLUTION *Atlantic K 11630*	15	8 wks
6 Feb 82	LET'S GET IT UP *Atlantic K 11706*	13	6 wks
3 Jul 82	FOR THOSE ABOUT TO ROCK (WE SALUTE YOU) *Atlantic K 11721*	15	6 wks
29 Oct 83	GUNS FOR HIRE *Atlantic A 9774*	37	4 wks
4 Aug 84	NERVOUS SHAKEDOWN *Atlantic A 9651*	35	5 wks
6 Jul 85	DANGER *Atlantic A 9532*	48	4 wks
18 Jan 86	SHAKE YOUR FOUNDATIONS *Atlantic A 9474*	24	5 wks
24 May 86	WHO MADE WHO *Atlantic A 9425*	16	5 wks
30 Aug 86	YOU SHOOK ME ALL NIGHT LONG (re-issue) *Atlantic A 9377*	46	4 wks
16 Jan 88	HEATSEEKER *Atlantic A 9136*	12	6 wks
2 Apr 88	THAT'S THE WAY I WANNA ROCK 'N' ROLL *Atlantic A 9098*	22	5 wks
22 Sep 90	THUNDERSTRUCK *Atco B 8907*	13	5 wks
24 Nov 90	MONEYTALKS *Atco B 8886*	36	5 wks
27 Apr 91	ARE YOU READY *Atco B 8830*	34	3 wks
17 Oct 92	HIGHWAY TO HELL (LIVE) *Atco B 8479*	14	4 wks

ACE *UK, male vocal/instrumental group* 10 wks

9 Nov 74	HOW LONG *Anchor ANC 1002*	20	10 wks

ABBA twice achieved three consecutive number ones.

Julian Lennon tells BRYAN ADAMS (left) "Sixteen weeks at number one? Great! Fifty-three more weeks and you equal my dad's group!"

Richard ACE *Jamaica, male vocalist* **2 wks**

2 Dec 78	STAYIN' ALIVE *Blue Inc. INC 2*	66	2 wks

ACEN *UK, male producer* **4 wks**

8 Aug 92	TRIP II THE MOON *Production House PNT 042*	38	3 wks
10 Oct 92	TRIP II THE MOON (re-mix) *Production House PNT 042RX*	71	1 wk

ACES – *See Desmond DEKKER and the ACES*

ACT *UK/Germany, male/female vocal/instrumental group* **2 wks**

23 May 87	SNOBBERY AND DECAY *ZTT ZTAS 28*	60	2 wks

ACT ONE *US, male/female vocal/instrumental group* **6 wks**

18 May 74	TOM THE PEEPER *Mercury 6008 005*	40	6 wks

Arthur ADAMS *US, male vocalist* **5 wks**

24 Oct 81	YOU GOT THE FLOOR *RCA 146*	38	5 wks

Bryan ADAMS *Canada, male vocalist/instrumentalist - guitar* **105 wks**

12 Jan 85	RUN TO YOU *A & M AM 224*	11	12 wks
16 Mar 85	SOMEBODY *A & M AM 236*	35	7 wks
25 May 85	HEAVEN *A & M AM 256*	38	5 wks
10 Aug 85	SUMMER OF '69 *A & M AM 267*	42	7 wks
2 Nov 85	IT'S ONLY LOVE *A & M AM 285 **	29	6 wks
21 Dec 85	CHRISTMAS TIME *A & M AM 297*	55	2 wks
22 Feb 86	THIS TIME *A & M AM 295*	41	7 wks
12 Jul 86	STRAIGHT FROM THE HEART *A & M AM 322*	51	3 wks
28 Mar 87	HEAT OF THE NIGHT *A & M ADAM 2*	50	2 wks
20 Jun 87	HEARTS ON FIRE *A & M ADAM 3*	57	3 wks
17 Oct 87	VICTIM OF LOVE *A & M AM 407*	68	2 wks
29 Jun 91 ★	(EVERYTHING I DO) I DO IT FOR YOU *A & M AM 789*	1	24 wks
14 Sep 91	CAN'T STOP THIS THING WE STARTED *A & M AM 612*	12	6 wks
23 Nov 91	THERE WILL NEVER BE ANOTHER TONIGHT *A & M AM 838*	32	3 wks
28 Dec 91	(EVERYTHING I DO) I DO IT FOR YOU (re-entry) *A & M AM 789*	73	1 wk
22 Feb 92 ●	THOUGHT I'D DIED AND GONE TO HEAVEN *A & M AM 848*	8	7 wks
18 Jul 92	ALL I WANT IS YOU *A & M AM 879*	22	5 wks
26 Sep 92	DO I HAVE TO SAY THE WORDS *A & M AM 0068*	30	3 wks

* Bryan Adams and Tina Turner

Cliff ADAMS *UK, orchestra* **2 wks**

28 Apr 60	LONELY MAN THEME *Pye International 7N 25056*	39	2 wks

Gayle ADAMS *US, female vocalist* **1 wk**

26 Jul 80	STRETCHIN' OUT *Epic EPC 8791*	64	1 wk

Marie ADAMS – *See Johnny OTIS SHOW*

Oleta ADAMS *US, female vocalist* **27 wks**

24 Mar 90	RHYTHM OF LIFE *Fontana OLETA 1*	52	2 wks
3 Nov 90	RHYTHM OF LIFE (re-entry) *Fontana OLETA 1*	56	3 wks
12 Jan 91 ●	GET HERE *Fontana OLETA 3*	4	12 wks
13 Apr 91	YOU'VE GOT TO GIVE ME ROOM/RHYTHM OF LIFE (re-issue) *Fontana OLETA 4*	49	3 wks
29 Jun 91	CIRCLE OF ONE *Fontana OLETA 5*	73	1 wk
28 Sep 91	DON'T LET THE SUN GO DOWN ON ME *Fontana TRIBO 1*	33	5 wks
25 Apr 92	WOMAN IN CHAINS (re-issue) *Fontana IDEA 16 **	57	1 wk

* Tears For Fears featuring Oleta Adams
The original release of Woman In Chains *credited Tears For Fears only.*

ADAMSKI *UK, male instrumentalist/producer* **38 wks**

20 Jan 90	N-R-G *MCA MCA 1386*	12	6 wks
7 Apr 90 ★	KILLER *MCA MCA 1400*	1	18 wks
8 Sep 90 ●	THE SPACE JUNGLE *MCA MCA 1435*	7	8 wks
17 Nov 90	FLASHBACK JACK *MCA MCA 1159*	16	3 wks
9 Nov 91	NEVER GOIN' DOWN/BORN TO BE ALIVE *MCA MCS 1578 **	51	2 wks
4 Apr 92	GET YOUR BODY *MCA MCS 1613 ***	68	1 wk
4 Jul 92	BACK TO FRONT *MCA MCS 1644*	63	1 wk

* Adamski featuring Jimi Polo/Adamski featuring Soho ** Adamski featuring Nina Hagen
Featured vocalist on Killer *was Seal.*

ADDAMS and GEE *UK, male instrumental duo* **1 wk**

20 Apr 91	CHUNG KUO (REVISITED) *Debut DEBT 3108*	72	1 wk

ADDRISI BROTHERS *US, male vocal duo* **3 wks**

6 Oct 79	GHOST DANCER *Scotti Brothers K 11361*	57	3 wks

ADEVA *US, female vocalist* **56 wks**

14 Jan 89	RESPECT *Cooltempo COOL 179*	17	9 wks
25 Mar 89	MUSICAL FREEDOM (MOVING ON UP) *Cooltempo COOL 182 **	22	8 wks
12 Aug 89	WARNING *Cooltempo COOL 185*	17	8 wks
21 Oct 89	I THANK YOU *Cooltempo COOL 192*	17	7 wks
16 Dec 89	BEAUTIFUL LOVE *Cooltempo COOL 195*	57	5 wks
28 Apr 90	TREAT ME RIGHT *Cooltempo COOL 200*	62	2 wks
6 Apr 91	RING MY BELL *Cooltempo COOL 224 ***	20	5 wks
19 Oct 91	IT SHOULD'VE BEEN ME *Cooltempo COOL 236*	48	3 wks
29 Feb 92	DON'T LET IT SHOW ON YOUR FACE *Cooltempo COOL 248*	34	4 wks
17 Oct 92	I'M THE ONE FOR YOU *Cooltempo COOL 264*	51	2 wks
6 Jun 92	UNTIL YOU COME BACK TO ME *Cooltempo COOL 254*	45	3 wks

* Paul Simpson featuring Adeva ** Monie Love vs Adeva

ADICTS *UK, male vocal/instrumental group* **1 wk**

14 May 83	BAD BOY *Razor RZS 104*	75	1 wk

ADONIS featuring 2 PUERTO RICANS, A BLACK MAN AND A DOMINICAN **4 wks**
US, male vocal/instrumental group

13 Jun 87	DO IT PROPERLY ('NO WAY BACK')/NO WAY BACK *London LON 136*	47	4 wks

ADRENALIN M.O.D. *US, male vocal/instrumental group* **5 wks**

8 Oct 88	O-O-O *MCA RAGAT 2*	49	5 wks

ADULT NET UK/US, *male/female vocal/instrumental group* — 2 wks

10 Jun 89	**WHERE WERE YOU** *Fontana BRX 2*	66	2 wks

ADVENTURES UK, *male vocal/instrumental group* — 24 wks

15 Sep 84	**ANOTHER SILENT DAY** *Chrysalis CHS 2000*	71	2 wks
1 Dec 84	**SEND MY HEART** *Chrysalis CHS 2001*	62	4 wks
13 Jul 85	**FEEL THE RAINDROPS** *Chrysalis AD 1*	58	3 wks
9 Apr 88	**BROKEN LAND** *Elektra EKR 69*	20	10 wks
2 Jul 88	**DROWNING IN THE SEA OF LOVE** *Elektra EKR 76*	44	4 wks
13 Jun 92	**RAINING ALL OVER THE WORLD** *Polydor PO 211*	68	1 wk

ADVENTURES OF STEVIE V — 21 wks
US, *male producer and vocalist*

21 Apr 90	● **DIRTY CASH** *Mercury MER 311*	2	13 wks
29 Sep 90	**BODY LANGUAGE** *Mercury MER 331*	29	5 wks
2 Mar 91	**JEALOUSY** *Mercury MER 337*	58	3 wks

ADVERTS UK, *male/female vocal/instrumental group* — 11 wks

27 Aug 77	**GARY GILMORE'S EYES** *Anchor ANC 1043*	18	7 wks
4 Feb 78	**NO TIME TO BE 21** *Bright BR1*	38	4 wks

AEROSMITH US, *male vocal/instrumental group* — 26 wks

17 Oct 87	**DUDE (LOOKS LIKE A LADY)** *Geffen GEF 29*	45	5 wks
16 Apr 88	**ANGEL** *Geffen GEF 34*	69	2 wks
9 Sep 89	**LOVE IN AN ELEVATOR** *Geffen GEF 63*	13	8 wks
24 Feb 90	**DUDE (LOOKS LIKE A LADY)** (re-issue) *Geffen GEF 72*	20	5 wks
14 Apr 90	**RAG DOLL** *Geffen GEF 76*	42	4 wks
1 Sep 90	**THE OTHER SIDE** *Geffen GEF 79*	46	2 wks

AFRICAN BUSINESS Italy, *male vocal/instrumental group* — 1 wk

17 Nov 90	**IN ZAIRE** *Urban URB 64*	73	1 wk

AFTER 7 US, *male vocal group* — 3 wks

3 Nov 90	**CAN'T STOP** *Virgin America VUS 31*	54	3 wks

AFTER THE FIRE UK, *male vocal/instrumental group* — 12 wks

9 Jun 79	**ONE RULE FOR YOU** *CBS 7025*	40	6 wks
8 Sep 79	**LASER LOVE** *CBS 7769*	62	2 wks
9 Apr 83	**DER KOMMISSAR** *CBS A 2399*	47	4 wks

AFTERNOON BOYS – *See Steve WRIGHT*

AGE OF CHANCE — 13 wks
UK, *male/female vocal/instrumental group*

17 Jan 87	**KISS** *Fon AGE 5*	50	6 wks
30 May 87	**WHO'S AFRAID OF THE BIG BAD NOISE!** *Fon VS 962*	65	2 wks
20 Jan 90	**HIGHER THAN HEAVEN** *Virgin VS 1228*	53	5 wks

A-HA Norway, *male vocal/instrumental group* — 121 wks

28 Sep 85	● **TAKE ON ME** *Warner Bros. W 9006*	2	19 wks
28 Dec 85	★ **THE SUN ALWAYS SHINES ON TV** *Warner Bros. W 8846*	1	12 wks
5 Apr 86	● **TRAIN OF THOUGHT** *Warner Bros. W 8736*	8	8 wks
14 Jun 86	● **HUNTING HIGH AND LOW** *Warner Bros. W 6663*	5	10 wks
4 Oct 86	● **I'VE BEEN LOSING YOU** *Warner Bros. W 8594*	8	7 wks
6 Dec 86	● **CRY WOLF** *Warner Bros. W 8500*	5	9 wks
28 Feb 87	**MANHATTAN SKYLINE** *Warner Bros. W 8405*	13	6 wks
4 Jul 87	**THE LIVING DAYLIGHTS** *Warner Bros. W 8305*	5	9 wks
26 Mar 88	● **STAY ON THESE ROADS** *Warner Bros. W 7936*	5	6 wks
18 Jun 88	**THE BLOOD THAT MOVES THE BODY** *Warner Bros. W 7840*	25	4 wks
27 Aug 88	**TOUCHY!** *Warner Bros. W 7749*	11	7 wks
8 Dec 88	**YOU ARE THE ONE** *Warner Bros. W 7636*	13	10 wks
13 Oct 90	**CRYING IN THE RAIN** *Warner Bros. W 9547*	13	7 wks
15 Dec 90	**I CALL YOUR NAME** *Warner Bros. W 9462*	44	5 wks
26 Oct 91	**MOVE TO MEMPHIS** *Warner Bros. W 0070*	47	2 wks

AIR SUPPLY UK/Australia, *male vocal/instrumental group* — 15 wks

27 Sep 80	**ALL OUT OF LOVE** *Arista ARIST 362*	11	11 wks
2 Oct 82	**EVEN THE NIGHTS ARE BETTER** *Arista ARIST 474*	44	4 wks

AIRHEAD UK, *male vocal/instrumental group* — 10 wks

5 Oct 91	**FUNNY HOW** *Korova KOW 47*	57	3 wks
21 Dec 91	**COUNTING SHEEP** *Korova KOW 48*	35	5 wks
7 Mar 92	**RIGHT NOW** *Korova KOW 49*	50	2 wks

Laurel AITKEN and the UNITONE — 3 wks
Jamaica/Cuba, *male vocal/instrumental group*

17 May 80	**RUDI GOT MARRIED** *I-Spy SEE 6*	60	3 wks

Jewel AKENS US, *male/vocalist* — 8 wks

25 Mar 65	**THE BIRDS AND THE BEES** *London HLN 9954*	29	8 wks

ALARM UK, *male vocal/instrumental group* — 64 wks

24 Sep 83	**68 GUNS** *IRS PFP 1023*	17	7 wks
21 Jan 84	**WHERE WERE YOU HIDING WHEN THE STORM BROKE** *IRS IRS 101*	22	6 wks
31 Mar 84	**THE DECEIVER** *IRS IRS 103*	51	4 wks
3 Nov 84	**THE CHANT HAS JUST BEGUN** *IRS IRS 104*	48	4 wks
2 Mar 85	**ABSOLUTE REALITY** *IRS ALARM 1*	35	6 wks
28 Sep 85	**STRENGTH** *IRS IRM 104*	40	4 wks
18 Jan 86	**SPIRIT OF '76** *IRS IRM 109*	22	5 wks
26 Apr 86	**KNIFE EDGE** *IRS IRM 112*	43	3 wks
17 Oct 87	**RAIN IN THE SUMMERTIME** *IRS IRM 144*	18	5 wks
12 Dec 87	**RESCUE ME** *IRS IRM 150*	48	2 wks
20 Feb 88	**PRESENCE OF LOVE (LAUGHERNE)** *IRS IRM 155*	44	3 wks
16 Sep 89	**SOLD ME DOWN THE RIVER** *IRS EIRS 123*	43	3 wks
4 Nov 89	**A NEW SOUTH WALES/THE ROCK** *IRS EIRS 129*	31	3 wks
3 Feb 90	**LOVE DON'T COME EASY** *IRS EIRS 134*	48	3 wks
27 Oct 90	**UNSAFE BUILDING 1990** *IRS ALARME 2*	54	2 wks
13 Apr 91	**RAW** *IRS ALARM 3*	51	2 wks

A New South Wales *features Morriston Orpheus Male Voice Choir.*

Morris ALBERT Brazil, *male vocalist* — 10 wks

27 Sep 75	● **FEELINGS** *Decca F 13591*	4	10 wks

ALBERTO Y LOST TRIOS PARANOIAS — 5 wks
UK, *male vocal/instrumental group*

23 Sep 78	**HEADS DOWN NO NONSENSE MINDLESS BOOGIE** *Logo GO 323*	47	5 wks

British Hit Singles Part One: Alphabetically by Artist
Date of chart entry/Title & catalogue no./Peak position reached/Weeks on chart
★ Number one   ● Top Ten   † still on chart at 31 Dec 1992
* = credited to act billed in footnote

ALESSI US, male vocal duo — 11 wks

11 Jun 77 ● OH LORI *A & M AMS 7289* ....8 11 wks

ALFI and HARRY — 5 wks
US, male vocalist, David Seville under two false names

23 Mar 56 THE TROUBLE WITH HARRY *London HLU 8242*...........15 5 wks
See also David Seville.

ALISHA US, female vocalist — 2 wks

25 Jan 86 BABY TALK *Total Control TOCO 6*............................67 2 wks

ALL ABOUT EVE UK, female/male vocal/instrumental group — 47 wks

31 Oct 87 IN THE CLOUDS *Mercury EVEN 5*...........................47 5 wks
23 Jan 88 WILD HEARTED WOMAN *Mercury EVEN 6*......................33 4 wks
9 Apr 88 EVERY ANGEL *Mercury EVEN 7*...........................30 5 wks
30 Jul 88 ● MARTHA'S HARBOUR *Mercury EVEN 8*........................10 8 wks
12 Nov 88 WHAT KIND OF FOOL *Mercury EVEN 9* ....29 4 wks
30 Sep 89 ROAD TO YOUR SOUL *Mercury EVEN 10* ....37 4 wks
16 Dec 89 DECEMBER *Mercury EVEN 11* ....34 5 wks
28 Apr 90 SCARLET *Mercury EVEN 12*.............................34 2 wks
15 Jun 91 FAREWELL MR SORROW *Mercury EVEN 14* ....36 2 wks
10 Aug 91 STRANGE WAY *Vertigo EVEN 15*..........................50 3 wks
19 Oct 91 THE DREAMER *Vertigo EVEN 16* ....41 2 wks
10 Oct 92 PHASED (EP) *MCA MCS 1688*.............................38 2 wks
28 Nov 92 SOME FINER DAY *MCA MCS 1706* ....57 1 wk
Tracks on Phased EP: Phased/Mine/Infra Red/Ascent-Descent.

ALL STARS – *See Louis ARMSTRONG*

ALL-STARS – *See Junior WALKER and the ALL-STARS*

ALL SYSTEMS GO UK, male vocal/instrumental group — 2 wks

18 Jun 88 POP MUZIK *Unique NIQ 03* ....63 2 wks

Richard ALLAN UK, male vocalist — 1 wk

24 Mar 60 AS TIME GOES BY *Parlophone R 4634* ....44 1 wk

Steve ALLAN UK, male vocalist — 2 wks

27 Jan 79 TOGETHER WE ARE BEAUTIFUL *Creole CR 164* ....67 1 wk
10 Feb 79 TOGETHER WE ARE BEAUTIFUL (re-entry)
Creole CR 164 ....70 1 wk

Donna ALLEN US, female vocalist — 22 wks

18 Apr 87 ● SERIOUS *Portrait PRT 650744 7* ....8 12 wks
3 Jun 89 ● JOY AND PAIN *BCM BCM 257* ....10 10 wks

ALLISONS UK, male vocal duo — 27 wks

23 Feb 61 ● ARE YOU SURE *Fontana H 294* ....2 16 wks

18 May 61 WORDS *Fontana H 304* ....34 5 wks
15 Feb 62 LESSONS IN LOVE *Fontana H 362* ....30 6 wks

ALLNIGHT BAND UK, male instrumental group — 3 wks

3 Feb 79 THE JOKER (THE WIGAN JOKER)
Casino Classics CC 6 ....50 3 wks

ALMIGHTY UK, male vocal/instrumental group — 8 wks

30 Jun 90 WILD AND WONDERFUL *Polydor PO 75* ....50 2 wks
2 Mar 91 FREE 'N' EASY *Polydor PO 127*........................35 2 wks
11 May 91 DEVIL'S TOY *Polydor PO 144* ....36 2 wks
29 Jun 91 LITTLE LOST SOMETIMES *Polydor PO 151* ....42 2 wks

Marc ALMOND UK, male vocalist — 99 wks

2 Jun 83 BLACK HEART *Some Bizzare BZS 19* * ....49 3 wks
2 Jun 84 THE BOY WHO CAME BACK *Some Bizzare BZS 23* ....52 5 wks
1 Sep 84 YOU HAVE *Some Bizzare BZS 24* ....57 3 wks
20 Apr 85 ● I FEEL LOVE (MEDLEY) *Forbidden Fruit BITE 4* ** ...3 12 wks
24 Aug 85 STORIES OF JOHNNY *Some Bizzare BONK 1* ....23 5 wks
26 Oct 85 LOVE LETTER *Some Bizzare BONK 2* ....68 3 wks
4 Jan 86 THE HOUSE IS HAUNTED (BY THE ECHO OF
YOUR LAST GOODBYE) *Some Bizzare GLOW 1* ...55 3 wks
7 Jun 86 A WOMAN'S STORY *Some Bizzare GLOW 2* *** ....41 5 wks
18 Oct 86 RUBY RED *Some Bizzare GLOW 3* ....47 3 wks
14 Feb 87 MELANCHOLY ROSE *Some Bizzare GLOW 4* ....71 1 wk
3 Sep 88 TEARS RUN RINGS *Parlophone R 6186* ....26 7 wks
5 Nov 88 BITTER SWEET *Some Bizzare R 6194* ....40 3 wks
14 Jan 89 ★ SOMETHING'S GOTTEN HOLD OF MY HEART
Parlophone R 6201 **** ....1 12 wks
8 Apr 89 ONLY THE MOMENT *Parlophone R 6210* ....45 2 wks
3 Mar 90 A LOVER SPURNED *Some Bizzare R 6229* ....29 4 wks
19 May 90 THE DESPERATE HOURS *Some Bizzare R 6252*...........45 2 wks
18 May 91 ● TAINTED LOVE *Mercury SOFT 2* ***** ....5 8 wks
28 Sep 91 JACKY *Some Bizzare YZ 610* ....17 6 wks
11 Jan 92 MY HAND OVER MY HEART *Some Bizzare YZ 633*.........33 5 wks
25 Apr 92 ● THE DAYS OF PEARLY SPENCER
Some Bizzare YZ 638 ....4 7 wks

* Marc and the Mambas ** Bronski Beat and Marc Almond *** Marc Almond
and the Willing Sinners **** Marc Almond featuring special guest star Gene
Pitney ***** Soft Cell/Marc Almond
*I Feel Love medley comprises I Feel Love/Love To Love You Baby/Johnny Remember Me.
Tainted Love is a re-recording of a Soft Cell hit.*

ALOOF UK, male vocal/instrumental group — 1 wk

19 Sep 92 ON A MISSION *Cowboy RODEO 5*.........................64 1 wk

Herb ALPERT US, male instrumentalist - trumpet — 106 wks

3 Jan 63 THE LONELY BULL *Stateside SS 138* * ....22 9 wks
9 Dec 65 ● SPANISH FLEA *Pye International 7 N 25335* ** ....3 20 wks
24 Mar 66 TIJUANA TAXI *Pye International 7 N 25352* ** ....37 4 wks
27 Apr 67 CASINO ROYALE *A & M AMS 700* ** ....27 14 wks
3 Jul 68 ● THIS GUY'S IN LOVE WITH YOU *A & M AMS 727*.........3 16 wks
26 Mar 69 THIS GUY'S IN LOVE WITH YOU (re-entry)
A & M AMS 727 ....47 1 wk
9 Apr 69 THIS GUY'S IN LOVE WITH YOU (2nd re-entry)
A & M AMS 727 ....49 1 wk
7 May 69 THIS GUY'S IN LOVE WITH YOU (3rd re-entry)
A & M AMS 727 ....50 1 wk
18 Jun 69 WITHOUT HER *A & M AMS 755* ** ....36 5 wks
12 Dec 70 JERUSALEM *A & M AMS 810* ** ....47 1 wk
2 Jan 71 JERUSALEM (re-entry) *A & M AMS 810* ** ....42 2 wks
13 Oct 79 RISE *A & M AMS 7465* ....13 13 wks
19 Jan 80 ROTATION *A & M AMS 7500* ....46 3 wks

| 21 Mar 87 | **KEEP YOUR EYE ON ME** *Breakout USA 602* | **19** | 9 wks |
| 6 Jun 87 | **DIAMONDS** *Breakout USA 605* | **27** | 7 wks |

* Tijuana Brass ** Herb Alpert and the Tijuana Brass
Alpert vocalises on This Guy's In Love With You *and* Without Her. *Janet Jackson provides uncredited vocals on* Diamonds.

ALPHABETA – *See Izhar* COHEN *and* ALPHABETA

ALPHAVILLE *Germany, male vocal/instrumental group* **13 wks**

| 18 Aug 84 ● | **BIG IN JAPAN** *WEA Int. X9505* | **8** | 13 wks |

Gerald ALSTON *US, male vocalist* **1 wk**

| 15 Apr 89 | **ACTIVATED** *RCA ZB 42681* | **73** | 1 wk |

ALTERED IMAGES **60 wks**
UK, male/female vocal/instrumental group

28 Mar 81	**DEAD POP STARS** *Epic EPC A 1023*	**67**	2 wks
26 Sep 81 ●	**HAPPY BIRTHDAY** *Epic EPC A 1522*	**2**	17 wks
12 Dec 81 ●	**I COULD BE HAPPY** *Epic EPC A 1834*	**7**	12 wks
27 Mar 82	**SEE THOSE EYES** *Epic EPC A 2198*	**11**	7 wks
22 May 82	**PINKY BLUE** *Epic EPC A 2426*	**35**	6 wks
19 Mar 83 ●	**DON'T TALK TO ME ABOUT LOVE**		
	Epic EPC A 3083	**7**	7 wks
28 May 83	**BRING ME CLOSER** *Epic EPC A 3398*	**29**	6 wks
16 Jul 83	**LOVE TO STAY** *Epic EPC A 3582*	**46**	3 wks

ALTERN 8 *UK, male instrumental/production duo* **31 wks**

13 Jul 91	**INFILTRATE 202** *Network NWK 24*	**28**	7 wks
16 Nov 91 ●	**ACTIV 8 (COME WITH ME)** *Network NWK 34*	**3**	9 wks
8 Feb 92	**FREQUENCY** *Network NWKT 37*	**41**	1 wk
11 Apr 92 ●	**EVAPOR 8** *Network NWK 38*	**6**	6 wks
4 Jul 92	**HYPNOTIC ST-8** *Network NWK 49*	**16**	4 wks
10 Oct 92	**SHAME** *Network NWKTEN 56 **	**74**	1 wk
12 Dec 92	**BRUTAL-8-E** *Network NWK 59*	**43**†	3 wks

* Altern 8 vs Evelyn King

ALTHIA and DONNA *Jamaica, female vocal duo* **11 wks**

| 24 Dec 77 ★ | **UP TOWN TOP RANKING** *Lightning LIG 506* | **1** | 11 wks |

ALVIN and the CHIPMUNKS – *See* CHIPMUNKS

ALY-US *US, male vocal/insrumental group* **2 wks**

| 21 Nov 92 | **FOLLOW ME** *Cooltempo COOL 266* | **43** | 2 wks |

AMAZULU *UK, female/male vocal/instrumental group* **57 wks**

6 Jul 85	**EXCITABLE** *Island IS 201*	**12**	13 wks
23 Nov 85	**DON'T YOU JUST KNOW IT** *Island IS 233*	**17**	11 wks
15 Mar 86	**THE THINGS THE LONELY DO** *Island IS 267*	**43**	6 wks
31 May 86 ●	**TOO GOOD TO BE FORGOTTEN** *Island IS 284*	**5**	13 wks
13 Sep 86	**MONTEGO BAY** *Island IS 293*	**16**	9 wks
10 Oct 87	**MONY MONY** *EMI EM 32*	**38**	5 wks

AMBASSADORS OF FUNK featuring MC **8 wks**
MARIO *US, male DJ and rapper – Simon Harris and Einstein*

| 31 Oct 92 ● | **SUPERMARIOLAND** *Living Beat SMASH 23* | **8** | 8 wks |

AMEN CORNER *UK, male vocal/instrumental group* **67 wks**

26 Jul 67	**GIN HOUSE BLUES** *Deram DM 136*	**12**	10 wks
11 Oct 67	**WORLD OF BROKEN HEARTS** *Deram DM 151*	**26**	6 wks
17 Jan 68 ●	**BEND ME SHAPE ME** *Deram DM 172*	**3**	12 wks
31 Jul 68 ●	**HIGH IN THE SKY** *Deram DM 197*	**6**	13 wks
29 Jan 69 ★	**(IF PARADISE IS) HALF AS NICE** *Immediate IM 073*	**1**	11 wks
25 Jun 69 ●	**HELLO SUZIE** *Immediate IM 081*	**4**	10 wks
14 Feb 76	**(IF PARADISE IS) HALF AS NICE (re-issue)**		
	Immediate IMS 103	**34**	5 wks

AMERICA *US, male vocal/instrumental group* **20 wks**

18 Dec 71	**HORSE WITH NO NAME** *Warner Bros. K 16128*	**49**	2 wks
8 Jan 72 ●	**HORSE WITH NO NAME (re-entry)**		
	Warner Bros. K 16128	**3**	11 wks
25 Nov 72	**VENTURA HIGHWAY** *Warner Bros. K 16219*	**43**	4 wks
6 Nov 82	**YOU CAN DO MAGIC** *Capitol CL 264*	**59**	3 wks

AMERICAN BREED *US, male vocal/instrumental group* **6 wks**

| 7 Feb 68 | **BEND ME SHAPE ME** *Stateside SS 2078* | **24** | 6 wks |

AMES BROTHERS *US, male vocal group* **6 wks**

| 4 Feb 55 ● | **NAUGHTY LADY OF SHADY LANE** *HMV B 10800* | **6** | 6 wks |

Tori AMOS *US, female vocalist* **19 wks**

23 Nov 91	**SILENT ALL THESE YEARS** *East West YZ 618*	**51**	3 wks
1 Feb 92	**CHINA** *East West YZ 7531*	**51**	2 wks
21 Mar 92	**WINTER** *East West A 7504*	**25**	4 wks
20 Jun 92	**CRUCIFY** *East West A 7479*	**15**	6 wks
22 Aug 92	**SILENT ALL THESE YEARS (re-issue)**		
	East West A 7433	**26**	4 wks

AND WHY NOT? *UK, male vocal/instrumental group* **18 wks**

14 Oct 89	**RESTLESS DAYS (SHE CRIES OUT LOUD)**		
	Island IS 426	**38**	7 wks
13 Jan 90	**THE FACE** *Island IS 444*	**13**	8 wks
21 Apr 90	**SOMETHING YOU GOT** *Island IS 452*	**39**	3 wks

Angry ANDERSON *Australia, male vocalist* **13 wks**

| 19 Nov 88 ● | **SUDDENLY** *Food For Thought YUM 113* | **3** | 13 wks |

John ANDERSON BIG BAND *UK, big band* **5 wks**

| 21 Dec 85 | **GLENN MILLER MEDLEY** *Modern GLEN 1* | **63** | 2 wks |
| 11 Jan 86 | **GLENN MILLER MEDLEY (re-entry)** *Modern GLEN 1* | **61** | 3 wks |

Glenn Miller Medley *comprises the following tracks:* In The Mood/American Patrol/Little Brown Jug/Pennsylvania 65000.

ANDERSON BRUFORD WAKEMAN **2 wks**
HOWE *UK, male vocal/instrumental group*

| 24 Jun 89 | **BROTHER OF MINE** *Arista 112379* | **63** | 2 wks |

Carl ANDERSON *US, male vocalist* **4 wks**

| 8 Jun 85 | **BUTTERCUP** *Streetwave KHAN 45* | **49** | 4 wks |

Laurie ANDERSON
US, female vocalist/multi-instrumentalist — **6 wks**

17 Oct 81	● O SUPERMAN *Warner Bros. K 17870*	**2**	6 wks

Leroy ANDERSON and his POPS CONCERT ORCHESTRA *US, orchestra* — **4 wks**

28 Jun 57	FORGOTTEN DREAMS *Brunswick 05485*	**28**	1 wk
12 Jul 57	FORGOTTEN DREAMS (re-entry) *Brunswick 05485*	**30**	1 wk
6 Sep 57	FORGOTTEN DREAMS (2nd re-entry) *Brunswick 05485*	**24**	2 wks

Lynn ANDERSON *US, female vocalist* — **20 wks**

20 Feb 71	● ROSE GARDEN *CBS 5360*	**3**	20 wks

Moira ANDERSON *UK, female vocalist* — **2 wks**

27 Dec 69	HOLY CITY *Decca F 12989*	**43**	2 wks

Chris ANDREWS *UK, male vocalist* — **36 wks**

7 Oct 65	● YESTERDAY MAN *Decca F 12236*	**3**	15 wks
2 Dec 65	TO WHOM IT CONCERNS *Decca F 22285*	**13**	10 wks
14 Apr 66	SOMETHING ON MY MIND *Decca F 22365*	**45**	1 wk
28 Apr 66	SOMETHING ON MY MIND (re-entry) *Decca F 22365*	**41**	2 wks
2 Jun 66	WHATCHA GONNA DO NOW *Decca F 22404*	**40**	4 wks
25 Aug 66	STOP THAT GIRL *Decca F 22472*	**36**	4 wks

Eamonn ANDREWS *Ireland, male vocalist* — **3 wks**

20 Jan 56	SHIFTING WHISPERING SANDS (PARTS 1 & 2) *Parlophone R 4106*	**18**	3 wks

Hit is 'with Ron Goodwin and his Orchestra and Chorus'.

ANEKA *UK, female vocalist* — **16 wks**

8 Aug 81	★ JAPANESE BOY *Hansa HANSA 5*	**1**	12 wks
7 Nov 81	LITTLE LADY *Hansa HANSA 8*	**50**	4 wks

ANGELETTES *UK, female vocal group* — **5 wks**

13 May 72	DON'T LET HIM TOUCH YOU *Decca F 13284*	**35**	5 wks

ANGELIC UPSTARTS
UK, male vocal/instrumental group — **30 wks**

21 Apr 79	I'M AN UPSTART *Warner Bros. K 17354*	**31**	8 wks
11 Aug 79	TEENAGE WARNING *Warner Bros. K 17426*	**29**	6 wks
3 Nov 79	NEVER 'AD NOTHIN' *Warner Bros. K 17476*	**52**	4 wks
9 Feb 80	OUT OF CONTROL *Warner Bros. K 17558*	**58**	3 wks
22 Mar 80	WE GOTTA GET OUT OF THIS PLACE *Warner Bros. K 17576*	**65**	2 wks
2 Aug 80	LAST NIGHT ANOTHER SOLDIER *Angelic Upstarts Z 7*	**51**	4 wks
7 Feb 81	KIDS ON THE STREET *Angelic Upstarts Z 16*	**57**	3 wks

Bobby ANGELO and the TUXEDOS — **6 wks**
UK, male vocal/instrumental group

10 Aug 61	BABY SITTIN' *HMV POP 892*	**30**	6 wks

ANGELS *US, female vocal group* — **1 wk**

3 Oct 63	MY BOYFRIEND'S BACK *Mercury AMT 1211*	**50**	1 wk

ANGELS OF LIGHT – *See PSYCHIC TV*

ANGELWITCH *UK, male vocal/instrumental group* — **1 wk**

7 Jun 80	SWEET DANGER *EMI 5064*	**75**	1 wk

ANIMAL NIGHTLIFE — **22 wks**
UK, male/female vocal/instrumental group

13 Aug 83	NATIVE BOY (UPTOWN) *Innervision A3584*	**60**	3 wks
18 Aug 84	MR. SOLITAIRE *Island IS 193*	**25**	12 wks
6 Jul 85	LOVE IS JUST THE GREAT PRETENDER *Island IS 200*	**28**	6 wks
5 Oct 85	PREACHER, PREACHER *Island IS 245*	**67**	1 wk

ANIMALS *UK, male vocal/instrumental group* — **147 wks**

16 Apr 64	BABY LET ME TAKE YOU HOME *Columbia DB 7247*	**21**	8 wks
25 Jun 64	★ HOUSE OF THE RISING SUN *Columbia DB 7301*	**1**	12 wks
17 Sep 64	● I'M CRYING *Columbia DB 7354*	**8**	10 wks
4 Feb 65	● DON'T LET ME BE MISUNDERSTOOD *Columbia DB 7445*	**3**	9 wks
8 Apr 65	● BRING IT ON HOME TO ME *Columbia DB 7539*	**7**	11 wks
15 Jul 65	● WE GOTTA GET OUT OF THIS PLACE *Columbia DB 7639*	**2**	12 wks
28 Oct 65	● IT'S MY LIFE *Columbia DB 7741*	**7**	11 wks
17 Feb 66	INSIDE - LOOKING OUT *Decca F 12332*	**12**	8 wks
2 Jun 66	● DON'T BRING ME DOWN *Decca F 12407*	**6**	8 wks
27 Oct 66	HELP ME GIRL *Decca F 12502* *	**14**	10 wks
15 Jun 67	WHEN I WAS YOUNG *MGM 1340* *	**45**	3 wks
6 Sep 67	GOOD TIMES *MGM 1344* *	**20**	11 wks
18 Oct 67	● SAN FRANCISCAN NIGHTS *MGM 1359* *	**7**	10 wks
14 Feb 68	SKY PILOT *MGM 1373* *	**40**	3 wks
15 Jan 69	RING OF FIRE *MGM 1461* *	**35**	5 wks
7 Oct 72	HOUSE OF THE RISING SUN (re-issue) *RAK RR 1*	**25**	6 wks
18 Sep 82	HOUSE OF THE RISING SUN (re-entry of re-issue) *RAK RR 1*	**11**	10 wks

* Eric Burdon and the Animals

ANIMOTION *US/UK, male/female vocal/instrumental group* — **12 wks**

11 May 85	● OBSESSION *Mercury PH 34*	**5**	12 wks

Paul ANKA *Canada, male vocalist* — **134 wks**

9 Aug 57	★ DIANA *Columbia DB 3980*	**1**	25 wks
8 Nov 57	● I LOVE YOU BABY *Columbia DB 4022*	**3**	15 wks
8 Nov 57	TELL ME THAT YOU LOVE ME *Columbia DB 4022*	**25**	2 wks
31 Jan 58	● YOU ARE MY DESTINY *Columbia DB 4063*	**6**	13 wks
30 May 58	CRAZY LOVE *Columbia DB 4110*	**26**	1 wk
26 Sep 58	MIDNIGHT *Columbia DB 4172*	**26**	1 wk
30 Jan 59	● (ALL OF A SUDDEN) MY HEART SINGS *Columbia DB 4241*	**10**	13 wks
10 Jul 59	● LONELY BOY *Columbia DB 4324*	**3**	17 wks
30 Oct 59	● PUT YOUR HEAD ON MY SHOULDER *Columbia DB 4355*	**7**	12 wks
26 Feb 60	IT'S TIME TO CRY *Columbia DB 4390*	**28**	1 wk
31 Mar 60	PUPPY LOVE *Columbia DB 4434*	**33**	4 wks
14 Apr 60	IT'S TIME TO CRY (re-entry) *Columbia DB 4390*	**47**	1 wk
5 May 60	PUPPY LOVE (re-entry) *Columbia DB 4434*	**37**	3 wks
15 Sep 60	HELLO YOUNG LOVERS *Columbia DB 4504*	**44**	1 wk
15 Mar 62	LOVE ME WARM AND TENDER *RCA 1276*	**19**	11 wks

26 Jul 62	**A STEEL GUITAR AND A GLASS OF WINE**		
	RCA 1292 ....**41**	4 wks
28 Sep 74 ●	**(YOU'RE) HAVING MY BABY**		
	United Artists UP 35713 * **6**	10 wks

Paul Anka featuring Odia Coates

ANNETTE – *See VARIOUS ARTISTS (EPs & LPs) - Further Adventures Of North EP*

ANOUCHKA – *See Terry HALL*

Adam ANT *UK, male vocalist*   188 wks

2 Aug 80	**KINGS OF THE WILD FRONTIER** *CBS 8877* * **48**	5 wks
11 Oct 80 ●	**DOG EAT DOG** *CBS 9039* * **4**	16 wks
6 Dec 80 ●	**ANTMUSIC** *CBS 9352* * **2**	18 wks
27 Dec 80 ●	**YOUNG PARISIANS** *Decca F13803* * **9**	7 wks
24 Jan 81	**CARTROUBLE** *Do It DUN 10* * **33**	9 wks
24 Jan 81	**ZEROX** *Do It DUN 8* * **45**	9 wks
21 Feb 81 ●	**KINGS OF THE WILD FRONTIER (re-entry)**		
	CBS 8877 * **2**	13 wks
9 May 81 ★	**STAND AND DELIVER** *CBS A 1065* * **1**	15 wks
12 Sep 81 ★	**PRINCE CHARMING** *CBS A 1408* * **1**	12 wks
12 Dec 81 ●	**ANT RAP** *CBS A 1738* * **3**	10 wks
27 Feb 82	**DEUTSCHER GIRLS** *Ego 5* * **13**	6 wks
13 Mar 82	**THE ANTMUSIC EP (THE B-SIDES)**		
	Do It DUN 20 * **46**	4 wks
22 May 82 ★	**GOODY TWO SHOES** *CBS A 2367*..............**1**	11 wks
18 Sep 82 ●	**FRIEND OR FOE** *CBS A 2736* **9**	8 wks
27 Nov 82	**DESPERATE BUT NOT SERIOUS** *CBS A 2892* ..**33**	7 wks
29 Oct 83 ●	**PUSS 'N BOOTS** *CBS A 3614* **5**	11 wks
10 Dec 83	**STRIP** *CBS A 3589*..**41**	6 wks
22 Sep 84	**APOLLO 9** *CBS A 4719* **13**	8 wks
13 Jul 85	**VIVE LE ROCK** *CBS A 6367*........................**50**	4 wks
17 Feb 90	**ROOM AT THE TOP** *MCA MCA 1387*..........**13**	7 wks
28 Apr 90	**CAN'T SET RULES ABOUT LOVE** *MCA MCA 1404*...**47**	2 wks

Adam and the Ants

Tracks on The Antmusic EP (The B-Sides): *Friends/Kick/Physical.*

Billie ANTHONY *UK, female vocalist*   16 wks

| 15 Oct 54 ● | **THIS OLE HOUSE** *Columbia DB 3519* ....**4** | 16 wks |

Marc ANTHONY – *See Louie VEGA and Marc ANTHONY*

Miki ANTHONY *UK, male vocalist*   7 wks

| 3 Feb 73 | **IF IT WASN'T FOR THE REASON THAT I LOVE** | | |
| | **YOU** *Bell 1275* ....**27** | 7 wks |

Ray ANTHONY *US, orchestra*   2 wks

| 4 Dec 53 ● | **DRAGNET** *Capitol CL 13983* ....**7** | 1 wk |
| 8 Jan 54 | **DRAGNET (re-entry)** *Capitol CL 13983* ....**11** | 1 wk |

Richard ANTHONY *France, male vocalist*   15 wks

12 Dec 63	**WALKING ALONE** *Columbia DB 7133* **37**	5 wks
2 Apr 64	**IF I LOVED YOU** *Columbia DB 7235* **48**	1 wk
23 Apr 64	**IF I LOVED YOU (re-entry)** *Columbia DB 7235* **18**	9 wks

ANTHRAX *US, male vocal/instrumental group*   32 wks

28 Feb 87	**I AM THE LAW** *Island IS LAW 1* **32**	5 wks
27 Jun 87	**INDIANS** *Island IS 325* **44**	4 wks
5 Dec 87	**I'M THE MAN** *Island IS 338* **20**	6 wks
10 Sep 88	**MAKE ME LAUGH** *Island IS 379* **26**	3 wks

British Hit Singles Part One: Alphabetically by Artist
Date of chart entry/ Title & catalogue no./ Peak position reached/ Weeks on chart

★ Number one   ● Top Ten   † still on chart at 31 Dec 1992

* = credited to act billed in footnote

18 Mar 89	**ANTI-SOCIAL** *Island IS 409*....................**44**	3 wks
1 Sep 90	**IN MY WORLD** *Island IS 470* **29**	2 wks
5 Jan 91	**GOT THE TIME** *Island IS 476* **16**	4 wks
6 Jul 91	**BRING THE NOISE** *Island IS 490* * **14**	5 wks

Anthrax featuring Chuck D

ANTI-NOWHERE LEAGUE   10 wks
UK, male vocal/instrumental group

23 Jan 82	**STREETS OF LONDON** *WXYZ ABCD 1* **48**	5 wks
20 Mar 82	**I HATE ... PEOPLE** *WXYZ ABCD 2* **46**	3 wks
3 Jul 82	**WOMAN** *WXYZ ABCD 4* **72**	2 wks

ANTI-PASTI – *See EXPLOITED*

ANTICAPPELLA   6 wks
Italy/UK, male/female vocal/instrumental group

| 16 Nov 91 | **2√231** *PWL Continental PWL 205* ....**24** | 4 wks |
| 18 Apr 92 | **EVERY DAY** *PWL Continental PWL 220* ....**45** | 2 wks |

ANTONIA – *See BOMB THE BASS*

ANTS – *See Adam ANT*

APACHE INDIAN – *See Maxi PRIEST*

APHEX TWIN *UK, male producer - Richard James*   2 wks

| 9 May 92 | **DIGERIDOO** *R&S RSUK 12* ....**55** | 2 wks |

APHRODITE'S CHILD   7 wks
Greece, male vocal/instrumental group

| 6 Nov 68 | **RAIN AND TEARS** *Mercury MF 1039* ....**30** | 7 wks |

Kim APPLEBY *UK, female vocalist*   27 wks

3 Nov 90 ●	**DON'T WORRY** *Parlophone R 6272*...................**2**	10 wks
9 Feb 91 ●	**G.L.A.D.** *Parlophone R 6281* **10**	6 wks
29 Jun 91	**MAMA** *Parlophone R 6291* **19**	8 wks
19 Oct 91	**IF YOU CARED** *Parlophone R 6297* **44**	3 wks

See also Mel and Kim.

APPLEJACKS *UK, male/female vocal/instrumental group*   29 wks

5 Mar 64 ●	**TELL ME WHEN** *Decca F 11833*.........................**7**	13 wks
11 Jun 64	**LIKE DREAMERS DO** *Decca F 11916* **20**	11 wks
15 Oct 64	**THREE LITTLE WORDS** *Decca F 11981* **23**	5 wks

APPLES *UK, male vocal/instrumental group*   1 wk

| 23 Mar 91 | **EYE WONDER** *Epic 6566717* ....**75** | 1 wk |

Charlie APPLEWHITE *US, male vocalist*   1 wk

| 23 Sep 55 | **BLUE STAR (THE MEDIC THEME)** *Brunswick 05416* ....**20** | 1 wk |

THE AMERICAN BREED were bred in Illinois.

LYNN ANDERSON recorded the Joe South song 'Rose Garden' over the objections of her advisers, who thought a woman would not say to a man "I could promise you things like big diamond rings".

With their imaginative uses of the number eight, ALTERN8 should have been around to help promote the previous edition of this book.

CHET ATKINS won numerous Grammy Awards in the 1970s and 80s, but his UK chart career was strictly teensville.

Anthony Gourdine (front) led LITTLE ANTHONY AND THE IMPERIALS.

Helen APRIL – *See John DUMMER and Helen APRIL*

APRIL WINE *Canada, male vocal/instrumental group*　　　**9 wks**

| 15 Mar 80 | | I LIKE TO ROCK *Capitol CL 16121* | 41 | 5 wks |
| 11 Apr 81 | | JUST BETWEEN YOU AND ME *Capitol CL 16184* | 52 | 4 wks |

AQUARIAN DREAM　　　**1 wk**
US, male/female vocal/instrumental group

| 24 Feb 79 | | YOU'RE A STAR *Elektra LV 7* | 67 | 1 wk |

ARCADIA *UK, male vocal/instrumental group*　　　**13 wks**

26 Oct 85	●	ELECTION DAY *Odeon NSR 1*	7	7 wks
25 Jan 86		THE PROMISE *Odeon NSR 2*	37	4 wks
26 Jul 86		THE FLAME *Odeon NSR 3*	58	2 wks

Tasmin ARCHER *UK, female vocalist*　　　**15 wks**

| 12 Sep 92 | ★ | SLEEPING SATELLITE *EMI EM 233* | 1 | 15 wks |

ARCHIES *US, male/female vocal group*　　　**26 wks**

| 11 Oct 69 | ★ | SUGAR SUGAR *RCA 1872* | 1 | 26 wks |

ARGENT *UK, male vocal/instrumental group*　　　**27 wks**

4 Mar 72	●	HOLD YOUR HEAD UP *Epic EPC 7786*	5	12 wks
10 Jun 72		TRAGEDY *Epic EPC 8115*	34	7 wks
24 Mar 73		GOD GAVE ROCK AND ROLL TO YOU *Epic EPC 1243*	18	8 wks

Ship's Company and Royal Marine Band of　　　**6 wks**
H.M.S. ARK ROYAL *UK, male choir and Marine band*

| 23 Dec 78 | | THE LAST FAREWELL *BBC RESL 61* | 46 | 6 wks |

Joan ARMATRADING *UK, female vocalist*　　　**53 wks**

16 Oct 76	●	LOVE AND AFFECTION *A & M AMS 7249*	10	9 wks
23 Feb 80		ROSIE *A & M AMS 7506*	49	5 wks
14 Jun 80		ME MYSELF I *A & M AMS 7527*	21	11 wks
6 Sep 80		ALL THE WAY FROM AMERICA *A & M AMS 7552*	54	3 wks
12 Sep 81		I'M LUCKY *A & M AMS 8163*	46	5 wks
16 Jan 82		NO LOVE *A & M AMS 8179*	50	5 wks
19 Feb 83		DROP THE PILOT *A & M AMS 8306*	11	10 wks
16 Mar 85		TEMPTATION *A & M AM 238*	65	2 wks
26 May 90		MORE THAN ONE KIND OF LOVE *A & M AM 561*	75	1 wk
23 May 92		WRAPPED AROUND HER *A & M AM 877*	56	2 wks

ARMOURY SHOW *UK, male vocal/instrumental group*　　　**6 wks**

25 Aug 84		CASTLES IN SPAIN *Parlophone R 6079*	69	2 wks
26 Jan 85		WE CAN BE BRAVE AGAIN *Parlophone R 6087*	66	1 wk
17 Jan 87		LOVE IN ANGER *Parlophone R 6149*	63	3 wks

Louis ARMSTRONG　　　**80 wks**
US, male jazz band leader, vocalist/instrumentalist - trumpet

19 Dec 52	●	TAKES TWO TO TANGO *Brunswick 04995*	6	10 wks
13 Apr 56	●	THEME FROM THE THREEPENNY OPERA *Philips PB 574 **	8	11 wks
15 Jun 56		TAKE IT SATCH EP *Philips BBE 12035 **	29	1 wk
13 Jul 56		THE FAITHFUL HUSSAR *Philips PB 604 **	27	2 wks
6 Nov 59		MACK THE KNIFE *Philips PB 967 **	24	1 wk
4 Jun 64		HELLO DOLLY *London HLR 9878*	4	14 wks
7 Feb 68	★	WHAT A WONDERFUL WORLD/CABARET *HMV POP 1615*	1	29 wks
26 Jun 68		SUNSHINE OF LOVE *Stateside SS 2116*	41	7 wks
16 Apr 88		WHAT A WONDERFUL WORLD (re-issue) *A & M AM 435*	53	5 wks

* Louis Armstrong with his All-Stars

Tracks on Take It Satch EP: Tiger Rag/Mack The Knife/The Faithful Hussar/Back O'Town Blues. Mack The Knife is a re-issue of Theme From Threepenny Opera under a different title. Cabaret was not listed with What A Wonderful World until 14 Feb 68.

ARMY OF LOVERS　　　**11 wks**
Sweden/France, male/female vocal/group

17 Aug 91		CRUCIFIED *Ton Son Ton WOK 2007*	47	4 wks
28 Dec 91		OBSESSION *Ton Son Ton WOK 2009*	67	1 wk
15 Feb 92		CRUCIFIED (re-issue) *Ton Son Ton WOK 2017*	31	5 wks
18 Apr 92		RIDE THE BULLET *Ton Son Ton WOK 2018*	67	1 wk

ARNEE and the TERMINATERS　　　**7 wks**
UK, male vocal/instrumental group

| 24 Aug 91 | ● | I'LL BE BACK *Epic 6574177* | 5 | 7 wks |

ARNIE'S LOVE *US, male/female vocal/instrumental group*　　　**3 wks**

| 26 Nov 83 | | I'M OUT OF YOUR LIFE *Streetwave WAVE 9* | 67 | 3 wks |

Eddy ARNOLD *US, male vocalist*　　　**21 wks**

17 Feb 66	●	MAKE THE WORLD GO AWAY *RCA 1496*	8	17 wks
26 May 66		I WANT TO GO WITH YOU *RCA 1519*	49	1 wk
9 Jun 66		I WANT TO GO WITH YOU (re-entry) *RCA 1519*	46	2 wks
28 Jul 66		IF YOU WERE MINE MARY *RCA 1529*	49	1 wk

P.P. ARNOLD *US, female vocalist*　　　**37 wks**

4 May 67		FIRST CUT IS THE DEEPEST *Immediate IM 047*	18	10 wks
2 Aug 67		THE TIME HAS COME *Immediate IM 055*	47	2 wks
24 Jan 68		(IF YOU THINK) YOU'RE GROOVY *Immediate IM 061*	41	4 wks
10 Jul 68		ANGEL OF THE MORNING *Immediate IM 067*	29	11 wks
24 Sep 88		BURN IT UP *Rhythm King LEFT 27 **	14	10 wks

* Beatmasters with P.P. Arnold

ARPEGGIO *US, male/female vocal group*　　　**3 wks**

| 31 Mar 79 | | LOVE AND DESIRE (PART 1) *Polydor POSP 40* | 63 | 3 wks |

ARRESTED DEVELOPMENT　　　**17 wks**
US, male/female vocal/instrumental group

16 May 92		TENNESSEE *Cooltempo COOL 253*	46	4 wks
11 Jul 92		TENNESSEE (re-entry) *Cooltempo COOL 253*	54	3 wks
24 Oct 92	●	PEOPLE EVERYDAY *Cooltempo COOL 265*	2†	10 wks

Steve ARRINGTON *US, male vocalist*　　　**19 wks**

27 Apr 85	●	FEEL SO REAL *Atlantic A 9576*	5	10 wks
6 Jul 85		DANCIN' IN THE KEY OF LIFE *Atlantic A 9534*	21	8 wks
7 Sep 85		DANCIN' IN THE KEY OF LIFE (re-entry) *Atlantic A 9534*	75	1 wk

British Hit Singles Part One: Alphabetically by Artist
Date of chart entry/Title & catalogue no./Peak position reached/Weeks on chart
★ Number one   ● Top Ten   † still on chart at 31 Dec 1992
* = credited to act billed in footnote

ARRIVAL UK, male/female vocal/instrumental group   20 wks

| 10 Jan 70 ● | **FRIENDS** Decca F 12986 | 8 | 9 wks |
| 6 Jun 70 | **I WILL SURVIVE** Decca F 13026 | 16 | 11 wks |

ARROW Montserrat, male vocalist   12 wks

| 28 Jul 84 | **HOT HOT HOT** Cooltempo ARROW 1 | 59 | 5 wks |
| 13 Jul 85 | **LONG TIME** London LON 70 | 30 | 7 wks |

ARROWS US/UK, male vocal/instrumental group   16 wks

| 25 May 74 ● | **A TOUCH TOO MUCH** RAK 171 | 8 | 9 wks |
| 1 Feb 75 | **MY LAST NIGHT WITH YOU** RAK 189 | 25 | 7 wks |

ARSENAL F.C. FIRST TEAM SQUAD   7 wks
UK, male football team vocalists

| 8 May 71 | **GOOD OLD ARSENAL** Pye 7N 45067 | 16 | 7 wks |

ART COMPANY Holland, male vocal/instrumental group   11 wks

| 26 May 84 | **SUSANNA** Epic A 4174 | 12 | 11 wks |

ART OF NOISE   64 wks
UK, male/female instrumental/production group

24 Nov 84 ●	**CLOSE (TO THE EDIT)** ZTT ZTPS 01	8	19 wks
13 Apr 85	**MOMENTS IN LOVE/BEAT BOX** ZTT ZTPS 02	51	4 wks
9 Nov 85	**LEGS** China WOK 5	69	1 wk
22 Mar 86 ●	**PETER GUNN** China WOK 6 *	8	9 wks
21 Jun 86	**PARANOIMIA** China WOK 9 **	12	9 wks
18 Jul 87	**DRAGNET** China WOK 14	60	4 wks
29 Oct 88 ●	**KISS** China CHINA 11 ***	5	7 wks
12 Aug 89	**YEBO** China CHINA 18 ****	63	3 wks
16 Jun 90	**ART OF LOVE** China CHINA 23	67	1 wk
11 Jan 92	**INSTRUMENTS OF DARKNESS (ALL OF US ARE ONE PEOPLE)** China WOK 2012	45	5 wks
29 Feb 92	**SHADES OF PARANOIMIA** China WOK 2014	53	2 wks

* Art Of Noise featuring Duane Eddy ** Art Of Noise featuring Max Headroom
*** Art Of Noise featuring Tom Jones **** Art Of Noise featuring Mahlathini and the Mahotella Queens

ARTISTS UNITED AGAINST APARTHEID   8 wks
Multi-national, male/female vocal/instrumental charity assembly

| 23 Nov 85 | **SUN CITY** Manhattan MT 7 | 21 | 8 wks |

ASAP UK, male vocal/instrumental group   4 wks

| 14 Oct 89 | **SILVER AND GOLD** EMI EM 107 | 60 | 2 wks |
| 3 Feb 90 | **DOWN THE WIRE** EMI EM 131 | 67 | 2 wks |

ASHAYE UK, male vocalist   3 wks

| 15 Oct 83 | **MICHAEL JACKSON MEDLEY** Record Shack SOHO 10 | 45 | 3 wks |

Tracks on medley: Don't Stop Til You Get Enough/Wanna Be Startin' Something/Shake Your Body Down To The Ground/Blame It On The Boogie.

John ASHER UK, male vocalist   6 wks

| 15 Nov 75 | **LET'S TWIST AGAIN** Creole CR 112 | 14 | 6 wks |

ASHFORD and SIMPSON US, male/female vocal duo   22 wks

18 Nov 78	**IT SEEMS TO HANG ON** Warner Bros. K 17237	48	4 wks
5 Jan 85 ●	**SOLID** Capitol CL 345	3	15 wks
20 Apr 85	**BABIES** Capitol CL 355	56	3 wks

ASHTON, GARDNER AND DYKE   14 wks
UK, male vocal/instrumental group

| 16 Jan 71 ● | **RESURRECTION SHUFFLE** Capitol CL 15665 | 3 | 14 wks |

ASIA UK, male vocal/instrumental group   13 wks

3 Jul 82	**HEAT OF THE MOMENT** Geffen GEF A2494	46	5 wks
18 Sep 82	**ONLY TIME WILL TELL** Geffen GEF A2228	54	3 wks
13 Aug 83	**DON'T CRY** Geffen A 3580	33	5 wks

ASIA BLUE UK, female vocal group   2 wks

| 27 Jun 92 | **ESCAPING** Atomic WNR 882 | 50 | 2 wks |

ASSEMBLY UK, male vocal/instrumental group   10 wks

| 12 Nov 83 ● | **NEVER NEVER** Mute TINY 1 | 4 | 10 wks |

ASSOCIATES UK, male vocal/instrumental group   47 wks

20 Feb 82 ●	**PARTY FEARS TWO** Associates ASC 1	9	10 wks
8 May 82	**CLUB COUNTRY** Associates ASC 2	13	10 wks
7 Aug 82	**LOVE HANGOVER/18 CARAT LOVE AFFAIR** Associates ASC 3	21	8 wks
16 Jun 84	**THOSE FIRST IMPRESSIONS** WEA YZ 6	43	6 wks
1 Sep 84	**WAITING FOR THE LOVEBOAT** WEA YZ 16	53	4 wks
19 Jan 85	**BREAKFAST** WEA YZ 28	49	6 wks
17 Sep 88	**HEART OF GLASS** WEA YZ 310	56	3 wks

18 Carat Love Affair listed until 28 Aug only. Act was duo on 1982 hits.

ASSOCIATION US, male vocal/instrumental group   8 wks

| 22 May 68 | **TIME FOR LIVING** Warner Bros. WB 7195 | 23 | 8 wks |

Rick ASTLEY UK, male vocalist   87 wks

8 Aug 87 ★	**NEVER GONNA GIVE YOU UP** RCA PB 41447	1	18 wks
31 Oct 87 ●	**WHENEVER YOU NEED SOMEBODY** RCA PB 41567	3	12 wks
12 Dec 87 ●	**WHEN I FALL IN LOVE/MY ARMS KEEP MISSING YOU** RCA PB 41683	2	10 wks
27 Feb 88 ●	**TOGETHER FOREVER** RCA PB 41817	2	9 wks
24 Sep 88 ●	**SHE WANTS TO DANCE WITH ME** RCA PB 42189	6	10 wks
26 Nov 88 ●	**TAKE ME TO YOUR HEART** RCA PB 42573	8	10 wks
11 Feb 89 ●	**HOLD ME IN YOUR ARMS** RCA PB 42615	10	8 wks
26 Jan 91 ●	**CRY FOR HELP** RCA PB 44247	7	7 wks
30 Mar 91	**MOVE RIGHT OUT** RCA PB 44407	58	2 wks
29 Jun 91	**NEVER KNEW LOVE** RCA PB 44737	70	1 wk

Before 9 Jan 88 When I Fall In Love was listed by itself. After that date My Arms Keep Missing You was the side listed.

ASWAD UK, male vocal/instrumental group   52 wks

| 3 Mar 84 | **CHASING FOR THE BREEZE** Island IS 160 | 51 | 3 wks |

Date	Title	Pos	Wks
6 Oct 84	**54-46 (WAS MY NUMBER)** *Island IS 170*	70	3 wks
27 Feb 88 ★	**DON'T TURN AROUND** *Mango IS 341*	1	12 wks
21 May 88	**GIVE A LITTLE LOVE** *Mango IS 358*	11	8 wks
24 Sep 88	**SET THEM FREE** *Mango IS 383*	70	2 wks
1 Apr 89	**BEAUTY'S ONLY SKIN DEEP** *Mango MNG 105*	31	6 wks
22 Jul 89	**ON AND ON** *Mango MNG 708*	25	8 wks
18 Aug 90	**NEXT TO YOU** *Mango MNG 753*	24	6 wks
17 Nov 90	**SMILE** *Mango MNG 767 **	53	2 wks
30 Mar 91	**TOO WICKED EP** *Mango MNG 771*	61	2 wks

* Aswad featuring Sweetie Irie

Tracks on Too Wicked EP: Best of My Love/Warrior Re-Charge/ Fire/I Shot The Sheriff.

Gali ATARI – *See MILK AND HONEY featuring Gali ATARI*

Chet ATKINS *US, male instrumentalist - guitar*   **2 wks**

Date	Title	Pos	Wks
17 Mar 60	**TEENSVILLE** *RCA 1174*	46	1 wk
5 May 60	**TEENSVILLE (re-entry)** *RCA 1174*	49	1 wk

ATLANTA RHYTHM SECTION   **4 wks**
US, male vocal/instrumental group

Date	Title	Pos	Wks
27 Oct 79	**SPOOKY** *Polydor POSP 74*	48	4 wks

ATLANTIC STARR   **46 wks**
US, male/female vocal/instrumental group

Date	Title	Pos	Wks
9 Sep 78	**GIMME YOUR LOVIN'** *A & M AMS 7380*	66	3 wks
29 Jun 85	**SILVER SHADOW** *A & M AM 260*	41	6 wks
7 Sep 85	**ONE LOVE** *A & M AM 273*	58	4 wks
15 Mar 86 ●	**SECRET LOVERS** *A & M AM 307*	10	12 wks
24 May 86	**IF YOUR HEART ISN'T IN IT** *A & M AM 319*	48	4 wks
13 Jun 87 ●	**ALWAYS** *Warner Bros. W 8455*	3	14 wks
12 Sep 87	**ONE LOVER AT A TIME** *Warner Bros. W 8327*	57	3 wks

ATMOSFEAR *UK, male vocal/instrumental group*   **7 wks**

Date	Title	Pos	Wks
17 Nov 79	**DANCING IN OUTER SPACE** *MCA 543*	46	7 wks

ATOMIC ROOSTER *UK, male vocal/instrumental group*   **25 wks**

Date	Title	Pos	Wks
6 Feb 71	**TOMORROW NIGHT** *B & C CB 131*	11	12 wks
10 Jul 71 ●	**THE DEVIL'S ANSWER** *B & C CB 157*	4	13 wks

ATTRACTIONS – *See Elvis COSTELLO and the ATTRACTIONS*

Winifred ATWELL *UK, female instrumentalist - piano*   **117 wks**

Date	Title	Pos	Wks
12 Dec 52	**BRITANNIA RAG** *Decca F 10015*	11	1 wk
9 Jan 53 ●	**BRITANNIA RAG (re-entry)** *Decca F 10015*	5	5 wks
15 May 53	**CORONATION RAG** *Decca F 10110*	12	1 wk
29 May 53 ●	**CORONATION RAG (re-entry)** *Decca F 10110*	5	5 wks
25 Sep 53	**FLIRTATION WALTZ** *Decca F 10161*	12	1 wk
9 Oct 53 ●	**FLIRTATION WALTZ (re-entry)** *Decca F 10161*	10	1 wk
6 Nov 53	**FLIRTATION WALTZ (2nd re-entry)** *Decca F10161*	12	1 wk
4 Dec 53 ●	**LET'S HAVE A PARTY** *Philips PB 213*	2	9 wks
23 Jul 54 ●	**RACHMANINOFF'S 18TH VARIATION ON A THEME BY PAGANINI (THE STORY OF THREE LOVES)** *Philips PB 234*	9	7 wks
1 Oct 54	**RACHMANINOFF'S 18TH VARIATION ON A THEME BY PAGANINI (THE STORY OF THREE LOVES) (re-entry)** *Philips PB 234*	19	2 wks
26 Nov 54 ★	**LET'S HAVE ANOTHER PARTY** *Philips PB 268*	1	8 wks
26 Nov 54	**LET'S HAVE A PARTY (re-entry)** *Philips PB 213*	14	6 wks
4 Nov 55 ●	**LET'S HAVE A DING DONG** *Decca F 10634*	3	10 wks
16 Mar 56 ★	**POOR PEOPLE OF PARIS** *Decca F 10681*	1	16 wks
18 May 56	**PORT AU PRINCE** *Decca F 10727 **	18	6 wks
20 Jul 56	**LEFT BANK** *Decca F 10762*	14	7 wks
26 Oct 56 ●	**MAKE IT A PARTY** *Decca F 10796*	7	12 wks
22 Feb 57	**LET'S ROCK 'N ROLL** *Decca F 10852*	28	2 wks
15 Mar 57	**LET'S ROCK 'N ROLL (re-entry)** *Decca F 10852*	24	2 wks
6 Dec 57 ●	**LET'S HAVE A BALL** *Decca F 10956*	4	6 wks
7 Aug 59	**SUMMER OF THE SEVENTEENTH DOLL** *Decca F 11143*	24	2 wks
27 Nov 59 ●	**PIANO PARTY** *Decca F 11183*	10	7 wks

* Winifred Atwell and Frank Chacksfield

Various hits listed above were medleys as follows: Let's Have a Party: Boomps A Daisy/Daisy Bell/If You Knew Suzie/Knees Up Mother Brown/The More We Are Together/She Was One Of The Early Birds/That's My Weakness Now/Three O'Clock In The Morning. Let's Have Another Party: Another Little Drink/Broken Doll/Bye Bye Blackbird/Honeysuckle And The Bee/I Wonder Where My Baby Is Tonight/Lily of Laguna/Nellie Dean/Sheik of Araby/Somebody Stole My Gal/When The Red Red Robin. Let's Have a Ding Dong: Happy Days Are Here Again/Oh Johnny Oh Johnny Oh/Oh You Beautiful Doll/Ain't She Sweet/Yes We Have No Bananas/I'm Forever Blowing Bubbles/I'll Be Your Sweetheart/If These Lips Could Only Speak/Who's Taking You Home Tonight. Make It a Party: Who Were You With Last Night/Hello Hello Who's Your Lady Friend/Yes Sir That's My Baby/Don't Dilly Dally On The Way/Beer Barrel Polka/After The Ball/Peggy O'Neil/Meet Me Tonight In Dreamland/I Belong To Glasgow/Down At The Old Bull And Bush. Let's Rock 'n Roll: Singin' The Blues/Green Door/See You Later Alligator/Shake Rattle And Roll/Rock Around The Clock/Razzle Dazzle. Let's Have a Ball: Music Music Music/This Ole House/Heartbreaker/Woody Woodpecker/Last Train To San Fernando/Bring A Little Water Sylvie/Puttin' On The Style/Don't You Rock Me Daddy-O. Piano Party: Baby Face/Comin' Thru' The Rye/Annie Laurie/Little Brown Jug/Let Him Go Let Him Tarry/Put Your Arms Around Me Honey/I'll Be With You In Apple Blossom Time/Shine On Harvest Moon/Blue Skies/I'll Never Say 'Never Again' Again/I'll See You In My Dreams. See also Various Artists (EPs & LPs) - All Star Hit Parade.

Brian AUGER – *See Julie DRISCOLL, Brian AUGER and the TRINITY*

AURRA *US, male/female vocal duo*   **18 wks**

Date	Title	Pos	Wks
4 May 85	**LIKE I LIKE IT** *10 TEN 45*	51	5 wks
19 Apr 86	**YOU AND ME TONIGHT** *10 TEN 71*	12	8 wks
21 Jun 86	**LIKE I LIKE IT (re-issue)** *10 TEN 126*	43	5 wks

David AUSTIN *UK, male vocalist*   **3 wks**

Date	Title	Pos	Wks
21 Jul 84	**TURN TO GOLD** *Parlophone R 6068*	68	3 wks

Patti AUSTIN *US, female vocalist*   **20 wks**

Date	Title	Pos	Wks
20 Jun 81	**RAZZAMATAZZ** *A & M AMS 8140 **	11	9 wks
12 Feb 83	**BABY COME TO ME** *Qwest K 15005 ***	11	10 wks
5 Sep 92	**I'LL KEEP YOUR DREAMS ALIVE** *Ammi AMMI 101 ****	68	1 wk

* Quincy Jones featuring Patti Austin ** Patti Austin and James Ingram
*** George Benson and Patti Austin

AUTUMN *UK, male vocal/instrumental group*   **6 wks**

Date	Title	Pos	Wks
16 Oct 71	**MY LITTLE GIRL** *Pye 7N 45090*	37	6 wks

Peter AUTY and the SINFONIA OF LONDON *UK, male vocalist with UK orchestra*   **9 wks**

Date	Title	Pos	Wks
14 Dec 85	**WALKING IN THE AIR** *Stiff LAD 1*	42	5 wks
19 Dec 87	**WALKING IN THE AIR (re-issue)** *CBS GA 3950*	37	4 wks

Label credits the Snowman featuring Peter Auty. See also Digital Dream Baby.

AVALON BOYS – *See LAUREL and HARDY with the AVALON BOYS*

Frankie AVALON *US, male vocalist*   **15 wks**

Date	Title	Pos	Wks
10 Oct 58	**GINGERBREAD** *HMV POP 517*	30	1 wk

24 Apr 59	VENUS *HMV POP 603*	16	6 wks
22 Jan 60	WHY *HMV POP 688*	20	4 wks
28 Apr 60	DON'T THROW AWAY ALL THOSE TEARDROPS *HMV POP 727*	37	4 wks

AVERAGE WHITE BAND　　45 wks
UK, male vocal/instrumental vocal group

22 Feb 75	● PICK UP THE PIECES *Atlantic K 10489*	6	9 wks
26 Apr 75	CUT THE CAKE *Atlantic K 10605*	31	4 wks
9 Oct 76	QUEEN OF MY SOUL *Atlantic K 10825*	23	7 wks
28 Apr 79	WALK ON BY *RCA XC 1087*	46	5 wks
25 Aug 79	WHEN WILL YOU BE MINE *RCA XB 1096*	49	5 wks
26 Apr 80	LET'S GO ROUND AGAIN PT.1 *RCA AWB 1*	12	11 wks
26 Jul 80	FOR YOU FOR LOVE *RCA AWB 2*	46	4 wks

AVONS　　22 wks
UK, male/female vocal group

13 Nov 59	● SEVEN LITTLE GIRLS SITTING IN THE BACK SEAT *Columbia DB 4363*	3	13 wks
7 Jul 60	WE'RE ONLY YOUNG ONCE *Columbia DB 4461*	49	1 wk
21 Jul 60	WE'RE ONLY YOUNG ONCE (re-entry) *Columbia DB 4461*	45	1 wk
27 Oct 60	FOUR LITTLE HEELS *Columbia DB 4522*	45	2 wks
1 Dec 60	FOUR LITTLE HEELS (re-entry) *Columbia DB 4522*	49	1 wk
26 Jan 61	RUBBER BALL *Columbia DB 4569*	30	4 wks

AWESOME 3　　4 wks
UK, male/female vocal/instrumental group

8 Sep 90	HARD UP *A & M AM 591*	55	3 wks
3 Oct 92	DON'T GO *Citybeat CBE 1271*	75	1 wk

Hoyt AXTON　　4 wks
US, male vocalist

7 Jun 80	DELLA AND THE DEALER *Young Blood YB 82*	48	4 wks

Roy AYERS　　12 wks
US, male vocalist/instrumentalist - vibraphone

21 Oct 78	GET ON UP, GET ON DOWN *Polydor AYERS 7*	41	4 wks
13 Jan 79	HEAT OF THE BEAT *Polydor POSP 16* *	43	5 wks
2 Feb 80	DON'T STOP THE FEELING *Polydor STEP 6*	56	3 wks

* Roy Ayers and Wayne Henderson

Charles AZNAVOUR　　29 wks
France, male vocalist

22 Sep 73	THE OLD FASHIONED WAY *Barclay BAR 20*	38	15 wks
22 Jun 74	★ SHE *Barclay BAR 26*	1	14 wks

AZTEC CAMERA　　72 wks
UK, male vocal/instrumental group

19 Feb 83	OBLIVIOUS *Rough Trade RT 122*	47	6 wks
4 Jun 83	WALK OUT TO WINTER *Rough Trade RT 132*	64	4 wks
5 Nov 83	OBLIVIOUS (re-issue) *WEA AZTEC 1*	18	11 wks
1 Sep 84	ALL I NEED IS EVERYTHING *WEA AC 1*	34	6 wks
13 Feb 88	HOW MEN ARE *WEA YZ 168*	25	9 wks
23 Apr 88	● SOMEWHERE IN MY HEART *WEA YZ 181*	3	14 wks
6 Aug 88	WORKING IN A GOLDMINE *WEA YZ 199*	31	5 wks
8 Oct 88	DEEP AND WIDE AND TALL *WEA YZ 154*	55	3 wks
7 Jul 90	THE CRYING SCENE *WEA YZ 492*	70	3 wks
6 Oct 90	GOOD MORNING BRITAIN *WEA YZ 521* *	19	8 wks
18 Jul 92	SPANISH HORSES *WEA YZ 688*	52	3 wks

* Aztec Camera and Mick Jones

AZYMUTH　　8 wks
Brazil, male instrumental group

12 Jan 80	JAZZ CARNIVAL *Milestone MRC 101*	19	8 wks

Bob AZZAM　　14 wks
Egypt, singing orchestra

26 May 60	MUSTAPHA *Decca F 21235*	23	14 wks

Derek B　　15 wks
UK, male rapper

27 Feb 88	GOODGROOVE *Music Of Life 7NOTE 12*	16	6 wks
7 May 88	BAD YOUNG BROTHER *Tuff Audio DRKB 1*	16	6 wks
2 Jul 88	WE'VE GOT THE JUICE *Tuff Audio DRKB 2*	56	3 wks

Eric B and RAKIM　　26 wks
US, male vocal/instrumental duo

7 Nov 87	PAID IN FULL *Fourth & Broadway BRW 78*	15	6 wks
20 Feb 88	MOVE THE CROWD *Fourth & Broadway BRW 88*	53	2 wks
12 Mar 88	I KNOW YOU GOT SOUL *Cooltempo COOL 146*	13	6 wks
2 Jul 88	FOLLOW THE LEADER *MCA MCA 1256*	21	5 wks
19 Nov 88	THE MICROPHONE FIEND *MCA MCA 1300*	74	1 wk
12 Aug 89	FRIENDS *MCA MCA 1352* *	21	6 wks

* Jody Watley with Eric B and Rakim

JAZZIE B – *See Maxi PRIEST; SOUL II SOUL*

Stevie B　　9 wks
US, male vocalist

23 Feb 91	● BECAUSE I LOVE YOU (THE POSTMAN SONG) *Polydor PO 126*	6	9 wks

Tairrie B　　2 wks
US, female rapper

1 Dec 90	MURDER SHE WROTE *MCA MCA 1455*	71	2 wks

B B and Q BAND　　15 wks
US, male vocal/instrumental group

18 Jul 81	ON THE BEAT *Capitol CL 202*	41	5 wks
6 Jul 85	GENIE *Cooltempo COOL 110* *	40	4 wks
20 Sep 86	(I'M A) DREAMER *Cooltempo COOL 132*	35	5 wks
17 Oct 87	RICOCHET *Cooltempo COOL 154*	71	1 wk

* Brooklyn Bronx and Queens

Alice BABS　　1 wk
Sweden, female vocalist

15 Aug 63	AFTER YOU'VE GONE *Fontana TF 409*	43	1 wk

BABY JUNE　　1 wk
UK, male vocalist - Tim Hegarty

15 Aug 92	HEY! WHAT'S YOUR NAME *Arista 115271*	75	1 wk

BABY O　　5 wks
US, male/female vocal/instrumental group

26 Jul 80	IN THE FOREST *Calibre CAB 505*	46	5 wks

BABY ROOTS　　1 wk
UK, male vocalist

1 Aug 92	ROCK ME BABY *ZYX ZYX 68027*	71	1 wk

BABYS US/UK, male vocal/instrumental group   **3 wks**

21 Jan 78	**ISN'T IT TIME** Chrysalis CHS 2173	45	3 wks

BACCARA Spain, female vocal duo   **25 wks**

17 Sep 77	★ **YES SIR I CAN BOOGIE** RCA PB 5526	1	16 wks
14 Jan 78	● **SORRY I'M A LADY** RCA PB 5555	8	9 wks

Burt BACHARACH US, orchestra and chorus   **11 wks**

20 May 65	● **TRAINS AND BOATS AND PLANES** London HL 9968	4	11 wks

BACHELORS Ireland, male vocal group   **187 wks**

24 Jan 63	● **CHARMAINE** Decca F 11559	.6	19 wks
4 Jul 63	**FARAWAY PLACES** Decca F 11666	.36	3 wks
29 Aug 63	**WHISPERING** Decca F 11712	.18	10 wks
23 Jan 64	★ **DIANE** Decca F 11799	.1	19 wks
19 Mar 64	● **I BELIEVE** Decca F 11857	.2	17 wks
4 Jun 64	● **RAMONA** Decca F 11910	.4	13 wks
13 Aug 64	● **I WOULDN'T TRADE YOU FOR THE WORLD** Decca F 11949	.4	16 wks
3 Dec 64	● **NO ARMS CAN EVER HOLD YOU** Decca F 12034	.7	12 wks
1 Apr 65	**TRUE LOVE FOR EVER MORE** Decca F 12108	.34	6 wks
20 May 65	● **MARIE** Decca F 12156	.9	12 wks
28 Oct 65	**IN THE CHAPEL IN THE MOONLIGHT** Decca F 12256	.27	10 wks
6 Jan 66	**HELLO DOLLY** Decca F 12309	.38	4 wks
17 Mar 66	● **THE SOUND OF SILENCE** Decca F 12351	.3	13 wks
7 Jul 66	**CAN I TRUST YOU** Decca F 12417	.26	7 wks
1 Dec 66	**WALK WITH FAITH IN YOUR HEART** Decca F 22523	.22	9 wks
6 Apr 67	**OH HOW I MISS YOU** Decca F 22592	.30	8 wks
5 Jul 67	**MARTA** Decca F 22634	.20	9 wks

BACHMAN-TURNER OVERDRIVE   **18 wks**
Canada, male vocal/instrumental group

16 Nov 74	● **YOU AIN'T SEEN NOTHIN' YET** Mercury 6167 025	2	12 wks
1 Feb 75	**ROLL ON DOWN THE HIGHWAY** Mercury 6167 071	.22	6 wks

BACKBEAT DISCIPLES – See Arthur BAKER

BACKROOM BOYS – See Frank IFIELD

BAD COMPANY UK, male vocal/instrumental group   **23 wks**

1 Jun 74	**CAN'T GET ENOUGH** Island WIP 6191	.15	8 wks
22 Mar 75	**GOOD LOVIN' GONE BAD** Island WIP 6223	.31	6 wks
30 Aug 75	**FEEL LIKE MAKIN' LOVE** Island WIP 6242	.20	9 wks

BAD ENGLISH UK/US, male vocal/instrumental group   **3 wks**

25 Nov 89	**WHEN I SEE YOU SMILE** Epic 655347 1	.61	3 wks

BAD MANNERS UK, male vocal/instrumental group   **111 wks**

1 Mar 80	**NE-NE NA-NA NA-NA NU-NU** Magnet MAG 164	.28	14 wks
14 Jun 80	**LIP UP FATTY** Magnet MAG 175	.15	14 wks
27 Sep 80	● **SPECIAL BREW** Magnet MAG 180	.3	13 wks
6 Dec 80	**LORRAINE** Magnet MAG 181	.21	12 wks
28 Mar 81	**JUST A FEELING** Magnet MAG 187	.13	9 wks
27 Jun 81	● **CAN CAN** Magnet MAG 190	.3	13 wks
26 Sep 81	● **WALKING IN THE SUNSHINE** Magnet MAG 197	.10	9 wks
21 Nov 81	**BUONA SERA** Magnet MAG 211	.34	9 wks

British Hit Singles Part One: Alphabetically by Artist
Date of chart entry/Title & catalogue no./Peak position reached/Weeks on chart
★ Number one   ● Top Ten   † still on chart at 31 Dec 1992
* = credited to act billed in footnote

1 May 82	**GOT NO BRAINS** Magnet MAG 216	.44	5 wks
31 Jul 82	● **MY GIRL LOLLIPOP (MY BOY LOLLIPOP)** Magnet MAG 232	.9	7 wks
30 Oct 82	**SAMSON AND DELILAH** Magnet MAG 236	.58	3 wks
14 May 83	**THAT'LL DO NICELY** Magnet MAG 243	.49	3 wks

BAD NEWS UK, male vocal group   **5 wks**

12 Sep 87	**BOHEMIAN RHAPSODY** EMI EM 24	.44	5 wks

BAD SEEDS – See Nick CAVE

Wally BADAROU France, male instrumentalist - keyboards   **6 wks**

19 Oct 85	**CHIEF INSPECTOR** Fourth & Broadway BRW 37	.46	6 wks

BADFINGER UK, male vocal/instrumental group   **34 wks**

10 Jan 70	● **COME AND GET IT** Apple 20	.4	11 wks
9 Jan 71	● **NO MATTER WHAT** Apple 31	.5	12 wks
29 Jan 72	● **DAY AFTER DAY** Apple 40	.10	11 wks

See also Various Artists (EPs and LPs) - The Apple EP.

BADMAN UK, male producer — Julian Brettle   **3 wks**

2 Feb 91	**MAGIC STYLE** Citybeat CBE 759	.61	3 wks

Joan BAEZ US, female vocalist   **47 wks**

6 May 65	**WE SHALL OVERCOME** Fontana TF 564	.26	10 wks
8 Jul 65	● **THERE BUT FOR FORTUNE** Fontana TF 587	.8	12 wks
2 Sep 65	**IT'S ALL OVER NOW BABY BLUE** Fontana TF 604	.22	8 wks
23 Dec 65	**FAREWELL ANGELINA** Fontana TF 639	.35	3 wks
20 Jan 66	**FAREWELL ANGELINA (re-entry)** Fontana TF 639	.49	1 wk
28 Jul 66	**PACK UP YOUR SORROWS** Fontana TF 727	.50	1 wk
9 Oct 71	● **THE NIGHT THEY DROVE OLD DIXIE DOWN** Vanguard VS 35138	.6	12 wks

Philip BAILEY US, male vocalist   **20 wks**

9 Mar 85	★ **EASY LOVER** CBS A 4915 *	.1	12 wks
18 May 85	**WALKING ON THE CHINESE WALL** CBS A 6202	.34	8 wks

* Philip Bailey (duet with Phil Collins)

Adrian BAKER UK, male vocalist   **8 wks**

19 Jul 75	● **SHERRY** Magnet MAG 34	.10	8 wks

See also Gidea Park.

Anita BAKER US, female vocalist   **20 wks**

15 Nov 86	**SWEET LOVE** Elektra EKR 44	.13	10 wks
31 Jan 87	**CAUGHT UP IN THE RAPTURE** Elektra EKR 49	.51	5 wks
8 Oct 88	**GIVING YOU THE BEST THAT I GOT** Elektra EKR 79	.55	3 wks
30 Jun 90	**TALK TO ME** Elektra EKR 111	.68	2 wks

Arthur BAKER US, male producer/multi-instrumentalist   7 wks

| 20 May 89 | IT'S YOUR TIME Breakout USA 654 * | 64 | 2 wks |
| 21 Oct 89 | THE MESSAGE IS LOVE Breakout USA 668 ** | 38 | 5 wks |

* Arthur Baker featuring Shirley Lewis ** Arthur Baker and the Backbeat Disciples featuring Al Green
See also Wally Jump Jr and the Criminal Element.

Hylda BAKER and Arthur MULLARD   6 wks
UK, female/male vocal duo

| 9 Sep 78 | YOU'RE THE ONE THAT I WANT Pye 7N 46121 | 22 | 6 wks |

George BAKER SELECTION   10 wks
Holland, male/female vocal/instrumental group

| 6 Sep 75 | ● PALOMA BLANCA Warner Bros. K 16541 | 10 | 10 wks |

BALAAM AND THE ANGEL   2 wks
UK, male vocal/instrumental group

| 29 Mar 86 | SHE KNOWS Virgin VS 842 | 70 | 2 wks |

Long John BALDRY UK, male vocalist   36 wks

8 Nov 67	★ LET THE HEARTACHES BEGIN Pye 7N 17385	1	13 wks
28 Aug 68	WHEN THE SUN COMES SHININ' THRU Pye 7N 17593	29	7 wks
23 Oct 68	MEXICO Pye 7N 17563	15	8 wks
29 Jan 69	IT'S TOO LATE NOW Pye 7N 17664	21	8 wks

Kenny BALL and his JAZZMEN   136 wks
UK, male jazz band, Kenny Ball vocals and trumpet

23 Feb 61	SAMANTHA Pye Jazz Today 7NJ 2040	13	15 wks
11 May 61	I STILL LOVE YOU ALL Pye Jazz 7NJ 2042	24	6 wks
31 Aug 61	SOMEDAY Pye Jazz 7NJ 2047	28	6 wks
9 Nov 61	● MIDNIGHT IN MOSCOW Pye Jazz 7NJ 2049	2	21 wks
15 Feb 62	● MARCH OF THE SIAMESE CHILDREN Pye Jazz 7NJ 2051	4	13 wks
17 May 62	● THE GREEN LEAVES OF SUMMER Pye Jazz 7NJ 2054	7	14 wks
23 Aug 62	SO DO I Pye Jazz 7NJ 2056	14	8 wks
18 Oct 62	THE PAY OFF Pye Jazz 7NJ 2061	23	6 wks
17 Jan 63	● SUKIYAKI Pye Jazz 7NJ 2062	10	13 wks
25 Apr 63	CASABLANCA Pye Jazz 7NJ 2064	21	11 wks
13 Jun 63	RONDO Pye Jazz 7NJ 2065	24	8 wks
22 Aug 63	ACAPULCO 1922 Pye Jazz 7NJ 2067	27	6 wks
11 Jun 64	HELLO DOLLY Pye Jazz 7NJ 2071	30	7 wks
19 Jul 67	WHEN I'M 64 Pye 7N 17348	43	2 wks

Michael BALL UK, male vocalist   27 wks

28 Jan 89	● LOVE CHANGES EVERYTHING Really Useful RUR 3	2	14 wks
28 Oct 89	THE FIRST MAN YOU REMEMBER Really Useful RUR 6 *	68	2 wks
10 Aug 91	IT'S STILL YOU Polydor PO 160	58	2 wks
25 Apr 92	ONE STEP OUT OF TIME Polydor PO 206	20	7 wks
12 Dec 92	IF I CAN DREAM (EP) Polydor PO 248	51	1 wk
26 Dec 92	IF I CAN DREAM (EP) (re-entry) Polydor PO 248	68†	1 wk

* Michael Ball and Diana Morrison
Tracks on If I Can Dream (EP): If I Can Dream/You Don't Have To Say You Love Me/Always On My Mind/Tell Me There's A Heaven.

BALTIMORA Ireland, male vocalist   12 wks

| 10 Aug 85 | ● TARZAN BOY Columbia DB 9102 | 3 | 12 wks |

BAM BAM US, male vocalist/multi-instrumentalist   2 wks

| 19 Mar 88 | GIVE IT TO ME Serious 7OUS 10 | 65 | 2 wks |

Afrika BAMBAATAA US, male vocalist   23 wks

28 Aug 82	PLANET ROCK Polydor POSP 497 *	53	3 wks
10 Mar 84	RENEGADES OF FUNK Tommy Boy AFR 1 *	30	4 wks
1 Sep 84	UNITY (PART 1 - THE THIRD COMING) Tommy Boy AFR 2 **	49	5 wks
27 Feb 88	RECKLESS EMI EM 41 ***	17	8 wks
12 Oct 91	JUST GET UP AND DANCE EMI USA MT 100	45	3 wks

* Afrika Bambaataa and the Soul Sonic Force ** Afrika Bambaataa and James Brown *** Afrika Bambaataa with UB40 and Family

BANANARAMA UK, female vocal group   198 wks

13 Feb 82	● IT AIN'T WHAT YOU DO IT'S THE WAY THAT YOU DO IT Chrysalis CHS 2570 *	4	10 wks
10 Apr 82	● REALLY SAYING SOMETHING Deram NANA 1 **	5	10 wks
3 Jul 82	● SHY BOY London NANA 2	4	11 wks
4 Dec 82	CHEERS THEN London NANA 3	45	7 wks
26 Feb 83	● NA NA HEY HEY KISS HIM GOODBYE London NANA 4	5	10 wks
9 Jul 83	● CRUEL SUMMER London NANA 5	8	10 wks
3 Mar 84	● ROBERT DE NIRO'S WAITING London NANA 6	3	11 wks
26 May 84	ROUGH JUSTICE London NANA 7	23	7 wks
24 Nov 84	HOTLINE TO HEAVEN London NANA 8	58	2 wks
24 Aug 85	DO NOT DISTURB London NANA 9	31	6 wks
31 May 86	● VENUS London NANA 10	8	13 wks
16 Aug 86	MORE THAN PHYSICAL London NANA 11	41	5 wks
14 Feb 87	TRICK OF THE NIGHT London NANA 12	32	5 wks
11 Jul 87	I HEARD A RUMOUR London NANA 13	14	9 wks
10 Oct 87	● LOVE IN THE FIRST DEGREE London NANA 14	3	12 wks
9 Jan 88	I CAN'T HELP IT London NANA 15	20	6 wks
9 Apr 88	● I WANT YOU BACK London NANA 16	5	10 wks
24 Sep 88	LOVE, TRUTH AND HONESTY London NANA 17	23	8 wks
19 Nov 88	NATHAN JONES London NANA 18	15	9 wks
25 Feb 89	● HELP London LON 222 ***	3	9 wks
10 Jun 89	CRUEL SUMMER (re-mix) London NANA 19	19	6 wks
28 Jul 90	ONLY YOUR LOVE London NANA 21	27	4 wks
5 Jan 91	PREACHER MAN London NANA 23	20	6 wks
20 Apr 91	LONG TRAIN RUNNING London NANA 24	30	5 wks
29 Aug 92	MOVIN' ON London NANA 25	24	5 wks
28 Nov 92	LAST THING ON MY MIND London NANA 26	71	2 wks

* Funboy Three and Bananarama ** Bananarama with Funboy Three
*** Bananarama/La Na Nee Nee Noo Noo
The listed flip side of Love In The First Degree was Mr Sleaze by Stock Aitken Waterman. Act were a duo for last two hits.

BAND Canada/US, male vocal/instrumental group   18 wks

| 18 Sep 68 | THE WEIGHT Capitol CL 15559 | 21 | 9 wks |
| 4 Apr 70 | RAG MAMA RAG Capitol CL 15629 | 16 | 9 wks |

BAND AID International, male/female vocal/instrumental group   26 wks

15 Dec 84	★ DO THEY KNOW IT'S CHRISTMAS? Mercury FEED 1	1	13 wks
7 Dec 85	● DO THEY KNOW IT'S CHRISTMAS? (re-entry) Mercury FEED 1	3	7 wks
23 Dec 89	★ DO THEY KNOW IT'S CHRISTMAS? PWL/Polydor FEED 2 *	1	6 wks

* Band Aid II

BAND AKA US, male vocal/instrumental group | 12 wks

15 May 82	GRACE *Epic EPC A 2376*	41	5 wks
5 Mar 83	JOY *Epic EPC A 3145*	24	7 wks

BAND OF GOLD | 11 wks
Holland, male/female vocal/instrumental group

14 Jul 84	LOVE SONGS ARE BACK AGAIN (MEDLEY) *RCA 428*	24	11 wks

BANDERAS UK, female vocal/instrumental duo | 16 wks

23 Feb 91	THIS IS YOUR LIFE *London LON 290*	16	10 wks
15 Jun 91	SHE SELLS *London LON 298*	41	6 wks

BANDWAGON – *See Johnny JOHNSON and the BANDWAGON*

Honey BANE UK, female vocalist | 8 wks

24 Jan 81	TURN ME ON TURN ME OFF *Zonophone Z 15*	37	5 wks
18 Apr 81	BABY LOVE *Zonophone Z 19*	58	3 wks

BANG UK, male vocal duo | 2 wks

6 May 89	YOU'RE THE ONE *RCA PB 42715*	74	2 wks

BANGLES US, female vocal/instrumental group | 94 wks

15 Feb 86 ●	MANIC MONDAY *CBS A 6796*	2	12 wks
26 Apr 86	IF SHE KNEW WHAT SHE WANTS *CBS A 7062*	31	7 wks
5 Jul 86	GOING DOWN TO LIVERPOOL *CBS A 7255*	56	3 wks
13 Sep 86 ●	WALK LIKE AN EGYPTIAN *CBS 650071 7*	3	19 wks
10 Jan 87	WALKING DOWN YOUR STREET *CBS BANGS 1*	16	6 wks
18 Apr 87	FOLLOWING *CBS BANGS 2*	55	3 wks
6 Feb 88	HAZY SHADE OF WINTER *Def Jam BANGS 3*	11	10 wks
5 Nov 88	IN YOUR ROOM *CBS BANGS 4*	35	6 wks
18 Feb 89 ★	ETERNAL FLAME *CBS BANGS 5*	1	18 wks
10 Jun 89	BE WITH YOU *CBS BANGS 6*	23	8 wks
14 Oct 89	I'LL SET YOU FREE *CBS BANGS 7*	74	1 wk
9 Jun 90	WALK LIKE AN EGYPTIAN (re-issue) *CBS BANGS 8*	73	1 wk

Tony BANKS – *See FISH*

BANNED UK, male vocal/instrumental group | 6 wks

17 Dec 77	LITTLE GIRL *Harvest HAR 5145*	36	6 wks

BANSHEES – *See SIOUXSIE and the BANSHEES*

BAR-KAYS US, male vocal/instrumental group | 15 wks

23 Aug 67	SOUL FINGER *Stax 601 014*	33	7 wks
22 Jan 77	SHAKE YOUR RUMP TO THE FUNK *Mercury 6167 417*	41	4 wks
12 Jan 85	SEXOMATIC *Club JAB 10*	51	4 wks

Chris BARBER'S JAZZ BAND | 30 wks
UK, male jazz band, Chris Barber - trombone

13 Feb 59 ●	PETITE FLEUR *Pye Nixa NJ 2026*	3	22 wks
31 Jul 59	PETITE FLEUR (re-entry) *Pye Nixa NJ 2026*	22	2 wks
4 Jan 62	REVIVAL *Columbia SCD 2166*	50	2 wks
1 Feb 62	REVIVAL (re-entry) *Columbia SCD 2166*	43	2 wks
9 Oct 62	LONESOME *Columbia DB 4333*	27	2 wks

BARBRA and NEIL – *See Barbra STREISAND; Neil DIAMOND*

BARCLAY JAMES HARVEST | 9 wks
UK, male vocal/instrumental group

2 Apr 77	LIVE EP *Polydor 2229 198*	49	1 wk
16 Apr 77	LIVE EP (re-entry) *Polydor 2229 198*	49	1 wk
26 Jan 80	LOVE ON THE LINE *Polydor POSP 97*	63	2 wks
22 Nov 80	LIFE IS FOR LIVING *Polydor POSP 195*	61	3 wks
21 May 83	JUST A DAY AWAY *Polydor POSP 585*	68	2 wks

Tracks on Live (EP): Rock'n'Roll Star/Medicine Man (Parts 1 & 2).

BARDO UK, male/female vocal duo | 8 wks

10 Apr 82 ●	ONE STEP FURTHER *Epic EPC A2265*	2	8 wks

BARNBRACK UK, male vocal/instrumental group | 7 wks

16 Mar 85	BELFAST *Homespun HS 092*	45	7 wks

Jimmy BARNES – *See INXS*

Richard BARNES UK, male vocalist | 10 wks

23 May 70	TAKE TO THE MOUNTAINS *Philips BF 1840*	35	6 wks
24 Oct 70	GO NORTH *Philips 6006 039*	49	1 wk
7 Nov 70	GO NORTH (re-entry) *Philips 6006 039*	38	3 wks

BARRACUDAS UK/US, male vocal/instrumental group | 6 wks

16 Aug 80	SUMMER FUN *EMI-Wipe Out Z 5*	37	6 wks

Wild Willy BARRETT – *See John OTWAY and Wild Willy BARRETT*

J. J. BARRIE Canada, male vocalist | 11 wks

24 Apr 76 ★	NO CHARGE *Power Exchange PX 209*	1	11 wks

Featured vocalist is Vicki Brown.

Ken BARRIE UK, male vocalist | 15 wks

10 Jul 82	POSTMAN PAT *Post Music PP 001*	44	8 wks
25 Dec 82	POSTMAN PAT (re-entry) *Post Music PP 001*	54	3 wks
24 Dec 83	POSTMAN PAT (2nd re-entry) *Post Music PP 001*	59	4 wks

BARRON KNIGHTS UK, male vocal/instrumental group | 94 wks

9 Jul 64 ●	CALL UP THE GROUPS *Columbia DB 7317*	3	13 wks
22 Oct 64	COME TO THE DANCE *Columbia DB 7375*	42	2 wks
25 Mar 65 ●	POP GO THE WORKERS *Columbia DB 7525*	5	13 wks
16 Dec 65 ●	MERRY GENTLE POPS *Columbia DB 7780*	9	7 wks
1 Dec 66	UNDER NEW MANAGEMENT *Columbia DB 8071*	15	9 wks
23 Oct 68	AN OLYMPIC RECORD *Columbia DB 8485*	35	4 wks
29 Oct 77 ●	LIVE IN TROUBLE *Epic EPC 5752*	7	10 wks
2 Dec 78 ●	A TASTE OF AGGRO *Epic EPC 6829*	3	10 wks
8 Dec 79	FOOD FOR THOUGHT *Epic EPC 8011*	46	6 wks
4 Oct 80	THE SIT SONG *Epic EPC 8994*	44	4 wks
6 Dec 80	NEVER MIND THE PRESENTS *Epic EPC 9070*	17	8 wks
5 Dec 81	BLACKBOARD JUMBLE *CBS A 1795*	52	5 wks
19 Mar 83	BUFFALO BILL'S LAST SCRATCH *Epic EPC A 3208*	49	3 wks

The front man played trombone in CHRIS BARBER'S JAZZ BAND, but Monty Sunshine was clarinetist on 'Petite Fleur'.

FONTELLA BASS is shown on 4 December, 1965, during a visit to promote 'Rescue Me'.

The BEE GEES are shown in a Florida studio in 1979 during their string of major hits.

Joe BARRY US, male vocalist — 1 wk

24 Aug 61	I'M A FOOL TO CARE *Mercury AMT 1149*	49	1 wk

John BARRY ORCHESTRA — 78 wks
UK, male instrumental group/orchestra

10 Mar 60	● HIT AND MISS *Columbia DB 4414* *	10	12 wks
28 Apr 60	BEAT FOR BEATNIKS *Columbia DB 4446*	40	2 wks
9 Jun 60	HIT AND MISS (re-entry) *Columbia DB 4414* *	45	1 wk
14 Jul 60	NEVER LET GO *Columbia DB 4480*	49	1 wk
18 Aug 60	BLUEBERRY HILL *Columbia DB 4480*	34	3 wks
8 Sep 60	WALK DON'T RUN *Columbia DB 4505* *	49	1 wk
22 Sep 60	WALK DON'T RUN (re-entry) *Columbia DB 4505* *	11	13 wks
8 Dec 60	BLACK STOCKINGS *Columbia DB 4554* *	27	9 wks
2 Mar 61	THE MAGNIFICENT SEVEN *Columbia DB 4598* *	48	1 wk
16 Mar 61	THE MAGNIFICENT SEVEN (re-entry) *Columbia DB 4598* *	45	2 wks
6 Apr 61	THE MAGNIFICENT SEVEN (2nd re-entry) *Columbia DB 4598* *	50	1 wk
8 Jun 61	THE MAGNIFICENT SEVEN (3rd re-entry) *Columbia DB 4598* *	47	1 wk
26 Apr 62	CUTTY SARK *Columbia DB 4806* *	35	2 wks
1 Nov 62	JAMES BOND THEME *Columbia DB 4898*	13	11 wks
21 Nov 63	FROM RUSSIA WITH LOVE *Ember S 181*	44	1 wk
19 Dec 63	FROM RUSSIA WITH LOVE (re-entry) *Ember S 181*	39	2 wks
11 Dec 71	THE PERSUADERS *CBS 7469*	13	15 wks

* John Barry Seven

Len BARRY US, male vocalist — 24 wks

4 Nov 65	● 1-2-3 *Brunswick 05942*	3	14 wks
13 Jan 66	● LIKE A BABY *Brunswick 05949*	10	10 wks

Lionel BART UK, male vocalist — 3 wks

25 Nov 89	HAPPY ENDINGS (GIVE YOURSELF A PINCH) *EMI EM 121*	68	1 wk
23 Dec 89	HAPPY ENDINGS (GIVE YOURSELF A PINCH) (re-entry) *EMI EM 121*	71	2 wks

BAS NOIR US, female vocal duo — 1 wk

11 Feb 89	MY LOVE IS MAGIC *10 TEN 257*	73	1 wk

Rob BASE and DJ E-Z ROCK US, male vocal duo — 19 wks

16 Apr 88	IT TAKES TWO *Citybeat CBE 724*	24	6 wks
14 Jan 89	GET ON THE DANCE FLOOR *Supreme SUPE 139*	14	7 wks
4 Mar 89	IT TAKES TWO (re-entry) *Citybeat CBE 724*	49	3 wks
22 Apr 89	JOY AND PAIN *Supreme SUPE 143*	47	3 wks

BASEMENT BOYS – *See Ultra NATE*

BASIA Poland, female vocalist — 7 wks

23 Jan 88	PROMISES *Epic BASH 4*	48	4 wks
28 May 88	TIME AND TIDE *Epic BASH 5*	61	3 wks

Count BASIE – *See Frank SINATRA*

Toni BASIL US, female vocalist — 16 wks

6 Feb 82	● MICKEY *Radialchoice TIC 4*	2	12 wks
1 May 82	NOBODY *Radialchoice TIC 2*	52	4 wks

Alfie BASS – *See Michael MEDWIN, Bernard BRESSLAW, Alfie BASS and Leslie FYSON*

Fontella BASS US, female vocalist — 15 wks

2 Dec 65	RESCUE ME *Chess CRS 8023*	11	10 wks
20 Jan 66	RECOVERY *Chess CRS 8027*	32	5 wks

BASS-O-MATIC UK, male multi-instrumentalist — 19 wks

12 May 90	IN THE REALM OF THE SENSES *Virgin VS 1265*	66	3 wks
1 Sep 90	● FASCINATING RHYTHM *Virgin VS 1274*	9	11 wks
22 Dec 90	EASE ON BY *Virgin VS 1295*	61	4 wks
3 Aug 91	FUNKY LOVE VIBRATIONS *Virgin VS 1355*	71	1 wk

Shirley BASSEY UK, female vocalist — 315 wks

15 Feb 57	● BANANA BOAT SONG *Philips PB 668*	8	10 wks
23 Aug 57	FIRE DOWN BELOW *Philips PB 723*	30	1 wk
6 Sep 57	YOU YOU ROMEO *Philips PB 723*	29	2 wks
19 Dec 58	AS I LOVE YOU *Philips PB 845*	27	2 wks
26 Dec 58	● KISS ME HONEY HONEY KISS ME *Philips PB 860*	3	17 wks
9 Jan 59	★ AS I LOVE YOU (re-entry) *Philips PB 845*	1	17 wks
31 Mar 60	WITH THESE HANDS *Columbia DB 4421*	38	2 wks
21 Apr 60	WITH THESE HANDS (re-entry) *Columbia DB 4421*	31	2 wks
12 May 60	WITH THESE HANDS (2nd re-entry) *Columbia DB 4421*	41	2 wks
4 Aug 60	● AS LONG AS HE NEEDS ME *Columbia DB 4490*	2	30 wks
11 May 61	● YOU'LL NEVER KNOW *Columbia DB 4643*	6	17 wks
27 Jul 61	★ REACH FOR THE STARS/CLIMB EV'RY MOUNTAIN *Columbia DB 4685*	1	16 wks
23 Nov 61	● I'LL GET BY *Columbia DB 4737*	10	8 wks
23 Nov 61	REACH FOR THE STARS/CLIMB EV'RY MOUNTAIN (re-entry) *Columbia DB 4685*	40	2 wks
15 Feb 62	TONIGHT *Columbia DB 4777*	21	8 wks
26 Apr 62	AVE MARIA *Columbia DB 4816*	34	4 wks
31 May 62	FAR AWAY *Columbia DB 4836*	24	13 wks
30 Aug 62	● WHAT NOW MY LOVE *Columbia DB 4882*	5	17 wks
28 Feb 63	WHAT KIND OF FOOL AM I? *Columbia DB 4974*	47	2 wks
26 Sep 63	● I (WHO HAVE NOTHING) *Columbia DB 7113*	6	20 wks
23 Jan 64	MY SPECIAL DREAM *Columbia DB 7185*	32	7 wks
9 Apr 64	GONE *Columbia DB 7248*	36	5 wks
15 Oct 64	GOLDFINGER *Columbia DB 7360*	21	9 wks
20 May 65	NO REGRETS *Columbia DB 7535*	39	4 wks
11 Oct 67	BIG SPENDER *United Artists UP 1192*	21	15 wks
20 Jun 70	● SOMETHING *United Artists UP 35125*	4	21 wks
2 Jan 71	THE FOOL ON THE HILL *United Artists UP 35156*	48	1 wk
23 Jan 71	SOMETHING (re-entry) *United Artists UP 35125*	50	1 wk
27 Mar 71	(WHERE DO I BEGIN) LOVE STORY *United Artists UP 35194*	34	9 wks
7 Aug 71	FOR ALL WE KNOW *United Artists UP 35267*	46	1 wk
21 Aug 71	● FOR ALL WE KNOW (re-entry) *United Artists UP 35267*	6	23 wks
15 Jan 72	DIAMONDS ARE FOREVER *United Artists UP 35293*	38	6 wks
3 Mar 73	● NEVER NEVER NEVER *United Artists UP 35490*	8	18 wks
14 Jul 73	NEVER NEVER NEVER (re-entry) *United Artists UP 35490*	48	1 wk
22 Aug 87	THE RHYTHM DIVINE *Mercury MER 253* *	54	2 wks

* Yello featuring Shirley Bassey

BASSHEADS UK, male/female vocal/instrumental group — 14 wks

16 Nov 91	● IS THERE ANYBODY OUT THERE *Deconstruction R 6303*	5	8 wks
30 May 92	BACK TO THE OLD SCHOOL *Deconstruction R 6310*	12	4 wks

28 Nov 92	WHO CAN MAKE ME FEEL GOOD		
	Deconstruction R 6326	38	2 wks

Mike BATT with the NEW EDITION   **8 wks**
UK, male vocalist with male/female vocal group

16 Aug 75	● SUMMERTIME CITY *Epic EPC 3460*	4	8 wks

BAUHAUS *UK, male vocal/instrumental group*   **35 wks**

18 Apr 81	KICK IN THE EYE *Beggars Banquet BEG 54*	59	3 wks
4 Jul 81	THE PASSIONS OF LOVERS *Beggars Banquet BEG 59*	56	2 wks
6 Mar 82	KICK IN THE EYE EP *Beggars Banquet BEG 74*	45	4 wks
19 Jun 82	SPIRIT *Beggars Banquet BEG 79*	42	5 wks
9 Oct 82	ZIGGY STARDUST *Beggars Banquet BEG 83*	15	7 wks
22 Jan 83	LAGARTIJA NICK *Beggars Banquet BEG 88*	44	4 wks
9 Apr 83	SHE'S IN PARTIES *Beggars Banquet BEG 91*	26	6 wks
29 Oct 83	THE SINGLES 1981-83 *Beggars Banquet BEG 100E*	52	4 wks

Tracks on Kick In The Eye (EP): *Kick In The Eye (Searching For Satori)/Harry/Earwax.*

Les BAXTER *US, orchestra and chorus*   **9 wks**

13 May 55	● UNCHAINED MELODY *Capitol CL 14257*	10	9 wks

BAY CITY ROLLERS *UK, male vocal/instrumental group* **113 wks**

18 Sep 71	● KEEP ON DANCING *Bell 1164*	9	13 wks
9 Feb 74	● REMEMBER (SHA-LA-LA) *Bell 1338*	6	12 wks
27 Apr 74	● SHANG-A-LANG *Bell 1355*	2	10 wks
27 Jul 74	● SUMMERLOVE SENSATION *Bell 1369*	3	10 wks
12 Oct 74	● ALL OF ME LOVES ALL OF YOU *Bell 1382*	4	10 wks
8 Mar 75	★ BYE BYE BABY *Bell 1409*	1	16 wks
12 Jul 75	★ GIVE A LITTLE LOVE *Bell 1425*	1	9 wks
22 Nov 75	● MONEY HONEY *Bell 1461*	3	9 wks
10 Apr 76	● LOVE ME LIKE I LOVE YOU *Bell 1477*	4	6 wks
11 Sep 76	● I ONLY WANNA BE WITH YOU *Bell 1493*	4	9 wks
7 May 77	IT'S A GAME *Arista 108*	16	6 wks
30 Jul 77	YOU MADE ME BELIEVE IN MAGIC *Arista 127*	34	3 wks

BBG *UK, male vocal/instrumental group*   **7 wks**

28 Apr 90	SNAPPINESS *Urban URB 54*	28	5 wks
11 Aug 90	SOME KIND OF HEAVEN *Urban URB 59*	65	2 wks

BE BOP DELUXE *UK, male vocal/instrumental group* **13 wks**

21 Feb 76	SHIPS IN THE NIGHT *Harvest HAR 5104*	23	8 wks
13 Nov 76	HOT VALVES EP *Harvest HAR 5117*	36	5 wks

Tracks on Hot Valves EP: *Maid In Heaven/Blazing Apostles/Jet Silver And The Dolls Of Venus/Bring Back The Spark.*

BEACH BOYS *US, male vocal/instrumental group* **277 wks**

1 Aug 63	SURFIN' USA *Capitol CL 15305*	34	7 wks
9 Jul 64	● I GET AROUND *Capitol CL 15350*	7	13 wks
29 Oct 64	WHEN I GROW UP (TO BE A MAN) *Capitol CL 15361*	44	2 wks
19 Nov 64	WHEN I GROW UP (TO BE A MAN) (re-entry) *Capitol CL 15361*	27	5 wks
21 Jan 65	DANCE DANCE DANCE *Capitol CL 15370*	24	4 wks
3 Jun 65	HELP ME RHONDA *Capitol CL 15392*	27	10 wks
2 Sep 65	CALIFORNIA GIRLS *Capitol CL 15409*	26	8 wks
17 Feb 66	● BARBARA ANN *Capitol CL 15432*	3	10 wks
21 Apr 66	● SLOOP JOHN B *Capitol CL 15441*	2	15 wks
28 Jul 66	● GOD ONLY KNOWS *Capitol CL 15459*	2	14 wks
3 Nov 66	★ GOOD VIBRATIONS *Capitol CL 15475*	1	13 wks
4 May 67	● THEN I KISSED HER *Capitol CL 15502*	4	11 wks
23 Aug 67	● HEROES AND VILLAINS *Capitol CL 15510*	8	9 wks
22 Nov 67	WILD HONEY *Capitol CL 15521*	29	6 wks
17 Jan 68	DARLIN' *Capitol CL 15527*	11	14 wks
8 May 68	FRIENDS *Capitol CL 15545*	25	7 wks
24 Jul 68	★ DO IT AGAIN *Capitol CL 15554*	1	14 wks
25 Dec 68	BLUEBIRDS OVER THE MOUNTAIN *Capitol CL 15572*	33	5 wks
26 Feb 69	● I CAN HEAR MUSIC *Capitol CL 15584*	10	13 wks
11 Jun 69	● BREAK AWAY *Capitol CL 15598*	6	11 wks
16 May 70	● COTTONFIELDS *Capitol CL 15640*	5	17 wks
3 Mar 73	CALIFORNIA SAGA - CALIFORNIA *Reprise K 14232*	37	5 wks
3 Jul 76	GOOD VIBRATIONS (re-issue) *Capitol CL 15875*	18	7 wks
10 Jul 76	ROCK AND ROLL MUSIC *Reprise K 14440*	36	4 wks
31 Mar 79	HERE COMES THE NIGHT *Caribou CRB 7204*	37	4 wks
16 Jun 79	● LADY LYNDA *Caribou CRB 7427*	6	11 wks
29 Sep 79	SUMAHAMA *Caribou CRB 7846*	45	4 wks
29 Aug 81	BEACH BOYS MEDLEY *Capitol CL 213*	47	4 wks
22 Aug 87	● WIPEOUT *Urban URB 5 *	2	12 wks
19 Nov 88	KOKOMO *Elektra EKR 85*	25	9 wks
2 Jun 90	WOULDN'T IT BE NICE *Capitol CL 579*	58	1 wk
29 Jun 91	DO IT AGAIN (re-issue) *Capitol EMCT 1*	61	2 wks

* Fat Boys and the Beach Boys

Walter BEASLEY *US, male vocalist*   **3 wks**

23 Jan 88	I'M SO HAPPY *Urban URB 14*	70	3 wks

BEASTIE BOYS *US, male rap group*   **33 wks**

28 Feb 87	(YOU GOTTA) FIGHT FOR YOUR RIGHT (TO PARTY) *Def Jam 650418 7*	11	11 wks
30 May 87	NO SLEEP TILL BROOKLYN *Def Jam BEAST 1*	14	7 wks
18 Jul 87	● SHE'S ON IT *Def Jam BEAST 2*	10	8 wks
3 Oct 87	GIRLS /SHE'S CRAFTY *Def Jam BEAST 3*	34	4 wks
11 Apr 92	PASS THE MIC *Capitol 12CL 653*	47	2 wks
4 Jul 92	FROZEN METAL HEAD EP *Capitol 12CL 665*	55	1 wk

Tracks on Frozen Metal Head EP: *Jimmy James/Jimmy James (Original)/Drinkin' Wine/The Blue Nun.*

BEAT *UK, male vocal/instrumental group*   **90 wks**

8 Dec 79	● TEARS OF A CLOWN/RANKING FULL STOP *2 Tone CHS TT 6*	6	11 wks
23 Feb 80	● HANDS OFF - SHE'S MINE *Go Feet FEET 1*	9	9 wks
3 May 80	● MIRROR IN THE BATHROOM *Go Feet FEET 2*	4	9 wks
16 Aug 80	BEST FRIEND/STAND DOWN MARGARET (DUB) *Go Feet FEET 3*	22	9 wks
13 Dec 80	● TOO NICE TO TALK TO *Go Feet FEET 4*	7	11 wks
18 Apr 81	DROWNING/ALL OUT TO GET YOU *Go Feet FEET 6*	22	8 wks
20 Jun 81	DOORS OF YOUR HEART *Go Feet FEET 9*	33	6 wks
5 Dec 81	HIT IT *Go Feet FEET 11*	70	2 wks
17 Apr 82	SAVE IT FOR LATER *Go Feet FEET 333*	47	4 wks
18 Sep 82	JEANETTE *Go Feet FEET 15*	45	3 wks
4 Dec 82	I CONFESS *Go Feet FEET 16*	54	3 wks
30 Apr 83	● CAN'T GET USED TO LOSING YOU *Go Feet FEET 17*	3	11 wks
2 Jul 83	ACKEE 1-2-3 *Go Feet FEET 18*	54	4 wks

BEAT SYSTEM *UK, male vocal/instrumental group* **2 wks**

3 Mar 90	WALK ON THE WILD SIDE *Fourth & Broadway BRW 163*	63	2 wks

BEATLES *UK, male vocal/instrumental group* **434 wks**

11 Oct 62	LOVE ME DO *Parlophone R 4949*	17	18 wks
17 Jan 63	● PLEASE PLEASE ME *Parlophone R 4983*	2	18 wks
18 Apr 63	★ FROM ME TO YOU *Parlophone R 5015*	1	21 wks

Date	Title	Position	Weeks
6 Jun 63	MY BONNIE *Polydor NH 66833* *	48	1 wk
29 Aug 63 ★	SHE LOVES YOU *Parlophone R 5055*	1	31 wks
5 Dec 63 ★	I WANT TO HOLD YOUR HAND *Parlophone R 5084*	1	21 wks
26 Mar 64 ★	CAN'T BUY ME LOVE *Parlophone R 5114*	1	14 wks
9 Apr 64	SHE LOVES YOU (re-entry) *Parlophone R 5055*	42	2 wks
14 May 64	I WANT TO HOLD YOUR HAND (re-entry) *Parlophone R 5084*	48	1 wk
11 Jun 64	AIN'T SHE SWEET *Polydor 52 317*	29	6 wks
9 Jul 64	CAN'T BUY ME LOVE (re-entry) *Parlophone R 5114*	47	1 wk
16 Jul 64 ★	A HARD DAY'S NIGHT *Parlophone R 5160*	1	13 wks
3 Dec 64 ★	I FEEL FINE *Parlophone R 5200*	1	13 wks
15 Apr 65 ★	TICKET TO RIDE *Parlophone R 5265*	1	12 wks
29 Jul 65 ★	HELP! *Parlophone R 5305*	1	14 wks
9 Dec 65 ★	DAY TRIPPER/WE CAN WORK IT OUT *Parlophone R 5389*	1	12 wks
16 Jun 66 ★	PAPERBACK WRITER *Parlophone R 5452*	1	11 wks
11 Aug 66 ★	YELLOW SUBMARINE/ELEANOR RIGBY *Parlophone R 5493*	1	13 wks
23 Feb 67 ●	PENNY LANE/STRAWBERRY FIELDS FOREVER *Parlophone R 5570*	2	11 wks
12 Jul 67 ★	ALL YOU NEED IS LOVE *Parlophone R 5620*	1	13 wks
29 Nov 67 ★	HELLO GOODBYE *Parlophone R 5655*	1	12 wks
13 Dec 67 ●	MAGICAL MYSTERY TOUR (DOUBLE EP) *Parlophone SMMT/MMT 1*	2	12 wks
20 Mar 68 ★	LADY MADONNA *Parlophone R 5675*	1	8 wks
4 Sep 68 ★	HEY JUDE *Apple R 5722*	1	16 wks
23 Apr 69 ★	GET BACK *Apple R 5777* **	1	17 wks
4 Jun 69 ★	BALLAD OF JOHN AND YOKO *Apple R 5786*	1	14 wks
8 Nov 69 ●	SOMETHING/COME TOGETHER *Apple R 5814*	4	12 wks
14 Mar 70 ●	LET IT BE *Apple R 5833*	2	9 wks
24 Oct 70	LET IT BE (re-entry) *Apple R 5833*	43	1 wk
13 Mar 76 ●	YESTERDAY *Apple R 6013*	8	7 wks
27 Mar 76	HEY JUDE (re-entry) *Apple R 5722*	12	7 wks
27 Mar 76	PAPERBACK WRITER (re-entry) *Parlophone R 5452*	23	5 wks
3 Apr 76	GET BACK (re-entry) *Apple R 5777* **	28	5 wks
3 Apr 76	STRAWBERRY FIELDS FOREVER (re-entry) *Parlophone R 5570*	32	3 wks
10 Apr 76	HELP! (re-entry) *Parlophone R 5305*	37	3 wks
10 Jul 76	BACK IN THE U.S.S.R. *Parlophone R 6016*	19	6 wks
7 Oct 78	SGT. PEPPER'S LONELY HEARTS CLUB BAND - WITH A LITTLE HELP FROM MY FRIENDS *Parlophone R 6022*	63	3 wks
5 Jun 82 ●	BEATLES MOVIE MEDLEY *Parlophone R 6055*	10	9 wks
16 Oct 82 ●	LOVE ME DO (re-entry) *Parlophone R 4949*	4	7 wks
22 Jan 83	PLEASE PLEASE ME (re-entry) *Parlophone R 4983*	29	4 wks
23 Apr 83	FROM ME TO YOU (re-entry) *Parlophone R 5015*	40	4 wks
3 Sep 83	SHE LOVES YOU (2nd re-entry) *Parlophone R 5055*	45	3 wks
26 Nov 83	I WANT TO HOLD YOUR HAND (2nd re-entry) *Parlophone R 5084*	62	2 wks
31 Mar 84	CAN'T BUY ME LOVE (2nd re-entry) *Parlophone R 5114*	53	2 wks
21 Jul 84	A HARD DAY'S NIGHT (re-entry) *Parlophone R 5160*	52	2 wks
8 Dec 84	I FEEL FINE (re-entry) *Parlophone R 5200*	65	1 wk
20 Apr 85	TICKET TO RIDE (re-entry) *Parlophone R 5265*	70	2 wks
30 Aug 86	ELEANOR RIGBY/YELLOW SUBMARINE (re-entry) *Parlophone R 5493*	63	1 wk
28 Feb 87	PENNY LANE/STRAWBERRY FIELDS FOREVER (2nd re-entry) *Parlophone R 5570*	65	2 wks
18 Jul 87	ALL YOU NEED IS LOVE (re-entry) *Parlophone R 5620*	47	3 wks
5 Dec 87	HELLO GOODBYE (re-entry) *Parlophone R 5655*	63	1 wk
26 Mar 88	LADY MADONNA (re-entry) *Parlophone R 5675*	67	1 wk
10 Sep 88	HEY JUDE (re-entry) *Apple 5722*	52	2 wks
22 Apr 89	GET BACK (2nd re-entry) *Apple R 5777* **	74	1 wk
17 Oct 92	LOVE ME DO (2nd re-entry) *Parlophone R 4949*	53	1 wk

* Tony Sheridan and the Beatles ** Beatles with Billy Preston

Tracks on Magical Mystery Tour (EP): *Magical Mystery Tour/Your Mother Should Know/I Am The Walrus/Fool On The Hill/Flying/Blue Jay Way.*

BEATMASTERS UK, *male/female instrumental group*   47 wks

Date	Title	Position	Weeks
9 Jan 88 ●	ROK DA HOUSE *Rhythm King LEFT 11* *	5	11 wks
24 Sep 88	BURN IT UP *Rhythm King LEFT 27* **	14	10 wks
22 Apr 89 ●	WHO'S IN THE HOUSE *Rhythm King LEFT 31* ***	8	9 wks
12 Aug 89 ●	HEY DJ I CAN'T DANCE TO THAT MUSIC YOU'RE PLAYING/SKA TRAIN *Rhythm King LEFT 34* ****	7	11 wks
2 Dec 89	WARM LOVE *Rhythm King LEFT 37* *****	51	2 wks

Date	Title	Position	Weeks
21 Sep 91	BOULEVARD OF BROKEN DREAMS *Rhythm King 6573617*	62	1 wk
16 May 92	DUNNO WHAT IT IS (ABOUT YOU) *Rhythm King 6580017* ******	43	3 wks

* Beatmasters featuring the Cookie Crew ** Beatmasters with P.P. Arnold *** Beatmasters featuring Merlin **** Beatmasters featuring Betty Boo ***** Beatmasters featuring Claudia Fontaine ****** Beatmasters featuring Elaine Vassell

BEATS INTERNATIONAL   30 wks
UK, *male/female vocal/instrumental group*

Date	Title	Position	Weeks
10 Feb 90 ★	DUB BE GOOD TO ME *Go Beat GOD 39* *	1	13 wks
12 May 90 ●	WON'T TALK ABOUT IT *Go Beat GOD 43*	9	7 wks
15 Sep 90	BURUNDI BLUES *Go Beat GOD 45*	51	3 wks
2 Mar 91	ECHO CHAMBER *Go Beat GOD 51*	60	2 wks
21 Sep 91	THE SUN DOESN'T SHINE *Go Beat GOD 59*	66	2 wks
23 Nov 91	IN THE GHETTO *Go Beat GOD 64*	44	3 wks

* Beats International featuring Lindy Layton

BEAUTIFUL SOUTH   65 wks
UK, *male/female vocal/instrumental group*

Date	Title	Position	Weeks
3 Jun 89 ●	SONG FOR WHOEVER *Go! Discs GOD 32*	2	11 wks
23 Sep 89 ●	YOU KEEP IT ALL IN *Go! Discs GOD 35*	8	8 wks
2 Dec 89	I'LL SAIL THIS SHIP ALONE *Go! Discs GOD 38*	31	8 wks
6 Oct 90 ★	A LITTLE TIME *Go! Discs GOD 47*	1	14 wks
8 Dec 90	MY BOOK *Go! Discs GOD 48*	43	6 wks
16 Mar 91	LET LOVE SPEAK UP ITSELF *Go! Discs GOD 53*	51	2 wks
11 Jan 92	OLD RED EYES IS BACK *Go! Discs GOD 66*	22	6 wks
14 Mar 92	WE ARE EACH OTHER *Go! Discs GOD 71*	30	3 wks
13 Jun 92	BELL BOTTOMED TEAR *Go! Discs GOD 78*	16	5 wks
26 Sep 92	36D *Go! Discs GOD 88*	46	2 wks

Gilbert BECAUD *France, male vocalist*   12 wks

Date	Title	Position	Weeks
29 Mar 75 ●	A LITTLE LOVE AND UNDERSTANDING *Decca F 13537*	10	12 wks

Jeff BECK *UK, male vocalist/instrumentalist - guitar*   57 wks

Date	Title	Position	Weeks
23 Mar 67	HI-HO SILVER LINING *Columbia DB 8151*	14	14 wks
2 Aug 67	TALLYMAN *Columbia DB 8227*	30	3 wks
28 Feb 68	LOVE IS BLUE *Columbia DB 8359*	23	7 wks
9 Jul 69	GOO GOO BARABAJAGAL (LOVE IS HOT) *Pye 7N 17778* *	12	9 wks
4 Nov 72	HI-HO SILVER LINING (re-issue) *RAK RR 3*	17	11 wks
5 May 73	I'VE BEEN DRINKING *RAK RR 4* **	27	6 wks
9 Oct 82	HI-HO SILVER LINING (re-entry of re-issue) *RAK RR 3*	62	4 wks
7 Mar 92	PEOPLE GET READY *Epic 6577567* **	49	3 wks

* Donovan with the Jeff Beck Group ** Jeff Beck and Rod Stewart

Robin BECK *US, female vocalist*   13 wks

Date	Title	Position	Weeks
22 Oct 88 ★	FIRST TIME *Mercury MER 270*	1	13 wks

Peter BECKETT – *See Barry GRAY ORCHESTRA*

BEDAZZLED UK, *male vocal/instrumental group*   1 wk

Date	Title	Position	Weeks
4 Jul 92	SUMMER SONG *Columbia 6581627*	73	1 wk

BEDROCKS UK, *male vocal/instrumental group*   7 wks

Date	Title	Position	Weeks
18 Dec 68	OB-LA-DI OB-LA-DA *Columbia DB 8516*	20	7 wks

Celi BEE and the BUZZY BUNCH

1 wk

US, male/female vocal/instrumental group

17 Jun 78   **HOLD YOUR HORSES BABE** *TK TKR 6032* ....**72** 1 wk

BEE GEES *UK, male vocal/instrumental group*

299 wks

27 Apr 67	**NEW YORK MINING DISASTER 1941** *Polydor 56 161* **12**	10 wks
12 Jul 67	**TO LOVE SOMEBODY** *Polydor 56 178* **50**	1 wk
26 Jul 67	**TO LOVE SOMEBODY (re-entry)** *Polydor 56 178* **41**	4 wks
20 Sep 67 ★	**MASSACHUSETTS** *Polydor 56 192* **1**	17 wks
22 Nov 67 ●	**WORLD** *Polydor 56 220* **9**	16 wks
31 Jan 68 ●	**WORDS** *Polydor 56 229* **8**	10 wks
27 Mar 68	**JUMBO/THE SINGER SANG HIS SONG**	
	Polydor 56 242 ....**25**	7 wks
7 Aug 68 ★	**I'VE GOTTA GET A MESSAGE TO YOU**	
	Polydor 56 273 ....**1**	15 wks
19 Feb 69 ●	**FIRST OF MAY** *Polydor 56 304* **6**	11 wks
4 Jun 69	**TOMORROW TOMORROW** *Polydor 56 331* **23**	8 wks
16 Aug 69 ●	**DON'T FORGET TO REMEMBER** *Polydor 56 343* **2**	15 wks
28 Mar 70	**I.O.I.O.** *Polydor 56 377* **49**	1 wk
5 Dec 70	**LONELY DAYS** *Polydor 2001 104* **33**	9 wks
29 Jan 72	**MY WORLD** *Polydor 2058 185* **16**	9 wks
22 Jul 72 ●	**RUN TO ME** *Polydor 2058 255* **9**	10 wks
28 Jun 75 ●	**JIVE TALKIN'** *RSO 2090 160* **5**	11 wks
31 Jul 76 ●	**YOU SHOULD BE DANCING** *RSO 2090 195* **5**	10 wks
13 Nov 76	**LOVE SO RIGHT** *RSO 2090 207* **41**	4 wks
29 Oct 77 ●	**HOW DEEP IS YOUR LOVE** *RSO 2090 259* **3**	15 wks
4 Feb 78 ●	**STAYIN' ALIVE** *RSO 2090 267* **4**	12 wks
15 Apr 78 ★	**NIGHT FEVER** *RSO 002* **1**	20 wks
13 May 78	**STAYIN' ALIVE (re-entry)** *RSO 2090 267* **63**	6 wks
25 Nov 78 ●	**TOO MUCH HEAVEN** *RSO 25* **3**	13 wks
17 Feb 79 ★	**TRAGEDY** *RSO 27* **1**	10 wks
14 Apr 79	**LOVE YOU INSIDE OUT** *RSO 31* **13**	9 wks
5 Jan 80	**SPIRITS (HAVING FLOWN)** *RSO 52* **16**	6 wks
17 Sep 83	**SOMEONE BELONGING TO SOMEONE** *RSO 96* **49**	4 wks
26 Sep 87 ★	**YOU WIN AGAIN** *Warner Bros. W 8351* **1**	15 wks
12 Dec 87	**E.S.P.** *Warner Bros. W 8139* **51**	5 wks
15 Apr 89	**ORDINARY LIVES** *Warner Bros. W 7523* **54**	3 wks
24 Jun 89	**ONE** *Warner Bros. W 2916* **71**	1 wk
2 Mar 91 ●	**SECRET LOVE** *Warner Bros. W 0014* **5**	11 wks

Act was UK/Australia up to and including Tomorrow Tomorrow.

BEF – *See Lalah HATHAWAY*

BEGGAR and CO *UK, male vocal/instrumental group*

15 wks

7 Feb 81	**(SOMEBODY) HELP ME OUT** *Ensign ENY 201* **15**	10 wks
12 Sep 81	**MULE (CHANT NO. 2)** *RCA 130* **37**	5 wks

BEGINNING OF THE END

6 wks

US, male vocal/instrumental group

23 Feb 74   **FUNKY NASSAU** *Atlantic K 10021* ....**31** 6 wks

Harry BELAFONTE *US, male vocalist*

87 wks

1 Mar 57 ●	**BANANA BOAT SONG** *HMV POP 308* **2**	18 wks
14 Jun 57 ●	**ISLAND IN THE SUN** *RCA 1007* **3**	25 wks
6 Sep 57	**SCARLET RIBBONS** *HMV POP 360* **18**	6 wks
1 Nov 57 ★	**MARY'S BOY CHILD** *RCA 1022* **1**	12 wks
22 Aug 58	**LITTLE BERNADETTE** *RCA 1072* **16**	7 wks
28 Nov 58 ●	**MARY'S BOY CHILD (re-entry)** *RCA 1022* **10**	6 wks
12 Dec 58	**SON OF MARY** *RCA 1084* **18**	4 wks
11 Dec 59	**MARY'S BOY CHILD (2nd re-entry)** *RCA 1022* **30**	1 wk
21 Sep 61	**HOLE IN THE BUCKET** *RCA 1247* * **32**	2 wks
12 Oct 61	**HOLE IN THE BUCKET (re-entry)** *RCA 1247* * **34**	6 wks

* Harry Belafonte and Odetta

Archie BELL and the DRELLS

33 wks

US, male vocal/instrumental group

7 Oct 72	**HERE I GO AGAIN** *Atlantic K 10210* **11**	10 wks
27 Jan 73	**THERE'S GONNA BE A SHOWDOWN**	
	Atlantic K 10263 ....**36**	5 wks
8 May 76	**SOUL CITY WALK** *Philadelphia International PIR 4250* **13**	10 wks
11 Jun 77	**EVERYBODY HAVE A GOOD TIME**	
	Philadelphia International PIR 5179 ....**43**	4 wks
28 Jun 86	**DON'T LET LOVE GET YOU DOWN** *Portrait A 7254* **49**	4 wks

Freddie BELL and the BELLBOYS

10 wks

US, male vocal/instrumental group

28 Sep 56 ● **GIDDY-UP-A-DING-DONG** *Mercury MT 122* ....**4** 10 wks

Maggie BELL *UK, female vocalist*

12 wks

15 Apr 78	**HAZELL** *Swansong SSK 19412* **37**	3 wks
13 May 78	**HAZELL (re-entry)** *Swansong SSK 19412* **74**	1 wk
17 Oct 81	**HOLD ME** *Swansong BAM 1* * **11**	8 wks

* B.A. Robertson and Maggie Bell

William BELL *US, male vocalist*

22 wks

29 May 68	**TRIBUTE TO A KING** *Stax 601 038* **31**	7 wks
20 Nov 68 ●	**PRIVATE NUMBER** *Stax 101* * **8**	14 wks
26 Apr 86	**HEADLINE NEWS** *Absolute LUTE 1* **70**	1 wk

* Judy Clay and William Bell

BELL and JAMES *US, male vocal duo*

3 wks

31 Mar 79	**LIVIN' IT UP (FRIDAY NIGHT)** *A & M AMS 7424* **68**	1 wk
14 Apr 79	**LIVIN' IT UP (FRIDAY NIGHT) (re-entry)**	
	A & M AMS 7424 ....**59**	2 wks

BELL BIV DEVOE *US, male vocal group*

14 wks

30 Jun 90	**POISON** *MCA MCA 1414* **19**	11 wks
22 Sep 90	**DO ME** *MCA MCA 1440* **56**	3 wks
15 Aug 92 ●	**THE BEST THINGS IN LIFE ARE FREE**	
	PERSS 7400 * **2**	13 wks

* Luther Vandross and Janet Jackson with special guests BBD and Ralph Tresvant

BELLAMY BROTHERS *US, male vocal duo*

29 wks

17 Apr 76 ●	**LET YOUR LOVE FLOW** *Warner Bros. K 16690* **7**	12 wks
21 Aug 76	**SATIN SHEETS** *Warner Bros. K 16775* **43**	3 wks
11 Aug 79 ●	**IF I SAID YOU HAVE A BEAUTIFUL BODY**	
	WOULD YOU HOLD IT AGAINST ME	
	Warner Bros. K 17405 ....**3**	14 wks

BELLBOYS – *See Freddie BELL and the BELLBOYS*

Regina BELLE *US, female vocalist*

1 wk

21 Oct 89   **GOOD LOVIN'** *CBS 655230* ....**73** 1 wk

BELLE and the DEVOTIONS *UK, female vocal group* **8 wks**

21 Apr 84   **LOVE GAMES** *CBS A 4332* ....**11** 8 wks

La BELLE EPOQUE *France, female vocal duo* — **14 wks**

27 Aug 77	**BLACK IS BLACK** *Harvest HAR 5133* 48	1 wk
10 Sep 77 ●	**BLACK IS BLACK (re-entry)** *Harvest HAR 5133* 2	13 wks

BELLE STARS *UK, female vocal/instrumental group* — **42 wks**

5 Jun 82	**IKO IKO** *Stiff BUY 150* 35	6 wks
17 Jul 82	**THE CLAPPING SONG** *Stiff BUY 155* 11	9 wks
16 Oct 82	**MOCKINGBIRD** *Stiff BUY 159* 51	3 wks
15 Jan 83 ●	**SIGN OF THE TIMES** *Stiff BUY 167* 3	11 wks
16 Apr 83	**SWEET MEMORY** *Stiff BUY 174* 22	9 wks
13 Aug 83	**INDIAN SUMMER** *Stiff BUY 185* 52	3 wks
14 Jul 84	**80'S ROMANCE** *Stiff BUY 200* 71	1 wk

BELMONTS – *See DION*

BELOVED *UK, male vocal/instrumental duo* — **24 wks**

21 Oct 89	**THE SUN RISING** *WEA YZ 414* 26	7 wks
27 Jan 90	**HELLO** *WEA YZ 426* 19	7 wks
24 Mar 90	**YOUR LOVE TAKES ME HIGHER** *East West YZ 463* 39	3 wks
9 Jun 90	**TIME AFTER TIME** *East West YZ 482* 46	4 wks
10 Nov 90	**IT'S ALRIGHT NOW** *East West YZ 541* 48	3 wks

BELTRAM *US, male producer - Joey Beltram* — **4 wks**

28 Sep 91	**ENERGY FLASH (EP)** *R&S RSUK 3* 52	2 wks
7 Dec 91	**THE OMEN** *R&S RSUK 7 ** 53	2 wks

* Program 2 Beltram

Tracks on Energy Flash (EP): *Energy Flash/Psycho Bass/My Sound/Sub-Base Experience.*

Pat BENATAR *US, female vocalist* — **52 wks**

21 Jan 84	**LOVE IS A BATTLEFIELD** *Chrysalis CHS 2747* 49	5 wks
12 Jan 85	**WE BELONG** *Chrysalis CHS 2821* 22	9 wks
23 Mar 85	**LOVE IS A BATTLEFIELD (re-issue)** *Chrysalis PAT 1* 17	10 wks
15 Jun 85	**SHADOWS OF THE NIGHT** *Chrysalis PAT 2* 50	4 wks
19 Oct 85	**INVINCIBLE (THEME FROM 'THE LEGEND OF BILLIE JEAN')** *Chrysalis PAT 3* 53	3 wks
15 Feb 86	**SEX AS A WEAPON** *Chrysalis PAT 4* 67	3 wks
2 Jul 88	**ALL FIRED UP** *Chrysalis PAT 5* 19	10 wks
1 Oct 88	**DON'T WALK AWAY** *Chrysalis PAT 6* 42	5 wks
14 Jan 89	**ONE LOVE** *Chrysalis PAT 7* 59	3 wks

David BENDETH — **5 wks**

Canada, male vocalist and multi-instrumentalist

8 Sep 79	**FEEL THE REAL** *Sidewalk SID 113* 44	5 wks

BENELUX and Nancy DEE — **4 wks**

Belgium/Holland/Luxembourg, female vocal group

25 Aug 79	**SWITCH** *Scope SC 4* 52	4 wks

Nigel BENN – *See PACK featuring Nigel BENN*

Boyd BENNETT *US, male vocalist* — **2 wks**

23 Dec 55	**SEVENTEEN** *Parlophone R 4063* 16	2 wks

Chris BENNETT – *See MUNICH MACHINE*

Cliff BENNETT and the REBEL ROUSERS — **23 wks**

UK, male vocal/instrumental group

1 Oct 64 ●	**ONE WAY LOVE** *Parlophone R 5173* 9	9 wks
4 Feb 65	**I'LL TAKE YOU HOME** *Parlophone R 5229* 42	3 wks
11 Aug 66 ●	**GOT TO GET YOU INTO MY LIFE** *Parlophone R 5489* 6	11 wks

Peter E. BENNETT *UK, male vocalist* — **1 wk**

7 Nov 70	**THE SEAGULL'S NAME WAS NELSON** *RCA 1991* 45	1 wk

Tony BENNETT *US, male vocalist* — **61 wks**

15 Apr 55 ★	**STRANGER IN PARADISE** *Philips PB 420* 1	16 wks
16 Sep 55	**CLOSE YOUR EYES** *Philips PB 445* 18	1 wk
13 Apr 56	**COME NEXT SPRING** *Philips PB 537* 29	1 wk
5 Jan 61	**TILL** *Philips PB 1079* 35	2 wks
18 Jul 63	**THE GOOD LIFE** *CBS AAG 153* 27	13 wks
6 May 65	**IF I RULED THE WORLD** *CBS 201735* 40	5 wks
27 May 65	**I LEFT MY HEART IN SAN FRANCISCO** *CBS 201730* 46	2 wks
30 Sep 65	**I LEFT MY HEART IN SAN FRANCISCO (re-entry)** *CBS 201730* 40	5 wks
9 Dec 65	**I LEFT MY HEART IN SAN FRANCISCO (2nd re-entry)** *CBS 201730* 25	7 wks
23 Dec 65	**THE VERY THOUGHT OF YOU** *CBS 202021* 21	9 wks

Gary BENSON *UK, male vocalist* — **8 wks**

9 Aug 75	**DON'T THROW IT ALL AWAY** *State STAT 10* 20	8 wks

George BENSON *US, male vocalist/instrumentalist - guitar* — **140 wks**

25 Oct 75	**SUPERSHIP** *CTI CTSP 002 ** 30	6 wks
4 Jun 77	**NATURE BOY** *Warner Bros. K 16921* 26	6 wks
24 Sep 77	**THE GREATEST LOVE OF ALL** *Arista 133* 27	7 wks
31 Mar 79	**LOVE BALLAD** *Warner Bros. K 17333* 29	9 wks
26 Jul 80 ●	**GIVE ME THE NIGHT** *Warner Bros. K 17673* 7	10 wks
4 Oct 80 ●	**LOVE X LOVE** *Warner Bros. K 17699* 10	8 wks
7 Feb 81	**WHAT'S ON YOUR MIND** *Warner Bros. K 17748* 45	5 wks
19 Sep 81	**LOVE ALL THE HURT AWAY** *Arista ARIST 428 *** 49	3 wks
14 Nov 81	**TURN YOUR LOVE AROUND** *Warner Bros. K 17877* 29	11 wks
23 Jan 82	**NEVER GIVE UP ON A GOOD THING** *Warner Bros. K 17902* 14	10 wks
21 May 83	**LADY LOVE ME (ONE MORE TIME)** *Warner Bros. W 9614* 11	10 wks
16 Jul 83	**FEEL LIKE MAKIN' LOVE** *Warner Bros. W 9551* 28	7 wks
24 Sep 83 ●	**IN YOUR EYES** *Warner Bros. W 9487* 7	10 wks
17 Dec 83	**INSIDE LOVE (SO PERSONAL)** *WEA Int. W 9427* 57	5 wks
19 Jan 85	**20/20** *Warner Bros. W 9120* 29	9 wks
20 Apr 85	**BEYOND THE SEA (LA MER)** *Warner Bros. W 9014* 60	3 wks
16 Aug 86	**KISSES IN THE MOONLIGHT** *Warner Bros. W 8640* 60	4 wks
29 Nov 86	**SHIVER** *Warner Bros. W 8523* 19	9 wks
14 Feb 87	**TEASER** *Warner Bros. W 8437* 45	4 wks
27 Aug 88	**LET'S DO IT AGAIN** *Warner Bros. W 7780* 56	3 wks
5 Sep 92	**I'LL KEEP YOUR DREAMS ALIVE** *Ammi AMMI 101 **** 68	1 wk

* George 'Bad' Benson ** Aretha Franklin and George Benson *** George Benson and Patti Austin

Brook BENTON *US, male vocalist* — **18 wks**

10 Jul 59	**ENDLESSLY** *Mercury AMT 1043* 28	2 wks

6 Oct 60	KIDDIO *Mercury AMT 1109*	42	3 wks
3 Nov 60	KIDDIO (re-entry) *Mercury AMT 1109*	41	3 wks
16 Feb 61	FOOLS RUSH IN *Mercury AMT 1121*	50	1 wk
13 Jul 61	BOLL WEEVIL SONG *Mercury AMT 1148*	30	9 wks

Ingrid BERGMAN – *See Dooley WILSON*

BERLIN *US, male/female vocal/instrumental group* **39 wks**

25 Oct 86 ★	TAKE MY BREATH AWAY (LOVE THEME FROM 'TOP GUN') *CBS A 7320*	1	15 wks
17 Jan 87	YOU DON'T KNOW *Mercury MER 237*	39	6 wks
14 Mar 87	LIKE FLAMES *Mercury MER 240*	47	3 wks
20 Feb 88	TAKE MY BREATH AWAY (LOVE THEME FROM 'TOP GUN') (re-entry) *CBS A 7320*	52	3 wks
13 Oct 90 ●	TAKE MY BREATH AWAY (re-issue) *CBS 656361 7*	3	12 wks

Elmer BERNSTEIN *US, orchestra* **11 wks**

18 Dec 59 ●	STACCATO'S THEME *Capitol CL 15101*	4	10 wks
10 Mar 60	STACCATO'S THEME (re-entry) *Capitol CL 15101*	40	1 wk

Chuck BERRY *US, male vocalist/instrumentalist - guitar* **91 wks**

21 Jun 57	SCHOOL DAY *Columbia DB 3951*	24	2 wks
12 Jul 57	SCHOOL DAY (re-entry) *Columbia DB 3951*	24	2 wks
25 Apr 58	SWEET LITTLE SIXTEEN *London HLM 8585*	16	5 wks
11 Jul 63	GO GO GO *Pye International 7N 25209*	38	6 wks
10 Oct 63 ●	LET IT ROCK/MEMPHIS TENNESSEE *Pye International 7N 25218*	6	13 wks
19 Dec 63	RUN RUDOLPH RUN *Pye International 7N 25228*	36	6 wks
13 Feb 64	NADINE (IS IT YOU) *Pye International 7N 25236*	27	6 wks
2 Apr 64	NADINE (IS IT YOU) (re-entry) *Pye International 7N 25236*	43	1 wk
7 May 64 ●	NO PARTICULAR PLACE TO GO *Pye International 7N 25242*	3	12 wks
20 Aug 64	YOU NEVER CAN TELL *Pye International 7N 25257*	23	8 wks
14 Jan 65	PROMISED LAND *Pye International 7N 25285*	26	6 wks
28 Oct 72 ★	MY DING-A-LING *Chess 6145 019*	1	17 wks
3 Feb 73	REELIN' AND ROCKIN' *Chess 6145 020*	18	7 wks

Dave BERRY *UK, male vocalist* **76 wks**

19 Sep 63	MEMPHIS TENNESSEE *Decca F 11734* *	19	13 wks
9 Jan 64	MY BABY LEFT ME *Decca F 11803* *	41	1 wk
23 Jan 64	MY BABY LEFT ME (re-entry) *Decca F 11803* *	37	8 wks
30 Apr 64	BABY IT'S YOU *Decca F 11876*	24	6 wks
6 Aug 64 ●	THE CRYING GAME *Decca F 11937*	5	12 wks
26 Nov 64	ONE HEART BETWEEN TWO *Decca F 12020*	41	2 wks
25 Mar 65 ●	LITTLE THINGS *Decca F 12103*	5	12 wks
22 Jul 65	THIS STRANGE EFFECT *Decca F 12188*	37	6 wks
30 Jun 66 ●	MAMA *Decca F 12435*	5	16 wks

* Dave Berry and the Cruisers

Mike BERRY *UK, male vocalist* **51 wks**

12 Oct 61	TRIBUTE TO BUDDY HOLLY *HMV POP 912* *	24	6 wks
3 Jan 63 ●	DON'T YOU THINK IT'S TIME *HMV POP 1105* *	6	12 wks
11 Apr 63	MY LITTLE BABY *HMV POP 1142* *	34	7 wks
2 Aug 80 ●	THE SUNSHINE OF YOUR SMILE *Polydor 2059 261*	9	12 wks
29 Nov 80	IF I COULD ONLY MAKE YOU CARE *Polydor POSP 202*	37	9 wks
5 Sep 81	MEMORIES *Polydor POSP 287*	55	5 wks

* Mike Berry with the Outlaws

Nick BERRY *UK, male vocalist* **24 wks**

4 Oct 86 ★	EVERY LOSER WINS *BBC RESL 204*	1	11 wks

27 Dec 86	EVERY LOSER WINS (re-entry) *BBC RESL 204*	72	2 wks
13 Jun 92 ●	HEARTBEAT *Columbia 6581517*	2	8 wks
31 Oct 92	LONG LIVE LOVE *Columbia 6587597*	47	3 wks

Adele BERTEI – *See JELLYBEAN*

BEVERLEY SISTERS *UK, female vocal trio* **34 wks**

27 Nov 53	I SAW MOMMY KISSING SANTA CLAUS *Philips PB 188*	11	1 wk
11 Dec 53 ●	I SAW MOMMY KISSING SANTA CLAUS (re-entry) *Philips PB 188*	6	4 wks
13 Apr 56	WILLIE CAN *Decca F 10705*	23	4 wks
1 Feb 57	I DREAMED *Decca F 10832*	24	2 wks
13 Feb 59 ●	LITTLE DRUMMER BOY *Decca F 11107*	6	13 wks
20 Nov 59	LITTLE DONKEY *Decca F 11172*	14	7 wks
23 Jun 60	GREEN FIELDS *Columbia DB 4444*	48	1 wk
7 Jul 60	GREEN FIELDS (re-entry) *Columbia DB 4444*	29	2 wks

See also Various Artists (EPs and LPs) - All Star Hit Parade No.2.

Frankie BEVERLY – *See MAZE featuring Frankie BEVERLY*

BEYOND *UK, male vocal/instrumental group* **1 wk**

21 Sep 91	RAGING EP *Harvest HARS 530*	68	1 wk

Tracks on Raging EP: *Great Indifference/Nail/Eve Of My Release.*

B-52s *US, male/female vocal/instrumental group* **48 wks**

11 Aug 79	ROCK LOBSTER *Island WIP 6506*	37	5 wks
9 Aug 80	GIVE ME BACK MY MAN *Island WIP 6579*	61	3 wks
7 May 83	FUTURE GENERATION *Island IS 107*	63	2 wks
10 May 86	ROCK LOBSTER (re-issue)/PLANET CLAIRE *Island BFT 1*	12	7 wks
3 Mar 90 ●	LOVE SHACK *Reprise W 9917*	2	13 wks
19 May 90	ROAM *Reprise W 9827*	17	7 wks
18 Aug 90	CHANNEL Z *Reprise W 9737*	61	2 wks
20 Jun 92	GOOD STUFF *Reprise W 0109*	21	6 wks
12 Sep 92	TELL IT LIKE IT T-I-IS *Reprise W 0130*	61	3 wks

Planet Claire only listed from 17 May '86.

BG THE PRINCE OF RAP *Germany, male rapper* **2 wks**

18 Jan 92	TAKE CONTROL OF THE PARTY *Columbia 6576330*	71	2 wks

BIBLE *UK, male vocal/instrumental group* **8 wks**

20 May 89	GRACELAND *Chrysalis BIB 4*	51	4 wks
26 Aug 89	HONEY BE GOOD *Ensign BIB 5*	54	4 wks

BIBLE OF DREAMS – *See Johnny PANIC and the BIBLE OF DREAMS*

BIDDU *UK, orchestra* **13 wks**

2 Aug 75	SUMMER OF '42 *Epic EPC 3318*	14	8 wks
17 Apr 76	RAIN FOREST *Epic EPC 4084*	39	4 wks
11 Feb 78	JOURNEY TO THE MOON *Epic EPC 5910*	41	1 wk

BIG APPLE BAND – *See Walter MURPHY and the BIG APPLE BAND*

BIG AUDIO DYNAMITE **25 wks**
UK/US, male vocal/instrumental group

22 Mar 86	E = MC^2 *CBS A 6963*	11	9 wks

7 Jun 86	**MEDICINE SHOW** CBS A 7181 ....**29**	5 wks
18 Oct 86	**C'MON EVERY BEATBOX** CBS 650147 ....**51**	3 wks
21 Feb 87	**V THIRTEEN** CBS BAAD 2 ....**49**	5 wks
28 May 88	**JUST PLAY MUSIC** CBS BAAD 4 ....**51**	3 wks

BIG BAD HORNS – *See LITTLE ANGELS*

BIG BAM BOO *UK/Canada, male vocal/instrumental duo*   **2 wks**

28 Jan 89	**SHOOTING FROM MY HEART** MCA MCA 1281...........**61**	2 wks

BIG BEN BANJO BAND *UK, instrumental group*   **6 wks**

10 Dec 54	● **LET'S GET TOGETHER NO. 1** Columbia DB 3549 ....**6**	4 wks
9 Dec 55	**LET'S GET TOGETHER AGAIN** Columbia DB 3676 ....**19**	1 wk
30 Dec 55	**LET'S GET TOGETHER AGAIN (re-entry)**	
	Columbia DB 3676..**18**	1 wk

These hits were both medleys as follows: Let's Get Together No.1: I'm Just Wild About Harry/April Showers/Rock-a-Bye Your Baby/Swanee/Darktown Strutters Ball/For Me And My Gal/Oh You Beautiful Doll/Yes Sir That's My Baby. Let's Get Together Again: I'm Looking Over A Four-leafed Clover/By The Light Of The Silvery Moon/Oh Susannah/Baby Face/I'm Sitting On Top Of The World/My Mammy/Dixie's Land/Margie.

BIG BOPPER *US, male vocalist*   **8 wks**

26 Dec 58	**CHANTILLY LACE** Mercury AMT 1002................................**30**	1 wk
9 Jan 59	**CHANTILLY LACE (re-entry)** Mercury AMT 1002.............**12**	7 wks

BIG COUNTRY *UK, male vocal/instrumental group*   **94 wks**

26 Feb 83	● **FIELDS OF FIRE (400 MILES)** Mercury COUNT 2 ....**10**	12 wks
28 May 83	**IN A BIG COUNTRY** Mercury COUNT 3 ....**17**	7 wks
3 Sep 83	● **CHANCE** Mercury COUNT 4 ....**9**	9 wks
21 Jan 84	● **WONDERLAND** Mercury COUNT 5 ....**8**	8 wks
29 Sep 84	**EAST OF EDEN** Mercury MER 175.....................................**17**	6 wks
1 Dec 84	**WHERE THE ROSE IS SOWN** Mercury MER 185.................**29**	7 wks
19 Jan 85	**JUST A SHADOW** Mercury BCO 8 ....**26**	4 wks
12 Apr 86	● **LOOK AWAY** Mercury BIGC 1 ....**7**	8 wks
21 Jun 86	**THE TEACHER** Mercury BIGC 2 ....**28**	4 wks
20 Sep 86	**ONE GREAT THING** Mercury BIGC 3 ....**19**	6 wks
29 Nov 86	**HOLD THE HEART** Mercury BIGC 4 ....**55**	2 wks
20 Aug 88	**KING OF EMOTION** Mercury BIGC 5 ....**16**	5 wks
1 Oct 88	**KING OF EMOTION (re-entry)** Mercury BIGC 5 ....**74**	1 wk
5 Nov 88	**BROKEN HEART (THIRTEEN VALLEYS)**	
	Mercury BIGC 6..**47**	4 wks
4 Feb 89	**PEACE IN OUR TIME** Mercury BIGC 8 ....**39**	3 wks
12 May 90	**SAVE ME** Mercury BIGC 8 ....**41**	3 wks
21 Jul 90	**HEART OF THE WORLD** Mercury BIGC 9 ....**50**	2 wks
31 Aug 91	**REPUBLICAN PARTY REPTILE (EP)** Vertigo BIC 1 ....**37**	2 wks
19 Oct 91	**BEAUTIFUL PEOPLE** Vertigo BIC 2................................**72**	1 wk

Tracks on Republican Party Reptile (EP): *Republican Party Reptile/Comes A Time/You And Me And The Truth.*

BIG DADDY *US, male vocal/instrumental group*   **8 wks**

9 Mar 85	**DANCING IN THE DARK** Making Waves SURF 1033.........**21**	8 wks

BIG DADDY KANE *US, male vocalist*   **6 wks**

13 May 89	**RAP SUMMARY/WRATH OF KANE**	
	Cold Chillin' W 2973 ....**52**	2 wks
26 Aug 89	**SMOOTH OPERATOR** Cold Chillin' W 2804 ....**65**	1 wk
13 Jan 90	**AIN'T NO STOPPIN' US NOW** Cold Chillin' W 2635.........**44**	3 wks

BIG DISH *UK, male vocal/instrumental group*   **5 wks**

12 Jan 91	**MISS AMERICA** East West YZ 529 ....**37**	5 wks

BIG FAMILY – *See JT and the BIG FAMILY*

BIG FUN *UK, male vocal group*   **33 wks**

12 Aug 89	● **BLAME IT ON THE BOOGIE** Jive JIVE 217 ....**4**	11 wks
25 Nov 89	● **CAN'T SHAKE THE FEELING** Jive JIVE 234 ....**8**	9 wks
17 Mar 90	**HANDFUL OF PROMISES** Jive JIVE 243 ....**21**	6 wks
23 Jun 90	**YOU'VE GOT A FRIEND** Jive CHILD 90 * **14**	6 wks
4 Aug 90	**HEY THERE LONELY GIRL** Jive JIVE 251 ....**62**	1 wk

* Big Fun and Sonia

BIG ROLL BAND – *See Zoot MONEY and the BIG ROLL BAND*

BIG SOUND – *See Simon DUPREE and the BIG SOUND*

BIG SOUND AUTHORITY   **12 wks**
UK, male/female vocal/instrumental group

19 Jan 85	**THIS HOUSE (IS WHERE YOUR LOVE STANDS)**	
	Source BSA 1...**21**	9 wks
8 Jun 85	**A BAD TOWN** Source BSA 2..**54**	3 wks

BIG SUPREME *UK, male vocal group*   **5 wks**

20 Sep 86	**DON'T WALK** Polydor POSP 809 ....**58**	3 wks
14 Mar 87	**PLEASE YOURSELF** Polydor POSP 840 ....**64**	2 wks

BIG THREE *UK, vocal/instrumental group*   **17 wks**

11 Apr 63	**SOME OTHER GUY** Decca F 11614 ....**37**	7 wks
11 Jul 63	**BY THE WAY** Decca F 11689 ....**22**	10 wks

Barry BIGGS *Jamaica, male vocalist*   **46 wks**

28 Aug 76	**WORK ALL DAY** Dynamic DYN 101 ....**38**	5 wks
4 Dec 76	● **SIDESHOW** Dynamic DYN 118 ....**3**	16 wks
23 Apr 77	**YOU'RE MY LIFE** Dynamic DYN 127 ....**36**	4 wks
9 Jul 77	**THREE RING CIRCUS** Dynamic DYN 128 ....**22**	8 wks
15 Dec 79	**WHAT'S YOUR SIGN GIRL** Dynamic DYN 150 ....**55**	7 wks
20 Jun 81	**WIDE AWAKE IN A DREAM** Dynamic DYN 10 ....**44**	6 wks

Ronald BIGGS – *See SEX PISTOLS*

Ivor BIGGUN *UK, male vocalist*   **15 wks**

2 Sep 78	**WINKER'S SONG (MISPRINT)**	
	Beggars Banquet BOP 1 * **22**	12 wks
12 Sep 81	**BRAS ON 45 (FAMILY VERSION)**	
	Dead Badger BOP 6 ** **50**	3 wks

* Ivor Biggun and the Red Nosed Burglars ** Ivor Biggun and the D Cups

BILBO *UK, male vocal/instrumental group*   **7 wks**

26 Aug 78	**SHE'S GONNA WIN** Lightning LIG 548 ....**42**	7 wks

Mr. Acker BILK and his PARAMOUNT JAZZ BAND   **171 wks**
UK, male jazz band leader, vocalist/instrumentalist - clarinet

22 Jan 60	● **SUMMER SET** Columbia DB 4382 ....**5**	19 wks
9 Jun 60	**GOODNIGHT SWEET PRINCE** Melodisc MEL 1547 ....**50**	1 wk
18 Aug 60	**WHITE CLIFFS OF DOVER** Columbia DB 4492 ....**30**	9 wks
8 Dec 60	● **BUONA SERA** Columbia DB 4544 ....**7**	18 wks

13 Jul 61 ●	THAT'S MY HOME *Columbia DB 4673*	7	17 wks
2 Nov 61	STARS AND STRIPES FOREVER/CREOLE JAZZ		
	Columbia SCD 2155 22		10 wks
30 Nov 61 ●	STRANGER ON THE SHORE *Columbia DB 4750* * 2		55 wks
15 Mar 62	FRANKIE AND JOHNNY *Columbia DB 4795*.....................42		2 wks
26 Jul 62	GOTTA SEE BABY TONIGHT *Columbia SCD 2176*.........24		9 wks
27 Sep 62	LONELY *Columbia DB 4897* * 14		11 wks
24 Jan 63	A TASTE OF HONEY *Columbia DB 4949* * 16		9 wks
21 Aug 76 ●	ARIA *Pye 7N 45607* ** 5		11 wks

* Mr. Acker Bilk with the Leon Young String Chorale ** Acker Bilk, his Clarinet and Strings

BILLY – *See S EXPRESS*

BIMBO JET *France, male/female vocal/instrumental group* **10 wks**

26 Jul 75	EL BIMBO *EMI 2317* 12	10 wks

Umberto BINDI *Italy, male vocalist* **1 wk**

10 Nov 60	IL NOSTRO CONCERTO *Oriole CB 1577* 47	1 wk

La BIONDA *Italy, male/female vocal group* **4 wks**

7 Oct 78	ONE FOR YOU ONE FOR ME *Philips 6198 227*.................54	4 wks

BIRDLAND *UK, male vocal/instrumental group* **7 wks**

1 Apr 89	HOLLOW HEART *Lazy LAZY 13* 70	1 wk
8 Jul 89	PARADISE *Lazy LAZY 14* 70	1 wk
3 Feb 90	SLEEP WITH ME *Lazy LAZY 17* 32	3 wks
22 Sep 90	ROCK AND ROLL NIGGER *Lazy LAZY 20* 47	1 wk
2 Feb 91	EVERYBODY NEEDS SOMEBODY *Lazy LAZY 24* 44	1 wk

BIRDS *UK, male vocal/instrumental group* **1 wk**

27 May 65	LEAVING HERE *Decca F 12140* 45	1 wk

Jane BIRKIN and Serge GAINSBOURG **34 wks**
UK/France, female/male vocal duo

30 Jul 69 ●	JE T'AIME... MOI NON PLUS *Fontana TF 1042*.................2	11 wks
4 Oct 69 ★	JE T'AIME... MOI NON PLUS (re-issue)	
	Major Minor MM 645 1	14 wks
7 Dec 74	JE T'AIME... MOI NON PLUS (2nd re-issue)	
	Antic K 11511 31	9 wks

Elvin BISHOP *US, male instrumentalist - guitar* **4 wks**

15 May 76	FOOLED AROUND AND FELL IN LOVE	
	Capricorn 2089 024 34	4 wks

Hit has vocal (uncredited) by Mickey Thomas.

BITI – *See DEGREES OF MOTION featuring BITI*

BIZARRE INC *UK, male instrumental/production group* **34 wks**

16 Mar 91	PLAYING WITH KNIVES *Vinyl Solution STORM 25R*.........43	5 wks
14 Sep 91	SUCH A FEELING *Vinyl Solution STORM 32S*.................13	9 wks
23 Nov 91 ●	PLAYING WITH KNIVES (re-entry)	
	Vinyl Solution STORM 25R 4	8 wks
3 Oct 92 ●	I'M GONNA GET YOU *Vinyl Solution STORM 46S* * 3	12 wks

* Bizarre Inc featuring Angie Brown

BIZZ NIZZ *US/Belgium, male/female vocal/instrumental group* **11 wks**

31 Mar 90 ●	DON'T MISS THE PARTY LINE *Cooltempo COOL 203* 7	11 wks

BJORK – *See 808 STATE*

BJORN AGAIN **6 wks**
Australia, male/female vocal/instrumental group

24 Oct 92	ERASURE-ISH (A LITTLE RESPECT/STOP!)	
	M&G MAGS 32 25	3 wks
12 Dec 92	SANTA CLAUS IS COMING TO TOWN	
	M&G MAGS 35 ....55†	3 wks

BLACK *UK, male vocalist - Colin Vearncombe* **32 wks**

27 Sep 86	WONDERFUL LIFE *Ugly Man JACK 71* 72	1 wk
27 Jun 87 ●	SWEETEST SMILE *A & M AM 394* 8	10 wks
22 Aug 87 ●	WONDERFUL LIFE *A & M AM 402* 8	9 wks
16 Jan 88	PARADISE *A & M AM 422* 38	3 wks
24 Sep 88	THE BIG ONE *A & M AM 468* 54	4 wks
21 Jan 89	NOW YOU'RE GONE *A & M AM 491* 66	2 wks
4 May 91	FEEL LIKE CHANGE *A & M AM 780* 56	2 wks
15 Jun 91	HERE IT COMES AGAIN *A & M AM 753* 70	1 wk

Wonderful Life *on A & M is a re-recording of his first hit.*

Cilla BLACK *UK, female vocalist* **192 wks**

17 Oct 63	LOVE OF THE LOVED *Parlophone R 5065* 35	6 wks
6 Feb 64 ★	ANYONE WHO HAD A HEART *Parlophone R 5101*...........1	17 wks
7 May 64 ●	YOU'RE MY WORLD *Parlophone R 5133* 1	17 wks
6 Aug 64 ●	IT'S FOR YOU *Parlophone R 5162* 7	10 wks
14 Jan 65 ●	YOU'VE LOST THAT LOVIN' FEELIN'	
	Parlophone R 5225 2	9 wks
22 Apr 65	I'VE BEEN WRONG BEFORE *Parlophone R 5269* 17	8 wks
13 Jan 66	LOVE'S JUST A BROKEN HEART *Parlophone R 5395* 5	11 wks
31 Mar 66 ●	ALFIE *Parlophone R 5427* 9	12 wks
9 Jun 66 ●	DON'T ANSWER ME *Parlophone R 5463* 6	10 wks
20 Oct 66	A FOOL AM I *Parlophone R 5515* 13	9 wks
8 Jun 67	WHAT GOOD AM I *Parlophone R 5608* 24	7 wks
29 Nov 67	I ONLY LIVE TO LOVE YOU *Parlophone R 5652* 26	11 wks
13 Mar 68 ●	STEP INSIDE LOVE *Parlophone R 5674* 8	9 wks
12 Jun 68	WHERE IS TOMORROW *Parlophone R 5706*.................39	3 wks
12 Feb 69 ●	SURROUND YOURSELF WITH SORROW	
	Parlophone R 5759 3	12 wks
9 Jul 69 ●	CONVERSATIONS *Parlophone R 5785* 7	12 wks
13 Dec 69	IF I THOUGHT YOU'D EVER CHANGE YOUR	
	MIND *Parlophone R 5820* 20	9 wks
20 Nov 71 ●	SOMETHING TELLS ME (SOMETHING IS	
	GONNA HAPPEN TONIGHT) *Parlophone R 5924* 3	14 wks
2 Feb 74	BABY WE CAN'T GO WRONG *EMI 2107* 36	6 wks

Jeanne BLACK *US, female vocalist* **4 wks**

23 Jun 60	HE'LL HAVE TO STAY *Capitol CL 15131* 41	4 wks

BLACK BOX *Italy, male/female vocal/instrumental group* **66 wks**

12 Aug 89 ★	RIDE ON TIME *deConstruction PB 43055*.....................1	22 wks
17 Feb 90 ●	I DON'T KNOW ANYBODY ELSE	
	deConstruction PB 43479 4	8 wks
2 Jun 90 ●	EVERYBODY EVERYBODY *deConstruction PB 43715*.......16	5 wks
3 Nov 90 ●	FANTASY *deConstruction PB 43895* 5	11 wks
15 Dec 90	THE TOTAL MIX *deConstruction PB 44235* 12	8 wks
6 Apr 91	STRIKE IT UP/RIDE ON TIME (re-mix)	
	deConstruction PB 44459 16	8 wks
14 Dec 91	OPEN YOUR EYES *deConstruction PB 45053*.................48	4 wks

BLACK CROWES *US, male vocal/instrumental group*　　　**22 wks**

1 Sep 90		HARD TO HANDLE *Def American DEFA 6*	45	5 wks
12 Jan 91		TWICE AS HARD *Def American DEFA 7*	47	3 wks
22 Jun 91		JEALOUS AGAIN/SHE TALKS TO ANGELS		
		Def American DEFA 8 (re-issue)	70	1 wk
24 Aug 91		HARD TO HANDLE (re-issue) *Def American DEFA 10*	39	4 wks
26 Oct 91		SEEING THINGS *Def American DEFA 13*	72	1 wk
2 May 92		REMEDY *Def American DEFA 16*	24	3 wks
26 Sep 92		STING ME *Def American DEFA 21*	42	2 wks
28 Nov 92		HOTEL ILLNESS *Def American DEFA 23*	47	3 wks

BLACK GORILLA　　　**6 wks**

UK, male/female vocal/instrumental group

27 Aug 77		GIMME DAT BANANA *Response SR 502*	29	6 wks

BLACK LACE *UK, male vocal/instrumental group*　　　**82 wks**

31 Mar 79		MARY ANN *EMI 2919*	42	4 wks
24 Sep 83	●	SUPERMAN (GIOCA JOUER) *Flair FLA 105*	9	18 wks
30 Jun 84	●	AGADOO *Flair FLA 107*	2	30 wks
24 Nov 84	●	DO THE CONGA *Flair FLA 108*	10	9 wks
1 Jun 85		EL VINO COLLAPSO *Flair LACE 1*	42	5 wks
7 Sep 85		I SPEAKA DA LINGO *Flair LACE 2*	49	4 wks
7 Dec 85		HOKEY COKEY *Flair LACE 3*	31	6 wks
20 Sep 86		WIG WAM BAM *Flair LACE 5*	63	3 wks
26 Aug 89		I AM THE MUSIC MAN *Flair LACE 10*	52	3 wks

BLACK RIOT *US, male producer*　　　**3 wks**

3 Dec 88		WARLOCK/A DAY IN THE LIFE		
		Champion CHAMP 75	68	3 wks

A Day In The Life *only listed from 17 Dec 88.*

BLACK SABBATH *UK/US, male vocal/instrumental group*　　　**70 wks**

29 Aug 70	●	PARANOID *Vertigo 6059 010*	4	18 wks
3 Jun 78		NEVER SAY DIE *Vertigo SAB 001*	21	8 wks
14 Oct 78		HARD ROAD *Vertigo SAB 002*	33	4 wks
5 Jul 80		NEON KNIGHTS *Vertigo SAB 3*	22	9 wks
16 Aug 80		PARANOID (re-issue) *Nems BSS 101*	14	12 wks
6 Dec 80		DIE YOUNG *Vertigo SAB 4*	41	7 wks
7 Nov 81		MOB RULES *Vertigo SAB 5*	46	4 wks
13 Feb 82		TURN UP THE NIGHT *Vertigo SAB 6*	37	5 wks
15 Apr 89		HEADLESS CROSS *IRS EIRS 107*	62	1 wk
13 Jun 92		TV CRIMES *IRS EIRSP 178*	33	2 wks

Group UK only for first three hits and re-issue of Paranoid.

BLACK SLATE *UK/Jamaica, male vocal/instrumental group*　　　**15 wks**

20 Sep 80	●	AMIGO *Ensign ENY 42*	9	9 wks
6 Dec 80		BOOM BOOM *Ensign ENY 47*	51	6 wks

BLACK UHURU *Jamaica, male vocal/instrumental group*　　　**9 wks**

8 Sep 84		WHAT IS LIFE? *Island IS 150*	56	6 wks
31 May 86		THE GREAT TRAIN ROBBERY		
		Real Authentic Sound RAS 7018	62	3 wks

Band of the BLACK WATCH *UK, military band*　　　**22 wks**

30 Aug 75	●	SCOTCH ON THE ROCKS *Spark SRL 1128*	8	14 wks
13 Dec 75		DANCE OF THE CUCKOOS *Spark SRL 1135*	37	8 wks

Bill BLACK'S COMBO　　　**8 wks**

US, male instrumental group, Bill Black, bass

8 Sep 60		WHITE SILVER SANDS *London HLU 9090*	50	1 wk
3 Nov 60		DON'T BE CRUEL *London HLU 9212*	32	7 wks

Tony BLACKBURN *UK, male vocalist*　　　**7 wks**

24 Jan 68		SO MUCH LOVE *MGM 1375*	31	4 wks
26 Mar 69		IT'S ONLY LOVE *MGM 1467*	42	3 wks

BLACKBYRDS *US, male vocal/instrumental group*　　　**6 wks**

31 May 75		WALKING IN RHYTHM *Fantasy FTC 114*	23	6 wks

BLACKFOOT *US, male vocal/instrumental group*　　　**5 wks**

6 Mar 82		DRY COUNTY *Atco K 11686*	43	4 wks
18 Jun 83		SEND ME AN ANGEL *Atco B 9880*	66	1 wk

J. BLACKFOOT *US, male vocalist*　　　**4 wks**

17 Mar 84		TAXI *Allegiance ALES 2*	48	4 wks

BLACKFOOT SUE *UK, male vocal/instrumental group*　　　**15 wks**

12 Aug 72	●	STANDING IN THE ROAD *Jam 13*	4	10 wks
16 Dec 72		SING DON'T SPEAK *Jam 29*	36	5 wks

BLACKHEARTS – *See Joan JETT and the BLACKHEARTS*

Honor BLACKMAN – *See Patrick MACNEE and Honor BLACKMAN*

BLACKWELLS *US, male vocal group*　　　**2 wks**

18 May 61		LOVE OR MONEY *London HLW 9334*	46	2 wks

Vivian BLAINE *US, female vocalist*　　　**1 wk**

10 Jul 53		BUSHEL AND A PECK *Brunswick 05100*	12	1 wk

BLAIR – *See Terry HALL*

Peter BLAKE *UK, male vocalist*　　　**4 wks**

8 Oct 77		LIPSMACKIN' ROCK 'N' ROLLIN' *Pepper UP 36295*	40	4 wks

BLAME *UK, male instrumental/production duo*　　　**2 wks**

11 Apr 92		MUSIC TAKES YOU *Moving Shadow SHADOW 11*	48	2 wks

BLANCMANGE *UK, male vocal/instrumental group*　　　**71 wks**

17 Apr 82		GOD'S KITCHEN/I'VE SEEN THE WORD		
		London BLANC 1	65	2 wks

31 Jul 82	FEEL ME *London BLANC 2*	**46**	5 wks
30 Oct 82 ●	LIVING ON THE CEILING *London BLANC 3*	**7**	14 wks
19 Feb 83	WAVES *London BLANC 4*	**19**	9 wks
7 May 83 ●	BLIND VISION *London BLANC 5*	**10**	8 wks
26 Nov 83	THAT'S LOVE, THAT IT IS *London BLANC 6*	**33**	8 wks
14 Apr 84 ●	DON'T TELL ME *London BLANC 7*	**8**	10 wks
21 Jul 84	THE DAY BEFORE YOU CAME *London BLANC 8* ..	**22**	8 wks
7 Sep 85	WHAT'S YOUR PROBLEM? *London BLANC 9*	**40**	5 wks
10 May 86	I CAN SEE IT *London BLANC 11*	**71**	2 wks

Billy BLAND *US, male vocalist* **10 wks**

19 May 60	LET THE LITTLE GIRL DANCE *London HL 9096*	**15**	10 wks

BLESSING *UK, male vocal/instrumental group* **12 wks**

11 May 91	HIGHWAY 5 *MCA MCS 1509*	**42**	6 wks
18 Jan 92	HIGHWAY 5 (re-mix) *MCA MCS 1603*	**30**	6 wks

Mary J BLIGE *US, female vocalist* **2 wks**

28 Nov 92	REAL LOVE *MCA MCS 1721*	**68**	2 wks

BLOCKHEADS – *See Ian DURY and the BLOCKHEADS*

BLONDIE *US/UK, female/male vocal/instrumental group* **145 wks**

18 Feb 78 ●	DENIS *Chrysalis CHS 2204*	**2**	14 wks
6 May 78 ●	(I'M ALWAYS TOUCHED BY YOUR) PRESENCE DEAR *Chrysalis CHS 2217*	**10**	9 wks
26 Aug 78	PICTURE THIS *Chrysalis CHS 2242*	**12**	11 wks
11 Nov 78 ●	HANGING ON THE TELEPHONE *Chrysalis CHR 2266*	**5**	12 wks
27 Jan 79 ★	HEART OF GLASS *Chrysalis CHS 2275*	**1**	12 wks
19 May 79 ★	SUNDAY GIRL *Chrysalis CHS 2320*	**1**	13 wks
29 Sep 79 ●	DREAMING *Chrysalis CHS 2350*	**2**	8 wks
24 Nov 79	UNION CITY BLUE *Chrysalis CHS 2400*	**13**	10 wks
23 Feb 80 ★	ATOMIC *Chrysalis CHS 2410*	**1**	9 wks
12 Apr 80 ★	CALL ME *Chrysalis CHS 2414*	**1**	9 wks
8 Nov 80 ★	THE TIDE IS HIGH *Chrysalis CHS 2465*	**1**	12 wks
24 Jan 81 ●	RAPTURE *Chrysalis CHS 2485*	**5**	8 wks
8 May 82	ISLAND OF LOST SOULS *Chrysalis CHS 2608* ..	**11**	9 wks
24 Jul 82	WAR CHILD *Chrysalis CHS 2624*	**39**	4 wks
3 Dec 88	DENIS (re-mix) *Chrysalis CHS 3328*	**50**	3 wks
11 Feb 89	CALL ME (re-mix) *Chrysalis CHS 3342*	**61**	2 wks

BLOOD SWEAT AND TEARS **6 wks**
US/Canada, male vocal/instrumental group

30 Apr 69	YOU'VE MADE ME SO VERY HAPPY *CBS 4116*	**35**	6 wks

BLOODSTONE *US, male vocal/instrumental group* **4 wks**

18 Aug 73	NATURAL HIGH *Decca F 13382*	**40**	4 wks

Bobby BLOOM *US, male vocalist* **24 wks**

29 Aug 70 ●	MONTEGO BAY *Polydor 2058 051*	**3**	14 wks
12 Dec 70	MONTEGO BAY (re-entry) *Polydor 2058 051* ...	**42**	3 wks
9 Jan 71	HEAVY MAKES YOU HAPPY *Polydor 2001 122* ..	**31**	5 wks
9 Jan 71	MONTEGO BAY (2nd re-entry) *Polydor 2058 051* ..	**47**	2 wks

BLOOMSBURY SET *UK, male vocal/instrumental group* **3 wks**

25 Jun 83	HANGING AROUND WITH THE BIG BOYS *Stiletto STL 13*	**56**	3 wks

Kurtis BLOW *US, male vocalist* **23 wks**

15 Dec 79	CHRISTMAS RAPPIN' *Mercury BLOW 7*	**30**	6 wks
11 Oct 80	THE BREAKS *Mercury BLOW 8*	**47**	4 wks
16 Mar 85	PARTY TIME (THE GO-GO EDIT) *Club JAB 12* ..	**67**	1 wk
15 Jun 85	SAVE YOUR LOVE (FOR NUMBER 1) *Club JAB 14 **	**66**	2 wks
18 Jan 86	IF I RULED THE WORLD *Club JAB 26*	**24**	8 wks
8 Nov 86	I'M CHILLIN' *Club JAB 42*	**64**	2 wks

* Rene and Angela featuring Kurtis Blow

BLOW MONKEYS *UK, male vocal/instrumental group* **46 wks**

1 Mar 86	DIGGING YOUR SCENE *RCA PB 40599*	**12**	10 wks
17 May 86	WICKED WAYS *RCA MONK 2*	**60**	2 wks
31 Jan 87 ●	IT DOESN'T HAVE TO BE THIS WAY *RCA MONK 4*	**5**	8 wks
28 Mar 87	OUT WITH HER *RCA MONK 5*	**30**	6 wks
30 May 87	(CELEBRATE) THE DAY AFTER YOU *RCA MONK 6 **	**52**	2 wks
15 Aug 87	SOME KIND OF WONDERFUL *RCA MONK 7* ...	**67**	1 wk
6 Aug 88	THIS IS YOUR LIFE *RCA PB 42149*	**70**	2 wks
8 Apr 89	THIS IS YOUR LIFE (re-mix) *RCA PB 42695* ...	**32**	5 wks
15 Jul 89	CHOICE? *RCA PB 42885 ***	**22**	6 wks
14 Oct 89	SLAVES NO MORE *RCA PB 43201 ***	**73**	2 wks
26 May 90	SPRINGTIME FOR THE WORLD *RCA PB 43623* ..	**69**	2 wks

* Blow Monkeys with Curtis Mayfield ** Blow Monkeys featuring Sylvia Tella

BLUE *UK, male vocal/instrumental group* **8 wks**

30 Apr 77	GONNA CAPTURE YOUR HEART *Rocket ROKN 522* ...	**18**	8 wks

Babbity BLUE *UK, female vocalist* **2 wks**

11 Feb 65	DON'T MAKE ME *Decca F 12053*	**48**	2 wks

Barry BLUE *UK, male vocalist* **48 wks**

28 Jul 73 ●	(DANCING) ON A SATURDAY NIGHT *Bell 1295* ..	**2**	15 wks
3 Nov 73 ●	DO YOU WANNA DANCE *Bell 1336*	**7**	12 wks
2 Mar 74	SCHOOL LOVE *Bell 1345*	**11**	9 wks
3 Aug 74	MISS HIT AND RUN *Bell 1364*	**26**	7 wks
26 Oct 74	HOT SHOT *Bell 1379*	**23**	5 wks

See also Cry Sisco!

BLUE AEROPLANES **3 wks**
UK, male/female vocal/instrumental group

17 Feb 89	JACKET HANGS *Ensign ENY 628*	**72**	1 wk
26 May 89	... AND STONES *Ensign ENY 632*	**63**	2 wks

BLUE FEATHER *Holland, male vocal/instrumental group* **4 wks**

3 Jul 82	LET'S FUNK TONIGHT *Mercury MER 109*	**50**	4 wks

BLUE FLAMES – *See Georgie FAME*

BLUE GRASS BOYS – *See Johnny DUNCAN and the BLUE GRASS BOYS*

BLUE HAZE *UK, male vocal/instrumental group* **6 wks**

18 Mar 72	SMOKE GETS IN YOUR EYES *A & M AMS 891*	**32**	6 wks

BLUE JEANS – *See Bob B. SOXX and the BLUE JEANS*

BLUE MERCEDES UK, male vocal/instrumental duo — 18 wks

10 Oct 87	I WANT TO BE YOUR PROPERTY MCA BONA 1	23	11 wks
13 Feb 88	SEE WANT MUST HAVE MCA BONA 2	57	2 wks
23 Jul 88	LOVE IS THE GUN MCA BONA 3	46	5 wks

BLUE MINK UK/US, male/female vocal/instrumental group — 83 wks

15 Nov 69 ●	MELTING POT Philips BF 1818	3	15 wks
28 Mar 70 ●	GOOD MORNING FREEDOM Philips BF 1838	10	10 wks
19 Sep 70	OUR WORLD Philips 6006 042	17	9 wks
29 May 71 ●	BANNER MAN Regal Zonophone RZ 3034	3	14 wks
11 Nov 72	STAY WITH ME Regal Zonophone RZ 3064	11	13 wks
17 Feb 73	STAY WITH ME (re-entry) Regal Zonophone RZ 3064	43	2 wks
3 Mar 73	BY THE DEVIL EMI 2007	26	9 wks
23 Jun 73 ●	RANDY EMI 2028	9	11 wks

BLUE NILE UK, male vocal/instrumental group — 4 wks

30 Sep 89	THE DOWNTOWN LIGHTS Linn LKS 3	67	1 wk
29 Sep 90	HEADLIGHTS ON THE PARADE Linn LKS 4	72	1 wk
19 Jan 91	SATURDAY NIGHT Linn LKS 5	50	2 wks

BLUE OYSTER CULT — 14 wks
US, male vocal/instrumental group

20 May 78	(DON'T FEAR) THE REAPER CBS 6333	16	14 wks

BLUE PEARL UK/US, male/female vocal/instrumental group — 26 wks

7 Jul 90 ●	NAKED IN THE RAIN Big Life BLR 23	4	13 wks
3 Nov 90	LITTLE BROTHER Big Life BLR 32	31	5 wks
11 Jan 92	(CAN YOU) FEEL THE PASSION Big Life BLR 67	14	6 wks
25 Jul 92	MOTHER DAWN Big Life BLR 73	50	2 wks

BLUE RONDO A LA TURK — 9 wks
UK, male vocal/instrumental group

14 Nov 81	ME AND MR SANCHEZ Virgin VS 463	40	4 wks
13 Mar 82	KLACTOVEESEDSTEIN Diable Noir VS 476	50	5 wks

BLUE ZOO UK, male vocal/instrumental group — 17 wks

12 Jun 82	I'M YOUR MAN Magnet MAG 224	55	3 wks
16 Oct 82	CRY BOY CRY Magnet MAG 234	13	10 wks
28 May 83	I JUST CAN'T (FORGIVE AND FORGET) Magnet MAG 241	60	4 wks

BLUEBELLS UK, male vocal/instrumental group — 37 wks

12 Mar 83	CATH London LON 20	62	2 wks
9 Jul 83	SUGAR BRIDGE (IT WILL STAND) London LON 27	72	1 wk
24 Mar 84	I'M FALLING London LON 45	11	12 wks
23 Jun 84 ●	YOUNG AT HEART London LON 49	8	12 wks
1 Sep 84	CATH (re-issue)/WILL SHE ALWAYS BE WAITING London LON 54	38	7 wks
9 Feb 85	ALL I AM (IS LOVING YOU) London LON 58	58	3 wks

BLUENOTES – See Harold MELVIN and the BLUENOTES

BLUES BAND UK, male vocal/instrumental group — 2 wks

12 Jul 80	BLUES BAND EP Arista BOOT 2	68	2 wks

Tracks on Blues Band EP: Maggie's Farm/Ain't it Tuff/Diddy Wah Diddy/Back Door Man.

BLUES BROTHERS US, male vocal duo — 8 wks

7 Apr 89	EVERYBODY NEEDS SOMEBODY TO LOVE East West A7591	12	8 wks

For the first two weeks, the flip side of Everybody Needs Somebody To Love was listed as Think by Aretha Franklin.

Colin BLUNSTONE UK, male vocalist — 29 wks

12 Feb 72	SAY YOU DON'T MIND Epic EPC 7765	15	9 wks
11 Nov 72	I DON'T BELIEVE IN MIRACLES Epic EPC 8434	31	6 wks
17 Feb 73	HOW COULD WE DARE TO BE WRONG Epic EPC 1197	45	2 wks
14 Mar 81	WHAT BECOMES OF THE BROKEN HEARTED Stiff BROKEN 1 *	13	10 wks
29 May 82	TRACKS OF MY TEARS PRT 7P 236	60	2 wks

* Dave Stewart. Guest vocals: Colin Blunstone
See also Neil MacArthur.

BLUR UK, male vocal/instrumental group — 19 wks

27 Oct 90	SHE'S SO HIGH Food FOOD 26	48	3 wks
27 Apr 91 ●	THERE'S NO OTHER WAY Food FOOD 29	8	8 wks
10 Aug 91	BANG Food FOOD 31	24	4 wks
11 Apr 92	POPSCENE Food FOOD 37	32	2 wks

B-MOVIE UK, male vocal/instrumental group — 7 wks

18 Apr 81	REMEMBRANCE DAY Deram DM 437	61	3 wks
27 Mar 82	NOWHERE GIRL Some Bizzare BZZ 8	67	4 wks

BOB and EARL US, male vocal duo — 13 wks

12 Mar 69 ●	HARLEM SHUFFLE Island WIP 6053	7	13 wks

BOB and MARCIA Jamaica, male/female vocal duo — 25 wks

14 Mar 70 ●	YOUNG GIFTED AND BLACK Harry J HJ 6605	5	12 wks
5 Jun 71	PIED PIPER Trojan TR 7818	11	13 wks

BOBBYSOCKS Norway/Sweden, female vocal duo — 4 wks

25 May 85	LET IT SWING RCA PB 40127	44	4 wks

Karen BODDINGTON and Mark WILLIAMS Australia, female/male vocal duo — 1 wk

2 Sep 89	HOME AND AWAY First Night SCORE 19	73	1 wk

BODYSNATCHERS UK, female vocal/instrumental group — 12 wks

15 Mar 80	LET'S DO ROCK STEADY 2 Tone CHS TT 9	22	9 wks
19 Jul 80	EASY LIFE 2 Tone CHS TT 12	50	3 wks

Humphrey BOGART – See Dooley WILSON

Hamilton BOHANNON — 38 wks
US, male vocalist/instrumentalist - drums

15 Feb 75	SOUTH AFRICAN MAN Brunswick BR 16	22	8 wks
24 May 75 ●	DISCO STOMP Brunswick BR 19	6	12 wks

5 Jul 75	FOOT STOMPIN' MUSIC *Brunswick BR 21*	23	6 wks
6 Sep 75	HAPPY FEELING *Brunswick BR 24*	49	3 wks
26 Aug 78	LET'S START THE DANCE *Mercury 6167 700*	56	4 wks
13 Feb 82	LET'S START TO DANCE AGAIN *London HL 10582*	49	5 wks

BOILING POINT *US, male vocal/instrumental group*   **6 wks**

| 27 May 78 | LET'S GET FUNKTIFIED *Bang BANG 1312* | 41 | 6 wks |

Marc BOLAN – *See T. REX*

Michael BOLTON *US, male vocalist*   **66 wks**

17 Feb 90 ●	HOW AM I SUPPOSED TO LIVE WITHOUT YOU		
	CBS 655397 7	3	10 wks
28 Apr 90 ●	HOW CAN WE BE LOVERS *CBS 655918 7*	10	10 wks
21 Jul 90	WHEN I'M BACK ON MY FEET AGAIN		
	CBS 656077 7	44	5 wks
20 Apr 91	LOVE IS A WONDERFUL THING *Columbia 6567717*	23	8 wks
27 Jul 91	TIME LOVE AND TENDERNESS *Columbia 6569897*	28	7 wks
9 Nov 91 ●	WHEN A MAN LOVES A WOMAN *Columbia 6574887*	6	9 wks
8 Feb 92	STEEL BARS *Columbia 6577257*	17	6 wks
9 May 92	MISSING YOU NOW *Columbia 6579917 **	28	4 wks
31 Oct 92	TO LOVE SOMEBODY *Columbia 6584557*	16	8 wks
26 Dec 92	DRIFT AWAY *Columbia 6588657*	19†	1 wk

* Michael Bolton featuring Kenny G

BOMB THE BASS *UK, male producer - Tim Simenon*   **42 wks**

20 Feb 88 ●	BEAT DIS *Mister-ron DOOD 1*	2	9 wks
27 Aug 88 ●	MEGABLAST/DON'T MAKE ME WAIT		
	Mister-ron DOOD 2 *	6	9 wks
26 Nov 88 ●	SAY A LITTLE PRAYER *Rhythm King DOOD 3 ***	10	10 wks
27 Jul 91 ●	WINTER IN JULY *Rhythm King 6572757*	7	9 wks
9 Nov 91	THE AIR YOU BREATHE *Rhythm King 6575387*	52	3 wks
2 May 92	KEEP GIVING ME LOVE *Rhythm King 6579887*	62	2 wks

* Bomb The Bass featuring Merlin and Antonia/Bomb The Bass featuring
Lorraine ** Bomb The Bass featuring Maureen

BOMBALURINA *UK, male/female vocal group*   **20 wks**

28 Jul 90 ★	ITSY BITSY TEENY WEENY YELLOW POLKA		
	DOT BIKINI *Carpet CRPT 1*	1	13 wks
24 Nov 90	SEVEN LITTLE GIRLS SITTING IN THE		
	BACKSEAT *Carpet CRPT 2 **	18	7 wks

* Bombalurina featuring Timmy Mallett

BOMBERS *Canada, male/female vocal/instrumental group*   **10 wks**

| 5 May 79 | (EVERYBODY) GET DANCIN' *Flamingo FM 1* | 37 | 7 wks |
| 18 Aug 79 | LET'S DANCE *Flamingo FM 4* | 58 | 3 wks |

BON JOVI *US, male vocal/instrumental group*   **77 wks**

31 Aug 85	HARDEST PART IS THE NIGHT *Vertigo VER 22*	68	1 wk
9 Aug 86	YOU GIVE LOVE A BAD NAME *Vertigo VER 26*	14	10 wks
25 Oct 86 ●	LIVIN' ON A PRAYER *Vertigo VER 28*	4	15 wks
11 Apr 87	WANTED DEAD OR ALIVE *Vertigo JOV 1*	13	7 wks
15 Aug 87	NEVER SAY GOODBYE *Vertigo JOV 2*	21	5 wks
24 Sep 88	BAD MEDICINE *Vertigo JOV 3*	17	7 wks
10 Dec 88	BORN TO BE MY BABY *Vertigo JOV 4*	22	7 wks
29 Apr 89	I'LL BE THERE FOR YOU *Vertigo JOV 5*	18	7 wks
26 Aug 89	LAY YOUR HANDS ON ME *Vertigo JOV 6*	18	6 wks
9 Dec 89	LIVING IN SIN *Vertigo JOV 7*	35	6 wks
24 Oct 92 ●	KEEP THE FAITH *Jambco JOV 8*	5	6 wks

Jon BON JOVI *US, male vocalist*   **13 wks**

| 4 Aug 90 | BLAZE OF GLORY *Vertigo JBJ 1* | 13 | 8 wks |
| 10 Nov 90 | MIRACLE *Vertigo JBVJ 2* | 29 | 5 wks |

Ronnie BOND *UK, male vocalist*   **5 wks**

| 31 May 80 | IT'S WRITTEN ON YOUR BODY *Mercury MER 13* | 52 | 5 wks |

Gary 'U.S.' BONDS *US, male vocalist*   **39 wks**

19 Jan 61	NEW ORLEANS *Top Rank JAR 527 **	16	11 wks
20 Jul 61	QUARTER TO THREE *Top Rank JAR 575 **	7	13 wks
30 May 81	THIS LITTLE GIRL *EMI America EA 122*	43	6 wks
22 Aug 81	JOLE BLON *EMI America EA 127*	51	3 wks
31 Oct 81	IT'S ONLY LOVE *EMI America EA 128*	43	3 wks
17 Jul 82	SOUL DEEP *EMI America EA 140*	59	3 wks

* U.S. Bonds

Elbow BONES and the RACKETEERS   **9 wks**
US, male group leader and female backing group

| 14 Jan 84 | A NIGHT IN NEW YORK *EMI America EA 165* | 33 | 9 wks |

BONEY M *Jamaica/Antilles/Montserrat, male/female vocal group* **159 wks**

18 Dec 76 ●	DADDY COOL *Atlantic K 10827*	6	13 wks
12 Mar 77 ●	SUNNY *Atlantic K 10892*	3	10 wks
25 Jun 77 ●	MA BAKER *Atlantic K 10965*	2	13 wks
29 Oct 77 ●	BELFAST *Atlantic K 11020*	8	13 wks
29 Apr 78 ★	RIVERS OF BABYLON/BROWN GIRL IN THE		
	RING *Atlantic/Hansa K 11120*	1	40 wks
7 Oct 78 ●	RASPUTIN *Atlantic/Hansa K 11192*	2	10 wks
2 Dec 78 ★	MARY'S BOY CHILD - OH MY LORD		
	Atlantic/Hansa K 11221	1	8 wks
3 Mar 79 ●	PAINTER MAN *Atlantic/Hansa K 11255*	10	6 wks
28 Apr 79	HOORAY HOORAY IT'S A HOLI-HOLIDAY		
	Atlantic/Hansa K 11279	3	9 wks
11 Aug 79	GOTTA GO HOME/EL LUTE *Atlantic/Hansa K 11351*	12	11 wks
15 Dec 79	I'M BORN AGAIN *Atlantic/Hansa K 11410*	35	7 wks
26 Apr 80	MY FRIEND JACK *Atlantic/Hansa K 11463*	57	5 wks
14 Feb 81	CHILDREN OF PARADISE *Atlantic/Hansa K 11637*	66	2 wks
21 Nov 81	WE KILL THE WORLD (DON'T KILL THE		
	WORLD) *Atlantic/Hansa K 11689*	39	5 wks
24 Dec 88	MEGAMIX/MARY'S BOY CHILD (re-mix)		
	Ariola 111947	52	3 wks
5 Dec 92 ●	BONEY M MEGAMIX *Arista 74321125127*	7†	4 wks

Brown Girl in The Ring *only listed with* Rivers of Babylon *from 5 Aug 78.* El Lute *only listed
with* Gotta Go Home *from 29 Sep 79. The megamixes are different.*

Graham BONNET *UK, male vocalist*   **15 wks**

| 21 Mar 81 ● | NIGHT GAMES *Vertigo VER 1* | 6 | 11 wks |
| 13 Jun 81 | LIAR *Vertigo VER 2* | 51 | 4 wks |

Graham BONNEY *UK, male vocalist*   **8 wks**

| 24 Mar 66 | SUPERGIRL *Columbia DB 7843* | 19 | 8 wks |

BONO – *See CLANNAD*

BONZO DOG DOO-DAH BAND   **14 wks**
UK, male vocal/instrumental group

| 6 Nov 68 ● | I'M THE URBAN SPACEMAN *Liberty LBF 15144* | 5 | 14 wks |

Betty BOO *UK, female rapper* **52 wks**

12 Aug 89 ●	HEY DJ I CAN'T DANCE TO THAT MUSIC YOU'RE PLAYING *Rhythm King LEFT 34* *	7	11 wks
19 May 90 ●	DOIN' THE DO *Rhythm King LEFT 39*	7	12 wks
11 Aug 90 ●	WHERE ARE YOU BABY *Rhythm King LEFT 43*	3	10 wks
1 Dec 90	24 HOURS *Rhythm King LEFT 45*	25	8 wks
8 Aug 92	LET ME TAKE YOU THERE *WEA YZ 677*	12	8 wks
3 Oct 92	I'M ON MY WAY *WEA YZ 693*	44	3 wks

* Beatmasters featuring Betty Boo

BOO RADLEYS *UK, male vocal/instrumental group* **1 wk**

20 Jun 92	DOES THIS HURT/BOO! FOREVER *Creation CRE 128*	67	1 wk

BOO-YAA T.R.I.B.E. *US, male rap group* **3 wks**

30 Jun 90	PSYKO FUNK *Fourth & Broadway BRW 179*	43	3 wks

BOOGIE BOX HIGH *UK, male vocal/instrumental duo* **11 wks**

4 Jul 87 ●	JIVE TALKIN' *Hardback 7BOSS 4*	7	11 wks

BOOGIE DOWN PRODUCTIONS **2 wks**
US, male rap/scratch duo

4 Jun 88	MY PHILOSOPHY/STOP THE VIOLENCE *Jive JIVEX 170*	69	2 wks

BOOKER T. and the M.G.'s **43 wks**
US, male instrumental group

11 Dec 68	SOUL LIMBO *Stax 102*	30	9 wks
7 May 69 ●	TIME IS TIGHT *Stax 119*	4	18 wks
30 Aug 69	SOUL CLAP '69 *Stax 127*	35	4 wks
15 Dec 79 ●	GREEN ONIONS *Atlantic K 10109*	7	12 wks

BOOM BOOM ROOM **1 wk**
UK, male vocal/instrumental group

8 Mar 86	HERE COMES THE MAN *Fun After All FUN 101*	74	1 wk

BOOMTOWN RATS **121 wks**
Ireland, male vocal/instrumental group

27 Aug 77	LOOKING AFTER NO. 1 *Ensign ENY 4*	11	9 wks
19 Nov 77	MARY OF THE FOURTH FORM *Ensign ENY 9*	15	9 wks
15 Apr 78	SHE'S SO MODERN *Ensign ENY 13*	12	11 wks
17 Jun 78 ●	LIKE CLOCKWORK *Ensign ENY 14*	6	13 wks
14 Oct 78 ★	RAT TRAP *Ensign ENY 16*	1	15 wks
21 Jul 79 ★	I DON'T LIKE MONDAYS *Ensign ENY 30*	1	12 wks
17 Nov 79	DIAMOND SMILES *Ensign ENY 33*	13	10 wks
26 Jan 80 ●	SOMEONE'S LOOKING AT YOU *Ensign ENY 34*	4	9 wks
22 Nov 80 ●	BANANA REPUBLIC *Ensign BONGO 1*	3	11 wks
31 Jan 81	THE ELEPHANT'S GRAVEYARD (GUILTY) *Ensign BONGO 2*	26	6 wks
12 Dec 81	NEVER IN A MILLION YEARS *Mercury MER 87*	62	4 wks
20 Mar 82	HOUSE ON FIRE *Mercury MER 91*	24	8 wks
18 Feb 84	TONIGHT *Mercury MER 154*	73	1 wk
19 May 84	DRAG ME DOWN *Mercury MER 163*	50	3 wks

British Hit Singles Part One: Alphabetically by Artist
Date of chart entry/Title & catalogue no./Peak position reached/Weeks on chart

★ Number one ● Top Ten † still on chart at 31 Dec 1992

* = credited to act billed in footnote

Daniel BOONE *UK, male vocalist* **25 wks**

14 Aug 71	DADDY DON'T YOU WALK SO FAST *Penny Farthing PEN 764*	17	15 wks
1 Apr 72	BEAUTIFUL SUNDAY *Penny Farthing PEN 781*	48	1 wk
15 Apr 72	BEAUTIFUL SUNDAY (re-entry) *Penny Farthing PEN 781*	21	9 wks

Debby BOONE *US, female vocalist* **2 wks**

24 Dec 77	YOU LIGHT UP MY LIFE *Warner Bros. K 17043*	48	2 wks

Pat BOONE *US, male vocalist* **296 wks**

18 Nov 55 ●	AIN'T THAT A SHAME *London HLD 8173*	7	9 wks
27 Apr 56 ★	I'LL BE HOME *London HLD 8253*	1	22 wks
27 Jul 56	LONG TALL SALLY *London HLD 8291*	27	3 wks
17 Aug 56	I ALMOST LOST MY MIND *London HLD 8303*	14	7 wks
24 Aug 56	LONG TALL SALLY (re-entry) *London HLD 8291*	18	4 wks
7 Dec 56 ●	FRIENDLY PERSUASION *London HLD 8346*	3	21 wks
11 Jan 57	AIN'T THAT A SHAME (re-entry) *London HLD 8173*	22	2 wks
11 Jan 57	I'LL BE HOME (re-entry) *London HLD 8253*	19	2 wks
1 Feb 57 ●	DON'T FORBID ME *London HLD 8370*	2	16 wks
26 Apr 57	WHY BABY WHY *London HLD 8404*	17	7 wks
5 Jul 57 ●	LOVE LETTERS IN THE SAND *London HLD 8445*	2	21 wks
27 Sep 57 ●	REMEMBER YOU'RE MINE/THERE'S A GOLDMINE IN THE SKY *London HLD 8479*	5	18 wks
6 Dec 57 ●	APRIL LOVE *London HLD 8512*	7	23 wks
13 Dec 57	WHITE CHRISTMAS *London HLD 8520*	29	1 wk
4 Apr 58 ●	A WONDERFUL TIME UP THERE *London HLD 8574*	2	17 wks
11 Apr 58 ●	IT'S TOO SOON TO KNOW *London HLD 8574*	7	12 wks
27 Jun 58 ●	SUGAR MOON *London HLD 8640*	6	12 wks
29 Aug 58	IF DREAMS CAME TRUE *London HLD 8675*	16	11 wks
5 Dec 58	GEE BUT IT'S LONELY *London HLD 8739*	30	1 wk
16 Jan 59	I'LL REMEMBER TONIGHT *London HLD 8775*	28	1 wk
6 Feb 59	I'LL REMEMBER TONIGHT (re-entry) *London HLD 8775*	21	1 wk
20 Feb 59	I'LL REMEMBER TONIGHT (2nd re-entry) *London HLD 8775*	18	7 wks
10 Apr 59	WITH THE WIND AND THE RAIN IN YOUR HAIR *London HLD 8824*	21	3 wks
22 May 59	FOR A PENNY *London HLD 8855*	28	3 wks
26 Jun 59	FOR A PENNY (re-entry) *London HLD 8855*	19	2 wks
31 Jul 59	'TWIXT TWELVE AND TWENTY *London HLD 8910*	18	6 wks
18 Sep 59	'TWIXT TWELVE AND TWENTY (re-entry) *London HLD 8910*	26	1 wk
23 Jun 60	WALKING THE FLOOR OVER YOU *London HLD 9138*	40	2 wks
14 Jul 60	WALKING THE FLOOR OVER YOU (re-entry) *London HLD 9138*	46	1 wk
4 Aug 60	WALKING THE FLOOR OVER YOU (2nd re-entry) *London HLD 9138*	39	2 wks
6 Jul 61	MOODY RIVER *London HLD 9350*	18	10 wks
7 Dec 61 ●	JOHNNY WILL *London HLD 9461*	4	13 wks
15 Feb 62	I'LL SEE YOU IN MY DREAMS *London HLD 9504*	27	9 wks
24 May 62	QUANDO QUANDO QUANDO *London HLD 9543*	41	4 wks
12 Jul 62 ●	SPEEDY GONZALES *London HLD 9573*	2	19 wks
15 Nov 62	THE MAIN ATTRACTION *London HLD 9620*	12	11 wks

There's A Goldmine In The Sky *was only credited for the week of 27 Sep 57.*

Duke BOOTEE – *See GRANDMASTER FLASH, Melle MEL and the FURIOUS FIVE*

Ken BOOTHE *Jamaica, male vocalist* **22 wks**

21 Sep 74 ★	EVERYTHING I OWN *Trojan TR 7920*	1	12 wks

BOOKER T. & THE M.G.'S cross a Memphis Street in a tribute to the Beatles' *Abbey Road*. The Stax studios can be seen top left.

BOY GEORGE also charted under the name emblazoned on his shirt, Jesus Loves You.

EDIE BRICKELL AND THE NEW BOHEMIANS sang 'A Hard Rain's A Gonna Fall' on the soundtrack of the film *Born On The Fourth Of July*.

| | 14 Dec 74 | CRYING OVER YOU *Trojan TR 7944* ....**11** | 10 wks |

BOOTHILL FOOTAPPERS
UK, male/female vocal/instrumental group **3 wks**

| 14 Jul 84 | GET YOUR FEET OUT OF MY SHOES
Go! Discs TAP 1 ....**64** | 3 wks |

BOOTSY'S RUBBER BAND
US, male vocal/instrumental group **3 wks**

| 8 Jul 78 | BOOTZILLA *Warner Bros. K 17196* ....**43** | 3 wks |

BOOTZILLA ORCHESTRA – *See Malcolm McLAREN*

BOSTON *US, male vocal/instrumental group* **13 wks**

| 29 Jan 77 | MORE THAN A FEELING *Epic EPC 4658* ....**22** | 8 wks |
| 7 Oct 78 | DON'T LOOK BACK *Epic EPC 6653* ....**43** | 5 wks |

Eve BOSWELL *Hungary, female vocalist* **13 wks**

30 Dec 55 ●	PICKIN' A CHICKEN *Parlophone R 4082* **9**	7 wks
2 Mar 56	PICKIN' A CHICKEN (re-entry) *Parlophone R 4082* **16**	3 wks
6 Apr 56	PICKIN' A CHICKEN (2nd re-entry) *Parlophone R 4082* **20**	3 wks

Judy BOUCHER *UK, female vocalist* **23 wks**

| 4 Apr 87 ● | CAN'T BE WITH YOU TONIGHT *Orbitone OR 721* ....**2** | 14 wks |
| 4 Jul 87 | YOU CAUGHT MY EYE *Orbitone OR 722* ....**18** | 9 wks |

Peter BOUNCER – *See SHUT UP AND DANCE*

BOUNCING CZECKS
UK, male vocal/instrumental group **1 wk**

| 29 Dec 84 | I'M A LITTLE CHRISTMAS CRACKER *RCA 463* ....**72** | 1 wk |

BOURGEOIS TAGG *US, male vocal/instrumental duo* **6 wks**

| 6 Feb 88 | I DON'T MIND AT ALL *Island IS 353* ....**35** | 6 wks |

BOURGIE BOURGIE *UK, male vocal/instrumental group* **4 wks**

| 3 Mar 84 | BREAKING POINT *MCA BOU 1* ....**48** | 4 wks |

BOW WOW WOW *UK, female/male vocal/instrumental group* **54 wks**

26 Jul 80	C30, C60, C90, GO *EMI 5088* **34**	7 wks
6 Dec 80	YOUR CASSETTE PET *EMI WOW 1* **58**	6 wks
28 Mar 81	W.O.R.K. (N.O. NAH NO NO MY DADDY DON'T) *EMI 5153* **62**	3 wks
15 Aug 81	PRINCE OF DARKNESS *RCA 100* **58**	4 wks
7 Nov 81	CHIHUAHUA *RCA 144* **51**	4 wks
30 Jan 82 ●	GO WILD IN THE COUNTRY *RCA 175* **7**	13 wks
1 May 82	SEE JUNGLE (JUNGLE BOY)/TV SAVAGE *RCA 220* ...**45**	3 wks
5 Jun 82 ●	I WANT CANDY *RCA 238* **9**	8 wks
31 Jul 82	LOUIS QUATORZE *RCA 263* **66**	2 wks
12 Mar 83	DO YOU WANNA HOLD ME *RCA 314* **47**	4 wks

Your Cassette Pet listed as Louis Quatorze on 6 Dec 80 only. Tracks on Your Cassette Pet (available only as a cassette) are: Louis Quatorze/Gold He Said/Umo-Sex-Al Apache/I Want My Baby On Mars/Sexy Eiffel Towers/Giant Sized Baby Thing/Fools Rush In/Radio G.String. RCA 263 is disc version of track on EMI WOW 1 Cassette.

BOWA featuring MALA
US, male/female vocal/instrumental duo **1 wk**

| 7 Dec 91 | DIFFERENT STORY *Dead Dead Good GOOD 8* ....**64** | 1 wk |

David BOWIE *UK, male vocalist* **405 wks**

6 Sep 69	SPACE ODDITY *Philips BF 1801* **48**	1 wk
20 Sep 69 ●	SPACE ODDITY (re-entry) *Philips BF 1801* **5**	13 wks
24 Jun 72 ●	STARMAN *RCA 2199* **10**	11 wks
16 Sep 72	JOHN I'M ONLY DANCING *RCA 2263* **12**	10 wks
9 Dec 72 ●	THE JEAN GENIE *RCA 2302* **2**	13 wks
14 Apr 73 ●	DRIVE-IN SATURDAY *RCA 2352* **3**	10 wks
30 Jun 73 ●	LIFE ON MARS *RCA 2316* **3**	13 wks
15 Sep 73	THE LAUGHING GNOME *Deram DM 123* **6**	12 wks
20 Oct 73 ●	SORROW *RCA 2424* **3**	15 wks
23 Feb 74 ●	REBEL REBEL *RCA LPBO 5009* **5**	7 wks
20 Apr 74	ROCK AND ROLL SUICIDE *RCA LPBO 5021* **22**	7 wks
22 Jun 74	DIAMOND DOGS *RCA APBO 0293* **21**	6 wks
28 Sep 74 ●	KNOCK ON WOOD *RCA 2466* **10**	6 wks
1 Mar 75	YOUNG AMERICANS *RCA 2523* **18**	7 wks
2 Aug 75	FAME *RCA 2579* **17**	8 wks
11 Oct 75 ★	SPACE ODDITY (re-issue) *RCA 2593* **1**	10 wks
29 Nov 75 ●	GOLDEN YEARS *RCA 2640* **8**	10 wks
22 May 76	TVC 15 *RCA 2682* **33**	4 wks
19 Feb 77 ●	SOUND AND VISION *RCA PB 0905* **3**	11 wks
15 Oct 77	HEROES *RCA PB 1121* **24**	8 wks
21 Jan 78	BEAUTY AND THE BEAST *RCA PB 1190* **39**	3 wks
2 Dec 78	BREAKING GLASS (EP) *RCA BOW 1* **54**	7 wks
5 May 79 ●	BOYS KEEP SWINGING *RCA BOW 2* **7**	10 wks
21 Jul 79	D.J. *RCA BOW 3* **29**	5 wks
15 Dec 79	JOHN I'M ONLY DANCING (AGAIN) (1975)/JOHN I'M ONLY DANCING (1972) *RCA BOW 4* **12**	8 wks
1 Mar 80	ALABAMA SONG *RCA BOW 5* **23**	5 wks
16 Aug 80 ★	ASHES TO ASHES *RCA BOW 6* **1**	10 wks
1 Nov 80 ●	FASHION *RCA BOW 7* **5**	12 wks
10 Jan 81	SCARY MONSTERS (AND SUPER CREEPS) *RCA BOW 8* **20**	6 wks
28 Mar 81	UP THE HILL BACKWARDS *RCA BOW 9* **32**	6 wks
14 Nov 81 ★	UNDER PRESSURE *EMI 5250 ** **1**	11 wks
28 Nov 81	WILD IS THE WIND *RCA BOW 10* **24**	10 wks
6 Mar 82	BAAL'S HYMN (EP) *RCA BOW 11* **29**	5 wks
10 Apr 82	CAT PEOPLE (PUTTING OUT FIRE) *MCA 770* **26**	6 wks
27 Nov 82 ●	PEACE ON EARTH - LITTLE DRUMMER BOY *RCA BOW 12 *** **3**	8 wks
26 Mar 83 ★	LET'S DANCE *EMI America EA 152* **1**	14 wks
11 Jun 83 ●	CHINA GIRL *EMI America EA 157* **2**	8 wks
24 Sep 83 ●	MODERN LOVE *EMI America EA 158* **2**	8 wks
5 Nov 83	WHITE LIGHT, WHITE HEAT *RCA 372* **46**	3 wks
22 Sep 84 ●	BLUE JEAN *EMI America EA 181* **6**	8 wks
8 Dec 84	TONIGHT *EMI America EA 187* **53**	4 wks
9 Feb 85	THIS IS NOT AMERICA *EMI America EA 190 **** **14**	7 wks
8 Jun 85	LOVING THE ALIEN *EMI America EA 195* **19**	6 wks
27 Jul 85	LOVING THE ALIEN (re-entry) *EMI America EA 195* **67**	1 wk
7 Sep 85 ★	DANCING IN THE STREET *EMI America EA 204 ***** **1**	12 wks
15 Mar 86 ●	ABSOLUTE BEGINNERS *Virgin VS 838* **2**	9 wks
21 Jun 86	UNDERGROUND *EMI America EA 216* **21**	6 wks
8 Nov 86	WHEN THE WIND BLOWS *Virgin VS 906* **44**	4 wks
4 Apr 87	DAY-IN DAY-OUT *EMI America EA 230* **17**	6 wks
27 Jun 87	TIME WILL CRAWL *EMI America EA 237* **33**	4 wks
29 Aug 87	NEVER LET ME DOWN *EMI America EA 239* **34**	6 wks
7 Apr 90	FAME (re-mix) *EMI-USA FAME 90* **28**	4 wks
22 Aug 92	REAL COOL WORLD *Warner Bros. W 0127* **53**	1 wk

* Queen and David Bowie ** David Bowie and Bing Crosby *** David Bowie and the Pat Metheny Group **** David Bowie and Mick Jagger

Tracks on Breaking Glass (EP): Breaking Glass/Art Decade/Ziggy Stardust. All three versions of John I'm Only Dancing are different. Tracks on Baal's Hymn (EP): Baal's Hymn/The Drowned Girl/Remembering Marie/The Dirty Song/Ballad of the Adventurers.

BOX TOPS *US, male vocal/instrumental group* **33 wks**

| 13 Sep 67 ● | THE LETTER *Stateside SS 2044* ....**5** | 12 wks |

| 20 Mar 68 | **CRY LIKE A BABY** *Bell 1001* | 15 | 12 wks |
| 23 Aug 69 | **SOUL DEEP** *Bell 1068* | 22 | 9 wks |

BOY GEORGE UK, male vocalist
38 wks

7 Mar 87	★	**EVERYTHING I OWN** *Virgin BOY 100*	1	9 wks
6 Jun 87		**KEEP ME IN MIND** *Virgin BOY 101*	29	4 wks
18 Jul 87		**SOLD** *Virgin BOY 102*	24	5 wks
21 Nov 87		**TO BE REBORN** *Virgin BOY 103*	13	7 wks
5 Mar 88		**LIVE MY LIFE** *Virgin BOY 105*	62	2 wks
18 Jun 88		**NO CLAUSE 28** *Virgin BOY 106*	57	3 wks
8 Oct 88		**DON'T CRY** *Virgin BOY 107*	60	2 wks
4 Mar 89		**DON'T TAKE MY MIND ON A TRIP** *Virgin BOY 108*	68	2 wks
19 Sep 92		**THE CRYING GAME** *Spaghetti CIAO 6*	22	4 wks

BOY MEETS GIRL US, male/female vocal duo
13 wks

| 3 Dec 88 | ● | **WAITING FOR A STAR TO FALL** *RCA PB 49519* | 9 | 13 wks |

Jimmy BOYD US, male vocalist
22 wks

8 May 53	●	**TELL ME A STORY** *Philips PB 126* *	5	15 wks
11 Sep 53		**TELL ME A STORY (re-entry)** *Philips PB 126* *	12	1 wk
27 Nov 53	●	**I SAW MOMMY KISSING SANTA CLAUS** *Columbia DB 3365*	3	6 wks

* Frankie Laine and Jimmy Boyd

Jacqueline BOYER France, female vocalist
2 wks

| 28 Apr 60 | **TOM PILLIBI** *Columbia DB 4452* | 33 | 2 wks |

BOYS US, male vocal group
3 wks

| 12 Nov 88 | **DIAL MY HEART** *Motown ZB 42245* | 61 | 2 wks |
| 29 Sep 90 | **CRAZY** *Motown ZB 44037* | 57 | 1 wk |

BOYS NEXT DOOR – *See June HUTTON and Axel STORDAHL with the BOYS NEXT DOOR*

BOYSTOWN GANG US, male/female vocal group
20 wks

22 Aug 81		**AIN'T NO MOUNTAIN HIGH ENOUGH - REMEMBER ME (MEDLEY)** *WEA DICK 1*	46	6 wks
31 Jul 82	●	**CAN'T TAKE MY EYES OFF YOU** *ERC 101*	4	11 wks
9 Oct 82		**SIGNED SEALED DELIVERED (I'M YOURS)** *ERC 102*	50	3 wks

BOYZ – *See HEAVY D and the BOYZ*

BOYZ II MEN US, male vocal group
19 wks

| 5 Sep 92 | ★ | **END OF THE ROAD** *Motown TMG 1411* | 1† | 17 wks |
| 19 Dec 92 | | **MOTOWNPHILLY** *Motown TMG 1402* | 23† | 2 wks |

Billy BRAGG UK, male vocalist
49 wks

16 Mar 85		**BETWEEN THE WARS (EP)** *Go! Discs AGOEP 1*	15	6 wks
28 Dec 85		**DAYS LIKE THESE** *Go! Discs GOD 8*	43	5 wks
28 Jun 86		**LEVI STUBBS TEARS** *Go! Discs GOD 12*	29	6 wks
15 Nov 86		**GREETINGS TO THE NEW BRUNETTE** *Go! Discs GOD 15*	58	2 wks
14 May 88	★	**SHE'S LEAVING HOME** *Childline CHILD 1* *	1	11 wks
10 Sep 88		**WAITING FOR THE GREAT LEAP FORWARDS** *Go! Discs GOD 23*	52	3 wks
8 Jul 89		**WON'T TALK ABOUT IT** *Go Beat GOD 33* **	29	6 wks
6 Jul 91		**SEXUALITY** *Go! Discs GOD 56*	27	5 wks
7 Sep 91		**YOU WOKE UP MY NEIGHBOURHOOD** *Go! Discs GOD 60*	54	2 wks

| 29 Feb 92 | | **ACCIDENT WAITING TO HAPPEN (EP)** *Go! Discs GOD 67* | 33 | 3 wks |

* Billy Bragg with Cara Tivey ** Norman Cook featuring Billy Bragg

Tracks on Between The Wars (EP): *Between The Wars/Which Side Are You On/World Turned Upside Down/It Says Here.* Tracks on Accident Waiting To Happen (EP): *Accident Waiting To Happen/Revolution/Sulk/The Warmest Room.* She's Leaving Home *was listed with the flip side* With A Little Help From My Friends *by Wet Wet Wet.* Won't Talk About It *was listed with the flip side* Blame It On The Bassline *by Norman Cook featuring MC Wildski.*

Wilfred BRAMBELL and Harry H. CORBETT UK, male vocal duo
12 wks

| 28 Nov 63 | **AT THE PALACE** (PARTS 1 & 2) *Pye 7N 15588* | 25 | 12 wks |

BRAND NEW HEAVIES
19 wks

UK, male/female vocal/instrumental group

5 Oct 91	**NEVER STOP** *ffrr F 165*	43	3 wks
15 Feb 92	**DREAM COME TRUE** *ffrr F 180*	24	4 wks
18 Apr 92	**ULTIMATE TRUNK FUNK EP** *ffrr F 185*	19	6 wks
1 Aug 92	**DON'T LET IT GO TO YOUR HEAD** *Acid Jazz BNH 1*	24	4 wks
19 Dec 92	**STAY THIS WAY** *Acid Jazz BNH 2*	40†	2 wks

All the above hits are credited 'featuring N'Dea Davenport' on either the sleeve or the label. Tracks on Ultimate Trunk Funk EP: *Never Stop/Stay This Way/Mr Tanaka/Never Stop (re-mix). BNH 2 is a remixed version to that on the EP.*

Johnny BRANDON UK, male vocalist
12 wks

11 Mar 55	●	**TOMORROW** *Polygon P 1131* *	8	6 wks
29 Apr 55		**TOMORROW (re-entry)** *Polygon P 1131* *	16	2 wks
1 Jul 55		**DON'T WORRY** *Polygon P 1163*	18	4 wks

* Johnny Brandon and the Phantoms

Laura BRANIGAN US, female vocalist
33 wks

18 Dec 82	●	**GLORIA** *Atlantic K 11759*	6	13 wks
7 Jul 84	●	**SELF CONTROL** *Atlantic A 9676*	5	17 wks
6 Oct 84		**THE LUCKY ONE** *Atlantic A 9636*	56	3 wks

BRASS CONSTRUCTION
35 wks

US, male vocal/instrumental group

3 Apr 76	**MOVIN'** *United Artists UP 36090*	23	6 wks
5 Feb 77	**HA CHA CHA (FUNKTION)** *United Artists UP 36205*	37	5 wks
26 Jan 80	**MUSIC MAKES YOU FEEL LIKE DANCING** *United Artists UP 615*	39	6 wks
28 May 83	**WALKIN' THE LINE** *Capitol CL 292*	47	3 wks
16 Jul 83	**WE CAN WORK IT OUT** *Capitol CL 299*	70	2 wks
7 Jul 84	**PARTYLINE** *Capitol CL 335*	56	4 wks
27 Oct 84	**INTERNATIONAL** *Capitol CL 341*	70	2 wks
9 Nov 85	**GIVE AND TAKE** *Capitol CL 377*	62	3 wks
28 May 88	**MOVIN' 1988 (re-mix)** *Syncopate SY 11*	24	4 wks

BRAT UK, male vocalist - Roger Kitter
8 wks

| 10 Jul 82 | **CHALK DUST - THE UMPIRE STRIKES BACK** *Hansa SMASH 1* | 19 | 8 wks |

Los BRAVOS Spain/Germany, male vocal/instrumental group
24 wks

| 30 Jun 66 | ● | **BLACK IS BLACK** *Decca F 22419* | 2 | 13 wks |
| 8 Sep 66 | | **I DON'T CARE** *Decca F 22484* | 16 | 11 wks |

Dhar BRAXTON US, female vocalist — 8 wks

31 May 86	**JUMP BACK (SET ME FREE)** Fourth & Broadway BRW 47	**32**	8 wks

BREAD US, male vocal/instrumental group — 46 wks

1 Aug 70 ●	**MAKE IT WITH YOU** Elektra 2101 010	**5**	14 wks
15 Jan 72	**BABY I'M A WANT YOU** Elektra K 12033	**14**	10 wks
29 Apr 72	**EVERYTHING I OWN** Elektra K 12041	**32**	6 wks
30 Sep 72	**GUITAR MAN** Elektra K 12066	**16**	9 wks
25 Dec 76	**LOST WITHOUT YOUR LOVE** Elektra K 12241	**27**	7 wks

BREAK MACHINE US, male vocal/dance group — 32 wks

4 Feb 84 ●	**STREET DANCE** Record Shack SOHO 13	**3**	14 wks
12 May 84 ●	**BREAKDANCE PARTY** Record Shack SOHO 20	**9**	8 wks
14 Jul 84	**BREAKDANCE PARTY (re-entry)** Record Shack SOHO 20	**65**	2 wks
11 Aug 84	**ARE YOU READY?** Record Shack SOHO 24	**27**	8 wks

BREAKFAST CLUB US, male vocal/instrumental group — 3 wks

27 Jun 87	**RIGHT ON TRACK** MCA MCA 1146	**54**	3 wks

BREATHE UK, male vocal/instrumental group — 27 wks

30 Jul 88 ●	**HANDS TO HEAVEN** Siren SRN 68	**4**	12 wks
22 Oct 88	**JONAH** Siren SRN 95	**60**	3 wks
3 Dec 88	**HOW CAN I FALL** Siren SRN 102	**48**	7 wks
11 Mar 89	**DON'T TELL ME LIES** Siren SRN 109	**45**	5 wks

Freddy BRECK Germany, male vocalist — 4 wks

13 Apr 74	**SO IN LOVE WITH YOU** Decca F 13481	**44**	4 wks

BRECKER BROTHERS
US, male vocal/instrumental group — 5 wks

4 Nov 78	**EAST RIVER** Arista ARIST 211	**34**	5 wks

BREEDERS US, female/male vocal/instrumental group — 1 wk

18 Apr 92	**SAFARI (EP)** 4AD BAD 2003	**69**	1 wk

Tracks on Safari (EP): Do You Love Me Now/Don't Call Home/Safari/So Sad About Us.

BREEKOUT KREW US, male vocal duo — 3 wks

24 Nov 84	**MATT'S MOOD** London LON 59	**51**	3 wks

Ann BREEN Ireland, female vocalist — 2 wks

19 Mar 83	**PAL OF MY CRADLE DAYS** Homespun HS 052	**69**	1 wk
7 Jan 84	**PAL OF MY CRADLE DAYS (re-entry)** Homespun HS 052	**74**	1 wk

BRENDON UK, male vocalist — 9 wks

19 Mar 77	**GIMME SOME** Magnet MAG 80	**14**	9 wks

Maire BRENNAN Ireland, female vocalist — 2 wks

16 May 92	**AGAINST THE WIND** RCA PB 45399	**64**	2 wks

Rose BRENNAN Ireland, female vocalist — 9 wks

7 Dec 61	**TALL DARK STRANGER** Philips PB 1193	**31**	9 wks

Walter BRENNAN US, male vocalist — 3 wks

28 Jun 62	**OLD RIVERS** Liberty LIB 55436	**38**	3 wks

Tony BRENT UK, male vocalist — 52 wks

19 Dec 52 ●	**WALKIN' TO MISSOURI** Columbia DB 3147	**9**	2 wks
2 Jan 53 ●	**MAKE IT SOON** Columbia DB 3187	**9**	4 wks
9 Jan 53 ●	**WALKIN' TO MISSOURI (re-entry)** Columbia DB 3147	**7**	5 wks
23 Jan 53	**GOT YOU ON MY MIND** Columbia DB 3226	**12**	1 wk
13 Mar 53	**MAKE IT SOON (re-entry)** Columbia DB 3187	**9**	3 wks
30 Nov 56	**CINDY OH CINDY** Columbia DB 3844	**16**	6 wks
8 Feb 57	**CINDY OH CINDY (re-entry)** Columbia DB 3844	**30**	1 wk
28 Jun 57	**DARK MOON** Columbia DB 3950	**17**	14 wks
28 Feb 58	**THE CLOUDS WILL SOON ROLL BY** Columbia DB 4066	**24**	3 wks
9 May 58	**THE CLOUDS WILL SOON ROLL BY (re-entry)** Columbia DB 4066	**20**	2 wks
5 Sep 58	**GIRL OF MY DREAMS** Columbia DB 4177	**16**	7 wks
24 Jul 59	**WHY SHOULD I BE LONELY** Columbia DB 4304	**24**	4 wks

Bernard BRESSLAW UK, male vocalist — 11 wks

5 Sep 58 ●	**MAD PASSIONATE LOVE** HMV POP 522	**6**	11 wks

See also Michael Medwin, Bernard Bresslaw, Alfie Bass and Leslie Fyson.

Teresa BREWER US, female vocalist — 53 wks

11 Feb 55 ●	**LET ME GO LOVER** Vogue/Coral Q 72043	**9**	10 wks
13 Apr 56 ●	**A TEAR FELL** Vogue/Coral Q 72146	**2**	15 wks
13 Jul 56 ●	**SWEET OLD-FASHIONED GIRL** Vogue/Coral Q 72172	**3**	15 wks
10 May 57	**NORA MALONE** Vogue/Coral Q 72224	**26**	2 wks
23 Jun 60	**HOW DO YOU KNOW IT'S LOVE** Coral Q 72396	**21**	11 wks

BRIAN and MICHAEL UK, male vocal duo — 19 wks

25 Feb 78 ★	**MATCHSTALK MEN AND MATCHSTALK CATS AND DOGS** Pye 7N 46035	**1**	19 wks

BRICK US, male vocal/instrumental group — 4 wks

5 Feb 77	**DAZZ** Bang 004	**36**	4 wks

Edie BRICKELL and the NEW BOHEMIANS — 8 wks
US, female/male vocal/instrumental group

4 Feb 89	**WHAT I AM** Geffen GEF 49	**31**	7 wks
27 May 89	**CIRCLE** Geffen GEF 51	**74**	1 wk

Alicia BRIDGES US, female vocalist — 10 wks

11 Nov 78	**I LOVE THE NIGHT LIFE (DISCO ROUND)** Polydor 2066 936	**32**	10 wks

BRIGHOUSE AND RASTRICK BRASS BAND *UK, male brass band*   **13 wks**

12 Nov 77 ●	THE FLORAL DANCE *Transatlantic BIG 548*	**2**	13 wks

Bette BRIGHT *UK, female vocalist*   **5 wks**

8 Mar 80	HELLO I AM YOUR HEART *Korova KOW 3*	**50**	5 wks

Sarah BRIGHTMAN *UK, female vocalist*   **79 wks**

11 Nov 78 ●	I LOST MY HEART TO A STARSHIP TROOPER *Ariola/Hansa AHA 527 ***	**6**	14 wks
7 Apr 79	THE ADVENTURES OF THE LOVE CRUSADER *Ariola/Hansa AHA 538 *** ***	**53**	5 wks
30 Jul 83	HIM *Polydor POSP 625 *** * **	**55**	4 wks
23 Mar 85 ●	PIE JESU *HMV WEBBER 1 *** ** **	**3**	8 wks
11 Jan 86 ●	THE PHANTOM OF THE OPERA *Polydor POSP 800 *** ** ** **	**7**	10 wks
4 Oct 86 ●	ALL I ASK OF YOU *Polydor POSP 802 *** ** ** ** **	**3**	16 wks
10 Jan 87 ●	WISHING YOU WERE SOMEHOW HERE AGAIN *Polydor POSP 803*	**7**	11 wks
11 Jul 92	AMIGOS PARA SIEMPRE (FRIENDS FOR LIFE) *Really Useful RUR 10 *** ** ** ** ** **	**11**	11 wks

* Sarah Brightman and Hot Gossip ** Sarah Brightman and the Starship Troopers *** Sarah Brightman and the Royal Philharmonic Orchestra **** Sarah Brightman and Paul Miles-Kingston ***** Sarah Brightman and Steve Harley ****** Cliff Richard and Sarah Brightman ******* Jose Carreras and Sarah Brightman

The listed flip side of Wishing You Were Somehow Here Again *was* The Music Of The Night *by Michael Crawford.*

BRIGHTON AND HOVE ALBION F.C.   **2 wks**
UK, male football team vocalists

28 May 83	THE BOYS IN THE OLD BRIGHTON BLUE *Energy NRG 2*	**65**	2 wks

BRILLIANT *UK, male/female vocal/instrumental group*   **13 wks**

19 Oct 85	IT'S A MAN'S MAN'S MAN'S WORLD *Food FOOD 5*	**58**	5 wks
22 Mar 86	LOVE IS WAR *Food FOOD 6*	**64**	4 wks
2 Aug 86	SOMEBODY *Food FOOD 7*	**67**	4 wks

Johnny BRISTOL *US, male vocalist*   **16 wks**

24 Aug 74 ●	HANG ON IN THERE BABY *MGM 2006 443*	**3**	11 wks
19 Jul 80	MY GUY - MY GIRL (MEDLEY) *Atlantic/Hansa K 11550 **	**39**	5 wks

* Amii Stewart and Johnny Bristol

BRITS – *See VARIOUS ARTISTS (MONTAGES)*

BROKEN ENGLISH *UK, male vocal/instrumental group*   **13 wks**

30 May 87	COMIN' ON STRONG *EMI EM 5*	**18**	10 wks
3 Oct 87	LOVE ON THE SIDE *EMI EM 55*	**69**	3 wks

BRONSKI BEAT *UK, male vocal/instrumental group*   **78 wks**

2 Jun 84 ●	SMALLTOWN BOY *Forbidden Fruit BITE 1*	**3**	13 wks
22 Sep 84 ●	WHY? *Forbidden Fruit BITE 2*	**6**	10 wks
1 Dec 84	IT AIN'T NECESSARILY SO *Forbidden Fruit BITE 3*	**16**	11 wks
20 Apr 85 ●	I FEEL LOVE (MEDLEY) *Forbidden Fruit BITE 4 **	**3**	12 wks
30 Nov 85 ●	HIT THAT PERFECT BEAT *Forbidden Fruit BITE 6*	**3**	14 wks
29 Mar 86	COME ON, COME ON *Forbidden Fruit BITE 7*	**20**	7 wks

1 Jul 89	CHA CHA HEELS *Arista 112331 ***	**32**	7 wks
2 Feb 91	SMALLTOWN BOY (re-mix) *London LON 287 *** ***	**32**	4 wks

* Bronski Beat and Marc Almond ** Eartha Kitt and Bronski Beat *** Jimmy Somerville with Bronski Beat

Tracks on medley: I Feel Love/Love To Love You Baby/Johnny Remember Me.

Jet BRONX and the FORBIDDEN   **1 wk**
UK, male vocal/instrumental group

17 Dec 77	AIN'T DOIN' NOTHIN' *Lightning LIG 50*	**49**	1 wk

BROOK BROTHERS *UK, male vocal duo*   **35 wks**

30 Mar 61 ●	WARPAINT *Pye 7N 15333*	**5**	14 wks
24 Aug 61	AIN'T GONNA WASH FOR A WEEK *Pye 7N 15369*	**13**	10 wks
25 Jan 62	HE'S OLD ENOUGH TO KNOW BETTER *Pye 7N 15409*	**37**	1 wk
16 Aug 62	WELCOME HOME BABY *Pye 7N 15453*	**33**	6 wks
21 Feb 63	TROUBLE IS MY MIDDLE NAME *Pye 7N 15498*	**38**	4 wks

Bruno BROOKES – *See Liz KERSHAW and Bruno BROOKES*

BROOKLYN, BRONX and QUEENS – *See BB and Q Band*

Elkie BROOKS *UK, female vocalist*   **91 wks**

2 Apr 77 ●	PEARL'S A SINGER *A & M AMS 7275*	**8**	9 wks
20 Aug 77 ●	SUNSHINE AFTER THE RAIN *A & M AMS 7306*	**10**	9 wks
25 Feb 78	LILAC WINE *A & M AMS 7333*	**16**	7 wks
3 Jun 78	ONLY LOVE CAN BREAK YOUR HEART *A & M AMS 7353*	**43**	5 wks
11 Nov 78	DON'T CRY OUT LOUD *A & M AMS 7395*	**12**	11 wks
5 May 79	THE RUNAWAY *A & M AMS 7428*	**50**	5 wks
16 Jan 82	FOOL IF YOU THINK IT'S OVER *A & M AMS 8187*	**17**	10 wks
1 May 82	OUR LOVE *A & M AMS 8214*	**43**	5 wks
17 Jul 82	NIGHTS IN WHITE SATIN *A & M AMS 8235*	**33**	5 wks
22 Jan 83	GASOLINE ALLEY *A & M AMS 8305*	**52**	5 wks
22 Nov 86 ●	NO MORE THE FOOL *Legend LM 4*	**5**	16 wks
4 Apr 87	BREAK THE CHAIN *Legend LM 8*	**55**	3 wks
11 Jul 87	WE'VE GOT TONIGHT *Legend LM 9*	**69**	1 wk

Garth BROOKS *US, male vocalist*   **1 wk**

1 Feb 92	SHAMELESS *Capitol CL 646*	**71**	1 wk

Mel BROOKS *US, male vocalist*   **10 wks**

18 Feb 84	TO BE OR NOT TO BE (THE HITLER RAP) *Island IS 158*	**12**	10 wks

Norman BROOKS *US, male vocalist*   **1 wk**

12 Nov 54	A SKY BLUE SHIRT AND A RAINBOW TIE *London L 1228*	**17**	1 wk

BROS *UK, male vocal/instrumental group*   **84 wks**

5 Dec 87	WHEN WILL I BE FAMOUS *CBS ATOM 2*	**62**	2 wks
9 Jan 88 ●	WHEN WILL I BE FAMOUS (re-entry) *CBS ATOM 2*	**2**	13 wks
19 Mar 88 ●	DROP THE BOY *CBS ATOM 3*	**2**	10 wks
18 Jun 88 ★	I OWE YOU NOTHING *CBS ATOM 4*	**1**	11 wks
17 Sep 88 ●	I QUIT *CBS ATOM 5*	**4**	8 wks
3 Dec 88 ●	CAT AMONG THE PIGEONS/SILENT NIGHT *CBS ATOM 6*	**2**	8 wks
29 Jul 89 ●	TOO MUCH *CBS ATOM 7*	**2**	7 wks
7 Oct 89 ●	CHOCOLATE BOX *CBS ATOM 8*	**9**	6 wks
16 Dec 89 ●	SISTER *CBS ATOM 9*	**10**	6 wks
10 Mar 90	MADLY IN LOVE *CBS ATOM 10*	**14**	4 wks
13 Jul 91	ARE YOU MINE *Columbia 6569707*	**12**	5 wks
21 Sep 91	TRY *Columbia 6574047*	**27**	4 wks

Act were duo for last six hits.

PATRICK MACNEE AND HONOR
BLACKMAN admire her kinky boots.

BREAD appear on the
1972 US TV
Valentine's Day special
Love Love Love.

Below: VIVIAN BLAINE (left), star of *Guys
And Dolls*, welcomes Diana Lynn to her party
for leading ladies on the West End stage in
1953, the year of her hit from the show.

Left: Although the
Hollies have had the
biggest UK hit with
'Stay', JACKSON
BROWNE did
outdistance the
original American
number one by
Maurice Williams and
the Zodiacs, and a
1982 version by
Barry Manilow.

BROTHER BEYOND *UK, male vocal/instrumental group* **58 wks**

4 Apr 87	HOW MANY TIMES *EMI EMI 5591*	62	3 wks
8 Aug 87	CHAIN-GANG SMILE *Parlophone R 6160*	57	3 wks
23 Jan 88	CAN YOU KEEP A SECRET *Parlophone R 6174*	56	4 wks
30 Jul 88	● THE HARDER I TRY *Parlophone R 6184*	2	14 wks
5 Nov 88	● HE AIN'T NO COMPETITION *Parlophone R 6193*	6	10 wks
21 Apr 89	BE MY TWIN *Parlophone R 6195*	14	6 wks
1 Apr 89	CAN YOU KEEP A SECRET (re-mix) *Parlophone R 6197*	22	5 wks
28 Oct 89	DRIVE ON *Parlophone R 6233*	39	4 wks
9 Dec 89	WHEN WILL I SEE YOU AGAIN *Parlophone R 6239*	43	5 wks
10 Mar 90	TRUST *Parlophone R 6245*	53	2 wks
19 Jan 91	THE GIRL I USED TO KNOW *Parlophone R 6265*	48	2 wks

BROTHERHOOD OF MAN **97 wks**
UK, male/female vocal group

14 Feb 70	● UNITED WE STAND *Deram DM 284*	10	9 wks
4 Jul 70	WHERE ARE YOU GOING TO MY LOVE *Deram DM 298*	22	10 wks
13 Mar 76	★ SAVE YOUR KISSES FOR ME *Pye 7N 45569*	1	16 wks
19 Jun 76	MY SWEET ROSALIE *Pye 7N 45602*	30	7 wks
26 Feb 77	● OH BOY (THE MOOD I'M IN) *Pye 7N 45656*	8	12 wks
9 Jul 77	★ ANGELO *Pye 7N 45699*	1	12 wks
14 Jan 78	★ FIGARO *Pye 7N 46037*	1	11 wks
27 May 78	BEAUTIFUL LOVER *Pye 7N 46071*	15	12 wks
30 Sep 78	MIDDLE OF THE NIGHT *Pye 7N 46117*	41	6 wks
3 Jul 82	LIGHTNING FLASH *EMI 5309*	67	2 wks

BROTHER LOVE – See PRATT and McCLAIN with BROTHER LOVE

BROTHERS *UK, male vocal group* **9 wks**

29 Jan 77	● SING ME *Bus Stop Bus 1054*	8	9 wks

BROTHERS FOUR *US, male vocal group* **2 wks**

23 Jun 60	GREENFIELDS *Philips PB 1009*	49	1 wk
7 Jul 60	GREENFIELDS (re-entry) *Philips PB 1009*	40	1 wk

BROTHERS GRIMM – See JAZZ and the BROTHERS GRIMM

BROTHERS IN RHYTHM **10 wks**
US, male vocal/instrumental group

16 Mar 91	SUCH A GOOD FEELING *4th + B'way BRW 228*	64	2 wks
14 Sep 91	SUCH A GOOD FEELING (re-entry) *4th + B'way BRW 228*	14	8 wks

BROTHERS JOHNSON **34 wks**
US, male vocal/instrumental duo

9 Jul 77	STRAWBERRY LETTER 23 *A & M AMS 7297*	35	5 wks
2 Sep 78	AIN'T WE FUNKIN' NOW *A & M AMS 7379*	43	6 wks
4 Nov 78	RIDE-O-ROCKET *A & M AMS 7400*	50	4 wks
23 Feb 80	● STOMP *A & M AMS 7509*	6	12 wks
31 May 80	LIGHT UP THE NIGHT *A & M AMS 7526*	47	4 wks
25 Jul 81	THE REAL THING *A & M AMS 8149*	50	3 wks

Edgar BROUGHTON BAND **10 wks**
UK, male vocal/instrumental group

18 Apr 70	OUT DEMONS OUT *Harvest HAR 5015*	39	5 wks
23 Jan 71	APACHE DROPOUT *Harvest HAR 5032*	49	1 wk
6 Feb 71	APACHE DROPOUT (re-entry) *Harvest HAR 5032*	35	2 wks
13 Mar 71	APACHE DROPOUT (2nd re-entry) *Harvest HAR 5032*	35	1 wk
27 Mar 71	APACHE DROPOUT (3rd re-entry) *Harvest HAR 5032*	33	1 wk

Angie BROWN – See BIZARRE INC

Bobby BROWN *US, male vocalist* **89 wks**

6 Aug 88	DON'T BE CRUEL *MCA MCA 1268*	42	7 wks
17 Dec 88	● MY PREROGATIVE *MCA MCA 1299*	6	17 wks
25 Mar 89	DON'T BE CRUEL (re-issue) *MCA MCA 1310*	13	8 wks
20 May 89	● EVERY LITTLE STEP *MCA MCA 1338*	6	9 wks
15 Jul 89	● ON OUR OWN (FROM GHOSTBUSTERS II) *MCA MCA 1350*	4	9 wks
23 Sep 89	ROCK WIT'CHA *MCA MCA 1367*	33	6 wks
25 Nov 89	RONI *MCA MCA 1384*	21	7 wks
9 Jun 90	THE FREE STYLE MEGA-MIX *MCA MCA 1421*	14	7 wks
30 Jun 90	SHE AIN'T WORTH IT *London LON 265* *	12	9 wks
22 Aug 92	HUMPIN' AROUND *MCA MCS 1680*	19	6 wks
17 Oct 92	GOOD ENOUGH *MCA MCS 1704*	41	4 wks

* Glenn Medeiros featuring Bobby Brown

Carl BROWN – See DOUBLE TROUBLE

Crazy World of Arthur BROWN **14 wks**
UK, male vocal/instrumental group

26 Jun 68	★ FIRE *Track 604 022*	1	14 wks

Dennis BROWN *Jamaica, male vocalist* **18 wks**

3 Mar 79	MONEY IN MY POCKET *Lightning LV 5*	14	9 wks
3 Jul 82	LOVE HAS FOUND ITS WAY *A & M AMS 8226*	47	6 wks
11 Sep 82	HALFWAY UP HALFWAY DOWN *A & M AMS 8250*	56	3 wks

Diana BROWN and Barrie K. SHARPE **11 wks**
UK, female/male vocal duo

2 Jun 90	THE MASTERPLAN *ffrr F 133*	39	6 wks
1 Sep 90	SUN WORSHIPPERS (POSITIVE THINKING) *ffrr F 144*	61	2 wks
23 Mar 91	LOVE OR NOTHING *ffrr F 152*	71	1 wk
27 Jun 92	EATING ME ALIVE *ffrr F 190*	53	2 wks

Errol BROWN *UK, male vocalist* **10 wks**

4 Jul 87	PERSONAL TOUCH *WEA YZ 130*	25	8 wks
28 Nov 87	BODY ROCKIN' *WEA YZ 162*	51	2 wks

Gloria D. BROWN *US, female vocalist* **3 wks**

8 Jun 85	THE MORE THEY KNOCK, THE MORE I LOVE YOU *10 TEN 52*	57	3 wks

James BROWN *US, male vocalist* **99 wks**

23 Sep 65	PAPA'S GOT A BRAND NEW BAG *London HL 9990* *	25	7 wks
24 Feb 66	I GOT YOU *Pye International 7N 25350* *	29	6 wks
16 Jun 66	IT'S A MAN'S MAN'S MAN'S WORLD *Pye International 7N 25371* *	13	9 wks
10 Oct 70	GET UP I FEEL LIKE BEING A SEX MACHINE *Polydor 2001 071*	32	7 wks
27 Nov 71	HEY AMERICA *Mojo 2093 006*	47	3 wks
18 Sep 76	GET UP OFFA THAT THING *Polydor 2066 687*	22	6 wks
29 Jan 77	BODY HEAT *Polydor 2066 763*	36	4 wks
10 Jan 81	RAPP PAYBACK (WHERE IZ MOSES?) *RCA 28*	39	5 wks
2 Jul 83	BRING IT ON ... BRING IT ON *Sonet SON 2258*	45	4 wks
1 Sep 84	UNITY (PART 1 - THE THIRD COMING) *Tommy Boy AFR 2* **	49	5 wks

27 Apr 85	FROGGY MIX Boiling Point FROG 1	50	3 wks
1 Jun 85	GET UP I FEEL LIKE BEING A SEX MACHINE (re-issue) Boiling Point POSP 751	47	5 wks
25 Jan 86 ●	LIVING IN AMERICA Scotti Brothers A 6701	5	10 wks
1 Mar 86	GET UP I FEEL LIKE BEING A SEX MACHINE (re-entry of re-issue) Boiling Point POSP 751	46	4 wks
18 Oct 86	GRAVITY Scotti Brothers 650059 7	65	2 wks
30 Jan 88	SHE'S THE ONE Urban URB 13	45	3 wks
23 Apr 88	THE PAYBACK MIX Urban URB 17	12	6 wks
4 Jun 88	I'M REAL Scotti Brothers JSB 1 ***	31	4 wks
23 Jul 88	I GOT YOU (I FEEL GOOD) (re-issue) A & M AM 444	52	3 wks
16 Nov 91	GET UP (I FEEL LIKE BEING A SEX MACHINE) (2nd re-issue) Polydor PO 185	69	2 wks
24 Oct 92	I GOT YOU (I FEEL GOOD) (re-mix) FBI FBI 9 ****	72	1 wk

* James Brown and The Famous Flames ** Afrika Bambaataa and James Brown
*** James Brown featuring Full Force **** James Brown v Dakeyne

Froggy Mix is a medley of twelve James Brown songs. The listed flip side of I Got You (I Feel good) was Nowhere To Run by Martha Reeves and the Vandellas.

Joanne BROWN – *See Tony OSBORNE*

Jocelyn BROWN *US, female vocalist* — 36 wks

21 Apr 84	SOMEBODY ELSE'S GUY Fourth & Broadway BRW 5	13	9 wks
22 Sep 84	I WISH YOU WOULD Fourth & Broadway BRW 14	51	3 wks
15 Mar 86	LOVE'S GONNA GET YOU Warner Bros. W 8889	70	1 wk
29 Jun 91 ●	ALWAYS THERE Talkin Loud TLK 10 *	6	9 wks
14 Sep 91	SHE GOT SOUL A & M AM 819 **	57	3 wks
7 Dec 91 ●	DON'T TALK JUST KISS Tug SNOG 2 ***	3	11 wks

* Incognito featuring Jocelyn Brown ** Jamestown featuring Jocelyn Brown
*** Right Said Fred. Guest vocals: Jocelyn Brown

Joe BROWN and the BRUVVERS — 92 wks
UK, male vocal/instrumental group

17 Mar 60	DARKTOWN STRUTTERS BALL Decca F 11207	34	6 wks
26 Jan 61	SHINE Pye 7N 15322 *	33	6 wks
11 Jan 62	WHAT A CRAZY WORLD WE'RE LIVING IN Piccadilly 7N 35024	37	2 wks
17 May 62 ●	A PICTURE OF YOU Piccadilly 7N 35047	2	19 wks
13 Sep 62	YOUR TENDER LOOK Piccadilly 7N 35058	31	6 wks
15 Nov 62 ●	IT ONLY TOOK A MINUTE Piccadilly 7N 35082	6	13 wks
7 Feb 63 ●	THAT'S WHAT LOVE WILL DO Piccadilly 7N 35106	3	14 wks
21 Feb 63	IT ONLY TOOK A MINUTE (re-entry) Piccadilly 7N 35082	50	1 wk
27 Jun 63	NATURE'S TIME FOR LOVE Piccadilly 7N 35129	26	6 wks
26 Sep 63	SALLY ANN Piccadilly 7N 35138	28	9 wks
29 Jun 67	WITH A LITTLE HELP FROM MY FRIENDS Pye 7N 17339 *	32	4 wks
14 Apr 73	HEY MAMA Ammo AMO 101 *	33	6 wks

* Joe Brown

Miquel BROWN *US, female vocalist* — 7 wks

18 Feb 84	HE'S A SAINT, HE'S A SINNER Record Shack SOHO 15	68	4 wks
24 Aug 85	CLOSE TO PERFECTION Record Shack SOHO 48	63	3 wks

Peter BROWN *US, male vocalist* — 9 wks

11 Feb 78	DO YA WANNA GET FUNKY WITH ME TK TKR 6009	43	4 wks
17 Jun 78	DANCE WITH ME TK TKR 6027	57	5 wks

Polly BROWN *UK, female vocalist* — 5 wks

14 Sep 74	UP IN A PUFF OF SMOKE GTO GT 2	43	5 wks

Sam BROWN *UK, female vocalist* — 34 wks

11 Jun 88	STOP A & M AM 440	52	3 wks
4 Feb 89 ●	STOP (re-entry) A & M AM 440	4	12 wks
13 May 89	CAN I GET A WITNESS A & M AM 509	15	7 wks
3 Mar 90	WITH A LITTLE LOVE A & M AM 539	44	4 wks
5 May 90	KISSING GATE A& M AM 549	23	8 wks

Sharon BROWN *US, female vocalist* — 9 wks

17 Apr 82	I SPECIALIZE IN LOVE Virgin VS 494	38	9 wks

BROWN SAUCE *UK, male/female vocal group* — 12 wks

12 Dec 81	I WANNA BE A WINNER BBC RESL 101	15	12 wks

Duncan BROWNE *UK, male vocalist* — 8 wks

19 Aug 72	JOURNEY RAK 135	23	6 wks
22 Dec 84	THEME FROM 'THE TRAVELLING MAN' Towerbell TOW 64	68	2 wks

Jackson BROWNE *US, male vocalist* — 13 wks

1 Jul 78	STAY Asylum K 13128	12	11 wks
18 Oct 86	IN THE SHAPE OF A HEART Elektra EKR 42	66	2 wks

Ronnie BROWNE – *See SCOTTISH RUGBY TEAM with Ronnie BROWNE*

Tom BROWNE *US, male vocalist* — 24 wks

19 Jul 80 ●	FUNKIN' FOR JAMAICA (N.Y.) Arista ARIST 357	10	11 wks
25 Oct 80	THIGHS HIGH (GRIP YOUR HIPS AND MOVE) Arista ARIST 367	45	5 wks
30 Jan 82	FUNGI MAMA (BEBOPAFUNKADISCOLYPSO) Arista ARIST 450	58	4 wks
11 Jan 92	FUNKIN' FOR JAMAICA (re-mix) Arista 114998	45	4 wks

BROWNS *US, male/female vocal group* — 13 wks

18 Sep 59 ●	THE THREE BELLS RCA 1140	6	13 wks

BROWNSVILLE STATION — 6 wks
US, male vocal/instrumental group

2 Mar 74	SMOKIN' IN THE BOYS' ROOM Philips 6073 834	27	6 wks

Dave BRUBECK QUARTET — 30 wks
US, male instrumental group

26 Oct 61 ●	TAKE FIVE Fontana H 339	6	15 wks
8 Feb 62	IT'S A RAGGY WALTZ Fontana H 352	36	3 wks
17 May 62	UNSQUARE DANCE CBS AAG 102	14	12 wks

Tommy BRUCE and the BRUISERS — 21 wks
UK, male vocal/instrumental group

26 May 60 ●	AIN'T MISBEHAVIN' Columbia DB 4453	3	16 wks
8 Sep 60	BROKEN DOLL Columbia DB 4498	36	4 wks
22 Feb 62	BABETTE Columbia DB 4776 *	50	1 wk

* Tommy Bruce

British Hit Singles Part One: Alphabetically by Artist
Date of chart entry/Title & catalogue no./Peak position reached/Weeks on chart
★ Number one   ● Top Ten   † still on chart at 31 Dec 1992
* = credited to act billed in footnote

Claudia BRUCKEN *Germany, female vocalist*   2 wks

1 Aug 90	ABSOLUT(E) *Island IS 471*	71	1 wk
16 Feb 91	KISS LIKE ETHER *Island IS 479*	63	1 wk

BRUISERS *UK, male instrumental group*   7 wks

8 Aug 63	BLUE GIRL *Parlophone R 5042*	31	6 wks
26 Sep 63	BLUE GIRL (re-entry) *Parlophone R 5042*	47	1 wk

See also Tommy Bruce.

BRUNO and LIZ – *See Liz KERSHAW and Bruno BROOKES*

Tyrone BRUNSON *US, male instrumentalist - bass*   5 wks

25 Dec 82	THE SMURF *Epic EPC A 3024*	52	5 wks

BRUVVERS – *See Joe BROWN and the BRUVVERS*

Dora BRYAN *UK, female vocalist*   6 wks

5 Dec 63	ALL I WANT FOR CHRISTMAS IS A BEATLE *Fontana TF 427*	20	6 wks

Anita BRYANT *US, female vocalist*   6 wks

26 May 60	PAPER ROSES *London HLL 9144*	49	1 wk
30 Jun 60	PAPER ROSES (re-entry) *London HLL 9144*	45	1 wk
14 Jul 60	PAPER ROSES (2nd re-entry) *London HLL 9144*	24	2 wks
6 Oct 60	MY LITTLE CORNER OF THE WORLD *London HLL 9171*	48	2 wks

Peabo BRYSON *US, male vocalist*   20 wks

20 Aug 83 ●	TONIGHT I CELEBRATE MY LOVE *Capitol CL 302* *	2	13 wks
16 May 92 ●	BEAUTY AND THE BEAST *Epic 6576607* **	9	7 wks

* Peabo Bryson and Roberta Flack ** Celine Dion and Peabo Bryson

B. T. EXPRESS *US, male instrumental/vocal group*   10 wks

29 Mar 75	EXPRESS *Pye International 7N 25674*	34	6 wks
26 Jul 80	DOES IT FEEL GOOD/GIVE UP THE FUNK (LET'S DANCE) *Calibre CAB 503*	52	4 wks

BUBBLEROCK – *See Jonathan KING*

Catherine BUCHANAN – *See JELLYBEAN*

Roy BUCHANAN *US, male instrumentalist - guitar*   3 wks

31 Mar 73	SWEET DREAMS *Polydor 2066 307*	40	3 wks

Lindsey BUCKINGHAM *US, male vocalist*   7 wks

16 Jan 82	TROUBLE *Mercury MER 85*	31	7 wks

BUCKS FIZZ *UK, male/female vocal group*   150 wks

28 Mar 81 ★	MAKING YOUR MIND UP *RCA 56*	1	12 wks
6 Jun 81	PIECE OF THE ACTION *RCA 88*	12	9 wks
15 Aug 81	ONE OF THOSE NIGHTS *RCA 114*	20	10 wks
28 Nov 81 ★	THE LAND OF MAKE BELIEVE *RCA 163*	1	16 wks
27 Mar 82 ★	MY CAMERA NEVER LIES *RCA 202*	1	8 wks
19 Jun 82 ●	NOW THOSE DAYS ARE GONE *RCA 241*	8	9 wks
27 Nov 82 ●	IF YOU CAN'T STAND THE HEAT *RCA 300*	10	11 wks
12 Mar 83	RUN FOR YOUR LIFE *RCA FIZ 1*	14	7 wks
18 Jun 83 ●	WHEN WE WERE YOUNG *RCA 342*	10	8 wks
1 Oct 83	LONDON TOWN *RCA 363*	34	6 wks
17 Dec 83	RULES OF THE GAME *RCA 380*	57	6 wks
25 Aug 84	TALKING IN YOUR SLEEP *RCA FIZ 2*	15	9 wks
27 Oct 84	GOLDEN DAYS *RCA FIZ 3*	42	4 wks
29 Dec 84	I HEAR TALK *RCA FIZ 4*	34	8 wks
22 Jun 85	YOU AND YOUR HEART SO BLUE *RCA PB 40233*	43	4 wks
14 Sep 85	MAGICAL *RCA PB 40367*	57	3 wks
7 Jun 86 ●	NEW BEGINNING (MAMBA SEYRA) *Polydor POSP 794*	8	10 wks
30 Aug 86	LOVE THE ONE YOU'RE WITH *Polydor POSP 813*	47	3 wks
15 Nov 86	KEEP EACH OTHER WARM *Polydor POSP 835*	45	4 wks
5 Nov 88	HEART OF STONE *RCA PB 42035*	50	3 wks

BUDGIE *UK, male vocal/instrumental group*   2 wks

3 Oct 81	KEEPING A RENDEZVOUS *RCA BUDGIE 3*	71	2 wks

BUG KANN and PLASTIC JAM featuring Patti LOW and DOOGIE   1 wk
UK, male/female vocal/instrumental group

31 Aug 91	MADE IN TWO MINUTES *Optimum Dance BKPJ 1S*	70	1 wk

BUGGLES *UK, male vocal/instrumental duo*   28 wks

22 Sep 79 ★	VIDEO KILLED THE RADIO STAR *Island WIP 6524*	1	11 wks
26 Jan 80	THE PLASTIC AGE *Island WIP 6540*	16	8 wks
5 Apr 80	CLEAN CLEAN *Island WIP 6584*	38	5 wks
8 Nov 80	ELSTREE *Island WIP 6624*	55	4 wks

B. BUMBLE and the STINGERS   26 wks
US, male instrumental group

19 Apr 62 ★	NUT ROCKER *Top Rank JAR 611*	1	15 wks
3 Jun 72	NUT ROCKER (re-issue) *Stateside SS 2203*	19	11 wks

BUMP *UK, male instrumental/production duo*   4 wks

4 Jul 92	I'M RUSHING *Good Boy EDGE7 1*	40	4 wks

BUNKER KRU – *See HARLEQUIN 4's/BUNKER KRU*

BUNNYMEN – *See ECHO and the BUNNYMEN*

Eric BURDON – *See ANIMALS*

Geoffrey BURGON *UK, orchestra*   4 wks

26 Dec 81	BRIDESHEAD THEME *Chrysalis CHS 2562*	48	4 wks

Keni BURKE *US, male vocalist*   4 wks

27 Jun 81	LET SOMEBODY LOVE YOU *RCA 93*	59	3 wks
18 Apr 92	RISIN' TO THE TOP *RCA PB 49103*	70	1 wk

Hank C. BURNETTE *Sweden, male multi-instrumentalist* **8 wks**

30 Oct 76	SPINNING ROCK BOOGIE *Sonet SON 2094*		21	8 wks

Johnny BURNETTE *US, male vocalist* **48 wks**

29 Sep 60 ●	DREAMIN' *London HLG 9172*		5	16 wks
12 Jan 61 ●	YOU'RE SIXTEEN *London HLG 9254*		3	12 wks
13 Apr 61	LITTLE BOY SAD *London HLG 9315*		12	12 wks
10 Aug 61	GIRLS *London HLG 9388*		37	5 wks
17 May 62	CLOWN SHOES *Liberty LIB 55416*		35	3 wks

Rocky BURNETTE *US, male vocalist* **7 wks**

17 Nov 79	TIRED OF TOEIN' THE LINE *EMI 2992*		58	7 wks

Jerry BURNS *UK, female vocalist* **1 wk**

25 Apr 92	PALE RED *Columbia 6579467*		64	1 wk

Ray BURNS *UK, male vocalist* **19 wks**

11 Feb 55 ●	MOBILE *Columbia DB 3563*		4	13 wks
26 Aug 55	THAT'S HOW A LOVE SONG WAS BORN *Columbia DB 3640* *		14	6 wks

* Ray Burns with the Coronets

Malandra BURROWS *UK, female vocalist* **8 wks**

1 Dec 90	JUST THIS SIDE OF LOVE *Yorkshire Television DALE 1*		11	8 wks

Jenny BURTON *US, female vocalist* **2 wks**

30 Mar 85	BAD HABITS *Atlantic A 9583*		68	2 wks

BURUNDI STEIPHENSON BLACK **14 wks**
Burundi, drummers and chanters with orchestral additions by Mike Steiphenson of France

13 Nov 71	BURUNDI BLACK *Barclay BAR 3*		31	14 wks

Lou BUSCH *US, orchestra and chorus* **17 wks**

27 Jan 56 ●	ZAMBESI *Capitol CL 14504*		2	17 wks

See also Joe 'Fingers' Carr.

Kate BUSH *UK, female vocalist* **153 wks**

11 Feb 78 ★	WUTHERING HEIGHTS *EMI 2719*		1	12 wks
13 May 78	WUTHERING HEIGHTS (re-entry) *EMI 2719*		75	1 wk
10 Jun 78 ●	MAN WITH THE CHILD IN HIS EYES *EMI 2806*		6	11 wks
11 Nov 78	HAMMER HORROR *EMI 2887*		44	6 wks
17 Mar 79	WOW *EMI 2911*		14	10 wks
15 Sep 79 ●	KATE BUSH ON STAGE EP *EMI MIEP 2991*		10	9 wks
26 Apr 80	BREATHING *EMI 5058*		16	7 wks
5 Jul 80 ●	BABOOSHKA *EMI 5085*		5	10 wks
4 Oct 80	ARMY DREAMERS *EMI 5106*		16	9 wks
6 Dec 80	DECEMBER WILL BE MAGIC AGAIN *EMI 5121*		29	7 wks
11 Jul 81	SAT IN YOUR LAP *EMI 5201*		11	7 wks
7 Aug 82	THE DREAMING *EMI 5296*		48	3 wks
17 Aug 85 ●	RUNNING UP THAT HILL *EMI KB 1*		3	11 wks
26 Oct 85	CLOUDBUSTING *EMI KB 2*		20	6 wks
1 Mar 86	HOUNDS OF LOVE *EMI KB 3*		18	5 wks
10 May 86	THE BIG SKY *EMI KB 4*		37	3 wks
8 Nov 86	EXPERIMENT IV *EMI KB 5*		23	4 wks
1 Nov 88 ●	DON'T GIVE UP *Virgin PGS 2* *		9	11 wks
30 Sep 89	THE SENSUAL WORLD *EMI EM 102*		12	5 wks
2 Dec 89	THIS WOMAN'S WORK *EMI EM 119*		25	5 wks
10 Mar 90	LOVE AND ANGER *EMI EM 134*		38	3 wks
7 Dec 91	ROCKET MAN (I THINK IT'S GOING TO BE A LONG LONG TIME) *Mercury TRIBO 2*		12	8 wks

* Peter Gabriel and Kate Bush

Tracks on On Stage EP: Them Heavy People/Don't Push Your Foot on the Heartbrake/James and the Cold Gun/L'Amour Looks Something Like You.

BUSTER *UK, male vocal/instrumental group* **1 wk**

19 Jun 76	SUNDAY *RCA 2678*		49	1 wk

Jonathan BUTLER **18 wks**
South Africa, male vocalist/instrumentalist - guitar

25 Jan 86	IF YOU'RE READY (COME GO WITH ME) *Jive JIVE 109* *		30	7 wks
8 Aug 87	LIES *Jive JIVE 141*		18	11 wks

* Ruby Turner featuring Jonathan Butler

BUTTERSCOTCH *UK, male vocal group* **11 wks**

2 May 70	DON'T YOU KNOW *RCA 1937*		17	11 wks

BUZZCOCKS *UK, male vocal/instrumental group* **53 wks**

18 Feb 78	WHAT DO I GET *United Artists UP 36348*		37	3 wks
13 May 78	I DON'T MIND *United Artists UP 36386*		55	2 wks
15 Jul 78	LOVE YOU MORE *United Artists UP 36433*		34	6 wks
23 Sep 78	EVER FALLEN IN LOVE (WITH SOMEONE YOU SHOULDN'T'VE) *United Artists UP 36455*		12	11 wks
25 Nov 78	PROMISES *United Artists UP 36471*		20	10 wks
10 Mar 79	EVERYBODY'S HAPPY NOWADAYS *United Artists UP 36499*		29	6 wks
21 Jul 79	HARMONY IN MY HEAD *United Artists UP 36541*		32	6 wks
25 Aug 79	SPIRAL SCRATCH EP *New Hormones ORG 1*		31	6 wks
6 Sep 80	ARE EVERYTHING/WHY SHE'S A GIRL FROM THE CHAINSTORE *United Artists BP 365*		61	3 wks

Tracks on Spiral Scratch EP: Breakdown/Time's Up/Boredom/Friends Of Mine. Sleeve of EP (not the label) credits 'Buzzcocks with Howard Devoto'. Why She's A Girl From The Chainstore listed from 13 Sep 80.

BUZZY BUNCH – See Celi BEE and the BUZZY BUNCH

B.V.S.M.P. *US, male vocal group* **12 wks**

23 Jul 88 ●	I NEED YOU *Debut DEBT 3044*		3	12 wks

BY ALL MEANS *US, male vocal group* **2 wks**

18 Jun 88	I SURRENDER TO YOUR LOVE *Fourth & Broadway BRW 102*		65	2 wks

Max BYGRAVES *UK, male vocalist* **131 wks**

14 Nov 52	COWPUNCHER'S CANTATA *HMV B 10250*		11	1 wk
2 Jan 53 ●	COWPUNCHER'S CANTATA (re-entry) *HMV B 10250*		8	1 wk
23 Jan 53 ●	COWPUNCHER'S CANTATA (2nd re-entry) *HMV B 10250*		6	5 wks
6 Mar 53 ●	COWPUNCHER'S CANTATA (3rd re-entry) *HMV B 10250*		10	1 wk

14 May 54 ●	HEART OF MY HEART *HMV B 10654*	7	8 wks
10 Sep 54 ●	GILLY GILLY OSSENFEFFER KATZENELLEN BOGEN BY THE SEA *HMV B 10734*	7	7 wks
5 Nov 54	GILLY GILLY OSSENFEFFER KATZENELLEN BOGEN BY THE SEA (re-entry) *HMV B 10734*	20	1 wk
21 Jan 55	MR. SANDMAN *HMV B 10801*	16	1 wk
18 Nov 55 ●	MEET ME ON THE CORNER *HMV POP 116*	2	11 wks
17 Feb 56	BALLAD OF DAVY CROCKETT *HMV POP 153*	20	1 wk
25 May 56	OUT OF TOWN *HMV POP 164*	18	7 wks
5 Apr 57	HEART *Decca F 10862*	14	8 wks
2 May 58 ●	YOU NEED HANDS/TULIPS FROM AMSTERDAM *Decca F 11004*	3	25 wks
22 Aug 58	LITTLE TRAIN/GOTTA HAVE RAIN *Decca F 11046*	28	2 wks
2 Jan 59	MY UKELELE *Decca F 11077*	19	4 wks
18 Dec 59 ●	JINGLE BELL ROCK *Decca F 11176*	7	4 wks
10 Mar 60 ●	FINGS AIN'T WOT THEY USED T'BE *Decca F 11214*	5	15 wks
28 Jul 60	CONSIDER YOURSELF *Decca F 11251*	50	1 wk
1 Jun 61	BELLS OF AVIGNON *Decca F 11350*	36	5 wks
19 Feb 69	YOU'RE MY EVERYTHING *Pye 7N 17705*	50	1 wk
5 Mar 69	YOU'RE MY EVERYTHING (re-entry) *Pye 7N 17705*	34	3 wks
6 Oct 73	DECK OF CARDS *Pye 7N 45276*	13	15 wks
9 Dec 89	WHITE CHRISTMAS *Parkfield PMS 5012*	71	4 wks

See also Various Artists (EPs & LPs) - All Star Hit Parade No. 2. Cowpuncher's Cantata is a medley with the following songs: Cry Of The Wild Goose/Riders In The Sky/Mule Train/Jezebel. You Need Hands was listed by itself on 2 May 58. Tulips From Amsterdam was first listed on 9 May 58 and both sides continued to be listed until the end of the record's chart run.

Charlie BYRD – *See Stan GETZ*

Donald BYRD *US, male vocalist/instrumentalist - trumpet* — 6 wks

26 Sep 81	LOVING YOU/LOVE HAS COME AROUND *Elektra K 12559*	41	6 wks

Gary BYRD and the GB EXPERIENCE — 9 wks
US, male vocalist and male/female instrumental group

23 Jul 83 ●	THE CROWN *Motown TMGT 1312*	6	9 wks

BYRDS *US, male vocal/instrumental group* — 52 wks

17 Jun 65 ★	MR. TAMBOURINE MAN *CBS 201765*	1	14 wks
12 Aug 65 ●	ALL I REALLY WANT TO DO *CBS 201796*	4	10 wks
11 Nov 65	TURN! TURN! TURN! *CBS 202008*	26	8 wks
5 May 66	EIGHT MILES HIGH *CBS 202067*	24	9 wks
5 Jun 68	YOU AIN'T GOIN' NOWHERE *CBS 3411*	45	3 wks
13 Feb 71	CHESTNUT MARE *CBS 5322*	19	8 wks

Edward BYRNES – *See Connie STEVENS*

BYSTANDERS *UK, male vocal/instrumental group* — 1 wk

9 Feb 67	98.6 *Piccadilly 7N 35363*	45	1 wk

C

Roy C *US, male vocalist* — 24 wks

21 Apr 66 ●	SHOTGUN WEDDING *Island WI 273*	6	11 wks
25 Nov 72 ●	SHOTGUN WEDDING (re-issue) *UK 19*	8	13 wks

C & C MUSIC FACTORY/CLIVILLES & COLE — 46 wks
US, male/female vocal/instrumental group

15 Dec 90 ●	GONNA MAKE YOU SWEAT (EVERYBODY DANCE NOW) *CBS 6564540 **	3	12 wks
30 Mar 91	HERE WE GO *Columbia 6566907 **	20	7 wks
6 Jul 91 ●	THINGS THAT MAKE YOU GO HMMM... *Columbia 6566907 **	4	11 wks
23 Nov 91	JUST A TOUCH OF LOVE EVERYDAY *Columbia 6575247 ****	31	3 wks
18 Jan 92	PRIDE (IN THE NAME OF LOVE) *Columbia 6577017 ******	15	5 wks
14 Mar 92	A DEEPER LOVE *Columbia 6578497 ******	15	5 wks
3 Oct 92	KEEP IT COMIN' (DANCE TILL YOU CAN'T DANCE NO MORE) *Columbia 6584307 ******	34	3 wks

* C & C Music Factory (featuring Freedom Williams) ** C & C Music Factory featuring Zelma Davis *** Clivilles and Cole **** C & C Music Factory featuring Q Unique and Deborah Cooper

ÇA VA ÇA VA *UK, male vocal/instrumental group* — 8 wks

18 Sep 82	WHERE'S ROMEO *Regard RG 103*	49	5 wks
19 Feb 83	BROTHER BRIGHT *Regard RG 105*	65	3 wks

Montserrat CABALLE – *See Freddie MERCURY*

CABARET VOLTAIRE — 8 wks
UK, male vocal/instrumental group

18 Jul 87	DON'T ARGUE *Parlophone R 6157*	69	2 wks
4 Nov 89	HYPNOTISED *Parlophone R 6227*	66	2 wks
12 May 90	KEEP ON *Parlophone R 6250*	55	2 wks
18 Aug 90	EASY LIFE *Parlophone R 6261*	61	2 wks

CACIQUE *UK, male/female vocal/instrumental group* — 1 wk

1 Jun 85	DEVOTED TO YOU *Diamond Duel DISC 1*	69	1 wk

CACTUS WORLD NEWS — 7 wks
Ireland, male vocal/instrumental group

8 Feb 86	YEARS LATER *MCA MCA 1024*	59	3 wks
26 Apr 86	WORLDS APART *MCA MCA 1040*	58	3 wks
20 Sep 86	THE BRIDGE *MCA MCA 1080*	74	1 wk

CADETS with Eileen READ — 1 wk
Ireland, male/female vocal group

3 Jun 65	JEALOUS HEART *Pye 7N 15852*	42	1 wk

Susan CADOGAN *UK, female vocalist* — 19 wks

5 Apr 75 ●	HURT SO GOOD *Magnet MAG 23*	4	12 wks
19 Jul 75	LOVE ME BABY *Magnet MAG 36*	22	7 wks

Al CAIOLA *US, orchestra* — 6 wks

15 Jun 61	THE MAGNIFICENT SEVEN *HMV POP 889*	34	6 wks

CALIBRE CUTS – *See VARIOUS ARTISTS (MONTAGES)*

CALL *US, male vocal/instrumental group* — 6 wks

30 Sep 89	LET THE DAY BEGIN *MCA MCA 1362*	42	6 wks

Eddie CALVERT *UK, male instrumentalist - trumpet* — 80 wks

18 Dec 53 ★	OH MEIN PAPA *Columbia DB 3337*	1	21 wks
8 Apr 55 ★	CHERRY PINK AND APPLE BLOSSOM WHITE *Columbia DB 3581*	1	21 wks
13 May 55	STRANGER IN PARADISE *Columbia DB 3594*	14	4 wks
29 Jul 55 ●	JOHN AND JULIE *Columbia DB 3624*	6	11 wks
2 Mar 56	ZAMBESI *Columbia DB 3747*	18	1 wk
23 Mar 56	ZAMBESI (re-entry) *Columbia DB 3747*	13	6 wks

7 Feb 58 ●	**MANDY** *Columbia DB 3956*	**9**	14 wks
20 Jun 58	**LITTLE SERENADE** *Columbia DB 4105*	**28**	2 wks

Donnie CALVIN – *See ROCKER'S REVENGE*

CAMEO *US, male vocal/instrumental group* — **66 wks**

31 Mar 84	**SHE'S STRANGE** *Club JAB 2*	**37**	8 wks
13 Jul 85	**ATTACK ME WITH YOUR LOVE** *Club JAB 16*	**65**	2 wks
14 Sep 85	**SINGLE LIFE** *Club JAB 21*	**15**	10 wks
7 Dec 85	**SHE'S STRANGE (re-issue)** *Club JAB 25*	**22**	8 wks
22 Mar 86	**A GOODBYE** *Club JAB 28*	**65**	2 wks
30 Aug 86 ●	**WORD UP** *Club JAB 38*	**3**	13 wks
29 Nov 86	**CANDY** *Club JAB 43*	**27**	9 wks
25 Apr 87	**BACK AND FORTH** *Club JAB 49*	**11**	9 wks
17 Oct 87	**SHE'S MINE** *Club JAB 57*	**35**	4 wks
29 Oct 88	**YOU MAKE ME WORK** *Club JAB 70*	**74**	1 wk

Andy CAMERON *UK, male vocalist* — **8 wks**

4 Mar 78 ●	**ALLY'S TARTAN ARMY** *Klub 03*	**6**	8 wks

Tony CAMILLO'S BAZUKA — **5 wks**
US, male instrumental/vocal group

31 May 75	**DYNOMITE** (PART 1) *A & M AMS 7168*	**28**	5 wks

---

CAMOUFLAGE featuring MYSTI — **3 wks**
UK, male/female vocal/instrumental group

24 Sep 77	**BEE STING** *State STAT 58*	**48**	3 wks

Ethna CAMPBELL *UK, female vocalist* — **11 wks**

27 Dec 75	**THE OLD RUGGED CROSS** *Philips 6006 475*	**33**	11 wks

---

Glen CAMPBELL *US, male vocalist* — **98 wks**

29 Jan 69 ●	**WICHITA LINEMAN** *Ember EMBS 261*	**7**	13 wks
7 May 69	**GALVESTON** *Ember EMBS 263*	**14**	10 wks
6 Dec 69	**ALL I HAVE TO DO IS DREAM** *Capitol CL 15619* *	**3**	14 wks
7 Feb 70	**TRY A LITTLE KINDNESS** *Capitol CL 15622*	**45**	2 wks
9 May 70 ●	**HONEY COME BACK** *Capitol CL 15638*	**4**	19 wks
26 Sep 70	**EVERYTHING A MAN COULD EVER NEED** *Capitol CL 15653*	**32**	5 wks
21 Nov 70 ●	**IT'S ONLY MAKE BELIEVE** *Capitol CL 15663*	**4**	14 wks
27 Mar 71	**DREAM BABY** *Capitol CL 15674*	**39**	3 wks
4 Oct 75 ●	**RHINESTONE COWBOY** *Capitol CL 15824*	**4**	12 wks
26 Mar 77	**SOUTHERN NIGHTS** *Capitol CL 15907*	**28**	6 wks

* Bobbie Gentry and Glen Campbell

Jo Ann CAMPBELL *US, female vocalist* — **3 wks**

8 Jun 61	**MOTORCYCLE MICHAEL** *HMV POP 873*	**41**	3 wks

Junior CAMPBELL *UK, male vocalist* — **18 wks**

14 Oct 72 ●	**HALLELUJAH FREEDOM** *Deram DM 364*	**10**	9 wks
2 Jun 73	**SWEET ILLUSION** *Deram DM 387*	**15**	9 wks

Pat CAMPBELL *Ireland, male vocalist* — **5 wks**

15 Nov 69	**THE DEAL** *Major Minor MM 648*	**31**	5 wks

Stan CAMPBELL *UK, male vocalist* — **3 wks**

6 Jun 87	**YEARS GO BY** *WEA YZ 127*	**65**	3 wks

Tevin CAMPBELL *US, male vocalist* — **2 wks**

18 Apr 92	**TELL ME WHAT YOU WANT ME TO DO** *Qwest W 0102*	**63**	2 wks

---

Ian CAMPBELL FOLK GROUP — **5 wks**
UK, male vocal/instrumental group

11 Mar 65	**THE TIMES THEY ARE A-CHANGIN'** *Transatlantic SP 5*	**42**	2 wks
1 Apr 65	**THE TIMES THEY ARE A-CHANGIN' (re-entry)** *Transatlantic SP 5*	**47**	1 wk
15 Apr 65	**THE TIMES THEY ARE A-CHANGIN' (2nd re-entry)** *Transatlantic SP 5*	**46**	2 wks

---

CAN *Germany, male vocal/instrumental group* — **10 wks**

28 Aug 76	**I WANT MORE** *Virgin VS 153*	**26**	10 wks

CANDIDO *US, male multi-instrumentalist* — **3 wks**

18 Jul 81	**JINGO** *Excaliber EXC 102*	**55**	3 wks

CANDLEWICK GREEN *UK, vocal/instrumental group* — **8 wks**

23 Feb 74	**WHO DO YOU THINK YOU ARE** *Decca F 13480*	**21**	8 wks

---

CANDY FLIP *UK, male vocal/instrumental duo* — **14 wks**

17 Mar 90 ●	**STRAWBERRY FIELDS FOREVER** *Debut DEBT 3092*	**3**	10 wks
14 Jul 90	**THIS CAN BE REAL** *Debut DEBT 3099*	**60**	4 wks

---

CANDYLAND *UK, male vocal/instrumental group* — **1 wk**

9 Mar 91	**FOUNTAIN O' YOUTH** *Non Fiction YES 4*	**72**	1 wk

---

CANNED HEAT *US, male vocal/instrumental group* — **41 wks**

24 Jul 68 ●	**ON THE ROAD AGAIN** *Liberty LBS 15090*	**8**	15 wks
1 Jan 69	**GOING UP THE COUNTRY** *Liberty LBF 15169*	**19**	10 wks
17 Jan 70 ●	**LET'S WORK TOGETHER** *Liberty LBF 15302*	**2**	15 wks
11 Jul 70	**SUGAR BEE** *Liberty LBF 15350*	**49**	1 wk

Freddy CANNON *US, male vocalist* — **51 wks**

14 Aug 59	**TALLAHASSEE LASSIE** *Top Rank JAR 135*	**17**	8 wks
1 Jan 60 ●	**WAY DOWN YONDER IN NEW ORLEANS** *Top Rank JAR 247*	**3**	16 wks
10 Mar 60	**CALIFORNIA HERE I COME** *Top Rank JAR 309*	**33**	1 wk
17 Mar 60	**INDIANA** *Top Rank JAR 309*	**42**	1 wk
24 Mar 60	**CALIFORNIA HERE I COME (re-entry)** *Top Rank JAR 309*	**46**	1 wk
19 May 60	**THE URGE** *Top Rank JAR 369*	**18**	10 wks
20 Apr 61	**MUSKRAT RAMBLE** *Top Rank JAR 548*	**32**	5 wks
28 Jun 62	**PALISADES PARK** *Stateside SS 101*	**20**	9 wks

Jim CAPALDI *UK, male vocalist* — **17 wks**

27 Jul 74	**IT'S ALL UP TO YOU** *Island WIP 6198*	**27**	6 wks
25 Oct 75 ●	**LOVE HURTS** *Island WIP 6246*	**4**	11 wks

CAPERCAILLIE *UK, male/female vocal/instrumental group*   **2 wks**

23 May 92   **A PRINCE AMONG ISLANDS EP** *Survival ZB 45393*........**39** 2 wks

Tracks on A Prince Among Islands EP: *Coisich A Ruin (Walk My Beloved)/Fagail Bhearnaraid (Leaving Bernaray)/The Lorn Theme/Gun Teann Mi Ris Na Ruinn Tha Seo (Remembrance).*

CAPPELLA *Italy, male vocalist*   **18 wks**

9 Apr 88	**PUSH THE BEAT/BAUHAUS** *Fast Globe FGL 1* **60**	2 wks
6 May 89	**HELYOM HALIB** *Music Man MMPS 7004* **11**	9 wks
23 Sep 89	**HOUSE ENERGY REVENGE** *Music Man MMPS 7009* **73**	1 wk
27 Apr 91	**EVERYBODY** *ffrr F158* **66**	1 wk
18 Jan 92	**TAKE ME AWAY** *PWL Continental PWL 210* * **25**	5 wks

* *Cappella featuring Loleatta Holloway*

Tony CAPSTICK and the CARLTON MAIN/FRICKLEY COLLIERY BAND   **8 wks**
UK, male vocalist and male instrumental band

21 Mar 81 ● **THE SHEFFIELD GRINDER/CAPSTICK COMES HOME** *Dingles SID 27* ....**3** 8 wks

---

CAPTAIN BEAKY – *See Keith MICHELL*

CAPTAIN HOLLYWOOD – *See TWENTY 4 SEVEN featuring CAPTAIN HOLLYWOOD*

CAPTAIN SENSIBLE *UK, male vocalist*   **30 wks**

26 Jun 82	★	**HAPPY TALK** *A & M CAP 1* **1**	8 wks
14 Aug 82		**WOT** *A & M CAP 2* **26**	7 wks
24 Mar 84	●	**GLAD IT'S ALL OVER/DAMNED ON 45** *A & M CAP 6* **6**	10 wks
28 Jul 84		**THERE ARE MORE SNAKES THAN LADDERS** *A & M CAP 7* **57**	5 wks

---

CAPTAIN and TENNILLE   **24 wks**
US, male instrumentalist - keyboards and female vocalist

2 Aug 75	**LOVE WILL KEEP US TOGETHER** *A & M AMS 7165* **32**	5 wks
24 Jan 76	**THE WAY I WANT TO TOUCH YOU** *A & M AMS 7203* **28**	6 wks
4 Nov 78	**YOU NEVER DONE IT LIKE THAT** *A & M AMS 7384* **63**	3 wks
16 Feb 80 ●	**DO THAT TO ME ONE MORE TIME** *Casablanca CAN 175* **7**	10 wks

---

Irene CARA *US, female vocalist*   **33 wks**

3 Jul 82	★	**FAME** *RSO 90*...**1**	16 wks
4 Sep 82		**OUT HERE ON MY OWN** *RSO 66*........................**58**	3 wks
4 Jun 83	●	**FLASHDANCE ... WHAT A FEELING** *Casablanca CAN 1016* **2**	14 wks

---

CARAMBA *Sweden, male vocalist/multi-instrumentalist*   **6 wks**
dog impersonator - Michael Tretow

12 Nov 83   **FEDORA (I'LL BE YOUR DAWG)** *Billco BILL 101* ....**56** 6 wks

---

CARAVELLES *UK, female vocal duo*   **13 wks**

8 Aug 63 ● **YOU DON'T HAVE TO BE A BABY TO CRY** *Decca F 11697* ....**6** 13 wks

---

British Hit Singles Part One: Alphabetically by Artist
Date of chart entry/Title & catalogue no./Peak position reached/Weeks on chart

★ Number one   ● Top Ten   † still on chart at 31 Dec 1992

* = credited to act billed in footnote

CARE *UK, male vocal/instrumental duo*   **4 wks**

12 Nov 83   **FLAMING SWORD** *Arista KBIRD 2*.......................**48** 4 wks

---

Mariah CAREY *US, female vocalist*   **58 wks**

4 Aug 90	●	**VISION OF LOVE** *CBS 6559320* **9**	12 wks
10 Nov 90		**LOVE TAKES TIME** *CBS 6563647* **37**	8 wks
26 Jan 91		**SOMEDAY** *Columbia 6565837* **38**	6 wks
1 Jun 91		**THERE'S GOT TO BE A WAY** *Columbia 6569317*........**54**	3 wks
5 Oct 91		**EMOTIONS** *Columbia 6574037* **17**	9 wks
11 Jan 92		**CAN'T LET GO** *Columbia 6576627* **20**	7 wks
18 Apr 92		**MAKE IT HAPPEN** *Columbia 6579417* **17**	5 wks
27 Jun 92	●	**I'LL BE THERE** *Columbia 6581377*........................**2**	9 wks

Although he is uncredited, I'll Be There *is a duet with Trey Lorenz.*

Belinda CARLISLE *US, female vocalist*   **114 wks**

12 Dec 87	★	**HEAVEN IS A PLACE ON EARTH** *Virgin VS 1036*............**1**	14 wks
27 Feb 88	●	**I GET WEAK** *Virgin VS 1046* **10**	9 wks
7 May 88	●	**CIRCLE IN THE SAND** *Virgin VS 1074* **4**	11 wks
6 Aug 88		**MAD ABOUT YOU** *IRS IRM 118*..........................**67**	3 wks
10 Sep 88		**WORLD WITHOUT YOU** *Virgin VS 1114* **34**	6 wks
10 Dec 88		**LOVE NEVER DIES...** *Virgin VS 1150* **54**	5 wks
7 Oct 89	●	**LEAVE A LIGHT ON** *Virgin VS 1210* **4**	10 wks
9 Dec 89		**LA LUNA** *Virgin VS 1230* **38**	6 wks
24 Feb 90		**RUNAWAY HORSES** *Virgin VS 1244* **40**	5 wks
26 May 90		**VISION OF YOU** *Virgin VS 1264* **41**	4 wks
13 Oct 90	●	**(WE WANT) THE SAME THING** *Virgin VS 1219* **6**	10 wks
22 Dec 90		**SUMMER RAIN** *Virgin VS 1323* **23**	10 wks
20 Apr 91		**VISION OF YOU (re-entry)** *Virgin VS 1264* **71**	1 wk
28 Sep 91		**LIVE YOUR LIFE BE FREE** *Virgin VS 1370* **12**	7 wks
16 Nov 91		**DO YOU FEEL LIKE I FEEL** *Virgin VS 1383* **29**	4 wks
11 Jan 92		**HALF THE WORLD** *Virgin VS 1388* **35**	4 wks
29 Aug 92		**LITTLE BLACK BOOK** *Virgin VS 1428*...................**28**	5 wks

---

Sara CARLSON – *See MANIC MC's featuring Sara CARLSON*

CARLTON *UK, male vocalist*   **2 wks**

16 Feb 91   **LOVE AND PAIN** *Smith & Mighty SNM 4* ....**56** 2 wks

---

Carl CARLTON *US, male vocalist*   **8 wks**

18 Jul 81   **SHE'S A BAD MAMA JAMA (SHE'S BUILT, SHE'S STACKED)** *20th Century TC 2488*........................**34** 8 wks

---

Larry CARLTON – *See Mike POST*

CARLTON MAIN/FRICKLEY COLLIERY BAND – *See Tony CAPSTICK and the CARLTON MAIN/FRICKLEY COLLIERY BAND*

CARMEL *UK, female/male vocal/instrumental group*   **19 wks**

6 Aug 83	**BAD DAY** *London LON 29* **15**	9 wks
11 Feb 84	**MORE, MORE, MORE** *London LON 44* **23**	7 wks
14 Jun 86	**SALLY** *London LON 90* **60**	3 wks

---

Eric CARMEN *US, male vocalist*   **7 wks**

10 Apr 76   **ALL BY MYSELF** *Arista 42* ....**12** 7 wks

Jean CARN – See Bobby M featuring Jean CARN

Kim CARNEGIE UK, female vocalist — 1 wk

19 Jan 91	JAZZ RAP Best ZB 44085	73	1 wk

Kim CARNES US, female vocalist — 15 wks

9 May 81	●	BETTE DAVIS EYES EMI America EA 121	10	9 wks
8 Aug 81		DRAW OF THE CARDS EMI America EA 125	49	4 wks
9 Oct 82		VOYEUR EMI America EA 143	68	2 wks

Renato CAROSONE and his SEXTET — 1 wk
Italy, male vocalist and instrumental backing group

4 Jul 58	TORERO - CHA CHA CHA Parlophone R 4433	25	1 wk

CARPENTERS US, male/female vocal/instrumental duo — 169 wks

5 Sep 70	●	(THEY LONG TO BE) CLOSE TO YOU A & M AMS 800	6	18 wks
9 Jan 71		WE'VE ONLY JUST BEGUN A & M AMS 813	28	7 wks
18 Sep 71		SUPERSTAR/FOR ALL WE KNOW A & M AMS 864	18	13 wks
1 Jan 72		MERRY CHRISTMAS DARLING A & M AME 601	45	1 wk
23 Sep 72	●	I WON'T LAST A DAY WITHOUT YOU/GOODBYE TO LOVE A & M AMS 7023	9	16 wks
7 Jul 73	●	YESTERDAY ONCE MORE A & M AMS 7073	2	17 wks
20 Oct 73	●	TOP OF THE WORLD A & M AMS 7086	5	18 wks
2 Mar 74		JAMBALAYA (ON THE BAYOU)/MR. GUDER A & M AMS 7098	12	11 wks
8 Jun 74		I WON'T LAST A DAY WITHOUT YOU (re-issue) A & M AMS 7111	32	5 wks
18 Jan 75	●	PLEASE MR. POSTMAN A & M AMS 7141	2	12 wks
19 Apr 75	●	ONLY YESTERDAY A & M AMS 7159	7	10 wks
30 Aug 75		SOLITAIRE A & M AMS 7187	32	5 wks
20 Dec 75		SANTA CLAUS IS COMIN' TO TOWN A & M AMS 7144	37	4 wks
27 Mar 76		THERE'S A KIND OF HUSH (ALL OVER THE WORLD) A & M AMS 7219	22	6 wks
3 Jul 76		I NEED TO BE IN LOVE A & M AMS 7238	36	5 wks
8 Oct 77		CALLING OCCUPANTS OF INTERPLANETARY CRAFT (THE RECOGNISED ANTHEM OF WORLD CONTACT DAY) A & M AMS 7318	9	9 wks
11 Feb 78		SWEET SWEET SMILE A & M AMS 7327	40	4 wks
22 Oct 83		MAKE BELIEVE IT'S YOUR FIRST TIME A & M AM 147	60	3 wks
8 Dec 90		MERRY CHRISTMAS DARLING/(THEY LONG TO BE) CLOSE TO YOU (re-issues) A & M AM 716	25	5 wks

I Won't Last A Day Without You *AMS 703 listed by itself 23 Sep 72. Goodbye To Love, the other side, listed by itself from 30 Sep 72 until the end of the record's chart run. Mr Guder listed with Jambalaya from 16 Mar 74 until the end of the record's chart run.*

Joe 'Fingers' CARR — 5 wks
US, male instrumentalist - piano, Lou Busch under a false name

29 Jun 56	PORTUGUESE WASHERWOMAN Capitol CL 14587	20	5 wks

See also Lou Busch.

Linda CARR US, female vocalist — 12 wks

12 Jul 75	HIGHWIRE Chelsea 2005 025 *	15	8 wks
5 Jun 76	SOLD MY ROCK 'N' ROLL (GAVE IT FOR FUNKY SOUL) Spark SRL 1139 **	36	4 wks

* Linda Carr and the Love Squad ** Linda and the Funky Boys

Pearl CARR and Teddy JOHNSON — 19 wks
UK, female/male vocal duo

20 Mar 59	SING LITTLE BIRDIE Columbia DB 4275	12	8 wks

6 Apr 61	HOW WONDERFUL TO KNOW Columbia DB 4603	23	11 wks

Valerie CARR UK, female vocalist — 2 wks

4 Jul 58	WHEN THE BOYS TALK ABOUT THE GIRLS Columbia DB 4131	29	1 wk
18 Jul 58	WHEN THE BOYS TALK ABOUT THE GIRLS (re-entry) Columbia DB 4131	30	1 wk

Vikki CARR US, female vocalist — 26 wks

1 Jun 67	●	IT MUST BE HIM (SEUL SUR SON ETOILE) Liberty LIB 55917	2	20 wks
30 Aug 67		THERE I GO Liberty LBF 15022	50	1 wk
12 Mar 69		WITH PEN IN HAND Liberty LBF 15166	43	1 wk
26 Mar 69		WITH PEN IN HAND (re-entry) Liberty LBF 15166	40	2 wks
30 Apr 69		WITH PEN IN HAND (2nd re-entry) Liberty LBF 15166	40	2 wks

Raffaella CARRA Italy, female vocalist — 12 wks

15 Apr 78	●	DO IT DO IT AGAIN Epic EPC 6094	9	12 wks

Paul CARRACK UK, male vocalist — 8 wks

16 May 87	WHEN YOU WALK IN THE ROOM Chrysalis CHS 3109	48	5 wks
18 Mar 89	DON'T SHED A TEAR Chrysalis CHS 3164	60	3 wks

Jose CARRERAS – See Sarah BRIGHTMAN

Tia CARRERE US, female vocalist — 6 wks

30 May 92	BALLROOM BLITZ Reprise W 0105	26	6 wks

Dina CARROLL UK, female vocalist — 34 wks

2 Feb 91	●	IT'S TOO LATE Mercury ITM 3 *	8	14 wks
15 Jun 91		NAKED LOVE (JUST SAY YOU WANT ME) Mercury ITM 4 **	39	3 wks
11 Jul 92		AIN'T NO MAN A & M AM 0001	16	8 wks
10 Oct 92		SPECIAL KIND OF LOVE A & M AM 0088	16	5 wks
5 Dec 92		SO CLOSE A & M AM 0101	20†	4 wks

* Quartz introducing Dina Carroll ** Quartz and Dina Carroll

Ronnie CARROLL UK, male vocalist — 50 wks

27 Jul 56		WALK HAND IN HAND Philips PB 605	13	8 wks
29 Mar 57		THE WISDOM OF A FOOL Philips PB 667	20	2 wks
31 Mar 60		FOOTSTEPS Philips PB 1004	36	3 wks
22 Feb 62		RING A DING GIRL Philips PB 1222	46	3 wks
2 Aug 62	●	ROSES ARE RED Philips 326532 BF	3	16 wks
15 Nov 62		IF ONLY TOMORROW Philips 326550 BF	33	4 wks
7 Mar 63	●	SAY WONDERFUL THINGS Philips 326574 BF	6	14 wks

Jasper CARROTT UK, male vocalist — 15 wks

16 Aug 75	●	FUNKY MOPED/MAGIC ROUNDABOUT DJM DJS 388	5	15 wks

CARS US, male vocal/instrumental group — 51 wks

11 Nov 78	●	MY BEST FRIEND'S GIRL Elektra K 12301	3	10 wks
17 Feb 79		JUST WHAT I NEEDED Elektra K 12312	17	10 wks
28 Jul 79		LET'S GO Elektra K 12371	51	4 wks

5 Jun 82	SINCE YOU'RE GONE Elektra K 13177	37	4 wks
29 Sep 84 ●	DRIVE Elektra E 9706	5	11 wks
3 Aug 85 ●	DRIVE (re-entry) Elektra E 9706	4	12 wks

CARTER - THE UNSTOPPABLE SEX MACHINE UK, male vocal/instrumental duo
30 wks

26 Jan 91	BLOODSPORTS FOR ALL Rough Trade R 20112687	48	2 wks
22 Jun 91	SHERIFF FATMAN Big Cat USM 1	23	7 wks
26 Oct 91	AFTER THE WATERSHED Big Cat USM 2	11	5 wks
11 Jan 92	RUBBISH Big Cat USM 3	14	5 wks
25 Apr 92 ●	THE ONLY LIVING BOY IN NEW CROSS Big Cat USM 4	7	5 wks
4 Jul 92	DO RE ME SO FAR SO GOOD Chrysalis USM 5	22	3 wks
28 Nov 92	THE IMPOSSIBLE DREAM Chrysalis USM 6	21	3 wks

Clarence CARTER US, male vocalist
13 wks

10 Oct 70 ●	PATCHES Atlantic 2091 030	2	13 wks

CARVELLS UK, male vocalist/instrumentalist - Alan Carvell
4 wks

26 Nov 77	THE L.A. RUN Creole CR 143	31	4 wks

CASCADES US, male vocal group
16 wks

28 Feb 63 ●	RHYTHM OF THE RAIN Warner Bros. WB 88	5	16 wks

Natalie CASEY UK, female vocalist
1 wk

7 Jan 84	CHICK CHICK CHICKEN Polydor CHICK 1	72	1 wk

Johnny CASH US, male vocalist
59 wks

3 Jun 65	IT AIN'T ME BABE CBS 201760	28	8 wks
6 Sep 69 ●	A BOY NAMED SUE CBS 4460	4	19 wks
23 May 70	WHAT IS TRUTH CBS 4934	21	11 wks
15 Apr 72 ●	A THING CALLED LOVE CBS 7797 *	4	13 wks
22 Jul 72	A THING CALLED LOVE (re-entry) CBS 7797 *	48	1 wk
3 Jul 76	ONE PIECE AT A TIME CBS 4287 **	32	7 wks

* Johnny Cash with the Evangel Temple Choir ** Johnny Cash with the Tennessee Three

Pat CASH – *See John McENROE and Pat CASH with the FULL METAL RACKETS*

CASHFLOW US, male vocal/instrumental group
8 wks

24 May 86	MINE ALL MINE/PARTY FREAK Club JAB 30	15	8 wks

CASHMERE US, male vocal/instrumental group
11 wks

19 Jan 85	CAN I Fourth & Broadway BRW 19	29	8 wks
23 Mar 85	WE NEED LOVE Fourth & Broadway BRW 22	52	3 wks

CASINOS US, male vocal group
7 wks

23 Feb 67	THEN YOU CAN TELL ME GOODBYE President PT 123	28	7 wks

David CASSIDY US, male vocalist
109 wks

8 Apr 72 ●	COULD IT BE FOREVER/CHERISH Bell 1224	2	17 wks
16 Sep 72 ★	HOW CAN I BE SURE Bell 1258	1	11 wks
25 Nov 72	ROCK ME BABY Bell 1268	11	9 wks
24 Mar 73 ●	I'M A CLOWN/SOME KIND OF A SUMMER Bell MABEL 4	3	12 wks
13 Oct 73 ★	DAYDREAMER/THE PUPPY SONG Bell 1334	1	15 wks
11 May 74	IF I DIDN'T CARE Bell 1350	9	8 wks
27 Jul 74	PLEASE PLEASE ME Bell 1371	16	6 wks
5 Jul 75	I WRITE THE SONGS/GET IT UP FOR LOVE RCA 2571	11	8 wks
25 Oct 75	DARLIN' RCA 2622	16	8 wks
23 Feb 85 ●	THE LAST KISS Arista ARIST 589	6	9 wks
11 May 85	ROMANCE (LET YOUR HEART GO) Arista ARIST 620	54	6 wks

See also Partridge Family starring Shirley Jones featuring David Cassidy.

Roy CASTLE UK, male vocalist
3 wks

22 Dec 60	LITTLE WHITE BERRY Philips PB 1087	40	3 wks

CASUALS UK, male vocal/instrumental group
26 wks

14 Aug 68 ●	JESAMINE Decca F 22784	2	18 wks
4 Dec 68	TOY Decca F 22852	30	8 wks

CATCH UK, male vocal/instrumental group
1 wk

17 Nov 90	FREE (C'MON) ffrr F 147	70	1 wk

CATHERINE WHEEL UK, male vocal/instrumental group
4 wks

23 Nov 91	BLACK METALLIC (EP) Fontana CW 1	68	1 wk
8 Feb 92	BALLOON Fontana CW 2	59	1 wk
18 Apr 92	I WANT TO TOUCH YOU Fontana CW 3	35	2 wks

Tracks on Black Metallic (EP): *Black Metallic/Crawling Over Me/Let Me Down Again/Saccharine.*

CATS UK, male instrumental group
2 wks

9 Apr 69	SWAN LAKE BAF 1	48	1 wk
21 May 69	SWAN LAKE (re-entry) BAF 1	50	1 wk

CATS U.K. UK, female vocal group
8 wks

6 Oct 79	LUTON AIRPORT WEA K 18075	22	8 wks

Nick CAVE Australia, male vocalist
2 wks

11 Apr 92	STRAIGHT TO YOU/JACK THE RIPPER Mute MUTE 140 *	68	1 wk
12 Dec 92	WHAT A WONDERFUL WORLD Mute MUTE 151 **	72	1 wk

* Nick Cave and the Bad Seeds ** Nick Cave and Shane McGowan

CAVEMAN UK, male rap group
2 wks

9 Mar 91	I'M READY Profile PROF 330	65	2 wks

C. C. S. UK, male vocal/instrumental group
55 wks

31 Oct 70	WHOLE LOTTA LOVE RAK 104	13	13 wks
27 Feb 71 ●	WALKIN' RAK 109	7	16 wks
4 Sep 71 ●	TAP TURNS ON THE WATER RAK 119	5	13 wks
4 Mar 72	BROTHER RAK 126	25	8 wks
4 Aug 73	BAND PLAYED THE BOOGIE RAK 154	36	5 wks

Because it followed his 1990 re-issue smash 'Blue Velvet', 'Roses Are Red' by Bobby Vinton received considerable airplay, re-inforcing the fact that he originated the song in 1962. However, RONNIE CARROLL had the biggest British version of the tune.

THE CASCADES used rain sound effects before Love Unlimited and Oran 'Juice' Jones.

MARIAH CAREY was there at the 1992 American Music Awards.

After sharing a number one with Sonny in 1965, CHER got her own 26 years later with 'The Shoop Shoop Song (It's In His Kiss)'.

CENTRAL LINE *UK, male vocal/instrumental group*   **30 wks**

31 Jan 81	(YOU KNOW) YOU CAN DO IT *Mercury LINE 7* **67**	3 wks
15 Aug 81	WALKING INTO SUNSHINE *Mercury MER 78* **42**	10 wks
30 Jan 82	DON'T TELL ME *Mercury MER 90* **55**	3 wks
20 Nov 82	YOU'VE SAID ENOUGH *Mercury MER 117* **58**	3 wks
22 Jan 83	NATURE BOY *Mercury MER 131* **21**	8 wks
11 Jun 83	SURPRISE SURPRISE *Mercury MER 133* **48**	3 wks

CERRONE *France, male producer/multi-instrumentalist*   **20 wks**

5 Mar 77	LOVE IN C MINOR *Atlantic K 10895* **31**	4 wks
29 Jul 78 ●	SUPER NATURE *Atlantic K 11089* **8**	12 wks
13 Jan 79	JE SUIS MUSIC *CBS 6918* **39**	4 wks

A CERTAIN RATIO *UK, male vocal/instrumental group*   **3 wks**

16 Jun 90	WON'T STOP LOVING YOU *A & M ACR 540* **55**	3 wks

Peter CETERA *US, male vocalist*   **13 wks**

2 Aug 86 ●	GLORY OF LOVE *Full Moon W 8662* **3**	13 wks

Frank CHACKSFIELD *UK, orchestra*   **41 wks**

3 Apr 53 ●	LITTLE RED MONKEY *Parlophone R 3658* * **10**	3 wks
22 May 53 ●	TERRY'S THEME FROM 'LIMELIGHT' *Decca F 10106* **2**	24 wks
12 Feb 54 ●	EBB TIDE *Decca F 10122* **9**	2 wks
24 Feb 56	IN OLD LISBON *Decca F 10689* **15**	4 wks
18 May 56	PORT AU PRINCE *Decca F 10727* ** **18**	6 wks
31 Aug 56	DONKEY CART *Decca F 10743* **26**	2 wks

* Frank Chacksfield's Tunesmiths, featuring Jack Jordan - clavioline ** Winifred Atwell and Frank Chacksfield

CHAIRMEN OF THE BOARD *US, male vocal group*   **77 wks**

22 Aug 70 ●	GIVE ME JUST A LITTLE MORE TIME *Invictus INV 501* **3**	13 wks
14 Nov 70 ●	YOU'VE GOT ME DANGLING ON A STRING *Invictus INV 504* **5**	13 wks
20 Feb 71	EVERYTHING'S TUESDAY *Invictus INV 507* **12**	9 wks
15 May 71	PAY TO THE PIPER *Invictus INV 511* **34**	7 wks
4 Sep 71	CHAIRMAN OF THE BOARD *Invictus INV 516* **48**	2 wks
15 Jul 72	WORKING ON A BUILDING OF LOVE *Invictus INV 519* **20**	8 wks
7 Oct 72	ELMO JAMES *Invictus INV 524* **21**	7 wks
16 Dec 72	I'M ON MY WAY TO A BETTER PLACE *Invictus INV 527* **38**	1 wk
13 Jan 73	I'M ON MY WAY TO A BETTER PLACE (re-entry) *Invictus INV 527* **30**	5 wks
23 Jun 73	FINDERS KEEPERS *Invictus INV 530* **21**	9 wks
13 Sep 86	LOVERBOY *EMI EMI 5585* * **56**	3 wks

* Chairmen Of The Board featuring General Johnson

CHAKACHAS *Belgium, male/female vocal/instrumental group*   **8 wks**

11 Jan 62	TWIST TWIST *RCA 1264* **48**	1 wk
27 May 72	JUNGLE FEVER *Polydor 2121 064* **29**	7 wks

George CHAKIRIS *US, male vocalist*   **1 wk**

2 Jun 60	HEART OF A TEENAGE GIRL *Triumph RGM 1010* **49**	1 wk

Richard CHAMBERLAIN *US, male vocalist*   **36 wks**

7 Jun 62	THEME FROM 'DR. KILDARE' (THREE STARS WILL SHINE TONIGHT) *MGM 1160* **12**	10 wks
1 Nov 62	LOVE ME TENDER *MGM 1173* **15**	11 wks
21 Feb 63	HI-LILI HI-LO *MGM 1189* **20**	9 wks
18 Jul 63	TRUE LOVE *MGM 1205* **30**	6 wks

CHAMELEONS – *See LORI and the CHAMELEONS*

CHAMPAIGN *US, male/female vocal/instrumental group*   **13 wks**

9 May 81 ●	HOW 'BOUT US *CBS A 1046* **5**	13 wks

CHAMPION LEGEND – *See VARIOUS ARTISTS (MONTAGES)*

CHAMPS *US, male instrumental group*   **10 wks**

4 Apr 58 ●	TEQUILA *London HLU 8580* **5**	9 wks
17 Mar 60	TOO MUCH TEQUILA *London HLH 9052* **49**	1 wk

CHAMPS BOYS *France, male instrumental group*   **6 wks**

19 Jun 76	TUBULAR BELLS *Philips 6006 519* **41**	6 wks

Gene CHANDLER *US, male vocalist*   **29 wks**

5 Jun 68	NOTHING CAN STOP ME *Soul City SC 102* **41**	4 wks
3 Feb 79	GET DOWN *20th Century BTC 1040* **11**	11 wks
1 Sep 79	WHEN YOU'RE NUMBER 1 *20th Century TC 2411* **43**	5 wks
28 Jun 80	DOES SHE HAVE A FRIEND *20th Century TC 2451* **28**	9 wks

CHANELLE *US, female vocalist*   **8 wks**

11 Mar 89	ONE MAN *Cooltempo COOL 183* **16**	8 wks

CHANGE *US, male/female vocal/instrumental group*   **43 wks**

28 Jun 80	A LOVER'S HOLIDAY/GLOW OF LOVE *WEA K 79141* **14**	8 wks
6 Sep 80	SEARCHING *WEA K 79156* **11**	10 wks
2 Jun 84	CHANGE OF HEART *WEA YZ 7* **17**	10 wks
11 Aug 84	YOU ARE MY MELODY *WEA YZ 14* **48**	4 wks
16 Mar 85	LET'S GO TOGETHER *Cooltempo COOL 107* **37**	7 wks
25 May 85	OH WHAT A FEELING *Cooltempo COOL 109* **56**	2 wks
13 Jul 85	MUTUAL ATTRACTION *Cooltempo COOL 111* **60**	2 wks

Bruce CHANNEL *US, male vocalist*   **28 wks**

22 Mar 62 ●	HEY! BABY *Mercury AMT 1171* **2**	12 wks
26 Jun 68	KEEP ON *Bell 1010* **12**	16 wks

CHANNEL X *Belgium, male/female vocal/instrumental group*   **1 wk**

14 Dec 91	GROOVE TO MOVE *PWL Continental PWL 209* **67**	1 wk

CHANSON *US, male/female vocal group*   **7 wks**

13 Jan 79	DON'T HOLD BACK *Ariola ARO 140* **33**	7 wks

CHANTAYS *US, male instrumental group*   **14 wks**

18 Apr 63	PIPELINE *London HLD 9696* **16**	14 wks

CHANTER SISTERS *UK, female vocal group*   **5 wks**

17 Jul 76	SIDE SHOW *Polydor 2058 735* **43**	5 wks

CHAOS UK, male vocal group — 2 wks

3 Oct 92	FAREWELL MY SUMMER LOVE *Arista 74321116397*	55	2 wks

Harry CHAPIN US, male vocalist — 5 wks

11 May 74	W.O.L.D. *Elektra K 12133*	34	5 wks

Tracy CHAPMAN US, female vocalist — 15 wks

11 Jun 88 ●	FAST CAR *Elektra EKR 73*	5	12 wks
30 Sep 89	CROSSROADS *Elektra EKR 95*	61	3 wks

CHAPTERHOUSE UK, male vocal/instrumental group — 3 wks

30 Mar 91	PEARL *Dedicated STONE 003*	67	1 wk
12 Oct 91	MESMERISE *Dedicated HOUSE 001*	60	2 wks

CHAQUITO UK, male arranger/conductor - Johnny Gregory — 1 wk

27 Oct 60	NEVER ON SUNDAY *Fontana H 265*	50	1 wk

CHARLATANS UK, male vocal/instrumental group — 29 wks

2 Jun 90 ●	THE ONLY ONE I KNOW *Situation Two SIT 70T*	9	9 wks
22 Sep 90	THEN *Situation Two SIT 74T*	12	5 wks
9 Mar 91	OVER RISING *Situation Two SIT 76*	15	5 wks
17 Aug 91	INDIAN ROPE *Dead Dead Good GOOD 1T*	57	1 wk
9 Nov 91	ME. IN TIME *Situation Two SIT 84*	28	3 wks
7 Mar 92	WEIRDO *Situation Two SIT 88*	19	4 wks
18 Jul 92	TREMELO SONG (EP) *Situation Two SIT 97T*	44	2 wks

Tracks on Tremelo Song (EP): *Tremelo Song/Happen To Die/Normality Swing.*

CHARLENE US, female vocalist — 12 wks

15 May 82 ★	I'VE NEVER BEEN TO ME *Motown TMG 1260*	1	12 wks

Don CHARLES UK, male vocalist — 5 wks

22 Feb 62	WALK WITH ME MY ANGEL *Decca F 11424*	39	5 wks

Ray CHARLES US, male vocalist/instrumentalist - piano — 130 wks

1 Dec 60	GEORGIA ON MY MIND *HMV POP 792*	47	1 wk
15 Dec 60	GEORGIA ON MY MIND (re-entry) *HMV POP 792*	24	7 wks
19 Oct 61 ●	HIT THE ROAD JACK *HMV POP 935*	6	12 wks
14 Jun 62 ★	I CAN'T STOP LOVING YOU *HMV POP 1034*	1	17 wks
13 Sep 62 ★	YOU DON'T KNOW ME *HMV POP 1064*	9	13 wks
13 Dec 62	YOUR CHEATING HEART *HMV POP 1099*	13	8 wks
28 Mar 63	DON'T SET ME FREE *HMV POP 1133*	37	3 wks
16 May 63 ●	TAKE THESE CHAINS FROM MY HEART *HMV POP 1161*	5	20 wks
12 Sep 63	NO ONE *HMV POP 1202*	35	7 wks
31 Oct 63	BUSTED *HMV POP 1221*	21	10 wks
24 Sep 64	NO ONE TO CRY TO *HMV POP 1333*	38	3 wks
21 Jan 65	MAKIN' WHOOPEE *HMV POP 1383*	42	4 wks
10 Feb 66	CRYIN' TIME *HMV POP 1502*	50	1 wk
21 Apr 66	TOGETHER AGAIN *HMV POP 1519*	48	1 wk
5 Jul 67	HERE WE GO AGAIN *HMV POP 1595*	38	1 wk
19 Jul 67	HERE WE GO AGAIN (re-entry) *HMV POP 1595*	45	2 wks
20 Dec 67	YESTERDAY *Stateside SS 2071*	44	4 wks
31 Jul 68	ELEANOR RIGBY *Stateside SS 2120*	36	9 wks
13 Jan 90	I'LL BE GOOD TO YOU *Qwest W 9992* *	21	7 wks

* Quincy Jones featuring Ray Charles and Chaka Khan

Tina CHARLES UK, female vocalist — 63 wks

7 Feb 76 ★	I LOVE TO LOVE (BUT MY BABY LOVES TO DANCE) *CBS 3937*	1	12 wks
1 May 76	LOVE ME LIKE A LOVER *CBS 4237*	28	7 wks
21 Aug 76 ●	DANCE LITTLE LADY DANCE *CBS 4480*	6	13 wks
4 Dec 76 ●	DR. LOVE *CBS 4779*	4	10 wks
14 May 77	RENDEZVOUS *CBS 5174*	27	6 wks
29 Oct 77	LOVE BUG-SWEETS FOR MY SWEET (MEDLEY) *CBS 5680*	26	4 wks
11 Mar 78	I'LL GO WHERE YOUR MUSIC TAKES ME *CBS 6062*	27	8 wks
30 Aug 86	I LOVE TO LOVE (re-mix) *DMC DECK 1*	67	3 wks

CHARLES and EDDIE US, male vocal duo — 9 wks

31 Oct 92 ★	WOULD I LIE TO YOU *Capitol CL 673*	1†	9 wks

Dick CHARLESWORTH and his CITY GENTS UK, male jazz band group, Dick Charlesworth clarinet — 1 wk

4 May 61	BILLY BOY *Top Rank JAR 558*	43	1 wk

CHARME US, male/female vocal group — 2 wks

17 Nov 84	GEORGY PORGY *RCA 464*	68	2 wks

CHARO and the SALSOUL ORCHESTRA US, female vocalist and orchestra — 4 wks

29 Apr 78	DANCE A LITTLE BIT CLOSER *Salsoul SSOL 101*	44	4 wks

CHAS and DAVE UK, male vocal/instrumental duo — 66 wks

11 Nov 78	STRUMMIN' *EMI 2874* *	52	3 wks
26 May 79	GERTCHA *EMI 2947*	20	8 wks
1 Sep 79	THE SIDEBOARD SONG (GOT MY BEER IN THE SIDEBOARD HERE) *EMI 2986*	55	3 wks
29 Nov 80 ●	RABBIT *Rockney 9*	8	11 wks
12 Dec 81	STARS OVER 45 *Rockney KOR 12*	21	8 wks
13 Mar 82 ●	AIN'T NO PLEASING YOU *Rockney KOR 14*	2	11 wks
17 Jul 82	MARGATE *Rockney KOR 15*	46	4 wks
19 Mar 83	LONDON GIRLS *Rockney KOR 17*	63	3 wks
3 Dec 83	MY MELANCHOLY BABY *Rockney KOR 21*	51	6 wks
3 May 86 ●	SNOOKER LOOPY *Rockney POT 147* **	6	9 wks

* Chas and Dave with Rockney ** Matchroom Mob with Chas and Dave
See also Tottenham Hotspur FA Cup Final Squad.

CHEAP TRICK US, male vocal/instrumental group — 14 wks

5 May 79	I WANT YOU TO WANT ME *Epic EPC 7258*	29	9 wks
2 Feb 80	WAY OF THE WORLD *Epic EPC 8114*	73	2 wks
31 Jul 82	IF YOU WANT MY LOVE *Epic EPC A 2406*	57	3 wks

Oliver CHEATHAM US, male vocalist — 5 wks

2 Jul 83	GET DOWN SATURDAY NIGHT *MCA 828*	38	5 wks

CHECK 1-2 – *See Craig McLACHLAN*

Chubby CHECKER US, male vocalist — 112 wks

22 Sep 60	THE TWIST *Columbia DB 4503*	49	1 wk
6 Oct 60	THE TWIST (re-entry) *Columbia DB 4503*	44	1 wk
30 Mar 61	PONY TIME *Columbia DB 4591*	27	6 wks

17 Aug 61		LET'S TWIST AGAIN *Columbia DB 4691*	37 3 wks
28 Dec 61	●	LET'S TWIST AGAIN (re-entry) *Columbia DB 4691*	2 27 wks
11 Jan 62		THE TWIST (2nd re-entry) *Columbia DB 4503*	14 10 wks
5 Apr 62		SLOW TWISTIN' *Columbia DB 4808*	23 8 wks
19 Apr 62		TEACH ME TO TWIST *Columbia DB 4802 *	45 1 wk
9 Aug 62		DANCIN' PARTY *Columbia DB 4876*	19 13 wks
23 Aug 62		LET'S TWIST AGAIN (2nd re-entry) *Columbia DB 4691*	46 1 wk
13 Sep 62		LET'S TWIST AGAIN (3rd re-entry) *Columbia DB 4691*	49 3 wks
1 Nov 62		LIMBO ROCK *Cameo-Parkway P 849*	32 10 wks
20 Dec 62		JINGLE BELL ROCK *Cameo-Parkway C 205 *	40 3 wks
31 Oct 63		WHAT DO YA SAY *Cameo-Parkway P 806*	37 4 wks
29 Nov 75	●	LET'S TWIST AGAIN/THE TWIST (re-issue) *London HL 10512*	5 10 wks
18 Jun 88	●	THE TWIST (YO, TWIST) *Urban URB 20 **	2 11 wks

* Chubby Checker and Bobby Rydell ** Fat Boys and Chubby Checker

CHECKMATES – *See Emile FORD and the CHECKMATES*

CHECKMATES LTD. *US, male vocal/instrumental group*   **8 wks**

15 Nov 69		PROUD MARY *A & M AMS 769*	30 8 wks

CHEETAHS *UK, male vocal/instrumental group*   **6 wks**

1 Oct 64		MECCA *Philips BF 1362*	36 3 wks
21 Jan 65		SOLDIER BOY *Philips BF 1383*	39 3 wks

CHELSEA F.C. *UK, male football team vocalists*   **12 wks**

26 Feb 72	●	BLUE IS THE COLOUR *Penny Farthing PEN 782*	5 12 wks

CHEQUERS *UK, male vocal/instrumental group*   **10 wks**

18 Oct 75		ROCK ON BROTHER *Creole CR 111*	21 5 wks
28 Feb 76		HEY MISS PAYNE *Creole CR 116*	32 5 wks

CHER *US, female vocalist*   **135 wks**

19 Aug 65	●	ALL I REALLY WANT TO DO *Liberty LIB 66114*	9 10 wks
31 Mar 66	●	BANG BANG (MY BABY SHOT ME DOWN) *Liberty LIB 66160*	3 12 wks
4 Aug 66		I FEEL SOMETHING IN THE AIR *Liberty LIB 12034*	43 2 wks
22 Sep 66		SUNNY *Liberty LIB 12083*	32 4 wks
6 Nov 71	●	GYPSYS TRAMPS AND THIEVES *MCA MU 1142*	4 13 wks
16 Feb 74		DARK LADY *MCA 101*	36 3 wks
16 Mar 74		DARK LADY (re-entry) *MCA 101*	45 1 wk
19 Dec 87	●	I FOUND SOMEONE *Geffen GEF 31*	5 10 wks
2 Apr 88		WE ALL SLEEP ALONE *Geffen GEF 35*	47 5 wks
2 Sep 89	●	IF I COULD TURN BACK TIME *Geffen GEF 59*	6 14 wks
13 Jan 90		JUST LIKE JESSE JAMES *Geffen GEF 69*	11 11 wks
7 Apr 90		HEART OF STONE *Geffen GEF 75*	43 5 wks
11 Aug 90		YOU WOULDN'T KNOW LOVE *Geffen GEF 77*	55 3 wks
13 Apr 91	★	THE SHOOP SHOOP SONG (IT'S IN HIS KISS) *Epic 6566737*	1 15 wks
13 Jul 91	●	LOVE AND UNDERSTANDING *Geffen GFS 5*	10 8 wks
12 Oct 91		SAVE UP ALL YOUR TEARS *Geffen GFS 11*	37 5 wks
7 Dec 91		LOVE HURTS *Geffen GFS 16*	43 5 wks
18 Apr 92		COULD'VE BEEN YOU *Geffen GFS 19*	31 4 wks
14 Nov 92		OH NO NOT MY BABY *Geffen GFS 29*	33 4 wks

See also Sonny and Cher; Meatloaf.

CHERELLE *US, female vocalist*   **25 wks**

28 Dec 85	●	SATURDAY LOVE *Tabu A 6829 *	6 11 wks
1 Mar 86		WILL YOU SATISFY? *Tabu A 6927*	57 3 wks
6 Feb 88		NEVER KNEW LOVE LIKE THIS *Tabu 6513827 **	26 7 wks
6 May 89		AFFAIR *Tabu 654673 7*	67 2 wks
24 Mar 90		SATURDAY LOVE (re-mix) *Tabu 6556807 *	55 2 wks

* Cherelle with Alexander O'Neal ** Alexander O'Neal featuring Cherelle

CHERI *Canada, female vocal duo*   **9 wks**

19 Jun 82		MURPHY'S LAW *Polydor POSP 459*	13 9 wks

CHEROKEES *UK, male vocal/instrumental group*   **5 wks**

3 Sep 64		SEVEN DAFFODILS *Columbia DB 7341*	33 5 wks

Don CHERRY *US, male vocalist*   **11 wks**

10 Feb 56	●	BAND OF GOLD *Philips PB 549*	6 11 wks

Neneh CHERRY *US, female vocalist*   **45 wks**

10 Dec 88	●	BUFFALO STANCE *Circa YR 21*	3 13 wks
20 May 89	●	MANCHILD *Circa YR 30*	5 10 wks
12 Aug 89		KISSES ON THE WIND *Circa YR 33*	20 6 wks
23 Dec 89		INNA CITY MAMMA *Circa YR 42*	31 7 wks
29 Sep 90		I'VE GOT YOU UNDER MY SKIN *Circa YR 53*	25 5 wks
3 Oct 92		MONEY LOVE *Circa YR 83*	23 4 wks

CHIC *US, male/female vocal/instrumental group*   **90 wks**

26 Nov 77	●	DANCE DANCE DANCE (YOWSAH YOWSAH YOWSAH) *Atlantic K 11038*	6 12 wks
1 Apr 78	●	EVERYBODY DANCE *Atlantic K 11097*	9 11 wks
18 Nov 78	●	LE FREAK *Atlantic K 11209*	7 16 wks
24 Feb 79	●	I WANT YOUR LOVE *Atlantic LV 16*	4 11 wks
30 Jun 79	●	GOOD TIMES *Atlantic K 11310*	5 11 wks
13 Oct 79		MY FORBIDDEN LOVER *Atlantic K 11385*	15 8 wks
8 Dec 79		MY FEET KEEP DANCING *Atlantic K 11415*	21 9 wks
12 Mar 83		HANGIN' *Atlantic A 9898*	64 1 wk
19 Sep 87		JACK LE FREAK *Atlantic A 9198*	19 6 wks
14 Jul 90		MEGACHIC - CHIC MEDLEY *East West A 7949*	58 2 wks
15 Feb 92		CHIC MYSTIQUE *Warner Bros. W 0083*	48 3 wks

CHICAGO *US, male vocal/instrumental group*   **81 wks**

10 Jan 70	●	I'M A MAN *CBS 4715*	8 11 wks
18 Jul 70	●	25 OR 6 TO 4 *CBS 5076*	7 13 wks
9 Oct 76	★	IF YOU LEAVE ME NOW *CBS 4603*	1 16 wks
5 Nov 77		BABY WHAT A BIG SURPRISE *CBS 5672*	41 7 wks
21 Aug 82	●	HARD TO SAY I'M SORRY *Full Moon K 79301*	4 15 wks
27 Oct 84	●	HARD HABIT TO BREAK *Full Moon W 9214*	8 13 wks
26 Jan 85		YOU'RE THE INSPIRATION *Warner Bros. W 9126*	14 10 wks

CHICKEN SHACK   **19 wks**
UK, male/female vocal/instrumental group

7 May 69		I'D RATHER GO BLIND *Blue Horizon 57-3153*	14 13 wks
6 Sep 69		TEARS IN THE WIND *Blue Horizon 57-3160*	29 6 wks

CHICORY TIP *UK, male vocal/instrumental group*   **34 wks**

29 Jan 72	★	SON OF MY FATHER *CBS 7737*	1 13 wks
20 May 72		WHAT'S YOUR NAME *CBS 8021*	13 8 wks
31 Mar 73		GOOD GRIEF CHRISTINA *CBS 1258*	17 13 wks

CHIFFONS *US, female vocal group*   **40 wks**

11 Apr 63		HE'S SO FINE *Stateside SS 172*	16 12 wks
18 Jul 63		ONE FINE DAY *Stateside SS 202*	29 6 wks

26 May 66	**SWEET TALKIN' GUY** *Stateside SS 512* **31**	8 wks
18 Mar 72 ●	**SWEET TALKIN' GUY (re-issue)** *London HL 10271* **4**	14 wks

CHILD *UK, male vocal/instrumental group* **22 wks**

29 Apr 78	**WHEN YOU WALK IN THE ROOM** *Ariola Hansa AHA 511* **38**	5 wks
22 Jul 78 ●	**IT'S ONLY MAKE BELIEVE** *Ariola Hansa AHA 522* **10**	12 wks
28 Apr 79	**ONLY YOU (AND YOU ALONE)** *Ariola Hansa AHA 536* **33**	5 wks

Jane CHILD *Canada, female vocalist* **8 wks**

12 May 90	**DON'T WANNA FALL IN LOVE** *Warner Bros. W 9817* **22**	8 wks

CHILDREN OF THE NIGHT **2 wks**
UK, male vocalist/producer

26 Nov 88	**IT'S A TRIP (TUNE IN, TURN ON, DROP OUT)** *Jive JIVE 189* **52**	2 wks

CHILDREN OF THE REVOLUTION – *See KLF*

Toni CHILDS *US, female vocalist* **4 wks**

25 Mar 89	**DON'T WALK AWAY** *A & M AM 462* **53**	4 wks

CHI-LITES *US, male vocal group* **89 wks**

28 Aug 71	**(FOR GOD'S SAKE) GIVE MORE POWER TO THE PEOPLE** *MCA MU 1138* **32**	6 wks
15 Jan 72 ●	**HAVE YOU SEEN HER** *MCA MU 1146* **3**	12 wks
27 May 72	**OH GIRL** *MCA MU 1156* **14**	9 wks
23 Mar 74 ●	**HOMELY GIRL** *Brunswick BR 9* **5**	13 wks
20 Jul 74	**I FOUND SUNSHINE** *Brunswick BR 12* **35**	5 wks
2 Nov 74 ●	**TOO GOOD TO BE FORGOTTEN** *Brunswick BR 13* **10**	11 wks
21 Jun 75 ●	**HAVE YOU SEEN HER/OH GIRL (re-issues)** *Brunswick BR 20* **5**	9 wks
13 Sep 75 ●	**IT'S TIME FOR LOVE** *Brunswick BR 25* **5**	10 wks
31 Jul 76 ●	**YOU DON'T HAVE TO GO** *Brunswick BR 34* **3**	11 wks
13 Aug 83	**CHANGING FOR YOU** *R & B RBS 215* **61**	3 wks

CHILL FAC-TORR *US, male vocal/instrumental group* **8 wks**

2 Apr 83	**TWIST (ROUND 'N' ROUND)** *Phillyworld PWS 109* **37**	8 wks

CHIMES *UK, male/female vocal/instrumental group* **28 wks**

19 Aug 89	**1-2-3** *CBS 655166 7* **60**	3 wks
2 Dec 89	**HEAVEN** *CBS 655432 7* **66**	2 wks
6 Jan 90	**HEAVEN (re-entry)** *CBS 655432 7* **69**	3 wks
19 May 90 ●	**STILL HAVEN'T FOUND WHAT I'M LOOKING FOR** *CBS CHIM 1* **6**	9 wks
28 Jul 90	**TRUE LOVE** *CBS CHIM 12* **48**	3 wks
29 Sep 90	**HEAVEN (re-issue)** *CBS CHIM 3* **24**	6 wks
1 Dec 90	**LOVE COMES TO MIND** *CBS CHIM 4* **49**	2 wks

CHINA CRISIS *UK, male vocal/instrumental group* **66 wks**

7 Aug 82	**AFRICAN AND WHITE** *Inevitable INEV 011* **45**	5 wks
22 Jan 83	**CHRISTIAN** *Virgin VS 562* **12**	9 wks
21 May 83	**TRAGEDY AND MYSTERY** *Virgin VS 587* **46**	6 wks
15 Oct 83	**WORKING WITH FIRE AND STEEL** *Virgin VS 620* **48**	5 wks
14 Jan 84 ●	**WISHFUL THINKING** *Virgin VS 647* **9**	8 wks
10 Mar 84	**HANNA HANNA** *Virgin VS 665* **44**	3 wks
30 Mar 85	**BLACK MAN RAY** *Virgin VS 752* **14**	9 wks
1 Jun 85	**KING IN A CATHOLIC STYLE (WAKE UP)** *Virgin VS 765* **19**	9 wks

7 Sep 85	**YOU DID CUT ME** *Virgin VS 799* **54**	3 wks
8 Nov 86	**ARIZONA SKY** *Virgin VS 898* **47**	4 wks
24 Jan 87	**BEST KEPT SECRET** *Virgin VS 926* **36**	5 wks

Jonny CHINGAS *US, male vocalist* **6 wks**

19 Feb 83	**PHONE HOME** *CBS A 3121* **43**	6 wks

CHIPMUNKS **10 wks**
US, male vocalist, David Seville as himself and a chipmunk vocal trio

24 Jul 59	**RAGTIME COWBOY JOE** *London HLU 8916* **11**	8 wks
19 Dec 92	**ACHY BREAKY HEART** *Epic 6588837 ** ....**53†**	2 wks

* Alvin and the Chipmunks featuring Billy Ray Cyrus

CHIPPENDALES *UK/US, male vocal group* **4 wks**

31 Oct 92	**GIVE ME YOUR BODY** *XS Rhythm XSR 3* **28**	4 wks

CHOPS-EMC + EXTENSIVE **1 wk**
UK, male instrumental group and rapper

8 Aug 92	**ME' ISRAELITES** *Faze 2 FAZE 6* **60**	1 wk

CHORDETTES *US, female vocal group* **25 wks**

17 Dec 54	**MR. SANDMAN** *Columbia DB 3553* **11**	8 wks
31 Aug 56 ●	**BORN TO BE WITH YOU** *London HLA 8302* **8**	9 wks
18 Apr 58 ●	**LOLLIPOP** *London HLD 8584* **6**	8 wks

CHORDS *UK, male vocal/instrumental group* **17 wks**

6 Oct 79	**NOW IT'S GONE** *Polydor 2059 141* **63**	2 wks
2 Feb 80	**MAYBE TOMORROW** *Polydor POSP 101* **40**	5 wks
26 Apr 80	**SOMETHING'S MISSING** *Polydor POSP 146* **55**	3 wks
12 Jul 80	**THE BRITISH WAY OF LIFE** *Polydor 2059 258* **54**	3 wks
18 Oct 80	**IN MY STREET** *Polydor POSP 185* **50**	4 wks

Neil CHRISTIAN *UK, male vocalist* **10 wks**

7 Apr 66	**THAT'S NICE** *Strike JH 301* **14**	10 wks

Roger CHRISTIAN *UK, male vocalist* **3 wks**

30 Sep 89	**TAKE IT FROM ME** *Island IS 427* **63**	3 wks

CHRISTIANS *UK, male vocal/instrumental group* **81 wks**

31 Jan 87	**FORGOTTEN TOWN** *Island IS 291* **22**	11 wks
13 Jun 87	**HOOVERVILLE (THEY PROMISED US THE WORLD)** *Island IS 326* **21**	10 wks
26 Sep 87	**WHEN THE FINGERS POINT** *Island IS 335* **34**	7 wks
5 Dec 87	**IDEAL WORLD** *Island IS 347* **14**	13 wks
23 Apr 88	**BORN AGAIN** *Island IS 365* **25**	7 wks
15 Oct 88 ●	**HARVEST FOR THE WORLD** *Island IS 395* **8**	7 wks
20 May 89 ★	**FERRY 'CROSS THE MERSEY** *PWL PWL 41 ** **1**	7 wks
23 Dec 89	**WORDS** *Island IS 450* **18**	8 wks
7 Apr 90	**I FOUND OUT** *Island IS 453* **56**	2 wks
15 Sep 90	**GREENBANK DRIVE** *Island IS 466* **63**	2 wks
5 Sep 92	**WHAT'S IN A WORD** *Island IS 536* **33**	5 wks
14 Nov 92	**FATHER** *Island IS 543* **55**	2 wks

* Christians, Holly Johnson, Paul McCartney, Gerry Marsden and Stock Aitken Waterman

CHRISTIE UK, male vocal/instrumental group — 37 wks

2 May 70 ★	YELLOW RIVER CBS 4911	1	22 wks
10 Oct 70	SAN BERNADINO CBS 5169	49	1 wk
24 Oct 70 ●	SAN BERNADINO (re-entry) CBS 5169	7	13 wks
25 Mar 72	IRON HORSE CBS 7747	47	1 wk

David CHRISTIE France, male vocalist — 12 wks

14 Aug 82 ●	SADDLE UP KR KR 9	9	12 wks

John CHRISTIE Australia, male vocalist — 6 wks

25 Dec 76	HERE'S TO LOVE (AULD LANG SYNE) EMI 2554	24	6 wks

Lou CHRISTIE US, male vocalist — 35 wks

24 Feb 66	LIGHTNIN' STRIKES MGM 1297	11	8 wks
28 Apr 66	RHAPSODY IN THE RAIN MGM 1308	37	2 wks
13 Sep 69 ●	I'M GONNA MAKE YOU MINE Buddah 201 057	2	17 wks
27 Dec 69	SHE SOLD ME MAGIC Buddah 201 073	25	8 wks

Tony CHRISTIE UK, male vocalist — 47 wks

9 Jan 71	LAS VEGAS MCA MK 5058	21	9 wks
8 May 71 ●	I DID WHAT I DID FOR MARIA MCA MK 5064	2	17 wks
20 Nov 71	IS THIS THE WAY TO AMARILLO MCA MKS 5073	18	13 wks
10 Feb 73	AVENUES AND ALLEYWAYS MCA MKS 5101	37	4 wks
17 Jan 76	DRIVE SAFELY DARLIN' MCA 219	35	4 wks

Shawn CHRISTOPHER US, female vocalist — 9 wks

4 May 91	ANOTHER SLEEPLESS NIGHT Arista 114186	50	4 wks
21 Mar 92	DON'T LOSE THE MAGIC Arista 115097	30	5 wks

CHUCKS UK, male/female vocal group — 7 wks

24 Jan 63	LOO-BE-LOO Decca F 11569	22	7 wks

CHYNA – See INCOGNITO

CICERO UK, male vocalist — 12 wks

18 Jan 92	LOVE IS EVERYWHERE Spaghetti CIAO 3	19	8 wks
18 Apr 92	THAT LOVING FEELING Spaghetti CIAO 4	46	3 wks
1 Aug 92	HEAVEN MUST HAVE SENT YOU BACK Spaghetti CIAO 5	70	1 wk

CINDERELLA US, male vocal/instrumental group — 7 wks

6 Aug 88	GYPSY ROAD Vertigo VER 40	54	2 wks
4 Mar 89	DON'T KNOW WHAT YOU GOT Vertigo VER 43	54	2 wks
17 Nov 90	SHELTER ME Vertigo VER 51	55	2 wks
27 Apr 91	HEARTBREAK STATION Vertigo VER 53	63	1 wk

CINDY and the SAFFRONS UK, female vocal group — 3 wks

15 Jan 83	PAST, PRESENT AND FUTURE Stilletto STL 9	56	3 wks

Gigliola CINQUETTI Italy, female vocalist — 27 wks

23 Apr 64	NON HO L'ETA PER AMARTI Decca F 21882	17	17 wks
4 May 74 ●	GO (BEFORE YOU BREAK MY HEART) CBS 2294	8	10 wks

CIRCUIT UK, male/female vocal/instrumental group — 2 wks

20 Jul 91	SHELTER ME Cooltempo COOL 237	44	2 wks

CIRRUS UK, male vocal group — 1 wk

30 Sep 78	ROLLIN' ON Jet 123	62	1 wk

CITY BOY UK, male vocal/instrumental group — 20 wks

8 Jul 78 ●	5-7-0-5 Vertigo 6059 207	8	12 wks
28 Oct 78	WHAT A NIGHT Vertigo 6059 211	39	5 wks
15 Sep 79	THE DAY THE EARTH CAUGHT FIRE Vertigo 6059 238	67	3 wks

CITY GENTS – See Dick CHARLESWORTH and his CITY GENTS

C.J. & CO. US, male vocal/instrumental group — 2 wks

30 Jul 77	DEVIL'S GUN Atlantic K 10956	43	2 wks

Gary CLAIL ON-U SOUND SYSTEM — 17 wks
UK, male producer

14 Jul 90	BEEF RCA PB 49265 *	64	2 wks
30 Mar 91 ●	HUMAN NATURE Perfecto PB 44401	10	9 wks
8 Jun 91	ESCAPE Perfecto PB 44563	44	3 wks
14 Nov 92	WHO PAYS THE PIPER Perfecto 74321117017	31	3 wks

* Gary Clail

CLAIRE and FRIENDS — 11 wks
UK, female vocalist and young male/female friends

7 Jun 86	IT'S 'ORRIBLE BEING IN LOVE (WHEN YOU'RE 8 1/2) BBC RESL 189	13	11 wks

CLANNAD Ireland, male/female vocal group — 29 wks

6 Nov 82 ●	THEME FROM HARRY'S GAME RCA 292	5	10 wks
2 Jul 83	NEW GRANGE RCA 340	65	1 wk
12 May 84	ROBIN (THE HOODED MAN) RCA HOOD 1	42	5 wks
25 Jan 86	IN A LIFETIME RCA PB 40535 *	20	5 wks
10 Jun 89	IN A LIFETIME (re-issue) RCA PB 42873 *	17	7 wks
10 Aug 91	BOTH SIDES NOW MCA MCS 1546 **	74	1 wk

* Clannad featuring Bono ** Clannad and Paul Young

Jimmy CLANTON US, male vocalist — 1 wk

21 Jul 60	ANOTHER SLEEPLESS NIGHT Top Rank JAR 382	50	1 wk

Eric CLAPTON UK, male vocalist/instrumentalist - guitar — 130 wks

20 Dec 69	COMIN' HOME Atlantic 584 308 *	16	9 wks
12 Aug 72 ●	LAYLA Polydor 2058 130 **	7	11 wks
27 Jul 74 ●	I SHOT THE SHERIFF RSO 2090 132	9	9 wks
10 May 75	SWING LOW SWEET CHARIOT RSO 2090 158	19	9 wks
16 Aug 75	KNOCKIN' ON HEAVEN'S DOOR RSO 2090 166	38	4 wks
24 Dec 77	LAY DOWN SALLY RSO 2090 264	39	6 wks
21 Oct 78	PROMISES RSO 21	37	7 wks
6 Mar 82 ●	LAYLA (re-issue) RSO 87 **	4	10 wks
5 Jun 82	I SHOT THE SHERIFF (re-issue) RSO 88	64	2 wks
23 Apr 83	THE SHAPE YOU'RE IN Duck W 9701	75	1 wk
16 Mar 85	FOREVER MAN Warner Bros. W 9069	51	4 wks
4 Jan 86	EDGE OF DARKNESS BBC RESL 178 ***	65	3 wks
17 Jan 87	BEHIND THE MASK Duck W 8461	15	11 wks

20 Jun 87		TEARING US APART *Duck W 8299* ****	....................**56**	3 wks
27 Jan 90		BAD LOVE *Duck W 2644*	....................**25**	7 wks
14 Apr 90		NO ALIBIS *Duck W 9981*	....................**53**	3 wks
16 Nov 91		WONDERFUL TONIGHT (LIVE) *Duck W 0069*	....**30**	7 wks
8 Feb 92		TEARS IN HEAVEN *Reprise W 0081*	..........**50**	3 wks
7 Mar 92	●	TEARS IN HEAVEN (re-entry) *Reprise W 0081*	....................**5**	9 wks
1 Aug 92		RUNAWAY TRAIN *Rocket EJS 29* *****	........**31**	4 wks
29 Aug 92		IT'S PROBABLY ME *A & M AM 883* ******	....**30**	5 wks
3 Oct 92		LAYLA (ACOUSTIC) *Duck W 0134*	....................**45**	3 wks

* Delaney and Bonnie and Friends featuring Eric Clapton ** Derek and the Dominoes *** Eric Clapton featuring Michael Kamen **** Eric Clapton and Tina Turner ***** Elton John and Eric Clapton ****** Sting with Eric Clapton
Layla (Acoustic) *is as its title suggests an acoustic re-recording of Layla.*

Dee CLARK *US, male vocalist*   9 wks

| 2 Oct 59 | | JUST KEEP IT UP *London HL 8915* | ....**26** | 1 wk |
| 11 Oct 75 | | RIDE A WILD HORSE *Chelsea 2005 037* | ....**16** | 8 wks |

Petula CLARK *UK, female vocalist*   247 wks

11 Jun 54		THE LITTLE SHOEMAKER *Polygon P 1117*	....**12**	1 wk
25 Jun 54	●	THE LITTLE SHOEMAKER (re-entry) *Polygon P 1117*	....**7**	9 wks
18 Feb 55		MAJORCA *Polygon P 1146*	....................**12**	4 wks
25 Mar 55		MAJORCA (re-entry) *Polygon P 1146*	..........**18**	1 wk
25 Nov 55	●	SUDDENLY THERE'S A VALLEY *Pye Nixa N 15013*	....**7**	10 wks
26 Jul 57	●	WITH ALL MY HEART *Pye Nixa N 15096*	....**4**	18 wks
15 Nov 57	●	ALONE *Pye Nixa N 15112*	....................**8**	12 wks
28 Feb 58		BABY LOVER *Pye Nixa N 15126*	..........**12**	7 wks
26 Jan 61	★	SAILOR *Pye 7N 15324*	....................**1**	15 wks
13 Apr 61		SOMETHING MISSING *Pye 7N 15337*	..........**44**	1 wk
13 Jul 61	●	ROMEO *Pye 7N 15361*	....................**3**	15 wks
16 Nov 61	●	MY FRIEND THE SEA *Pye 7N 15389*	..........**7**	13 wks
8 Feb 62		I'M COUNTING ON YOU *Pye 7N 15407*	..........**41**	2 wks
28 Jun 62		YA YA TWIST *Pye 7N 15448*	....................**14**	11 wks
20 Sep 62		YA YA TWIST (re-entry) *Pye 7N 15448*	........**45**	1 wk
2 May 63		CASANOVA /CHARIOT *Pye 7N 15522*	..........**39**	7 wks
12 Nov 64	●	DOWNTOWN *Pye 7N 15722*	....................**2**	15 wks
11 Mar 65		I KNOW A PLACE *Pye 7N 15772*	..........**17**	8 wks
12 Aug 65		YOU BETTER COME HOME *Pye 7N 15864*	....**44**	4 wks
14 Oct 65		ROUND EVERY CORNER *Pye 7N 15945*	........**43**	3 wks
4 Nov 65		YOU'RE THE ONE *Pye 7N 15991*	..........**23**	9 wks
10 Feb 66	●	MY LOVE *Pye 7N 17038*	....................**4**	9 wks
21 Apr 66		A SIGN OF THE TIMES *Pye 7N 17071*	..........**49**	1 wk
30 Jun 66	●	I COULDN'T LIVE WITHOUT YOUR LOVE *Pye 7N 17133*	....................**6**	11 wks
2 Feb 67	★	THIS IS MY SONG *Pye 7N 17258*	..........**1**	14 wks
25 May 67		DON'T SLEEP IN THE SUBWAY *Pye 7N 17325*	....**12**	11 wks
13 Dec 67		THE OTHER MAN'S GRASS *Pye 7N 17416*	......**20**	9 wks
6 Mar 68		KISS ME GOODBYE *Pye 7N 17466*	..........**50**	1 wk
30 Jan 71		THE SONG OF MY LIFE *Pye 7N 45026*	..........**41**	1 wk
13 Feb 71		THE SONG OF MY LIFE (re-entry) *Pye 7N 45026*	....**32**	11 wks
15 Jan 72		I DON'T KNOW HOW TO LOVE HIM *Pye 7N 45112*	....**47**	1 wk
29 Jan 72		I DON'T KNOW HOW TO LOVE HIM (re-entry) *Pye 7N 45112*	....................**49**	1 wk
19 Nov 88	●	DOWNTOWN '88 (re-mix) *PRT PYS 19*	..........**10**	11 wks

Dave CLARK FIVE *UK, male vocal/instrumental group*   171 wks

3 Oct 63		DO YOU LOVE ME *Columbia DB 7112*	..........**30**	6 wks
21 Nov 63	★	GLAD ALL OVER *Columbia DB 7154*	..........**1**	19 wks
20 Feb 64	●	BITS AND PIECES *Columbia DB 7210*	..........**2**	11 wks
28 May 64	●	CAN'T YOU SEE THAT SHE'S MINE *Columbia DB 7291*	....................**10**	11 wks
13 Aug 64		THINKING OF YOU BABY *Columbia DB 7335*	....**26**	4 wks
22 Oct 64		ANYWAY YOU WANT IT *Columbia DB 7377*	....**25**	5 wks
14 Jan 65		EVERYBODY KNOWS *Columbia DB 7453*	........**37**	4 wks
11 Mar 65		REELIN' AND ROCKIN' *Columbia DB 7503*	....**24**	8 wks
27 May 65		COME HOME *Columbia DB 7580*	..........**16**	8 wks
15 Jul 65	●	CATCH US IF YOU CAN *Columbia DB 7625*	....**5**	11 wks
11 Nov 65		OVER AND OVER *Columbia DB 7744*	..........**45**	4 wks
19 May 66		LOOK BEFORE YOU LEAP *Columbia DB 7909*	....**50**	1 wk
16 Mar 67		YOU GOT WHAT IT TAKES *Columbia DB 8152*	....**28**	8 wks
1 Nov 67	●	EVERYBODY KNOWS *Columbia DB 8286*	........**2**	14 wks

28 Feb 68		NO ONE CAN BREAK A HEART LIKE YOU *Columbia DB 8342*	....................**28**	7 wks
18 Sep 68	●	RED BALLOON *Columbia DB 8465*	..........**7**	11 wks
27 Nov 68		LIVE IN THE SKY *Columbia DB 8505*	..........**39**	6 wks
25 Oct 69		PUT A LITTLE LOVE IN YOUR HEART *Columbia DB 8624*	....................**31**	4 wks
6 Dec 69	●	GOOD OLD ROCK 'N ROLL *Columbia DB 8638*	....**7**	12 wks
7 Mar 70	●	EVERYBODY GET TOGETHER *Columbia DB 8660*	....**8**	8 wks
4 Jul 70		HERE COMES SUMMER *Columbia DB 8689*	....**44**	3 wks
7 Nov 70		MORE GOOD OLD ROCK 'N ROLL *Columbia DB 8724*	....................**34**	6 wks

Everybody Knows *on DB 7453 and* Everybody Knows *on DB 8286 are two different songs. The two Rock 'N Roll titles are medleys as follows: Good Old Rock 'N Roll/Sweet Little Sixteen/Long Tall Sally/Whole Lotta Shakin' Goin' On/Blue Suede Shoes/Lucille/Reelin' And Rockin'/Memphis Tennessee. More Good Old Rock and Roll: Rock And Roll Music/Blueberry Hill/Good Golly Miss Molly/My Blue Heaven/Keep A Knockin'/Loving You/One Night/Lawdy Miss Clawdy.*

John Cooper CLARKE *UK, male vocalist*   3 wks

| 10 Mar 79 | | GIMMIX! PLAY LOUD *Epic EPC 7009* | ....**39** | 3 wks |

Rick CLARKE *UK, male vocalist*   2 wks

| 30 Apr 88 | | I'LL SEE YOU ALONG THE WAY *WA WA 1* | ......**63** | 2 wks |

Sharon D. CLARKE – *See FPI PROJECT*

Julian CLARY – *See JOAN COLLINS FAN CLUB*

CLASH *UK, male vocal/instrumental group*   135 wks

2 Apr 77		WHITE RIOT *CBS 5058*	..........**38**	3 wks
8 Oct 77		COMPLETE CONTROL *CBS 5664*	..........**28**	2 wks
4 Mar 78		CLASH CITY ROCKERS *CBS 5834*	..........**35**	4 wks
24 Jun 78		(WHITE MAN) IN HAMMERSMITH PALAIS *CBS 6383*	....................**32**	7 wks
2 Dec 78		TOMMY GUN *CBS 6788*	..........**19**	10 wks
3 Mar 79		ENGLISH CIVIL WAR (JOHNNY COMES MARCHING HOME) *CBS 7082*	....................**25**	6 wks
19 May 79		THE COST OF LIVING EP *CBS 7324*	..........**22**	8 wks
15 Dec 79		LONDON CALLING *CBS 8087*	..........**11**	10 wks
9 Aug 80		BANKROBBER *CBS 8323*	..........**12**	10 wks
6 Dec 80		THE CALL UP *CBS 9339*	..........**40**	6 wks
24 Jan 81		HITSVILLE UK *CBS 9480*	..........**56**	4 wks
25 Apr 81		THE MAGNIFICENT SEVEN *CBS 1133*	..........**34**	5 wks
28 Nov 81		THIS IS RADIO CLASH *CBS A 1797*	..........**47**	6 wks
1 May 82		KNOW YOUR RIGHTS *CBS A 2309*	..........**43**	3 wks
26 Jun 82		ROCK THE CASBAH *CBS A 2429*	..........**30**	10 wks
25 Sep 82		SHOULD I STAY OR SHOULD I GO/STRAIGHT TO HELL *CBS A 2646*	....................**17**	9 wks
12 Oct 85		THIS IS ENGLAND *CBS A 6122*	..........**24**	5 wks
12 Mar 88		I FOUGHT THE LAW *CBS CLASH 1*	..........**29**	5 wks
7 May 88		LONDON CALLING (re-issue) *CBS CLASH 2*	....**46**	3 wks
21 Jul 90		RETURN TO BRIXTON *CBS 656072 7*	..........**57**	2 wks
2 Mar 91	★	SHOULD I STAY OR SHOULD I GO (re-issue) *Columbia 6566677*	....................**1**	9 wks
13 Apr 91		ROCK THE CASBAH (re-issue) *Columbia 6568147*	....**15**	6 wks
8 Jun 91		LONDON CALLING (re-issue) *Columbia 6569467*	....**64**	3 wks

Tracks on The Cost Of Living EP: *I Fought The Law/Groovy Times/Gates Of The West/Capital Radio. CBS CLASH 1 is a re-issue of a track from* The Cost of Living EP.

CLASS ACTION featuring Chris WILTSHIRE *US, female vocal group*   3 wks

| 7 May 83 | | WEEKEND *Jive JIVE 35* | ....**49** | 3 wks |

CLASSICS IV *US, male vocal/instrumental group*   1 wk

| 28 Feb 68 | | SPOOKY *Liberty LBS 15051* | ....**46** | 1 wk |

The biggest country hit of the early 90s, 'Achy Breaky Heart' by BILLY RAY CYRUS was nominated for the Record of the Year Grammy Award.

Nineteen-sixty-three was a fine year for THE CHIFFONS.

Above: The first hit by COLOR ME BADD came from the film *New Jack City*.

For years THE CLASH had the most hits without a top ten hit. After they disbanded, AC/DC overtook them. There was no longer any point in not having a big hit, so they had a number one with a re-issue popularized by a jeans commercial.

CLASSIX NOUVEAUX
34 wks
UK, male vocal/instrumental group

28 Feb 81	GUILTY *Liberty BP 388*	43	7 wks
16 May 81	TOKYO *Liberty BP 397*	67	3 wks
8 Aug 81	INSIDE OUTSIDE *Liberty BP 403*	45	5 wks
7 Nov 81	NEVER AGAIN (THE DAYS TIME ERASED) *Liberty BP 406*	44	4 wks
13 Mar 82	IS IT A DREAM *Liberty BP 409*	11	9 wks
29 May 82	BECAUSE YOU'RE YOUNG *Liberty BP 411*	43	4 wks
30 Oct 82	THE END ... OR THE BEGINNING *Liberty BP 414*	60	2 wks

Judy CLAY – *See William BELL*

Merry CLAYTON *US, female vocalist*
1 wk

21 May 88	YES *RCA PB 49563*	70	1 wk

CLAYTOWN TROUPE
3 wks
UK, male vocal/instrumental group

16 Jun 90	WAYS OF LOVE *Island IS 464*	57	2 wks
14 Mar 92	WANTED IT ALL *EMI USA MT 102*	74	1 wk

Johnny CLEGG and SAVUKA
1 wk
UK/South Africa, male vocal/instrumental group

16 May 87	SCATTERLINGS OF AFRICA *EMI EMI 5605*	75	1 wk

Jimmy CLIFF *Jamaica, male vocalist*
28 wks

25 Oct 69 ●	WONDERFUL WORLD BEAUTIFUL PEOPLE *Trojan TR 690*	6	13 wks
14 Feb 70	VIETNAM *Trojan TR 7722*	47	1 wk
28 Feb 70	VIETNAM (re-entry) *Trojan TR 7722*	46	2 wks
8 Aug 70 ●	WILD WORLD *Island WIP 6087*	8	12 wks

Buzz CLIFFORD *US, male vocalist*
13 wks

2 Mar 61	BABY SITTIN' BOOGIE *Fontana H 297*	17	13 wks

Linda CLIFFORD *US, female vocalist*
12 wks

10 Jun 78	IF MY FRIENDS COULD SEE ME NOW *Curtom K 17163*	50	5 wks
5 May 79	BRIDGE OVER TROUBLED WATER *RSO 30*	28	7 wks

CLIMAX BLUES BAND
9 wks
UK, male vocal/instrumental group

9 Oct 76 ●	COULDN'T GET IT RIGHT *BTM SBT 105*	10	9 wks

Simon CLIMIE *UK, male vocalist*
2 wks

19 Sep 92	SOUL INSPIRATION *Epic 6582837*	60	2 wks

CLIMIE FISHER *UK, male vocal/instrumental duo*
44 wks

5 Sep 87	LOVE CHANGES (EVERYTHING) *EMI EM 15*	67	2 wks
12 Dec 87 ●	RISE TO THE OCCASION *EMI EM 33*	10	11 wks
12 Mar 88 ●	LOVE CHANGES (EVERYTHING) (re-mix) *EMI EM 47*	2	12 wks
21 May 88	THIS IS ME *EMI EM 58*	22	5 wks
20 Aug 88	I WON'T BLEED FOR YOU *EMI EM 66*	35	4 wks
24 Dec 88	LOVE LIKE A RIVER *EMI EM 81*	22	7 wks
23 Sep 89	FACTS OF LOVE *EMI EMI 103*	50	3 wks

Patsy CLINE *US, female vocalist*
17 wks

26 Apr 62	SHE'S GOT YOU *Brunswick 05866*	43	1 wk
29 Nov 62	HEARTACHES *Brunswick 05878*	31	5 wks
8 Dec 90	CRAZY *MCA MCA 1465*	14	11 wks

George CLINTON *US, male vocalist*
7 wks

4 Dec 82	LOOPZILLA *Capitol CL 271*	57	5 wks
26 Apr 86	DO FRIES GO WITH THAT SHAKE *Capitol CL 402*	57	2 wks

CLIVILLES & COLE – *See C & C MUSIC FACTORY*

Rosemary CLOONEY *US, female vocalist*
81 wks

14 Nov 52 ●	HALF AS MUCH *Columbia DB 3129*	3	9 wks
5 Feb 54 ●	MAN *Philips PB 220*	7	5 wks
8 Oct 54 ★	THIS OLE HOUSE *Philips PB 336*	1	18 wks
17 Dec 54 ★	MAMBO ITALIANO *Philips PB 382*	1	16 wks
20 May 55 ●	WHERE WILL THE BABY'S DIMPLE BE *Philips PB 428*	6	13 wks
30 Sep 55 ●	HEY THERE *Philips PB 494*	4	11 wks
29 Mar 57	MANGOS *Philips PB 671*	25	2 wks
26 Apr 57	MANGOS (re-entry) *Philips PB 671*	17	7 wks

From 19 Feb 54 other side of Man, Woman *by José Ferrer was also credited.*

CLOUD *UK, male instrumental group*
1 wk

31 Jan 81	ALL NIGHT LONG/TAKE IT TO THE TOP *UK Champagne FUNK 1*	72	1 wk

CLOUT *South Africa, female vocal/instrumental group*
15 wks

17 Jun 78 ●	SUBSTITUTE *Carrere EMI 2788*	2	15 wks

CLUB NOUVEAU
12 wks
US, male/female vocal/instrumental group

21 Mar 87 ●	LEAN ON ME *King Jay W 8430*	3	12 wks

CLUB 69 *Austria/US, male/female vocal/instrumental duo*
4 wks

5 Dec 92	LET ME BE YOUR UNDERWEAR *ffrr F 204*	33†	4 wks

CLUBHOUSE *Italy, male vocal/instrumental group*
16 wks

23 Jul 83	DO IT AGAIN - BILLIE JEAN (MEDLEY) *Island IS 132*	11	6 wks
3 Dec 83	SUPERSTITION - GOOD TIMES (MEDLEY) *Island IS 147*	59	3 wks
1 Jul 89	I'M A MAN - YE KE YE KE (MEDLEY) *Music Man MMPS 7003*	69	3 wks
20 Apr 91	DEEP IN MY HEART *ffrr F 157*	59	2 wks
22 Jun 91	DEEP IN MY HEART (re-entry) *ffrr F 157*	55	2 wks

Jeremy CLYDE – *See Chad STUART and Jeremy CLYDE*

CLYDE VALLEY STOMPERS
UK, male instrumental group — **8 wks**

9 Aug 62	PETER AND THE WOLF *Parlophone R 4928*	25	8 wks

COAST TO COAST *UK, male vocal/instrumental group* — **22 wks**

31 Jan 81 ●	(DO) THE HUCKLEBUCK *Polydor POSP 214*	5	15 wks
23 May 81	LET'S JUMP THE BROOMSTICK *Polydor POSP 249*	28	7 wks

COASTERS *US, male vocal group* — **28 wks**

27 Sep 57	SEARCHIN' *London HLE 8450*	30	1 wk
15 Aug 58	YAKETY YAK *London HLE 8665*	12	8 wks
27 Mar 59 ●	CHARLIE BROWN *London HLE 8819*	6	12 wks
30 Oct 59	POISON IVY *London HLE 8938*	15	7 wks

Odia COATES – *See Paul ANKA*

Luis COBOS – *See Placido DOMINGO*

Eddie COCHRAN *US, male vocalist* — **90 wks**

7 Nov 58	SUMMERTIME BLUES *London HLU 8702*	18	6 wks
13 Mar 59 ●	C'MON EVERYBODY *London HLU 8792*	6	13 wks
16 Oct 59	SOMETHIN' ELSE *London HLU 8944*	22	3 wks
22 Jan 60	HALLELUJAH I LOVE HER SO *London HLW 9022*	28	1 wk
5 Feb 60	HALLELUJAH I LOVE HER SO (re-entry) *London HLW 9022*	22	3 wks
12 May 60 ★	THREE STEPS TO HEAVEN *London HLG 9115*	1	15 wks
6 Oct 60	SWEETIE PIE *London HLG 9196*	38	3 wks
3 Nov 60	LONELY *London HLG 9196*	41	1 wk
15 Jun 61	WEEKEND *London HLG 9362*	15	16 wks
30 Nov 61	JEANNIE, JEANNIE, JEANNIE *London HLG 9460*	31	4 wks
25 Apr 63	MY WAY *Liberty LIB 10088*	23	10 wks
24 Apr 68	SUMMERTIME BLUES (re-issue) *Liberty LBF 15071*	34	8 wks
13 Feb 88	C'MON EVERYBODY (re-issue) *Liberty EDDIE 501*	14	7 wks

Tom COCHRANE *Canada, male vocalist* — **2 wks**

27 Jun 92	LIFE IS A HIGHWAY *Capitol CL 660*	62	2 wks

COCK ROBIN *US, male/female vocal/instrumental group* — **12 wks**

31 May 86	THE PROMISE YOU MADE *CBS A 6764*	28	12 wks

Joe COCKER *UK, male vocalist* — **73 wks**

22 May 68	MARJORINE *Regal-Zonophone RZ 3006*	48	1 wk
2 Oct 68 ★	WITH A LITTLE HELP FROM MY FRIENDS *Regal-Zonophone RZ 3013*	1	13 wks
27 Sep 69 ●	DELTA LADY *Regal-Zonophone RZ 3024*	10	11 wks
4 Jul 70	THE LETTER *Regal-Zonophone RZ 3027*	39	6 wks
26 Sep 81	I'M SO GLAD I'M STANDING HERE TODAY *MCA 741 **	61	3 wks
15 Jan 83 ●	UP WHERE WE BELONG *Island WIP 6831 ***	7	13 wks
14 Nov 87	UNCHAIN MY HEART *Capitol CL 465*	46	4 wks
13 Jan 90	WHEN THE NIGHT COMES *Capitol CL 535*	65	2 wks
7 Mar 92	(ALL I KNOW) FEELS LIKE FOREVER *Capitol CL 645*	25	5 wks
9 May 92	NOW THAT THE MAGIC HAS GONE *Capitol CL 657*	28	6 wks
4 Jul 92	UNCHAIN MY HEART (re-issue) *Capitol CL 664*	17	6 wks
21 Nov 92	WHEN THE NIGHT COMES *Capitol CL 674*	61	3 wks

* Crusaders, featured vocalist Joe Cocker ** Joe Cocker and Jennifer Warnes

COCKEREL CHORUS *UK, male vocal group* — **12 wks**

24 Feb 73	NICE ONE CYRIL *Youngblood YB 1017*	14	12 wks

COCKNEY REBEL – *See Steve HARLEY*

COCKNEY REJECTS *UK, male vocal/instrumental group* — **22 wks**

1 Dec 79	I'M NOT A FOOL *EMI 5008*	65	2 wks
16 Feb 80	BADMAN *EMI 5035*	65	3 wks
26 Apr 80	THE GREATEST COCKNEY RIPOFF *EMI Z 2*	21	7 wks
17 May 80	I'M FOREVER BLOWING BUBBLES *EMI Z 4*	35	5 wks
12 Jul 80	WE CAN DO ANYTHING *EMI Z 6*	65	2 wks
25 Oct 80	WE ARE THE FIRM *EMI Z 10*	54	3 wks

CO-CO *UK, male/female vocal/instrumental group* — **7 wks**

22 Apr 78	BAD OLD DAYS *Ariola Hansa AHA 513*	13	7 wks

El COCO *US, male vocal/instrumental group* — **4 wks**

14 Jan 78	COCOMOTION *Pye International 7N 25761*	31	4 wks

COCONUTS *US, female vocal group* — **3 wks**

11 Jun 83	DID YOU HAVE TO LOVE ME LIKE YOU DID *EMI America EA 156*	60	3 wks

See also Kid Creole and the Coconuts.

COCTEAU TWINS — **15 wks**
UK, male/female vocal/instrumental group

28 Apr 84	PEARLY-DEWDROPS' DROPS *4AD 405*	29	5 wks
30 Mar 85	AIKEA-GUINEA *4AD AD 501*	41	3 wks
23 Nov 85	TINY DYNAMINE EP *4AD BAD 510*	52	2 wks
7 Dec 85	ECHOES IN A SHALLOW BAY EP *4AD BAD 511*	65	1 wk
25 Oct 86	LOVE'S EASY TEARS *4AD AD 610*	53	1 wk
8 Sep 90	ICEBLINK LUCK *4AD AD 0011*	38	3 wks

Tracks on Tiny Dynamine EP: *Pink Orange Red/Ribbed and Veined/Plain Tiger/Sultitan Itan.*
Tracks on Echoes In A Shallow Bay EP: *Great Spangled Fritillary/Melonella/Pale Clouded White/Eggs and Their Shells.*

C.O.D. *US, male vocal/instrumental group* — **2 wks**

14 May 83	IN THE BOTTLE *Streetwave WAVE 2*	54	2 wks

COFFEE *US, female vocal group* — **13 wks**

27 Sep 80	CASANOVA *De-Lite MER 38*	13	10 wks
6 Dec 80	SLIP AND DIP/I WANNA BE WITH YOU *De-Lite DE 1*	57	3 wks

Alma COGAN *UK, female vocalist* — **110 wks**

19 Mar 54 ●	BELL BOTTOM BLUES *HMV B 10653*	4	9 wks
27 Aug 54	LITTLE THINGS MEAN A LOT *HMV B 10717*	11	2 wks
8 Oct 54	LITTLE THINGS MEAN A LOT (re-entry) *HMV B 10717*	19	1 wk
22 Oct 54	LITTLE THINGS MEAN A LOT (2nd re-entry) *HMV B 10717*	18	2 wks
3 Dec 54 ●	I CAN'T TELL A WALTZ FROM A TANGO *HMV B 10786*	6	11 wks
27 May 55 ★	DREAMBOAT *HMV B 10872*	1	16 wks
23 Sep 55	BANJO'S BACK IN TOWN *HMV B 10917*	17	1 wk
14 Oct 55	GO ON BY *HMV B 10917*	16	4 wks
16 Dec 55	TWENTY TINY FINGERS *HMV POP 129*	17	1 wk
23 Dec 55 ●	NEVER DO A TANGO WITH AN ESKIMO *HMV POP 129*	6	5 wks
30 Mar 56	WILLIE CAN *HMV POP 187 **	13	8 wks
13 Jul 56	THE BIRDS AND THE BEES *HMV POP 223*	25	4 wks
10 Aug 56	WHY DO FOOLS FALL IN LOVE *HMV POP 223*	22	3 wks

2 Nov 56	**IN THE MIDDLE OF THE HOUSE** *HMV POP 261*........26	1 wk
23 Nov 56	**IN THE MIDDLE OF THE HOUSE (re-entry)**	
	HMV POP 261 20	3 wks
18 Jan 57	**YOU ME AND US** *HMV POP 284* 18	6 wks
29 Mar 57	**WHATEVER LOLA WANTS** *HMV POP 317*.........26	2 wks
31 Jan 58	**THE STORY OF MY LIFE** *HMV POP 433*..........25	2 wks
14 Feb 58	**SUGARTIME** *HMV POP 450* 16	10 wks
2 May 58	**SUGARTIME (re-entry)** *HMV POP 450*.............30	1 wk
23 Jan 59	**LAST NIGHT ON THE BACK PORCH**	
	HMV POP 573 27	2 wks
18 Dec 59	**WE GOT LOVE** *HMV POP 670*....................26	4 wks
12 May 60	**DREAM TALK** *HMV POP 728* 48	1 wk
11 Aug 60	**TRAIN OF LOVE** *HMV POP 760* 27	5 wks
20 Apr 61	**COWBOY JIMMY JOE** *Columbia DB 4607*.........37	6 wks

* Alma Cogan with Desmond Lane - penny whistle

Shaye COGAN *US, female vocalist* **1 wk**

24 Mar 60	**MEAN TO ME** *MGM 1063* 40	1 wk

Izhar COHEN and ALPHABETA **7 wks**
Israel, male/female vocal group

13 May 78	**A BA NI BI** *Polydor 2001 781* 20	7 wks

Marc COHN *US, male vocalist* **12 wks**

25 May 91	**WALKING IN MEMPHIS** *Atlantic A 7747*.........66	4 wks
10 Aug 91	**SILVER THUNDERBIRD** *Atlantic A 7657* 54	3 wks
12 Oct 91	**WALKING IN MEMPHIS (re-issue)** *Atlantic A 7585*...22	5 wks

COLA BOY *UK, male/female vocal/instrumental duo* **7 wks**

6 Jul 91 ●	**7 WAYS TO LOVE** *Arista 114526* 8	7 wks

COLD JAM featuring GRACE **2 wks**
US, male/female vocal/instrumental group

28 Jul 90	**LAST NIGHT A DJ SAVED MY LIFE**	
	Big Wave BWR 39 64	2 wks

COLDCUT *UK, male production duo* **32 wks**

20 Feb 88 ●	**DOCTORIN' THE HOUSE**	
	Ahead Of Our Time CCUT 27 * 6	9 wks
10 Sep 88	**STOP THIS CRAZY THING**	
	Ahead Of Our Time CCUT 4 ** 21	7 wks
25 Mar 89	**PEOPLE HOLD ON** *Ahead Of Our Time CCUT 5* ***...11	9 wks
3 Jun 89	**MY TELEPHONE** *Ahead Of Our Time CCUT 6* ...52	2 wks
16 Dec 89	**COLDCUT'S CHRISTMAS BREAK**	
	Ahead Of Our Time CCUT 7........................67	3 wks
26 May 90	**FIND A WAY** *Ahead Of Our Time CCUT 8* ****...52	2 wks

* Coldcut featuring Yazz and the Plastic Population ** Coldcut featuring Junior Reid and the ahead of our Time Orchestra *** Coldcut featuring Lisa Stansfield **** Coldcut featuring Queen Latifah

Cozy COLE *US, male instrumentalist - drums* **1 wk**

5 Dec 58	**TOPSY** (PARTS 1 AND 2) *London HL 8750*...........29	1 wk

George COLE – *See Dennis WATERMAN*

Lloyd COLE *UK, male vocalist* **56 wks**

26 May 84	**PERFECT SKIN** *Polydor COLE 1* * 71	1 wk
9 Jun 84	**PERFECT SKIN (re-entry)** *Polydor COLE 1* * 26	8 wks
25 Aug 84	**FOREST FIRE** *Polydor COLE 2* * 41	6 wks

17 Nov 84	**RATTLESNAKES** *Poldor COLE 3* * 65	2 wks
14 Sep 85	**BRAND NEW FRIEND** *Polydor COLE 4* * 19	8 wks
9 Nov 85	**LOST WEEKEND** *Polydor COLE 5* * 17	7 wks
18 Jan 86	**CUT ME DOWN** *Polydor COLE 6* * 38	4 wks
3 Oct 87	**MY BAG** *Polydor COLE 7* * 46	4 wks
9 Jan 88	**JENNIFER SHE SAID** *Polydor COLE 8* * 31	5 wks
23 Apr 88	**FROM THE HIP EP** *Polydor COLE 9* * 59	2 wks
3 Feb 90	**NO BLUE SKIES** *Polydor COLE 11* 42	4 wks
7 Apr 90	**DON'T LOOK BACK** *Polydor COLE 12* 59	3 wks
31 Aug 91	**SHE'S A GIRL AND I'M A MAN** *Polydor COLE 14*...55	2 wks

* Lloyd Cole and the Commotions
Tracks on From The Hip EP: *From The Hip/Please/Lonely Mile/Love Your Wife.*

Nat 'King' COLE *US, male vocalist* **237 wks**

14 Nov 52 ●	**SOMEWHERE ALONG THE WAY** *Capitol CL 13774*.........3	7 wks
19 Dec 52 ●	**BECAUSE YOU'RE MINE** *Capitol CL 13811*........6	2 wks
2 Jan 53	**FAITH CAN MOVE MOUNTAINS** *Capitol CL 13811*......11	1 wk
16 Jan 53	**FAITH CAN MOVE MOUNTAINS (re-entry)**	
	Capitol CL 13811...................12	2 wks
23 Jan 53 ●	**BECAUSE YOU'RE MINE (re-entry)** *Capitol CL 13811* 10	1 wk
6 Feb 53 ●	**FAITH CAN MOVE MOUNTAINS (2nd re-entry)**	
	Capitol CL 13811..................10	1 wk
13 Feb 53	**BECAUSE YOU'RE MINE (2nd re-entry)**	
	Capitol CL 13811..................11	1 wk
24 Apr 53 ●	**PRETEND** *Capitol CL 13878*......................2	18 wks
14 Aug 53 ●	**CAN'T I?** *Capitol CL 13937*......................9	3 wks
18 Sep 53 ●	**CAN'T I? (re-entry)** *Capitol CL 13937*.............6	4 wks
18 Sep 53 ●	**MOTHER NATURE AND FATHER TIME**	
	Capitol CL 13912...................7	7 wks
30 Oct 53 ●	**CAN'T I? (2nd re-entry)** *Capitol CL 13937*........10	1 wk
16 Apr 54 ●	**TENDERLY** *Capitol CL 14061*....................10	1 wk
10 Sep 54 ●	**SMILE** *Capitol CL 14149*.........................2	14 wks
8 Oct 54	**MAKE HER MINE** *Capitol CL 14149*.............11	2 wks
25 Feb 55 ●	**A BLOSSOM FELL** *Capitol CL 14235*..............3	10 wks
26 Aug 55	**MY ONE SIN** *Capitol CL 14327*..................18	1 wk
16 Sep 55	**MY ONE SIN (re-entry)** *Capitol CL 14327*........17	1 wk
27 Jan 56 ●	**DREAMS CAN TELL A LIE** *Capitol CL 14513*.....10	9 wks
11 May 56 ●	**TOO YOUNG TO GO STEADY** *Capitol CL 14573* ...8	14 wks
14 Sep 56	**LOVE ME AS THOUGH THERE WERE NO**	
	TOMORROW *Capitol CL 14621*......24	2 wks
5 Oct 56	**LOVE ME AS IF THERE WERE NO**	
	TOMORROW (re-entry) *Capitol CL 14621*.........11	13 wks
19 Apr 57 ●	**WHEN I FALL IN LOVE** *Capitol CL 14709*.........2	20 wks
5 Jul 57	**WHEN ROCK 'N ROLL CAME TO TRINIDAD**	
	Capitol CL 14733...................28	1 wk
18 Oct 57	**MY PERSONAL POSSESSION** *Capitol CL 14765*....21	2 wks
25 Oct 57	**STARDUST** *Capitol CL 14787*....................24	2 wks
29 May 59	**YOU MADE ME LOVE YOU** *Capitol CL 15017*.....22	3 wks
4 Sep 59	**MIDNIGHT FLYER** *Capitol CL 15056*..............27	1 wk
18 Sep 59	**MIDNIGHT FLYER (re-entry)** *Capitol CL 15056*.....23	3 wks
12 Feb 60	**TIME AND THE RIVER** *Capitol CL 15111*..........29	1 wk
26 Feb 60	**TIME AND THE RIVER (re-entry)** *Capitol CL 15111*...23	2 wks
31 Mar 60	**TIME AND THE RIVER (2nd re-entry)**	
	Capitol CL 15111...................47	1 wk
26 May 60 ●	**THAT'S YOU** *Capitol CL 15129*...................10	8 wks
10 Nov 60	**JUST AS MUCH AS EVER** *Capitol CL 15163*.......18	10 wks
2 Feb 61	**THE WORLD IN MY ARMS** *Capitol CL 15178*.....36	10 wks
16 Nov 61	**LET TRUE LOVE BEGIN** *Capitol CL 15224*........29	10 wks
22 Mar 62	**BRAZILIAN LOVE SONG** *Capitol CL 15241*........34	4 wks
31 May 62	**THE RIGHT THING TO SAY** *Capitol CL 15250*.....42	4 wks
19 Jul 62	**LET THERE BE LOVE** *Capitol CL 15257* *.........11	14 wks
27 Sep 62 ●	**RAMBLIN' ROSE** *Capitol CL 15270*................5	14 wks
20 Dec 62	**DEAR LONELY HEARTS** *Capitol CL 15280*.........37	3 wks
12 Dec 87 ●	**WHEN I FALL IN LOVE (re-issue)** *Capitol CL 15975*...4	7 wks
14 Dec 91	**THE CHRISTMAS SONG** *Capitol CL 641*...........69	2 wks

* Nat 'King' Cole with George Shearing
See also Natalie Cole.

Natalie COLE *US, female vocalist* **87 wks**

11 Oct 75	**THIS WILL BE** *Capitol CL 15834* 32	5 wks
8 Aug 87	**JUMP START** *Manhattan MT 22* 44	8 wks
26 Mar 88 ●	**PINK CADILLAC** *Manhattan MT 35* 5	12 wks
25 Jun 88	**EVERLASTING** *Manhattan MT 46* 28	6 wks
20 Aug 88	**JUMP START (re-issue)** *Manhattan MT 50* 36	5 wks

26 Nov 88	I LIVE FOR YOUR LOVE *Manhattan MT 57*	23	14 wks
15 Apr 89 ●	MISS YOU LIKE CRAZY *EMI-USA MT 63*	2	15 wks
22 Jul 89	BEST OF THE NIGHT *EMI-USA MT 69*	56	2 wks
16 Dec 89	STARTING OVER AGAIN *EMI-USA MT 77*	56	4 wks
21 Apr 90	WILD WOMEN DO *EMI-USA MT 81*	16	7 wks
22 Jun 91	UNFORGETTABLE *Elektra EKR 128*	19	8 wks
16 May 92	THE VERY THOUGHT OF YOU *Elektra EKR 147*	71	1 wk

Unforgettable *features the uncredited vocals of Nat 'King' Cole.*

John Ford COLEY – *See ENGLAND DAN and John Ford COLEY*

COLLAGE 5 wks
US/Canada/Philippines, male vocal/instrumental group

21 Sep 85	ROMEO WHERE'S JULIET? *MCA MCA 1006*	46	5 wks

Dave and Ansil COLLINS 27 wks
Jamaica, male vocal/instrumental duo

27 Mar 71 ★	DOUBLE BARREL *Technique TE 901*	1	15 wks
26 Jun 71 ●	MONKEY SPANNER *Technique TE 914*	7	12 wks

Edwyn COLLINS – *See Paul QUINN and Edwyn COLLINS*

Jeff COLLINS *UK, male vocalist* 8 wks

18 Nov 72	ONLY YOU *Polydor 2058 287*	40	8 wks

Judy COLLINS *US, female vocalist* 86 wks

17 Jan 70	BOTH SIDES NOW *Elektra EKSN 45043*	14	11 wks
5 Dec 70 ●	AMAZING GRACE *Elektra 2101 020*	5	32 wks
24 Jul 71	AMAZING GRACE (re-entry) *Elektra 2101 020*	48	1 wk
4 Sep 71	AMAZING GRACE (2nd re-entry) *Elektra 2101 020*	40	7 wks
20 Nov 71	AMAZING GRACE (3rd re-entry) *Elektra 2101 020*	50	1 wk
18 Dec 71	AMAZING GRACE (4th re-entry) *Elektra 2101 020*	48	2 wks
22 Apr 72	AMAZING GRACE (5th re-entry) *Elektra 2101 020*	20	19 wks
9 Sep 72	AMAZING GRACE (6th re-entry) *Elektra 2101 020*	46	2 wks
23 Dec 72	AMAZING GRACE (7th re-entry) *Elektra 2101 020*	49	3 wks
17 May 75 ●	SEND IN THE CLOWNS *Elektra K 12177*	6	8 wks

Phil COLLINS *UK, male vocalist* 188 wks

17 Jan 81 ●	IN THE AIR TONIGHT *Virgin VSK 102*	2	10 wks
7 Mar 81	I MISSED AGAIN *Virgin VS 402*	14	8 wks
30 May 81	IF LEAVING ME IS EASY *Virgin VS 423*	17	8 wks
23 Oct 82	THRU' THESE WALLS *Virgin VS 524*	56	2 wks
4 Dec 82 ★	YOU CAN'T HURRY LOVE *Virgin VS 531*	1	16 wks
19 Mar 83	DON'T LET HIM STEAL YOUR HEART AWAY *Virgin VS 572*	45	5 wks
7 Apr 84 ●	AGAINST ALL ODDS (TAKE A LOOK AT ME NOW) *Virgin VS 674*	2	14 wks
26 Jan 85	SUSSUDIO *Virgin VS 736*	12	9 wks
9 Mar 85 ★	EASY LOVER *CBS A 4915 *	1	12 wks
13 Apr 85 ●	ONE MORE NIGHT *Virgin VS 755*	4	9 wks
27 Jul 85	TAKE ME HOME *Virgin VS 777*	19	9 wks
23 Nov 85 ●	SEPARATE LIVES *Virgin VS 818 **	4	13 wks
18 Jun 88 ●	IN THE AIR TONIGHT (re-mix) *Virgin VS 102*	4	9 wks
3 Sep 88 ★	A GROOVY KIND OF LOVE *Virgin VS 1117*	1	13 wks
26 Nov 88 ●	TWO HEARTS *Virgin VS 1141*	6	11 wks
4 Nov 89 ●	ANOTHER DAY IN PARADISE *Virgin VS 1234*	2	11 wks
27 Jan 90 ●	I WISH IT WOULD RAIN DOWN *Virgin VS 1240*	7	9 wks
28 Apr 90	SOMETHING HAPPENED ON THE WAY TO HEAVEN *Virgin VS 1251*	15	7 wks
28 Jul 90	THAT'S JUST THE WAY IT IS *Virgin VS 1277*	26	5 wks
6 Oct 90	HANG IN LONG ENOUGH *Virgin VS 1300*	34	3 wks
8 Dec 90	DO YOU REMEMBER (LIVE) *Virgin VS 1305*	57	5 wks

* Philip Bailey (duet with Phil Collins) ** Phil Collins and Marilyn Martin

Rodger COLLINS *US, male vocalist* 6 wks

3 Apr 76	YOU SEXY SUGAR PLUM (BUT I LIKE IT) *Fantasy FTC 132*	22	6 wks

Willie COLLINS *US, male vocalist* 4 wks

28 Jun 86	WHERE YOU GONNA BE TONIGHT? *Capitol CL 410*	46	4 wks

Willie COLON *US, male vocalist* 7 wks

28 Jun 86	SET FIRE TO ME *A & M AM 330*	41	7 wks

COLOR ME BADD *US, male vocal group* 29 wks

18 May 91 ★	I WANNA SEX YOU UP *Giant W 0036*	1	14 wks
3 Aug 91 ●	ALL 4 LOVE *Giant W 0053*	5	10 wks
12 Oct 91	I ADORE MI AMOR *Giant W 0067*	44	2 wks
9 Nov 91	I ADORE MI AMOR (re-issue) *Giant W 0076*	59	2 wks
22 Feb 92	HEARTBREAKER *Giant W 0078*	58	1 wk

COLORADO *UK, female vocal group* 3 wks

21 Oct 78	CALIFORNIA DREAMIN' *Pinnacle PIN 67*	45	3 wks

COLOUR FIELD *UK, male vocal/instrumental group* 18 wks

21 Jan 84	THE COLOUR FIELD *Chrysalis COLF 1*	43	4 wks
28 Jul 84	TAKE *Chrysalis COLF 2*	70	1 wk
26 Jan 85	THINKING OF YOU *Chrysalis COLF 3*	12	10 wks
13 Apr 85	CASTLES IN THE AIR *Chrysalis COLF 4*	51	3 wks

COMETS – *See Bill HALEY and his COMETS*

COMMENTATORS 7 wks
UK, male impressionist - Rory Bremner

22 Jun 85	N-N-NINETEEN NOT OUT *Oval 100*	13	7 wks

COMMITMENTS 1 wk
Ireland, male/female vocal/instrumental group

30 Nov 91	MUSTANG SALLY *MCA MCS 1598*	63	1 wk

COMMODORES *US, male vocal/instrumental group* 121 wks

24 Aug 74	MACHINE GUN *Tamla Motown TMG 902*	20	11 wks
23 Nov 74	THE ZOO (THE HUMAN ZOO) *Tamla Motown TMG 924*	44	2 wks
2 Jul 77 ●	EASY *Motown TMG 1073*	9	10 wks
8 Oct 77	SWEET LOVE/BRICK HOUSE *Motown TMG 1086*	32	6 wks
11 Mar 78	TOO HOT TO TROT/ZOOM *Motown TMG 1096*	38	4 wks
24 Jun 78	FLYING HIGH *Motown TMG 1111*	37	7 wks
5 Aug 78 ★	THREE TIMES A LADY *Motown TMG 1113*	1	14 wks
25 Nov 78	JUST TO BE CLOSE TO YOU *Motown TMG 1127*	62	4 wks
25 Aug 79 ●	SAIL ON *Motown TMG 1155*	8	10 wks
3 Nov 79 ●	STILL *Motown TMG 1166*	4	11 wks
19 Jan 80	WONDERLAND *Motown TMG 1172*	40	4 wks
1 Aug 81	LADY (YOU BRING ME UP) *Motown TMG 1238*	56	5 wks
21 Nov 81	OH NO *Motown TMG 1245*	44	3 wks
26 Jan 85 ●	NIGHTSHIFT *Motown TMG 1371*	3	14 wks
11 May 85	ANIMAL INSTINCT *Motown ZB 40097*	74	1 wk
25 Oct 86	GOIN' TO THE BANK *Polydor POSPA 826*	43	4 wks
13 Aug 88	EASY (re-issue) *Motown ZB 41793*	15	11 wks

Group were US/UK for 1985 and 1986 hits.

COMMUNARDS *UK, male vocal/instrumental duo* **76 wks**

12 Oct 85	**YOU ARE MY WORLD** *London LON 77*	30	8 wks
24 May 86	**DISENCHANTED** *London LON 89*	29	5 wks
23 Aug 86	★ **DON'T LEAVE ME THIS WAY** *London LON 103* *	1	14 wks
29 Nov 86	● **SO COLD THE NIGHT** *London LON 110*	8	10 wks
21 Feb 87	**YOU ARE MY WORLD ('87) (re-mix)** *London LON 123*	21	6 wks
12 Sep 87	**TOMORROW** *London LON 143*	23	7 wks
7 Nov 87	● **NEVER CAN SAY GOODBYE** *London LON 158*	4	11 wks
20 Feb 88	**FOR A FRIEND** *London LON 166*	28	7 wks
11 Jun 88	**THERE'S MORE TO LOVE** *London LON 173*	20	8 wks

* Communards with Sarah Jane Morris

Perry COMO *US, male vocalist* **298 wks**

16 Jan 53	★ **DON'T LET THE STARS GET IN YOUR EYES** *HMV B 10400*	1	15 wks
4 Jun 54	● **WANTED** *HMV B 10667*	4	14 wks
25 Jun 54	● **IDLE GOSSIP** *HMV B 10710*	3	15 wks
1 Oct 54	**WANTED (re-entry)** *HMV B 10667*	18	1 wk
10 Dec 54	**PAPA LOVES MAMBO** *HMV B 10776*	16	1 wk
30 Dec 55	**TINA MARIE** *HMV POP 103*	24	1 wk
27 Apr 56	**JUKE BOX BABY** *HMV POP 191*	22	6 wks
25 May 56	● **HOT DIGGITY** *HMV POP 221*	4	13 wks
21 Sep 56	● **MORE** *HMV POP 240*	10	11 wks
28 Sep 56	**GLENDORA** *HMV POP 240*	18	6 wks
14 Dec 56	**MORE (re-entry)** *HMV POP 240*	29	1 wk
7 Feb 58	★ **MAGIC MOMENTS** *RCA 1036*	1	17 wks
7 Mar 58	● **CATCH A FALLING STAR** *RCA 1036*	9	10 wks
9 May 58	● **KEWPIE DOLL** *RCA 1055*	9	7 wks
30 May 58	**I MAY NEVER PASS THIS WAY AGAIN** *RCA 1062*	15	8 wks
5 Sep 58	**MOON TALK** *RCA 1071*	17	11 wks
7 Nov 58	● **LOVE MAKES THE WORLD GO ROUND** *RCA 1086*	6	14 wks
21 Nov 58	**MANDOLINS IN THE MOONLIGHT** *RCA 1086*	13	12 wks
27 Feb 59	● **TOMBOY** *RCA 1111*	10	12 wks
10 Jul 59	**I KNOW** *RCA 1126*	13	16 wks
26 Feb 60	● **DELAWARE** *RCA 1170*	3	13 wks
10 May 62	**CATERINA** *RCA 1283*	37	4 wks
14 Jun 62	**CATERINA (re-entry)** *RCA 1283*	45	2 wks
30 Jan 71	● **IT'S IMPOSSIBLE** *RCA 2043*	4	23 wks
15 May 71	**I THINK OF YOU** *RCA 2075*	14	11 wks
21 Apr 73	● **AND I LOVE YOU SO** *RCA 2346*	3	31 wks
25 Aug 73	● **FOR THE GOOD TIMES** *RCA 2402*	7	27 wks
8 Dec 73	**WALK RIGHT BACK** *RCA 2432*	33	10 wks
12 Jan 74	**AND I LOVE YOU SO (re-entry)** *RCA 2346*	40	4 wks
25 May 74	**I WANT TO GIVE** *RCA LPBO 7518*	31	6 wks

COMPAGNONS DE LA CHANSON **3 wks**

France, male vocal group

9 Oct 59	**THE THREE BELLS (THE JIMMY BROWN SONG)** *Columbia DB 4358*	27	1 wk
23 Oct 59	**THE THREE BELLS (THE JIMMY BROWN SONG) (re-entry)** *Columbia DB 4358*	21	2 wks

COMSAT ANGELS *UK, male vocal/instrumental group* **2 wks**

21 Jan 84	**INDEPENDENCE DAY** *Jive JIVE 54*	75	1 wk
4 Feb 84	**INDEPENDENCE DAY (re-entry)** *Jive JIVE 54*	71	1 wk

CON FUNK SHUN *US, male vocal/instrumental group* **2 wks**

19 Jul 86	**BURNIN' LOVE** *Club JAB 32*	68	2 wks

CONCEPT *US, male vocalist/instrumentalist - keyboards* **6 wks**

14 Dec 85	**MR. DJ** *Fourth & Broadway BRW 40*	27	6 wks

CONGREGATION *UK, male/female choir* **14 wks**

27 Nov 71	● **SOFTLY WHISPERING I LOVE YOU** *Columbia DB 8830*	4	14 wks

CONGRESS *UK, male/female vocal/instrumental group* **4 wks**

26 Oct 91	**40 MILES** *Inner Rhythm 7HEART 01*	26	4 wks

Arthur CONLEY *US, male vocalist* **15 wks**

27 Apr 67	● **SWEET SOUL MUSIC** *Atlantic 584 083*	7	14 wks
10 Apr 68	**FUNKY STREET** *Atlantic 583 175*	46	1 wk

Harry CONNICK Jr *US, male vocalist* **11 wks**

25 May 91	**RECIPE FOR LOVE/IT HAD TO BE YOU** *Columbia 6568907*	32	6 wks
3 Aug 91	**WE ARE IN LOVE** *Columbia 6572847*	62	2 wks
23 Nov 91	**BLUE LIGHT RED LIGHT (SOMEONE'S THERE)** *Columbia 6575367*	54	3 wks

Billy CONNOLLY *UK, male vocalist* **31 wks**

1 Nov 75	★ **D.I.V.O.R.C.E.** *Polydor 2058 652*	1	10 wks
17 Jul 76	**NO CHANCE (NO CHARGE)** *Polydor 2058 748*	24	5 wks
25 Aug 79	**IN THE BROWNIES** *Polydor 2059 160*	38	7 wks
9 Mar 85	**SUPER GRAN** *Stiff BUY 218*	32	9 wks

Jess CONRAD *UK, male vocalist* **13 wks**

30 Jun 60	**CHERRY PIE** *Decca F 11236*	39	1 wk
26 Jan 61	**MYSTERY GIRL** *Decca F 11315*	44	1 wk
9 Feb 61	**MYSTERY GIRL (re-entry)** *Decca F 11315*	18	9 wks
11 Oct 62	**PRETTY JENNY** *Decca F 11511*	50	2 wks

CONSORTIUM *UK, male vocal group* **9 wks**

12 Feb 69	**ALL THE LOVE IN THE WORLD** *Pye 7N 17635*	22	9 wks

CONTOURS *US, male vocal group* **6 wks**

24 Jan 70	**JUST A LITTLE MISUNDERSTANDING** *Tamla Motown TMG 723*	31	6 wks

CONTRABAND **2 wks**

Germany/US, male/female vocal/instrumental group

20 Jul 91	**ALL THE WAY FROM MEMPHIS** *Impact American EM 195*	65	2 wks

CONTROL *UK, male/female vocal/instrumental group* **5 wks**

2 Nov 91	**DANCE WITH ME** *All Around The World GLOBE 105*	17	5 wks

CONVERT *Belgium, male instrumental/production duo* **4 wks**

11 Jan 92	**NIGHTBIRD** *A & M AM 845*	39	4 wks

CONWAY BROTHERS *US, male vocal group* **10 wks**

22 Jun 85	**TURN IT UP** *10 TEN 57*	11	10 wks

Russ CONWAY *UK, male instrumentalist - piano*   **178 wks**

29 Nov 57	**PARTY POPS** Columbia DB 4031	**24**	5 wks
29 Aug 58	**GOT A MATCH** Columbia DB 4166	**30**	1 wk
28 Nov 58 ●	**MORE PARTY POPS** Columbia DB 4204	**10**	7 wks
23 Jan 59	**THE WORLD OUTSIDE** Columbia DB 4234	**24**	1 wk
20 Feb 59 ★	**SIDE SADDLE** Columbia DB 4256	**1**	30 wks
6 Mar 59	**THE WORLD OUTSIDE (re-entry)** Columbia DB 4234 ...	**24**	3 wks
15 May 59 ★	**ROULETTE** Columbia DB 4298	**1**	19 wks
21 Aug 59 ●	**CHINA TEA** Columbia DB 4337	**5**	13 wks
13 Nov 59 ●	**SNOW COACH** Columbia DB 4368	**7**	9 wks
20 Nov 59 ●	**MORE AND MORE PARTY POPS** Columbia DB 4373....	**5**	8 wks
10 Mar 60	**ROYAL EVENT** Columbia DB 4418	**15**	7 wks
21 Apr 60	**FINGS AIN'T WOT THEY USED T'BE**		
	Columbia DB 4422	**47**	1 wk
19 May 60	**LUCKY FIVE** Columbia DB 4457	**14**	9 wks
29 Sep 60	**PASSING BREEZE** Columbia DB 4508	**16**	10 wks
24 Nov 60	**EVEN MORE PARTY POPS** Columbia DB 1535	**27**	9 wks
19 Jan 61	**PEPE** Columbia DB 4564	**19**	9 wks
25 May 61	**PABLO** Columbia DB 4649	**45**	2 wks
24 Aug 61	**SAY IT WITH FLOWERS** Columbia DB 4665 *	**23**	10 wks
30 Nov 61 ●	**TOY BALLOONS** Columbia DB 4738	**7**	11 wks
22 Feb 62	**LESSON ONE** Columbia DB 4784	**21**	7 wks
29 Nov 62	**ALWAYS YOU AND ME** Columbia DB 4934	**33**	4 wks
3 Jan 63	**ALWAYS YOU AND ME (re-entry)** Columbia DB 4934	**35**	3 wks

* Dorothy Squires and Russ Conway

Always You And Me featured Russ Conway talking as well as playing piano. Several of the discs were medleys as follows: Party Pops: When You're Smiling/I'm Looking Over a Four-Leafed Clover/When You Wore a Tulip/Row Row Row/For Me And My Girl/Shine On Harvest Moon/By The Light Of The Silvery Moon/Side By Side. More Party Pops: Music Music Music/If You Were The Only Girl In The World/Nobody's Sweetheart/Yes Sir That's My Baby/Some Of These Days/Honeysuckle And The Bee/Hello Hello Who's Your Lady Friend/Shanty In Old Shanty Town. More And More Party Pops: Sheik of Araby/Who Were You With Last Night/Any Old Iron/Tiptoe Through The Tulips/If You Were The Only Girl In The World/When I Leave The World Behind. Even More Party Pops: Ain't She Sweet/I Can't Give You Anything But Love/Yes We Have No Bananas/I May Be Wrong/Happy Days And Lonely Nights/Glad Rag Doll. He really did feature If You Were The Only Girl In The World *on two different hits.*

Martin COOK – *See Richard DENTON and Martin COOK*

Norman COOK *UK, male producer/multi-instrumentalist*   **10 wks**

8 Jul 89	**WON'T TALK ABOUT IT/BLAME IT ON THE**		
	BASSLINE Go Beat GOD 33 *	**29**	6 wks
21 Oct 89	**FOR SPACIOUS LIES** Go Beat GOD 37 **	**48**	4 wks

* Norman Cook featuring Billy Bragg/Norman Cook featuring MC Wildski
** Norman Cook featuring Lester

Peter COOK *UK, male vocalist*   **15 wks**

17 Jun 65	**GOODBYE-EE** Decca F 12158 *	**18**	10 wks
15 Jul 65	**THE BALLAD OF SPOTTY MULDOON**		
	Decca F 12182	**34**	5 wks

* Peter Cook and Dudley Moore

Brandon COOKE – *See Roxanne SHANTE*

Sam COOKE *US, male vocalist*   **82 wks**

17 Jan 58	**YOU SEND ME** London HLU 8506	**29**	1 wk
14 Aug 59	**ONLY SIXTEEN** HMV POP 642	**23**	4 wks
7 Jul 60	**WONDERFUL WORLD** HMV POP 754	**27**	8 wks
29 Sep 60 ●	**CHAIN GANG** RCA 1202	**9**	11 wks
27 Jul 61 ●	**CUPID** RCA 1242	**7**	14 wks
8 Mar 62 ●	**TWISTIN' THE NIGHT AWAY** RCA 1277	**6**	14 wks
16 May 63	**ANOTHER SATURDAY NIGHT** RCA 1341	**23**	12 wks
5 Sep 63	**FRANKIE AND JOHNNY** RCA 1361	**30**	6 wks
22 Mar 86 ●	**WONDERFUL WORLD (re-issue)** RCA PB 49871	**2**	11 wks
10 May 86	**ANOTHER SATURDAY NIGHT (re-issue)**		
	RCA PB 49849	**75**	1 wk

British Hit Singles Part One: Alphabetically by Artist
Date of chart entry/Title & catalogue no./Peak position reached/Weeks on chart
★ Number one   ● Top Ten   † still on chart at 31 Dec 1992
* = credited to act billed in footnote

COOKIE CREW *UK, female vocal group*   **31 wks**

9 Jan 88 ●	**ROK DA HOUSE** Rhythm King LEFT 11 *	**5**	11 wks
7 Jan 89	**BORN THIS WAY (LET'S DANCE)** ffrr FFR 19	**23**	5 wks
1 Apr 89	**GOT TO KEEP ON** ffrr FFR 25	**17**	9 wks
15 Jul 89	**COME AND GET SOME** ffrr F 110	**42**	3 wks
27 Jul 91	**SECRETS OF SUCCESS** ffrr F159 **	**53**	3 wks

* Beatmasters featuring the Cookie Crew ** Cookie Crew featuring Danny D

COOKIES *US, female vocal group*   **1 wk**

10 Jan 63	**CHAINS** London HLU 9634	**50**	1 wk

COOL DOWN ZONE   **4 wks**
UK, male/female vocal/instrumental group

30 Jun 90	**HEAVEN KNOWS** 10 TEN 309	**52**	4 wks

Rita COOLIDGE *US, female vocalist*   **24 wks**

25 Jun 77 ●	**WE'RE ALL ALONE** A & M AMS 7295	**6**	13 wks
15 Oct 77	**(YOUR LOVE HAS LIFTED ME) HIGHER AND**		
	HIGHER A & M AMS 7315	**49**	1 wk
29 Oct 77	**(YOUR LOVE HAS LIFTED ME) HIGHER AND**		
	HIGHER (re-entry) A & M AMS 7315	**48**	1 wk
4 Feb 78	**WORDS** A & M AMS 7330	**25**	8 wks
25 Jun 83	**ALL TIME HIGH** A & M AM 007	**75**	1 wk

COOLNOTES *UK, male/female vocal/instrumental group*   **28 wks**

18 Aug 84	**YOU'RE NEVER TOO YOUNG** Abstract Dance AD 1	**42**	5 wks
17 Nov 84	**I FORGOT** Abstract Dance AD 2	**63**	2 wks
23 Mar 85	**SPEND THE NIGHT** Abstract Dance AD 3	**11**	9 wks
13 Jul 85	**IN YOUR CAR** Abstract Dance AD 4	**13**	9 wks
19 Oct 85	**HAVE A GOOD FOREVER** Abstract Dance AD 5	**73**	1 wk
17 May 86	**INTO THE MOTION** Abstract Dance AD 8	**66**	2 wks

Alice COOPER *US, male vocalist*   **99 wks**

15 Jul 72 ★	**SCHOOL'S OUT** Warner Bros. K 16188	**1**	12 wks
7 Oct 72 ●	**ELECTED** Warner Bros. K 16214	**4**	10 wks
10 Feb 73 ●	**HELLO HURRAY** Warner Bros. K 16248	**6**	12 wks
21 Apr 73 ●	**NO MORE MR. NICE GUY** Warner Bros. K 16262	**10**	10 wks
19 Jan 74	**TEENAGE LAMENT '74** Warner Bros. K 16345	**12**	7 wks
21 May 77	**(NO MORE) LOVE AT YOUR CONVENIENCE**		
	Warner Bros. K 16935	**44**	2 wks
23 Dec 78	**HOW YOU GONNA SEE ME NOW**		
	Warner Bros. K 17270	**61**	6 wks
6 Mar 82	**SEVEN AND SEVEN IS** (LIVE VERSION)		
	Warner Bros. K 17924	**62**	3 wks
8 May 82	**FOR BRITAIN ONLY/UNDER MY WHEELS**		
	Warner Bros. K 17940	**66**	2 wks
18 Oct 86	**HE'S BACK (THE MAN BEHIND THE MASK)**		
	MCA MCA 1090	**61**	2 wks
9 Apr 88	**FREEDOM** MCA MCA 1241	**50**	3 wks
29 Jul 89 ●	**POISON** Epic 655061 7	**2**	11 wks
7 Oct 89	**BED OF NAILS** Epic ALICE 3	**38**	5 wks
2 Dec 89	**HOUSE OF FIRE** Epic ALICE 4	**65**	2 wks
22 Jun 91	**HEY STOOPID** Epic 6569837	**21**	6 wks
5 Oct 91	**LOVE'S A LOADED GUN** Epic 6574387	**38**	3 wks
6 Jun 92	**FEED MY FRANKENSTEIN** Epic 6580927	**27**	3 wks

For the first five hits, 'Alice Cooper' was the name of the entire group, not just of the lead vocalist.

Deborah COOPER – See C & C MUSIC FACTORY/CLIVILLES & COLE

Tommy COOPER UK, male vocalist · 3 wks

| 29 Jun 61 | DON'T JUMP OFF THE ROOF DAD Palette PG 9019 | 40 | 2 wks |
| 20 Jul 61 | DON'T JUMP OFF THE ROOF DAD (re-entry) Palette PG 9019 | 50 | 1 wk |

Julian COPE UK, male vocalist · 53 wks

19 Nov 83	SUNSHINE PLAYROOM Mercury COPE 1	64	1 wk
31 Mar 84	THE GREATNESS AND PERFECTION OF LOVE Mercury MER 155	52	5 wks
27 Sep 86	WORLD SHUT YOUR MOUTH Island IS 290	19	8 wks
17 Jan 87	TRAMPOLENE Island IS 305	31	6 wks
11 Apr 87	EVE'S VOLCANO (COVERED IN SIN) Island IS 318	41	5 wks
24 Sep 88	CHARLOTTE ANNE Island IS 380	35	6 wks
21 Jan 89	5 O'CLOCK WORLD Island IS 399	42	4 wks
24 Jun 89	CHINA DOLL Island IS 406	53	2 wks
9 Feb 91	BEAUTIFUL LOVE Island IS 483	32	6 wks
20 Apr 91	EAST EASY RIDER Island IS 492	51	3 wks
3 Aug 91	HEAD Island IS 497	57	2 wks
8 Aug 92	WORLD SHUT YOUR MOUTH (re-issue) Island IS 534	44	3 wks
17 Oct 92	FEAR LOVES THIS PLACE Island IS 545	42	2 wks

Harry H. CORBETT – See Wilfred BRAMBELL and Harry H. CORBETT

Frank CORDELL UK, orchestra · 4 wks

| 24 Aug 56 | SADIE'S SHAWL HMV POP 229 | 29 | 2 wks |
| 16 Feb 61 | BLACK BEAR HMV POP 824 | 44 | 2 wks |

Louise CORDET France, female vocalist · 13 wks

| 5 Jul 62 | I'M JUST A BABY Decca F 11476 | 13 | 13 wks |

Don CORNELL US, male vocalist · 23 wks

| 3 Sep 54 | ★ HOLD MY HAND Vogue Q 2013 | 1 | 21 wks |
| 22 Apr 55 | STRANGER IN PARADISE Vogue Q 72073 | 19 | 2 wks |

Lynn CORNELL UK, female vocalist · 9 wks

| 20 Oct 60 | NEVER ON SUNDAY Decca F 11277 | 30 | 9 wks |

Charlotte CORNWELL – See Julie COVINGTON, Rula LENSKA, Charlotte CORNWELL and Sue JONES-DAVIES

Hugh CORNWELL
UK, male vocalist/instrumentalist - guitar · 3 wks

| 24 Jan 87 | FACTS + FIGURES Virgin VS 922 | 61 | 2 wks |
| 7 May 88 | ANOTHER KIND OF LOVE Virgin VS 945 | 71 | 1 wk |

CORO featuring TARLISA
Germany, male/female vocal/production group · 1 wk

| 12 Dec 92 | BECAUSE THE NIGHT ZYX ZYX 68227 | 61 | 1 wk |

CORONETS UK, male/female vocal group · 7 wks

| 26 Aug 55 | THAT'S HOW A LOVE SONG WAS BORN Columbia DB 3640 * | 14 | 6 wks |
| 25 Nov 55 | TWENTY TINY FINGERS Columbia DB 3671 | 20 | 1 wk |

* Ray Burns with the Coronets

Vladimir COSMA Hungary, orchestra · 1 wk

| 14 Jul 79 | DAVID'S SONG (MAIN THEME FROM 'KIDNAPPED') Decca FR 13841 | 64 | 1 wk |

Don COSTA US, orchestra · 10 wks

| 13 Oct 60 | NEVER ON SUNDAY London HLT 9195 | 27 | 9 wks |
| 22 Dec 60 | NEVER ON SUNDAY (re-entry) London HLT 9195 | 41 | 1 wk |

Elvis COSTELLO UK, male vocalist · 161 wks

5 Nov 77	WATCHING THE DETECTIVES Stiff BUY 20	15	11 wks
11 Mar 78	(I DON'T WANNA GO TO) CHELSEA Radar ADA 3 *	16	10 wks
13 May 78	PUMP IT UP Radar ADA 10 *	24	10 wks
28 Oct 78	RADIO RADIO Radar ADA 24 *	29	7 wks
10 Feb 79	● OLIVER'S ARMY Radar ADA 31 *	2	12 wks
12 May 79	ACCIDENTS WILL HAPPEN Radar ADA 35 *	28	8 wks
16 Feb 80	● I CAN'T STAND UP FOR FALLING DOWN F. Beat XX 1	4	8 wks
12 Apr 80	HI FIDELITY F. Beat XX 3	30	5 wks
7 Jun 80	NEW AMSTERDAM F. Beat XX 5	36	6 wks
20 Dec 80	CLUBLAND F. Beat XX 12 *	60	4 wks
3 Oct 81	A GOOD YEAR FOR THE ROSES F. Beat XX 17	6	11 wks
12 Dec 81	SWEET DREAMS F. Beat XX 19	42	8 wks
10 Apr 82	I'M YOUR TOY F. Beat XX 21 **	51	3 wks
19 Jun 82	YOU LITTLE FOOL F. Beat XX 26	52	3 wks
31 Jul 82	MAN OUT OF TIME F. Beat XX 28	58	2 wks
25 Sep 82	FROM HEAD TO TOE F. Beat XX 30	43	4 wks
11 Dec 82	PARTY PARTY A & M AMS 8267	48	6 wks
11 Jun 83	PILLS AND SOAP Imp IMP 001 ***	16	4 wks
9 Jul 83	EVERYDAY I WRITE THE BOOK F. Beat XX 32	28	8 wks
17 Sep 83	LET THEM ALL TALK F. Beat XX 33	59	2 wks
28 Apr 84	PEACE IN OUR TIME Imposter TRUCE 1 ***	48	3 wks
16 Jun 84	I WANNA BE LOVED /TURNING THE TOWN RED F. Beat XX 35	25	6 wks
25 Aug 84	THE ONLY FLAME IN TOWN F. Beat XX 37	71	2 wks
4 May 85	GREEN SHIRT F. Beat ZB 40085	71	1 wk
18 May 85	GREEN SHIRT (re-entry) F. Beat ZB 40085	68	1 wk
1 Feb 86	DON'T LET ME BE MISUNDERSTOOD F. Beat ZB 40555 ****	33	4 wks
30 Aug 86	TOKYO STORM WARNING Imp IMP 007	73	1 wk
4 Mar 89	VERONICA Warner Bros. W 7558	31	6 wks
20 May 89	BABY PLAYS AROUND EP Warner Bros. W 2949	65	1 wk
4 May 91	THE OTHER SIDE OF SUMMER Warner Bros. W 0025	43	4 wks

* Elvis Costello and the Attractions ** Elvis Costello and the Attractions with the Royal Philharmonic Orchestra *** Imposter **** Costello Show featuring the Confederates

Tracks on Baby Plays Around (EP): Baby Plays Around/Poisoned Rose/Almost Blue/My Funny Valentine.

COTTAGERS – See Tony REES and the COTTAGERS

Billy COTTON and his BAND · 25 wks
UK, male bandleader, vocalist, with band and chorus

1 May 53	● IN A GOLDEN COACH Decca F 10058 *	3	10 wks
18 Dec 53	I SAW MOMMY KISSING SANTA CLAUS Decca F 10206 **	11	3 wks
30 Apr 54	FRIENDS AND NEIGHBOURS Decca F 10299 ***	12	1 wk
14 May 54	● FRIENDS AND NEIGHBOURS (re-entry) Decca F 10299 ***	3	11 wks

* Billy Cotton and his Band, vocals by Doreen Stephens ** Billy Cotton and his Band, vocals by the Mill Girls and the Bandits *** Billy Cotton and his Band, vocals by the Bandits
See also Various Artists (EPs and LPs) - All Stars Hit Parade No. 2.

Mike COTTON'S JAZZMEN · 4 wks
UK, male instrumental band, Mike Cotton trumpet

| 20 Jun 63 | SWING THAT HAMMER Columbia DB 7029 | 36 | 4 wks |

John COUGAR – *See John Cougar MELLENCAMP*

COUGARS UK, *male instrumental group* — **8 wks**

28 Feb 63	SATURDAY NITE AT THE DUCK POND *Parlophone R 4989*		33	8 wks

COUNCIL COLLECTIVE — **6 wks**
UK/US, *male/female vocal/instrumental group*

22 Dec 84	SOUL DEEP (PART 1) *Polydor MINE 1*		24	6 wks

COUNTRYMEN UK, *male vocal group* — **2 wks**

3 May 62	I KNOW WHERE I'M GOING *Piccadilly 7N 35029*		45	2 wks

Don COVAY US, *male vocalist* — **6 wks**

7 Sep 74	IT'S BETTER TO HAVE (AND DON'T NEED) *Mercury 6052 634*		29	6 wks

COVENTRY CITY CUP FINAL SQUAD — **2 wks**
UK, *male football team vocalists*

23 May 87	GO FOR IT! *Sky Blue SKB 1*		61	2 wks

COVER GIRLS US, *female vocal group* — **4 wks**

1 Aug 92	WISHING ON A STAR *Epic 6581437*		38	4 wks

Julie COVINGTON UK, *female vocalist* — **29 wks**

25 Dec 76	★	DON'T CRY FOR ME ARGENTINA *MCA 260*	1	15 wks
3 Dec 77		ONLY WOMEN BLEED *Virgin VS 196*	12	11 wks
15 Jul 78		DON'T CRY FOR ME ARGENTINA (re-entry) *MCA 260*	63	3 wks

See also Julie Covington, Rula Lenska, Charlotte Cornwell and Sue Jones-Davies.

Julie COVINGTON, Rula LENSKA, Charlotte CORNWELL and Sue JONES-DAVIES UK, *female vocal group* — **6 wks**

21 May 77	●	O.K? *Polydor 2001 714*	10	6 wks

See also Julie Covington.

Warren COVINGTON – *See Tommy DORSEY ORCHESTRA starring Warren COVINGTON*

Patrick COWLEY – *See SYLVESTER*

Michael COX UK, *male vocalist* — **15 wks**

9 Jun 60	●	ANGELA JONES *Triumph RGM 1011*	7	13 wks
20 Oct 60		ALONG CAME CAROLINE *HMV POP 789*	41	2 wks

Floyd CRAMER US, *male instrumentalist – piano* — **24 wks**

13 Apr 61	★	ON THE REBOUND *RCA 1231*	1	14 wks
20 Jul 61		SAN ANTONIO ROSE *RCA 1241*	36	8 wks
23 Aug 62		HOT PEPPER *RCA 1301*	46	2 wks

CRAMPS US, *male/female vocal/instrumental group* — **4 wks**

9 Nov 85	CAN YOUR PUSSY DO THE DOG? *Big Beat NS 110*		68	1 wk
10 Feb 90	BIKINI GIRLS WITH MACHINE GUNS *Enigma ENV 17*		35	3 wks

Les CRANE US, *male vocalist* — **14 wks**

19 Feb 72	●	DESIDERATA *Warner Bros. K 16119*	7	14 wks

Beverley CRAVEN UK, *female vocalist* — **27 wks**

20 Apr 91	●	PROMISE ME *Epic 6559437*	3	13 wks
20 Jul 91		HOLDING ON *Epic 6565507*	32	7 wks
5 Oct 91		WOMAN TO WOMAN *Epic 6574647*	40	5 wks
7 Dec 91		MEMORIES *Epic 6576617*	68	2 wks

Jimmy CRAWFORD UK, *male vocalist* — **11 wks**

8 Jun 61	LOVE OR MONEY *Columbia DB 4633*		49	1 wk
16 Nov 61	I LOVE HOW YOU LOVE ME *Columbia DB 4717*		18	10 wks

Michael CRAWFORD UK, *male vocalist* — **11 wks**

10 Jan 87	●	THE MUSIC OF THE NIGHT *Polydor POSP 803*	7	11 wks

The flip side of The Music Of The Night *was* Wishing You Were Somehow Here Again *by Sarah Brightman.*

Randy CRAWFORD US, *female vocalist* — **74 wks**

21 Jun 80		LAST NIGHT AT DANCELAND *Warner Bros. K 17631*	61	2 wks
30 Aug 80	●	ONE DAY I'LL FLY AWAY *Warner Bros. K 17680*	2	11 wks
30 May 81		YOU MIGHT NEED SOMEBODY *Warner Bros. K 17803*	11	13 wks
8 Aug 81		RAINY NIGHT IN GEORGIA *Warner Bros. K 17840*	18	9 wks
31 Oct 81		SECRET COMBINATION *Warner Bros. K 17872*	48	3 wks
30 Jan 82		IMAGINE *Warner Bros. K 17906*	60	1 wk
13 Feb 82		IMAGINE (re-entry) *Warner Bros. K 17906*	75	1 wk
5 Jun 82		ONE HELLO *Warner Bros. K 17948*	48	4 wks
19 Feb 83		HE REMINDS ME *Warner Bros. K 17970*	65	2 wks
8 Oct 83		NIGHT LINE *Warner Bros. W 9530*	51	4 wks
29 Nov 86	●	ALMAZ *Warner Bros. W 8583*	4	17 wks
18 Jan 92		DIAMANTE *London LON 313* *	44	7 wks

* Zucchero with Randy Crawford

See also Crusaders.

Robert CRAY BAND US, *male vocal/instrumental group* — **4 wks**

20 Jun 87	RIGHT NEXT DOOR (BECAUSE OF ME) *Mercury CRAY 3*		50	4 wks

CRAZY ELEPHANT US, *male vocal group* — **13 wks**

21 May 69	GIMME GIMME GOOD LOVIN' *Major Minor MM 609*		12	13 wks

CRAZYHEAD UK, *male vocal/instrumental group* — **4 wks**

16 Jul 88	TIME HAS TAKEN ITS TOLL ON YOU *Food FOOD 12*		65	2 wks
25 Feb 89	HAVE LOVE, WILL TRAVEL EP *Food SGE 2025*		68	2 wks

Tracks on Have Love, Will Travel *(EP): Have Love Will Travel/Out On A Limb (Live)/Baby Turpentine (Live)/Snake Eyes (Live). See also Various Artists (EPs & LPs) - The Food Christmas EP.*

CREAM UK, *male vocal/instrumental group* — **59 wks**

20 Oct 66	WRAPPING PAPER *Reaction 591 007*		34	6 wks

LOUISE CORDET was the first Frenchwoman to reach the British top twenty. **Left:** DORIS DAY, shown here in 1950, had 29 American hits before the British charts began, among them the number ones 'Love Somebody', 'A Guy Is A Guy' and the original version of 'When I Fall In Love'.

Left: BEVERLEY CRAVEN was chosen Best British Newcomer in the 1992 Brit Awards.

JUDY COLLINS still holds the amazing record for most weeks on chart by a recording by a female vocalist.

15 Dec 66	I FEEL FREE *Reaction 591 011*	11	12 wks
8 Jun 67	STRANGE BREW *Reaction 591 015*	17	9 wks
5 Jun 68	ANYONE FOR TENNIS (THE SAVAGE SEVEN THEME) *Polydor 56 258*	40	3 wks
9 Oct 68	SUNSHINE OF YOUR LOVE *Polydor 56 286*	25	7 wks
15 Jan 69	WHITE ROOM *Polydor 56 300*	28	8 wks
9 Apr 69	BADGE *Polydor 56 315*	18	10 wks
28 Oct 72	BADGE (re-issue) *Polydor 2058 285*	42	4 wks

CREATION *UK, male vocal/instrumental group* — 3 wks

| 7 Jul 66 | MAKING TIME *Planet PLF 116* | 49 | 1 wk |
| 3 Nov 66 | PAINTER MAN *Planet PLF 119* | 36 | 2 wks |

CREATURES *UK, male/female vocal/instrumental group* — 26 wks

3 Oct 81	MAD EYED SCREAMER *Polydor POSPD 354*	24	7 wks
23 Apr 83	MISS THE GIRL *Wonderland SHE 1*	21	7 wks
16 Jul 83	RIGHT NOW *Wonderland SHE 2*	14	10 wks
14 Oct 89	STANDING THERE *Wonderland SHE 17*	53	2 wks

CREEDENCE CLEARWATER REVIVAL — 94 wks
US, male vocal/instrumental group

28 May 69	● PROUD MARY *Liberty LBF 15223*	8	13 wks
16 Aug 69	★ BAD MOON RISING *Liberty LBF 15230*	1	15 wks
15 Nov 69	GREEN RIVER *Liberty LBF 15250*	19	11 wks
14 Feb 70	DOWN ON THE CORNER *Liberty LBF 15283*	31	6 wks
4 Apr 70	● TRAVELLIN' BAND *Liberty LBF 15310*	8	12 wks
20 Jun 70	● UP AROUND THE BEND *Liberty LBF 15354*	3	12 wks
4 Jul 70	TRAVELLIN' BAND (re-entry) *Liberty LBF 15310*	46	1 wk
5 Sep 70	LONG AS I CAN SEE THE LIGHT *Liberty LBF 15384*	20	9 wks
20 Mar 71	HAVE YOU EVER SEEN THE RAIN *Liberty LBF 15440*	36	6 wks
24 Jul 71	SWEET HITCH-HIKER *United Artists UP 35261*	36	8 wks
2 May 92	BAD MOON RISING (re-issue) *Epic 6580047*	71	1 wk

Kid CREOLE and the COCONUTS — 56 wks
US, male vocalist and female vocal group

13 Jun 81	ME NO POP I *Ze WIP 6711* *	32	7 wks
15 May 82	● I'M A WONDERFUL THING, BABY *Ze WIP 6756*	4	11 wks
24 Jul 82	● STOOL PIGEON *Ze WIP 6793*	7	9 wks
9 Oct 82	● ANNIE I'M NOT YOUR DADDY *Ze WIP 6801*	2	8 wks
11 Dec 82	DEAR ADDY *Ze WIP 6840*	29	7 wks
10 Sep 83	THERE'S SOMETHING WRONG IN PARADISE *Island IS 130*	35	5 wks
19 Nov 83	THE LIFEBOAT PARTY *Island IS 142*	49	4 wks
14 Apr 90	THE SEX OF IT *CBS 655698 7*	29	5 wks

* Kid Creole and the Coconuts present Coati Mundi

See also Coconuts.

CREW CUTS *Canada, male vocal group* — 29 wks

| 1 Oct 54 | SH-BOOM *Mercury MB 3140* | 12 | 9 wks |
| 15 Apr 55 | ● EARTH ANGEL *Mercury MB 3202* | 4 | 20 wks |

Bernard CRIBBINS *UK, male vocalist* — 29 wks

15 Feb 62	● HOLE IN THE GROUND *Parlophone R 4869*	9	13 wks
5 Jul 62	● RIGHT SAID FRED *Parlophone R 4923*	10	10 wks
13 Dec 62	GOSSIP CALYPSO *Parlophone R 4961*	25	6 wks

CRICKETS *US, male vocal/instrumental group* — 97 wks

27 Sep 57	★ THAT'LL BE THE DAY *Vogue Coral Q 72279*	1	14 wks
27 Dec 57	● OH BOY *Coral Q 72298*	3	15 wks
10 Jan 58	THAT'LL BE THE DAY (re-entry) *Vogue Coral Q 72279*	29	1 wk
14 Mar 58	● MAYBE BABY *Coral Q 72307*	4	10 wks
25 Jul 58	THINK IT OVER *Coral Q 72329*	11	7 wks
24 Apr 59	LOVE'S MADE A FOOL OF YOU *Coral Q 72365*	26	1 wk
8 May 59	LOVE'S MADE A FOOL OF YOU (re-entry) *Coral Q 72365*	30	1 wk
15 Jan 60	WHEN YOU ASK ABOUT LOVE *Coral Q 72382*	27	1 wk
12 May 60	MORE THAN I CAN SAY *Coral Q 72395*	42	1 wk
26 May 60	BABY MY HEART *Coral Q 72395*	33	4 wks
21 Jun 62	● DON'T EVER CHANGE *Liberty LIB 55441*	5	13 wks
24 Jan 63	MY LITTLE GIRL *Liberty LIB 10067*	17	9 wks
6 Jun 63	DON'T TRY TO CHANGE ME *Liberty LIB 10092*	37	4 wks
14 May 64	YOU'VE GOT LOVE *Coral Q 72472* *	40	6 wks
2 Jul 64	(THEY CALL HER) LA BAMBA *Liberty LIB 55696*	21	10 wks

* Buddy Holly and the Crickets

Although not credited on the records, Buddy Holly was featured on the first four hits.

CRIMINAL ELEMENT ORCHESTRA = See Wally JUMP Jr and the CRIMINAL ELEMENT

CRISPY AND COMPANY — 11 wks
US, male vocal/instrumental group

| 16 Aug 75 | BRAZIL *Creole CR 109* | 26 | 5 wks |
| 27 Dec 75 | GET IT TOGETHER *Creole CR 114* | 21 | 6 wks |

CRITTERS *US, male vocal/instrumental group* — 5 wks

| 30 Jun 66 | YOUNGER GIRL *London HL 10047* | 38 | 5 wks |

Tony CROMBIE and his ROCKETS — 2 wks
UK, male vocal/instrumental group, Tony Crombie-drums

| 19 Oct 56 | TEACH YOU TO ROCK/SHORT'NIN' BREAD *Columbia DB 3822* | 25 | 2 wks |

Bing CROSBY *US, male vocalist* — 93 wks

14 Nov 52	● ISLE OF INNISFREE *Brunswick 04900*	3	12 wks
5 Dec 52	● ZING A LITTLE ZONG *Brunswick 04981* *	10	2 wks
19 Dec 52	● SILENT NIGHT *Brunswick 03929*	8	2 wks
19 Mar 54	● CHANGING PARTNERS *Brunswick 05244*	10	1 wk
2 Apr 54	● CHANGING PARTNERS (re-entry) *Brunswick 05244*	9	1 wk
23 Apr 54	CHANGING PARTNERS (2nd re-entry) *Brunswick 05244*	11	1 wk
7 Jan 55	COUNT YOUR BLESSINGS *Brunswick 05339*	18	1 wk
21 Jan 55	COUNT YOUR BLESSINGS (re-entry) *Brunswick 05339*	11	2 wks
29 Apr 55	STRANGER IN PARADISE *Brunswick 05410*	17	2 wks
27 Apr 56	IN A LITTLE SPANISH TOWN *Brunswick 05543*	22	3 wks
23 Nov 56	● TRUE LOVE *Capitol CL 14645* **	4	27 wks
24 May 57	● AROUND THE WORLD *Brunswick 05674*	5	15 wks
9 Aug 75	THAT'S WHAT LIFE IS ALL ABOUT *United Artists UP 35852*	41	4 wks
3 Dec 77	● WHITE CHRISTMAS *MCA 111*	5	7 wks
27 Nov 82	● PEACE ON EARTH - LITTLE DRUMMER BOY *RCA BOW 12* ***	3	8 wks
17 Dec 83	TRUE LOVE (re-issue) *Capitol CL 315* **	70	3 wks
21 Dec 85	WHITE CHRISTMAS (re-issue) *MCA BING 1*	69	2 wks

* Bing Crosby and Jane Wyman ** Bing Crosby and Grace Kelly *** David Bowie and Bing Crosby

CROSBY STILLS NASH and YOUNG — 12 wks
US/UK/Canada, male vocal/instrumental group

| 16 Aug 69 | MARRAKESH EXPRESS *Atlantic 584 283* * | 17 | 9 wks |
| 21 Jan 89 | AMERICAN DREAM *Atlantic A 9003* | 55 | 3 wks |

* Crosby, Stills and Nash

See also Stephen Stills; Neil Young.

CROSS UK/US, male vocal/instrumental group   1 wk

17 Oct 87	**COWBOYS AND INDIANS** *Virgin VS 1007*........................**74**	1 wk

Christopher CROSS US, male vocalist   27 wks

19 Apr 80	**RIDE LIKE THE WIND** *Warner Bros. K 17582* **69**	1 wk
14 Feb 81	**SAILING** *Warner Bros. K 17695*..................................**48**	6 wks
17 Oct 81	**ARTHUR'S THEME (BEST THAT YOU CAN DO)** *Warner Bros. K 17847* **56**	4 wks
9 Jan 82 ●	**ARTHUR'S THEME (BEST THAT YOU CAN DO) (re-entry)** *Warner Bros. K 17847*...................**7**	11 wks
5 Feb 83	**ALL RIGHT** *Warner Bros. W 9843* **51**	5 wks

CROWD   11 wks
Multi-national, male/female vocal/instrumental charity assembly

1 Jun 85 ★	**YOU'LL NEVER WALK ALONE** *Spartan BRAD 1* **1**	11 wks

CROWDED HOUSE   35 wks
Australia/New Zealand, male vocal/instrumental group

6 Jun 87	**DON'T DREAM IT'S OVER** *Capitol CL 438* **27**	8 wks
22 Jun 91	**CHOCOLATE CAKE** *Capitol CL 618* **69**	2 wks
2 Nov 91	**FALL AT YOUR FEET** *Capitol CL 626* **17**	7 wks
29 Feb 92 ●	**WEATHER WITH YOU** *Capitol CL 643* **7**	9 wks
20 Feb 92	**FOUR SEASONS IN ONE DAY** *Capitol CL 655* **26**	5 wks
26 Sep 92	**IT'S ONLY NATURAL** *Capitol CL 661* **24**	4 wks

CROWN HEIGHTS AFFAIR   34 wks
US, male vocal/instrumental group

19 Aug 78	**GALAXY OF LOVE** *Philips 6168 801* **24**	10 wks
11 Nov 78	**I'M GONNA LOVE YOU FOREVER** *Mercury 6168 803*......**47**	4 wks
14 Apr 79	**DANCE LADY DANCE** *Mercury 6168 804*........................**44**	4 wks
3 May 80 ●	**YOU GAVE ME LOVE** *De-Lite MER 9*..............................**10**	12 wks
9 Aug 80	**YOU'VE BEEN GONE** *De-Lite MER 28* **44**	4 wks

Julee CRUISE US, female vocalist   12 wks

10 Nov 90 ●	**FALLING** *Warner Bros. W 9544* **7**	10 wks
2 Mar 91	**ROCKIN' BACK INSIDE MY HEART** *Warner Bros. W 0004*.................................**66**	2 wks

CRUISERS – *See Dave BERRY*

CRUSADERS US, male vocal/instrumental group   16 wks

18 Aug 79 ●	**STREET LIFE** *MCA 513* **5**	11 wks
26 Sep 81	**I'M SO GLAD I'M STANDING HERE TODAY** *MCA 741* * **61**	3 wks
7 Apr 84	**NIGHT LADIES** *MCA MCA 853* **55**	2 wks

* Crusaders, featured vocalist Joe Cocker
Vocalist on Street Life *was Randy Crawford, though uncredited.*

Bobby CRUSH UK, male instrumentalist - piano   4 wks

4 Nov 72	**BORSALINO** *Philips 6006 248* **37**	4 wks

CRY BEFORE DAWN   2 wks
Ireland, male vocal/instrumental group

17 Jun 89	**WITNESS FOR THE WORLD** *Epic GONE 3* **67**	2 wks

CRY SISCO! UK, male producer - Barry Blue   9 wks

2 Sep 89	**AFRO DIZZI ACT** *Escape AWOL 1*.................................**42**	8 wks
20 Jan 90	**AFRO DIZZI ACT (re-entry)** *Escape AWOL 1*..................**70**	1 wk

CRYIN' SHAMES UK, male vocal/instrumental group   7 wks

31 Mar 66	**PLEASE STAY** *Decca F 12340*......................................**26**	7 wks

CRYPT-KICKERS – *See Bobby 'Boris' PICKETT and the CRYPT-KICKERS*

CRYSTAL PALACE UK, male football team vocalists   2 wks

12 May 90	**GLAD ALL OVER/WHERE EAGLES FLY** *Parkfield PMS 5019* **50**	2 wks

CRYSTALS US, female vocal group   54 wks

22 Nov 62	**HE'S A REBEL** *London HLU 9611* **19**	13 wks
20 Jun 63 ●	**DA DOO RON RON** *London HLU 9732*............................**5**	16 wks
19 Sep 63 ●	**THEN HE KISSED ME** *London HLU 9773* **2**	14 wks
5 Mar 64	**I WONDER** *London HLU 9852* **36**	3 wks
19 Oct 74	**DA DOO RON RON (re-issue)** *Warner Spector K 19010* **15**	8 wks

CUBIC 22 Belgium, male production duo   7 wks

22 Jun 91	**NIGHT IN MOTION** *XL XLS 20*.....................................**15**	7 wks

CUD UK, male vocal/instrumental group   11 wks

19 Oct 91	**OH NO WON'T DO (EP)** *A & M AMB 829* **49**	2 wks
28 Mar 92	**THROUGH THE ROOF** *A & M AM 857* **44**	2 wks
30 May 92	**RICH AND STRANGE** *A & M AM 871* **24**	3 wks
15 Aug 92	**PURPLE LOVE BALLOON** *A & M AM 0024* **27**	3 wks
10 Oct 92	**ONCE AGAIN** *A & M AM 0081* **45**	1 wk

Tracks on Oh No Won't Do (EP): *Oh No Won't Do/Profession/Ariel/Price Of Love.*

CUFFLINKS US, male vocal group   30 wks

29 Nov 69 ●	**TRACY** *MCA MU 1101* **4**	16 wks
14 Mar 70 ●	**WHEN JULIE COMES AROUND** *MCA MU 1112*.............**10**	14 wks

CULT UK, male vocal/instrumental group   74 wks

22 Dec 84	**RESURRECTION JOE** *Beggars Banquet BEG 122* **74**	2 wks
25 May 85	**SHE SELLS SANCTUARY** *Beggars Banquet BEG 135* **15**	17 wks
28 Sep 85	**SHE SELLS SANCTUARY (re-entry)** *Beggars Banquet BEG 135* **61**	2 wks
5 Oct 85	**RAIN** *Beggars Banquet BEG 147* **17**	8 wks
30 Nov 85	**REVOLUTION** *Beggars Banquet BEG 152* **30**	7 wks
28 Feb 87	**LOVE REMOVAL MACHINE** *Beggars Banquet BEG 182*......**18**	7 wks
2 May 87	**LIL' DEVIL** *Beggars Banquet BEG 188* **11**	7 wks
22 Aug 87	**WILD FLOWER (DOUBLE SINGLE)** *Beggars Banquet BEG 195D* **24**	2 wks
29 Aug 87	**WILD FLOWER** *Beggars Banquet BEG 195* **30**	4 wks
1 Apr 89	**FIRE WOMAN** *Beggars Banquet BEG 228* **15**	4 wks
8 Jul 89	**EDIE (CIAO BABY)** *Beggars Banquet BEG 230* **32**	5 wks
18 Nov 89	**SUN KING/EDIE (CIAO BABY) (re-issue)** *Beggars Banquet BEG 235* **39**	2 wks
10 Mar 90	**SWEET SOUL SISTER** *Beggars Banquet BEG 241* **42**	4 wks
14 Sep 91	**WILD HEARTED SON** *Beggars Banquet BEG 255* **40**	2 wks
29 Feb 92	**HEART OF SOUL** *Beggars Banquet BEG 260* **51**	1 wk

Tracks on double single: Wild Flower/Love Trooper/Outlaw/Horse Nation.

CULT JAM – *See LISA LISA and CULT JAM*

CULTURE BEAT
3 wks

Germany, male/female vocal/instrumental group

3 Feb 90	(CHERRY LIPS) DER ERDBEERMUND *Epic 655633 7* 55	3 wks

CULTURE CLUB *UK, male vocal/instrumental group*
103 wks

18 Sep 82 ★	DO YOU REALLY WANT TO HURT ME *Virgin VS 518*.....................1	18 wks
27 Nov 82 ●	TIME (CLOCK OF THE HEART) *Virgin VS 558*.........3	12 wks
9 Apr 83 ●	CHURCH OF THE POISON MIND *Virgin VS 571* 2	9 wks
17 Sep 83 ★	KARMA CHAMELEON *Virgin VS 612*.................1	20 wks
10 Dec 83 ●	VICTIMS *Virgin VS 641* 3	10 wks
24 Mar 84 ●	IT'S A MIRACLE *Virgin VS 662*................4	9 wks
6 Oct 84 ●	THE WAR SONG *Virgin VS 694* 2	8 wks
1 Dec 84	THE MEDAL SONG *Virgin VS 730*................32	4 wks
5 Jan 85	THE MEDAL SONG (re-entry) *Virgin VS 730* 74	1 wk
15 Mar 86 ●	MOVE AWAY *Virgin VS 845*............7	7 wks
31 May 86	GOD THANK YOU WOMAN *Virgin VS 861*.............31	5 wks

Smiley CULTURE *UK, male vocalist*
13 wks

15 Dec 84	POLICE OFFICER *Fashion FAD 7012* 12	10 wks
6 Apr 85	COCKNEY TRANSLATION *Fashion FAD 7028* 71	1 wk
13 Sep 86	SCHOOLTIME CHRONICLE *Polydor POSP 815* 59	2 wks

Larry CUNNINGHAM and the MIGHTY AVONS *Ireland, male vocal/instrumental group*
11 wks

10 Dec 64	TRIBUTE TO JIM REEVES *King KG 1016*............40	8 wks
25 Feb 65	TRIBUTE TO JIM REEVES (re-entry) *King KG 1016*........46	3 wks

CUPID'S INSPIRATION
19 wks

UK, male vocal/instrumental group

19 Jun 68 ●	YESTERDAY HAS GONE *Nems 56 3500* 4	11 wks
2 Oct 68	MY WORLD *Nems 56 3702* 33	8 wks

CURE *UK, male vocal/instrumental group*
138 wks

12 Apr 80	A FOREST *Fiction FICS 10* 31	8 wks
4 Apr 81	PRIMARY *Fiction FICS 12* 43	6 wks
17 Oct 81	CHARLOTTE SOMETIMES *Fiction FICS 14* 44	4 wks
24 Jul 82	HANGING GARDEN *Fiction FICS 15*............34	4 wks
27 Nov 82	LET'S GO TO BED *Fiction FICS 17*............44	4 wks
8 Jan 83	LET'S GO TO BED (re-entry) *Fiction FICS 17*............75	1 wk
9 Jul 83	THE WALK *Fiction FICS 18* 12	8 wks
29 Oct 83 ●	THE LOVE CATS *Fiction FICS 19* 7	11 wks
7 Apr 84	THE CATERPILLAR *Fiction FICS 20* 14	7 wks
27 Jul 85	IN BETWEEN DAYS *Fiction FICS 22* 15	10 wks
21 Sep 85	CLOSE TO ME *Fiction FICS 23* 24	8 wks
3 May 86	BOYS DON'T CRY *Fiction FICS 24* 22	6 wks
18 Apr 87	WHY CAN'T I BE YOU *Fiction FICS 25* 21	5 wks
4 Jul 87	CATCH *Fiction FICS 26* 27	6 wks
17 Oct 87	JUST LIKE HEAVEN *Fiction FICS 27* 29	5 wks
20 Feb 88	HOT HOT HOT!!! *Fiction FICSX 28* 45	3 wks
22 Apr 89 ●	LULLABY *Fiction FICS 29* 5	6 wks
2 Sep 89	LOVESONG *Fiction FICS 30* 18	7 wks
31 Mar 90	PICTURES OF YOU *Fiction FICS 34* 24	6 wks
29 Sep 90	NEVER ENOUGH *Fiction FICS 35* 13	5 wks
3 Nov 90	CLOSE TO ME (re-mix) *Fiction FICS 36* 13	5 wks
28 Mar 92 ●	HIGH *Fiction FICS 39* 8	3 wks
11 Apr 92	HIGH (re-mix) *Fiction FICXS 41* 44	1 wk
23 May 92 ●	FRIDAY I'M IN LOVE *Fiction FICS 42* 6	7 wks
17 Oct 92	A LETTER TO ELISE *Fiction FICS 46* 28	2 wks

CURIOSITY *UK, male vocal/instrumental group*
57 wks

13 Dec 86 ●	DOWN TO EARTH *Mercury CAT 2* * 3	18 wks
4 Apr 87 ●	ORDINARY DAY *Mercury CAT 3* * 11	7 wks
20 Jun 87 ●	MISFIT *Mercury CAT 4* * 7	9 wks

British Hit Singles Part One: Alphabetically by Artist
Date of chart entry/Title & catalogue no./Peak position reached/Weeks on chart

★ Number one ● Top Ten † still on chart at 31 Dec 1992

* = credited to act billed in footnote

19 Sep 87	FREE *Mercury CAT 5* * 56	2 wks
16 Sep 89	NAME AND NUMBER *Mercury CAT 6* 14	9 wks
25 Apr 92 ●	HANG ON IN THERE BABY *RCA PB 45377* 3	10 wks
29 Aug 92	I NEED YOUR LOVIN' *RCA 74321111377* 47	2 wks

*Curiosity Killed The Cat

CURLS – *See Paul EVANS and the CURLS*

Chantal CURTIS *France, female vocalist*
3 wks

14 Jul 79	GET ANOTHER LOVE *Pye 7P 5003* 51	3 wks

T.C. CURTIS *Jamaica, male vocalist/instrumentalist*
4 wks

23 Feb 85	YOU SHOULD HAVE KNOWN BETTER *Hot Melt VS 754* 50	4 wks

CURVE *UK, male/female vocal/instrumental duo*
11 wks

16 Mar 91	THE BLINDFOLD (EP) *AnXious ANX 27* 68	1 wk
25 May 91	COAST IS CLEAR *AnXious ANX 30* 34	3 wks
9 Nov 91	CLIPPED *AnXious ANX 35* 36	1 wk
7 Mar 92	FAIT ACCOMPLI (EP) *AnXious ANXT 36* 22	3 wks
18 Jul 92	HORROR HEAD *AnXious ANXT 38* 31	2 wks

Tracks on The Blindfold EP: *Ten Little Girls/I Speak Your Every Word/Blindfold/No Escape From Heaven. Tracks on* Horror Head (EP): *Horror Head/Falling Free/Mission From God/Today Is Not The Day.*

CURVED AIR *UK, male/female vocal/instrumental group*
12 wks

7 Aug 71 ●	BACK STREET LUV *Warner Bros. K 16092* 4	12 wks

Adge CUTLER – *See WURZELS*

CUTTING CREW
37 wks

UK/Canada, male vocal/instrumental group

16 Aug 86 ●	(I JUST) DIED IN YOUR ARMS *Siren SIREN 21* 4	12 wks
25 Oct 86	I'VE BEEN IN LOVE BEFORE *Siren SIREN 29* 31	9 wks
10 Jan 87	I'VE BEEN IN LOVE BEFORE (re-entry) *Siren SIREN 29* 70	1 wk
7 Mar 87	ONE FOR THE MOCKINGBIRD *Siren SIREN 40* 52	5 wks
21 Nov 87	I'VE BEEN IN LOVE BEFORE (2nd re-entry) *Siren SIREN 29* 24	8 wks
22 Jul 89	(BETWEEN A) ROCK AND A HARD PLACE *Siren SRN 108* 66	2 wks

CYBERSONIK *US, male sampling group*
1 wk

10 Nov 90	TECHNARCHY *Champion CHAMP 264* 73	1 wk

Johnny CYMBAL *UK, male vocalist*
10 wks

14 Mar 63	MR. BASS MAN *London HLR 9682* 24	10 wks

Billy Ray CYRUS *US, male vocalist*
17 wks

25 Jul 92 ●	ACHY BREAKY HEART *Mercury MER 373* 3	10 wks
10 Oct 92	COULD'VE BEEN ME *Mercury MER 378* 24	4 wks
28 Nov 92	THESE BOOTS ARE MADE FOR WALKIN' *Mercury MER 384* 63	1 wk
19 Dec 92	ACHY BREAKY HEART *Epic 6588837* * ....53†	2 wks

*Alvin and the Chipmunks featuring Billy Ray Cyrus

British Hit Singles Part One: Alphabetically by Artist
Date of chart entry/Title & catalogue no./Peak position reached/Weeks on chart
★ Number one   ● Top Ten   † still on chart at 31 Dec 1992
* = credited to act billed in footnote

Chuck D – See ANTHRAX

Dimples D *US, female rapper* — **10 wks**

17 Nov 90	SUCKER DJ *FBI FBI 11*	....	**17**	10 wks

Longsy D *UK, male vocalist* — **7 wks**

4 Mar 89	THIS IS SKA *Big One BIG 13*	....	**56**	7 wks

Nikki D *US, female rapper* — **6 wks**

6 May 89	MY LOVE IS SO RAW *Def Jam 6548987* *	....	**34**	5 wks
30 Mar 91	DADDY'S LITTLE GIRL *Def Jam 6567347*	....	**75**	1 wk

* Alyson Williams featuring Nikki D

Vicky D *US, female vocalist* — **6 wks**

13 Mar 82	THIS BEAT IS MINE *Virgin VS 486*	....	**42**	6 wks

D.B.M. *Germany, male/female vocal/instrumental group* — **3 wks**

12 Nov 77	DISCO BEATLEMANIA *Atlantic K 11027*	....	**45**	3 wks

D, B, M and T *UK, male vocal/instrumental group* — **8 wks**

1 Aug 70	MR. PRESIDENT *Fontana 6007 022*	....	**33**	8 wks

See also Dave Dee, Dozy, Beaky, Mick and Tich.

D MOB *UK, male producer – Danny D.* — **43 wks**

15 Oct 88	● WE CALL IT ACIEED *ffrr FFR 13* *	....	**3**	12 wks
3 Jun 89	● IT IS TIME TO GET FUNKY *ffrr F 107* **	....	**9**	10 wks
21 Oct 89	● C'MON AND GET MY LOVE *ffrr F 117* ***	....	**15**	10 wks
6 Jan 90	● PUT YOUR HANDS TOGETHER *ffrr F 124* ****	....	**7**	8 wks
7 Apr 90	THAT'S THE WAY OF THE WORLD *ffrr F 132* ***	....	**48**	3 wks

* D Mob featuring Gary Haisman ** D Mob featuring LRS *** D Mob featuring Cathy Dennis **** D Mob featuring Nuff Juice

D TRAIN *US, male vocal/instrumental duo* — **36 wks**

6 Feb 82	YOU'RE THE ONE FOR ME *Epic EPC A 2016*	....	**30**	8 wks
8 May 82	WALK ON BY *Epic EPC A 2298*	....	**44**	6 wks
7 May 83	MUSIC PART 1 *Prelude A 3332*	....	**23**	7 wks
16 Jul 83	KEEP GIVING ME LOVE *Prelude A 3497*	....	**65**	2 wks
27 Jul 85	YOU'RE THE ONE FOR ME (re-mix) *Prelude ZB 40302*	....	**15**	11 wks
12 Oct 85	MUSIC *Prelude ZB 40431*	....	**62**	2 wks

D-INFLUENCE *UK, male/female vocal/instrumental group* — **2 wks**

20 Jun 92	GOOD LOVER *East West A 8573*	....	**46**	2 wks

D:REAM *UK, male/female vocal/instrumental group* — **1 wk**

4 Jul 92	U R THE BEST THING *FXU FXU 3*	....	**72**	1 wk

D-SHAKE *Holland, male production duo* — **8 wks**

2 Jun 90	YAAAH/TECHNO TRANCE *Cooltempo COOL 213*	....	**20**	6 wks
2 Feb 91	MY HEART THE BEAT *Cooltempo COOL 228*	....	**42**	2 wks

Paul DA VINCI *UK, male vocalist* — **8 wks**

20 Jul 74	YOUR BABY AIN'T YOUR BABY ANYMORE *Penny Farthing PEN 843*	....	**20**	8 wks

Terry DACTYL and the DINOSAURS — **16 wks**
UK, male vocal/instrumental group

15 Jul 72	● SEASIDE SHUFFLE *UK 5*	....	**2**	12 wks
13 Jan 73	ON A SATURDAY NIGHT *UK 21*	....	**45**	4 wks

Terry Dactyl is Jona Lewie.

DADDY FREDDY – See Simon HARRIS

DAFFY DUCK featuring the GROOVE GANG — **3 wks**
Germany, male instrumental/production group

6 Jul 91	PARTY ZONE *East West YZ 592*	....	**58**	3 wks

DAINTEES – See Martin STEPHENSON and the DAINTEES

DAISY CHAINSAW — **6 wks**
UK, male/female vocal/instrumental group

18 Jan 92	LOVE YOUR MONEY *Deva DEVA 001*	....	**26**	5 wks
28 Mar 92	PINK FLOWER/ROOM ELEVEN *Deva 82 TP7*	....	**65**	1 wk

DAKEYNE – See James BROWN

DAKOTAS *UK, male instrumental group* — **13 wks**

11 Jul 63	THE CRUEL SEA *Parlophone R 5044*	....	**18**	13 wks

See also Billy J. Kramer and the Dakotas.

Jim DALE *UK, male vocalist* — **22 wks**

11 Oct 57	● BE MY GIRL *Parlophone R 4343*	....	**2**	16 wks
10 Jan 58	JUST BORN *Parlophone R 4376*	....	**27**	1 wk
17 Jan 58	CRAZY DREAM *Parlophone R 4376*	....	**24**	2 wks
7 Mar 58	SUGARTIME *Parlophone R 4402*	....	**25**	3 wks

DALE and GRACE *US, male/female vocal duo* — **2 wks**

9 Jan 64	I'M LEAVING IT UP TO YOU *London HL 9807*	....	**42**	2 wks

DALE SISTERS *UK, female vocal group* — **6 wks**

23 Nov 61	MY SUNDAY BABY *Ember S 140*	....	**36**	6 wks

DALI'S CAR *UK, male vocal/instrumental duo* — **2 wks**

3 Nov 84	THE JUDGEMENT IS THE MIRROR *Paradox DOX 1*	....	**66**	2 wks

Roger DALTREY *UK, male vocalist* — **46 wks**

14 Apr 73	● GIVING IT ALL AWAY *Track 2094 110*	....	**5**	11 wks
4 Aug 73	I'M FREE *Ode ODS 66302*	....	**13**	10 wks

14 May 77	**WRITTEN ON THE WIND** *Polydor 2121 319*	**46**	2 wks
2 Aug 80	**FREE ME** *Polydor 2001 980*	**39**	4 wks
11 Oct 80	**WITHOUT YOUR LOVE** *Polydor POSP 181*	**55**	4 wks
3 Mar 84	**WALKING IN MY SLEEP** *WEA U 9686*	**56**	3 wks
5 Oct 85	**AFTER THE FIRE** *10 TEN 69*	**50**	5 wks
8 Mar 86	**UNDER A RAGING MOON** *10 TEN 81*	**43**	5 wks

Carolina DAMAS – *See SUENO LATINO featuring Carolina DAMAS*

DAMIAN *UK, male vocalist* — 26 wks

26 Dec 87	**THE TIME WARP 2** *Jive JIVE 160*	**51**	6 wks
27 Aug 88	**THE TIME WARP 2 (re-issue)** *Jive JIVE 182*	**64**	3 wks
19 Aug 89 ●	**THE TIME WARP (re-mix)** *Jive JIVE 209*	**7**	13 wks
16 Dec 89	**WIG WAM BAM** *Jive JIVE 236*	**49**	4 wks

DAMNED *UK, male vocal/instrumental group* — 77 wks

5 May 79	**LOVE SONG** *Chiswick CHIS 112*	**20**	8 wks
20 Oct 79	**SMASH IT UP** *Chiswick CHIS 116*	**35**	5 wks
1 Dec 79	**I JUST CAN'T BE HAPPY TODAY** *Chiswick CHIS 120*	**46**	5 wks
4 Oct 80	**HISTORY OF THE WORLD** (PART 1) *Chiswick CHIS 135*	**51**	4 wks
28 Nov 81	**FRIDAY 13TH EP** *Stale One TRY 1*	**50**	4 wks
10 Jul 82	**LOVELY MONEY** *Bronze BRO 149*	**42**	4 wks
9 Jun 84	**THANKS FOR THE NIGHT** *Damned DAMNED 1*	**43**	4 wks
30 Mar 85	**GRIMLY FIENDISH** *MCA GRIM 1*	**21**	7 wks
22 Jun 85	**THE SHADOW OF LOVE** *MCA GRIM 2*	**25**	8 wks
21 Sep 85	**IS IT A DREAM** *MCA GRIM 3*	**34**	4 wks
8 Feb 86 ●	**ELOISE** *MCA GRIM 4*	**3**	9 wks
19 Apr 86	**ELOISE (re-entry)** *MCA GRIM 4*	**72**	1 wk
22 Nov 86	**ANYTHING** *MCA GRIM 5*	**32**	4 wks
7 Feb 87	**GIGOLO** *MCA GRIM 6*	**29**	3 wks
25 Apr 87	**ALONE AGAIN OR** *MCA GRIM 7*	**27**	6 wks
28 Nov 87	**IN DULCE DECORUM** *MCA GRIM 8*	**72**	1 wk

Tracks on Friday 13th EP: *Disco Man/Limit Club/Billy Bad Breaks/Citadel.*

Kenny DAMON *US, male vocalist* — 1 wk

19 May 66	**WHILE I LIVE** *Mercury MF 907*	**48**	1 wk

Vic DAMONE *US, male vocalist* — 22 wks

6 Dec 57	**AN AFFAIR TO REMEMBER** *Philips PB 745*	**29**	1 wk
31 Jan 58	**AN AFFAIR TO REMEMBER (re-entry)** *Philips PB 745*	**30**	1 wk
9 May 58 ★	**ON THE STREET WHERE YOU LIVE** *Philips PB 819*	**1**	17 wks
1 Aug 58	**THE ONLY MAN ON THE ISLAND** *Philips PB 837*	**24**	3 wks

DANA *UK, female vocalist* — 75 wks

4 Apr 70 ★	**ALL KINDS OF EVERYTHING** *Rex R 11054*	**1**	15 wks
25 Jul 70	**ALL KINDS OF EVERYTHING (re-entry)** *Rex R 11054*	**47**	1 wk
13 Feb 71	**WHO PUT THE LIGHTS OUT** *Rex R 11062*	**14**	11 wks
25 Jan 75 ●	**PLEASE TELL HIM THAT I SAID HELLO** *GTO GT 6*	**8**	14 wks
13 Dec 75 ●	**IT'S GONNA BE A COLD COLD CHRISTMAS** *GTO GT 45*	**4**	6 wks
6 Mar 76	**NEVER GONNA FALL IN LOVE AGAIN** *GTO GT 55*	**31**	4 wks
16 Oct 76	**FAIRYTALE** *GTO GT 66*	**13**	16 wks
31 Mar 79	**SOMETHING'S COOKIN' IN THE KITCHEN** *GTO GT 243*	**44**	5 wks
15 May 82	**I FEEL LOVE COMIN' ON** *Creole CR 32*	**66**	3 wks

DANCE CONSPIRACY — 1 wk
UK, male instrumental/production duo

3 Oct 92	**DUB WAR** *XL XLT 34*	**72**	1 wk

DANGER DANGER *US, male vocal/instrumental group* — 5 wks

8 Feb 92	**MONKEY BUSINESS** *Epic 6577517*	**42**	2 wks
28 Mar 92	**I STILL THINK ABOUT YOU** *Epic 6578387*	**46**	2 wks
13 Jun 92	**COMIN' HOME** *Epic 6581337*	**75**	1 wk

DAN-I *UK, male vocalist* — 9 wks

10 Nov 79	**MONKEY CHOP** *Island WIP 6520*	**30**	9 wks

Charlie DANIELS BAND — 10 wks
US, male vocal/instrumental group

22 Sep 79	**THE DEVIL WENT DOWN TO GEORGIA** *Epic EPC 7737*	**14**	10 wks

Johnny DANKWORTH — 33 wks
UK, male orchestral/group leader/instrumentalist - alto sax

22 Jun 56 ●	**EXPERIMENTS WITH MICE** *Parlophone R 4185*	**7**	12 wks
23 Feb 61 ●	**AFRICAN WALTZ** *Columbia DB 4590*	**9**	21 wks

DANNY and the JUNIORS *US, male vocal group* — 19 wks

17 Jan 58 ●	**AT THE HOP** *HMV POP 436*	**3**	14 wks
10 Jul 76	**AT THE HOP (re-issue)** *ABC 4123*	**39**	5 wks

DANNY WILSON *UK, male vocal/instrumental group* — 28 wks

22 Aug 87	**MARY'S PRAYER** *Virgin VS 934*	**42**	7 wks
2 Apr 88 ●	**MARY'S PRAYER (re-entry)** *Virgin VS 934*	**3**	11 wks
17 Jun 89	**THE SECOND SUMMER OF LOVE** *Virgin VS 1186*	**23**	9 wks
16 Sep 89	**NEVER GONNA BE THE SAME** *Virgin VS 1203*	**69**	1 wk

DANSE SOCIETY *UK, male vocal/instrumental group* — 5 wks

27 Aug 83	**WAKE UP** *Society SOC 5*	**61**	3 wks
5 Nov 83	**HEAVEN IS WAITING** *Society SOC 6*	**60**	2 wks

Steven DANTE *UK, male vocalist* — 16 wks

26 Sep 87	**THE REAL THING** *Chrysalis CHS 3167* *	**13**	10 wks
9 Jul 88	**I'M TOO SCARED** *Cooltempo DANTE 1*	**34**	6 wks

*Jellybean featuring Steven Dante

DANY – *See DOUBLE DEE featuring DANY*

Terence Trent D'ARBY *US, male vocalist* — 44 wks

14 Mar 87 ●	**IF YOU LET ME STAY** *CBS TRENT 1*	**7**	13 wks
20 Jun 87 ●	**WISHING WELL** *CBS TRENT 2*	**4**	11 wks
10 Oct 87	**DANCE LITTLE SISTER (PART ONE)** *CBS TRENT 3*	**20**	7 wks
9 Jan 88 ●	**SIGN YOUR NAME** *CBS TRENT 4*	**2**	10 wks
20 Jan 90	**TO KNOW SOMEONE DEEPLY IS TO KNOW SOMEONE SOFTLY** *CBS TRENT 6*	**55**	3 wks

Richard DARBYSHIRE – *See JELLYBEAN*

DARE *UK, male vocal/instrumental group* — 7 wks

29 Apr 89	**THE RAINDANCE** *A & M AM 483*	**62**	2 wks
29 Jul 89	**ABANDON** *A & M AM 519*	**71**	2 wks

| 10 Aug 91 | WE DON'T NEED A REASON *A & M AM 755* | 52 | 2 wks |
| 5 Oct 91 | REAL LOVE *A & M AM 824* | 67 | 1 wk |

Bobby DARIN US, male vocalist — 161 wks

1 Aug 58	SPLISH SPLASH *London HLE 8666*	28	1 wk
15 Aug 58	SPLISH SPLASH (re-entry) *London HLE 8666*	18	6 wks
9 Jan 59	QUEEN OF THE HOP *London HLE 8737*	24	2 wks
29 May 59 ★	DREAM LOVER *London HLE 8867*	1	19 wks
25 Sep 59 ★	MACK THE KNIFE *London HLK 8939*	1	16 wks
22 Jan 60	MACK THE KNIFE (re-entry) *London HLK 8939*	30	1 wk
29 Jan 60 ●	LA MER (BEYOND THE SEA) *London HLK 9034*	8	10 wks
10 Mar 60	MACK THE KNIFE (2nd re-entry) *London HLE 8939*	50	1 wk
31 Mar 60 ●	CLEMENTINE *London HLK 9086*	8	12 wks
21 Apr 60	LA MER (BEYOND THE SEA) (re-entry) *London HLE 9034*	40	2 wks
30 Jun 60	BILL BAILEY *London HLK 9142*	36	1 wk
14 Jul 60	BILL BAILEY (re-entry) *London HLK 9142*	34	1 wk
16 Mar 61 ●	LAZY RIVER *London HLK 9303*	2	13 wks
6 Jul 61	NATURE BOY *London HLK 9375*	24	7 wks
12 Oct 61 ●	YOU MUST HAVE BEEN A BEAUTIFUL BABY *London HLK 9429*	10	11 wks
26 Oct 61	COME SEPTEMBER *London HLK 9407 *	50	1 wk
21 Dec 61 ●	MULTIPLICATION *London HLK 9474*	5	13 wks
19 Jul 62 ●	THINGS *London HLK 9575*	2	17 wks
4 Oct 62	IF A MAN ANSWERS *Capitol CL 15272*	24	6 wks
29 Nov 62	BABY FACE *London HLK 9624*	40	4 wks
25 Jul 63	EIGHTEEN YELLOW ROSES *Capitol CL 15306*	37	4 wks
13 Oct 66 ●	IF I WERE A CARPENTER *Atlantic 584 051*	9	12 wks
14 Apr 79	DREAM LOVER/MACK THE KNIFE (re-issue) *Lightning LIG 9017*	64	1 wk

* Bobby Darin Orchestra

DARLING BUDS UK, male/female vocal/instrumental group — 20 wks

8 Oct 88	BURST *Epic BLOND 1*	50	5 wks
7 Jan 89	HIT THE GROUND *CBS BLOND 2*	27	5 wks
25 Mar 89	LET'S GO ROUND THERE *CBS BLOND 3*	49	4 wks
22 Jul 89	YOU'VE GOT TO CHOOSE *CBS BLOND 4*	45	3 wks
2 Jun 90	TINY MACHINE *CBS BLOND 5*	60	2 wks
12 Sep 92	SURE THING *Epic 6582157*	71	1 wk

Guy DARRELL UK, male vocalist — 13 wks

| 18 Aug 73 | I'VE BEEN HURT *Santa Ponsa PNS 4* | 12 | 13 wks |

James DARREN US, male vocalist — 25 wks

11 Aug 60	BECAUSE THEY'RE YOUNG *Pye International 7N 25059*	29	7 wks
14 Dec 61	GOODBYE CRUEL WORLD *Pye International 7N 25116*	28	9 wks
29 Mar 62	HER ROYAL MAJESTY *Pye International 7N 25125*	36	13 wks
21 Jun 62	CONSCIENCE *Pye International 7N 25138*	30	6 wks

DARTS UK, male/female vocal/instrumental group — 117 wks

5 Nov 77 ●	DADDY COOL/THE GIRL CAN'T HELP IT *Magnet MAG 100*	6	13 wks
28 Jan 78 ●	COME BACK MY LOVE *Magnet MAG 110*	2	12 wks
6 May 78 ●	BOY FROM NEW YORK CITY *Magnet MAG 116*	2	13 wks
5 Aug 78 ●	IT'S RAINING *Magnet MAG 126*	2	11 wks
11 Nov 78	DON'T LET IT FADE AWAY *Magnet MAG 134*	18	11 wks
10 Feb 79 ●	GET IT *Magnet MAG 140*	10	9 wks
21 Jul 79 ●	DUKE OF EARL *Magnet MAG 147*	6	11 wks

20 Oct 79	CAN'T GET ENOUGH OF YOUR LOVE *Magnet MAG 156*	43	6 wks
1 Dec 79	REET PETITE *Magnet MAG 160*	51	7 wks
31 May 80	LET'S HANG ON *Magnet MAG 174*	11	14 wks
6 Sep 80	PEACHES *Magnet MAG 179*	66	3 wks
29 Nov 80	WHITE CHRISTMAS/SH-BOOM (LIFE COULD BE A DREAM) *Magnet MAG 184*	48	7 wks

N'Dea DAVENPORT – See BRAND NEW HEAVIES

Anne-Marie DAVID France, female vocalist — 9 wks

| 28 Apr 73 | WONDERFUL DREAM *Epic EPC 1446* | 13 | 9 wks |

F.R. DAVID France, male vocalist — 13 wks

| 2 Apr 83 ● | WORDS *Carrere CAR 248* | 2 | 12 wks |
| 18 Jun 83 | MUSIC *Carrere CAR 282* | 71 | 1 wk |

DAVID and JONATHAN UK, male vocal duo — 22 wks

| 13 Jan 66 | MICHELLE *Columbia DB 7800* | 11 | 6 wks |
| 7 Jul 66 ● | LOVERS OF THE WORLD UNITE *Columbia DB 7950* | 7 | 16 wks |

Jim DAVIDSON UK, male vocalist — 4 wks

| 27 Dec 80 | WHITE CHRISTMAS/TOO RISKY *Scratch SCR 001* | 52 | 4 wks |

Paul DAVIDSON Jamaica, male vocalist — 10 wks

| 27 Dec 75 ● | MIDNIGHT RIDER *Tropical ALO 56* | 10 | 10 wks |

Dave DAVIES UK, male vocalist — 17 wks

| 19 Jul 67 ● | DEATH OF A CLOWN *Pye 7N 17356* | 3 | 10 wks |
| 6 Dec 67 | SUSANNAH'S STILL ALIVE *Pye 7N 17429* | 20 | 7 wks |

Windsor DAVIES and Don ESTELLE UK, male vocal duo — 16 wks

| 17 May 75 ★ | WHISPERING GRASS *EMI 2290* | 1 | 12 wks |
| 25 Oct 75 | PAPER DOLL *EMI 2361* | 41 | 4 wks |

Billie DAVIS UK, female vocalist — 33 wks

30 Aug 62	WILL I WHAT *Parlophone R 4932 *	18	10 wks
7 Feb 63 ●	TELL HIM *Decca F 11572*	10	12 wks
30 May 63	HE'S THE ONE *Decca F 11658*	40	3 wks
9 Oct 68	I WANT YOU TO BE MY BABY *Decca F 12823*	33	8 wks

* Mike Sarne with Billie Davis

Billy DAVIS Jr. – See Marilyn McCOO and Billy DAVIS Jr.

Darlene DAVIS US, female vocalist — 5 wks

| 7 Feb 87 | I FOUND LOVE *Serious 7OUS 1* | 55 | 5 wks |

John DAVIS and the MONSTER ORCHESTRA US, male vocal/instrumental group — 2 wks

| 10 Feb 79 | AIN'T THAT ENOUGH FOR YOU *Miracle M 2* | 70 | 2 wks |

Mac DAVIS US, male vocalist — 22 wks

4 Nov 72	**BABY DON'T GET HOOKED ON ME** CBS 8250	29	6 wks
15 Nov 80	**IT'S HARD TO BE HUMBLE** Casablanca CAN 210	27	16 wks

Ruth DAVIS – See Bo KIRKLAND and Ruth DAVIS

Sammy DAVIS Jr. US, male vocalist — 37 wks

29 Jul 55	**SOMETHING'S GOTTA GIVE** Brunswick 05428	19	2 wks
19 Aug 55	**SOMETHING'S GOTTA GIVE (re-entry)** Brunswick 05428	11	5 wks
9 Sep 55 ●	**LOVE ME OR LEAVE ME** Brunswick 05428	8	6 wks
30 Sep 55	**THAT OLD BLACK MAGIC** Brunswick 05450	16	1 wk
7 Oct 55	**HEY THERE** Brunswick 05469	19	1 wk
4 Nov 55	**LOVE ME OR LEAVE ME (re-entry)** Brunswick 05428	18	2 wks
20 Apr 56	**IN A PERSIAN MARKET** Brunswick 05518	29	1 wk
28 Dec 56	**ALL OF YOU** Brunswick 05629	28	1 wk
16 Jun 60	**HAPPY TO MAKE YOUR ACQUAINTANCE** Brunswick 05830 *	46	1 wk
22 Mar 62	**WHAT KIND OF FOOL AM I?/GONNA BUILD A MOUNTAIN** Reprise R 20048	26	8 wks
13 Dec 62	**ME AND MY SHADOW** Reprise R 20128 **	20	7 wks
7 Feb 63	**ME AND MY SHADOW (re-entry)** Reprise R 20128 **	47	2 wks

* Sammy Davis Jr. and Carmen McRae ** Frank Sinatra and Sammy Davis Jr.

Skeeter DAVIS US, female vocalist — 13 wks

14 Mar 63	**END OF THE WORLD** RCA 1328	18	13 wks

Zelma DAVIS – See C & C MUSIC FACTORY/CLIVILLES & COLE

Spencer DAVIS GROUP
UK, male vocal/instrumental group — 71 wks

5 Nov 64	**I CAN'T STAND IT** Fontana TF 499	47	3 wks
25 Feb 65	**EVERY LITTLE BIT HURTS** Fontana TF 530	43	2 wks
18 Mar 65	**EVERY LITTLE BIT HURTS (re-entry)** Fontana TF 530	41	1 wk
10 Jun 65	**STRONG LOVE** Fontana TF 571	50	1 wk
24 Jun 65	**STRONG LOVE (re-entry)** Fontana TF 571	44	3 wks
2 Dec 65 ★	**KEEP ON RUNNING** Fontana TF 632	1	14 wks
24 Mar 66 ★	**SOMEBODY HELP ME** Fontana TF 679	1	10 wks
1 Sep 66	**WHEN I COME HOME** Fontana TF 739	12	9 wks
3 Nov 66 ●	**GIMME SOME LOVING** Fontana TF 762	2	12 wks
26 Jan 67 ●	**I'M A MAN** Fontana TF 785	9	7 wks
9 Aug 67	**TIME SELLER** Fontana TF 854	30	5 wks
10 Jan 68	**MR. SECOND CLASS** United Artists UP 1203	35	4 wks

DAVIS PINCKNEY PROJECT – See GO GO LORENZO and the DAVIS PINCKNEY PROJECT

DAWN US, male/female vocal group — 109 wks

16 Jan 71 ●	**CANDIDA** Bell 1118	9	11 wks
10 Apr 71 ★	**KNOCK THREE TIMES** Bell 1146	1	27 wks
31 Jul 71 ●	**WHAT ARE YOU DOING SUNDAY** Bell 1169 *	3	12 wks
10 Mar 73 ★	**TIE A YELLOW RIBBON ROUND THE OLD OAK TREE** Bell 1287 *	1	39 wks
4 Aug 73	**SAY, HAS ANYBODY SEEN MY SWEET GYPSY ROSE** Bell 1322 *	12	15 wks
5 Jan 74	**TIE A YELLOW RIBBON ROUND THE OLD OAK TREE (re-entry)** Bell 1287 *	41	1 wk
9 Mar 74	**WHO'S IN THE STRAWBERRY PATCH WITH SALLY** Bell 1343 **	37	4 wks

* Dawn featuring Tony Orlando ** Tony Orlando and Dawn

Julie DAWN – See Cyril STAPLETON

Bobby DAY US, male vocalist — 2 wks

7 Nov 58	**ROCKIN' ROBIN** London HL 8726	29	2 wks

Doris DAY US, female vocalist — 146 wks

14 Nov 52 ●	**SUGARBUSH** Columbia DB 3123 *	8	2 wks
21 Nov 52 ●	**MY LOVE AND DEVOTION** Columbia DB 3157	10	2 wks
5 Dec 52 ●	**SUGARBUSH (re-entry)** Columbia DB 3123 *	8	6 wks
3 Apr 53	**MA SAYS PA SAYS** Columbia DB 3242 **	12	1 wk
17 Apr 53	**FULL TIME JOB** Columbia DB 3242 **	11	1 wk
24 Jul 53	**LET'S WALK THATA-WAY** Philips PB 157 **	4	14 wks
2 Apr 54 ★	**SECRET LOVE** Philips PB 230	1	29 wks
27 Aug 54 ●	**BLACK HILLS OF DAKOTA** Philips PB 287	7	8 wks
1 Oct 54 ●	**IF I GIVE MY HEART TO YOU** Philips PB 325	4	11 wks
8 Apr 55 ●	**READY WILLING AND ABLE** Philips PB 402	7	9 wks
9 Sep 55	**LOVE ME OR LEAVE ME** Philips PB 479	20	1 wk
21 Oct 55	**I'LL NEVER STOP LOVING YOU** Philips PB 497	17	2 wks
25 Nov 55	**I'LL NEVER STOP LOVING YOU (re-entry)** Philips PB 497	19	1 wk
29 Jun 56 ★	**WHATEVER WILL BE WILL BE** Philips PB 586	1	22 wks
13 Jun 58	**A VERY PRECIOUS LOVE** Philips PB 799	16	11 wks
15 Aug 58	**EVERYBODY LOVES A LOVER** Philips PB 843	25	3 wks
26 Sep 58	**EVERYBODY LOVES A LOVER (re-entry)** Philips PB 843	27	1 wk
12 Mar 64 ●	**MOVE OVER DARLING** CBS AAG 183	8	16 wks
18 Apr 87	**MOVE OVER DARLING (re-issue)** CBS LEGS 1	45	6 wks

* Doris Day and Frankie Laine ** Doris Day and Johnnie Ray

Patti DAY US, female vocalist — 1 wk

9 Dec 89	**RIGHT BEFORE MY EYES** Debut DEBT 3080	69	1 wk

Taylor DAYNE US, female vocalist — 38 wks

23 Jan 88 ●	**TELL IT TO MY HEART** Arista 109616	3	13 wks
19 Mar 88 ●	**PROVE YOUR LOVE** Arista 109830	8	10 wks
11 Jun 88	**I'LL ALWAYS LOVE YOU** Arista 111536	41	7 wks
18 Nov 89	**WITH EVERY BEAT OF MY HEART** Arista 112760	53	2 wks
14 Apr 90	**I'LL BE YOUR SHELTER** Arista 112966	43	5 wks
4 Aug 90	**LOVE WILL LEAD YOU BACK** Arista 113277	69	1 wk

DAYTON US, male vocalist — 1 wk

10 Dec 83	**THE SOUND OF MUSIC** Capitol CL 318	75	1 wk

DAZZ BAND US, male vocal/instrumental group — 12 wks

3 Nov 84	**LET IT ALL BLOW** Motown TMG 1361	12	12 wks

D'BORA US, female vocalist — 1 wk

14 Sep 91	**DREAM ABOUT YOU** Polydor PO 161	75	1 wk

Nino DE ANGELO Germany, male vocalist — 5 wks

21 Jul 84	**GUARDIAN ANGEL** Carrere CAR 335	57	5 wks

Chris DE BURGH Ireland, male vocalist — 64 wks

23 Oct 82	**DON'T PAY THE FERRYMAN** A & M AMS 8256	48	5 wks
12 May 84	**HIGH ON EMOTION** A & M AM 190	44	5 wks
12 Jul 86 ★	**THE LADY IN RED** A & M AM 331	1	14 wks
20 Sep 86	**FATAL HESITATION** A & M AM 348	44	4 wks
13 Dec 86	**A SPACEMAN CAME TRAVELLING/THE BALLROOM OF ROMANCE** A & M AM 365	40	5 wks
21 Feb 87	**THE LADY IN RED (re-entry)** A & M AM 331	74	1 wk
12 Dec 87	**THE SIMPLE TRUTH (A CHILD IS BORN)** A & M AM 427	69	2 wks
2 Jan 88	**THE SIMPLE TRUTH (A CHILD IS BORN) (re-entry)** A & M AM 427	55	1 wk
29 Oct 88 ●	**MISSING YOU** A & M AM 474	3	12 wks
7 Jan 89	**TENDER HANDS** A & M AM 486	43	6 wks
14 Oct 89	**THIS WAITING HEART** A & M AM 528	59	3 wks

25 May 91	THE SIMPLE TRUTH (A CHILD IS BORN) (re-issue) *A & M RELF 1*	36	2 wks
11 Apr 92	SEPARATE TABLES *A & M AM 863*	30	4 wks

DE CASTRO SISTERS *US, female vocal group* — 1 wk

11 Feb 55	TEACH ME TONIGHT *London HL 8104*	20	1 wk

DE LA SOUL *US, male rap/sampling group* — 51 wks

8 Apr 89	ME MYSELF AND I *Big Life BLR 7*	22	8 wks
8 Jul 89	SAY NO GO *Big Life BLR 10*	18	7 wks
21 Oct 89	EYE KNOW *Big Life BLR 13*	14	7 wks
23 Dec 89 ●	THE MAGIC NUMBER/BUDDY *Big Life BLR 14*	7	8 wks
24 Mar 90	MAMA GAVE BIRTH TO THE SOUL CHILDREN *Gee Street GEE 26* *	14	7 wks
27 Apr 91 ●	RING RING RING (HA HA HEY) *Big Life BLR 42*	10	7 wks
3 Aug 91	A ROLLER SKATING JAM NAMED 'SATURDAYS' *Big Life BLR 55*	22	5 wks
23 Nov 91	KEEPIN' THE FAITH *Big Life BLR 64*	50	2 wks

* Queen Latifah + De La Soul

Buddy *only listed for first four weeks. See also Jungle Brothers.*

Lynsey DE PAUL *UK, female vocalist* — 54 wks

19 Aug 72 ●	SUGAR ME *MAM 81*	5	11 wks
2 Dec 72	GETTING A DRAG *MAM 88*	18	8 wks
27 Oct 73	WON'T SOMEBODY DANCE WITH ME *MAM 109*	14	7 wks
8 Jun 74	OOH I DO *Warner Bros. K 16401*	25	6 wks
2 Nov 74 ●	NO HONESTLY *Jet 747*	7	11 wks
22 Mar 75	MY MAN AND ME *Jet 750*	40	4 wks
26 Mar 77	ROCK BOTTOM *Polydor 2058 859* *	19	7 wks

* Lynsey De Paul and Mike Moran

Tullio DE PISCOPO *Italy, male vocalist* — 4 wks

28 Feb 87	STOP BAJON...PRIMAVERA *Greyhound GREY 9*	58	4 wks

Teri DE SARIO *US, female vocalist* — 5 wks

2 Sep 78	AIN'T NOTHIN' (GONNA KEEP ME FROM YOU) *Casablanca CAN 128*	52	5 wks

Stephanie DE SYKES *UK, female vocalist* — 17 wks

20 Jul 74 ●	BORN WITH A SMILE ON MY FACE *Bradley's BRAD 7409* *	2	10 wks
19 Apr 75	WE'LL FIND OUR DAY *Bradley's BRAD 7509*	17	7 wks

* Stephanie De Sykes with Rain

William DE VAUGHN *US, male vocalist* — 10 wks

6 Jul 74	BE THANKFUL FOR WHAT YOU'VE GOT *Chelsea 2005 002*	31	5 wks
20 Sep 80	BE THANKFUL FOR WHAT YOU'VE GOT *EMI 5101*	44	5 wks

EMI version of hit is a new recording.

DEACON BLUE *UK, male/female vocal/instrumental group* — 91 wks

23 Jan 88	DIGNITY *CBS DEAC 4*	31	8 wks
9 Apr 88	WHEN WILL YOU MAKE MY TELEPHONE RING *CBS DEAC 5*	34	7 wks
16 Jul 88	CHOCOLATE GIRL *CBS DEAC 6*	43	7 wks
15 Oct 88 ●	REAL GONE KID *CBS DEAC 7*	8	13 wks
4 Mar 89	WAGES DAY *CBS DEAC 8*	18	6 wks
20 May 89	FERGUS SINGS THE BLUES *CBS DEAC 9*	14	6 wks
16 Sep 89	LOVE AND REGRET *CBS DEAC 10*	28	5 wks
6 Jan 90	QUEEN OF THE NEW YEAR *CBS DEAC 11*	21	5 wks
25 Aug 90 ●	FOUR BACHARACH AND DAVID SONGS EP *CBS DEAC 12*	2	9 wks
25 May 91	YOUR SWAYING ARMS *Columbia 6568937*	23	4 wks
27 Jul 91 ●	TWIST AND SHOUT *Columbia 6573027*	10	9 wks
12 Oct 91	CLOSING TIME *Columbia 6575027*	42	3 wks
14 Dec 91	COVER FROM THE SKY *Columbia 6576737*	31	4 wks
28 Nov 92	YOUR TOWN *Columbia 6587867*	14†	5 wks

Tracks on Four Bacharach and David Songs EP: I'll Never Fall In Love Again/The Look Of Love/Message To Michael/Are You There (With Another Girl).

DEAD END KIDS *UK, male vocal/instrumental group* — 10 wks

26 Mar 77 ●	HAVE I THE RIGHT *CBS 4972*	6	10 wks

DEAD KENNEDYS *US, male vocal/instrumental group* — 9 wks

1 Nov 80	KILL THE POOR *Cherry Red CHERRY 16*	49	3 wks
30 May 81	TOO DRUNK TO FUCK *Cherry Red CHERRY 24*	36	6 wks

DEAD OR ALIVE *UK, male vocal/instrumental group* — 70 wks

24 Mar 84	THAT'S THE WAY (I LIKE IT) *Epic A 4271*	22	9 wks
1 Dec 84 ★	YOU SPIN ME ROUND (LIKE A RECORD) *Epic A 4861*	1	23 wks
20 Apr 85	LOVER COME BACK TO ME *Epic A 6086*	11	8 wks
29 Jun 85	IN TOO DEEP *Epic A 6360*	14	8 wks
21 Sep 85	MY HEART GOES BANG (GET ME TO THE DOCTOR) *Epic A 6571*	23	6 wks
20 Sep 86	BRAND NEW LOVER *Epic A 650075 7*	31	4 wks
10 Jan 87	SOMETHING IN MY HOUSE *Epic BURNS 1*	12	7 wks
4 Apr 87	HOOKED ON LOVE *Epic BURNS 2*	69	2 wks
3 Sep 88	TURN ROUND AND COUNT 2 TEN *Epic BURNS 4*	70	1 wk
22 Jul 89	COME HOME WITH ME BABY *Epic BURNS 5*	62	2 wks

Hazell DEAN *UK, female vocalist* — 71 wks

18 Feb 84	EVERGREEN/JEALOUS LOVE *Proto ENA 114*	63	3 wks
21 Apr 84 ●	SEARCHIN' (I GOTTA FIND A MAN) *Proto ENA 109*	6	15 wks
28 Jul 84 ●	WHATEVER I DO (WHEREVER I GO) *Proto ENA 119*	4	11 wks
3 Nov 84	BACK IN MY ARMS(ONCE AGAIN) *Proto ENA 122*	41	4 wks
2 Mar 85	NO FOOL (FOR LOVE) *Proto ENA 123*	41	5 wks
12 Oct 85	THEY SAY IT'S GONNA RAIN *Parlophone R 6107*	58	4 wks
2 Apr 88 ●	WHO'S LEAVING WHO *EMI EM 45*	4	11 wks
25 Jun 88	MAYBE (WE SHOULD CALL IT A DAY) *EMI EM 62*	15	6 wks
24 Sep 88	TURN IT INTO LOVE *EMI EM 71*	21	7 wks
26 Aug 89	LOVE PAINS *Lisson DOLE 12*	48	4 wks
23 Mar 91	BETTER OFF WITHOUT YOU *Lisson DOLE 19*	72	1 wk

Jimmy DEAN *US, male vocalist* — 17 wks

26 Oct 61 ●	BIG BAD JOHN *Philips PB 1187*	2	13 wks
8 Nov 62	LITTLE BLACK BOOK *CBS AAG 122*	33	4 wks

Letitia DEAN and Paul MEDFORD — 7 wks
UK, female/male vocal duo

25 Oct 86	SOMETHING OUTA NOTHING *BBC RESL 203*	12	7 wks

DeBARGE *US, male/female vocal group* — 17 wks

6 Apr 85 ●	RHYTHM OF THE NIGHT *Gordy TMG 1376*	4	14 wks
21 Sep 85	YOU WEAR IT WELL *Gordy ZB 40345* *	54	3 wks

* El DeBarge with Debarge

El DeBARGE US, male vocalist | 3 wks

28 Jun 86	WHO'S JOHNNY ('SHORT CIRCUIT' THEME) Gordy ELD 1	60	2 wks
31 Mar 90	SECRET GARDEN Qwest W 9992 *	67	1 wk

* Quincy Jones featuring Al B Sure, James Ingram, El DeBarge and Barry White
See also DeBarge.

Diana DECKER US, female vocalist | 10 wks

23 Oct 53 ●	POPPA PICCOLINO Columbia DB 3325	2	8 wks
8 Jan 54 ●	POPPA PICCOLINO (re-entry) Columbia DB 3325	5	2 wks

Dave DEE UK, male vocalist | 4 wks

14 Mar 70	MY WOMAN'S MAN Fontana TF 1074	42	4 wks

See also Dave Dee, Dozy, Beaky, Mick and Tich.

Dave DEE, DOZY, BEAKY, MICK and TICH UK, male vocal/instrumental group | 141 wks

23 Dec 65	YOU MAKE IT MOVE Fontana TF 630	26	8 wks
3 Mar 66 ●	HOLD TIGHT Fontana TF 671	4	17 wks
9 Jun 66 ●	HIDEAWAY Fontana TF 711	10	11 wks
15 Sep 66 ●	BEND IT Fontana TF 746	2	12 wks
8 Dec 66 ●	SAVE ME Fontana TF 775	4	10 wks
9 Mar 67	TOUCH ME TOUCH ME Fontana TF 798	13	9 wks
18 May 67 ●	OKAY! Fontana TF 830	4	11 wks
11 Oct 67 ●	ZABADAK! Fontana TF 873	3	14 wks
14 Feb 68 ★	LEGEND OF XANADU Fontana TF 903	1	12 wks
3 Jul 68 ●	LAST NIGHT IN SOHO Fontana TF 953	8	11 wks
2 Oct 68	WRECK OF THE ANTOINETTE Fontana TF 971	14	9 wks
5 Mar 69	DON JUAN Fontana TF 1000	23	9 wks
14 May 69	SNAKE IN THE GRASS Fontana TF 1020	23	8 wks

See also Dave Dee; D, B, M and T.

Jazzy DEE US, male vocalist | 5 wks

5 Mar 83	GET ON UP Laurie LRS 101	53	5 wks

Joey DEE and the STARLITERS US, male vocal/instrumental group | 8 wks

8 Feb 62	PEPPERMINT TWIST Columbia DB 4758	33	8 wks

Kiki DEE UK, female vocalist | 69 wks

10 Nov 73	AMOUREUSE Rocket PIG 4	13	13 wks
7 Sep 74	I GOT THE MUSIC IN ME Rocket PIG 12 *	19	8 wks
12 Apr 75	(YOU DONT KNOW) HOW GLAD I AM Rocket PIG 16 *	33	4 wks
3 Jul 76 ★	DON'T GO BREAKING MY HEART Rocket ROKN 512 **	1	14 wks
11 Sep 76	LOVING AND FREE/AMOUREUSE (re-issue) Rocket ROKN 515	13	8 wks
19 Feb 77	FIRST THING IN THE MORNING Rocket ROKN 520	32	5 wks
11 Jun 77	CHICAGO Rocket ROKN 526	28	4 wks
21 Feb 81	STAR Ariola ARO 251	13	10 wks
23 May 81	PERFECT TIMING Ariola ARO 257	66	3 wks

* Kiki Dee Band ** Elton John and Kiki Dee
On 18 Sep, 25 Sep and 2 Oct 1976, Loving And Free was listed by itself. Chicago was one side of a double sided chart entry, the other being Bite Your Lip (Get Up And Dance) by Elton John.

Nancy DEE – See BENELUX and Nancy DEE

DEEE-LITE US/Russia/Japan, male/female vocal/instrumental group | 28 wks

18 Aug 90 ●	GROOVE IS IN THE HEART/WHAT IS LOVE Elektra EKR 114	2	13 wks
24 Nov 90	POWER OF LOVE/DEEE-LITE THEME Elektra EKR 117	25	7 wks
23 Feb 91	HOW DO YOU SAY...LOVE/GROOVE IS IN THE HEART (re-mix) Elektra EKR 118	52	2 wks
27 Apr 91	GOOD BEAT/RIDING ON THROUGH Elektra EKR 122	53	3 wks
13 Jun 92	RUNAWAY Elektra EKR 148	45	3 wks

What Is Love only listed from 25 Aug 90.

Carol DEENE UK, female vocalist | 25 wks

26 Oct 61	SAD MOVIES HMV POP 922	44	3 wks
25 Jan 62	NORMAN HMV POP 973	24	8 wks
5 Jul 62	JOHNNY GET ANGRY HMV POP 1027	32	4 wks
23 Aug 62	SOME PEOPLE HMV POP 1058	25	10 wks

DEEP C UK, male/female vocal/instrumental group | 3 wks

19 Jan 91	AFRICAN REIGN M&G MAGS 4	75	1 wk
8 Jun 91	CHILL TO THE PANIC M&G MAGS 10	73	2 wks

DEEP FEELING UK, male vocal/instrumental group | 5 wks

25 Apr 70	DO YOU LOVE ME Page One POF 165	45	1 wk
9 May 70	DO YOU LOVE ME (re-entry) Page One POF 165	34	4 wks

DEEP PURPLE UK, male vocal/instrumental group | 84 wks

15 Aug 70 ●	BLACK NIGHT Harvest HAR 5020	2	21 wks
27 Feb 71 ●	STRANGE KIND OF WOMAN Harvest HAR 5033	8	12 wks
13 Nov 71	FIREBALL Harvest HAR 5045	15	13 wks
1 Apr 72	NEVER BEFORE Purple PUR 102	35	6 wks
16 Apr 77	SMOKE ON THE WATER Purple PUR 132	21	7 wks
15 Oct 77	NEW LIVE AND RARE EP Purple PUR 135	31	4 wks
7 Oct 78	NEW LIVE AND RARE II EP Purple PUR 137	45	3 wks
2 Aug 80	BLACK NIGHT (re-issue) Harvest HAR 5210	43	6 wks
1 Nov 80	NEW LIVE AND RARE VOLUME 3 EP Harvest SHEP 101	48	3 wks
26 Jan 85	PERFECT STRANGERS Polydor POSP 719	48	3 wks
15 Jun 85	KNOCKING AT YOUR BACK DOOR/PERFECT STRANGERS Polydor POSP 749	68	1 wk
18 Jun 88	HUSH Polydor PO 4	62	2 wks
20 Oct 90	KING OF DREAMS RCA PB 49247	70	1 wk
2 Mar 91	LOVE CONQUERS ALL RCA PB 49225	57	2 wks

Tracks on New Live And Rare EP: Black Night (Live)/Painted Horse/When A Blind Man Cries. New Live And Rare II EP: Burn (Edited Version)/Coronarias Redig/Mistreated (Live)/Rock Me Baby. New Live And Rare Volume 3 EP: Smoke On The Water/Bird Has Flown/Grabsplatter.

DEEP RIVER BOYS US, male vocal group | 1 wk

7 Dec 56	THAT'S RIGHT HMV POP 263	29	1 wk

Rick DEES and his CAST OF IDIOTS US, male vocalist with male/female vocal/instrumental group | 9 wks

18 Sep 76 ●	DISCO DUCK (PART ONE) RSO 2090 204	6	9 wks

DEF LEPPARD UK, male vocal/instrumental group | 72 wks

17 Nov 79	WASTED Vertigo 6059 247	61	3 wks

23 Feb 80	HELLO AMERICA *Vertigo LEPP 1*................................	45	4 wks
5 Feb 83	PHOTOGRAPH *Vertigo VER 5*................................	66	3 wks
27 Aug 83	ROCK OF AGES *Vertigo VER 6*................................	41	4 wks
1 Aug 87 ●	ANIMAL *Bludgeon Riffola LEP 1*................................	6	9 wks
19 Sep 87	POUR SOME SUGAR ON ME *Bludgeon Riffola LEP 2*.........18		6 wks
28 Nov 87	HYSTERIA *Bludgeon Riffola LEP 3*................................	26	5 wks
9 Jan 88	HYSTERIA (re-entry) *Bludgeon Riffola LEP 3*.................	74	1 wk
9 Apr 88	ARMAGEDDON IT *Bludgeon Riffola LEP 4*.....................	20	5 wks
16 Jul 88	LOVE BITES *Bludgeon Riffola LEP 5*.............................	11	8 wks
11 Feb 89	ROCKET *Bludgeon Riffola LEP 6*.................................	15	7 wks
28 Mar 92 ●	LET'S GET ROCKED *Bludgeon Riffola DEF 7*.................	2	7 wks
27 Jun 92	MAKE LOVE LIKE A MAN *Bludgeon Riffola LEP 7*.........12		5 wks
12 Sep 92	HAVE YOU EVER NEEDED SOMEONE SO BAD		
	Bludgeon Riffola LEP 8................................	16	5 wks

DEFINITION OF SOUND *UK, male rap duo*   **20 wks**

9 Mar 91	WEAR YOUR LOVE LIKE HEAVEN *Circa YR 61* 17		9 wks
1 Jun 91	NOW IS TOMORROW *Circa YR 66*...............................	48	4 wks
8 Feb 92	MOIRA JANE'S CAFE *Circa YR 80*..............................	34	4 wks
19 Sep 92	WHAT ARE YOU UNDER *Circa YR 95*.........................	68	1 wk
14 Nov 92	CAN I GET OVER *Circa YR 97*...................................	61	2 wks

DEGREES OF MOTION featuring BITI   **9 wks**
US, female vocal group

25 Apr 92	DO YOU WANT IT RIGHT NOW *ffrr F 184* 31		5 wks
18 Jul 92	SHINE ON *ffrr F 192* *................................	43	3 wks
7 Nov 92	SOUL FREEDOM - FREE YOUR SOUL *ffrr FX 201*......64		1 wk

* Degrees Of Motion featuring Biti with Kit West

DEJA *US, male/female vocal duo*   **1 wk**

29 Aug 87	SERIOUS *10 TEN 132*................................	75	1 wk

Desmond DEKKER and the ACES   **71 wks**
Jamaica, male vocal/instrumental group

12 Jul 67	007 *Pyramid PYR 6004*................................	14	11 wks
19 Mar 69 ★	ISRAELITES *Pyramid PYR 6058*...............................	1	14 wks
25 Jun 69 ●	IT MIEK *Pyramid PYR 6068*................................	7	11 wks
2 Jul 69	ISRAELITES (re-entry) *Pyramid PYR 6058*..................45		1 wk
10 Jan 70	PICKNEY GAL *Pyramid PYR 6078*.............................	42	3 wks
22 Aug 70	YOU CAN GET IT IF YOU REALLY WANT		
	Trojan TR 7777 *................................	2	15 wks
10 May 75 ●	ISRAELITES (re-issue) *Cactus CT 57*.......................	10	9 wks
30 Aug 75	SING A LITTLE SONG *Cactus CT 73*.........................	16	7 wks

* Desmond Dekker

DEL AMITRI *UK, male vocal/instrumental group*   **42 wks**

19 Aug 89	KISS THIS THING GOODBYE *A & M AM 515*...............59		2 wks
13 Jan 90	NOTHING EVER HAPPENS *A & M AM 536*.................	11	9 wks
24 Mar 90	KISS THIS THING GOODBYE (re-issue)		
	A & M AM 551................................	43	4 wks
16 Jun 90	MOVE AWAY JIMMY BLUE *A & M AM 555*...............	36	6 wks
3 Nov 90	SPIT IN THE RAIN *A & M AM 589*.............................	21	6 wks
9 May 92	ALWAYS THE LAST TO KNOW *A & M AM 870*...........13		7 wks
11 Jul 92	BE MY DOWNFALL *A & M AM 884*	30	4 wks
12 Sep 92	JUST LIKE A MAN *A & M AM 0057*	25	4 wks

DELAGE *UK, female vocal group*   **2 wks**

15 Dec 90	ROCK THE BOAT *PWL/Polydor PO 113*	63	2 wks

DELANEY and BONNIE and FRIENDS featuring Eric CLAPTON – *See Eric CLAPTON*

British Hit Singles Part One: Alphabetically by Artist
Date of chart entry/Title & catalogue no./Peak position reached/Weeks on chart
★ Number one   ● Top Ten   † still on chart at 31 Dec 1992
* = credited to act billed in footnote

DELEGATION *UK, male vocal/instrumental group*   **7 wks**

23 Apr 77	WHERE IS THE LOVE (WE USED TO KNOW)		
	State STAT 40................................	22	6 wks
20 Aug 77	YOU'VE BEEN DOING ME WRONG *State STAT 55*........49		1 wk

DELFONICS *US, male vocal group*   **23 wks**

10 Apr 71	DIDN'T I (BLOW YOUR MIND THIS TIME)		
	Bell 1099................................	43	1 wk
24 Apr 71	DIDN'T I (BLOW YOUR MIND THIS TIME)		
	(re-entry) *Bell 1099*................................	22	8 wks
10 Jul 71	LA-LA MEANS I LOVE YOU *Bell 1165*.....................	19	10 wks
16 Oct 71	READY OR NOT HERE I COME *Bell 1175*	41	4 wks

'DELIVERANCE' SOUNDTRACK   **7 wks**
US, male instrumental duo, Eric Weissberg - banjo and Steve Mandell - guitar

31 Mar 73	DUELLING BANJOS *Warner Bros. K 16223*......................	17	7 wks

DELLS *US, male vocal group*   **9 wks**

16 Jul 69	I CAN SING A RAINBOW - LOVE IS BLUE		
	(MEDLEY) *Chess CRS 8099*................................	15	9 wks

DELRONS – *See REPARATA and the DELRONS*

DELUXE *US, female vocalist*   **1 wk**

18 Mar 89	JUST A LITTLE MORE *Unyque UNQ 5* 74		1 wk

Terry DENE *UK, male vocalist*   **20 wks**

7 Jun 57	A WHITE SPORT COAT *Decca F 10895*.....................	18	6 wks
19 Jul 57	START MOVIN' *Decca F 10914*................................	15	8 wks
26 Jul 57	A WHITE SPORT COAT (re-entry) *Decca F 10895*..........30		1 wk
16 May 58	STAIRWAY OF LOVE *Decca F 11016*	16	5 wks

Cathy DENNIS *UK, female vocalist*   **55 wks**

21 Oct 89	C'MON AND GET MY LOVE *ffrr F 117* * 15		10 wks
7 Apr 90	THAT'S THE WAY OF THE WORLD *ffrr F 132* * 48		3 wks
4 May 91 ●	TOUCH ME (ALL NIGHT LONG) *Polydor CATH 3* 5		10 wks
20 Jul 91	JUST ANOTHER DREAM *Polydor CATH 2* 13		7 wks
5 Oct 91	TOO MANY WALLS *Polydor CATH 4* 17		7 wks
7 Dec 91	EVERYBODY MOVE *Polydor CATH 5* 25		8 wks
29 Aug 92	YOU LIED TO ME *Polydor CATH 6* 34		4 wks
21 Nov 92	IRRESISTIBLE *Polydor CATH 7* 24		6 wks

* D Mob featuring Cathy Dennis

Jackie DENNIS *UK, male vocalist*   **10 wks**

14 Mar 58 ●	LA DEE DAH *Decca F 10992*................................	4	9 wks
27 Jun 58	PURPLE PEOPLE EATER *Decca F 11033*.....................29		1 wk

Stefan DENNIS *Australia, male vocalist*   **8 wks**

6 May 89	DON'T IT MAKE YOU FEEL GOOD		
	Sublime LIME 105................................	16	7 wks
7 Oct 89	THIS LOVE AFFAIR *Sublime LIME 113* 67		1 wk

DENNISONS UK, male vocal/instrumental group — 13 wks

15 Aug 63	BE MY GIRL *Decca F 11691* 46	6 wks
7 May 64	WALKIN' THE DOG *Decca F 11880* 36	7 wks

Richard DENTON and Martin COOK — 7 wks
UK, male orchestra leaders/instrumental duo, guitar and keyboards

15 Apr 78	THEME FROM 'THE HONG KONG BEAT' *BBC RESL 52* 25	7 wks

John DENVER US, male vocalist — 22 wks

17 Aug 74 ★	ANNIE'S SONG *RCA APBO 0295* 1	13 wks
12 Dec 81	PERHAPS LOVE *CBS A 1905* * 46	9 wks

* Placido Domingo with John Denver

Karl DENVER UK, male vocalist — 127 wks

22 Jun 61 ●	MARCHETA *Decca F 11360* 8	20 wks
19 Oct 61 ●	MEXICALI ROSE *Decca F 11395* 8	11 wks
25 Jan 62 ●	WIMOWEH *Decca F 11420* 4	17 wks
22 Feb 62 ●	NEVER GOODBYE *Decca F 11431* 9	18 wks
7 Jun 62	A LITTLE LOVE A LITTLE KISS *Decca F 11470* 19	10 wks
20 Sep 62	BLUE WEEKEND *Decca F 11505* 33	5 wks
21 Mar 63	CAN YOU FORGIVE ME *Decca F 11608* 32	8 wks
13 Jun 63	INDIAN LOVE CALL *Decca F 11674* 32	8 wks
22 Aug 63	STILL *Decca F 11720* 13	15 wks
5 Mar 64	MY WORLD OF BLUE *Decca F 11828* 29	6 wks
4 Jun 64	LOVE ME WITH ALL YOUR HEART *Decca F 11905* 37	6 wks
9 Jun 90	LAZYITIS - ONE ARMED BOXER *Factory FAC 2227* * 46	3 wks

* Happy Mondays and Karl Denver

DEODATO US, male multi-instrumentalist — 9 wks

5 May 73 ●	ALSO SPRACH ZARATHUSTRA (2001) *Creed Taylor CTI 4000* 7	9 wks

DEPARTMENT S UK, male vocal/instrumental group — 13 wks

4 Apr 81	IS VIC THERE? *Demon D 1003* 22	10 wks
11 Jul 81	GOING LEFT RIGHT *Stiff BUY 118* 55	3 wks

DEPECHE MODE UK, male vocal/instrumental group — 189 wks

4 Apr 81	DREAMING OF ME *Mute MUTE 013* 57	4 wks
13 Jun 81	NEW LIFE *Mute MUTE 014* 11	15 wks
19 Sep 81 ●	JUST CAN'T GET ENOUGH *Mute MUTE 016* 8	10 wks
13 Feb 82 ●	SEE YOU *Mute MUTE 018* 6	10 wks
8 May 82	THE MEANING OF LOVE *Mute MUTE 022* 12	8 wks
28 Aug 82	LEAVE IN SILENCE *Mute BONG 1* 18	10 wks
12 Feb 83	GET THE BALANCE RIGHT *Mute BONG 2* 13	8 wks
23 Jul 83 ●	EVERYTHING COUNTS *Mute 7BONG 3* 6	11 wks
1 Oct 83	LOVE IN ITSELF.2 *Mute 7BONG 4* 21	7 wks
24 Mar 84 ●	PEOPLE ARE PEOPLE *Mute 7BONG 5* 4	10 wks
1 Sep 84 ●	MASTER AND SERVANT *Mute 7BONG 6* 9	9 wks
10 Nov 84	SOMEBODY/BLASPHEMOUS RUMOURS *Mute 7BONG 7* 16	6 wks
11 May 85	SHAKE THE DISEASE *Mute BONG 8* 18	9 wks
28 Sep 85	IT'S CALLED A HEART *Mute BONG 9* 18	4 wks
22 Feb 86	STRIPPED *Mute BONG 10* 15	5 wks
26 Apr 86	A QUESTION OF LUST *Mute BONG 11* 28	5 wks
23 Aug 86	A QUESTION OF TIME *Mute BONG 12* 17	6 wks
9 May 87	STRANGELOVE *Mute BONG 13* 16	5 wks
5 Sep 87	NEVER LET ME DOWN AGAIN *Mute BONG 14* 22	5 wks
9 Jan 88	BEHIND THE WHEEL *Mute BONG 15* 21	5 wks
28 May 88	LITTLE 15 (IMPORT) *Mute LITTLE 15* 60	2 wks
25 Feb 89	EVERYTHING COUNTS *Mute BONG 16* 22	7 wks
9 Sep 89	PERSONAL JESUS *Mute BONG 17* 13	8 wks
17 Feb 90 ●	ENJOY THE SILENCE *Mute BONG 18* 6	9 wks
19 May 90	POLICY OF TRUTH *Mute BONG 19* 16	6 wks
29 Sep 90	WORLD IN MY EYES *Mute BONG 20* 17	6 wks

BONG 16 is a live version of BONG 3.

DEREK and the DOMINOES – *See Eric CLAPTON*

DESIRELESS France, female vocalist — 19 wks

31 Oct 87	VOYAGE VOYAGE *CBS DESI 1* 53	6 wks
14 May 88 ●	VOYAGE VOYAGE (re-mix) *CBS DESI 2* 5	13 wks

DESIYA featuring Melissa YIANNAKOU — 1 wk
UK, male/female vocal/instrumental duo

1 Feb 92	COMIN' ON STRONG *Blackmarket 12MKT 2* 74	1 wk

DESKEE UK, male instrumentalist — 3 wks

3 Feb 90	LET THERE BE HOUSE *Big One VBIG 19* 52	2 wks
8 Sep 90	DANCE, DANCE *Big One VBIG 22* 74	1 wk

DES'REE UK, female vocalist — 18 wks

31 Aug 91	FEEL SO HIGH *Dusted Sound 6573667* 51	5 wks
11 May 92	FEEL SO HIGH (re-issue) *Dusted Sound 6576897* 13	7 wks
21 Mar 92	MIND ADVENTURES *Dusted Sound 6578637* 43	3 wks
27 Jun 92	WHY SHOULD I LOVE YOU *Sony S2 6580917* 44	3 wks

DESTRY – *See ZOO EXPERIENCE featuring DESTRY*

DETROIT EMERALDS US, male vocal group — 44 wks

10 Feb 73 ●	FEEL THE NEED IN ME *Janus 6146 020* 4	15 wks
5 May 73	YOU WANT IT YOU GOT IT *Westbound 6146 103* 12	9 wks
11 Aug 73	I THINK OF YOU *Westbound 6146 104* 27	9 wks
18 Jun 77	FEEL THE NEED IN ME *Atlantic K 10945* 12	11 wks

The second Feel The Need In Me was a re-recording.

DETROIT SPINNERS US, male vocal group — 89 wks

14 Nov 70	IT'S A SHAME *Tamla Motown TMG 755* * 20	11 wks
21 Apr 73	COULD IT BE I'M FALLING IN LOVE *Atlantic K 10283* 11	11 wks
29 Sep 73 ●	GHETTO CHILD *Atlantic K 10359* 7	10 wks
19 Oct 74	THEN CAME YOU *Atlantic K 10495* ** 29	6 wks
11 Sep 76	THE RUBBERBAND MAN *Atlantic K 10807* 16	11 wks
29 Jan 77	WAKE UP SUSAN *Atlantic K 10799* 29	6 wks
7 May 77	COULD IT BE I'M FALLING IN LOVE EP *Atlantic K 10935* 32	3 wks
23 Feb 80 ★	WORKING MY WAY BACK TO YOU - FORGIVE ME GIRL - (MEDLEY) *Atlantic K 11432* 1	14 wks
10 May 80	BODY LANGUAGE *Atlantic K 11392* 40	7 wks
28 Jun 80 ●	CUPID - I'VE LOVED YOU FOR A LONG TIME (MEDLEY) *Atlantic K 11498* 4	10 wks

* Motown Spinners ** Dionne Warwicke and the Detroit Spinners
Group is known simply as the Spinners in the US. Tracks on Could It Be I'm Falling In Love *EP:* Could It Be I'm Falling In Love/You're Throwing A Good Love Away/Games People Play/Lazy Susan.

DETROIT WHEELS – *See Mitch RYDER and the DETROIT WHEELS*

Sidney DEVINE UK, male vocalist — 1 wk

1 Apr 78	SCOTLAND FOREVER *Philips SCOT 1* 48	1 wk

DEVO *US, male vocal/instrumental group* — **23 wks**

22 Apr 78	**(I CAN'T ME GET NO) SATISFACTION** *Stiff BOY 1*......**41**	8 wks
13 May 78	**JOCKO HOMO** *Stiff DEV 1*..........**62**	3 wks
12 Aug 78	**BE STIFF** *Stiff BOY 2*..........**71**	1 wk
2 Sep 78	**COME BACK JONEE** *Virgin VS 223*..........**60**	4 wks
22 Nov 80	**WHIP IT** *Virgin VS 383*..........**51**	7 wks

Sheila B. DEVOTION *France, female vocalist* — **33 wks**

11 Mar 78	**SINGIN' IN THE RAIN** PART 1 *Carrere EMI 2751*..........**11**	13 wks
22 Jul 78	**YOU LIGHT MY FIRE** *Carrere EMI 2828*..........**44**	6 wks
24 Nov 79	**SPACER** *Carrere CAR 128* *..........**18**	14 wks

* Sheila and B. Devotion

DEVOTIONS – *See BELLE and the DEVOTIONS*

Howard DEVOTO – *See BUZZCOCKS*

DEXY'S MIDNIGHT RUNNERS — **93 wks**
UK, male vocal/instrumental group

19 Jan 80	**DANCE STANCE** *Oddball Productions R 6028*..........**40**	6 wks
22 Mar 80 ★	**GENO** *Late Night Feelings R 6033*..........**1**	14 wks
12 Jul 80 ●	**THERE THERE MY DEAR** *Late Night Feelings R 6038*..........**7**	9 wks
21 Mar 81	**PLAN B** *Parlophone R 6046*..........**58**	2 wks
11 Jul 81	**SHOW ME** *Mercury DEXYS 6*..........**16**	9 wks
20 Mar 82	**THE CELTIC SOUL BROTHERS** *Mercury DEXYS 8* * **45**	4 wks
3 Jul 82 ★	**COME ON EILEEN** *Mercury DEXYS 9* *....**1**	17 wks
2 Oct 82 ●	**JACKIE WILSON SAID** *Mercury DEXYS 10* **..........**5**	7 wks
4 Dec 82	**LET'S GET THIS STRAIGHT (FROM THE START)/OLD** *Mercury DEXYS 11* **..........**17**	9 wks
2 Apr 83	**THE CELTIC SOUL BROTHERS** *Mercury DEXYS 12* **..........**20**	6 wks
22 Nov 86	**BECAUSE OF YOU** *Mercury BRUSH 1*..........**13**	10 wks

* Dexy's Midnight Runners with the Emerald Express ** Kevin Rowland and Dexy's Midnight Runners
DEXYS 12 is a different version from DEXYS 8.

Jim DIAMOND *UK, male vocalist* — **30 wks**

3 Nov 84 ★	**I SHOULD HAVE KNOWN BETTER** *A & M AM 220*..........**1**	13 wks
2 Feb 85	**I SLEEP ALONE AT NIGHT** *A & M AM 229*..........**72**	1 wk
18 May 85	**REMEMBER I LOVE YOU** *A & M AM 247*..........**42**	5 wks
22 Feb 86 ●	**HI HO SILVER** *A & M AM 296*..........**5**	11 wks

Neil DIAMOND *US, male vocalist* — **121 wks**

7 Nov 70 ●	**CRACKLIN' ROSIE** *Uni UN 529*..........**3**	17 wks
20 Feb 71 ●	**SWEET CAROLINE** *Uni UN 531*..........**8**	11 wks
8 May 71 ●	**I AM . . . I SAID** *Uni UN 532*..........**4**	12 wks
13 May 72	**SONG SUNG BLUE** *Uni UN 538*..........**14**	13 wks
14 Aug 76	**IF YOU KNOW WHAT I MEAN** *CBS 4398*..........**35**	4 wks
23 Oct 76	**BEAUTIFUL NOISE** *CBS 4601*..........**13**	9 wks
24 Dec 77	**DESIREE** *CBS 5869*..........**39**	6 wks
25 Nov 78 ●	**YOU DON'T BRING ME FLOWERS** *CBS 6803* *..........**5**	12 wks
3 Mar 79	**FOREVER IN BLUE JEANS** *CBS 7047*..........**16**	12 wks
15 Nov 80	**LOVE ON THE ROCKS** *Capitol CL 16173*..........**17**	12 wks
14 Feb 81	**HELLO AGAIN** *Capitol CL 16176*..........**51**	4 wks
20 Nov 82	**HEARTLIGHT** *CBS A 2814*..........**47**	7 wks
21 Nov 92	**MORNING HAS BROKEN** *Columbia 6588267*..........**36**	2 wks

* Barbra and Neil

Gregg DIAMOND BIONIC BOOGIE — **3 wks**
US, male/female vocal group

20 Jan 79	**CREAM (ALWAYS RISES TO THE TOP)** *Polydor POSP 18*..........**61**	3 wks

DIAMOND HEAD *UK, male vocal/instrumental group* — **2 wks**

11 Sep 82	**IN THE HEAT OF THE NIGHT** *MCA DHM 102*..........**67**	2 wks

DIAMONDS *Canada, male vocal group* — **17 wks**

31 May 57 ●	**LITTLE DARLIN'** *Mercury MT 148*..........**3**	17 wks

DICK and DEEDEE *US, male/female vocal duo* — **3 wks**

26 Oct 61	**THE MOUNTAIN'S HIGH** *London HLG 9408*..........**37**	3 wks

Charles DICKENS *UK, male vocalist* — **8 wks**

1 Jul 65	**THAT'S THE WAY LOVE GOES** *Pye 7N 15887*..........**37**	8 wks

Gwen DICKEY *US, female vocalist* — **2 wks**

27 Jan 90	**CAR WASH** *Swanyard SYR 7*..........**72**	2 wks

Neville DICKIE *UK, male instrumentalist - piano* — **10 wks**

25 Oct 69	**ROBIN'S RETURN** *Major Minor MM 644*..........**33**	7 wks
20 Dec 69	**ROBIN'S RETURN (re-entry)** *Major Minor MM 644*..........**43**	3 wks

DICKIES *US, male vocal/instrumental group* — **28 wks**

16 Dec 78	**SILENT NIGHT** *A & M AMS 7403*..........**47**	4 wks
21 Apr 79 ●	**BANANA SPLITS (TRA LA LA SONG)** *A & M AMS 7431*..........**7**	8 wks
21 Jul 79	**PARANOID** *A & M AMS 7368*..........**45**	6 wks
15 Sep 79	**NIGHTS IN WHITE SATIN** *A & M AMS 7469*..........**39**	4 wks
16 Feb 80	**FAN MAIL** *A & M AMS 7504*..........**57**	3 wks
19 Jul 80	**GIGANTOR** *A & M AMS 7544*..........**72**	2 wks

Bruce DICKINSON *UK, male vocalist* — **17 wks**

28 Apr 90	**TATTOOED MILLIONAIRE** *EMI EM 138*..........**18**	5 wks
23 Jun 90	**ALL THE YOUNG DUDES** *EMI EM 142*..........**23**	5 wks
25 Aug 90	**DIVE! DIVE! DIVE!** *EMI EM 151*..........**45**	2 wks
4 Apr 92 ●	**(I WANT TO BE) ELECTED** *London LON 319* *..........**9**	5 wks

* Mr Bean and Smear Campaign featuring Bruce Dickinson

Barbara DICKSON *UK, female vocalist* — **49 wks**

17 Jan 76 ●	**ANSWER ME** *RSO 2090 174*..........**9**	7 wks
26 Feb 77	**ANOTHER SUITCASE IN ANOTHER HALL** *MCA 266*..........**18**	7 wks
19 Jan 80	**CARAVAN SONG** *Epic EPC 8103*..........**41**	7 wks
15 Mar 80	**JANUARY FEBRUARY** *Epic EPC 8115*..........**11**	10 wks
14 Jun 80	**IN THE NIGHT** *Epic EPC 8593*..........**48**	2 wks
5 Jan 85 ★	**I KNOW HIM SO WELL** *RCA CHESS 3* *..........**1**	16 wks

* Elaine Paige and Barbara Dickson

DICTATORS *US, male vocal/instrumental group* — **2 wks**

17 Sep 77	**SEARCH AND DESTROY** *Asylum K 13091*..........**49**	1 wk
1 Oct 77	**SEARCH AND DESTROY (re-entry)** *Asylum K 13091*..........**50**	1 wk

Bo DIDDLEY *US, male vocalist/instrumentalist - guitar* — **10 wks**

10 Oct 63	**PRETTY THING** *Pye International 7N 25217*..........**34**	6 wks
18 Mar 65	**HEY GOOD LOOKIN'** *Chess 8000*..........**39**	4 wks

DIESEL PARK WEST *UK, male vocal/instrumental group* **15 wks**

4 Feb 89	**ALL THE MYTHS ON SUNDAY** *Food FOOD 17* **66**	2 wks
1 Apr 89	**LIKE PRINCES DO** *Food FOOD 19* **58**	3 wks
5 Aug 89	**WHEN THE HOODOO COMES** *Food FOOD 20* **62**	2 wks
18 Jan 92	**FALL TO LOVE** *Food FOOD 35* **48**	3 wks
21 Mar 92	**BOY ON TOP OF THE NEWS** *Food FOOD 36* **58**	2 wks
5 Sep 92	**GOD ONLY KNOWS** *Food FOOD 39* **57**	3 wks

See also Various Artists (EPs and LPs) - The Food Christmas EP.

DIFFORD and TILBROOK **2 wks**
UK, male vocal/instrumental duo

30 Jun 84	**LOVE'S CRASHING WAVES** *A & M AM 193* **57**	2 wks

DIGITAL DREAM BABY **4 wks**
UK, male vocalist - Peter Auty

14 Dec 91	**WALKING IN THE AIR** *Columbia 6576067* **49**	4 wks

Hit is a dance re-mix of Walking in the Air by Peter Auty.

DIGITAL EXCITATION **2 wks**
Belgium, male producer - Frank De Wulf

29 Feb 92	**PURE PLEASURE** *R&S RSUK 10* **37**	2 wks

DIGITAL ORGASM **14 wks**
Belgium, male/female vocal/instrumental group

7 Dec 91	**RUNNING OUT OF TIME** *Dead Dead Good GOOD 009* **16**	9 wks
18 Apr 92	**STARTOUCHERS** *DDG International GOOD 13* **31**	3 wks
25 Jul 92	**MOOG ERUPTION** *DDG International GOOD 17* **62**	2 wks

DIGITAL UNDERGROUND *US, male vocal group* **4 wks**

16 Mar 91	**SAME SONG** *Big Life BLR 40* **52**	4 wks

Paolo DINI – *See FPI PROJECT*

Mark DINNING *US, male vocalist* **4 wks**

10 Mar 60	**TEEN ANGEL** *MGM 1053* **37**	3 wks
7 Apr 60	**TEEN ANGEL (re-entry)** *MGM 1053* **42**	1 wk

DINOSAUR Jr *US, male vocal/instrumental group* **3 wks**

2 Feb 91	**THE WAGON** *blanco y negro NEG 48* **49**	2 wks
14 Nov 92	**GET ME** *blanco y negro NEG 60* **44**	1 wk

DINOSAURS – *See Terry DACTYL and the DINOSAURS*

DIO *UK/US, male vocal/instrumental group* **22 wks**

20 Aug 83	**HOLY DIVER** *Vertigo DIO 1* **72**	2 wks
29 Oct 83	**RAINBOW IN THE DARK** *Vertigo DIO 2* **46**	3 wks
11 Aug 84	**WE ROCK** *Vertigo DIO 3* **42**	3 wks
29 Sep 84	**MYSTERY** *Vertigo DIO 4* **34**	4 wks
10 Aug 85	**ROCK 'N' ROLL CHILDREN** *Vertigo DIO 5* **26**	6 wks
2 Nov 85	**HUNGRY FOR HEAVEN** *Vertigo DIO 6* **72**	1 wk
17 May 86	**HUNGRY FOR HEAVEN (re-issue)** *Vertigo DIO 7* **56**	2 wks
1 Aug 87	**I COULD HAVE BEEN A DREAMER** *Vertigo DIO 8* **69**	1 wk

DION *US, male vocalist* **35 wks**

26 Jun 59	**A TEENAGER IN LOVE** *London HLU 8874* * **28**	2 wks
19 Jan 61	**LONELY TEENAGER** *Top Rank JAR 521* **47**	1 wk
2 Nov 61	**RUNAROUND SUE** *Top Rank JAR 586* **11**	9 wks
15 Feb 62 ●	**THE WANDERER** *HMV POP 971* **10**	12 wks
22 May 76	**THE WANDERER (re-issue)** *Philips 6146 700* **16**	9 wks
19 May 89	**KING OF THE NEW YORK STREET** *Arista 112556* **74**	2 wks

* Dion and the Belmonts

Celine DION *Canada, female vocalist* **12 wks**

16 May 92 ●	**BEAUTY AND THE BEAST** *Epic 6576607* * **9**	7 wks
4 Jul 92	**IF YOU ASKED ME TO** *Epic 6581927* **60**	2 wks
14 Nov 92	**LOVE CAN MOVE MOUNTAINS** *Epic 6587787* **46**	2 wks
26 Dec 92	**IF YOU ASKED ME TO (re-entry)** *Epic 6581927* ....**71†**	1 wk

* Celine Dion and Peabo Bryson

DIONNE *Canada, female vocalist* **2 wks**

23 Sep 89	**COME GET MY LOVIN'** *Citybeat CBC 745* **69**	2 wks

DIRE STRAITS *UK, male vocal/instrumental group* **116 wks**

10 Mar 79 ●	**SULTANS OF SWING** *Vertigo 6059 206* **8**	11 wks
28 Jul 79	**LADY WRITER** *Vertigo 6059 230* **51**	6 wks
17 Jan 81 ●	**ROMEO AND JULIET** *Vertigo MOVIE 1* **8**	11 wks
4 Apr 81	**SKATEAWAY** *Vertigo MOVIE 2* **37**	5 wks
10 Oct 81	**TUNNEL OF LOVE** *Vertigo MUSIC 3* **54**	3 wks
4 Sep 82 ●	**PRIVATE INVESTIGATIONS** *Vertigo DSTR 1* **2**	8 wks
22 Jan 83	**TWISTING BY THE POOL** *Vertigo DSTR 2* **14**	7 wks
18 Feb 84	**LOVE OVER GOLD (LIVE)/SOLID ROCK (LIVE)** *Vertigo DSTR 6* **50**	3 wks
20 Apr 85	**SO FAR AWAY** *Vertigo DSTR 9* **20**	6 wks
6 Jul 85 ●	**MONEY FOR NOTHING** *Vertigo DSTR 10* **4**	16 wks
26 Oct 85	**BROTHERS IN ARMS** *Vertigo DSTR 11* **16**	13 wks
11 Jan 86 ●	**WALK OF LIFE** *Vertigo DSTR 12* **2**	11 wks
3 May 86	**YOUR LATEST TRICK** *Vertigo DSTR 13* **26**	6 wks
5 Nov 88	**SULTANS OF SWING (re-issue)** *Vertigo DSTR 15* **62**	1 wk
31 Aug 91	**CALLING ELVIS** *Vertigo DSTR 16* **21**	4 wks
2 Nov 91	**HEAVY FUEL** *Vertigo DSTR 17* **55**	2 wks
29 Feb 92	**ON EVERY STREET** *Vertigo DSTR 18* **42**	2 wks
27 Jun 92	**THE BUG** *Vertigo DSTR 19* **67**	1 wk

DIRECT DRIVE *UK, male/female vocal/instrumental group* **3 wks**

26 Jan 85	**ANYTHING?** *Polydor POSP 728* **67**	2 wks
4 May 85	**A.B.C. (FALLING IN LOVE'S NOT EASY)** *Boiling Point POSP 742* **75**	1 wk

DISCHARGE *UK, male vocal/instrumental group* **3 wks**

24 Oct 81	**NEVER AGAIN** *Clay CLAY 6* **64**	3 wks

DISCO TEX and the SEX-O-LETTES **22 wks**
US, male vocalist/female vocal group

23 Nov 74 ●	**GET DANCING** *Chelsea 2005 013* **8**	12 wks
26 Apr 75 ●	**I WANNA DANCE WIT CHOO** *Chelsea 2005 024* * **6**	10 wks

* Disco Tex and the Sex-O-Lettes featuring Sir Monti Rock III

DISPOSABLE HEROES OF HIPHOPRISY **5 wks**
US, male vocal/instrumental duo

4 Apr 92	**TELEVISION THE DRUG OF THE NATION** *4th + Broadway BRW 241* **57**	2 wks
30 May 92	**LANGUAGE OF VIOLENCE** *4th + Broadway 12BRW 248* **68**	1 wk
19 Dec 92	**TELEVISION THE DRUG OF THE NATION (re-entry)** *4th + Broadway BRW 241* ....**44†**	2 wks

Sacha DISTEL *France, male vocalist* **27 wks**

10 Jan 70	**RAINDROPS KEEP FALLING ON MY HEAD** *Warner Bros. WB 7345* **50**	1 wk

British Hit Singles Part One: Alphabetically by Artist
Date of chart entry/Title & catalogue no./Peak position reached/Weeks on chart
★ Number one   ● Top Ten   † still on chart at 31 Dec 1992
* = credited to act billed in footnote

24 Jan 70 ●	**RAINDROPS KEEP FALLING ON MY HEAD (re-entry)** *Warner Bros. WB 7345*	10	20 wks
27 Jun 70	**RAINDROPS KEEP FALLING ON MY HEAD (2nd re-entry)** *Warner Bros. WB 7345*	43	4 wks
1 Aug 70	**RAINDROPS KEEP FALLING ON MY HEAD (3rd re-entry)** *Warner Bros. WB 7345*	47	1 wk
15 Aug 70	**RAINDROPS KEEP FALLING ON MY HEAD (4th re-entry)** *Warner Bros. WB 7345*	44	1 wk

DIVERSIONS *UK, male/female vocal/instrumental group*   **3 wks**

20 Sep 75	**FATTIE BUM BUM** *Gull GULS 18*	34	3 wks

DIVINE *US, male vocalist*   **24 wks**

15 Oct 83	**LOVE REACTION** *Design Communications DES 4*	65	2 wks
14 Jul 84	**YOU THINK YOU'RE A MAN** *Proto ENA 118*	16	10 wks
20 Oct 84	**I'M SO BEAUTIFUL** *Proto ENA 121*	52	2 wks
27 Apr 85	**WALK LIKE A MAN** *Proto ENA 125*	23	7 wks
20 Jul 85	**TWISTIN' THE NIGHT AWAY** *Proto ENA 127*	47	3 wks

DIVINYLS *Australia, male/female vocal/instrumental duo*   **12 wks**

18 May 91 ●	**I TOUCH MYSELF** *Virgin America VUS 36*	10	12 wks

DIXIE CUPS *US, female vocal group*   **16 wks**

18 Jun 64	**CHAPEL OF LOVE** *Pye International 7N 25245*	22	8 wks
13 May 65	**IKO IKO** *Red Bird RB 10024*	23	8 wks

DIZZY HEIGHTS *UK, male vocal/instrumental group*   **4 wks**

18 Dec 82	**CHRISTMAS RAPPING** *Polydor WRAP 1*	49	4 wks

DJ Carl COX *UK, male producer*   **10 wks**

28 Sep 91	**I WANT YOU (FOREVER)** *Perfecto PB 44885*	23	7 wks
8 Aug 92	**DOES IT FEEL GOOD TO YOU** *Perfecto PB 74321102877*	35	3 wks

DJ 'Fast' EDDIE *US, male producer*   **15 wks**

11 Apr 87	**CAN U DANCE** *Champion CHAMP 41* *	71	2 wks
14 Nov 87	**CAN U DANCE (re-entry)** *Champion CHAMP 41* *	67	2 wks
21 Jan 89	**HIP HOUSE/I CAN DANCE** *DJ International DJIN 5*	47	4 wks
11 Mar 89	**YO YO GET FUNKY** *DJ International DJIN 7*	54	3 wks
28 Oct 89	**GIT ON UP** *DJ International 655366 7* **	49	4 wks

* Kenny 'Jammin'' Jason and 'Fast' Eddie Smith   ** DJ 'Fast' Eddie featuring Sundance

DJ E-Z ROCK – *See Rob BASE and DJ E-Z ROCK*

DJ JAZZY JEFF and the FRESH PRINCE   **18 wks**
US, male vocal/instrumental rap duo

4 Oct 86	**GIRLS AIN'T NOTHING BUT TROUBLE** *Champion CHAMP 18*	21	8 wks
3 Aug 91 ●	**SUMMERTIME** *Jive JIVE 279*	8	8 wks
9 Nov 91	**RING MY BELL** *Jive JIVE 288*	53	2 wks

DJ POWER *Italy, male producer - Steve Gambaroli*   **2 wks**

7 Mar 92	**EVERYBODY PUMP** *Cooltempo COOL 252*	46	2 wks

DJ PROFESSOR *Italy, male producer*   **4 wks**

10 Aug 91	**WE GOTTA DO IT** *4th + Broadway BRW 225* *	57	2 wks
28 Mar 92	**ROCK ME STEADY** *PWL Continental PWL 219*	49	2 wks

* DJ Professor featuring Francesco Zappala

DJ Doc SCOTT *UK, male producer*   **2 wks**

1 Feb 92	**NHS EP** *Absolute 2 ABS 001DJ*	64	2 wks

Tracks on NHS EP: Surgery/Night Nurse.

DJ SEDUCTION *UK, male producer - John Kallum*   **8 wks**

22 Feb 92	**HARDCORE HEAVEN/YOU AND ME** *Ffrreedom TAB 103*	26	5 wks
11 Jul 92	**COME ON** *Ffrreedom TAB 111*	37	3 wks

DJAIMIN *Switzerland, male producer*   **2 wks**

19 Sep 92	**GIVE YOU** *Cooltempo COOL 262*	45	2 wks

DJH featuring STEFY   **14 wks**
Italy, male instrumental/production group

16 Feb 91	**THINK ABOUT...** *RCA PB 44385*	22	6 wks
13 Jul 91	**I LIKE IT** *RCA PB 44741*	16	7 wks
18 Oct 91	**MOVE YOUR LOVE** *RCA PB 44965*	73	1 wk

DJPC *Belgium, male producer*   **5 wks**

26 Oct 91	**INSSOMNIAK** *Hype 7PUM 005*	62	4 wks
29 Feb 92	**INSSOMNIAK (re-issue)** *Hype PUMR 005*	64	1 wk

DNA *UK, male production duo*   **29 wks**

28 Jul 90 ●	**TOM'S DINER** *A & M AM 592* *	2	10 wks
18 Aug 90	**LA SERENISSIMA** *Raw Bass RBASS 006*	34	8 wks
3 Aug 91	**REBEL WOMAN** *DNA 7DNA 001* **	42	4 wks
1 Feb 92	**CAN YOU HANDLE IT** *EMI EM 219* ***	17	5 wks
9 May 92	**BLUE LOVE (CALL MY NAME)** *EMI EM 226* ****	66	2 wks

* DNA featuring Suzanne Vega   ** DNA performed by Jazzi P.   *** DNA featuring Sharon Redd   **** DNA featuring Joe Nye

Carl DOBKINS Jr. *US, male vocalist*   **1 wk**

31 Mar 60	**LUCKY DEVIL** *Brunswick 05817*	44	1 wk

Anita DOBSON *UK, female vocalist*   **13 wks**

9 Aug 86 ●	**ANYONE CAN FALL IN LOVE** *BBC RESL 191* *	4	9 wks
18 Jul 87	**TALKING OF LOVE** *Parlophone R 6159*	43	4 wks

* Anita Dobson featuring the Simon May Orchestra

DOCTOR and the MEDICS   **25 wks**
UK, male/female vocal/instrumental group

10 May 86 ★	**SPIRIT IN THE SKY** *IRS IRM 113*	1	15 wks

DR ALBAN and KIM
APPLEBY both con-
template having missed
number one by just
one position.

Left: The first two hits by SAMMY DAVIS JR. were both film tunes, coming from the movies *Daddy Long Legs* and *Love Me Or Leave Me* respectively.

Far left: VAL DOONICAN walked in and out of the top ten for four years in the mid-60s.

DEF LEPPARD had half a dozen hits from their number one album *Hysteria*.

JASON DONOVAN is shown without his dream coat at a concert in Jersey.

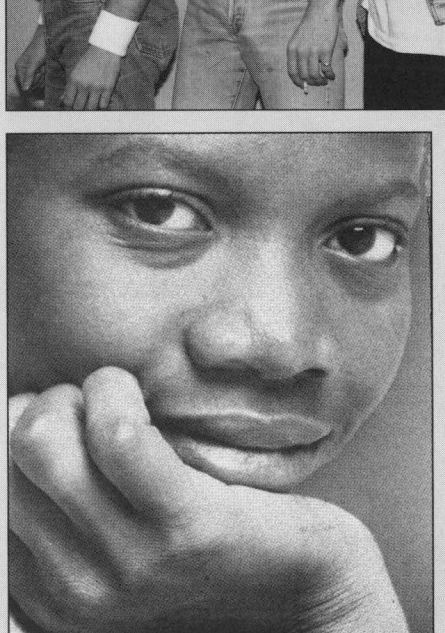

RONNIE DYSON, who died in 1990, originated the song 'Aquarius' in the Broadway musical *Hair*.

9 Aug 86	**BURN** IRS IRM 119	.29	6 wks
22 Nov 86	**WATERLOO** IRS IRM 125 *	.45	4 wks

* Doctor and the Medics featuring Roy Wood

DR. ALBAN Nigeria, male producer — 14 wks

5 Sep 92 ●	**IT'S MY LIFE** Arista 115330	.2	12 wks
14 Nov 92	**ONE LOVE** Arista 74321108727	.45	2 wks

DR. FEELGOOD UK, male vocal/instrumental group — 29 wks

11 Jun 77	**SNEAKIN' SUSPICION** United Artists UP 36255	.47	3 wks
24 Sep 77	**SHE'S A WIND UP** United Artists UP 36304	.34	5 wks
30 Sep 78	**DOWN AT THE DOCTOR'S** United Artists UP 36444	.48	5 wks
20 Jan 79 ●	**MILK AND ALCOHOL** United Artists UP 36468	.9	9 wks
5 May 79	**AS LONG AS THE PRICE IS RIGHT** United Artists YUP 36506	.40	6 wks
8 Dec 79	**PUT HIM OUT OF YOUR MIND** United Artists BP 306	.73	1 wk

DR. HOOK US, male vocal/instrumental group — 104 wks

24 Jun 72 ●	**SYLVIA'S MOTHER** CBS 7929 *	.2	13 wks
26 Jun 76 ●	**A LITTLE BIT MORE** Capitol CL 15871	.2	14 wks
30 Oct 76 ●	**IF NOT YOU** Capitol CL 15885	.5	10 wks
25 Mar 78	**MORE LIKE THE MOVIES** Capitol CL 15967	.14	10 wks
22 Sep 79 ★	**WHEN YOU'RE IN LOVE WITH A BEAUTIFUL WOMAN** Capitol CL 16039	.1	17 wks
5 Jan 80 ●	**BETTER LOVE NEXT TIME** Capitol CL 16112	.8	8 wks
29 Mar 80 ●	**SEXY EYES** Capitol CL 16127	.4	9 wks
23 Aug 80	**YEARS FROM NOW** Capitol CL 16154	.47	6 wks
8 Nov 80	**SHARING THE NIGHT TOGETHER** Capitol CL 16171	.43	4 wks
22 Nov 80	**GIRLS CAN GET IT** Mercury MER 51	.40	5 wks
1 Feb 92	**WHEN YOU'RE IN LOVE WITH A BEAUTIFUL WOMAN (re-issue)** Capitol EMCT 4	.44	4 wks
6 Jun 92	**A LITTLE BIT MORE (re-issue)** EMI EMCT 6	.47	4 wks

* Dr. Hook and The Medicine Show

DOCTOR SPIN UK, male instrumental/production duo — 8 wks

3 Oct 92 ●	**TETRIS** Carpet CRPT 4	.6	8 wks

Ken DODD UK, male vocalist — 233 wks

7 Jul 60 ●	**LOVE IS LIKE A VIOLIN** Decca F 11248	.8	18 wks
15 Jun 61	**ONCE IN EVERY LIFETIME** Decca F 11355	.28	7 wks
10 Aug 61	**ONCE IN EVERY LIFETIME (re-entry)** Decca F 11355	.47	1 wk
24 Aug 61	**ONCE IN EVERY LIFETIME (2nd re-entry)** Decca F 11355	.31	10 wks
1 Feb 62	**PIANISSIMO** Decca F 11422	.21	15 wks
29 Aug 63	**STILL** Columbia DB 7094	.35	10 wks
6 Feb 64	**EIGHT BY TEN** Columbia DB 7191	.22	11 wks
23 Jul 64	**HAPPINESS** Columbia DB 7325	.31	13 wks
26 Nov 64	**SO DEEP IS THE NIGHT** Columbia DB 7398	.31	7 wks
2 Sep 65 ★	**TEARS** Columbia DB 7659	.1	24 wks
18 Nov 65 ●	**THE RIVER (LE COLLINE SONO IN FIORO)** Columbia DB 7750	.3	14 wks
12 May 66 ●	**PROMISES** Columbia DB 7914	.6	14 wks
4 Aug 66	**MORE THAN LOVE** Columbia DB 7976	.14	11 wks
27 Oct 66	**IT'S LOVE** Columbia DB 8031	.36	7 wks
19 Jan 67	**LET ME CRY ON YOUR SHOULDER** Columbia DB 8101	.11	10 wks
30 Jul 69	**TEARS WON'T WASH AWAY MY HEARTACHE** Columbia DB 8600	.22	11 wks
5 Dec 70	**BROKEN HEARTED** Columbia DB 8725	.15	9 wks
13 Feb 71	**BROKEN HEARTED (re-entry)** Columbia DB 8725	.38	1 wk
10 Jul 71	**WHEN LOVE COMES ROUND AGAIN (L'ARCA DI NOE)** Columbia DB 8796	.19	16 wks
18 Nov 72	**JUST OUT OF REACH (OF MY TWO EMPTY ARMS)** Columbia DB 8947	.29	11 wks

29 Nov 75	**(THINK OF ME) WHEREVER YOU ARE** EMI 2342	.21	8 wks
26 Dec 81	**HOLD MY HAND** Images IMGS 0002	.44	5 wks

Rory DODD – See Jim STEINMAN

DOGS D'AMOUR UK, male vocal/instrumental group — 14 wks

4 Feb 89	**HOW COME IT NEVER RAINS** China CHINA 13	.44	3 wks
5 Aug 89	**SATELLITE KID** China CHINA 17	.26	3 wks
14 Oct 89	**TRAIL OF TEARS** China CHINA 20	.47	3 wks
23 Jun 90	**VICTIMS OF SUCCESS** China CHINA 24	.36	3 wks
15 Sep 90	**EMPTY WORLD** China CHINA 27	.61	2 wks

Joe DOLAN Ireland, male vocalist — 40 wks

25 Jun 69 ●	**MAKE ME AN ISLAND** Pye 7N 17738	.3	18 wks
1 Nov 69	**TERESA** Pye 7N 17833	.20	7 wks
8 Nov 69	**MAKE ME AN ISLAND (re-entry)** Pye 7N 17738	.48	1 wk
28 Feb 70	**YOU'RE SUCH A GOOD LOOKING WOMAN** Pye 7N 17891	.17	13 wks
17 Sep 77	**I NEED YOU** Pye 7N 45702	.43	1 wk

Thomas DOLBY UK, male vocalist/multi-instrumentalist — 47 wks

3 Oct 81	**EUROPA AND THE PIRATE TWINS** Parlophone R 6051	.48	3 wks
14 Aug 82	**WINDPOWER** Venice In Peril VIPS 103	.31	8 wks
6 Nov 82	**SHE BLINDED ME WITH SCIENCE** Venice In Peril VIPS 104	.49	4 wks
16 Jul 83	**SHE BLINDED ME WITH SCIENCE (re-issue)** Venice In Peril VIP 105	.56	4 wks
21 Jan 84	**HYPERACTIVE** Parlophone Odeon R 6065	.17	9 wks
31 Mar 84	**I SCARE MYSELF** Parlophone Odeon R 6067	.46	5 wks
16 Apr 88	**AIRHEAD** Manhattan MT 38	.53	3 wks
9 May 92	**CLOSE BUT NO CIGAR** Virgin VS 1410	.22	5 wks
11 Jul 92	**I LOVE YOU GOODBYE** Virgin VS 1417	.36	4 wks
26 Sep 92	**SILK PYJAMAS** Virgin VS 1430	.62	2 wks

Joe DOLCE MUSIC THEATRE US, male vocalist — 10 wks

7 Feb 81 ★	**SHADDAP YOU FACE** Epic EPC 9518	.1	10 wks

DOLL UK, male/female vocal/instrumental group — 8 wks

13 Jan 79	**DESIRE ME** Beggars Banquet BEG 11	.28	8 wks

DOLLAR UK, male/female vocal duo — 128 wks

11 Nov 78	**SHOOTING STAR** EMI 2871	.14	12 wks
19 May 79	**WHO WERE YOU WITH IN THE MOONLIGHT** Carrere CAR 110	.14	12 wks
18 Aug 79 ●	**LOVE'S GOTTA HOLD ON ME** Carrere CAR 122	.4	13 wks
24 Nov 79 ●	**I WANNA HOLD YOUR HAND** Carrere CAR 131	.9	14 wks
25 Oct 80	**TAKIN' A CHANCE ON YOU** WEA K 18353	.62	3 wks
15 Aug 81	**HAND HELD IN BLACK AND WHITE** WEA BUCK 1	.19	12 wks
14 Nov 81 ●	**MIRROR MIRROR (MON AMOUR)** WEA BUCK 2	.4	17 wks
20 Mar 82	**RING RING** Carrere CAR 225	.61	2 wks
27 Mar 82 ●	**GIVE ME BACK MY HEART** WEA BUCK 3	.4	9 wks
19 Jun 82	**VIDEOTHEQUE** WEA BUCK 4	.17	10 wks
18 Sep 82	**GIVE ME SOME KINDA MAGIC** WEA BUCK 5	.34	6 wks
16 Aug 86	**WE WALKED IN LOVE** Arista DIME 1	.61	4 wks
26 Dec 87 ●	**O L'AMOUR** London LON 146	.7	11 wks
16 Jul 88	**IT'S NATURE'S WAY (NO PROBLEM)** London LON 179	.58	3 wks

Placido DOMINGO Spain, male vocalist — 20 wks

12 Dec 81	**PERHAPS LOVE** CBS A 1905 *	.46	9 wks

27 May 89	**TILL I LOVED YOU** CBS 654843 7 **	...24	9 wks
16 Jun 90	**NESSUN DORMA FROM 'TURANDOT'**		
	Epic 656005 7 ***	...59	2 wks

* Placido Domingo with John Denver ** Placido Domingo and Jennifer Rush
*** Luis Cobos featuring Placido Domingo

Fats DOMINO *US, male vocalist/instrumentalist – piano*   **109 wks**

27 Jul 56	**I'M IN LOVE AGAIN** London HLU 8280	...28	1 wk
17 Aug 56	**I'M IN LOVE AGAIN (re-entry)** London HLU 8280	...12	13 wks
30 Nov 56	**BLUEBERRY HILL** London HLU 8330	...26	1 wk
21 Dec 56 ●	**BLUEBERRY HILL (re-entry)** London HLU 8330	...6	14 wks
25 Jan 57	**AIN'T THAT A SHAME** London HLU 8173	...23	2 wks
1 Feb 57	**HONEY CHILE** London HLU 8356	...29	1 wk
29 Mar 57	**BLUE MONDAY** London HLP 8377	...23	1 wk
19 Apr 57	**BLUE MONDAY (re-entry)** London HLP 8377	...30	1 wk
19 Apr 57	**I'M WALKIN'** London HLP 8407	...19	7 wks
19 Jul 57	**VALLEY OF TEARS** London HLP 8449	...25	1 wk
28 Mar 58	**THE BIG BEAT** London HLP 8575	...20	4 wks
4 Jul 58	**SICK AND TIRED** London HLP 8628	...26	1 wk
22 May 59	**MARGIE** London HLP 8865	...18	5 wks
16 Oct 59	**I WANT TO WALK YOU HOME** London HLP 8942	...14	5 wks
18 Dec 59	**BE MY GUEST** London HLP 9005	...11	8 wks
19 Feb 60	**BE MY GUEST (re-entry)** London HLP 9005	...19	3 wks
17 Mar 60	**COUNTRY BOY** London HLP 9073	...19	11 wks
21 Jul 60	**WALKING TO NEW ORLEANS** London HLP 9163	...19	10 wks
10 Nov 60	**THREE NIGHTS A WEEK** London HLP 9198	...45	2 wks
5 Jan 61	**MY GIRL JOSEPHINE** London HLP 9244	...32	4 wks
27 Jul 61	**IT KEEPS RAININ'** London HLP 9374	...49	1 wk
30 Nov 61	**WHAT A PARTY** London HLP 9456	...43	1 wk
29 Mar 62	**JAMBALAYA** London HLP 9520	...41	1 wk
31 Oct 63	**RED SAILS IN THE SUNSET** HMV POP 1219	...34	6 wks
24 Apr 76	**BLUEBERRY HILL (re-issue)** United Artists UP 35797	...41	5 wks

DON PABLO'S ANIMALS   **10 wks**

Italy, male instrumental group

| 19 May 90 ● | **VENUS** Rumour RUMA 18 | ...4 | 10 wks |

DON-E *UK, male vocalist*   **7 wks**

9 May 92	**LOVE MAKES THE WORLD GO ROUND**		
	4th + B'way BRW 242	...18	6 wks
25 Jul 92	**PEACE IN THE WORLD** 4th + B'way BRW 256	...41	1 wk

Lonnie DONEGAN *UK, male vocalist*   **321 wks**

6 Jan 56 ●	**ROCK ISLAND LINE** Decca F 10647	...8	13 wks
13 Apr 56	**ROCK ISLAND LINE (re-entry)** Decca F 10647	...16	3 wks
20 Apr 56	**STEWBALL** Pye Nixa N 15036	...27	1 wk
27 Apr 56 ●	**LOST JOHN/STEWBALL** Pye Nixa N 15036	...2	17 wks
11 May 56	**ROCK ISLAND LINE (2nd re-entry)** Decca F 10647	...19	6 wks
6 Jul 56	**SKIFFLE SESSION EP** Pye Nixa NJE 1017	...20	2 wks
7 Sep 56	**BRING A LITTLE WATER SYLVIE/DEAD OR**		
	ALIVE Pye Nixa N 15071	...7	12 wks
21 Dec 56	**LONNIE DONEGAN SHOWCASE (LP)**		
	Pye Nixa NPT 19012	...26	3 wks
11 Jan 57	**BRING A LITTLE WATER SYLVIE/DEAD OR**		
	ALIVE (re-entry) Pye Nixa N 15071	...30	1 wk
18 Jan 57 ●	**DON'T YOU ROCK ME DADDY-O** Pye Nixa N 15080	...4	17 wks
5 Apr 57 ★	**CUMBERLAND GAP** Pye Nixa N 15087	...1	12 wks
7 Jun 57 ★	**GAMBLIN' MAN/PUTTING ON THE STYLE**		
	Pye Nixa N 15093	...1	19 wks
11 Oct 57 ●	**MY DIXIE DARLING** Pye Nixa N 15108	...10	15 wks
20 Dec 57	**JACK O' DIAMONDS** Pye Nixa N 15116	...14	7 wks
11 Apr 58 ●	**GRAND COOLIE DAM** Pye Nixa N 15129	...6	15 wks
11 Jul 58	**SALLY DON'T YOU GRIEVE/BETTY BETTY**		
	BETTY Pye Nixa 7N 15148	...11	7 wks
26 Sep 58	**LONESOME TRAVELLER** Pye Nixa 7N 15158	...28	1 wk
14 Nov 58	**LONNIE'S SKIFFLE PARTY** Pye Nixa 7N 15165	...23	5 wks
21 Nov 58 ●	**TOM DOOLEY** Pye Nixa 7N 15172	...3	14 wks
6 Feb 59 ●	**DOES YOUR CHEWING GUM LOSE ITS**		
	FLAVOUR Pye Nixa 7N 15181	...3	12 wks

8 May 59	**FORT WORTH JAIL** Pye Nixa 7N 15198	...14	5 wks
26 Jun 59 ●	**BATTLE OF NEW ORLEANS** Pye Nixa 7N 15206	...2	16 wks
11 Sep 59	**SAL'S GOT A SUGAR LIP** Pye Nixa 7N 15223	...13	4 wks
4 Dec 59	**SAN MIGUEL** Pye Nixa 7N 15237	...19	4 wks
24 Mar 60 ★	**MY OLD MAN'S A DUSTMAN** Pye Nixa 7N 15256	...1	13 wks
26 May 60	**I WANNA GO HOME** Pye Nixa 7N 15267	...5	17 wks
25 Aug 60	**LORELEI** Pye Nixa 7N 15275	...10	8 wks
24 Nov 60	**LIVELY** Pye Nixa 7N 15312	...13	9 wks
8 Dec 60	**VIRGIN MARY** Pye Nixa 7N 15315	...27	5 wks
11 May 61	**HAVE A DRINK ON ME** Pye Nixa 7N 15354	...8	15 wks
31 Aug 61 ●	**MICHAEL ROW THE BOAT/LUMBERED**		
	Pye 7N 15371	...6	11 wks
18 Jan 62	**THE COMANCHEROS** Pye 7N 15410	...14	11 wks
5 Apr 62	**THE PARTY'S OVER** Pye 7N 15424	...9	12 wks
16 Aug 62	**PICK A BALE OF COTTON** Pye 7N 15455	...11	10 wks

Stewball *had one week on the chart by itself on 20 Apr 56. Lost John, the other side, replaced it on 27 Apr 56 but* Stewball *was given co-billing with* Lost John *for the weeks of 11, 18 and 25 May 56 only during* Lost John's *17-week run.* Dead Or Alive *was not listed with* Bring A Little Water Sylvie *for the week 7 Sep 56.* Putting On The Style *was not listed with* Gamblin' Man *for the weeks of 7 and 14 Jun 56. Tracks on* Skiffle Session (EP): Railroad Bill/Stockalee/Ballad of Jesse James/Ol' Riley. *Tracks on* Lonnie Donegan Showcase (LP): Wabash Cannonball/How Long How Long Blues/Nobody's Child/I Shall Not Be Moved/I'm Alabammy Bound/I'm A Rambling Man/Wreck Of The Old '97/Frankie And Johnny. Lonnie's Skiffle Party *was a medley as follows:* Little Liza Jane/Putting On The Style/Camptown Races/Knees Up Mother Brown/So Long/On Top Of Old Smokey/Down In The Valley/So Long. *Yes, there are two versions of* So Long *on this disc.*

Ral DONNER *US, male vocalist*   **10 wks**

| 21 Sep 61 | **YOU DON'T KNOW WHAT YOU'VE GOT** | | |
| | *Parlophone R 4820* | ...25 | 10 wks |

DONOVAN *UK, male vocalist*   **100 wks**

25 Mar 65 ●	**CATCH THE WIND** Pye 7N 15801	...4	13 wks
3 Jun 65 ●	**COLOURS** Pye 7N 15866	...4	12 wks
11 Nov 65	**TURQUOISE** Pye 7N 15984	...30	6 wks
8 Dec 66 ●	**SUNSHINE SUPERMAN** Pye 7N 17241	...2	11 wks
9 Feb 67 ●	**MELLOW YELLOW** Pye 7N 17267	...8	8 wks
25 Oct 67 ●	**THERE IS A MOUNTAIN** Pye 7N 17403	...8	11 wks
21 Feb 68 ●	**JENNIFER JUNIPER** Pye 7N 17457	...5	11 wks
29 May 68 ●	**HURDY GURDY MAN** Pye 7N 17537	...4	10 wks
4 Dec 68	**ATLANTIS** Pye 7N 17660	...23	8 wks
9 Jul 69	**GOO GOO BARABAJAGAL (LOVE IS HOT)**		
	Pye 7N 17778 *	...12	9 wks
1 Dec 90	**JENNIFER JUNIPER** Fontana SYP 1 **	...68	1 wk

* Donovan with the Jeff Beck Group ** Singing Corner meets Donovan

Jason DONOVAN *Australia, male vocalist*   **133 wks**

10 Sep 88 ●	**NOTHING CAN DIVIDE US** PWL PWL 17	...5	12 wks
10 Dec 88 ★	**ESPECIALLY FOR YOU** PWL PWL 24 *	...1	14 wks
4 Mar 89 ★	**TOO MANY BROKEN HEARTS** PWL PWL 32	...1	13 wks
10 Jun 89	**SEALED WITH A KISS** PWL PWL 39	...1	10 wks
9 Sep 89	**EVERY DAY (I LOVE YOU MORE)** PWL PWL 43	...2	9 wks
9 Dec 89 ●	**WHEN YOU COME BACK TO ME** PWL PWL 46	...2	11 wks
7 Apr 90	**HANG ON TO YOUR LOVE** PWL PWL 51	...8	7 wks
30 Jun 90	**ANOTHER NIGHT** PWL PWL 58	...18	5 wks
1 Sep 90	**RHYTHM OF THE RAIN** PWL PWL 60	...9	6 wks
27 Oct 90	**I'M DOING FINE** PWL PWL 69	...22	6 wks
18 May 91	**RSVP** PWL PWL 80	...17	5 wks
22 Jun 91 ★	**ANY DREAM WILL DO** Really Useful RUR 7	...1	12 wks
24 Aug 91 ●	**HAPPY TOGETHER** PWL PWL 203	...10	6 wks
7 Dec 91	**JOSEPH MEGA REMIX** Really Useful RUR 9 **	...13	8 wks
18 Jul 92	**MISSION OF LOVE** Polydor PO 222	...26	4 wks
28 Nov 92	**AS TIME GOES BY** Polydor PO 245	...26†	5 wks

* Kylie Minogue and Jason Donovan ** Jason Donovan and Original London Cast featuring Linzi Hately, David Easter and Johnny Amobi

DOOBIE BROTHERS *US, male vocal/instrumental group*   **32 wks**

| 9 Mar 74 | **LISTEN TO THE MUSIC** Warner Bros. K 16208 | ...29 | 7 wks |

7 Jun 75	TAKE ME IN YOUR ARMS *Warner Bros. K 16559*	**29**	5 wks
17 Feb 79	WHAT A FOOL BELIEVES *Warner Bros. K 17314*	**31**	10 wks
5 May 79	WHAT A FOOL BELIEVES (re-entry)		
	Warner Bros. K 17314	**72**	1 wk
14 Jul 79	MINUTE BY MINUTE *Warner Bros. K 17411*	**47**	4 wks
24 Jan 87	WHAT A FOOL BELIEVES (re-issue)		
	*Warner Bros. W 8451 *	**57**	3 wks
29 Jul 89	THE DOCTOR *Capitol CL 536*	**73**	2 wks

* Doobie Brothers featuring Michael McDonald

DOOGIE – *See BUG KANN and PLASTIC JAM featuring Patti LOW and DOOGIE*

DOOLEYS *UK, male/female vocal/instrumental group*   **83 wks**

13 Aug 77	THINK I'M GONNA FALL IN LOVE WITH YOU		
	GTO GT 95	**13**	10 wks
12 Nov 77	● LOVE OF MY LIFE *GTO GT 110*	**9**	11 wks
13 May 78	DON'T TAKE IT LYIN' DOWN *GTO GT 220*	**60**	3 wks
2 Sep 78	A ROSE HAS TO DIE *GTO GT 229*	**11**	11 wks
10 Feb 79	HONEY I'M LOST *GTO GT 242*	**24**	9 wks
16 Jun 79	● WANTED *GTO GT 249*	**3**	14 wks
22 Sep 79	THE CHOSEN FEW *GTO GT 258*	**7**	11 wks
8 Mar 80	LOVE PATROL *GTO GT 260*	**29**	7 wks
6 Sep 80	BODY LANGUAGE *GTO GT 276*	**46**	4 wks
10 Oct 81	AND I WISH *GTO GT 300*	**52**	3 wks

Val DOONICAN *Ireland, male vocalist*   **143 wks**

15 Oct 64	● WALK TALL *Decca F 11982*	**3**	21 wks
21 Jan 65	THE SPECIAL YEARS *Decca F 12049*	**7**	12 wks
8 Apr 65	I'M GONNA GET THERE SOMEHOW *Decca F 12118*	**25**	5 wks
22 Apr 65	THE SPECIAL YEARS (re-entry) *Decca F 12049*	**49**	1 wk
17 Mar 66	● ELUSIVE BUTTERFLY *Decca F 12358*	**5**	12 wks
3 Nov 66	● WHAT WOULD I BE *Decca F 12505*	**2**	17 wks
23 Feb 67	MEMORIES ARE MADE OF THIS *Decca F 12566*	**11**	12 wks
25 May 67	TWO STREETS *Decca F 12608*	**39**	4 wks
18 Oct 67	● IF THE WHOLE WORLD STOPPED LOVING		
	Pye 7N 17396	**3**	19 wks
21 Feb 68	YOU'RE THE ONLY ONE *Pye 7N 17465*	**37**	4 wks
12 Jun 68	NOW *Pye 7N 17534*	**43**	2 wks
23 Oct 68	IF I KNEW THEN WHAT I KNOW NOW		
	Pye 7N 17616	**14**	13 wks
23 Apr 69	RING OF BRIGHT WATER *Pye 7N 17713*	**48**	1 wk
4 Dec 71	MORNING *Philips 6006 177*	**12**	13 wks
10 Mar 73	HEAVEN IS MY WOMAN'S LOVE *Philips 6028 031*	**34**	6 wks
28 Apr 73	HEAVEN IS MY WOMAN'S LOVE (re-entry)		
	Philips 6028 031	**47**	1 wk

DOORS *US, male vocal/instrumental group*   **42 wks**

16 Aug 67	LIGHT MY FIRE *Elektra EKSN 45014*	**49**	1 wk
28 Aug 68	HELLO I LOVE YOU *Elektra EKSN 45037*	**15**	12 wks
16 Oct 71	RIDERS ON THE STORM *Elektra K 12021*	**50**	1 wk
30 Oct 71	RIDERS ON THE STORM (re-entry) *Elektra K 12021*	**22**	10 wks
20 Mar 76	RIDERS ON THE STORM (re-issue) *Elektra K 12203*	**33**	5 wks
3 Feb 79	HELLO I LOVE YOU (re-issue) *Elektra K 12215*	**71**	1 wk
27 Apr 91	BREAK ON THROUGH *Elektra EKR 121*	**64**	2 wks
1 Jun 91	● LIGHT MY FIRE (re-issue) *Elektra EKR 125*	**7**	8 wks
10 Aug 91	RIDERS ON THE STORM (re-issue) *Elektra EKR 131*	**68**	1 wk

Charlie DORE *UK, female vocalist*   **2 wks**

17 Nov 79	PILOT OF THE AIRWAVES *Island WIP 6526*	**66**	2 wks

Lee DORSEY *US, male vocalist*   **36 wks**

3 Feb 66	GET OUT OF MY LIFE WOMAN *Stateside SS 485*	**22**	7 wks
5 May 66	CONFUSION *Stateside SS 506*	**38**	6 wks
11 Aug 66	● WORKING IN THE COALMINE *Stateside SS 528*	**8**	11 wks
27 Oct 66	● HOLY COW *Stateside SS 552*	**6**	12 wks

Tommy DORSEY ORCHESTRA starring Warren COVINGTON   **19 wks**
US, orchestra Warren Covington, male instrumentalist – trombone

17 Oct 58	● TEA FOR TWO CHA CHA *Brunswick 05757*	**3**	19 wks

DOUBLE *Switzerland, male vocal/instrumental duo*   **10 wks**

25 Jan 86	● THE CAPTAIN OF HER HEART *Polydor POSP 779*	**8**	9 wks
5 Dec 87	DEVIL'S BALL *Polydor POSP 888*	**71**	1 wk

DOUBLE DEE featuring DANY   **2 wks**
US, male vocal/instrumental group

1 Dec 90	FOUND LOVE *Epic 6563766*	**63**	2 wks

DOUBLE TROUBLE   **35 wks**
UK, male instrumental/production duo

27 May 89	JUST KEEP ROCKIN' *Desire WANT 9 *	**11**	12 wks
7 Oct 89	● STREET TUFF *Desire WANT 18 *	**3**	14 wks
12 May 90	TALK BACK *Desire WANT 27 **	**71**	1 wk
30 Jun 90	LOVE DON'T LIVE HERE ANYMORE		
	*Desire WANT 32 ***	**21**	6 wks
15 Jun 91	RUB-A-DUB *Desire WANT 41*	**66**	2 wks

* Double Trouble and the Rebel MC ** Double Trouble featuring Janette Sewell
*** Double Trouble featuring Janette Sewell and Carl Brown

DOUBLE YOU? *Italy, male vocalist – Willie Morales*   **3 wks**

2 May 92	PLEASE DON'T GO *ZYX ZYX 67487*	**41**	3 wks

Carl DOUGLAS *Jamaica, male vocalist*   **28 wks**

17 Aug 74	★ KUNG FU FIGHTING *Pye 7N 45377*	**1**	13 wks
30 Nov 74	DANCE THE KUNG FU *Pye 7N 45418*	**35**	5 wks
3 Dec 77	RUN BACK *Pye 7N 46018*	**25**	10 wks

Carol DOUGLAS *US, female vocalist*   **4 wks**

22 Jul 78	NIGHT FEVER *Gull GULS 61*	**66**	4 wks

Craig DOUGLAS *UK, male vocalist*   **112 wks**

12 Jun 59	A TEENAGER IN LOVE *Top Rank JAR 133*	**13**	11 wks
7 Aug 59	★ ONLY SIXTEEN *Top Rank JAR 159*	**1**	15 wks
22 Jan 60	● PRETTY BLUE EYES *Top Rank JAR 268*	**4**	14 wks
28 Apr 60	● THE HEART OF A TEENAGE GIRL		
	Top Rank JAR 340	**10**	9 wks
11 Aug 60	OH! WHAT A DAY *Top Rank JAR 406*	**43**	1 wk
20 Apr 61	● A HUNDRED POUNDS OF CLAY *Top Rank JAR 555*	**9**	9 wks
29 Jun 61	● TIME *Top Rank JAR 569*	**9**	14 wks
22 Mar 62	● WHEN MY LITTLE GIRL IS SMILING		
	Top Rank JAR 610	**9**	13 wks
28 Jun 62	● OUR FAVOURITE MELODIES *Columbia DB 4854*	**9**	10 wks
18 Oct 62	OH LONESOME ME *Decca F 11523*	**15**	12 wks
28 Feb 63	TOWN CRIER *Decca F 11575*	**36**	4 wks

DOWLANDS *UK, male vocal duo*   **7 wks**

9 Jan 64	ALL MY LOVING *Oriole CB 1897*	**33**	7 wks

Don DOWNING US, male vocalist — 10 wks

10 Nov 73	**LONELY DAYS, LONELY NIGHTS** People PEO 102	32	10 wks

Will DOWNING US, male vocalist — 34 wks

2 Apr 88	**A LOVE SUPREME** Fourth & Broadway BRW 90	14	10 wks
25 Jun 88	**IN MY DREAMS** Fourth & Broadway BRW 104	34	6 wks
1 Oct 88	**FREE** Fourth & Broadway BRW 112	58	5 wks
21 Jan 89	**WHERE IS THE LOVE** Fourth & Broadway BRW 122 *	19	7 wks
28 Oct 89	**TEST OF TIME** Fourth & Broadway BRW 146	67	2 wks
24 Feb 90	**COME TOGETHER AS ONE** Fourth & Broadway BRW 159	48	4 wks

* Mica Paris and Will Downing

Lamont DOZIER – See HOLLAND-DOZIER featuring Lamont DOZIER

Charlie DRAKE UK, male vocalist — 37 wks

8 Aug 58 ●	**SPLISH SPLASH** Parlophone R 4461	7	11 wks
24 Oct 58	**VOLARE** Parlophone R 4478	28	2 wks
27 Oct 60	**MR. CUSTER** Parlophone R 4701	12	12 wks
5 Oct 61	**MY BOOMERANG WON'T COME BACK** Parlophone R 4824	14	11 wks
1 Jan 72	**PUCKWUDGIE** Columbia DB 8829	47	1 wk

DRAMATIS UK, male vocal/instrumental group — 8 wks

5 Dec 81	**LOVE NEEDS NO DISGUISE** Beggars Banquet BEG 68 *	33	7 wks
13 Nov 82	**I CAN SEE HER NOW** Rocket XPRES 83	57	1 wk

* Gary Numan and Dramatis

Rusty DRAPER US, male vocalist — 4 wks

11 Aug 60	**MULE SKINNER BLUES** Mercury AMT 1101	39	4 wks

DREAD ZEPPELIN US, male vocal/instrumental group — 3 wks

1 Dec 90	**YOUR TIME IS GONNA COME** IRS DREAD 1	59	1 wk
13 Jul 91	**STAIRWAY TO HEAVEN** IRS DREAD 2	62	2 wks

DREAM ACADEMY
UK, male/female vocal/instrumental group — 10 wks

30 Mar 85	**LIFE IN A NORTHERN TOWN** blanco y negro NEG 10	15	8 wks
14 Sep 85	**THE LOVE PARADE** blanco y negro NEG 16	68	2 wks

DREAM FREQUENCY UK, male producer - Ian Bland — 10 wks

12 Jan 91	**LOVE PEACE AND HARMONY** Citybeat CBE 756	71	2 wks
25 Jan 92	**FEEL SO REAL** Citybeat CBE 763 *	23	5 wks
25 Apr 92	**TAKE ME** Citybeat CBE 768	39	3 wks

* Dream Frequency featuring Debbie Sharp

DREAM WARRIORS Canada, male rap group — 19 wks

14 Jul 90	**WASH YOUR FACE IN MY SINK** Fourth & Broadway BRW 183	16	8 wks
24 Nov 90	**MY DEFINITION OF A BOOMBASTIC JAZZ STYLE** Fourth & Broadway BRW 197	13	8 wks
25 Apr 92	**LUDI** Fourth & Broadway BRW 206	39	3 wks

DREAMERS – See FREDDIE and the DREAMERS

British Hit Singles Part One: Alphabetically by Artist
Date of chart entry/Title & catalogue no./Peak position reached/Weeks on chart
★ Number one ● Top Ten † still on chart at 31 Dec 1992
* = credited to act billed in footnote

DREAMWEAVERS US, male/female vocal group — 18 wks

10 Feb 56 ★	**IT'S ALMOST TOMORROW** Brunswick 05515	1	18 wks

DRELLS – See Archie BELL and the DRELLS

Eddie DRENNON and B.B.S. UNLIMITED — 6 wks
US, male vocal/instrumental group

28 Feb 76	**LET'S DO THE LATIN HUSTLE** Pye International 7N 25702	20	6 wks

Alan DREW UK, male vocalist — 2 wks

26 Sep 63	**ALWAYS THE LONELY ONE** Columbia DB 7090	48	2 wks

DRIFTERS US, male vocal group — 176 wks

8 Jan 60	**DANCE WITH ME** London HLE 8988	17	4 wks
10 Mar 60	**DANCE WITH ME (re-entry)** London HLE 8988	35	1 wk
3 Nov 60 ●	**SAVE THE LAST DANCE FOR ME** London HLK 9201	2	18 wks
16 Mar 61	**I COUNT THE TEARS** London HLK 9287	28	6 wks
5 Apr 62	**WHEN MY LITTLE GIRL IS SMILING** London HLK 9522	31	3 wks
10 Oct 63	**I'LL TAKE YOU HOME** London HLK 9785	37	5 wks
24 Sep 64	**UNDER THE BOARDWALK** Atlantic AT 4001	45	4 wks
8 Apr 65	**AT THE CLUB** Atlantic AT 4019	35	7 wks
29 Apr 65	**COME ON OVER TO MY PLACE** Atlantic AT 4023	40	5 wks
2 Feb 67	**BABY WHAT I MEAN** Atlantic 584 065	49	1 wk
25 Mar 72	**AT THE CLUB (re-issue)** Atlantic K 10148	39	1 wk
8 Apr 72 ●	**AT THE CLUB/SATURDAY NIGHT AT THE MOVIES (re-entry of re-issue)** Atlantic K 10148	3	19 wks
26 Aug 72 ●	**COME ON OVER TO MY PLACE (re-issue)** Atlantic K 10216	9	11 wks
4 Aug 73 ●	**LIKE SISTER AND BROTHER** Bell 1313	7	12 wks
15 Jun 74 ●	**KISSIN' IN THE BACK ROW OF THE MOVIES** Bell 1358	2	13 wks
12 Oct 74 ●	**DOWN ON THE BEACH TONIGHT** Bell 1381	7	9 wks
8 Feb 75	**LOVE GAMES** Bell 1396	33	6 wks
6 Sep 75 ●	**THERE GOES MY FIRST LOVE** Bell 1433	3	12 wks
29 Nov 75 ●	**CAN I TAKE YOU HOME LITTLE GIRL** Bell 1462	10	10 wks
13 Mar 76	**HELLO HAPPINESS** Bell 1469	12	8 wks
11 Sep 76	**EVERY NITE'S A SATURDAY NIGHT WITH YOU** Bell 1491	29	7 wks
18 Dec 76 ●	**YOU'RE MORE THAN A NUMBER IN MY LITTLE RED BOOK** Arista 78	5	12 wks
14 Apr 79	**SAVE THE LAST DANCE FOR ME/WHEN MY LITTLE GIRL IS SMILING (re-issue)** Lightning LIG 9014	69	2 wks

Saturday Night At The Movies only received chart credit with At The Club after the re-issue's return to the chart on 8 Apr 72.

Julie DRISCOLL, Brian AUGER and the — 16 wks
TRINITY UK, female vocalist/male instrumental group

17 Apr 68 ●	**THIS WHEEL'S ON FIRE** Marmalade 598 006	5	16 wks

DRIVER 67 UK, male vocalist - Paul Phillips — 12 wks

23 Dec 78 ●	**CAR 67** Logo GO 336	7	12 wks

DRIZA BONE UK, male instrumental/production duo   **2 wks**

26 Oct 91	**CATCH THE FIRE** 4th + Broadway BRW 232	**54**	2 wks

Frank D'RONE US, male vocalist   **6 wks**

22 Dec 60	**STRAWBERRY BLONDE** Mercury AMT 1123	**24**	6 wks

DRUM THEATRE UK, male vocal/instrumental group   **8 wks**

15 Feb 86	**LIVING IN THE PAST** Epic A 6798	**67**	2 wks
17 Jan 87	**ELDORADO** Epic EMU 1	**44**	6 wks

DRUPI Italy, male vocalist   **12 wks**

1 Dec 73	**VADO VIA** A & M AMS 7083	**17**	12 wks

DSK UK, male instrumental/production group   **3 wks**

31 Aug 91	**WHAT WOULD WE DO/READ MY LIPS** Boys' Own BOI 6	**46**	3 wks

D.S.M. US, male rap group   **4 wks**

7 Dec 85	**WARRIOR GROOVE** 10 DAZZ 45-7	**68**	4 wks

D T I US, male vocal/instrumental group   **1 wk**

16 Apr 88	**KEEP THIS FREQUENCY CLEAR/KEEP IT CLEAR** Premiere UK GRE 501	**73**	1 wk

DTOX UK, male/female vocal/instrumental group   **1 wk**

21 Nov 92	**SHATTERED GLASS** Vitality VITAL 1	**75**	1 wk

John DU CANN UK, male vocalist   **6 wks**

22 Sep 79	**DON'T BE A DUMMY** Vertigo 6059 241	**33**	6 wks

John DU PREZ – See MODERN ROMANCE

DUBLINERS Ireland, male vocal/instrumental group   **45 wks**

30 Mar 67 ●	**SEVEN DRUNKEN NIGHTS** Major Minor MM 506	**7**	17 wks
30 Aug 67	**BLACK VELVET BAND** Major Minor MM 530	**15**	15 wks
20 Dec 67	**NEVER WED AN OLD MAN** Major Minor MM 551	**43**	3 wks
28 Mar 87 ●	**THE IRISH ROVER** Stiff BUY 258 *	**8**	8 wks
16 Jun 90	**JACK'S HEROES/WHISKEY IN THE JAR** Pogue Mahone YZ 500 *	**63**	2 wks

* Pogues and the Dubliners

DUFFO Australia, male vocalist   **2 wks**

24 Mar 79	**GIVE ME BACK ME BRAIN** Beggars Banquet BEG 15	**60**	2 wks

Stephen 'Tin Tin' DUFFY UK, male vocalist   **24 wks**

9 Jul 83	**HOLD IT** Curve X 9763 *	**55**	4 wks
2 Mar 85 ●	**KISS ME** 10 TIN 2	**4**	11 wks
18 May 85	**ICING ON THE CAKE** 10 TIN 3	**14**	9 wks

* Tin Tin

George DUKE US, male vocalist/instrumentalist   **6 wks**

12 Jul 80	**BRAZILIAN LOVE AFFAIR** Epic EPC 8751	**36**	6 wks

DUKES UK, male vocal duo   **13 wks**

17 Oct 81	**MYSTERY GIRL** WEA K 18867	**47**	7 wks
1 May 82	**THANK YOU FOR THE PARTY** WEA K 19136	**53**	6 wks

Candy DULFER Holland, female instrumentalist - saxophone   **14 wks**

24 Feb 90 ●	**LILY WAS HERE** RCA ZB 43045 *	**6**	12 wks
4 Aug 90	**SAXUALITY** RCA PB 43769	**60**	2 wks

* David A. Stewart featuring Candy Dulfer

Thuli DUMAKUDE South Africa, male vocalist   **1 wk**

2 Jan 88	**THE FUNERAL (SEPTEMBER 25, 1977)** MCA MCA 1228	**75**	1 wk

The listed flip side of The Funeral was Cry Freedom by George Fenton and Jonas Gwangwa.

John DUMMER and Helen APRIL   **3 wks**
UK, male/female vocal duo

28 Aug 82	**BLUE SKIES** Speed SPEED 8	**54**	3 wks

Johnny DUNCAN and the BLUE GRASS BOYS US, male vocal/instrumental group   **20 wks**

26 Jul 57 ●	**LAST TRAIN TO SAN FERNANDO** Columbia DB 3959	**2**	17 wks
25 Oct 57	**BLUE BLUE HEARTACHES** Columbia DB 3996	**27**	1 wk
29 Nov 57	**FOOTPRINTS IN THE SNOW** Columbia DB 4029	**27**	1 wk
3 Jan 58	**FOOTPRINTS IN THE SNOW (re-entry)** Columbia DB 4029	**28**	1 wk

David DUNDAS UK, male vocalist   **14 wks**

24 Jul 76 ●	**JEANS ON** Air CHS 2094	**3**	9 wks
9 Apr 77	**ANOTHER FUNNY HONEYMOON** Air CHS 2136	**29**	5 wks

Erroll DUNKLEY Jamaica, male vocalist   **14 wks**

22 Sep 79	**O.K. FRED** Scope SC 6	**11**	11 wks
2 Feb 80	**SIT DOWN AND CRY** Scope SC 11	**52**	3 wks

Clive DUNN UK, male vocalist   **28 wks**

28 Nov 70 ★	**GRANDAD** Columbia DB 8726	**1**	27 wks
26 Jun 71	**GRANDAD (re-entry)** Columbia D8 8726	**50**	1 wk

Simon DUPREE and the BIG SOUND   **16 wks**
UK, male vocal/instrumental group

22 Nov 67 ●	**KITES** Parlophone R 5646	**9**	13 wks
3 Apr 68	**FOR WHOM THE BELL TOLLS** Parlophone R 5670	**43**	3 wks

DURAN DURAN UK, male vocal/instrumental group   **187 wks**

21 Feb 81	**PLANET EARTH** EMI 5137	**12**	11 wks

9 May 81	CARELESS MEMORIES *EMI 5168*	37	7 wks
25 Jul 81 ●	GIRLS ON FILM *EMI 5206*	5	11 wks
28 Nov 81	MY OWN WAY *EMI 5254*	14	11 wks
15 May 82 ●	HUNGRY LIKE THE WOLF *EMI 5295*	5	12 wks
21 Aug 82 ●	SAVE A PRAYER *EMI 5327*	2	9 wks
13 Nov 82 ●	RIO *EMI 5346*	9	11 wks
26 Mar 83 ★	IS THERE SOMETHING I SHOULD KNOW *EMI 5371*	1	9 wks
29 Oct 83 ●	UNION OF THE SNAKE *EMI 5429*	3	7 wks
24 Dec 83	UNION OF THE SNAKE (re-entry) *EMI 5429*	66	4 wks
4 Feb 84 ●	NEW MOON ON MONDAY *EMI DURAN 1*	9	7 wks
28 Apr 84 ★	THE REFLEX *EMI DURAN 2*	1	14 wks
3 Nov 84 ●	WILD BOYS *Parlophone DURAN 3*	2	14 wks
18 May 85 ●	A VIEW TO A KILL *Parlophone DURAN 007*	2	16 wks
1 Nov 86 ●	NOTORIOUS *EMI DDN 45*	7	6 wks
3 Jan 87	NOTORIOUS (re-entry) *EMI DDN 5*	73	1 wk
21 Feb 87	SKIN TRADE *EMI TRADE 1*	22	6 wks
25 Apr 87	MEET EL PRESIDENTE *EMI TOUR 1*	24	5 wks
1 Oct 88	I DON'T WANT YOUR LOVE *EMI YOUR 1*	14	5 wks
7 Jan 89 ●	ALL SHE WANTS IS *EMI DD 11*	9	5 wks
22 Apr 89	DO YOU BELIEVE IN SHAME *EMI DD 12*	30	4 wks
16 Dec 89	BURNING THE GROUND *EMI DD 13*	31	5 wks
4 Aug 90	VIOLENCE OF SUMMER (LOVE'S TAKING OVER) *Parlophone DD 14*	20	4 wks
17 Nov 90	SERIOUS *Parlophone DD 15*	48	3 wks

Judith DURHAM *Australia, female vocalist* — 5 wks

15 Jun 67	OLIVE TREE *Columbia DB 8207*	33	5 wks

Ian DURY and the BLOCKHEADS — 55 wks
UK, male vocal/instrumental group

29 Apr 78 ●	WHAT A WASTE *Stiff BUY 27*	9	12 wks
9 Dec 78 ★	HIT ME WITH YOUR RHYTHM STICK *Stiff BUY 38 ***	1	15 wks
4 Aug 79 ●	REASONS TO BE CHEERFUL (PT. 3) *Stiff BUY 50*	3	8 wks
30 Aug 80	I WANT TO BE STRAIGHT *Stiff BUY 90*	22	7 wks
15 Nov 80	SUEPERMAN'S BIG SISTER *Stiff BUY 100*	51	3 wks
25 May 85	HIT ME WITH YOUR RHYTHM STICK (re-mix) *Stiff BUY 214*	55	4 wks
26 Oct 85	PROFOUNDLY IN LOVE WITH PANDORA *EMI EMI 5534 ****	45	5 wks
27 Jul 91	HIT ME WITH YOUR RHYTHM STICK (2nd re-mix) *Flying FLYR 1*	73	1 wk

* Ian and the Blockheads ** Ian Dury

Slim DUSTY *Australia, male vocalist* — 15 wks

30 Jan 59 ●	A PUB WITH NO BEER *Columbia DB 4212*	3	15 wks

Bob DYLAN *US, male vocalist* — 133 wks

25 Mar 65 ●	TIMES THEY ARE A-CHANGIN' *CBS 201751*	9	11 wks
29 Apr 65 ●	SUBTERRANEAN HOMESICK BLUES *CBS 201753*	9	9 wks
17 Jun 65	MAGGIE'S FARM *CBS 201781*	22	8 wks
19 Aug 65 ●	LIKE A ROLLING STONE *CBS 201811*	4	12 wks
28 Oct 65 ●	POSITIVELY FOURTH STREET *CBS 201824*	8	12 wks
27 Jan 66	CAN YOU PLEASE CRAWL OUT YOUR WINDOW *CBS 201900*	17	5 wks
14 Apr 66	ONE OF US MUST KNOW (SOONER OR LATER) *CBS 202053*	33	5 wks
12 May 66 ●	RAINY DAY WOMEN NOS. 12 & 35 *CBS 202307*	7	8 wks
21 Jul 66	I WANT YOU *CBS 202258*	16	9 wks
14 May 69	I THREW IT ALL AWAY *CBS 4219*	30	6 wks
13 Sep 69 ●	LAY LADY LAY *CBS 4434*	5	12 wks
10 Jul 71	WATCHING THE RIVER FLOW *CBS 7329*	24	9 wks
6 Oct 73	KNOCKIN' ON HEAVEN'S DOOR *CBS 1762*	14	9 wks
7 Feb 76	HURRICANE *CBS 3878*	43	4 wks
29 Jul 78	BABY STOP CRYING *CBS 6499*	13	11 wks
28 Oct 78	IS YOUR LOVE IN VAIN *CBS 6718*	56	3 wks

DYNAMIX II featuring TOO TOUGH TEE — 4 wks
US, male vocal/instrumental group

8 Aug 87	JUST GIVE THE DJ A BREAK *Cooltempo COOL 151*	50	4 wks

DYNASTY *US, male vocal/instrumental group* — 20 wks

13 Oct 79	I DON'T WANT TO BE A FREAK (BUT I CAN'T HELP MYSELF) *Solar FB 1694*	20	13 wks
9 Aug 80	I'VE JUST BEGUN TO LOVE YOU *Solar SO 10*	51	4 wks
21 May 83	DOES THAT RING A BELL *Solar E 9911*	53	3 wks

DYNASTY OF TWO featuring ROWETTA – *See VARIOUS ARTISTS (EPs & LPs) - The Further Adventures Of North EP*

Ronnie DYSON *US, male vocalist* — 6 wks

4 Dec 71	WHEN YOU GET RIGHT DOWN TO IT *CBS 7449*	34	6 wks

E

Katherine E *US, female vocalist* — 7 wks

6 Apr 91	I'M ALRIGHT *Dead Dead Good GOOD 2*	41	5 wks
18 Jan 92	THEN I FEEL GOOD *PWL Continental PWL 13*	56	2 wks

Lizz E – *See FRESH 4 featuring Lizz E*

Sheila E *US, female vocalist/instrumentalist - percussion* — 9 wks

23 Feb 85	THE BELLE OF ST MARK *Warner Bros. W 9180*	18	9 wks

EAGLES *US, male vocal/instrumental group* — 50 wks

9 Aug 75	ONE OF THESE NIGHTS *Asylum AYM 543*	23	7 wks
1 Nov 75	LYIN' EYES *Asylum AYM 548*	23	7 wks
6 Mar 76	TAKE IT TO THE LIMIT *Asylum K 13029*	12	7 wks
15 Jan 77	NEW KID IN TOWN *Asylum K 13069*	20	7 wks
16 Apr 77 ●	HOTEL CALIFORNIA *Asylum K 13079*	8	10 wks
16 Dec 78	PLEASE COME HOME FOR CHRISTMAS *Asylum K 13145*	30	5 wks
13 Oct 79	HEARTACHE TONIGHT *Asylum K 12394*	40	5 wks
1 Dec 79	THE LONG RUN *Elektra K 12404*	66	2 wks

Robert EARL *UK, male vocalist* — 27 wks

25 Apr 58	I MAY NEVER PASS THIS WAY AGAIN *Philips PB 805*	14	13 wks
24 Oct 58	MORE THAN EVER (COME PRIMA) *Philips PB 867*	26	2 wks
21 Nov 58	MORE THAN EVER (COME PRIMA) (re-entry) *Philips PB 867*	28	2 wks
13 Feb 59	WONDERFUL SECRET OF LOVE *Philips PB 891*	17	10 wks

Charles EARLAND *US, male instrumentalist - keyboards* — 5 wks

19 Aug 78	LET THE MUSIC PLAY *Mercury 6167 703*	46	5 wks

Hit features uncredited male vocalist.

Steve EARLE *US, male vocalist/instrumentalist - guitar* — 7 wks

15 Oct 88	COPPERHEAD ROAD *MCA MCA 1280*	45	6 wks

| 31 Dec 88 | JOHNNY COME LATELY MCA MCA 1301 | 75 | 1 wk |

EARLY MUSIC CONSORT, directed by David MUNROW *UK, male/female instrumental group*

1 wk

| 3 Apr 71 | HENRY VIII SUITE EP *BBC RESL 1* | 49 | 1 wk |

Tracks on Henry VIII Suite EP: Fanfare Passomezo Du Roy, Gaillard De Escosse/Pavane, Mille Ducats/Larocque Gaillarde/Allemande/Wedding March, La Morisque/If Love Now Reigned/Ronde, Pourquoi.

EARTH WIND AND FIRE

125 wks

US, male vocal/instrumental group

12 Feb 77	SATURDAY NITE *CBS 4835*	17	9 wks
11 Feb 78	FANTASY *CBS 6056*	14	10 wks
13 May 78	JUPITER *CBS 6267*	41	5 wks
29 Jul 78	MAGIC MIND *CBS 6490*	75	1 wk
12 Aug 78	MAGIC MIND (re-entry) *CBS 6490*	54	4 wks
7 Oct 78	GOT TO GET YOU INTO MY LIFE *CBS 6553*	33	7 wks
9 Dec 78 ●	SEPTEMBER *CBS 6922*	3	13 wks
12 May 79 ●	BOOGIE WONDERLAND *CBS 7292 **	4	13 wks
28 Jul 79 ▲	AFTER THE LOVE HAS GONE *CBS 7721*	4	10 wks
6 Oct 79	STAR *CBS 7092*	16	8 wks
15 Dec 79	CAN'T LET GO *CBS 8077*	46	7 wks
8 Mar 80	IN THE STONE *CBS 8252*	53	3 wks
11 Oct 80	LET ME TALK *CBS 8982*	29	5 wks
20 Dec 80	BACK ON THE ROAD *CBS 9377*	63	4 wks
7 Nov 81 ●	LET'S GROOVE *CBS A 1679*	3	13 wks
6 Feb 82	I'VE HAD ENOUGH *CBS A 1959*	29	6 wks
5 Feb 83	FALL IN LOVE WITH ME *CBS A 2927*	47	4 wks
7 Nov 87	SYSTEM OF SURVIVAL *CBS EWF 1*	54	3 wks

* Earth Wind and Fire with the Emotions

EAST OF EDEN *UK, male instrumental group*

12 wks

| 17 Apr 71 ● | JIG A JIG *Deram DM 297* | 7 | 12 wks |

EAST 17 *UK, male vocal/instrumental group*

15 wks

29 Aug 92 ●	HOUSE OF LOVE *London LON 325*	10	9 wks
14 Nov 92	GOLD *London LON 331*	28	4 wks
19 Dec 92	GOLD (re-entry) *London LON 331*	71†	2 wks

EAST SIDE BEAT *Italy, male vocal/instrumental duo*

13 wks

| 30 Nov 91 ● | RIDE LIKE THE WIND *ffrr F 176* | 3 | 11 wks |
| 19 Dec 92 | ALIVE AND KICKING *ffrr F 206* | 26† | 2 wks |

Sheena EASTON *UK, female vocalist*

103 wks

5 Apr 80	MODERN GIRL *EMI 5042*	56	3 wks
19 Jul 80 ●	9 TO 5 *EMI 5066*	3	15 wks
9 Aug 80 ●	MODERN GIRL (re-entry) *EMI 5042*	8	12 wks
25 Oct 80	ONE MAN WOMAN *EMI 5114*	14	6 wks
14 Feb 81	TAKE MY TIME *EMI 5135*	44	5 wks
2 May 81	WHEN HE SHINES *EMI 5166*	12	8 wks
27 Jun 81 ●	FOR YOUR EYES ONLY *EMI 5195*	8	13 wks
12 Sep 81	JUST ANOTHER BROKEN HEART *EMI 5232*	33	8 wks
5 Dec 81	YOU COULD HAVE BEEN WITH ME *EMI 5252*	54	3 wks
31 Jul 82	MACHINERY *EMI 5326*	38	5 wks
12 Feb 83	WE'VE GOT TONIGHT *Liberty UP 658 **	28	7 wks
21 Jan 89	THE LOVER IN ME *MCA MCA 1289*	15	8 wks
18 Mar 89	DAYS LIKE THIS *MCA MCA 1325*	43	3 wks
15 Jul 89	101 *MCA MCA 1348*	54	2 wks
18 Nov 89	THE ARMS OF ORION *Warner Bros. W 2757 ***	27	5 wks

* Kenny Rogers and Sheena Easton ** Prince with Sheena Easton

See also Prince

EASTSIDE CONNECTION *US, disco aggregation*

3 wks

| 8 Apr 78 | YOU'RE SO RIGHT FOR ME *Creole CR 149* | 44 | 3 wks |

Clint EASTWOOD *US, male vocalist*

2 wks

| 7 Feb 70 | I TALK TO THE TREES *Paramount PARA 3004* | 18 | 2 wks |

This is the flip of Wand'rin Star by Lee Marvin and was listed with Marvin's A-side for 2 weeks only.

Clint EASTWOOD and General SAINT

3 wks

UK, male vocal duo

| 29 Sep 84 | LAST PLANE (ONE WAY TICKET) *MCA MCA 910* | 51 | 3 wks |

EASYBEATS *Australia, male vocal/instrumental group*

24 wks

| 27 Oct 66 ● | FRIDAY ON MY MIND *United Artists UP 1157* | 6 | 15 wks |
| 10 Apr 68 | HELLO HOW ARE YOU *United Artists UP 2209* | 20 | 9 wks |

Cleveland EATON *US, male instrumentalist - keyboards*

6 wks

| 23 Sep 78 | BAMA BOOGIE WOOGIE *Gull GULS 63* | 35 | 6 wks |

EAV *Austria, male vocal/instrumental group*

4 wks

| 27 Sep 86 | BA-BA-BANKROBBERY (ENGLISH VERSION??) *Columbia DB 9139* | 63 | 4 wks |

EAV is short for Erste Allgemeine Verunsicherung.

ECHO and the BUNNYMEN

73 wks

UK, male vocal/instrumental group

17 May 80	RESCUE *Korova KOW 1*	62	1 wk
18 Apr 81	CROCODILES *Korova ECHO 1*	37	4 wks
18 Jul 81	A PROMISE *Korova KOW 15*	49	4 wks
29 May 82	THE BACK OF LOVE *Korova KOW 24*	19	7 wks
22 Jan 83 ●	THE CUTTER *Korova KOW 26*	8	8 wks
16 Jul 83	NEVER STOP *Korova KOW 28*	15	7 wks
28 Jan 84 ●	THE KILLING MOON *Korova KOW 32*	9	6 wks
21 Apr 84	SILVER *Korova KOW 34*	30	5 wks
14 Jul 84	SEVEN SEAS *Korova KOW 35*	16	7 wks
19 Oct 85	BRING ON THE DANCING HORSES *Korova KOW 43*	21	7 wks
13 Jun 87	THE GAME *WEA YZ 134*	28	4 wks
1 Aug 87	LIPS LIKE SUGAR *WEA YZ 144*	36	4 wks
20 Feb 88	PEOPLE ARE STRANGE *WEA YZ 175*	29	5 wks
2 Mar 91	PEOPLE ARE STRANGE (re-issue) *East West YZ 567*	34	4 wks

Billy ECKSTINE *US, male vocalist*

48 wks

12 Nov 54 ●	NO ONE BUT YOU *MGM 763*	3	17 wks
27 Sep 57	PASSING STRANGERS *Mercury MT 164 **	22	2 wks
13 Feb 59 ●	GIGI *Mercury AMT 1018*	8	14 wks
12 Mar 69	PASSING STRANGERS (re-issue) *Mercury MF 1082 **	20	15 wks

* Billy Eckstine and Sarah Vaughan

EDDIE and the HOTRODS

26 wks

UK, male vocal/instrumental group

11 Sep 76	LIVE AT THE MARQUEE EP *Island IEP 2*	43	5 wks
13 Nov 76	TEENAGE DEPRESSION *Island WIP 6354*	35	4 wks
23 Apr 77	I MIGHT BE LYING *Island WIP 6388*	44	3 wks
13 Aug 77 ●	DO ANYTHING YOU WANNA DO *Island WIP 6401 **	9	10 wks
21 Jan 78	QUIT THIS TOWN *Island WIP 6411*	36	4 wks

* Rods

Tracks on Live At The Marquee EP: 96 Tears/Get Out Of Denver/Medley: Gloria/Satisfaction.

Left: ERASURE vocalist Andy Bell comtemplates partner Vince Clarke's studio domain.

Right: DEON ESTUS got the chart help he asked for from uncredited vocalist George Michael.

Left: EMF hold a press conference at Tower Records in West Hollywood during 1991.

Left: Television host Johnny Carson (centre) discusses the Grammy with multiple winners DUKE ELLINGTON (left) and Ella Fitzgerald.

Above: THE ELECTRIC PRUNES were from Seattle a quarter of a century before it became fashionable to originate from that Washington city.

Duane EDDY and the REBELS
201 wks

US, male instrumentalist - guitar and male instrumental group

5 Sep 58		REBEL ROUSER *London HL 8669*	19	10 wks
2 Jan 59		CANNONBALL *London HL 8764*	22	4 wks
19 Jun 59	●	PETER GUNN THEME *London HLW 8879*	6	10 wks
24 Jul 59		YEP *London HLW 8879*	17	5 wks
4 Sep 59		FORTY MILES OF BAD ROAD *London HLW 8929*	11	9 wks
11 Sep 59		PETER GUNN THEME (re-entry) *London HLW 8879*	27	1 wk
10 Dec 59		SOME KINDA EARTHQUAKE *London HLW 9007*	12	5 wks
19 Feb 60		BONNIE CAME BACK *London HLW 9050*	12	6 wks
28 Apr 60	●	SHAZAM! *London HLW 9104*	4	13 wks
21 Jul 60	●	BECAUSE THEY'RE YOUNG *London HLW 9162*	2	18 wks
10 Nov 60		KOMMOTION *London HLW 9225*	13	10 wks
12 Jan 61	●	PEPE *London HLW 9257*	2	14 wks
20 Apr 61	●	THEME FROM DIXIE *London HLW 9324*	7	10 wks
22 Jun 61		RING OF FIRE *London HLW 9370*	17	10 wks
14 Sep 61		DRIVIN' HOME *London HLW 9406*	30	4 wks
5 Oct 61		CARAVAN *Parlophone R 4826 ***	42	3 wks
24 May 62		DEEP IN THE HEART OF TEXAS *RCA 1288 ***	19	8 wks
23 Aug 62	●	BALLAD OF PALADIN *RCA 1300 ***	10	10 wks
8 Nov 62	●	DANCE WITH THE GUITAR MAN *RCA 1316 ****	4	16 wks
14 Feb 63		BOSS GUITAR *RCA 1329 ****	27	8 wks
30 May 63		LONELY BOY LONELY GUITAR *RCA 1344 ***	35	4 wks
29 Aug 63		YOUR BABY'S GONE SURFIN' *RCA 1357 ***	49	1 wk
8 Mar 75	●	PLAY ME LIKE YOU PLAY YOUR GUITAR *GTO GT 11 ****	9	9 wks
22 Mar 86	●	PETER GUNN *China WOK 6 *****	8	9 wks

* Duane Eddy ** Duane Eddy and the Rebelettes *** Art Of Noise featuring Duane Eddy

EDDY and the SOUL BAND
7 wks

US, male vocal/instrumental group

23 Feb 85		THE THEME FROM 'SHAFT' *Club JAB 11*	13	7 wks

Randy EDELMAN
US, male vocalist
18 wks

6 Mar 76		CONCRETE AND CLAY *20th Century BTC 2261*	11	7 wks
18 Sep 76		UPTOWN UPTEMPO WOMAN *20th Century BTC 2225*	25	7 wks
15 Jan 77		YOU *20th Century BTC 2253*	49	2 wks
17 Jul 82		NOBODY MADE ME *Rocket XPRES 81*	60	2 wks

EDELWEISS
Switzerland, male/female vocal/instrumental group 10 wks

29 Apr 89	●	BRING ME EDELWEISS *WEA YZ 353*	5	10 wks

EDISON LIGHTHOUSE
13 wks

UK, male vocal/instrumental group

24 Jan 70	★	LOVE GROWS (WHERE MY ROSEMARY GOES) *Bell 1091*	1	12 wks
30 Jan 71		IT'S UP TO YOU PETULA *Bell 1136*	49	1 wk

Dave EDMUNDS
UK, male vocalist/multi-instrumentalist
93 wks

21 Nov 70	★	I HEAR YOU KNOCKING *MAM 1*	1	14 wks
20 Jan 73	●	BABY I LOVE YOU *Rockfield ROC 1*	8	13 wks
9 Jun 73	●	BORN TO BE WITH YOU *Rockfield ROC 2*	5	12 wks
2 Jul 77		I KNEW THE BRIDE *Swansong SSK 19411*	26	8 wks
30 Jun 79	●	GIRLS TALK *Swansong SSK 19418*	4	11 wks
22 Sep 79		QUEEN OF HEARTS *Swansong SSK 19419*	11	9 wks
24 Nov 79		CRAWLING FROM THE WRECKAGE *Swansong SSK 19420*	59	4 wks
9 Feb 80		SINGING THE BLUES *Swansong SSK 19422*	28	8 wks
28 Mar 81		ALMOST SATURDAY NIGHT *Swansong SSK 19424*	58	3 wks
20 Jun 81		THE RACE IS ON *Swansong SSK 19425 ***	34	6 wks
26 Mar 83		SLIPPING AWAY *Arista ARIST 522*	60	4 wks
7 Apr 90		KING OF LOVE *Capitol CL 568*	68	1 wk

* Dave Edmunds and the Stray Cats

Alton EDWARDS
South Africa, male vocalist
9 wks

9 Jan 82		I JUST WANNA (SPEND SOME TIME WITH YOU) *Streetwave STRA 1897*	20	9 wks

Dennis EDWARDS featuring Siedah GARRETT
US, male/female vocal duo
10 wks

24 Mar 84		DON'T LOOK ANY FURTHER *Gordy TMG 1334*	45	5 wks
20 Jun 87		DON'T LOOK ANY FURTHER (re-entry) *Gordy TMG 1334*	55	5 wks

See also Michael Jackson.

Rupie EDWARDS
Jamaica, male vocalist
16 wks

23 Nov 74	●	IRE FEELINGS (SKANGA) *Cactus CT 38*	9	10 wks
8 Feb 75		LEGO SKANGA *Cactus CT 51*	32	6 wks

Tommy EDWARDS
US, male vocalist
18 wks

3 Oct 58	★	IT'S ALL IN THE GAME *MGM 989*	1	17 wks
7 Aug 59		MY MELANCHOLY BABY *MGM 1020*	29	1 wk

EGYPTIAN EMPIRE
UK, male producer - Tim Taylor
2 wks

24 Oct 92		THE HORN TRACK *Ffrreedom TAB 115*	61	2 wks

808 STATE
UK, male instrumental group
54 wks

18 Nov 89	●	PACIFIC STATE *ZTT ZANG 1*	10	9 wks
31 Mar 90		THE EXTENDED PLEASURE OF DANCE EP *ZTT 2T*	56	1 wk
2 Jun 90	●	THE ONLY RHYME THAT BITES *ZTT ZANG 3 ***	10	10 wks
15 Sep 90		TUNES SPLITS THE ATOM *ZTT ZANG 6 ***	18	7 wks
10 Nov 90	●	CUBIK/OLYMPIC *ZTT ZANG 5*	10	10 wks
16 Feb 91		IN YER FACE *ZTT ZANG 14*	9	6 wks
27 Apr 91		OOOPS *ZTT ZANG 19 ****	42	3 wks
17 Aug 91		LIFT/OPEN YOUR MIND *ZTT ZANG 20*	38	4 wks
29 Aug 92		TIME BOMB/NIMBUS *ZTT ZANG 33*	59	1 wk
12 Dec 92		ONE IN TEN *ZTT ZANG 39 *****	17†	3 wks

* MC Tunes versus 808 State ** 808 State featuring Bjork *** 808 State vs UB40
Tracks on The Extended Pleasure Of Dance EP: Ancodia/Cubik/Cuba Bora. Cubik is a re-issue of one of the tracks from The Extended Pleasure Of Dance EP.

EIGHTH WONDER
UK, male/female vocal/instrumental group
25 wks

2 Nov 85		STAY WITH ME *CBS A 6594*	65	2 wks
20 Feb 88	●	I'M NOT SCARED *CBS SCARE 1*	7	13 wks
25 Jun 88		CROSS MY HEART *CBS 651552 7*	13	8 wks
1 Oct 88		BABY BABY *CBS BABE 1*	65	2 wks

EINSTEIN – *See AMBASSADORS OF FUNK featuring MC MARIO; Simon HARRIS; TECHNOTRONIC*

Donnie ELBERT
US, male vocalist
29 wks

8 Jan 72	●	WHERE DID OUR LOVE GO? *London HL 10352*	8	10 wks

26 Feb 72	**I CAN'T HELP MYSELF** *Avco 6105 009*	11	10 wks
29 Apr 72	**LITTLE PIECE OF LEATHER** *London HL 10370*	27	9 wks

ELECTRA *UK, male vocal/instrumental group* — 7 wks

6 Aug 88	**JIBARO** *FFRR FFR 9*	54	3 wks
30 Dec 89	**IT'S YOUR DESTINY/AUTUMN LOVE** *London F 121*	...51	4 wks

ELECTRIBE 101 — 13 wks
UK/Germany, male/female vocal/instrumental group

28 Oct 89	**TELL ME WHEN THE FEVER ENDED** *Mercury MER 310*	32	5 wks
24 Feb 90	**TALKING WITH MYSELF** *Mercury MER 316*	23	5 wks
22 Sep 90	**YOU'RE WALKING** *Mercury MER 328*	50	3 wks

ELECTRIC LIGHT ORCHESTRA — 255 wks
UK, male vocal/instrumental group

29 Jul 72	● **10538 OVERTURE** *Harvest HAR 5053*	9	8 wks
27 Jan 73	● **ROLL OVER BEETHOVEN** *Harvest HAR 5063*	6	10 wks
6 Oct 73	**SHOWDOWN** *Harvest HAR 5077*	12	10 wks
9 Mar 74	**MA-MA-MA-BELLE** *Warner Bros. K 16349*	22	8 wks
10 Jan 76	● **EVIL WOMAN** *Jet 764*	10	8 wks
3 Jul 76	**STRANGE MAGIC** *Jet 779*	38	3 wks
13 Nov 76	● **LIVIN' THING** *Jet UP 36184*	4	12 wks
19 Feb 77	● **ROCKARIA!** *Jet UP 36209*	9	9 wks
21 May 77	● **TELEPHONE LINE** *Jet UP 36254*	8	10 wks
29 Oct 77	**TURN TO STONE** *Jet UP 36313*	18	12 wks
28 Jan 78	● **MR. BLUE SKY** *Jet UP 36342*	6	11 wks
10 Jun 78	● **WILD WEST HERO** *Jet JET 109*	6	14 wks
7 Oct 78	● **SWEET TALKIN' WOMAN** *Jet 121*	6	8 wks
9 Dec 78	**ELO EP** *Jet ELO 1*	34	8 wks
19 May 79	● **SHINE A LITTLE LOVE** *Jet 144*	6	10 wks
21 Jul 79	● **THE DIARY OF HORACE WIMP** *Jet 150*	8	9 wks
1 Sep 79	● **DON'T BRING ME DOWN** *Jet 153*	3	9 wks
17 Nov 79	● **CONFUSION/LAST TRAIN TO LONDON** *Jet 166*	8	10 wks
24 May 80	**I'M ALIVE** *Jet 179*	20	9 wks
21 Jun 80	★ **XANADU** *Jet 185 **	1	11 wks
2 Aug 80	**ALL OVER THE WORLD** *Jet 195*	11	8 wks
22 Nov 80	**DON'T WALK AWAY** *Jet 7004*	21	10 wks
1 Aug 81	● **HOLD ON TIGHT** *Jet 7011*	4	12 wks
24 Oct 81	**TWILIGHT** *Jet 7015*	30	7 wks
9 Jan 82	**TICKET TO THE MOON/HERE IS THE NEWS** *Jet 7018*	24	8 wks
18 Jun 83	**ROCK 'N' ROLL IS KING** *Jet A 3500*	13	9 wks
3 Sep 83	**SECRET MESSAGES** *Jet A 3720*	48	3 wks
1 Mar 86	**CALLING AMERICA** *Epic A 6844*	28	7 wks
11 May 91	**HONEST MEN** *Telstar ELO 100 ***	60	1 wk

* Olivia Newton-John and Electric Light Orchestra ** Electric Light Orchestra Part 2
Here Is The News *listed from 16 Jan 82. Tracks on ELO EP:* Out of My Head/Strange Magic/Ma-Ma-Ma-Belle/Evil Woman.

ELECTRIC PRUNES *US, male vocal/instrumental group* — 5 wks

9 Feb 67	**I HAD TOO MUCH TO DREAM LAST NIGHT** *Reprise RS 20532*	49	1 wk
11 May 67	**GET ME TO THE WORLD ON TIME** *Reprise RS 20564*	42	4 wks

ELECTRONIC *UK, male vocal/instrumental group* — 25 wks

16 Dec 89	**GETTING AWAY WITH IT** *Factory FAC 2577*	12	9 wks
27 Apr 91	● **GET THE MESSAGE** *Factory FAC 2877*	8	7 wks
21 Sep 91	**FEEL EVERY BEAT** *Factory FAC 3287*	39	4 wks
4 Jul 92	● **DISAPPOINTED** *Parlophone R 6311*	6	5 wks

ELECTRONICAS *Holland, male instrumental group* — 8 wks

19 Sep 81	**ORIGINAL BIRD DANCE** *Polydor POSP 360*	22	8 wks

ELECTROSET *UK, male instrumental production group* — 3 wks

21 Nov 92	**HOW DOES IT FEEL** *ffrr F 203*	27	3 wks

ELEGANTS *US, male vocal group* — 2 wks

26 Sep 58	**LITTLE STAR** *HMV POP 520*	25	2 wks

ELEVATION *UK, male instrumental/production duo* — 1 wk

23 May 92	**CAN YOU FEEL IT** *Nova Mute 12NOMU 3*	62	1 wk

ELGINS *US, male/female vocal group* — 20 wks

1 May 71	● **HEAVEN MUST HAVE SENT YOU** *Tamla Motown TMG 771*	3	13 wks
9 Oct 71	**PUT YOURSELF IN MY PLACE** *Tamla Motown TMG 787*	28	7 wks

ELIAS and his ZIGZAG JIVE FLUTES — 14 wks
South Africa, male instrumental group

25 Apr 58	● **TOM HARK** *Columbia DB 4109*	2	14 wks

Yvonne ELLIMAN *US, female vocalist* — 44 wks

29 Jan 72	**I DON'T KNOW HOW TO LOVE HIM** *MCA MMKS 5077*	47	1 wk
6 Nov 76	● **LOVE ME** *RSO 2090 205*	6	13 wks
7 May 77	**HELLO STRANGER** *RSO 2090 236*	26	5 wks
13 Aug 77	**I CAN'T GET YOU OUT OF MY MIND** *RSO 2090 251*	17	13 wks
6 May 78	● **IF I CAN'T HAVE YOU** *RSO 2090 266*	4	12 wks

I Don't Know How To Love Him *was one of four tracks on a Maxi-Single, two of which were credited during the disc's one week on the chart. The other track credited was* Superstar *by Murray Head.*

Duke ELLINGTON *US, orchestra* — 4 wks

5 Mar 54	● **SKIN DEEP** *Philips PB 243*	7	4 wks

Ray ELLINGTON *UK, orchestra* — 4 wks

15 Nov 62	**THE MADISON** *Ember S 102*	41	2 wks
20 Dec 62	**THE MADISON (re-entry)** *Ember S 102*	36	2 wks

Bern ELLIOTT and the FENMEN — 22 wks
UK, male vocalist and male vocal/instrumental backing group

21 Nov 63	**MONEY** *Decca F 11770*	14	13 wks
19 Mar 64	**NEW ORLEANS** *Decca F 11852*	24	9 wks

ELLIS, BEGGS AND HOWARD — 8 wks
UK, male vocal/instrumental group

2 Jul 88	**BIG BUBBLES, NO TROUBLES** *RCA PB 42089*	59	3 wks
11 Mar 89	**BIG BUBBLES, NO TROUBLES (re-entry)** *RCA PB 42089*	41	5 wks

Joey B ELLIS US, male vocalist — 10 wks

16 Feb 91		GO FOR IT (HEART AND FIRE) Capitol CL 601 *	20	8 wks
18 May 91		THOUGHT YOU WERE THE ONE FOR ME		
		Capitol CL 614	58	2 wks

* Rocky V featuring Joey B Ellis and Tynetta Hare

Shirley ELLIS US, female vocalist — 17 wks

| 6 May 65 | ● | THE CLAPPING SONG London HLR 9961 | 6 | 13 wks |
| 8 Jul 78 | | THE CLAPPING SONG (EP) MCA MCEP 1 | 59 | 4 wks |

Tracks on The Clapping Song (EP): The Clapping Song/Ever See A Diver Kiss His Wife While
The Bubbles Bounce Above The Water/The Name Game/The Nitty Gritty. The Clapping Song
itself qualifies as a re-issue.

E-LUSTRIOUS featuring Deborah FRENCH — 1 wk
UK, male/female vocal/instrumental group

| 15 Feb 92 | | DANCE NO MORE MOS MOS 001T | 58 | 1 wk |

Keith EMERSON UK, male instrumentalist - piano — 5 wks

| 10 Apr 76 | | HONKY TONK TRAIN BLUES Manticore K 13513 | 21 | 5 wks |

EMERSON, LAKE AND PALMER — 13 wks
UK, male instrumental group

| 4 Jun 77 | ● | FANFARE FOR THE COMMON MAN | | |
| | | Atlantic K 10946 | 2 | 13 wks |

See also Keith Emerson; Greg Lake.

Dick EMERY UK, male vocalist — 8 wks

| 26 Feb 69 | | IF YOU LOVE HER Pye 7N 17644 | 32 | 4 wks |
| 13 Jan 73 | | YOU ARE AWFUL Pye 7N 45202 | 43 | 4 wks |

EMF UK, male vocal/instrumental group — 38 wks

3 Nov 90	●	UNBELIEVABLE Parlophone R 6273	3	13 wks
2 Feb 91	●	I BELIEVE Parlophone R 6279	6	7 wks
27 Apr 91		CHILDREN Parlophone R 6288	19	5 wks
31 Aug 91		LIES Parlophone R 6295	28	3 wks
2 May 92		UNEXPLAINED EP Parlophone SGE 2026	18	4 wks
19 Sep 92		THEY'RE HERE Parlophone R 6321	29	3 wks
21 Nov 92		IT'S YOU Parlophone R 6327	23	3 wks

Tracks on Unexplained EP: Getting Through/Far From Me/The Same/Search And Destroy

EMMA UK, female vocalist — 6 wks

| 28 Apr 90 | | GIVE A LITTLE LOVE BACK TO THE WORLD | | |
| | | Big Wave BWR 33 | 33 | 6 wks |

An EMOTIONAL FISH UK, male vocal/instrumental group — 5 wks

| 23 Jun 90 | | CELEBRATE East West YZ 489 | 46 | 5 wks |

EMOTIONS US, female vocal group — 28 wks

10 Sep 77	●	BEST OF MY LOVE CBS 5555	4	10 wks
24 Dec 77		I DON'T WANNA LOSE YOUR LOVE CBS 5819	40	5 wks
12 May 79	●	BOOGIE WONDERLAND CBS 7292 *	4	13 wks

* Earth Wind and Fire with the Emotions

EN VOGUE US, female vocal/instrumental group — 38 wks

| 5 May 90 | ● | HOLD ON East West America 7908 | 5 | 11 wks |

21 Jul 90		LIES East West America 7893	44	4 wks
4 Apr 92		MY LOVIN' East West America A 8578	69	3 wks
9 May 92	●	MY LOVIN' (re-entry) East West America A 8578	4	9 wks
15 Aug 92		GIVING HIM SOMETHING HE CAN FEEL		
		East West America A 8524	44	3 wks
7 Nov 92		GIVING HIM SOMETHING HE CAN FEEL		
		(re-issue)/FREE YOUR MIND East West America A 8468	16†	8 wks

ENERGISE UK, male vocal/instrumental group — 1 wk

| 16 Feb 91 | | REPORT TO THE DANCEFLOOR | | |
| | | Network NWKT 16 | 69 | 1 wk |

ENERGY ORCHARD — 6 wks
Ireland, male vocal/instrumental group

| 27 Jan 90 | | BELFAST MCA MCA 1392 | 52 | 4 wks |
| 7 Apr 90 | | SAILORTOWN MCA MCA 1402 | 73 | 2 wks |

Harry ENFIELD UK, male vocalist — 7 wks

| 7 May 88 | ● | LOADSAMONEY (DOIN' UP THE HOUSE) | | |
| | | Mercury DOSH 1 | 4 | 7 wks |

ENGLAND DAN and John Ford COLEY — 12 wks
US, male vocal duo

25 Sep 76		I'D REALLY LOVE TO SEE YOU TONIGHT		
		Atlantic K 10810	26	7 wks
23 Jun 79		LOVE IS THE ANSWER Big Tree K 11296	45	5 wks

ENGLAND SISTERS UK, female vocal group — 1 wk

| 17 Mar 60 | | HEARTBEAT HMV POP 710 | 33 | 1 wk |

ENGLAND WORLD CUP SQUAD — 46 wks
UK, male football team vocalists

18 Apr 70	★	BACK HOME Pye 7N 17920	1	16 wks
15 Aug 70		BACK HOME (re-entry) Pye 7N 17920	46	1 wk
10 Apr 82	●	THIS TIME (WE'LL GET IT RIGHT)/ENGLAND		
		WE'LL FLY THE FLAG England ER 1	2	13 wks
19 Apr 86		WE'VE GOT THE WHOLE WORLD AT OUR		
		FEET/WHEN WE ARE FAR FROM HOME		
		Columbia DB 9128	66	2 wks
21 May 88		ALL THE WAY MCA GOAL 1 *	64	2 wks
2 Jun 90	★	WORLD IN MOTION... Factory/MCA FAC 2937 **	1	12 wks

* England Football Team and the 'sound' of Stock, Aitken and Waterman
** Englandneworder

ENGLAND WORLD CUP SQUAD – See UNION featuring the ENGLAND
WORLD CUP SQUAD

Scott ENGLISH US, male vocalist — 10 wks

| 9 Oct 71 | | BRANDY Horse HOSS 7 | 12 | 10 wks |

ENIGMA UK, male vocal/instrumental group — 15 wks

| 23 May 81 | | AIN'T NO STOPPING Creole CR 9 | 11 | 8 wks |
| 8 Aug 81 | | I LOVE MUSIC Creole CR 14 | 25 | 7 wks |

ENIGMA — 19 wks
Germany/Romania, male/female vocal/instrumental group

| 15 Dec 90 | ★ | SADNESS PART 1 Virgin International DINS 101 | 1 | 12 wks |

30 Mar 91	MEA CULPA PART II *Virgin International DINS 104*	55	3 wks
10 Aug 91	PRICIPLES OF LUST *Virgin International DINS 110*	59	2 wks
11 Jan 92	THE RIVERS OF BELIEF *Virgin International DINS 112*	68	2 wks

British Hit Singles Part One: Alphabetically by Artist
Date of chart entry/Title & catalogue no./Peak position reached/Weeks on chart
★ Number one ● Top Ten † still on chart at 31 Dec 1992
* = credited to act billed in footnote

ENYA *Ireland, female vocalist* **43 wks**

15 Oct 88	★ ORINOCO FLOW *WEA YZ 312*	1	13 wks
24 Dec 88	EVENING FALLS... *WEA YZ 356*	20	4 wks
10 Jun 89	STORMS IN AFRICA (PART II) *WEA YZ 368*	41	4 wks
19 Oct 91	CARIBBEAN BLUE *WEA YZ 604*	13	7 wks
7 Dec 91	HOW CAN I KEEP FROM SINGING *WEA YZ 365*	32	5 wks
1 Aug 92	● BOOK OF DAYS *WEA YZ 640*	10	6 wks
14 Nov 92	THE CELTS *WEA YZ 705*	29	4 wks

EON *UK, male producer - Ian Bela* **1 wk**

| 17 Aug 91 | FEAR: THE MINDKILLER *Vinyl Solution STORM 33* | 63 | 1 wk |

EQUALS *UK/Guyana, male vocal/instrumental group* **69 wks**

21 Feb 68	I GET SO EXCITED *President PT 180*	44	4 wks
1 May 68	BABY COME BACK *President PT 135*	50	1 wk
15 May 68	★ BABY COME BACK (re-entry) *President PT 135*	1	17 wks
21 Aug 68	LAUREL AND HARDY *President PT 200*	35	5 wks
27 Nov 68	SOFTLY SOFTLY *President PT 222*	48	3 wks
2 Apr 69	MICHAEL AND THE SLIPPER TREE *President PT 240*	24	7 wks
30 Jul 69	● VIVA BOBBY JOE *President PT 260*	6	14 wks
27 Dec 69	RUB A DUB DUB *President PT 275*	34	7 wks
19 Dec 70	● BLACK SKIN BLUE EYED BOYS *President PT 325*	9	11 wks

ERASURE *UK, male vocal/instrumental duo* **168 wks**

5 Oct 85	WHO NEEDS LOVE LIKE THAT *Mute MUTE 40*	55	2 wks
25 Oct 86	● SOMETIMES *Mute MUTE 51*	2	17 wks
28 Feb 87	IT DOESN'T HAVE TO BE *Mute MUTE 56*	12	9 wks
30 May 87	● VICTIM OF LOVE *Mute MUTE 61*	7	9 wks
3 Oct 87	● THE CIRCUS *Mute MUTE 66*	6	10 wks
5 Mar 88	● SHIP OF FOOLS *Mute MUTE 74*	6	8 wks
11 Jun 88	CHAINS OF LOVE *Mute MUTE 83*	11	7 wks
1 Oct 88	● A LITTLE RESPECT *Mute MUTE 85*	4	10 wks
10 Dec 88	● CRACKERS INTERNATIONAL EP *Mute MUTE 93*	2	13 wks
30 Sep 89	● DRAMA! *Mute MUTE 89*	4	8 wks
9 Dec 89	YOU SURROUND ME *Mute MUTE 99*	15	9 wks
10 Mar 90	● BLUE SAVANNAH *Mute MUTE 109*	3	10 wks
2 Jun 90	STAR *Mute MUTE 111*	11	7 wks
29 Jun 91	● CHORUS *Mute MUTE 125*	3	9 wks
21 Sep 91	● LOVE TO HATE YOU *Mute MUTE 131*	4	9 wks
7 Dec 91	AM I RIGHT (EP) *Mute MUTE 134*	15	6 wks
11 Jan 92	AM I RIGHT (EP) (re-mix) *Mute L12MUTE 134*	22	3 wks
28 Mar 92	● BREATH OF LIFE *Mute MUTE 142*	8	6 wks
13 Jun 92	★ ABBA-ESQUE EP *Mute MUTE 144*	1	12 wks
7 Nov 92	● WHO NEEDS LOVE (LIKE THAT) (re-mix) *Mute MUTE 150*	10	4 wks

Tracks on Crackers International EP: Stop/The Hardest Part/Knocking On Your Door/She Won't Be Home. Tracks on Am I Right EP: Am I Right/Carry On Clangers/Let It Flow/Waiting For Sex. Tracks on Am I Right (Re-mix EP): Am I Right/Chorus/Love To Hate You/Perfect Stranger. Tracks on Abba-esque EP: Lay All Your Love On Me/SOS/Take A Chance On Me/Voulez-Vous.

ERIC and the GOOD GOOD FEELING **1 wk**
UK, male/female vocal/instrumental group

| 3 Jun 89 | GOOD GOOD FEELING *Equinox EQN 1* | 73 | 1 wk |

See also S Express.

EROTIC DRUM BAND **3 wks**
Canada, male/female vocal/instrumental group

| 9 Jun 79 | LOVE DISCO STYLE *Scope SC 1* | 47 | 3 wks |

ERUPTION *US, male/female vocal/instrumental group* **21 wks**

| 18 Feb 78 | ● I CAN'T STAND THE RAIN *Atlantic K 11068* * | 5 | 11 wks |
| 21 Apr 79 | ● ONE WAY TICKET *Atlantic/Hansa K 11266* | 9 | 10 wks |

* Eruption featuring Precious Wilson

ESCORTS *UK, male vocal/instrumental group* **2 wks**

| 2 Jul 64 | THE ONE TO CRY *Fontana TF 474* | 49 | 2 wks |

ESSEX *US, male/female vocal group* **5 wks**

| 8 Aug 63 | EASIER SAID THAN DONE *Columbia DB 7077* | 41 | 5 wks |

David ESSEX *UK, male vocalist* **196 wks**

18 Aug 73	● ROCK ON *CBS 1693*	3	11 wks
10 Nov 73	● LAMPLIGHT *CBS 1902*	7	15 wks
11 May 74	AMERICA *CBS 2176*	32	5 wks
12 Oct 74	★ GONNA MAKE YOU A STAR *CBS 2492*	1	17 wks
14 Dec 74	STARDUST *CBS 2828*	7	10 wks
5 Jul 75	● ROLLIN' STONE *CBS 3425*	5	7 wks
13 Sep 75	★ HOLD ME CLOSE *CBS 3572*	1	10 wks
6 Dec 75	IF I COULD *CBS 3776*	13	8 wks
20 Mar 76	CITY LIGHTS *CBS 4050*	24	4 wks
16 Oct 76	COMING HOME *CBS 4486*	24	6 wks
17 Sep 77	COOL OUT TONIGHT *CBS 5495*	23	6 wks
11 Mar 78	STAY WITH ME BABY *CBS 6063*	45	5 wks
19 Aug 78	● OH WHAT A CIRCUS *Mercury 6007 185*	3	11 wks
21 Oct 78	BRAVE NEW WORLD *CBS 6705*	55	3 wks
3 Mar 79	IMPERIAL WIZARD *Mercury 6007 202*	32	8 wks
5 Apr 80	● SILVER DREAM MACHINE (PART 1) *Mercury BIKE 1*	4	11 wks
14 Jun 80	HOT LOVE *Mercury HOT 11*	57	4 wks
26 Jun 82	ME AND MY GIRL (NIGHT-CLUBBING) *Mercury MER 107*	13	10 wks
11 Dec 82	● A WINTER'S TALE *Mercury MER 127*	2	10 wks
4 Jun 83	THE SMILE *Mercury ESSEX 1*	52	4 wks
27 Aug 83	● TAHITI *Mercury BOUNT 1*	8	11 wks
26 Nov 83	YOU'RE IN MY HEART *Mercury ESSEX 2*	67	2 wks
17 Dec 83	YOU'RE IN MY HEART (re-entry) *Mercury ESSEX 2*	59	4 wks
23 Feb 85	FALLING ANGELS RIDING *Mercury ESSEX 5*	29	7 wks
18 Apr 87	MYFANWY *Arista RIS 11*	41	7 wks

Gloria ESTEFAN *US, female vocalist* **138 wks**

11 Aug 84	● DR BEAT *Epic A 4614* *	6	14 wks
17 May 86	BAD BOY *Epic A 6537* *	16	11 wks
16 Jul 88	● ANYTHING FOR YOU *Epic 651673 7* **	10	16 wks
22 Oct 88	1-2-3 *Epic 652958 7* **	9	9 wks
17 Dec 88	RHYTHM IS GONNA GET YOU *Epic 654514 7* **	16	9 wks
31 Dec 88	1-2-3 (re-entry) *Epic 652958 7* **	72	1 wk
11 Feb 89	● CAN'T STAY AWAY FROM YOU *Epic 651444 7* **	7	12 wks
15 Jul 89	● DON'T WANNA LOSE YOU *Epic 655054 0*	6	10 wks
16 Sep 89	OYE MI CANTO (HEAR MY VOICE) *Epic 655287 7*	16	8 wks
25 Nov 89	GET ON YOUR FEET *Epic 655450 7*	23	7 wks
3 Mar 90	HERE WE ARE *Epic 655473 9*	23	6 wks
26 May 90	CUTS BOTH WAYS *Epic 655982 7*	49	5 wks

26 Jan 91		COMING OUT OF THE DARK Epic 6565747	25	5 wks
6 Apr 91		SEAL OUR FATE Epic 6567737	24	7 wks
8 Jun 91		REMEMBER ME WITH LOVE Epic 6569687	22	6 wks
21 Sep 91		LIVE FOR LOVING YOU Epic 6573827	33	5 wks
24 Oct 92		ALWAYS TOMORROW Epic 6583977	24	4 wks
12 Dec 92	●	MIAMI HIT MIX/CHRISTMAS THROUGH YOUR EYES Epic 6588377	8†	3 wks

* Miami Sound Machine ** Gloria Estefan and Miami Sound Machine
Christmas Through Your Eyes *only listed from 19 Dec '92.*

Don ESTELLE – *See Windsor DAVIES and Don ESTELLE*

Deon ESTUS US, *male vocalist/instrumentalist - bass* **7 wks**

25 Jan 86		MY GUY - MY GIRL Sedition EDIT 3310 *	63	3 wks
29 Apr 89		HEAVEN HELP ME Mika MIKA 2	41	4 wks

* Amii Stewart and Deon Estus

ETHIOPIANS Jamaica, *male vocal/instrumental group* **6 wks**

13 Sep 67		TRAIN TO SKAVILLE Rio RIO 130	40	6 wks

Tony ETORIA UK, *male vocalist* **8 wks**

4 Jun 77		I CAN PROVE IT GTO GT 89	21	8 wks

E.U. – *See SALT-N-PEPA*

EUROPE Sweden, *male vocal/instrumental group* **46 wks**

1 Nov 86	★	THE FINAL COUNTDOWN Epic A 7127	1	15 wks
31 Jan 87		ROCK THE NIGHT Epic EUR 1	12	9 wks
18 Apr 87		CARRIE Epic EUR 2	22	8 wks
20 Aug 88		SUPERSTITIOUS Epic EUR 3	34	5 wks
1 Feb 92		I'LL CRY FOR YOU Epic 6576977	28	5 wks
21 Mar 92		HALFWAY TO HEAVEN Epic 6578517	42	4 wks

EURYTHMICS UK, *male/female vocal/instrumental duo* **198 wks**

4 Jul 81		NEVER GONNA CRY AGAIN RCA 68	63	3 wks
20 Nov 82		LOVE IS A STRANGER RCA DA 1	54	5 wks
12 Feb 83	●	SWEET DREAMS (ARE MADE OF THIS) RCA DA 2	2	14 wks
9 Apr 83	●	LOVE IS A STRANGER (re-entry) RCA DA 1	6	8 wks
9 Jul 83	●	WHO'S THAT GIRL? RCA DA 3	3	10 wks
5 Nov 83	●	RIGHT BY YOUR SIDE RCA DA 4	10	11 wks
21 Jan 84	●	HERE COMES THE RAIN AGAIN RCA DA 5	8	8 wks
3 Nov 84	●	SEXCRIME (NINETEEN EIGHTY FOUR) Virgin VS 728	4	13 wks
19 Jan 85		JULIA Virgin VS 734	44	4 wks
20 Apr 85		WOULD I LIE TO YOU? RCA PB 40101	17	8 wks
6 Jul 85	★	THERE MUST BE AN ANGEL (PLAYING WITH MY HEART) RCA PB 40247	1	13 wks
2 Nov 85	●	SISTERS ARE DOIN' IT FOR THEMSELVES RCA PB 40339 *	9	11 wks
11 Jan 86		IT'S ALRIGHT (BABY'S COMING BACK) RCA PB 40375	12	8 wks
14 Jun 86		WHEN TOMORROW COMES RCA DA 7	30	6 wks
6 Sep 86	●	THORN IN MY SIDE RCA DA 8	5	11 wks
29 Nov 86		THE MIRACLE OF LOVE RCA DA 9	23	9 wks
28 Feb 87		MISSIONARY MAN RCA DA 10	31	4 wks
24 Oct 87		BEETHOVEN (I LOVE TO LISTEN TO) RCA DA 11	25	5 wks
26 Dec 87		SHAME RCA DA 14	41	6 wks
9 Apr 88		I NEED A MAN RCA DA 15	26	5 wks
11 Jun 88		YOU HAVE PLACED A CHILL IN MY HEART RCA DA 16	16	8 wks
26 Aug 89		REVIVAL RCA DA 17	26	6 wks
4 Nov 89		DON'T ASK ME WHY RCA DA 19	25	6 wks
3 Feb 90		THE KING AND QUEEN OF AMERICA RCA DA 20	29	5 wks
12 May 90		ANGEL RCA DA 21	23	6 wks

9 Mar 91		LOVE IS A STRANGER (re-issue) RCA PB 44265	46	3 wks
16 Nov 91		SWEET DREAMS (ARE MADE OF THIS) (re-mix) RCA PB 45031	48	2 wks

* Eurythmics and Aretha Franklin

EVANGEL TEMPLE CHOIR – *See Johnny CASH*

Maureen EVANS UK, *female vocalist* **37 wks**

22 Jan 60		THE BIG HURT Oriole CB 1533	26	2 wks
17 Mar 60		LOVE KISSES AND HEARTACHES Oriole CB 1540	44	1 wk
2 Jun 60		PAPER ROSES Oriole CB 1550	40	5 wks
29 Nov 62	●	LIKE I DO Oriole CB 1760	3	18 wks
27 Feb 64		I LOVE HOW YOU LOVE ME Oriole CB 1906	34	10 wks
14 May 64		I LOVE HOW YOU LOVE ME (re-entry) Oriole CB 1906	50	1 wk

Paul EVANS US, *male vocalist* **14 wks**

27 Nov 59		SEVEN LITTLE GIRLS SITTING IN THE BACK SEAT London HLL 8968 *	25	1 wk
31 Mar 60		MIDNIGHT SPECIAL London HLL 9045	41	1 wk
16 Dec 78	●	HELLO THIS IS JOANIE (THE TELEPHONE ANSWERING MACHINE SONG) Spring 2066 932	6	12 wks

* Paul Evans and the Curls

EVASIONS UK, *male/female vocal/instrumental group* **8 wks**

13 Jun 81		WIKKA WRAP Groove GP 107	20	8 wks

Betty EVERETT US, *female vocalist* **14 wks**

14 Jan 65		GETTING MIGHTY CROWDED Fontana TF 520	29	7 wks
30 Oct 68		IT'S IN HIS KISS President PT 215	34	7 wks

Kenny EVERETT UK, *male vocalist* **12 wks**

12 Nov 77		CAPTAIN KREMMEN (RETRIBUTION) DJM DJS 10810 *	32	4 wks
26 Mar 83	●	SNOT RAP RCA KEN 1	9	8 wks

* Kenny Everett and Mike Vickers

Phil EVERLY US, *male vocalist* **15 wks**

6 Nov 82		LOUISE Capitol CL 266	47	6 wks
19 Feb 83	●	SHE MEANS NOTHING TO ME Capitol CL 276 *	9	9 wks

* Phil Everly and Cliff Richard

EVERLY BROTHERS US, *male vocal duo* **344 wks**

12 Jul 57	●	BYE BYE LOVE London HLA 8440	6	16 wks
8 Nov 57	●	WAKE UP LITTLE SUSIE London HLA 8498	2	13 wks
23 May 58	★	ALL I HAVE TO DO IS DREAM/CLAUDETTE London HLA 8618	1	21 wks
12 Sep 58	●	BIRD DOG London HLA 8685	2	16 wks
23 Jan 59	●	PROBLEMS London HLA 8781	6	12 wks
22 May 59		TAKE A MESSAGE TO MARY London HLA 8863	29	1 wk
29 May 59		POOR JENNY London HLA 8863	14	11 wks
19 Jun 59		TAKE A MESSAGE TO MARY (re-entry) London HLA 8863	27	1 wk
3 Jul 59		TAKE A MESSAGE TO MARY (2nd re-entry) London HLA 8863	20	8 wks
11 Sep 59	●	('TIL) I KISSED YOU London HLA 8934	2	15 wks
12 Feb 60		LET IT BE ME London HLA 9039	13	5 wks
31 Mar 60		LET IT BE ME (re-entry) London HLA 9039	26	4 wks
14 Apr 60	★	CATHY'S CLOWN Warner Bros. WB 1	1	18 wks

14 Jul 60 ●	WHEN WILL I BE LOVED *London HLA 9157*	4	16 wks
22 Sep 60 ●	LUCILLE /SO SAD (TO WATCH GOOD LOVE GO BAD) *Warner Bros. WB 19*	4	15 wks
15 Dec 60	LIKE STRANGERS *London HLA 9250*	11	10 wks
9 Feb 61 ★	WALK RIGHT BACK/EBONY EYES *Warner Bros. WB 33*	1	16 wks
15 Jun 61 ★	TEMPTATION *Warner Bros. WB 42*	1	15 wks
5 Oct 61	MUSKRAT/DON'T BLAME ME *Warner Bros. WB 50*	20	6 wks
18 Jan 62 ●	CRYIN' IN THE RAIN *Warner Bros. WB 56*	6	15 wks
17 May 62	HOW CAN I MEET HER *Warner Bros. WB 67*	12	10 wks
25 Oct 62	NO ONE CAN MAKE MY SUNSHINE SMILE *Warner Bros. WB 79*	11	11 wks
21 Mar 63	SO IT WILL ALWAYS BE *Warner Bros. WB 94*	23	11 wks
13 Jun 63	IT'S BEEN NICE *Warner Bros. WB 99*	26	5 wks
17 Oct 63	THE GIRL SANG THE BLUES *Warner Bros. WB 109*	25	9 wks
16 Jul 64	FERRIS WHEEL *Warner Bros. WB 135*	22	10 wks
3 Dec 64	GONE GONE GONE *Warner Bros. WB 146*	36	7 wks
6 May 65	THAT'LL BE THE DAY *Warner Bros. WB 158*	30	4 wks
20 May 65 ●	THE PRICE OF LOVE *Warner Bros. WB 161*	2	14 wks
26 Aug 65	I'LL NEVER GET OVER YOU *Warner Bros. WB 5639*	35	5 wks
21 Oct 65	LOVE IS STRANGE *Warner Bros. WB 5649*	11	9 wks
8 May 68	IT'S MY TIME *Warner Bros. WB 7192*	39	6 wks
22 Sep 84	ON THE WINGS OF A NIGHTINGALE *Mercury MER 170*	41	9 wks

All I Have To Do Is Dream was listed without Claudette for its first week on the chart, but from 30 May 58 both sides were charted for 20 more weeks. See also Phil Everly.

EVERTON 1985 *UK, male football team vocalists* **5 wks**

11 May 85	HERE WE GO *Columbia DB 9106*	14	5 wks

EVERYTHING BUT THE GIRL **38 wks**
UK, male/female vocal/instrumental duo

12 May 84	EACH AND EVERYONE *blanco y negro NEG 1*	28	7 wks
21 Jul 84	MINE *blanco y negro NEG 3*	58	2 wks
6 Oct 84	NATIVE LAND *blanco y negro NEG 6*	73	2 wks
2 Aug 86	COME ON HOME *blanco y negro NEG 21*	44	7 wks
11 Oct 86	DON'T LEAVE ME BEHIND *blanco y negro NEG 23*	72	2 wks
13 Feb 88	THESE EARLY DAYS *blanco y negro NEG 30*	75	1 wk
9 Jul 88 ●	I DON'T WANT TO TALK ABOUT IT *blanco y negro NEG 34*	3	9 wks
27 Jan 90	DRIVING *blanco y negro NEG 40*	54	2 wks
22 Feb 92	COVERS EP *blanco y negro NEG 54*	13	6 wks

Tracks on Covers EP: *Love Is Strange/Tougher Than The Rest/Time After Time/Alison.*

EX PISTOLS *UK, male vocal/instrumental group* **2 wks**

2 Feb 85	LAND OF HOPE AND GLORY *Virginia PISTOL 76*	69	2 wks

EXCITERS *US, male/female vocal group* **7 wks**

21 Feb 63	TELL HIM *United Artists UP 1011*	46	1 wk
4 Oct 75	REACHING FOR THE BEST *20th Century BTC 1005*	31	6 wks

EXILE *US, male vocal/instrumental group* **18 wks**

19 Aug 78 ●	KISS YOU ALL OVER *RAK 279*	6	12 wks
12 May 79	HOW COULD THIS GO WRONG *RAK 293*	67	2 wks
12 Sep 81	HEART AND SOUL *RAK 333*	54	4 wks

EXPLOITED *UK, male vocal/instrumental group* **13 wks**

18 Apr 81	DOGS OF WAR *Secret SHH 110*	63	4 wks
17 Oct 81	DEAD CITIES *Secret SHH 120*	31	5 wks
5 Dec 81	DON'T LET 'EM GRIND YOU DOWN *Superville EXP 1003 **	70	1 wk
8 May 82	ATTACK *Secret SHH 130*	50	3 wks

* Exploited and Anti-Pasti

EXPRESSOS *UK, male/female vocal/instrumental group* **5 wks**

21 Jun 80	HEY GIRL *WEA K 18246*	60	3 wks
14 Mar 81	TANGO IN MONO *WEA K 18431*	70	2 wks

EXTENSIVE – *See CHOPS-EMC + EXTENSIVE*

EXTREME *US, male vocal/instrumental group* **41 wks**

8 Jun 91	GET THE FUNK OUT *A & M AM 737*	19	7 wks
27 Jul 91 ●	MORE THAN WORDS *A & M AM 792*	2	11 wks
12 Oct 91	DECADENCE DANCE *A & M AM 773*	36	3 wks
23 Nov 91	HOLE HEARTED *A & M AM 839*	12	7 wks
2 May 92	SONG FOR LOVE *A & M AM 698*	12	6 wks
5 Sep 92	REST IN PEACE *A & M AM 0055*	13	5 wks
14 Nov 92	STOP THE WORLD *A & M AM 0096*	22	2 wks

E-ZEE POSSEE *UK, male/female vocal/instrumental group* **16 wks**

26 Aug 89	EVERYTHING STARTS WITH AN 'E' *More Protein PROT 1*	69	1 wk
20 Jan 90	LOVE ON LOVE *More Protein PROT 3*	59	3 wks
17 Mar 90	EVERYTHING STARTS WITH AN 'E' (re-entry) *More Protein PROT 1*	15	8 wks
30 Jun 90	THE SUN MACHINE *More Protein PROT 4*	62	3 wks
21 Sep 91	BREATHING IS E-ZEE *More Protein PROT 12 **	72	1 wk

* E-Zee Possee featuring Tara Newley

F

FAB *UK, male producers* **11 wks**

7 Jul 90 ●	THUNDERBIRDS ARE GO *Brothers Organisation FAB 1 **	5	8 wks
20 Oct 90	THE PRISONER *Brothers Organisation FAB 6 ***	56	2 wks
1 Dec 90	THE STINGRAY MEGAMIX *Brothers Organisation FAB 2 ****	66	1 wk

* FAB featuring MC Parker ** FAB featuring MC Number 6 *** FAB featuring Aqua Marina

Shelley FABARES *US, female vocalist* **4 wks**

26 Apr 62	JOHNNY ANGEL *Pye International 7N 25132*	41	4 wks

FABIAN *US, male vocalist* **1 wk**

10 Mar 60	HOUND DOG MAN *HMV POP 695*	46	1 wk

FACES *UK, male vocal/instrumental group* **46 wks**

18 Dec 71 ●	STAY WITH ME *Warner Bros. K 16136*	6	14 wks
17 Feb 73 ●	CINDY INCIDENTALLY *Warner Bros. K 16247*	2	9 wks
8 Dec 73 ●	POOL HALL RICHARD/I WISH IT WOULD RAIN *Warner Bros. K 16341*	8	11 wks
7 Dec 74	YOU CAN MAKE ME DANCE SING OR ANYTHING *Warner Bros. K 16494 **	12	9 wks
4 Jun 77	THE FACES EP *Riva 8*	41	3 wks

* Rod Stewart and the Faces
Tracks on The Faces EP: *Memphis/You Can Make Me Dance Sing Or Anything/Stay With Me/Cindy Incidentally.*

Joe FAGIN *UK, male vocalist* **20 wks**

7 Jan 84 ●	THAT'S LIVIN' ALRIGHT *Towerbell TOW 46*	3	11 wks

5 Apr 86	**BACK WITH THE BOYS AGAIN/GET IT RIGHT** Towerbell TOW 84	53	9 wks

Yvonne FAIR US, female vocalist   11 wks

24 Jan 76 ●	**IT SHOULD HAVE BEEN ME** Tamla Motown TMG 1013	5	11 wks

FAIR WEATHER UK, male vocal/instrumental group   12 wks

18 Jul 70 ●	**NATURAL SINNER** RCA 1977	6	12 wks

Fair Weather is led by Andy Fairweather-Low.

FAIRGROUND ATTRACTION   27 wks
UK, female/male vocal/instrumental group

16 Apr 88 ★	**PERFECT** RCA PB 41845	1	13 wks
30 Jul 88 ●	**FIND MY LOVE** RCA PB 42079	7	10 wks
19 Nov 88	**A SMILE IN A WHISPER** RCA PB 42249	75	1 wk
28 Jan 89	**CLARE** RCA PB 42607	49	3 wks

FAIRPORT CONVENTION   9 wks
UK, male/female vocal/instrumental group

23 Jul 69	**SI TU DOIS PARTIR** Island WIP 6064	21	8 wks
27 Sep 69	**SI TU DOIS PARTIR (re-entry)** Island WIP 6064	49	1 wk

Andy FAIRWEATHER-LOW UK, male vocalist   18 wks

21 Sep 74 ●	**REGGAE TUNE** A & M AMS 7129	10	8 wks
6 Dec 75 ●	**WIDE EYED AND LEGLESS** A & M AMS 7202	6	10 wks

Adam FAITH UK, male vocalist   251 wks

20 Nov 59 ★	**WHAT DO YOU WANT** Parlophone R 4591	1	19 wks
22 Jan 60 ★	**POOR ME** Parlophone R 4623	1	17 wks
14 Apr 60 ●	**SOMEONE ELSE'S BABY** Parlophone R 4643	2	13 wks
30 Jun 60 ●	**WHEN JOHNNY COMES MARCHING HOME/MADE YOU** Parlophone R 4665	5	13 wks
15 Sep 60 ●	**HOW ABOUT THAT** Parlophone R 4689	4	14 wks
17 Nov 60 ●	**LONELY PUP (IN A CHRISTMAS SHOP)** Parlophone R 4708	4	11 wks
9 Feb 61 ●	**WHO AM I/THIS IS IT!** Parlophone R 4735	5	14 wks
27 Apr 61	**EASY GOING ME** Parlophone R 4766	12	11 wks
20 Jul 61 ●	**DON'T YOU KNOW IT** Parlophone R 4807	12	10 wks
26 Oct 61 ●	**THE TIME HAS COME** Parlophone R 4837	4	14 wks
18 Jan 62	**LONESOME** Parlophone R 4864	12	9 wks
3 May 62 ●	**AS YOU LIKE IT** Parlophone R 4896	5	15 wks
30 Aug 62 ●	**DON'T THAT BEAT ALL** Parlophone R 4930	8	11 wks
13 Dec 62	**BABY TAKE A BOW** Parlophone R 4964	22	6 wks
31 Jan 63	**WHAT NOW** Parlophone R 4990	31	5 wks
11 Jul 63	**WALKIN' TALL** Parlophone R 5039	23	6 wks
19 Sep 63 ●	**THE FIRST TIME** Parlophone R 5061 *	5	13 wks
12 Dec 63	**WE ARE IN LOVE** Parlophone R 5091 *	11	12 wks
12 Mar 64	**IF HE TELLS YOU** Parlophone R 5109 *	25	9 wks
28 May 64	**I LOVE BEING IN LOVE WITH YOU** Parlophone R 5138 *	33	6 wks
26 Nov 64	**MESSAGE TO MARTHA (KENTUCKY BLUEBIRD)** Parlophone R 5201	12	11 wks
11 Feb 65	**STOP FEELING SORRY FOR YOURSELF** Parlophone R 5235	23	6 wks
17 Jun 65	**SOMEONE'S TAKEN MARIA AWAY** Parlophone R 5289	34	5 wks
20 Oct 66	**CHERYL'S GOIN' HOME** Parlophone R 5516	46	2 wks

* Adam Faith and the Roulettes

Horace FAITH Jamaica, male vocalist   10 wks

12 Sep 70	**BLACK PEARL** Trojan TR 7790	13	10 wks

Percy FAITH Canada, orchestra   30 wks

10 Mar 60 ●	**THEME FROM 'A SUMMER PLACE'** Philips PB 989	2	30 wks

FAITH BROTHERS UK, male vocal/instrumental group   6 wks

13 Apr 85	**THE COUNTRY OF THE BLIND** Siren SIREN 2	63	3 wks
6 Jul 85	**A STRANGER ON HOME GROUND** Siren SIREN 4	69	3 wks

FAITH, HOPE and CHARITY   4 wks
US, male/female vocal group

31 Jan 76	**JUST ONE LOOK** RCA 2632	38	4 wks

FAITH, HOPE and CHARITY   3 wks
UK, female vocal group

23 Jun 90	**BATTLE OF THE SEXES** WEA YZ 480	53	3 wks

FAITH NO MORE US, male vocal/instrumental group   35 wks

6 Feb 88	**WE CARE A LOT** Slash LASH 17	53	3 wks
10 Feb 90	**EPIC** Slash LASH 21	37	4 wks
14 Apr 90	**FROM OUT OF NOWHERE** Slash LASH 24	23	6 wks
14 Jul 90	**FALLING TO PIECES** Slash LASH 25	41	3 wks
8 Sep 90	**EPIC (re-issue)** Slash LASH 26	25	5 wks
6 Jun 92 ●	**MIDLIFE CRISIS** Slash LASH 37	10	5 wks
15 Aug 92	**A SMALL VICTORY** Slash LASH 39	29	5 wks
12 Sep 92	**A SMALL VICTORY (re-mix)** Slash LASHX 40	55	1 wk
21 Nov 92	**EVERYTHING'S RUINED** Slash LASH 43	28	3 wks

Marianne FAITHFULL UK, female vocalist   59 wks

13 Aug 64 ●	**AS TEARS GO BY** Decca F 11923	9	13 wks
18 Feb 65 ●	**COME AND STAY WITH ME** Decca F 12075	4	13 wks
6 May 65 ●	**THIS LITTLE BIRD** Decca F 12162	6	11 wks
22 Jul 65 ●	**SUMMER NIGHTS** Decca F 12193	10	10 wks
4 Nov 65	**YESTERDAY** Decca F 12268	36	4 wks
9 Mar 67	**IS THIS WHAT I GET FOR LOVING YOU** Decca F 22524	43	2 wks
24 Nov 79	**THE BALLAD OF LUCY JORDAN** Island WIP 6491	48	6 wks

FALCO Austria, male vocalist   26 wks

22 Mar 86 ★	**ROCK ME AMADEUS** A & M AM 278	1	15 wks
31 May 86 ●	**VIENNA CALLING** A & M AM 318	10	8 wks
2 Aug 86	**JEANNY** A & M AM 333	68	1 wk
27 Sep 86	**THE SOUND OF MUSIK** WEA U 8591	61	2 wks

FALL UK, male vocalist/multi-instrumentalist — Mark E. Smith   20 wks

13 Sep 86	**MR. PHARMACIST** Beggars Banquet BEG 168	75	1 wk
20 Dec 86	**HEY! LUCIANI** Beggars Banquet BEG 176	59	1 wk
9 May 87	**THERE'S A GHOST IN MY HOUSE** Beggars Banquet BEG 187	30	4 wks
31 Oct 87	**HIT THE NORTH** Beggars Banquet BEG 200	57	5 wks
30 Jan 88	**VICTORIA** Beggars Banquet BEG 206	35	3 wks
26 Nov 88	**BIG NEW PRINZ/JERUSALEM (DOUBLE SINGLE)** Beggars Banquet FALL 2/3	59	2 wks
27 Jan 90	**TELEPHONE THING** Cog Sinister SIN 4	58	1 wk
8 Sep 90	**WHITE LIGHTNING** Cog Sinister SIN 6	56	2 wks
14 Mar 92	**FREE RANGE** Cog Sinister SINS 8	40	1 wk

Tracks on Big New Prinz/Jerusalem double single: Big New Prinz/Wrong Place Right Time Number Two/Jerusalem/Acid Priest 2088.

British Hit Singles Part One: Alphabetically by Artist
Date of chart entry/Title & catalogue no./Peak position reached/Weeks on chart
★ Number one ● Top Ten † still on chart at 31 Dec 1992
* = credited to act billed in footnote

Harold FALTERMEYER
23 wks

Germany, male instrumentalist - keyboards

23 Mar 85	AXEL F *MCA MCA 949*..**62**	4 wks
1 Jun 85 ●	AXEL F (re-entry) *MCA MCA 949*..**2**	18 wks
24 Aug 85	FLETCH THEME *MCA MCA 991*...**74**	1 wk

Agnetha FALTSKOG *Sweden, female vocalist*
12 wks

28 May 83	THE HEAT IS ON *Epic A 3436* **35**	6 wks
13 Aug 83	WRAP YOUR ARMS AROUND ME *Epic A 3622* **44**	5 wks
22 Oct 83	CAN'T SHAKE LOOSE *Epic A 3812* **63**	1 wk

Georgie FAME *UK, male vocalist*
115 wks

17 Dec 64 ★	YEH YEH *Columbia DB 7428* * **1**	12 wks
4 Mar 65	IN THE MEANTIME *Columbia DB 7494* * **22**	8 wks
29 Jul 65	LIKE WE USED TO BE *Columbia DB 7633* * **33**	7 wks
28 Oct 65	SOMETHING *Columbia DB 7727* * **23**	7 wks
23 Jun 66 ★	GET AWAY *Columbia DB 7946* * **1**	11 wks
22 Sep 66	SUNNY *Columbia DB 8015* * **13**	8 wks
22 Dec 66	SITTING IN THE PARK *Columbia DB 8096* * **12**	10 wks
23 Mar 67	BECAUSE I LOVE YOU *CBS 202587* **15**	8 wks
13 Sep 67	TRY MY WORLD *CBS 2945* **37**	5 wks
13 Dec 67 ★	BALLAD OF BONNIE AND CLYDE *CBS 3124*..................**1**	13 wks
9 Jul 69	PEACEFUL *CBS 4295* **16**	9 wks
13 Dec 69	SEVENTH SON *CBS 4659* **25**	7 wks
10 Apr 71	ROSETTA *CBS 7108* * * **11**	10 wks

* Georgie Fame and the Blue Flames ** Fame and Price Together

FAMILY *UK, male vocal/instrumental group*
44 wks

1 Nov 69	NO MULE'S FOOL *Reprise RS 27001* **29**	7 wks
22 Aug 70	STRANGE BAND *Reprise RS 27009* **11**	12 wks
17 Jul 71 ●	IN MY OWN TIME *Reprise K 14090* **4**	13 wks
23 Sep 72	BURLESQUE *Reprise K 14196*...**13**	12 wks

FAMILY COOKIN' – *See LIMMIE and the FAMILY COOKIN'*

FAMILY DOGG *UK, male/female vocal group*
14 wks

28 May 69 ●	WAY OF LIFE *Bell 1055* **6**	14 wks

FAMILY FOUNDATION
4 wks

UK, male/female vocal/instrumental group

13 Jun 92	XPRESS YOURSELF *380 PEW 1* **42**	4 wks

FAMILY STAND *US, male/female vocal/instrumental group*
11 wks

31 Mar 90 ●	GHETTO HEAVEN *East West A 7997* **10**	11 wks

FAMILY STONE – *See SLY and the FAMILY STONE*

FAMOUS FLAMES – *See James BROWN*

FANTASTIC FOUR *US, male vocal group*
4 wks

24 Feb 79	B.Y.O.F. (BRING YOUR OWN FUNK) *Atlantic LV 14* **62**	4 wks

FANTASTICS *US, male vocal group*
12 wks

27 Mar 71 ●	SOMETHING OLD, SOMETHING NEW *Bell 1141* **9**	12 wks

FANTASY U.F.O. *UK, male instrumental group*
6 wks

29 Sep 90	FANTASY *XL XLT 15*..**56**	3 wks
10 Aug 91	MIND BODY SOUL *Strictly Underground YZ 591* * **50**	3 wks

* Fantasy U.F.O. featuring Jay Groove

FAR CORPORATION
11 wks

UK/US/Germany/Switzerland, male vocal/instrumental group

26 Oct 85 ●	STAIRWAY TO HEAVEN *Arista ARIST 639* **8**	11 wks

Don FARDON *UK, male vocalist*
22 wks

18 Apr 70	BELFAST BOY *Young Blood YB 1010* **32**	5 wks
10 Oct 70 ●	INDIAN RESERVATION *Young Blood YB 1015* **3**	17 wks

Chris FARLOWE *UK, male vocalist*
36 wks

27 Jan 66	THINK *Immediate IM 023* **49**	1 wk
10 Feb 66	THINK (re-entry) *Immediate IM 023* **37**	2 wks
23 Jun 66 ★	OUT OF TIME *Immediate IM 035* **1**	13 wks
27 Oct 66	RIDE ON BABY *Immediate IM 038* **31**	7 wks
16 Feb 67	MY WAY OF GIVING IN *Immediate IM 041*.......................**48**	1 wk
29 Jun 67	MOANIN' *Immediate IM 056* **46**	2 wks
13 Dec 67	HANDBAGS AND GLADRAGS *Immediate IM 065*............**33**	6 wks
27 Sep 75	OUT OF TIME (re-issue) *Immediate IMS 101* **44**	4 wks

FARM *UK, male vocal/instrumental group*
50 wks

5 May 90	STEPPING STONE/FAMILY OF MAN		
	Produce MILK 101 ....**58**	4 wks
1 Sep 90 ●	GROOVY TRAIN *Produce MILK 102* **6**	10 wks
8 Dec 90 ●	ALL TOGETHER NOW *Produce MILK 103* **4**	12 wks
13 Apr 91	SINFUL! *Siren SRN 138* * **28**	5 wks
4 May 91	DON'T LET ME DOWN *Produce MILK 104* **36**	3 wks
24 Aug 91	MIND *Produce MILK 105* **31**	4 wks
14 Dec 91	LOVE SEE NO COLOUR *Produce MILK 106* **58**	4 wks
4 Jul 92	RISING SUN *End Product 6581737* **48**	3 wks
17 Oct 92	DON'T YOU WANT ME *End Product 6584687*....................**18**	5 wks

* Pete Wylie with the Farm

FARMERS BOYS *UK, male vocal/instrumental group*
17 wks

9 Apr 83	MUCK IT OUT *EMI 5380* **48**	6 wks
30 Jul 83	FOR YOU *EMI 5401* **66**	3 wks
4 Aug 84	IN THE COUNTRY *EMI FAB 2* **44**	5 wks
3 Nov 84	PHEW WOW *EMI FAB 3*..**59**	3 wks

John FARNHAM *Australia, male vocalist*
17 wks

25 Apr 87 ●	YOU'RE THE VOICE *Wheatley PB 41093* **6**	17 wks

Joe FARRELL *US, male instrumentalist - saxophone*
4 wks

16 Dec 78	NIGHT DANCING *Warner Bros. LV 2* **57**	4 wks

Gene FARROW and G.F. BAND
8 wks

UK, male vocal/instrumental group

1 Apr 78	MOVE YOUR BODY *Magnet MAG 109*.................................**33**	5 wks

13 May 78	MOVE YOUR BODY (re-entry) *Magnet MAG 109*	67	1 wk
5 Aug 78	DON'T STOP NOW *Magnet MAG 125*	71	1 wk
19 Aug 78	DON'T STOP NOW (re-entry) *Magnet MAG 125*	74	1 wk

FASCINATIONS US, female vocal group — 6 wks

| 3 Jul 71 | GIRLS ARE OUT TO GET YOU *Mojo 2092 004* | 32 | 6 wks |

FASHION UK, male vocal/instrumental group — 12 wks

3 Apr 82	STREETPLAYER (MECHANIK) *Arista ARIST 456*	46	5 wks
21 Aug 82	LOVE SHADOW *Arista ARIST 483*	51	5 wks
18 Feb 84	EYE TALK *De Stijl A 4106*	69	2 wks

Susan FASSBENDER UK, female vocalist — 8 wks

| 17 Jan 81 | TWILIGHT CAFE *CBS 9468* | 21 | 8 wks |

FASTWAY UK, male vocal/instrumental group — 1 wk

| 2 Apr 83 | EASY LIVIN' *CBS A 3196* | 74 | 1 wk |

FAT BOYS US, male vocal rap group — 29 wks

4 May 85	JAIL HOUSE RAP *Sultra U 9123*	63	2 wks
22 Aug 87 ●	WIPEOUT *Urban URB 5* *	2	12 wks
18 Jun 88 ●	THE TWIST (YO, TWIST) *Urban URB 20* **	2	11 wks
5 Nov 88	LOUIE LOUIE *Urban URB 26*	46	4 wks

* Fat Boys and the Beach Boys ** Fat Boys and Chubby Checker

FAT LARRY'S BAND US, male vocal/instrumental group — 26 wks

2 Jul 77	CENTER CITY *Atlantic K 10951*	31	5 wks
10 Mar 79	BOOGIE TOWN *Fantasy FTC 168* *	46	4 wks
18 Aug 79	LOOKING FOR LOVE TONIGHT *Fantasy FTC 179*	46	6 wks
18 Sep 82 ●	ZOOM *Virgin VS 546*	2	11 wks

* F.L.B.

FATBACK BAND US, male vocal/instrumental group — 67 wks

6 Sep 75	YUM YUM (GIMME SOME) *Polydor 2066 590*	40	6 wks
6 Dec 75	(ARE YOU READY) DO THE BUS STOP *Polydor 2066 637*	18	10 wks
21 Feb 76 ●	(DO THE) SPANISH HUSTLE *Polydor 2066 656*	10	7 wks
29 May 76	PARTY TIME *Polydor 2066 682*	41	4 wks
14 Aug 76	NIGHT FEVER *Spring 2066 706*	38	4 wks
12 Mar 77	DOUBLE DUTCH *Spring 2066 777*	31	4 wks
9 Aug 80	BACKSTROKIN' *Spring POSP 149* *	41	9 wks
23 Jun 84	I FOUND LOVIN' *Master Mix CME 8401*	49	4 wks
4 May 85	GIRLS ON MY MIND *Atlantic/Cotillion FBACK 1* *	69	2 wks
6 Sep 86	I FOUND LOVIN' (re-mix) *Important TAN 10*	55	5 wks
5 Sep 87 ●	I FOUND LOVIN' (re-issue) *Master Mix CHE 8401*	7	12 wks

* Fatback

FATHER ABRAHAM and the SMURFS — 36 wks
Holland, male vocalist as himself and Smurfs

3 Jun 78 ●	THE SMURF SONG *Decca F 13759*	2	17 wks
30 Sep 78	DIPPETY DAY *Decca F 13798*	13	12 wks
2 Dec 78	CHRISTMAS IN SMURFLAND *Decca F 13819*	19	7 wks

FATHER ABRAPHART and the SMURPS – *See Jonathan KING*

FATIMA MANSIONS — 10 wks
Ireland, male/female vocal/instrumental group

| 23 May 92 | EVIL MAN *Radioactive SKX 56* | 59 | 1 wk |

| 1 Aug 92 | 1000% *Radioactive SKX 59* | 61 | 3 wks |
| 19 Sep 92 ● | (EVERYTHING I DO) I DO IT FOR YOU *Columbia 6583827* | 7 | 6 wks |

(Everything I Do) I Do It For You *was listed with* Theme From M.A.S.H. (Suicide Is Painless) *by Manic Street Preachers.*

FBI – *See REDHEAD KINGPIN and the FBI*

Phil FEARON UK, vocalist — 63 wks

23 Apr 83 ●	DANCING TIGHT *Ensign ENY 501* *	4	11 wks
30 Jul 83	WAIT UNTIL TONIGHT (MY LOVE) *Ensign ENY 503* *	20	8 wks
22 Oct 83	FANTASY REAL *Ensign ENY 507* **	41	6 wks
10 Mar 84 ●	WHAT DO I DO *Ensign ENY 510* **	5	10 wks
14 Jul 84 ●	EVERYBODY'S LAUGHING *Ensign ENY 514* **	10	10 wks
15 Jun 85	YOU DON'T NEED A REASON *Ensign ENY 517* **	42	4 wks
27 Jul 85	THIS KIND OF LOVE *Ensign ENY 521* ***	70	3 wks
2 Aug 86 ●	I CAN PROVE IT *Ensign PF 1*	8	9 wks
15 Nov 86	AIN'T NOTHING BUT A HOUSEPARTY *Ensign PF 2*	60	2 wks

* Galaxy featuring Phil Fearon ** Phil Fearon and Galaxy *** Phil Fearon and Galaxy featuring Dee Galdes

Wilton FELDER US, male instrumentalist - tenor sax — 7 wks

| 1 Nov 80 | INHERIT THE WIND *MCA 646* | 39 | 5 wks |
| 16 Feb 85 | (NO MATTER HOW HIGH I GET) I'LL STILL BE LOOKIN' UP TO YOU *MCA MCA 919* | 63 | 2 wks |

Bobby Womack is the uncredited lead vocalist on both hits, Altrina Grayson co-vocalises on MCA 919.

José FELICIANO US, male vocalist/instrumentalist - guitar — 23 wks

| 18 Sep 68 ● | LIGHT MY FIRE *RCA 1715* | 6 | 16 wks |
| 18 Oct 69 | AND THE SUN WILL SHINE *RCA 1871* | 25 | 7 wks |

FELIX UK, male producer — 17 wks

| 8 Aug 92 ● | DON'T YOU WANT ME *deConstruction 74321110507* | 6 | 11 wks |
| 24 Oct 92 | IT WILL MAKE ME CRAZY *deConstruction 74321118137* | 11 | 6 wks |

Julie FELIX US, female vocalist — 19 wks

| 18 Apr 70 | IF I COULD (EL CONDOR PASA) *RAK 101* | 19 | 11 wks |
| 17 Oct 70 | HEAVEN IS HERE *RAK 105* | 22 | 8 wks |

FELLY – *See TECHNOTRONIC*

FEMME FATALE US, male/female vocal/instrumental group — 2 wks

| 11 Feb 89 | FALLING IN AND OUT OF LOVE *MCA MCA 1309* | 69 | 2 wks |

FENDERMEN US, male vocal/instrumental duo - guitars — 9 wks

18 Aug 60	MULE SKINNER BLUES *Top Rank JAR 395*	50	1 wk
1 Sep 60	MULE SKINNER BLUES (re-entry) *Top Rank JAR 395*	37	2 wks
29 Sep 60	MULE SKINNER BLUES (2nd re-entry) *Top Rank JAR 395*	32	6 wks

FENMEN – *See Bern ELLIOTT and the FENMEN*

George FENTON and Jonas GWANGWA — 1 wk
UK/South Africa, male instrumental production duo

| 2 Jan 88 | CRY FREEDOM *MCA MCA 1228* | 75 | 1 wk |

The listed flip side of Cry Freedom *was* The Funeral *by Thuli Dumakude.*

Peter FENTON UK, male vocalist — **3 wks**

10 Nov 66	**MARBLE BREAKS IRON BENDS** *Fontana TF 748*	**46**	3 wks

Shane FENTON and the FENTONES — **28 wks**
UK, male vocal/instrumental group

26 Oct 61	**I'M A MOODY GUY** *Parlophone R 4827*	**22**	8 wks
1 Feb 62	**WALK AWAY** *Parlophone R 4866*	**38**	5 wks
5 Apr 62	**IT'S ALL OVER NOW** *Parlophone R 4883*	**29**	7 wks
12 Jul 62	**CINDY'S BIRTHDAY** *Parlophone R 4921*	**19**	8 wks

Fenton later became Alvin Stardust.

FENTONES UK, male instrumental group — **4 wks**

19 Apr 62	**THE MEXICAN** *Parlophone R 4899*	**41**	3 wks
27 Sep 62	**THE BREEZE AND I** *Parlophone R 4937*	**48**	1 wk

FERKO STRING BAND — **2 wks**
US, male vocal/instrumental group

12 Aug 55	**ALABAMA JUBILEE** *London HL 8140*	**20**	2 wks

Luisa FERNANDEZ Spain, female vocalist — **8 wks**

11 Nov 78	**LAY LOVE ON YOU** *Warner Bros. K 17061*	**31**	8 wks

FERRANTE and TEICHER — **18 wks**
US, male instrumental duo - pianos

18 Aug 60	**THEME FROM 'THE APARTMENT'** *London HLT 9164*	**44**	1 wk
9 Mar 61 ●	**THEME FROM 'EXODUS'** *London HLT 9298 and HMV POP 881*	**6**	17 wks

Theme From 'Exodus' available first on London, then on HMV when the American label, United Artists, changed its UK outlet.

José FERRER US, male vocalist — **3 wks**

19 Feb 54 ●	**WOMAN** *Philips PB 220*	**7**	3 wks

Woman coupled with Man by Rosemary Clooney.

FERRY AID International, male/female charity ensemble — **7 wks**

4 Apr 87 ★	**LET IT BE** *The Sun AID 1*	**1**	7 wks

Bryan FERRY UK, male vocalist — **119 wks**

29 Sep 73 ●	**A HARD RAIN'S GONNA FALL** *Island WIP 6170*	**10**	9 wks
25 May 74	**THE IN CROWD** *Island WIP 6196*	**13**	6 wks
31 Aug 74	**SMOKE GETS IN YOUR EYES** *Island WIP 6205*	**17**	8 wks
5 Jul 75	**YOU GO TO MY HEAD** *Island WIP 6234*	**33**	3 wks
12 Jun 76 ●	**LET'S STICK TOGETHER** *Island WIP 6307*	**4**	10 wks
7 Aug 76 ●	**EXTENDED PLAY EP** *Island IEP 1*	**7**	9 wks
5 Feb 77 ●	**THIS IS TOMORROW** *Polydor 2001 704*	**9**	9 wks
14 May 77	**TOKYO JOE** *Polydor 2001 711*	**15**	7 wks
13 May 78	**WHAT GOES ON** *Polydor POSP 3*	**67**	2 wks
5 Aug 78	**SIGN OF THE TIMES** *Polydor 2001 798*	**37**	8 wks
11 May 85 ●	**SLAVE TO LOVE** *EG FERRY 1*	**10**	9 wks
31 Aug 85	**DON'T STOP THE DANCE** *EG FERRY 2*	**21**	7 wks
7 Dec 85	**WINDSWEPT** *EG FERRY 3*	**46**	3 wks
29 Mar 86	**IS YOUR LOVE STRONG ENOUGH?** *EG FERRY 4*	**22**	7 wks
10 Oct 87	**THE RIGHT STUFF** *Virgin VS 940*	**37**	6 wks
13 Feb 88	**KISS AND TELL** *Virgin VS 1034*	**41**	5 wks
29 Oct 88	**LET'S STICK TOGETHER (re-mix)** *EG EGO 44*	**12**	7 wks

11 Feb 89	**THE PRICE OF LOVE (re-mix)** *EG EGO 46*	**49**	3 wks
22 Apr 89	**HE'LL HAVE TO GO** *EG EGO 48*	**63**	1 wk

Tracks on EP: Price Of Love/Shame Shame Shame/Heart On My Sleeve/It's Only Love.

Karel FIALKA UK, male vocalist/multi-instrumentalist — **12 wks**

17 May 80	**THE EYES HAVE IT** *Blueprint BLU 2005*	**52**	4 wks
5 Sep 87 ●	**HEY MATTHEW** *IRS IRM 140*	**9**	8 wks

FIAT LUX UK, male vocal/instrumental group — **4 wks**

28 Jan 84	**SECRETS** *Polydor FIAT 2*	**65**	3 wks
17 Mar 84	**BLUE EMOTION** *Polydor FIAT 3*	**59**	1 wk

FICTION FACTORY UK, male vocal/instrumental group — **11 wks**

14 Jan 84 ●	**(FEELS LIKE) HEAVEN** *CBS A 3996*	**6**	9 wks
17 Mar 84	**GHOST OF LOVE** *CBS A 3819*	**64**	2 wks

FIDDLER'S DRAM — **9 wks**
UK, male/female vocal/instrumental group

15 Dec 79 ●	**DAY TRIP TO BANGOR (DIDN'T WE HAVE A LOVELY TIME)** *Dingles SID 211*	**3**	9 wks

FIDELFATTI featuring RONNETTE — **1 wk**
Italy, male producer and female vocalist

27 Jan 90	**JUST WANNA TOUCH ME** *Urban URB 46*	**65**	1 wk

Billy FIELD Australia, male vocalist — **3 wks**

12 Jun 82	**YOU WEREN'T IN LOVE WITH ME** *CBS A 2344*	**67**	3 wks

Ernie FIELDS US, orchestra — **8 wks**

25 Dec 59	**IN THE MOOD** *London HL 8985*	**13**	8 wks

Gracie FIELDS UK, female vocalist — **15 wks**

31 May 57 ●	**AROUND THE WORLD** *Columbia DB 3953*	**8**	8 wks
2 Aug 57	**AROUND THE WORLD (re-entry)** *Columbia DB 3953*	**24**	1 wk
6 Nov 59	**LITTLE DONKEY** *Columbia DB 4360*	**30**	1 wk
20 Nov 59	**LITTLE DONKEY (re-entry)** *Columbia DB 4360*	**20**	5 wks

FIELDS OF THE NEPHILIM — **9 wks**
UK, male vocal/instrumental group

24 Oct 87	**BLUE WATER** *Situation Two SIT 48*	**75**	1 wk
4 Jun 88	**MOONCHILD** *Situation Two SIT 52*	**28**	3 wks
27 May 89	**PSYCHONAUT** *Situation Two ST 57*	**35**	3 wks
4 Aug 90	**FOR HER LIGHT** *Beggars Banquet BEG 244T*	**54**	1 wk
24 Nov 90	**SUMERLAND (DREAMED)** *Beggars Banquet BEG 250*	**37**	1 wk

Richard 'Dimples' FIELDS US, male vocalist — **4 wks**

20 Feb 82	**I'VE GOT TO LEARN TO SAY NO** *Epic EPC A 1918*	**56**	4 wks

FIFTH DIMENSION US, male/female vocal group — **21 wks**

16 Apr 69	**AQUARIUS/LET THE SUNSHINE IN (MEDLEY)** *Liberty LBF 15193*	**11**	12 wks
17 Jan 70	**WEDDING BELL BLUES** *Liberty LBF 15288*	**16**	9 wks

52ND STREET UK, male/female vocal/instrumental group   **13 wks**

2 Nov 85	TELL ME (HOW IT FEELS) 10 TEN 74	54	5 wks
11 Jan 86	YOU'RE MY LAST CHANCE 10 TEN 89	49	4 wks
8 Mar 86	I CAN'T LET YOU GO 10 TEN 114	57	4 wks

53RD AND THIRD – See Jonathan KING

FINAL CUT – See TRUE FAITH with FINAL CUT

FINE YOUNG CANNIBALS   **76 wks**
UK, male vocal/instrumental group

8 Jun 85 ●	JOHNNY COME HOME London LON 68	8	13 wks
9 Nov 85	BLUE London LON 79	41	6 wks
11 Jan 86 ●	SUSPICIOUS MINDS London LON 82	8	9 wks
12 Apr 86	FUNNY HOW LOVE IS London LON 88	58	4 wks
21 Mar 87 ●	EVER FALLEN IN LOVE London LON 121	9	10 wks
7 Jan 89 ●	SHE DRIVES ME CRAZY London LON 199	5	11 wks
15 Apr 89 ●	GOOD THING London LON 218	7	8 wks
19 Aug 89	DON'T LOOK BACK London LON 220	34	4 wks
18 Nov 89	I'M NOT THE MAN I USED TO BE London LON 244	20	8 wks
24 Feb 90	I'M NOT SATISFIED London LON 252	46	3 wks

FINITRIBE UK, male/female vocal/instrumental group   **1 wk**

| 11 Jul 92 | FOREVERGREEN One Little Indian 74 TP12F | 51 | 1 wk |

FINK BROTHERS UK, male vocal/instrumental duo   **4 wks**

| 9 Feb 85 | MUTANTS IN MEGA CITY ONE Zarjazz JAZZ 2 | 50 | 4 wks |

Micky FINN – See URBAN SHAKEDOWN featuring Micky FINN

Elisa FIORILLO US, female vocalist   **14 wks**

| 28 Nov 87 ● | WHO FOUND WHO Chrysalis CHS JEL 1 * | 10 | 10 wks |
| 13 Feb 88 | HOW CAN I FORGET YOU Chrysalis ELISA 1 | 50 | 4 wks |

* Jellybean featuring Elisa Fiorillo

FIRE INC. – See Jim STEINMAN

FIRE ISLAND UK, male instrumental/production group   **1 wk**

| 8 Aug 92 | IN YOUR BONES/FIRE ISLAND Boys Own BOIX 11 | 66 | 1 wk |

FIREBALLS US, male instrumental group   **17 wks**

27 Jul 61	QUITE A PARTY Pye International 7N 25092	29	9 wks
14 Nov 63	SUGAR SHACK London HLD 9789 *	45	4 wks
19 Dec 63	SUGAR SHACK (re-entry) London HLD 9789 *	46	4 wks

* Jimmy Gilmer and the Fireballs

FIREHOUSE US, male vocal/instrumental group   **2 wks**

| 13 Jul 91 | DON'T TREAT ME BAD Epic 6567807 | 71 | 1 wk |
| 19 Dec 92 | WHEN I LOOK INTO YOUR EYES Epic 6588347 | 65 | 1 wk |

FIRM UK, male vocal/instrumental group   **21 wks**

| 17 Jul 82 | ARTHUR DALEY ('E'S ALRIGHT) Bark HID 1 | 14 | 9 wks |
| 6 Jun 87 ★ | STAR TREKKIN' Bark TREK 1 | 1 | 12 wks |

FIRST CHOICE US, female vocal group   **21 wks**

| 19 May 73 | ARMED AND EXTREMELY DANGEROUS Bell 1297 | 16 | 10 wks |
| 4 Aug 73 ● | SMARTY PANTS Bell 1324 | 9 | 11 wks |

FIRST CLASS UK, male vocal group   **10 wks**

| 15 Jun 74 | BEACH BABY UK 66 | 13 | 10 wks |

FIRST EDITION – See Kenny ROGERS

FIRST LIGHT UK, male vocal/instrumental duo   **5 wks**

| 21 May 83 | EXPLAIN THE REASONS London LON 26 | 65 | 3 wks |
| 28 Jan 84 | WISH YOU WERE HERE London LON 43 | 71 | 2 wks |

FISCHER-Z UK, male vocal/instrumental group   **7 wks**

| 26 May 79 | THE WORKER United Artists UP 36509 | 53 | 5 wks |
| 3 May 80 | SO LONG United Artists BP 342 | 72 | 2 wks |

FISH UK, male vocalist   **17 wks**

18 Oct 86	SHORT CUT TO SOMEWHERE Charisma CB 426 *	75	1 wk
28 Oct 89	STATE OF MIND EMI EM 109	32	3 wks
6 Jan 90	BIG WEDGE EMI EM 125	25	4 wks
17 Mar 90	A GENTLEMAN'S EXCUSE ME EMI EM 135	30	3 wks
28 Sep 91	INTERNAL EXILE Polydor FISHY 1	37	2 wks
11 Jan 92	CREDO Polydor FISHY 2	38	2 wks
4 Jul 92	SOMETHING IN THE AIR Polydor FISHY 3	51	2 wks

* Fish and Tony Banks

FISHBONE US, male vocal/instrumental group   **2 wks**

| 1 Aug 92 | EVERYDAY SUNSHINE/FIGHT THE YOUTH Columbia 6581937 | 60 | 2 wks |

Eddie FISHER US, male vocalist   **105 wks**

2 Jan 53 ★	OUTSIDE OF HEAVEN HMV B 10362	1	16 wks
23 Jan 53	EVERYTHING I HAVE IS YOURS HMV B 10398	12	1 wk
6 Feb 53 ●	EVERYTHING I HAVE IS YOURS (re-entry) HMV B 10398	8	4 wks
1 May 53 ●	DOWNHEARTED HMV B 10450	3	15 wks
1 May 53 ●	OUTSIDE OF HEAVEN (re-entry) HMV B 10362	12	1 wk
22 May 53 ★	I'M WALKING BEHIND YOU HMV B 10489 *	1	18 wks
6 Nov 53 ●	WISH YOU WERE HERE HMV B 10564	8	9 wks
22 Jan 54 ●	OH MY PAPA HMV B 10614	9	1 wk
5 Feb 54 ●	OH MY PAPA (re-entry) HMV B 10614	11	1 wk
26 Feb 54 ●	OH MY PAPA (2nd re-entry) HMV B 10614	10	1 wk
12 Mar 54 ●	OH MY PAPA (3rd re-entry) HMV B 10614	11	1 wk
29 Oct 54	I NEED YOU NOW HMV B 10755	16	2 wks
19 Nov 54	I NEED YOU NOW (re-entry) HMV B 10755	13	7 wks
21 Jan 55	I NEED YOU NOW (2nd re-entry) HMV B 10755	19	1 wk
18 Mar 55 ●	WEDDING BELLS HMV B 10839	5	11 wks
23 Nov 56 ●	CINDY OH CINDY HMV POP 273	5	16 wks

* Eddie Fisher with Sally Sweetland (soprano)

Mark FISHER featuring Dotty GREEN   **2 wks**
UK, male instrumentalist - keyboards and female vocalist

| 29 Jun 85 | LOVE SITUATION Total Control TOCO 3 | 59 | 2 wks |

Toni FISHER US, female vocalist   **1 wk**

| 12 Feb 60 | THE BIG HURT Top Rank JAR 261 | 30 | 1 wk |

Ella FITZGERALD US, female vocalist — 29 wks

23 May 58	**SWINGIN' SHEPHERD BLUES** HMV POP 486 15		5 wks
16 Oct 59	**BUT NOT FOR ME** HMV POP 657 25		2 wks
25 Dec 59	**BUT NOT FOR ME (re-entry)** HMV POP 657 29		1 wk
21 Apr 60	**MACK THE KNIFE** HMV POP 736 19		9 wks
6 Oct 60	**HOW HIGH THE MOON** HMV POP 782 46		1 wk
22 Nov 62	**DESAFINADO** Verve VS 502 38		4 wks
27 Dec 62	**DESAFINADO (re-entry)** Verve VS 502 41		2 wks
30 Apr 64	**CAN'T BUY ME LOVE** Verve VS 519 34		5 wks

Scott FITZGERALD UK, male vocalist — 12 wks

14 Jan 78 ●	**IF I HAD WORDS** Pepper UP 36333 * 3		10 wks
7 May 88	**GO** PRT PYS 10 52		2 wks

* Scott Fitzgerald and Yvonne Keeley and the St Thomas More School Choir

FIVE SMITH BROTHERS UK, male vocal group — 1 wk

22 Jul 55	**I'M IN FAVOUR OF FRIENDSHIP** Decca F 10527 20		1 wk

FIVE STAR UK, male/female vocal group — 140 wks

4 May 85	**ALL FALL DOWN** Tent PB 40039 15		12 wks
20 Jul 85	**LET ME BE THE ONE** Tent PB 40193 18		9 wks
14 Sep 85	**LOVE TAKE OVER** Tent PB 40353 25		9 wks
16 Nov 85	**R.S.V.P.** Tent PB 40445 45		5 wks
11 Jan 86 ●	**SYSTEM ADDICT** Tent PB 40515 3		11 wks
12 Apr 86 ●	**CAN'T WAIT ANOTHER MINUTE** Tent PB 40697 7		10 wks
26 Jul 86 ●	**FIND THE TIME** Tent PB 40799 7		10 wks
13 Sep 86 ●	**RAIN OR SHINE** Tent PB 40901 2		11 wks
22 Nov 86	**IF I SAY YES** Tent PB 40981 15		9 wks
7 Feb 87 ●	**STAY OUT OF MY LIFE** Tent PB 41131 9		8 wks
18 Apr 87 ●	**THE SLIGHTEST TOUCH** Tent PB 41265 4		9 wks
22 Aug 87	**WHENEVER YOU'RE READY** Tent PB 41477 11		6 wks
10 Oct 87	**STRONG AS STEEL** Tent PB 41565 16		7 wks
5 Dec 87	**SOMEWHERE SOMEBODY** Tent PB 41661 23		6 wks
4 Jun 88	**ANOTHER WEEKEND** Tent PB 42081 18		4 wks
6 Aug 88	**ROCK MY WORLD** Tent PB 42145 28		4 wks
17 Sep 88	**THERE'S A BRAND NEW WORLD** Tent PB 42235 61		2 wks
19 Nov 88	**LET ME BE YOURS** Tent PB 42343 51		3 wks
8 Apr 89	**WITH EVERY HEARTBEAT** Tent PB 42693 49		2 wks
10 Mar 90	**TREAT ME LIKE A LADY** Tent FIVE 1 54		2 wks
7 Jul 90	**HOT LOVE** Tent FIVE 2 68		1 wk

FIVE THIRTY UK, male vocal/instrumental group — 4 wks

4 Aug 90	**ABSTAIN** East West YZ 530 75		1 wk
25 May 91	**13TH DISCIPLE** East West YZ 577 67		1 wk
3 Aug 91	**SUPERNOVA** East West YZ 594 75		1 wk
2 Nov 91	**YOU (EP)** East West YZ 624 72		1 wk

Tracks on You (EP): You/Cuddly Drug/Slow Train Into The Ocean.

5000 VOLTS UK, male/female vocal/instrumental group — 18 wks

6 Sep 75 ●	**I'M ON FIRE** Philips 6006 464 4		9 wks
24 Jul 76 ●	**DR. KISS KISS** Philips 6006 533 8		9 wks

FIXX UK, male vocal/instrumental group — 8 wks

24 Apr 82	**STAND OR FALL** MCA FIXX 2 54		4 wks
17 Jul 82	**RED SKIES** MCA FIXX 3 57		4 wks

Roberta FLACK US, female vocalist — 79 wks

27 May 72	**THE FIRST TIME EVER I SAW YOUR FACE** Atlantic K 10161 14		14 wks
5 Aug 72	**WHERE IS THE LOVE** Atlantic K 10202 * 29		7 wks
17 Feb 73 ●	**KILLING ME SOFTLY WITH HIS SONG** Atlantic K 10282 6		14 wks
24 Aug 74	**FEEL LIKE MAKING LOVE** Atlantic K 10467 34		7 wks
6 May 78	**THE CLOSER I GET TO YOU** Atlantic K 11099 * 42		4 wks
17 May 80 ●	**BACK TOGETHER AGAIN** Atlantic K 11481 * 3		11 wks
30 Aug 80	**DON'T MAKE ME WAIT TOO LONG** Atlantic K 11555 44		7 wks
20 Aug 83 ●	**TONIGHT I CELEBRATE MY LOVE** Capitol CL 302 ** 2		13 wks
29 Jul 89	**UH-UH OOH OOH LOOK OUT (HERE IT COMES)** Atlantic A 8941 72		2 wks

* Roberta Flack and Donny Hathaway ** Peabo Bryson and Roberta Flack

FLAMINGOS US, male vocal group — 5 wks

4 Jun 69	**BOOGALOO PARTY** Philips BF 1786 26		5 wks

Michael FLANDERS UK, male vocalist — 3 wks

27 Feb 59	**LITTLE DRUMMER BOY** Parlophone R 4528 20		2 wks
17 Apr 59	**LITTLE DRUMMER BOY (re-entry)** Parlophone R 4528 24		1 wk

FLASH AND THE PAN — 15 wks
Australia, male vocal/instrumental group

23 Sep 78	**AND THE BAND PLAYED ON (DOWN AMONG THE DEAD MEN)** Ensign ENY 15 54		4 wks
21 May 83 ●	**WAITING FOR A TRAIN** Easybeat EASY 1 7		11 wks

Lester FLATT and Earl SCRUGGS — 6 wks
US, male instrumental duo - banjos

15 Nov 67	**FOGGY MOUNTAIN BREAKDOWN** CBS 3038 and Mercury MF 1007 39		6 wks

The versions on the two labels were not the same cuts; CBS had a 1965 recording, Mercury a 1967. The chart did not differentiate and listed both together.

Fogwell FLAX and the ANKLEBITERS from FREEHOLD JUNIOR SCHOOL — 2 wks
UK, male vocalist and school choir

26 Dec 81	**ONE NINE FOR SANTA** EMI 5255 68		2 wks

F.L.B. – See FAT LARRY'S BAND

FLEE-REKKERS UK, male instrumental group — 13 wks

19 May 60	**GREEN JEANS** Triumph RGM 1008 23		13 wks

FLEETWOOD MAC — 223 wks
UK/US, male/female vocal/instrumental group

10 Apr 68	**BLACK MAGIC WOMAN** Blue Horizon 57 3138 37		7 wks
17 Jul 68	**NEED YOUR LOVE SO BAD** Blue Horizon 57 3139 31		13 wks
4 Dec 68 ★	**ALBATROSS** Blue Horizon 57 3145 1		20 wks
16 Apr 69	**MAN OF THE WORLD** Immediate IM 080 2		14 wks
23 Jul 69	**NEED YOUR LOVE SO BAD (re-issue)** Blue Horizon 57 3157 32		6 wks
13 Sep 69	**NEED YOUR LOVE SO BAD (re-entry of re-issue)** Blue Horizon 57 3157 42		3 wks
4 Oct 69 ●	**OH WELL** Reprise RS 27000 2		16 wks
23 May 70 ●	**THE GREEN MANALISHI (WITH THE TWO-PRONG CROWN)** Reprise RS 27007 10		12 wks
12 May 73 ●	**ALBATROSS (re-issue)** CBS 8306 2		15 wks
13 Nov 76	**SAY YOU LOVE ME** Reprise K 14447 40		4 wks
19 Feb 77	**GO YOUR OWN WAY** Warner Bros. K 16872 38		4 wks
30 Apr 77	**DON'T STOP** Warner Bros. K 16930 32		5 wks
9 Jul 77	**DREAMS** Warner Bros. K 16969 24		9 wks
22 Oct 77	**YOU MAKE LOVING FUN** Warner Bros. K 17013 45		2 wks
11 Mar 78	**RHIANNON** Reprise K 14430 46		3 wks

FIELDS OF THE
NEPHILIM pose in,
what else, a field.

GEORGE FORMBY
(left), shown with
comedian Terry-
Thomas, had his only
hit single one year
before his death.

Date	Title	Peak	Weeks
6 Oct 79 ●	**TUSK** *Warner Bros. K 17468*	6	10 wks
22 Dec 79	**SARA** *Warner Bros. K 17533*	37	8 wks
25 Sep 82	**GYPSY** *Warner Bros. K 17997*	46	3 wks
18 Dec 82 ●	**OH DIANE** *Warner Bros. FLEET 1*	9	15 wks
4 Apr 87 ●	**BIG LOVE** *Warner Bros. W 8398*	9	14 wks
11 Jul 87	**SEVEN WONDERS** *Warner Bros. W 8317*	56	4 wks
26 Sep 87 ●	**LITTLE LIES** *Warner Bros. W 8291*	5	12 wks
26 Dec 87	**FAMILY MAN** *Warner Bros. W 8114*	54	5 wks
2 Apr 88 ●	**EVERYWHERE** *Warner Bros. W 8143*	4	10 wks
18 Jun 88	**ISN'T IT MIDNIGHT** *Warner Bros. W 7860*	60	2 wks
17 Dec 88	**AS LONG AS YOU FOLLOW** *Warner Bros. W 7644*	66	3 wks
5 May 90	**SAVE ME** *Warner Bros. W 9866*	53	3 wks
25 Aug 90	**IN THE BACK OF MY MIND** *Warner Bros. W 9739*	58	3 wks

Group were UK and male only up to and including the re-issue of Albatross.

FLEETWOODS *US, male/female vocal group*   **8 wks**

24 Apr 59 ●	**COME SOFTLY TO ME** *London HLU 8841*	6	8 wks

La FLEUR *Holland, male/female vocal/instrumental group*   **4 wks**

30 Jul 83	**BOOGIE NIGHTS** *Proto ENA 111*	51	4 wks

K.C. FLIGHTT *US, male rapper*   **4 wks**

1 Apr 89	**PLANET E** *RCA PT 49404*	48	4 wks

Dread FLIMSTONE and the NEW TONE AGE FAMILY *US, male vocal/instrumental group*   **1 wk**

30 Nov 91	**FROM THE GHETTO** *Urban URB 87*	66	1 wk

Berni FLINT *UK, male vocalist*   **11 wks**

19 Mar 77 ●	**I DON'T WANT TO PUT A HOLD ON YOU** *EMI 2599*	3	10 wks
23 Jul 77	**SOUTHERN COMFORT** *EMI 2621*	48	1 wk

FLINTLOCK *UK, male vocal/instrumental group*   **5 wks**

29 May 76	**DAWN** *Pinnacle P 8419*	30	5 wks

F.L.O. – *See Rahni HARRIS and F.L.O.*

FLOATERS *US, male vocal/instrumental group*   **11 wks**

23 Jul 77 ★	**FLOAT ON** *ABC 4187*	1	11 wks

A FLOCK OF SEAGULLS
UK, male vocal/instrumental group   **46 wks**

27 Mar 82	**I RAN** *Jive JIVE 14*	43	6 wks
12 Jun 82	**SPACE AGE LOVE SONG** *Jive JIVE 17*	34	6 wks
6 Nov 82 ●	**WISHING (IF I HAD A PHOTOGRAPH OF YOU)** *Jive JIVE 25*	10	12 wks
23 Apr 83	**NIGHTMARES** *Jive JIVE 33*	53	3 wks
25 Jun 83	**TRANSFER AFFECTION** *Jive JIVE 41*	38	5 wks
14 Jul 84	**THE MORE YOU LIVE, THE MORE YOU LOVE** *Jive JIVE 62*	26	11 wks
19 Oct 85	**WHO'S THAT GIRL (SHE'S GOT IT)** *Jive JIVE 106*	66	3 wks

FLOWERED UP *UK, male vocal/instrumental group*   **17 wks**

28 Jul 90	**IT'S ON** *Heavenly HVN 3*	54	4 wks

24 Nov 90	**PHOBIA** *Heavenly HVN 7*	75	1 wk
11 May 91	**TAKE IT** *London FUP 1*	34	4 wks
17 Aug 91	**IT'S ON/EGG RUSH** *London FUP 2*	38	3 wks
2 May 92	**WEEKENDER** *Heavenly HVN 16*	20	5 wks

See also Various Artists (EPs & LPs) - The Fred EP.

FLOWERPOT MEN *UK, male vocal group*   **12 wks**

23 Aug 67 ●	**LET'S GO TO SAN FRANCISCO** *Deram DM 142*	4	12 wks

Eddie FLOYD *US, male vocalist*   **29 wks**

2 Feb 67	**KNOCK ON WOOD** *Atlantic 584 041*	50	1 wk
2 Mar 67	**KNOCK ON WOOD (re-entry)** *Atlantic 584 041*	19	17 wks
16 Mar 67	**RAISE YOUR HAND** *Stax 601 001*	42	3 wks
9 Aug 67	**THINGS GET BETTER** *Stax 601 016*	31	8 wks

Tenor FLY – *See REBEL MC*

FLYING LIZARDS   **16 wks**
UK, male/female vocal/instrumental group

4 Aug 79 ●	**MONEY** *Virgin VS 276*	5	10 wks
9 Feb 80	**T.V.** *Virgin VS 325*	43	6 wks

FLYING PICKETS *UK, male vocal group*   **20 wks**

26 Nov 83 ★	**ONLY YOU** *10 TEN 14*	1	11 wks
21 Apr 84 ●	**WHEN YOU'RE YOUNG AND IN LOVE** *10 TEN 20*	7	8 wks
8 Dec 84	**WHO'S THAT GIRL** *10 GIRL 1*	71	1 wk

FM *UK, male vocal/instrumental group*   **11 wks**

31 Jan 87	**FROZEN HEART** *Portrait DIDGE 1*	64	2 wks
20 Jun 87	**LET LOVE BE THE LEADER** *Portrait MERV 1*	71	2 wks
5 Aug 89	**BAD LUCK** *Epic 655031 7*	54	4 wks
7 Oct 89	**SOMEDAY (YOU'LL COME RUNNING)** *CBS DINK 1*	64	2 wks
10 Feb 90	**EVERYTIME I THINK OF YOU** *Epic DINK 2*	73	1 wk

FOCUS *Holland, male instrumental group*   **21 wks**

20 Jan 73	**HOCUS POCUS** *Polydor 2001 211*	20	10 wks
27 Jan 73 ●	**SYLVIA** *Polydor 2001 422*	4	11 wks

Dan FOGELBERG *US, male vocalist*   **4 wks**

15 Mar 80	**LONGER** *Epic EPC 8230*	59	4 wks

Claudia FONTAINE – *See BEATMASTERS*

Wayne FONTANA *UK, male vocalist*   **31 wks**

9 Dec 65	**IT WAS EASIER TO HURT HER** *Fontana TF 642*	36	6 wks
21 Apr 66	**COME ON HOME** *Fontana TF 684*	16	12 wks
25 Aug 66	**GOODBYE BLUEBIRD** *Fontana TF 737*	49	1 wk
8 Dec 66	**PAMELA PAMELA** *Fontana TF 770*	11	12 wks

See also Wayne Fontana and the Mindbenders.

Wayne FONTANA and the MINDBENDERS 45 wks
UK, male vocalist, male vocal/instrumental backing group

11 Jul 63	**HELLO JOSEPHINE** *Fontana TF 404*	46	2 wks
28 May 64	**STOP LOOK AND LISTEN** *Fontana TF 451*	37	4 wks
8 Oct 64 ●	**UM UM UM UM UM UM** *Fontana TF 497*	5	15 wks
4 Feb 65 ●	**GAME OF LOVE** *Fontana TF 535*	2	11 wks
17 Jun 65	**JUST A LITTLE BIT TOO LATE** *Fontana TF 579*	20	7 wks
30 Sep 65	**SHE NEEDS LOVE** *Fontana TF 611*	32	6 wks

See also Wayne Fontana; Mindbenders.

Bill FORBES *UK, male vocalist* 1 wk

15 Jan 60	**TOO YOUNG** *Columbia DB 4386*	29	1 wk

FORBIDDEN – *See Jet BRONX and the FORBIDDEN*

FORCE M.D.s *US, male vocal group* 9 wks

12 Apr 86	**TENDER LOVE** *Tommy Boy IS 269*	23	9 wks

Baby FORD *UK, male instrumentalist - keyboards* 16 wks

10 Sep 88	**OOCHY KOOCHY** *Rhythm King 7BFORD 1*	58	6 wks
24 Dec 88	**CHIKKI CHIKKI AHH AHH** *Rhythm King 7BFORD 2*	75	1 wk
7 Jan 89	**CHIKKI CHIKKI AHH AHH (re-entry)** *Rhythm King 7BFORD 2*	54	3 wks
17 Jun 89	**CHILDREN OF THE REVOLUTION** *Rhythm King 7BFORD 4*	53	4 wks
17 Feb 90	**BEACH BUMP** *Rhythm King 7BFORD 6*	68	2 wks

Clinton FORD *UK, male vocalist* 25 wks

23 Oct 59	**OLD SHEP** *Oriole CB 1500*	27	1 wk
17 Aug 61	**TOO MANY BEAUTIFUL GIRLS** *Oriole CB 1623*	48	1 wk
8 Mar 62	**FANLIGHT FANNY** *Oriole CB 1706*	22	10 wks
5 Jan 67	**RUN TO THE DOOR** *Piccadilly 7N 35361*	25	13 wks

Emile FORD and the CHECKMATES 87 wks
UK, male vocal/instrumental group

30 Oct 59 ★	**WHAT DO YOU WANT TO MAKE THOSE EYES AT ME FOR** *Pye 7N 15225*	1	25 wks
5 Feb 60 ●	**ON A SLOW BOAT TO CHINA** *Pye 7N 15245*	3	14 wks
26 May 60	**YOU'LL NEVER KNOW WHAT YOU'RE MISSING** *Pye 7N 15268*	12	9 wks
1 Sep 60	**THEM THERE EYES** *Pye 7N 15282 **	18	16 wks
8 Dec 60 ●	**COUNTING TEARDROPS** *Pye 7N 15314*	4	12 wks
2 Mar 61	**WHAT AM I GONNA DO** *Pye 7N 15331*	33	6 wks
18 May 61	**HALF OF MY HEART** *Piccadilly 7N 35003 **	50	1 wk
22 Jun 61	**HALF OF MY HEART (re-entry)** *Piccadilly 7N 35003 **	42	3 wks
8 Mar 62	**I WONDER WHO'S KISSING HER NOW** *Piccadilly 7N 35033 **	43	1 wk

* Emile Ford

Lita FORD *US, female vocalist* 7 wks

17 Dec 88	**KISS ME DEADLY** *RCA PB 49575*	75	1 wk
20 May 89	**CLOSE MY EYES FOREVER** *Dreamland PB 49409 **	47	3 wks
11 Jan 92	**SHOT OF POISON** *RCA PB 49145*	63	3 wks

* Lita Ford duet with Ozzy Osbourne

Martyn FORD *UK, orchestra* 3 wks

14 May 77	**LET YOUR BODY GO DOWNTOWN** *Mountain TOP 26*	38	3 wks

Mary FORD – *See Les PAUL and Mary FORD*

Pennye FORD *US, female vocalist* 5 wks

4 May 85	**DANGEROUS** *Total Experience FB 49975*	43	5 wks

Tennessee Ernie FORD *US, male vocalist* 42 wks

21 Jan 55 ★	**GIVE ME YOUR WORD** *Capitol CL 14005*	1	24 wks
6 Jan 56 ★	**SIXTEEN TONS** *Capitol CL 14500*	1	11 wks
13 Jan 56 ●	**THE BALLAD OF DAVY CROCKETT** *Capitol CL 14506*	3	7 wks

Julia FORDHAM *UK, female vocalist* 28 wks

2 Jul 88	**HAPPY EVER AFTER** *Circa YR 15*	27	9 wks
25 May 89	**WHERE DOES THE TIME GO** *Circa YR 23*	41	5 wks
31 Aug 91	**I THOUGHT IT WAS YOU** *Circa YR 69*	64	2 wks
18 Jan 92	**LOVE MOVES (IN MYSTERIOUS WAYS)** *Circa YR 73*	19	9 wks
30 May 92	**I THOUGHT IT WAS YOU (re-mix)** *Circa YR 90*	45	3 wks

FOREIGNER *UK/US, male vocal/instrumental group* 77 wks

6 May 78	**FEELS LIKE THE FIRST TIME** *Atlantic K 11086*	39	6 wks
15 Jul 78	**COLD AS ICE** *Atlantic K 10986*	24	10 wks
28 Oct 78	**HOT BLOODED** *Atlantic K 11167*	42	3 wks
24 Feb 79	**BLUE MORNING BLUE DAY** *Atlantic K 11236*	45	4 wks
29 Aug 81	**URGENT** *Atlantic K 11665*	54	4 wks
10 Oct 81	**JUKE BOX HERO** *Atlantic K 11678*	48	4 wks
12 Dec 81 ●	**WAITING FOR A GIRL LIKE YOU** *Atlantic K 11696*	8	13 wks
8 May 82	**URGENT (re-issue)** *Atlantic K 11728*	45	5 wks
8 Dec 84 ★	**I WANT TO KNOW WHAT LOVE IS** *Atlantic A 9596*	1	16 wks
6 Apr 85	**THAT WAS YESTERDAY** *Atlantic A 9571*	28	6 wks
22 Jun 85	**COLD AS ICE (re-mix)** *Atlantic A 9539*	64	2 wks
19 Dec 87	**SAY YOU WILL** *Atlantic A 9169*	71	4 wks

FORMATIONS *US, male vocal group* 11 wks

31 Jul 71	**AT THE TOP OF THE STAIRS** *Mojo 2027 001*	50	1 wk
14 Aug 71	**AT THE TOP OF THE STAIRS (re-entry)** *Mojo 2027 001*	28	10 wks

George FORMBY *UK, male vocalist/instrumentalist - ukelele* 3 wks

21 Jul 60	**HAPPY GO LUCKY ME/BANJO BOY** *Pye 7N 15269*	40	3 wks

FORREST *US, male vocalist* 20 wks

26 Feb 83 ●	**ROCK THE BOAT** *CBS A 3121*	4	10 wks
14 May 83	**FEEL THE NEED IN ME** *CBS A 3411*	17	8 wks
17 Sep 83	**ONE LOVER (DON'T STOP THE SHOW)** *CBS A 3734*	67	2 wks

Lance FORTUNE *UK, male vocalist* 17 wks

19 Feb 60 ●	**BE MINE** *Pye 7N 15240*	4	12 wks
5 May 60	**THIS LOVE I HAVE FOR YOU** *Pye 7N 15260*	26	5 wks

FORTUNES *UK, male vocal/instrumental group* 65 wks

8 Jul 65 ●	**YOU'VE GOT YOUR TROUBLES** *Decca F 12173*	2	14 wks
7 Oct 65 ●	**HERE IT COMES AGAIN** *Decca F 12243*	4	14 wks
3 Feb 66	**THIS GOLDEN RING** *Decca F 12321*	15	9 wks
11 Sep 71 ●	**FREEDOM COME FREEDOM GO** *Capitol CL 15693*	6	17 wks
29 Jan 72 ●	**STORM IN A TEACUP** *Capitol CL 15707*	7	11 wks

45 KING *US, male producer - Mark King* 6 wks

28 Oct 89	**THE KING IS HERE/THE 900 NUMBER** *Dance Trax DRX 9*	60	5 wks

11 Aug 90	THE KING IS HERE/THE 900 NUMBER (re-entry)		
	Dance Trax DRX 9 73	1 wk

49ERS *Italy, male producer – Gianfranco Bortolotti*   **25 wks**

16 Dec 89	●	TOUCH ME *Fourth & Broadway BRW 157* 3	13 wks
17 Mar 90		DON'T YOU LOVE ME *Fourth & Broadway BRW 167* 12	6 wks
9 Jun 90		GIRL TO GIRL *Fourth & Broadway BRW 174* 31	3 wks
6 Jun 92		GOT TO BE FREE *Fourth & Broadway BRW 255* 46	2 wks
29 Aug 92		THE MESSAGE *Fourth & Broadway BRW 257* 68	1 wk

FOSTER and ALLEN *Ireland, male vocal duo*   **47 wks**

27 Feb 82	A BUNCH OF THYME *Ritz RITZ 5* 18	11 wks
30 Oct 82	OLD FLAMES *Ritz RITZ 028* 51	8 wks
19 Feb 83	MAGGIE *Ritz RITZ 023* 27	9 wks
29 Oct 83	I WILL LOVE YOU ALL MY LIFE *Ritz RITZ 056* 49	6 wks
30 Jun 84	JUST FOR OLD TIME'S SAKE *Ritz RITZ 066* 47	6 wks
29 Mar 86	AFTER ALL THESE YEARS *Ritz RITZ 106* 43	7 wks

FOUNDATIONS *UK, male vocal/instrumental group*   **56 wks**

27 Sep 67	★	BABY NOW THAT I'VE FOUND YOU *Pye 7N 17366* 1	16 wks
24 Jan 68		BACK ON MY FEET AGAIN *Pye 7N 17417* 18	10 wks
1 May 68		ANY OLD TIME *Pye 7N 17503* 48	1 wk
15 May 68		ANY OLD TIME (re-entry) *Pye 7N 17503* 50	1 wk
20 Nov 68	●	BUILD ME UP BUTTERCUP *Pye 7N 17636* 2	15 wks
12 Mar 69	●	IN THE BAD BAD OLD DAYS *Pye 7N 17702* 8	10 wks
13 Sep 69		BORN TO LIVE AND BORN TO DIE *Pye 7N 17809* 46	3 wks

FOUR ACES *US, male vocal group*   **40 wks**

30 Jul 54	●	THREE COINS IN THE FOUNTAIN		
		Brunswick 05308 * 5	5 wks
22 Oct 54		THREE COINS IN THE FOUNTAIN (re-entry)		
		Brunswick 05308 * 17	1 wk
7 Jan 55	●	MR. SANDMAN *Brunswick 05355* * 9	5 wks
20 May 55	●	STRANGER IN PARADISE *Brunswick 05418* 6	6 wks
18 Nov 55	●	LOVE IS A MANY SPLENDOURED THING		
		Brunswick 05480 * 2	13 wks
19 Oct 56		WOMAN IN LOVE *Brunswick 05589* * 19	3 wks
4 Jan 57		FRIENDLY PERSUASION *Brunswick 05623* * 29	1 wk
23 Jan 59		THE WORLD OUTSIDE *Brunswick 05773* 18	6 wks

* Four Aces featuring Al Roberts

FOUR BUCKETEERS *UK, male/female vocal group*   **6 wks**

3 May 80	BUCKET OF WATER SONG *CBS 8393* 26	6 wks

FOUR ESQUIRES *US, male vocal group*   **2 wks**

31 Jan 58	LOVE ME FOREVER *London HLO 8533* 23	2 wks

4 HERO *UK, male instrumental group*   **4 wks**

24 Nov 90	MR. KIRK'S NIGHTMARE *Reinforced RIVET 1203* 73	2 wks
9 May 92	COOKIN' UP YAH BRAIN *Reinforced RIVET 1216* 59	2 wks

400 BLOWS *UK, male vocal/instrumental duo*   **4 wks**

29 Jun 85	MOVIN' *Illuminated ILL 61* 54	4 wks

FOUR KNIGHTS *US, male vocal group*   **11 wks**

4 Jun 54	●	I GET SO LONELY *Capitol CL 14076* 5	7 wks
30 Jul 54	●	I GET SO LONELY (re-entry) *Capitol CL 14076* 10	4 wks

FOUR LADS *Canada, male vocal group*   **23 wks**

19 Dec 52	●	FAITH CAN MOVE MOUNTAINS		
		Columbia DB 3154 * 7	2 wks
9 Jan 53	●	FAITH CAN MOVE MOUNTAINS (re-entry)		
		Columbia DB 3154 * 9	1 wk
22 Oct 54	●	RAIN RAIN RAIN *Philips PB 311* ** 8	16 wks
28 Apr 60		STANDING ON THE CORNER *Philips PB 1000* 34	4 wks

* Johnnie Ray and the Four Lads   ** Frankie Laine and the Four Lads

FOUR PENNIES *UK, male vocal/instrumental group*   **56 wks**

16 Jan 64	DO YOU WANT ME TO *Philips BF 1296* 47	1 wk
6 Feb 64	DO YOU WANT ME TO (re-entry) *Philips BF 1296* 49	1 wk
2 Apr 64	★ JULIET *Philips BF 1322* 1	15 wks
16 Jul 64	I FOUND OUT THE HARD WAY *Philips BF 1349* 14	11 wks
29 Oct 64	BLACK GIRL *Philips BF 1366* 20	12 wks
7 Oct 65	UNTIL IT'S TIME FOR YOU TO GO *Philips BF 1435* 19	11 wks
17 Feb 66	TROUBLE IS MY MIDDLE NAME *Philips BF 1469* 32	5 wks

FOUR PREPS *US, male vocal group*   **23 wks**

13 Jun 58	●	BIG MAN *Capitol CL 14873* 2	13 wks
19 Sep 58		BIG MAN (re-entry) *Capitol CL 14873* 22	1 wk
26 May 60		GOT A GIRL *Capitol CL 15128* 28	6 wks
14 Jul 60		GOT A GIRL (re-entry) *Capitol CL 15128* 47	1 wk
2 Nov 61		MORE MONEY FOR YOU AND ME (MEDLEY)		
		Capitol CL 15217 39	2 wks

Tracks of medley: Mr. Blue/Alley Oop/Smoke Gets In Your Eyes/In This Whole Wide World/A Worried Man/Tom Dooley/A Teenager In Love, all with new lyrics.

FOUR SEASONS *US, male vocal group*   **151 wks**

4 Oct 62	●	SHERRY *Stateside SS 122* 8	16 wks
17 Jan 63		BIG GIRLS DON'T CRY *Stateside SS 145* 13	10 wks
28 Mar 63		WALK LIKE A MAN *Stateside SS 169* 12	12 wks
27 Jun 63		AIN'T THAT A SHAME *Stateside SS 194* 38	3 wks
27 Aug 64		RAG DOLL *Philips BF 1347* * 2	13 wks
18 Nov 65	●	LET'S HANG ON *Philips BF 1439* * 4	16 wks
31 Mar 66		WORKIN' MY WAY BACK TO YOU		
		Philips BF 1474 ** 50	3 wks
2 Jun 66		OPUS 17 (DON'T YOU WORRY 'BOUT ME)		
		Philips BF 1493 ** 20	9 wks
29 Sep 66		I'VE GOT YOU UNDER MY SKIN *Philips BF 1511* ** ...12	11 wks
12 Jan 67		TELL IT TO THE RAIN *Philips BF 1538* ** 37	5 wks
19 Apr 75	●	NIGHT *Mowest MW 3024* *** 7	9 wks
20 Sep 75	●	WHO LOVES YOU *Warner Bros. K 16602* 6	9 wks
31 Jan 76	★	DECEMBER '63 (OH WHAT A NIGHT)		
		Warner Bros. K 16688 1	10 wks
24 Apr 76	●	SILVER STAR *Warner Bros. K 16742* 3	9 wks
27 Nov 76		WE CAN WORK IT OUT *Warner Bros. K 16845* 34	4 wks
18 Jun 77		RHAPSODY *Warner Bros. K 16932* 37	3 wks
20 Aug 77		DOWN THE HALL *Warner Bros. K 16982* 34	5 wks
29 Oct 88		DECEMBER '63 (OH WHAT A NIGHT) (re-mix)		
		BR 45277 *** 49	4 wks

* Four Seasons with the sound of Frankie Valli   ** Four Seasons with Frankie Valli
*** Frankie Valli and the Four Seasons

FOUR TOPS *US, male vocal group*   **318 wks**

1 Jul 65	I CAN'T HELP MYSELF *Tamla Motown TMG 515* 23	9 wks
2 Sep 65	IT'S THE SAME OLD SONG *Tamla Motown TMG 528* 34	8 wks
21 Jul 66	LOVING YOU IS SWEETER THAN EVER		
	Tamla Motown TMG 568 21	12 wks
13 Oct 66	★ REACH OUT I'LL BE THERE *Tamla Motown TMG 579* 1	16 wks
12 Jan 67	● STANDING IN THE SHADOWS OF LOVE		
	Tamla Motown TMG 589 6	8 wks
30 Mar 67	● BERNADETTE *Tamla Motown TMG 601* 8	10 wks
15 Jun 67	SEVEN ROOMS OF GLOOM *Tamla Motown TMG 612* 12	9 wks
11 Oct 67	YOU KEEP RUNNING AWAY *Tamla Motown TMG 623* 26	7 wks
13 Dec 67	● WALK AWAY RENEE *Tamla Motown TMG 634* 3	11 wks

13 Mar 68	● IF I WERE A CARPENTER *Tamla Motown TMG 647* **7**	11 wks
21 Aug 68	YESTERDAY'S DREAMS *Tamla Motown TMG 665* **23**	15 wks
13 Nov 68	I'M IN A DIFFERENT WORLD *Tamla Motown TMG 675* **27**	13 wks
28 May 69	WHAT IS A MAN *Tamla Motown TMG 698* **16**	11 wks
27 Sep 69	DO WHAT YOU GOTTA DO *Tamla Motown TMG 710* **11**	11 wks
21 Mar 70	● I CAN'T HELP MYSELF (re-issue) *Tamla Motown TMG 732* **10**	11 wks
30 May 70	IT'S ALL IN THE GAME *Tamla Motown TMG 736* **5**	14 wks
12 Sep 70	IT'S ALL IN THE GAME (re-entry) *Tamla Motown TMG 736* **48**	2 wks
3 Oct 70	● STILL WATER (LOVE) *Tamla Motown TMG 752* **10**	10 wks
19 Dec 70	STILL WATER (LOVE) (re-entry) *Tamla Motown TMG 752* **44**	2 wks
1 May 71	JUST SEVEN NUMBERS (CAN STRAIGHTEN OUT MY LIFE) *Tamla Motown TMG 770* **36**	5 wks
26 Jun 71	RIVER DEEP MOUNTAIN HIGH *Tamla Motown TMG 777 *** **11**	10 wks
25 Sep 71	● SIMPLE GAME *Tamla Motown TMG 785* **3**	11 wks
20 Nov 71	YOU GOTTA HAVE LOVE IN YOUR HEART *Tamla Motown TMG 793 *** **25**	10 wks
11 Mar 72	BERNADETTE (re-issue) *Tamla Motown TMG 803* **23**	7 wks
5 Aug 72	WALK WITH ME TALK WITH ME DARLING *Tamla Motown TMG 823* **32**	6 wks
18 Nov 72	KEEPER OF THE CASTLE *Probe PRO 575* **18**	9 wks
10 Nov 73	SWEET UNDERSTANDING LOVE *Probe PRO 604* **29**	10 wks
17 Oct 81	● WHEN SHE WAS MY GIRL *Casablanca CAN 1005* **3**	10 wks
19 Dec 81	DON'T WALK AWAY *Casablanca CAN 1006* **16**	11 wks
6 Mar 82	TONIGHT I'M GONNA LOVE YOU ALL OVER *Casablanca CAN 1008* **43**	4 wks
26 Jun 82	BACK TO SCHOOL AGAIN *RSO 89* **62**	2 wks
23 Jul 88	REACH OUT I'LL BE THERE (re-mix) *Motown ZB 41943* **11**	9 wks
17 Sep 88	INDESTRUCTIBLE *Arista 111717* **55**	4 wks
3 Dec 88	● LOCO IN ACAPULCO *Arista 111850* **7**	13 wks
25 Feb 89	INDESTRUCTIBLE *Arista 112074 **** **30**	7 wks

* Supremes and the Four Tops ** Four Tops featuring Smokey Robinson
The original US recording of Indestructible was not issued until after the chart run of the UK-only mix.

FOURMOST *UK, male vocal/instrumental group* **64 wks**

12 Sep 63	● HELLO LITTLE GIRL *Parlophone R 5056* **9**	17 wks
26 Dec 63	I'M IN LOVE *Parlophone R 5078* **17**	12 wks
23 Apr 64	● A LITTLE LOVING *Parlophone R 5128* **6**	13 wks
13 Aug 64	HOW CAN I TELL HER *Parlophone R 5157* **33**	4 wks
26 Nov 64	BABY I NEED YOUR LOVIN' *Parlophone R 5194* **24**	12 wks
9 Dec 65	GIRLS GIRLS GIRLS *Parlophone R 5379* **33**	6 wks

14-18 *UK, male vocalist – Peter Waterman* **4 wks**

1 Nov 75	GOODBYE-EE *Magnet MAG 48* **33**	4 wks

FOX *UK/US, male/female vocal/instrumental group* **29 wks**

15 Feb 75	● ONLY YOU CAN *GTO GT 8* **3**	11 wks
10 May 75	IMAGINE ME IMAGINE YOU *GTO GT 21* **15**	8 wks
10 Apr 76	● S-S-S-SINGLE BED *GTO GT 57* **4**	10 wks

Noosha FOX *UK, female vocalist* **6 wks**

12 Nov 77	GEORGINA BAILEY *GTO GT 106* **31**	6 wks

Samantha FOX *UK, female vocalist* **71 wks**

22 Mar 86	● TOUCH ME (I WANT YOUR BODY) *Jive FOXY 1*............**3**	10 wks
28 Jun 86	● DO YA DO YA (WANNA PLEASE ME) *Jive FOXY 2*........**10**	7 wks
6 Sep 86	HOLD ON TIGHT *Jive FOXY 3* **26**	5 wks
13 Dec 86	I'M ALL YOU NEED *Jive FOXY 4* **41**	6 wks
30 May 87	● NOTHING'S GONNA STOP ME NOW *Jive FOXY 5*........**8**	9 wks
25 Jul 87	I SURRENDER (TO THE SPIRIT OF THE NIGHT) *Jive FOXY 6* **25**	7 wks

17 Oct 87	I PROMISE YOU (GET READY) *Jive FOXY 7* **58**	3 wks
19 Dec 87	TRUE DEVOTION *Jive FOXY 8* **62**	3 wks
21 May 88	NAUGHTY GIRLS *Jive FOXY 9 ** **31**	5 wks
19 Nov 88	LOVE HOUSE *Jive FOXY 10* **32**	6 wks
28 Jan 89	I ONLY WANNA BE WITH YOU *Jive FOXY 11* **16**	8 wks
17 Jun 89	I WANNA HAVE SOME FUN *Jive FOXY 12* **63**	2 wks

* Samantha Fox featuring Full Force

Bruce FOXTON *UK, male vocalist* **9 wks**

30 Jul 83	FREAK *Arista BFOX 1* **23**	5 wks
29 Oct 83	THIS IS THE WAY *Arista BFOX 2* **56**	3 wks
21 Apr 84	IT MAKES ME WONDER *Arista BFOX 3* **74**	1 wk

Inez FOXX *US, female vocalist* **8 wks**

23 Jul 64	HURT BY LOVE *Sue WI 323* **40**	3 wks
19 Feb 69	MOCKINGBIRD *United Artists UP 2269 ** **36**	2 wks
19 Mar 69	MOCKINGBIRD (re-entry) *United Artists UP 2269 ** **34**	3 wks

* Inez and Charlie Foxx

John FOXX *UK, male vocalist* **31 wks**

26 Jan 80	UNDERPASS *Virgin VS 318* **31**	8 wks
29 Mar 80	NO-ONE DRIVING (DOUBLE SINGLE) *Virgin VS 338* **32**	4 wks
19 Jul 80	BURNING CAR *Virgin VS 360* **35**	7 wks
8 Nov 80	MILES AWAY *Virgin VS 382* **51**	3 wks
29 Aug 81	EUROPE (AFTER THE RAIN) *Virgin VS 393* **40**	5 wks
2 Jul 83	ENDLESSLY *Virgin VS 543* **66**	3 wks
17 Sep 83	YOUR DRESS *Virgin VS 615* **61**	1 wk

Tracks on double single: No-One Driving/Glimmer/Mr. No/This City.

FPI PROJECT *Italy, male instrumental/production group* **15 wks**

9 Dec 89	● GOING BACK TO MY ROOTS/RICH IN PARADISE *Rumour RUMAT 9* **9**	12 wks
9 Mar 91	EVERYBODY (ALL OVER THE WORLD) *Rumour RUMA 29* **65**	3 wks

Going Back To My Roots was a vocal track available in two formats and featured either Paolo Dini or Sharon D. Clarke.

FRAGGLES *UK/US, puppets* **8 wks**

18 Feb 84	'FRAGGLE ROCK' THEME *RCA 389* **33**	8 wks

Peter FRAMPTON *UK, male vocalist* **24 wks**

1 May 76	● SHOW ME THE WAY *A & M AMS 7218* **10**	12 wks
11 Sep 76	BABY I LOVE YOUR WAY *A & M AMS 7246* **43**	5 wks
6 Nov 76	DO YOU FEEL LIKE WE DO *A & M AMS 7260* **39**	4 wks
23 Jul 77	I'M IN YOU *A & M AMS 7298* **41**	3 wks

Connie FRANCIS *US, female vocalist* **241 wks**

4 Apr 58	★ WHO'S SORRY NOW *MGM 975* **1**	25 wks
27 Jun 58	I'M SORRY I MADE YOU CRY *MGM 982* **11**	10 wks
22 Aug 58	★ CAROLINA MOON/STUPID CUPID *MGM 985* **1**	19 wks
31 Oct 58	I'LL GET BY *MGM 993* **19**	6 wks
21 Nov 58	FALLIN' *MGM 993* **20**	5 wks
26 Dec 58	YOU ALWAYS HURT THE ONE YOU LOVE *MGM 998* **13**	7 wks
13 Feb 59	● MY HAPPINESS *MGM 1001* **4**	14 wks
29 May 59	MY HAPPINESS (re-entry) *MGM 1001* **30**	1 wk
3 Jul 59	● LIPSTICK ON YOUR COLLAR *MGM 1018* **3**	16 wks
11 Sep 59	PLENTY GOOD LOVIN' *MGM 1036* **18**	6 wks
4 Dec 59	AMONG MY SOUVENIRS *MGM 1046* **11**	10 wks
17 Mar 60	VALENTINO *MGM 1060* **27**	8 wks

19 May 60	● MAMA /ROBOT MAN MGM 1076	2	19 wks
18 Aug 60	● EVERYBODY'S SOMEBODY'S FOOL MGM 1086	5	13 wks
3 Nov 60	● MY HEART HAS A MIND OF ITS OWN MGM 1100	3	15 wks
12 Jan 61	MANY TEARS AGO MGM 1111	12	9 wks
16 Mar 61	● WHERE THE BOYS ARE/BABY ROO MGM 1121	5	14 wks
15 Jun 61	BREAKIN' IN A BRAND NEW BROKEN HEART MGM 1136	12	11 wks
14 Sep 61	● TOGETHER MGM 1138	6	11 wks
14 Dec 61	BABY'S FIRST CHRISTMAS MGM 1145	30	4 wks
26 Apr 62	DON'T BREAK THE HEART THAT LOVES YOU MGM 1157	39	3 wks
2 Aug 62	● VACATION MGM 1165	10	9 wks
20 Dec 62	I'M GONNA BE WARM THIS WINTER MGM 1185	48	1 wk
10 Jun 65	MY CHILD MGM 1271	26	6 wks
20 Jan 66	JEALOUS HEART MGM 1293	44	2 wks

Baby Roo listed with Where The Boys Are for first eight weeks only.

Claude FRANCOIS France, male vocalist — **4 wks**

| 10 Jan 76 | TEARS ON THE TELEPHONE Bradley's BRAD 7528 | ....35 | 4 wks |

Joe FRANK – See HAMILTON, Joe FRANK and REYNOLDS

FRANK AND WALTERS — **5 wks**
Ireland, male vocal/instrumental group

| 21 Mar 92 | HAPPY BUSMAN Setanta HOO 2 | ....49 | 2 wks |
| 12 Sep 92 | THIS IS NOT A SONG Setanta HOO 3 | ....46 | 3 wks |

FRANKË UK, male vocalist – Frankë Pharoah — **2 wks**

| 7 Nov 92 | UNDERSTAND THIS GROOVE China WOK 2028 | ....60 | 2 wks |

FRANKIE GOES TO HOLLYWOOD — **117 wks**
UK, male vocal/instrumental group

26 Nov 83	★ RELAX ZTT ZTAS 1	1	48 wks
16 Jun 84	★ TWO TRIBES ZTT ZTAS 3	1	20 wks
10 Nov 84	TWO TRIBES (re-entry) ZTT ZTAS 3	73	1 wk
1 Dec 84	★ THE POWER OF LOVE ZTT ZTAS 5	1	11 wks
16 Feb 85	RELAX (re-entry) ZTT ZTAS 1	58	4 wks
23 Feb 85	THE POWER OF LOVE (re-entry) ZTT ZTAS 5	64	1 wk
30 Mar 85	● WELCOME TO THE PLEASURE DOME ZTT ZTAS 7	2	11 wks
6 Sep 86	● RAGE HARD ZTT ZTAS 22	4	7 wks
22 Nov 86	WARRIORS (OF THE WASTELAND) ZTT ZTAS 25	19	8 wks
7 Mar 87	WATCHING THE WILDLIFE ZTT ZTAS 26	28	6 wks

Aretha FRANKLIN US, female vocalist — **163 wks**

8 Jun 67	● RESPECT Atlantic 584 115	10	14 wks
23 Aug 67	BABY I LOVE YOU Atlantic 584 127	39	4 wks
20 Dec 67	CHAIN OF FOOLS/SATISFACTION Atlantic 584 157	43	2 wks
10 Jan 68	SATISFACTION (re-entry) Atlantic 584 157	37	5 wks
13 Mar 68	SINCE YOU'VE BEEN GONE Atlantic 584 172	47	1 wk
22 May 68	THINK Atlantic 584 186	26	9 wks
7 Aug 68	● I SAY A LITTLE PRAYER Atlantic 584 206	4	14 wks
22 Aug 70	DON'T PLAY THAT SONG Atlantic 2091 027	13	11 wks
2 Oct 71	SPANISH HARLEM Atlantic 2091 138	14	9 wks
8 Sep 73	ANGEL Atlantic K 10346	37	5 wks
16 Feb 74	UNTIL YOU COME BACK TO ME (THAT'S WHAT I'M GONNA DO) Atlantic K 10399	26	8 wks
6 Dec 80	WHAT A FOOL BELIEVES Arista ARIST 377	46	7 wks
19 Sep 81	LOVE ALL THE HURT AWAY Arista ARIST 428 *	49	3 wks
4 Sep 82	JUMP TO IT Arista ARIST 479	42	5 wks
23 Jul 83	GET IT RIGHT Arista ARIST 537	74	2 wks
13 Jul 85	FREEWAY OF LOVE Arista ARIST 624	68	3 wks
2 Nov 85	● SISTERS ARE DOIN' IT FOR THEMSELVES RCA PB 40339 **	9	11 wks
23 Nov 85	WHO'S ZOOMIN' WHO Arista ARIST 633	11	14 wks
22 Feb 86	ANOTHER NIGHT Arista ARIST 657	54	6 wks
10 May 86	FREEWAY OF LOVE (re-entry) Arista ARIST 624	51	3 wks
25 Oct 86	JUMPIN' JACK FLASH Arista ARIST 678	58	3 wks
31 Jan 87	★ I KNEW YOU WERE WAITING (FOR ME) Epic DUET 1 ***	1	9 wks
14 Mar 87	JIMMY LEE Arista RIS 6	46	4 wks
6 May 89	THROUGH THE STORM Arista 112185 ****	41	3 wks
9 Sep 89	IT ISN'T, IT WASN'T, IT AIN'T NEVER GONNA BE Arista 112545 *****	29	5 wks
7 Apr 90	THINK East West A 7951	31	2 wks
27 Jul 91	EVERYDAY PEOPLE Arista 114420	69	1 wk

* Aretha Franklin and George Benson ** Eurythmics and Aretha Franklin
*** Aretha Franklin and George Michael **** Aretha Franklin and Elton John
***** Aretha Franklin and Whitney Houston

Think on East West is a re-recording. It was the flip side of Everybody Needs Somebody To Love by Blues Brothers and was listed for the first two weeks of the record's run.

Erma FRANKLIN US, female vocalist — **10 wks**

| 10 Oct 92 | ● (TAKE A LITTLE) PIECE OF MY HEART Epic 6583847 | .....9 | 10 wks |

Rodney FRANKLIN US, male instrumentalist - piano — **9 wks**

| 19 Apr 80 | ● THE GROOVE CBS 8529 | .....7 | 9 wks |

FRANTIC FIVE – See Don LANG

FRANTIQUE US, female vocal group — **12 wks**

| 11 Aug 79 | ● STRUT YOUR FUNKY STUFF Philadelphia International PIR 7728 | ....10 | 12 wks |

Elizabeth FRASER – See Ian McCULLOCH

Wendy FRASER – See Patrick SWAYZE featuring Wendy FRASER

FRAZIER CHORUS — **14 wks**
UK, male/female vocal/instrumental group

4 Feb 89	DREAM KITCHEN Virgin VS 1145	57	3 wks
15 Apr 89	TYPICAL! Virgin VS 1174	53	2 wks
15 Jul 89	SLOPPY HEART Virgin VS 1192	73	1 wk
9 Jun 90	CLOUD 8 Virgin VS 1252	52	3 wks
25 Aug 90	NOTHING Virgin VS 1284	51	3 wks
16 Feb 91	WALKING ON AIR Virgin VS 1330	60	2 wks

Stan FREBERG US, male vocalist — **5 wks**

19 Nov 54	SH-BOOM Capitol CL 14187 *	15	2 wks
27 Jul 56	ROCK ISLAND LINE/HEARTBREAK HOTEL Capitol CL 14608	24	1 wk
10 Aug 56	ROCK ISLAND LINE/HEARTBREAK HOTEL (re-entry) Capitol CL 14608	29	1 wk
12 May 60	THE OLD PAYOLA ROLL BLUES Capitol CL 15122	40	1 wk

* Stan Freberg with the Toads

John FRED and the PLAYBOY BAND — **12 wks**
US, male vocal/instrumental group

| 3 Jan 68 | ● JUDY IN DISGUISE (WITH GLASSES) Pye International 7N 25442 | .....3 | 12 wks |

FREDDIE and the DREAMERS — **85 wks**
UK, male vocal/instrumental group

| 9 May 63 | ● IF YOU GOTTA MAKE A FOOL OF SOMEBODY Columbia DB 7032 | .....3 | 14 wks |

British Hit Singles Part One: Alphabetically by Artist
Date of chart entry/Title & catalogue no./Peak position reached/Weeks on chart
★ Number one ● Top Ten † still on chart at 31 Dec 1992
* = credited to act billed in footnote

8 Aug 63 ●	I'M TELLING YOU NOW *Columbia DB 7086*	2	11 wks
7 Nov 63 ●	YOU WERE MADE FOR ME *Columbia DB 7147*	3	15 wks
20 Feb 64	OVER YOU *Columbia DB 7214*	13	11 wks
14 May 64	I LOVE YOU BABY *Columbia DB 7286*	16	8 wks
16 Jul 64	JUST FOR YOU *Columbia DB 7322*	41	3 wks
5 Nov 64 ●	I UNDERSTAND *Columbia DB 7381*	5	15 wks
22 Apr 65	A LITTLE YOU *Columbia DB 7526*	26	5 wks
4 Nov 65	THOU SHALT NOT STEAL *Columbia DB 7720*	44	3 wks

FREDERICK – *See NINA and FREDERICK*

FREE *UK, male vocal/instrumental group* — 75 wks

6 Jun 70 ●	ALL RIGHT NOW *Island WIP 6082*	2	16 wks
1 May 71 ●	MY BROTHER JAKE *Island WIP 6100*	4	11 wks
27 May 72	LITTLE BIT OF LOVE *Island WIP 6129*	13	10 wks
13 Jan 73 ●	WISHING WELL *Island WIP 6146*	7	10 wks
21 Jul 73	ALL RIGHT NOW (re-entry) *Island WIP 6082*	15	9 wks
18 Feb 78	FREE EP *Island IEP 6*	11	7 wks
23 Oct 82	FREE EP (re-entry) *Island IEP 6*	57	3 wks
9 Feb 91 ●	ALL RIGHT NOW (re-mix) *Island IS 486*	8	9 wks

Tracks on Free EP: All Right Now/My Brother Jake/Wishing Well.

FREEEZ *UK, male vocal/instrumental group* — 48 wks

7 Jun 80	KEEP IN TOUCH *Calibre CAB 103*	49	3 wks
7 Feb 81 ●	SOUTHERN FREEEZ *Beggars Banquet BEG 51*	8	11 wks
18 Apr 81	FLYING HIGH *Beggars Banquet BEG 55*	35	5 wks
18 Jun 83	I.O.U. *Beggars Banquet BEG 96*	2	15 wks
1 Oct 83	POP GOES MY LOVE *Beggars Banquet BEG 98*	26	6 wks
17 Jan 87	I.O.U. (re-mix) *Citybeat CBE 709* *	23	6 wks
30 May 87	SOUTHERN FREEEZ (re-mix) *Total Control TOCO 14*	63	2 wks

* *Freeez featuring John Rocca*

FREEFALL featuring PSYCHOTROPIC — 1 wk
UK/US, male instrumental/production group

27 Jul 91	FEEL SURREAL *ffr FX 160*	63	1 wk

FREEHOLD JUNIOR SCHOOL – *See Fogwell FLAX and the ANKLEBITERS from FREEHOLD JUNIOR SCHOOL*

FREIHEIT *Germany, male vocal/instrumental duo* — 9 wks

17 Dec 88	KEEPING THE DREAM ALIVE *CBS 652989 7*	14	9 wks

Deborah FRENCH – *See E-LUSTRIOUS featuring Deborah FRENCH*

FREQUENCY 9 – *See VARIOUS ARTISTS (EPs & LPs) - The Further Adventures Of North EP*

Doug E. FRESH and the GET FRESH CREW — 11 wks
US, male vocalist and rap/scratch group

9 Nov 85 ●	THE SHOW *Cooltempo COOL 116*	7	11 wks

FRESH 4 featuring Lizz E — 9 wks
UK, male scratch group and female vocal group

7 Oct 89 ●	WISHING ON A STAR *10 TEN 287*	10	9 wks

FRESH PRINCE – *See DJ JAZZY JEFF and FRESH PRINCE*

FRESHIES *UK, male vocal/instrumental group* — 3 wks

14 Feb 81	I'M IN LOVE WITH THE GIRL ON A CERTAIN MANCHESTER MEGASTORE CHECKOUT DESK *MCA 670*	54	3 wks

Matt FRETTON *UK, male vocalist* — 5 wks

11 Jun 83	IT'S SO HIGH *Chrysalis MATT 1*	50	5 wks

~~~○ FREUR *UK, male vocal/instrumental group* — 4 wks

23 Apr 83	DOOT DOOT *CBS A 3141*	59	4 wks

Glenn FREY *US, male vocalist* — 20 wks

2 Mar 85	THE HEAT IS ON *MCA MCA 941*	12	12 wks
22 Jun 85	SMUGGLER'S BLUES *BBC RESL 170*	22	8 wks

FRIDA *Norway, female vocalist* — 12 wks

21 Aug 82	I KNOW THERE'S SOMETHING GOING ON *Epic EPC A2603*	43	7 wks
17 Dec 83	TIME *Epic A 3983* *	45	5 wks

* *Frida and B.A. Robertson*

Dean FRIEDMAN *US, male vocalist* — 22 wks

3 Jun 78	WOMAN OF MINE *Lifesong LS 401*	52	5 wks
23 Sep 78 ●	LUCKY STARS *Lifesong LS 402*	3	10 wks
18 Nov 78	LYDIA *Lifesong LS 403*	31	7 wks

FRIENDS AGAIN *UK, male vocal/instrumental group* — 3 wks

4 Aug 84	THE FRIENDS AGAIN EP *Mercury FA 1*	59	3 wks

Tracks on EP: Lullaby On Board/Wand You Wave/Thank You For Being an Angel.

FRIJID PINK *US, male vocal/instrumental group* — 16 wks

28 Mar 70 ●	HOUSE OF THE RISING SUN *Deram DM 288*	4	16 wks

Jane FROMAN *US, female vocalist* — 4 wks

17 Jun 55	I WONDER *Capitol CL 14254*	14	4 wks

FULL CIRCLE *US, male vocal group* — 5 wks

7 Mar 87	WORKIN' UP A SWEAT *EMI America EA 229*	41	5 wks

FULL FORCE *US, male vocal/instrumental group* — 37 wks

4 May 85	I WONDER IF I TAKE YOU HOME *CBS A 6057* *	53	6 wks
3 Aug 85	I WONDER IF I TAKE YOU HOME (re-entry) *CBS A 6057* *	12	11 wks
21 Dec 85 ●	ALICE I WANT YOU JUST FOR ME *CBS A 6640*	9	11 wks
21 May 88	NAUGHTY GIRLS *Jive FOXY 9* **	31	5 wks
4 Jun 88	I'M REAL *Scotti Brothers JSB 1* ***	31	4 wks

* *Lisa Lisa and Cult Jam with Full Force* ** *Samantha Fox featuring Full Force*
*** *James Brown featuring Full Force*

FULL METAL RACKETS – *See John McENROE and Pat CASH with the FULL METAL RACKETS*

Bobby FULLER FOUR *US, male vocal/instrumental group* — **4 wks**

14 Apr 66	I FOUGHT THE LAW *London HL 10030*	33	4 wks

FUN BOY THREE *UK, male vocal/instrumental group* — **70 wks**

7 Nov 81	THE LUNATICS (HAVE TAKEN OVER THE ASYLUM) *Chrysalis CHS 2563*	20	12 wks
13 Feb 82 ●	IT AIN'T WHAT YOU DO IT'S THE WAY THAT YOU DO IT *Chrysalis CHS 2570 **	4	10 wks
10 Apr 82 ●	REALLY SAYING SOMETHING *Deram NANA 1 ****	5	10 wks
8 May 82	THE TELEPHONE ALWAYS RINGS *Chrysalis CHS 2609*	17	9 wks
31 Jul 82	SUMMERTIME *Chrysalis CHS 2629*	18	8 wks
15 Jan 83	THE MORE I SEE (THE LESS I BELIEVE) *Chrysalis CHS 2554*	68	1 wk
5 Feb 83 ●	TUNNEL OF LOVE *Chrysalis CHS 2678*	10	10 wks
30 Apr 83 ●	OUR LIPS ARE SEALED *Chrysalis FUNB 1*	7	10 wks

*Fun Boy Three and Bananarama ** Bananarama with the Fun Boy Three

Farley 'Jackmaster' FUNK *US, male producer* — **14 wks**

23 Aug 86 ●	LOVE CAN'T TURN AROUND *D.J. International LON 105*	10	12 wks
11 Feb 89	AS ALWAYS *Champion CHAMP 90*	49	2 wks

FUNK MASTERS *UK, male/female vocal/instrumental group* — **12 wks**

18 Jun 83 ●	IT'S OVER *Master Funk Records 7MP 004*	8	12 wks

FUNKADELIC *US, male vocal/instrumental group* — **12 wks**

9 Dec 78 ●	ONE NATION UNDER A GROOVE (PART 1) *Warner Bros. K 17246*	9	12 wks

FUNKAPOLITAN *UK, male vocal/instrumental group* — **7 wks**

22 Aug 81	AS TIME GOES BY *London LON 001*	41	7 wks

FUNKY BOYS – *See Linda CARR*

FUNKY BUNCH – *See MARKY MARK and the FUNKY BUNCH*

FUNKY WORM *UK, male/female vocal/instrumental group* — **14 wks**

30 Jul 88	HUSTLE! (TO THE MUSIC...) *Fon FON 15*	13	8 wks
26 Nov 88	THE SPELL! *Fon FON 16*	61	3 wks
20 May 89	U + ME = LOVE *Fon FON 19*	46	3 wks

FUREYS *Ireland, male vocal group* — **14 wks**

10 Oct 81	WHEN YOU WERE SWEET SIXTEEN *Ritz RITZ 003 **	14	11 wks
3 Apr 82	I WILL LOVE YOU (EV'RY TIME WHEN WE ARE GONE) *Ritz RITZ 012*	54	3 wks

*Fureys with Davey Arthur

FURIOUS FIVE – *See GRANDMASTER FLASH, Melle MEL and the FURIOUS FIVE*

FURNITURE *UK, male/female vocal/instrumental group* — **10 wks**

14 Jun 86	BRILLIANT MIND *Stiff BUY 251*	21	10 wks

Billy FURY *UK, male vocalist* — **281 wks**

27 Feb 59	MAYBE TOMORROW *Decca F 11102*	22	3 wks
27 Mar 59	MAYBE TOMORROW (re-entry) *Decca F 11102*	18	6 wks
26 Jun 59	MARGO *Decca F 11128*	28	1 wk
10 Mar 60 ●	COLETTE *Decca F 11200*	9	10 wks
26 May 60	THAT'S LOVE *Decca F 11237*	19	11 wks
22 Sep 60	WONDROUS PLACE *Decca F 11267*	25	9 wks
19 Jan 61	A THOUSAND STARS *Decca F 11311*	14	10 wks
27 Apr 61	DON'T WORRY *Decca F 11334*	40	2 wks
11 May 61 ●	HALFWAY TO PARADISE *Decca F 11349*	3	23 wks
7 Sep 61	JEALOUSY *Decca F 11384*	2	12 wks
14 Dec 61	I'D NEVER FIND ANOTHER YOU *Decca F 11409*	5	15 wks
15 Mar 62	LETTER FULL OF TEARS *Decca F 11437*	32	6 wks
3 May 62 ●	LAST NIGHT WAS MADE FOR LOVE *Decca F 11458*	4	16 wks
19 Jul 62	ONCE UPON A DREAM *Decca F 11485*	7	13 wks
25 Oct 62	BECAUSE OF LOVE *Decca F 11508*	18	14 wks
14 Feb 63 ●	LIKE I'VE NEVER BEEN GONE *Decca F 11582*	3	15 wks
16 May 63 ●	WHEN WILL YOU SAY I LOVE YOU *Decca F 11655*	3	12 wks
25 Jul 63	IN SUMMER *Decca F 11701*	5	11 wks
3 Oct 63	SOMEBODY ELSE'S GIRL *Decca F 11744*	18	7 wks
2 Jan 64	DO YOU REALLY LOVE ME TOO *Decca F 11792*	13	10 wks
30 Apr 64	I WILL *Decca F 11888*	14	12 wks
23 Jul 64	IT'S ONLY MAKE BELIEVE *Decca F 11939*	10	10 wks
14 Jan 65	I'M LOST WITHOUT YOU *Decca F 12048*	16	10 wks
22 Jul 65 ●	IN THOUGHTS OF YOU *Decca F 12178*	9	11 wks
16 Sep 65	RUN TO MY LOVIN' ARMS *Decca F 12230*	25	7 wks
10 Feb 66	I'LL NEVER QUITE GET OVER YOU *Decca F 12325*	35	5 wks
4 Aug 66	GIVE ME YOUR WORD *Decca F 12459*	27	7 wks
4 Sep 82	LOVE OR MONEY *Polydor POSP 488*	57	5 wks
13 Nov 82	DEVIL OR ANGEL *Polydor POSP 528*	58	4 wks
4 Jun 83	FORGET HIM *Polydor POSP 558*	59	4 wks

FUTURE SOUND OF LONDON — **6 wks**
UK, male instrumental/production duo

23 May 92	PAPUA NEW GUINEA *Jumpin' & Pumpin' TOT 17*	22	6 wks

FUZZBOX – *See WE'VE GOT A FUZZBOX AND WE'RE GONNA USE IT*

Leslie FYSON – *See Michael MEDWIN, Bernard BRESSLAW, Alfie BASS and Leslie FYSON*

G

Bobby G *UK, male vocalist* — **12 wks**

1 Dec 84	BIG DEAL *BBC RESL 151*	75	1 wk
15 Dec 84	BIG DEAL (re-entry) *BBC RESL 151*	65	5 wks
19 Oct 85	BIG DEAL (2nd re-entry) *BBC RESL 151*	46	6 wks

Kenny G *US, male instrumentalist - saxophone* — **16 wks**

21 Apr 84	HI! HOW YA DOIN'? *Arista ARIST 561*	70	3 wks
30 Aug 86	WHAT DOES IT TAKE (TO WIN YOUR LOVE) *Arista ARIST 672*	64	2 wks
4 Jul 87	SONGBIRD *Arista RIS 18*	22	7 wks
9 May 92	MISSING YOU NOW *Columbia 6579917 **	28	4 wks

* Michael Bolton featuring Kenny G

Peter GABRIEL *UK, male vocalist* — **94 wks**

9 Apr 77	SOLSBURY HILL *Charisma CB 301*	13	9 wks
9 Feb 80 ●	GAMES WITHOUT FRONTIERS *Charisma CB 354*	4	11 wks

10 May 80	**NO SELF CONTROL** *Charisma CB 360* **33**	6 wks
23 Aug 80	**BIKO** *Charisma CB 370* **38**	3 wks
25 Sep 82	**SHOCK THE MONKEY** *Charisma SHOCK 1* **58**	5 wks
9 Jul 83	**I DON'T REMEMBER** *Charisma GAB 1* **62**	3 wks
2 Jun 84	**WALK THROUGH THE FIRE** *Virgin VS 689* **69**	3 wks
26 Apr 86 ●	**SLEDGEHAMMER** *Virgin PGS 1* **4**	16 wks
1 Nov 86 ●	**DON'T GIVE UP** *Virgin PGS 2 ** **9**	11 wks
28 Mar 87	**BIG TIME** *Charisma PGS 3* **13**	7 wks
11 Jul 87	**RED RAIN** *Charisma PGS 4* **46**	3 wks
21 Nov 87	**BIKO (LIVE)** *Charisma PGS 6* **49**	6 wks
3 Jun 89	**SHAKING THE TREE** *Virgin VS 1167 *** **61**	3 wks
22 Dec 90	**SOLSBURY HILL/SHAKING THE TREE (re-issue)** *Virgin VS 1322 **** **57**	4 wks
19 Sep 92	**DIGGING IN THE DIRT** *Realworld PGS 7* **24**	4 wks

* Peter Gabriel and Kate Bush **Youssou N'Dour and Peter Gabriel *** Peter Gabriel/Youssou N'Dour and Peter Gabriel

---

Yvonne GAGE *US, female vocalist*   **4 wks**

16 Jun 84	**DOIN' IT IN A HAUNTED HOUSE** *Epic A 4519* **45**	4 wks

---

Danni'elle GAHA *Australia, female vocalist*   **2 wks**

1 Aug 92	**STUCK IN THE MIDDLE** *Epic 6581247* **68**	2 wks

---

Serge GAINSBOURG – *See Jane BIRKIN and Serge GAINSBOURG*

GALAXY – *See Phil FEARON*

Dee GALDES – *See Phil FEARON*

Eve GALLAGHER *UK, female vocalist*   **4 wks**

1 Dec 90	**LOVE COME DOWN** *More Protein PROT 6* **61**	3 wks
29 Dec 90	**LOVE COME DOWN (re-entry)** *More Protein PROT 6* **68**	1 wk

---

GALLAGHER and LYLE   **27 wks**
UK, male vocal/instrumental duo

28 Feb 76 ●	**I WANNA STAY WITH YOU** *A & M AMS 7211* **6**	9 wks
22 May 76 ●	**HEART ON MY SLEEVE** *A & M AMS 7227* **6**	10 wks
11 Sep 76	**BREAKAWAY** *A & M AMS 7245* **35**	4 wks
29 Jan 77	**EVERY LITTLE TEARDROP** *A & M AMS 7274* **32**	4 wks

---

Patsy GALLANT *Canada, female vocalist*   **9 wks**

10 Sep 77 ●	**FROM NEW YORK TO L.A.** *EMI 2620* **6**	9 wks

---

GALLIANO *UK, male/female vocal/instrumental group*   **7 wks**

30 May 92	**SKUNK FUNK** *Talkin Loud TLK 23* **41**	2 wks
1 Aug 92	**PRINCE OF PEACE** *Talkin Loud TLK 24* **47**	3 wks
10 Oct 92	**JUS' REACH (RECYCLED)** *Talkin Loud TLK 29* **66**	2 wks

---

James GALWAY *UK, male instrumentalist - flute*   **13 wks**

27 May 78 ●	**ANNIE'S SONG** *RCA Red Seal RB 5085* **3**	13 wks

---

GANG OF FOUR *UK, male vocal/instrumental group*   **5 wks**

16 Jun 79	**AT HOME HE'S A TOURIST** *EMI 2956* **58**	3 wks
22 May 82	**I LOVE A MAN IN UNIFORM** *EMI 5299* **65**	2 wks

---

GANG STARR *US, male rap group*   **8 wks**

13 Oct 90	**JAZZ THING** *CBS 356377 7* **66**	2 wks

---

23 Feb 91	**TAKE A REST** *Cooltempo COOL 230* **63**	1 wk
25 May 91	**LOVESICK** *Cooltempo COOL 234* **50**	3 wks
13 Jun 92	**2 DEEP** *Cooltempo COOL 256* **67**	2 wks

---

GAP BAND *US, male vocal/instrumental group*   **82 wks**

12 Jul 80 ●	**OOPS UP SIDE YOUR HEAD** *Mercury MER 22* **6**	14 wks
27 Sep 80	**PARTY LIGHTS** *Mercury MER 37* **30**	8 wks
27 Dec 80	**BURN RUBBER ON ME (WHY YOU WANNA HURT ME)** *Mercury MER 52* **22**	11 wks
11 Apr 81	**HUMPIN'** *Mercury MER 63* **36**	6 wks
27 Jun 81	**YEARNING FOR YOUR LOVE** *Mercury MER 73* **47**	4 wks
5 Jun 82	**EARLY IN THE MORNING** *Mercury MER 97* **55**	4 wks
19 Feb 83	**OUTSTANDING** *Total Experience TE 001* **68**	2 wks
31 Mar 84	**SOMEDAY** *Total Experience TE 5* **17**	8 wks
23 Jun 84	**JAMMIN' IN AMERICA** *Total Experience TE 6* **64**	2 wks
13 Dec 86 ●	**BIG FUN** *Total Experience FB 49779* **4**	12 wks
14 Mar 87	**HOW MUSIC CAME ABOUT (BOP B DA B DA DA)** *Total Experience FB 49755* **61**	2 wks
11 Jul 87	**OOPS UPSIDE YOUR HEAD (re-mix)** *Club JAB 54* **20**	8 wks
18 Feb 89	**I'M GONNA GIT YOU SUCKA** *Arista 112016* **63**	2 wks

---

Boris GARDINER *Jamaica, male vocalist/instrumentalist*   **38 wks**

17 Jan 70	**ELIZABETHAN REGGAE** *Duke DU 39* **48**	1 wk
31 Jan 70	**ELIZABETHAN REGGAE (re-entry)** *Duke DU 39* **14**	13 wks
26 Jul 86 ★	**I WANT TO WAKE UP WITH YOU** *Revue REV 733* **1**	15 wks
4 Oct 86	**YOU'RE EVERYTHING TO ME** *Revue REV 735* **11**	8 wks
27 Dec 86	**THE MEANING OF CHRISTMAS** *Revue REV 740* **69**	1 wk

The first copies of Elizabethan Reggae, an instrumental, were printed with the label incorrectly crediting Byron Lee as the performer. The charts for the first entry, and the first four weeks of the re-entry, all reprinted this error. All charts and discs printed after 28 Feb 1970 gave Boris Gardiner the credit he deserved.

Paul GARDINER *UK, male instrumentalist - bass*   **4 wks**

25 Jul 81	**STORMTROOPER IN DRAG** *Beggars Banquet BEG 61* **49**	4 wks

Uncredited vocalist is Gary Numan.

Art GARFUNKEL *US, male vocalist*   **37 wks**

13 Sep 75 ★	**I ONLY HAVE EYES FOR YOU** *CBS 3575* **1**	11 wks
3 Mar 79 ★	**BRIGHT EYES** *CBS 6947* **1**	19 wks
7 Jul 79	**SINCE I DON'T HAVE YOU** *CBS 7371* **38**	7 wks

---

Judy GARLAND *US, female vocalist*   **2 wks**

10 Jun 55	**THE MAN THAT GOT AWAY** *Philips PB 366* **18**	2 wks

---

Lee GARRETT *US, male vocalist*   **7 wks**

29 May 76	**YOU'RE MY EVERYTHING** *Chrysalis CHS 2087* **15**	7 wks

---

Leif GARRETT *US, male vocalist*   **14 wks**

20 Jan 79 ●	**I WAS MADE FOR DANCIN'** *Scotti Brothers K 11202* **4**	10 wks
21 Apr 79	**FEEL THE NEED** *Scotti Brothers K 11274* **38**	4 wks

---

Siedah GARRETT – *See Dennis EDWARDS; Michael JACKSON*

David GARRICK *UK, male vocalist*   **16 wks**

9 Jun 66	**LADY JANE** *Piccadilly 7N 35317* **28**	7 wks
22 Sep 66	**DEAR MRS. APPLEBEE** *Piccadilly 7N 35335* **22**	9 wks

---

GARY'S GANG *US, male vocal/instrumental group*   **18 wks**

24 Feb 79 ●	**KEEP ON DANCIN'** *CBS 7109* **8**	10 wks

2 Jun 79	LET'S LOVE DANCE TONIGHT *CBS 7328*	49 4 wks
6 Nov 82	KNOCK ME OUT *Arista ARIST 499*	45 4 wks

Barbara GASKIN – *See Dave STEWART*

GAT DECOR *UK, male instrumental group* **4 wks**

16 May 92	PASSION *Effective EFFS 1*	29 4 wks

David GATES *US, male vocalist* **2 wks**

22 Jul 78	TOOK THE LAST TRAIN *Elektra K 12307*	50 2 wks

GAY GORDON and the MINCE PIES **5 wks**
UK, male/female vocal/instrumental group

6 Dec 86	THE ESSENTIAL WALLY PARTY MEDLEY *Lifestyle XY 2*	60 5 wks

---

GAYE BYKERS ON ACID **2 wks**
UK, male vocal/instrumental group

31 Oct 87	GIT DOWN (SHAKE YOUR THANG) *Purple Fluid VS 1008*	54 2 wks

---

Marvin GAYE *US, male vocalist* **199 wks**

30 Jul 64	ONCE UPON A TIME *Stateside SS 316* *	50 1 wk
10 Dec 64	HOW SWEET IT IS *Stateside SS 360*	49 1 wk
29 Sep 66	LITTLE DARLIN' *Tamla Motown TMG 574*	50 1 wk
26 Jan 67	IT TAKES TWO *Tamla Motown TMG 590* **	16 11 wks
17 Jan 68	IF I COULD BUILD MY WHOLE WORLD AROUND YOU *Tamla Motown TMG 635* ***	41 7 wks
12 Jun 68	AIN'T NOTHIN' LIKE THE REAL THING *Tamla Motown TMG 655* ***	34 7 wks
2 Oct 68	YOU'RE ALL I NEED TO GET BY *Tamla Motown TMG 668* ***	19 19 wks
22 Jan 69	YOU AIN'T LIVIN' TILL YOU'RE LOVIN' *Tamla Motown TMG 681* ***	21 8 wks
12 Feb 69	★ I HEARD IT THROUGH THE GRAPEVINE *Tamla Motown TMG 686*	1 15 wks
4 Jun 69	GOOD LOVIN' AIN'T EASY TO COME BY *Tamla Motown TMG 697* ***	26 7 wks
23 Jul 69	● TOO BUSY THINKING 'BOUT MY BABY *Tamla Motown TMG 705*	5 16 wks
30 Jul 69	GOOD LOVIN' AIN'T EASY TO COME BY (re-entry) *Tamla Motown TMG 697* ***	48 1 wk
15 Nov 69	● ONION SONG *Tamla Motown TMG 715* ***	9 12 wks
9 May 70	● ABRAHAM MARTIN AND JOHN *Tamla Motown TMG 734*	9 14 wks
11 Dec 71	SAVE THE CHILDREN *Tamla Motown TMG 796*	41 6 wks
22 Sep 73	LET'S GET IT ON *Tamla Motown TMG 868*	31 7 wks
23 Mar 74	● YOU ARE EVERYTHING *Tamla Motown TMG 890* ****	5 12 wks
20 Jul 74	STOP LOOK LISTEN (TO YOUR HEART) *Tamla Motown TMG 906* ****	25 8 wks
7 May 77	● GOT TO GIVE IT UP *Motown TMG 1069*	7 10 wks
24 Feb 79	POPS WE LOVE YOU *Motown TMG 1136* *****	66 5 wks
30 Oct 82	● (SEXUAL) HEALING *CBS A 2855*	4 14 wks
8 Jan 83	MY LOVE IS WAITING *CBS A 3048*	34 5 wks
18 May 85	SANCTIFIED LADY *CBS A 4894*	51 4 wks
26 Apr 86	● I HEARD IT THRU THE GRAPEVINE (re-issue) *Tamla Motown ZB 40701*	8 8 wks

* Marvin Gaye and Mary Wells ** Marvin Gaye and Kim Weston *** Marvin Gaye and Tammi Terrell **** Diana Ross and Marvin Gaye ***** Diana Ross, Marvin Gaye, Smokey Robinson and Stevie Wonder

---

Crystal GAYLE *US, female vocalist* **28 wks**

12 Nov 77	● DON'T IT MAKE MY BROWN EYES BLUE *United Artists UP 36307*	5 14 wks

26 Aug 78	TALKING IN YOUR SLEEP *United Artists UP 36422*	11 14 wks

Roy GAYLE – *See MIRAGE*

Gloria GAYNOR *US, female vocalist* **62 wks**

7 Dec 74	● NEVER CAN SAY GOODBYE *MGM 2006 463*	2 13 wks
8 Mar 75	REACH OUT I'LL BE THERE *MGM 2006 499*	14 8 wks
9 Aug 75	ALL I NEED IS YOUR SWEET LOVIN' *MGM 2006 531*	44 3 wks
17 Jan 76	HOW HIGH THE MOON *MGM 2006 558*	33 4 wks
3 Feb 79	★ I WILL SURVIVE *Polydor 2095 017*	1 15 wks
6 Oct 79	LET ME KNOW (I HAVE A RIGHT) *Polydor STEP 5*	32 7 wks
24 Dec 83	I AM WHAT I AM *Chrysalis CHS 2765*	13 12 wks

GAZ *US, male vocal/instrumental group* **4 wks**

24 Feb 79	SING SING *Salsoul SSOL 116*	60 4 wks

GAZZA *UK, male vocalist – Paul Gascoigne* **14 wks**

10 Nov 90	● FOG ON THE TYNE (REVISITED) *Best ZB 44083* *	2 9 wks
22 Dec 90	GEORDIE BOYS (GAZZA RAP) *Best ZB 44229*	31 5 wks

* Gazza and Lindisfarne

GBH *UK, male vocal/instrumental group* **5 wks**

6 Feb 82	NO SURVIVORS *Clay CLAY 8*	63 2 wks
20 Nov 82	GIVE ME FIRE *Clay CLAY 16*	69 3 wks

G-CLEFS *US, male vocal group* **12 wks**

30 Nov 61	I UNDERSTAND *London HLU 9433*	17 12 wks

J. GEILS BAND *US, male vocal/instrumental group* **20 wks**

9 Jun 79	ONE LAST KISS *EMI America AM 507*	74 1 wk
13 Feb 82	● CENTERFOLD *EMI America EA 135*	3 9 wks
10 Apr 82	FREEZE-FRAME *EMI America EA 134*	27 7 wks
26 Jun 82	ANGEL IN BLUE *EMI America EA 138*	55 3 wks

Bob GELDOF *Ireland, male vocalist* **14 wks**

1 Nov 86	THIS IS THE WORLD CALLING *Mercury BOB 101*	25 5 wks
21 Feb 87	LOVE LIKE A ROCKET *Mercury BOB 102*	61 3 wks
23 Jun 90	THE GREAT SONG OF INDIFFERENCE *Mercury BOB 104*	15 6 wks

---

GEM – *See ONE TRIBE featuring GEM*

GENE AND JIM ARE INTO SHAKES **2 wks**
UK, male vocal/instrumental duo

19 Mar 88	SHAKE! (HOW ABOUT A SAMPLING GENE) *Rough Trade RT 216*	68 2 wks

---

GENE LOVES JEZEBEL **7 wks**
UK, male vocal/instrumental group

29 Mar 86	SWEETEST THING *Beggars Banquet BEG 156*	75 1 wk
14 Jun 86	HEARTACHE *Beggars Banquet BEG 161*	71 2 wks
5 Sep 87	THE MOTION OF LOVE *Beggars Banquet BEG 192*	56 3 wks
5 Dec 87	GORGEOUS *Beggars Banquet BEG 202*	68 1 wk

GENERAL PUBLIC *UK, male vocal/instrumental group* **3 wks**

10 Mar 84	**GENERAL PUBLIC** *Virgin VS 659*..**60**	3 wks

GENERATION X *UK, male vocal/instrumental group* **31 wks**

17 Sep 77	**YOUR GENERATION** *Chrysalis CHS 2165*.....................**36**	4 wks
11 Mar 78	**READY STEADY GO** *Chrysalis CHS 2207*.....................**47**	3 wks
20 Jan 79	**KING ROCKER** *Chrysalis CHS 2261*.............................**11**	9 wks
7 Apr 79	**VALLEY OF THE DOLLS** *Chrysalis CHS 2310* **23**	7 wks
30 Jun 79	**FRIDAY'S ANGELS** *Chrysalis CHS 2330*.....................**62**	2 wks
18 Oct 80	**DANCING WITH MYSELF** *Chrysalis CHS 2444* *..........**62**	2 wks
24 Jan 81	**DANCING WITH MYSELF (EP)** *Chrysalis CHS 2488* * **60**	4 wks

* Gen X

Tracks on Dancing With Myself (EP): *Dancing With Myself/Untouchables/Rock On/ King Rocker.*

GENESIS *UK, male vocal/instrumental group* **180 wks**

6 Apr 74	**I KNOW WHAT I LIKE (IN YOUR WARDROBE)** *Charisma CB 224* **21**	7 wks
26 Feb 77	**YOUR OWN SPECIAL WAY** *Charisma CB 300* **43**	3 wks
28 May 77	**SPOT THE PIGEON EP** *Charisma GEN 001* **14**	7 wks
11 Mar 78	● **FOLLOW YOU FOLLOW ME** *Charisma CB 309*.................**7**	13 wks
8 Jul 78	**MANY TOO MANY** *Charisma CB 315* **43**	5 wks
15 Mar 80	● **TURN IT ON AGAIN** *Charisma CB 356* **8**	10 wks
17 May 80	**DUCHESS** *Charisma CB 363* **46**	5 wks
13 Sep 80	**MISUNDERSTANDING** *Charisma CB 369* **42**	5 wks
22 Aug 81	● **ABACAB** *Charisma CB 388* **9**	8 wks
31 Oct 81	**KEEP IT DARK** *Charisma CB 391* **33**	4 wks
13 Mar 82	**MAN ON THE CORNER** *Charisma CB 393* **41**	5 wks
22 May 82	● **3 X 3 EP** *Charisma GEN 1* **10**	8 wks
3 Sep 83	● **MAMA** *Virgin/Charisma MAMA 1* **4**	10 wks
12 Nov 83	**THAT'S ALL** *Charisma/Virgin TATA 1* **16**	11 wks
11 Feb 84	**ILLEGAL ALIEN** *Charisma/Virgin AL1* **46**	3 wks
10 Mar 84	**ILLEGAL ALIEN (re-entry)** *Charisma/Virgin AL1* **70**	1 wk
31 May 86	**INVISIBLE TOUCH** *Virgin GENS 1* **15**	8 wks
30 Aug 86	**IN TOO DEEP** *Virgin GENS 2* **19**	9 wks
22 Nov 86	**LAND OF CONFUSION** *Virgin GENS 3* **14**	12 wks
14 Mar 87	**TONIGHT TONIGHT TONIGHT** *Virgin GENS 4*..........**18**	6 wks
20 Jun 87	**THROWING IT ALL AWAY** *Virgin GENS 5* **22**	8 wks
2 Nov 91	● **NO SON OF MINE** *Virgin GENS 6* **6**	6 wks
4 Jan 92	**NO SON OF MINE (re-entry)** *Virgin GENS 6* **70**	1 wk
11 Jan 92	● **I CAN'T DANCE** *Virgin GENS 7* **7**	9 wks
18 Apr 92	**HOLD ON MY HEART** *Virgin GENS 8*..........................**16**	5 wks
25 Jul 92	**JESUS HE KNOWS ME** *Virgin GENS 9* **20**	7 wks
21 Nov 92	● **INVISIBLE TOUCH (LIVE)** *Virgin GENS 10* **7**	4 wks

Tracks on Spot The Pigeon EP: *Match Of The Day/Pigeons/Inside and Out. Tracks on 3 X 3 EP: Paperlate/You Might Recall/Me And Virgil.*

GENEVIEVE *France, female vocalist* **1 wk**

5 May 66	**ONCE** *CBS 202061* **43**	1 wk

Bobbie GENTRY *US, female vocalist* **48 wks**

13 Sep 67	**ODE TO BILLY JOE** *Capitol CL 15511* **13**	11 wks
30 Aug 69	★ **I'LL NEVER FALL IN LOVE AGAIN** *Capitol CL 15606* **1**	19 wks
6 Dec 69	● **ALL I HAVE TO DO IS DREAM** *Capitol CL 15619* * **3**	14 wks
21 Feb 70	**RAINDROPS KEEP FALLIN' ON MY HEAD** *Capitol CL 15626* **40**	4 wks

* Bobbie Gentry and Glen Campbell

GEORDIE *UK, vocal/instrumental group* **35 wks**

2 Dec 72	**DON'T DO THAT** *Regal Zonophone RZ 3067* **32**	7 wks
17 Mar 73	● **ALL BECAUSE OF YOU** *EMI 2008* **6**	13 wks
16 Jun 73	**CAN YOU DO IT** *EMI 2031* **13**	9 wks
25 Aug 73	**ELECTRIC LADY** *EMI 2048* **32**	6 wks

British Hit Singles Part One: Alphabetically by Artist
Date of chart entry/Title & catalogue no./Peak position reached/Weeks on chart
★ Number one ● Top Ten † still on chart at 31 Dec 1992
* = credited to act billed in footnote

Robin GEORGE *UK, male vocalist/instrumentalist - guitar* **2 wks**

27 Apr 85	**HEARTLINE** *Bronze BRO 191* **68**	2 wks

Sophia GEORGE *Jamaica, female vocalist* **11 wks**

7 Dec 85	● **GIRLIE GIRLIE** *Winner WIN 01* **7**	11 wks

GEORGIA SATELLITES **8 wks**
US, male vocal/instrumental group

7 Feb 87	**KEEP YOUR HANDS TO YOURSELF** *Elektra EKR 50* **69**	1 wk
16 May 87	**BATTLESHIP CHAINS** *Elektra EKR 58* **44**	4 wks
21 Jan 89	**HIPPY HIPPY SHAKE** *Elektra EKR 86* **63**	3 wks

GEORGIO *US, male vocalist* **3 wks**

20 Feb 88	**LOVER'S LANE** *Motown ZB 41611* **54**	3 wks

Danyel GERARD *France, male vocalist* **12 wks**

18 Sep 71	**BUTTERFLY** *CBS 7454* **11**	12 wks

GERRY and the PACEMAKERS **114 wks**
UK, male vocal/instrumental group

14 Mar 63	★ **HOW DO YOU DO IT?** *Columbia DB 4987* **1**	18 wks
30 May 63	★ **I LIKE IT** *Columbia DB 7041* **1**	15 wks
10 Oct 63	★ **YOU'LL NEVER WALK ALONE** *Columbia DB 7126* **1**	19 wks
16 Jan 64	● **I'M THE ONE** *Columbia DB 7189* **2**	15 wks
16 Apr 64	● **DON'T LET THE SUN CATCH YOU CRYING** *Columbia DB 7268* **6**	11 wks
3 Sep 64	**IT'S GONNA BE ALL RIGHT** *Columbia DB 7353* **24**	7 wks
17 Dec 64	● **FERRY ACROSS THE MERSEY** *Columbia DB 7437* **8**	13 wks
25 Mar 65	**I'LL BE THERE** *Columbia DB 7504* **15**	9 wks
18 Nov 65	**WALK HAND IN HAND** *Columbia DB 7738* **29**	7 wks

GET FRESH CREW – *See Doug E. FRESH and the GET FRESH CREW*

Stan GETZ *US, male instrumentalist - tenor sax* **29 wks**

8 Nov 62	**DESAFINADO** *HMV POP 1061* * **11**	13 wks
23 Jul 64	**THE GIRL FROM IPANEMA (GAROTA DE IPANEMA)** *Verve VS 520* ** **29**	10 wks
25 Aug 84	**THE GIRL FROM IPANEMA (re-issue)** *Verve IPA 1* *** **55**	6 wks

* Stan Getz and Charlie Byrd ** Stan Getz and Joao Gilberto *** Astrud Gilberto

The re-issue of The Girl From Ipanema was credited only to Astrud Gilberto, the vocalist, even though it was exactly the same recording as the original hit.

GHOST DANCE *UK, male vocal/instrumental group* **2 wks**

17 Jun 89	**DOWN TO THE WIRE** *Chrysalis CHS 3376* **66**	2 wks

Andy GIBB *UK, male vocalist* **30 wks**

25 Jun 77	**I JUST WANNA BE YOUR EVERYTHING** *RSO 2090 237* **26**	7 wks

13 May 78		SHADOW DANCING *RSO 001*	42	6 wks
12 Aug 78	●	AN EVERLASTING LOVE *RSO 015*	10	10 wks
27 Jan 79		(OUR LOVE) DON'T THROW IT ALL AWAY *RSO 26*	32	7 wks

Barry GIBB – *See Barbra STREISAND*

Robin GIBB *UK, male vocalist* **21 wks**

9 Jul 69	●	SAVED BY THE BELL *Polydor 56-337*	2	16 wks
15 Nov 69		SAVED BY THE BELL (re-entry) *Polydor 56-337*	49	1 wk
7 Feb 70		AUGUST OCTOBER *Polydor 56-371*	45	3 wks
11 Feb 84		ANOTHER LONELY NIGHT IN NEW YORK *Polydor POSP 668*	71	1 wk

Steve GIBBONS BAND **14 wks**
UK, male vocal/instrumental group

6 Aug 77		TULANE *Polydor 2058 889*	12	10 wks
13 May 78		EDDY VORTEX *Polydor 2059 017*	56	4 wks

Georgia GIBBS *US, female vocalist* **2 wks**

22 Apr 55		TWEEDLE DEE *Mercury MB 3196*	20	1 wk
13 Jul 56		KISS ME ANOTHER *Mercury MT 110*	24	1 wk

Debbie GIBSON *US, female vocalist* **63 wks**

26 Sep 87		ONLY IN MY DREAMS *Atlantic A 9322*	54	5 wks
23 Jan 88	●	SHAKE YOUR LOVE *Atlantic A 9187*	7	8 wks
19 Mar 88		ONLY IN MY DREAMS (re-entry) *Atlantic A 9322*	11	7 wks
7 May 88		OUT OF THE BLUE *Atlantic A 9091*	19	7 wks
9 Jul 88	●	FOOLISH BEAT *Atlantic A 9059*	9	9 wks
15 Oct 88		STAYING TOGETHER *Atlantic A 9020*	53	2 wks
28 Jan 89		LOST IN YOUR EYES *Atlantic A 8970*	34	7 wks
29 Apr 89		ELECTRIC YOUTH *Atlantic A 8919*	14	8 wks
19 Aug 89		WE COULD BE TOGETHER *Atlantic A 8896*	22	8 wks
9 Mar 91		ANYTHING IS POSSIBLE *Atlantic A 7735*	51	2 wks

Don GIBSON *US, male vocalist* **16 wks**

31 Aug 61		SEA OF HEARTBREAK *RCA 1243*	14	13 wks
1 Feb 62		LONESOME NUMBER ONE *RCA 1272*	47	3 wks

Wayne GIBSON *UK, male vocalist* **13 wks**

3 Sep 64		KELLY *Pye 7N 15680*	48	2 wks
23 Nov 74		UNDER MY THUMB *Pye Disco Demand DDS 2001*	17	11 wks

GIBSON BROTHERS **54 wks**
Martinique, male vocal/instrumental group

10 Mar 79		CUBA *Island WIP 6483*	41	9 wks
21 Jul 79	●	OOH! WHAT A LIFE *Island WIP 6503*	10	12 wks
17 Nov 79	●	QUE SERA MI VIDA (IF YOU SHOULD GO) *Island WIP 6525*	5	11 wks
23 Feb 80		CUBA/BETTER DO IT SALSA (re-issue) *Island WIP 6561*	12	9 wks
12 Jul 80		MARIANA *Island WIP 6617*	11	10 wks
9 Jul 83		MY HEART'S BEATING WILD (TIC TAC TIC TAC) *Stiff BUY 184*	56	3 wks

GIDEA PARK *UK, male vocal/instrumentalist - Adrian Baker* **19 wks**

4 Jul 81		BEACHBOY GOLD *Stone SON 2162*	11	13 wks
12 Sep 81		SEASONS OF GOLD *Polo POLO 14*	28	6 wks

Astrud GILBERTO – *See Stan GETZ*

Joao GILBERTO – *See Stan GETZ*

Johnny GILL *US, male vocalist* **7 wks**

23 Feb 91		WRAP MY BODY TIGHT *Motown ZB 44271*	57	2 wks
28 Nov 92		SLOW AND SEXY *Epic 6587727* *	17†	5 wks

* Shabba Ranks featuring Johnny Gill

GILLAN *UK, male vocal/instrumental group* **46 wks**

14 Jun 80		SLEEPIN' ON THE JOB *Virgin VS 355*	55	3 wks
4 Oct 80		TROUBLE *Virgin VS 377*	14	6 wks
14 Feb 81		MUTUALLY ASSURED DESTRUCTION *Virgin VS 103*	32	5 wks
21 Mar 81		NEW ORLEANS *Virgin VS 406*	17	10 wks
20 Jun 81		NO LAUGHING IN HEAVEN *Virgin VS 425*	31	6 wks
10 Oct 81		NIGHTMARE *Virgin VS 441*	36	6 wks
23 Jan 82		RESTLESS *Virgin VS 465*	25	7 wks
4 Sep 82		LIVING FOR THE CITY *Virgin VS 519*	50	3 wks

Stuart GILLIES *UK, male vocalist* **10 wks**

31 Mar 73		AMANDA *Philips 6006 293*	13	10 wks

Jimmy GILMER – *See FIREBALLS*

James GILREATH *US, male vocalist* **10 wks**

2 May 63		LITTLE BAND OF GOLD *Pye International 7N 25190*	29	10 wks

Jim GILSTRAP *US, male vocalist* **11 wks**

15 Mar 75	●	SWING YOUR DADDY *Chelsea 2005 021*	4	11 wks

Gordon GILTRAP *UK, male instrumentalist - guitar* **10 wks**

14 Jan 78		HEARTSONG *Electric WOT 19*	21	7 wks
28 Apr 79		FEAR OF THE DARK *Electric WOT 29* *	58	3 wks

* Gordon Giltrap Band

GINGERBREADS – *See GOLDIE and the GINGERBREADS*

Martine GIRAULT *US, female vocalist* **2 wks**

29 Aug 92		REVIVAL *ffrr FX 195*	53	2 wks

GIRL *UK, male vocal/instrumental group* **3 wks**

12 Apr 80		HOLLYWOOD TEASE *Jet 176*	50	3 wks

GIRLSCHOOL *UK, female vocal/instrumental group* **25 wks**

2 Aug 80		RACE WITH THE DEVIL *Bronze BRO 100*	49	6 wks
21 Feb 81	●	ST. VALENTINE'S DAY MASSACRE EP *Bronze BRO 116* *	5	8 wks
11 Apr 81		HIT AND RUN *Bronze BRO 118*	32	6 wks
11 Jul 81		C'MON LET'S GO *Bronze BRO 126*	42	3 wks
3 Apr 82		WILDLIFE (EP) *Bronze BRO 144*	58	2 wks

* Motorhead and Girlschool (also known as Headgirl)

Tracks on St. Valentine's Day Massacre EP: *Please Don't Touch/Emergency/Bomber. Tracks on* Wildlife (EP): *Don't Call It Love/Wildlife/Don't Stop.*

Junior GISCOMBE – *See JUNIOR*

GLADIATORS – *See NERO and the GLADIATORS*

LESLEY GORE wrote
Irene Cara's 1982 hit
'Out Here On My
Own' with her brother
Michael.

The GLITTER
BAND celebrated half
a dozen top ten hits in
under two years.

GLASS TIGER *Canada, male vocal/instrumental group*   **18 wks**

18 Oct 86	**DON'T FORGET ME (WHEN I'M GONE)** *Manhattan MT 13*	29	9 wks
31 Jan 87	**SOMEDAY** *Manhattan MT 17*	66	2 wks
26 Oct 91	**MY TOWN** *EMI EM 212*	33	7 wks

My Town features the uncredited vocals of Rod Stewart.

Mayson GLEN ORCHESTRA – *See Paul HENRY and the Mayson GLEN ORCHESTRA*

GLENN and CHRIS *UK, male vocal duo*   **8 wks**

18 Apr 87	**DIAMOND LIGHTS** *Record Shack KICK 1*	12	8 wks

Gary GLITTER *UK, male vocalist*   **168 wks**

10 Jun 72	● **ROCK AND ROLL (PARTS 1 & 2)** *Bell 1216*	2	15 wks
23 Sep 72	● **I DIDN'T KNOW I LOVED YOU (TILL I SAW YOU ROCK 'N' ROLL)** *Bell 1259*	4	11 wks
20 Jan 73	● **DO YOU WANNA TOUCH ME? (OH YEAH)** *Bell 1280*	2	11 wks
7 Apr 73	● **HELLO HELLO I'M BACK AGAIN** *Bell 1299*	2	14 wks
21 Jul 73	● **I'M THE LEADER OF THE GANG (I AM)** *Bell 1321*	1	12 wks
17 Nov 73	★ **I LOVE YOU LOVE ME LOVE** *Bell 1337*	1	14 wks
30 Mar 74	● **REMEMBER ME THIS WAY** *Bell 1349*	3	8 wks
15 Jun 74	★ **ALWAYS YOURS** *Bell 1359*	1	9 wks
23 Nov 74	● **OH YES! YOU'RE BEAUTIFUL** *Bell 1391*	2	10 wks
3 May 75	● **LOVE LIKE YOU AND ME** *Bell 1423*	10	6 wks
21 Jun 75	● **DOING ALRIGHT WITH THE BOYS** *Bell 1429*	6	7 wks
8 Nov 75	● **PAPA OOM MOW MOW** *Bell 1451*	38	5 wks
13 Mar 76	**YOU BELONG TO ME** *Bell 1473*	40	5 wks
22 Jan 77	**IT TAKES ALL NIGHT LONG** *Arista 85*	25	6 wks
16 Jul 77	**A LITTLE BOOGIE WOOGIE IN THE BACK OF MY MIND** *Arista 112*	31	5 wks
20 Sep 80	**GARY GLITTER EP** *GTO GT 282*	57	3 wks
10 Oct 81	**AND THEN SHE KISSED ME** *Bell BELL 1497*	39	5 wks
5 Dec 81	**ALL THAT GLITTERS** *Bell BELL 1498*	48	5 wks
23 Jun 84	**DANCE ME UP** *Arista ARIST 570*	25	5 wks
1 Dec 84	● **ANOTHER ROCK AND ROLL CHRISTMAS** *Arista ARIST 592*	7	7 wks
10 Oct 92	**AND THE LEADER ROCKS ON** *EMI EM 252*	58	2 wks
21 Nov 92	**THROUGH THE YEARS** *EMI EM 256*	49	3 wks

Rock And Roll Part 1 *not listed with Part 2 for weeks of 10 and 17 Jan 72. Tracks on* Gary Glitter EP: *I'm The Leader Of The Gang (I Am)/Rock And Roll (Part 2)/Hello Hello I'm Back Again/Do You Wanna Touch Me?(Oh Yeah). All were re-issues.*

GLITTER BAND *UK, male vocal/instrumental group*   **60 wks**

23 Mar 74	● **ANGEL FACE** *Bell 1348*	4	10 wks
3 Aug 74	● **JUST FOR YOU** *Bell 1368*	10	8 wks
19 Oct 74	● **LET'S GET TOGETHER AGAIN** *Bell 1383*	8	8 wks
18 Jan 75	● **GOODBYE MY LOVE** *Bell 1395*	2	9 wks
12 Apr 75	● **THE TEARS I CRIED** *Bell 1416*	8	8 wks
9 Aug 75	**LOVE IN THE SUN** *Bell 1437*	15	8 wks
28 Feb 76	● **PEOPLE LIKE YOU AND PEOPLE LIKE ME** *Bell 1471*	5	9 wks

GLOVE *UK, male vocal/instrumental group*   **3 wks**

20 Aug 83	**LIKE AN ANIMAL** *Wonderland SHE 3*	52	3 wks

GO GO LORENZO and the DAVIS PINCKNEY PROJECT   **8 wks**
US, male vocal/instrumental group

6 Dec 86	**YOU CAN DANCE (IF YOU WANT TO)** *Boiling Point POSP 836*	46	8 wks

GO-GOS *US, female vocal/instrumental group*   **7 wks**

15 May 82	**OUR LIPS ARE SEALED** *IRS GDN 102*	47	6 wks
26 Jan 91	**COOL JERK** *IRS AM 712*	60	1 wk

GO WEST *UK, male vocal/instrumental duo*   **69 wks**

23 Feb 85	● **WE CLOSE OUR EYES** *Chrysalis CHS 2850*	5	14 wks
11 May 85	**CALL ME** *Chrysalis GOW 1*	12	9 wks
3 Aug 85	**GOODBYE GIRL** *Chrysalis GOW 2*	25	7 wks
23 Nov 85	**DON'T LOOK DOWN - THE SEQUEL** *Chrysalis GOW 3*	13	10 wks
29 Nov 86	**TRUE COLOURS** *Chrysalis GOW 4*	48	7 wks
9 May 87	**I WANT TO HEAR IT FROM YOU** *Chrysalis GOW 5*	43	3 wks
12 Sep 87	**THE KING IS DEAD** *Chrysalis GOW 6*	67	2 wks
28 Jul 90	**THE KING OF WISHFUL THINKING** *Chrysalis GOW 8*	18	10 wks
17 Oct 92	**FAITHFUL** *Chrysalis GOW 9*	13	6 wks

GODIEGO *Japan/US, male vocal/instrumental group*   **11 wks**

15 Oct 77	**THE WATER MARGIN** *BBC RESL 50*	37	4 wks
16 Feb 80	**GANDHARA** *BBC RESL 66*	56	7 wks

The Water Margin is the English version of the song, which shared chart credit with the Japanese language version by Pete Mac Jr.

GODLEY and CREME *UK, male vocal/instrumental duo*   **36 wks**

12 Sep 81	● **UNDER YOUR THUMB** *Polydor POSP 322*	3	11 wks
21 Nov 81	● **WEDDING BELLS** *Polydor POSP 369*	7	11 wks
30 Mar 85	**CRY** *Polydor POSP 732*	19	11 wks
16 Aug 86	**CRY (re-entry)** *Polydor POSP 732*	66	3 wks

Andrew GOLD *US, male vocalist/instrumentalist - piano*   **36 wks**

2 Apr 77	**LONELY BOY** *Asylum K 13076*	11	9 wks
25 Mar 78	● **NEVER LET HER SLIP AWAY** *Asylum K 13112*	5	13 wks
24 Jun 78	**HOW CAN THIS BE LOVE** *Asylum K 13126*	19	10 wks
14 Oct 78	**THANK YOU FOR BEING A FRIEND** *Asylum K 13135*	42	4 wks

GOLDEN EARRING   **16 wks**
Holland, male vocal/instrumental group

8 Dec 73	● **RADAR LOVE** *Track 2094 116*	7	13 wks
8 Oct 77	**RADAR LOVE** *Polydor 2121 335*	44	3 wks

These are two different recordings of the same song.

GOLDIE *UK, male vocal/instrumental group*   **11 wks**

27 May 78	● **MAKING UP AGAIN** *Bronze BRO 50*	7	11 wks

GOLDIE and the GINGERBREADS   **5 wks**
US, female vocal/instrumental group

25 Feb 65	**CAN'T YOU HEAR MY HEART BEAT?** *Decca F 12070*	25	5 wks

Bobby GOLDSBORO *US, male vocalist*   **47 wks**

17 Apr 68	● **HONEY** *United Artists UP2215*	2	15 wks
4 Aug 73	● **SUMMER (THE FIRST TIME)** *United Artists UP35558*	9	10 wks
3 Aug 74	**HELLO SUMMERTIME** *United Artists UP35705*	14	10 wks
29 Mar 75	● **HONEY (re-issue)** *United Artists UP35633*	2	12 wks

Glen GOLDSMITH US, male vocalist — 24 wks

7 Nov 87	I WON'T CRY Reproduction PB 41493	34	7 wks
12 Mar 88	DREAMING Reproduction PB 41711	12	11 wks
11 Jun 88	WHAT YOU SEE IS WHAT YOU GET Reproduction PB 42075	33	5 wks
3 Sep 88	SAVE A LITTLE BIT Reproduction PB 42147	73	1 wk

Leroy GOMEZ – See SANTA ESMERALDA and Leroy GOMEZ

GONZALEZ UK/US, male vocal/instrumental group — 11 wks

31 Mar 79	HAVEN'T STOPPED DANCING YET Sidewalk SID 102	15	11 wks

GOODBYE MR. MACKENZIE
UK, male/female vocal/instrumental group — 13 wks

20 Aug 88	GOODBYE MR MACKENZIE Capitol CL 501	62	2 wks
11 Mar 89	THE RATTLER Capitol CL 522	37	6 wks
29 Jul 89	GOODWILL CITY/I'M SICK OF YOU Capitol CL 538	49	2 wks
21 Apr 90	LOVE CHILD Parlophone R 6247	52	2 wks
23 Jun 90	BLACKER THAN BLACK Parlophone R 6257	61	1 wk

GOODIES UK, male vocal group — 38 wks

7 Dec 74 ●	THE IN BETWEENIES/FATHER CHRISTMAS DO NOT TOUCH ME Bradley's BRAD 7421	7	9 wks
15 Mar 75 ●	FUNKY GIBBON/SICK MAN BLUES Bradley's BRAD 7504	4	10 wks
21 Jun 75	BLACK PUDDING BERTHA Bradley's BRAD 7517	19	7 wks
27 Sep 75	NAPPY LOVE/WILD THING Bradley's BRAD 7524	21	6 wks
13 Dec 75	MAKE A DAFT NOISE FOR CHRISTMAS Bradley's BRAD 7533	20	6 wks

Cuba GOODING US, male vocalist — 2 wks

19 Nov 83	HAPPINESS IS JUST AROUND THE BEND London LON 41	72	2 wks

Ron GOODWIN UK, orchestra — 24 wks

15 May 53 ●	TERRY'S THEME FROM 'LIMELIGHT' Parlophone R 3686	3	23 wks
28 Oct 55	BLUE STAR (THE MEDIC THEME) Parlophone R 4074	20	1 wk

See also Eamonn Andrews.

GOODY GOODY US, female vocal duo — 5 wks

2 Dec 78	NUMBER ONE DEE JAY Atlantic LV 3	55	5 wks

GOOMBAY DANCE BAND — 16 wks
Germany/Montserrat, male/female vocal/instrumental group

27 Feb 82 ★	SEVEN TEARS Epic EPC A 1242	1	12 wks
15 May 82	SUN OF JAMAICA Epic EPC A 2345	50	4 wks

GOONS UK, male vocal group — 30 wks

29 Jun 56 ●	I'M WALKING BACKWARDS FOR CHRISTMAS/BLUEBOTTLE BLUES Decca F 10756	4	10 wks
14 Sep 56 ●	BLOODNOK'S ROCK 'N' ROLL CALL/YING TONG SONG Decca E 10780	3	10 wks
21 Jul 73 ●	YING TONG SONG (re-issue) Decca F 13414	9	10 wks

Bluebottle Blues only listed from 13 Jul 56.

Lonnie GORDON US, female vocalist — 21 wks

24 Jun 89	(I'VE GOT YOUR) PLEASURE CONTROL ffrr F 106 *	60	3 wks
27 Jan 90 ●	HAPPENIN' ALL OVER AGAIN Supreme SUPE 159	4	10 wks
11 Aug 90	BEYOND YOUR WILDEST DREAMS Supreme SUPE 167	48	2 wks
17 Nov 90	IF I HAVE TO STAND ALONE Supreme SUPE 181	68	1 wk
4 May 91	GONNA CATCH YOU Supreme SUPE 185	32	5 wks

* Simon Harris featuring Lonnie Gordon

Lesley GORE US, female vocalist — 20 wks

20 Jun 63 ●	IT'S MY PARTY Mercury AMT 1205	9	12 wks
24 Sep 64	MAYBE I KNOW Mercury MF 829	20	8 wks

Eydie GORMÉ US, female vocalist — 33 wks

24 Jan 58	LOVE ME FOREVER HMV POP 432	21	5 wks
21 Jun 62 ●	YES MY DARLING DAUGHTER CBS AAG 105	10	9 wks
31 Jan 63	BLAME IT ON THE BOSSA NOVA CBS AAG 131	32	6 wks
22 Aug 63 ●	I WANT TO STAY HERE CBS AAG 163 *	3	13 wks

* Steve and Eydie

G.O.S.H. UK, male/female charity ensemble — 11 wks

28 Nov 87	THE WISHING WELL MBS GOSH 1	22	11 wks

Nigel GOULDING – See Abigail MEAD and Nigel GOULDING

Graham GOULDMAN UK, male vocalist — 4 wks

23 Jun 79	SUNBURN Mercury SUNNY 1	52	4 wks

G.Q. US, male vocal/instrumental group — 6 wks

10 Mar 79	DISCO NIGHTS (ROCK FREAK) Arista ARIST 245	42	6 wks

Charlie GRACIE US, male vocalist — 41 wks

19 Apr 57	BUTTERFLY Parlophone R 4290	12	8 wks
14 Jun 57 ●	FABULOUS Parlophone R 4313	8	16 wks
23 Aug 57	I LOVE YOU SO MUCH IT HURTS/WANDERIN' EYES London HLU 8467	14	2 wks
6 Sep 57 ●	WANDERIN' EYES London HLU 8467	6	12 wks
6 Sep 57	I LOVE YOU SO MUCH IT HURTS London HLU 8467	20	2 wks
10 Jan 58	COOL BABY London HLU 8521	26	1 wk

I Love You So Much It Hurts and Wanderin' Eyes were listed together for 2 weeks, then listed separately for a further 2 and 12 weeks respectively.

Eve GRAHAM – See NEW SEEKERS

Jaki GRAHAM UK, female vocalist — 71 wks

23 Mar 85 ●	COULD IT BE I'M FALLING IN LOVE Chrysalis GRAN 6 *	5	11 wks
29 Jun 85 ●	ROUND AND ROUND EMI JAKI 4	9	11 wks
31 Aug 85	HEAVEN KNOWS EMI JAKI 5	59	3 wks
16 Nov 85	MATED EMI JAKI 6 *	20	10 wks
3 May 86 ●	SET ME FREE EMI JAKI 7	7	12 wks
9 Aug 86	BREAKING AWAY EMI JAKI 8	16	8 wks
15 Nov 86	STEP RIGHT UP EMI JAKI 9	15	12 wks
9 Jul 88	NO MORE TEARS EMI JAKI 12	60	2 wks
24 Jun 89	FROM NOW ON EMI JAKI 15	73	2 wks

* David Grant and Jaki Graham

British Hit Singles Part One: Alphabetically by Artist
Date of chart entry/Title & catalogue no./Peak position reached/Weeks on chart
★ Number one   ● Top Ten   † still on chart at 31 Dec 1992
* = credited to act billed in footnote

Larry GRAHAM US, male vocalist — 4 wks

3 Jul 82	SOONER OR LATER Warner Bros. K 17925	54	4 wks

Ron GRAINER ORCHESTRA UK, orchestra — 7 wks

9 Dec 78	A TOUCH OF VELVET A STING OF BRASS Casino Classics CC 5	60	7 wks

GRAND FUNK RAILROAD
US, male vocal/instrumental group — 1 wk

6 Feb 71	INSIDE LOOKING OUT Capitol CL 15668	40	1 wk

GRAND PLAZ UK, production group — 4 wks

8 Sep 90	WOW WOW - NA NA Urban URB 6 0	41	4 wks

GRAND PRIX UK, male vocal/instrumental group — 1 wk

27 Feb 82	KEEP ON BELIEVING RCA 162	75	1 wk

GRANDMASTER FLASH, Melle MEL and the FURIOUS FIVE — 84 wks
US, male vocal duo and male vocal group

28 Aug 82	● THE MESSAGE Sugarhill SHL 117 *	8	9 wks
22 Jan 83	MESSAGE II (SURVIVAL) Sugarhill SH 119 **	74	2 wks
19 Nov 83	WHITE LINES (DON'T DON'T DO IT) Sugarhill SH 130 ***	60	3 wks
11 Feb 84	WHITE LINES (DON'T DON'T DO IT) (re-entry) Sugarhill SH 130 ***	7	38 wks
30 Jun 84	BEAT STREET BREAKDOWN Atlantic A9659 ****	42	7 wks
22 Sep 84	WE DON'T WORK FOR FREE Sugarhill SH 136 ****	45	4 wks
24 Nov 84	WHITE LINES (DON'T DON'T DO IT) (2nd re-entry) Sugarhill SH 130 ***	75	1 wk
15 Dec 84	● STEP OFF (PART 1) Sugarhill SH 139 ****	8	12 wks
5 Jan 85	WHITE LINES (DON'T DON'T DO IT) (3rd re-entry) Sugarhill SH 130 ***	73	1 wk
16 Feb 85	SIGN OF THE TIMES Elektra E 9677 *****	72	1 wk
16 Mar 85	PUMP ME UP Sugarhill SH 141 ****	45	6 wks

* Grandmaster Flash and the Furious Five ** Melle Mel and Duke Bootee
*** Grandmaster Flash and Melle Mel **** Grandmaster Melle Mel and the
Furious Five ***** Grandmaster Flash

GRANDMIXER US, male 'scratch' DJ — 3 wks

24 Dec 83	CRAZY CUTS Island IS 146	73	2 wks
14 Jan 84	CRAZY CUTS (re-entry) Island IS 146	71	1 wk

GRANGE HILL CAST — 6 wks
UK, male/female vocal charity assembly

19 Apr 86	● JUST SAY NO BBC RESL 183	5	6 wks

Gerri GRANGER US, female vocalist — 3 wks

30 Sep 78	I GO TO PIECES (EVERYTIME) Casino Classics CC3	50	3 wks

Amy GRANT US, female vocalist — 24 wks

11 May 91	● BABY BABY A & M AM 727	2	13 wks
3 Aug 91	EVERY HEARTBEAT A & M AM 783	25	7 wks
2 Nov 91	THAT'S WHAT LOVE IS FOR A & M AM 666	60	3 wks
15 Feb 92	GOOD FOR ME A & M AM 810	60	1 wk

Boysie GRANT – See Ezz RECO and the LAUNCHERS with Boysie GRANT

David GRANT UK, male vocalist — 59 wks

30 Apr 83	STOP AND GO Chrysalis GRAN 1	19	9 wks
16 Jul 83	● WATCHING YOU WATCHING ME Chrysalis GRAN 2	10	13 wks
8 Oct 83	LOVE WILL FIND A WAY Chrysalis GRAN 3	24	6 wks
26 Nov 83	ROCK THE MIDNIGHT Chrysalis GRAN 4	46	4 wks
23 Mar 85	● COULD IT BE I'M FALLING IN LOVE Chrysalis GRAN 6 *	5	11 wks
16 Nov 85	MATED EMI JAKI 6 *	20	10 wks
1 Aug 87	CHANGE Polydor POSP 871	55	4 wks
12 May 90	KEEP IT TOGETHER Fourth & Broadway BRW 169	56	2 wks

* David Grant and Jaki Graham

Eddy GRANT Guyana, male vocalist/multi-instrumentalist — 94 wks

2 Jun 79	LIVING ON THE FRONT LINE Ensign ENY 26	11	11 wks
15 Nov 80	● DO YOU FEEL MY LOVE Ensign ENY 45	8	11 wks
4 Apr 81	CAN'T GET ENOUGH OF YOU Ensign ENY 207	13	10 wks
25 Jul 81	I LOVE YOU, YES I LOVE YOU Ensign ENY 216	37	6 wks
16 Oct 82	★ I DON'T WANNA DANCE Ice ICE 56	1	15 wks
15 Jan 83	● ELECTRIC AVENUE Ice ICE 57	2	9 wks
19 Mar 83	LIVING ON THE FRONT LINE/DO YOU FEEL MY LOVE (re-issues) Mercury MER 135	47	4 wks
23 Apr 83	WAR PARTY Ice ICE 58	42	4 wks
29 Oct 83	TILL I CAN'T TAKE LOVE NO MORE Ice ICE 60	42	7 wks
19 May 84	ROMANCING THE STONE Ice ICE 61	52	3 wks
23 Jan 88	● GIMME HOPE JO'ANNA Ice ICE 78701	7	12 wks
27 May 89	WALKING ON SUNSHINE Blue Wave R 6217	63	2 wks

Gogi GRANT US, female vocalist — 11 wks

29 Jun 56	● WAYWARD WIND London HLB 8282	9	11 wks

Julie GRANT UK, female vocalist — 17 wks

3 Jan 63	UP ON THE ROOF Pye 7N 15483	33	3 wks
28 Mar 63	COUNT ON ME Pye 7N 15508	24	9 wks
24 Sep 64	COME TO ME Pye 7N 15684	31	5 wks

Rudy GRANT Guyana, male vocalist — 3 wks

14 Feb 81	LATELY Ensign ENY 202	58	3 wks

GRAPEFRUIT UK, male vocal/instrumental group — 19 wks

14 Feb 68	DEAR DELILAH RCA 1656	21	9 wks
14 Aug 68	C'MON MARIANNE RCA 1716	31	10 wks

Dobie GRAY US, male vocalist — 11 wks

25 Feb 65	THE IN CROWD London HL 9953	25	7 wks
27 Sep 75	OUT ON THE FLOOR Black Magic BM 107	42	4 wks

Dorian GRAY UK, male vocalist   **7 wks**

27 Mar 68   **I'VE GOT YOU ON MY MIND** Parlophone R 5667 ....**36** 7 wks

Les GRAY UK, male vocalist   **5 wks**

26 Feb 77   **A GROOVY KIND OF LOVE** Warner Bros. K 16883 ....**32** 5 wks

Barry GRAY ORCHESTRA UK, orchestra   **8 wks**

11 Jul 81   **THUNDERBIRDS** PRT 7P 216 ....**61** 2 wks
14 Jun 86   **JOE 90/CAPTAIN SCARLET THEME**
       PRT 7PX 345 * ....**53** 6 wks

* Barry Gray Orchestra with Peter Beckett - keyboards

Altrina GRAYSON – See Wilton FELDER

GREAT WHITE US, male vocal/instrumental group   **5 wks**

24 Feb 90   **HOUSE OF BROKEN LOVE** Capitol CL 562 ....**44** 2 wks
16 Feb 91   **CONGO SQUARE** Capitol CL 605 ....**62** 1 wk
7 Sep 91   **CALL IT ROCK 'N' ROLL** Capitol CL 625 ....**67** 2 wks

Buddy GRECO US, male vocalist   **8 wks**

7 Jul 60   **LADY IS A TRAMP** Fontana H 225 ....**26** 8 wks

GREEDIES Ireland/UK/US, male vocal/instrumental group   **5 wks**

15 Dec 79   **A MERRY JINGLE** Vertigo GREED 1 ....**28** 5 wks

Al GREEN US, male vocalist   **66 wks**

9 Oct 71 ● **TIRED OF BEING ALONE** London HL 10337 ....**4** 13 wks
8 Jan 72 ● **LET'S STAY TOGETHER** London HL 10348 ....**7** 12 wks
20 May 72   **LOOK WHAT YOU DONE FOR ME** London HL 10369 ....**44** 4 wks
19 Aug 72   **I'M STILL IN LOVE WITH YOU** London HL 10382 ....**35** 5 wks
16 Nov 74   **SHA-LA-LA (MAKE ME HAPPY)** London HL 10470 ....**20** 11 wks
15 Mar 75   **L. O. V. E.** London HL 10482 ....**24** 8 wks
3 Dec 88   **PUT A LITTLE LOVE IN YOUR HEART**
       A & M AM 484 * ....**28** 8 wks
21 Oct 89   **THE MESSAGE IS LOVE** Breakout USA 668 ** ....**38** 5 wks

* Annie Lennox and Al Green ** Arthur Baker and the Backbeat Disciples
featuring Al Green

Dotty GREEN – See Mark FISHER featuring Dotty GREEN

Jesse GREEN US, male vocalist   **26 wks**

7 Aug 76   **NICE AND SLOW** EMI 2492 ....**17** 12 wks
18 Dec 76   **FLIP** EMI 2564 ....**26** 8 wks
11 Jun 77   **COME WITH ME** EMI 2615 ....**29** 6 wks

Norman GREENBAUM US, male vocalist   **20 wks**

21 Mar 70 ★ **SPIRIT IN THE SKY** Reprise RS 20885 ....**1** 20 wks

Lorne GREENE Canada, male vocalist   **8 wks**

17 Dec 64   **RINGO** RCA 1428 ....**22** 8 wks

Lee GREENWOOD US, male vocalist   **6 wks**

19 May 84   **THE WIND BENEATH MY WINGS** MCA 877 ....**49** 6 wks

Iain GREGORY UK, male vocalist   **2 wks**

4 Jan 62   **CAN'T YOU HEAR THE BEAT OF A BROKEN
       HEART** Pye 7N 15397 ....**39** 2 wks

Johnny GREGORY – See CHAQUITO

Band of the GRENADIER GUARDS – See ST. JOHN'S COLLEGE SCHOOL
CHOIR and the Band of the GRENADIER GUARDS

GREYHOUND Jamaica, male vocal/instrumental group   **33 wks**

26 Jun 71 ● **BLACK AND WHITE** Trojan TR 7820 ....**6** 13 wks
8 Jan 72   **MOON RIVER** Trojan TR 7848 ....**12** 11 wks
25 Mar 72   **I AM WHAT I AM** Trojan TR 7853 ....**20** 9 wks

GRID UK, male vocal/instrumental duo   **11 wks**

7 Jul 90   **FLOATATION** East West YZ 475 ....**60** 2 wks
29 Sep 90   **A BEAT CALLED LOVE** East West YZ 498 ....**64** 4 wks
25 Jul 92   **FIGURE OF 8** Virgin VSTG 1421 ....**50** 3 wks
3 Oct 92   **HEARTBEAT** Virgin VST 1427 ....**72** 2 wks

Zaine GRIFF New Zealand, male vocalist   **6 wks**

16 Feb 80   **TONIGHT** Automatic K 17547 ....**54** 3 wks
31 May 80   **ASHES AND DIAMONDS** Automatic K 17610 ....**68** 3 wks

Billy GRIFFIN US, male vocalist   **12 wks**

8 Jan 83   **HOLD ME TIGHTER IN THE RAIN** CBS A 2935 ....**17** 9 wks
14 Jan 84   **SERIOUS** CBS A 4053 ....**64** 3 wks

Clive GRIFFIN UK, male vocalist   **5 wks**

24 Jun 89   **HEAD ABOVE WATER** Mercury STEP 4 ....**60** 2 wks
11 May 91   **I'LL BE WAITING** Mercury STEP 6 ....**56** 3 wks

Ronnie GRIFFITH US, female vocalist   **4 wks**

30 Jun 84   **(THE BEST PART OF) BREAKING UP**
       Making Waves SURF 101 ....**63** 4 wks

GRIMETHORPE COLLIERY BAND – See Peter SKELLERN

Jay GROOVE – See FANTASY U.F.O.

GROOVE GANG – See DAFFY DUCK featuring the GROOVE GANG

Henry GROSS US, male vocalist   **4 wks**

28 Aug 76   **SHANNON** Life Song ELS 45002 ....**32** 4 wks

Boring Bob GROVER – See PIRANHAS

GSP UK, male instrumental/production duo   **3 wks**

3 Oct 92   **THE BANANA SONG** Yoyo YOYO 1 ....**37** 3 wks

G.T.O. Holland, male instrumental group   **7 wks**

4 Aug 90   **PURE** Cooltempo COOL 218....................**57** 3 wks
7 Sep 91   **LISTEN TO THE RHYTHM FLOW/BULLFROG**
       React REACT 7001 ....**72** 2 wks

| 2 May 92 | **ELEVATION** React REACT 4 | 59 | 2 wks |

GUESS WHO *Canada, male vocal/instrumental group* — 14 wks

16 Feb 67	**HIS GIRL** King KG 1044	45	1 wk
9 May 70	**AMERICAN WOMAN** RCA 1943	45	2 wks
30 May 70	**AMERICAN WOMAN (re-entry)** RCA 1943	19	11 wks

GUN *UK, male vocal/instrumental group* — 11 wks

| 20 Nov 68 | ● **RACE WITH THE DEVIL** CBS 3734 | 8 | 11 wks |

GUN *UK, male vocal/instrumental group* — 28 wks

1 Jul 89	**BETTER DAYS** A & M AM 505	33	9 wks
16 Sep 89	**MONEY (EVERYBODY LOVES HER)** A & M AM 520	73	2 wks
11 Nov 89	**INSIDE OUT** A & M AM 531	57	2 wks
10 Feb 90	**TAKING ON THE WORLD** A & M AM 541	50	3 wks
14 Jul 90	**SHAME ON YOU** A & M AM 573	33	4 wks
14 Mar 92	**STEAL YOUR FIRE** A & M AM 851	24	4 wks
2 May 92	**HIGHER GROUND** A & M AM 869	48	2 wks
4 Jul 92	**WELCOME TO THE REAL WORLD** A & M AM 885	43	2 wks

GUNS N' ROSES *US, male vocal/instrumental group* — 86 wks

3 Oct 87	**WELCOME TO THE JUNGLE** Geffen GEF 30	67	2 wks
20 Aug 88	**SWEET CHILD O' MINE** Geffen GEF 43	24	8 wks
29 Oct 88	**WELCOME TO THE JUNGLE/ NIGHTRAIN (re-issue)** Geffen GEF 47	24	5 wks
18 Mar 89	● **PARADISE CITY** Geffen GEF 50	6	9 wks
3 Jun 89	● **SWEET CHILD O' MINE (re-mix)** Geffen GEF 55	6	9 wks
1 Jul 89	● **PATIENCE** Geffen GEF 56	10	7 wks
2 Sep 89	● **NIGHTRAIN (re-issue)** Geffen GEF 60	17	5 wks
13 Jul 91	● **YOU COULD BE MINE** Geffen GFS 6	3	10 wks
21 Sep 91	● **DON'T CRY** Geffen GFS 9	8	4 wks
21 Dec 91	● **LIVE AND LET DIE** Geffen GFS 17	5	7 wks
7 Mar 92	● **NOVEMBER RAIN** Geffen GFS 18	4	5 wks
23 May 92	● **KNOCKIN' ON HEAVEN'S DOOR** Geffen GFS 21	2	9 wks
21 Nov 92	● **YESTERDAYS/NOVEMBER RAIN (re-issue)** Geffen GFS 27	8†	6 wks

The re-issue of November Rain *only listed from 28 Nov '92.*

GURU JOSH *UK, male vocal/instrumental group* — 14 wks

| 24 Feb 90 | ● **INFINITY** deConstruction PB 43475 | 5 | 10 wks |
| 16 Jun 90 | **WHOSE LAW (IS IT ANYWAY)** deConstruction PB 43647 | 26 | 4 wks |

Adrian GURVITZ *UK, male vocalist* — 16 wks

| 30 Jan 82 | ● **CLASSIC** RAK 339 | 8 | 13 wks |
| 12 Jun 82 | **YOUR DREAM** RAK 343 | 61 | 3 wks |

Gwen GUTHRIE *US, female vocalist* — 23 wks

19 Jul 86	● **AIN'T NOTHING GOIN' ON BUT THE RENT** Boiling Point POSP 807	5	12 wks
11 Oct 86	**(THEY LONG TO BE) CLOSE TO YOU** Boiling Point POSP 822	25	7 wks
14 Feb 87	**GOOD TO GO LOVER/OUTSIDE IN THE RAIN** Boiling Point POSP 841	37	4 wks

GUY *US, male vocal group* — 4 wks

| 4 May 91 | **HER** MCA MCS 1575 | 58 | 4 wks |

A GUY CALLED GERALD — 23 wks
UK, male producer - Gerald Simpson

| 8 Apr 89 | **VOODOO RAY** Rham! RS 804 | 55 | 8 wks |

| 24 Jun 89 | **VOODOO RAY (re-entry)** Rham! RS 804 | 12 | 10 wks |
| 16 Dec 89 | **FX/EYES OF SORROW** Subscape AGCG 1 | 52 | 5 wks |

GUYS and DOLLS *UK, male/female vocal group* — 33 wks

1 Mar 75	● **THERE'S A WHOLE LOT OF LOVING** Magnet MAG 20	2	11 wks
17 May 75	**HERE I GO AGAIN** Magnet MAG 30	33	5 wks
21 Feb 76	● **YOU DON'T HAVE TO SAY YOU LOVE ME** Magnet MAG 50	5	8 wks
6 Nov 76	**STONEY GROUND** Magnet MAG 76	38	4 wks
13 May 78	**ONLY LOVIN' DOES IT** Magnet MAG 115	42	5 wks

Jonas GWANGWA – *See George FENTON and Jonas GWANGWA*

HABIT *UK, male vocal/instrumental group* — 2 wks

| 30 Apr 88 | **LUCY** Virgin VS 1063 | 56 | 2 wks |

Steve HACKETT *UK, male vocalist/instrumentalist - guitar* — 2 wks

| 2 Apr 83 | **CELL 151** Charisma CELL 1 | 66 | 2 wks |

Tony HADLEY *UK, male vocalist* — 6 wks

| 7 Mar 92 | **LOST IN YOUR LOVE** EMI EM 222 | 42 | 4 wks |
| 29 Aug 92 | **FOR YOUR BLUE EYES ONLY** EMI EM 234 | 67 | 2 wks |

Sammy HAGAR *US, male vocalist/instrumentalist - guitar* — 15 wks

15 Dec 79	**THIS PLANET'S ON FIRE/SPACE STATION NO. 5** Capitol CL 16114	52	5 wks
16 Feb 80	**I'VE DONE EVERYTHING FOR YOU** Capitol CL 16120	36	5 wks
24 May 80	**HEARTBEAT /LOVE OR MONEY** Capitol RED 1	67	2 wks
16 Jan 82	**PIECE OF MY HEART** Geffen GEFA 1884	67	1 wk
30 Jan 82	**PIECE OF MY HEART (re-entry)** Geffen GEFA 1884	67	2 wks

Paul HAIG *UK, male vocalist* — 3 wks

| 28 May 83 | **HEAVEN SENT** Island IS 111 | 74 | 3 wks |

HAIRCUT 100 *UK, male vocal/instrumental group* — 47 wks

24 Oct 81	● **FAVOURITE SHIRTS (BOY MEETS GIRL)** Arista CLIP 1	4	14 wks
30 Jan 82	● **LOVE PLUS ONE** Arista CLIP 2	3	12 wks
10 Apr 82	● **FANTASTIC DAY** Arista CLIP 3	9	9 wks
21 Aug 82	● **NOBODY'S FOOL** Arista CLIP 4	9	7 wks
6 Aug 83	**PRIME TIME** Polydor HC 1	46	5 wks

Curtis HAIRSTON *US, male vocalist* — 16 wks

15 Oct 83	**I WANT YOU (ALL TONIGHT)** RCA 368	44	5 wks
27 Apr 85	**I WANT YOUR LOVIN' (JUST A LITTLE BIT)** London LON 66	13	7 wks
6 Dec 86	**CHILLIN' OUT** Atlantic A 9335	57	4 wks

Gary HAISMAN – *See D MOB*

Below: ISAAC HAYES won both Grammy and Oscar for his 'Theme From Shaft'.

Above: Inspirational singer AMY GRANT scored an international pop hit with 'Baby Baby'.

GEORGIA GIBBS was known as 'Her Nibs, Miss Georgia Gibbs', even by people who had no idea what 'Nibs' meant.

JET HARRIS signs an autograph after a show at the 400 Ballroom on 16 February 1963. (He and Tony Meehan were number one at the time with 'Diamonds'.)

Left: Axl Rose of GUNS N' ROSES was welcomed to the British chart in 1987.

HALE and PACE and the STONKERS
UK, male comedy duo and backing group **7 wks**

| 9 Mar 91 ★ | THE STONK *London LON 296* | 1 | 7 wks |

Bill HALEY and his COMETS
US, male vocal/instrumental group **199 wks**

17 Dec 54 ●	SHAKE RATTLE AND ROLL *Brunswick 05338*	4	14 wks
7 Jan 55	ROCK AROUND THE CLOCK *Brunswick 05317*	17	2 wks
15 Apr 55	MAMBO ROCK *Brunswick 05405*	14	2 wks
14 Oct 55 ★	ROCK AROUND THE CLOCK (re-entry) *Brunswick 05317*	1	17 wks
30 Dec 55 ●	ROCK-A-BEATIN' BOOGIE *Brunswick 05509*	4	9 wks
9 Mar 56 ●	SEE YOU LATER ALLIGATOR *Brunswick 05530*	7	13 wks
25 May 56 ●	THE SAINTS ROCK 'N ROLL *Brunswick 05565*	5	24 wks
17 Aug 56 ●	ROCKIN' THROUGH THE RYE *Brunswick 05582*	3	18 wks
14 Sep 56 ●	RAZZLE DAZZLE *Brunswick 05453*	13	8 wks
21 Sep 56 ●	ROCK AROUND THE CLOCK (2nd re-entry) *Brunswick 05317*	5	11 wks
21 Sep 56	SEE YOU LATER ALLIGATOR (re-entry) *Brunswick 05530*	12	8 wks
9 Nov 56 ●	RIP IT UP *Brunswick 05615*	4	18 wks
9 Nov 56	ROCK 'N ROLL STAGE SHOW (LP) *Brunswick LAT 8139*	30	1 wk
23 Nov 56	RUDY'S ROCK *Brunswick 05616*	30	1 wk
14 Dec 56	ROCK AROUND THE CLOCK (3rd re-entry) *Brunswick 05317*	24	2 wks
14 Dec 56	RUDY'S ROCK (re-entry) *Brunswick 05616*	26	4 wks
4 Jan 57	ROCK AROUND THE CLOCK (4th re-entry) *Brunswick 05317*	25	2 wks
4 Jan 57	ROCKIN' THROUGH THE RYE (re-entry) *Brunswick 05582*	19	5 wks
25 Jan 57	ROCK AROUND THE CLOCK (5th re-entry) *Brunswick 05317*	22	2 wks
1 Feb 57	ROCK THE JOINT *London HLF 8371*	20	4 wks
8 Feb 57 ●	DON'T KNOCK THE ROCK *Brunswick 05640*	7	8 wks
3 Apr 68	ROCK AROUND THE CLOCK (re-issue) *MCA MU 1013*	20	11 wks
16 Mar 74	ROCK AROUND THE CLOCK (2nd re-issue) *MCA 128*	12	10 wks
25 Apr 81	HALEY'S GOLDEN MEDLEY *MCA 694*	50	5 wks

Tracks on Rock 'N Roll Stage Show LP: Calling All Comets/Rockin' Through The Rye/A Rockin' Little Tune/Hide And Seek/Hey There Now/Goofin' Around/Hook Line and Sinker/Rudy's Rock/Choo Choo Ch'Boogie/Blue Comets Rock/Hot Dog Buddy Buddy/Tonight's The Night. Occasionally, some of the Rock Around The Clock labels billed the song as (We're Gonna) Rock Around The Clock.

Aaron HALL
US, male vocalist **2 wks**

| 13 Jun 92 | DON'T BE AFRAID *MCA MCS 1632* | 56 | 2 wks |

Audrey HALL
Jamaica, female vocalist **20 wks**

| 25 Jan 86 | ONE DANCE WON'T DO *Germain DG7-1985* | 20 | 11 wks |
| 5 Jul 86 | SMILE *Germain DG 15* | 14 | 9 wks |

Daryl HALL
US, male vocalist **8 wks**

| 2 Aug 86 | DREAMTIME *RCA HALL 1* | 28 | 8 wks |

See also Daryl Hall and John Oates.

Daryl HALL and John OATES
US, male vocal/instrumental duo **84 wks**

16 Oct 76	SHE'S GONE *Atlantic K 10828*	42	4 wks
14 Jun 80	RUNNING FROM PARADISE *RCA RUN 1*	41	6 wks
20 Sep 80	YOU'VE LOST THAT LOVIN' FEELIN' *RCA 1*	55	3 wks
15 Nov 80	KISS ON MY LIST *RCA 15*	33	8 wks
23 Jan 82 ●	I CAN'T GO FOR THAT (NO CAN DO) *RCA 172*	8	10 wks
10 Apr 82	PRIVATE EYES *RCA 134*	32	7 wks
30 Oct 82 ●	MANEATER *RCA 290*	6	11 wks
22 Jan 83	ONE ON ONE *RCA 305*	63	3 wks
30 Apr 83	FAMILY MAN *RCA 323*	15	7 wks
12 Nov 83	SAY IT ISN'T SO *RCA 375*	69	3 wks
10 Mar 84	ADULT EDUCATION *RCA 396*	63	2 wks
20 Oct 84	OUT OF TOUCH *RCA 449*	48	5 wks
9 Feb 85	METHOD OF MODERN LOVE *RCA RCA 472*	21	8 wks
22 Jun 85	OUT OF TOUCH (re-mix) *RCA PB 4 9967*	62	3 wks
21 Sep 85	A NIGHT AT THE APOLLO LIVE! *RCA PB 49935* *	58	2 wks
29 Sep 90	SO CLOSE *Arista 113600* **	69	1 wk
26 Jan 91	EVERYWHERE I LOOK *Arista 113980*	74	1 wk

** Daryl Hall and John Oates featuring David Ruffin and Eddie Kendrick ** Hall and Oates*

A Night At The Apollo Live! is a medley of The Way You Do The Things You Do/My Girl. See also Daryl Hall.

Pam HALL
Jamaica, female vocalist **4 wks**

| 16 Aug 86 | DEAR BOOPSIE *Bluemountain BM 027* | 54 | 4 wks |

Terry HALL
UK, male vocalist **1 wk**

| 11 Nov 89 | MISSING *Chrysalis CHS 3381* | 75 | 1 wk |

The sleeve, not the label, of Missing credits Terry, Blair and Anouchka.

HALO JAMES
UK, male vocal/instrumental group **24 wks**

7 Oct 89	WANTED *Epic HALO 1*	45	5 wks
23 Dec 89 ●	COULD HAVE TOLD YOU SO *Epic HALO 2*	6	12 wks
17 Mar 90	BABY *Epic HALO 3*	43	4 wks
19 May 90	MAGIC HOUR *Epic HALO 4*	59	3 wks

HAMILTON, Joe FRANK and REYNOLDS
US, male vocal group **6 wks**

| 13 Sep 75 | FALLIN' IN LOVE *Pye International 7N 25690* | 33 | 6 wks |

George HAMILTON IV
US, male vocalist **13 wks**

7 Mar 58	WHY DON'T THEY UNDERSTAND *HMV POP 429*	22	9 wks
18 Jul 58	I KNOW WHERE I'M GOING *HMV POP 505*	29	1 wk
8 Aug 58	I KNOW WHERE I'M GOING (re-entry) *HMV POP 505*	23	3 wks

Lynne HAMILTON
Australia, female vocalist **11 wks**

| 29 Apr 89 ● | ON THE INSIDE (THEME FROM 'PRISONER CELL BLOCK H') *A.1. A1 311* | 3 | 11 wks |

Russ HAMILTON
UK, male vocalist **26 wks**

| 24 May 57 ● | WE WILL MAKE LOVE *Oriole CB 1359* | 2 | 20 wks |
| 27 Sep 57 | WEDDING RING *Oriole CB 1388* | 20 | 6 wks |

Marvin HAMLISCH
US, male instrumentalist - piano **13 wks**

| 30 Mar 74 | THE ENTERTAINER *MCA 121* | 25 | 13 wks |

HAMMER
US, male rapper **64 wks**

| 9 Jun 90 ● | U CAN'T TOUCH THIS *Capitol CL 578* * | 3 | 16 wks |

6 Oct 90 ●	HAVE YOU SEEN HER *Capitol CL 590 *...............*	8	7 wks
8 Dec 90 ●	PRAY *Capitol CL 599 *...............*	8	10 wks
23 Feb 91	HERE COMES THE HAMMER *Capitol CL 610 *...........*	15	5 wks
1 Jun 91	YO!! SWEETNESS *Capitol CL 616 *...............*	16	5 wks
20 Jul 91	(HAMMER HAMMER) THEY PUT ME IN THE MIX *Capitol CL 607 *...............*	20	4 wks
26 Oct 91	2 LEGIT 2 QUIT *Capitol CL 636*...............*	60	2 wks
21 Dec 91 ●	ADDAMS GROOVE *Capitol CL 642*...............*	4	9 wks
21 Mar 92	DO NOT PASS ME BY *Capitol CL 650*...............*	14	6 wks

* MC Hammer

Jan HAMMER   26 wks
Czechoslovakia, male instrumentalist - keyboards

12 Oct 85 ●	MIAMI VICE THEME *MCA MCA 1000*...............*	5	8 wks
19 Sep 87 ●	CROCKETT'S THEME *MCA MCA 1193*...............*	2	12 wks
1 Jun 91	CROCKETT'S THEME (re-issue)/CHANCER *MCA MCS 1541*...............*	47	6 wks

Albert HAMMOND *UK, male vocalist*   11 wks

30 Jun 73	FREE ELECTRIC BAND *Mums 1494*...............*	19	11 wks

Beres HAMMOND – *See Maxi PRIEST*

Herbie HANCOCK   41 wks
US, male vocalist/instrumentalist - keyboards

26 Aug 78	I THOUGHT IT WAS YOU *CBS 6530*...............*	15	9 wks
3 Feb 79	YOU BET YOUR LOVE *CBS 7010*...............*	18	10 wks
30 Jul 83 ●	ROCKIT *CBS A 3577*...............*	8	12 wks
8 Oct 83	AUTO DRIVE *CBS A 3802*...............*	33	4 wks
21 Jan 84	FUTURE SHOCK *CBS A 4075*...............*	54	3 wks
4 Aug 84	HARDROCK *CBS A 4616*...............*	65	3 wks

HANDLEY FAMILY *UK, male/female vocal group*   7 wks

7 Apr 73	WAM BAM *GL 100*...............*	30	7 wks

HANNAH – *See PJB featuring HANNAH and her SISTERS*

HANOI ROCKS *Finland/UK, male vocal/instrumental group*   2 wks

7 Jul 84	UP AROUND THE BEND *CBS A 4513*...............*	61	2 wks

HAPPENINGS *US, male vocal group*   14 wks

18 May 67	I GOT RHYTHM *Stateside SS 2013*...............*	28	9 wks
16 Aug 67	MY MAMMY *Pye International 7N 25501 & B.T. Puppy BTS 45530*...............*	34	5 wks

Pye gave the American B.T. Puppy label its own identification halfway through the success of My Mammy.

HAPPY MONDAYS *UK, male vocal/instrumental group*   51 wks

30 Sep 89	WFL *Factory FAC 2327*...............*	68	2 wks
25 Nov 89	MADCHESTER RAVE ON EP *Factory FAC 2427*...............*	19	14 wks
7 Apr 90 ●	STEP ON *Factory FAC 2727*...............*	5	11 wks
9 Jun 90	LAZYITIS - ONE ARMED BOXER *Factory FAC 2227 *...............*	46	3 wks
20 Oct 90 ●	KINKY AFRO *Factory FAC 3027*...............*	5	7 wks
9 Mar 91	LOOSE FIT *Factory FAC 3127*...............*	17	7 wks
30 Nov 91	JUDGE FUDGE *Factory FAC 3327*...............*	24	3 wks
19 Sep 92	STINKIN THINKIN *Factory FAC 3627*...............*	31	3 wks
21 Nov 92	SUNSHINE AND LOVE *Factory FAC 3727*...............*	62	1 wk

* Happy Mondays and Karl Denver

Tracks on Madchester Rave On EP: Hallelujah/Holy Ghost/Clap Your Hands/Rave On.

Paul HARDCASTLE *UK, male producer*   66 wks

7 Apr 84	YOU'RE THE ONE FOR ME - DAYBREAK - A.M. *Total Control TOCO 1*...............*	41	4 wks
28 Jul 84	GUILTY *Total Control TOCO 2*...............*	55	3 wks
22 Sep 84	RAIN FOREST *Bluebird BR 8*...............*	41	5 wks
17 Nov 84	EAT YOUR HEART OUT *Cool Tempo COOL 102*...............*	59	4 wks
4 May 85 ★	NINETEEN *Chrysalis CHS 2860*...............*	1	16 wks
15 Jun 85	RAIN FOREST (re-issue) *Bluebird 10 BR 15*...............*	53	4 wks
9 Nov 85	JUST FOR MONEY *Chrysalis CASH 1*...............*	19	5 wks
1 Feb 86 ●	DON'T WASTE MY TIME *Chrysalis PAUL 1 *...............*	8	11 wks
21 Jun 86	FOOLIN' YOURSELF *Chrysalis PAUL 2*...............*	51	5 wks
11 Oct 86	THE WIZARD *Chrysalis PAUL 3*...............*	15	6 wks
9 Apr 88	WALK IN THE NIGHT *Chrysalis PAUL 4*...............*	54	3 wks
4 Jun 88	40 YEARS *Chrysalis PAUL 5*...............*	53	2 wks

* Paul Hardcastle featuring Carol Kenyon

Just for Money features the voices of Laurence Olivier, Bob Hoskins, Ed O'Ross and Alan Talbot, who are credited on the sleeve only. See also Silent Underdog.

HARDCORE RHYTHM TEAM   1 wk
UK, male vocal/production group

14 Mar 92	HARDCORE - THE FINAL CONFLICT *Furious FRUT 001*...............*	69	1 wk

HARDFLOOR *Germany, male production group*   1 wk

26 Dec 92	HARDTRANCE ACPERIENCE *Harthouse HARTUK 1*...*	65†	1 wk

Tim HARDIN *US, male vocalist*   1 wk

5 Jan 67	HANG ON TO A DREAM *Verve VS 1504*...............*	50	1 wk

Mike HARDING *UK, male vocalist*   8 wks

2 Aug 75	ROCHDALE COWBOY *Rubber ADUB 3*...............*	22	8 wks

Francoise HARDY *France, female vocalist*   26 wks

25 Jun 64	TOUS LES GARCONS ET LES FILLES *Pye 7N 15653*....*	36	7 wks
7 Jan 65	ET MEME *Pye 7N 15740*...............*	31	4 wks
25 Mar 65	ALL OVER THE WORLD *Pye 7N 15802*...............*	16	15 wks

Tynetta HARE – *See Joey B ELLIS*

HARLEM COMMUNITY CHOIR – *See John LENNON*

HARLEQUIN 4's/BUNKER KRU   4 wks
US, male vocal/instrumental group with UK, male production duo

19 Mar 88	SET IT OFF *Champion CHAMP 64*...............*	55	4 wks

Steve HARLEY and COCKNEY REBEL   66 wks
UK, male vocalist and male vocal/instrumental backing group

11 May 74 ●	JUDY TEEN *EMI 2128 *...............*	5	11 wks
10 Aug 74 ●	MR. SOFT *EMI 2191 *...............*	8	9 wks
8 Feb 75 ★	MAKE ME SMILE (COME UP AND SEE ME) *EMI 2263*...............*	1	9 wks
7 Jun 75	MR. RAFFLES (MAN IT WAS MEAN) *EMI 2299*...............*	13	6 wks
31 Jul 76 ●	HERE COMES THE SUN *EMI 2505 **...............*	10	7 wks
6 Nov 76	LOVE'S A PRIMA DONNA *EMI 2539 **...............*	41	4 wks
20 Oct 79	FREEDOM'S PRISONER *EMI 2994 **...............*	58	5 wks
13 Aug 83	BALLERINA (PRIMA DONNA) *Stilletto STL 14 **...............*	51	5 wks
11 Jan 86 ●	THE PHANTOM OF THE OPERA *Polydor POSP 800 ***...............*	7	10 wks

| 25 Apr 92 | MAKE ME SMILE (COME UP AND SEE ME) (re-issue) *EMI EMCT 5* ** | 46 | 2 wks |

*Cockney Rebel **Steve Harley ***Sarah Brightman and Steve Harley

---

HARLEY QUINNE UK, male vocal group — 8 wks

| 14 Oct 72 | NEW ORLEANS *Bell 1255* | 19 | 8 wks |

HARMONY GRASS UK, male vocal/instrumental group — 7 wks

| 29 Jan 69 | MOVE IN A LITTLE CLOSER *RCA 1772* | 24 | 7 wks |

Charlie HARPER UK, male vocalist — 1 wk

| 19 Jul 80 | BARMY LONDON ARMY *Gem GEMS 35* | 68 | 1 wk |

HARPERS BIZARRE US, male vocal group — 13 wks

| 30 Mar 67 | 59TH STREET BRIDGE SONG (FEELING GROOVY) *Warner Bros. WB 5890* | 34 | 7 wks |
| 4 Oct 67 | ANYTHING GOES *Warner Bros. WB 7063* | 33 | 6 wks |

HARPO Sweden, male vocalist — 6 wks

| 17 Apr 76 | MOVIE STAR *DJM DJS 400* | 24 | 6 wks |

T. HARRINGTON – See Rahni HARRIS and F.L.O.

Anita HARRIS UK, female vocalist — 50 wks

29 Jun 67	● JUST LOVING YOU *CBS 2724*	6	30 wks
11 Oct 67	PLAYGROUND *CBS 2991*	46	3 wks
24 Jan 68	ANNIVERSARY WALTZ *CBS 3211*	21	9 wks
14 Aug 68	DREAM A LITTLE DREAM OF ME *CBS 3637*	33	8 wks

Emmylou HARRIS US, female vocalist — 6 wks

| 6 Mar 76 | HERE THERE AND EVERYWHERE *Reprise K 14415* | 30 | 6 wks |

Jet HARRIS UK, male instrumentalist - bass guitar — 18 wks

| 24 May 62 | BESAME MUCHO *Decca F 11466* | 22 | 7 wks |
| 16 Aug 62 | MAIN TITLE THEME FROM 'MAN WITH THE GOLDEN ARM' *Decca F 11488* | 12 | 11 wks |

See also Jet Harris and Tony Meehan.

Jet HARRIS and Tony MEEHAN — 39 wks
UK, male instrumental duo - bass guitar and drums

10 Jan 63	★ DIAMONDS *Decca F 11563*	1	13 wks
25 Apr 63	● SCARLETT O'HARA *Decca F 11644*	2	13 wks
5 Sep 63	● APPLEJACK *Decca F 11710*	4	13 wks

See also Jet Harris; Tony Meehan.

Keith HARRIS and ORVILLE — 20 wks
UK, male ventriloquist vocalist with feathered dummy

18 Dec 82	● ORVILLE'S SONG *BBC RESL 124*	4	11 wks
24 Dec 83	COME TO MY PARTY *BBC RESL 138* *	44	4 wks
14 Dec 85	WHITE CHRISTMAS *Columbia DB 9121*	40	5 wks

* Keith Harris and Orville with Dippy

British Hit Singles Part One: Alphabetically by Artist

Date of chart entry/Title & catalogue no./Peak position reached/Weeks on chart

★ Number one   ● Top Ten   † still on chart at 31 Dec 1992
* = credited to act billed in footnote

Major HARRIS US, male vocalist — 9 wks

| 9 Aug 75 | LOVE WON'T LET ME WAIT *Atlantic K 10585* | 37 | 7 wks |
| 5 Nov 83 | ALL MY LIFE *London LON 37* | 61 | 2 wks |

Max HARRIS UK, orchestra — 10 wks

| 1 Dec 60 | GURNEY SLADE *Fontana H 282* | 11 | 10 wks |

Rahni HARRIS and F.L.O. US, male instrumental group — 7 wks

| 16 Dec 78 | SIX MILLION STEPS (WEST RUNS SOUTH) *Mercury 6007 198* | 43 | 7 wks |

Hit has credit 'vocals by T. Harrington and O. Rasbury'.

Richard HARRIS Ireland, male vocalist — 18 wks

| 26 Jun 68 | ● MACARTHUR PARK *RCA 1699* | 4 | 12 wks |
| 8 Jul 72 | MACARTHUR PARK (re-issue) *Probe GFF 101* | 38 | 6 wks |

Rolf HARRIS Australia, male vocalist — 64 wks

21 Jul 60	● TIE ME KANGAROO DOWN SPORT *Columbia DB 4483*	9	13 wks
25 Oct 62	● SUN ARISE *Columbia DB 4888*	3	16 wks
28 Feb 63	JOHNNY DAY *Columbia DB 4979*	44	2 wks
16 Apr 69	BLUER THAN BLUE *Columbia DB 8553*	30	8 wks
22 Nov 69	★ TWO LITTLE BOYS *Columbia DB 8630*	1	24 wks
20 Jun 70	TWO LITTLE BOYS (re-entry) *Columbia DB 8630*	50	1 wk

---

Ronnie HARRIS UK, male vocalist — 3 wks

| 24 Sep 54 | STORY OF TINA *Columbia DB 3499* | 12 | 3 wks |

Sam HARRIS US, male vocalist — 2 wks

| 9 Feb 85 | HEARTS ON FIRE/OVER THE RAINBOW *Motown TMG 1370* | 67 | 2 wks |

Simon HARRIS US, male producer — 17 wks

19 Mar 88	BASS (HOW LOW CAN YOU GO) *ffrr FFR 4*	12	6 wks
29 Oct 88	HERE COMES THAT SOUND *ffrr FFR 12*	38	4 wks
24 Jun 89	(I'VE GOT YOUR) PLEASURE CONTROL *ffrr F 106* *	60	3 wks
18 Nov 89	ANOTHER MONSTERJAM *ffrr F 116* **	65	1 wk
10 Mar 90	RAGGA HOUSE (ALL NIGHT LONG) *Living Beat 7SMASH 9* ***	56	3 wks

* Simon Harris featuring Lonnie Gordon ** Simon Harris featuring Einstein
*** Simon Harris featuring Daddy Freddy

George HARRISON UK, male vocalist — 82 wks

23 Jan 71	★ MY SWEET LORD *Apple R 5884*	1	17 wks
14 Aug 71	● BANGLA DESH *Apple R 5912*	10	9 wks
2 Jun 73	● GIVE ME LOVE (GIVE ME PEACE ON EARTH) *Apple R 5988*	8	10 wks
21 Dec 74	DING DONG *Apple R 6002*	38	5 wks

CHESNEY HAWKES reached number one two dozen years after his dad Chip, who sang lead on the Tremeloes' 'Silence Is Golden'.

HALE AND PACE would do and show nearly everything for a good cause.

HEAVY D AND THE BOYZ had their greatest success with a rap re-make of Third World's 1978 success.

Date	Title	Pos	Weeks
11 Oct 75	**YOU** Apple R 6007	38	5 wks
10 Mar 79	**BLOW AWAY** Dark Horse K 17327	51	5 wks
23 May 81	**ALL THOSE YEARS AGO** Dark Horse 3 K 17807	13	7 wks
24 Oct 87 ●	**GOT MY MIND SET ON YOU** Dark Horse W 8178	2	14 wks
6 Feb 88	**WHEN WE WAS FAB** Dark Horse W 8131	25	7 wks
25 Jun 88	**THIS IS LOVE** Dark Horse W 7913	55	3 wks

Noel HARRISON UK, male vocalist — 14 wks

Date	Title	Pos	Weeks
26 Feb 69 ●	**WINDMILLS OF YOUR MIND** Reprise RS 20758	8	14 wks

Deborah HARRY US, female vocalist — 46 wks

Date	Title	Pos	Weeks
1 Aug 81	**BACKFIRED** Chrysalis CHS 2526 *	32	6 wks
15 Nov 86 ●	**FRENCH KISSIN' IN THE USA** Chrysalis CHS 3066 *	8	10 wks
28 Feb 87	**FREE TO FALL** Chrysalis CHS 3093 *	46	4 wks
9 May 87	**IN LOVE WITH LOVE** Chrysalis CHS 3128 *	45	5 wks
7 Oct 89	**I WANT THAT MAN** Chrysalis CHS 3369	13	10 wks
2 Dec 89	**BRITE SIDE** Chrysalis CHS 3452	59	4 wks
31 Mar 90	**SWEET AND LOW** Chrysalis CHS 3491	57	3 wks
5 Jan 91	**WELL DID YOU EVAH!** Chrysalis CHS 3646 **	42	4 wks

* Debbie Harry ** Deborah Harry and Iggy Pop

HARRY J. ALL STARS Jamaica, male instrumental group — 25 wks

Date	Title	Pos	Weeks
25 Oct 69 ●	**LIQUIDATOR** Trojan TR 675	9	20 wks
29 Mar 80	**LIQUIDATOR (re-issue)** Trojan TRO 9063	42	5 wks

Re-issue of Liquidator coupled with re-issue of Long Shot Kick De Bucket by the Pioneers.

Richard HARTLEY/Michael REED ORCHESTRA UK, male instrumentalist - synthesizer, orchestra — 10 wks

Date	Title	Pos	Weeks
25 Feb 84 ●	**THE MUSIC OF TORVILL AND DEAN EP** Safari SKATE 1	9	10 wks

Tracks on EP: Bolero/Capriccio Espagnole Opus. 34 (Nos.4 and 5) by Richard Hartley; Barnum On Ice/Discoskate by the Michael Reed Orchestra.

Dan HARTMAN US, male vocalist — 33 wks

Date	Title	Pos	Weeks
21 Oct 78 ●	**INSTANT REPLAY** Sky 6706	8	15 wks
13 Jan 79	**THIS IS IT** Blue Sky SKY 6999	17	8 wks
18 May 85	**SECOND NATURE** MCA MCA 957	66	2 wks
24 Aug 85	**I CAN DREAM ABOUT YOU** MCA MCA 988	12	8 wks

Sensational Alex HARVEY BAND
UK, male vocal/instrumental group — 25 wks

Date	Title	Pos	Weeks
26 Jul 75 ●	**DELILAH** Vertigo ALEX 001	7	7 wks
22 Nov 75	**GAMBLIN' BAR ROOM BLUES** Vertigo ALEX 002	38	8 wks
19 Jun 76	**THE BOSTON TEA PARTY** Mountain TOP 12	13	10 wks

PJ HARVEY UK, female/male vocal/instrumental group — 1 wks

Date	Title	Pos	Weeks
29 Feb 92 ●	**SHEELA-NA-GIG** Too Pure PURE 008	69	1 wk

Steve HARVEY UK, male vocalist — 6 wks

Date	Title	Pos	Weeks
28 May 83	**SOMETHING SPECIAL** London LON 25	46	4 wks
29 Oct 83	**TONIGHT** London LON 36	63	2 wks

Tony HATCH UK, orchestra — 1 wk

Date	Title	Pos	Weeks
4 Oct 62	**OUT OF THIS WORLD** Pye 7N 15460	50	1 wk

Donny HATHAWAY – See Roberta FLACK

Lalah HATHAWAY US, female vocalist — 10 wks

Date	Title	Pos	Weeks
1 Sep 90	**HEAVEN KNOWS** Virgin America VUS 28	66	2 wks
2 Feb 91	**BABY DON'T CRY** Virgin America VUS 35	54	3 wks
17 Jul 91	**FAMILY AFFAIR** Ten TEN 369 *	37	5 wks

* BEF featuring Lalah Hathaway

Chesney HAWKES UK, male vocalist — 24 wks

Date	Title	Pos	Weeks
23 Feb 91 ★	**THE ONE AND ONLY** Chrysalis CHS 3627	1	16 wks
22 Jun 91	**I'M A MAN NOT A BOY** Chrysalis CHS 3708	27	5 wks
28 Sep 91	**SECRETS OF THE HEART** Chrysalis CHS 3681	57	3 wks

Edwin HAWKINS SINGERS featuring Dorothy Combs MORRISON
US, male/female vocal group — 13 wks

Date	Title	Pos	Weeks
21 May 69 ●	**OH HAPPY DAY** Buddah 201 048	2	12 wks
23 Aug 69	**OH HAPPY DAY (re-entry)** Buddah 201 048	43	1 wk

Sophie B. HAWKINS US, female vocalist — 12 wks

Date	Title	Pos	Weeks
4 Jul 92	**DAMN I WISH I WAS YOUR LOVER** Columbia 6581077	14	9 wks
12 Sep 92	**CALIFORNIA HERE I COME** Columbia 6583177	53	3 wks

HAWKWIND
UK, male vocal/instrumental group with female dancer — 28 wks

Date	Title	Pos	Weeks
1 Jul 72 ●	**SILVER MACHINE** United Artists UP 35381	3	15 wks
11 Aug 73	**URBAN GUERRILLA** United Artists UP 35566	39	3 wks
21 Oct 78	**SILVER MACHINE (re-entry)** United Artists UP 35381	34	5 wks
19 Jul 80	**SHOT DOWN IN THE NIGHT** Bronze BRO 98	59	3 wks
15 Jan 83	**SILVER MACHINE (2nd re-entry)** United Artists UP 35381	67	2 wks

Bill HAYES US, male vocalist — 9 wks

Date	Title	Pos	Weeks
6 Jan 56 ●	**BALLAD OF DAVY CROCKETT** London HLA 8220	2	9 wks

Isaac HAYES US, male vocalist/multi-instrumentalist — 21 wks

Date	Title	Pos	Weeks
4 Dec 71 ●	**THEME FROM 'SHAFT'** Stax 2025 069	4	12 wks
3 Apr 76 ●	**DISCO CONNECTION** ABC 4100 *	10	9 wks

* Isaac Hayes Movement

HAYSI FANTAYZEE UK, male/female vocal duo — 25 wks

Date	Title	Pos	Weeks
24 Jul 82	**JOHN WAYNE IS BIG LEGGY** Regard RG 100	11	10 wks
13 Nov 82	**HOLY JOE** Regard RG 104	51	3 wks
22 Jan 83	**SHINY SHINY** Regard RG 106	16	10 wks
25 Jun 83	**SISTER FRICTION** Regard RG 108	62	2 wks

Justin HAYWARD UK, male vocalist — 20 wks

Date	Title	Pos	Weeks
25 Oct 75 ●	**BLUE GUITAR** Threshold TH 21 *	8	7 wks
8 Jul 78 ●	**FOREVER AUTUMN** CBS 6368	5	13 wks

* Justin Hayward and John Lodge

Leon HAYWOOD US, male vocalist — 11 wks

Date	Title	Pos	Weeks
15 Mar 80	**DON'T PUSH IT, DON'T FORCE IT** 20th Century Fox TC 2443	12	11 wks

HAYWOODE UK, female vocalist — 31 wks

17 Sep 83	**A TIME LIKE THIS** CBS A 3651	**48**	7 wks
29 Sep 84	**I CAN'T LET YOU GO** CBS A 4664	**63**	4 wks
13 Apr 85	**ROSES** CBS A 6069	**65**	3 wks
5 Oct 85	**GETTING CLOSER** CBS A 6582	**67**	2 wks
21 Jun 86	**ROSES (re-issue)** CBS A 7224	**11**	11 wks
13 Sep 86	**I CAN'T LET YOU GO (re-issue)** CBS 650076 7	**50**	4 wks

Ofra HAZA Israel, female vocalist — 8 wks

30 Apr 88	**IM NIN'ALU** WEA YZ 190	**15**	8 wks

Lee HAZLEWOOD – See Nancy SINATRA

Murray HEAD UK, male vocalist — 15 wks

29 Jan 72	**SUPERSTAR** MCA MMKS 5077	**47**	1 wk
10 Nov 84	**ONE NIGHT IN BANGKOK** RCA CHESS 1	**12**	13 wks
16 Feb 85	**ONE NIGHT IN BANGKOK (re-entry)** RCA CHESS 1	**74**	1 wk

Superstar *was one of four tracks on a maxi single, two of which were credited during the disc's one week on the chart. The other track credited was* I Don't Know How To Love Him *by Yvonne Elliman.*

Roy HEAD US, male vocalist — 5 wks

4 Nov 65	**TREAT HER RIGHT** Vocalion V-P 9248	**30**	5 wks

HEADBANGERS UK, male vocal/instrumental group — 3 wks

10 Oct 81	**STATUS ROCK** Magnet MAG 206	**60**	3 wks

HEADBOYS UK, male vocal/instrumental group — 8 wks

22 Sep 79	**THE SHAPE OF THINGS TO COME** RSO 40	**45**	8 wks

HEADGIRL – See MOTORHEAD; GIRLSCHOOL

Max HEADROOM – See ART OF NOISE

HEADS UK, male instrumental group — 4 wks

21 Jun 86	**AZTEC LIGHTNING (THEME FROM BBC WORLD CUP GRANDSTAND)** BBC RESL 184	**45**	4 wks

HEAR 'N AID International, male/female vocal/instrumental charity assembly — 6 wks

19 Apr 86	**STARS** Vertigo HEAR 1	**26**	6 wks

HEART US, female/male vocal/instrumental group — 72 wks

29 Mar 86	**THESE DREAMS** Capitol CL 394	**62**	4 wks
13 Jun 87 ●	**ALONE** Capitol CL 448	**3**	16 wks
19 Sep 87	**WHO WILL YOU RUN TO** Capitol CL 457	**30**	7 wks
12 Dec 87	**THERE'S THE GIRL** Capitol CL 473	**34**	7 wks
5 Mar 88 ●	**NEVER/THESE DREAMS (re-issue)** Capitol CL 482	**8**	9 wks
14 May 88	**WHAT ABOUT LOVE** Capitol CL 487	**14**	6 wks
22 Oct 88	**NOTHIN' AT ALL** Capitol CL 507	**38**	3 wks
24 Mar 90 ●	**ALL I WANNA DO IS MAKE LOVE TO YOU** Capitol CL 569	**8**	13 wks
28 Jul 90	**I DIDN'T WANT TO NEED YOU** Capitol CL 580	**47**	3 wks
17 Nov 90	**STRANDED** Capitol CL 595	**60**	2 wks
14 Sep 91	**YOU'RE THE VOICE** Capitol CLS 624	**56**	2 wks

HEARTBEAT UK, male/female vocal/instrumental group — 5 wks

24 Oct 87	**TEARS FROM HEAVEN** Priority P 17	**32**	4 wks
23 Apr 88	**THE WINNER** Priority P 19	**70**	1 wk

HEARTBREAKERS – See Tom PETTY and the HEARTBREAKERS; Stevie NICKS

Ted HEATH UK, orchestra — 56 wks

16 Jan 53	**VANESSA** Decca F 9983	**11**	1 wk
3 Jul 53 ●	**HOT TODDY** Decca F 10093	**6**	11 wks
23 Oct 53	**DRAGNET** Decca F 10176	**12**	1 wk
27 Nov 53	**DRAGNET (re-entry)** Decca F 10176	**9**	1 wk
11 Dec 53	**DRAGNET (2nd re-entry)** Decca F 10176	**11**	1 wk
15 Jan 54	**DRAGNET (3rd re-entry)** Decca F 10176	**11**	1 wk
5 Feb 54	**DRAGNET (4th re-entry)** Decca F 10176	**12**	1 wk
12 Feb 54 ●	**SKIN DEEP** Decca F 10246	**9**	3 wks
6 Jul 56	**THE FAITHFUL HUSSAR** Decca F 10746	**18**	9 wks
14 Mar 58 ●	**SWINGIN' SHEPHERD BLUES** Decca F 11000	**3**	14 wks
11 Apr 58	**TEQUILA** Decca F 11003	**21**	6 wks
4 Jul 58	**TOM HARK** Decca F 11025	**24**	2 wks
5 Oct 61	**SUCU SUCU** Decca F 11392	**36**	4 wks
9 Nov 61	**SUCU SUCU (re-entry)** Decca F 11392	**47**	1 wk

HEATWAVE UK/US, male vocal/instrumental group — 80 wks

22 Jan 77 ●	**BOOGIE NIGHTS** GTO GT 77	**2**	14 wks
7 May 77	**TOO HOT TO HANDLE/SLIP YOUR DISC TO THIS** GTO GT 91	**15**	11 wks
14 Jan 78	**THE GROOVE LINE** GTO GT 115	**12**	8 wks
3 Jun 78	**MIND BLOWING DECISIONS** GTO GT 226	**12**	11 wks
4 Nov 78 ●	**ALWAYS AND FOREVER/MIND BLOWING DECISIONS (re-mix)** GTO GT 236	**9**	14 wks
26 May 79	**RAZZLE DAZZLE** GTO GT 248	**43**	5 wks
17 Jan 81	**GANGSTERS OF THE GROOVE** GTO GT 285	**19**	8 wks
21 Mar 81	**JITTERBUGGIN'** GTO GT 290	**34**	7 wks
1 Sep 90	**MIND BLOWING DECISIONS (re-issue)** Brothers Organisation HW 1	**65**	2 wks

Mind Blowing Decisions *on GT 236 is an extended remixed version of GT 226.*

HEAVEN 17 UK, male vocal/instrumental group — 79 wks

21 Mar 81	**(WE DON'T NEED THIS) FASCIST GROOVE THANG** Virgin VS 400	**45**	5 wks
5 Sep 81	**PLAY TO WIN** Virgin VS 433	**46**	7 wks
14 Nov 81	**PENTHOUSE AND PAVEMENT** Virgin VS 455	**57**	3 wks
30 Oct 82	**LET ME GO** Virgin VS 532	**41**	6 wks
16 Apr 83 ●	**TEMPTATION** Virgin VS 570	**2**	13 wks
25 Jun 83 ●	**COME LIVE WITH ME** Virgin VS 607	**5**	11 wks
10 Sep 83	**CRUSHED BY THE WHEELS OF INDUSTRY** Virgin VS 628	**17**	7 wks
1 Sep 84	**SUNSET NOW** Virgin VS 708	**24**	6 wks
27 Oct 84	**THIS IS MINE** Virgin VS 722	**23**	7 wks
19 Jan 85	**...(AND THAT'S NO LIE)** Virgin VS 740	**52**	5 wks
17 Jan 87	**TROUBLE** Virgin VS 920	**51**	3 wks
21 Nov 92 ●	**TEMPTATION (re-mix)** Virgin VS 1446	**4†**	6 wks

Carol Kenyon *is the uncredited vocalist on* Temptation.

HEAVY D. and the BOYZ Jamaica/US, male vocal/instrumental group — 25 wks

6 Dec 86	**MR. BIG STUFF** MCA MCA 1106	**61**	8 wks
15 Jul 89	**WE GOT OUR OWN THANG** MCA MCA 23942	**69**	2 wks
6 Jul 91 ●	**NOW THAT WE FOUND LOVE** MCA MCS 1550	**2**	12 wks
28 Sep 91	**IS IT GOOD TO YOU** MCA MCS 1564	**46**	3 wks

HEAVY PETTIN' UK, male vocal/instrumental group — 2 wks

17 Mar 84	**LOVE TIMES LOVE** Polydor HEP 3	**69**	2 wks

Bobby HEBB US, male vocalist   **15 wks**

8 Sep 66	**SUNNY** *Philips BF 1503*	.12	9 wks
19 Aug 72	**LOVE LOVE LOVE** *Philips 6051 023*	.32	6 wks

HEDGEHOPPERS ANONYMOUS   **12 wks**
UK, male vocal/instrumental group

30 Sep 65 ●	**IT'S GOOD NEWS WEEK** *Decca F 12241*	.5	12 wks

Neal HEFTI US, male orchestra   **4 wks**

9 Apr 88	**BATMAN THEME** *RCA PB 49571*	.55	4 wks

Den HEGARTY UK, male vocalist   **2 wks**

31 Mar 79	**VOODOO VOODOO** *Magnet MAG 143*	.73	2 wks

Anita HEGERLAND – *See Mike OLDFIELD*

HEINZ UK, male vocalist   **35 wks**

8 Aug 63 ●	**JUST LIKE EDDIE** *Decca F 11693*	.5	15 wks
28 Nov 63	**COUNTRY BOY** *Decca F 11768*	.26	9 wks
27 Feb 64	**YOU WERE THERE** *Decca F 11831*	.26	8 wks
15 Oct 64	**QUESTIONS I CAN'T ANSWER** *Columbia DB 7374*	.39	2 wks
18 Mar 65	**DIGGIN' MY POTATOES** *Columbia DB 7482*	.49	1 wk

HELLO UK, male vocal/instrumental group   **21 wks**

9 Nov 74 ●	**TELL HIM** *Bell 1377*	.6	12 wks
18 Oct 75 ●	**NEW YORK GROOVE** *Bell 1438*	.9	9 wks

HELLOWEEN US, male vocal/instrumental group   **7 wks**

27 Aug 88	**DR STEIN** *Noise International 7HELLO 1*	.57	3 wks
12 Nov 88	**I WANT OUT** *Noise International 7HELLO 2*	.69	2 wks
2 Mar 91	**KIDS OF THE CENTURY** *EMI EM 178*	.56	2 wks

Bobby HELMS US, male vocalist   **7 wks**

29 Nov 57	**MY SPECIAL ANGEL** *Brunswick 05721*	.22	3 wks
21 Feb 58	**NO OTHER BABY** *Brunswick 05730*	.30	1 wk
1 Aug 58	**JACQUELINE** *Brunswick 05748*	.20	3 wks

Jimmy HELMS UK, male vocalist   **10 wks**

24 Feb 73 ●	**GONNA MAKE YOU AN OFFER YOU CAN'T REFUSE** *Cube BUG 27*	.8	10 wks

Eddie HENDERSON   **6 wks**
US, male vocalist/instrumentalist - trumpet

28 Oct 78	**PRANCE ON** *Capitol CL 16015*	.44	6 wks

Joe 'Mr. Piano' HENDERSON   **23 wks**
UK, male instrumentalist - piano

3 Jun 55	**SING IT WITH JOE** *Polygon P 1167*	.14	4 wks
2 Sep 55	**SING IT AGAIN WITH JOE** *Polygon P 1184*	.18	3 wks
25 Jul 58	**TRUDIE** *Pye Nixa N 15147*	.14	12 wks
24 Oct 58	**TRUDIE (re-entry)** *Pye Nixa N 15147*	.23	2 wks

23 Oct 59	**TREBLE CHANCE** *Pye 7N 15224*	.28	1 wk
24 Mar 60	**OOH LA LA** *Pye 7N 15257*	.46	1 wk

First two hits are medleys as follows: Sing It With Joe: Margie/I'm Nobody's Sweetheart/Somebody Stole My Gal/Moonlight Bay/By The Light Of The Silvery Moon/Cuddle Up A Little Closer. Sing It Again With Joe: Put Your Arms Around Me Honey/Ain't She Sweet/When You're Smiling/Shine On Harvest Moon/My Blue Heaven/Show Me The Way To Go Home.

Wayne HENDERSON – *See Roy AYERS*

Jimi HENDRIX EXPERIENCE   **87 wks**
US/UK, male vocal/instrumental group, Jimi Hendrix, vocalist/instrumentalist - guitar

5 Jan 67 ●	**HEY JOE** *Polydor 56 139* *	.6	10 wks
23 Mar 67 ●	**PURPLE HAZE** *Track 604 001*	.3	14 wks
11 May 67 ●	**THE WIND CRIES MARY** *Track 604 004*	.6	11 wks
30 Aug 67	**BURNING OF THE MIDNIGHT LAMP** *Track 604 007*	.18	9 wks
23 Oct 68 ●	**ALL ALONG THE WATCHTOWER** *Track 604 025*	.5	11 wks
16 Apr 69	**CROSSTOWN TRAFFIC** *Track 604 029*	.37	3 wks
7 Nov 70 ★	**VOODOO CHILE** *Track 2095 001*	.1	13 wks
30 Oct 71	**GYPSY EYES/REMEMBER** *Track 2094 010*	.35	5 wks
12 Feb 72	**JOHNNY B. GOODE** *Polydor 2001 277* *	.35	5 wks
21 Apr 90	**CROSSTOWN TRAFFIC (re-issue)** *Polydor PO 71* *	.61	3 wks
20 Oct 90	**ALL ALONG THE WATCHTOWER (EP)** *Polydor PO 100* *	.52	3 wks

* Jimi Hendrix

Tracks on All Along The Watchtower (EP): All Along The Watchtower/Voodoo Chile/Hey Joe.

Nona HENDRYX US, female vocalist   **2 wks**

16 May 87	**WHY SHOULD I CRY** *EMI America EA 234*	.60	2 wks

Don HENLEY US, male vocalist   **24 wks**

12 Feb 83	**DIRTY LAUNDRY** *Asylum E 9894*	.59	3 wks
9 Feb 85	**THE BOYS OF SUMMER** *Geffen A 4945*	.12	10 wks
29 Jul 89	**THE END OF THE INNOCENCE** *Geffen GEF 57*	.48	5 wks
3 Oct 92	**SOMETIMES LOVE JUST AIN'T ENOUGH** *MCA MCS 1692* *	.22	6 wks

* Patty Smyth with Don Henley

Clarence 'Frogman' HENRY US, male vocalist   **33 wks**

4 May 61 ●	**BUT I DO** *Pye International 7N 25078*	.3	19 wks
13 Jul 61 ●	**YOU ALWAYS HURT THE ONE YOU LOVE** *Pye International 7N 25089*	.6	12 wks
21 Sep 61	**LONELY STREET/WHY CAN'T YOU** *Pye International 7N 25108*	.42	2 wks

Kevin HENRY – *See L.A. MIX*

Paul HENRY and the Mayson GLEN ORCHESTRA   **2 wks**
UK, male vocalist/orchestra

14 Jan 78	**BENNY'S THEME** *Pye 7N 46027*	.39	2 wks

HERD UK, male vocal/instrumental group   **35 wks**

13 Sep 67 ●	**FROM THE UNDERWORLD** *Fontana TF 856*	.6	13 wks
20 Dec 67	**PARADISE LOST** *Fontana TF 887*	.15	9 wks
10 Apr 68 ●	**I DON'T WANT OUR LOVING TO DIE** *Fontana TF 925*	.5	13 wks

HERMAN'S HERMITS   **211 wks**
UK, male vocal/instrumental group

20 Aug 64 ★	**I'M INTO SOMETHING GOOD** *Columbia DB 7338*	.1	15 wks
19 Nov 64	**SHOW ME GIRL** *Columbia DB 7408*	.19	9 wks

18 Feb 65 ●	SILHOUETTES *Columbia DB 7475*	3	12 wks
29 Apr 65 ●	WONDERFUL WORLD *Columbia DB 7546*	7	9 wks
2 Sep 65	JUST A LITTLE BIT BETTER *Columbia DB 7670*	15	9 wks
23 Dec 65 ●	A MUST TO AVOID *Columbia DB 7791*	6	11 wks
24 Mar 66	YOU WON'T BE LEAVING *Columbia DB 7861*	20	7 wks
23 Jun 66	THIS DOOR SWINGS BOTH WAYS *Columbia DB 7947*	18	7 wks
6 Oct 66 ●	NO MILK TODAY *Columbia DB 8012*	7	11 wks
1 Dec 66	EAST WEST *Columbia DB 8076*	37	7 wks
9 Feb 67 ●	THERE'S A KIND OF HUSH *Columbia DB 8123*	7	11 wks
17 Jan 68	I CAN TAKE OR LEAVE YOUR LOVING *Columbia DB 8327*	11	9 wks
1 May 68 ●	SLEEPY JOE *Columbia DB 8404*	12	10 wks
17 Jul 68 ●	SUNSHINE GIRL *Columbia DB 8446*	8	14 wks
18 Dec 68 ●	SOMETHING'S HAPPENING *Columbia DB 8504*	6	15 wks
23 Apr 69 ●	MY SENTIMENTAL FRIEND *Columbia DB 8563*	2	12 wks
8 Nov 69	HERE COMES THE STAR *Columbia DB 8626*	33	9 wks
7 Feb 70 ●	YEARS MAY COME, YEARS MAY GO *Columbia DB 8656*	7	11 wks
2 May 70	YEARS MAY COME, YEARS MAY GO (re-entry) *Columbia DB 8656*	45	1 wk
23 May 70	BET YER LIFE I DO *RAK 102*	22	10 wks
14 Nov 70	LADY BARBARA *RAK 106* *	13	12 wks

* Peter Noone and Herman's Hermits

See also Peter Noone.

HERNANDEZ *UK, male vocalist*   **3 wks**

15 Apr 89	ALL MY LOVE *Epic HER 1*	58	3 wks

Patrick HERNANDEZ *Guadeloupe, male vocalist*   **14 wks**

16 Jun 79 ●	BORN TO BE ALIVE *Gem GEM 4*	10	14 wks

HERREYS *Sweden, male vocal group*   **3 wks**

26 May 84	DIGGI LOO-DIGGI LEY *Panther PAN 5*	46	3 wks

Nick HEYWARD *UK, male vocalist*   **57 wks**

19 Mar 83	WHISTLE DOWN THE WIND *Arista HEY 1*	13	8 wks
4 Jun 83	TAKE THAT SITUATION *Arista HEY 2*	11	10 wks
24 Sep 83	BLUE HAT FOR A BLUE DAY *Arista HEY 3*	14	8 wks
3 Dec 83	ON A SUNDAY *Arista HEY 4*	52	5 wks
2 Jun 84	LOVE ALL DAY *Arista HEY 5*	31	6 wks
3 Nov 84	WARNING SIGN *Arista HEY 6*	25	8 wks
5 Jan 85	WARNING SIGN (re-entry) *Arista HEY 6*	72	1 wk
8 Jun 85	LAURA *Arista HEY 8*	45	4 wks
10 May 86	OVER THE WEEKEND *Arista HEY 9*	43	5 wks
10 Sep 88	YOU'RE MY WORLD *Warner Bros. W 7758*	67	2 wks

HI GLOSS *US, disco aggregation*   **13 wks**

8 Aug 81	YOU'LL NEVER KNOW *Epic EPC A 1387*	12	13 wks

HI POWER *Germany, male rap group*   **1 wk**

1 Sep 90	CULT OF SNAP/SIMBA GROOVE *Rumour RUMAT 24*	73	1 wk

HI TENSION *UK, male vocal/instrumental group*   **23 wks**

6 May 78	HI TENSION *Island WIP 6422*	13	12 wks
12 Aug 78 ●	BRITISH HUSTLE/PEACE ON EARTH *Island WIP 6446*	8	11 wks

Peace On Earth *credited with* British Hustle *from 2 Sep 78 to end of record's chart run.*

Al HIBBLER *US, male vocalist*   **17 wks**

13 May 55 ●	UNCHAINED MELODY *Brunswick 05420*	2	17 wks

HI-FIVE *US, male vocal group*   **8 wks**

1 Jun 91	I LIKE THE WAY (THE KISSING GAME) *Jive JIVE 271*	43	6 wks
24 Oct 92	SHE'S PLAYING HARD TO GET *Jive JIVE 316*	55	2 wks

Bertie HIGGINS *US, male vocalist*   **4 wks**

5 Jun 82	KEY LARGO *Epic EPC A 2168*	60	4 wks

HIGH *UK, male vocal group*   **10 wks**

25 Aug 90	UP AND DOWN *London LON 272*	53	4 wks
27 Oct 90	TAKE YOUR TIME *London LON 280*	56	2 wks
12 Jan 91	BOX SET GO *London LONG 286*	28	3 wks
8 Apr 91	MORE... *London LON 297*	67	1 wk

HIGH NUMBERS *UK, male vocal/instrumental group*   **4 wks**

5 Apr 80	I'M THE FACE *Back Door DOOR 4*	49	4 wks

The High Numbers were an early version of the Who. See also the Who.

HIGH SOCIETY *UK, male vocal/instrumental group*   **4 wks**

15 Nov 80	I NEVER GO OUT IN THE RAIN *Eagle ERS 002*	53	4 wks

---

HIGHLY LIKELY *UK, male vocal/instrumental group*   **4 wks**

21 Apr 73	WHATEVER HAPPENED TO YOU ('LIKELY LADS' THEME) *BBC RESL 10*	35	4 wks

---

HIGHWAYMEN *US, male vocal group*   **18 wks**

7 Sep 61 ★	MICHAEL *HMV POP 910*	1	14 wks
7 Dec 61	GYPSY ROVER *HMV POP 948*	41	3 wks
11 Jan 62	GYPSY ROVER (re-entry) *HMV POP 948*	43	1 wk

HIJACK *UK, male producer*   **3 wks**

6 Jan 90	THE BADMAN IS ROBBIN' *Rhyme Syndicate 655517 7*	56	3 wks

---

Benny HILL *UK, male vocalist*   **43 wks**

16 Feb 61	GATHER IN THE MUSHROOMS *Pye 7N 15327*	12	8 wks
1 Jun 61	TRANSISTOR RADIO *Pye 7N 15359*	24	6 wks
16 May 63	HARVEST OF LOVE *Pye 7N 15520*	20	8 wks
13 Nov 71 ★	ERNIE (THE FASTEST MILKMAN IN THE WEST) *Columbia DB 8833*	1	17 wks
30 May 92	ERNIE (THE FASTEST MILKMAN IN THE WEST) (re-issue) *EMI ERN 1*	29	4 wks

---

Chris HILL *UK, male vocalist/producer*   **14 wks**

6 Dec 75 ●	RENTA SANTA *Philips 6006 491*	10	7 wks
4 Dec 76 ●	BIONIC SANTA *Philips 6006 551*	10	7 wks

Dan HILL *Canada, male vocalist*   **13 wks**

18 Feb 78	SOMETIMES WHEN WE TOUCH *20th Century BTC 2355*	46	1 wk

4 Mar 78	SOMETIMES WHEN WE TOUCH (re-entry)		
	20th Century BTC 2355 ....**13**	12 wks

Lonnie HILL US, male vocalist — 4 wks

22 Mar 86	GALVESTON BAY 10 TEN 111 ....**51**	4 wks

Roni HILL US, female vocalist — 4 wks

7 May 77	YOU KEEP ME HANGIN' ON - STOP IN THE		
	NAME OF LOVE (MEDLEY) Creole CR 138 ....**36**	4 wks

Vince HILL UK, male vocalist — 91 wks

7 Jun 62	THE RIVER'S RUN DRY Piccadilly 7N 35043 ....**49**	1 wk
28 Jun 62	THE RIVER'S RUN DRY (re-entry) Piccadilly 7N 35043 ....**41**	1 wk
6 Jan 66	TAKE ME TO YOUR HEART AGAIN	
	Columbia DB 7781 ....**13**	11 wks
17 Mar 66	HEARTACHES Columbia DB 7852 ....**28**	5 wks
2 Jun 66	MERCI CHERI Columbia DB 7924 ....**36**	6 wks
9 Feb 67 ●	EDELWEISS Columbia DB 8127 ....**2**	17 wks
11 May 67	ROSES OF PICARDY Columbia DB 8185 ....**13**	11 wks
27 Sep 67	LOVE LETTERS IN THE SAND Columbia DB 8268 ....**23**	9 wks
26 Jun 68	IMPORTANCE OF YOUR LOVE Columbia DB 8414 ....**32**	12 wks
12 Feb 69	DOESN'T ANYBODY KNOW MY NAME?	
	Columbia DB 8515 ....**50**	1 wk
25 Oct 69	LITTLE BLUE BIRD Columbia DB 8616 ....**42**	1 wk
25 Sep 71	LOOK AROUND Columbia DB 8804 ....**12**	16 wks

HILLTOPPERS US, male vocal group — 30 wks

27 Jan 56 ●	ONLY YOU London HLD 8221 ....**3**	22 wks
10 Aug 56	ONLY YOU (re-entry) London HLD 8221 ....**24**	1 wk
14 Sep 56	TRYIN' London HLD 8298 ....**30**	1 wk
5 Apr 57	MARIANNE London HLD 8381 ....**20**	2 wks
26 Apr 57	MARIANNE (re-entry) London HLD 8381 ....**23**	4 wks

Ronnie HILTON UK, male vocalist — 136 wks

26 Nov 54 ●	I STILL BELIEVE HMV B 10785 ....**3**	14 wks
10 Dec 54	VENI VIDI VICI HMV B 10785 ....**12**	8 wks
11 Mar 55 ●	A BLOSSOM FELL HMV B 10808 ....**10**	5 wks
26 Aug 55	STARS SHINE IN YOUR EYES HMV B 10901 ....**13**	7 wks
11 Nov 55	YELLOW ROSE OF TEXAS HMV B 10924 ....**15**	2 wks
10 Feb 56	YOUNG AND FOOLISH HMV POP 154 ....**17**	1 wk
24 Feb 56	YOUNG AND FOOLISH (re-entry) HMV POP 154 ....**20**	1 wk
9 Mar 56	YOUNG AND FOOLISH (2nd re-entry)	
	HMV POP 154 ....**19**	1 wk
20 Apr 56 ★	NO OTHER LOVE HMV POP 198 ....**1**	14 wks
29 Jun 56 ●	WHO ARE WE HMV POP 221 ....**6**	12 wks
21 Sep 56	WOMAN IN LOVE HMV POP 248 ....**30**	1 wk
9 Nov 56	TWO DIFFERENT WORLDS HMV POP 274 ....**13**	13 wks
24 May 57 ●	AROUND THE WORLD HMV POP 338 ....**4**	18 wks
2 Aug 57	WONDERFUL WONDERFUL HMV POP 364 ....**27**	2 wks
21 Feb 58	MAGIC MOMENTS HMV POP 446 ....**22**	2 wks
18 Apr 58	I MAY NEVER PASS THIS WAY AGAIN	
	HMV POP 468 * **30**	1 wk
2 May 58	I MAY NEVER PASS THIS WAY AGAIN (re-entry)	
	HMV POP 468 * **30**	1 wk
6 Jun 58	I MAY NEVER PASS THIS WAY AGAIN (2nd	
	re-entry) HMV POP 468 * **27**	1 wk
9 Jan 59	THE WORLD OUTSIDE HMV POP 559 * **18**	6 wks
21 Aug 59	THE WONDER OF YOU HMV POP 638 ....**22**	3 wks
21 May 64	DON'T LET THE RAIN COME DOWN	
	HMV POP 1291 ....**21**	10 wks

11 Feb 65	A WINDMILL IN OLD AMSTERDAM		
	HMV POP 1378 ....**23**	13 wks

* Ronnie Hilton with the Michael Sammes Singers

HINDSIGHT UK, male vocal/instrumental group — 3 wks

5 Sep 87	LOWDOWN Circa YR 5 ....**62**	3 wks

Gregory HINES – See Luther VANDROSS

HIPSWAY UK, male vocal/instrumental group — 21 wks

13 Jul 85	THE BROKEN YEARS Mercury MER 193 ....**72**	3 wks
14 Sep 85	ASK THE LORD Mercury MER 195 ....**72**	1 wk
22 Feb 86	THE HONEYTHIEF Mercury MER 212 ....**17**	9 wks
10 May 86	ASK THE LORD Mercury LORD 1 ....**50**	5 wks
20 Sep 86	LONG WHITE CAR Mercury MER 230 ....**55**	2 wks
1 Apr 89	YOUR LOVE Mercury MER 279 ....**66**	1 wk

LORD 1 was a re-recording of MER 195.

HISTORY featuring Q-TEE — 5 wks
US, male/female rap group

21 Apr 90	AFRIKA SBK SBK 7008 ....**42**	5 wks

Carol HITCHCOCK Australia, female vocalist — 5 wks

30 May 87	GET READY A & M AM 391 ....**56**	5 wks

HI-TEK 3 featuring YA KID K — 10 wks
Belgium, male/female vocal/instrumental group

3 Feb 90	SPIN THAT WHEEL Brothers Organisation BORG 1 ....**69**	3 wks
29 Sep 90	SPIN THAT WHEEL (TURTLES GET	
	REAL) (re-issue) Brothers Organisation BORG 16 ....**15**	7 wks

See also Technotronic.

HITHOUSE Holland, male producer - Peter Slaghuis — 13 wks

5 Nov 88	JACK TO THE SOUND OF THE UNDERGROUND	
	Supreme SUPE 137 ....**14**	12 wks
19 Aug 89	MOVE YOUR FEET TO THE RHYTHM OF THE	
	BEAT Supreme SUPE 149 ....**69**	1 wk

HITMAN HOWIE TEE – See REAL ROXANNE

Edmund HOCKRIDGE Canada, male vocalist — 18 wks

17 Feb 56 ●	YOUNG AND FOOLISH Nixa N 15039 ....**10**	7 wks
13 Apr 56	YOUNG AND FOOLISH (re-entry) Nixa N 15039 ....**28**	1 wk
4 May 56	YOUNG AND FOOLISH (2nd re-entry) Nixa N 15039 ...**26**	1 wk
11 May 56	NO OTHER LOVE Nixa N 15048 ....**24**	2 wks
1 Jun 56	NO OTHER LOVE (re-entry) Nixa N 15048 ....**29**	1 wk
15 Jun 56	NO OTHER LOVE (2nd re-entry) Nixa N 15048 ....**30**	1 wk
31 Aug 56	BY THE FOUNTAINS OF ROME Pye Nixa N 15063 ....**17**	5 wks

Eddie HODGES US, male vocalist — 10 wks

28 Sep 61	I'M GONNA KNOCK ON YOUR DOOR	
	London HLA 9369 ....**37**	6 wks
9 Aug 62	MADE TO LOVE (GIRLS GIRLS GIRLS)	
	London HLA 9576 ....**37**	4 wks

Roger HODGSON – See SUPERTRAMP

Susanna HOFFS US, female vocalist — 6 wks

2 Mar 91	MY SIDE OF THE BED Columbia 6565547	44	4 wks
11 May 91	UNCONDITIONAL LOVE Columbia 6567827	65	2 wks

HOLLAND-DOZIER featuring Lamont DOZIER US, male vocal duo — 5 wks

28 Oct 72	WHY CAN'T WE BE LOVERS Invictus INV 525	29	5 wks

Jennifer HOLLIDAY US, female vocalist — 6 wks

4 Sep 82	AND I'M TELLING YOU I'M NOT GOING Geffen GEF A 2644	32	6 wks

Michael HOLLIDAY UK, male vocalist — 65 wks

30 Mar 56	NOTHIN' TO DO Columbia DB 3746	20	1 wk
27 Apr 56	NOTHIN' TO DO (re-entry) Columbia DB 3746	23	2 wks
15 Jun 56	GAL WITH THE YALLER SHOES Columbia DB 3783	13	3 wks
22 Jun 56	HOT DIGGITY Columbia DB 3783	14	5 wks
3 Aug 56	HOT DIGGITY/GAL WITH THE YALLER SHOES (re-entry) Columbia DB 3783	17	3 wks
5 Oct 56	TEN THOUSAND MILES Columbia DB 3813	24	3 wks
17 Jan 58 ★	THE STORY OF MY LIFE Columbia DB 4058	1	15 wks
14 Mar 58	IN LOVE Columbia DB 4087	26	3 wks
16 May 58 ●	STAIRWAY OF LOVE Columbia DB 4121	3	13 wks
11 Jul 58	I'LL ALWAYS BE IN LOVE WITH YOU Columbia DB 4155	27	1 wk
1 Jan 60 ★	STARRY EYED Columbia DB 4378	1	12 wks
14 Apr 60	SKYLARK Columbia DB 4437	39	3 wks
1 Sep 60	LITTLE BOY LOST Columbia DB 4475	50	1 wk

When Hot Diggity/Gal With The Yaller Shoes re-entered the chart on 3 Aug 56 Hot Diggity was listed by itself on 3 Aug and 10 Aug. Both sides were listed on 17 Aug.

HOLLIES UK, male vocal/instrumental group — 316 wks

30 May 63	JUST LIKE ME Parlophone R 5030	25	10 wks
29 Aug 63	SEARCHIN' Parlophone R 5052	12	14 wks
21 Nov 63 ●	STAY Parlophone R 5077	8	16 wks
27 Feb 64 ●	JUST ONE LOOK Parlophone R 5104	2	13 wks
21 May 64 ●	HERE I GO AGAIN Parlophone R 5137	4	12 wks
17 Sep 64 ●	WE'RE THROUGH Parlophone R 5178	7	11 wks
28 Jan 65	YES I WILL Parlophone R 5232	9	13 wks
27 May 65 ★	I'M ALIVE Parlophone R 5287	1	14 wks
2 Sep 65 ●	LOOK THROUGH ANY WINDOW Parlophone R 5322	4	11 wks
9 Dec 65	IF I NEEDED SOMEONE Parlophone R 5392	20	9 wks
24 Feb 66 ●	I CAN'T LET GO Parlophone R 5409	2	10 wks
23 Jun 66 ●	BUS STOP Parlophone R 5469	5	9 wks
13 Oct 66 ●	STOP STOP STOP Parlophone R 5508	2	12 wks
16 Feb 67 ●	ON A CAROUSEL Parlophone R 5562	4	11 wks
1 Jun 67 ●	CARRIE-ANNE Parlophone R 5602	3	11 wks
27 Sep 67	KING MIDAS IN REVERSE Parlophone R 5637	18	8 wks
27 Mar 68 ●	JENNIFER ECCLES Parlophone R 5680	7	11 wks
2 Oct 68	LISTEN TO ME Parlophone R 5733	11	11 wks
5 Mar 69 ●	SORRY SUZANNE Parlophone R 5765	3	12 wks
4 Oct 69 ●	HE AIN'T HEAVY, HE'S MY BROTHER Parlophone R 5806	3	15 wks
18 Apr 70 ●	I CAN'T TELL THE BOTTOM FROM THE TOP Parlophone R 5837	7	10 wks
3 Oct 70	GASOLINE ALLEY BRED Parlophone R 5862	14	7 wks
22 May 71	HEY WILLY Parlophone R 5905	22	7 wks
26 Feb 72	THE BABY Polydor 2058 199	26	6 wks
2 Sep 72	LONG COOL WOMAN IN A BLACK DRESS Parlophone R 5939	32	8 wks
13 Oct 73	THE DAY THAT CURLY BILLY SHOT DOWN CRAZY SAM MCGHEE Polydor 2058 403	24	6 wks
9 Feb 74 ●	THE AIR THAT I BREATHE Polydor 2058 435	2	13 wks
14 Jun 80	SOLDIER'S SONG Polydor 2059 246	58	3 wks
29 Aug 81	HOLLIEDAZE (MEDLEY) EMI 5229	28	7 wks
3 Sep 88 ★	HE AIN'T HEAVY, HE'S MY BROTHER (re-issue) EMI EM 74	1	11 wks
3 Dec 88	THE AIR THAT I BREATHE (re-issue) EMI EM 80	60	5 wks

Loleatta HOLLOWAY – *See MARKY MARK and the FUNKY BUNCH; CAPPELLA*

Buddy HOLLY US, male vocalist — 190 wks

6 Dec 57 ●	PEGGY SUE Coral Q 72293	6	17 wks
14 Mar 58	LISTEN TO ME Coral Q 72288	16	2 wks
20 Jun 58 ●	RAVE ON Coral Q 72325	5	14 wks
29 Aug 58	EARLY IN THE MORNING Coral Q 72333	17	4 wks
16 Jan 59	HEARTBEAT Coral Q 72346	30	1 wk
27 Feb 59 ★	IT DOESN'T MATTER ANYMORE Coral Q 72360	1	21 wks
31 Jul 59	MIDNIGHT SHIFT Brunswick 05800	26	3 wks
11 Sep 59	PEGGY SUE GOT MARRIED Coral Q 72376	13	10 wks
28 Apr 60	HEARTBEAT (re-issue) Coral Q 72392	30	3 wks
26 May 60	TRUE LOVE WAYS Coral Q 72397	25	7 wks
20 Oct 60	LEARNIN' THE GAME Coral Q 72411	36	3 wks
26 Jan 61	WHAT TO DO Coral Q 72419	34	6 wks
6 Jul 61	BABY I DON'T CARE/VALLEY OF TEARS Coral Q 72432	12	14 wks
15 Mar 62	LISTEN TO ME (re-issue) Coral Q 72449	48	1 wk
13 Sep 62	REMINISCING Coral Q 72455	17	11 wks
14 Mar 63 ●	BROWN-EYED HANDSOME MAN Coral Q 72459	3	10 wks
6 Jun 63 ●	BO DIDDLEY Coral Q 72463	4	12 wks
5 Sep 63 ●	WISHING Coral Q 72466	10	11 wks
19 Dec 63	WHAT TO DO Coral Q 72469	27	8 wks
14 May 64	YOU'VE GOT LOVE Coral Q 72472 *	40	6 wks
10 Jun 64	LOVE'S MADE A FOOL OF YOU Coral Q 72475 *	39	6 wks
3 Apr 68	PEGGY SUE/RAVE ON (re-issue) MCA MU 1012	32	9 wks
10 Dec 88	TRUE LOVE WAYS (re-issue) MCA MCA 1302	65	4 wks

* Buddy Holly and the Crickets

Buddy Holly's version of Love's Made A Fool Of You is not the same version as the Crickets' hit of 1959, on which Holly did not appear. Valley Of Tears was not listed together with Baby I Don't Care until 13 Jul 61. What To Do on Q 72469 was a re-recording.

HOLLY and the IVYS — 4 wks
UK, male/female vocal/instrumental group

19 Dec 81	CHRISTMAS ON 45 Decca SANTA 1	40	4 wks

HOLLYWOOD ARGYLES US, male vocal group — 10 wks

21 Jul 60	ALLEY OOP London HLU 9146	24	10 wks

HOLLYWOOD BEYOND UK, male vocalist — 14 wks

12 Jul 86 ●	WHAT'S THE COLOUR OF MONEY? WEA YZ 76	7	10 wks
20 Sep 86	NO MORE TEARS WEA YZ 81	47	4 wks

Eddie HOLMAN US, male vocalist — 13 wks

19 Oct 74 ●	(HEY THERE) LONELY GIRL ABC 4012	4	13 wks

Rupert HOLMES US, male vocalist — 14 wks

12 Jan 80	ESCAPE (THE PINA COLADA SONG) Infinity INF 120	23	7 wks
22 Mar 80	HIM MCA 565	31	7 wks

John HOLT Jamaica, male vocalist — 14 wks

14 Dec 74 ●	HELP ME MAKE IT THROUGH THE NIGHT Trojan TR 7909	6	14 wks

A HOMEBOY, A HIPPIE and A FUNKI DREDD UK, male vocal/instrumental group — 7 wks

13 Oct 90	TOTAL CONFUSION Tam Tam 7TTT 031	56	3 wks
29 Dec 90	FREEDOM Tam Tam 7TTT 039	68	4 wks

HONEYBUS UK, male vocal/instrumental group — 12 wks

20 Mar 68	●	I CAN'T LET MAGGIE GO *Deram DM 182*	8	12 wks

HONEYCOMBS UK, male/female vocal/instrumental group — 39 wks

23 Jul 64	★	HAVE I THE RIGHT *Pye 7N 15664*	1	15 wks
22 Oct 64		IS IT BECAUSE *Pye 7N 15705*	38	6 wks
29 Apr 65		SOMETHING BETTER BEGINNING *Pye 7N 15827*	39	4 wks
5 Aug 65		THAT'S THE WAY *Pye 7N 15890*	12	14 wks

HONEYDRIPPERS UK/US, male vocal/instrumental group — 3 wks

2 Feb 85		SEA OF LOVE *Es Paranza YZ 33 YZ 33*	56	3 wks

HONKY UK, male vocal/instrumental group — 5 wks

28 May 77		JOIN THE PARTY *Creole CR 137*	28	5 wks

Frank HOOKER and POSITIVE PEOPLE — 4 wks
US, male vocal/instrumental group

5 Jul 80		THIS FEELIN' *DJM DJS 10947*	48	4 wks

John Lee HOOKER US, male vocalist — 15 wks

11 Jun 64		DIMPLES *Stateside SS 297*	23	10 wks
24 Oct 92		BOOM BOOM *Pointblank POB 3*	16	5 wks

HOOTERS US, male vocal/instrumental group — 9 wks

21 Nov 87		SATELLITE *CBS 651168 7*	22	9 wks

Mary HOPKIN UK, female vocalist — 74 wks

4 Sep 68	★	THOSE WERE THE DAYS *Apple 2*	1	21 wks
2 Apr 69	●	GOODBYE *Apple 10*	2	14 wks
31 Jan 70	●	TEMMA HARBOUR *Apple 22*	6	11 wks
28 Mar 70	●	KNOCK KNOCK WHO'S THERE *Apple 26*	2	14 wks
31 Oct 70		THINK ABOUT YOUR CHILDREN *Apple 30*	19	7 wks
2 Jan 71		THINK ABOUT YOUR CHILDREN (re-entry) *Apple 30*	46	2 wks
31 Jul 71		LET MY NAME BE SORROW *Apple 34*	46	1 wk
20 Mar 76		IF YOU LOVE ME *Good Earth GD 2*	32	4 wks

See also Various Artists (EPs & LPs) - The Apple EP.

Anthony HOPKINS UK, male vocalist — 1 wk

27 Dec 86		DISTANT STAR *Juice AA 5*	75	1 wk

Bruce HORNSBY and the RANGE — 15 wks
US, male vocal/instrumental group

2 Aug 86		THE WAY IT IS *RCA PB 49805*	15	10 wks
25 Apr 87		MANDOLIN RAIN *RCA PB 49769*	70	1 wk
28 May 88		THE VALLEY ROAD *RCA PB 49561*	44	4 wks

HORSE UK, male/female vocal/instrumental group — 3 wks

24 Nov 90		CAREFUL *Capitol CL 587*	52	3 wks

Johnny HORTON US, male vocalist — 15 wks

26 Jun 59		BATTLE OF NEW ORLEANS *Philips PB 932*	16	4 wks
19 Jan 61		NORTH TO ALASKA *Philips PB 1062*	23	11 wks

HOT BLOOD France, male instrumental group — 5 wks

9 Oct 76		SOUL DRACULA *Creole CR 132*	32	5 wks

HOT BUTTER US, male instrumental group — 19 wks

22 Jul 72	●	POPCORN *Pye International 7N 25583*	5	16 wks
23 Dec 72		POPCORN (re-entry) *Pye International 7N 25583*	50	3 wks

HOT CHOCOLATE UK, male vocal/instrumental group — 267 wks

15 Aug 70	●	LOVE IS LIFE *RAK 103*	6	12 wks
6 Mar 71		YOU COULD HAVE BEEN A LADY *RAK 110*	22	9 wks
28 Aug 71	●	I BELIEVE (IN LOVE) *RAK 118*	8	11 wks
28 Oct 72		YOU'LL ALWAYS BE A FRIEND *RAK 139*	23	8 wks
14 Apr 73	●	BROTHER LOUIE *RAK 149*	7	10 wks
18 Aug 73		RUMOURS *RAK 157*	44	3 wks
16 Mar 74	●	EMMA *RAK 168*	3	10 wks
30 Nov 74		CHERI BABE *RAK 188*	31	9 wks
24 May 75		DISCO QUEEN *RAK 202*	11	7 wks
9 Aug 75	●	A CHILD'S PRAYER *RAK 212*	7	10 wks
8 Nov 75	●	YOU SEXY THING *RAK 221*	2	12 wks
20 Mar 76		DON'T STOP IT NOW *RAK 230*	11	8 wks
26 Jun 76		MAN TO MAN *RAK 238*	14	8 wks
21 Aug 76		HEAVEN IS IN THE BACK SEAT OF MY CADILLAC *RAK 240*	25	8 wks
18 Jun 77	★	SO YOU WIN AGAIN *RAK 259*	1	11 wks
26 Nov 77	●	PUT YOUR LOVE IN ME *RAK 266*	10	9 wks
4 Mar 78		EVERY 1'S A WINNER *RAK 270*	12	11 wks
2 Dec 78		I'LL PUT YOU TOGETHER AGAIN *RAK 286*	13	11 wks
19 May 79		MINDLESS BOOGIE *RAK 292*	46	5 wks
28 Jul 79		GOING THROUGH THE MOTIONS *RAK 296*	53	4 wks
3 May 80	●	NO DOUBT ABOUT IT *RAK 310*	2	11 wks
19 Jul 80		ARE YOU GETTING ENOUGH OF WHAT MAKES YOU HAPPY *RAK 318*	17	7 wks
13 Dec 80		LOVE ME TO SLEEP *RAK 324*	50	5 wks
30 May 81		YOU'LL NEVER BE SO WRONG *RAK 331*	52	4 wks
17 Apr 82	●	GIRL CRAZY *RAK 341*	7	11 wks
10 Jul 82	●	IT STARTED WITH A KISS *RAK 344*	5	12 wks
25 Sep 82		CHANCES *RAK 350*	32	5 wks
7 May 83	●	WHAT KINDA BOY YOU LOOKING FOR (GIRL) *RAK 357*	10	9 wks
17 Sep 83		TEARS ON THE TELEPHONE *RAK 363*	37	5 wks
4 Feb 84		I GAVE YOU MY HEART (DIDN'T I) *RAK 369*	13	10 wks
17 Jan 87	●	YOU SEXY THING (re-mix) *EMI 5592*	10	10 wks
4 Apr 87		EVERY 1'S A WINNER (re-mix) *EMI 5607*	69	2 wks

HOT GOSSIP – *See Sarah BRIGHTMAN*

HOT HOUSE UK, male/female vocal/instrumental group — 3 wks

14 Feb 87		DON'T COME TO STAY *deConstruction CHEZ 1*	74	1 wk
24 Sep 88		DON'T COME TO STAY (re-issue) *deConstruction PB 42233*	70	2 wks

HOT STREAK US, male vocal/instrumental group — 8 wks

10 Sep 83		BODY WORK *Polydor POSP 642*	19	8 wks

HOTHOUSE FLOWERS — 25 wks
Ireland, male vocal/instrumental group

14 May 88		DON'T GO *London LON 174*	11	8 wks

23 Jul 88		I'M SORRY *London LON 187*	....	53	3 wks
12 May 90		GIVE IT UP *London LON 258*	....	30	5 wks
28 Jul 90		I CAN SEE CLEARLY NOW *London LON 269*	....	23	7 wks
20 Oct 90		MOVIES *London LON 276*	....	68	2 wks

HOTLEGS *UK, male vocal/instrumental group* — **14 wks**

| 4 Jul 70 | ● | NEANDERTHAL MAN *Fontana 6007 019* | .... | 2 | 14 wks |

HOTRODS – *See EDDIE and the HOTRODS*

HOTSHOTS *UK, male vocal group* — **15 wks**

| 2 Jun 73 | ● | SNOOPY VS. THE RED BARON *Mooncrest MOON 5* | .... | 4 | 15 wks |

A HOUSE *Ireland, male vocal/instrumental group* — **5 wks**

| 13 Jun 92 | | ENDLESS ART *Setanta AHOU 1* | .... | 46 | 3 wks |
| 8 Aug 92 | | TAKE IT EASY ON ME *Setanta AHOU 2* | .... | 55 | 2 wks |

HOUSE ENGINEERS *UK, male vocal/instrumental duo* — **2 wks**

| 5 Dec 87 | | GHOST HOUSE *Syncopate SY 8* | .... | 69 | 2 wks |

HOUSE OF LOVE *UK, male vocal/instrumental group* — **21 wks**

22 Apr 89		NEVER *Fontana HOL 1*	....	41	2 wks
18 Nov 89		I DON'T KNOW WHY I LOVE YOU *Fontana HOL 2*	....	41	3 wks
3 Feb 90		SHINE ON *Fontana HOL 3*	....	20	4 wks
7 Apr 90		BEATLES AND THE STONES *Fontana HOL 4*	....	36	4 wks
26 Oct 91		THE GIRL WITH THE LONELIEST EYES *Fontana HOL 5*	....	58	1 wk
2 May 92		FEEL *Fontana HOL 6*	....	45	3 wks
27 Jun 92		YOU DON'T UNDERSTAND *Fontana HOL 7*	....	46	3 wks
5 Dec 92		CRUSH ME *Fontana HOL 810*	....	67	1 wk

HOUSE OF PAIN *US, male rap group* — **4 wks**

| 10 Oct 92 | | JUMP AROUND *Ruffness XLS 32* | .... | 32 | 4 wks |

HOUSEMARTINS *UK, male vocal/instrumental group* — **59 wks**

8 Mar 86		SHEEP *Go! Discs GOD 9*	....	54	3 wks
5 Apr 86		SHEEP (re-entry) *Go! Discs GOD 9*	....	71	1 wk
7 Jun 86	●	HAPPY HOUR *Go! Discs GOD 11*	....	3	13 wks
4 Oct 86		THINK FOR A MINUTE *Go! Discs GOD 13*	....	18	8 wks
6 Dec 86	★	CARAVAN OF LOVE *Go! Discs GOD 16*	....	1	11 wks
23 May 87		FIVE GET OVER EXCITED *Go! Discs GOD 18*	....	11	6 wks
5 Sep 87		ME AND THE FARMER *Go! Discs GOD 19*	....	15	5 wks
21 Nov 87		BUILD *Go! Discs GOD 21*	....	15	8 wks
23 Apr 88		THERE IS ALWAYS SOMETHING THERE TO REMIND ME *Go! Discs GOD 22*	....	35	4 wks

HOUSEMASTER BOYZ and the RUDE BOY OF HOUSE *US, male vocal/instrumental group* — **14 wks**

| 9 May 87 | | HOUSE NATION *Magnetic Dance MAGD 1* | .... | 48 | 6 wks |
| 12 Sep 87 | ● | HOUSE NATION (re-entry) *Magnetic Dance MAGD 1* | .... | 8 | 8 wks |

Thelma HOUSTON *US, female vocalist* — **20 wks**

5 Feb 77		DON'T LEAVE ME THIS WAY *Motown TMG 1060*	....	13	8 wks
27 Jun 81		IF YOU FEEL IT *RCA 77*	....	48	4 wks
1 Dec 84		YOU USED TO HOLD ME SO TIGHT *MCA MCA 932*	....	49	8 wks

Whitney HOUSTON *US, female vocalist* — **145 wks**

16 Nov 85	★	SAVING ALL MY LOVE FOR YOU *Arista ARIST 640*	....	1	16 wks
25 Jan 86	●	HOW WILL I KNOW *Arista ARIST 656*	....	5	12 wks
25 Jan 86		HOLD ME *Asylum EKR 32 **	....	44	5 wks
12 Apr 86	●	GREATEST LOVE OF ALL *Arista ARIST 658*	....	8	11 wks
23 May 87	★	I WANNA DANCE WITH SOMEBODY (WHO LOVES ME) *Arista RIS 1*	....	1	16 wks
22 Aug 87		DIDN'T WE ALMOST HAVE IT ALL *Arista RIS 31*	....	14	8 wks
14 Nov 87	●	SO EMOTIONAL *Arista RIS 43*	....	5	11 wks
12 Mar 88		WHERE DO BROKEN HEARTS GO *Arista 109793*	....	14	8 wks
28 May 88	●	LOVE WILL SAVE THE DAY *Arista 111516*	....	10	7 wks
24 Sep 88	★	ONE MOMENT IN TIME *Arista 111613*	....	1	12 wks
9 Sep 89		IT ISN'T, IT WASN'T, IT AIN'T NEVER GONNA BE *Arista 112545 ***	....	29	5 wks
20 Oct 90	●	I'M YOUR BABY TONIGHT *Arista 113594*	....	5	9 wks
22 Dec 90		ALL THE MAN THAT I NEED *Arista 114000*	....	13	10 wks
29 Dec 90		I'M YOUR BABY TONIGHT (re-entry) *Arista 113594*	....	69	1 wk
6 Jul 91		MY NAME IS NOT SUSAN *Arista 114510*	....	29	5 wks
28 Sep 91		I BELONG TO YOU *Arista 114727*	....	54	2 wks
14 Nov 92	★	I WILL ALWAYS LOVE YOU *Arista 74321120657*	....	1†	7 wks

* Teddy Pendergrass with Whitney Houston ** Aretha Franklin and Whitney Houston

Billy HOWARD *UK, male vocalist* — **12 wks**

| 13 Dec 75 | ● | KING OF THE COPS *Penny Farthing PEN 892* | .... | 6 | 12 wks |

Miki HOWARD *US, female vocalist* — **2 wks**

| 26 May 90 | | UNTIL YOU COME BACK (THAT'S WHAT I'M GONNA DO) *East West 7935* | .... | 67 | 2 wks |

Robert HOWARD – *See Kym MAZELLE*

HOWLIN' WOLF *US, male vocalist* — **5 wks**

| 4 Jun 64 | | SMOKESTACK LIGHTNIN' *Pye International 7N 25244* | .... | 42 | 5 wks |

H₂O *UK, male vocal/instrumental group* — **16 wks**

H_2O *UK, male vocal/instrumental group* — **16 wks**

| 21 May 83 | | DREAM TO SLEEP *RCA 330* | .... | 17 | 10 wks |
| 13 Aug 83 | | JUST OUTSIDE OF HEAVEN *RCA 349* | .... | 38 | 6 wks |

Al HUDSON *US, male vocalist* — **22 wks**

9 Sep 78		DANCE, GET DOWN/HOW DO YOU DO *ABC 4229*	....	57	4 wks
15 Sep 79		YOU CAN DO IT *MCA 511 **	....	15	10 wks
8 Dec 79		MUSIC *MCA 542 ***	....	56	6 wks
29 Jun 85		LET'S TALK *MCA 972 ***	....	64	2 wks

* Al Hudson and the Partners ** One Way featuring Al Hudson

Lavine HUDSON *UK, female vocalist* — **3 wks**

| 21 May 88 | | INTERVENTION *Virgin VS 1067* | .... | 57 | 3 wks |

HUDSON-FORD *UK, male vocal/instrumental duo* — **20 wks**

18 Aug 73	●	PICK UP THE PIECES *A & M AMS 7078*	....	8	9 wks
16 Feb 74		BURN BABY BURN *A & M AMS 7096*	....	15	9 wks
29 Jun 74		FLOATING IN THE WIND *A & M AMS 7116*	....	35	2 wks

See also Monks.

HUE AND CRY *UK, male vocal/instrumental duo* — **55 wks**

| 13 Jun 87 | ● | LABOUR OF LOVE *Circa YR 4* | .... | 6 | 16 wks |
| 19 Sep 87 | | STRENGTH TO STRENGTH *Circa YR 6* | .... | 46 | 5 wks |

HOTLEGS (left to right: Eric Stewart, Kevin Godley and Lol Creme) perform 'Neanderthal Man' on television.

Right: WHITNEY HOUSTON holds the record for Most Consecutive Number Ones on the *US Billboard* Hot 100, seven.

The business practice of target marketing was best exemplified by EMI's promotion of IRON MAIDEN, who in the early 90s combined high positions with low weeks on chart.

JULIO IGLESIAS AND WILLIE NELSON give a live performance of 'To All the Girls I've Loved Before'.

30 Jan 88	**I REFUSE** Circa YR 8 ....**47**	3 wks
22 Oct 88	**ORDINARY ANGEL** Circa YR 18 ....**42**	6 wks
28 Jan 89	**LOOKING FOR LINDA** Circa YR 24 ....**15**	9 wks
6 May 89	**VIOLENTLY (EP)** Circa YR 29 ....**21**	6 wks
30 Sep 89	**SWEET INVISIBILITY** Circa YR 37 ....**55**	3 wks
25 May 91	**MY SALT HEART** Circa YR 64 ....**47**	3 wks
3 Aug 91	**LONG TERM LOVERS OF PAIN (EP)** Circa YR 71 .....**48**	3 wks
11 Jul 92	**PROFOUNDLY YOURS** Fidelity FIDEL 1 ....**74**	1 wk

Tracks on Violently (EP): *Violently/The Man With The Child In His Eyes/Calamity John.*
Tracks on Long Term Lovers Of Pain (EP): *Long Term Lovers Of Pain/Heart Of Saturday Night/Remember And Gold/Stars Crash Down.*

HUES CORPORATION *US, male/female vocal group* **16 wks**

27 Jul 74	● **ROCK THE BOAT** RCA APBO 0232 ....**6**	10 wks
19 Oct 74	**ROCKIN' SOUL** RCA PB 10066 ....**24**	6 wks

David HUGHES *UK, male vocalist* **1 wk**

21 Sep 56	**BY THE FOUNTAINS OF ROME** Philips PB 606 ....**27**	1 wk

HUGO and LUIGI *US, male vocal duo* **2 wks**

24 Jul 59	**LA PLUME DE MA TANTE** RCA 1127 ....**29**	2 wks

HUMAN LEAGUE **131 wks**
UK, male/female vocal/instrumental group

3 May 80	**HOLIDAY 80 (DOUBLE SINGLE)** Virgin SV 105 ....**56**	5 wks
21 Jun 80	**EMPIRE STATE HUMAN** Virgin VS 351 ....**62**	2 wks
28 Feb 81	**BOYS AND GIRLS** Virgin VS 395 ....**48**	4 wks
2 May 81	**THE SOUND OF THE CROWD** Virgin VS 416 ....**12**	10 wks
8 Aug 81	● **LOVE ACTION (I BELIEVE IN LOVE)** Virgin VS 435 ....**3**	13 wks
10 Oct 81	● **OPEN YOUR HEART** Virgin VS 453 ....**6**	9 wks
5 Dec 81	★ **DON'T YOU WANT ME** Virgin VS 466 ......**1**	13 wks
9 Jan 82	● **BEING BOILED** EMI FAST 4 ....**6**	9 wks
6 Feb 82	**HOLIDAY 80** (DOUBLE SINGLE) **(re-entry)** Virgin SV 105 ....**46**	5 wks
20 Nov 82	● **MIRROR MAN** Virgin VS 522 ....**2**	10 wks
23 Apr 83	● **(KEEP FEELING) FASCINATION** Virgin VS 569 ....**2**	9 wks
5 May 84	**THE LEBANON** Virgin VS 672 ....**11**	6 wks
23 Jun 84	**THE LEBANON (re-entry)** Virgin VS 672 .....**75**	1 wk
30 Jun 84	**LIFE ON YOUR OWN** Virgin VS 688 ....**16**	6 wks
17 Nov 84	**LOUISE** Virgin VS 723 ....**13**	10 wks
23 Aug 86	● **HUMAN** Virgin VS 880 ....**8**	8 wks
22 Nov 86	**I NEED YOUR LOVING** Virgin VS 900 ....**72**	1 wk
15 Oct 88	**LOVE IS ALL THAT MATTERS** Virgin VS 1025 ......**41**	5 wks
18 Aug 90	**HEART LIKE A WHEEL** Virgin VS 1262 ....**29**	5 wks

Tracks on double single: Being Boiled/Marianne/Rock And Roll - Nightclubbing/Dancevision.

HUMAN RESOURCE **14 wks**
Holland, male instrumental/production group

14 Sep 91	**DOMINATOR** R&S RSUK 4 ....**36**	7 wks
21 Dec 91	**THE COMPLETE DOMINATOR (re-mix)** R&S RSUK 4X **18**	7 wks

HUMANOID *UK, male producer* **13 wks**

26 Nov 88	**STAKKER HUMANOID** Westside WSR 12 .....**17**	8 wks
22 Apr 89	**SLAM** Westside WSR 14 ....**54**	2 wks
8 Aug 92	**STAKKER HUMANOID (re-issue)** Jumpin' + Pumpin' TOT 27 ....**40**	3 wks

HUMBLE PIE *UK, male vocal/instrumental group* **10 wks**

23 Aug 69	● **NATURAL BORN BUGIE** Immediate IM 082 ....**4**	10 wks

British Hit Singles Part One: Alphabetically by Artist
Date of chart entry/Title & catalogue no./Peak position reached/Weeks on chart
★ Number one ● Top Ten † still on chart at 31 Dec 1992
* = credited to act billed in footnote

Engelbert HUMPERDINCK *UK, male vocalist* **235 wks**

26 Jan 67	★ **RELEASE ME** Decca F 12541 ....**1**	56 wks
25 May 67	● **THERE GOES MY EVERYTHING** Decca F 12610 ...**2**	29 wks
23 Aug 67	★ **THE LAST WALTZ** Decca F 12655 ....**1**	27 wks
10 Jan 68	● **AM I THAT EASY TO FORGET** Decca F 12722 ....**3**	13 wks
24 Apr 68	● **A MAN WITHOUT LOVE** Decca F 12770 ....**2**	15 wks
25 Sep 68	● **LES BICYCLETTES DE BELSIZE** Decca F 12834 ...**5**	15 wks
5 Feb 69	● **THE WAY IT USED TO BE** Decca F 12879 ....**3**	14 wks
9 Aug 69	**I'M A BETTER MAN** Decca F 12957 ....**15**	13 wks
15 Nov 69	● **WINTER WORLD OF LOVE** Decca F 12980 ....**7**	13 wks
30 May 70	**MY MARIE** Decca F 13032 ....**31**	7 wks
12 Sep 70	**SWEETHEART** Decca F 13068 ....**22**	6 wks
31 Oct 70	**SWEETHEART (re-entry)** Decca F 13068 ....**50**	1 wk
11 Sep 71	**ANOTHER TIME ANOTHER PLACE** Decca F 13212 ...**13**	12 wks
4 Mar 72	**TOO BEAUTIFUL TO LAST** Decca F 13281 ....**14**	10 wks
20 Oct 73	**LOVE IS ALL** Decca F 13443 ....**44**	3 wks
17 Nov 73	**LOVE IS ALL (re-entry)** Decca F 13443 ....**45**	1 wk

Geraldine HUNT *Canada, female vocalist* **5 wks**

25 Oct 80	**CAN'T FAKE THE FEELING** Champagne FIZZ 501 ....**44**	5 wks

Marsha HUNT *US, female vocalist* **3 wks**

21 May 69	**WALK ON GILDED SPLINTERS** Track 604 030 .....**46**	2 wks
2 May 70	**KEEP THE CUSTOMER SATISFIED** Track 604 037 ....**41**	1 wk

Tommy HUNT *US, male vocalist* **17 wks**

11 Oct 75	**CRACKIN' UP** Spark SRL 1132 ....**39**	5 wks
21 Aug 76	**LOVING ON THE LOSING SIDE** Spark SRL 1146 ....**28**	9 wks
4 Dec 76	**ONE FINE MORNING** Spark SRL 1148 ....**44**	3 wks

Ian HUNTER *UK, male vocalist* **10 wks**

3 May 75	**ONCE BITTEN TWICE SHY** CBS 3194 ....**14**	10 wks

Tab HUNTER *US, male vocalist* **30 wks**

8 Feb 57	★ **YOUNG LOVE** London HLD 8380 ....**1**	18 wks
12 Apr 57	● **99 WAYS** London HLD 8410 ....**5**	11 wks
5 Jul 57	**99 WAYS (re-entry)** London HLD 8410 ....**29**	1 wk

Steve 'Silk' HURLEY *US, male vocalist* **9 wks**

10 Jan 87	★ **JACK YOUR BODY** DJ International LON 117 ....**1**	9 wks

HURRICANES – *See JOHNNY and the HURRICANES*

Phil HURTT *US, male vocalist* **5 wks**

11 Nov 78	**GIVING IT BACK** Fantasy FTC 161 ....**36**	5 wks

Willie HUTCH *US, male vocalist* **8 wks**

4 Dec 82	**IN AND OUT** Motown TMG 1285 ....**51**	7 wks
6 Jul 85	**KEEP ON JAMMIN'** Motown ZB 40173 ....**73**	1 wk

June HUTTON and Axel STORDAHL with the BOYS NEXT DOOR — 7 wks

US, female vocalist and male orchestra with male vocal group

7 Aug 53	●	SAY YOU'RE MINE AGAIN *Capitol CL 13918*	10	3 wks
4 Sep 53	●	SAY YOU'RE MINE AGAIN (re-entry) *Capitol CL 13918*	6	4 wks

HWA featuring SONIC THE HEDGEHOG — 4 wks

UK, male producer - Jeremy Healey

5 Dec 92	SUPERSONIC *Internal Affairs*	33†	4 wks

Brian HYLAND — US, male vocalist — 72 wks

7 Jul 60	●	ITSY BITSY TEENY WEENY YELLOW POLKA DOT BIKINI *London HLR 9161*	8	13 wks
20 Oct 60		FOUR LITTLE HEELS *London HLR 9203*	29	6 wks
10 May 62	●	GINNY COME LATELY *HMV POP 1013*	5	15 wks
2 Aug 62	●	SEALED WITH A KISS *HMV POP 1051*	3	15 wks
8 Nov 62		WARMED OVER KISSES *HMV POP 1079*	28	6 wks
27 Mar 71		GYPSY WOMAN *Uni UN 530*	45	1 wk
10 Apr 71		GYPSY WOMAN (re-entry) *Uni UN 530*	42	5 wks
28 Jun 75	●	SEALED WITH A KISS (re-issue) *ABC 4059*	7	11 wks

Sheila HYLTON — Jamaica, female vocalist — 12 wks

15 Sep 79	BREAKFAST IN BED *United Artists BP 304*	57	5 wks
17 Jan 81	THE BED'S TOO BIG WITHOUT YOU *Island WIP 6671*	35	7 wks

Phyllis HYMAN — US, female vocalist — 9 wks

16 Feb 80	YOU KNOW HOW TO LOVE ME *Arista ARIST 323*	47	6 wks
12 Sep 81	YOU SURE LOOK GOOD TO ME *Arista ARIST 424*	56	3 wks

Dick HYMAN TRIO — 10 wks

US, male instrumental group, Dick Hyman, keyboards

16 Mar 56	●	THEME FROM 'THE THREEPENNY OPERA' *MGM 890*	9	10 wks

Chrissie HYNDE – *See MOODSWINGS featuring Chrissie HYNDE; UB40*

HYPER GO GO — UK, male instrumental/production duo — 5 wks

22 Aug 92	HIGH *Deconstruction 74321110497*	30	5 wks

HYPNOTIST — UK, male producer - Caspar Pound — 5 wks

28 Sep 91	THE HOUSE IS MINE *Rising High RSN 4*	68	2 wks
21 Dec 91	THE HARDCORE EP *Rising High RSN 13*	65	3 wks

Tracks on The Hardcore EP: Hardcore U Know The Score/The Ride/Night Of The Livin' E Heads/God Of The Universe.

HYSTERICS — UK, male vocal/instrumental group — 5 wks

12 Dec 81	JINGLE BELLS LAUGHING ALL THE WAY *Record Delivery KA 5*	44	5 wks

Janis IAN — US, female vocalist — 10 wks

17 Nov 79	FLY TOO HIGH *CBS 7936*	44	7 wks
28 Jun 80	THE OTHER SIDE OF THE SUN *CBS 8611*	44	3 wks

ICEHOUSE — New Zealand, male vocal/instrumental group — 28 wks

5 Feb 83	HEY LITTLE GIRL *Chrysalis CHS 2670*	17	10 wks
23 Apr 83	STREET CAFE *Chrysalis COOL 1*	62	4 wks
3 May 86	NO PROMISES *Chrysalis CHS 2978*	72	1 wk
29 Aug 87	CRAZY *Chrysalis CHS 3156*	74	1 wk
13 Feb 88	CRAZY (re-entry) *Chrysalis CHS 3156*	38	8 wks
14 May 88	ELECTRIC BLUE *Chrysalis CHS 3239*	53	4 wks

ICE-T — US, male rapper — 7 wks

18 Mar 89	HIGH ROLLERS *Sire W 7574*	63	2 wks
17 Feb 90	YOU PLAYED YOURSELF *Sire W 9994*	64	2 wks
29 Sep 90	SUPERFLY 1990 *Capitol CL 586* *	48	3 wks

* Curtis Mayfield and Ice-T

ICICLE WORKS — UK, male vocal/instrumental group — 28 wks

24 Dec 83	LOVE IS A WONDERFUL COLOUR *Beggars Banquet BEG 99*	15	8 wks
10 Mar 84	BIRDS FLY (WHISPER TO A SCREAM)/IN THE CAULDRON OF LOVE *Beggars Banquet BEG 108*	53	4 wks
26 Jul 86	UNDERSTANDING JANE *Beggars Banquet BEG 160*	52	3 wks
4 Oct 86	WHO DO YOU WANT FOR YOUR LOVE *Beggars Banquet BEG 172*	54	4 wks
14 Feb 87	EVANGELINE *Beggars Banquet BEG 181*	53	4 wks
30 Apr 88	LITTLE GIRL LOST *Beggars Banquet BEG 215*	59	4 wks
17 Mar 90	MOTORCYCLE RIDER *Epic WORKS 100*	73	1 wk

IDES OF MARCH — US, male vocal/instrumental group — 9 wks

6 Jun 70	VEHICLE *Warner Bros. WB 7378*	31	9 wks

Billy IDOL — UK, male vocalist — 101 wks

11 Sep 82		HOT IN THE CITY *Chrysalis CHS 2625*	58	4 wks
24 Mar 84		REBEL YELL *Chrysalis IDOL 2*	62	2 wks
30 Jun 84		EYES WITHOUT A FACE *Chrysalis IDOL 3*	18	11 wks
29 Sep 84		FLESH FOR FANTASY *Chrysalis IDOL 4*	54	3 wks
13 Jul 85	●	WHITE WEDDING *Chrysalis IDOL 5*	6	15 wks
14 Sep 85	●	REBEL YELL (re-issue) *Chrysalis IDOL 6*	6	12 wks
4 Oct 86		TO BE A LOVER *Chrysalis IDOL 8*	22	8 wks
7 Mar 87		DON'T NEED A GUN *Chrysalis IDOL 9*	26	5 wks
13 Jun 87		SWEET SIXTEEN *Chrysalis IDOL 10*	17	9 wks
3 Oct 87	●	MONY MONY *Chrysalis IDOL 11*	7	10 wks
16 Jan 88		HOT IN THE CITY (re-mix) *Chrysalis IDOL 12*	13	9 wks
13 Aug 88		CATCH MY FALL *Chrysalis IDOL 13*	63	3 wks
28 Apr 90		CRADLE OF LOVE *Chrysalis IDOL 14*	34	4 wks
11 Aug 90		L.A. WOMAN *Chrysalis IDOL 15*	70	2 wks
22 Dec 90		PRODIGAL BLUES *Chrysalis IDOL 16*	47	4 wks

Frank IFIELD — UK, male vocalist — 162 wks

19 Feb 60	LUCKY DEVIL *Columbia DB 4399*	22	5 wks
7 Apr 60	LUCKY DEVIL (re-entry) *Columbia DB 4399*	33	2 wks
29 Sep 60	GOTTA GET A DATE *Columbia DB 4496*	49	1 wk

5 Jul 62 ★	**I REMEMBER YOU** *Columbia DB 4856*	**1**	28 wks
25 Oct 62 ★	**LOVESICK BLUES** *Columbia DB 4913*	**1**	17 wks
24 Jan 63 ★	**WAYWARD WIND** *Columbia DB 4960*	**1**	13 wks
11 Apr 63 ●	**NOBODY'S DARLIN' BUT MINE** *Columbia DB 7007*	**4**	16 wks
27 Jun 63 ★	**CONFESSIN'** *Columbia DB 7062*	**1**	16 wks
17 Oct 63	**MULE TRAIN** *Columbia DB 7131*	**22**	6 wks
9 Jan 64 ●	**DON'T BLAME ME** *Columbia DB 7184*	**8**	13 wks
23 Apr 64	**ANGRY AT THE BIG OAK TREE** *Columbia DB 7263*	**25**	8 wks
23 Jul 64	**I SHOULD CARE** *Columbia DB 7319*	**33**	3 wks
1 Oct 64	**SUMMER IS OVER** *Columbia DB 7355*	**25**	6 wks
19 Aug 65	**PARADISE** *Columbia DB 7655*	**26**	9 wks
23 Jun 66	**NO ONE WILL EVER KNOW** *Columbia DB 7940*	**25**	4 wks
8 Dec 66	**CALL HER YOUR SWEETHEART** *Columbia DB 8078*	**24**	11 wks
7 Dec 91	**THE YODELLING SONG** *EMI 7YODEL 1 **	**40**	4 wks

* Frank Ifield featuring the Backroom Boys

Julio IGLESIAS *Spain, male vocalist*   **66 wks**

24 Oct 81 ★	**BEGIN THE BEGUINE (VOLVER A EMPEZAR)** *CBS A 1612*	**1**	14 wks
6 Mar 82 ●	**QUIEREME MUCHO (YOURS)** *CBS A 1939*	**3**	9 wks
9 Oct 82	**AMOR** *CBS A 2801*	**32**	7 wks
9 Apr 83	**HEY!** *CBS JULIO 1*	**31**	7 wks
7 Apr 84	**TO ALL THE GIRLS I'VE LOVED BEFORE** *CBS A 4252 **	**17**	10 wks
7 Jul 84	**ALL OF YOU** *CBS A 4522 ***	**43**	8 wks
6 Aug 88 ●	**MY LOVE** *CBS JULIO 2 ****	**5**	11 wks

* Julio Iglesias and Willie Nelson ** Julio Iglesias and Diana Ross *** Julio Iglesias featuring Stevie Wonder

I-LEVEL *UK, male vocal/instrumental group*   **9 wks**

16 Apr 83	**MINEFIELD** *Virgin VS 563*	**52**	6 wks
18 Jun 83	**TEACHER** *Virgin VS 595*	**56**	3 wks

IMAGINATION *UK, male vocal/instrumental group*   **105 wks**

16 May 81 ●	**BODY TALK** *R & B RBS 201*	**4**	18 wks
5 Sep 81	**IN AND OUT OF LOVE** *R & B RBS 202*	**16**	9 wks
14 Nov 81	**FLASHBACK** *R & B RBS 206*	**16**	13 wks
6 Mar 82 ●	**JUST AN ILLUSION** *R & B RBS 208*	**2**	11 wks
26 Jun 82 ●	**MUSIC AND LIGHTS** *R & B RBS 210*	**5**	9 wks
25 Sep 82	**IN THE HEAT OF THE NIGHT** *R & B RBS 211*	**22**	8 wks
11 Dec 82	**CHANGES** *R & B RBS 213*	**31**	8 wks
4 Jun 83	**LOOKING AT MIDNIGHT** *R & B RBS 214*	**29**	7 wks
5 Nov 83	**NEW DIMENSIONS** *R & B RBS 216*	**56**	3 wks
26 May 84	**STATE OF LOVE** *R & B RBS 218*	**67**	2 wks
24 Nov 84	**THANK YOU MY LOVE** *R & B RBS 219*	**22**	15 wks
16 Jan 88	**INSTINCTUAL** *RCA PB 41697*	**62**	2 wks

IMMACULATE FOOLS   **4 wks**
UK, male vocal/instrumental group

26 Jan 85	**IMMACULATE FOOLS** *A & M AM 227*	**51**	4 wks

IMPALAS *US, male vocal group*   **1 wk**

21 Aug 59	**SORRY (I RAN ALL THE WAY HOME)** *MGM 1015*	**28**	1 wk

IMPEDANCE *UK, male producer - Daniel Haydon*   **4 wks**

11 Nov 89	**TAINTED LOVE** *Jumpin' & Pumpin' TOT 4*	**54**	4 wks

IMPERIALS – *See LITTLE ANTHONY and the IMPERIALS*

IMPOSTER – *See Elvis COSTELLO*

IMPRESSIONS *US, male vocal group*   **10 wks**

22 Nov 75	**FIRST IMPRESSIONS** *Curtom K 16638*	**16**	10 wks

IN CROWD *UK, male vocal/instrumental group*   **1 wk**

20 May 65	**THAT'S HOW STRONG MY LOVE IS** *Parlophone R 5276*	**48**	1 wk

IN TUA NUA *Ireland, male/female vocal/instrumental group*   **2 wks**

14 May 88	**ALL I WANTED** *Virgin VS 1072*	**69**	2 wks

INCANTATION *UK, male instrumental group*   **12 wks**

4 Dec 82	**CACHARPAYA (ANDES PUMPSA DAESI)** *Beggars Banquet BEG 84*	**12**	12 wks

INCOGNITO *France/UK, male/female instrumental group*   **21 wks**

15 Nov 80	**PARISIENNE GIRL** *Ensign ENY 44*	**73**	2 wks
29 Jun 91 ●	**ALWAYS THERE** *Talkin Loud TLK 10 **	**6**	9 wks
14 Sep 91	**CRAZY FOR YOU** *Talkin Loud TLK 14 ***	**59**	2 wks
6 Jun 92	**DON'T YOU WORRY 'BOUT A THING** *Talkin Loud TLK 21*	**19**	6 wks
15 Aug 92	**CHANGE** *Talkin Loud TLK 26*	**52**	2 wks

* Incognito featuring Jocelyn Brown ** Incognito featuring Chyna

INDEEP *US, male/female vocal duo*   **11 wks**

22 Jan 83	**LAST NIGHT A DJ SAVED MY LIFE** *Sound of New York SNY 1*	**13**	9 wks
14 May 83	**WHEN BOYS TALK** *Sound of New York SNY 3*	**67**	2 wks

Los INDIOS TABAJARAS   **17 wks**
Brazil, male instrumental duo - guitars

31 Oct 63 ●	**MARIA ELENA** *RCA 1365*	**5**	17 wks

INGRAM *US, male vocal/instrumental group*   **2 wks**

11 Jun 83	**SMOOTHIN' GROOVIN'** *Streetwave WAVE 3*	**56**	2 wks

James INGRAM *US, male vocalist*   **40 wks**

12 Feb 83	**BABY COME TO ME** *Qwest K 15005 **	**11**	10 wks
18 Feb 84	**YAH MO B THERE** *Qwest W 9394 ***	**44**	5 wks
7 Apr 84	**YAH MO B THERE (re-entry)** *Qwest W 9394 ***	**69**	3 wks
12 Jan 85	**YAH MO B THERE (re-mix)** *Qwest W 9394 ***	**12**	8 wks
11 Jul 87 ●	**SOMEWHERE OUT THERE** *MCA MCA 1132 ****	**8**	13 wks
31 Mar 90	**SECRET GARDEN** *Qwest W 9992 *****	**67**	1 wk

* Patti Austin and James Ingram ** James Ingram with Michael McDonald *** Linda Ronstadt and James Ingram **** Quincy Jones featuring Al B Sure!, James Ingram, El DeBarge and Barry White

INK SPOTS *US, male vocal group*   **4 wks**

29 Apr 55 ●	**MELODY OF LOVE** *Parlophone R 3977*	**10**	4 wks

John INMAN *UK, male vocalist*   **6 wks**

25 Oct 75	**ARE YOU BEING SERVED SIR** *DJM DJS 602*	**39**	6 wks

INMATES *UK, male vocal/instrumental group*   **9 wks**

8 Dec 79	**THE WALK** *Radar ADA 47*	**36**	9 wks

INNER CIRCLE *Jamaica, male vocal/instrumental group* **16 wks**

24 Feb 79	**EVERYTHING IS GREAT** *Island WIP 6472*	37	8 wks
12 May 79	**STOP BREAKING MY HEART** *Island WIP 6488*	50	3 wks
31 Oct 92	**SWEAT (A LA LA LA LA LONG)** *Magnet 9031776802*	43	5 wks

INNER CITY *US, male/female vocal/instrumental duo* **67 wks**

3 Sep 88 ●	**BIG FUN** *10 TEN 240 **	8	14 wks
10 Dec 88 ●	**GOOD LIFE** *10 TEN 249*	4	12 wks
22 Apr 89 ●	**AIN'T NOBODY BETTER** *10 TEN 252*	10	7 wks
29 Jul 89	**DO YOU LOVE WHAT YOU FEEL** *10 TEN 237*	16	7 wks
18 Nov 89	**WATCHA GONNA DO WITH MY LOVIN'** *10 TEN 290*	12	9 wks
13 Oct 90	**THAT MAN (HE'S ALL MINE)** *10 TEN 334*	42	4 wks
23 Feb 91	**TILL WE MEET AGAIN** *Ten TEN 337*	47	2 wks
7 Dec 91	**LET IT REIGN** *Ten TEN 392*	51	1 wk
4 Apr 92	**HALLELUJAH '92** *Ten TEN 398*	22	4 wks
13 Jun 92	**PENNIES FROM HEAVEN** *Ten TEN 405*	24	4 wks
12 Sep 92	**PRAISE** *Ten TENX 408*	59	2 wks

* Inner City featuring Kevin Saunderson

INNOCENCE *UK, male/female vocal/instrumental group* **33 wks**

3 Mar 90	**NATURAL THING** *Cooltempo COOL 201*	16	7 wks
21 Jul 90	**SILENT VOICE** *Cooltempo COOL 212*	37	5 wks
13 Oct 90	**LET'S PUSH IT** *Cooltempo COOL 220*	25	6 wks
8 Dec 90	**A MATTER OF FACT** *Cooltempo COOL 223*	37	7 wks
30 Mar 91	**REMEMBER THE DAY** *Cooltempo COOL 226*	56	2 wks
20 Jun 92	**I'LL BE THERE** *Cooltempo COOL 255*	26	3 wks
3 Oct 92	**ONE LOVE IN MY LIFETIME** *Cooltempo COOL 263*	40	2 wks
21 Nov 92	**BUILD** *Cooltempo COOL 267*	72	1 wk

INSPIRAL CARPETS *UK, male vocal/instrumental group* **39 wks**

18 Nov 89	**MOVE** *Cow DUNG 6*	49	2 wks
17 Mar 90	**THIS IS HOW IT FEELS** *Cow DUNG 7*	14	8 wks
30 Jun 90	**SHE COMES IN THE FALL** *Cow DUNG 10*	27	6 wks
17 Nov 90	**ISLAND HEAD EP** *Cow DUNG 11*	21	4 wks
30 Mar 91	**CARAVAN** *Cow DUNG 13*	30	7 wks
22 Jun 91	**PLEASE BE CRUEL** *Cow DUNG 15*	50	2 wks
29 Feb 92	**DRAGGING ME DOWN** *Cow DUNG 16*	12	5 wks
30 May 92	**TWO WORLDS COLLIDE** *Cow DUNG 17*	32	2 wks
19 Sep 92	**GENERATIONS** *Cow DUNG 18T*	28	3 wks
14 Nov 92	**BITCHES BREW** *Cow DUNG 20T*	36	2 wks

Tracks on Island Head EP: *Biggest Mountain/Gold Top/Weakness/I'll Keep It In Mind*.

INSPIRATIONAL CHOIR *US, male/female choir* **11 wks**

22 Dec 84	**ABIDE WITH ME** *Epic A 4997*	44	5 wks
14 Dec 85	**ABIDE WITH ME (re-issue)** *Portrait A 4997*	36	6 wks

Label credits the Royal Choral Society.

INSTANT FUNK *US, male vocal/instrumental group* **5 wks**

20 Jan 79	**GOT MY MIND MADE UP** *Salsoul SSOL 114*	46	5 wks

INTASTELLA *UK, male/female vocal/instrumental group* **5 wks**

25 May 91	**DREAM SOME PARADISE** *MCA MCS 1520*	69	1 wk
24 Aug 91	**PEOPLE** *MCA MCS 1559*	74	2 wks
16 Nov 91	**CENTURY** *MCA MCS 1585*	70	2 wks

INTELLIGENT HOODLUM *US, male rap group* **3 wks**

6 Oct 90	**BACK TO REALITY** *A & M AM 598*	55	3 wks

INTRUDERS *US, male vocal group* **21 wks**

13 Apr 74	**I'LL ALWAYS LOVE MY MAMA** *Philadelphia International PIR 2149*	32	7 wks
6 Jul 74	**(WIN PLACE OR SHOW) SHE'S A WINNER** *Philadelphia International PIR 2212*	14	9 wks
22 Dec 84	**WHO DO YOU LOVE?** *Streetwave KHAN 34*	65	5 wks

INVADERS OF THE HEART – See Jah WOBBLE'S INVADERS OF THE HEART

INVISIBLE GIRLS – See Pauline MURRAY and the INVISIBLE GIRLS

INXS *Australia, male vocal/instrumental group* **99 wks**

19 Apr 86	**WHAT YOU NEED** *Mercury INXS 5*	51	6 wks
28 Jun 86	**LISTEN LIKE THIEVES** *Mercury INXS 6*	46	7 wks
30 Aug 86	**KISS THE DIRT (FALLING DOWN THE MOUNTAIN)** *Mercury INXS 7*	54	3 wks
24 Oct 87	**NEED YOU TONIGHT** *Mercury INXS 8*	58	3 wks
9 Jan 88	**NEW SENSATION** *Mercury INXS 9*	25	6 wks
12 Mar 88	**DEVIL INSIDE** *Mercury INXS 10*	47	5 wks
25 Jun 88	**NEVER TEAR US APART** *Mecury INXS 11*	24	7 wks
12 Nov 88 ●	**NEED YOU TONIGHT (re-issue)** *Mercury INXS 12*	2	11 wks
8 Apr 89	**MYSTIFY** *Mercury INXS 13*	14	7 wks
15 Sep 90	**SUICIDE BLONDE** *Mercury INXS 14*	11	6 wks
8 Dec 90	**DISAPPEAR** *Mercury INXS 15*	21	8 wks
26 Jan 91	**GOOD TIMES** *Atlantic A 7751 **	18	8 wks
30 Mar 91	**BY MY SIDE** *Mercury INXS 16*	42	4 wks
13 Jul 91	**BITTER TEARS** *Mercury INXS 17*	30	3 wks
2 Nov 91	**SHINING STAR (EP)** *Mercury INXS 18*	27	3 wks
18 Jul 92	**HEAVEN SENT** *Mercury INXS 19*	31	3 wks
5 Sep 92	**BABY DON'T CRY** *Mercury INXS 20*	20	5 wks
14 Nov 92	**TASTE IT** *Mercury INXS 23*	21	4 wks

* Jimmy Barnes and INXS

Tracks on Shining Star (EP): *Shining Star/Send A Message (Live)/Faith In Each Other (Live)/Bitter Tears (Live)*.

Sweetie IRIE – See ASWAD; SCRITTI POLITTI

Tippa IRIE *UK, male vocalist* **10 wks**

22 Mar 86	**HELLO DARLING** *Greensleeves/UK Bubblers TIPPA 4*	22	7 wks
19 Jul 86	**HEARTBEAT** *Greensleeves/UK Bubblers TIPPA 5*	59	3 wks

IRON MAIDEN *UK, male vocal/instrumental group* **132 wks**

23 Feb 80	**RUNNING FREE** *EMI 5032*	34	5 wks
7 Jun 80	**SANCTUARY** *EMI 5065*	29	5 wks
8 Nov 80	**WOMEN IN UNIFORM** *EMI 5105*	35	4 wks
14 Mar 81	**TWILIGHT ZONE/WRATH CHILD** *EMI 5145*	31	5 wks
27 Jun 81	**PURGATORY** *EMI 5184*	52	3 wks
26 Sep 81	**MAIDEN JAPAN** *EMI 5219*	43	4 wks
20 Feb 82 ●	**RUN TO THE HILLS** *EMI 5263*	7	10 wks
15 May 82	**THE NUMBER OF THE BEAST** *EMI 5287*	18	8 wks
23 Apr 83	**FLIGHT OF ICARUS** *EMI 5378*	11	6 wks
2 Jul 83	**THE TROOPER** *EMI 5397*	12	7 wks
18 Aug 84	**2 MINUTES TO MIDNIGHT** *EMI 5849*	11	6 wks
3 Nov 84	**ACES HIGH** *EMI 5502*	20	5 wks
5 Oct 85	**RUNNING FREE (LIVE)** *EMI 5532*	19	5 wks
14 Dec 85	**RUN TO THE HILLS (LIVE)** *EMI 5542*	26	6 wks
6 Sep 86	**WASTED YEARS** *EMI EMI 5583*	18	4 wks
22 Nov 86	**STRANGER IN A STRANGE LAND** *EMI EMI 5589*	22	4 wks
27 Dec 86	**STRANGER IN A STRANGE LAND (re-entry)** *EMI EMI 5589*	71	2 wks
26 Mar 88 ●	**CAN I PLAY WITH MADNESS** *EMI EM 49*	3	6 wks
13 Aug 88 ●	**THE EVIL THAT MEN DO** *EMI EM 64*	5	6 wks
19 Nov 88 ●	**THE CLAIRVOYANT** *EMI EM 79*	6	8 wks
18 Nov 89 ●	**INFINITE DREAMS** *EMI EM 117*	6	5 wks
30 Dec 89	**INFINITE DREAMS (re-entry)** *EMI EM 117*	74	1 wk

22 Sep 90	● HOLY SMOKE EMI EM 153	3	4 wks
5 Jan 91	★ BRING YOUR DAUGHTER...TO THE SLAUGHTER EMI EMPD 171	1	5 wks
25 Apr 92	● BE QUICK OR BE DEAD EMI EM 229	2	4 wks
11 Jul 92	FROM HERE TO ETERNITY EMI EMS 240	21	4 wks

IRONHORSE Canada, male vocal/instrumental group — 3 wks

5 May 79	SWEET LUI-LOUISE Scotti Brothers K 11271	60	3 wks

Big Dee IRWIN US, male vocalist — 17 wks

21 Nov 63	● SWINGING ON A STAR Colpix PX 11010	7	17 wks

This hit was in fact a vocal duet by Big Dee Irwin and Little Eva, though she was not credited.

Chris ISAAK US, male vocalist — 17 wks

24 Nov 90	● WICKED GAME London LON 279	10	10 wks
2 Feb 91	BLUE HOTEL Reprise W 0005	17	7 wks

Ronald ISLEY – See Rod STEWART

ISLEY BROTHERS US, male vocal/instrumental group — 108 wks

25 Jul 63	TWIST AND SHOUT Stateside SS 112	42	1 wk
28 Apr 66	THIS OLD HEART OF MINE Tamla Motown TMG 555	47	1 wk
1 Sep 66	I GUESS I'LL ALWAYS LOVE YOU Tamla Motown TMG 572	45	2 wks
23 Oct 68	● THIS OLD HEART OF MINE (re-entry) Tamla Motown TMG 555	3	16 wks
15 Jan 69	I GUESS I'LL ALWAYS LOVE YOU (re-issue) Tamla Motown TMG 683	11	9 wks
16 Apr 69	● BEHIND A PAINTED SMILE Tamla Motown TMG 693	5	12 wks
25 Jun 69	IT'S YOUR THING Major Minor MM 621	30	5 wks
30 Aug 69	PUT YOURSELF IN MY PLACE Tamla Motown TMG 708	13	11 wks
22 Sep 73	THAT LADY Epic EPC 1704	14	9 wks
19 Jan 74	HIGHWAY OF MY LIFE Epic EPC 1980	25	8 wks
25 May 74	SUMMER BREEZE Epic EPC 2244	16	8 wks
10 Jul 76	● HARVEST FOR THE WORLD Epic EPC 4369	10	8 wks
13 May 78	TAKE ME TO THE NEXT PHASE Epic EPC 6292	50	4 wks
3 Nov 79	IT'S A DISCO NIGHT (ROCK DON'T STOP) Epic EPC 7911	14	11 wks
16 Jul 83	BETWEEN THE SHEETS Epic A 3513	52	3 wks

ISLEY JASPER ISLEY US, male vocal/instrumental group — 5 wks

23 Nov 85	CARAVAN OF LOVE Epic A 6612	52	5 wks

ISOTONIK UK, male producer - Chris Paul — 9 wks

11 Jan 92	DIFFERENT STROKES Ffrreedom TAB 101	12	5 wks
2 May 92	EVERYWHERE I GO/LET'S GET DOWN Ffrreedom TAB 108	25	4 wks

Let's Get Down only listed from 9 May 92.

IT BITES UK, male vocal/instrumental group — 21 wks

12 Jul 86	● CALLING ALL THE HEROES Virgin VS 872	6	12 wks
18 Oct 86	WHOLE NEW WORLD Virgin VS 896	54	3 wks
23 May 87	THE OLD MAN AND THE ANGEL Virgin VS 941	72	1 wk
13 May 89	STILL TOO YOUNG TO REMEMBER Virgin VS 1184	66	3 wks
24 Feb 90	STILL TOO YOUNG TO REMEMBER (re-issue) Virgin VS 1238	60	2 wks

IT'S IMMATERIAL UK, male vocal/instrumental group — 10 wks

12 Apr 86	DRIVING AWAY FROM HOME (JIM'S TUNE) Siren SIREN 15	18	7 wks

2 Aug 86	ED'S FUNKY DINER (FRIDAY NIGHT, SATURDAY MORNING) Siren SIREN 24	65	3 wks

Burl IVES US, male vocalist — 25 wks

25 Jan 62	● A LITTLE BITTY TEAR Brunswick 05863	9	15 wks
17 May 62	FUNNY WAY OF LAUGHIN' Brunswick 05868	29	10 wks

IVY LEAGUE UK, male vocal group — 31 wks

4 Feb 65	● FUNNY HOW LOVE CAN BE Piccadilly 7N 35222	8	9 wks
6 May 65	THAT'S WHY I'M CRYING Piccadilly 7N 35228	22	8 wks
24 Jun 65	● TOSSING AND TURNING Piccadilly 7N 35251	3	13 wks
14 Jul 66	WILLOW TREE Piccadilly 7N 35326	50	1 wk

IZIT UK, male/female vocal/instrumental group — 3 wks

2 Dec 89	STORIES ffrr F 122	52	3 wks

J

Lady J and SECRETARY of ENTERTAINMENT – See RAZE

JACK 'N' CHILL UK, male instrumental group — 21 wks

6 Jun 87	THE JACK THAT HOUSE BUILT Oval TEN 174	48	5 wks
9 Jan 88	● THE JACK THAT HOUSE BUILT (re-entry) Oval TEN 174	6	11 wks
9 Jul 88	BEATIN' THE HEAT 10 TEN 234	42	5 wks

Terry JACKS Canada, male vocalist — 21 wks

23 Mar 74	★ SEASONS IN THE SUN Bell 1344	1	12 wks
29 Jun 74	● IF YOU GO AWAY Bell 1362	8	9 wks

Chad JACKSON UK, male producer — 10 wks

2 Jun 90	● HEAR THE DRUMMER (GET WICKED) Big Wave BWR 36	3	10 wks

Dee D. JACKSON UK, female vocalist — 14 wks

22 Apr 78	● AUTOMATIC LOVER Mercury 6007 171	4	9 wks
2 Sep 78	METEOR MAN Mercury 6007 182	48	5 wks

Freddie JACKSON US, male vocalist — 30 wks

23 Nov 85	YOU ARE MY LADY Capitol CL 379	49	4 wks
22 Feb 86	ROCK ME TONIGHT (FOR OLD TIME'S SAKE) Capitol CL 358	18	9 wks
11 Oct 86	TASTY LOVE Capitol CL 428	73	1 wk
7 Feb 87	HAVE YOU EVER LOVED SOMEBODY Capitol CL 437	33	6 wks
9 Jul 88	NICE 'N' SLOW Capitol CL 502	56	2 wks
15 Oct 88	CRAZY (FOR ME) Capitol CL 510	41	3 wks
5 Sep 92	ME AND MRS JONES Capitol CL 668	32	5 wks

Janet JACKSON US, female vocalist — 109 wks

22 Mar 86	● WHAT HAVE YOU DONE FOR ME LATELY A & M AM 308	3	14 wks

31 May 86		NASTY *A & M AM 316*	19	9 wks
9 Aug 86	●	WHEN I THINK OF YOU *A & M AM 337*	10	10 wks
1 Nov 86		CONTROL *A & M AM 359*	42	5 wks
21 Mar 87	●	LET'S WAIT AWHILE *Breakout USA 601*	3	10 wks
13 Jun 87		PLEASURE PRINCIPLE *Breakout USA 604*	24	5 wks
14 Nov 87		FUNNY HOW TIME FLIES (WHEN YOU'RE HAVING FUN) *Breakout USA 613*	59	2 wks
2 Sep 89		MISS YOU MUCH *Breakout USA 663*	22	7 wks
4 Nov 89		RHYTHM NATION *Breakout USA 673*	23	5 wks
27 Jan 90		COME BACK TO ME *Breakout USA 681*	20	7 wks
31 Mar 90		ESCAPADE *Breakout USA 684*	17	7 wks
7 Jul 90		ALRIGHT *A & M USA 693*	20	5 wks
8 Sep 90		BLACK CAT *A & M EM 587*	15	6 wks
27 Oct 90		LOVE WILL NEVER DO (WITHOUT YOU) *A & M EM 700*	34	4 wks
15 Aug 92	●	THE BEST THINGS IN LIFE ARE FREE *Perspective PERSS 7400* *	2	13 wks

* Luther Vandross and Janet Jackson with special guests BBD and Ralph Tresvant

---

Jermaine JACKSON *US, male vocalist*   **43 wks**

10 May 80	●	LET'S GET SERIOUS *Motown TMG 1183*	8	11 wks
26 Jul 80		BURNIN' HOT *Motown TMG 1194*	32	6 wks
30 May 81		YOU LIKE ME DON'T YOU *Motown TMG 1222*	41	5 wks
12 May 84		SWEETEST SWEETEST *Arista JJK 1*	52	4 wks
27 Oct 84		WHEN THE RAIN BEGINS TO FALL *Arista ARIST 584* *	68	2 wks
16 Feb 85	●	DO WHAT YOU DO *Arista ARIST 609*	6	13 wks
21 Oct 89		DON'T TAKE IT PERSONAL *Arista 112634*	69	2 wks

* Jermaine Jackson and Pia Zadora

Joe JACKSON *UK, male vocalist*   **49 wks**

4 Aug 79		IS SHE REALLY GOING OUT WITH HIM? *A & M AMS 7459*	13	9 wks
12 Jan 80	●	IT'S DIFFERENT FOR GIRLS *A & M AMS 7493*	5	9 wks
4 Jul 81		JUMPIN' JIVE *A & M AMS 8145* *	43	5 wks
8 Jan 83	●	STEPPIN' OUT *A & M AMS 8262*	6	8 wks
12 Mar 83		BREAKING US IN TWO *A & M AM 101*	59	4 wks
28 Apr 84		HAPPY ENDING *A & M AM 186*	58	3 wks
7 Jul 84		BE MY NUMBER TWO *A & M AM 200*	70	2 wks
7 Jun 86		LEFT OF CENTER *A & M AM 320* **	32	9 wks

* Joe Jackson's Jumpin' Jive ** Suzanne Vega featuring Joe Jackson

---

Michael JACKSON *US, male vocalist*   **349 wks**

12 Feb 72	●	GOT TO BE THERE *Tamla Motown TMG 797*	5	11 wks
20 May 72	●	ROCKIN' ROBIN *Tamla Motown TMG 816*	3	14 wks
19 Aug 72	●	AIN'T NO SUNSHINE *Tamla Motown TMG 826*	8	11 wks
25 Nov 72	●	BEN *Tamla Motown TMG 834*	7	14 wks
18 Nov 78		EASE ON DOWN THE ROAD *MCA 396* *	45	4 wks
15 Sep 79	●	DON'T STOP TILL YOU GET ENOUGH *Epic EPC 7763*	3	12 wks
24 Nov 79	●	OFF THE WALL *Epic EPC 8045*	7	10 wks
9 Feb 80	●	ROCK WITH YOU *Epic EPC 8206*	7	9 wks
3 May 80	●	SHE'S OUT OF MY LIFE *Epic EPC 8384*	3	9 wks
26 Jul 80		GIRLFRIEND *Epic EPC 8782*	41	5 wks
23 May 81	★	ONE DAY IN YOUR LIFE *Motown TMG 976*	1	14 wks
1 Aug 81		WE'RE ALMOST THERE *Motown TMG 977*	46	4 wks
6 Nov 82	●	THE GIRL IS MINE *Epic EPC A 2729* **	8	9 wks
15 Jan 83		THE GIRL IS MINE (re-entry) *Epic EPC A 2729* **	75	1 wk
29 Jan 83	★	BILLIE JEAN *Epic EPC A 3084*	1	15 wks
9 Apr 83	●	BEAT IT *Epic EPC A 3258*	3	12 wks
11 Jun 83	●	WANNA BE STARTIN' SOMETHING *Epic A 3427*	8	9 wks
23 Jul 83		HAPPY (LOVE THEME FROM 'LADY SINGS THE BLUES') *Tamla Motown TMG 986*	52	3 wks

15 Oct 83	●	SAY SAY SAY *Parlophone R 6062* ***	2	15 wks
19 Nov 83	●	THRILLER *Epic A 3643*	10	18 wks
31 Mar 84	●	P.Y.T. (PRETTY YOUNG THING) *Epic A 4136*	11	8 wks
2 Jun 84	●	FAREWELL MY SUMMER LOVE *Motown TMG 1342*	7	12 wks
11 Aug 84		GIRL YOU'RE SO TOGETHER *Motown TMG 1355*	33	8 wks
8 Aug 87	★	I JUST CAN'T STOP LOVING YOU *Epic 650202 7*	1	9 wks
26 Sep 87	●	BAD *Epic 651155 7*	3	11 wks
5 Dec 87	●	THE WAY YOU MAKE ME FEEL *Epic 651275 7*	3	10 wks
20 Feb 88		MAN IN THE MIRROR *Epic 651388 7*	21	5 wks
28 May 88		GET IT *Motown ZB 41883* ****	37	4 wks
16 Jul 88	●	DIRTY DIANA *Epic 651546 7*	4	8 wks
10 Sep 88		ANOTHER PART OF ME *Epic 652844 7*	15	6 wks
26 Nov 88	●	SMOOTH CRIMINAL *Epic 653026 7*	8	10 wks
25 Feb 89	●	LEAVE ME ALONE *Epic 654672 7*	2	8 wks
15 Jul 89		LIBERIAN GIRL *Epic 654947 0*	13	6 wks
23 Nov 91	★	BLACK OR WHITE *Epic 6575987*	1	10 wks
18 Jan 92		BLACK OR WHITE (re-mix) *Epic 6577316*	14	4 wks
15 Feb 92	●	REMEMBER THE TIME/COME TOGETHER *Epic 6577747*	3	8 wks
2 May 92	●	IN THE CLOSET *Epic 6580187*	8	6 wks
25 Jul 92	●	WHO IS IT *Epic 6581797*	10	7 wks
12 Sep 92		JAM *Epic 6583607*	13	5 wks
5 Dec 92	●	HEAL THE WORLD *Epic 6584887*	2†	4 wks

* Diana Ross and Michael Jackson ** Michael Jackson and Paul McCartney *** Paul McCartney and Michael Jackson **** Stevie Wonder and Michael Jackson

Only the sleeve of I Just Can't Stop Loving You *credits Siedah Garrett.* Come Together *only listed from 7 Mar 92.*

Mick JACKSON *UK, male vocalist*   **16 wks**

30 Sep 78		BLAME IT ON THE BOOGIE *Atlantic K 11102*	15	8 wks
3 Feb 79		WEEKEND *Atlantic K 11224*	38	8 wks

Millie JACKSON *US, female vocalist*   **8 wks**

18 Nov 72		MY MAN A SWEET MAN *Mojo 2093 022*	50	1 wk
10 Mar 84		I FEEL LIKE WALKIN' IN THE RAIN *Sire W 9348*	55	2 wks
15 Jun 85		ACT OF WAR *Rocket EJS 8* *	32	5 wks

* Elton John and Millie Jackson

Stonewall JACKSON *US, male vocalist*   **2 wks**

17 Jul 59		WATERLOO *Philips PB 941*	24	2 wks

Tony JACKSON and the VIBRATIONS   **3 wks**
UK, male vocal/instrumental group

8 Oct 64		BYE BYE BABY *Pye 7N 15685*	38	3 wks

Wanda JACKSON *US, female vocalist*   **11 wks**

1 Sep 60		LET'S HAVE A PARTY *Capitol CL 15147*	32	8 wks
26 Jan 61		MEAN MEAN MAN *Capitol CL 15176*	46	1 wk
9 Feb 61		MEAN MEAN MAN (re-entry) *Capitol CL 15176*	40	2 wks

---

JACKSON SISTERS *US, female vocal group*   **2 wks**

20 Jun 87		I BELIEVE IN MIRACLES *Urban URB 4*	72	2 wks

JACKSONS *US, male vocal group*   **235 wks**

31 Jan 70	●	I WANT YOU BACK *Tamla Motown TMG 724* *	2	13 wks
16 May 70	●	ABC *Tamla Motown TMG 738* *	8	11 wks
1 Aug 70	●	THE LOVE YOU SAVE *Tamla Motown TMG 746* *	7	9 wks
21 Nov 70	●	I'LL BE THERE *Tamla Motown TMG 758* *	4	16 wks
10 Apr 71		MAMA'S PEARL *Tamla Motown TMG 769* *	25	7 wks
17 Jul 71		NEVER CAN SAY GOODBYE *Tamla Motown TMG 778* *	33	7 wks

The KAYE SISTERS were not related at all. They were (left to right) Sheila Jones, Shan Palmer and Carol Lindsay.

STONEWALL JACKSON got his name from an ancestor, Civil War General 'Stonewall' Jackson.

Madonna drives MICHAEL JACKSON to dinner in West Hollywood during 1991.

It's high time we had a solo picture of PAUL JONES in this book.

11 Nov 72 ●	LOOKIN' THROUGH THE WINDOWS		
	Tamla Motown TMG 833 * 9		11 wks
23 Dec 72	SANTA CLAUS IS COMING TO TOWN		
	Tamla Motown TMG 837 * 43		3 wks
17 Feb 73 ●	DOCTOR MY EYES *Tamla Motown TMG 842* * 9		10 wks
9 Jun 73	HALLELUJAH DAY *Tamla Motown TMG 856* * 20		9 wks
8 Sep 73	SKYWRITER *Tamla Motown TMG 865* * 25		8 wks
9 Apr 77	ENJOY YOURSELF *Epic EPC 5063* 42		4 wks
4 Jun 77 ★	SHOW YOU THE WAY TO GO *Epic EPC 5266* 1		10 wks
13 Aug 77	DREAMER *Epic EPC 5458* 22		9 wks
5 Nov 77	GOIN' PLACES *Epic EPC 5732* 26		7 wks
11 Feb 78	EVEN THOUGH YOU'VE GONE *Epic EPC 5919* 31		4 wks
23 Sep 78 ●	BLAME IT ON THE BOOGIE *Epic EPC 6683* 8		12 wks
3 Feb 79	DESTINY *Epic EPC 6983* 39		6 wks
24 Mar 79 ●	SHAKE YOUR BODY (DOWN TO THE GROUND)		
	Epic EPC 7181 4		12 wks
25 Oct 80	LOVELY ONE *Epic EPC 9302* 29		6 wks
13 Dec 80	HEARTBREAK HOTEL *Epic EPC 9391* 44		6 wks
20 Feb 81 ●	CAN YOU FEEL IT *Epic EPC 9554* 6		15 wks
4 Jul 81 ●	WALK RIGHT NOW *Epic EPC A 1294* 7		11 wks
7 Jul 84	STATE OF SHOCK *Epic A 4431* ** 14		8 wks
8 Sep 84	TORTURE *Epic A 4675* 26		6 wks
16 Apr 88 ●	I WANT YOU BACK (re-mix) *Motown ZB 41913* *** 8		9 wks
13 May 89	NOTHIN' (THAT COMPARES 2 U) *Epic 654808 7* 33		6 wks

* Jackson Five **Jacksons, lead vocals Mick Jagger and Michael Jackson
***Michael Jackson with the Jackson Five

JACKY – *See Jackie LEE*

JADE 4 U – *See Praga KHAN*

JAGGED EDGE *UK, male vocal/instrumental group* **2 wks**

15 Sep 90	YOU DON'T LOVE ME *Polydor PO 97* 66		2 wks

---

Mick JAGGER *UK, male vocalist* **38 wks**

14 Nov 70	MEMO FROM TURNER *Decca F 13067* 32		5 wks
7 Jul 84	STATE OF SHOCK *Epic A 4431* * 14		8 wks
16 Feb 85	JUST ANOTHER NIGHT *CBS A 4722* 32		6 wks
7 Sep 85 ★	DANCING IN THE STREET *EMI America EA 204* ** 1		12 wks
12 Sep 87	LET'S WORK *CBS 651028 7* 31		7 wks

* Jacksons, lead vocals Mick Jagger and Michael Jackson ** David Bowie and Mick Jagger

---

JAGS *UK, male vocal/instrumental group* **11 wks**

8 Sep 79	BACK OF MY HAND *Island WIP 6501* 17		10 wks
2 Feb 80	WOMAN'S WORLD *Island WIP 6531* 75		1 wk

J.A.L.N. BAND *UK/Jamaica, male vocal/instrumental group* **17 wks**

11 Sep 76	DISCO MUSIC/I LIKE IT *Magnet MAG 73* 21		9 wks
27 Aug 77	I GOT TO SING *Magnet MAG 97* 40		4 wks
1 Jul 78	GET UP *Magnet MAG 118* 53		4 wks

JAM *UK, male vocal/instrumental group* **203 wks**

7 May 77	IN THE CITY *Polydor 2058 866* 40		6 wks
23 Jul 77	ALL AROUND THE WORLD *Polydor 2058 903* 13		8 wks
5 Nov 77	THE MODERN WORLD *Polydor 2058 945* 36		4 wks
11 Mar 78	NEWS OF THE WORLD *Polydor 2058 995* 27		5 wks
26 Aug 78	DAVID WATTS/'A' BOMB IN WARDOUR STREET		
	Polydor 2059 054 25		8 wks
21 Oct 78	DOWN IN THE TUBE STATION AT MIDNIGHT		
	Polydor POSP 8 15		7 wks
17 Mar 79	STRANGE TOWN *Polydor POSP 34* 15		9 wks
25 Aug 79	WHEN YOU'RE YOUNG *Polydor POSP 69* 17		7 wks
3 Nov 79 ●	THE ETON RIFLES *Polydor POSP 83* 3		12 wks
22 Mar 80 ★	GOING UNDERGROUND/DREAMS OF CHILDREN *Polydor POSP 113* 1		9 wks

---

26 Apr 80	ALL AROUND THE WORLD (re-entry)		
	Polydor 2058 903 43		3 wks
26 Apr 80	DAVID WATTS/'A' BOMB IN WARDOUR STREET (re-entry) *Polydor 2059 054* 54		3 wks
26 Apr 80	IN THE CITY (re-entry) *Polydor 2058 866* 40		4 wks
26 Apr 80	NEWS OF THE WORLD (re-entry) *Polydor 2058 995* 53		3 wks
26 Apr 80	STRANGE TOWN (re-entry) *Polydor POSP 34* 44		3 wks
26 Apr 80	THE MODERN WORLD (re-entry) *Polydor 2058 945* 52		3 wks
23 Aug 80 ★	START *Polydor 2059 266* 1		8 wks
7 Feb 81	THAT'S ENTERTAINMENT (IMPORT)		
	Metronome 0030 364 21		7 wks
6 Jun 81 ●	FUNERAL PYRE *Polydor POSP 257* 4		6 wks
24 Oct 81 ●	ABSOLUTE BEGINNERS *Polydor POSP 350* 4		6 wks
13 Feb 82 ★	TOWN CALLED MALICE/PRECIOUS *Polydor POSP 400* 1		8 wks
3 Jul 82 ●	JUST WHO IS THE FIVE O'CLOCK HERO *Polydor 2059 504* 8		5 wks
18 Sep 82 ●	THE BITTEREST PILL (I EVER HAD TO SWALLOW) *Polydor POSP 505* 2		7 wks
4 Dec 82 ★	BEAT SURRENDER *Polydor POSP 540* 1		9 wks
22 Jan 83	ALL AROUND THE WORLD (2nd re-entry)		
	Polydor 2058 903 38		4 wks
22 Jan 83	DAVID WATTS/'A' BOMB IN WARDOUR STREET (2nd re-entry) *Polydor 2059 054* 50		4 wks
22 Jan 83	DOWN IN THE TUBE STATION AT MIDNIGHT (re-entry) *Polydor POSP 8* 30		6 wks
22 Jan 83	GOING UNDERGROUND/DREAMS OF CHILDREN (re-entry) *Polydor POSP 113* 21		6 wks
22 Jan 83	IN THE CITY (2nd re-entry) *Polydor 2058 866* 47		4 wks
22 Jan 83	NEWS OF THE WORLD (2nd re-entry)		
	Polydor 2058 995 39		4 wks
22 Jan 83	STRANGE TOWN (2nd re-entry) *Polydor POSP 34* 42		5 wks
22 Jan 83	THE MODERN WORLD (2nd re-entry)		
	Polydor 2058 945 51		4 wks
22 Jan 83	WHEN YOU'RE YOUNG (re-entry) *Polydor POSP 69* 53		4 wks
29 Jan 83	THAT'S ENTERTAINMENT (re-issue)		
	Polydor POSP 482 60		3 wks
5 Feb 83	START (re-entry) *Polydor 2059 266* 62		2 wks
5 Feb 83	THE ETON RIFLES (re-entry) *Polydor POSP 83* 54		3 wks
5 Feb 83	TOWN CALLED MALICE/PRECIOUS (re-entry)		
	Polydor POSP 400 73		1 wk
29 Jun 91	THAT'S ENTERTAINMENT (2nd re-issue)		
	Polydor PO 155 57		2 wks

Dreams of Children was only listed with the re-entry of Going Underground *from 5 Feb 83.*

JAM AND SPOON **3 wks**
Germany, male instrumental/production duo

2 May 92	TALES FROM A DANCEOGRAPHIC OCEAN EP		
	R&S RSUK 14 49		1 wk
6 Jun 92	THE COMPLETE STELLA (re-mix) *R&S RSUK 14X* 66		2 wks

Tracks on Tales From A Danceographic Ocean EP: *Stella/Keep On Movin'/My First Fantastic FF.* The Complete Stella *is a re-mix of a track from the EP.*

JAM MACHINE *Italy/US, male vocal/instrumental group* **1 wk**

23 Dec 89	EVERYDAY *deConstruction PB 43299* 68		1 wk

---

JAM ON THE MUTHA **2 wks**
UK, male vocal/instrumental group

11 Aug 90	HOTEL CALIFORNIA *M & G MAGS 3* 62		2 wks

---

JAM TRONIK *Germany, male/female vocal/instrumental group* **7 wks**

24 Mar 90	ANOTHER DAY IN PARADISE *Debut DEBT 3093* 19		7 wks

---

JAMES *UK, male vocal/instrumental group* **39 wks**

12 May 90	HOW WAS IT FOR YOU *Fontana JIM 5* 32		3 wks
7 Jul 90	COME HOME *Fontana JIM 6* 32		4 wks

8 Dec 90		LOSE CONTROL *Fontana JIM 7*	38	5 wks
30 Mar 91	●	SIT DOWN *Fontana JIM 8*	2	10 wks
30 Nov 91	●	SOUND *Fontana JIM 9*	9	7 wks
1 Feb 92		BORN OF FRUSTRATION *Fontana JIM 10*	13	6 wks
4 Apr 92		RING THE BELLS *Fontana JIM 11*	37	2 wks
18 Jul 92		SEVEN (EP) *Fontana JIM 12*	46	2 wks

Tracks on Seven (EP): Seven/Goalie's Ball/William Burroughs/Still Alive

Dick JAMES *UK, male vocalist* 13 wks

20 Jan 56	ROBIN HOOD *Parlophone R 4117*	14	8 wks
18 May 56	ROBIN HOOD/BALLAD OF DAVY CROCKETT (re-entry) *Parlophone R 4117*	29	1 wk
11 Jan 57	GARDEN OF EDEN *Parlophone R 4255*	18	4 wks

Robin Hood is with Stephen James and his Chums.

Freddie JAMES *Canada, male vocalist* 3 wks

| 24 Nov 79 | GET UP AND BOOGIE *Warner Bros. K 17478* | 54 | 3 wks |

Jimmy JAMES and the VAGABONDS 25 wks
UK, male vocal/instrumental group

11 Sep 68		RED RED WINE *Pye 7N 17579*	36	8 wks
24 Apr 76		I'LL GO WHERE YOUR MUSIC TAKES ME *Pye 7N 45585*	23	8 wks
17 Jul 76	●	NOW IS THE TIME *Pye 7N 45606*	5	9 wks

Joni JAMES *US, female vocalist* 2 wks

| 6 Mar 53 | WHY DON'T YOU BELIEVE ME *MGM 582* | 11 | 1 wk |
| 30 Jan 59 | THERE MUST BE A WAY *MGM 1002* | 24 | 1 wk |

Rick JAMES *US, male vocalist* 30 wks

8 Jul 78	YOU AND I *Motown TMG 1110*	46	7 wks
7 Jul 79	I'M A SUCKER FOR YOUR LOVE *Motown TMG 1146 **	43	8 wks
6 Sep 80	BIG TIME *Motown TMG 1198*	41	6 wks
4 Jul 81	GIVE IT TO ME BABY *Motown TMG 1229*	47	3 wks
12 Jun 82	STANDING ON THE TOP (PART 1) *Motown TMG 1263 ***	53	3 wks
3 Jul 82	DANCE WIT' ME *Motown TMG 1266*	53	3 wks

* Teena Marie, co-lead vocals Rick James ** Temptations featuring Rick James

Sonny JAMES *US, male vocalist* 8 wks

| 30 Nov 56 | THE CAT CAME BACK *Capitol CL 14635* | 30 | 1 wk |
| 8 Feb 57 | YOUNG LOVE *Capitol CL 14683* | 11 | 7 wks |

Tommy JAMES and the SHONDELLS 25 wks
US, male vocal/instrumental group

| 21 Jul 66 | | HANKY PANKY *Roulette RK 7000* | 38 | 7 wks |
| 5 Jun 68 | ★ | MONY MONY *Major Minor MM 567* | 1 | 18 wks |

JAMES BOYS *UK, male vocal duo* 6 wks

| 19 May 73 | OVER AND OVER *Penny Farthing PEN 806* | 39 | 6 wks |

JAMESTOWN – *See Jocelyn BROWN*

JAMIROQUAI *UK, male producer - Jason Kay* 2 wks

| 31 Oct 92 | WHEN YOU GONNA LEARN *Acid Jazz JAZID 46T* | 52 | 2 wks |

JAMMERS *US, male vocal/instrumental group* 2 wks

| 29 Jan 83 | BE MINE TONIGHT *Salsoul SAL 101* | 65 | 2 wks |

Kenny 'Jammin' JASON – *See DJ 'FAST' EDDIE*

JAN and DEAN *US, male vocal duo* 18 wks

| 24 Aug 61 | HEART AND SOUL *London HLH 9395* | 24 | 8 wks |
| 15 Aug 63 | SURF CITY *Liberty LIB 55580* | 26 | 10 wks |

JAN and KJELD *Denmark, male vocal duo* 4 wks

| 21 Jul 60 | BANJO BOY *Ember S 101* | 36 | 4 wks |

JANE'S ADDICTION *US, male vocal/instrumental group* 4 wks

| 23 Mar 91 | BEEN CAUGHT STEALING *Warner Bros. W 0011* | 34 | 3 wks |
| 1 Jun 91 | CLASSIC GIRL *Warner Bros. W 0031* | 60 | 1 wk |

Horst JANKOWSKI *Germany, male instrumentalist - piano* 18 wks

| 29 Jul 65 | ● | A WALK IN THE BLACK FOREST *Mercury MF 861* | 3 | 18 wks |

Samantha JANUS *UK, female vocalist* 3 wks

| 11 May 91 | A MESSAGE TO YOUR HEART *Hollywood HWD 104* | 30 | 3 wks |

Philip JAP *UK, male vocalist* 8 wks

| 31 Jul 82 | SAVE US *A & M AMS 8217* | 53 | 4 wks |
| 25 Sep 82 | TOTAL ERASURE *A & M JAP 1* | 41 | 4 wks |

JAPAN *UK, male vocal/instrumental group* 81 wks

18 Oct 80		GENTLEMEN TAKE POLAROIDS *Virgin VS 379*	60	2 wks
9 May 81		THE ART OF PARTIES *Virgin VS 409*	48	5 wks
19 Sep 81		QUIET LIFE *Hansa HANSA 6*	19	9 wks
7 Nov 81		VISIONS OF CHINA *Virgin VS 436*	32	12 wks
23 Jan 82		EUROPEAN SON *Hansa HANSA 10*	31	6 wks
20 Mar 82	●	GHOSTS *Virgin VS 472*	5	8 wks
22 May 82		CANTONESE BOY *Virgin VS 502*	24	6 wks
3 Jul 82	●	I SECOND THAT EMOTION *Hansa HANSA 12*	9	11 wks
9 Oct 82		LIFE IN TOKYO *Hansa HANSA 17*	28	6 wks
20 Nov 82		NIGHT PORTER *Virgin VS 554*	29	9 wks
12 Mar 83		ALL TOMORROW'S PARTIES *Hansa HANSA 18*	38	4 wks
21 May 83		CANTON (LIVE) *Virgin VS 581*	42	3 wks

Jean-Michel JARRE *France, male instrumentalist/producer* 25 wks

27 Aug 77	●	OXYGENE PART IV *Polydor 2001 721*	4	9 wks
20 Jan 79		EQUINOXE PART 5 *Polydor POSP 20*	45	5 wks
23 Aug 86		FOURTH RENDEZ-VOUS *Polydor POSP 788*	65	4 wks
5 Nov 88		REVOLUTIONS *Polydor PO 25*	52	2 wks
7 Jan 89		LONDON KID *Polydor PO 32 **	52	3 wks
7 Oct 89		OXYGENE PART IV (re-mix) *Polydor PO 55*	65	2 wks

* Jean-Michel Jarre featuring Hank Marvin

Al JARREAU *US, male vocalist* 30 wks

26 Sep 81	WE'RE IN THIS LOVE TOGETHER *Warner Bros. K 17849*	55	4 wks
14 May 83	MORNIN' *WEA U9929*	28	6 wks
16 Jul 83	TROUBLE IN PARADISE *WEA Int. U9871*	36	5 wks

24 Sep 83		BOOGIE DOWN WEA U9814	63	3 wks
16 Nov 85		DAY BY DAY Polydor POSP 770 *	53	3 wks
5 Apr 86		THE MUSIC OF GOODBYE (LOVE THEME FROM 'OUT OF AFRICA') MCA MCA 1038 **	75	1 wk
7 Mar 87	●	'MOONLIGHTING' THEME WEA U8407	8	8 wks

* Shakatak featuring Al Jarreau ** Melissa Manchester and Al Jarreau

JAVELLS featuring Nosmo KING   8 wks
UK, male/female vocal group

9 Nov 74		GOODBYE NOTHING TO SAY *Pye Disco Demand DDS 2003*	26	8 wks

Peter JAY and the JAYWALKERS   11 wks
UK, male instrumental group, Peter Jay – drums

8 Nov 62		CAN CAN 62 Decca F 11531	31	11 wks

JAZZ and the BROTHERS GRIMM   2 wks
UK, male vocal/instrumental group

9 Jul 88		(LET'S ALL GO BACK) DISCO NIGHTS *Ensign ENY 616*	57	2 wks

JB's ALL STARS *UK, male/female vocal/instrumental group*   4 wks

11 Feb 84		BACKFIELD IN MOTION RCA Victor RCA 384	48	4 wks

JEFFERSON *UK, male vocalist*   8 wks

9 Apr 69		COLOUR OF MY LOVE Pye 7N 17706	22	8 wks

JEFFERSON STARSHIP – *See STARSHIP*

Garland JEFFREYS *US, male vocalist*   1 wk

8 Feb 92		HAIL HAIL ROCK 'N' ROLL RCA PB 49171	72	1 wk

JELLYBEAN *US, male producer*   47 wks

1 Feb 86		SIDEWALK TALK EMI America EA 210 *	47	4 wks
26 Sep 87		THE REAL THING Chrysalis CHS 3167 **	13	10 wks
28 Nov 87	●	WHO FOUND WHO Chrysalis CHS JEL 1 ***	10	10 wks
12 Dec 87		JINGO Chrysalis JEL 2	12	10 wks
12 Mar 88		JUST A MIRAGE Chrysalis JEL 3 ****	13	10 wks
20 Aug 88		COMING BACK FOR MORE Chrysalis JEL 4 *****	41	3 wks

* Jellybean featuring Catherine Buchanan ** Jellybean featuring Steven Dante
*** Jellybean featuring Elisa Fiorillo **** Jellybean featuring Adele Bertei
***** Jellybean featuring Richard Darbyshire

JELLYFISH *US, male vocal/instrumental group*   15 wks

26 Jan 91		THE KING IS HALF UNDRESSED Charisma CUSS 1	39	6 wks
27 Apr 91		BABY'S COMING BACK Charisma CUSS 2	51	4 wks
3 Aug 91		THE SCARY-GO-ROUND EP Charisma CUSS 3	49	3 wks
26 Oct 91		I WANNA STAY HOME Charisma CUSS 4	59	2 wks

Tracks on The Scary-Go-Round EP: Now She Knows She's Wrong/Bedspring Kiss/She Still Loves Him (Live)/Baby's Coming Back (Live).

JESUS AND MARY CHAIN   48 wks
UK, male vocal/instrumental group

2 Mar 85		NEVER UNDERSTAND blanco y negro NEG 8	47	4 wks

8 Jun 85		YOU TRIP ME UP blanco y negro NEG 13	55	3 wks
12 Oct 85		JUST LIKE HONEY blanco y negro NEG 17	45	3 wks
26 Jul 86		SOME CANDY TALKING blanco y negro NEG 19	13	5 wks
2 May 87	●	APRIL SKIES blanco y negro NEG 24	8	6 wks
15 Aug 87		HAPPY WHEN IT RAINS blanco y negro NEG 25	25	5 wks
7 Nov 87		DARKLANDS blanco y negro NEG 29	33	4 wks
9 Apr 88		SIDEWALKING blanco y negro NEG 32	30	3 wks
23 Sep 89		BLUES FROM A GUN blanco y negro NEG 41	32	2 wks
18 Nov 89		HEAD ON blanco y negro NEG 42	57	2 wks
8 Sep 90		ROLLERCOASTER (EP) blanco y negro NEG 45	46	2 wks
15 Feb 92	●	REVERENCE blanco y negro NEG 55	10	4 wks
14 Mar 92		FAR GONE AND OUT blanco y negro NEG 56	23	3 wks
4 Jul 92		ALMOST GOLD blanco y negro NEG 57	41	2 wks

Tracks on Rollercoaster (EP): Rollercoaster/Silverblade/Lowlife/Tower Of Song.

JESUS JONES *UK, male vocal/instrumental group*   39 wks

25 Feb 89		INFO-FREAKO Food FOOD 18	42	3 wks
8 Jul 89		NEVER ENOUGH Food FOOD 21	42	3 wks
23 Sep 89		BRING IT ON DOWN Food FOOD 22	46	3 wks
7 Apr 90		REAL REAL REAL Food FOOD 24	19	8 wks
6 Oct 90		RIGHT HERE RIGHT NOW Food FOOD 25	31	4 wks
12 Jan 91	●	INTERNATIONAL BRIGHT YOUNG THING *Food FOOD 27*	7	7 wks
2 Mar 91		WHO WHERE WHEN Food FOOD 28	21	7 wks
20 Jul 91		RIGHT HERE RIGHT NOW (re-issue) Food FOOD 30	31	4 wks

See also Various Artists (EPs & LPs) - The Food Christmas EP.

JESUS LOVES YOU *UK, male vocalist - Boy George*   18 wks

11 Nov 89		AFTER THE LOVE More Protein PROT 2	68	1 wk
23 Feb 91		BOW DOWN MISTER More Protein PROT 8	27	8 wks
8 Jun 91		GENERATIONS OF LOVE More Protein PROT 10	35	8 wks
12 Dec 92		SWEET TOXIC LOVE Virgin VS 1449	65	1 wk

JETHRO TULL *UK, male vocal/instrumental group*   65 wks

1 Jan 69		LOVE STORY Island WIP 6048	29	8 wks
14 May 69	●	LIVING IN THE PAST Island WIP 6056	3	14 wks
1 Nov 69	●	SWEET DREAM Chrysalis WIP 6070	7	11 wks
24 Jan 70	●	TEACHER/THE WITCH'S PROMISE *Chrysalis WIP 6077*	4	9 wks
18 Sep 71		LIFE IS A LONG SONG/UP THE POOL *Chrysalis WIP 6106*	11	8 wks
11 Dec 76		RING OUT SOLSTICE BELLS (EP) Chrysalis CXP 2	28	6 wks
15 Sep 84		LAP OF LUXURY Chrysalis TULL 1	70	2 wks
16 Jan 87		SAID SHE WAS A DANCER Chrysalis TULL 4	55	4 wks
21 Mar 92		ROCKS ON THE ROAD Chrysalis TULLX 7	47	3 wks

Tracks on EP: Ring Out Solstice Bells/March the Mad Scientist/The Christmas Song/Pan Dance.

JETS *UK, male vocal/instrumental group*   38 wks

22 Aug 81		SUGAR DOLL EMI 5211	55	3 wks
31 Oct 81		YES TONIGHT JOSEPHINE EMI 5247	25	11 wks
6 Feb 82		LOVE MAKES THE WORLD GO ROUND EMI 5262	21	9 wks
24 Apr 82		THE HONEYDRIPPER EMI 5289	58	3 wks
9 Oct 82		SOMEBODY TO LOVE EMI 5342	56	3 wks
6 Aug 83		BLUE SKIES EMI 5405	53	3 wks
17 Dec 83		ROCKIN' AROUND THE CHRISTMAS TREE *PRT 7P 297*	62	4 wks
13 Oct 84		PARTY DOLL PRT JETS 2	72	2 wks

JETS *US, male/female vocal/instrumental group*   19 wks

31 Jan 87	●	CRUSH ON YOU MCA MCA 1048	5	13 wks
25 Apr 87		CURIOSITY MCA MCA 1119	41	4 wks
28 May 88		ROCKET 2 U MCA MCA 1226	69	2 wks

Joan JETT and the BLACKHEARTS   20 wks
US, female vocalist with male vocal/instrumental group

24 Apr 82	●	I LOVE ROCK 'N' ROLL Epic EPC A 2087	4	10 wks

10 Jul 82	CRIMSON AND CLOVER *Epic EPC A 2485*	60	3 wks
20 Aug 88	I HATE MYSELF FOR LOVING YOU		
	London LON 195	46	6 wks
31 Mar 90	DIRTY DEEDS *Chrysalis CHS 3518* *	69	1 wk

* Joan Jett

JIGSAW UK, male vocal/instrumental group **16 wks**

1 Nov 75 ●	SKY HIGH *Splash CP1 1*	9	11 wks
6 Aug 77	IF I HAVE TO GO AWAY *Splash CP 11*	36	5 wks

JILTED JOHN UK, male vocalist **12 wks**

12 Aug 78 ●	JILTED JOHN *EMI International INT 567*	4	12 wks

JIMMY THE HOOVER **8 wks**
UK, male/female vocal/instrumental group

25 Jun 83	TANTALISE (WO WO EE YEH YEH)		
	Innervision A 3406	18	8 wks

JINGLE BELLES US/UK, female vocal group **4 wks**

17 Dec 83	CHRISTMAS SPECTRE *Passion PASH 14*	37	4 wks

JINNY Italy, female vocalist **3 wks**

29 Jun 91	KEEP WARM *Virgin VS 1356*	68	3 wks

JIVE BUNNY and the MASTERMIXERS **68 wks**
UK, male production/mixing group

15 Jul 89 ★	SWING THE MOOD *Music Factory Dance MFD 001*	1	19 wks
14 Oct 89 ★	THAT'S WHAT I LIKE *Music Factory Dance MFD 002*	1	12 wks
16 Dec 89 ★	LET'S PARTY *Music Factory Dance MFD 003*	1	6 wks
17 Mar 90 ●	THAT SOUNDS GOOD TO ME		
	Music Factory Dance MFD 004	4	6 wks
25 Aug 90 ●	CAN CAN YOU PARTY *Music Factory Dance MFD 007*	8	6 wks
17 Nov 90	LET'S SWING AGAIN *Music Factory Dance MFD 009*	19	5 wks
22 Dec 90	THE CRAZY PARTY MIXES		
	Music Factory Dance MFD 010	13	5 wks
23 Mar 91	OVER TO YOU JOHN (HERE WE GO AGAIN)		
	Music Factory Dance MFD 012	28	5 wks
20 Jul 91	HOT SUMMER SALSA *Music Factory Dance MFD 013*	43	2 wks
23 Nov 91	ROCK 'N' ROLL DANCE PARTY		
	Music Factory Dance MFD 015	48	2 wks

See also Liz Kershaw and Bruno Brookes.

JJ UK, male/female vocal/instumental duo **3 wks**

9 Feb 91	IF THIS IS LOVE *Columbia 6566097*	55	3 wks

JKD BAND UK, male vocal/instrumental group **4 wks**

1 Jul 78	DRAGON POWER *Satril SAT 132*	58	4 wks

J.M. SILK US, male vocal/instrumental duo **6 wks**

25 Oct 86	I CAN'T TURN AROUND *RCA PB 49793*	62	3 wks
7 Mar 87	LET THE MUSIC TAKE CONTROL *RCA PB 49767*	47	3 wks

J.M.D. – *See TYREE*

JO BOXERS UK, male vocal/instrumental group **33 wks**

19 Feb 83 ●	BOXER BEAT *RCA BOXX 1*	3	15 wks

21 May 83 ●	JUST GOT LUCKY *RCA BOXX 2*	7	9 wks
13 Aug 83	JOHNNY FRIENDLY *RCA BOXX 3*	31	8 wks
12 Nov 83	JEALOUS LOVE *RCA BOXX 4*	72	1 wk

JO JO GUNNE US, male vocal/instrumental group **12 wks**

25 Mar 72 ●	RUN RUN RUN *Asylum AYM 501*	6	12 wks

JOAN COLLINS FAN CLUB **3 wks**
UK, male vocalist – Julian Clary

18 Jun 88	LEADER OF THE PACK *10 TEN 227*	60	3 wks

John Paul JOANS UK, male vocalist **7 wks**

19 Dec 70	MAN FROM NAZARETH *RAK 107*	41	3 wks
16 Jan 71	MAN FROM NAZARETH (re-entry) *RAK 107*	25	4 wks

JOCKMASTER B.A. – *See MAD JOCKS featuring JOCKMASTER B.A.*

JOCKO US, male vocalist **3 wks**

23 Feb 80	RHYTHM TALK *Philadelphia International PIR 8222*	56	3 wks

JOE PUBLIC US, male rap group **5 wks**

11 Jul 92	LIVE AND LEARN *Columbia 6575267*	43	4 wks
28 Nov 92	I'VE BEEN WATCHIN' *Columbia 6587657*	75	1 wk

Billy JOEL US, male vocalist/instrumentalist - piano **125 wks**

11 Feb 78	JUST THE WAY YOU ARE *CBS 5872*	19	9 wks
24 Jun 78	MOVIN' OUT (ANTHONY'S SONG) *CBS 6412*	35	6 wks
2 Dec 78	MY LIFE *CBS 6821*	12	15 wks
28 Apr 79	UNTIL THE NIGHT *CBS 7242*	50	3 wks
12 Apr 80	ALL FOR LEYNA *CBS 8325*	40	4 wks
9 Aug 80	IT'S STILL ROCK AND ROLL TO ME *CBS 8753*	14	11 wks
15 Oct 83 ★	UPTOWN GIRL *CBS A 3775*	1	17 wks
10 Dec 83 ●	TELL HER ABOUT IT *CBS A 3655*	4	10 wks
18 Feb 84 ●	AN INNOCENT MAN *CBS A 4142*	8	10 wks
28 Apr 84	THE LONGEST TIME *CBS A 4280*	25	8 wks
23 Jun 84	LEAVE A TENDER MOMENT		
	ALONE/GOODNIGHT SAIGON *CBS A 4521*	29	7 wks
22 Feb 86	SHE'S ALWAYS A WOMAN/JUST THE WAY YOU		
	ARE (re-issue)*CBS A 6862*	53	1 wk
20 Sep 86	A MATTER OF TRUST *CBS 650057 7*	52	4 wks
30 Sep 89 ●	WE DIDN'T START THE FIRE *CBS JOEL 1*	7	10 wks
16 Dec 89	LENINGRAD *CBS JOEL 3*	53	4 wks
10 Mar 90	I GO TO EXTREMES *CBS JOEL 2*	70	2 wks
29 Aug 92	ALL SHOOK UP *Columbia 6583437*	27	4 wks

Goodnight Saigon only listed from 30 Jun 84.

Elton JOHN UK, male vocalist/instrumentalist - piano **464 wks**

23 Jan 71 ●	YOUR SONG *DJM DJS 233*	7	12 wks
22 Apr 72 ●	ROCKET MAN *DJM DJX 501*	2	13 wks
9 Sep 72	HONKY CAT *DJM DJS*	31	6 wks
4 Nov 72 ●	CROCODILE ROCK *DJM DJS 271*	5	14 wks
20 Jan 73 ●	DANIEL *DJM DJS 275*	4	10 wks
7 Jul 73 ●	SATURDAY NIGHT'S ALRIGHT FOR FIGHTING		
	DJM DJX 502	7	9 wks
29 Sep 73 ●	GOODBYE YELLOW BRICK ROAD *DJM DJS 285*	6	16 wks
8 Dec 73	STEP INTO CHRISTMAS *DJM DJS 290*	24	7 wks
2 Mar 74	CANDLE IN THE WIND *DJM DJS 297*	11	9 wks
1 Jun 74	DON'T LET THE SUN GO DOWN ON ME		
	DJM DJS 302	16	8 wks
14 Sep 74	THE BITCH IS BACK *DJM DJS 322*	15	7 wks

Date		Title / Catalogue	Peak	Weeks
23 Nov 74	●	LUCY IN THE SKY WITH DIAMONDS *DJM DJS 340*	10	10 wks
8 Mar 75		PHILADELPHIA FREEDOM *DJM DJS 354* *	12	9 wks
28 Jun 75		SOMEONE SAVED MY LIFE TONIGHT *DJM DJS 385*	22	5 wks
4 Oct 75		ISLAND GIRL *DJM DJS 610*	14	8 wks
20 Mar 76	●	PINBALL WIZARD *DJM DJS 652*	7	7 wks
3 Jul 76	★	DON'T GO BREAKING MY HEART *Rocket ROKN 512* **	1	14 wks
25 Sep 76		BENNIE AND THE JETS *DJM DJS 10705*	37	5 wks
13 Nov 76		SORRY SEEMS TO BE THE HARDEST WORD *Rocket ROKN 517*	11	10 wks
26 Feb 77		CRAZY WATER *Rocket ROKN 521*	27	6 wks
11 Jun 77		BITE YOUR LIP (GET UP AND DANCE) *Rocket ROKN 526*	28	4 wks
15 Apr 78		EGO *Rocket ROKN 538*	34	6 wks
21 Oct 78		PART TIME LOVE *Rocket XPRES 1*	15	13 wks
16 Dec 78	●	SONG FOR GUY *Rocket XPRES 5*	4	10 wks
12 May 79		ARE YOU READY FOR LOVE *Rocket XPRES 13*	42	6 wks
24 May 80		LITTLE JEANNIE *Rocket XPRES 32*	33	7 wks
23 Aug 80		SARTORIAL ELOQUENCE *Rocket XPRES 41*	44	5 wks
21 Mar 81		I SAW HER STANDING THERE *DJM DJS 10965* ***	40	4 wks
23 May 81		NOBODY WINS *Rocket XPRES 54*	42	5 wks
27 Mar 82	●	BLUE EYES *Rocket XPRES 71*	8	10 wks
12 Jun 82		EMPTY GARDEN *Rocket XPRES 77*	51	4 wks
30 Apr 83	●	I GUESS THAT'S WHY THEY CALL IT THE BLUES *Rocket XPRES 91*	5	15 wks
30 Jul 83		I'M STILL STANDING *Rocket EJS 1*	4	11 wks
15 Oct 83		KISS THE BRIDE *Rocket EJS 2*	20	7 wks
10 Dec 83		COLD AS CHRISTMAS *Rocket EJS 3*	33	6 wks
26 May 84	●	SAD SONGS (SAY SO MUCH) *Rocket PH 7*	7	12 wks
11 Aug 84	●	PASSENGERS *Rocket EJS 5*	5	11 wks
20 Oct 84		WHO WEARS THESE SHOES *Rocket EJS 6*	50	3 wks
2 Mar 85		BREAKING HEARTS (AIN'T WHAT IT USED TO BE) *Rocket EJS 7*	59	3 wks
15 Jun 85		ACT OF WAR *Rocket EJS 8* ****	32	5 wks
12 Oct 85	●	NIKITA *Rocket EJS 9*	3	13 wks
9 Nov 85		THAT'S WHAT FRIENDS ARE FOR *Arista ARIST 638* *****	16	9 wks
7 Dec 85		WRAP HER UP *Rocket EJS 10*	12	10 wks
1 Mar 86		CRY TO HEAVEN *Rocket EJS 11*	47	4 wks
4 Oct 86		HEARTACHE ALL OVER THE WORLD *Rocket EJS 12*	45	4 wks
29 Nov 86		SLOW RIVERS *Rocket EJS 13* ******	44	8 wks
20 Jun 87		FLAMES OF PARADISE *CBS 6508657* *******	59	3 wks
16 Jan 88	●	CANDLE IN THE WIND *Rocket EJS 15*	5	11 wks
4 Jun 88		I DON'T WANNA GO ON WITH YOU LIKE THAT *Rocket EJS 16*	30	8 wks
3 Sep 88		TOWN OF PLENTY *Rocket EJS 17*	74	1 wk
6 May 89		THROUGH THE STORM *Arista 112185* ********	41	5 wks
26 Aug 89		HEALING HANDS *Rocket EJS 19*	45	5 wks
4 Nov 89		SACRIFICE *Rocket EJS 20*	55	3 wks
9 Jun 90	★	SACRIFICE/HEALING HANDS (re-issues) *Rocket EJS 22*	1	15 wks
18 Aug 90		CLUB AT THE END OF THE STREET/WHISPERS *Rocket EJS 23*	47	3 wks
20 Oct 90		YOU GOTTA LOVE SOMEONE *Rocket EJS 24*	33	4 wks
15 Dec 90		EASIER TO WALK AWAY *Rocket EJS 25*	67	1 wk
29 Dec 90		EASIER TO WALK AWAY (re-entry) *Rocket EJS 25*	63	1 wk
7 Dec 91	★	DON'T LET THE SUN GO DOWN ON ME *Epic 6576467* *********	1	10 wks
6 Jun 92	●	THE ONE *Rocket EJS 28*	10	8 wks
1 Aug 92		RUNAWAY TRAIN *Rocket EJS 29* **********	31	4 wks
7 Nov 92		THE LAST SONG *Rocket EJS 30*	21	4 wks

* Elton John Band ** Elton John and Kiki Dee *** Elton John Band featuring John Lennon and the Muscle Shoals Horns **** Elton John and Millie Jackson ***** Dionne Warwick and Friends featuring Elton John, Stevie Wonder and Gladys Knight ****** Elton John and Cliff Richard ******* Jennifer Rush and Elton John ******** Aretha Franklin and Elton John ********* George Michael and Elton John ********** Elton John and Eric Clapton

Bite Your Lip (Get Up And Dance) *was one side of a double-sided chart entry, the other being* Chicago *by Kiki Dee.* Wrap Her Up *features George Michael as uncredited co-vocalist. The 1988 version of* Candle In The Wind *was a live recording.*

British Hit Singles Part One: Alphabetically by Artist

Date of chart entry/Title & catalogue no./Peak position reached/Weeks on chart

★ Number one ● Top Ten † still on chart at 31 Dec 1992

* = credited to act billed in footnote

Robert JOHN *US, male vocalist* — 13 wks

17 Jul 68		IF YOU DON'T WANT MY LOVE *CBS 3436*	42	5 wks
20 Oct 79		SAD EYES *EMI American EA 101*	31	8 wks

JOHNNY and CHARLEY *Spain, male vocal duo* — 1 wk

14 Oct 65		LA YENKA *Pye International 7N 25326*	49	1 wk

JOHNNY HATES JAZZ — 45 wks
UK, male vocal/instrumental group

11 Apr 87	●	SHATTERED DREAMS *Virgin VS 948*	5	14 wks
29 Aug 87		I DON'T WANT TO BE A HERO *Virgin VS 1000*	11	10 wks
21 Nov 87		TURN BACK THE CLOCK *Virgin VS 1017*	12	11 wks
27 Feb 88		HEART OF GOLD *Virgin VS 1045*	19	7 wks
9 Jul 88		DON'T SAY IT'S LOVE *Virgin VS 1081*	48	3 wks

JOHNNY and the HURRICANES — 88 wks
US, male instrumental group

9 Oct 59	●	RED RIVER ROCK *London HL 8948*	3	16 wks
25 Dec 59		REVEILLE ROCK *London HL 9017*	14	5 wks
17 Mar 60	●	BEATNIK FLY *London HLI 9072*	8	19 wks
16 Jun 60	●	DOWN YONDER *London HLX 9134*	8	11 wks
29 Sep 60	●	ROCKING GOOSE *London HLX 9190*	3	20 wks
2 Mar 61		JA-DA *London HLX 9289*	14	9 wks
6 Jul 61		OLD SMOKEY/HIGH VOLTAGE *London HLX 9378*	24	8 wks

Bryan JOHNSON *UK, male vocalist* — 11 wks

10 Mar 60		LOOKING HIGH HIGH HIGH *Decca F 11213*	20	11 wks

Carey JOHNSON *Australia, male vocalist* — 8 wks

25 Apr 87		REAL FASHION REGGAE STYLE *Oval TEN 170*	19	8 wks

Denise JOHNSON – *See PRIMAL SCREAM*

Don JOHNSON *US, male vocalist* — 12 wks

18 Oct 86		HEARTBEAT *Epic 650064 7*	46	5 wks
5 Nov 88		TILL I LOVED YOU (LOVE THEME FROM 'GOYA') *CBS BARB 2* *	16	7 wks

* Barbra Streisand and Don Johnson

General JOHNSON – *See CHAIRMEN OF THE BOARD*

Holly JOHNSON *UK, male vocalist* — 36 wks

14 Jan 89	●	LOVE TRAIN *MCA MCA 1306*	4	11 wks
1 Apr 89	●	AMERICANOS *MCA MCA 1323*	4	11 wks
20 May 89	★	FERRY 'CROSS THE MERSEY *PWL PWL 41* *	1	7 wks
24 Jun 89		ATOMIC CITY *MCA MCA 1342*	18	4 wks
30 Sep 89		HEAVEN'S HERE *MCA MCA 1365*	62	2 wks
1 Dec 90		WHERE HAS LOVE GONE *MCA MCA 1460*	73	1 wk

* Christians, Holly Johnson, Paul McCartney, Gerry Marsden and Stock Aitken Waterman

Howard JOHNSON US, male vocalist — 6 wks

4 Sep 82	KEEPIN' LOVE NEW/SO FINE A & M USA 1221	45	6 wks

Keepin' Love New listed 4 Sep 82 only.

Johnny JOHNSON and the BANDWAGON — 50 wks
US, male vocal group

16 Oct 68 ●	BREAKIN' DOWN THE WALLS OF HEARTACHE Direction 58-3670 *	4	15 wks
5 Feb 69	YOU Direction 58-3923 *	34	4 wks
28 May 69	LET'S HANG ON Direction 58-4180 *	36	6 wks
25 Jul 70 ●	SWEET INSPIRATION Bell 1111	10	12 wks
24 Oct 70	SWEET INSPIRATION (re-entry) Bell 1111	46	1 wk
28 Nov 70 ●	BLAME IT ON THE PONY EXPRESS Bell 1128	7	12 wks

* Bandwagon

Kevin JOHNSON Australia, male vocalist — 6 wks

11 Jan 75	ROCK 'N ROLL (I GAVE YOU THE BEST YEARS OF MY LIFE) UK UKR 84	23	6 wks

Laurie JOHNSON UK, orchestra — 12 wks

28 Sep 61 ●	SUCU SUCU Pye 7N 15383	9	12 wks

L. J. JOHNSON US, male vocalist — 6 wks

7 Feb 76	YOUR MAGIC PUT A SPELL ON ME Philips 6006 492	27	6 wks

Lou JOHNSON US, male vocalist — 2 wks

26 Nov 64	MESSAGE TO MARTHA London HL 9929	36	2 wks

Marv JOHNSON US, male vocalist — 39 wks

12 Feb 60 ●	YOU GOT WHAT IT TAKES London HLT 9013	5	16 wks
5 May 60	I LOVE THE WAY YOU LOVE London HLT 9109	35	3 wks
11 Aug 60	AIN'T GONNA BE THAT WAY London HLT 9165	50	1 wk
22 Jan 69 ●	I'LL PICK A ROSE FOR MY ROSE Tamla Motown TMG 680	10	11 wks
25 Oct 69	I MISS YOU BABY Tamla Motown TMG 713	25	8 wks

Orlando JOHNSON – See SECCHI featuring Orlando JOHNSON

Paul JOHNSON UK, male vocalist — 7 wks

21 Feb 87	WHEN LOVE COMES CALLING CBS PJOHN 1	52	5 wks
25 Feb 89	NO MORE TOMORROWS CBS PJOHN 7	67	2 wks

Teddy JOHNSON – See Pearl CARR and Teddy JOHNSON

Bruce JOHNSTON US, male instrumentalist - keyboards — 4 wks

27 Aug 77	PIPELINE CBS 5514	33	4 wks

JOHNSTON BROTHERS UK, male vocal group — 33 wks

3 Apr 53 ●	OH HAPPY DAY Decca F 10071	4	8 wks
5 Nov 54	WAIT FOR ME DARLING Decca F 10362 *	18	1 wk
21 Jan 55	HAPPY DAYS AND LONELY NIGHTS Decca F 10389 **	14	2 wks
7 Oct 55 ★	HERNANDO'S HIDEAWAY Decca F 10608	1	13 wks
30 Dec 55 ●	JOIN IN AND SING AGAIN Decca F 10636	9	1 wk
13 Apr 56	NO OTHER LOVE Decca F 10721	22	1 wk
30 Nov 56	IN THE MIDDLE OF THE HOUSE Decca F 10781	27	1 wk
7 Dec 56	JOIN IN AND SING (NO. 3) Decca F 10814	30	1 wk
28 Dec 56	JOIN IN AND SING (NO. 3) (re-entry) Decca F 10814	24	1 wk
8 Feb 57	GIVE HER MY LOVE Decca F 10828	27	1 wk
19 Apr 57	HEART Decca F 10860	23	3 wks

* Joan Regan and the Johnston Brothers ** Suzi Miller and the Johnston Brothers
The following two hits were medleys: Join In And Sing Again: Sheik Of Araby/Yes Sir That's My Baby/California Here I Come/Some Of These Days/Charleston/Margie. Join In And Sing (No.3): Coal Black Morning/When You're Smiling/Alexander's Ragtime Band/Sweet Sue Just You/When You Wore A Tulip/If You Were The Only Girl In The World. See also Various Artists (EPs & LPs) - All Star Hit Parade No. 2.

Sabrina JOHNSTON US, female vocalist — 18 wks

7 Sep 91 ●	PEACE East West YZ 616	8	10 wks
7 Dec 91	FRIENDSHIP East West YZ 637	58	4 wks
11 Jul 92	I WANNA SING East West YZ 661	46	2 wks
3 Oct 92	PEACE (re-mix) Epic 6584377	35	2 wks

The listed flipside of Peace (re-mix) *was* Gypsy Woman (re-mix) *by Crystal Waters.*

JOLLY BROTHERS Jamaica, male vocal/instrumental group — 7 wks

28 Jul 79	CONSCIOUS MAN United Artists UP 36415	46	7 wks

JOLLY ROGER UK, male vocalist — 12 wks

10 Sep 88	ACID MAN 10 TEN 236	23	12 wks

JOMANDA US, female vocalist — 7 wks

22 Apr 89	MAKE MY BODY ROCK RCA PB 42749	44	3 wks
29 Jun 91	GOT A LOVE FOR YOU Giant W 0040	43	4 wks

JON and VANGELIS — 28 wks
UK, male vocalist/Greece, male multi-instrumentalist

5 Jan 80 ●	I HEAR YOU NOW Polydor POSP 96	8	11 wks
12 Dec 81 ●	I'LL FIND MY WAY HOME Polydor JV 1	6	13 wks
30 Jul 83	HE IS SAILING Polydor JV 4	61	2 wks
18 Aug 84	STATE OF INDEPENDENCE Polydor JV 5	67	2 wks

See also Vangelis.

Aled JONES UK, male vocalist — 24 wks

20 Jul 85	MEMORY BBC RESL 175	42	4 wks
30 Nov 85 ●	WALKING IN THE AIR HMV ALED 1	5	11 wks
14 Dec 85	PICTURES IN THE DARK Virgin VS 836 *	50	6 wks
20 Dec 86	A WINTER STORY HMV ALED 2	51	3 wks

* Mike Oldfield featuring Aled Jones, Anita Hegerland and Barry Palmer

Barbara JONES Jamaica, female vocalist — 7 wks

31 Jan 81	JUST WHEN I NEEDED YOU MOST Sonet SON 2221	31	7 wks

Catherine Zeta JONES UK, female vocalist — 5 wks

19 Sep 92	FOR ALL TIME Columbia 6583547	36	5 wks

Grace JONES US, female vocalist — 43 wks

26 Jul 80	PRIVATE LIFE Island WIP 6629	17	8 wks
20 Jun 81	PULL UP TO THE BUMPER Island WIP 6696	53	4 wks
30 Oct 82	THE APPLE STRETCHING/NIPPLE TO THE BOTTLE Island WIP 6779	50	4 wks
9 Apr 83	MY JAMAICAN GUY Island IS 103	56	3 wks

12 Oct 85	SLAVE TO THE RHYTHM *ZTT IS 206*	12	8 wks
18 Jan 86	PULL UP TO THE BUMPER (re-issue)/		
	LA VIE ENROSE *Island IS 240*	12	9 wks
1 Mar 86	LOVE IS THE DRUG *Island IS 266*	35	4 wks
15 Nov 86	I'M NOT PERFECT (BUT I'M PERFECT FOR YOU)		
	Manhattan MT 15	56	3 wks

La Vie En Rose *was only listed from 1 Feb 86.*

Howard JONES *UK, male vocalist* · 103 wks

17 Sep 83	●	NEW SONG *WEA HOW 1*	3	12 wks
26 Nov 83	●	WHAT IS LOVE *WEA HOW 2*	2	15 wks
14 Jan 84		NEW SONG (re-entry) *WEA HOW 1*	60	3 wks
18 Feb 84		HIDE AND SEEK *WEA HOW 3*	12	9 wks
26 May 84	●	PEARL IN THE SHELL *WEA HOW 4*	7	10 wks
11 Aug 84	●	LIKE TO GET TO KNOW YOU WELL *WEA HOW 5*	4	12 wks
9 Feb 85	●	THINGS CAN ONLY GET BETTER *WEA HOW 6*	6	8 wks
20 Apr 85	●	LOOK MAMA *WEA HOW 7*	10	6 wks
29 Jun 85		LIFE IN ONE DAY *WEA HOW 8*	14	7 wks
15 Mar 86		NO ONE IS TO BLAME *WEA HOW 9*	16	7 wks
4 Oct 86		ALL I WANT *WEA HOW 10*	35	4 wks
29 Nov 86		YOU KNOW I LOVE YOU...DON'T YOU?		
		WEA HOW 11	43	3 wks
21 Mar 87		A LITTLE BIT OF SNOW *WEA HOW 12*	70	1 wk
4 Mar 89		EVERLASTING LOVE *WEA HOW 13*	62	3 wks
11 Apr 92		LIFT ME UP *East West HOW 15*	52	3 wks

Janie JONES *UK, female vocalist* · 3 wks

| 27 Jan 66 | WITCHES' BREW *HMV POP 1495* | 46 | 3 wks |

Jimmy JONES *US, male vocalist* · 47 wks

17 Mar 60	●	HANDY MAN *MGM 1051*	3	21 wks
16 Jun 60	★	GOOD TIMIN' *MGM 1078*	1	15 wks
18 Aug 60		HANDY MAN (re-entry) *MGM 1051*	32	3 wks
8 Sep 60		I JUST GO FOR YOU *MGM 1091*	35	4 wks
17 Nov 60		READY FOR LOVE *MGM 1103*	46	1 wk
30 Mar 61		I TOLD YOU SO *MGM 1123*	33	3 wks

Juggy JONES *US, male multi-instrumentalist* · 4 wks

| 7 Feb 76 | INSIDE AMERICA *Contempo CS 2080* | 39 | 4 wks |

Mick JONES – *See AZTEC CAMERA*

Oran 'Juice' JONES *US, male vocalist* · 14 wks

| 15 Nov 86 | ● | THE RAIN *Def Jam A 7303* | 4 | 14 wks |

Paul JONES *UK, male vocalist* · 34 wks

6 Oct 66	●	HIGH TIME *HMV POP 1554*	4	15 wks
19 Jan 67	●	I'VE BEEN A BAD BAD BOY *HMV POP 1576*	5	9 wks
23 Aug 67		THINKIN' AIN'T FOR ME *HMV POP 1602*	47	1 wk
13 Sep 67		THINKIN' AIN'T FOR ME (re-entry) *HMV POP 1602*	32	7 wks
5 Feb 69		AQUARIUS *Columbia DB 8514*	45	2 wks

Quincy JONES *US, male producer/instrumentalist - keyboards* · 39 wks

29 Jul 78		STUFF LIKE THAT *A & M AMS 7367*	34	9 wks
11 Apr 81		AI NO CORRIDA (I-NO-KO-REE-DA)		
		A & M AMS 8109	14	10 wks
20 Jun 81		RAZZAMATAZZ *A & M AMS 8140* *	11	9 wks
5 Sep 81		BETCHA' WOULDN'T HURT ME *A & M AMS 8157*	52	3 wks

| 13 Jan 90 | I'LL BE GOOD TO YOU *Quest W 2697* ** | 21 | 7 wks |
| 31 Mar 90 | SECRET GARDEN *Quest W 9992* *** | 67 | 1 wk |

* Quincy Jones featuring Patti Austin ** Quincy Jones featuring Ray Charles and Chaka Khan *** Quincy Jones featuring Al B Sure!, James Ingram, El DeBarge and Barry White

Uncredited vocals on Stuff Like That *were by Ashford and Simpson and Chaka Khan, and on* Ai No Corrida *by Dune.*

Rickie Lee JONES *US, female vocalist* · 9 wks

| 23 Jun 79 | CHUCK E.'S IN LOVE *Warner Bros. K 17390* | 18 | 9 wks |

Shirley JONES – *See PARTRIDGE FAMILY starring Shirley JONES featuring David CASSIDY; VARIOUS ARTISTS (EPs & LPs) - Carousel Soundtrack*

Tammy JONES *UK, female vocalist* · 10 wks

| 26 Apr 75 | ● | LET ME TRY AGAIN *Epic EPC 3211* | 5 | 10 wks |

Tom JONES *UK, male vocalist* · 343 wks

11 Feb 65	★	IT'S NOT UNUSUAL *Decca F 12062*	1	14 wks
6 May 65		ONCE UPON A TIME *Decca F 12121*	32	4 wks
8 Jul 65		WITH THESE HANDS *Decca F 12191*	13	11 wks
12 Aug 65		WHAT'S NEW PUSSYCAT *Decca F 12203*	11	10 wks
13 Jan 66		THUNDERBALL *Decca F 12292*	35	4 wks
19 May 66		ONCE THERE WAS A TIME/NOT RESPONSIBLE		
		Decca F 12390	18	9 wks
18 Aug 66		THIS AND THAT *Decca F 12461*	44	3 wks
10 Nov 66	★	GREEN GREEN GRASS OF HOME *Decca F 22511*	1	22 wks
16 Feb 67	●	DETROIT CITY *Decca F 22555*	8	10 wks
13 Apr 67	●	FUNNY FAMILIAR FORGOTTEN FEELINGS		
		Decca F 12599	7	15 wks
26 Jul 67	●	I'LL NEVER FALL IN LOVE AGAIN *Decca F 12639*	2	25 wks
22 Nov 67	●	I'M COMING HOME *Decca F 12693*	2	16 wks
28 Feb 68	●	DELILAH *Decca F 12747*	2	17 wks
17 Jul 68	●	HELP YOURSELF *Decca F 12812*	5	26 wks
27 Nov 68		A MINUTE OF YOUR TIME *Decca F 12854*	14	15 wks
14 May 69	●	LOVE ME TONIGHT *Decca F 12924*	9	12 wks
13 Dec 69	●	WITHOUT LOVE *Decca F 12990*	10	11 wks
14 Mar 70		WITHOUT LOVE (re-entry) *Decca F 12990*	49	1 wk
18 Apr 70	●	DAUGHTER OF DARKNESS *Decca F 13013*	5	15 wks
15 Aug 70		I (WHO HAVE NOTHING) *Decca F 13061*	16	8 wks
17 Oct 70		I (WHO HAVE NOTHING) (re-entry) *Decca F 13061*	47	3 wks
16 Jan 71		SHE'S A LADY *Decca F 13113*	13	9 wks
27 Mar 71		SHE'S A LADY (re-entry) *Decca F 13113*	47	1 wk
5 Jun 71		PUPPET MAN *Decca F 13183*	49	1 wk
19 Jun 71		PUPPET MAN (re-entry) *Decca F 13183*	50	1 wk
23 Oct 71	●	TILL *Decca F 13236*	2	15 wks
1 Apr 72	●	THE YOUNG NEW MEXICAN PUPPETEER		
		Decca F 13298	6	12 wks
14 Apr 73		LETTER TO LUCILLE *Decca F 13393*	31	8 wks
7 Sep 74		SOMETHING 'BOUT YOU BABY I LIKE		
		Decca F 13550	36	5 wks
16 Apr 77		SAY YOU'LL STAY UNTIL TOMORROW *EMI 2583*	40	3 wks
18 Apr 87	●	A BOY FROM NOWHERE *Epic OLE 1*	2	12 wks
30 May 87		IT'S NOT UNUSUAL (re-issue) *Decca F 103*	17	8 wks
2 Jan 88		I WAS BORN TO BE ME *Epic OLE 4*	61	1 wk
29 Oct 88	●	KISS *China CHINA 11* *	5	7 wks
29 Apr 89		MOVE CLOSER *Jive JIVE 203*	49	3 wks
26 Jan 91		COULDN'T SAY GOODBYE *Dover ROJ 10*	51	2 wks
16 Mar 91		CARRYING A TORCH *Dover ROJ 12*	57	2 wks
4 Jul 92		DELILAH (re-issue) *The Hit Label TOM 10*	68	2 wks

* Art Of Noise featuring Tom Jones

Sue JONES-DAVIES – *See Julie COVINGTON, Rula LENSKA, Charlotte CORNWELL and Sue JONES-DAVIES*

Alison JORDAN *UK, female vocalist* · 4 wks

| 9 May 92 | BOY FROM NEW YORK CITY *Arista 74321100427* | 23 | 4 wks |

Dick JORDAN UK, male vocalist — 4 wks

17 Mar 60	HALLELUJAH I LOVE HER SO *Oriole CB 1534*	47	1 wk
9 Jun 60	LITTLE CHRISTINE *Oriole CB 1548*	39	3 wks

Jack JORDAN – *See Frank CHACKSFIELD*

Ronny JORDAN UK, male vocalist — 4 wks

1 Feb 92	SO WHAT! *Antilles ANN 14*	32	4 wks

David JOSEPH UK, male vocalist — 21 wks

26 Feb 83	YOU CAN'T HIDE (YOUR LOVE FROM ME) *Island IS 101*	13	9 wks
28 May 83	LET'S LIVE IT UP (NITE PEOPLE) *Island IS 116*	26	5 wks
18 Feb 84	JOYS OF LIFE *Island IS 153*	61	2 wks
31 May 86	EXPANSIONS '86 (EXPAND YOUR MIND) *Fourth & Broadway BRW 48* *	58	5 wks

* Chris Paul featuring David Joseph

Martyn JOSEPH UK, male vocalist — 5 wks

20 Jun 92	DOLPHINS MAKE ME CRY *Epic 6581347*	34	4 wks
12 Sep 92	WORKING MOTHER *Epic 6582937*	65	1 wk

JOURNEY US, male vocal/instrumental group — 9 wks

27 Feb 82	DON'T STOP BELIEVIN' *CBS A 1728*	62	4 wks
11 Sep 82	WHO'S CRYING NOW *CBS A 2725*	46	5 wks

Ruth JOY UK, female vocalist — 3 wks

26 Aug 89	DON'T PUSH IT *MCA RJOY 1*	66	2 wks
22 Feb 92	FEEL *MCA MCS 1574*	67	1 wk

JOY DIVISION UK, male vocal/instrumental group — 21 wks

28 Jun 80	LOVE WILL TEAR US APART *Factory FAC 23*	13	9 wks
29 Oct 83	LOVE WILL TEAR US APART (re-entry) *Factory FAC 23*	19	7 wks
18 Jun 88	ATMOSPHERE *Factory FAC 2137*	34	5 wks

JOY STRINGS UK, male/female vocal/instrumental group — 11 wks

27 Feb 64	IT'S AN OPEN SECRET *Regal-Zonophone RZ 501*	32	7 wks
17 Dec 64	A STARRY NIGHT *Regal-Zonophone RZ 504*	35	4 wks

JT and the BIG FAMILY
Italy, male/female vocal/instrumental group — 8 wks

3 Mar 90	● MOMENTS IN SOUL *Champion CHAMP 237*	7	8 wks

JUDAS PRIEST UK, male vocal/instrumental group — 50 wks

20 Jan 79	TAKE ON THE WORLD *CBS 6915*	14	10 wks
12 May 79	EVENING STAR *CBS 7312*	53	4 wks
29 Mar 80	LIVING AFTER MIDNIGHT *CBS 8379*	12	7 wks
7 Jun 80	BREAKING THE LAW *CBS 8644*	12	6 wks
23 Aug 80	UNITED *CBS 8897*	26	8 wks
21 Feb 81	DON'T GO *CBS 9520*	51	3 wks
25 Apr 81	HOT ROCKIN' *CBS 1153*	60	3 wks
21 Aug 82	YOU'VE GOT ANOTHER THING COMIN' *CBS A 2611*	66	2 wks
21 Jan 84	FREEWHEEL BURNIN' *CBS A 4054*	42	3 wks
23 Apr 88	JOHNNY B. GOODE *Atlantic A 9114*	64	2 wks
15 Sep 90	PAINKILLER *CBS 656273 7*	74	1 wk
23 Mar 91	A TOUCH OF EVIL *Columbia 6565897*	58	1 wk

JUDGE DREAD UK, male vocalist — 95 wks

26 Aug 72	BIG SIX *Big Shot BI 608*	11	27 wks
9 Dec 72	● BIG SEVEN *Big Shot BI 613*	8	18 wks
21 Apr 73	BIG EIGHT *Big Shot BI 619*	14	10 wks
5 Jul 75	● JE T'AIME (MOI NON PLUS) *Cactus CT 65*	9	9 wks
27 Sep 75	BIG TEN *Cactus CT 77*	14	7 wks
6 Dec 75	CHRISTMAS IN DREADLAND/COME OUTSIDE *Cactus CT 80*	14	7 wks
8 May 76	THE WINKLE MAN *Cactus CT 90*	35	4 wks
28 Aug 76	Y VIVA SUSPENDERS *Cactus CT 99*	27	4 wks
2 Apr 77	5TH ANNIVERSARY EP *Cactus CT 98*	31	4 wks
14 Jan 78	UP WITH THE COCK/BIG PUNK *Cactus CT 110*	49	1 wk
16 Dec 78	HOKEY COKEY/JINGLE BELLS *EMI 2881*	59	4 wks

Tracks on 5th Anniversary EP: Jamaica Jerk (off)/Bring Back The Skins/End Of The World/Big Everything.

JUICY US, male/female vocal duo — 5 wks

22 Feb 86	SUGAR FREE *Epic A 6917*	45	5 wks

JUICY LUCY UK, male vocal/instrumental group — 17 wks

7 Mar 70	WHO DO YOU LOVE *Vertigo V 1*	14	12 wks
10 Oct 70	PRETTY WOMAN *Vertigo 6059 015*	45	2 wks
31 Oct 70	PRETTY WOMAN (re-entry) *Vertigo 6059 015*	44	3 wks

JULIA and COMPANY US, male/female vocal group — 10 wks

3 Mar 84	BREAKIN' DOWN (SUGAR SAMBA) *London LON 46*	15	8 wks
23 Feb 85	I'M SO HAPPY *Next Plateau LON 61*	56	2 wks

JULUKA UK/South Africa, male/female vocal/instrumental group — 4 wks

12 Feb 83	SCATTERLINGS OF AFRICA *Safari ZULU 1*	44	4 wks

Wally JUMP Jr. and the CRIMINAL ELEMENT US, male producer - Arthur Baker — 19 wks

28 Feb 87	TURN ME LOOSE *London LON 126*	60	2 wks
5 Sep 87	PUT THE NEEDLE TO THE RECORD *Cooltempo COOL 150* *	63	3 wks
12 Dec 87	TIGHTEN UP - I JUST CAN'T STOP DANCING *Breakout USA 621*	24	7 wks
19 Mar 88	PRIVATE PARTY *Breakout USA 624*	57	3 wks
6 Oct 90	EVERYBODY (RAP) *deConstruction PB 44701* **	30	4 wks

* Criminal Element Orchestra ** Criminal Element Orchestra and Wendell Williams

JUMPING JACKS – *See Danny PEPPERMINT and the JUMPING JACKS*

Rosemary JUNE US, female vocalist — 9 wks

23 Jan 59	I'LL BE WITH YOU IN APPLE BLOSSOM TIME *Pye International 7N 25005*	14	9 wks

JUNGLE BROTHERS US, male rap group — 17 wks

22 Oct 88	I'LL HOUSE YOU *Gee Street GEE 003* *	22	5 wks
18 Mar 89	BLACK IS BLACK/STRAIGHT OUT OF THE JUNGLE *Gee Street GEE 15*	72	1 wk

| 31 Mar 90 | WHAT 'U' WAITIN' '4' *Eternal W 9865* | 35 | 5 wks |
| 21 Jul 90 | DOIN' OUR OWN DANG *Eternal W 9754* | 33 | 6 wks |

* Richie Rich meets the Jungle Brothers

Doin' Our Own Dang *features the uncredited De La Soul and Monie Love.*

JUNIOR *UK, male vocalist*   57 wks

24 Apr 82	● MAMA USED TO SAY *Mercury MER 98*	7	13 wks
10 Jul 82	TOO LATE *Mercury MER 112*	20	9 wks
25 Sep 82	LET ME KNOW/I CAN'T HELP IT *Mercury MER 116*	53	3 wks
23 Apr 83	COMMUNICATION BREAKDOWN *Mercury MER 134*	57	3 wks
8 Sep 84	SOMEBODY *London LON 50*	64	2 wks
9 Feb 85	DO YOU REALLY (WANT MY LOVE) *London LON 60*	47	4 wks
30 Nov 85	OH LOUISE *London LON 75*	74	3 wks
4 Apr 87	● ANOTHER STEP CLOSER TO YOU *MCA KIM 5* *	6	11 wks
25 Aug 90	STEP OFF *MCA MCA 1432* **	63	3 wks
15 Aug 92	THEN CAME YOU *MCA MCS 1676* **	32	5 wks
31 Oct 92	ALL OVER THE WORLD *MCA MCS 1691* **	74	1 wk

* Kim Wilde and Junior ** Junior Giscombe

JUNIORS – *See DANNY and the JUNIORS*

Jimmy JUSTICE *UK, male vocalist*   35 wks

29 Mar 62	● WHEN MY LITTLE GIRL IS SMILING *Pye 7N 15421*	9	13 wks
14 Jun 62	● AIN'T THAT FUNNY *Pye 7N 15443*	8	11 wks
23 Aug 62	SPANISH HARLEM *Pye 7N 15457*	20	11 wks

JUSTIFIED ANCIENTS OF MU MU   6 wks
UK, male production duo - The KLF under an assumed name

| 9 Nov 91 | ● IT'S GRIM UP NORTH *KLF Communications JAMS 028* | 10 | 5 wks |
| 4 Jan 92 | IT'S GRIM UP NORTH (re-entry) *KLF Communications JAMS 028* | 67 | 1 wk |

Bill JUSTIS *US, male instrumentalist - alto sax*   8 wks

| 10 Jan 58 | RAUNCHY *London HLS 8517* | 24 | 2 wks |
| 31 Jan 58 | RAUNCHY (re-entry) *London HLS 8517* | 11 | 6 wks |

Patrick JUVET *France, male vocalist*   19 wks

| 2 Sep 78 | GOT A FEELING *Casablanca CAN 127* | 34 | 7 wks |
| 4 Nov 78 | I LOVE AMERICA *Casablanca CAN 132* | 12 | 12 wks |

Frank K featuring Wiston OFFICE   1 wk
Italy/US, male vocal/instrumental duo

| 26 Jan 91 | EVERYBODY LET'S SOMEBODY LOVE *Urban URB 66* | 61 | 1 wk |

Leila K – *See ROB 'N' RAZ featuring Leila K*

K-CREATIVE *UK, male vocal/instrumental group*   2 wks

| 7 Mar 92 | THREE TIMES A MAYBE *Talkin Loud TLK 17* | 58 | 2 wks |

The listed flipside of Three Times A Maybe *was* Feed The Feeling *by Perception.*

K-KLASS *UK, male/female vocal/instrumental group*   20 wks

4 May 91	RHYTHM IS A MYSTERY *Deconstruction CREED 11*	61	2 wks
8 Nov 91	● RHYTHM IS A MYSTERY (re-issue) *Deconstruction R 6302*	3	10 wks
25 Apr 92	SO RIGHT *Deconstruction R 6309*	20	5 wks
7 Nov 92	DON'T STOP *Deconstruction R 6325*	32	3 wks

Bert KAEMPFERT *Germany, orchestra*   10 wks

| 23 Dec 65 | BYE BYE BLUES *Polydor BM 56 504* | 24 | 10 wks |

KAJAGOOGOO *UK, male vocal/instrumental group*   50 wks

22 Jan 83	★ TOO SHY *EMI 5359*	1	13 wks
2 Apr 83	● OOH TO BE AH *EMI 5383*	7	8 wks
4 Jun 83	HANG ON NOW *EMI 5394*	13	7 wks
17 Sep 83	● BIG APPLE *EMI 5423*	8	8 wks
3 Mar 84	THE LION'S MOUTH *EMI 5449*	25	7 wks
5 May 84	TURN YOUR BACK ON ME *EMI 5646*	47	4 wks
21 Sep 85	SHOULDN'T DO THAT *Parlophone R 6106* *	63	3 wks

* Kaja

KALIN TWINS *US, male vocal duo*   18 wks

| 18 Jul 58 | ★ WHEN *Brunswick 05751* | 1 | 18 wks |

Kitty KALLEN *US, female vocalist*   23 wks

| 2 Jul 54 | ★ LITTLE THINGS MEAN A LOT *Brunswick 05287* | 1 | 23 wks |

Gunther KALLMAN CHOIR   3 wks
Germany, male/female vocal group

| 24 Dec 64 | ELISABETH SERENADE *Polydor NH 24678* | 45 | 3 wks |

Nick KAMEN *UK, male vocalist*   33 wks

8 Nov 86	● EACH TIME YOU BREAK MY HEART *WEA YZ 90*	5	12 wks
28 Feb 87	LOVING YOU IS SWEETER THAN EVER *WEA YZ 106*	16	9 wks
16 May 87	NOBODY ELSE *WEA YZ 122*	47	3 wks
28 May 88	TELL ME *WEA YZ 184*	40	5 wks
28 Apr 90	I PROMISED MYSELF *WEA YZ 454*	50	4 wks

KANDIDATE *UK, male vocal/instrumental group*   28 wks

19 Aug 78	DON'T WANNA SAY GOODNIGHT *RAK 280*	47	6 wks
17 Mar 79	I DON'T WANNA LOSE YOU *RAK 289*	11	12 wks
4 Aug 79	GIRLS GIRLS GIRLS *RAK 295*	34	7 wks
22 Mar 80	LET ME ROCK YOU *RAK 306*	58	3 wks

Eden KANE *UK, male vocalist*   73 wks

1 Jun 61	★ WELL I ASK YOU *Decca F 11353*	1	21 wks
14 Sep 61	● GET LOST *Decca F 11381*	10	11 wks
18 Jan 62	● FORGET ME NOT *Decca F 11418*	3	14 wks
10 May 62	● I DON'T KNOW WHY *Decca F 11460*	7	13 wks
30 Jan 64	● BOYS CRY *Fontana TF 438*	8	14 wks

KANE GANG UK, male vocal/instrumental group — 37 wks

19 May 84	**SMALL TOWN CREED** Kitchenware SK 11	**60**	2 wks
7 Jul 84	**CLOSEST THING TO HEAVEN** Kitchenware SK 15	**12**	11 wks
10 Nov 84	**RESPECT YOURSELF** Kitchenware SK 16	**21**	10 wks
26 Jan 85	**RESPECT YOURSELF (re-entry)** Kitchenware SK 16	**75**	1 wk
9 Mar 85	**GUN LAW** Kitchenware SK 20	**53**	4 wks
27 Jun 87	**MOTORTOWN** Kitchenware SK 30	**45**	5 wks
16 Apr 88	**DON'T LOOK ANY FURTHER** Kitchenware SK 33	**52**	4 wks

KANSAS US, male vocal/instrumental group — 7 wks

1 Jul 78	**CARRY ON WAYWARD SON** Kirshner KIR 4932	**51**	7 wks

Mory KANTÉ Guinea, male vocalist — 9 wks

23 Jul 88	**YE KE YE KE** London LON 171	**29**	9 wks

KAOMA France, male/female vocal/instrumental group — 20 wks

21 Oct 89 ●	**LAMBADA** CBS 655011 7	**4**	18 wks
27 Jan 90	**DANCANDO LAMBADA** CBS 655235 7	**62**	2 wks

KAOTIC CHEMISTRY — 1 wk
UK, male instrumental/production group

31 Oct 92	**LSD (EP)** Moving Shadow SHADOW 20	**68**	1 wk

Tracks on LSD (EP): Space Cakes/LSD/Illegal Substances/Drumtrip II.

KARIN – See UNIQUE 3

KARIYA US, female vocalist — 9 wks

8 Jul 89	**LET ME LOVE YOU FOR TONIGHT** Sleeping Bag SBUK 4	**44**	6 wks
21 Oct 89	**LET ME LOVE YOU FOR TONIGHT (re-entry)** Sleeping Bag SBUK 4	**57**	3 wks

Mick KARN UK, male instrumentalist - saxophone — 6 wks

9 Jul 83	**AFTER A FASHION** Musicfest FEST 1 *	**39**	4 wks
17 Jan 87	**BUOY** Virgin VS 910 **	**63**	2 wks

* Midge Ure and Mick Karn ** Mick Karn featuring David Sylvian

KARTOON KREW US, male vocal/instrumental group — 6 wks

7 Dec 85	**INSPECTOR GADGET** Champion CHAMP 6	**58**	6 wks

KASENETZ-KATZ SINGING ORCHESTRAL CIRCUS — 15 wks
US, male vocal/instrumental group

20 Nov 68	**QUICK JOEY SMALL (RUN JOEY RUN)** Buddah 201 022	**19**	15 wks

KATRINA and the WAVES — 21 wks
UK/US, male/female vocal/instrumental group

4 May 85 ●	**WALKING ON SUNSHINE** Capitol CL 354	**8**	12 wks
5 Jul 86	**SUN STREET** Capitol CL 407	**22**	9 wks

Janet KAY UK, female vocalist — 24 wks

9 Jun 79 ●	**SILLY GAMES** Scope SC 2	**2**	14 wks
11 Aug 90	**SILLY GAMES** Arista 113452 *	**22**	7 wks
11 Aug 90	**SILLY GAMES (re-mix)** Music Factory Dance MFD 006	**62**	3 wks

* Lindy Layton featuring Janet Kay

Danny KAYE US, male vocalist — 10 wks

27 Feb 53 ●	**WONDERFUL COPENHAGEN** Brunswick 05023	**5**	10 wks

KAYE SISTERS UK, female vocal group — 45 wks

25 May 56	**IVORY TOWER** HMV POP 209 *	**20**	5 wks
1 Nov 57 ●	**GOTTA HAVE SOMETHING IN THE BANK FRANK** Philips PB 751 **	**8**	11 wks
3 Jan 58	**SHAKE ME I RATTLE/ALONE** Philips PB 752	**27**	1 wk
1 May 59 ●	**COME SOFTLY TO ME** Philips PB 913 **	**9**	9 wks
7 Jul 60 ●	**PAPER ROSES** Philips PB 1024	**7**	19 wks

* Three Kayes ** Frankie Vaughan and The Kaye Sisters

KC and the SUNSHINE BAND — 104 wks
US, male vocal/instrumental group

17 Aug 74 ●	**QUEEN OF CLUBS** Jayboy BOY 88	**7**	12 wks
23 Nov 74	**SOUND YOUR FUNKY HORN** Jayboy BOY 83	**17**	9 wks
29 Mar 75	**GET DOWN TONIGHT** Jayboy BOY 93	**21**	9 wks
2 Aug 75	**THAT'S THE WAY (I LIKE IT)** Jayboy BOY 99	**4**	10 wks
22 Nov 75	**I'M SO CRAZY** Jayboy BOY 101	**34**	3 wks
17 Jul 76	**(SHAKE SHAKE SHAKE) SHAKE YOUR BOOTY** Jayboy BOY 110	**22**	8 wks
11 Dec 76	**KEEP IT COMIN' LOVE** Jayboy BOY 112	**31**	8 wks
30 Apr 77	**I'M YOUR BOOGIE MAN** TK XB 2167	**41**	4 wks
6 May 78	**BOOGIE SHOES** TK TKR 6025	**34**	5 wks
22 Jul 78	**IT'S THE SAME OLD SONG** TK TKR 6037	**49**	5 wks
8 Dec 79 ●	**PLEASE DON'T GO** TK TKR 7558	**3**	12 wks
16 Jul 83 ★	**GIVE IT UP** Epic EPC A 3017	**1**	14 wks
24 Sep 83	**(YOU SAID) YOU'D GIMME SOME MORE** Epic A 2760	**41**	3 wks
11 May 91	**THAT'S THE WAY I LIKE IT (re-mix)** Music Factory Dance M7FAC 2	**59**	2 wks

Ernie K-DOE US, male vocalist — 7 wks

11 May 61	**MOTHER-IN-LAW** London HLU 9330	**29**	7 wks

Johnny KEATING UK, orchestra — 14 wks

1 Mar 62 ●	**THEME FROM 'Z CARS'** Piccadilly 7N 35032	**8**	14 wks

Kevin KEEGAN UK, male vocalist — 6 wks

9 Jun 79	**HEAD OVER HEELS IN LOVE** EMI 2965	**31**	6 wks

Yvonne KEELEY – See Scott FITZGERALD

Nelson KEENE UK, male vocalist — 5 wks

25 Aug 60	**IMAGE OF A GIRL** HMV POP 771	**37**	4 wks
29 Sep 60	**IMAGE OF A GIRL (re-entry)** HMV POP 771	**45**	1 wk

KEITH US, male vocalist — 8 wks

26 Jan 67	**98.6** Mercury MF 955	**24**	7 wks
16 Mar 67	**TELL ME TO MY FACE** Mercury MF 968	**50**	1 wk

Jerry KELLER US, male vocalist — 14 wks

28 Aug 59 ★	HERE COMES SUMMER London HLR 8890	1	14 wks

Frank KELLY Ireland, male vocalist — 5 wks

| 24 Dec 83 | CHRISTMAS COUNTDOWN Ritz RITZ 062 | 26 | 4 wks |
| 29 Dec 84 | CHRISTMAS COUNTDOWN (re-entry) Ritz RITZ 062 | 54 | 1 wk |

Frankie KELLY US, male vocalist/instrumentalist — 2 wks

| 2 Nov 85 | AIN'T THAT THE TRUTH 10 TEN 87 | 65 | 2 wks |

Grace KELLY – See Bing CROSBY

Keith KELLY UK, male vocalist — 5 wks

5 May 60	TEASE ME Parlophone R 4640	46	1 wk
19 May 60	TEASE ME (re-entry) Parlophone R 4640	27	3 wks
18 Aug 60	LISTEN LITTLE GIRL Parlophone R 4676	47	1 wk

R KELLY and PUBLIC ANNOUNCEMENT — 2 wks
US, male/female vocal/instrumental group

| 9 May 92 | SHE'S GOT THAT VIBE Jive JIVET 292 | 57 | 2 wks |

Roberta KELLY US, female vocalist — 3 wks

| 21 Jan 78 | ZODIACS Oasis/Hansa 3 | 48 | 1 wk |
| 4 Feb 78 | ZODIACS (re-entry) Oasis/Hansa 3 | 44 | 2 wks |

Johnny KEMP Barbados, male vocalist — 1 wk

| 27 Aug 88 | JUST GOT PAID CBS 651470 7 | 68 | 1 wk |

Tara KEMP US, female vocalist — 2 wks

| 20 Apr 91 | HOLD YOU TIGHT Giant W 0020 | 69 | 2 wks |

Graham KENDRICK UK, male vocalist — 4 wks

| 9 Sep 89 | LET THE FLAME BURN BRIGHTER Power P 30 | 55 | 4 wks |

Eddie KENDRICKS US, male vocalist — 20 wks

3 Nov 73	KEEP ON TRUCKIN' Tamla Motown TMG 873	18	14 wks
16 Mar 74	BOOGIE DOWN Tamla Motown TMG 888	39	4 wks
21 Sep 85	A NIGHT AT THE APOLLO LIVE! RCA PB 49935 *	58	2 wks

*Daryl Hall and John Oates featuring David Ruffin and Eddie Kendrick
A Night At The Apollo Live! is a medley of The Way You Do The Things You Do/My Girl.
Kendricks dropped the 's' from his name for last hit.

Jane KENNAWAY and STRANGE BEHAVIOUR — 3 wks
UK, female vocalist, male instrumental group

| 24 Jan 81 | I.O.U. Deram DM 436 | 65 | 3 wks |

KENNY Ireland, male vocalist — 16 wks

| 3 Mar 73 | HEART OF STONE RAK 144 | 11 | 13 wks |
| 30 Jun 73 | GIVE IT TO ME NOW RAK 153 | 38 | 3 wks |

KENNY UK, male vocal/instrumental group — 39 wks

7 Dec 74 ●	THE BUMP RAK 186	3	15 wks
8 Mar 75 ●	FANCY PANTS RAK 196	4	9 wks
7 Jun 75	BABY I LOVE YOU OK RAK 207	12	7 wks
16 Aug 75 ●	JULIE ANN RAK 214	10	8 wks

Gerard KENNY US, male vocalist — 21 wks

9 Dec 78	NEW YORK, NEW YORK RCA PB 5117	43	8 wks
21 Jun 80	FANTASY RCA PB 5256	65	1 wk
5 Jul 80	FANTASY (re-entry) RCA PB 5256	34	5 wks
18 Feb 84	THE OTHER WOMAN, THE OTHER MAN Impression IMS 3	69	4 wks
4 May 85	NO MAN'S LAND WEA YZ 38	56	3 wks

Klark KENT US, male vocalist/multi-instrumentalist — 4 wks

| 26 Aug 78 | DON'T CARE A & M AMS 7376 | 48 | 4 wks |

Carol KENYON – See Paul HARDCASTLE; HEAVEN 17

KERRI and MICK Australia, female/male vocal duo — 3 wks

| 28 Apr 84 | 'SONS AND DAUGHTERS' THEME A-1 A1 286 | 68 | 3 wks |

Liz KERSHAW and Bruno BROOKES — 3 wks
UK, male/female vocal duo

| 2 Dec 89 | IT TAKES TWO BABY Spartan CIN 101 * | 53 | 2 wks |
| 1 Dec 90 | LET'S DANCE Jive BRUNO 1 ** | 54 | 1 wk |

* Liz Kershaw, Bruno Brookes, Jive Bunny and Londonbeat ** Bruno and Liz
and the Radio 1 DJ Posse
See also Jive Bunny and the Mastermixers; Londonbeat.

Nik KERSHAW UK, male vocalist — 87 wks

19 Nov 83	I WON'T LET THE SUN GO DOWN ON ME MCA MCA 816	47	5 wks
28 Jan 84 ●	WOULDN'T IT BE GOOD MCA NIK 2	4	14 wks
14 Apr 84	DANCING GIRLS MCA NIK 3	13	9 wks
16 Jun 84 ●	I WON'T LET THE SUN GO DOWN ON ME (re-issue) MCA NIK 4	2	13 wks
15 Sep 84	HUMAN RACING MCA NIK 5	19	7 wks
17 Nov 84 ●	THE RIDDLE MCA NIK 6	3	11 wks
16 Mar 85 ●	WIDE BOY MCA NIK 7	9	8 wks
3 Aug 85 ●	DON QUIXOTE MCA NIK 8	10	7 wks
30 Nov 85	WHEN A HEART BEATS MCA NIK 9	27	7 wks
11 Oct 86	NOBODY KNOWS MCA NIK 10	44	3 wks
13 Dec 86	RADIO MUSICOLA MCA NIK 11	43	2 wks
4 Feb 89	ONE STEP AHEAD MCA NIK 12	55	1 wk

KEVIN THE GERBIL UK, male gerbil vocalist — 6 wks

| 4 Aug 84 | SUMMER HOLIDAY Magnet RAT 3 | 50 | 6 wks |

KEYNOTES – See Dave KING

Chaka KHAN US, female vocalist — 89 wks

2 Dec 78	I'M EVERY WOMAN Warner Bros. K 17269	11	13 wks
31 Mar 84 ●	AIN'T NOBODY Warner Bros. RCK 1 *	8	12 wks
20 Oct 84 ★	I FEEL FOR YOU Warner Bros. W 9209	1	16 wks
19 Jan 85	THIS IS MY NIGHT Warner Bros. W 9097	14	6 wks
20 Apr 85	EYE TO EYE Warner Bros. W 9009	16	7 wks

12 Jul 86		LOVE OF A LIFETIME *Warner Bros. W 8671*	52	4 wks
21 Jan 89		IT'S MY PARTY *Warner Bros. W 7678*	71	2 wks
6 May 89	●	I'M EVERY WOMAN (re-mix) *Warner Bros. W 2963*	8	8 wks
8 Jul 89	●	AIN'T NOBODY (re-mix) *Warner Bros. W 2880 **	6	9 wks
7 Oct 89		I FEEL FOR YOU (re-mix) *Warner Bros. W 2764*	45	2 wks
13 Jan 90		I'LL BE GOOD TO YOU *Qwest W 2697 ***	21	7 wks
28 Mar 92		LOVE YOU ALL MY LIFETIME *Warner Bros. W 0087*	49	3 wks

* Rufus and Chaka Khan ** Quincy Jones featuring Ray Charles and Chaka Khan
See also Quincy Jones.

Praga KHAN *Belgium, male producer* 8 wks

4 Apr 92		FREE YOUR BODY/INJECTED WITH A POISON *Profile PROFT 347 *	16	6 wks
11 Jul 92		RAVE ALERT *Profile PROF 369*	39	2 wks

* Praga Khan featuring Jade 4 U

KICK SQUAD *UK/Germany, male vocal/instrumental group* 2 wks

10 Nov 90	SOUND CLASH (CHAMPION SOUND) *Kickin KICK 2*	59	2 wks

KICKING BACK with TAXMAN 8 wks
UK, male/female vocal/instrumental duo with male rapper

17 Mar 90	DEVOTION *10 TEN 297*	47	4 wks
7 Jul 90	EVERYTHING *10 TEN 307*	54	4 wks

KICKS LIKE A MULE 6 wks
UK, male instrumental/production duo

1 Feb 92	●	THE BOUNCER *Tribal Bass TRIBE 3S*	7	6 wks

K.I.D. *Antilles, male/female vocal/instrumental group* 4 wks

28 Feb 81	DON'T STOP *EMI 5143*	49	4 wks

KID 'N' PLAY *US, male vocal/instrumental duo* 7 wks

18 Jul 87	LAST NIGHT *Cooltempo COOL 148*	71	1 wk
26 Mar 88	DO THIS MY WAY *Cooltempo COOL 164*	48	3 wks
17 Sep 88	GITTIN' FUNKY *Cooltempo COOL 168*	55	3 wks

KID UNKNOWN *UK, male producer - Paul Fitzpatrick* 1 wk

2 May 92	NIGHTMARE *Warp WAP 20CD*	64	1 wk

Carol KIDD featuring Terry WAITE 3 wks
UK, female/male vocal duo

17 Oct 92	WHEN I DREAM *The Hit Label HLS 1*	58	3 wks

Johnny KIDD and the PIRATES 62 wks
UK, male vocal/instrumental group

12 Jun 59	PLEASE DON'T TOUCH *HMV POP 615 *	26	3 wks
17 Jul 59	PLEASE DON'T TOUCH (re-entry) *HMV POP 615 *	25	2 wks
12 Feb 60	YOU GOT WHAT IT TAKES *HMV POP 698*	25	3 wks
16 Jun 60 ★	SHAKIN' ALL OVER *HMV POP 753*	1	19 wks
6 Oct 60	RESTLESS *HMV POP 790*	22	7 wks
13 Apr 61	LINDA LU *HMV POP 853*	47	1 wk
10 Jan 63	SHOT OF RHYTHM AND BLUES *HMV POP 1088*	48	1 wk

25 Jul 63	●	I'LL NEVER GET OVER YOU *HMV POP 1173*	4	15 wks
28 Nov 63		HUNGRY FOR LOVE *HMV POP 1228*	20	10 wks
30 Apr 64		ALWAYS AND EVER *HMV POP 1269*	46	1 wk

* Johnny Kidd

KIDS FROM 'FAME' *US, male/female vocal group* 36 wks

14 Aug 82	●	HI-FIDELITY *RCA 254 *	5	10 wks
2 Oct 82	●	STARMAKER *RCA 280*	3	10 wks
11 Dec 82		MANNEQUIN *RCA 299 ***	50	6 wks
9 Apr 83		FRIDAY NIGHT (LIVE VERSION) *RCA 320*	13	10 wks

* Kids From Fame featuring Valerie Landsberg ** Kids From Fame featuring Gene Anthony Ray

Greg KIHN BAND *US, male vocal/instrumental group* 2 wks

23 Apr 83	JEOPARDY *Beserkley E 9847*	63	2 wks

KILLING JOKE *UK, male vocal/instrumental group* 41 wks

23 May 81	FOLLOW THE LEADERS *Malicious Damage EGMDS 101*	55	5 wks
20 Mar 82	EMPIRE SONG *Malicious Damage EGO 4*	43	4 wks
30 Oct 82	BIRDS OF A FEATHER *EG EGO 10*	64	2 wks
25 Jun 83	LET'S ALL (GO TO THE FIRE DANCES) *EG EGO 11*	51	3 wks
15 Oct 83	ME OR YOU? *EG EGO 14*	57	1 wk
7 Apr 84	EIGHTIES *EG EGO 16*	60	5 wks
21 Jul 84	A NEW DAY *EG EGO 17*	56	2 wks
2 Feb 85	LOVE LIKE BLOOD *EG EGO 20*	16	9 wks
30 Mar 85	KINGS AND QUEENS *EG EGO 21*	58	3 wks
16 Aug 86	ADORATIONS *EG EGO 27*	42	6 wks
18 Oct 86	SANITY *EG EGO 30*	70	1 wk

Andy KIM *Canada, male vocalist* 12 wks

24 Aug 74	●	ROCK ME GENTLY *Capitol CL 15787*	2	12 wks

KING *UK/Ireland, male vocal/instrumental group* 44 wks

12 Jan 85	●	LOVE AND PRIDE *CBS A 4988*	2	14 wks
23 Mar 85		WON'T YOU HOLD MY HAND NOW *CBS A 6094*	24	8 wks
17 Aug 85	●	ALONE WITHOUT YOU *CBS A 6308*	8	9 wks
19 Oct 85		THE TASTE OF YOUR TEARS *CBS A 6618*	11	9 wks
11 Jan 86		TORTURE *CBS A 6761*	23	4 wks

Albert KING – *See Gary MOORE*

B.B. KING *US, male vocalist/instrumentalist - guitar* 10 wks

15 Apr 89	●	WHEN LOVE COMES TO TOWN *Island IS 411 *	6	7 wks
18 Jul 92		SINCE I MET YOU BABY *Virgin VS 1423 ***	59	3 wks

* U2 with B.B. King ** Gary Moore and B.B. King

Ben E. KING *US, male vocalist* 35 wks

2 Feb 61		FIRST TASTE OF LOVE *London HLK 9258*	27	11 wks
22 Jun 61		STAND BY ME *London HLK 9358*	50	1 wk
6 Jul 61		STAND BY ME (re-entry) *London HLK 9358*	27	6 wks
5 Oct 61		AMOR AMOR *London HLK 9416*	38	4 wks
14 Feb 87	★	STAND BY ME (re-issue) *Atlantic A 9361*	1	11 wks
4 Jul 87		SAVE THE LAST DANCE FOR ME *Manhattan MT 25*	69	2 wks

Carole KING *US, female vocalist* 29 wks

20 Sep 62	●	IT MIGHT AS WELL RAIN UNTIL SEPTEMBER *London HLU 9591*	3	13 wks

| 7 Aug 71 ● | IT'S TOO LATE A & M AMS 849 | 6 | 12 wks |
| 28 Oct 72 | IT MIGHT AS WELL RAIN UNTIL SEPTEMBER (re-issue) London HL 10391 | 43 | 4 wks |

Dave KING Canada, male vocalist — 29 wks

17 Feb 56 ●	MEMORIES ARE MADE OF THIS Decca F 10684 *	5	15 wks
13 Apr 56	YOU CAN'T BE TRUE TO TWO Decca F 10720 *	11	9 wks
21 Dec 56	CHRISTMAS AND YOU Decca F 10791	23	2 wks
24 Jan 58	THE STORY OF MY LIFE Decca F 10973	20	3 wks

* Dave King featuring The Keynotes
See also Various Artists (EPs & LPs) - All Star Hit Parade.

Denis KING – See STUTZ BEARCATS and the Denis KING ORCHESTRA

Evelyn 'Champagne' KING US, female vocalist — 76 wks

13 May 78	SHAME RCA PC 1122	39	23 wks
3 Feb 79	I DON'T KNOW IF IT'S RIGHT RCA PB 1386	67	2 wks
27 Jun 81	I'M IN LOVE RCA 95 *	27	11 wks
26 Sep 81	IF YOU WANT MY LOVIN' RCA 131 *	43	6 wks
28 Aug 82 ●	LOVE COME DOWN RCA 249 *	7	13 wks
20 Nov 82	BACK TO LOVE RCA 287 *	40	4 wks
19 Feb 83	GET LOOSE RCA 315 *	45	5 wks
9 Nov 85	YOUR PERSONAL TOUCH RCA PB 49915	37	5 wks
29 Mar 86	HIGH HORSE RCA PB 49891	55	3 wks
23 Jul 88	HOLD ON TO WHAT YOU'VE GOT Manhattan MT 49	47	3 wks
10 Oct 92	SHAME (re-mix) Network NWKTEN 156 **	74	1 wk

* Evelyn King ** Altern 8 vs Evelyn King

Jonathan KING UK, male vocalist — 128 wks

29 Jul 65 ●	EVERYONE'S GONE TO THE MOON Decca F 12187	4	11 wks
10 Jan 70	LET IT ALL HANG OUT Decca F 12988	26	7 wks
16 Jan 71	IT'S THE SAME OLD SONG B and C CB 139 *	19	9 wks
3 Apr 71	SUGAR SUGAR RCA 2064 **	12	14 wks
29 May 71	LAZY BONES Decca F 13177	23	8 wks
20 Nov 71	HOOKED ON A FEELING Decca F 13241	23	10 wks
5 Feb 72	FLIRT Decca F 13276	22	9 wks
14 Oct 72 ●	LOOP DI LOVE UK 7 ***	4	13 wks
26 Jan 74	(I CAN'T GET NO) SATISFACTION UK 53 ****	29	5 wks
6 Sep 75 ●	UNA PALOMA BLANCA UK 105	5	11 wks
20 Sep 75	CHICK-A-BOOM (DON'T YA JES LOVE IT) UK 2012 002 *****	36	4 wks
7 Feb 76	IN THE MOOD UK 121 ******	46	3 wks
26 Jun 76 ●	IT ONLY TAKES A MINUTE UK 135 *******	9	9 wks
7 Oct 78	ONE FOR YOU ONE FOR ME GTO GT 237	29	6 wks
16 Dec 78	LICK A SMURP FOR CHRISTMAS (ALL FALL DOWN) Petrol GAS 1 ********	58	4 wks
16 Jun 79	YOU'RE THE GREATEST LOVER UK International INT 586	67	2 wks
3 Nov 79	GLORIA Ariola ARO 198	65	3 wks

* Weathermen ** Sakkarin *** Shag **** Bubblerock ***** 53rd and 3rd featuring the Sound Of Shag ****** Sound 9418 ******* One Hundred Ton And A Feather ******** Father Abraphart and the Smurps
Petrol GAS 1 transferred to Magnet MAG 139 after the first week on chart.

Nosmo KING – See JAVELLS featuring Nosmo KING

Paul KING UK, male vocalist — 3 wks

| 2 May 87 | I KNOW CBS PKING 1 | 59 | 3 wks |

Solomon KING US, male vocalist — 28 wks

| 3 Jan 68 ● | SHE WEARS MY RING Columbia DB 8325 | 3 | 18 wks |
| 1 May 68 | WHEN WE WERE YOUNG Columbia DB 8402 | 21 | 10 wks |

Tony KING – See Kylie MINOGUE

British Hit Singles Part One: Alphabetically by Artist
Date of chart entry/Title & catalogue no./Peak position reached/Weeks on chart
★ Number one ● Top Ten † still on chart at 31 Dec 1992
* = credited to act billed in footnote

KING BEE UK, male rapper — 5 wks

| 26 Jan 91 | MUST BEE THE MUSIC Columbia 6565827 | 44 | 3 wks |
| 23 Mar 91 | BACK BY DOPE DEMAND First Bass 7RUFF 6X | 61 | 2 wks |

KING BROTHERS UK, male vocal/instrumental group — 74 wks

31 May 57 ●	A WHITE SPORT COAT Parlophone R 4310	6	14 wks
9 Aug 57	IN THE MIDDLE OF AN ISLAND Parlophone R 4338	19	13 wks
6 Dec 57	WAKE UP LITTLE SUSIE Parlophone R 4367	22	3 wks
31 Jan 58	PUT A LIGHT IN THE WINDOW Parlophone R 4389	29	1 wk
14 Feb 58	PUT A LIGHT IN THE WINDOW (re-entry) Parlophone R 4389	28	1 wk
28 Feb 58	PUT A LIGHT IN THE WINDOW (2nd re-entry) Parlophone R 4389	25	2 wks
14 Apr 60 ●	STANDING ON THE CORNER Parlophone R 4639	4	11 wks
28 Jul 60	MAIS OUI Parlophone R 4672	16	10 wks
12 Jan 61	DOLL HOUSE Parlophone R 4715	21	8 wks
2 Mar 61	76 TROMBONES Parlophone R 4737	19	11 wks

KING KURT UK, male vocal/instrumental group — 16 wks

15 Oct 83	DESTINATION ZULULAND Stiff BUY 189	36	6 wks
28 Apr 84	MACK THE KNIFE Stiff BUY 199	55	4 wks
4 Aug 84	BANANA BANANA Stiff BUY 206	54	4 wks
15 Nov 86	AMERICA Polydor KURT 1	73	1 wk
2 May 87	THE LAND OF RING DANG DO Polydor KURT 2	67	1 wk

KING SUN-D'MOET US, male rap/scratch duo — 3 wks

| 11 Jul 87 | HEY LOVE Flame MELT 5 | 66 | 3 wks |

KING TRIGGER UK, male/female vocal/instrumental group — 4 wks

| 14 Aug 82 | THE RIVER Chrysalis CHS 2623 | 57 | 4 wks |

KINGDOM COME US, male vocal/instrumental group — 2 wks

| 16 Apr 88 | GET IT ON Polydor KCS 1 | 75 | 1 wk |
| 6 May 89 | DO YOU LIKE IT Polydor KCS 3 | 73 | 1 wk |

KINGMAKER UK, male vocal/instrumental group — 8 wks

18 Jan 92	IDIOTS AT THE WHEEL EP Scorch SCORCH 3	30	3 wks
23 May 92	EAT YOURSELF WHOLE Scorch SCORCHG 5	15	3 wks
31 Oct 92	ARMCHAIR ANARCHIST Scorch SCORCHG 6	47	2 wks

Tracks on Idiots At The Wheel EP: Really Scrape The Sky/Revelation/Every Teenage Suicide/Strip Away.

KINGS OF SWING ORCHESTRA — 5 wks
Australia, orchestra

| 1 May 82 | SWITCHED ON SWING Philips Swing 1 | 48 | 5 wks |

KINGSMEN US, male vocal/instrumental group — 7 wks

| 30 Jan 64 | LOUIE LOUIE Pye International 7N 25231 | 26 | 7 wks |

KINGSTON TRIO US, male vocal/instrumental group — **15 wks**

21 Nov 58 ●	TOM DOOLEY *Capitol CL 14951*	5	14 wks
4 Dec 59	SAN MIGUEL *Capitol CL 15073*	29	1 wk

KINKS UK, male vocal/instrumental group — **213 wks**

13 Aug 64 ★	YOU REALLY GOT ME *Pye 7N 15673*	1	12 wks
29 Oct 64 ●	ALL DAY AND ALL OF THE NIGHT *Pye 7N 15714*	2	14 wks
21 Jan 65 ★	TIRED OF WAITING FOR YOU *Pye 7N 15759*	1	10 wks
25 Mar 65	EVERYBODY'S GONNA BE HAPPY *Pye 7N 15813*	17	8 wks
27 May 65 ●	SET ME FREE *Pye 7N 15854*	9	11 wks
5 Aug 65 ●	SEE MY FRIEND *Pye 7N 15919*	10	9 wks
2 Dec 65 ●	TILL THE END OF THE DAY *Pye 7N 15981*	8	12 wks
3 Mar 66 ●	DEDICATED FOLLOWER OF FASHION *Pye 7N 17064*	4	11 wks
9 Jun 66 ★	SUNNY AFTERNOON *Pye 7N 17125*	1	13 wks
24 Nov 66 ●	DEAD END STREET *Pye 7N 17222*	5	11 wks
11 May 67 ●	WATERLOO SUNSET *Pye 7N 17321*	2	11 wks
18 Oct 67 ●	AUTUMN ALMANAC *Pye 7N 17400*	3	11 wks
17 Apr 68	WONDERBOY *Pye 7N 17468*	36	5 wks
17 Jul 68	DAYS *Pye 7N 17573*	12	10 wks
16 Apr 69	PLASTIC MAN *Pye 7N 17724*	31	4 wks
10 Jan 70	VICTORIA *Pye 7N 17865*	33	4 wks
4 Jul 70 ●	LOLA *Pye 7N 17961*	2	14 wks
12 Dec 70 ●	APEMAN *Pye 7N 45016*	5	14 wks
27 May 72	SUPERSONIC ROCKET SHIP *RCA 2211*	16	8 wks
27 Jun 81	BETTER THINGS *Arista ARIST 415*	46	5 wks
6 Aug 83	COME DANCING *Arista ARIST 502*	12	9 wks
15 Oct 83	DON'T FORGET TO DANCE *Arista ARIST 524*	58	3 wks
15 Oct 83	YOU REALLY GOT ME (re-issue) *PRT KD1*	47	4 wks

Fern KINNEY US, female vocalist — **11 wks**

16 Feb 80 ★	TOGETHER WE ARE BEAUTIFUL *WEA K 79111*	1	11 wks

KINSHASA BAND – *See Johnny WAKELIN*

Kathy KIRBY UK, female vocalist — **54 wks**

15 Aug 63	DANCE ON *Decca F 11682*	11	13 wks
7 Nov 63 ●	SECRET LOVE *Decca F 11759*	4	18 wks
20 Feb 64 ●	LET ME GO LOVER *Decca F 11832*	10	11 wks
7 May 64	YOU'RE THE ONE *Decca F 11892*	17	9 wks
4 Mar 65	I BELONG *Decca F 12087*	36	3 wks

Bo KIRKLAND and Ruth DAVIS
US, male/female vocal duo — **9 wks**

4 Jun 77	YOU'RE GONNA GET NEXT TO ME *EMI International INT 532*	12	9 wks

KISS US, male vocal/instrumental group — **57 wks**

30 Jun 79	I WAS MADE FOR LOVIN' YOU *Casablanca CAN 152*	50	7 wks
20 Feb 82	A WORLD WITHOUT HEROES *Casablanca KISS 002*	55	3 wks
30 Apr 83	CREATURES OF THE NIGHT *Casablanca KISS 4*	34	4 wks
29 Oct 83	LICK IT UP *Vertigo KISS 5*	31	5 wks
8 Sep 84	HEAVEN'S ON FIRE *Vertigo VER 12*	43	3 wks
9 Nov 85	TEARS ARE FALLING *Vertigo KISS 6*	57	2 wks
3 Oct 87 ●	CRAZY CRAZY NIGHTS *Vertigo KISS 7*	4	9 wks
5 Dec 87	REASON TO LIVE *Vertigo KISS 8*	33	7 wks
10 Sep 88	TURN ON THE NIGHT *Vertigo KISS 9*	41	3 wks
18 Nov 89	HIDE YOUR HEART *Vertigo KISS 10*	59	2 wks
31 Mar 90	FOREVER *Vertigo KISS 11*	65	2 wks
11 Jan 92 ●	GOD GAVE ROCK AND ROLL TO YOU II *Interscope A 8696*	4	8 wks
9 May 92	UNHOLY *Mercury KISS 12*	26	2 wks

KISS AMC UK, female vocal duo — **5 wks**

1 Jul 89	A BIT OF... *Syncopate SY 29*	58	2 wks

19 Aug 89	A BIT OF U2 (re-entry) *Syncopate SY 29*	58	2 wks
3 Feb 90	MY DOCS *Syncopate XAMC 1*	66	1 wk

Before the re-entry of A BIT OF U2, *copyright problems meant that the disc was unable to be given its full title.*

KISSING THE PINK — **14 wks**
UK, male/female vocal/instrumental group

5 Mar 83	LAST FILM *Magnet KTP 3*	19	14 wks

Mac and Katie KISSOON UK, male/female vocal duo — **33 wks**

19 Jun 71	CHIRPY CHIRPY CHEEP CHEEP *Young Blood YB 1026*	41	1 wk
18 Jan 75 ●	SUGAR CANDY KISSES *Polydor 2058 531*	3	10 wks
3 May 75 ●	DON'T DO IT BABY *State STAT 4*	9	8 wks
30 Aug 75	LIKE A BUTTERFLY *State STAT 9*	18	9 wks
15 May 76	THE TWO OF US *State STAT 21*	46	5 wks

Kevin KITCHEN UK, male vocalist — **3 wks**

20 Apr 85	PUT MY ARMS AROUND YOU *China WOK 1*	64	3 wks

Eartha KITT US, female vocalist — **32 wks**

1 Apr 55 ●	UNDER THE BRIDGES OF PARIS *HMV B 10647*	7	9 wks
10 Jun 55	UNDER THE BRIDGES OF PARIS (re-entry) *HMV B 10647*	20	1 wk
3 Dec 83	WHERE IS MY MAN *Record Shack SOHO 11*	36	11 wks
7 Jul 84	I LOVE MEN *Record Shack SOHO 21*	50	3 wks
12 Apr 86	THIS IS MY LIFE *Record Shack SOHO 61*	73	1 wk
1 Jul 89	CHA CHA HEELS *Arista 112331* *	32	7 wks

* *Eartha Kitt and Bronski Beat*

KLAXONS Belgium, male vocal/instrumental group — **6 wks**

10 Dec 83	THE CLAP CLAP SOUND *PRT 7P 290*	45	6 wks

KLEEER US, male/female vocal/instrumental group — **10 wks**

17 Mar 79	KEEEP YOUR BODY WORKING *Atlantic LV 21*	51	6 wks
14 Mar 81	GET TOUGH *Atlantic 11560*	49	4 wks

KLF UK, male vocal/instrumental duo — **51 wks**

11 Aug 90 ●	WHAT TIME IS LOVE (LIVE AT TRANCENTRAL) *KLF Commmunications KLF 004* *	5	12 wks
19 Jan 91 ★	3 AM ETERNAL *KLF Communications KLF 005* *	1	11 wks
4 May 91 ●	LAST TRAIN TO TRANCENTRAL *KLF Communications KLF 008* *	2	9 wks
7 Dec 91 ●	JUSTIFIED AND ANCIENT *KLF Communications KLF 099* **	2	12 wks
7 Mar 92 ●	AMERICA: WHAT TIME IS LOVE *KLF Communications KLFUSA 004*	4	7 wks

* *KLF featuring the Children Of The Revolution* ** *KLF Guest vocals: Tammy Wynette*

See also Justified Ancients Of Mu Mu.

KNACK US, male vocal/instrumental group — **12 wks**

30 Jun 79 ●	MY SHARONA *Capitol CL 16087*	6	10 wks
13 Oct 79	GOOD GIRLS DON'T *Capitol CL 16097*	66	2 wks

Frederick KNIGHT US, male vocalist — **10 wks**

10 Jun 72	I'VE BEEN LONELY SO LONG *Stax 2025 098*	22	10 wks

Gladys KNIGHT and the PIPS
US, female vocalist and male vocal backing group — **187 wks**

8 Jun 67	TAKE ME IN YOUR ARMS AND LOVE ME		
	Tamla Motown TMG 604	13	15 wks
27 Dec 67	I HEARD IT THROUGH THE GRAPEVINE		
	Tamla Motown TMG 629	47	1 wk
17 Jun 72	JUST WALK IN MY SHOES *Tamla Motown TMG 813*	35	8 wks
25 Nov 72	HELP ME MAKE IT THROUGH THE NIGHT		
	Tamla Motown TMG 830	11	17 wks
3 Mar 73	LOOK OF LOVE *Tamla Motown TMG 844*	21	9 wks
26 May 73	NEITHER ONE OF US *Tamla Motown TMG 855*	31	7 wks
5 Apr 75 ●	THE WAY WE WERE - TRY TO REMEMBER		
	Buddah BDS 428	4	15 wks
2 Aug 75 ●	BEST THING THAT EVER HAPPENED TO ME		
	Buddah BDS 432	7	10 wks
15 Nov 75	PART TIME LOVER *Buddah BDS 438*	30	5 wks
8 May 76 ●	MIDNIGHT TRAIN TO GEORGIA *Buddah BDS 444*	10	9 wks
21 Aug 76	MAKE YOURS A HAPPY HOME *Buddah BDS 447*	35	4 wks
6 Nov 76	SO SAD THE SONG *Buddah BDS 448*	20	9 wks
15 Jan 77	NOBODY BUT YOU *Buddah BDS 451*	34	2 wks
28 May 77 ●	BABY DON'T CHANGE YOUR MIND		
	Buddah BDS 458	4	12 wks
24 Sep 77	HOME IS WHERE THE HEART IS *Buddah BDS 460*	35	4 wks
8 Apr 78	THE ONE AND ONLY *Buddah BDS 470*	32	4 wks
13 May 78	THE ONE AND ONLY (re-entry) *Buddah BDS 470*	66	1 wk
24 Jun 78	COME BACK AND FINISH WHAT YOU STARTED		
	Buddah BDS 473	15	13 wks
30 Sep 78	IT'S A BETTER THAN GOOD TIME		
	Buddah BDS 478	59	4 wks
30 Aug 80	TASTE OF BITTER LOVE *CBS 8890*	35	6 wks
8 Nov 80	BOURGIE BOURGIE *CBS 9081*	32	6 wks
26 Dec 81	WHEN A CHILD IS BORN *CBS S 1758* *	74	2 wks
9 Nov 85	THAT'S WHAT FRIENDS ARE FOR		
	Arista ARIST 638 **	16	9 wks
16 Jan 88	LOVE OVERBOARD *MCA MCA 1223*	42	4 wks
10 Jun 89 ●	LICENCE TO KILL *MCA MCA 1339* ***	6	11 wks

*Johnny Mathis and Gladys Knight **Dionne Warwick and Friends featuring Elton John, Stevie Wonder and Gladys Knight ***Gladys Knight

Robert KNIGHT *US, male vocalist* — **26 wks**

17 Jan 68	EVERLASTING LOVE *Monument MON 1008*	40	2 wks
24 Nov 73 ●	LOVE ON A MOUNTAIN TOP *Monument MNT 1875*	10	16 wks
9 Mar 74	EVERLASTING LOVE (re-issue) *Monument MNT 2106*	19	8 wks

Mark KNOPFLER *UK, male vocalist/instrumentalist - guitar* — **3 wks**

| 12 Mar 83 | GOING HOME (THEME OF 'LOCAL HERO') | | |
| | *Vertigo DSTR 4* | 56 | 3 wks |

Buddy KNOX *US, male vocalist* — **5 wks**

| 10 May 57 | PARTY DOLL *Columbia DB 3914* | 29 | 3 wks |
| 16 Aug 62 | SHE'S GONE *Liberty LIB 55473* | 45 | 2 wks |

Frankie KNUCKLES *US, male producer* — **15 wks**

17 Jun 89	TEARS *ffrr F 108* *	50	3 wks
21 Oct 89	YOUR LOVE *Trax TRAXT 3*	59	4 wks
27 Jul 91	THE WHISTLE SONG *Virgin America VUS 47*	17	5 wks
23 Nov 91	IT'S HARD SOMETIMES *Virgin America VUS 52*	67	1 wk
6 Jun 92	RAIN FALLS *Virgin America VUST 60* **	48	2 wks

*Frankie Knuckles presents Satoshi Tomiie **Frankie Knuckles featuring Lisa Michaelis

Moe KOFFMAN QUARTETTE — **2 wks**
Canada, male instrumental group, Moe Koffman - flute

| 28 Mar 58 | SWINGIN' SHEPHERD BLUES *London HLJ 8549* | 23 | 2 wks |

KOKOMO *US, male instrumentalist - piano* — **7 wks**

| 13 Apr 61 | ASIA MINOR *London HLU 9305* | 35 | 7 wks |

KOKOMO *UK, male/female vocal/instrumental group* — **3 wks**

| 29 May 82 | A LITTLE BIT FURTHER AWAY *CBS A 2064* | 45 | 3 wks |

KON KAN *Canada, male vocal/instrumental duo* — **13 wks**

| 4 Mar 89 ● | I BEG YOUR PARDON *Atlantic A 8969* | 5 | 13 wks |

John KONGOS — **25 wks**
South Africa, male vocalist/multi-instrumentalist

| 22 May 71 ● | HE'S GONNA STEP ON YOU AGAIN *Fly BUG 8* | 4 | 14 wks |
| 20 Nov 71 ● | TOKOLOSHE MAN *Fly BUG 14* | 4 | 11 wks |

KOOL and the GANG *US, male vocal/instrumental group* **207 wks**

27 Oct 79 ●	LADIES NIGHT *Mercury KOOL 7*	9	12 wks
19 Jan 80	TOO HOT *Mercury KOOL 8*	23	8 wks
12 Jul 80	HANGIN' OUT *De-Lite KOOL 9*	52	4 wks
1 Nov 80 ●	CELEBRATION *De-Lite KOOL 10*	7	13 wks
21 Feb 81	JONES VS JONES/SUMMER MADNESS		
	De-Lite KOOL 11	17	11 wks
30 May 81	TAKE IT TO THE TOP *De-Lite DE 2*	15	9 wks
31 Oct 81	STEPPIN' OUT *De-Lite DE 4*	12	13 wks
19 Dec 81 ●	GET DOWN ON IT *De-Lite DE 5*	3	12 wks
6 Mar 82	TAKE MY HEART (YOU CAN HAVE IT IF YOU		
	WANT IT) *De-Lite DE 6*	29	7 wks
7 Aug 82	BIG FUN *De-Lite DE 7*	14	8 wks
16 Oct 82 ●	OOH LA LA LA (LET'S GO DANCIN') *De-Lite DE 9*	6	9 wks
4 Dec 82	HI DE HI, HI DE HO *De-Lite DE 14*	29	8 wks
10 Dec 83	STRAIGHT AHEAD *De-Lite DE 15*	15	10 wks
11 Feb 84 ●	JOANNA /TONIGHT *De-Lite DE 16*	2	11 wks
14 Apr 84 ●	(WHEN YOU SAY YOU LOVE SOMEBODY) IN		
	THE HEART *De-Lite DE 17*	7	8 wks
24 Nov 84	FRESH *De-Lite DE 18*	11	12 wks
9 Feb 85	MISLED *De-Lite DE 19*	28	5 wks
11 May 85 ●	CHERISH *De-Lite DE 20*	4	22 wks
2 Nov 85	EMERGENCY *De-Lite DE 21*	50	3 wks
22 Nov 86	VICTORY *Club JAB 44*	67	2 wks
20 Dec 86	VICTORY (re-entry) *Club JAB 44*	30	10 wks
21 Mar 87	STONE LOVE *Club JAB 47*	45	4 wks
31 Dec 88	CELEBRATION (re-mix) *Club JAB 78*	56	5 wks
6 Jul 91	GET DOWN ON IT (re-mix) *Mercury MER 346*	69	1 wk

Funky Stuff and Hollywood Swinging only appeared on 12-inch and EP versions of Kool 11, although the chart listed all four songs.

KOOLROCK STEADY – *See TYREE*

KORGIS *UK, male vocal/instrumental duo* — **27 wks**

23 Jun 79	IF I HAD YOU *Rialto TREB 103*	13	12 wks
24 May 80 ●	EVERYBODY'S GOT TO LEARN SOMETIME		
	Rialto TREB 115	5	12 wks
30 Aug 80	IF IT'S ALRIGHT WITH YOU BABY *Rialto TREB 118*	56	3 wks

KRAFTWERK *Germany, male instrumental/vocal group* — **69 wks**

10 May 75	AUTOBAHN *Vertigo 6147 012*	11	9 wks
28 Oct 78	NEON LIGHTS *Capitol CL 15998*	53	3 wks
9 May 81	POCKET CALCULATOR *EMI 5175*	39	6 wks
11 Jul 81	COMPUTER LOVE/THE MODEL *EMI 5207*	36	8 wks
26 Dec 81 ★	COMPUTER LOVE/THE MODEL (re-entry)		
	EMI 5207	1	13 wks

In 1992 the young Atlanta rap duo KRIS KROSS joined the Pointer Sisters and Van Halen as artists with a top ten song titled 'Jump'.

Left: The hit albums of JAMES LAST have outnumbered his chart single 56 to 1.

'Please Don't Go' by KC and the Sunshine Band was America's first number one of the 80s. KWS took the song to the top in Britain in 1992.

CYNDI LAUPER (left) is defeated by Cher in the battle of the see-through garments at the 1987 MTV Awards.

20 Feb 82	**SHOWROOM DUMMIES** *EMI 5272* **25**	5 wks
6 Aug 83	**TOUR DE FRANCE** *EMI 5413* **22**	8 wks
25 Aug 84	**TOUR DE FRANCE (re-entry)** *EMI 5413* **24**	11 wks
1 Jun 91	**THE ROBOTS** *EMI EM 192* **20**	4 wks
2 Nov 91	**RADIOACTIVITY** *EMI EM 201* **43**	2 wks

Billy J. KRAMER and the DAKOTAS   71 wks
UK, male vocalist and male instrumental backing group

2 May 63 ●	**DO YOU WANT TO KNOW A SECRET?** *Parlophone R 5023* **2**	15 wks
1 Aug 63 ★	**BAD TO ME** *Parlophone R 5049* **1**	14 wks
7 Nov 63 ●	**I'LL KEEP YOU SATISFIED** *Parlophone R 5073* **4**	13 wks
27 Feb 64 ★	**LITTLE CHILDREN** *Parlophone R 5105* **1**	13 wks
23 Jul 64 ●	**FROM A WINDOW** *Parlophone R 5156* **10**	8 wks
20 May 65	**TRAINS AND BOATS AND PLANES** *Parlophone R 5285* **12**	8 wks

KRANKIES *UK, male/female vocal duo*   6 wks

7 Feb 81	**FAN'DABI'DOZI** *Monarch MON 21* **71**	1 wk
7 Mar 81	**FAN'DABI'DOZI (re-entry)** *Monarch MON 21* **46**	5 wks

Lenny KRAVITZ *US, male vocalist*   20 wks

2 Jun 90	**MR. CABDRIVER** *Virgin America VUS 20* **58**	2 wks
4 Aug 90	**LET LOVE RULE** *Virgin America VUS 26* **39**	4 wks
30 Mar 91	**ALWAYS ON THE RUN** *Virgin America VUS 34* **41**	3 wks
15 Jun 91	**IT AIN'T OVER TIL IT'S OVER** *Virgin America VUS 43* ...**11**	8 wks
14 Sep 91	**STAND BY MY WOMAN** *Virgin America VUS 45* **55**	3 wks

KRAZE *US, male/female vocal/instrumental group*   6 wks

22 Oct 88	**THE PARTY** *MCA MCA 1288* **29**	5 wks
17 Jun 89	**LET'S PLAY HOUSE** *MCA MCA 1337* **71**	1 wk

KREW-KATS *UK, male instrumental group*   10 wks

9 Mar 61	**TRAMBONE** *HMV POP 840* **33**	9 wks
18 May 61	**TRAMBONE (re-entry)** *HMV POP 840* **49**	1 wk

KRIS KROSS *US, male vocal duo*   17 wks

30 May 92 ●	**JUMP** *Ruff House 6578547* **2**	8 wks
25 Jul 92	**WARM IT UP** *Columbia 6582187* **16**	6 wks
17 Oct 92	**I MISSED THE BUS** *Columbia 6583927* **57**	1 wk
19 Dec 92	**IT'S A SHAME** *Columbia 6588587* ....**31†**	2 wks

Marty KRISTIAN – *See NEW SEEKERS*

KROKUS *Switzerland/Argentina, male vocal/instrumental group*   2 wks

16 May 81	**INDUSTRIAL STRENGTH EP** *Ariola ARO 258* **62**	2 wks

Tracks on Industrial Strength EP: *Bedside Radio/Easy Rocker/Celebration/Bye Bye Baby.*

KRUSH *UK, male/female vocal/instrumental group*   16 wks

5 Dec 87 ●	**HOUSE ARREST** *Club JAB 63* **3**	15 wks
14 Nov 92	**WALKING ON SUNSHINE** *Network NWK 55* **71**	1 wk

K3M *Italy, male/female vocal/instrumental duo*   1 wk

21 Mar 92	**LISTEN TO THE RHYTHM** *PWL Continental PWL 214* ...**71**	1 wk

Charlie KUNZ *US, male instrumentalist - piano*   4 wks

17 Dec 54	**PIANO MEDLEY NO. 114** *Decca F 10419* **20**	3 wks

14 Jan 55	**PIANO MEDLEY NO. 114 (re-entry)** *Decca F 10419* **16**	1 wk

Medley titles: There Must Be A Reason/Hold My Hand/If I Give My Heart To You/Little Things Mean A Lot/Make Her Mine/My Son My Son.

KURSAAL FLYERS *UK, male vocal/instrumental group*   10 wks

20 Nov 76	**LITTLE DOES SHE KNOW** *CBS 4689* **14**	10 wks

KWS *UK, male vocal/instrumental group*   26 wks

25 Apr 92 ★	**PLEASE DON'T GO/GAME BOY** *Network NWK 46* ...**1**	16 wks
22 Aug 92 ●	**ROCK YOUR BABY** *Network NWK 54* **8**	7 wks
12 Dec 92	**HOLD BACK THE NIGHT** *Network NWK 65* * ....**30†**	3 wks

* *KWS features guest vocal from the Trammps*
Game Boy only listed from 9 May 92.

L.A. GUNS *US, male/female vocal/instrumental group*   4 wks

30 Nov 91	**SOME LIE 4 LOVE** *Mercury MER 358* **61**	1 wk
21 Dec 91	**THE BALLAD OF JAYNE** *Mercury MER 361* **53**	3 wks

L.A. MIX *UK, male/female vocal/instrumental duo*   25 wks

10 Oct 87	**DON'T STOP (JAMMIN')** *Breakout USA 615* **47**	4 wks
21 May 88 ●	**CHECK THIS OUT** *Breakout USA 629* **6**	7 wks
8 Jul 89	**GET LOOSE** *Breakout USA 659* * **25**	6 wks
16 Sep 89	**LOVE TOGETHER** *Breakout USA 662* ** **66**	2 wks
15 Sep 90	**COMING BACK FOR MORE** *A & M AM 579* **50**	3 wks
19 Jan 91	**MYSTERIES OF LOVE** *A & M AM 707* **46**	2 wks
23 Mar 91	**WE SHOULDN'T HOLD HANDS IN THE DARK** *A & M AM 755* **69**	1 wk

* *L.A. Mix performed by Jazzi P* ** *L.A. Mix featuring Kevin Henry*

LA NA NEE NEE NOO NOO – *See BANANARAMA*

Danny LA RUE *UK, male vocalist*   9 wks

18 Dec 68	**ON MOTHER KELLY'S DOORSTEP** *Page One POF 108* **33**	9 wks

Denise LA SALLE *US, female vocalist*   13 wks

15 Jun 85 ●	**MY TOOT TOOT** *Epic A 6334* **6**	13 wks

LABELLE *US, female vocal group*   9 wks

22 Mar 75	**LADY MARMALADE (VOULEZ-VOUS COUCHER AVEC MOI CE SOIR?)** *Epic EPC 2852* **17**	9 wks

See also Patti Labelle.

Patti LABELLE *US, female vocalist*   19 wks

3 May 86 ●	**ON MY OWN** *MCA MCA 1045* * **2**	13 wks
2 Aug 86	**OH, PEOPLE** *MCA MCA 1075* **26**	6 wks

* *Patti Labelle and Michael McDonald*
See also Labelle.

LADIES CHOICE UK, male vocalist   4 wks

25 Jan 86   FUNKY SENSATION Sure Delight SD 01 41   4 wks

LAID BACK Norway, male vocal/instrumental duo   4 wks

5 May 90   BAKERMAN Arista 112356...........................44   4 wks

Cleo LAINE UK, female vocalist   14 wks

29 Dec 60   LET'S SLIP AWAY Fontana H 269...................42   1 wk
14 Sep 61 ● YOU'LL ANSWER TO ME Fontana H 326 ....5 13 wks

Frankie LAINE US, male vocalist   281 wks

14 Nov 52 ● HIGH NOON Columbia DB 3113 7   7 wks
14 Nov 52 ● SUGARBUSH Columbia DB 3123 * 8   2 wks
5 Dec 52 ●   SUGARBUSH (re-entry) Columbia DB 3123 * 8   6 wks
20 Mar 53   GIRL IN THE WOOD Columbia DB 2907.............11   1 wk
3 Apr 53 ★   I BELIEVE Philips PB 117 ....1 36 wks
8 May 53 ●   TELL ME A STORY Philips PB 126 ** ....5 15 wks
4 Sep 53 ●   WHERE THE WINDS BLOW Philips PB 167 ....12 12 wks
11 Sep 53   TELL ME A STORY (re-entry) Philips PB 126 ** ...12   1 wk
16 Oct 53 ★ HEY JOE Philips PB 172 1   8 wks
30 Oct 53 ★ ANSWER ME Philips PB 196 ....1 17 wks
8 Jan 54 ●   BLOWING WILD Philips PB 207 ....2 12 wks
26 Mar 54 ● GRANADA Philips PB 242 10   1 wk
9 Apr 54 ●   GRANADA (re-entry) Philips PB 242 9   1 wk
16 Apr 54 ● THE KID'S LAST FIGHT Philips PB 258 ....3 10 wks
13 Aug 54 ● MY FRIEND Philips PB 316 3   9 wks
8 Oct 54 ●   THERE MUST BE A REASON Philips PB 306 9   9 wks
22 Oct 54 ● RAIN RAIN RAIN Philips PB 311 *** ....8 16 wks
11 Mar 55   IN THE BEGINNING Philips PB 404 20   1 wk
24 Jun 55 ● COOL WATER Philips PB 465 ....2 22 wks
15 Jul 55 ● STRANGE LADY IN TOWN Philips PB 478 ....6 13 wks
11 Nov 55   HUMMING BIRD Philips PB 498 16   1 wk
25 Nov 55 ● HAWKEYE Philips PB 519 7   8 wks
20 Jan 56 ● SIXTEEN TONS Philips PB 539 10   3 wks
4 May 56   HELL HATH NO FURY Philips PB 585 28   1 wk
7 Sep 56 ★   A WOMAN IN LOVE Philips PB 617 ....1 21 wks
28 Dec 56 ● MOONLIGHT GAMBLER Philips PB 638 ....13 12 wks
29 Mar 57   MOONLIGHT GAMBLER (re-entry) Philips PB 638 ...28   1 wk
26 Apr 57   LOVE IS A GOLDEN RING Philips PB 676 19   5 wks
4 Oct 57   GOOD EVENING FRIENDS/UP ABOVE MY HEAD
             Philips PB 708 **** 25   4 wks
13 Nov 59 ● RAWHIDE Philips PB 965...........................6 17 wks
31 Mar 60   RAWHIDE (re-entry) Philips PB 965..............41   2 wks
11 May 61   GUNSLINGER Philips PB 1135......................50   1 wk

* Doris Day and Frankie Laine ** Frankie Laine and Jimmy Boyd *** Frankie
Laine and the Four Lads **** Frankie Laine and Johnnie Ray

Greg LAKE UK, male vocalist   12 wks

6 Dec 75 ●   I BELIEVE IN FATHER CHRISTMAS
             Manticore K 13511............................2   7 wks
25 Dec 82   I BELIEVE IN FATHER CHRISTMAS (re-entry)
             Manticore K 13511................................72   3 wks
24 Dec 83   I BELIEVE IN FATHER CHRISTMAS (2nd re-entry)
             Manticore K 13511................................65   2 wks

See also Emerson, Lake and Palmer.

Annabel LAMB UK, female vocalist   7 wks

27 Aug 83   RIDERS ON THE STORM A & M AM 131 27   7 wks

LAMBRETTAS UK, male vocal/instrumental group   24 wks

1 Mar 80 ●   POISON IVY Rocket XPRESS 25 ....7 12 wks
24 May 80 ● D-A-A-ANCE Rocket XPRESS 33 12   8 wks
23 Aug 80   ANOTHER DAY (ANOTHER GIRL)
             Rocket XPRESS 36 49   4 wks

LANCASTRIANS UK, male vocal/instrumental group   2 wks

24 Dec 64   WE'LL SING IN THE SUNSHINE Pye 7N 15732 47   2 wks

Major LANCE US, male vocalist   2 wks

13 Feb 64   UM UM UM UM UM UM Columbia DB 7205......40   2 wks

Valerie LANDSBERG – See KIDS FROM FAME

LANDSCAPE UK, male vocal/instrumental group   20 wks

28 Feb 81 ● EINSTEIN A GO-GO RCA 22 ....5 13 wks
23 May 81   NORMAN BATES RCA 60 40   7 wks

Desmond LANE – See Alma COGAN; Cyril STAPLETON

Ronnie LANE and SLIM CHANCE   12 wks
UK, male vocalist and male instrumental group

12 Jan 74   HOW COME GM GMS 011 11   8 wks
15 Jun 74   THE POACHER GM GMS 024 36   4 wks

Don LANG UK, male vocalist   18 wks

4 Nov 55   CLOUDBURST HMV POP 115........................16   2 wks
2 Dec 55   CLOUDBURST (re-entry) HMV POP 115............18   1 wk
13 Jan 56   CLOUDBURST (2nd re-entry) HMV POP 115.......20   1 wk
5 Jul 57   SCHOOL DAY HMV POP 350 * 26   2 wks
23 May 58 ● WITCH DOCTOR HMV POP 488 * ....5 11 wks
10 Mar 60   SINK THE BISMARCK HMV POP 714................43   1 wk

* Don Lang and his Frantic Five

k.d. lang Canada, female vocalist   10 wks

16 May 92   CONSTANT CRAVING Sire W 0100.................52   4 wks
22 Aug 92   CRYING Virgin America VUS 63 * 13   6 wks

* Roy Orbison (duet with kd lang)

Thomas LANG UK, male vocalist   3 wks

30 Jan 88   THE HAPPY MAN Epic VOW 4.......................67   3 wks

Mario LANZA US, male vocalist   32 wks

14 Nov 52 ● BECAUSE YOU'RE MINE HMV DA 2017...............3 24 wks
4 Feb 55   DRINKING SONG HMV DA 2065....................13   1 wk
18 Feb 55   I'LL WALK WITH GOD HMV DA 2062 18   1 wk
22 Apr 55   SERENADE HMV DA 2065 19   1 wk
6 May 55   I'LL WALK WITH GOD (re-entry) HMV DA 2062 ...20   1 wk
6 May 55   SERENADE (re-entry) HMV DA 2065..............15   2 wks
14 Sep 56   SERENADE HMV DA 2085 25   1 wk
12 Oct 56   SERENADE (re-entry) HMV DA 2085..............29   1 wk

DA 2065 and DA 2085 are two different songs.

Julius LAROSA US, male vocalist   9 wks

4 Jul 58   TORERO RCA 1063 15   9 wks

LA'S UK, male vocal/instrumental group — **18 wks**

Date	Title	Pos	Wks
14 Jan 89	**THERE SHE GOES** Go! Discs GOLAS 2	59	4 wks
15 Sep 90	**TIMELESS MELODY** Go! Discs GOLAS 4	57	2 wks
3 Nov 90	**THERE SHE GOES (re-issue)** Go! Discs GOLAS 5	13	9 wks
16 Feb 91	**FEELIN'** Go! Discs GOLAS 6	43	3 wks

James LAST BAND Germany, male orchestra — **4 wks**

Date	Title	Pos	Wks
3 May 80	**THE SEDUCTION (LOVE THEME)** Polydor PD 2071	48	4 wks

LATE SHOW UK, male vocal/instrumental group — **6 wks**

Date	Title	Pos	Wks
3 Mar 79	**BRISTOL STOMP** Decca F 13822	40	6 wks

LATIN QUARTER
UK, male/female vocal/instrumental group — **10 wks**

Date	Title	Pos	Wks
18 Jan 86	**RADIO AFRICA** Rockin' Horse RH 102	19	9 wks
18 Apr 87	**NOMZAMO (ONE PEOPLE ONE CAUSE)** Rockin' Horse RH 113	73	1 wk

Gino LATINO Italy, male producer — **7 wks**

Date	Title	Pos	Wks
20 Jan 90	**WELCOME** FFRR F 126	17	7 wks

LATINO RAVE – See VARIOUS ARTISTS (MONTAGES)

LATOUR US, male vocalist/producer — **7 wks**

Date	Title	Pos	Wks
8 Jun 91	**PEOPLE ARE STILL HAVING SEX** Polydor PO 147	15	7 wks

Stacy LATTISAW US, female vocalist — **14 wks**

Date	Title	Pos	Wks
14 Jun 80 ●	**JUMP TO THE BEAT** Atlantic/Cotillion K 11496	3	11 wks
30 Aug 80	**DYNAMITE** Atlantic K 11554	51	3 wks

LAUNCHERS – See Ezz RECO and the LAUNCHERS with Boysie GRANT

Cyndi LAUPER US, female vocalist — **76 wks**

Date	Title	Pos	Wks
14 Jan 84 ●	**GIRLS JUST WANT TO HAVE FUN** Portrait A 3943	2	12 wks
24 Mar 84	**TIME AFTER TIME** Portrait A 4290	54	4 wks
16 Jun 84 ●	**TIME AFTER TIME (re-entry)** Portrait A 4290	3	13 wks
1 Sep 84	**SHE BOP** Portrait A 4620	46	5 wks
17 Nov 84	**ALL THROUGH THE NIGHT** Portrait A 4849	64	2 wks
20 Sep 86	**TRUE COLOURS** Portrait 650026 7	12	11 wks
27 Dec 86	**CHANGE OF HEART** Portrait CYNDI 1	74	1 wk
10 Jan 87	**CHANGE OF HEART (re-entry)** Portrait CYNDI 1	67	1 wk
28 Mar 87	**WHAT'S GOING ON** Portrait CYN 1	57	3 wks
20 May 89 ●	**I DROVE ALL NIGHT** Epic CYN 4	7	12 wks
5 Aug 89	**MY FIRST NIGHT WITHOUT YOU** Epic CYN 5	53	4 wks
30 Dec 89	**HEADING WEST** Epic CYN 6	68	1 wk
6 Jun 92	**THE WORLD IS STONE** Epic 6579707	15	7 wks

LAUREL and HARDY UK, male vocal/instrumental duo — **2 wks**

Date	Title	Pos	Wks
2 Apr 83	**CLUNK CLINK** CBS A 3213	65	2 wks

LAUREL and HARDY with the AVALON BOYS featuring Chill WILLS — **10 wks**
UK/US, male vocal duo with US, male vocal group

Date	Title	Pos	Wks
22 Nov 75 ●	**THE TRAIL OF THE LONESOME PINE** United Artists UP 36026	2	10 wks

Joanna LAW UK, female vocalist — **3 wks**

Date	Title	Pos	Wks
7 Jul 90	**FIRST TIME EVER** Citybeat CBE 752	67	3 wks

Lee LAWRENCE UK, male vocalist — **10 wks**

Date	Title	Pos	Wks
20 Nov 53	**CRYING IN THE CHAPEL** Decca F 10177	11	1 wk
11 Dec 53 ●	**CRYING IN THE CHAPEL (re-entry)** Decca F 10177	7	5 wks
2 Dec 55	**SUDDENLY THERE'S A VALLEY** Columbia DB 3681	19	1 wk
16 Dec 55	**SUDDENLY THERE'S A VALLEY (re-entry)** Columbia DB 3681	14	3 wks

Sophie LAWRENCE UK, female vocalist — **7 wks**

Date	Title	Pos	Wks
3 Aug 91	**LOVE'S UNKIND** IQ ZB 44821	21	7 wks

Steve LAWRENCE US, male vocalist — **27 wks**

Date	Title	Pos	Wks
21 Apr 60 ●	**FOOTSTEPS** HMV POP 726	4	13 wks
18 Aug 60	**GIRLS GIRLS GIRLS** London HLT 9166	49	1 wk
22 Aug 63 ●	**I WANT TO STAY HERE** CBS AAG 163 *	3	13 wks

* Steve and Eydie

Lindy LAYTON UK, female vocalist — **11 wks**

Date	Title	Pos	Wks
11 Aug 90	**SILLY GAMES** Arista 113452 *	22	7 wks
26 Jan 91	**ECHO MY HEART** Arista 113845	42	2 wks
31 Aug 91	**WITHOUT YOU (ONE AND ONE)** Arista 114636	71	2 wks

* Lindy Layton featuring Janet Kay

See also Beats International.

Doug LAZY US, male vocalist — **9 wks**

Date	Title	Pos	Wks
15 Jul 89	**LET IT ROLL** Atlantic A 8866 *	27	5 wks
4 Nov 89	**LET THE RHYTHM PUMP** Atlantic A 8784	45	3 wks
26 May 90	**LET THE RHYTHM PUMP (re-mix)** East West A 7919	63	1 wk

* Raze presents Doug Lazy

Keith LE BLANC – See Malcolm X

Vicky LEANDROS Greece, female vocalist — **29 wks**

Date	Title	Pos	Wks
8 Apr 72 ●	**COME WHAT MAY** Philips 6000 049	2	16 wks
23 Dec 72	**THE LOVE IN YOUR EYES** Philips 6000 081	48	3 wks
20 Jan 73	**THE LOVE IN YOUR EYES (re-entry)** Philips 6000 081	40	4 wks
7 Apr 73	**THE LOVE IN YOUR EYES (2nd re-entry)** Philips 6000 081	46	1 wk
7 Jul 73	**WHEN BOUZOUKIS PLAYED** Philips 6000 111	44	2 wks
28 Jul 73	**WHEN BOUZOUKIS PLAYED (re-entry)** Philips 6000 111	45	3 wks

Brenda LEE US, female vocalist — **210 wks**

Date	Title	Pos	Wks
17 Mar 60	**SWEET NOTHIN'S** Brunswick 05819	45	1 wk
7 Apr 60 ●	**SWEET NOTHIN'S (re-entry)** Brunswick 05819	4	18 wks
30 Jun 60	**I'M SORRY** Brunswick 05833	12	16 wks
20 Oct 60	**I WANT TO BE WANTED** Brunswick 05839	31	6 wks
19 Jan 61	**LET'S JUMP THE BROOMSTICK** Brunswick 05823	12	15 wks
6 Apr 61	**EMOTIONS** Brunswick 05847	45	1 wk
20 Jul 61	**DUM DUM** Brunswick 05854	22	8 wks
16 Nov 61	**FOOL NUMBER ONE** Brunswick 05860	38	5 wks
8 Feb 62	**BREAK IT TO ME GENTLY** Brunswick 05864	46	2 wks
5 Apr 62 ●	**SPEAK TO ME PRETTY** Brunswick 05867	3	12 wks
21 Jun 62 ●	**HERE COMES THAT FEELING** Brunswick 05871	5	12 wks
13 Sep 62	**IT STARTED ALL OVER AGAIN** Brunswick 05876	15	11 wks
29 Nov 62 ●	**ROCKIN' AROUND THE CHRISTMAS TREE** Brunswick 05880	6	7 wks

17 Jan 63 ●	**ALL ALONE AM I** Brunswick 05882 ....**7**	17 wks
28 Mar 63 ●	**LOSING YOU** Brunswick 05886 ....**10**	16 wks
18 Jul 63	**I WONDER** Brunswick 05891 ....**14**	9 wks
31 Oct 63	**SWEET IMPOSSIBLE YOU** Brunswick 05896 ...**28**	6 wks
9 Jan 64 ●	**AS USUAL** Brunswick 05899 ....**5**	15 wks
9 Apr 64	**THINK** Brunswick 05903 ....**26**	8 wks
10 Sep 64	**IS IT TRUE** Brunswick 05915 ....**17**	8 wks
10 Dec 64	**CHRISTMAS WILL BE JUST ANOTHER LONELY**	
	DAY Brunswick 05921 ....**29**	5 wks
4 Feb 65	**THANKS A LOT** Brunswick 05927 ....**41**	2 wks
29 Jul 65	**TOO MANY RIVERS** Brunswick 05936 ....**22**	12 wks

Byron LEE – *See Boris GARDINER*

Curtis LEE US, *male vocalist*　　　　　　　**2 wks**

31 Aug 61	**PRETTY LITTLE ANGEL EYES** London HLX 9397 ....**47**	1 wk
14 Sep 61	**PRETTY LITTLE ANGEL EYES (re-entry)**	
	London HLX 9397 ....**48**	1 wk

Dee C. LEE UK, *female vocalist*　　　　　**17 wks**

9 Nov 85 ●	**SEE THE DAY** CBS A 6570 ....**3**	12 wks
8 Mar 86	**COME HELL OR WATERS HIGH** CBS A 6869 ....**46**	5 wks

Jackie LEE UK, *female vocalist*　　　　　**31 wks**

10 Apr 68 ●	**WHITE HORSES** Philips BF 1674 * **10**	14 wks
2 Jan 71	**RUPERT** Pye 7N 45003 ....**14**	17 wks

* Jacky

Leapy LEE UK, *male vocalist*　　　　　　**28 wks**

21 Aug 68 ●	**LITTLE ARROWS** MCA MU 1028 ....**2**	21 wks
20 Dec 69	**GOOD MORNING** MCA MK 5021 ....**47**	1 wk
10 Jan 70	**GOOD MORNING (re-entry)** MCA MK 5021 ....**29**	6 wks

Peggy LEE US, *female vocalist*　　　　　**29 wks**

24 May 57 ●	**MR. WONDERFUL** Brunswick 05671 ....**5**	13 wks
15 Aug 58 ●	**FEVER** Capitol CL 14902 ....**5**	11 wks
23 Mar 61	**TILL THERE WAS YOU** Capitol CL 15184 ....**40**	1 wk
6 Apr 61	**TILL THERE WAS YOU (re-entry)** Capitol CL 15184 ....**30**	3 wks
22 Aug 92	**FEVER (re-issue)** Capitol PEG 1 ....**75**	1 wk

Toney LEE US, *male vocalist*　　　　　　**4 wks**

29 Jan 83	**REACH UP** TMT TMT 2 ....**64**	4 wks

LEEDS UNITED FC UK, *male football team vocalists*　　　**13 wks**

29 Apr 72 ●	**LEEDS UNITED** Chapter One SCH 168 ....**10**	10 wks
25 Apr 92	**LEEDS LEEDS LEEDS** Q Music LUFC 2 ....**61**	1 wk
9 May 92	**LEEDS LEEDS LEEDS (re-entry)** Q Music LUFC 2 ....**54**	2 wks

Raymond LEFEVRE France, *orchestra*　　　**2 wks**

15 May 68	**SOUL COAXING** Major Minor MM 559 ....**46**	2 wks

LEFTFIELD UK, *male vocal/instrumental group*　　　**1 wk**

12 Dec 92	**SONG OF LIFE** Hard Hands HAND 002T **59**	1 wk

Paul LEKAKIS US, *male vocalist*　　　　　**4 wks**

30 May 87	**BOOM BOOM (LET'S GO BACK TO MY ROOM)**	
	Champion CHAMP 43 ....**60**	4 wks

LEMON PIPERS US, *male vocal/instrumental group*　　　**16 wks**

7 Feb 68 ●	**GREEN TAMBOURINE** Pye International 7N 25444 ....**7**	11 wks
1 May 68	**RICE IS NICE** Pye International 7N 25454 ....**41**	5 wks

LEMON TREES UK, *male vocal/instrumental group*　　　**3 wks**

26 Sep 92	**LOVE IS IN YOUR EYES** Oxygen GASP 1 ....**75**	1 wk
7 Nov 92	**THE WAY I FEEL** Oxygen GASP 2 ....**62**	2 wks

LEMONHEADS US, *male vocal/instrumental group*　　　**5 wks**

17 Oct 92	**IT'S A SHAME ABOUT RAY** Atlantic A 7423 ....**70**	1 wk
5 Dec 92	**MRS ROBINSON/BEIN' AROUND** Atlantic A 7401 ....**20†**	4 wks

John LENNON UK, *male vocalist*　　　　**184 wks**

9 Jul 69 ●	**GIVE PEACE A CHANCE** Apple 13 * **2**	13 wks
1 Nov 69	**COLD TURKEY** Apple APPLES 1001 * **14**	8 wks
21 Feb 70 ●	**INSTANT KARMA** Apple APPLES 1003 ** **5**	9 wks
20 Mar 71 ●	**POWER TO THE PEOPLE** Apple R 5892 *** **7**	9 wks
9 Dec 72 ●	**HAPPY XMAS (WAR IS OVER)** Apple R 5970 **** **4**	8 wks
24 Nov 73	**MIND GAMES** Apple R 5994 ....**26**	9 wks
19 Oct 74	**WHATEVER GETS YOU THROUGH THE NIGHT**	
	Apple R 5998 ***** **36**	4 wks
4 Jan 75	**HAPPY XMAS (WAR IS OVER) (re-entry)**	
	Apple R 5970 **** **48**	1 wk
8 Feb 75	**NUMBER 9 DREAM** Apple R 6003 ....**23**	8 wks
3 May 75	**STAND BY ME** Apple R 6005 ....**30**	7 wks
1 Nov 75 ●	**IMAGINE** Apple R 6009 ....**6**	11 wks
8 Nov 80 ★	**(JUST LIKE) STARTING OVER** Geffen K 79186 ....**1**	15 wks
20 Dec 80 ●	**HAPPY XMAS (WAR IS OVER) (2nd re-entry)**	
	Apple R 5970 **** **2**	9 wks
27 Dec 80 ★	**IMAGINE (re-entry)** Apple R 6009 ....**1**	13 wks
24 Jan 81 ★	**WOMAN** Geffen K 79195 ....**1**	11 wks
24 Jan 81	**GIVE PEACE A CHANCE (re-entry)** Apple 13 ....**33**	5 wks
21 Mar 81	**I SAW HER STANDING THERE**	
	DJM DJS 10965 ****** **40**	4 wks
4 Apr 81	**WATCHING THE WHEELS** Geffen K 79207 ....**30**	6 wks
19 Dec 81	**HAPPY XMAS (WAR IS OVER) (3rd re-entry)**	
	Apple R 5970 **** **28**	5 wks
20 Nov 82	**LOVE** Parlophone R 6059 ....**41**	7 wks
25 Dec 82	**HAPPY XMAS (WAR IS OVER) (4th re-entry)**	
	Apple R 5970 **** **56**	3 wks
21 Jan 84 ●	**NOBODY TOLD ME** Ono Music/Polydor POSP 700 ....**6**	6 wks
17 Mar 84	**BORROWED TIME** Polydor POSP 701 ....**32**	6 wks
30 Nov 85	**JEALOUS GUY** Parlophone R 6117 ....**65**	2 wks
10 Dec 88	**IMAGINE/JEALOUS GUY/HAPPY XMAS (WAR IS**	
	OVER) (re-issues) Parlophone R 6199 ....**45**	5 wks

* Plastic Ono Band ** Lennon, Ono and the Plastic Ono Band *** John
Lennon and the Plastic Ono Band **** John and Yoko and the Plastic Ono Band
with the Harlem Community Choir ***** John Lennon with the Plastic Ono
Nuclear Band ****** The Elton John Band featuring John Lennon and the
Muscle Shoals Horns

Julian LENNON UK, *male vocalist*　　　　**46 wks**

6 Oct 84 ●	**TOO LATE FOR GOODBYES** Charisma JL 1 ....**6**	11 wks
15 Dec 84	**VALOTTE** Charisma JL 2 ....**55**	6 wks
9 Mar 85	**SAY YOU'RE WRONG** Charisma JL 3 ....**75**	1 wk
7 Dec 85	**BECAUSE** EMI 5538 ....**40**	7 wks
11 Mar 89	**NOW YOU'RE IN HEAVEN** Virgin VS 1154 ....**59**	3 wks
24 Aug 91	**SALTWATER** Virgin VS 1361 ....**6**	13 wks
30 Nov 91	**HELP YOURSELF** Virgin VS 1379 ....**53**	2 wks
25 Apr 92	**GET A LIFE** Virgin VS 1398 ....**56**	3 wks

Annie LENNOX UK, *female vocalist*　　　**33 wks**

3 Dec 88	**PUT A LITTLE LOVE IN YOUR HEART**	
	A & M AM 484 * **28**	8 wks

Comedian JERRY LEWIS had a bigger hit in 1957 than his former partner Dean Martin.

Above right: JULIUS LaROSA was famously fired on air in 1953 from his job as a regular vocalist on the US television show *Arthur Godfrey And His Friends*. He went on to have several hits, including one in Britain; Godfrey, who had previously been a chart star in the US, never had another hit.

JERRY LEE LEWIS celebrates the first four country hits of his late 60s C&W period with producer Jerry Kennedy.

Right: The hits of KENNY LOGGINS appeared in the films *Footloose* and *Top Gun*.

28 Mar 92	● WHY RCA PB 45317	5	8 wks
6 Jun 92	PRECIOUS RCA 74321100257	23	5 wks
22 Aug 92	● WALKING ON BROKEN GLASS RCA 74321107227	8	8 wks
31 Oct 92	COLD RCA 74321116902	26	4 wks

Annie Lennox and Al Green

Rula LENSKA – *See Julie COVINGTON, Rula LENSKA, Charlotte CORNWELL and Sue JONES-DAVIES*

LESTER – *See Norman COOK*

Ketty LESTER *US, female vocalist*   16 wks

| 19 Apr 62 | ● LOVE LETTERS London HLN 9527 | 4 | 12 wks |
| 19 Jul 62 | BUT NOT FOR ME London HLN 9574 | 45 | 4 wks |

LETTERMEN *US, male vocal group*   3 wks

| 23 Nov 61 | THE WAY YOU LOOK TONIGHT Capitol CL 15222 | 36 | 3 wks |

LEVEL 42 *UK, male vocal/instrumental group*   168 wks

30 Aug 80	LOVE MEETING LOVE Polydor POSP 170	61	4 wks
18 Apr 81	LOVE GAMES Polydor POSP 234	38	6 wks
8 Aug 81	TURN IT ON Polydor POSP 286	57	6 wks
14 Nov 81	STARCHILD Polydor POSP 343	47	4 wks
8 May 82	ARE YOU HEARING (WHAT I HEAR)? Polydor POSP 396	49	5 wks
2 Oct 82	WEAVE YOUR SPELL Polydor POSP 500	43	4 wks
15 Jan 83	THE CHINESE WAY Polydor POSP 538	24	8 wks
16 Apr 83	OUT OF SIGHT, OUT OF MIND Polydor POSP 570	41	4 wks
30 Jul 83	● THE SUN GOES DOWN (LIVING IT UP) Polydor POSP 622	10	12 wks
22 Oct 83	MICRO KID Polydor POSP 643	37	5 wks
1 Sep 84	HOT WATER Polydor POSP 697	18	9 wks
3 Nov 84	THE CHANT HAS BEGUN Polydor POSP 710	41	5 wks
21 Sep 85	● SOMETHING ABOUT YOU Polydor POSP 759	6	17 wks
7 Dec 85	LEAVING ME NOW Polydor POSP 776	15	11 wks
26 Apr 86	● LESSONS IN LOVE Polydor POSP 790	3	13 wks
14 Feb 87	● RUNNING IN THE FAMILY Polydor POSP 842	6	10 wks
25 Apr 87	● TO BE WITH YOU AGAIN Polydor POSP 855	10	7 wks
12 Sep 87	● IT'S OVER Polydor POSP 900	10	8 wks
12 Dec 87	CHILDREN SAY Polydor POSP 911	22	6 wks
3 Sep 88	HEAVEN IN MY HANDS Polydor PO 14	12	5 wks
29 Oct 88	TAKE A LOOK Polydor PO 24	32	4 wks
21 Jan 89	TRACIE Polydor PO 34	25	5 wks
28 Oct 89	TAKE CARE OF YOURSELF Polydor PO 58	39	3 wks
17 Aug 91	GUARANTEED RCA PB 44745	17	4 wks
19 Oct 91	OVERTIME RCA PB 44997	62	2 wks
18 Apr 92	MY FATHER'S SHOES RCA PB 45271	55	1 wk

LEVELLERS *UK, male vocal/instrumental group*   8 wks

21 Sep 91	ONE WAY China WOK 2008	51	2 wks
7 Dec 91	FAR FROM HOME China WOK 2010	71	1 wk
23 May 92	15 YEARS (EP) China WOKX 2020	11	5 wks

Tracks on 15 Years (EP): 15 Years/Dance Before The Storm/The River Flow (Live)/Plastic Jeezus.

LEVERT *UK, male vocal group*   10 wks

| 22 Aug 87 | ● CASANOVA Atlantic A 9217 | 9 | 10 wks |

Hank LEVINE *US, orchestra*   4 wks

| 21 Dec 61 | IMAGE HMV POP 947 | 45 | 4 wks |

Barrington LEVY *Jamaica, male vocalist*   10 wks

| 2 Feb 85 | HERE I COME London LON 62 | 41 | 4 wks |

| 15 Jun 91 | TRIBAL BASS Desire WANT 44 * | 20 | 6 wks |

* Rebel MC featuring Tenor Fly and Barrington Levy

Jona LEWIE *UK, male vocalist*   20 wks

| 10 May 80 | YOU'LL ALWAYS FIND ME IN THE KITCHEN AT PARTIES Stiff BUY 73 | 16 | 9 wks |
| 29 Nov 80 | ● STOP THE CAVALRY Stiff BUY 104 | 3 | 11 wks |

On some copies first title was simply Kitchen At Parties. See also Terry Dactyl and the Dinosaurs.

Dee LEWIS *UK, female vocalist*   5 wks

| 18 Jun 88 | BEST OF MY LOVE Mercury DEE 3 | 47 | 5 wks |

Gary LEWIS and the PLAYBOYS   7 wks
US, male vocal/instrumental group

| 8 Feb 75 | MY HEART'S SYMPHONY United Artists UP 35780 | 36 | 7 wks |

Huey LEWIS and the NEWS   66 wks
US, male vocal/instrumental group

27 Oct 84	IF THIS IS IT Chrysalis CHS 2829	39	6 wks
31 Aug 85	THE POWER OF LOVE Chrysalis HUEY 1	11	10 wks
23 Nov 85	HEART AND SOUL (EP) Chrysalis HUEY 2	61	4 wks
8 Feb 86	● THE POWER OF LOVE (re-issue)/DO YOU BELIEVE IN LOVE Chrysalis HUEY 3	9	12 wks
10 May 86	THE HEART OF ROCK AND ROLL Chrysalis HUEY 4	49	3 wks
23 Aug 86	STUCK WITH YOU Chrysalis HUEY 5	12	12 wks
6 Dec 86	HIP TO BE SQUARE Chrysalis HUEY 6	41	8 wks
21 Mar 87	SIMPLE AS THAT Chrysalis HUEY 7	47	5 wks
16 Jul 88	PERFECT WORLD Chrysalis HUEY 10	48	6 wks

Tracks on EP: Heart and Soul/Hope You Love Me Like You Say You Do/Heart of Rock And Roll/Buzz Buzz Buzz. Do You Believe In Love only listed from 15 Feb 86.

Jerry LEWIS *US, male vocalist*   8 wks

| 8 Feb 57 | ROCK-A-BYE YOUR BABY (WITH A DIXIE MELODY) Brunswick 05636 | 12 | 7 wks |
| 5 Apr 57 | ROCK-A-BYE YOUR BABY (WITH A DIXIE MELODY) (re-entry) Brunswick 05636 | 22 | 1 wk |

Jerry Lee LEWIS *US, male vocalist/instrumentalist – piano*   68 wks

27 Sep 57	● WHOLE LOTTA SHAKIN' GOIN' ON London HLS 8457	8	10 wks
20 Dec 57	★ GREAT BALLS OF FIRE London HLS 8529	1	12 wks
27 Dec 57	WHOLE LOTTA SHAKIN' GOIN' ON (re-entry) London HLS 8457	26	1 wk
11 Apr 58	● BREATHLESS London HLS 8592	8	7 wks
23 Jan 59	HIGH SCHOOL CONFIDENTIAL London HLS 8780	12	6 wks
1 May 59	LOVIN' UP A STORM London HLS 8840	28	1 wk
9 Jun 60	BABY BABY BYE BYE London HLS 9131	47	1 wk
4 May 61	● WHAT'D I SAY London HLS 9335	10	12 wks
3 Aug 61	WHAT'D I SAY (re-entry) London HLS 9335	49	2 wks
6 Sep 62	SWEET LITTLE SIXTEEN London HLS 9584	38	5 wks
14 Mar 63	GOOD GOLLY MISS MOLLY London HLS 9688	31	6 wks
6 May 72	CHANTILLY LACE Mercury 6052 141	33	5 wks

Linda LEWIS *UK, female vocalist*   30 wks

2 Jun 73	ROCK-A-DOODLE-DOO Raft RA 18502	15	11 wks
12 Jul 75	● IT'S IN HIS KISS Arista 17	6	8 wks
17 Apr 76	BABY I'M YOURS Arista 43	33	6 wks
2 Jun 79	I'D BE SURPRISINGLY GOOD FOR YOU Ariola ARO 166	40	5 wks

Ramsey LEWIS US, male instrumentalist - piano — 8 wks

15 Apr 72	WADE IN THE WATER Chess 6145 004	31	8 wks

Shirley LEWIS – See Arthur BAKER

John LEYTON UK, male vocalist — 70 wks

3 Aug 61 ★	JOHNNY REMEMBER ME Top Rank JAR 577	1	15 wks
5 Oct 61 ●	WILD WIND Top Rank JAR 585	2	10 wks
28 Dec 61	SON THIS IS SHE HMV POP 956	15	10 wks
15 Mar 62	LONE RIDER HMV POP 992	40	5 wks
3 May 62	LONELY CITY HMV POP 1014	14	11 wks
23 Aug 62	DOWN THE RIVER NILE HMV POP 1054	42	3 wks
21 Feb 63	CUPBOARD LOVE HMV POP 1122	22	12 wks
18 Jul 63	I'LL CUT YOUR TAIL OFF HMV POP 1175	50	1 wk
8 Aug 63	I'LL CUT YOUR TAIL OFF (re-entry) HMV POP 1175	36	2 wks
20 Feb 64	MAKE LOVE TO ME HMV POP 1264	49	1 wk

LEYTON BUZZARDS — 5 wks
UK, male vocal/instrumental group

3 Mar 79	SATURDAY NIGHT (BENEATH THE PLASTIC PALM TREES) Chrysalis CHS 2288	53	5 wks

LFO UK, male instrumental group — 15 wks

14 Jul 90	LFO Warp WAP 5	12	10 wks
6 Jul 91	WE ARE BACK/NURTURE Warp 7WAP 14	47	3 wks
1 Feb 92	WHAT IS HOUSE (EP) Warp WAP 17	62	2 wks

Tracks on What Is House (EP): Tan Ta Ra/Mashed Potato/What Is House/Syndrome.

LIBERACE US, male instrumentalist - piano — 2 wks

17 Jun 55	UNCHAINED MELODY Philips PB 430	20	1 wk
19 Oct 56	I DON'T CARE Columbia DB 3834	28	1 wk

I Don't Care featured Liberace as vocalist too.

LIBERATION UK, male instrumental/production duo — 3 wks

24 Oct 92	LIBERATION ZYX ZYX 68657	28	3 wks

LICK THE TINS UK, male/female vocal/instrumental group — 8 wks

29 Mar 86	CAN'T HELP FALLING IN LOVE Sedition EDIT 3308	42	8 wks

Ben LIEBRAND — 2 wks
Holland, male producer/multi-instrumentalist

9 Jun 90	PULS(T)AR Epic LIEB 1	68	2 wks

LIEUTENANT PIGEON — 29 wks
UK, male/female instrumental group

16 Sep 72 ★	MOULDY OLD DOUGH Decca F 13278	1	19 wks
16 Dec 72	DESPERATE DAN Decca F 13365	17	10 wks

LIGHT OF THE WORLD — 25 wks
UK, male vocal/instrumental group

14 Apr 79	SWINGIN' Ensign ENY 22	45	5 wks
14 Jul 79	MIDNIGHT GROOVIN' Ensign ENY 29	72	1 wk

18 Oct 80	LONDON TOWN Ensign ENY 43	41	5 wks
17 Jan 81	I SHOT THE SHERIFF Ensign ENY 46	40	5 wks
28 Mar 81	I'M SO HAPPY Ensign MER 64	35	6 wks
21 Nov 81	RIDE THE LOVE TRAIN EMI 5242	49	3 wks

Gordon LIGHTFOOT Canada, male vocalist — 26 wks

19 Jun 71	IF YOU COULD READ MY MIND Reprise RS 20974	30	9 wks
3 Aug 74	SUNDOWN Reprise K 14327	33	7 wks
15 Jan 77	THE WRECK OF THE EDMUND FITZGERALD Reprise K 14451	40	4 wks
16 Sep 78	DAYLIGHT KATY Warner Bros. K 17214	41	6 wks

Terry LIGHTFOOT and his NEW ORLEANS JAZZMEN — 17 wks
UK, male jazz band, Terry Lightfoot vocalist/instrumentalist - clarinet

7 Sep 61	TRUE LOVE Columbia DB 4696	33	4 wks
23 Nov 61	KING KONG Columbia SCD 2165	29	12 wks
3 May 62	TAVERN IN THE TOWN Columbia DB 4822	49	1 wk

LIGHTNING SEEDS UK, male vocalist - Ian Broudie — 19 wks

22 Jul 89	PURE Ghetto GTG 4	16	8 wks
14 Mar 92	THE LIFE OF RILEY Virgin VS 1402	28	6 wks
30 May 92	SENSE Virgin VS 1414	31	5 wks

LIL' LOUIS US, male producer — 18 wks

29 Jul 89 ●	FRENCH KISS ffrr FX 115	2	11 wks
13 Jan 90	I CALLED U ffrr F 123	16	6 wks
26 Sep 92	SAVED MY LIFE ffrr FX 197 *	74	1 wk

* Lil' Louis and the World

LIMAHL UK, male vocalist — 25 wks

5 Nov 83	ONLY FOR LOVE EMI LML 1	16	7 wks
7 Jan 84	ONLY FOR LOVE (re-entry) EMI LML 1	75	1 wk
2 Jun 84	TOO MUCH TROUBLE EMI LML 2	64	3 wks
13 Oct 84 ●	NEVER ENDING STORY EMI LML 3	4	14 wks

Alison LIMERICK UK, female vocalist — 23 wks

30 Mar 91	WHERE LOVE LIVES Arista 144208	27	8 wks
12 Oct 91	COME BACK (FOR REAL LOVE) EMI 114530	53	2 wks
21 Dec 91	MAGIC'S BACK (THEME FROM THE GHOSTS OF OXFORD STREET) RCA PB 45223 *	42	4 wks
29 Feb 92	MAKE IT ON MY OWN Arista 114990	16	6 wks
18 Jul 92	GETTIN' IT RIGHT Arista 74321102867	57	2 wks
28 Nov 92	HEAR MY CALL Arista 115337	73	1 wk

* Malcolm McLaren featuring Alison Limerick

LIMIT Holland, male vocal/instrumental duo — 8 wks

5 Jan 85	SAY YEAH Portrait A 4808	17	8 wks

LIMMIE and the FAMILY COOKIN' — 28 wks
US, male/female vocal group

21 Jul 73 ●	YOU CAN DO MAGIC Avco 6105 019	3	13 wks
20 Oct 73	DREAMBOAT Avco 6105 025	31	5 wks
6 Apr 74 ●	A WALKIN' MIRACLE Avco 6105 027	6	10 wks

Bob LIND US, male vocalist — 10 wks

10 Mar 66 ●	ELUSIVE BUTTERFLY Fontana TF 670	5	9 wks
26 May 66	REMEMBER THE RAIN Fontana TF 702	46	1 wk

LINDA and the FUNKY BOYS – *See Linda CARR*

LINDISFARNE *UK, male vocal/instrumental group*   **55 wks**

26 Feb 72 ●	MEET ME ON THE CORNER *Charisma CB 173*	**5**	11 wks
13 May 72 ●	LADY ELEANOR *Charisma CB 153*	**3**	11 wks
23 Sep 72	ALL FALL DOWN *Charisma CB 191*	**34**	5 wks
3 Jun 78 ●	RUN FOR HOME *Mercury 6007 177*	**10**	15 wks
7 Oct 78	JUKE BOX GYPSY *Mercury 6007 187*	**56**	4 wks
10 Nov 90 ●	FOG ON THE TYNE (REVISITED) *Best ZB 44083 * *	**2**	9 wks

* Gazza and Lindisfarne

LINER *UK, male vocal/instrumental group*   **6 wks**

10 Mar 79	KEEP REACHING OUT FOR LOVE *Atlantic K 11235*	**49**	3 wks
26 May 79	YOU AND ME *Atlantic K 11285*	**44**	3 wks

Laurie LINGO and the DIPSTICKS   **7 wks**
UK, male vocal duo, disc jockeys Dave Lee Travis and Paul Burnett

17 Apr 76 ●	CONVOY G. B. *State STAT 23*	**4**	7 wks

LINX *UK, male vocal/instrumental duo*   **45 wks**

20 Sep 80	YOU'RE LYING *Chrysalis CHS 2461*	**15**	10 wks
7 Mar 81 ●	INTUITION *Chrysalis CHS 2500*	**7**	11 wks
13 Jun 81	THROW AWAY THE KEY *Chrysalis CHS 2519*	**21**	9 wks
5 Sep 81	SO THIS IS ROMANCE *Chrysalis CHS 2546*	**15**	9 wks
21 Nov 81	CAN'T HELP MYSELF *Chrysalis CHS 2565*	**55**	3 wks
10 Jul 82	PLAYTHING *Chrysalis CHS 2621*	**48**	3 wks

LION ROCK *UK, male producer - Justin Robertson*   **1 wk**

5 Dec 92	LIONROCK *Deconstruction 74321124381*	**63**	1 wk

LIPPS INC. *US, male/female vocal/instrumental group*   **13 wks**

17 May 80 ●	FUNKYTOWN *Casablanca CAN 194*	**2**	13 wks

LIQUID *UK, male instrumental/production duo*   **8 wks**

21 Mar 92	SWEET HARMONY *XL XLS 28*	**15**	6 wks
5 Sep 92	THE FUTURE MUSIC EP *XL XLT 33*	**59**	2 wks

Tracks on The Future Music EP: *Liquid Is Liquid/Music/House (Is A Feeling)/The Year 3000.*

LIQUID GOLD *UK, male/female vocal/instrumental group*   **46 wks**

2 Dec 78	ANYWAY YOU DO IT *Creole CR 159*	**41**	7 wks
23 Feb 80 ●	DANCE YOURSELF DIZZY *Polo POLO 1*	**2**	14 wks
31 May 80 ●	SUBSTITUTE *Polo POLO 4*	**8**	9 wks
1 Nov 80	THE NIGHT THE WINE AND THE ROSES *POLO 6*	**32**	7 wks
28 Mar 81	DON'T PANIC *Polo POLO 8*	**42**	5 wks
21 Aug 82	WHERE DID WE GO WRONG *Polo POLO 23*	**56**	4 wks

LIQUID OXYGEN *US, male producer*   **2 wks**

28 Apr 90	THE PLANET DANCE *Champion CHAMP 242*	**56**	2 wks

LISA LISA and CULT JAM   **29 wks**
US, female/male vocal/instrumental group

4 May 85	I WONDER IF I TAKE YOU HOME *CBS A 6057 * *	**53**	6 wks

British Hit Singles Part One: Alphabetically by Artist
Date of chart entry/Title & catalogue no./Peak position reached/Weeks on chart
★ Number one   ● Top Ten   † still on chart at 31 Dec 1992
* = credited to act billed in footnote

3 Aug 85	I WONDER IF I TAKE YOU HOME (re-entry) *CBS A 6057 * *	**12**	11 wks
31 Oct 87	LOST IN EMOTION *CBS 651036 7*	**58**	4 wks
13 Jul 91	LET THE BEAT HIT 'EM *Columbia 6572867*	**17**	6 wks
24 Aug 91	LET THE BEAT HIT 'EM PART 2 *Columbia 6573747*	**49**	2 wks

* Lisa Lisa and Cult Jam with Full Force

LISA MARIE – *See Malcolm McLAREN*

De Etta LITTLE and Nelson PIGFORD   **5 wks**
US, female/male vocal duo

13 Aug 77	YOU TAKE MY HEART AWAY *United Artists UP 36257*	**35**	5 wks

LITTLE ANGELS *UK, male vocal/instrumental group*   **26 wks**

4 Mar 89	BIG BAD EP *Polydor LTLEP 2*	**74**	1 wk
24 Feb 90	KICKING UP DUST *Polydor LTL 5*	**46**	4 wks
12 May 90	RADICAL YOUR LOVER *Polydor LTL 6 * *	**34**	4 wks
4 Aug 90	SHE'S A LITTLE ANGEL *Polydor LTL 7*	**21**	3 wks
2 Feb 91	BONEYARD *Polydor LTL 8*	**33**	4 wks
30 Apr 91	PRODUCT OF THE WORKING CLASS *Polydor LTL 9*	**40**	2 wks
1 Jun 91	YOUNG GODS *Polydor LTL 10*	**34**	2 wks
20 Jul 91	I AIN'T GONNA CRY *Polydor LTL 11*	**26**	3 wks
7 Nov 92	TOO MUCH TOO YOUNG *Polydor LTL 12*	**22**	3 wks

* Little Angels featuring the Big Bad Horns
Tracks on Big Bad EP: *She's A Little Angel/Don't Waste My Time/Better Than The Rest/Sex In Cars.*

LITTLE ANTHONY and the IMPERIALS   **17 wks**
US, male vocal group

31 Jul 76	BETTER USE YOUR HEAD *United Artists UP 36141*	**42**	4 wks
24 Dec 77	WHO'S GONNA LOVE ME *Power Exchange PX 266 * *	**17**	9 wks

* Imperials

LITTLE BENNY and the MASTERS   **7 wks**
US, male rapper/instrumentalist - trumpet, and male instrumental group

2 Feb 85	WHO COMES TO BOOGIE *Bluebird 10 BR 13*	**33**	7 wks

LITTLE CAESAR *UK, male vocalist*   **3 wks**

9 Jun 90	THE WHOLE OF THE MOON *A1 EAU 1*	**68**	3 wks

LITTLE EVA *US, female vocalist*   **45 wks**

6 Sep 62 ●	THE LOCO-MOTION *London HL 9581*	**2**	17 wks
3 Jan 63	KEEP YOUR HANDS OFF MY BABY *London HLU 9633*	**30**	5 wks
7 Mar 63	LET'S TURKEY TROT *London HLU 9687*	**13**	12 wks
29 Jul 72	THE LOCO-MOTION (re-entry) *London HL 9581*	**11**	11 wks

See also Big Dee Irwin.

LITTLE RICHARD   **116 wks**
US, male vocalist/instrumentalist - piano

14 Dec 56	RIP IT UP *London HLO 8336*	**30**	1 wk

LITTLE RICHARD
had seven rock-'n'-roll
hits in 1957, more than
anyone except Elvis
Presley.

8 Feb 57 ●	**LONG TALL SALLY** London HLO 8366	3	16 wks
22 Feb 57	**TUTTI FRUTTI** London HLO 8366	29	1 wk
8 Mar 57	**SHE'S GOT IT** London HLO 8382	15	7 wks
15 Mar 57 ●	**THE GIRL CAN'T HELP IT** London HLO 8382	9	11 wks
24 May 57	**SHE'S GOT IT (re-entry)** London HLO 8382	28	2 wks
28 Jun 57 ●	**LUCILLE** London HLO 8446	10	9 wks
13 Sep 57	**JENNY JENNY** London HLO 8470	11	5 wks
29 Nov 57	**KEEP A KNOCKIN'** London HLO 8509	21	7 wks
28 Feb 58 ●	**GOOD GOLLY MISS MOLLY** London HLU 8560	8	9 wks
11 Jul 58	**OOH MY SOUL** London HLO 8647	30	1 wk
25 Jul 58	**OOH MY SOUL (re-entry)** London HLO 8647	22	3 wks
2 Jan 59 ●	**BABY FACE** London HLU 8770	2	15 wks
3 Apr 59	**BY THE LIGHT OF THE SILVERY MOON** London HLU 8831	17	5 wks
5 Jun 59	**KANSAS CITY** London HLU 8868	26	5 wks
11 Oct 62	**HE GOT WHAT HE WANTED** Mercury AMT 1189	38	4 wks
4 Jun 64	**BAMA LAMA BAMA LOO** London HL 9896	20	7 wks
2 Jul 77	**GOOD GOLLY MISS MOLLY/RIP IT UP** Creole CR 140	37	4 wks
14 Jun 86	**GREAT GOSH A'MIGHTY (IT'S A MATTER OF TIME)** MCA MCA 1049	62	2 wks
25 Oct 86	**OPERATOR** WEA YZ 89	67	2 wks

The versions of Good Golly Miss Molly *and* Rip It Up *on Creole are re-recordings.*

LITTLE STEVEN US, male vocalist/instrumentalist - guitar   3 wks

23 May 87	**BITTER FRUIT** Manhattan MT 21	66	3 wks

LITTLE T – *See* REBEL MC

LITTLE TONY Italy, male vocalist   3 wks

15 Jan 60	**TOO GOOD** Decca F 11190	19	3 wks

LIVE REPORT UK, male vocal/instrumental group   1 wk

20 May 89	**WHY DO I ALWAYS GET IT WRONG** Brouhaha CUE 7	73	1 wk

LIVERPOOL EXPRESS
UK, male vocal/instrumental group   26 wks

26 Jun 76	**YOU ARE MY LOVE** Warner Bros. K 16743	11	9 wks
16 Oct 76	**HOLD TIGHT** Warner Bros. K 16799	46	2 wks
18 Dec 76	**EVERY MAN MUST HAVE A DREAM** Warner Bros. K 16854	17	11 wks
4 Jun 77	**DREAMIN'** Warner Bros. K 16933	40	4 wks

LIVERPOOL FC UK, male football team vocalists   16 wks

28 May 77	**WE CAN DO IT (EP)** State STAT 50	15	4 wks
23 Apr 83	**LIVERPOOL (WE'RE NEVER GONNA...)/LIVERPOOL (ANTHEM)** Mean MEAN 102	54	4 wks
17 May 86	**SITTING ON THE TOP OF THE WORLD** Columbia DB 9116	50	2 wks
14 May 88 ●	**ANFIELD RAP (RED MACHINE IN FULL EFFECT)** Virgin LFC 1	3	6 wks

Tracks on We Can Do It (EP): We Can Do It/Liverpool Lou/We Shall Not Be Moved/You'll Never Walk Alone.

LIVING COLOR US, male vocal/instrumental group   19 wks

27 Oct 90	**TYPE** Epic LCL 7	75	1 wk
2 Feb 91	**LOVE REARS ITS UGLY HEAD** Epic 6565937	12	11 wks
1 Jun 91	**SOLACE OF YOU** Epic 6569087	33	5 wks
26 Oct 91	**CULT OF PERSONALITY** Epic 6575357	67	2 wks

LIVING IN A BOX UK, male vocal/instrumental group   62 wks

4 Apr 87 ●	**LIVING IN A BOX** Chrysalis LIB 1	5	13 wks

13 Jun 87	**SCALES OF JUSTICE** Chrysalis LIB 2	30	6 wks
26 Sep 87	**SO THE STORY GOES** Chrysalis LIB 3 *	34	8 wks
30 Jan 88	**LOVE IS THE ART** Chrysalis LIB 4	45	4 wks
18 Feb 89 ●	**BLOW THE HOUSE DOWN** Chrysalis LIB 5	10	9 wks
10 Jun 89	**GATECRASHING** Chrysalis LIB 6	36	6 wks
23 Sep 89 ●	**ROOM IN YOUR HEART** Chrysalis LIB 7	5	13 wks
30 Dec 89	**DIFFERENT AIR** Chrysalis LIB 8	64	1 wk
13 Jan 90	**DIFFERENT AIR (re-entry)** Chrysalis LIB 8	57	2 wks

* Living In A Box featuring Bobby Womack

Dandy LIVINGSTONE Jamaica, male vocalist   19 wks

2 Sep 72	**SUZANNE BEWARE OF THE DEVIL** Horse HOSS 16	14	11 wks
13 Jan 73	**BIG CITY/THINK ABOUT THAT** Horse HOSS 25	26	8 wks

LL COOL J US, male rapper   30 wks

4 Jul 87	**I'M BAD** Def Jam 650856 7	71	1 wk
12 Sep 87 ●	**I NEED LOVE** Def Jam 651101 7	8	10 wks
21 Nov 87	**GO CUT CREATOR GO** Def Jam LLCJ 1	66	2 wks
13 Feb 88	**GOING BACK TO CALI/JACK THE RIPPER** Def Jam LLCJ 2	37	4 wks
10 Jun 89	**I'M THAT TYPE OF GUY** Def Jam LLCJ 3	43	5 wks
1 Dec 90	**AROUND THE WAY GIRL/MAMA SAID KNOCK YOU OUT** Def Jam 6564470	41	4 wks
9 Mar 91	**AROUND THE WAY GIRL (re-issue)** Columbia 6564470	36	4 wks

Jack The Ripper *only listed from 27 Feb 88.*

LNR US, male vocal/instrumental duo   2 wks

3 Jun 89	**WORK IT TO THE BONE** Kool Kat KOOL 501	64	2 wks

LOBO US, male vocalist   25 wks

19 Jun 71 ●	**ME AND YOU AND A DOG NAMED BOO** Philips 6073 801	4	14 wks
8 Jun 74 ●	**I'D LOVE YOU TO WANT ME** UK 68	5	11 wks

LOBO Holland, male vocalist   11 wks

25 Jul 81 ●	**THE CARIBBEAN DISCO SHOW** Polydor POSP 302	8	11 wks

Los LOBOS US, male vocal/instrumental group   24 wks

6 Apr 85	**DON'T WORRY BABY/WILL THE WOLF SURVIVE** London LASH 4	57	4 wks
18 Jul 87 ★	**LA BAMBA** Slash LASH 13	1	11 wks
26 Sep 87	**COME ON LET'S GO** Slash LASH 14	18	9 wks

Tone LOC US, male rapper   19 wks

11 Feb 89	**WILD THING/LOC'ED AFTER DARK** Fourth & Broadway BRW 121	21	8 wks
20 May 89	**FUNKY COLD MEDINA/ON FIRE** Fourth & Broadway BRW 129	13	9 wks
5 Aug 89	**I GOT IT GOIN' ON** Fourth & Broadway BRW 140	55	2 wks

Hank LOCKLIN US, male vocalist   41 wks

11 Aug 60 ●	**PLEASE HELP ME I'M FALLING** RCA 1188	9	19 wks
15 Feb 62	**FROM HERE TO THERE TO YOU** RCA 1273	44	3 wks
15 Nov 62	**WE'RE GONNA GO FISHIN'** RCA 1305	18	11 wks
5 May 66	**I FEEL A CRY COMING ON** RCA 1510	29	8 wks

LOCKSMITH US, male vocal/instrumental group   6 wks

23 Aug 80	**UNLOCK THE FUNK** Arista ARIST 364	42	6 wks

LOCOMOTIVE UK, *male vocal/instrumental group*   **8 wks**

16 Oct 68   **RUDI'S IN LOVE** *Parlophone R 5718* ....**25**   8 wks

John LODGE – *See Justin HAYWARD*

Nils LOFGREN US, *male vocalist/instrumentalist - guitar*   **3 wks**

8 Jun 85   **SECRETS IN THE STREET** *Towerbell TOW 68*.................**53**   3 wks

Johnny LOGAN Ireland, *male vocalist*   **24 wks**

3 May 80 ★ **WHAT'S ANOTHER YEAR** *Epic EPC 8572*...............**1**   8 wks
23 May 87 ● **HOLD ME NOW** *Epic LOG 1* ....**2**   11 wks
22 Aug 87   **I'M NOT IN LOVE** *Epic LOG 2* ....**31**   5 wks

Kenny LOGGINS US, *male vocalist*   **21 wks**

28 Apr 84 ● **FOOTLOOSE** *CBS A 4101* ....**6**   10 wks
1 Nov 86   **DANGER ZONE** *CBS A 7188* ....**45**   11 wks

LOLA US, *female vocalist*   **1 wk**

28 Mar 87   **WAX THE VAN** *Syncopate SY 1* ....**65**   1 wk

Jackie LOMAX – *See VARIOUS ARTISTS (EPs & LPs)* - The Apple EP

Alain LOMBARD – *See Mady MÉSPLE and Danielle MILLET*

Julie LONDON US, *female vocalist*   **3 wks**

5 Apr 57   **CRY ME A RIVER** *London HLU 8240* ....**22**   3 wks

Laurie LONDON UK, *male vocalist*   **12 wks**

8 Nov 57   **HE'S GOT THE WHOLE WORLD IN HIS HANDS**
      Parlophone R 4359 ....**12**   12 wks

LONDON BOYS UK, *male vocal duo*   **46 wks**

10 Dec 88   **REQUIEM** *WEA YZ 345* ....**59**   6 wks
1 Apr 89 ● **REQUIEM (re-entry)** *WEA YZ 345* ....**4**   15 wks
1 Jul 89 ● **LONDON NIGHTS** *WEA YZ 393* ....**2**   9 wks
16 Sep 89   **HARLEM DESIRE** *WEA YZ 415* ....**17**   7 wks
2 Dec 89   **MY LOVE** *WEA YZ 433* ....**46**   6 wks
16 Jun 90   **CHAPEL OF LOVE** *East West YZ 458* ....**75**   1 wk
19 Jan 91   **FREEDOM** *East West YZ 554* ....**54**   2 wks

LONDON COMMUNITY GOSPEL CHOIR – *See Sal SOLO*

LONDON PHILHARMONIC ORCHESTRA – *See Cliff RICHARD*

LONDON STRING CHORALE UK, *orchestra/choir*   **13 wks**

15 Dec 73   **GALLOPING HOME** *Polydor 2058 280* ....**49**   3 wks
19 Jan 74   **GALLOPING HOME (re-entry)** *Polydor 2058 280* ....**31**   10 wks

LONDON SYMPHONY ORCHESTRA   **5 wks**
UK, orchestra

6 Jan 79   **THEME FROM 'SUPERMAN' (MAIN TITLE)**
      Warner Bros. K 17292 ....**32**   5 wks

Orchestra conducted by John Williams.

LONDONBEAT UK/US, *male vocal group*   **43 wks**

26 Nov 88   **9 A.M. (THE COMFORT ZONE)** *AnXious ANX 008* ....**19**   10 wks
18 Feb 89   **FAILING IN LOVE AGAIN** *AnXious ANX 007* ....**60**   2 wks
1 Sep 90 ● **I'VE BEEN THINKING ABOUT YOU**
      AnXious ANX 14 ....**2**   13 wks
24 Nov 90   **A BETTER LOVE** *AnXious ANX 21*......................**52**   5 wks
2 Mar 91   **NO WOMAN NO CRY** *AnXious ANX 25* ....**64**   2 wks
20 Jul 91   **A BETTER LOVE (re-issue)** *AnXious ANX 32*......**23**   6 wks
27 Jun 92   **YOU BRING ON THE SUN** *AnXious ANX 37* ....**32**   4 wks
24 Oct 92   **THAT'S HOW I FEEL ABOUT YOU** *AnXious ANX 40*......**69**   1 wk

See also Liz Kershaw and Bruno Brookes.

LONE JUSTICE US, *female/male vocal/instrumental group*   **4 wks**

7 Mar 87   **I FOUND LOVE** *Geffen GEF 18* ....**45**   4 wks

Shorty LONG US, *male vocalist*   **7 wks**

17 Jul 68   **HERE COMES THE JUDGE** *Tamla Motown TMG 663*........**30**   7 wks

LONG AND THE SHORT   **8 wks**
UK, male vocal/instrumental group

10 Sep 64   **THE LETTER** *Decca F 11964* ....**30**   5 wks
24 Dec 64   **CHOC ICE** *Decca F 12043* ....**49**   3 wks

LONG RYDERS US, *male vocal/instrumental group*   **4 wks**

5 Oct 85   **LOOKING FOR LEWIS AND CLARK** *Island IS 237*..........**59**   4 wks

LOOK UK, *male vocal/instrumental group*   **15 wks**

20 Dec 80 ● **I AM THE BEAT** *MCA 647* ....**6**   12 wks
29 Aug 81   **FEEDING TIME** *MCA 736* ....**50**   3 wks

LOOSE ENDS UK, *male/female vocal/instrumental group*   **76 wks**

25 Feb 84   **TELL ME WHAT YOU WANT** *Virgin VS 658*.................**74**   1 wk
28 Apr 84   **EMERGENCY (DIAL 999)** *Virgin VS 677* ....**41**   6 wks
21 Jul 84   **CHOOSE ME (RESCUE ME)** *Virgin VS 697*.................**59**   3 wks
23 Feb 85   **HANGIN' ON A STRING (CONTEMPLATING)**
      Virgin VS 748 ....**13**   13 wks
11 May 85   **MAGIC TOUCH** *Virgin VS 761*..........................**16**   7 wks
27 Jul 85   **GOLDEN YEARS** *Virgin VS 795* ....**59**   4 wks
14 Jun 86   **STAY A LITTLE WHILE, CHILD** *Virgin VS 819* ....**52**   5 wks
20 Sep 86   **SLOW DOWN** *Virgin VS 884* ....**27**   7 wks
29 Nov 86   **NIGHTS OF PLEASURE** *Virgin VS 919* ....**42**   7 wks
4 Jun 88   **MR BACHELOR** *Virgin VS 1080* ....**50**   4 wks
25 Aug 90   **DON'T BE A FOOL** *10 TEN 312* ....**13**   9 wks
17 Nov 90   **LOVE'S GOT ME** *10 TEN 330* ....**40**   4 wks
20 Jun 92   **HANGIN' ON A STRING (re-mix)** *Ten TEN 406*..........**25**   5 wks
5 Sep 92   **MAGIC TOUCH (re-mix)** *Ten TEN 409* ....**75**   1 wk

Trini LOPEZ US, *male vocalist*   **37 wks**

12 Sep 63 ● **IF I HAD A HAMMER** *Reprise R 20198* ....**4**   17 wks
12 Dec 63   **KANSAS CITY** *Reprise R 20236* ....**35**   5 wks
12 May 66   **I'M COMING HOME CINDY** *Reprise R 20455* ....**28**   5 wks
6 Apr 67   **GONNA GET ALONG WITHOUT YA NOW**
      Reprise R 20547 ....**41**   5 wks
19 Dec 81   **TRINI TRACKS** *RCA 154* ....**59**   5 wks

LORD TANAMO Trinidad, *male vocalist*   **2 wks**

1 Dec 90   **I'M IN THE MOOD FOR LOVE** *Mooncrest MOON 1009*....**58**   2 wks

Jerry LORDAN UK, male vocalist — 15 wks

8 Jan 60	I'LL STAY SINGLE *Parlophone R 4588*	26	2 wks
26 Feb 60	WHO COULD BE BLUER *Parlophone R 4627*	17	9 wks
10 Mar 60	I'LL STAY SINGLE (re-entry) *Parlophone R 4588*	41	1 wk
19 May 60	WHO COULD BE BLUER (re-entry) *Parlophone R 4627*	45	1 wk
2 Jun 60	SING LIKE AN ANGEL *Parlophone R 4653*	36	2 wks

Sophia LOREN – *See Peter SELLERS*

Trey LORENZ US, male vocalist — 2 wks

| 21 Nov 92 | SOMEONE TO HOLD *Epic 6587857* | 65 | 2 wks |

See also Mariah Carey.

LORI and the CHAMELEONS — 1 wk
UK, female/male vocal/instrumental group

| 8 Dec 79 | TOUCH *Sire SIR 4025* | 70 | 1 wk |

LORRAINE – *See BOMB THE BASS*

Joe LOSS UK, orchestra — 53 wks

29 Jun 61	WHEELS CHA CHA *HMV POP 880*	21	21 wks
19 Oct 61	SUCU SUCU *HMV POP 937*	48	1 wk
29 Mar 62	THE MAIGRET THEME *HMV POP 995*	20	10 wks
1 Nov 62	MUST BE MADISON *HMV POP 1075*	20	13 wks
5 Nov 64	MARCH OF THE MODS *HMV POP 1351*	35	4 wks
24 Dec 64	MARCH OF THE MODS (re-entry) *HMV POP 1351*	31	4 wks

LOST UK, male/instrumental/production duo — 1 wk

| 22 Jun 91 | TECHNO FUNK *Perfecto PT 44560* | 75 | 1 wk |

LOTUS EATERS UK, male vocal/instrumental duo — 16 wks

| 2 Jul 83 | FIRST PICTURE OF YOU *Sylvan SYL 1* | 15 | 12 wks |
| 8 Oct 83 | YOU DON'T NEED SOMEONE NEW *Sylvan SYL 2* | 53 | 4 wks |

Bonnie LOU US, female vocalist — 10 wks

| 5 Feb 54 ● | TENNESSEE WIG WALK *Parlophone R 3730* | 4 | 10 wks |

LOUD UK, male vocal/instrumental group — 2 wks

| 28 Mar 92 | EASY *China WOK 2016* | 67 | 2 wks |

John D. LOUDERMILK US, male vocalist — 10 wks

| 4 Jan 62 | THE LANGUAGE OF LOVE *RCA 1269* | 13 | 10 wks |

Louie LOUIE US, male vocalist — 2 wks

| 19 Dec 92 | THE THOUGHT OF IT *Hardback YZ 724* | 38† | 2 wks |

Darlene LOVE US, female vocalist — 2 wks

| 19 Dec 92 | ALL ALONE ON CHRISTMAS *Arista 74321124767* | 34† | 2 wks |

Geoff LOVE – *See MANUEL and his MUSIC OF THE MOUNTAINS*

Monie LOVE UK, female rapper — 39 wks

4 Feb 89	I CAN DO THIS *Cooltempo COOL 177*	37	4 wks
24 Jun 89	GRANDPA'S PARTY *Cooltempo COOL 184*	16	9 wks
14 Jul 90	MONIE IN THE MIDDLE *Cooltempo COOL 210*	46	3 wks
22 Sep 90	IT'S A SHAME (MY SISTER) *Cooltempo COOL 219* *	12	8 wks
1 Dec 90	DOWN TO EARTH *Cooltempo COOL 222*	31	6 wks
6 Apr 91	RING MY BELL *Cooltempo COOL 224* **	20	5 wks
25 Jul 92	FULL TERM LOVE *Cooltempo COOL 258*	34	4 wks

* Monie Love featuring True Image ** Monie Love vs Adeva
See also Jungle Brothers.

Vikki LOVE – *See NUANCE featuring Vikki LOVE*

LOVE AFFAIR UK, male vocal/instrumental group — 56 wks

3 Jan 68 ★	EVERLASTING LOVE *CBS 3125*	1	12 wks
17 Apr 68 ●	RAINBOW VALLEY *CBS 3366*	5	13 wks
11 Sep 68 ●	A DAY WITHOUT LOVE *CBS 3674*	6	12 wks
19 Feb 69	ONE ROAD *CBS 3994*	16	9 wks
16 Jul 69 ●	BRINGING ON BACK THE GOOD TIMES *CBS 4300*	9	10 wks

LOVE AND MONEY UK, male vocal/instrumental group — 23 wks

24 May 86	CANDYBAR EXPRESS *Mercury MONEY 1*	56	4 wks
25 Apr 87	LOVE AND MONEY *Mercury MONEY 4*	68	4 wks
17 Sep 88	HALLELUJAH MAN *Fontana MONEY 5*	63	4 wks
14 Jan 89	STRANGE KIND OF LOVE *Fontana MONEY 6*	45	5 wks
25 Mar 89	JOCELYN SQUARE *Fontana MONEY 7*	51	4 wks
16 Nov 91	WINTER *Fontana MONEY 9*	52	2 wks

LOVE DECADE UK, male/female vocal/instrumental group — 12 wks

6 Jul 91	DREAM ON (IS THIS A DREAM) *All Around The World GLOBE 100*	52	2 wks
23 Nov 91	SO REAL *All Around The World GLOBE 106*	14	7 wks
11 Apr 92	I FEEL YOU *All Around The World GLOBE 107*	34	3 wks

LOVE DECREE UK, male vocal/instrumental group — 4 wks

| 16 Sep 89 | SOMETHING SO REAL (CHINHEADS THEME) *Ariola 112642* | 61 | 4 wks |

LOVE/HATE US, male vocal/instrumental group — 4 wks

| 30 Nov 91 | EVIL TWIN *Columbia 6575967* | 59 | 1 wk |
| 4 Apr 92 | WASTED IN AMERICA *Columbia 6578897* | 38 | 3 wks |

LOVE INC UK, male vocal/production duo — 3 wks

| 9 Feb 91 | LOVE IS THE MESSAGE *Love EVOL 1* | 59 | 3 wks |

LOVE REACTION – *See Zodiac MINDWARP and the LOVE REACTION*

LOVE SCULPTURE UK, instrumental group — 14 wks

| 27 Nov 68 ● | SABRE DANCE *Parlophone R 5744* | 5 | 14 wks |

LOVE SQUAD – *See Linda CARR*

LOVE UNLIMITED US, female vocal group — 19 wks

| 17 Jun 72 | WALKIN' IN THE RAIN WITH THE ONE I LOVE *Uni UN 539* | 14 | 10 wks |

25 Jan 75   **IT MAY BE WINTER OUTSIDE (BUT IN MY HEART IT'S SPRING)** *20th Century BTC 2149* ....**11**   9 wks

LOVE UNLIMITED ORCHESTRA *US, orchestra*   **10 wks**

2 Feb 74 ● **LOVE'S THEME** *Pye International 7N 25635* ....**10**   10 wks

LOVEBUG STARSKI *US, male vocalist*   **9 wks**

31 May 86   **AMITYVILLE (THE HOUSE ON THE HILL)** *Epic A 7182* ....**12**   9 wks

Bill LOVELADY *UK, male vocalist*   **10 wks**

18 Aug 79   **REGGAE FOR IT NOW** *Charisma CB 337* ....**12**   10 wks

LOVER SPEAKS *UK, male vocal/instrumental duo*   **5 wks**

16 Aug 86   **NO MORE 'I LOVE YOU'S** *A & M AM 326* ....**58**   5 wks

Michael LOVESMITH *US, male vocalist*   **1 wk**

5 Oct 85   **AIN'T NOTHIN' LIKE IT** *Motown ZB 40369* ....**75**   1 wk

Lene LOVICH *US, female vocalist*   **38 wks**

17 Feb 79 ● **LUCKY NUMBER** *Stiff BUY 42* ....**3**   11 wks
12 May 79   **SAY WHEN** *Stiff BUY 46* ....**19**   10 wks
20 Oct 79   **BIRD SONG** *Stiff BUY 53* ....**39**   7 wks
29 Mar 80   **WHAT WILL I DO WITHOUT YOU** *Stiff BUY 69* ....**58**   3 wks
14 Mar 81   **NEW TOY** *Stiff BUY 97* ....**53**   5 wks
27 Nov 82   **IT'S YOU, ONLY YOU (MEIN SCHMERZ)** *Stiff BUY 164* ....**68**   2 wks

LOVIN' SPOONFUL   **33 wks**
US/Canada, male vocal/instrumental group

14 Apr 66 ● **DAYDREAM** *Pye International 7N 25361* ....**2**   13 wks
14 Jul 66 ● **SUMMER IN THE CITY** *Kama Sutra KAS 200* ....**8**   11 wks
5 Jan 67   **NASHVILLE CATS** *Kama Sutra KAS 204* ....**26**   7 wks
9 Mar 67   **DARLING BE HOME SOON** *Kama Sutra KAS 207* ....**44**   2 wks

LOVINDEER *UK, male vocalist*   **3 wks**

27 Sep 86   **MAN SHORTAGE** *TSOJ TS 1* ....**69**   3 wks

Gary LOW *Italy, male vocalist*   **3 wks**

8 Oct 83   **I WANT YOU** *Savoir Faire FAIS 004* ....**52**   3 wks

Patti LOW – *See BUG KHAN and PLASTIC JAM featuring Patti LOW and DOOGIE*

Jim LOWE *US, male vocalist*   **9 wks**

26 Oct 56 ● **THE GREEN DOOR** *London HLD 8317* ....**8**   9 wks

Nick LOWE *UK, male vocalist*   **27 wks**

11 Mar 78 ● **I LOVE THE SOUND OF BREAKING GLASS** *Radar ADA 1* ....**7**   8 wks

9 Jun 79   **CRACKIN' UP** *Radar ADA 34* ....**34**   5 wks
25 Aug 79   **CRUEL TO BE KIND** *Radar ADA 43* ....**12**   11 wks
26 May 84   **HALF A BOY HALF A MAN** *F. Beat XX 34* ....**53**   3 wks

LOWRELL *US, male vocalist*   **9 wks**

24 Nov 79   **MELLOW MELLOW RIGHT ON** *AVI AVIS 108* ....**37**   9 wks

LRS – *See D MOB*

L7 *US, female vocal/instrumental group*   **16 wks**

4 Apr 92   **PRETEND WE'RE DEAD** *Slash LASH 34* ....**21**   7 wks
30 May 92   **EVERGLADE** *Slash LASH 36* ....**27**   3 wks
12 Sep 92   **MONSTER** *Slash LASH 38* ....**33**   3 wks
28 Nov 92   **PRETEND WE'RE DEAD (re-issue)** *Slash LASH 42* ....**50**   3 wks

L.T.D. *US, male vocal/instrumental group*   **3 wks**

9 Sep 78   **HOLDING ON (WHEN LOVE IS GONE)** *A & M AMS 7378* ....**70**   3 wks

Carrie LUCAS *US, female vocalist*   **6 wks**

16 Jun 79   **DANCE WITH YOU** *Solar FB 1482* ....**40**   6 wks

Tammy LUCAS – *See Teddy RILEY featuring Tammy LUCAS*

Robin LUKE *US, male vocalist*   **6 wks**

17 Oct 58   **SUSIE DARLIN'** *London HLD 8676* ....**24**   3 wks
21 Nov 58   **SUSIE DARLIN' (re-entry)** *London HLD 8676* ....**23**   1 wk
5 Dec 58   **SUSIE DARLIN' (2nd re-entry)** *London HLD 8676* ....**23**   2 wks

LUKK featuring Felicia COLLINS   **1 wk**
US, male/female vocal/instrumental group

28 Sep 85   **ON THE ONE** *Important TAN 6* ....**72**   1 wk

LULU *UK, female vocalist*   **133 wks**

14 May 64 ● **SHOUT** *Decca F 11884* * ....**7**   13 wks
12 Nov 64   **HERE COMES THE NIGHT** *Decca F 12017* ....**50**   1 wk
17 Jun 65 ● **LEAVE A LITTLE LOVE** *Decca F 12169* ....**8**   11 wks
2 Sep 65   **TRY TO UNDERSTAND** *Decca F 12214* ....**25**   8 wks
13 Apr 67 ● **THE BOAT THAT I ROW** *Columbia DB 8169* ....**6**   11 wks
29 Jun 67   **LET'S PRETEND** *Columbia DB 8221* ....**11**   11 wks
8 Nov 67   **LOVE LOVES TO LOVE LOVE** *Columbia DB 8295* ....**32**   6 wks
28 Feb 68 ● **ME THE PEACEFUL HEART** *Columbia DB 8358* ....**9**   9 wks
5 Jun 68   **BOY** *Columbia DB 8425* ....**15**   7 wks
6 Nov 68 ● **I'M A TIGER** *Columbia DB 8500* ....**9**   13 wks
12 Mar 69 ● **BOOM BANG-A-BANG** *Columbia DB 8550* ....**2**   13 wks
22 Nov 69   **OH ME OH MY (I'M A FOOL FOR YOU BABY)** *Atco 226 008* ....**47**   2 wks
26 Jan 74 ● **THE MAN WHO SOLD THE WORLD** *Polydor 2001 490* ....**3**   9 wks
19 Apr 75   **TAKE YOUR MAMA FOR A RIDE** *Chelsea 2005 022* ....**37**   4 wks
12 Dec 81   **I COULD NEVER MISS YOU (MORE THAN I DO)** *Alfa ALFA 1700* ....**62**   4 wks
16 Jan 82   **I COULD NEVER MISS YOU (MORE THAN I DO) (re-entry)** *Alfa ALFA 1700* ....**63**   1 wk
19 Jul 86 ● **SHOUT** *Jive LULU 1/Decca SHOUT 1* ....**8**   10 wks

* Lulu and the Luvvers

The newly recorded Shout entered the chart 19 Jul 86, and the next week the original Decca version by Lulu and the Luvvers also charted. For all subsequent weeks Gallup amalgamated both versions under one entry.

Bob LUMAN *US, male vocalist*   **21 wks**

8 Sep 60 ● **LET'S THINK ABOUT LIVING** *Warner Bros. WB 18* ....**6**   18 wks

| 15 Dec 60 | | WHY WHY BYE BYE *Warner Bros. WB 28* .... | 46 | 1 wk |
| 4 May 61 | | THE GREAT SNOWMAN *Warner Bros. WB 37* .... | 49 | 2 wks |

LURKERS *UK, male vocal/instrumental group*   **11 wks**

3 Jun 78		AIN'T GOT A CLUE *Beggars Banquet BEG 6*	45	3 wks
5 Aug 78		I DON'T NEED TO TELL HER *Beggars Banquet BEG 9*	49	4 wks
3 Feb 79		JUST THIRTEEN *Beggars Banquet BEG 14*	66	2 wks
9 Jun 79		OUT IN THE DARK/CYANIDE		
		Beggars Banquet BEG 19	72	1 wk
17 Nov 79		NEW GUITAR IN TOWN *Beggars Banquet BEG 28*	72	1 wk

LUSH *UK, male/female vocal/instrumental group*   **6 wks**

10 Mar 90		MAD LOVE EP *4AD BAD 003*	55	1 wk
27 Oct 90		SWEETNESS AND LIGHT *4AD BAD 0013*	47	2 wks
19 Oct 91		NOTHING NATURAL *4AD AD 1016*	43	1 wk
11 Jan 92		FOR LOVE (EP) *4AD BAD 2001*	35	2 wks

Tracks on Mad Love EP: *De-Luxe/Leaves Me Cold/Downer/Thoughtforms.* Tracks on For Love (EP): *For Love/Starlust/Outdoor Miner/Astronaut.*

LUVVERS – See LULU

Frankie LYMON and the TEENAGERS   **38 wks**
US, male vocal group

29 Jun 56	★	WHY DO FOOLS FALL IN LOVE		
		Columbia DB 3772 *	1	16 wks
29 Mar 57		I'M NOT A JUVENILE DELINQUENT		
		Columbia DB 3878	12	7 wks
12 Apr 57	●	BABY BABY *Columbia DB 3878*	4	12 wks
20 Sep 57		GOODY GOODY *Columbia DB 3983*	24	3 wks

* Teenagers featuring Frankie Lymon

Kenny LYNCH *UK, male vocalist*   **59 wks**

30 Jun 60		MOUNTAIN OF LOVE *HMV POP 751*	33	3 wks
13 Sep 62		PUFF *HMV POP 1057*	33	5 wks
25 Oct 62		PUFF (re-entry) *HMV POP 1057*	46	1 wk
6 Dec 62	●	UP ON THE ROOF *HMV POP 1090*	10	12 wks
20 Jun 63	●	YOU CAN NEVER STOP ME LOVING YOU		
		HMV POP 1165	10	14 wks
16 Apr 64		STAND BY ME *HMV POP 1280*	39	7 wks
27 Aug 64		WHAT AM I TO YOU *HMV POP 1321*	37	4 wks
1 Oct 64		WHAT AM I TO YOU (re-entry) *HMV POP 1321*	44	2 wks
17 Jun 65		I'LL STAY BY YOU *HMV POP 1430*	29	7 wks
20 Aug 83		HALF THE DAY'S GONE AND WE HAVEN'T		
		EARNT A PENNY *Satril SAT 510*	50	4 wks

Cheryl LYNN *US, female vocalist*   **2 wks**

| 8 Sep 84 | | ENCORE *Streetwave KHAN 23* .... | 68 | 2 wks |

Patti LYNN *UK, female vocalist*   **5 wks**

| 10 May 62 | | JOHNNY ANGEL *Fontana H 391* .... | 37 | 5 wks |

Tami LYNN *US, female vocalist*   **20 wks**

22 May 71	●	I'M GONNA RUN AWAY FROM YOU *Mojo 2092 001*	4	14 wks
3 May 75		I'M GONNA RUN AWAY FROM YOU (re-issue)		
		Contempo Raries CS 9026	36	6 wks

Vera LYNN *UK, female vocalist*   **46 wks**

14 Nov 52	●	AUF WIEDERSEHEN *Decca F 9927*	10	1 wk
14 Nov 52	●	FORGET ME NOT *Decca F 9985*	7	1 wk
14 Nov 52	●	HOMING WALTZ *Decca F 9959*	9	3 wks

28 Nov 52	●	FORGET ME NOT (re-entry) *Decca F 9985*	5	5 wks
5 Jun 53		WINDSOR WALTZ *Decca F 10092*	11	1 wk
15 Oct 54	★	MY SON MY SON *Decca F 10372 **	1	14 wks
8 Jun 56		WHO ARE WE *Decca F 10715*	30	1 wk
26 Oct 56		A HOUSE WITH LOVE IN IT *Decca F 10799*	17	13 wks
15 Mar 57		THE FAITHFUL HUSSAR (DON'T CRY MY LOVE)		
		Decca F 10846	29	2 wks
21 Jun 57		TRAVELLIN' HOME *Decca F 10903*	20	5 wks

* Vera Lynn with Frank Weir, his saxophone, his Orchestra and Chorus.

Jeff LYNNE *UK, male vocalist*   **4 wks**

| 30 Jun 90 | | EVERY LITTLE THING *Reprise W 9799* .... | 59 | 4 wks |

Philip LYNOTT *Ireland, male vocalist*   **36 wks**

5 Apr 80		DEAR MISS LONELY HEARTS *Vertigo SOLO 1*	32	6 wks
21 Jun 80		KING'S CALL *Vertigo SOLO 2*	35	6 wks
21 Mar 81		YELLOW PEARL *Vertigo SOLO 3*	56	3 wks
26 Dec 81		YELLOW PEARL (re-entry) *Vertigo SOLO 3*	14	9 wks
18 May 85	●	OUT IN THE FIELDS *10 TEN 49 **	5	10 wks
24 Jan 87		KING'S CALL (re-mix) *Vertigo LYN 1*	68	2 wks

* Gary Moore and Phil Lynott

See also Gary Moore.

LYNYRD SKYNYRD *US, male vocal/instrumental group*   **21 wks**

11 Sep 76		FREE BIRD EP *MCA 251*	31	4 wks
22 Dec 79		FREE BIRD EP (re-entry) *MCA 251*	43	8 wks
19 Jun 82		FREE BIRD EP (2nd re-entry) *MCA 251*	21	9 wks

Tracks on EP: *Free Bird/Sweet Home Alabama/Double Trouble.*

Barbara LYON *US, female vocalist*   **12 wks**

| 24 Jun 55 | | STOWAWAY *Columbia DB 3619* .... | 12 | 8 wks |
| 21 Dec 56 | | LETTER TO A SOLDIER *Columbia DB 3865* .... | 27 | 4 wks |

Humphrey LYTTELTON BAND   **6 wks**
UK, male jazz band, Humphrey Lyttelton - trumpet

| 13 Jul 56 | | BAD PENNY BLUES *Parlophone R 4184* .... | 19 | 6 wks |

M *UK, male vocalist/multi-instrumentalist - Robin Scott*   **39 wks**

7 Apr 79	●	POP MUZIK *MCA 413*	2	14 wks
8 Dec 79		MOONLIGHT AND MUZAK *MCA 541*	33	9 wks
15 Mar 80		THAT'S THE WAY THE MONEY GOES *MCA 570*	45	5 wks
22 Nov 80		OFFICIAL SECRETS *MCA 650*	64	2 wks
10 Jun 89		POP MUZIK (re-mix) *Freestyle FRS 1*	15	9 wks

Bobby M featuring Jean CARN   **3 wks**
US, male/female vocal/instrumental duo

| 29 Jan 83 | | LET'S STAY TOGETHER *Gordy TMG 1288* .... | 53 | 3 wks |

M + M *Canada, male/female vocal duo*   **4 wks**

| 28 Jul 84 | | BLACK STATIONS WHITE STATIONS *RCA 426* .... | 46 | 4 wks |

See also Martha and the Muffins.

M-D-EMM UK, male producer - Mark Ryder   **3 wks**

22 Feb 92	GET DOWN Strictly Underground 7STUR 13	55	2 wks
30 May 92	MOVE YOUR FEET Strictly Underground STUR 15	67	1 wk

M and O BAND UK, male vocal/instrumental group   **6 wks**

28 Feb 76	LET'S DO THE LATIN HUSTLE Creole CR 120	16	6 wks

M-PEOPLE UK, male/female vocal/instrumental group   **21 wks**

26 Oct 91	HOW CAN I LOVE YOU MORE Deconstruction PB 44855	29	9 wks
7 Mar 92	COLOUR MY LIFE Deconstruction PB 45241	35	4 wks
18 Apr 92	SOMEDAY Deconstruction PB 45369 *	38	3 wks
10 Oct 92	EXCITED Deconstruction 71321116337	29	5 wks

* M-People with Heather Small

Pete MAC Jr US, male vocalist   **4 wks**

15 Oct 77	THE WATER MARGIN BBC RESL 50	37	4 wks

This is the Japanese version of the song which shared chart credit with the English language version by Godiego. See also Godiego.

MAC BAND featuring the McCAMPBELL BROTHERS US, male vocal group   **17 wks**

18 Jun 88	● ROSES ARE RED MCA MCA 1264	8	13 wks
10 Sep 88	STALEMATE MCA MCA 1271	40	4 wks

Stalemate credits the McCampbell Brothers on the sleeve only, not on the label.

Neil MacARTHUR UK, male vocalist   **5 wks**

5 Feb 69	SHE'S NOT THERE Deram DM 225	34	5 wks

Neil MacArthur is Colin Blunstone under a false name.

David MacBETH UK, male vocalist   **4 wks**

30 Oct 59	MR. BLUE Pye 7N 15231	18	4 wks

Nicko McBRAIN UK, male vocalist/instrumentalist - drums   **1 wk**

13 Jul 91	RHYTHM OF THE BEAST EMI NICK 01	72	1 wk

Frankie McBRIDE Ireland, male vocalist   **15 wks**

9 Aug 67	FIVE LITTLE FINGERS Emerald MD 1081	19	15 wks

Dan McCAFFERTY UK, male vocalist   **3 wks**

13 Sep 75	OUT OF TIME Mountain TOP 1	41	3 wks

C.W. McCALL US, male vocalist   **10 wks**

14 Feb 76	● CONVOY MGM 2006 560	2	10 wks

David McCALLUM UK, male vocalist   **4 wks**

14 Apr 66	COMMUNICATION Capitol CL 15439	32	4 wks

McCAMPBELL BROTHERS – See MAC BAND featuring the McCAMPBELL BROTHERS

Paul McCARTNEY UK, male vocalist   **388 wks**

27 Feb 71	● ANOTHER DAY Apple R 5889	2	12 wks
28 Aug 71	BACK SEAT OF MY CAR Apple R 5914 *	39	5 wks
26 Feb 72	GIVE IRELAND BACK TO THE IRISH Apple R 5936 *	16	8 wks
27 May 72	● MARY HAD A LITTLE LAMB Apple R 5949 **	9	11 wks
9 Dec 72	HI HI HI/C MOON Apple R 5973 **	5	13 wks
7 Apr 73	● MY LOVE Apple R 5985 ***	9	11 wks
9 Jun 73	LIVE AND LET DIE Apple R 5987 **	9	13 wks
15 Sep 73	LIVE AND LET DIE (re-entry) Apple R 5987 **	49	1 wk
3 Nov 73	HELEN WHEELS Apple R 5993 ***	12	12 wks
2 Mar 74	● JET Apple R 5996 ***	7	9 wks
6 Jul 74	BAND ON THE RUN Apple R 5997 ***	3	11 wks
9 Nov 74	JUNIOR'S FARM Apple R 5999 ***	16	10 wks
31 May 75	LISTEN TO WHAT THE MAN SAID Capitol R 6006 **	6	8 wks
18 Oct 75	LETTING GO Capitol R 6008 **	41	3 wks
15 May 76	● SILLY LOVE SONGS Parlophone R 6014 **	2	11 wks
7 Aug 76	LET 'EM IN Parlophone R 6015 **	2	10 wks
19 Feb 77	MAYBE I'M AMAZED Parlophone R 6017 **	28	5 wks
19 Nov 77	★ MULL OF KINTYRE/GIRLS' SCHOOL Capitol R 6018 **	1	17 wks
1 Apr 78	● WITH A LITTLE LUCK Parlophone R 6019 **	5	9 wks
1 Jul 78	I'VE HAD ENOUGH Parlophone R 6020 **	42	7 wks
9 Sep 78	LONDON TOWN Parlophone R 6021 **	60	4 wks
7 Apr 79	● GOODNIGHT TONIGHT Parlophone R 6023 **	5	10 wks
16 Jun 79	OLD SIAM SIR MPL R 6026 **	35	6 wks
1 Sep 79	GETTING CLOSER/BABY'S REQUEST R 6027 **	60	3 wks
1 Dec 79	WONDERFUL CHRISTMASTIME Parlophone R 6029	6	8 wks
19 Apr 80	● COMING UP Parlophone R 6035	2	9 wks
21 Jun 80	WATERFALLS Parlophone R 6037	9	8 wks
10 Apr 82	★ EBONY AND IVORY Parlophone R 6054 ****	1	10 wks
3 Jul 82	TAKE IT AWAY Parlophone R 6056	15	10 wks
9 Oct 82	TUG OF WAR Parlophone R 6057	53	3 wks
6 Nov 82	THE GIRL IS MINE Epic EPC A 2729 *****	8	9 wks
15 Jan 83	THE GIRL IS MINE (re-entry) Epic EPC A 2729 *****	75	1 wk
15 Oct 83	SAY SAY SAY Parlophone R 6062 ******	2	15 wks
17 Dec 83	★ PIPES OF PEACE Parlophone R 6064	1	12 wks
6 Oct 84	● NO MORE LONELY NIGHTS Parlophone R 6080	2	15 wks
24 Nov 84	● WE ALL STAND TOGETHER Parlophone R 6086 *******	3	13 wks
30 Nov 85	SPIES LIKE US Parlophone R 6118	16	10 wks
21 Dec 85	WE ALL STAND TOGETHER (re-entry) Parlophone R 6086	32	5 wks
26 Jul 86	PRESS Parlophone R 6133	25	8 wks
13 Dec 86	ONLY LOVE REMAINS Parlophone R 6148	34	5 wks
28 Nov 87	● ONCE UPON A LONG AGO Parlophone R 6170	10	7 wks
20 May 89	★ FERRY 'CROSS THE MERSEY PWL PWL 41 ********	1	7 wks
20 May 89	MY BRAVE FACE Parlophone R 6213	18	5 wks
29 Jul 89	THIS ONE Parlophone R 6223	18	6 wks
25 Nov 89	FIGURE OF EIGHT Parlophone R 6235	42	3 wks
17 Feb 90	PUT IT THERE Parlophone R 6246	32	2 wks
20 Oct 90	BIRTHDAY Parlophone R 6271	29	3 wks
8 Dec 90	ALL MY TRIALS Parlophone R 6278	35	5 wks

* Paul and Linda McCartney ** Wings *** Paul McCartney and Wings **** Paul McCartney with Stevie Wonder ***** Michael Jackson and Paul McCartney ****** Paul McCartney and Michael Jackson ******* Paul McCartney and the Frog Chorus ******** Christians, Holly Johnson, Paul McCartney, Gerry Marsden and Stock Aitken Waterman

R 6027 credits no label at all, although the number is a Parlophone one.

Kirsty MacCOLL UK, female vocalist   **56 wks**

13 Jun 81	THERE'S A GUY WORKS DOWN THE CHIPSHOP SWEARS HE'S ELVIS Polydor POSP 250	14	9 wks
19 Jan 85	● A NEW ENGLAND Stiff BUY 216	7	10 wks
5 Dec 87	● FAIRYTALE OF NEW YORK Pogue Mahone NY 7 *	2	9 wks
8 Apr 89	FREE WORLD Virgin KMA 1	43	6 wks
1 Jul 89	DAYS Virgin KMA 2	12	9 wks
25 May 91	WALKING DOWN MADISON Virgin VS 1348	23	7 wks
24 Aug 91	MY AFFAIR Virgin VS 1354	68	1 wk
14 Dec 91	FAIRYTALE OF NEW YORK (re-issue) PM YZ 628 *	36	5 wks

* Pogues featuring Kirsty MacColl

Marilyn McCOO and Billy DAVIS Jr.   **9 wks**
US, female/male vocal duo

19 Mar 77 ●	YOU DON'T HAVE TO BE A STAR (TO BE IN MY SHOW) *ABC 4147*	7	9 wks

Van McCOY *US, orchestra*   **36 wks**

31 May 75 ●	THE HUSTLE *Avco 6105 038 *￼	3	12 wks
1 Nov 75	CHANGE WITH THE TIMES *Avco 6105 042*	36	4 wks
12 Feb 77	SOUL CHA CHA *H & L 6105 065*	34	6 wks
9 Apr 77	THE SHUFFLE *H & L 6105 076*	4	14 wks

*Van McCoy with the Soul City Symphony

McCOYS *US, male vocal/instrumental group*   **18 wks**

2 Sep 65 ●	HANG ON SLOOPY *Immediate IM 001*	5	14 wks
16 Dec 65	FEVER *Immediate IM 021*	44	4 wks

George McCRAE *US, male vocalist*   **62 wks**

29 Jun 74 ★	ROCK YOUR BABY *Jayboy BOY 85*	1	14 wks
5 Oct 74 ●	I CAN'T LEAVE YOU ALONE *Jayboy BOY 90*	9	9 wks
14 Dec 74	YOU CAN HAVE IT ALL *Jayboy BOY 92*	23	9 wks
22 Mar 75	SING A HAPPY SONG *Jayboy BOY 95*	38	4 wks
19 Jul 75 ●	IT'S BEEN SO LONG *Jayboy BOY 100*	4	11 wks
18 Oct 75	I AIN'T LYIN' *Jayboy BOY 105*	12	7 wks
24 Jan 76	HONEY I *Jayboy BOY 107*	33	4 wks
25 Feb 84	ONE STEP CLOSER (TO LOVE) *President PT 522*	57	4 wks

Gwen McCRAE *US, female vocalist*   **2 wks**

30 Apr 88	ALL THIS LOVE THAT I'M GIVING *Flame MELT 7*	63	2 wks

MacCRARYS *US, male vocal/instrumental group*   **4 wks**

31 Jul 82	LOVE ON A SUMMER NIGHT *Capitol CL 251*	52	4 wks

Ian McCULLOCH *UK, male vocalist*   **14 wks**

15 Dec 84	SEPTEMBER SONG *Korova KOW 40*	51	5 wks
2 Sep 89	PROUD TO FALL *WEA YZ 417*	51	4 wks
12 May 90	CANDLELAND (THE SECOND COMING) *East West YZ 452 *￼	75	1 wk
22 Feb 92	LOVER LOVER LOVER *East West YZ 643*	47	4 wks

*Ian McCulloch featuring Elizabeth Fraser

Gene McDANIELS *US, male vocalist*   **2 wks**

16 Nov 61	TOWER OF STRENGTH *London HLG 9448*	49	1 wk
30 Nov 61	TOWER OF STRENGTH (re-entry) *London HLG 9448*	49	1 wk

Charles McDEVITT SKIFFLE GROUP featuring Nancy WHISKEY   **20 wks**
UK, male/female vocal/instrumental group

12 Apr 57 ●	FREIGHT TRAIN *Oriole CB 1352*	5	17 wks
14 Jun 57	GREENBACK DOLLAR *Oriole CB 1371*	28	1 wk
5 Jul 57	GREENBACK DOLLAR (re-entry) *Oriole CB 1371*	30	1 wk
20 Sep 57	FREIGHT TRAIN (re-entry) *Oriole CB 1352*	27	1 wk

Michael McDONALD *US, male vocalist*   **45 wks**

18 Feb 84	YAH MO B THERE *Qwest W 9394 *￼	44	5 wks
7 Apr 84	YAH MO B THERE (re-entry) *Qwest W 9394 *￼	69	3 wks
12 Jan 85	YAH MO B THERE (2nd re-entry) *Qwest W 9394 *￼	12	8 wks
3 May 86 ●	ON MY OWN *MCA MCA 1045 **￼	2	13 wks
26 Jul 86	I KEEP FORGETTIN' *Warner Bros K 17992*	43	6 wks
6 Sep 86	SWEET FREEDOM *MCA MCA 1073*	12	10 wks

*James Ingram with Michael McDonald **Patti Labelle and Michael McDonald
The 85 entry of Yah Mo B There is a re-mix of the original hit with the same catalogue number. See also Doobie Brothers.

Carrie McDOWELL *US, female vocalist*   **3 wks**

26 Sep 87	UH UH NO NO CASUAL SEX *Motown ZV 41501*	68	3 wks

John McENROE and Pat CASH with the FULL METAL RACKETS   **1 wk**
US/Australia, male vocal/instrumental duo with UK backing group

13 Jul 91	ROCK 'N' ROLL *Music For Nations KUT 141*	66	1 wk

MACEO and the MACS   **5 wks**
US, male vocal/instrumental group

16 May 87	CROSS THE TRACK (WE BETTER GO BACK) *Urban URBX 1*	54	5 wks

McFADDEN and WHITEHEAD *US, male vocal duo* **10 wks**

19 May 79 ●	AIN'T NO STOPPIN' US NOW *Philadelphia International PIR 7365*	5	10 wks

Bobby McFERRIN *US, male vocalist*   **15 wks**

24 Sep 88 ●	DON'T WORRY BE HAPPY *Manhattan MT 56*	2	11 wks
17 Dec 88	THINKIN' ABOUT YOUR BODY *Manhattan BLUE 6*	46	4 wks

Mike McGEAR *UK, male vocalist*   **4 wks**

5 Oct 74	LEAVE IT *Warner Bros. K 16446*	36	4 wks

Maureen McGOVERN *US, female vocalist*   **8 wks**

5 Jun 76	THE CONTINENTAL *20th Century BTC 2222*	16	8 wks

Shane McGOWAN – *See Nick CAVE*

Freddie McGREGOR *Jamaica, male vocalist*   **16 wks**

27 Jun 87 ●	JUST DON'T WANT TO BE LONELY *Germain DG 24*	9	11 wks
19 Sep 87	THAT GIRL (GROOVY SITUATION) *Polydor POSP 884*	47	5 wks

Mary MacGREGOR *US, female vocalist*   **10 wks**

19 Feb 77 ●	TORN BETWEEN TWO LOVERS *Ariola America AA 111*	4	10 wks

McGUINNESS FLINT *UK, male vocal/instrumental group* **26 wks**

21 Nov 70 ●	WHEN I'M DEAD AND GONE *Capitol CL 15662*	2	14 wks
1 May 71 ●	MALT AND BARLEY BLUES *Capitol CL 15682*	5	12 wks

MADONNA gets into
the groove at a 1991
AIDS dance-a-thon at
the Los Angeles Sports
Arena.

Barry McGUIRE US, male vocalist — 13 wks

9 Sep 65 ● EVE OF DESTRUCTION RCA 1469	3	13 wks

McGUIRE SISTERS US, female vocal group — 24 wks

1 Apr 55	NO MORE Vogue Coral Q 72050	20	1 wk
15 Jul 55	SINCERELY Vogue Coral Q 72050	14	4 wks
1 Jun 56	DELILAH JONES Vogue Coral Q 72161	24	2 wks
14 Feb 58	SUGARTIME Coral Q 72305	14	6 wks
1 May 59	MAY YOU ALWAYS Coral Q 72356	15	10 wks
17 Jul 59	MAY YOU ALWAYS (re-entry) Coral Q 72356	28	1 wk

Lonnie MACK US, male instrumentalist - guitar — 3 wks

14 Apr 79	MEMPHIS Lightning LIG 9011	47	3 wks

Memphis *was coupled with* Let's Dance *by Chris Montez as a double A-side.*

Maria McKEE US, female vocalist — 19 wks

15 Sep 90 ★	SHOW ME HEAVEN Epic 656303 7	1	14 wks
26 Jan 91	BREATHE Geffen GFS 1	59	1 wk
1 Aug 92	SWEETEST CHILD Geffen GFS 23	45	4 wks

Kenneth McKELLAR UK, male vocalist — 4 wks

10 Mar 66	A MAN WITHOUT LOVE Decca F 12341	30	4 wks

Gisele McKENZIE Canada, female vocalist — 6 wks

17 Jul 53	SEVEN LONELY DAYS Capitol CL 13920	12	1 wk
31 Jul 53	SEVEN LONELY DAYS (re-entry) Capitol CL 13920	11	1 wk
21 Aug 53 ●	SEVEN LONELY DAYS (2nd re-entry) Capitol CL 13920	6	4 wks

Scott McKENZIE US, male vocalist — 18 wks

12 Jul 67 ★	SAN FRANCISCO (BE SURE TO WEAR SOME FLOWERS IN YOUR HAIR) CBS 2816	1	17 wks
1 Nov 67	LIKE AN OLD TIME MOVIE CBS 3009 *	50	1 wk

* The Voice Of Scott McKenzie

Ken MACKINTOSH UK, orchestra — 9 wks

15 Jan 54	THE CREEP HMV BD 1295	12	1 wk
29 Jan 54 ●	THE CREEP (re-entry) HMV BD 1295	10	1 wk
7 Feb 58	RAUNCHY HMV POP 426	19	6 wks
10 Mar 60	NO HIDING PLACE HMV POP 713	45	1 wk

Vivienne McKONE UK, female vocalist — 5 wks

25 Jul 92	SING (OOH-EE-OOH) ffrr F 183	47	4 wks
31 Oct 92	BEWARE ffrr F 202	69	1 wk

Craig McLACHLAN Australia, male vocalist — 28 wks

16 Jun 90 ●	MONA Epic 655784 7 *	2	11 wks
4 Aug 90	AMANDA Epic 656170 7 *	19	6 wks
10 Nov 90	I ALMOST FELT LIKE CRYING Epic 656310 7 *	50	3 wks
23 May 92	ONE REASON WHY Epic 6580677	29	6 wks
14 Nov 92	ON MY OWN Epic 6584677	59	2 wks

* Craig McLachlan and Check 1-2

British Hit Singles Part One: Alphabetically by Artist
Date of chart entry/Title & catalogue no./Peak position reached/Weeks on chart
★ Number one ● Top Ten † still on chart at 31 Dec 1992
* = credited to act billed in footnote

Tommy McLAIN US, male vocalist — 1 wk

8 Sep 66	SWEET DREAMS London HL 10065	49	1 wk

Malcolm McLAREN UK, male vocalist — 64 wks

4 Dec 82 ●	BUFFALO GALS Charisma MALC 1 *	9	12 wks
26 Feb 83	SOWETO Charisma MALC 2 **	32	5 wks
2 Jul 83 ●	DOUBLE DUTCH Charisma MALC 3	3	13 wks
17 Dec 83	DUCK FOR THE OYSTER Charisma MALC 4	54	5 wks
1 Sep 84	MADAM BUTTERFLY (UN BEL DI VEDREMO) Charisma MALC 5	13	9 wks
27 May 89	WALTZ DARLING Epic WALTZ 2 ***	31	8 wks
19 Aug 89	SOMETHING'S JUMPIN' IN YOUR SHIRT Epic WALTZ 3 ****	29	7 wks
25 Nov 89	HOUSE OF THE BLUE DANUBE Epic WALTZ 4 ****	73	1 wk
21 Dec 91	MAGIC'S BACK (THEME FROM THE GHOSTS OF OXFORD STREET) RCA PB 45223 *****	42	4 wks

* Malcolm McLaren and the World's Famous Supreme Team ** Malcolm McLaren and the McLarenettes *** Malcolm McLaren and the Bootzilla Orchestra **** Malcolm McLaren and the Bootzilla Orchestra featuring Lisa Marie ***** Malcolm McLaren featuring Alison Limerick

Don McLEAN US, male vocalist — 68 wks

22 Jan 72 ●	AMERICAN PIE United Artists UP 35325	2	16 wks
13 May 72 ★	VINCENT United Artists UP 35359	1	15 wks
14 Apr 73	EVERYDAY United Artists UP 35519	38	5 wks
10 May 80 ★	CRYING EMI 5051	1	14 wks
17 Apr 82	CASTLES IN THE AIR EMI 5258	47	8 wks
5 Oct 91	AMERICAN PIE (re-issue) Liberty EMCT 3	12	10 wks

Jackie McLEAN US, male instrumentalist - alto sax — 4 wks

7 Jul 79	DR. JACKYLL AND MISTER FUNK RCA PB 1575	53	4 wks

Phil McLEAN US, male vocalist — 4 wks

18 Jan 62	SMALL SAD SAM Top Rank JAR 597	34	4 wks

Patrick MACNEE and Honor BLACKMAN — 7 wks
UK, male/female vocal duo

1 Dec 90 ●	KINKY BOOTS Deram KINKY 1	5	7 wks

Rita MacNEIL Canada, female vocalist — 10 wks

6 Oct 90	WORKING MAN Polydor PO 98	11	10 wks

Clyde McPHATTER US, male vocalist — 1 wk

24 Aug 56	TREASURE OF LOVE London HLE 8293	27	1 wk

Carmen McRAE – See Sammy DAVIS Jr

Gordon MacRAE – See VARIOUS ARTISTS (EPs & LPs) - Carousel Soundtrack

Ralph McTELL UK, male vocalist — **18 wks**

7 Dec 74 ●	STREETS OF LONDON Reprise K 14380	2	12 wks
20 Dec 75	DREAMS OF YOU Warner Bros. K 16648	36	6 wks

MAD JOCKS featuring JOCKMASTER B.A. — **5 wks**
UK, male vocal/instrumental group

19 Dec 87	JOCK MIX 1 Debut DEBT 3037	46	5 wks

Danny MADDEN US, male vocalist — **2 wks**

14 Jul 90	THE FACTS OF LIFE Eternal YZ 473	72	2 wks

MADNESS UK, male vocal/instrumental group — **256 wks**

1 Sep 79	THE PRINCE 2-Tone TT 3	16	11 wks
10 Nov 79 ●	ONE STEP BEYOND Stiff BUY 56	7	14 wks
5 Jan 80 ●	MY GIRL Stiff BUY 62	3	10 wks
5 Apr 80 ●	WORK REST AND PLAY EP Stiff BUY 71	6	8 wks
13 Sep 80 ●	BAGGY TROUSERS Stiff BUY 84	3	20 wks
22 Nov 80 ●	EMBARRASSMENT Stiff BUY 102	4	12 wks
24 Jan 81 ●	THE RETURN OF THE LOS PALMAS SEVEN Stiff BUY 108	7	11 wks
25 Apr 81 ●	GREY DAY Stiff BUY 112	4	10 wks
26 Sep 81 ●	SHUT UP Stiff BUY 126	7	9 wks
5 Dec 81 ●	IT MUST BE LOVE Stiff BUY 134	4	12 wks
20 Feb 82	CARDIAC ARREST Stiff BUY 140	14	10 wks
22 May 82 ★	HOUSE OF FUN Stiff BUY 146	1	9 wks
24 Jul 82 ●	DRIVING IN MY CAR Stiff BUY 153	4	8 wks
27 Nov 82 ●	OUR HOUSE Stiff BUY 163	5	13 wks
19 Feb 83 ●	TOMORROW'S (JUST ANOTHER DAY)/MADNESS (IS ALL IN THE MIND) Stiff BUY 169	8	9 wks
20 Aug 83 ●	WINGS OF A DOVE Stiff BUY 181	2	10 wks
5 Nov 83 ●	THE SUN AND THE RAIN Stiff BUY 192	5	10 wks
11 Feb 84	MICHAEL CAINE Stiff BUY 196	11	8 wks
2 Jun 84	ONE BETTER DAY Stiff BUY 201	17	7 wks
31 Aug 85	YESTERDAY'S MEN Zarjazz JAZZ 5	18	7 wks
26 Oct 85	UNCLE SAM Zarjazz JAZZ 7	21	11 wks
1 Feb 86	SWEETEST GIRL Zarjazz JAZZ 8	35	6 wks
8 Nov 86	(WAITING FOR) THE GHOST TRAIN Zarjazz JAZZ 9	18	7 wks
3 Jan 87	(WAITING FOR) THE GHOST TRAIN (re-entry) Zarjazz JAZZ 9	74	1 wk
19 Mar 88	I PRONOUNCE YOU Virgin VS 1054 *	44	4 wks
15 Feb 92 ●	IT MUST BE LOVE (re-issue) Virgin VS 1405	6	9 wks
25 Apr 92	HOUSE OF FUN (re-issue) Virgin VS 1413	40	3 wks
8 Aug 92	MY GIRL (re-issue) Virgin VS 1425	27	4 wks
28 Nov 92	THE HARDER THEY COME Go! Discs GOD 93	44	3 wks

* The Madness

Tracks on Work Rest and Play EP: Night Boat to Cairo/Deceives The Eye/The Young And The Old/Don't Quote Me On That.

MADONNA US, female vocalist — **334 wks**

14 Jan 84 ●	HOLIDAY Sire W 9405	6	11 wks
17 Mar 84	LUCKY STAR Sire W 9522	14	9 wks
2 Jun 84	BORDERLINE Sire W 9260	56	4 wks
17 Nov 84 ●	LIKE A VIRGIN Sire W 9210	3	18 wks
2 Mar 85 ●	MATERIAL GIRL Sire W 9083	3	10 wks
8 Jun 85 ●	CRAZY FOR YOU Geffen A 6323	2	15 wks
27 Jul 85 ★	INTO THE GROOVE Sire W 8934	1	14 wks
3 Aug 85 ●	HOLIDAY (re-entry) Sire W 9405	2	10 wks
21 Sep 85 ●	ANGEL Sire W 8881	5	9 wks
12 Oct 85 ●	GAMBLER Geffen A 6585	4	11 wks
7 Dec 85 ●	DRESS YOU UP Sire W 8848	5	11 wks
4 Jan 86	GAMBLER (re-entry) Geffen A 6585	61	1 wk
25 Jan 86	BORDERLINE (re-entry) Sire W 9260	2	9 wks
26 Apr 86 ●	LIVE TO TELL Sire W 8717	2	12 wks

MAGAZINE UK, male vocal/instrumental group — **7 wks**

11 Feb 78	SHOT BY BOTH SIDES Virgin VS 200	41	4 wks
26 Jul 80	SWEET HEART CONTRACT Virgin VS 368	54	3 wks

MAGIC LADY US, female vocal duo — **3 wks**

14 May 88	BETCHA CAN'T LOSE (WITH MY LOVE) Motown ZB 42003	58	3 wks

MAGIC LANTERNS UK, male vocal/instrumental group — **3 wks**

7 Jul 66	EXCUSE ME BABY CBS 202094	46	1 wk
28 Jul 66	EXCUSE ME BABY (re-entry) CBS 202094	44	1 wk
11 Aug 66	EXCUSE ME BABY (2nd re-entry) CBS 202094	46	1 wk

MAGNUM UK, male vocal/instrumental group — **26 wks**

22 Mar 80	MAGNUM (DOUBLE SINGLE) Jet 175	47	6 wks
12 Jul 86	LONELY NIGHT Polydor POSP 798	70	2 wks
19 Mar 88	DAYS OF NO TRUST Polydor POSP 910	32	4 wks
7 May 88	START TALKING LOVE Polydor POSP 920	22	4 wks
2 Jul 88	IT MUST HAVE BEEN LOVE Polydor POSP 930	33	4 wks
23 Jun 90	ROCKIN' CHAIR Polydor PO 88	27	4 wks
25 Aug 90	HEARTBROKE AND BUSTED Polydor PO 94	49	2 wks

Tracks on double single: Invasion/Kingdom of Madness/All of My Life/Great Adventure.

Siobhan MAHER – See OCEANIC

MAHLATHINI and the MAHOTELLA QUEENS – See ART OF NOISE

MAI TAI Holland, female vocal group — **30 wks**

25 May 85 ●	HISTORY Virgin VS 773	8	13 wks
3 Aug 85 ●	BODY AND SOUL Virgin VS 801	9	13 wks
15 Feb 86	FEMALE INTUITION Virgin VS 844	54	4 wks

MAIN INGREDIENT US, male vocal group — **7 wks**

29 Jun 74	JUST DON'T WANT TO BE LONELY RCA APBO 0205	27	7 wks

MAISONETTES UK, male/female vocal group — **12 wks**

11 Dec 82 ●	HEARTACHE AVENUE Ready Steady Go! RSG 1	7	12 wks

(continued from the MADONNA column)

28 Jun 86 ★	PAPA DON'T PREACH Sire W 8636	1	14 wks
4 Oct 86 ★	TRUE BLUE Sire W 8550	1	15 wks
13 Dec 86 ●	OPEN YOUR HEART Sire W 8480	4	9 wks
4 Apr 87 ★	LA ISLA BONITA Sire W 8378	1	11 wks
18 Jul 87 ★	WHO'S THAT GIRL Sire W 8341	1	10 wks
19 Sep 87 ●	CAUSING A COMMOTION Sire W 8224	4	9 wks
12 Dec 87 ●	THE LOOK OF LOVE Sire W 8115	9	7 wks
18 Mar 89 ★	LIKE A PRAYER Sire W 7539	1	12 wks
3 Jun 89 ●	EXPRESS YOURSELF Sire W 2948	5	10 wks
16 Sep 89 ●	CHERISH Sire W 2883	3	8 wks
16 Dec 89 ●	DEAR JESSIE Sire W 2668	5	9 wks
7 Apr 90 ★	VOGUE Sire W 9851	1	14 wks
21 Jul 90 ●	HANKY PANKY Sire W 9789	2	9 wks
8 Dec 90 ●	JUSTIFY MY LOVE Sire W 9000	2	10 wks
2 Mar 91 ●	CRAZY FOR YOU (re-mix) Sire W 0008	2	8 wks
13 Apr 91 ●	RESCUE ME Sire W 0024	3	8 wks
8 Jun 91 ●	HOLIDAY (re-issue) Sire W 0037	5	7 wks
25 Jul 92 ●	THIS USED TO BE MY PLAYGROUND Sire W 0122	3	9 wks
17 Oct 92 ●	EROTICA Maverick W 0138	3	8 wks
12 Dec 92 ●	DEEPER AND DEEPER Maverick W 0146	6†	3 wks

Raven MAIZE US, male vocalist — 1 wk

Date	Title	Label	Pos	Wks
5 Aug 89	FOREVER TOGETHER	Republic LIC 014	67	1 wk

MAKADOPOULOS and his GREEK SERENADERS Greece, male vocal/instrumental group — 14 wks

Date	Title	Label	Pos	Wks
20 Oct 60	NEVER ON SUNDAY	Palette PG 9005	36	14 wks

Jack E. MAKOSSA Kenya, male producer — 5 wks

Date	Title	Label	Pos	Wks
12 Sep 87	THE OPERA HOUSE	Champion CHAMP 50	48	5 wks

MALA – See BOWA featuring MALA

Carl MALCOLM Jamaica, male vocalist — 8 wks

Date	Title	Label	Pos	Wks
13 Sep 75	● FATTIE BUM BUM	UK 108	8	8 wks

Timmy MALLETT – See BOMBALURINA

MAMA CASS US, female vocalist — 27 wks

Date	Title	Label	Pos	Wks
14 Aug 68	DREAM A LITTLE DREAM OF ME	RCA 1726	11	12 wks
16 Aug 69	● IT'S GETTING BETTER	Stateside SS 8021	8	15 wks

See also Mamas and the Papas.

MAMAS and the PAPAS US, female/male vocal group — 64 wks

Date	Title	Label	Pos	Wks
28 Apr 66	CALIFORNIA DREAMIN'	RCA 1503	23	9 wks
12 May 66	● MONDAY MONDAY	RCA 1516	3	13 wks
28 Jul 66	I SAW HER AGAIN	RCA 1533	11	11 wks
9 Feb 67	WORDS OF LOVE	RCA 1564	47	3 wks
6 Apr 67	● DEDICATED TO THE ONE I LOVE	RCA 1576	2	17 wks
26 Jul 67	● CREEQUE ALLEY	RCA 1613	9	11 wks

See also Mama Cass.

MAMBAS – See Marc ALMOND

A MAN CALLED ADAM
UK, male/female vocal/instrumental group — 4 wks

Date	Title	Label	Pos	Wks
29 Sep 90	BAREFOOT IN THE HEAD	Big Life BLR 28	70	2 wks
20 Oct 90	BAREFOOT IN THE HEAD (re-entry) Big Life BLR 28		60	2 wks

MAN TO MAN US, male vocal/instrumental duo — 19 wks

Date	Title	Label	Pos	Wks
13 Sep 86	MALE STRIPPER	Bolts BOLTS 4 *	64	3 wks
3 Jan 87	MALE STRIPPER (re-entry) Bolts BOLTS 4 *		63	1 wk
7 Feb 87	● MALE STRIPPER (2nd re-entry) Bolts BOLTS 4 *		4	12 wks
4 Jul 87	I NEED A MAN /ENERGY IS EUROBEAT Bolts BOLTS 5		43	3 wks

* Man 2 Man meet Man Parrish

Melissa MANCHESTER – See Al JARREAU

MANCHESTER UNITED FOOTBALL CLUB UK, male football team vocalists — 11 wks

Date	Title	Label	Pos	Wks
8 May 76	MANCHESTER UNITED	Decca F 13633	50	1 wk
21 May 83	GLORY GLORY MAN. UNITED	EMI 5390	13	5 wks
18 May 85	● WE ALL FOLLOW MAN. UNITED	Columbia DB 9107	10	5 wks

Henry MANCINI US, orchestra/chorus — 23 wks

Date	Title	Label	Pos	Wks
7 Dec 61	MOON RIVER	RCA 1256	46	2 wks
28 Dec 61	MOON RIVER (re-entry)	RCA 1256	44	1 wk
24 Sep 64	● HOW SOON	RCA 1414	10	12 wks
25 Mar 72	THEME FROM 'CADE'S COUNTY'	RCA 2182	42	1 wk
11 Feb 84	MAIN THEME FROM 'THE THORNBIRDS' Warner Bros. 9677		23	7 wks

Steve MANDELL – See 'DELIVERANCE' SOUNDTRACK

MANFRED MANN — 217 wks
South Africa/UK, male vocal/instrumental group

Date	Title	Label	Pos	Wks
23 Jan 64	● 5-4-3-2-1	HMV POP 1252	5	13 wks
16 Apr 64	HUBBLE BUBBLE TOIL AND TROUBLE HMV POP 1282		11	8 wks
16 Jul 64	★ DO WAH DIDDY DIDDY	HMV POP 1320	1	14 wks
15 Oct 64	● SHA LA LA	HMV POP 1346	3	12 wks
14 Jan 65	● COME TOMORROW	HMV POP 1381	4	9 wks
15 Apr 65	OH NO NOT MY BABY	HMV POP 1413	11	10 wks
16 Sep 65	● IF YOU GOTTA GO GO NOW	HMV POP 1466	2	12 wks
21 Apr 66	★ PRETTY FLAMINGO	HMV POP 1523	1	12 wks
7 Jul 66	YOU GAVE ME SOMEBODY TO LOVE HMV POP 1541		36	4 wks
4 Aug 66	● JUST LIKE A WOMAN	Fontana TF 730	10	10 wks
27 Oct 66	● SEMI-DETACHED SUBURBAN MR. JAMES Fontana TF 757		2	12 wks
30 Mar 67	● HA HA SAID THE CLOWN	Fontana TF 812	4	11 wks
25 May 67	SWEET PEA	Fontana TF 828	36	4 wks
24 Jan 68	★ MIGHTY QUINN	Fontana TF 897	1	11 wks
12 Jun 68	● MY NAME IS JACK	Fontana TF 943	8	11 wks
18 Dec 68	● FOX ON THE RUN	Fontana TF 985	5	12 wks
30 Apr 69	● RAGAMUFFIN MAN	Fontana TF 1013	8	11 wks
8 Sep 73	● JOYBRINGER	Vertigo 6059 083 *	9	10 wks
28 Aug 76	● BLINDED BY THE LIGHT	Bronze BRO 29 *	6	10 wks
20 May 78	● DAVY'S ON THE ROAD AGAIN	Bronze BRO 52 *	6	12 wks
17 Mar 79	YOU ANGEL YOU	Bronze BRO 68 *	54	5 wks
7 Jul 79	DON'T KILL IT CAROL	Bronze BRO 77 *	45	4 wks

* Manfred Mann's Earth Band

MANHATTAN TRANSFER — 72 wks
US, male/female vocal group

Date	Title	Label	Pos	Wks
7 Feb 76	TUXEDO JUNCTION	Atlantic K 10670	24	6 wks
5 Feb 77	★ CHANSON D'AMOUR	Atlantic K 10886	1	13 wks
28 May 77	DON'T LET GO	Atlantic K 10930	32	6 wks
18 Feb 78	WALK IN LOVE	Atlantic K 11075	48	1 wk
4 Mar 78	WALK IN LOVE (re-entry)	Atlantic K 11075	12	11 wks
20 May 78	ON A LITTLE STREET IN SINGAPORE Atlantic K 11136		20	9 wks
16 Sep 78	WHERE DID OUR LOVE GO/JE VOULAIS TE DIRE (QUE JE T'ATTENDS) Atlantic K 11182		40	4 wks
23 Dec 78	WHO WHAT WHEN WHERE WHY	Atlantic K 11233	49	6 wks
17 May 80	TWILIGHT ZONE-TWILIGHT TONE (MEDLEY) Atlantic K 11476		25	8 wks
21 Jan 84	SPICE OF LIFE	Atlantic A 9728	19	8 wks

MANHATTANS US, male vocal group — 31 wks

Date	Title	Label	Pos	Wks
19 Jun 76	● KISS AND SAY GOODBYE	CBS 4317	4	11 wks
2 Oct 76	● HURT	CBS 4562	4	11 wks
23 Apr 77	IT'S YOU	CBS 5093	43	3 wks
26 Jul 80	SHINING STAR	CBS 8624	45	4 wks
6 Aug 83	CRAZY	CBS A 3578	63	2 wks

M.A.N.I.C. UK, male vocal/production duo — 1 wk

Date	Title	Label	Pos	Wks
18 Apr 92	I'M COMIN' HARDCORE	Union City UCRT 2	60	1 wk

MANIC MC's featuring Sara CARLSON
UK, male production duo and female vocalist — **5 wks**

12 Aug 89	**MENTAL** *RCA PB 43037*	30	5 wks

MANIC STREET PREACHERS
UK, male vocal/instrumental group — **31 wks**

25 May 91	**YOU LOVE US** *Heavenly HVN 10*	62	2 wks
10 Aug 91	**STAY BEAUTIFUL** *Columbia 6573377*	40	3 wks
9 Nov 91	**LOVE'S SWEET EXILE** *Columbia 6575827*	26	3 wks
1 Feb 92	**YOU LOVE US (re-issue)** *Columbia 6577247*	16	4 wks
28 Mar 92	**SLASH 'N' BURN** *Columbia 6578737*	20	4 wks
13 Jun 92	**MOTORCYCLE EMPTINESS** *Columbia 6580837*	17	6 wks
19 Sep 92 ●	**THEME FROM M.A.S.H. (SUICIDE IS PAINLESS)** *Columbia 6583827*	7	6 wks
21 Nov 92	**LITTLE BABY NOTHING** *Columbia 6587967*	29	3 wks

The listed flipside of Theme From M.A.S.H. (Suicide Is Painless) *was with (Everything I Do) I Do It For You by Fatima Mansions.*

Barry MANILOW *US, male vocalist* — **128 wks**

22 Feb 75	**MANDY** *Arista 1*	11	9 wks
6 May 78	**CAN'T SMILE WITHOUT YOU** *Arista 176*	43	7 wks
29 Jul 78	**SOMEWHERE IN THE NIGHT/COPACABANA (AT THE COPA)** *Arista 196*	42	10 wks
23 Dec 78	**COULD IT BE MAGIC** *Arista ARIST 229*	25	10 wks
8 Nov 80	**LONELY TOGETHER** *Arista ARIST 373*	21	13 wks
7 Feb 81	**I MADE IT THROUGH THE RAIN** *Arista ARIST 384*	37	6 wks
11 Apr 81	**BERMUDA TRIANGLE** *Arista ARIST 406*	15	9 wks
26 Sep 81	**LET'S HANG ON** *Arista ARIST 429*	12	11 wks
12 Dec 81	**THE OLD SONGS** *Arista ARIST 443*	48	8 wks
20 Feb 82	**IF I SHOULD LOVE AGAIN** *Arista ARIST 453*	66	2 wks
17 Apr 82	**STAY** *Arista ARIST 464*	23	8 wks
16 Oct 82 ●	**I WANNA DO IT WITH YOU** *Arista ARIST 495*	8	8 wks
4 Dec 82	**I'M GONNA SIT RIGHT DOWN AND WRITE MYSELF A LETTER** *Arista ARIST 503*	36	7 wks
25 Jun 83	**SOME KIND OF FRIEND** *Arista ARIST 516*	48	2 wks
27 Aug 83	**YOU'RE LOOKING HOT TONIGHT** *Arista ARIST 542*	47	6 wks
10 Dec 83	**READ 'EM AND WEEP** *Arista ARIST 551*	17	7 wks
8 Apr 89	**PLEASE DON'T BE SCARED** *Arista 112186*	35	5 wks

ARIST 464 was available as both a live and studio recording.

MANIX *UK, male/female vocal/instrumental group* — **6 wks**

23 Nov 91	**MANIC MINDS** *Reinforced RIVET 1209*	63	2 wks
7 Mar 92	**OBLIVION (HEAD IN THE CLOUDS)(EP)** *Reinforced RIVET 1212*	43	3 wks
8 Aug 92	**RAINBOW PEOPLE** *Reinforced RIVET 1221*	57	1 wk

Tracks on Oblivion (Head In The Clouds) (EP): *Oblivion (Head In The Clouds)/Never Been To Belgium (Gotta Rush)/I Can't Stand It/You Held My Hand.*

MANKIND *UK, male instrumental group* — **12 wks**

25 Nov 78	**DR. WHO** *Pinnacle PIN 71*	25	12 wks

Aimee MANN – *See RUSH*

Johnny MANN SINGERS *US, male/female vocal group* — **13 wks**

12 Jul 67 ●	**UP, UP AND AWAY** *Liberty LIB 55972*	6	13 wks

MANTOVANI *UK, orchestra* — **52 wks**

19 Dec 52 ●	**WHITE CHRISTMAS** *Decca F 10017*	6	3 wks
29 May 53 ★	**MOULIN ROUGE** *Decca F 10094*	1	21 wks
23 Oct 53 ●	**SWEDISH RHAPSODY** *Decca F 10168*	2	17 wks
13 Nov 53	**MOULIN ROUGE (re-entry)** *Decca F 10094*	10	1 wk
4 Dec 53	**MOULIN ROUGE (2nd re-entry)** *Decca F 10094*	12	1 wk
26 Feb 54	**SWEDISH RHAPSODY (re-entry)** *Decca F 10168*	12	1 wk
11 Feb 55	**LONELY BALLERINA** *Decca F 10395*	16	3 wks
18 Mar 55	**LONELY BALLERINA (re-entry)** *Decca F 10395*	18	1 wk
31 May 57	**AROUND THE WORLD** *Decca F 10888*	20	4 wks

See also David Whitfield.

MANTRONIX *US/Jamaica, male vocal/instrumental duo* — **48 wks**

22 Feb 86	**LADIES** *10 TEN 116*	55	4 wks
17 May 86	**BASSLINE** *10 TEN 118*	34	6 wks
7 Feb 87	**WHO IS IT** *10 TEN 137*	40	6 wks
4 Jul 87	**SCREAM (PRIMAL SCREAM)** *10 TEN 169*	46	4 wks
30 Jan 88	**SING A SONG (BREAK IT DOWN)** *10 TEN 206*	61	2 wks
12 Mar 88	**SIMPLE SIMON (YOU GOTTA REGARD)** *10 TEN 217*	72	2 wks
6 Jan 90 ●	**GOT TO HAVE YOUR LOVE** *Capitol CL 559 **	4	11 wks
12 May 90 ●	**TAKE YOUR TIME** *Capitol CL 573 **	10	7 wks
2 Mar 91	**DON'T GO MESSIN' WITH MY HEART** *Capitol CL 608*	22	5 wks
22 Jun 91	**STEP TO ME (DO ME)** *Capitol CL 613*	59	1 wk

* Mantronix featuring Wondress

MANUEL and his MUSIC OF THE MOUNTAINS *UK, orchestra, leader Geoff Love* — **31 wks**

28 Aug 59	**THEME FROM HONEYMOON** *Columbia DB 4323*	29	2 wks
25 Sep 59	**THEME FROM HONEYMOON (re-entry)** *Columbia DB 4323*	22	5 wks
6 Nov 59	**THEME FROM HONEYMOON (2nd re-entry)** *Columbia DB 4323*	27	2 wks
13 Oct 60	**NEVER ON SUNDAY** *Columbia DB 4515*	29	10 wks
13 Oct 66	**SOMEWHERE MY LOVE** *Columbia DB 7969*	42	2 wks
31 Jan 76 ●	**RODRIGO'S GUITAR CONCERTO DE ARANJUEZ (THEME FROM 2ND MOVEMENT)** *EMI 2383*	3	10 wks

MARATHON *Germany/UK, male vocal/instrumental group* — **3 wks**

25 Jan 92	**MOVIN'** *Ten TEN 395*	36	3 wks

MARAUDERS *UK, male vocal/instrumental group* — **4 wks**

8 Aug 63	**THAT'S WHAT I WANT** *Decca F 11695*	48	1 wk
22 Aug 63	**THAT'S WHAT I WANT (re-entry)** *Decca F 11695*	43	3 wks

MARBLES *UK, male vocal duo* — **18 wks**

25 Sep 68 ●	**ONLY ONE WOMAN** *Polydor 56 272*	5	12 wks
26 Mar 69	**THE WALLS FELL DOWN** *Polydor 56 310*	28	6 wks

MARC and the MAMBAS – *See Marc ALMOND*

MARCELS *US, male vocal group* — **17 wks**

13 Apr 61 ★	**BLUE MOON** *Pye International 7N 25073*	1	13 wks
8 Jun 61	**SUMMERTIME** *Pye International 7N 25083*	46	4 wks

Little Peggy MARCH *US, female vocalist* — **7 wks**

12 Sep 63	**HELLO HEARTACHE GOODBYE LOVE** *RCA 1362*	29	7 wks

MARDI GRAS *UK, male vocal/instrumental group* — **9 wks**

5 Aug 72	**TOO BUSY THINKING 'BOUT MY BABY** *Bell 1226*	19	9 wks

The multiple Grammy winner HENRY MANCINI seems bemused that his biggest UK hit was not one of his award winners.

RICHARD MARX meets Kenny G. in 1991 at a children's charity softball game in El Monte, California.

Though the first two British hits of THE MANHATTANS were equal in terms of peak position and weeks on chart, the first was an American number one and the second a 97.

This distinctive logo was used to promote original recordings of the MASH theme 'Suicide Is Painless'.

Kelly MARIE UK, female vocalist — 36 wks

2 Aug 80	★ FEELS LIKE I'M IN LOVE *Calibre PLUS 1*	1	16 wks
18 Oct 80	LOVING JUST FOR FUN *Calibre PLUS 4*	21	7 wks
7 Feb 81	HOT LOVE *Calibre PLUS 5*	22	10 wks
30 May 81	LOVE TRIAL *Calibre PLUS 7*	51	3 wks

Teena MARIE US, female vocalist — 28 wks

7 Jul 79	I'M A SUCKER FOR YOUR LOVE *Motown TMG 1146* *	43	8 wks
31 May 80	● BEHIND THE GROOVE *Motown TMG 1185*	6	10 wks
11 Oct 80	I NEED YOUR LOVIN' *Motown TMG 1203*	28	6 wks
26 Mar 88	OO LA LA LA *Epic 651423 7*	74	2 wks
10 Nov 90	SINCE DAY ONE *Epic 656429 7*	69	2 wks

* Teena Marie, co-lead vocals Rick James

MARILLION UK, male vocal/instrumental group — 96 wks

20 Nov 82	MARKET SQUARE HEROES *EMI 5351*	60	2 wks
12 Feb 83	HE KNOWS YOU KNOW *EMI 5362*	35	4 wks
16 Apr 83	MARKET SQUARE HEROES (re-entry) *EMI 5351*	53	6 wks
18 Jun 83	GARDEN PARTY *EMI 5393*	16	5 wks
11 Feb 84	PUNCH AND JUDY *EMI MARIL 1*	29	4 wks
12 May 84	ASSASSING *EMI MARIL 2*	22	5 wks
18 May 85	● KAYLEIGH *EMI MARIL 3*	2	14 wks
7 Sep 85	● LAVENDER *EMI MARIL 4*	5	9 wks
30 Nov 85	HEART OF LOTHIAN *EMI MARIL 5*	29	6 wks
23 May 87	● INCOMMUNICADO *EMI MARIL 6*	6	5 wks
25 Jul 87	SUGAR MICE *EMI MARIL 7*	22	5 wks
7 Nov 87	WARM WET CIRCLES *EMI MARIL 8*	22	4 wks
26 Nov 88	FREAKS (LIVE) *EMI MARIL 9*	24	3 wks
9 Sep 89	HOOKS IN YOU *Capitol MARIL 10*	30	3 wks
9 Dec 89	UNINVITED GUEST *EMI MARIL 11*	53	2 wks
14 Apr 90	EASTER *EMI MARIL 12*	34	2 wks
8 Jun 91	COVER MY EYES (PAIN AND HEAVEN) *EMI MARIL 13*	34	4 wks
3 Aug 91	NO ONE CAN *EMI MARIL 14*	33	4 wks
5 Oct 91	DRY LAND *EMI MARIL 15*	34	2 wks
23 May 92	SYMPATHY *EMI MARIL 16*	17	3 wks
1 Aug 92	NO ONE CAN (re-issue) *EMI MARIL 17*	26	4 wks

MARILYN UK, male vocalist — 26 wks

5 Nov 83	● CALLING YOUR NAME *Mercury MAZ 1*	4	12 wks
11 Feb 84	CRY AND BE FREE *Mercury MAZ 2*	31	6 wks
21 Apr 84	YOU DON'T LOVE ME *Mercury MAZ 3*	40	7 wks
13 Apr 85	BABY U LEFT ME (IN THE COLD) *Mercury MAZ 4*	70	1 wk

Marino MARINI and his QUARTET — 23 wks
Italy, male vocalist and instrumental group

3 Oct 58	VOLARE *Durium DC 16632*	13	7 wks
10 Oct 58	● COME PRIMA *Durium DC 16632*	2	14 wks
20 Mar 59	CIAO CIAO BAMBINA *Durium DC 16636*	25	1 wk
3 Apr 59	CIAO CIAO BAMBINA (re-entry) *Durium DC 16636*	24	1 wk

Pigmeat MARKHAM US, male vocalist — 8 wks

17 Jul 68	HERE COMES THE JUDGE *Chess CRS 8077*	19	8 wks

Biz MARKIE US, male rapper — * 2 wks

26 May 90	JUST A FRIEND *Cold Chillin' W 9823*	55	2 wks

Yannis MARKOPOULOS Greece, orchestra — 8 wks

17 Dec 77	WHO PAYS THE FERRYMAN *BBC RESL 51*	11	8 wks

Guy MARKS Australia, male vocalist — 8 wks

13 May 78	LOVING YOU HAS MADE ME BANANAS *ABC 4211*	25	8 wks

MARKY MARK and the FUNKY BUNCH — 13 wks
US, male/female vocal/instrumental group

31 Aug 91	GOOD VIBRATIONS *Interscope A 8764* *	14	7 wks
2 Nov 91	WILDSIDE *Interscope A 8674*	42	3 wks
12 Dec 92	YOU GOTTA BELIEVE *Interscope A 8480*	54†	3 wks

* Marky Mark and the Funky Bunch featuring Loleatta Holloway

Bob MARLEY and the WAILERS — 136 wks
Jamaica, male vocal/instrumental group

27 Sep 75	NO WOMAN NO CRY *Island WIP 6244*	22	7 wks
25 Jun 77	EXODUS *Island WIP 6390*	14	9 wks
10 Sep 77	WAITING IN VAIN *Island WIP 6402*	27	6 wks
10 Dec 77	● JAMMING/PUNKY REGGAE PARTY *Island WIP 6410*	9	12 wks
25 Feb 78	● IS THIS LOVE *Island WIP 6420*	9	9 wks
10 Jun 78	SATISFY MY SOUL *Island WIP 6440*	21	10 wks
20 Oct 79	SO MUCH TROUBLE IN THE WORLD *Island WIP 6510*	56	4 wks
21 Jun 80	● COULD YOU BE LOVED *Island WIP 6610*	5	12 wks
13 Sep 80	THREE LITTLE BIRDS *Island WIP 6641*	17	9 wks
13 Jun 81	● NO WOMAN NO CRY (re-entry) *Island WIP 6244*	8	11 wks
7 May 83	● BUFFALO SOLDIER *Island/Tuff Gong IS 108*	4	12 wks
21 Apr 84	● ONE LOVE - PEOPLE GET READY *Island IS 169*	5	11 wks
23 Jun 84	WAITING IN VAIN (re-issue) *Island IS 180*	31	7 wks
8 Dec 84	COULD YOU BE LOVED (re-issue) *Island IS 210*	71	2 wks
18 May 91	ONE LOVE - PEOPLE GET READY (re-issue) *Tuff Gong TGX 1*	42	3 wks
19 Sep 92	● IRON LION ZION *Tuff Gong TGX 2*	5	9 wks
28 Nov 92	WHY SHOULD I/EXODUS *Tuff Gong TGX 3*	42	3 wks

Exodus on Tuff Gong TGX 3 only listed with Why Should I from 5 Dec 92 and is a different version from the Island hit.

Ziggy MARLEY and the MELODY MAKERS — 11 wks
Jamaica, male/female vocal/instrumental group

11 Jun 88	TOMORROW PEOPLE *Virgin VS 1049*	22	10 wks
23 Sep 89	LOOK WHO'S DANCING *Virgin America VUS 5*	65	1 wk

MARMALADE UK, male vocal/instrumental group — 130 wks

22 May 68	● LOVIN' THINGS *CBS 3412*	6	13 wks
23 Oct 68	WAIT FOR ME MARIANNE *CBS 3708*	30	5 wks
4 Dec 68	★ OB-LA-DI OB-LA-DA *CBS 3892*	1	20 wks
11 Jun 69	● BABY MAKE IT SOON *CBS 4287*	9	13 wks
20 Dec 69	● REFLECTIONS OF MY LIFE *Decca F 12982*	3	12 wks
18 Jul 70	● RAINBOW *Decca F 13035*	3	14 wks
27 Mar 71	MY LITTLE ONE *Decca F 13135*	15	11 wks
4 Sep 71	● COUSIN NORMAN *Decca F 13214*	6	11 wks
27 Nov 71	BACK ON THE ROAD *Decca F 13251*	35	7 wks
22 Jan 72	BACK ON THE ROAD (re-entry) *Decca F 13251*	50	1 wk
1 Apr 72	● RADANCER *Decca F 13297*	6	12 wks
21 Feb 76	● FALLING APART AT THE SEAMS *Target TGT 105*	9	11 wks

M/A/R/S UK, male instrumental/scratch group   **14 wks**

5 Sep 87 ★	PUMP UP THE VOLUME/ANITINA (THE FIRST TIME I SEE SHE DANCE) *4AD AD 70* **1**	14 wks

The b-side of this record was listed on the chart at the record company's request without evidence of consumer interest.

Gerry MARSDEN – *See CHRISTIANS; Holly JOHNSON; Paul McCARTNEY; STOCK AITKEN WATERMAN; GERRY and the PACEMAKERS*

Stevie MARSH UK, female vocalist   **4 wks**

4 Dec 59	THE ONLY BOY IN THE WORLD *Decca F 11181*.............**29**	2 wks
25 Dec 59	THE ONLY BOY IN THE WORLD (re-entry) *Decca F 11181* **24**	2 wks

Joy MARSHALL UK, female vocalist   **2 wks**

23 Jun 66	THE MORE I SEE YOU *Decca F 12422*.................**34**	2 wks

Keith MARSHALL UK, male vocalist   **10 wks**

4 Apr 81	ONLY CRYING *Arrival PIK 2* **12**	10 wks

MARSHALL HAIN UK, male/female vocal/instrumental duo   **19 wks**

3 Jun 78 ●	DANCING IN THE CITY *Harvest HAR 5157* **3**	15 wks
14 Oct 78	COMING HOME *Harvest HAR 5168* **39**	4 wks

Lena MARTELL UK, female vocalist   **18 wks**

29 Sep 79 ★	ONE DAY AT A TIME *Pye 7N 46021* **1**	18 wks

MARTHA and the MUFFINS   **10 wks**
Canada, female/male vocal/instrumental group

1 Mar 80 ●	ECHO BEACH *Dindisc DIN 9* **10**	10 wks

See also M + M, who are Martha and a Muffin.

MARTHA and the VANDELLAS – *See Martha REEVES and the VANDELLAS*

MARTIKA US, female vocalist   **57 wks**

29 Jul 89 ●	TOY SOLDIERS *CBS 655049 7* **5**	11 wks
14 Oct 89 ●	I FEEL THE EARTH MOVE *CBS 655294 7* **7**	14 wks
13 Jan 90	MORE THAN YOU KNOW *CBS 655526 7* **15**	7 wks
17 Mar 90	WATER *CBS 655731 7* **59**	3 wks
17 Aug 91 ●	LOVE...THY WILL BE DONE *Columbia 6573137*.................**9**	9 wks
30 Nov 91	MARTIKA'S KITCHEN *Columbia 6575687* **17**	10 wks
22 Feb 92	COLOURED KISSES *Columbia 6577097*.................**41**	3 wks

Dean MARTIN US, male vocalist   **160 wks**

18 Sep 53 ●	KISS *Capitol CL 13893* **9**	1 wk
2 Oct 53 ●	KISS (re-entry) *Capitol CL 13893* **5**	7 wks
22 Jan 54 ●	THAT'S AMORE *Capitol CL 14008* **2**	11 wks
1 Oct 54 ●	SWAY *Capitol CL 14138* **6**	7 wks
22 Oct 54	HOW DO YOU SPEAK TO AN ANGEL *Capitol CL 14150* **15**	2 wks
19 Nov 54	HOW DO YOU SPEAK TO AN ANGEL (re-entry) *Capitol CL 14150* **17**	4 wks
28 Jan 55 ●	NAUGHTY LADY OF SHADY LANE *Capitol CL 14226* **5**	10 wks

4 Feb 55	MAMBO ITALIANO *Capitol CL 14227* **14**	2 wks
25 Feb 55 ●	LET ME GO LOVER *Capitol CL 14226* **3**	9 wks
1 Apr 55 ●	UNDER THE BRIDGES OF PARIS *Capitol CL 14255* **6**	8 wks
10 Feb 56 ★	MEMORIES ARE MADE OF THIS *Capitol CL 14523*.................**1**	16 wks
2 Mar 56	YOUNG AND FOOLISH *Capitol CL 14519* **20**	1 wk
27 Apr 56	INNAMORATA *Capitol CL 14507* **21**	3 wks
22 Mar 57	THE MAN WHO PLAYS THE MANDOLINO *Capitol CL 14690* **21**	2 wks
13 Jun 58 ●	RETURN TO ME *Capitol CL 14844* **2**	22 wks
29 Aug 58 ●	VOLARE *Capitol CL 14910* **2**	14 wks
27 Aug 64	EVERYBODY LOVES SOMEBODY *Reprise R 20281* **11**	13 wks
12 Nov 64	THE DOOR IS STILL OPEN TO MY HEART *Reprise R 20307* **42**	4 wks
5 Feb 69 ●	GENTLE ON MY MIND *Reprise RS 23343* **2**	23 wks
30 Aug 69	GENTLE ON MY MIND (re-entry) *Reprise RS 23343*.................**49**	1 wk

Juan MARTIN Spain, male instrumentalist - guitar   **7 wks**

28 Jan 84 ●	LOVE THEME FROM 'THE THORN BIRDS' *WEA X 9518* **10**	7 wks

Linda MARTIN Ireland, female vocalist   **2 wks**

30 May 92	WHY ME *Columbia 6581317* **59**	2 wks

Marilyn MARTIN – *See Phil COLLINS*

Ray MARTIN UK, orchestra   **11 wks**

14 Nov 52 ●	BLUE TANGO *Columbia DB 3051* **8**	1 wk
28 Nov 52 ●	BLUE TANGO (re-entry) *Columbia DB 3051* **10**	3 wks
4 Dec 53 ●	SWEDISH RHAPSODY *Columbia DB 3346* **10**	1 wk
18 Dec 53 ●	SWEDISH RHAPSODY (re-entry) *Columbia DB 3346* **4**	3 wks
15 Jun 56	CAROUSEL WALTZ *Columbia DB 3771* **28**	1 wk
3 Aug 56	CAROUSEL WALTZ (re-entry) *Columbia DB 3771*.................**24**	2 wks

Tony MARTIN US, male vocalist   **28 wks**

22 Apr 55 ●	STRANGER IN PARADISE *HMV B 10849* **6**	13 wks
13 Jul 56 ●	WALK HAND IN HAND *HMV POP 222* **2**	15 wks

Vince MARTIN – *See TARRIERS*

Wink MARTINDALE US, male vocalist   **41 wks**

4 Dec 59	DECK OF CARDS *London HLD 8962* **18**	5 wks
15 Jan 60	DECK OF CARDS (re-entry) *London HLD 8962* **28**	2 wks
31 Mar 60	DECK OF CARDS (2nd re-entry) *London HLD 8962* **45**	1 wk
18 Apr 63 ●	DECK OF CARDS (3rd re-entry) *London HLD 8962* **5**	21 wks
20 Oct 73	DECK OF CARDS (re-issue) *Dot DOT 109* **22**	12 wks

Al MARTINO US, male vocalist   **87 wks**

14 Nov 52 ★	HERE IN MY HEART *Capitol CL 13779* **1**	18 wks
21 Nov 52 ●	TAKE MY HEART *Capitol CL 13769* **9**	1 wk
30 Jan 53 ●	NOW *Capitol CL 13835*.................**3**	12 wks
10 Jul 53 ●	RACHEL *Capitol CL 13879*.................**10**	4 wks
11 Sep 53	RACHEL (re-entry) *Capitol CL 13879* **12**	1 wk
4 Jun 54	WANTED *Capitol CL 14128* **12**	1 wk
18 Jun 54 ●	WANTED (re-entry) *Capitol CL 14128* **4**	14 wks
1 Oct 54	THE STORY OF TINA *Capitol CL 14163* **10**	8 wks
1 Oct 54	WANTED (2nd re-entry) *Capitol CL 14128* **17**	1 wk
23 Sep 55	THE MAN FROM LARAMIE *Capitol CL 14343* **19**	2 wks
28 Oct 55	THE MAN FROM LARAMIE (re-entry) *Capitol CL 14343* **20**	1 wk
31 Mar 60	SUMMERTIME *Top Rank JAR 312* **49**	1 wk
29 Aug 63	I LOVE YOU BECAUSE *Capitol CL 15300* **48**	1 wk
22 Aug 70	SPANISH EYES *Capitol CL 15430* **49**	1 wk
14 Jul 73 ●	SPANISH EYES (re-entry) *Capitol CL 15430* **5**	21 wks

MARVELETTES US, female vocal group — 10 wks

15 Jun 67	WHEN YOU'RE YOUNG AND IN LOVE		
	Tamla Motown TMG 609	13	10 wks

Hank MARVIN UK, male vocalist/instrumentalist - guitar — 36 wks

13 Sep 69 ●	THROW DOWN A LINE Columbia DB 8615 *	7	9 wks
21 Feb 70	JOY OF LIVING Columbia DB 8657 *	25	8 wks
6 Mar 82	DON'T TALK Polydor POSP 420	49	4 wks
22 Mar 86 ★	LIVING DOLL WEA YZ 65 **	1	11 wks
7 Jan 89	LONDON KID Polydor PO 32 ***	52	3 wks
17 Oct 92	WE ARE THE CHAMPIONS	66	1 wk
	PolyGram TV PO 229 ****		

* Cliff and Hank ** Cliff Richard and the Young Ones featuring Hank B. Marvin
*** Jean-Michel Jarre featuring Hank Marvin **** Hank Marvin featuring Brian May

Lee MARVIN US, male vocalist — 23 wks

7 Feb 70 ★	WAND'RIN' STAR Paramount PARA 3004	1	18 wks
20 Jun 70	WAND'RIN' STAR (re-entry) Paramount PARA 3004	42	3 wks
15 Aug 70	WAND'RIN' STAR (2nd re-entry)	47	2 wks
	Paramount PARA 3004		

I Talk To The Trees by Clint Eastwood, the flip side of Wand'rin' Star was listed with Wand'rin' Star for 7 Feb 70 and 14 Feb 70 only.

MARVIN THE PARANOID ANDROID — 4 wks
UK, robot

16 May 81	MARVIN Polydor POSP 261	53	4 wks

Richard MARX US, male vocalist — 61 wks

27 Feb 88	SHOULD'VE KNOWN BETTER Manhattan MT 32	50	5 wks
14 May 88	ENDLESS SUMMER NIGHTS Manhattan MT 39	50	3 wks
17 Jun 89	SATISFIED EMI-USA MT 64	52	4 wks
2 Sep 89 ●	RIGHT HERE WAITING EMI-USA MT 72	2	10 wks
11 Nov 89	ANGELIA EMI-USA MT 74	45	4 wks
24 Mar 90	TOO LATE TO SAY GOODBYE EMI-USA MT 80	38	3 wks
7 Jul 90	CHILDREN OF THE NIGHT EMI-USA MT 84	54	2 wks
1 Sep 90	ENDLESS SUMMER NIGHTS (re-issue)/HOLD ON		
	TO THE NIGHTS EMI-USA MT 89	60	2 wks
19 Oct 91	KEEP COMING BACK Capitol CL 634	55	2 wks
9 May 92 ●	HAZARD Capitol CL 654	3	15 wks
29 Aug 92	TAKE THIS HEART Capitol CL 667	13	6 wks
28 Nov 92	CHAINS AROUND MY HEART Capitol CL 676	29†	5 wks

MARY JANE GIRLS US, female vocal group — 14 wks

21 May 83	CANDY MAN Motown TMG 1301	60	4 wks
25 Jun 83	ALL NIGHT LONG Gordy TMG 1309	13	9 wks
8 Oct 83	BOYS Gordy TMG 1315	74	1 wk

Carolyne MAS US, female vocalist — 2 wks

2 Feb 80	QUOTE GOODBYE QUOTE Mercury 6167 873	71	2 wks

MASH US, male vocal/instrumental group — 12 wks

10 May 80 ★	THEME FROM M * A * S * H * (SUICIDE IS		
	PAINLESS) CBS 8536	1	12 wks

Barbara MASON US, female vocalist — 5 wks

21 Jan 84	ANOTHER MAN Streetwave KHAN 3	45	5 wks

Glen MASON UK, male vocalist — 7 wks

28 Sep 56	GLENDORA Parlophone R 4203	28	2 wks
16 Nov 56	GREEN DOOR Parlophone R 4244	24	5 wks

Mary MASON UK, female vocalist — 6 wks

8 Oct 77	ANGEL OF THE MORNING - ANY WAY THAT		
	YOU WANT ME (MEDLEY) Epic EPC 5552	27	6 wks

MASQUERADE UK, male/female vocal group — 10 wks

11 Jan 86	ONE NATION Streetwave KHAN 59	54	6 wks
5 Jul 86	(SOLUTION TO) THE PROBLEM	65	2 wks
	Streetwave KHAN 67		
26 Jul 86	(SOLUTION TO) THE PROBLEM (re-entry)	64	2 wks
	Streetwave KHAN 67		

MASS ORDER US, male vocal/instrumental duo — 5 wks

14 Mar 92	LIFT EVERY VOICE (TAKE ME AWAY)		
	Columbia 6577487	35	3 wks
23 May 92	LET'S GET HAPPY Columbia 6580737	45	2 wks

MASS PRODUCTION US, male vocal/instrumental group — 7 wks

12 Mar 77	WELCOME TO OUR WORLD (OF MERRY MUSIC)		
	Atlantic K 10898	44	3 wks
17 May 80	SHANTE Atlantic K 11475	59	4 wks

MASSIEL Spain, female vocalist — 4 wks

24 Apr 68	LA LA LA Philips BF 1667	35	4 wks

MASSIVE ATTACK — 19 wks
UK, male/female vocal/instrumental group

23 Feb 91	UNFINISHED SYMPATHY Wild Bunch WBRS 2 *	13	9 wks
8 Jun 91	SAFE FROM HARM Wild Bunch WBRS 3	25	6 wks
22 Feb 92	MASSIVE ATTACK EP Wild Bunch WBRS 4	27	4 wks

* Massive

Tracks on Massive Attack EP: Hymn Of The Big Wheel/Home Of The Whale/Be Thankful/Any Love.

MASSIVO featuring TRACY — 11 wks
UK, male/female vocal/instrumental group

26 May 90	LOVING YOU Debut DEBT 3097	25	11 wks

MASTER SINGERS UK, male vocal group — 7 wks

14 Apr 66	HIGHWAY CODE Parlophone R 5428	25	6 wks
17 Nov 66	WEATHER FORECAST Parlophone R 5523	50	1 wk

MASTERMIXERS – See JIVE BUNNY and the MASTERMIXERS

Sammy MASTERS US, male vocalist — 5 wks

9 Jun 60	ROCKIN' RED WING Warner Bros. WB 10	36	5 wks

MATCH UK, male vocal/instrumental group — 3 wks

16 Jun 79	BOOGIE MAN Flamingo FM 2	48	3 wks

MATCHBOX *UK, male vocal/instrumental group* — 66 wks

3 Nov 79		ROCKABILLY REBEL *Magnet MAG 155*	18	12 wks
19 Jan 80		BUZZ BUZZ A DIDDLE IT *Magnet MAG 157*	22	8 wks
10 May 80		MIDNITE DYNAMOS *Magnet MAG 169*	14	8 wks
27 Sep 80	●	WHEN YOU ASK ABOUT LOVE *Magnet MAG 191*	4	12 wks
29 Nov 80		OVER THE RAINBOW - YOU BELONG TO ME (MEDLEY) *Magnet MAG 192*	15	11 wks
4 Apr 81		BABES IN THE WOOD *Magnet MAG 193*	46	6 wks
1 Aug 81		LOVE'S MADE A FOOL OF YOU *Magnet MAG 194*	63	3 wks
29 May 82		ONE MORE SATURDAY NIGHT *Magnet MAG 223*	63	2 wks

MATCHROOM MOB – *See CHAS and DAVE*

Mireille MATHIEU *France, female vocalist* — 7 wks

13 Dec 67	LA DERNIERE VALSE *Columbia DB 8323*	26	7 wks

Johnny MATHIS *US, male vocalist* — 137 wks

23 May 58		TEACHER TEACHER *Fontana H 130*	27	5 wks
26 Sep 58	●	A CERTAIN SMILE *Fontana H 142*	4	16 wks
19 Dec 58		WINTER WONDERLAND *Fontana H 165*	17	3 wks
7 Aug 59	●	SOMEONE *Fontana H 199*	6	15 wks
27 Nov 59		THE BEST OF EVERYTHING *Fontana H 218*	30	1 wk
29 Jan 60		MISTY *Fontana H 219*	12	9 wks
24 Mar 60		YOU ARE BEAUTIFUL *Fontana H 234*	38	8 wks
14 Apr 60		MISTY (re-entry) *Fontana H 219*	46	1 wk
26 May 60		YOU ARE BEAUTIFUL (re-entry) *Fontana H 234*	46	1 wk
28 Jul 60		STARBRIGHT *Fontana H 254*	47	2 wks
6 Oct 60	●	MY LOVE FOR YOU *Fontana H 267*	9	18 wks
4 Apr 63		WHAT WILL MARY SAY *Fontana H 267* AAG 135	49	1 wk
25 Jan 75	●	I'M STONE IN LOVE WITH YOU *CBS 2653*	10	12 wks
13 Nov 76	★	WHEN A CHILD IS BORN (SOLEADO) *CBS 4599*	1	12 wks
25 Mar 78	●	TOO MUCH TOO LITTLE TOO LATE *CBS 6164* *	3	14 wks
29 Jul 78		YOU'RE ALL I NEED TO GET BY *CBS 6483* *	45	6 wks
11 Aug 79		GONE GONE GONE *CBS 7730*	15	10 wks
26 Dec 81		WHEN A CHILD IS BORN *CBS S 1758* **	74	2 wks

* Johnny Mathis and Deniece Williams ** Johnny Mathis and Gladys Knight

MATT BIANCO *UK, male vocalist* — 65 wks

11 Feb 84	GET OUT OF YOUR LAZY BED *WEA BIANCO 1*	15	8 wks
14 Apr 84	SNEAKING OUT THE BACK DOOR/MATT'S MOOD *WEA YZ 3*	44	7 wks
10 Nov 84	HALF A MINUTE *WEA YZ 26*	23	10 wks
2 Mar 85	MORE THAN I CAN BEAR *WEA YZ 34*	50	7 wks
5 Oct 85	YEH YEH *WEA YZ 46*	13	10 wks
1 Mar 86	JUST CAN'T STAND IT *WEA YZ 62*	66	2 wks
14 Jun 86	DANCING IN THE STREET *WEA YZ 72*	64	3 wks
4 Jun 88	DON'T BLAME IT ON THAT GIRL/WAP-BAM-BOOGIE *WEA YZ 188*	11	13 wks
27 Aug 88	GOOD TIMES *WEA YZ 302*	55	3 wks
4 Feb 89	NERVOUS/WAP BAM BOOGIE (re-mix) *WEA YZ 328*	59	2 wks

Matt's Mood *only credited from 5 May 84. Act was a UK/Poland male/female vocal/instrumental group on first five hits.*

Al MATTHEWS *US, male vocalist* — 8 wks

23 Aug 75	FOOL *CBS 3429*	16	8 wks

MATTHEWS SOUTHERN COMFORT
UK, male vocal/instrumental group — 18 wks

26 Sep 70	★	WOODSTOCK *Uni UNS 526*	1	18 wks

MATUMBI *UK, male vocal/instrumental group* — 7 wks

29 Sep 79	POINT OF VIEW *Matumbi RIC 101*	35	7 wks

Susan MAUGHAN *UK, female vocalist* — 25 wks

11 Oct 62	●	BOBBY'S GIRL *Philips 326544 BF*	3	19 wks
14 Feb 63		HAND A HANDKERCHIEF TO HELEN *Philips 326562 BF*	41	3 wks
9 May 63		SHE'S NEW TO YOU *Philips 326586 BF*	45	3 wks

MAUREEN *UK, female vocalist* — 22 wks

26 Nov 88	●	SAY A LITTLE PRAYER *Rhythm King DOOD 3* *	10	10 wks
16 Jun 90		THINKING OF YOU *Urban URB 55*	11	9 wks
12 Jan 91		WHERE HAS ALL THE LOVE GONE *Urban URB 65*	51	3 wks

* Bomb The Bass featuring Maureen
Some copies of Thinking Of You *are credited to the fuller name of Maureen Walsh.*

Paul MAURIAT *France, orchestra* — 14 wks

21 Feb 68	LOVE IS BLUE (L'AMOUR EST BLEU) *Philips BF 1637*	12	14 wks

MAX Q *Australia, male vocal/instrumental duo* — 3 wks

17 Feb 90	SOMETIMES *Mercury MXQ 2*	53	3 wks

MAX WEBSTER *Canada, male vocal/instrumental group* — 3 wks

19 May 79	PARADISE SKIES *Capitol CL 16079*	43	3 wks

Billy MAY *US, orchestra* — 10 wks

27 Apr 56	●	MAIN TITLE THEME FROM 'MAN WITH THE GOLDEN ARM' *Capitol CL 14551*	9	10 wks

Brian MAY *UK, male vocalist/instrumentalist - guitar* — 26 wks

5 Nov 83		STAR FLEET *EMI 5436* *	65	3 wks
7 Dec 91	●	DRIVEN BY YOU *Parlophone R 6304*	6	9 wks
5 Sep 92	●	TOO MUCH LOVE WILL KILL YOU *Parlophone R 6320*	5	9 wks
17 Oct 92		WE ARE THE CHAMPIONS *PolyGram TV PO 229* **	66	1 wk
21 Nov 92		BACK TO THE LIGHT *Parlophone R 6329*	19	4 wks

* Brian May and Friends ** Hank Marvin featuring Brian May

Mary MAY *UK, female vocalist* — 1 wk

27 Feb 64	ANYONE WHO HAD A HEART *Fontana TF 440*	49	1 wk

Simon MAY *UK, male vocalist* — 21 wks

9 Oct 76	●	SUMMER OF MY LIFE *Pye 7N 45627*	7	8 wks
21 May 77		WE'LL GATHER LILACS - ALL MY LOVING (MEDLEY) *Pye 7N 45688*	49	1 wk
4 Jun 77		WE'LL GATHER LILACS - ALL MY LOVING (MEDLEY) (re-entry) *Pye 7N 45688*	50	1 wk
26 Oct 85		HOWARD'S WAY *BBC RESL 174* *	21	11 wks

* Simon May Orchestra
See also Anita Dobson; Marti Webb.

Curtis MAYFIELD *US, male vocalist* — 18 wks

31 Jul 71	MOVE ON UP *Buddah 2011 080*	12	10 wks
2 Dec 78	NO GOODBYES *Atlantic LV 1*	65	3 wks
30 May 87	(CELEBRATE) THE DAY AFTER YOU *RCA MONK 6* *	52	2 wks
29 Sep 90	SUPERFLY 1990 *Capitol CL 586* **	48	3 wks

* Blow Monkeys with Curtis Mayfield ** Curtis Mayfield and Ice-T

MAYTALS   Jamaica, male vocal/instrumental group   4 wks

25 Apr 70	**MONKEY MAN** *Trojan TR 7711* **50**	1 wk
9 May 70	**MONKEY MAN (re-entry)** *Trojan TR 7711* **47**	3 wks

MAZE featuring Frankie BEVERLY   14 wks
US, male vocal/instrumental group

20 Jul 85	**TOO MANY GAMES** *Capitol CL 363*.....................**36**	7 wks
23 Aug 86	**I WANNA BE WITH YOU** *Capitol CL 421*...........**55**	3 wks
27 May 89	**JOY AND PAIN** *Capitol CL 531* * **57**	4 wks

* Maze

Kym MAZELLE *US, female vocalist*   38 wks

12 Nov 88	**USELESS (I DON'T NEED YOU NOW)** *Syncopate SY 18*..**53**	3 wks
14 Jan 89 ●	**WAIT** *RCA PB 42595* * **7**	10 wks
25 Mar 89	**GOT TO GET YOU BACK** *Syncopate SY 25* **29**	4 wks
7 Oct 89	**LOVE STRAIN** *Syncopate SY 30*.........................**52**	3 wks
20 Jan 90	**WAS THAT ALL IT WAS** *Syncopate SY 32*.........**33**	6 wks
26 May 90	**USELESS (I DON'T NEED YOU NOW) (re-mix)** *Syncopate SY 36*.......................................**48**	2 wks
24 Nov 90	**MISSING YOU** *Ten TEN 345* ** **22**	7 wks
25 May 91	**NO ONE CAN LOVE YOU MORE THAN ME** *Parlophone R 6287*.....................................**62**	2 wks
26 Dec 92	**LOVE ME THE RIGHT WAY** *Arista 74321128097* *** .**52**†	1 wk

* Robert Howard and Kym Mazelle ** Soul II Soul featuring Kym Mazelle
*** Rapination and Kym Mazelle

MC DUKE *US, male rapper*   1 wk

11 Mar 89	**I'M RIFFIN (ENGLISH RASTA)** *Music Of Life 7NOTE 25*................................**75**	1 wk

MC ERIC – *See* TECHNOTRONIC

MC Mikee FREEDOM – *See* NOMAD

MC HAMMER – *See* HAMMER

MC LETHAL *UK, male producer*   1 wk

14 Nov 92	**THE RAVE DIGGER** *Network NWKT 60* **66**	1 wk

MC MARIO – *See* AMBASSADORS OF FUNK *featuring* MC MARIO

MC MIKER 'G' and Deejay SVEN   7 wks
Holland, male vocal/instrumental rap duo

6 Sep 86 ●	**HOLIDAY RAP** *Debut DEBT 3008* **6**	7 wks

MC SKAT KAT and the STRAY MOB   2 wks
US, male vocal/instrumental group

9 Nov 91	**SKAT STRUT** *Virgin America VUS 51* **64**	2 wks

MC TUNES *UK, male rapper*   18 wks

2 Jun 90 ●	**THE ONLY RHYME THAT BITES** *ZTT ZANG 3* * **10**	10 wks
15 Sep 90	**TUNES SPLITS THE ATOM** *ZTT ZANG 6* * **18**	7 wks
1 Dec 90	**PRIMARY RHYMING** *ZTT ZANG 10* * **67**	1 wk

* MC Tunes versus 808 State

British Hit Singles Part One: Alphabetically by Artist
Date of chart entry/Title & catalogue no./Peak position reached/Weeks on chart
★ Number one   ● Top Ten   † still on chart at 31 Dec 1992
* = credited to act billed in footnote

MC WILDSKI *UK, male rapper*   10 wks

8 Jul 89	**BLAME IT ON THE BASSLINE** *Go Beat GOD 33* * **29**	6 wks
3 Mar 90	**WARRIOR** *Arista 112956*....................................**49**	4 wks

* Norman Cook featuring MC Wildski
Blame It On The Bassline *was listed with* Won't Talk About It *by Norman Cook featuring Billy Bragg.*

ME AND YOU featuring WE THE PEOPLE BAND *Jamaica/UK, male/female vocal/instrumental group*   9 wks

28 Jul 79	**YOU NEVER KNOW WHAT YOU'VE GOT** *Laser LAS 8* **31**	9 wks

Abigail MEAD and Nigel GOULDING   10 wks
UK/US, female/male producers

26 Sep 87 ●	**FULL METAL JACKET (I WANNA BE YOUR DRILL INSTRUCTOR)** *Warner Bros. W 8187*......................**2**	10 wks

MEAT LOAF *US, male vocalist*   83 wks

20 May 78	**YOU TOOK THE WORDS RIGHT OUT OF MY MOUTH** *Epic EPC 5980*.......................................**33**	8 wks
19 Aug 78	**TWO OUT OF THREE AIN'T BAD** *Epic EPC 6281* **32**	8 wks
10 Feb 79	**BAT OUT OF HELL** *Epic EPC 7018*.......................**15**	7 wks
26 Sep 81	**I'M GONNA LOVE HER FOR BOTH OF US** *Epic EPCA 1580*.......................................**62**	3 wks
28 Nov 81 ●	**DEAD RINGER FOR LOVE** *Epic EPCA 1697* * **5**	17 wks
28 May 83	**IF YOU REALLY WANT TO** *Epic A 3357*.................**59**	2 wks
24 Sep 83	**MIDNIGHT AT THE LOST AND FOUND** *Epic A 3748*..**17**	8 wks
14 Jan 84	**RAZOR'S EDGE** *Epic A 4080* **41**	3 wks
6 Oct 84	**MODERN GIRL** *Arista ARIST 585*.......................**17**	9 wks
22 Dec 84	**NOWHERE FAST** *Arista ARIST 600* **67**	4 wks
23 Mar 85	**PIECE OF THE ACTION** *Arista ARIST 603* **47**	5 wks
30 Aug 86	**ROCK 'N' ROLL MERCENARIES** *Arista ARIST 666* * **31**	6 wks
22 Jun 91	**DEAD RINGER FOR LOVE (re-issue)** *Epic 6569827*.........**53**	2 wks
27 Jun 92	**TWO OUT OF THREE AIN'T BAD (re-issue)** *Epic 6574917*......................................**69**	1 wk

* Meat Loaf featuring John Parr
Dead Ringer For Love *features* Cher *as uncredited co-vocalist.*

MECHANICS – *See* MIKE + *the* MECHANICS

MECO *US, orchestra*   9 wks

1 Oct 77 ●	**STAR WARS THEME-CANTINA BAND** *RCA XB 1028*...**7**	9 wks

Glenn MEDEIROS *US, male vocalist*   26 wks

18 Jun 88 ★	**NOTHING'S GONNA CHANGE MY LOVE FOR YOU** *London LON 184*....................................**1**	13 wks
3 Sep 88	**LONG AND LASTING LOVE (ONCE IN A LIFETIME)** *London LON 202*..........................**42**	4 wks
30 Jun 90	**SHE AIN'T WORTH IT** *London LON 265* * **12**	9 wks

* Glenn Medeiros featuring Bobby Brown

Paul MEDFORD – *See* Letitia DEAN and Paul MEDFORD

Teddy Pendergrass (top right) was the lead singer on all Philadelphia International hits by HAROLD MELVIN AND THE BLUENOTES.

SERGIO MENDES (third from left) is shown in the days he led Brasil '66.

The song FREDDIE MERCURY AND MONTSERRAT CABALLE recorded to support Barcelona's bid to host the Olympics became a bigger hit when the Games were actually held there.

MEDICINE HEAD UK, male vocal/instrumental duo — 37 wks

26 Jun 71	(AND THE) PICTURES IN THE SKY Dandelion DAN 7003	22	8 wks
5 May 73 ●	ONE AND ONE IS ONE Polydor 2001 432	3	13 wks
4 Aug 73	RISING SUN Polydor 2058 389	11	9 wks
9 Feb 74	SLIP AND SLIDE Polydor 2058 436	22	7 wks

MEDICINE SHOW – See DR. HOOK

Bill MEDLEY US, male vocalist — 29 wks

31 Oct 87 ●	(I'VE HAD) THE TIME OF MY LIFE RCA PB 49625 *	6	12 wks
27 Aug 88	HE AIN'T HEAVY, HE'S MY BROTHER Scotti Brothers PO 10	25	6 wks
15 Dec 90 ●	(I'VE HAD) THE TIME THE TIME OF MY LIFE (re-entry) RCA PB 49625 *	8	11 wks

* Bill Medley and Jennifer Warnes

Michael MEDWIN, Bernard BRESSLAW, Alfie BASS and Leslie FYSON UK, male vocal group — 9 wks

30 May 58 ●	THE SIGNATURE TUNE OF 'THE 'ARMY GAME' HMV POP 490	5	9 wks

See also Bernard Bresslaw.

Tony MEEHAN COMBO
UK, male instrumental group, Tony Meehan – drums — 4 wks

16 Jan 64	SONG OF MEXICO Decca F 11801	39	4 wks

See also Jet Harris and Tony Meehan.

MEGA CITY FOUR UK, male vocal/instrumental group — 5 wks

19 Oct 91	WORDS THAT SAY Big Life MEGA 2	66	1 wk
8 Feb 92	STOP (EP) Big Life MEGA 3	36	2 wks
16 May 92	SHIVERING SAND Big Life MEGA 4	35	2 wks

Tracks on Stop (EP): Stop/Desert Song/Back To Zero/Overlap.

MEGABASS – See VARIOUS ARTISTS (MONTAGES)

MEGADETH US, male vocal/instrumental group — 26 wks

19 Dec 87	WAKE UP DEAD Capitol CL 476	65	2 wks
27 Feb 88	ANARCHY IN THE UK Capitol CL 480	45	3 wks
21 May 88	MARY JANE Capitol CL 489	46	2 wks
13 Jan 90	NO MORE MR. NICE GUY SBK SBK 4	13	6 wks
29 Sep 90	HOLY WARS...THE PUNISHMENT DUE Capitol CLP 588	24	3 wks
16 Mar 91	HANGAR 18 Capitol CLS 604	26	4 wks
27 Jun 92	SYMPHONY OF DESTRUCTION Capitol CLS 662	15	3 wks
24 Oct 92	SKIN O' MY TEETH Capitol CLP 669	13	3 wks

Melle MEL – See GRANDMASTER FLASH, Melle MEL and the FURIOUS FIVE

MEL and KIM – See Mel SMITH; Kim WILDE

MEL and KIM UK, female vocal duo — 51 wks

20 Sep 86 ●	SHOWING OUT (GET FRESH AT THE WEEKEND) Supreme SUPE 107	3	19 wks
7 Mar 87 ★	RESPECTABLE Supreme SUPE 111	1	15 wks
11 Jul 87 ●	F.L.M. Supreme SUPE 113	7	10 wks
27 Feb 88 ●	THAT'S THE WAY IT IS Supreme SUPE 117	10	7 wks

George MELACHRINO ORCHESTRA — 9 wks
UK, orchestra

12 Oct 56	AUTUMN CONCERTO HMV B 10958	18	9 wks

MELANIE US, female vocalist — 35 wks

26 Sep 70 ●	RUBY TUESDAY Buddah 2011 038	9	14 wks
9 Jan 71	RUBY TUESDAY (re-entry) Buddah 2011 038	43	1 wk
16 Jan 71	WHAT HAVE THEY DONE TO MY SONG MA Buddah 2011 038	39	1 wk
1 Jan 72 ●	BRAND NEW KEY Buddah 2011 105	4	12 wks
16 Feb 74	WILL YOU LOVE ME TOMORROW Neighbourhood NBH 9	37	5 wks
24 Sep 83	EVERY BREATH OF THE WAY Neighbourhood HOOD NB1	70	2 wks

John Cougar MELLENCAMP US, male vocalist — 15 wks

23 Oct 82	JACK AND DIANE Riva RIVA 37 *	25	8 wks
1 Feb 86	SMALL TOWN Riva JCM 5	53	4 wks
10 May 86	R.O.C.K. IN THE U.S.A. Riva JCM 6	67	3 wks

* John Cougar

MELODIANS Jamaica, male vocal/instrumental group — 1 wk

10 Jan 70	SWEET SENSATION Trojan TR 695	41	1 wk

MELODY MAKERS – See Ziggy MARLEY and the MELODY MAKERS

Harold MELVIN and the BLUENOTES — 52 wks
US, male vocal group

13 Jan 73 ●	IF YOU DON'T KNOW ME BY NOW CBS 8496	9	9 wks
12 Jan 74	THE LOVE I LOST Philadelphia International PIR 1879	21	8 wks
13 Apr 74	SATISFACTION GUARANTEED (OR TAKE YOUR LOVE BACK) Philadelphia International PIR 2187	32	6 wks
31 May 75	GET OUT Route RT 06	35	5 wks
28 Feb 76	WAKE UP EVERYBODY Philadelphia PIR 3866	23	7 wks
22 Jan 77 ●	DON'T LEAVE ME THIS WAY Philadelphia International PIR 4909	5	10 wks
2 Apr 77	REACHING FOR THE WORLD ABC 4161	48	1 wk
28 Apr 84	DON'T GIVE ME UP London LON 47	59	4 wks
4 Aug 84	TODAY'S YOUR LUCKY DAY London LON 52	66	2 wks

MEMBERS UK, male vocal/instrumental group — 14 wks

3 Feb 79	THE SOUND OF THE SUBURBS Virgin VS 242	12	9 wks
7 Apr 79	OFFSHORE BANKING BUSINESS Virgin VS 248	31	5 wks

MEN AT WORK Australia, male vocal/instrumental group — 39 wks

30 Oct 82	WHO CAN IT BE NOW? Epic EPC A 2392	45	5 wks
8 Jan 83 ★	DOWN UNDER Epic EPC A 1980	1	12 wks
9 Apr 83	OVERKILL Epic EPC A 3220	21	10 wks
2 Jul 83	IT'S A MISTAKE Epic EPC A 3475	33	6 wks
10 Sep 83	DR. HECKYLL AND MR. JIVE Epic EPC A 3668	31	6 wks

MEN THEY COULDN'T HANG — 4 wks
UK, male vocal/instrumental group

2 Apr 88	THE COLOURS Magnet SELL 6	61	4 wks

MEN WITHOUT HATS
Canada, male vocal/instrumental group — 11 wks

8 Oct 83 ● THE SAFETY DANCE *Statik TAK 1* ....**6** 11 wks

Sergio MENDES *Brazil, male conductor* — 5 wks

9 Jul 83 NEVER GONNA LET YOU GO *A & M AM 118* ....**45** 5 wks
Uncredited vocals by Joe Pizzulo and Leza Miller.

MENTAL AS ANYTHING — 13 wks
Australia, male vocal/instrumental group

7 Feb 87 ● LIVE IT UP *Epic ANY 1* ....**3** 13 wks

Freddie MERCURY *UK, male vocalist* — 59 wks

22 Sep 84 ● LOVE KILLS *CBS A 4735* ....**10** 8 wks
20 Apr 85 I WAS BORN TO LOVE YOU *CBS A 6019* ....**11** 10 wks
13 Jul 85 MADE IN HEAVEN *CBS A 6413* ....**57** 4 wks
21 Sep 85 LIVING ON MY OWN *CBS A 6555* ....**50** 3 wks
24 May 86 TIME *EMI EMI 5559* ....**32** 5 wks
7 Mar 87 ● THE GREAT PRETENDER *Parlophone R 6151* .....**4** 9 wks
7 Nov 87 ● BARCELONA *Polydor POSP 887 ** ....**8** 9 wks
8 Aug 92 ● BARCELONA (re-issue) *Polydor PO 221 ** ....**2** 8 wks
12 Dec 92 ● IN MY DEFENCE *Parlophone R 6331* ....**8†** 3 wks

* Freddie Mercury and Montserrat Caballe

MERCY MERCY *UK, male vocal/instrumental group* — 2 wks

21 Sep 85 WHAT ARE WE GONNA DO ABOUT IT?
Ensign ENY 522 ....**59** 2 wks

Tony MERRICK *UK, male vocalist* — 1 wk

2 Jun 66 LADY JANE *Columbia DB 7913* ....**49** 1 wk

MERSEYBEATS *UK, male vocal/instrumental group* — 64 wks

12 Sep 63 IT'S LOVE THAT REALLY COUNTS *Fontana TF 412* ....**24** 12 wks
16 Jan 64 ● I THINK OF YOU *Fontana TF 431* ....**5** 17 wks
16 Apr 64 DON'T TURN AROUND *Fontana TF 459* ....**13** 11 wks
9 Jul 64 WISHIN' AND HOPIN' *Fontana TF 482* ....**13** 10 wks
5 Nov 64 LAST NIGHT *Fontana TF 504* ....**40** 3 wks
14 Oct 65 I LOVE YOU, YES I DO *Fontana TF 607* ....**22** 8 wks
20 Jan 66 I STAND ACCUSED *Fontana TF 645* ....**38** 3 wks

MERSEYS *UK, male vocal duo* — 13 wks

28 Apr 66 ● SORROW *Fontana TF 694* ....**4** 13 wks

MERTON PARKAS *UK, male vocal/instrumental group* — 6 wks

4 Aug 79 YOU NEED WHEELS *Beggars Banquet BEG 22* ....**40** 6 wks

Mady MESPLÉ and Danielle MILLET with the PARIS OPERA-COMIQUE ORCHESTRA conducted by Alain LOMBARD *France, female vocal duo and orchestra* — 4 wks

6 Apr 85 FLOWER DUET (FROM LAKME) *EMI 5481* ....**47** 4 wks

MESSIAH *UK, male instrumental/production group* — 10 wks

20 Jun 92 TEMPLE OF DREAMS *Kickin KICK 12S* ....**20** 5 wks
26 Sep 92 I FEEL LOVE *Kickin KICK 22S ** ....**19** 5 wks
* Messiah featuring Precious Wilson

METAL GURUS *UK, male vocal/instrumental group* — 2 wks

8 Dec 90 MERRY XMAS EVERYBODY *Mercury GURU 1* ....**55** 2 wks

METALLICA *US/Denmark, male vocal/instrumental group* — 32 wks

22 Aug 87 THE $5.98 E.P. - GARAGE DAYS REVISITED
Vertigo METAL 112 ....**27** 4 wks
3 Sep 88 HARVESTER OF SORROW *Vertigo METAL 212* ....**20** 4 wks
22 Apr 89 ONE *Vertigo METAL 5* ....**13** 7 wks
10 Aug 91 ● ENTER SANDMAN *Vertigo METAL 7* ....**5** 4 wks
9 Nov 91 THE UNFORGIVEN *Vertigo METAL 8* ....**15** 4 wks
2 May 92 ● NOTHING ELSE MATTERS *Vertigo METAL 10* ....**6** 6 wks
31 Oct 92 WHEREVER I MAY ROAM *Vertigo METAL 9* ....**25** 4 wks
Tracks on The $5.98 EP: Garage Days Revisited/Helpless/Crash Course in Brain Surgery/The Small Hours/Last Caress/Green Hell.

METEORS *UK, male vocal/instrumental group* — 2 wks

26 Feb 83 JOHNNY REMEMBER ME *I.D. EYE 1* ....**66** 2 wks

Pat METHENY GROUP – *See David BOWIE*

MEZZOFORTE *Iceland, male instrumental group* — 10 wks

5 Mar 83 GARDEN PARTY *Steinar STE 705* ....**17** 9 wks
11 Jun 83 ROCKALL *Steinar STE 710* ....**75** 1 wk

MFSB *US, orchestra* — 18 wks

27 Apr 74 TSOP (THE SOUND OF PHILADELPHIA)
Philadelphia International PIR 2289 * ....**22** 9 wks
26 Jul 75 SEXY *Philadelphia International PIR 3381* ....**37** 5 wks
31 Jan 81 MYSTERIES OF THE WORLD
The Sound of Philadelphia PIR 9501 ....**41** 4 wks

* MFSB featuring the Three Degrees

M.G.'s – *See BOOKER T. and the M.G.'s*

MIAMI SOUND MACHINE – *See Gloria ESTEFAN*

George MICHAEL *UK, male vocalist* — 127 wks

4 Aug 84 ★ CARELESS WHISPER *Epic A 4603* ....**1** 17 wks
5 Apr 86 ★ A DIFFERENT CORNER *Epic A 7033* ....**1** 10 wks
31 Jan 87 ★ I KNEW YOU WERE WAITING (FOR ME)
Epic DUET 2 * ....**1** 9 wks
13 Jun 87 ● I WANT YOUR SEX *Epic LUST 1* ....**3** 10 wks
24 Oct 87 ● FAITH *Epic EMU 3* ....**2** 12 wks
9 Jan 88 FATHER FIGURE *Epic EMU 4* ....**11** 6 wks
23 Apr 88 ● ONE MORE TRY *Epic EMU 5* ....**8** 7 wks
16 Jul 88 MONKEY *Epic EMU 6* ....**13** 6 wks
3 Dec 88 KISSING A FOOL *Epic EMU 7* ....**18** 6 wks
25 Aug 90 ● PRAYING FOR TIME *Epic GEO 1* ....**6** 7 wks
27 Oct 90 WAITING FOR THAT DAY *Epic GEO 2* ....**23** 5 wks
15 Dec 90 FREEDOM 90 *Epic GEO 3* ....**28** 6 wks
16 Feb 91 HEAL THE PAIN *Epic 6566477* ....**31** 4 wks
30 Mar 91 COWBOYS AND ANGELS *Epic 6567747* ....**45** 3 wks
7 Dec 91 ★ DON'T LET THE SUN GO DOWN ON ME
Epic 6576467 ** ....**1** 10 wks
13 Jun 92 ● TOOFUNKY *Epic 6580587* ....**4** 9 wks
* Aretha Franklin and George Michael ** George Michael and Elton John
See also Elton John.

MICHAELA UK, female vocalist — 6 wks

| 2 Sep 89 | -H-A-P-P-Y-RADIO London H 1 | 62 | 4 wks |
| 28 Apr 90 | TAKE GOOD CARE OF MY HEART London WAC 90 | 66 | 2 wks |

Lisa MICHAELIS – See Frankie KNUCKLES

Keith MICHELL Australia, male vocalist — 25 wks

27 Mar 71	I'LL GIVE YOU THE EARTH (TOUS LES BATEAUX, TOUS LES OISEAUX) Spark SRL 1046	43	1 wk
17 Apr 71	I'LL GIVE YOU THE EARTH (TOUS LES BATEAUX, TOUS LES OISEAUX) (re-entry) Spark SRL 1046	30	10 wks
26 Jan 80 ●	CAPTAIN BEAKY/WILFRED THE WEASEL Polydor POSP 106	5	10 wks
29 Mar 80	THE TRIAL OF HISSING SID Polydor HISS 1 *	53	4 wks

* Keith Michell, Captain Beaky and his Band

Lloyd MICHELS – See MISTURA featuring Lloyd MICHELS

MICK and PAT – See PAT and MICK

MICROBE UK, male vocalist — 7 wks

| 14 May 69 | GROOVY BABY CBS 4158 | 29 | 7 wks |

MICRODISNEY Ireland, male vocal/instrumental group — 3 wks

| 21 Feb 87 | TOWN TO TOWN Virgin VS 927 | 55 | 3 wks |

MIDDLE OF THE ROAD UK, male/female vocal/instrumental group — 76 wks

5 Jun 71 ★	CHIRPY CHIRPY CHEEP CHEEP RCA 2047	1	34 wks
4 Sep 71 ●	TWEEDLE DEE TWEEDLE DUM RCA 2110	2	17 wks
11 Dec 71 ●	SOLEY SOLEY RCA 2151	5	12 wks
25 Mar 72	SACRAMENTO RCA 2184	49	1 wk
8 Apr 72	SACRAMENTO (re-entry) RCA 2184	23	6 wks
29 Jul 72	SAMSON AND DELILAH RCA 2237	26	6 wks

Bette MIDLER US, female vocalist — 26 wks

17 Jun 89 ●	WIND BENEATH MY WINGS Atlantic A 8972	5	12 wks
13 Oct 90	FROM A DISTANCE Atlantic A 7820	45	5 wks
15 Jun 91 ●	FROM A DISTANCE (re-entry) Atlantic A 7820	6	9 wks

MIDNIGHT BAND – See Tony RALLO and the MIDNIGHT BAND

MIDNIGHT COWBOY SOUNDTRACK — 4 wks
US, orchestra

| 8 Nov 80 | MIDNIGHT COWBOY United Artists UP 634 | 47 | 4 wks |

MIDNIGHT OIL Australia, male vocal/instrumental group — 26 wks

23 Apr 88	BEDS ARE BURNING Sprint OIL 1	48	5 wks
2 Jul 88	THE DEAD HEART Spring OIL 2	68	2 wks
25 Mar 89 ●	BEDS ARE BURNING (re-issue) Sprint OIL 3	6	13 wks
1 Jul 89	THE DEAD HEART (re-issue) Sprint OIL 4	62	4 wks
10 Feb 90	BLUE SKY MINE CBS OIL 5	66	2 wks

MIDNIGHT STAR — 26 wks
US, male/female vocal/instrumental group

23 Feb 85	OPERATOR Solar MCA 942	66	2 wks
28 Jun 86	HEADLINES Solar MCA 1065	16	8 wks
4 Oct 86 ●	MIDAS TOUCH Solar MCA 1096	8	10 wks
7 Feb 87	ENGINE NO.9 Solar MCA 1117	64	3 wks
2 May 87	WET MY WHISTLE Solar MCA 1127	60	3 wks

MIGHTY AVENGERS UK, male vocal/instrumental group — 2 wks

| 26 Nov 64 | SO MUCH IN LOVE Decca F 11962 | 46 | 2 wks |

MIGHTY AVONS – See Larry CUNNINGHAM and the MIGHTY AVONS

MIGHTY LEMON DROPS — 6 wks
UK, male vocal/instrumental group

13 Sep 86	THE OTHER SIDE OF YOU Blue Guitar AZUR 1	67	1 wk
18 Apr 87	OUT OF HAND Blue Guitar AZUR 4	66	3 wks
23 Jan 88	INSIDE OUT Blue Guitar AZUR 6	74	2 wks

MIGHTY WAH – See WAH!

MIGIL FIVE UK, male vocal/instrumental group — 20 wks

| 19 Mar 64 ● | MOCKINGBIRD HILL Pye 7N 15597 | 10 | 13 wks |
| 4 Jun 64 | NEAR YOU Pye 7N 15645 | 31 | 7 wks |

MIG29 Italy, male instrumental/production group — 2 wks

| 22 Feb 92 | MIG29 Champion CHAMP 292 | 62 | 2 wks |

MIKE + the MECHANICS — 41 wks
UK, male vocal/instrumental group

15 Feb 86	SILENT RUNNING (ON DANGEROUS GROUND) WEA U 8908	21	9 wks
31 May 86	ALL I NEED IS A MIRACLE WEA U 8765	53	4 wks
14 Jan 89 ●	THE LIVING YEARS WEA U 7717	2	11 wks
16 Mar 91	WORD OF MOUTH Virgin VS 1345	13	10 wks
15 Jun 91	A TIME AND PLACE Virgin VS 1351	58	3 wks
8 Feb 92	EVERYBODY GETS A SECOND CHANCE Virgin VS 1396	56	4 wks

MIKI and GRIFF UK, female/male vocal duo — 25 wks

2 Oct 59	HOLD BACK TOMORROW Pye 7N 15213	26	2 wks
13 Oct 60	ROCKIN' ALONE Pye 7N 15296	44	3 wks
1 Feb 62	LITTLE BITTY TEAR Pye 7N 15412	16	13 wks
22 Aug 63	I WANNA STAY HERE Pye 7N 15555	23	7 wks

John MILES UK, male vocalist/multi-instrumentalist — 30 wks

18 Oct 75	HIGH FLY Decca F 13595	17	6 wks
20 Mar 76 ●	MUSIC Decca F 13627	3	9 wks
16 Oct 76	REMEMBER YESTERDAY Decca F 13667	32	5 wks
18 Jun 77 ●	SLOW DOWN Decca F 13709	10	10 wks

June MILES-KINGSTON – See Jimmy SOMERVILLE

Paul MILES-KINGSTON – See Sarah BRIGHTMAN

MILK AND HONEY featuring Gali ATARI   8 wks

Israel, male/female vocal/instrumental group

14 Apr 79	● HALLELUJAH *Polydor 2001 870*	....	5	8 wks

MILL GIRLS – *See Billy COTTON*

Frankie MILLER *UK, male vocalist*   32 wks

4 Jun 77	BE GOOD TO YOURSELF *Chrysalis CHS 2147*	....	27	6 wks
14 Oct 78	● DARLIN' *Chrysalis CHS 2255*	....	6	15 wks
20 Jan 79	WHEN I'M AWAY FROM YOU *Chrysalis CHS 2276*	......	42	5 wks
21 Mar 92	CALEDONIA *MCS MCS 2001*	....	45	6 wks

Gary MILLER *UK, male vocalist*   35 wks

21 Oct 55	YELLOW ROSE OF TEXAS *Nixa N 15004*	....	13	5 wks
13 Jan 56	● ROBIN HOOD *Nixa N 15020*	....	10	6 wks
11 Jan 57	GARDEN OF EDEN *Pye Nixa N 15070*	....	14	6 wks
1 Mar 57	GARDEN OF EDEN (re-entry) *Pye Nixa N 15070*	......	27	1 wk
19 Jul 57	WONDERFUL WONDERFUL *Pye Nixa N 15094*	......	29	1 wk
17 Jan 58	STORY OF MY LIFE *Pye Nixa N 15120*	....	14	6 wks
21 Dec 61	THERE GOES THAT SONG AGAIN/THE NIGHT			
	IS YOUNG *Pye 7N 15404*	....	29	9 wks
1 Mar 62	THERE GOES THAT SONG AGAIN (re-entry)			
	Pye 7N 15404	....	48	1 wk

The Night Is Young *only listed with* There Goes That Song Again *for weeks 21 and 28 Dec 61 and 4 Jan 62.*

Glenn MILLER *US, orchestra, Glenn Miller, trombone*   9 wks

12 Mar 54	MOONLIGHT SERENADE *HMV BD 5942*	....	12	1 wk
24 Jan 76	MOONLIGHT SERENADE/LITTLE BROWN			
	JUG/IN THE MOOD (re-issue) *RCA 2644*	......	13	8 wks

Jody MILLER *US, female vocalist*   1 wk

21 Oct 65	HOME OF THE BRAVE *Capitol CL 15415*	....	49	1 wk

Leza MILLER – *See Sergio MENDES*

Mitch MILLER *US, orchestra and chorus*   13 wks

7 Oct 55	● YELLOW ROSE OF TEXAS *Philips PB 505*	....	2	13 wks

Ned MILLER *US, male vocalist*   22 wks

14 Feb 63	● FROM A JACK TO A KING *London HL 9658*	....	2	21 wks
18 Feb 65	DO WHAT YOU DO DO WELL *London HL 9937*	......	48	1 wk

Roger MILLER *US, male vocalist*   42 wks

18 Mar 65	★ KING OF THE ROAD *Philips BF 1397*	....	1	15 wks
3 Jun 65	ENGINE ENGINE NO. 9 *Philips BF 1416*	....	33	5 wks
21 Oct 65	KANSAS CITY STAR *Philips BF 1437*	....	48	1 wk
16 Dec 65	ENGLAND SWINGS *Philips BF 1456*	....	45	1 wk
6 Jan 66	ENGLAND SWINGS (re-entry) *Philips BF 1456*	......	13	7 wks

27 Mar 68	LITTLE GREEN APPLES *Mercury MF 1021*	....	19	10 wks
2 Apr 69	LITTLE GREEN APPLES (re-entry) *Mercury MF 1021*	......	48	1 wk
7 May 69	LITTLE GREEN APPLES (2nd re-entry)			
	Mercury MF 1021	....	39	2 wks

Suzi MILLER – *See JOHNSTON BROTHERS*

Steve MILLER BAND *US, male vocal/instrumental group*   36 wks

23 Oct 76	ROCK 'N ME *Mercury 6078 804*	....	11	9 wks
19 Jun 82	● ABRACADABRA *Mercury STEVE 3*	....	2	11 wks
4 Sep 82	KEEPS ME WONDERING WHY *Mercury STEVE 4*	......	52	3 wks
11 Aug 90	★ THE JOKER *Capitol CL 583*	....	1	13 wks

MILLI VANILLI *France/Germany, male duo*   50 wks

1 Oct 88	● GIRL YOU KNOW IT'S TRUE *Cooltempo COOL 170*	....	3	13 wks
17 Dec 88	BABY DON'T FORGET MY NUMBER			
	Cooltempo COOL 178	....	16	11 wks
22 Jul 89	BLAME IT ON THE RAIN *Cooltempo COOL 180*	......	53	5 wks
30 Sep 89	● GIRL I'M GONNA MISS YOU *Cooltempo COOL 191*	......	2	15 wks
2 Dec 89	BLAME IT ON THE RAIN (re-entry)			
	Cooltempo COOL 180	....	52	5 wks
10 Mar 90	ALL OR NOTHING *Cooltempo COOL 199*	....	74	1 wk

MILLICAN and NESBITT *UK, male vocal duo*   14 wks

1 Dec 73	VAYA CON DIOS *Pye 7N 45310*	....	20	11 wks
18 May 74	FOR OLD TIME'S SAKE *Pye 7N 45357*	....	38	3 wks

MILLIE *Jamaica, female vocalist*   33 wks

12 Mar 64	● MY BOY LOLLIPOP *Fontana TF 449*	....	2	18 wks
25 Jun 64	SWEET WILLIAM *Fontana TF 479*	....	30	9 wks
11 Nov 65	BLOODSHOT EYES *Fontana TF 617*	....	48	1 wk
25 Jul 87	MY BOY LOLLIPOP (re-issue) *Island WIP 6574*	......	46	5 wks

Garry MILLS *UK, male vocalist*   31 wks

7 Jul 60	● LOOK FOR A STAR *Top Rank JAR 336*	....	7	14 wks
20 Oct 60	TOP TEEN BABY *Top Rank JAR 500*	....	24	12 wks
22 Jun 61	I'LL STEP DOWN *Decca F 11358*	....	39	5 wks

Hayley MILLS *UK, female vocalist*   11 wks

19 Oct 61	LET'S GET TOGETHER *Decca F 21396*	....	17	11 wks

Mrs. MILLS *UK, female instrumentalist - piano*   5 wks

14 Dec 61	MRS MILLS' MEDLEY *Parlophone R 4856*	....	18	5 wks

Mrs Mills' Medley *consisted of the following tunes: I Want To Be Happy/Sheik Of Araby/Baby Face/Somebody Stole My Gal/Ma (He's Making Eyes At Me)/Swanee/Ain't She Sweet/California Here I Come.*

Stephanie MILLS *US, female vocalist*   30 wks

18 Oct 80	● NEVER KNEW LOVE LIKE THIS BEFORE			
	20th Century TC 2460	....	4	14 wks
23 May 81	TWO HEARTS *20th Century TC 2492 **	....	49	5 wks
15 Sep 84	THE MEDICINE SONG *Club JAB 8*	....	29	9 wks
5 Sep 87	(YOU'RE PUTTIN') A RUSH ON ME			
	MCA MCA 1187	....	62	2 wks

* Stephanie Mills featuring Teddy Pendergrass

Warren MILLS *Zambia, male vocalist*   1 wk

28 Sep 85	SUNSHINE *Jive JIVE 99*	....	74	1 wk

WILLIE MITCHELL found his greatest chart success producing Al Green.

Top: THE MONKEES, shown here in 1966, are taught their parts for next week's show.

Right: KYLIE MINOGUE reached the top five with her first ten hits, the best such career start of any artist.

The teenage Broadway star STEPHANIE MILLS is shown reading her high school yearbook with a selection of Bronx and Manhattan phone books behind her.

MILLS BROTHERS US, male vocal group   1 wk

30 Jan 53 ● GLOW WORM Brunswick 05007 ....**10** 1 wk

MILLTOWN BROTHERS   13 wks
UK, male vocal/instrumental group

2 Feb 91   WHICH WAY SHOULD I JUMP A & M AM 711 ....**38** 5 wks
13 Apr 91   HERE I STAND A & M AM 758 ....**41** 4 wks
8 Jul 91   APPLE GREEN A & M AM 787 ....**43** 4 wks

Garnet MIMMS and TRUCKIN' CO.   1 wk
US, male vocalist and male instrumental group

25 Jun 77   WHAT IT IS Arista 109 ....**44** 1 wk

MIND OF KANE UK, male producer - David Hope   1 wk

27 Jul 91   STABBED IN THE BACK Deja Vu DJV 007 ....**64** 1 wk

MINDBENDERS UK, male vocal/instrumental group   34 wks

13 Jan 66 ● A GROOVY KIND OF LOVE Fontana TF 644 ....**2** 14 wks
5 May 66   CAN'T LIVE WITH YOU (CAN'T LIVE WITHOUT
    YOU) Fontana TF 697 ....**28** 7 wks
25 Aug 66   ASHES TO ASHES Fontana TF 731 ....**14** 9 wks
20 Sep 67   THE LETTER Fontana TF 869 ....**42** 4 wks

See also Wayne Fontana and the Mindbenders.

Zodiac MINDWARP and the LOVE REACTION   11 wks
UK, male/female vocal/instrumental group

9 May 87   PRIME MOVER Mercury ZOD 1 ....**18** 6 wks
14 Nov 87   BACKSEAT EDUCATION Mercury ZOD 2 ....**49** 3 wks
2 Apr 88   PLANET GIRL Mercury ZOD 3 ....**63** 2 wks

Sal MINEO US, male vocalist   11 wks

12 Jul 57   START MOVIN' Philips PB 707 ....**16** 11 wks

Marcello MINERBI Italy, orchestra   16 wks

22 Jul 65 ● ZORBA'S DANCE Durium DRS 54001 ....**6** 16 wks

MINI POPS UK, male/female vocal group   2 wks

26 Dec 87   SONGS FOR CHRISTMAS '87 EP Bright BULB 9 ....**39** 2 wks

Tracks on Songs For Christmas '87 EP: Thanks For Giving Us Christmas/The Man In
Red/Christmas Time Around The World/Shine On.

MINISTRY US, male vocal/instrumental group   1 wk

8 Aug 92   NWO Sire W 0125TE ....**49** 1 wk

MINK DE VILLE US, male vocal/instrumental group   9 wks

6 Aug 77   SPANISH STROLL Capitol CLX 103 ....**20** 9 wks

Liza MINNELLI US, female vocalist   15 wks

12 Aug 89 ● LOSING MY MIND Epic ZEE 1 ....**6** 7 wks

7 Oct 89   DON'T DROP BOMBS Epic ZEE 2 ....**46** 3 wks
25 Nov 89   SO SORRY I SAID Epic ZEE 3 ....**62** 2 wks
3 Mar 90   LOVE PAINS Epic ZEE 4 ....**41** 3 wks

Dannii MINOGUE Australia, female vocalist   38 wks

30 Mar 91 ● LOVE AND KISSES MCA MCS 1529 ....**8** 8 wks
18 May 91   SUCCESS MCA MCS 1538 ....**11** 7 wks
27 Jul 91 ● JUMP TO THE BEAT MCA MCS 1556 ....**8** 6 wks
19 Oct 91   BABY LOVE MCA MCS 1580 ....**14** 6 wks
14 Dec 91   I DON'T WANNA TAKE THIS PAIN
    MCA MCS 1600 ....**40** 5 wks
1 Aug 92   SHOW YOU THE WAY TO GO MCA MCS 1671 ....**30** 3 wks
12 Dec 92   LOVE'S ON EVERY CORNER MCA MCSR 1723 ...**44**† 3 wks

Kylie MINOGUE Australia, female vocalist   174 wks

23 Jan 88 ★ I SHOULD BE SO LUCKY PWL PWL 8 ....**1** 16 wks
14 May 88 ● GOT TO BE CERTAIN PWL PWL 12 ....**2** 12 wks
6 Aug 88 ● THE LOCO-MOTION PWL PWL 14 ....**2** 11 wks
22 Oct 88 ● JE NE SAIS PAS POURQUOI PWL PWL 21 ....**2** 13 wks
10 Dec 88 ★ ESPECIALLY FOR YOU PWL PWL 24 * ....**1** 14 wks
6 May 89 ★ HAND ON YOUR HEART PWL PWL 35 ....**1** 11 wks
5 Aug 89 ● WOULDN'T CHANGE A THING PWL PWL 42 ....**2** 9 wks
4 Nov 89 ● NEVER TOO LATE PWL PWL 45 ....**4** 10 wks
20 Jan 90 ★ TEARS ON MY PILLOW PWL PWL 47 ....**1** 8 wks
12 May 90 ● BETTER THE DEVIL YOU KNOW PWL PWL 56 ....**2** 10 wks
3 Nov 90 ● STEP BACK IN TIME PWL PWL 64 ....**4** 8 wks
2 Feb 91 ● WHAT DO I HAVE TO DO PWL PWL 72 ....**6** 8 wks
1 Jun 91 ● SHOCKED PWL PWL 81 ....**6** 7 wks
7 Sep 91   WORD IS OUT PWL PWL 204 ....**16** 5 wks
2 Nov 91 ● IF YOU WERE WITH ME NOW PWL PWL 208 ** ....**4** 7 wks
30 Nov 91   KEEP ON PUMPIN' IT PWL PWL 207 *** ....**49** 1 wk
25 Jan 92 ● GIVE ME JUST A LITTLE MORE TIME
    PWL PWL 212 ....**2** 8 wks
25 Apr 92   FINER FEELINGS PWL Int PWL 227 ....**11** 6 wks
22 Aug 92   WHAT KIND OF FOOL (HEARD IT ALL BEFORE)
    PWL Int PWL 241 ....**14** 5 wks
28 Nov 92   CELEBRATION PWL Int PWL 257 ....**20**† 5 wks

* Kylie Minogue and Jason Donovan ** Kylie Minogue and Keith Washington
*** Visionmasters with Tony King featuring Kylie Minogue

Morris MINOR and the MAJORS   11 wks
UK, male vocal group

19 Dec 87 ● STUTTER RAP (NO SLEEP 'TIL BEDTIME)
    10 TEN 203 ....**4** 11 wks

Sugar MINOTT UK, male vocalist   16 wks

28 Mar 81 ● GOOD THING GOING (WE'VE GOT A GOOD
    THING GOING) RCA 58 ....**4** 12 wks
17 Oct 81   NEVER MY LOVE RCA 138 ....**52** 4 wks

MINT JULEPS UK, female vocal group   7 wks

22 Mar 86   ONLY LOVE CAN BREAK YOUR HEART
    Stiff BUY 241 ....**62** 2 wks
30 May 87   EVERY KINDA PEOPLE Stiff BUY 257 ....**58** 5 wks

MIRACLES US, male vocal group   10 wks

10 Jan 76 ● LOVE MACHINE Tamla Motown TMG 1015 ....**3** 10 wks

See also Smokey Robinson and the Miracles.

MIRAGE UK, male vocal/instrumental group   35 wks

14 Jan 84   GIVE ME THE NIGHT Passion PASH 15 * ....**49** 4 wks

9 May 87 ●	**JACK MIX II/III** Debut DEBT 3022	4	11 wks
25 Jul 87	**SERIOUS MIX** Debut DEBT 3028	42	4 wks
7 Nov 87 ●	**JACK MIX IV** Debut DEBT 3035	8	10 wks
27 Feb 88	**JACK MIX VII** Debut DEBT 3042	50	3 wks
2 Jul 88	**PUSH THE BEAT** Debut DEBT 3050	67	2 wks
11 Nov 89	**LATINO HOUSE** Debut DEBT 3085	70	1 wk

* Mirage featuring Roy Gayle
Jack Mix III *only listed with Jack Mix II from 6 Jun 87.*

Danny MIRROR *Holland, male vocalist*　　9 wks

| 17 Sep 77 ● | **I REMEMBER ELVIS PRESLEY (THE KING IS DEAD)** Sonet SON 2121 | 4 | 9 wks |

MISSION *UK, male vocal/instrumental group*　　53 wks

14 Jun 86	**SERPENTS KISS** Chapter 22 CHAP 6	70	3 wks
26 Jul 86	**GARDEN OF DELIGHT/LIKE A HURRICANE** Chapter 22 CHAP 7	50	4 wks
18 Oct 86	**STAY WITH ME** Mercury MYTH 1	30	4 wks
17 Jan 87	**WASTELAND** Mercury MYTH 2	11	6 wks
14 Mar 87	**SEVERINA** Mercury MYTH 3	25	5 wks
13 Feb 88	**TOWER OF STRENGTH** Mercury MYTH 4	12	7 wks
23 Apr 88	**BEYOND THE PALE** Mercury MYTH 6	32	4 wks
13 Jan 90	**BUTTERFLY ON A WHEEL** Mercury MYTH 8	12	4 wks
10 Mar 90	**DELIVERANCE** Mercury MYTH 9	27	4 wks
2 Jun 90	**INTO THE BLUE** Mercury MYTH 10	32	3 wks
17 Nov 90	**HANDS ACROSS THE OCEAN** Mercury MYTH 11	28	2 wks
25 Apr 92	**NEVER AGAIN** Mercury MYTH 12	34	3 wks
20 Jun 92	**LIKE A CHILD AGAIN** Mercury MYTH 13	30	2 wks
17 Oct 92	**SHADES OF GREEN** Vertigo MYTH 14	49	2 wks

MISTA E *UK, male producer - Damon Rochort*　　5 wks

| 10 Dec 88 | **DON'T BELIEVE THE HYPE** Urban URB 28 | 41 | 5 wks |

MR. BEAN and SMEAR CAMPAIGN featuring Bruce DICKINSON　　5 wks
UK, male comedians and male vocalist

| 4 Apr 92 ● | **(I WANT TO BE) ELECTED** London LON 319 | 9 | 5 wks |

MR. BIG *UK, male vocal/instrumental group*　　14 wks

| 12 Feb 77 ● | **ROMEO** EMI 2567 | 4 | 10 wks |
| 21 May 77 | **FEEL LIKE CALLING HOME** EMI 2610 | 35 | 4 wks |

MR. BIG *US, male vocal/instrumental group*　　16 wks

7 Mar 92 ●	**TO BE WITH YOU** Atlantic A 7514	3	11 wks
23 May 92	**JUST TAKE MY HEART** Atlantic A 7490	26	4 wks
8 Aug 92	**GREEN TINTED SIXTIES MIND** Atlantic A 7468	72	1 wk

MR. BLOE *UK, male instrumentalist - harmonica*　　18 wks

| 9 May 70 ● | **GROOVIN' WITH MR. BLOE** DJM DJS 216 | 2 | 18 wks |

MR. FINGERS *US, male producer - Larry Heard*　　5 wks

17 Mar 90	**WHAT ABOUT THIS LOVE** ffrr F 131	74	1 wk
7 Mar 92	**CLOSER** MCA MCS 1601	50	3 wks
23 May 92	**ON MY WAY** MCA MCS 1630	71	1 wk

MR. FOOD *UK, male vocalist*　　3 wks

| 9 Jun 90 | **...AND THAT'S BEFORE ME TEA!** Tangible TGB 005 | 62 | 3 wks |

MR. LEE *US, male producer - Leroy Haggard*　　6 wks

6 Aug 88	**PUMP UP LONDON** Breakout USA 639	64	2 wks
11 Nov 89	**GET BUSY** Jive JIVE 231	71	1 wk
24 Feb 90	**GET BUSY (re-entry)** Jive JIVE 231	41	3 wks

MR. MISTER *US, male vocal/instrumental group*　　22 wks

| 21 Dec 85 ● | **BROKEN WINGS** RCA PB 49945 | 4 | 13 wks |
| 1 Mar 86 | **KYRIE** RCA PB 49927 | 11 | 9 wks |

MISTURA featuring Lloyd MICHELS　　10 wks
US, male instrumental group, Lloyd Michels - trumpet

| 15 May 76 | **THE FLASHER** Route RT 30 | 23 | 10 wks |

Cameron MITCHELL – *See VARIOUS ARTISTS (EPs & LPs) -* Carousel Soundtrack

Guy MITCHELL *US, male vocalist*　　164 wks

14 Nov 52 ●	**FEET UP** Columbia DB 3151	2	10 wks
13 Feb 53 ★	**SHE WEARS RED FEATHERS** Columbia DB 3238	1	15 wks
24 Apr 53 ●	**PRETTY LITTLE BLACK EYED SUSIE** Columbia DB 3255	2	11 wks
12 Jun 53	**SHE WEARS RED FEATHERS (re-entry)** Columbia DB 3238	12	1 wk
28 Aug 53 ★	**LOOK AT THAT GIRL** Philips PB 162	1	14 wks
6 Nov 53 ●	**CHICKA BOOM** Philips PB 178	5	9 wks
18 Dec 53 ●	**CLOUD LUCKY SEVEN** Philips PB 210	2	16 wks
15 Jan 54 ●	**CHICKA BOOM (re-entry)** Philips PB 178	4	6 wks
19 Feb 54 ●	**CUFF OF MY SHIRT** Philips PB 225	9	1 wk
26 Feb 54	**SIPPIN' SODA** Philips PB 210	11	1 wk
19 Mar 54	**CUFF OF MY SHIRT (re-entry)** Philips PB 225	12	1 wk
2 Apr 54	**CUFF OF MY SHIRT (2nd re-entry)** Philips PB 225	11	1 wk
30 Apr 54 ●	**DIME AND A DOLLAR** Philips PB 248	8	1 wk
14 May 54 ●	**DIME AND A DOLLAR (re-entry)** Philips PB 248	8	4 wks
7 Dec 56 ★	**SINGING THE BLUES** Philips PB 650	1	22 wks
15 Feb 57 ●	**KNEE DEEP IN THE BLUES** Philips PB 669	3	12 wks
26 Apr 57 ★	**ROCK-A-BILLY** Philips PB 685	1	14 wks
26 Jul 57	**IN THE MIDDLE OF A DARK DARK NIGHT/SWEET STUFF** Philips PB 712	27	2 wks
23 Aug 57	**IN THE MIDDLE OF A DARK DARK NIGHT/SWEET STUFF (re-entry)** Philips PB 712	25	2 wks
11 Oct 57	**CALL ROSIE ON THE PHONE** Philips PB 743	17	6 wks
27 Nov 59	**HEARTACHES BY THE NUMBER** Philips PB 964	26	2 wks
18 Dec 59 ●	**HEARTACHES BY THE NUMBER (re-entry)** Philips PB 964	5	13 wks

Joni MITCHELL *Canada, female vocalist*　　15 wks

| 13 Jun 70 | **BIG YELLOW TAXI** Reprise RS 20906 | 11 | 15 wks |

Willie MITCHELL *US, male instrumentalist - guitar*　　3 wks

| 24 Apr 68 | **SOUL SERENADE** London HLU 10186 | 43 | 1 wk |
| 11 Dec 76 | **THE CHAMPION** London HL 10545 | 47 | 2 wks |

MIXMASTER *Italy, male producer - Daniele Daroli*　　10 wks

| 4 Nov 89 ● | **GRAND PIANO** BCM BCM 344 | 9 | 10 wks |

MIXTURES *Australia, male vocal/instrumental group*　　21 wks

| 16 Jan 71 ● | **THE PUSHBIKE SONG** Polydor 2058 083 | 2 | 21 wks |

Hank MIZELL *US, male vocalist*　　13 wks

| 20 Mar 76 ● | **JUNGLE ROCK** Charly CS 1005 | 3 | 13 wks |

MNO Belgium, male instrumental/production group · 2 wks

28 Sep 91	GOD OF ABRAHAM A & M AM 820	66	2 wks

MOBILES UK, male/female vocal/instrumental group · 14 wks

9 Jan 82 ●	DROWNING IN BERLIN Rialto RIA 3	9	10 wks
27 Mar 82	AMOUR AMOUR Rialto RIA 5	45	4 wks

MOBY US, male producer - Richard Hall · 10 wks

27 Jul 91	GO Outer Rhythm FOOT 15	46	3 wks
19 Oct 91 ●	GO (re-entry) Outer Rhythm FOOT 15	10	7 wks

MOCK TURTLES UK, male vocal/instrumental group · 15 wks

9 Mar 91	CAN YOU DIG IT Siren SRN 136	18	11 wks
29 Jun 91	AND THEN SHE SMILES Siren SRN 139	44	4 wks

MODERN LOVERS – See Jonathan RICHMAN and the MODERN LOVERS

MODERN ROMANCE · 77 wks
UK, male vocal/instrumental group

15 Aug 81	EVERYBODY SALSA WEA K 18815	12	10 wks
7 Nov 81 ●	AY AY AY AY MOOSEY WEA K 18883	10	12 wks
30 Jan 82	QUEEN OF THE RAPPING SCENE (NOTHING EVER GOES THE WAY YOU PLAN) WEA K 18928	37	8 wks
14 Aug 82	CHERRY PINK AND APPLE BLOSSOM WHITE WEA K 19245 *	15	8 wks
13 Nov 82 ●	BEST YEARS OF OUR LIVES WEA ROM 1	4	13 wks
26 Feb 83 ●	HIGH LIFE WEA ROM 2	8	8 wks
7 May 83	DON'T STOP THAT CRAZY RHYTHM WEA ROM 3	14	6 wks
6 Aug 83 ●	WALKING IN THE RAIN WEA X 9733	7	12 wks

* Modern Romance featuring John du Prez

MODERN TALKING · 22 wks
Germany, male vocal/instrumental duo

15 Jun 85	YOU'RE MY HEART, YOU'RE MY SOUL Magnet MAG 277	69	2 wks
17 Aug 85	YOU'RE MY HEART, YOU'RE MY SOUL (re-entry) Magnet MAG 277	56	5 wks
12 Oct 85	YOU CAN WIN IF YOU WANT Magnet MAG 282	70	2 wks
16 Aug 86 ●	BROTHER LOUIE RCA PB 40875	4	10 wks
4 Oct 86	ATLANTIS IS CALLING (S.O.S. FOR LOVE) RCA PB 40969	55	3 wks

MODETTES UK, female vocal/instrumental group · 6 wks

12 Jul 80	PAINT IT BLACK Deram DET-R 1	42	5 wks
18 Jul 81	TONIGHT Deram DET 3	68	1 wk

Domenico MODUGNO Italy, male vocalist · 13 wks

5 Sep 58 ●	VOLARE Oriole ICB 5000	10	12 wks
27 Mar 59	CIAO CIAO BAMBINA Oriole CB 1489	29	1 wk

MOHAWKS Jamaica, male vocal/instrumental group · 2 wks

24 Jan 87	THE CHAMP Pama PM 1	58	2 wks

MOJO UK, male instrumental group · 3 wks

22 Aug 81	DANCE ON Creole CR 17	70	3 wks

MOJOS UK, male vocal/instrumental group · 26 wks

26 Mar 64 ●	EVERYTHING'S ALRIGHT Decca F 11853	9	11 wks
11 Jun 64	WHY NOT TONIGHT Decca F 11918	25	10 wks
10 Sep 64	SEVEN DAFFODILS Decca F 11959	30	5 wks

MOMENTS US, male vocal group · 32 wks

8 Mar 75 ●	GIRLS All Platinum 6146 302 *	3	10 wks
19 Jul 75 ●	DOLLY MY LOVE All Platinum 6146 306	10	9 wks
25 Oct 75	LOOK AT ME (I'M IN LOVE) All Platinum 6146 309	42	4 wks
22 Jan 77	JACK IN THE BOX All Platinum 6146 318	7	9 wks

* Moments and Whatnauts

Jay MONDI and the LIVING BASS · 3 wks
US, male/female vocal/instrumental group

24 Mar 90	ALL NIGHT LONG 10 TEN 304	63	3 wks

MONDO KANE UK, male vocal/instrumental group · 2 wks

16 Aug 86	NEW YORK AFTERNOON Lisson DOLE 2	70	2 wks

Zoot MONEY and the BIG ROLL BAND · 8 wks
UK, male vocal/instrumental

18 Aug 66	BIG TIME OPERATOR Columbia DB 7975	25	8 wks

T.S. MONK US, male/female vocal/instrumental group · 6 wks

7 Mar 81	BON BON VIE Mirage K 11653	63	2 wks
25 Apr 81	CANDIDATE FOR LOVE Mirage K 11648	58	4 wks

MONKEES US/UK, male vocal/instrumental group · 101 wks

5 Jan 67 ★	I'M A BELIEVER RCA 1560	1	17 wks
26 Jan 67	LAST TRAIN TO CLARKSVILLE RCA 1547	23	7 wks
6 Apr 67 ●	A LITTLE BIT ME A LITTLE BIT YOU RCA 1580	3	12 wks
22 Jun 67 ●	ALTERNATE TITLE RCA 1604	2	12 wks
16 Aug 67	PLEASANT VALLEY SUNDAY RC 1620	11	8 wks
15 Nov 67 ●	DAYDREAM BELIEVER RCA 1645	5	17 wks
27 Mar 68	VALLERI RCA 1673	12	8 wks
26 Jun 68	D.W. WASHBURN RCA 1706	17	6 wks
26 Mar 69	TEARDROP CITY RCA 1802	46	1 wk
25 Jun 69	SOMEDAY MAN RCA 1824	47	1 wk
15 Mar 80	THE MONKEES EP Arista ARIST 326	33	9 wks
18 Oct 86	THAT WAS THEN, THIS IS NOW Arista ARIST 673	68	1 wk
1 Apr 89	THE MONKEES EP Arista 112157	62	2 wks

Tracks on Arista 326 EP: I'm a Believer/Daydream Believer/Last Train to Clarksville/A Little Bit Me A Little Bit You. Tracks on Arista 112157 EP: Daydream Believer/Monkees Theme/Last Train To Clarksville.

MONKS UK, male vocal/instrumental duo · 9 wks

21 Apr 79	NICE LEGS SHAME ABOUT HER FACE Carrere CAR 104	19	9 wks

The Monks were Hudson-Ford under a different name.

Matt MONRO UK, male vocalist · 127 wks

15 Dec 60 ●	PORTRAIT OF MY LOVE Parlophone R 4714	3	16 wks
9 Mar 61 ●	MY KIND OF GIRL Parlophone R 4755	5	12 wks

18 May 61		WHY NOT NOW/CAN THIS BE LOVE		
		Parlophone R 4775	24	9 wks
28 Sep 61		GONNA BUILD A MOUNTAIN Parlophone R 4819	44	3 wks
8 Feb 62	●	SOFTLY AS I LEAVE YOU Parlophone R 4868	10	18 wks
14 Jun 62		WHEN LOVE COMES ALONG Parlophone R 4911	46	3 wks
8 Nov 62		MY LOVE AND DEVOTION Parlophone R 4954	29	5 wks
14 Nov 63		FROM RUSSIA WITH LOVE Parlophone R 5068	20	13 wks
17 Sep 64	●	WALK AWAY Parlophone R 5171	4	20 wks
24 Dec 64		FOR MAMA Parlophone R 5215	36	4 wks
25 Mar 65		WITHOUT YOU Parlophone R 5251	37	4 wks
21 Oct 65	●	YESTERDAY Parlophone R 5348	8	12 wks
24 Nov 73		AND YOU SMILED EMI 2091	28	8 wks

Gerry MONROE UK, male vocalist — 57 wks

23 May 70	●	SALLY Chapter One CH 122	4	20 wks
19 Sep 70		CRY Chapter One CH 128	38	5 wks
14 Nov 70		MY PRAYER Chapter One CH 132	9	12 wks
17 Apr 71		IT'S A SIN TO TELL A LIE Chapter One CH 144	13	12 wks
21 Aug 71		LITTLE DROPS OF SILVER Chapter One CH 152	37	6 wks
12 Feb 72		GIRL OF MY DREAMS Chapter One CH 159	43	2 wks

MONSOON UK, male/female vocal/instrumental group — 12 wks

3 Apr 82		EVER SO LONELY Mobile Suit Corp CORP 2	12	9 wks
5 Jun 82		SHAKTI (THE MEANING OF WITHIN)		
		Mobile Suit Corp CORP 4	41	3 wks

MONTANA SEXTET — 1 wk
US, male/female vocal/instrumental group

15 Jan 83		HEAVY VIBES Virgin VS 560	59	1 wk

Hugo MONTENEGRO US, orchestra — 26 wks

11 Sep 68	★	THE GOOD THE BAD AND THE UGLY RCA 1727	1	24 wks
8 Jan 69		HANG 'EM HIGH RCA 1771	50	1 wk
19 Mar 69		THE GOOD THE BAD AND THE UGLY (re-entry)		
		RCA 1727	48	1 wk

Chris MONTEZ US, male vocalist — 61 wks

4 Oct 62	●	LET'S DANCE London HLU 9596	2	18 wks
17 Jan 63	●	SOME KINDA FUN London HLU 9650	10	9 wks
30 Jun 66	●	THE MORE I SEE YOU Pye International 7N 25369	3	13 wks
22 Sep 66		THERE WILL NEVER BE ANOTHER YOU		
		Pye International 7N 25381	37	4 wks
14 Oct 72	●	LET'S DANCE (re-issue) London HL 10205	9	14 wks
14 Apr 79		LET'S DANCE (2nd re-issue) Lightning LIG 9011	47	3 wks

The second re-issue of Let's Dance on Lightning was coupled with Memphis by Lonnie Mack as a double A-side.

MONTROSE US, male vocal/instrumental group — 2 wks

28 Jun 80		SPACE STATION NO. 5/GOOD ROCKIN'		
		TONIGHT WB HM 9	71	2 wks

MONTY PYTHON UK, male comedy group — 9 wks

5 Oct 91	●	ALWAYS LOOK ON THE BRIGHT SIDE OF LIFE		
		Virgin PYTH 1	3	9 wks

MONYAKA US/Jamaica, male vocal/instrumental group — 8 wks

10 Sep 83		GO DEH YAKA (GO TO THE TOP)		
		Polydor POSP 641	14	8 wks

MOOD UK, male vocal/instrumental group — 10 wks

6 Feb 82		DON'T STOP RCA 171	59	4 wks
22 May 82		PARIS IS ONE DAY AWAY RCA 211	42	5 wks
30 Oct 82		PASSION IN DARK ROOMS RCA 276	74	1 wk

MOODSWINGS featuring Chrissie HYNDE — 2 wks
UK/US, male/female vocal/instrumental group

12 Oct 91		SPIRITUAL HIGH (STATE OF INDEPENDENCE)		
		Arista 114528	66	2 wks

MOODY BLUES UK, male vocal/instrumental group — 114 wks

10 Dec 64	★	GO NOW Decca F 12022	1	14 wks
4 Mar 65		I DON'T WANT TO GO ON WITHOUT YOU		
		Decca F 12095	33	9 wks
10 Jun 65		FROM THE BOTTOM OF MY HEART Decca F 12166	22	9 wks
18 Nov 65		EVERYDAY Decca F 12266	44	2 wks
27 Dec 67		NIGHTS IN WHITE SATIN Deram DM 161	19	11 wks
7 Aug 68		VOICES IN THE SKY Deram DM 196	27	10 wks
4 Dec 68		RIDE MY SEE-SAW Deram DM 213	42	1 wk
2 May 70		QUESTION Threshold TH 4	2	12 wks
6 May 72		ISN'T LIFE STRANGE Threshold TH 9	13	10 wks
2 Dec 72	●	NIGHTS IN WHITE SATIN (re-entry) Deram DM 161	9	11 wks
10 Feb 73		I'M JUST A SINGER (IN A ROCK 'N' ROLL BAND)		
		Threshold TH 13	36	4 wks
10 Nov 79		NIGHTS IN WHITE SATIN (2nd re-entry)		
		Deram DM 161	14	12 wks
20 Aug 83		BLUE WORLD Threshold TH 30	35	5 wks
25 Jun 88		I KNOW YOU'RE OUT THERE SOMEWHERE		
		Polydor POSP 921	52	4 wks

MOONTREKKERS UK, male instrumental group — 1 wk

2 Nov 61		NIGHT OF THE VAMPIRE Parlophone R 4814	50	1 wk

Dorothy MOORE US, female vocalist — 24 wks

19 Jun 76	●	MISTY BLUE Contempo CS 2087	5	12 wks
16 Oct 76		FUNNY HOW TIME SLIPS AWAY Contempo CS 2092	38	3 wks
15 Oct 77		I BELIEVE YOU Epic EPC 5573	20	9 wks

Dudley MOORE – See Peter COOK

Gary MOORE UK, male vocalist/instrumentalist - guitar — 97 wks

21 Apr 79	●	PARISIENNE WALKWAYS MCA 419	8	11 wks
21 Jan 84		HOLD ON TO LOVE 10 TEN 13	65	3 wks
11 Aug 84		EMPTY ROOMS 10 TEN 25	51	5 wks
18 May 85	●	OUT IN THE FIELDS 10 TEN 49 *	5	10 wks
27 Jul 85		EMPTY ROOMS (re-issue) 10 TEN 58	23	8 wks
20 Dec 86		OVER THE HILLS AND FAR AWAY 10 TEN 134	20	8 wks
28 Feb 87		WILD FRONTIER 10 TEN 159	35	5 wks
9 May 87		FRIDAY ON MY MIND 10 TEN 164	26	6 wks
29 Aug 87		THE LONER 10 TEN 178	53	5 wks
5 Dec 87		TAKE A LITTLE TIME (DOUBLE SINGLE)		
		10 TEN 190	75	1 wk
14 Jan 89		AFTER THE WAR Virgin GMS 1	37	4 wks
18 Mar 89		READY FOR LOVE Virgin GMS 2	56	2 wks
24 Mar 90		OH PRETTY WOMAN Virgin VS 1233 **	48	3 wks
12 May 90		STILL GOT THE BLUES (FOR YOU) Virgin VS 1267	31	7 wks
18 Aug 90		WALKING BY MYSELF Virgin VS 1281	48	5 wks
15 Dec 90		TOO TIRED Virgin VS 1306	71	1 wk
22 Feb 92		COLD DAY IN HELL Virgin VS 1393	24	5 wks
9 May 92		STORY OF THE BLUES Virgin VS 1412	40	4 wks
18 Jul 92		SINCE I MET YOU BABY Virgin VS 1423 ***	59	3 wks
24 Oct 92		SEPARATE WAYS Virgin VS 1437	59	1 wk

* Gary Moore and Phil Lynott ** Gary Moore featuring Albert King *** Gary Moore and B.B. King

Parisienne Walkways features uncredited vocals by Phil Lynott. Tracks on double single: Take A Little Time/Out In The Fields/All Messed Up/Thunder Rising.

Jackie MOORE US, female vocalist — 5 wks

15 Sep 79	**THIS TIME BABY** CBS 7722	....	49	5 wks

Melba MOORE US, female vocalist — 29 wks

15 May 76 ●	**THIS IS IT** Buddah BDS 443	....	9	8 wks
26 May 79	**PICK ME UP I'LL DANCE** Epic EPC 7234	....	48	5 wks
9 Oct 82	**LOVE'S COMIN' AT YA** EMI America EA 146	....	15	8 wks
15 Jan 83	**MIND UP TONIGHT** Capitol CL 272	....	22	6 wks
5 Mar 83	**UNDERLOVE** Capitol CL 281	....	60	2 wks

Ray MOORE UK, male vocalist — 9 wks

29 Nov 86	**O' MY FATHER HAD A RABBIT** Play PLAY 213	....	24	7 wks
5 Dec 87	**BOG EYED JOG** Play PLAY 224	....	61	2 wks

Sam MOORE – See SAM and DAVE; Lou REED

Mike MORAN – See Lynsey DE PAUL

MORE UK, male vocal/instrumental group — 2 wks

14 Mar 81	**WE ARE THE BAND** Atlantic K 11561	....	59	2 wks

Derrick MORGAN Jamaica, male vocalist — 1 wk

17 Jan 70	**MOON HOP** Crab 32	....	49	1 wk

Jamie J. MORGAN US, male vocalist — 6 wks

10 Feb 90	**WALK ON THE WILD SIDE** Tabu 655596 7	....	27	6 wks

Jane MORGAN US, female vocalist — 22 wks

5 Dec 58 ★	**THE DAY THE RAINS CAME** London HLR 8751	....	1	16 wks
22 May 59	**IF ONLY I COULD LIVE MY LIFE AGAIN** London HLR 8810	....	27	1 wk
21 Jul 60	**ROMANTICA** London HLR 9120	....	39	5 wks

Meli'sa MORGAN US, female vocalist — 7 wks

9 Aug 86	**FOOL'S PARADISE** Capitol CL 415	....	41	5 wks
25 Jun 88	**GOOD LOVE** Capitol CL 483	....	59	2 wks

Ray MORGAN UK, male vocalist — 6 wks

25 Jul 70	**THE LONG AND WINDING ROAD** B & C CB 128	....	32	6 wks

Giorgio MORODER

Italy, male instrumentalist - synthesizer — 34 wks

24 Sep 77	**FROM HERE TO ETERNITY** Oasis 1 *	....	16	10 wks
17 Mar 79	**CHASE** Casablanca CAN 144	....	48	6 wks
22 Sep 84 ●	**TOGETHER IN ELECTRIC DREAMS** Virgin VS 713 **	....	3	13 wks
29 Jun 85	**GOODBYE BAD TIMES** Virgin VS 772 **	....	44	5 wks

* Giorgio ** Giorgio Moroder and Phil Oakey

Ennio MORRICONE Italy, orchestra — 12 wks

11 Apr 81 ●	**CHI MAI (THEME FROM THE TV SERIES 'THE LIFE AND TIMES OF DAVID LLOYD GEORGE')** BBC RESL 92	....	2	12 wks

---

British Hit Singles Part One: Alphabetically by Artist

Date of chart entry/Title & catalogue no./Peak position reached/Weeks on chart

★ Number one   ● Top Ten   † still on chart at 31 Dec 1992

* = credited to act billed in footnote

Sarah Jane MORRIS – See COMMUNARDS

Diana MORRISON – See Michael BALL

Dorothy Combs MORRISON – See Edwin HAWKINS SINGERS featuring Dorothy Combs MORRISON

Van MORRISON UK, male vocalist — 10 wks

20 Oct 79	**BRIGHT SIDE OF THE ROAD** Mercury 6001 121	....	63	3 wks
1 Jul 89	**HAVE I TOLD YOU LATELY** Polydor VANS 1	....	74	1 wk
9 Dec 89	**WHENEVER GOD SHINES HIS LIGHT** Polydor VANS 2 *	....	20	6 wks

* Van Morrison with Cliff Richard

MORRISSEY UK, male vocalist — 50 wks

27 Feb 88 ●	**SUEDEHEAD** HMV POP 1618	....	5	6 wks
11 Jun 88 ●	**EVERYDAY IS LIKE SUNDAY** HMV POP 1619	....	9	6 wks
11 Feb 89 ●	**LAST OF THE FAMOUS INTERNATIONAL PLAYBOYS** HMV POP 1620	....	6	5 wks
29 Apr 89 ●	**INTERESTING DRUG** HMV POP 1621	....	9	4 wks
25 Nov 89	**OUIJA BOARD OUIJA BOARD** HMV POP 1622	....	18	4 wks
5 May 90	**NOVEMBER SPAWNED A MONSTER** HMV POP 1623	....	12	4 wks
20 Oct 90	**PICCADILLY PALARE** HMV POP 1624	....	18	2 wks
23 Feb 91	**OUR FRANK** HMV POP 1625	....	26	3 wks
13 Apr 91	**SING YOUR LIFE** HMV POP 1626	....	33	2 wks
27 Jul 91	**PREGNANT FOR THE LAST TIME** HMV POP 1627	....	25	4 wks
12 Oct 91	**MY LOVE LIFE** HMV POP 1628	....	29	2 wks
9 May 92	**WE HATE IT WHEN OUR FRIENDS BECOME SUCCESSFUL** HMV POP 1629	....	17	3 wks
18 Jul 92	**YOU'RE THE ONE FOR ME, FATTY** HMV POP 1630	....	19	3 wks
19 Dec 92	**CERTAIN PEOPLE I KNOW** HMV POP 1631	....	35†	2 wks

MORRISTON ORPHEUS MALE VOICE CHOIR – See ALARM

Buddy MORROW US, orchestra — 1 wk

20 Mar 53	**NIGHT TRAIN** HMV B 10347	....	12	1 wk

Mickie MOST UK, male vocalist — 1 wk

25 Jul 63	**MISTER PORTER** Decca F 11664	....	45	1 wk

MOTELS US/UK, male/female vocal/instrumental group — 7 wks

11 Oct 80	**WHOSE PROBLEM?** Capitol CL 16162	....	42	4 wks
10 Jan 81	**DAYS ARE O.K.** Capitol CL 16149	....	41	3 wks

MOTLEY CRUE US, male vocal/instrumental group — 25 wks

24 Aug 85	**SMOKIN' IN THE BOYS ROOM** Elektra EKR 16	....	71	2 wks
8 Feb 86	**HOME SWEET HOME/SMOKIN' IN THE BOYS ROOM (re-issue)** Elektra EKR 33	....	51	3 wks
1 Aug 87	**GIRLS GIRLS GIRLS** Elektra EKR 59	....	26	6 wks
16 Jan 88	**YOU'RE ALL I NEED/WILD SIDE** Elektra EKR 65	....	23	4 wks
4 Nov 89	**DR. FEELGOOD** Elektra EKR 97	....	50	3 wks

12 May 90		WITHOUT YOU *Elektra EKR 109*	39	3 wks
7 Sep 91		PRIMAL SCREAM *Elektra EKR 133*	32	2 wks
11 Jan 92		HOME SWEET HOME (re-mix) *Elektra EKR 136*	37	2 wks

Wild Side only listed with You're All I Need from 30 Jan 88.

MOTORHEAD *UK, male vocal/instrumental group*   74 wks

16 Sep 78		LOUIE LOUIE *Bronze BRO 60*	75	1 wk
30 Sep 78		LOUIE LOUIE (re-entry) *Bronze BRO 60*	68	1 wk
10 Mar 79		OVERKILL *Bronze BRO 67*	39	4 wks
14 Apr 79		OVERKILL (re-entry) *Bronze BRO 67*	57	3 wks
30 Jun 79		NO CLASS *Bronze BRO 78*	61	4 wks
1 Dec 79		BOMBER *Bronze BRO 85*	34	7 wks
3 May 80	●	THE GOLDEN YEARS EP *Bronze BRO 92*	8	7 wks
1 Nov 80		ACE OF SPADES *Bronze BRO 106*	15	12 wks
22 Nov 80		BEER DRINKERS AND HELL RAISERS *Big Beat SWT 61*	43	4 wks
21 Feb 81	●	ST. VALENTINE'S DAY MASSACRE EP *Bronze BRO 116 **	5	8 wks
11 Jul 81	●	MOTORHEAD LIVE *Bronze BRO 124*	6	7 wks
3 Apr 82		IRON FIST *Bronze BRO 146*	29	5 wks
21 May 83		I GOT MINE *Bronze BRO 165*	46	2 wks
30 Jul 83		SHINE *Bronze BRO 167*	59	2 wks
1 Sep 84		KILLED BY DEATH *Bronze BRO 185*	51	2 wks
5 Jul 86		DEAF FOREVER *GWR GWR 2*	67	1 wk
5 Jan 91		THE ONE TO SING THE BLUES *Epic 6565787*	45	3 wks
14 Nov 92		'92 TOUR EP *Epic 6588096*	63	1 wk

* Motorhead and Girlschool (also known as Headgirl)

Tracks on The Golden Years EP: Dead Men Tell No Tales/Too Late Too Late/Leaving Here/Stone Dead Forever. Tracks on St. Valentine's Day Massacre EP: Please Don't Touch/Emergency/Bomber. Tracks on '92 Tour EP: Hellraiser/You Better Run/Going To Brazil/Ramones.

MOTORS *UK, male vocal/instrumental group*   29 wks

24 Sep 77		DANCING THE NIGHT AWAY *Virgin VS 186*	42	4 wks
10 Jun 78	●	AIRPORT *Virgin VS 219*	4	13 wks
19 Aug 78		FORGET ABOUT YOU *Virgin VS 222*	13	9 wks
12 Apr 80		LOVE AND LONELINESS *Virgin VS 263*	58	3 wks

MOTOWN SPINNERS – *See* **DETROIT SPINNERS**

MOTT THE HOOPLE   55 wks
UK, male vocal/instrumental group

12 Aug 72	●	ALL THE YOUNG DUDES *CBS 8271*	3	11 wks
16 Jun 73		HONALOOCHIE BOOGIE *CBS 1530*	12	9 wks
8 Sep 73	●	ALL THE WAY FROM MEMPHIS *CBS 1764*	10	8 wks
24 Nov 73	●	ROLL AWAY THE STONE *CBS 1895*	8	12 wks
30 Mar 74		GOLDEN AGE OF ROCK AND ROLL *CBS 2177*	16	7 wks
22 Jun 74		FOXY FOXY *CBS 2439*	33	5 wks
2 Nov 74		SATURDAY GIGS *CBS 2754*	41	3 wks

Nana MOUSKOURI *Greece, female vocalist*   11 wks

| 11 Jan 86 | ● | ONLY LOVE *Philips PH 38* | 2 | 11 wks |

MOUTH and MACNEAL   10 wks
Holland, male/female vocal duo

| 4 May 74 | ● | I SEE A STAR *Decca F 13504* | 8 | 10 wks |

MOVE *UK, male vocal/instrumental group*   110 wks

5 Jan 67	●	NIGHT OF FEAR *Deram DM 109*	2	10 wks
6 Apr 67	●	I CAN HEAR THE GRASS GROW *Deram DM 117*	5	10 wks
6 Sep 67	●	FLOWERS IN THE RAIN *Regal Zonophone RZ3001*	2	13 wks

7 Feb 68	●	FIRE BRIGADE *Regal Zonophone RZ3005*	3	11 wks
25 Dec 68	★	BLACKBERRY WAY *Regal Zonophone RZ3015*	1	12 wks
23 Jul 69		CURLY *Regal Zonophone RZ3021*	12	12 wks
25 Apr 70	●	BRONTOSAURUS *Regal Zonophone RZ3026*	7	10 wks
3 Jul 71		TONIGHT *Harvest HAR 5038*	11	10 wks
23 Oct 71		CHINATOWN *Harvest HAR 5043*	23	8 wks
13 May 72	●	CALIFORNIA MAN *Harvest HAR 5050*	7	14 wks

MOVEMENT *US, male vocal/instrumental group*   2 wks

| 24 Oct 92 | | JUMP! *Arista 74321116677* | 57 | 2 wks |

MOVEMENT 98 featuring Carroll   8 wks
THOMPSON *UK, male/female vocal/instrumental group*

| 19 May 90 | | JOY AND HEARTBREAK *Circa YR 45* | 27 | 5 wks |
| 15 Sep 90 | | SUNRISE *Circa YR 51* | 58 | 3 wks |

See also Courtney Pine.

Alison MOYET *UK, female vocalist*   92 wks

23 Jun 84	●	LOVE RESURRECTION *CBS A 4497*	10	11 wks
13 Oct 84	●	ALL CRIED OUT *CBS A 4757*	8	11 wks
1 Dec 84		INVISIBLE *CBS A 4930*	21	10 wks
16 Mar 85	●	THAT OLE DEVIL CALLED LOVE *CBS A 6044*	2	10 wks
29 Nov 86	●	IS THIS LOVE? *CBS MOYET 1*	3	16 wks
7 Mar 87	●	WEAK IN THE PRESENCE OF BEAUTY *CBS MOYET 2*	6	10 wks
30 May 87		ORDINARY GIRL *CBS MOYET 3*	43	4 wks
28 Nov 87	●	LOVE LETTERS *CBS MOYET 5*	4	10 wks
6 Apr 91		IT WON'T BE LONG *Columbia 6567577*	50	4 wks
1 Jun 91		WISHING YOU WERE HERE *Columbia 6569397*	72	1 wk
12 Oct 91		THIS HOUSE *Columbia 6575157*	40	5 wks

MTUME *US, male/female vocal/instrumental group*   12 wks

| 14 May 83 | | JUICY FRUIT *Epic A 3424* | 34 | 9 wks |
| 22 Sep 84 | | PRIME TIME *Epic A 4720* | 57 | 3 wks |

MUD *UK, male vocal/instrumental group*   139 wks

10 Mar 73		CRAZY *RAK 146*	12	12 wks
23 Jun 73		HYPNOSIS *RAK 152*	16	13 wks
27 Oct 73	●	DYNA-MITE *RAK 159*	4	12 wks
19 Jan 74	★	TIGER FEET *RAK 166*	1	11 wks
13 Apr 74	●	THE CAT CREPT IN *RAK 170*	2	9 wks
27 Jul 74	●	ROCKET *RAK 178*	6	9 wks
30 Nov 74	★	LONELY THIS CHRISTMAS *RAK 187*	1	10 wks
15 Feb 75	●	THE SECRETS THAT YOU KEEP *RAK 194*	3	9 wks
26 Apr 75	★	OH BOY *RAK 201*	1	9 wks
21 Jun 75	●	MOONSHINE SALLY *RAK 208*	10	7 wks
2 Aug 75		ONE NIGHT *RAK 213*	32	4 wks
4 Oct 75	●	L-L-LUCY *Private Stock PVT 41*	10	6 wks
29 Nov 75	●	SHOW ME YOU'RE A WOMAN *Private Stock PVT 45*	8	8 wks
15 May 76		SHAKE IT DOWN *Private Stock PVT 65*	12	8 wks
27 Nov 76	●	LEAN ON ME *Private Stock PVT 85*	7	9 wks
21 Dec 85		LONELY THIS CHRISTMAS (re-entry) *RAK 187*	61	3 wks

MUDHONEY *US, male vocal/instrumental group*   2 wks

| 17 Aug 91 | | LET IT SLIDE *Subpop SP 15154* | 60 | 1 wk |
| 24 Oct 92 | | SUCK YOU DRY *Reprise W 0137* | 65 | 1 wk |

MUDLARKS *UK, male/female vocal group*   19 wks

2 May 58	●	LOLLIPOP *Columbia DB 4099*	2	9 wks
6 Jun 58	●	BOOK OF LOVE *Columbia DB 4133*	8	9 wks
27 Feb 59		THE LOVE GAME *Columbia DB 4250*	30	1 wk

MUFFINS – See MARTHA and the MUFFINS

Idris MUHAMMAD *US, male vocalist* — 3 wks

17 Sep 77	**COULD HEAVEN EVER BE LIKE THIS** *Kudu 935* 42	3 wks

Maria MULDAUR *US, female vocalist* — 8 wks

29 Jun 74	**MIDNIGHT AT THE OASIS** *Reprise K 14331* 21	8 wks

Arthur MULLARD – See Hylda BAKER and Arthur MULLARD

Coati MUNDI – See Kid CREOLE and the COCONUTS

MUNGO JERRY *UK, male vocal/instrumental group* — 87 wks

6 Jun 70 ★	**IN THE SUMMERTIME** *Dawn DNX 2502* 1	20 wks
6 Feb 71	**BABY JUMP** *Dawn DNX 2505* 32	1 wk
20 Feb 71 ★	**BABY JUMP (re-entry)** *Dawn DNX 2505* 1	12 wks
29 May 71 ●	**LADY ROSE** *Dawn DNX 2510* 5	12 wks
18 Sep 71	**YOU DON'T HAVE TO BE IN THE ARMY TO FIGHT IN THE WAR** *Dawn DNX 2513* 13	8 wks
22 Apr 72	**OPEN UP** *Dawn DNX 2514* 21	8 wks
7 Jul 73 ●	**ALRIGHT ALRIGHT ALRIGHT** *Dawn DNS 1037* 3	12 wks
10 Nov 73	**WILD LOVE** *Dawn DNS 1051* 32	5 wks
6 Apr 74	**LONGLEGGED WOMAN DRESSED IN BLACK** *Dawn DNS 1061* 13	9 wks

MUNICH MACHINE *Germany, male instrumental group* — 8 wks

10 Dec 77	**GET ON THE FUNK TRAIN** *Oasis OASIS 2* 41	4 wks
4 Nov 78	**A WHITER SHADE OF PALE** *Oasis OASIS 5* * 42	4 wks

* Munich Machine introducing Chris Bennett

David MUNROW – See EARLY MUSIC CONSORT

MUPPETS *US, puppets* — 15 wks

28 May 77 ●	**HALFWAY DOWN THE STAIRS** *Pye 7N 45698* 7	8 wks
17 Dec 77	**THE MUPPET SHOW MUSIC HALL EP** *Pye 7NX 8004* 19	7 wks

Halfway Down the Stairs *is sung by Jerry Nelson as Kermit the Frog's nephew, Robin. Tracks on EP: Don't Dilly Dally On The Way/Waiting At The Church/The Boy In The Gallery/Wotcher (Knocked 'Em In The Old Kent Road).*

Lydia MURDOCK *US, female vocalist* — 9 wks

24 Sep 83	**SUPERSTAR** *Korova KOW 30* 14	9 wks

Shirley MURDOCK *US, female vocalist* — 2 wks

12 Apr 86	**TRUTH OR DARE** *Elektra EKR 36* 60	2 wks

Noel MURPHY *Ireland, male vocalist* — 4 wks

27 Jun 87	**MURPHY AND THE BRICKS** *Murphy's STACK 1* 57	4 wks

Walter MURPHY and the BIG APPLE BAND *US, orchestra* — 9 wks

10 Jul 76	**A FIFTH OF BEETHOVEN** *Private Stock PVT 59* 28	9 wks

Anne MURRAY *Canada, female vocalist* — 40 wks

24 Oct 70	**SNOWBIRD** *Capitol CL 15654* 23	17 wks
21 Oct 72	**DESTINY** *Capitol CL 15734* 41	4 wks
9 Dec 78	**YOU NEEDED ME** *Capitol CL 16011* 22	14 wks
21 Apr 79	**I JUST FALL IN LOVE AGAIN** *Capitol CL 16069* 58	2 wks
19 Apr 80	**DAYDREAM BELIEVER** *Capitol CL 16123* 61	3 wks

Pauline MURRAY and the INVISIBLE GIRLS — 2 wks
UK, female vocalist with male (really) vocal/instrumental group

2 Aug 80	**DREAM SEQUENCE (ONE)** *Illusive IVE 1* 67	2 wks

Ruby MURRAY *UK, female vocalist* — 114 wks

3 Dec 54 ●	**HEARTBEAT** *Columbia DB 3542* 3	16 wks
28 Jan 55 ★	**SOFTLY SOFTLY** *Columbia DB 3558* 1	22 wks
4 Feb 55 ●	**HAPPY DAYS AND LONELY NIGHTS** *Columbia DB 3577* 6	8 wks
4 Mar 55 ●	**LET ME GO LOVER** *Columbia DB 3577* 5	7 wks
18 Mar 55 ●	**IF ANYONE FINDS THIS I LOVE YOU** *Columbia DB 3580* * 4	11 wks
1 Jul 55 ●	**EVERMORE** *Columbia DB 3617* 3	17 wks
8 Jul 55	**SOFTLY SOFTLY (re-entry)** *Columbia DB 3558* 20	1 wk
14 Oct 55 ●	**I'LL COME WHEN YOU CALL** *Columbia DB 3643* 6	7 wks
31 Aug 56	**YOU ARE MY FIRST LOVE** *Columbia DB 3770* 16	4 wks
5 Oct 56	**YOU ARE MY FIRST LOVE (re-entry)** *Columbia DB 3770* 21	1 wk
12 Dec 58	**REAL LOVE** *Columbia DB 4192* 18	6 wks
5 Jun 59 ●	**GOODBYE JIMMY GOODBYE** *Columbia DB 4305* 10	13 wks
9 Oct 59	**GOODBYE JIMMY GOODBYE (re-entry)** *Columbia DB 4305* 26	1 wk

* Ruby Murray with Anne Warren

Junior MURVIN *Jamaica, male vocalist* — 9 wks

3 May 80	**POLICE AND THIEVES** *Island WIP 6539* 23	9 wks

MUSICAL YOUTH *UK, male vocal/instrumental group* — 55 wks

25 Sep 82 ★	**PASS THE DUTCHIE** *MCA YOU 1* 1	12 wks
20 Nov 82	**YOUTH OF TODAY** *MCA YOU 2* 13	9 wks
8 Jan 83	**PASS THE DUTCHIE (re-entry)** *MCA YOU 1* 65	1 wk
12 Feb 83 ●	**NEVER GONNA GIVE YOU UP** *MCA YOU 3* 6	10 wks
16 Apr 83	**HEARTBREAKER** *MCA YOU 4* 44	3 wks
9 Jul 83	**TELL ME WHY** *MCA YOU 5* 33	6 wks
22 Oct 83	**007** *MCA YOU 6* 26	6 wks
14 Jan 84	**SIXTEEN** *MCA YOU 7* 23	8 wks

See also Donna Summer.

MUSIQUE *US, female vocal group* — 12 wks

18 Nov 78	**IN THE BUSH** *CBS 6791* 16	12 wks

MUSTAFAS – See STAIFFI and his MUSTAFAS

MXM *Italy, male/female vocal/instrumental group* — 1 wk

2 Jun 90	**NOTHING COMPARES 2 U** *London LON 267* 68	1 wk

MY BLOODY VALENTINE — 5 wks
UK, male/female vocal/instrumental group

5 May 90	**SOON** *Creation CRE 073* 41	3 wks
18 Feb 91	**TO HERE KNOWS WHEN** *Creation CRE 085* 29	2 wks

Tim MYCROFT – *See SOUNDS NICE*

Alicia MYERS *US, female vocalist*   **3 wks**

1 Sep 84	YOU GET THE BEST FROM ME (SAY SAY SAY) *MCA MCA 914*	58	3 wks

Richard MYHILL *UK, male vocalist*   **9 wks**

1 Apr 78	IT TAKES TWO TO TANGO *Mercury 6007 167*	17	9 wks

Alannah MYLES *Canada, female vocalist*   **17 wks**

17 Mar 90 ●	BLACK VELVET *East West A 8742*	2	15 wks
16 Jun 90	LOVE IS *East West A 8918*	61	2 wks

Marie MYRIAM *France, female vocalist*   **4 wks**

28 May 77	L'OISEAU ET L'ENFANT *Polydor 2056 634*	42	4 wks

MYSTERIANS – *See ?(QUESTION MARK) and the MYSTERIANS*

MYSTI – *See CAMOUFLAGE featuring MYSTI*

MYSTIC MERLIN   **9 wks**
US, male vocal/instrumental and magic group

26 Apr 80	JUST CAN'T GIVE YOU UP *Capitol CL 16133*	20	9 wks

N-JOI *UK, male instrumental/production group*   **23 wks**

27 Oct 90	ANTHEM *Deconstruction PB 44041*	45	5 wks
2 Mar 91	ADRENALIN (EP) *Deconstruction PT 44344*	23	5 wks
6 Apr 91 ●	ANTHEM (re-entry) *Deconstruction PB 44041*	8	8 wks
22 Feb 92	LIVE IN MANCHESTER (PARTS 1 + 2) *Deconstruction PT 45252*	12	5 wks

Tracks on Adrenalin (EP): *Adrenalin/The Kraken/Rhythm Zone/Phoenix.*

Jimmy NAIL *UK, male vocalist*   **25 wks**

27 Apr 85 ●	LOVE DON'T LIVE HERE ANYMORE *Virgin VS 764*	3	11 wks
11 Jul 92 ★	AIN'T NO DOUBT *East West YZ 686*	1	12 wks
3 Oct 92	LAURA *East West YZ 702*	58	2 wks

NAKED EYES *UK, male vocal/instrumental duo*   **3 wks**

23 Jul 83	ALWAYS SOMETHING THERE TO REMIND ME *RCA 348*	59	3 wks

NAPOLEON XIV *US, male vocalist*   **10 wks**

4 Aug 66 ●	THEY'RE COMING TO TAKE ME AWAY HA-HAAA! *Warner Bros. WB 5831*	4	10 wks

NARADA – *See Narada Michael WALDEN*

Johnny NASH *US, male vocalist*   **106 wks**

7 Aug 68 ●	HOLD ME TIGHT *Regal Zonophone RZ 3010*	5	16 wks
8 Jan 69 ●	YOU GOT SOUL *Major Minor MM 586*	6	12 wks
2 Apr 69 ●	CUPID *Major Minor MM 603*	6	11 wks
25 Jun 69	CUPID (re-entry) *Major Minor MM 603*	50	1 wk
1 Apr 72	STIR IT UP *CBS 7800*	13	12 wks
24 Jun 72 ●	I CAN SEE CLEARLY NOW *CBS 8113*	5	15 wks
7 Oct 72 ●	THERE ARE MORE QUESTIONS THAN ANSWERS *CBS 8351*	9	9 wks
14 Jun 75 ★	TEARS ON MY PILLOW *CBS 3220*	1	11 wks
11 Oct 75	LET'S BE FRIENDS *CBS 3597*	42	3 wks
12 Jun 76	(WHAT A) WONDERFUL WORLD *Epic EPC 4294*	25	7 wks
9 Nov 85	ROCK ME BABY *2000 A.D. FED 19*	47	4 wks
15 Apr 89	I CAN SEE CLEARLY NOW (re-mix) *Epic JN 1*	54	5 wks

NASHVILLE TEENS *UK, male vocal/instrumental group*   **37 wks**

9 Jul 64 ●	TOBACCO ROAD *Decca F 11930*	6	13 wks
22 Oct 64 ●	GOOGLE EYE *Decca F 12000*	10	11 wks
4 Mar 65	FIND MY WAY BACK HOME *Decca F 12089*	34	6 wks
20 May 65	THIS LITTLE BIRD *Decca F 12143*	38	4 wks
3 Feb 66	THE HARD WAY *Decca F 12316*	45	2 wks
24 Feb 66	THE HARD WAY (re-entry) *Decca F 12316*	48	1 wk

NATASHA *UK, female vocalist*   **16 wks**

5 Jun 82 ●	IKO IKO *Towerbell TOW 22*	10	11 wks
4 Sep 82	THE BOOM BOOM ROOM *Towerbell TOW 25*	44	5 wks

Ultra NATÉ *US, female vocalist*   **4 wks**

9 Dec 89	IT'S OVER NOW *Eternal YZ 440*	62	3 wks
23 Feb 91	IS IT LOVE *Eternal YZ 509*	71	1 wk

NATURAL LIFE *UK, male/female vocal/instrumental group*   **3 wks**

7 Mar 92	NATURAL LIFE *Tribe NLIFE 3*	47	3 wks

NATURAL SELECTION   **2 wks**
US, male vocal/instrumental duo

9 Nov 91	DO ANYTHING *East West A 8724*	69	2 wks

NATURALS *UK, male vocal/instrumental group*   **9 wks**

20 Aug 64	I SHOULD HAVE KNOWN BETTER *Parlophone R 5165*	24	9 wks

David NAUGHTON *US, male vocalist*   **6 wks**

25 Aug 79	MAKIN' IT *RSO 32*	44	6 wks

NAUGHTY BY NATURE *US, male rap group*   **4 wks**

9 Nov 91	OPP *Big Life BLR 62*	73	1 wk
20 Jun 92	OPP (re-issue) *Big Life BLR 74*	35	3 wks

NAZARETH *UK, male vocal/instrumental group*   **75 wks**

5 May 73 ●	BROKEN DOWN ANGEL *Mooncrest MOON 1*	9	11 wks
21 Jul 73 ●	BAD BAD BOY *Mooncrest MOON 9*	10	9 wks
13 Oct 73	THIS FLIGHT TONIGHT *Mooncrest MOON 14*	11	13 wks
23 Mar 74	SHANGHAI'D IN SHANGHAI *Mooncrest MOON 22*	41	4 wks

14 Jun 75	**MY WHITE BICYCLE** Mooncrest MOON 47	.........**14**	8 wks
15 Nov 75	**HOLY ROLLER** Mountain TOP 3	.........**36**	4 wks
24 Sep 77	**HOT TRACKS EP** Mountain NAZ 1	.........**15**	11 wks
18 Feb 78	**GONE DEAD TRAIN** Mountain NAZ 002	.........**49**	2 wks
13 May 78	**PLACE IN YOUR HEART** Mountain TOP 37	.........**70**	1 wk
27 May 78	**PLACE IN YOUR HEART (re-entry)** Mountain TOP 37	.........**74**	1 wk
27 Jan 79	**MAY THE SUN SHINE** Mountain NAZ 003	.........**22**	8 wks
28 Jul 79	**STAR** Mountain TOP 45	.........**54**	3 wks

Tracks on Hot Tracks EP: Love Hurts/This Flight Tonight/Broken Down Angel/Hair of the Dog.

Youssou N'DOUR – *See Peter GABRIEL*

NEBULA II *UK, male instrumental/production group*   **3 wks**

| 1 Feb 92 | **SEANCE/ATHEAMA** Reinforced RIVET 1211 | ....**55** | 2 wks |
| 16 May 92 | **FLATLINERS** J4M 12NEBULA 2 | ....**54** | 1 wk |

NED'S ATOMIC DUSTBIN   **19 wks**
UK, male vocal/instrumental group

14 Jul 90	**KILL YOUR TELEVISION** Chapter 22 CHAP 48	.........**53**	2 wks
27 Oct 90	**UNTIL YOU FIND OUT** Chapter 22 CHAP 52	.........**51**	2 wks
9 Mar 91	**HAPPY** Columbia 6566807	.........**16**	4 wks
21 Sep 91	**TRUST** Furtive 6574627	.........**21**	4 wks
10 Oct 92	**NOT SLEEPING AROUND** Furtive 6583866	.........**19**	3 wks
5 Dec 92	**INTACT** Furtive 6588166	.........**36†**	4 wks

Joey NEGRO *UK, male producer - Dave Lee*   **8 wks**

18 Mar 89	**REACHIN'** Republic LIC 006 *	.........**70**	1 wk
16 Nov 91	**DO WHAT YOU FEEL** Ten TEN 391	.........**36**	3 wks
21 Dec 91	**REACHIN' (re-mix)** Republic LIC 160 **	.........**70**	1 wk
18 Jul 92	**ENTER YOUR FANTASY EP** Ten TEN 397	.........**35**	3 wks

* Phase II ** Joey Negro presents Phase II

Tracks on Enter Your Fantasy EP: Love Fantasy/Get Up/Enter Your Mind/Everybody.

neil *UK, male vocalist*   **10 wks**

| 14 Jul 84 | ● **HOLE IN MY SHOE** WEA YZ 10 | ....**2** | 10 wks |

Vince NEIL *US, male vocalist*   **1 wk**

| 3 Oct 92 | **YOU'RE INVITED (BUT YOUR FRIEND CAN'T COME)** Hollywood HWD 123 | ....**63** | 1 wk |

NELSON *US, male vocal duo*   **3 wks**

| 27 Oct 90 | **(CAN'T LIVE WITHOUT YOUR) LOVE AND AFFECTION** DGC GEF 82 | ....**54** | 3 wks |

Bill NELSON   **12 wks**
UK, male vocalist/instrumentalist - guitar and synthesizer

24 Feb 79	**FURNITURE MUSIC** Harvest HAR 5176 *	.........**59**	3 wks
5 May 79	**REVOLT INTO STYLE** Harvest HAR 5183 *	.........**69**	2 wks
5 Jul 80	**DO YOU DREAM IN COLOUR?** Cocteau COQ 1	.........**52**	4 wks
13 Jun 81	**YOUTH OF NATION ON FIRE** Mercury WILL 2	.........**73**	3 wks

* Bill Nelson's Red Noise

Phyllis NELSON *US, female vocalist*   **21 wks**

| 23 Feb 85 | ★ **MOVE CLOSER** Carrere CAR 337 | ....**1** | 21 wks |

Ricky NELSON *US, male vocalist*   **150 wks**

| 21 Feb 58 | **STOOD UP** London HLP 8542 | ....**27** | 1 wk |

7 Mar 58	**STOOD UP (re-entry)** London HLP 8542	.........**29**	1 wk
22 Aug 58	● **POOR LITTLE FOOL** London HLP 8670	.........**4**	13 wks
7 Nov 58	● **SOMEDAY** London HLP 8732	.........**9**	13 wks
21 Nov 58	**I GOT A FEELING** London HLP 8732	.........**27**	1 wk
28 Nov 58	**POOR LITTLE FOOL (re-entry)** London HLP 8670	.........**28**	1 wk
17 Apr 59	● **IT'S LATE** London HLP 8817	.........**3**	20 wks
15 May 59	**NEVER BE ANYONE ELSE BUT YOU** London HLP 8817	.........**19**	1 wk
5 Jun 59	**NEVER BE ANYONE ELSE BUT YOU (re-entry)** London HLP 8817	.........**14**	9 wks
4 Sep 59	**SWEETER THAN YOU** London HLP 8927	.........**19**	3 wks
11 Sep 59	**JUST A LITTLE TOO MUCH** London HLP 8927	.........**11**	8 wks
15 Jan 60	**I WANNA BE LOVED** London HLP 9021	.........**30**	1 wk
7 Jul 60	**YOUNG EMOTIONS** London HLP 9121	.........**48**	1 wk
1 Jun 61	● **HELLO MARY LOU/TRAVELLIN' MAN** London HLP 9347	.........**2**	18 wks
16 Nov 61	**EVERLOVIN'** London HLP 9440 *	.........**23**	5 wks
29 Mar 62	**YOUNG WORLD** London HLP 9524 *	.........**19**	13 wks
30 Aug 62	**TEENAGE IDOL** London HLP 9583 *	.........**39**	4 wks
17 Jan 63	**IT'S UP TO YOU** London HLP 9648 *	.........**22**	9 wks
17 Oct 63	**FOOLS RUSH IN** Brunswick 05895 *	.........**12**	9 wks
30 Jan 64	**FOR YOU** Brunswick 05900 *	.........**14**	10 wks
21 Oct 72	**GARDEN PARTY** MCA MU 1165 *	.........**41**	4 wks
24 Aug 91	**HELLO MARY LOU (GOODBYE HEART) (re-issue)** Liberty EMCT 2	.........**45**	5 wks

* Rick Nelson

Sandy NELSON *US, male instrumentalist - drums*   **42 wks**

6 Nov 59	● **TEEN BEAT** Top Rank JAR 197	.........**9**	11 wks
5 Feb 60	**TEEN BEAT (re-entry)** Top Rank JAR 197	.........**25**	1 wk
14 Dec 61	● **LET THERE BE DRUMS** London HLP 9466	.........**3**	16 wks
22 Mar 62	**DRUMS ARE MY BEAT** London HLP 9521	.........**30**	6 wks
7 Jun 62	**DRUMMIN' UP A STORM** London HLP 9558	.........**39**	8 wks

Willie NELSON *US, male vocalist*   **13 wks**

| 31 Jul 82 | **ALWAYS ON MY MIND** CBS A 2511 | ....**49** | 3 wks |
| 7 Apr 84 | **TO ALL THE GIRLS I'VE LOVED BEFORE** CBS A 4252 * | ....**17** | 10 wks |

* Julio Iglesias and Willie Nelson

NENA *Germany, female/male vocal/instrumental group*   **14 wks**

| 4 Feb 84 | ★ **99 RED BALLOONS** Epic A 4074 | ....**1** | 12 wks |
| 5 May 84 | **JUST A DREAM** Epic H 3249 | ....**70** | 2 wks |

Frances NERO *US, female vocalist*   **9 wks**

| 13 Apr 91 | **FOOTSTEPS FOLLOWING ME** Debut DEBT 3109 | ....**17** | 9 wks |

NERO and the GLADIATORS   **6 wks**
UK, male instrumental group

23 Mar 61	**ENTRY OF THE GLADIATORS** Decca F 11329	.........**50**	1 wk
6 Apr 61	**ENTRY OF THE GLADIATORS (re-entry)** Decca F 11329	.........**37**	4 wks
27 Jul 61	**IN THE HALL OF THE MOUNTAIN KING** Decca F 11367	.........**48**	1 wk

Michael NESMITH *US, male vocalist*   **6 wks**

| 26 Mar 77 | **RIO** Island WIP 6373 | ....**28** | 6 wks |

NETWORK *UK, male vocal/instrumental group*   **3 wks**

| 12 Dec 92 | **BROKEN WINGS** Chrysalis CHS 3923 | ....**46†** | 3 wks |

NEVADA UK, male/female vocal/instrumental group — 1 wk

8 Jan 83	IN THE BLEAK MID WINTER *Polydor POSP 203*	71	1 wk

Robbie NEVIL US, male vocalist — 24 wks

20 Dec 86 ●	C'EST LA VIE *Manhattan MT 14*	3	11 wks
2 May 87	DOMINOES *Manhattan MT 19*	26	6 wks
11 Jul 87	WOT'S IT TO YA *Manhattan MT 24*	43	7 wks

Aaron NEVILLE – *See Linda RONSTADT*

NEVILLE BROTHERS — 7 wks
US, male vocal/instrumental group

25 Nov 89	WITH GOD ON OUR SIDE *A & M AM 545*	47	6 wks
7 Jul 90	BIRD ON A WIRE *A & M AM 568*	72	1 wk

NEW ATLANTIC UK, male instrumental/production duo — 8 wks

29 Feb 92	I KNOW *3 Beat 3BT 1*	12	7 wks
3 Oct 92	INTO THE FUTURE *3 Beat 3BT 2*	70	1 wk

NEW BOHEMIANS – *See Edie BRICKELL and the NEW BOHEMIANS*

NEW EDITION US, male vocal group — 28 wks

16 Apr 83 ★	CANDY GIRL *London LON 21*	1	13 wks
13 Aug 83	POPCORN LOVE *London LON 31*	43	5 wks
23 Feb 85	MR TELEPHONE MAN *MCA MCA 938*	19	9 wks
15 Apr 89	CRUCIAL *MCA MCA 23934*	70	1 wk

NEW GENERATION UK, male vocal/instrumental group — 5 wks

26 Jun 68	SMOKEY BLUES AWAY *Spark SRL 1007*	38	5 wks

NEW KIDS ON THE BLOCK US, male vocal group — 85 wks

16 Sep 89	HANGIN' TOUGH *CBS BLOCK 1*	52	4 wks
11 Nov 89 ★	YOU GOT IT (THE RIGHT STUFF) *CBS BLOCK 2*	1	13 wks
6 Jan 90 ★	HANGIN' TOUGH (re-issue) *CBS BLOCK 3*	1	9 wks
17 Mar 90 ●	I'LL BE LOVING YOU (FOREVER) *CBS BLOCK 4*	5	8 wks
12 May 90 ●	COVER GIRL *CBS BLOCK 5*	4	8 wks
16 Jun 90 ●	STEP BY STEP *CBS BLOCK 6*	2	7 wks
4 Aug 90 ●	TONIGHT *CBS BLOCK 7*	3	10 wks
13 Oct 90 ●	LET'S TRY AGAIN/DIDN'T I BLOW YOUR MIND *CBS BLOCK 8*	8	5 wks
8 Dec 90 ●	THIS ONE'S FOR THE CHILDREN *CBS BLOCK 9*	9	7 wks
9 Feb 91	GAMES *CBS 6566267*	14	4 wks
18 May 91	CALL IT WHAT YOU WANT *Columbia 6567857*	12	5 wks
14 Dec 91 ●	IF YOU GO AWAY *Columbia 6576667*	9	5 wks

NEW MODEL ARMY UK, male vocal/instrumental group — 30 wks

27 Apr 85	NO REST *EMI NMA 1*	28	5 wks
3 Aug 85	BETTER THAN THEM/NO SENSE *EMI NMA 2*	49	2 wks
30 Nov 85	BRAVE NEW WORLD *EMI NMA 3*	57	1 wk
8 Nov 86	FIFTY-FIRST STATE *EMI NMA 4*	71	2 wks
28 Feb 87	POISON STREET *EMI NMA 5*	64	1 wk
26 Sep 87	WHITE COATS EP *EMI NMA 6*	50	3 wks
21 Jan 89	STUPID QUESTION *EMI NMA 7*	31	3 wks
11 Mar 89	VAGABONDS *EMI NMA 8*	37	3 wks
10 Jun 89	GREEN AND GREY *EMI NMA 9*	37	3 wks
8 Sep 90	GET ME OUT *EMI NMA 10*	34	3 wks
3 Nov 90	PURITY *EMI NMA 11*	61	2 wks
8 Jun 91	SPACE *EMI NMA 12*	39	2 wks

Tracks on White Coats EP: *The Charge/Chinese Whispers/My Country.*

NEW MUSIK UK, male vocal/instrumental group — 27 wks

6 Oct 79	STRAIGHT LINES *GTO GT 255*	53	5 wks
19 Jan 80	LIVING BY NUMBERS *GTO GT 261*	13	8 wks
26 Apr 80	THIS WORLD OF WATER *GTO GT 268*	31	7 wks
12 Jul 80	SANCTUARY *GTO GT 275*	31	7 wks

NEW ORDER UK, male/female vocal/instrumental group — 143 wks

14 Mar 81	CEREMONY *Factory FAC 33*	34	5 wks
3 Oct 81	PROCESSION/EVERYTHING'S GONE GREEN *Factory FAC 53*	38	5 wks
22 May 82	TEMPTATION *Factory FAC 63*	29	7 wks
19 Mar 83	BLUE MONDAY *Factory FAC 73*	12	17 wks
13 Aug 83 ●	BLUE MONDAY (re-entry) *Factory FAC 73*	9	17 wks
3 Sep 83	CONFUSION *Factory FAC 93*	12	9 wks
7 Jan 84	BLUE MONDAY (2nd re-entry) *Factory FAC 73*	52	4 wks
28 Apr 84	THIEVES LIKE US *Factory FAC 103*	18	5 wks
25 May 85	THE PERFECT KISS *Factory FAC 123*	46	4 wks
9 Nov 85	SUB-CULTURE *Factory FAC 133*	63	4 wks
29 Mar 86	SHELLSHOCK *Factory FAC 143*	28	5 wks
27 Sep 86	STATE OF THE NATION *Factory FAC 153*	30	3 wks
27 Sep 86	THE PEEL SESSIONS (1ST JUNE 1982) *Strange Fruit SFPS 001*	54	1 wk
15 Nov 86	BIZARRE LOVE TRIANGLE *Factory FAC 163*	56	2 wks
1 Aug 87 ●	TRUE FAITH *Factory FAC 183/7*	4	10 wks
19 Dec 87	TOUCHED BY THE HAND OF GOD *Factory FAC 1937*	20	7 wks
7 May 88 ●	BLUE MONDAY 1988 (re-mix) *Factory FAC 737*	3	11 wks
10 Dec 88	FINE TIME *Factory FAC 2237*	11	8 wks
11 Mar 89	ROUND AND ROUND *Factory FAC 2637*	21	7 wks
9 Sep 89	RUN 2 *Factory FAC 273*	49	2 wks
2 Jun 90 ★	WORLD IN MOTION... *Factory/MCA FAC 2937* *	1	12 wks

* Englandneworder

Group male only on first hit. Blue Monday 1988 is a re-mixed version of the original 1983 hit which was made available on 7 inch for the first time, hence the slight difference in catalogue number. Sales for the re-mix and the original were combined from 7 May 1988 onwards when calculating its chart position.

NEW ORLEANS JAZZMEN – *See Terry LIGHTFOOT and his NEW ORLEANS JAZZMEN*

NEW POWER GENERATION – *See PRINCE*

NEW SEEKERS UK, male/female vocal/instrumental group — 144 wks

17 Oct 70	WHAT HAVE THEY DONE TO MY SONG MA *Philips 6006 027*	48	1 wk
31 Oct 70	WHAT HAVE THEY DONE TO MY SONG MA (re-entry) *Philips 6006 027*	44	1 wk
16 Jan 71	WHAT HAVE THEY DONE TO MY SONG MA (2nd re-entry) *Philips 6006 027*	39	1 wk
10 Jul 71 ●	NEVER ENDING SONG OF LOVE *Philips 6006 125*	2	19 wks
18 Dec 71 ★	I'D LIKE TO TEACH THE WORLD TO SING (IN PERFECT HARMONY) *Polydor 2058 184*	1	21 wks
4 Mar 72 ●	BEG STEAL OR BORROW *Polydor 2058 201*	2	13 wks
10 Jun 72 ●	CIRCLES *Polydor 2058 242*	4	16 wks
2 Dec 72	COME SOFTLY TO ME *Polydor 2058 315* *	20	11 wks
24 Feb 73	PINBALL WIZARD - SEE ME FEEL ME (MEDLEY) *Polydor 2058 338*	16	8 wks
7 Apr 73	NEVERTHELESS *Polydor 2068 340* **	34	5 wks
16 Jun 73	GOODBYE IS JUST ANOTHER WORD *Polydor 2058 368*	36	5 wks

The 1992 number one by JIMMY NAIL ended his seven-year chart exile.

MICHAEL NESMITH is shown with the First National Band, the group he formed after the Monkees disbanded.

MICKEY NEWBURY originally arranged and recorded 'American Trilogy', which became an Elvis Presley fan favourite.

ALANNAH MYLES is honoured at the 1990 Billboard Awards for her tribute to Elvis Presley, 'Black Velvet'.

24 Nov 73 ★	YOU WON'T FIND ANOTHER FOOL LIKE ME		
	Polydor 2058 421	1	16 wks
9 Mar 74 ●	I GET A LITTLE SENTIMENTAL OVER YOU		
	Polydor 2058 439	5	9 wks
14 Aug 76	IT'S SO NICE (TO HAVE YOU HOME) *CBS 4391*	44	4 wks
29 Jan 77	I WANNA GO BACK *CBS 4786*	25	4 wks
15 Jul 78	ANTHEM (ONE DAY IN EVERY WEEK) *CBS 6413*	21	10 wks

* New Seekers featuring Marty Kristian ** Eve Graham and the New Seekers

NEW TONE AGE FAMILY – *See Dread FLIMSTONE and the NEW TONE AGE FAMILY*

NEW VAUDEVILLE BAND
UK, male vocal/instrumental group   **43 wks**

8 Sep 66 ●	WINCHESTER CATHEDRAL *Fontana TF 741*	4	19 wks
26 Jan 67 ●	PEEK-A-BOO *Fontana TF 784* *	7	11 wks
11 May 67	FINCHLEY CENTRAL *Fontana TF 824*	11	9 wks
2 Aug 67	GREEN STREET GREEN *Fontana TF 853*	37	4 wks

* New Vaudeville Band featuring Tristram

NEW WORLD *Australia, male vocal/instrumental group*   **53 wks**

27 Feb 71	ROSE GARDEN *RAK 111*	15	11 wks
3 Jul 71 ●	TOM TOM TURNAROUND *RAK 117*	6	15 wks
4 Dec 71	KARA KARA *RAK 123*	17	13 wks
13 May 72 ●	SISTER JANE *RAK 130*	9	13 wks
12 May 73	ROOF TOP SINGING *RAK 148*	50	1 wk

NEW YORK CITY *US, male vocal group*   **11 wks**

21 Jul 73	I'M DOING FINE NOW *RCA 2351*	20	11 wks

NEW YORK SKYY
US, male/female vocal/instrumental group   **2 wks**

16 Jan 82	LET'S CELEBRATE *Epic EPC A 1898*	71	1 wk
30 Jan 82	LET'S CELEBRATE (re-entry) *Epic EPC A 1898*	67	1 wk

NEWBEATS *US, male vocal group*   **22 wks**

10 Sep 64	BREAD AND BUTTER *Hickory 1269*	15	9 wks
23 Oct 71 ●	RUN BABY RUN *London HL 10341*	10	13 wks

Booker NEWBURY III *US, male vocalist*   **11 wks**

28 May 83 ●	LOVE TOWN *Polydor POSP 613*	6	8 wks
8 Oct 83	TEDDY BEAR *Polydor POSP 637*	44	3 wks

Mickey NEWBURY *US, male vocalist*   **5 wks**

1 Jul 72	AMERICAN TRILOGY *Elektra K 12047*	42	5 wks

NEWCLEUS *US, male vocal/instrumental group*   **6 wks**

3 Sep 83	JAM ON REVENGE (THE WIKKI WIKKI SONG)		
	Beckett BKS 8	44	6 wks

Anthony NEWLEY *UK, male vocalist*   **129 wks**

1 May 59 ●	I'VE WAITED SO LONG *Decca F 11127*	3	15 wks
8 May 59	IDLE ON PARADE EP *Decca DFE 6566*	13	4 wks
12 Jun 59 ●	PERSONALITY *Decca F 11142*	6	12 wks

15 Jan 60 ★	WHY *Decca F 11194*	1	17 wks
24 Mar 60 ★	DO YOU MIND *Decca F 11220*	1	15 wks
14 Jul 60 ●	IF SHE SHOULD COME TO YOU *Decca F 11254*	6	15 wks
24 Nov 60 ●	STRAWBERRY FAIR *Decca F 11295*	3	11 wks
16 Mar 61 ●	AND THE HEAVENS CRIED *Decca F 11331*	6	12 wks
15 Jun 61	POP GOES THE WEASEL/BEE BOM *Decca F 11362*	12	9 wks
3 Aug 61	WHAT KIND OF FOOL AM I? *Decca F 11376*	36	8 wks
25 Jan 62	D-DARLING *Decca F 11419*	25	6 wks
26 Jul 62	THAT NOISE *Decca F 11486*	34	5 wks

Bee Bom *only listed together with Pop Goes The Weasel for weeks of 15 and 22 June 61. Tracks on Idle On Parade EP: I've Waited So Long/Idle Rock-A-Boogie/Idle On Parade/Saturday Night Rock-A-Boogie.*

Tara NEWLEY – *See E-ZEE POSSEE*

Alfred NEWMAN – *See VARIOUS ARTISTS (EPs & LPs) - Carousel Soundtrack*

Brad NEWMAN *UK, male vocalist*   **1 wk**

22 Feb 62	SOMEBODY TO LOVE *Fontana H 357*	47	1 wk

Dave NEWMAN *UK, male vocalist*   **6 wks**

15 Apr 72	THE LION SLEEPS TONIGHT *Pye 7N 45134*	48	1 wk
29 Apr 72	THE LION SLEEPS TONIGHT (re-entry)		
	Pye 7N 45134	34	5 wks

NEWS – *See Huey LEWIS and the NEWS*

NEWS *UK, male vocal/instrumental group*   **3 wks**

29 Aug 81	AUDIO VIDEO *George GEORGE 1*	52	3 wks

Juice NEWTON *US, female vocalist*   **6 wks**

2 May 81	ANGEL OF THE MORNING *Capitol CL 16189*	43	6 wks

Olivia NEWTON-JOHN *UK, female vocalist*   **221 wks**

20 Mar 71 ●	IF NOT FOR YOU *Pye International 7N 25543*	7	11 wks
23 Oct 71 ●	BANKS OF THE OHIO *Pye International 7N 25568*	6	17 wks
11 Mar 72	WHAT IS LIFE *Pye International 7N 25575*	16	8 wks
13 Jan 73	TAKE ME HOME COUNTRY ROADS		
	Pye International 7N 25599	15	13 wks
16 Mar 74	LONG LIVE LOVE *Pye International 7N 25638*	11	8 wks
12 Oct 74	I HONESTLY LOVE YOU *EMI 2216*	22	6 wks
11 Jun 77 ●	SAM *EMI 2616*	6	11 wks
20 May 78 ★	YOU'RE THE ONE THAT I WANT *RSO 006* *	1	26 wks
16 Sep 78 ★	SUMMER NIGHTS *RSO 18* *	1	19 wks
4 Nov 78 ●	HOPELESSLY DEVOTED TO YOU *RSO 17*	2	11 wks
16 Dec 78 ●	A LITTLE MORE LOVE *EMI 2879*	4	12 wks
30 Jun 79	DEEPER THAN THE NIGHT *EMI 2954*	64	3 wks
21 Jun 80 ★	XANADU *Jet 185* **	1	11 wks
23 Aug 80	MAGIC *Jet 196*	32	7 wks
25 Oct 80	SUDDENLY *Jet 7002* ***	15	7 wks
10 Oct 81 ●	PHYSICAL *EMI 5234*	7	16 wks
16 Jan 82	LANDSLIDE *EMI 5257*	18	9 wks
17 Apr 82	MAKE A MOVE ON ME *EMI 5291*	43	3 wks
23 Oct 82	HEART ATTACK *EMI 5347*	46	4 wks
15 Jan 83	I HONESTLY LOVE YOU (re-issue) *EMI 5360*	52	4 wks
12 Nov 83	TWIST OF FATE *EMI 5438*	57	4 wks
22 Dec 90 ●	THE GREASE MEGAMIX *Polydor PO 114* *	3	10 wks
23 Mar 91	GREASE - THE DREAM MIX *PWL/Polydor PO 136* *	47	2 wks
4 Jul 92	I NEED LOVE *Mercury MER 370*	75	1 wk

* John Travolta and Olivia Newton-John ** Olivia Newton-John and Electric Light Orchestra *** Olivia Newton-John and Cliff Richard

NICE *UK, male instrumental group*   **15 wks**

10 Jul 68	AMERICA *Immediate IM 068*	21	15 wks

Paul NICHOLAS UK, male vocalist — 31 wks

17 Apr 76		REGGAE LIKE IT USED TO BE RSO 2090 185	17	8 wks
9 Oct 76	●	DANCING WITH THE CAPTAIN RSO 2090 206	8	9 wks
4 Dec 76	●	GRANDMA'S PARTY RSO 2090 216	9	11 wks
9 Jul 77		HEAVEN ON THE 7TH FLOOR RSO 2090 249	40	3 wks

Sue NICHOLLS UK, female vocalist — 8 wks

3 Jul 68	WHERE WILL YOU BE Pye 7N 17565	17	8 wks

Stevie NICKS US, female vocalist — 27 wks

15 Aug 81	STOP DRAGGIN' MY HEART AROUND WEA K 79231 *	50	4 wks
25 Jan 86	I CAN'T WAIT Parlophone R 6110	54	4 wks
29 Mar 86	TALK TO ME Parlophone R 6124	68	2 wks
6 May 89	ROOMS ON FIRE EMI EM 90	16	7 wks
12 Aug 89	LONG WAY TO GO EMI EM 97	60	2 wks
11 Nov 89	WHOLE LOTTA TROUBLE EMI EM 114	62	2 wks
24 Aug 91	SOMETIMES IT'S A BITCH EMI EM 203	40	4 wks
9 Nov 91	I CAN'T WAIT (re-issue) EMI EM 214	47	2 wks

* Stevie Nicks with Tom Petty and the Heartbreakers

NICOLE Germany, female vocalist — 10 wks

8 May 82	★	A LITTLE PEACE CBS A 2365	1	9 wks
21 Aug 82		GIVE ME MORE TIME CBS A 2467	75	1 wk

NICOLE – See SOURCE; Timmy THOMAS

NIKKE? NICOLE! US, female rapper — 1 wk

1 Jun 91	NIKKE DOES IT BETTER Love EVOL 5	73	1 wk

Maxine NIGHTINGALE UK, female vocalist — 16 wks

1 Nov 75	●	RIGHT BACK WHERE WE STARTED FROM United Artists UP 36015	8	8 wks
12 Mar 77		LOVE HIT ME United Artists UP 36215	11	8 wks

NIGHTMARES ON WAX UK, male instrumental group — 5 wks

27 Oct 90	AFTERMATH/I'M FOR REAL Warp WAP 6	38	5 wks

NIGHTWRITERS US, male vocal/instrumental duo — 2 wks

23 May 92	LET THE MUSIC USE YOU Ffrreedom TABX 112	51	2 wks

NILSSON US, male vocalist — 51 wks

27 Sep 69		EVERYBODY'S TALKIN' RCA 1876	50	1 wk
11 Oct 69		EVERYBODY'S TALKIN' (re-entry) RCA 1876	23	9 wks
14 Mar 70		EVERYBODY'S TALKIN' (2nd re-entry) RCA 1876	39	5 wks
5 Feb 72	★	WITHOUT YOU RCA 2165	1	20 wks
3 Jun 72		COCONUT RCA 2214	42	5 wks
16 Oct 76		WITHOUT YOU (re-issue) RCA 2733	22	8 wks
20 Aug 77		ALL I THINK ABOUT IS YOU RCA PB 9104	43	3 wks

NINA and FREDERICK Denmark, female/male vocal duo — 29 wks

18 Dec 59	MARY'S BOY CHILD Columbia DB 4375	26	1 wk
10 Mar 60	LISTEN TO THE OCEAN Columbia DB 4332	47	1 wk
7 Apr 60	LISTEN TO THE OCEAN (re-entry) Columbia DB 4332	46	1 wk

17 Nov 60	●	LITTLE DONKEY Columbia DB 4536	3	10 wks
28 Sep 61		LONGTIME BOY Columbia DB 4703	43	3 wks
5 Oct 61		SUCU SUCU Columbia DB 4632	23	13 wks

NINE INCH NAILS — 6 wks
US, male vocalist/multi-instrumentalist - Trent Reznor

14 Sep 91	HEAD LIKE A HOLE TVT IS 484	45	4 wks
16 Nov 91	SIN TVT IS 508	35	2 wks

999 UK, male vocal/instrumental group — 13 wks

25 Nov 78	HOMICIDE United Artists UP 36467	40	3 wks
27 Oct 79	FOUND OUT TOO LATE Radar ADA 46	69	2 wks
16 May 81	OBSESSED Albion ION 1011	71	1 wk
18 Jul 81	LIL RED RIDING HOOD Albion ION 1017	59	4 wks
14 Nov 81	INDIAN RESERVATION Albion ION 1023	51	4 wks

9.9 US, female/male vocal group — 3 wks

6 Jul 85	ALL OF ME FOR ALL OF YOU RCA PB 49951	53	3 wks

1910 FRUITGUM CO. US, male vocal/instrumental group — 16 wks

20 Mar 68	●	SIMON SAYS Pye International 7N 25447	2	16 wks

1927 Australia, male vocal/instrumental group — 6 wks

22 Apr 89	THAT'S WHEN I THINK OF YOU WEA YZ 351	46	6 wks

NIRVANA UK/Ireland, male vocal/instrumental duo — 6 wks

15 May 68	RAINBOW CHASER Island WIP 6029	34	6 wks

NIRVANA US, male vocal/instrumental group — 20 wks

30 Nov 91	●	SMELLS LIKE TEEN SPIRIT DGC DGCS 5	7	6 wks
14 Mar 92	●	COME AS YOU ARE DGC DGCS 7	9	5 wks
25 Jul 92		LITHIUM DGC DGCS 9	11	6 wks
12 Dec 92		IN BLOOM Geffen GFS 34	28†	3 wks

NITRO DELUXE US, male multi-instrumentalist - — 16 wks
Lee Junior

14 Feb 87	THIS BRUTAL HOUSE Cooltempo COOL 142	47	7 wks
13 Jun 87	THIS BRUTAL HOUSE (re-entry) Cooltempo COOL 142	62	4 wks
6 Feb 88	LET'S GET BRUTAL Cooltempo COOL 142	24	5 wks

Let's Get Brutal is a re-mixed version of This Brutal House.

NITZER EBB UK, male vocal/instrumental group — 2 wks

11 Jan 92	GODHEAD Mute 1MUTE 135T	56	1 wk
11 Apr 92	ASCEND Mute 110MUTE 145	52	1 wk

NO DICE UK, male vocal/instrumental group — 2 wks

5 May 79	COME DANCING EMI 2927	65	2 wks

NO SWEAT Ireland, male vocal/instrumental group — 5 wks

13 Oct 90	HEART AND SOUL London LON 274	64	4 wks
2 Feb 91	TEAR DOWN THE WALLS London LON 288	61	1 wk

NO WAY JOSE US, male instrumental group — 6 wks

3 Aug 85	TEQUILA Fourth & Broadway BRW 28	47	6 wks

NOLANS Ireland, female vocal group — 89 wks

6 Oct 79	SPIRIT BODY AND SOUL Epic EPC 7796 *	34	6 wks
22 Dec 79 ●	I'M IN THE MOOD FOR DANCING Epic EPC 8068	3	15 wks
12 Apr 80	DON'T MAKE WAVES Epic EPC 8349	12	11 wks
13 Sep 80 ●	GOTTA PULL MYSELF TOGETHER Epic EPC 8878	9	13 wks
6 Dec 80	WHO'S GONNA ROCK YOU Epic EPC 9325	12	11 wks
14 Mar 81 ●	ATTENTION TO ME Epic EPC 9571	9	13 wks
15 Aug 81	CHEMISTRY Epic EPC A1485	15	8 wks
20 Feb 82	DON'T LOVE ME TOO HARD Epic EPC A 1927	14	12 wks

* Nolan Sisters

NOMAD UK, male/female vocal/instrumental duo — 20 wks

2 Feb 91 ●	(I WANNA GIVE YOU) DEVOTION Rumour RUMA 25 *	2	10 wks
4 May 91	JUST A GROOVE Rumour RUMA 33	16	6 wks
28 Sep 91	SOMETHING SPECIAL Rumour RUMA 35	73	1 wk
25 Apr 92	YOUR LOVE IS LIFTING ME Rumour RUMA 48	60	2 wks
7 Nov 92	24 HOURS A DAY Rumour RUMA 60	61	1 wk

* Nomad featuring MC Mikee Freedom

Peter NOONE UK, male vocalist — 9 wks

22 May 71	OH YOU PRETTY THING RAK 114	12	9 wks

See also Herman's Hermits.

Ken NORDENE – See Billy VAUGHN

Chris NORMAN – See Suzi QUATRO

NORTHSIDE UK, male vocal/instrumental group — 12 wks

9 Jun 90	SHALL WE TAKE A TRIP/MOODY PLACES Factory FAC 268	50	5 wks
3 Nov 90	MY RISING STAR Factory FAC 2987	32	3 wks
1 Jun 91	TAKE 5 Factory FAC 3087	40	4 wks

Freddie NOTES and the RUDIES — 2 wks
Jamaica, male vocal/instrumental group

10 Oct 70	MONTEGO BAY Trojan TR 7791	45	2 wks

NOTTINGHAM FOREST F.C. and PAPER LACE UK, football team vocalists and male vocal/instrumental group — 6 wks

4 Mar 78	WE'VE GOT THE WHOLE WORLD IN OUR HANDS Warner Bros. K 17110	24	6 wks

See also Paper Lace.

Nancy NOVA UK, female vocalist — 2 wks

4 Sep 82	NO NO NO EMI 5328	63	2 wks

N.T. GANG Germany, male vocal/instrumental group — 1 wk

2 Apr 88	WAM BAM Cooltempo COOL 163	71	1 wk

NU COLOURS UK, male/female vocal/instrumental group — 3 wks

6 Jun 92	TEARS Wild Card CARD 1	55	2 wks
10 Oct 92	POWER Wild Card CARD 3	64	1 wk

NU MATIC UK, male instrumental/production duo — 1 wk

8 Aug 92	SPRING IN MY STEP XL XLS 31	58	1 wk

NU SHOOZ US, male/female vocal duo — 17 wks

24 May 86 ●	I CAN'T WAIT Atlantic A 9446	2	14 wks
26 Jul 86	POINT OF NO RETURN Atlantic A 9392	48	3 wks

NUANCE featuring Vikki LOVE — 3 wks
US, male/female vocal/instrumental group

19 Jan 85	LOVERIDE Fourth & Broadway BRW 20	59	3 wks

NUBIAN PRINZ – See POWERCUT featuring NUBIAN PRINZ

NUFF JUICE – See D MOB

Gary NUMAN UK, male vocalist — 159 wks

19 May 79 ★	ARE 'FRIENDS' ELECTRIC Beggars Banquet BEG 18 *	1	16 wks
1 Sep 79 ★	CARS Beggars Banquet BEG 23	1	11 wks
24 Nov 79 ●	COMPLEX Beggars Banquet BEG 29	6	9 wks
24 May 80 ●	WE ARE GLASS Beggars Banquet BEG 35	5	7 wks
30 Aug 80	I DIE: YOU DIE Beggars Banquet BEG 46	6	7 wks
20 Dec 80	THIS WRECKAGE Beggars Banquet BEG 50	20	7 wks
29 Aug 81 ●	SHE'S GOT CLAWS Beggars Banquet BEG 62	6	6 wks
5 Dec 81	LOVE NEEDS NO DISGUISE Beggars Banquet BEG 68 **	33	7 wks
6 Mar 82	MUSIC FOR CHAMELEONS Beggars Banquet BEG 70	19	7 wks
19 Jun 82 ●	WE TAKE MYSTERY (TO BED) Beggars Banquet BEG 77	9	4 wks
28 Aug 82	WHITE BOYS AND HEROES Beggars Banquet BEG 81	20	4 wks
3 Sep 83	WARRIORS Beggars Banquet BEG 95	20	5 wks
22 Oct 83	SISTER SURPRISE Beggars Banquet BEG 101	32	3 wks
3 Nov 84	BERSERKER Numa NU 4	32	5 wks
22 Dec 84	MY DYING MACHINE Numa NU 6	66	1 wk
9 Feb 85	CHANGE YOUR MIND Polydor POSP 722 ***	17	8 wks
25 May 85	THE LIVE EP Numa NUM 7	27	4 wks
10 Aug 85	YOUR FASCINATION Numa NU 9	46	5 wks
21 Sep 85	CALL OUT THE DOGS Numa NU 11	49	2 wks
16 Nov 85	MIRACLES Numa NU 13	49	3 wks
19 Apr 86	THIS IS LOVE Numa NU 16	28	3 wks
28 Jun 86	I CAN'T STOP Numa NU 17	27	4 wks
4 Oct 86	NEW THING FROM LONDON TOWN Numa NU 19 ***	52	3 wks
6 Dec 86	I STILL REMEMBER Numa NU 21	74	1 wk
28 Mar 87	RADIO HEART GFM GFM 109 ****	35	6 wks
13 Jun 87	LONDON TIMES GFM GFM 112 ****	48	2 wks
19 Sep 87	CARS (E REG MODEL)/ARE 'FRIENDS' ELECTRIC (re-mixes) Beggars Banquet BEG 199	16	7 wks
30 Jan 88	NO MORE LIES Polydor POSP 894 ***	34	3 wks
1 Oct 88	NEW ANGER Illegal ILS 1003	46	2 wks
3 Dec 88	AMERICA Illegal ILS 1004	49	1 wk
3 Jun 89	I'M ON AUTOMATIC Polydor PO 43 ***	44	2 wks
16 Mar 91	HEART IRS NUMAN 1	43	2 wks
21 Mar 92	THE SKIN GAME Numa NU 23	68	1 wk
1 Aug 92	MACHINE + SOUL Numa NUM 124	72	1 wk

* Tubeway Army ** Gary Numan and Dramatis *** Sharpe and Numan
**** Radio Heart featuring Gary Numan

Tracks on The Live EP: Are 'Friends' Electric/Berserker/Cars/We Are Glass. See also Paul Gardiner.

Bobby NUNN US, male vocalist/multi-instrumentalist — 3 wks

4 Feb 84	DON'T KNOCK IT (UNTIL YOU TRY IT) Motown TMG 1323	65	3 wks

N.W.A. US, male rap group — 15 wks

9 Sep 89	EXPRESS YOURSELF Fourth & Broadway BRW 144	50	4 wks
26 May 90	EXPRESS YOURSELF (re-entry) Fourth & Broadway BRW 144	26	5 wks
1 Sep 90	GANGSTA, GANGSTA Fourth & Broadway BRW 191	70	1 wk
10 Nov 90	100 MILES AND RUNNIN' Fourth & Broadway BRW 200	38	3 wks
23 Nov 91	ALWAYZ INTO SOMETHIN' Fourth & Broadway BRW 238	60	2 wks

Joe NYE – See DNA

Phil OAKEY – See Giorgio MORODER

John OATES – See Daryl HALL and John OATES

OBERNKIRCHEN CHILDREN'S CHOIR — 26 wks
Germany, children's choir

22 Jan 54 ●	HAPPY WANDERER Parlophone R 3799	2	23 wks
9 Jul 54 ●	HAPPY WANDERER (re-entry) Parlophone R 3799	8	3 wks

Dermot O'BRIEN Ireland, male vocalist — 2 wks

20 Oct 66	THE MERRY PLOUGHBOY Envoy ENV 016	46	1 wk
3 Nov 66	THE MERRY PLOUGHBOY (re-entry) Envoy ENV 016	50	1 wk

Billy OCEAN UK, male vocalist — 151 wks

21 Feb 76 ●	LOVE REALLY HURTS WITHOUT YOU GTO GT 52	2	10 wks
10 Jul 76	L.O.D. (LOVE ON DELIVERY) GTO GT 62	19	8 wks
13 Nov 76	STOP ME (IF YOU'VE HEARD IT ALL BEFORE) GTO GT 72	12	11 wks
19 Mar 77 ●	RED LIGHT SPELLS DANGER GTO GT 85	2	10 wks
1 Sep 79	AMERICAN HEARTS GTO GT 244	54	5 wks
19 Jan 80	ARE YOU READY GTO GT 259	42	7 wks
13 Oct 84 ●	CARIBBEAN QUEEN (NO MORE LOVE ON THE RUN) Jive JIVE 77	6	14 wks
19 Jan 85	LOVERBOY Jive JIVE 80	15	10 wks
11 May 85 ●	SUDDENLY Jive JIVE 90	4	14 wks
17 Aug 85	MYSTERY LADY Jive JIVE 98	49	4 wks
25 Jan 86 ★	WHEN THE GOING GETS TOUGH, THE TOUGH GET GOING Jive JIVE 114	1	13 wks
12 Apr 86	THERE'LL BE SAD SONGS (TO MAKE YOU CRY) Jive JIVE 117	12	13 wks
9 Aug 86	LOVE ZONE Jive JIVE 124	49	3 wks
11 Oct 86	BITTERSWEET Jive JIVE 133	44	4 wks
10 Jan 87	LOVE IS FOREVER Jive JIVE 134	34	7 wks
6 Feb 88 ●	GET OUTTA MY DREAMS GET INTO MY CAR Jive BOS 1	3	11 wks
7 May 88	CALYPSO CRAZY Jive BOS 2	35	4 wks
6 Aug 88	THE COLOUR OF LOVE Jive BOS 3	65	3 wks

OCEAN COLOUR SCENE — 1 wk
UK, male vocal/instrumental group

23 Mar 91	YESTERDAY TODAY !Phfft FIT 2	49	1 wk

OCEANIC UK, male/female vocal/instrumental group — 26 wks

24 Aug 91 ●	INSANITY Dead Dead Good GOOD 4	3	15 wks
30 Nov 91	WICKED LOVE Dead Dead Good GOOD 5	25	3 wks
28 Dec 91	WICKED LOVE (re-entry) Dead Dead Good GOOD 5	65	2 wks
13 Jun 92	CONTROLLING ME Dead Dead Good GOOD 14	14	5 wks
14 Nov 92	IGNORANCE Dead Dead Good GOOD 22 *	72	1 wk

* Oceanic featuring Siobhan Maher

Des O'CONNOR UK, male vocalist — 117 wks

1 Nov 67 ●	CARELESS HANDS Columbia DB 8275	6	17 wks
8 May 68 ★	I PRETEND Columbia DB 8397	1	36 wks
20 Nov 68	1-2-3 O'LEARY Columbia DB 8492	4	11 wks
7 May 69	DICK-A-DUM-DUM (KING'S ROAD) Columbia DB 8566	14	10 wks
29 Nov 69	LONELINESS Columbia DB 8632	18	11 wks
14 Mar 70	I'LL GO ON HOPING Columbia DB 8661	30	7 wks
26 Sep 70	THE TIPS OF MY FINGERS Columbia DB 8713	15	15 wks
8 Nov 86 ●	THE SKYE BOAT SONG Tembo TML 119 *	10	10 wks

* Roger Whittaker and Des O'Connor

Hazel O'CONNOR UK, female vocalist — 46 wks

16 Aug 80 ●	EIGHTH DAY A & M AMS 7553	5	11 wks
25 Oct 80	GIVE ME AN INCH A & M AMS 7569	41	4 wks
21 Mar 81 ●	D-DAYS Albion ION 1009	10	9 wks
23 May 81 ●	WILL YOU A & M AMS 8131	8	10 wks
1 Aug 81	(COVER PLUS) WE'RE ALL GROWN UP Albion ION 1018	41	6 wks
3 Oct 81	HANGING AROUND Albion ION 1022	45	3 wks
23 Jan 82	CALLS THE TUNE A & M AMS 8203	60	3 wks

Sinead O'CONNOR Ireland, female vocalist — 46 wks

16 Jan 88	MANDINKA Ensign ENY 611	17	9 wks
20 Jan 90 ★	NOTHING COMPARES 2 U Ensign ENY 630	1	14 wks
21 Jul 90	THE EMPEROR'S NEW CLOTHES Ensign ENY 633	31	5 wks
20 Oct 90	THREE BABIES Ensign ENY 635	42	4 wks
8 Jun 91	MY SPECIAL CHILD Ensign ENY 646	42	4 wks
14 Dec 91	SILENT NIGHT Ensign ENY 652	60	4 wks
12 Sep 92	SUCCESS HAS MADE A FAILURE OF OUR HOME Ensign ENY 656	18	4 wks
12 Dec 92	DON'T CRY FOR ME ARGENTINA Ensign ENY 657	53†	3 wks

See also Jah Wobble's Invaders Of The Heart.

Alan O'DAY US, male vocalist — 3 wks

2 Jul 77	UNDERCOVER ANGEL Atlantic K 10926	43	3 wks

ODETTA – See Harry BELAFONTE

Daniel O'DONNELL Ireland, male vocalist — 7 wks

12 Sep 92	I JUST WANT TO DANCE WITH YOU Ritz RITZ 250P	20	7 wks

ODYSSEY US, male/female vocal group   82 wks

24 Dec 77	● NATIVE NEW YORKER RCA PC 1129	5	11 wks
21 Jun 80	★ USE IT UP AND WEAR IT OUT RCA PB 1962	1	12 wks
13 Sep 80	● IF YOU'RE LOOKIN' FOR A WAY OUT RCA 5	6	15 wks
17 Jan 81	HANG TOGETHER RCA 23	36	7 wks
30 May 81	● GOING BACK TO MY ROOTS RCA 85	4	12 wks
19 Sep 81	IT WILL BE ALRIGHT RCA 128	43	5 wks
12 Jun 82	● INSIDE OUT RCA 226	3	11 wks
11 Sep 82	MAGIC TOUCH RCA 275	41	5 wks
17 Aug 85	(JOY) I KNOW IT Mirror BUTCH 12	51	4 wks

Esther and Abi OFARIM Israel, female/male vocal duo   22 wks

14 Feb 68	★ CINDERELLA ROCKEFELLA Philips BF 1640	1	13 wks
19 Jun 68	ONE MORE DANCE Philips BF 1678	13	9 wks

OFF-SHORE Germany, male instrumental/production duo   12 wks

22 Dec 90	● I CAN'T TAKE THE POWER CBS 6565707	7	11 wks
17 Aug 91	I GOT A LITTLE SONG Dance Pool 6568257	64	1 wk

Wiston OFFICE – See Frank K featuring Wiston OFFICE

OH WELL Germany, male producer - Ackim Faulker   7 wks

14 Oct 89	OH WELL Parlophone R 6236	28	6 wks
3 Mar 90	RADAR LOVE Parlophone R 6244	65	1 wk

OHIO EXPRESS US, male vocal/instrumental group   15 wks

5 Jun 68	● YUMMY YUMMY YUMMY Pye International 7N 25459	5	15 wks

OHIO PLAYERS US, male vocal/instrumental group   4 wks

10 Jul 76	WHO'D SHE COO Mercury PLAY 001	43	4 wks

O'JAYS US, male vocal group   72 wks

23 Sep 72	BACK STABBERS CBS 8270	14	9 wks
3 Mar 73	● LOVE TRAIN CBS 1181	9	13 wks
31 Jan 76	I LOVE MUSIC Philadelphia International PIR 3879	13	9 wks
12 Feb 77	DARLIN' DARLIN' BABY (SWEET, TENDER, LOVE) Philadelphia International PIR 4834	24	6 wks
8 Apr 78	I LOVE MUSIC (re-issue) Philadelphia International PIR 6093	36	3 wks
17 Jun 78	USED TA BE MY GIRL Philadelphia International PIR 6332	12	12 wks
30 Sep 78	BRANDY Philadelphia International PIR 6658	21	9 wks
29 Sep 79	SING A HAPPY SONG Philadelphia International PIR 7825	39	6 wks
30 Jul 83	PUT OUR HEADS TOGETHER Philadelphia International A 3642	45	5 wks

John O'KANE UK, male vocalist   4 wks

9 May 92	STAY WITH ME Circa YR 88	41	4 wks

Mike OLDFIELD UK, male multi-instrumentalist/vocalist   100 wks

13 Jul 74	MIKE OLDFIELD'S SINGLE (THEME FROM TUBULAR BELLS) Virgin VS 101	31	6 wks
20 Dec 75	● IN DULCE JUBILO/ON HORSEBACK Virgin VS 131	4	10 wks
27 Nov 76	● PORTSMOUTH Virgin VS 163	3	12 wks
23 Dec 78	TAKE 4 EP Virgin VS 238	72	3 wks
21 Apr 79	GUILTY Virgin VS 245	22	8 wks
8 Dec 79	BLUE PETER Virgin VS 317	19	9 wks
20 Mar 82	FIVE MILES OUT Virgin VS 464 *	43	5 wks
12 Jun 82	FAMILY MAN Virgin VS 489 *	45	6 wks
28 May 83	● MOONLIGHT SHADOW Virgin VS 586 *	4	17 wks
14 Jan 84	CRIME OF PASSION Virgin VS 648 *	61	3 wks
30 Jun 84	TO FRANCE Virgin VS 686 *	48	7 wks
14 Dec 85	PICTURES IN THE DARK Virgin VS 836 **	50	6 wks
3 Oct 92	● SENTINEL WEA YZ 698	10	6 wks
19 Dec 92	TATTOO WEA YZ 708	33†	2 wks

* Mike Oldfield featuring Maggie Reilly ** Mike Oldfield featuring Aled Jones, Anita Hegerland and Barry Palmer

Tracks on Take 4 EP: Portsmouth/In Dulce Jubilo/Wrekorder Wrondo/Sailors Hornpipe.

Sally OLDFIELD UK, female vocalist   13 wks

9 Dec 78	MIRRORS Bronze BRO 66	19	13 wks

OLIVER US, male vocalist   18 wks

9 Aug 69	● GOOD MORNING STARSHINE CBS 4435	6	16 wks
27 Dec 69	GOOD MORNING STARSHINE (re-entry) CBS 4435	39	2 wks

OLLIE and JERRY US, male vocal duo   14 wks

23 Jun 84	● BREAKIN'...THERE'S NO STOPPING US Polydor POSP 690	5	11 wks
9 Mar 85	ELECTRIC BOOGALOO Polydor POSP 730	57	3 wks

OLYMPIC ORCHESTRA UK, orchestra   15 wks

1 Oct 83	REILLY Red Bus RBUS 82	26	15 wks

OLYMPIC RUNNERS UK, male vocal/instrumental group   21 wks

13 May 78	WHATEVER IT TAKES RCA PC 5078	61	2 wks
14 Oct 78	GET IT WHILE YOU CAN Polydor RUN 7	35	6 wks
20 Jan 79	SIR DANCEALOT Polydor POSP 17	35	6 wks
28 Jul 79	THE BITCH Polydor POSP 63	37	7 wks

OLYMPICS US, male vocal group   9 wks

3 Oct 58	WESTERN MOVIES HMV POP 528	12	8 wks
19 Jan 61	I WISH I COULD SHIMMY LIKE MY SISTER KATE Vogue V 9174	40	1 wk

OMAR UK, male vocalist   11 wks

22 Jun 91	THERE'S NOTHING LIKE THIS Talkin Loud TLK 9	14	7 wks
23 May 92	YOUR LOSS MY GAIN Talkin Loud TLK 22	47	2 wks
26 Sep 92	MUSIC Talkin Loud TLK 28	53	2 wks

OMD – See ORCHESTRAL MANOEUVRES IN THE DARK

ONE HUNDRED TON AND A FEATHER – See Jonathan KING

ONE THE JUGGLER UK, male vocal/instrumental group   1 wk

19 Feb 83	PASSION KILLER Regard RG 107	71	1 wk

ONE TRIBE featuring GEM   2 wks
UK, male/female vocal/instrumental duo

20 Jun 92	WHAT HAVE YOU DONE (IS THIS ALL) Inner Rhythm HEART 03	52	2 wks

ONE 2 MANY *Norway, male/female vocal/instrumental group* **11 wks**

| 12 Nov 88 | DOWNTOWN *A & M AM 476* | 65 | 4 wks |
| 3 Jun 89 | DOWNTOWN (re-issue) *A & M AM 456* | 43 | 7 wks |

ONE WAY featuring Al HUDSON – *See Al HUDSON*

Alexander O'NEAL *US, male vocalist* **96 wks**

28 Dec 85 ●	SATURDAY LOVE *Tabu A 6829 *	6	11 wks
15 Feb 86	IF YOU WERE HERE TONIGHT *Tabu A 6391*	13	10 wks
5 Apr 86	A BROKEN HEART CAN MEND *Tabu A 6244*	53	4 wks
6 Jun 87	FAKE *Tabu 650891 7*	33	6 wks
31 Oct 87 ●	CRITICIZE *Tabu 651211 7*	4	14 wks
6 Feb 88	NEVER KNEW LOVE LIKE THIS *Tabu 651382 7 **	26	7 wks
28 May 88	THE LOVERS *Tabu 651595 7*	28	4 wks
23 Jul 88	(WHAT CAN I SAY) TO MAKE YOU LOVE ME *Tabu 652852 7*	27	5 wks
24 Sep 88	FAKE '88 (re-mix) *Tabu 652949 7*	16	7 wks
10 Dec 88	CHRISTMAS SONG/THANK YOU FOR A GOOD YEAR *Tabu 653182 7*	30	5 wks
25 Feb 89	HEARSAY '89 *Tabu 654466 7*	56	2 wks
2 Sep 89	SUNSHINE *Tabu 655191 7*	72	1 wk
9 Dec 89	HITMIX (OFFICIAL BOOTLEG MEGA-MIX) *Tabu 655504 7*	19	7 wks
24 Mar 90	SATURDAY LOVE (re-mix) *Tabu 655680 7 *	55	2 wks
12 Jan 91	ALL TRUE MAN *Tabu 6565717*	18	6 wks
23 Mar 91	WHAT IS THIS THING CALLED LOVE *Tabu 6567317*	53	2 wks
11 May 91	SHAME ON ME *Tabu 6568737*	71	1 wk
9 May 92	SENTIMENTAL *Tabu 6580147*	53	2 wks

* Cherelle with Alexander O'Neal ** Alexander O'Neal featuring Cherelle

ONLY ONES *UK, male vocal/instrumental group* **2 wks**

| 1 Feb 92 | ANOTHER GIRL - ANOTHER PLANET *Columbia 6577507* | 57 | 2 wks |

Yoko ONO *Japan, female vocalist* **5 wks**

| 28 Feb 81 | WALKING ON THIN ICE *Geffen K 79202* | 35 | 5 wks |

See also John Lennon.

ONSLAUGHT *UK, male vocal/instrumental group* **3 wks**

| 6 May 89 | LET THERE BE ROCK *London LON 224* | 50 | 3 wks |

OO LA LA *UK, male vocal/instrumental group* **2 wks**

| 5 Sep 92 | OO...AH...CANTONA *North Speed OOAH 1* | 64 | 2 wks |

OPUS *Austria, male vocal/instrumental group* **15 wks**

| 15 Jun 85 ● | LIVE IS LIFE *Polydor POSP 743* | 6 | 15 wks |

OPUS III *UK, male/female vocal/instrumental group* **9 wks**

| 22 Feb 92 ● | IT'S A FINE DAY *PWL International PWL 215* | 5 | 8 wks |
| 27 Jun 92 | I TALK TO THE WIND *PWL Continental PWL 235* | 52 | 1 wk |

ORANGE JUICE *UK, male vocal/instrumental group* **34 wks**

7 Nov 81	L.O.V.E...LOVE *Polydor POSP 357*	65	2 wks
30 Jan 82	FELICITY *Polydor POSP 386*	63	3 wks
21 Aug 82	TWO HEARTS TOGETHER/HOKOYO *Polydor POSP 470*	60	2 wks

23 Oct 82	I CAN'T HELP MYSELF *Polydor POSP 522*	42	3 wks
19 Feb 83 ●	RIP IT UP *Polydor POSP 547*	8	11 wks
4 Jun 83	FLESH OF MY FLESH *Polydor OJ 4*	41	6 wks
25 Feb 84	BRIDGE *Polydor OJ 5*	67	2 wks
12 May 84	WHAT PRESENCE? *Polydor OJ 6*	47	4 wks
27 Oct 84	LEAN PERIOD *Polydor OJ 7*	74	1 wk

ORB *UK, male instrumental/production duo* **12 wks**

15 Jun 91	PERPETUAL DAWN *Big Life BLR 46*	61	1 wk
20 Jun 92 ●	BLUE ROOM *Big Life BLRT 75*	8	6 wks
17 Oct 92	ASSASSIN *Big Life BLRT 81*	12	5 wks

Roy ORBISON *US, male vocalist* **343 wks**

28 Jul 60	ONLY THE LONELY *London HLU 9149*	36	1 wk
11 Aug 60 ★	ONLY THE LONELY (re-entry) *London HLU 9149*	1	23 wks
27 Oct 60	BLUE ANGEL *London HLU 9207*	11	16 wks
25 May 61 ●	RUNNING SCARED *London HLU 9342*	9	15 wks
21 Sep 61	CRYIN' *London HLU 9405*	25	9 wks
8 Mar 62 ●	DREAM BABY *London HLU 9511*	2	14 wks
28 Jun 62	THE CROWD *London HLU 9561*	40	4 wks
8 Nov 62	WORKIN' FOR THE MAN *London HLU 9607*	50	1 wk
28 Feb 63 ●	IN DREAMS *London HLU 9676*	6	23 wks
30 May 63 ●	FALLING *London HLU 9727*	9	11 wks
19 Sep 63	BLUE BAYOU/MEAN WOMAN BLUES *London HLU 9777*	3	19 wks
20 Feb 64	BORNE ON THE WIND *London HLU 9845*	15	10 wks
30 Apr 64 ★	IT'S OVER *London HLU 9882*	1	18 wks
10 Sep 64 ★	OH PRETTY WOMAN *London HLU 9919*	1	18 wks
19 Nov 64	PRETTY PAPER *London HLU 9930*	6	11 wks
11 Feb 65	GOODNIGHT *London HLU 9951*	14	9 wks
22 Jul 65	(SAY) YOU'RE MY GIRL *London HLU 9978*	23	8 wks
9 Sep 65	RIDE AWAY *London HLU 9986*	34	6 wks
4 Nov 65	CRAWLIN' BACK *London HLU 10000*	19	9 wks
27 Jan 66	BREAKIN' UP IS BREAKIN' MY HEART *London HL 10015*	22	6 wks
7 Apr 66	TWINKLE TOES *London HLU 10034*	29	5 wks
16 Jun 66	LANA *London HL 10051*	15	9 wks
18 Aug 66 ●	TOO SOON TO KNOW *London HLU 10067*	3	17 wks
1 Dec 66	THERE WON'T BE MANY COMING HOME *London HL 10096*	18	9 wks
23 Feb 67	SO GOOD *London HL 10113*	32	6 wks
24 Jul 68	WALK ON *London HLU 10206*	39	10 wks
25 Sep 68	HEARTACHE *London HLU 10222*	44	4 wks
30 Apr 69	MY FRIEND *London HL 10261*	35	4 wks
13 Sep 69	PENNY ARCADE *London HL 10285*	40	3 wks
11 Oct 69	PENNY ARCADE (re-entry) *London HL 10285*	27	11 wks
14 Jan 89 ●	YOU GOT IT *Virgin VS 1166*	3	10 wks
1 Apr 89	SHE'S A MYSTERY TO ME *Virgin VS 1173*	27	5 wks
4 Jul 92 ●	I DROVE ALL NIGHT *MCA MCS 1652*	7	10 wks
22 Aug 92	CRYING *Virgin America VUS 63 *	13	6 wks
7 Nov 92	HEARTBREAK RADIO *Virgin America VUS 68*	36	3 wks

* Roy Orbison (duet with k.d. lang)

ORBITAL *UK, male instrumental duo* **19 wks**

24 Mar 90	CHIME *ffrr F B5*	17	7 wks
22 Sep 90	OMEN *ffrr F 145*	46	3 wks
19 Jan 91	SATAN *ffrr FX 149*	31	4 wks
15 Feb 92	MUTATIONS EP *ffrr FX 181*	24	3 wks
26 Sep 92	RADICCIO EP *Internal LIARX 1*	37	2 wks

Tracks on Mutations EP: *Chime Chime/Oolaa/Farenheit 3D 3/Speed Freak. Tracks on* Radiccio EP: *Halcyon/The Naked And The Dead/Sunday.*

ORCHESTRA ON THE HALF SHELL **9 wks**
US, male vocal/instrumental group

| 15 Dec 90 | TURTLE RHAPSODY *SBK SBK 17* | 36 | 9 wks |

ROY ORBISON steps into the spotlight on the 1960s television show *Thank Your Lucky Stars*.

Andy McCluskey is the last remaining original member of ORCHESTRAL MANOEUVRES IN THE DARK.

The full name of OLIVER was William Oliver Swofford.

THE O'JAYS had more hits than any other act on the Philadelphia International label.

ORCHESTRAL MANOEUVRES IN THE DARK UK, male vocal/instrumental group   182 wks

9 Feb 80	RED FRAME WHITE LIGHT Dindisc DIN 6	67	2 wks
10 May 80	MESSAGES Dindisc DIN 15	13	11 wks
4 Oct 80 ●	ENOLA GAY Dindisc DIN 22	8	15 wks
29 Aug 81 ●	SOUVENIR Dindisc DIN 24	3	12 wks
24 Oct 81 ●	JOAN OF ARC Dindisc DIN 36	5	14 wks
23 Jan 82 ●	MAID OF ORLEANS (THE WALTZ JOAN OF ARC) Dindisc DIN 40	4	10 wks
19 Feb 83	GENETIC ENGINEERING Virgin VS 527	20	8 wks
9 Apr 83	TELEGRAPH Virgin VS 580	42	4 wks
14 Apr 84 ●	LOCOMOTION Virgin VS 660	5	11 wks
16 Jun 84	TALKING LOUD AND CLEAR Virgin VS 685	11	10 wks
8 Sep 84	TESLA GIRLS Virgin VS 705	21	8 wks
10 Nov 84	NEVER TURN AWAY Virgin VS 727	70	2 wks
25 May 85	SO IN LOVE Virgin VS 766	27	7 wks
20 Jul 85	SECRET Virgin VS 796	34	7 wks
26 Oct 85	LA FEMME ACCIDENT Virgin VS 811	42	4 wks
3 May 86	IF YOU LEAVE Virgin VS 843	48	4 wks
6 Sep 86	(FOREVER) LIVE AND DIE Virgin VS 888	11	10 wks
15 Nov 86	WE LOVE YOU Virgin VS 911	54	5 wks
2 May 87	SHAME Virgin VS 938	52	3 wks
6 Feb 88	DREAMING Virgin VS 987	50	3 wks
2 Jul 88	DREAMING (re-entry) Virgin VS 987	60	3 wks
30 Mar 91 ●	SAILING ON THE SEVEN SEAS Virgin VS 1310	3	13 wks
6 Jul 91 ●	PANDORA'S BOX Virgin VS 1331	7	10 wks
14 Sep 91	THEN YOU TURN AWAY Virgin VS 1368	50	4 wks
7 Dec 91	CALL MY NAME Virgin VS 1380	50	2 wks

Group often known as OMD.

ORCHESTRE DE CHAMBRE Jean-Francois PAILLARD France, male conductor and orchestra   3 wks

20 Aug 88	THEME FROM 'VIETNAM'(CANON IN D) Debut DEBT 3053	61	3 wks

Raul ORELLANA Italy, male producer   8 wks

30 Sep 89	THE REAL WILD HOUSE RCA BCM 322	29	8 wks

Tony ORLANDO US, male vocalist   11 wks

5 Oct 61 ●	BLESS YOU Fontana H 330	5	11 wks

See also Dawn.

ORLONS US, female/male vocal group   3 wks

27 Dec 62	DON'T HANG UP Cameo Parkway C 231	50	1 wk
10 Jan 63	DON'T HANG UP (re-entry) Cameo Parkway C 231	39	2 wks

ORVILLE – See Keith HARRIS

Jeffrey OSBORNE US, male vocalist   38 wks

17 Sep 83	DON'T YOU GET SO MAD A & M AM 140	54	2 wks
14 Apr 84	STAY WITH ME TONIGHT A & M AM 188	18	11 wks
23 Jun 84	ON THE WINGS OF LOVE A & M AM 198	11	14 wks
20 Oct 84	DON'T STOP A & M AM 222	61	2 wks
26 Jul 86	SOWETO A & M AM 334	44	5 wks
6 Sep 86	SOWETO (re-entry) A & M AM 334	75	1 wk
15 Aug 87	LOVE POWER Arista RIS 27 *	63	3 wks

* Dionne Warwick and Jeffrey Osborne

Tony OSBORNE SOUND UK, orchestra   3 wks

23 Feb 61	MAN FROM MADRID HMV POP 827 *	50	1 wk
3 Feb 73	THE SHEPHERD'S SONG Philips 6006 266	46	2 wks

* Tony Osborne Sound featuring Joanne Brown

Ozzy OSBOURNE UK, male vocalist   39 wks

13 Sep 80	CRAZY TRAIN Jet 197 *	49	4 wks
15 Nov 80	MR. CROWLEY Jet 7003 *	46	3 wks
26 Nov 83	BARK AT THE MOON Epic A 3915	21	8 wks
2 Jun 84	SO TIRED Epic A 4452	20	9 wks
1 Feb 86	SHOT IN THE DARK Epic A 6859	20	6 wks
9 Aug 86	THE ULTIMATE SIN/LIGHTNING STRIKES Epic A 7311	72	1 wk
20 May 89	CLOSE MY EYES FOREVER Dreamland PB 49409 **	47	3 wks
28 Sep 91	NO MORE TEARS Epic 6574407	32	3 wks
30 Nov 91	MAMA I'M COMING HOME Epic 6576177	46	2 wks

* Ozzy Osbourne's Blizzard of Ozz ** Lita Ford duet with Ozzy Osbourne

OSIBISA Ghana/Nigeria, male vocal/instrumental group   12 wks

17 Jan 76	SUNSHINE DAY Bronze BRO 20	17	6 wks
5 Jun 76	DANCE THE BODY MUSIC Bronze BRO 26	31	6 wks

OSMOND BOYS US, male vocal group   6 wks

9 Nov 91	BOYS WILL BE BOYS Curb 6573847	65	2 wks
11 Jan 92	SHOW ME THE WAY Curb 6577227	60	4 wks

Donny OSMOND US, male vocalist   118 wks

17 Jun 72 ★	PUPPY LOVE MGM 2006 104	1	17 wks
16 Sep 72 ●	TOO YOUNG MGM 2006 113	5	12 wks
21 Oct 72	PUPPY LOVE (re-entry) MGM 2006 104	45	2 wks
11 Nov 72 ●	WHY MGM 2006 119	3	20 wks
23 Dec 72	PUPPY LOVE (2nd re-entry) MGM 2006 104	46	3 wks
23 Dec 72	TOO YOUNG (re-entry) MGM 2006 113	47	3 wks
27 Jan 73	PUPPY LOVE (3rd re-entry) MGM 2006 104	48	1 wk
10 Mar 73 ★	THE TWELFTH OF NEVER MGM 2006 199	1	14 wks
18 Aug 73 ★	YOUNG LOVE MGM 2006 300	1	10 wks
10 Nov 73 ●	WHEN I FALL IN LOVE MGM 2006 365	4	13 wks
9 Nov 74	WHERE DID ALL THE GOOD TIMES GO MGM 2006 468	18	10 wks
26 Sep 87	I'M IN IT FOR LOVE Virgin VS 994	70	1 wk
6 Aug 88	SOLDIER OF LOVE Virgin VS 1094	29	8 wks
12 Nov 88	IF IT'S LOVE THAT YOU WANT Virgin VS 1140	70	2 wks
9 Feb 91	MY LOVE IS A FIRE Capitol CL 600	64	2 wks

See also Donny and Marie Osmond; Osmonds.

Donny and Marie OSMOND   37 wks
US, male/female vocal duo

3 Aug 74 ●	I'M LEAVING IT (ALL) UP TO YOU MGM 2006 446	2	12 wks
14 Dec 74 ●	MORNING SIDE OF THE MOUNTAIN MGM 2006 274	5	12 wks
21 Jun 75	MAKE THE WORLD GO AWAY MGM 2006 523	18	6 wks
17 Jan 76	DEEP PURPLE MGM 2006 561	25	7 wks

See also Donny Osmond; Marie Osmond.

Little Jimmy OSMOND US, male vocalist   50 wks

25 Nov 72 ★	LONG HAIRED LOVER FROM LIVERPOOL MGM 2006 109	1	24 wks
31 Mar 73 ●	TWEEDLE DEE MGM 2006 175	4	13 wks
19 May 73	LONG HAIRED LOVER FROM LIVERPOOL (re-entry) MGM 2006 109	41	3 wks
23 Mar 74	I'M GONNA KNOCK ON YOUR DOOR MGM 2006 389	11	10 wks

Marie OSMOND *US, female vocalist* **15 wks**

17 Nov 73 ●	PAPER ROSES *MGM 2006 315*	2	15 wks

See also Donny and Marie Osmond.

OSMONDS *US, male vocal/instrumental group* **91 wks**

25 Mar 72	DOWN BY THE LAZY RIVER *MGM 2006 096*	40	5 wks
11 Nov 72 ●	CRAZY HORSES *MGM 2006 142*	2	18 wks
14 Jul 73 ●	GOING HOME *MGM 2006 288*	4	10 wks
27 Oct 73 ●	LET ME IN *MGM 2006 321*	2	14 wks
20 Apr 74	I CAN'T STOP *MCA 129*	12	10 wks
24 Aug 74 ★	LOVE ME FOR A REASON *MGM 2006 458*	1	9 wks
1 Mar 75	HAVING A PARTY *MGM 2006 492*	28	8 wks
24 May 75 ●	THE PROUD ONE *MGM 2006 520*	5	8 wks
15 Nov 75	I'M STILL GONNA NEED YOU *MGM 2006 551*	32	4 wks
30 Oct 76	I CAN'T LIVE A DREAM *Polydor 2066 726*	37	5 wks

Gilbert O'SULLIVAN *Ireland, male vocalist* **145 wks**

28 Nov 70 ●	NOTHING RHYMED *MAM 3*	8	11 wks
3 Apr 71	UNDERNEATH THE BLANKET GO *MAM 13*	40	1 wk
17 Apr 71	UNDERNEATH THE BLANKET GO (re-entry) *MAM 13*	42	3 wks
24 Jul 71	WE WILL *MAM 30*	16	11 wks
27 Nov 71 ●	NO MATTER HOW I TRY *MAM 53*	5	15 wks
4 Mar 72 ●	ALONE AGAIN (NATURALLY) *MAM 66*	3	12 wks
17 Jun 72 ●	OOH-WAKKA-DOO-WAKKA-DAY *MAM 78*	8	11 wks
21 Oct 72 ★	CLAIR *MAM 84*	1	14 wks
17 Mar 73 ★	GET DOWN *MAM 96*	1	13 wks
15 Sep 73	OOH BABY *MAM 107*	18	7 wks
10 Nov 73 ●	WHY OH WHY OH WHY *MAM 111*	6	14 wks
9 Feb 74	HAPPINESS IS ME AND YOU *MAM 114*	19	7 wks
24 Aug 74	A WOMAN'S PLACE *MAM 122*	42	3 wks
14 Dec 74	CHRISTMAS SONG *MAM 124*	12	6 wks
14 Jun 75	I DON'T LOVE YOU BUT I THINK I LIKE YOU *MAM 130*	14	6 wks
27 Sep 80	WHAT'S IN A KISS? *CBS 8929*	19	9 wks
24 Feb 90	SO WHAT *Dover ROJ 3*	70	2 wks

OTHER TWO *UK, male/female vocal/instrumental duo* **3 wks**

9 Nov 91	TASTY FISH *Factory FAC 3297*	41	3 wks

Johnny OTIS SHOW *US, orchestra and chorus* **22 wks**

22 Nov 57 ●	MA HE'S MAKING EYES AT ME *Capitol CL 14794* *	2	15 wks
10 Jan 58	BYE BYE BABY *Capitol CL 14817* **	20	7 wks

*Johnny Otis and his orchestra with Marie Adams and the Three Tons of Joy
**Johnny Otis Show, vocals by Marie Adams and Johnny Otis

OTTAWAN *France, male/female vocal duo* **45 wks**

13 Sep 80 ●	D.I.S.C.O. *Carrere CAR 161*	2	18 wks
13 Dec 80	YOU'RE O.K. *Carrere CAR 168*	56	6 wks
29 Aug 81 ●	HANDS UP (GIVE ME YOUR HEART) *Carrere CAR 183*	3	15 wks
5 Dec 81	HELP, GET ME SOME HELP! *Carrere CAR 215*	49	6 wks

John OTWAY and Wild Willy BARRETT **12 wks**
UK, male vocal/instrumental duo

3 Dec 77	REALLY FREE *Polydor 2058 951*	27	8 wks
5 Jul 80	DK 50-80 *Polydor 2059 250* *	45	4 wks

* Otway and Barrett

OUR DAUGHTER'S WEDDING **6 wks**
US, male vocal/instrumental group

1 Aug 81	LAWNCHAIRS *EMI America EA 124*	49	6 wks

OUR KID *UK, male vocal group* **11 wks**

29 May 76 ●	YOU JUST MIGHT SEE ME CRY *Polydor 2058 729*	2	11 wks

OUTLANDER *Belgium, male producer - Marcos Salon* **2 wks**

31 Aug 91	VAMP *R&S RSUK 1*	51	2 wks

OUTLAWS *UK, male instrumental group* **4 wks**

13 Apr 61	SWINGIN' LOW *HMV POP 844*	46	2 wks
8 Jun 61	AMBUSH *HMV POP 877*	43	2 wks

See also Mike Berry.

OVERLANDERS *UK, male vocal/instrumental group* **10 wks**

13 Jan 66 ★	MICHELLE *Pye 7N 17034*	1	10 wks

OVERWEIGHT POOCH – *See Ce Ce PENISTON*

Reg OWEN *UK, orchestra* **10 wks**

27 Feb 59	MANHATTAN SPIRITUAL *Pye International 7N 25009*	20	8 wks
27 Oct 60	OBSESSION *Palette PG 9004*	43	2 wks

Robert OWENS *US, male vocalist* **2 wks**

7 Dec 91	I'LL BE YOUR FRIEND *Perfecto PB 45161*	75	2 wks

Jazzi P *US, female vocalist* **12 wks**

8 Jul 89	GET LOOSE *Breakout USA 659* *	25	6 wks
9 Jun 90	FEEL THE RHYTHM *A & M AM USA 691*	51	2 wks
3 Aug 91	REBEL WOMAN *DNA 7DNA 001* **	42	4 wks

* L.A. Mix performed by Jazzi P ** DNA performed by Jazzi P

Thom PACE *US, male vocalist* **15 wks**

19 May 79	MAYBE *RSO 34*	14	15 wks

Top: Finally the American success of CE CE PENISTON reached Britain.

Above: ANN PEEBLES carried an umbrella on stage to perform 'I Can't Stand The Rain'.

The chart career of BILLY PAUL ended in America with 'Let's Make A Baby' but continued in Britain for four more hits.

Peri McKissack found fame as PEBBLES.

22 Mar 62   **THEME FROM 'Z CARS'** *Columbia DB 4789*.......................**33** 6 wks

PARAMOUNT JAZZ BAND – *See Mr. Acker BILK and his PARAMOUNT JAZZ BAND*

PARAMOUNTS *UK, male vocal/instrumental group*   **7 wks**

16 Jan 64   **POISON IVY** *Parlophone R 5093*.................................**35** 7 wks

PARCHMENT *UK, male/female vocal/instrumental group*   **5 wks**

16 Sep 72   **LIGHT UP THE FIRE** *Pye 7N 45178* ....**31** 5 wks

PARIS *UK, male/female vocal group*   **4 wks**

19 Jun 82   **NO GETTING OVER YOU** *RCA 222* ....**49** 4 wks

Mica PARIS *UK, female vocalist*   **45 wks**

7 May 88 ● **MY ONE TEMPTATION** *Fourth & Broadway BRW 85*...........**7** 11 wks
30 Jul 88   **LIKE DREAMERS DO** *Fourth & Broadway BRW 108* *.........**26** 5 wks
22 Oct 88   **BREATHE LIFE INTO ME** *Fourth & Broadway BRW 115* .....**26** 10 wks
21 Jan 89   **WHERE IS THE LOVE** *Fourth & Broadway BRW 122* ** ....**19** 7 wks
6 Oct 90   **CONTRIBUTION** *Fourth & Broadway BRW 188* ....**33** 4 wks
1 Dec 90   **SOUTH OF THE RIVER** *Fourth & Broadway BRW 199*........**50** 2 wks
23 Feb 91   **IF I LOVE U 2 NITE** *Fourth & Broadway BRW 207* ....**43** 3 wks
31 Aug 91   **YOUNG SOUL REBELS** *Big Life BLR 57* ....**61** 3 wks

* Mica Paris featuring Courtney Pine ** Mica Paris and Will Downing

Ryan PARIS *France, male vocalist*   **10 wks**

3 Sep 83 ● **DOLCE VITA** *Carrere CAR 289* ....**5** 10 wks

PARIS ANGELS *Ireland, male vocal/instrumental group*   **15 wks**

3 Nov 90   **SCOPE** *Sheer Joy SHEER 0047* ....**75** 1 wk
20 Jul 91   **PERFUME** *Virgin VS 1360*...................................**55** 3 wks
21 Sep 91   **FADE** *Virgin VS 1365* ....**70** 1 wk

PARIS RED *US/Germany, male/female vocal/instrumental duo*   **1 wk**

29 Feb 92   **GOOD FRIEND** *Columbia 6569417* ....**61** 1 wk

Simon PARK *UK, orchestra*   **23 wks**

25 Nov 72   **EYE LEVEL** *Columbia DB 8946* ....**41** 2 wks
15 Sep 73 ★ **EYE LEVEL (re-entry)** *Columbia DB 8946* ....**1** 21 wks

Graham PARKER and the RUMOUR   **16 wks**
UK, male vocal/instrumental group

19 Mar 77   **THE PINK PARKER EP** *Vertigo PARK 001*...........................**24** 5 wks
22 Apr 78   **HEY LORD DON'T ASK ME QUESTIONS**
             Vertigo PARK 002 ....**32** 7 wks
20 Mar 82   **TEMPORARY BEAUTY** *RCA PARK 100* * ....**50** 4 wks

* Graham Parker
Tracks on The Pink Parker EP: Hold Back The Night/(Let Me Get) Sweet On You/White Honey/Soul Shoes.

Ray PARKER Jr *US, male vocalist*   **47 wks**

25 Aug 84 ● **GHOSTBUSTERS** *Arista ARIST 580*........................**2** 31 wks

18 Jan 86   **GIRLS ARE MORE FUN** *Arista ARIST 641* ....**46** 4 wks
3 Oct 87   **I DON'T THINK THAT MAN SHOULD SLEEP**
             ALONE *Geffen GEF 27* ....**13** 10 wks
30 Jan 88   **OVER YOU** *Geffen GEF 33* ....**65** 2 wks

Robert PARKER *US, male vocalist*   **8 wks**

4 Aug 66   **BAREFOOTIN'** *Island WI 286* ....**24** 8 wks

Jimmy PARKINSON *Australia, male vocalist*   **19 wks**

2 Mar 56 ● **THE GREAT PRETENDER** *Columbia DB 3729* ....**9** 13 wks
17 Aug 56   **WALK HAND IN HAND** *Columbia DB 3775*.......................**30** 1 wk
5 Oct 56   **WALK HAND IN HAND (re-entry)** *Columbia DB 3775*.....**26** 1 wk
9 Nov 56   **IN THE MIDDLE OF THE HOUSE** *Columbia DB 3833* .....**26** 2 wks
30 Nov 56   **IN THE MIDDLE OF THE HOUSE (re-entry)**
             Columbia DB 3833 ....**20** 2 wks

John PARR *UK, male vocalist*   **22 wks**

14 Sep 85 ● **ST ELMOS'S FIRE (MAN IN MOTION)**
             London LON 73 ....**6** 13 wks
18 Jan 86   **NAUGHTY NAUGHTY** *London LON 80* ....**58** 3 wks
30 Aug 86   **ROCK 'N' ROLL MERCENARIES** *Arista ARIST 666* * ......**31** 6 wks

* Meat Loaf featuring John Parr

Dean PARRISH *US, male vocalist*   **5 wks**

8 Feb 75   **I'M ON MY WAY** *UK USA 2* ....**38** 5 wks

Man PARRISH *US, mixer*   **26 wks**

26 Mar 83   **HOP HOP, BE BOP (DON'T STOP)**
             Polydor POSP 575 ....**41** 6 wks
23 Mar 85   **BOOGIE DOWN (BRONX)** *Boiling Point POSP 731*...........**56** 4 wks
13 Sep 86   **MALE STRIPPER** *Bolts BOLTS 4* * ....**64** 3 wks
3 Jan 87   **MALE STRIPPER (re-entry)** *Bolts BOLTS 4* * ....**63** 1 wk
7 Feb 87 ● **MALE STRIPPER (2nd re-entry)** *Bolts BOLTS 4* * ....**4** 12 wks

* Man 2 Man meet Man Parrish

Bill PARSONS *US, male vocalist*   **2 wks**

10 Apr 59   **ALL AMERICAN BOY** *London HL 8798* ....**22** 2 wks
Record erroneously credited to Bill Parsons, actual vocalist is Bobby Bare.

Alan PARSONS PROJECT   **4 wks**
UK, male vocal/instrumental group

15 Jan 83   **OLD AND WISE** *Arista ARIST 494*...............................**74** 1 wk
10 Mar 84   **DON'T ANSWER ME** *Arista ARIST 553*..............................**58** 3 wks

PARTNERS – *See Al HUDSON*

PARTNERS IN KRYME   **10 wks**
US, male vocal/instrumental duo

21 Jul 90 ★ **TURTLE POWER** *SBK TURTLE 1*..............................**1** 10 wks

David PARTON *UK, male vocalist*   **9 wks**

15 Jan 77 ● **ISN'T SHE LOVELY** *Pye 7N 45663* ....**4** 9 wks

Dolly PARTON *US, female vocalist*   **31 wks**

15 May 76 ● **JOLENE** *RCA 2675* ....**7** 10 wks

21 Feb 81	9 TO 5 *RCA 25*	47	5 wks
12 Nov 83	● ISLANDS IN THE STREAM *RCA 378* *	7	15 wks
7 Apr 84	HERE YOU COME AGAIN *RCA 395*	75	1 wk

* Kenny Rogers and Dolly Parton

Stella PARTON US, *female vocalist*   **4 wks**

| 22 Oct 77 | THE DANGER OF A STRANGER *Elektra K 12272* .... | 35 | 4 wks |

Don PARTRIDGE UK, *male vocalist*   **32 wks**

7 Feb 68	● ROSIE *Columbia DB 8330*	4	12 wks
29 May 68	● BLUE EYES *Columbia DB 8416*	3	13 wks
19 Feb 69	BREAKFAST ON PLUTO *Columbia DB 8538*	26	7 wks

PARTRIDGE FAMILY US, *male/female vocal group*   **53 wks**

13 Feb 71	I THINK I LOVE YOU *Bell 1130* *	18	9 wks
26 Feb 72	IT'S ONE OF THOSE NIGHTS (YES LOVE)		
	Bell 1203	11	11 wks
8 Jul 72	● BREAKING UP IS HARD TO DO *Bell MABEL 1* *	3	13 wks
3 Feb 73	● LOOKING THROUGH THE EYES OF LOVE		
	Bell 1278 **	9	9 wks
19 May 73	● WALKING IN THE RAIN *Bell 1293* **	10	11 wks

* Partridge Family starring Shirley Jones featuring David Cassidy ** Partridge
Family starring David Cassidy

PASADENAS UK, *male vocal group*   **57 wks**

28 May 88	● TRIBUTE (RIGHT ON) *CBS PASA 1*	5	14 wks
17 Sep 88	RIDING ON A TRAIN *CBS PASA 2*	13	9 wks
26 Nov 88	ENCHANTED LADY *CBS PASA 3*	31	6 wks
12 May 90	LOVE THING *CBS PASA 4*	22	5 wks
14 Jul 90	REELING *CBS PASA 5*	75	1 wk
1 Feb 92	● I'M DOING FINE NOW *Columbia 6577187*	4	10 wks
4 Apr 92	MAKE IT WITH YOU *Columbia 6579257*	20	4 wks
6 Jun 92	I BELIEVE IN MIRACLES *Columbia 6580567*	34	3 wks
29 Aug 92	MOVING IN THE RIGHT DIRECTION		
	Columbia 6583417	49	2 wks
21 Nov 92	LET'S STAY TOGETHER *Columbia 6587747*	22	3 wks

PASSIONS UK, *male/female vocal/instrumental group*   **8 wks**

| 31 Jan 81 | I'M IN LOVE WITH A GERMAN FILM STAR | | |
| | *Polydor POSP 222* .... | 25 | 8 wks |

PAT and MICK UK, *male vocal duo*   **25 wks**

9 Apr 88	LET'S ALL CHANT/ON THE NIGHT		
	PWL PWL 10 *	11	9 wks
25 Mar 89	● I HAVEN'T STOPPED DANCING YET		
	PWL PWL 33	9	8 wks
14 Apr 90	USE IT UP AND WEAR IT OUT *PWL PWL 55*	22	6 wks
23 Mar 91	GIMME SOME *PWL PWL 75*	53	2 wks

* Mick and Pat

On The Night *only listed from 4 Jun 88.*

PATIENCE and PRUDENCE US, *female vocal duo*   **8 wks**

2 Nov 56	TONIGHT YOU BELONG TO ME *London HLU 8321*	28	3 wks
1 Mar 57	GONNA GET ALONG WITHOUT YA NOW		
	London HLU 8369	22	4 wks
12 Apr 57	GONNA GET ALONG WITHOUT YA		
	NOW (re-entry) *London HLU 8369*	24	1 wk

Kellee PATTERSON US, *female vocalist*   **7 wks**

| 18 Feb 78 | IF IT DON'T FIT DON'T FORCE IT | | |
| | *EMI International INT 544* .... | 44 | 7 wks |

Billy PAUL US, *male vocalist*   **44 wks**

13 Jan 73	ME AND MRS JONES *Epic EPC 1055*	12	9 wks
12 Jan 74	THANKS FOR SAVING MY LIFE		
	Philadelphia International PIR 1928	33	6 wks
22 May 76	LET'S MAKE A BABY *Philadelphia International PIR 4144* ..	30	5 wks
30 Apr 77	LET 'EM IN *Philadelphia International PIR 5143*	26	5 wks
16 Jul 77	YOUR SONG *Philadelphia International PIR 5391*	37	7 wks
19 Nov 77	ONLY THE STRONG SURVIVE		
	Philadelphia International PIR 5699	33	7 wks
14 Jul 79	BRING THE FAMILY BACK		
	Philadelphia International PIR 7456	51	5 wks

Chris PAUL UK, *male instrumentalist - guitar*   **8 wks**

31 May 86	EXPANSIONS '86 (EXPAND YOUR MIND)		
	Fourth & Broadway BRW 48 *	58	5 wks
21 Nov 87	BACK IN MY ARMS *Syncopate SY 5*	74	2 wks
13 Aug 88	TURN THE MUSIC UP *Syncopate SY 13*	73	1 wk

* Chris Paul featuring David Joseph

Les PAUL and Mary FORD   **4 wks**
US, *male instrumentalist - guitar, and female vocalist*

| 20 Nov 53 | ● VAYA CON DIOS *Capitol CL 13943* .... | 7 | 4 wks |

Lyn PAUL UK, *female vocalist*   **6 wks**

| 28 Jun 75 | IT OUGHTA SELL A MILLION *Polydor 2058 602* .... | 37 | 6 wks |

Owen PAUL UK, *male vocalist*   **14 wks**

| 31 May 86 | ● MY FAVOURITE WASTE OF TIME *Epic A 7125* .... | 3 | 14 wks |

PAUL and PAULA US, *male/female vocal duo*   **31 wks**

14 Feb 63	● HEY PAULA *Philips 304012 BF*	8	12 wks
18 Apr 63	● YOUNG LOVERS *Philips 304016 BF*	9	14 wks
16 May 63	HEY PAULA (re-entry) *Philips 304012 BF*	37	5 wks

Luciano PAVAROTTI Italy, *male operatic vocalist*   **16 wks**

| 16 Jun 90 | ● NESSUN DORMA *Decca PAV 03* .... | 2 | 11 wks |
| 24 Oct 92 | MISERERE *London LON 329* * .... | 15 | 5 wks |

* Zucchero with Luciano Pavarotti

PAVEMENT UK, *male vocal/instrumental group*   **1 wk**

| 28 Nov 92 | WATERY DOMESTIC EP *Big Cat ABB 38T* .... | 58 | 1 wk |

Tracks on Watery Domestic EP*: Brick Wall/Sick Profile/Annual Report/Fear The Panzers.*

Rita PAVONE Italy, *female vocalist*   **19 wks**

| 1 Dec 66 | HEART *RCA 1553* .... | 27 | 12 wks |
| 19 Jan 67 | YOU ONLY YOU *RCA 1561* .... | 21 | 7 wks |

Freda PAYNE US, *female vocalist*   **30 wks**

| 5 Sep 70 | ★ BAND OF GOLD *Invictus INV 502* .... | 1 | 19 wks |

| 21 Nov 70 | DEEPER AND DEEPER *Invictus INV 505* | **33** | 9 wks |
| 27 Mar 71 | CHERISH WHAT IS DEAR TO YOU *Invictus INV 509* | **46** | 2 wks |

Tammy PAYNE *UK, female vocalist*　2 wks

| 20 Jul 91 | TAKE ME NOW *Talkin Loud TLK 12* | **55** | 2 wks |

PEACHES and HERB *US, female/male vocal duo*　23 wks

| 20 Jan 79 | SHAKE YOUR GROOVE THING *Polydor 2066 992* | **26** | 10 wks |
| 21 Apr 79 ● | REUNITED *Polydor POSP 43* | **4** | 13 wks |

PEARL JAM *US, male vocal/instrumental group*　13 wks

15 Feb 92	ALIVE *Epic 6575727*	**16**	6 wks
18 Apr 92	EVEN FLOW *Epic 6578577*	**27**	3 wks
26 Sep 92	JEREMY *Epic 6582587*	**15**	4 wks

PEARLS *UK, female vocal duo*　24 wks

27 May 72	THIRD FINGER, LEFT HAND *Bell 1217*	**31**	6 wks
23 Sep 72	YOU CAME YOU SAW YOU CONQUERED *Bell 1254*	**32**	5 wks
24 Mar 73	YOU ARE EVERYTHING *Bell 1284*	**41**	3 wks
1 Jun 74 ●	GUILTY *Bell 1352*	**10**	10 wks

Johnny PEARSON　15 wks
UK, orchestra, Johnny Pearson featured pianist

| 18 Dec 71 ● | SLEEPY SHORES *Penny Farthing PEN 778* | **8** | 15 wks |

PEBBLES *US, female vocalist*　17 wks

19 Mar 88 ●	GIRLFRIEND *MCA MCA 1233*	**8**	11 wks
28 May 88	MERCEDES BOY *MCA MCA 1248*	**42**	4 wks
27 Oct 90	GIVING YOU THE BENEFIT *MCA MCA 1448*	**73**	2 wks

PEDDLERS *UK, male vocal/instrumental group*　14 wks

7 Jan 65	LET THE SUNSHINE IN *Philips BF 1375*	**50**	1 wk
23 Aug 69	BIRTH *CBS 4449*	**17**	9 wks
31 Jan 70	GIRLIE *CBS 4720*	**34**	4 wks

PEE BEE SQUAD *UK, male vocalist – Paul Burnett*　3 wks

| 5 Oct 85 | RUGGED AND MEAN, BUTCH AND ON SCREEN *Project PRO 3* | **52** | 3 wks |

Ann PEEBLES *US, female vocalist*　3 wks

| 20 Apr 74 | I CAN'T STAND THE RAIN *London HL 10428* | **50** | 1 wk |
| 4 May 74 | I CAN'T STAND THE RAIN (re-entry) *London HL 10428* | **41** | 2 wks |

PEECH BOYS *UK, male vocal/instrumental group*　3 wks

| 30 Oct 82 | DON'T MAKE ME WAIT *TMT QTMT 7001* | **49** | 3 wks |

Donald PEERS *UK, male vocalist*　27 wks

| 18 Dec 68 ● | PLEASE DON'T GO *Columbia DB 8502* | **3** | 18 wks |

| 30 Apr 69 | PLEASE DON'T GO (re-entry) *Columbia DB 8502* | **38** | 3 wks |
| 24 Jun 72 | GIVE ME ONE MORE CHANCE *Decca F 13302* | **36** | 6 wks |

PELE *UK, male/female vocal/instrumental group*　2 wks

| 15 Feb 92 | MEGALOMANIA *M&G MAGS 20* | **73** | 1 wk |
| 13 Jun 92 | FAIR BLOWS THE WIND FOR FRANCE *M&G MAGS 24* | **62** | 1 wk |

Teddy PENDERGRASS *US, male vocalist*　22 wks

21 May 77	THE WHOLE TOWN'S LAUGHING AT ME *Philadelphia International PIR 5116*	**44**	3 wks
28 Oct 78	ONLY YOU/CLOSE THE DOOR *Philadelphia International S PIR 6713*	**41**	6 wks
23 May 81	TWO HEARTS *20th Century TC 2492* *	**49**	5 wks
25 Jan 86	HOLD ME *Asylum EKR 32* **	**44**	5 wks
28 May 88	JOY *Elektra EKR 75*	**58**	3 wks

* Stephanie Mills featuring Teddy Pendergrass ** Teddy Pendergrass with Whitney Houston

Ce Ce PENISTON *US, female vocalist*　36 wks

12 Oct 91	FINALLY *A & M AM 822*	**29**	7 wks
11 Jan 92 ●	WE GOT A LOVE THANG *A & M AM 846*	**6**	8 wks
18 Jan 92	I LIKE IT *A & M AM 847* *	**58**	2 wks
21 Mar 92 ●	FINALLY (re-issue) *A & M AM 858*	**2**	8 wks
23 May 92 ●	KEEP ON WALKIN' *A & M AM 878*	**10**	6 wks
5 Sep 92	CRAZY LOVE *A & M AM 0060*	**44**	3 wks
12 Dec 92	INSIDE THAT I CRIED *A & M AM 0121*	**42†**	2 wks

* Overweight Pooch featuring Ce Ce Peniston

Barbara PENNINGTON *US, female vocalist*　8 wks

| 27 Apr 85 | FAN THE FLAME *Record Shack SOHO 37* | **62** | 3 wks |
| 27 Jul 85 | ON A CROWDED STREET *Record Shack SOHO 49* | **57** | 5 wks |

PENTANGLE *UK, male/female vocal/instrumental group*　4 wks

28 May 69	ONCE I HAD A SWEETHEART *Big T BIG 124*	**46**	1 wk
14 Feb 70	LIGHT FLIGHT *Big T BIG 128*	**43**	1 wk
28 Feb 70	LIGHT FLIGHT (re-entry) *Big T BIG 128*	**45**	2 wks

PENTHOUSE 4 *UK, male vocal/instrumental duo*　3 wks

| 23 Apr 88 | BUST THIS HOUSE DOWN *Syncopate SY 10* | **56** | 3 wks |

PEOPLES CHOICE *US, male vocal/instrumental group*　9 wks

| 20 Sep 75 | DO IT ANYWAY YOU WANNA *Philadelphia International PIR 3500* | **36** | 5 wks |
| 21 Jan 78 | JAM JAM JAM *Philadelphia International PIR 5891* | **40** | 4 wks |

Danny PEPPERMINT and the JUMPING JACKS *US, male vocal/instrumental group*　8 wks

| 18 Jan 62 | PEPPERMINT TWIST *London HLL 9478* | **26** | 8 wks |

PEPPERS *France, male instrumental group* **12 wks**

26 Oct 74 ● **PEPPER BOX** *Spark SRL 1100* ....6 12 wks

PEPSI and SHIRLIE *UK, female vocal duo* **24 wks**

17 Jan 87 ● **HEARTACHE** *Polydor POSP 837* ....2 12 wks
30 May 87 ● **GOODBYE STRANGER** *Polydor POSP 865* ....9 7 wks
26 Sep 87 **CAN'T GIVE ME LOVE** *Polydor POSP 885* ....58 3 wks
12 Dec 87 **ALL RIGHT NOW** *Polydor POSP 896* ....50 2 wks

PERCEPTION *UK, male vocal group* **2 wks**

7 Mar 92 **FEED THE FEELING** *Talkin Loud TLK 17* ....58 2 wks

The listed flip side of Feed The Feeling *was* Three Times A Maybe *by K-Creative.*

Lance PERCIVAL *UK, male vocalist* **3 wks**

28 Oct 65 **SHAME AND SCANDAL IN THE FAMILY**
Parlophone R 5335 ....37 3 wks

PERFECT DAY *UK, male vocal/instrumental group* **4 wks**

21 Jan 89 **LIBERTY TOWN** *London LON 214* ....58 3 wks
1 Apr 89 **JANE** *London LON 188* ....68 1 wk

PERFECTLY ORDINARY PEOPLE **3 wks**
UK, male vocal/instrumental group

22 Oct 88 **THEME FROM P.O.P.** *Urban URB 25* ....61 3 wks

Emilio PERICOLI *Italy, male vocalist* **14 wks**

28 Jun 62 **AL DI LA** *Warner Bros. WB 69* ....30 14 wks

Carl PERKINS *US, male vocalist* **8 wks**

18 May 56 ● **BLUE SUEDE SHOES** *London HLU 8271* ....10 8 wks

Steve PERRY *UK, male vocalist* **1 wk**

4 Aug 60 **STEP BY STEP** *HMV POP 745* ....41 1 wk

Jon PERTWEE *UK, male vocalist* **7 wks**

1 Mar 80 **WORZEL'S SONG** *Decca F 13885* ....33 7 wks

PET SHOP BOYS *UK, male vocal/instrumental duo* **149 wks**

23 Nov 85 ★ **WEST END GIRLS** *Parlophone R 6115* ....1 15 wks
8 Mar 86 **LOVE COMES QUICKLY** *Parlophone R 6116* ....19 9 wks
31 May 86 **OPPORTUNITIES (LET'S MAKE LOTS OF
MONEY)** *Parlophone R 6129* ....11 8 wks
4 Oct 86 ● **SUBURBIA** *Parlophone R 6140* ....8 9 wks
27 Jun 87 ★ **IT'S A SIN** *Parlophone R 6158* ....1 11 wks
22 Aug 87 ● **WHAT HAVE I DONE TO DESERVE THIS**
Parlophone R 6163 * ....2 9 wks
24 Oct 87 ● **RENT** *Parlophone R 6168* ....8 7 wks
12 Dec 87 ★ **ALWAYS ON MY MIND** *Parlophone R 6171* ....1 11 wks
2 Apr 88 ★ **HEART** *Parlophone R 6177* ....1 10 wks
24 Sep 88 ● **DOMINO DANCING** *Parlophone R 6190* ....7 8 wks
26 Nov 88 ● **LEFT TO MY OWN DEVICES** *Parlophone R 6198* ....4 8 wks
8 Jul 89 ● **IT'S ALRIGHT** *Parlophone R 6220* ....5 8 wks

6 Oct 90 ● **SO HARD** *Parlophone R 6269* ....4 6 wks
24 Nov 90 **BEING BORING** *Parlophone R 6275* ....20 8 wks
23 Mar 91 ● **WHERE THE STREETS HAVE NO NAME - CAN'T
TAKE MY EYES OFF YOU/HOW CAN YOU
EXPECT TO BE TAKEN SERIOUSLY**
Parlophone R 6285 ....4 8 wks
8 Jun 91 **JEALOUSY** *Parlophone R 6283* ....12 5 wks
26 Oct 91 **DJ CULTURE** *Parlophone R 6301* ....13 3 wks
23 Nov 91 **DJ CULTURE (re-mix)** *Parlophone 12RX 6301* ....40 2 wks
21 Dec 91 **WAS IT WORTH IT** *Parlophone R 6306* ....24 4 wks

* Pet Shop Boys and Dusty Springfield

PETER and GORDON *UK, male vocal duo* **77 wks**

12 Mar 64 ★ **A WORLD WITHOUT LOVE** *Columbia DB 7225* ....1 14 wks
4 Jun 64 **NOBODY I KNOW** *Columbia DB 7292* ....10 11 wks
8 Apr 65 ● **TRUE LOVE WAYS** *Columbia DB 7524* ....2 15 wks
24 Jun 65 ● **TO KNOW YOU IS TO LOVE YOU** *Columbia DB 7617* ....5 10 wks
21 Oct 65 **BABY I'M YOURS** *Columbia DB 7729* ....19 9 wks
24 Feb 66 **WOMAN** *Columbia DB 7834* ....28 7 wks
22 Sep 66 **LADY GODIVA** *Columbia DB 8003* ....16 11 wks

PETER, PAUL and MARY **38 wks**
US, male/female vocal/instrumental group

10 Oct 63 **BLOWING IN THE WIND** *Warner Bros. WB 104* ....13 16 wks
16 Apr 64 **TELL IT ON THE MOUNTAIN** *Warner Bros. WB 127* ....33 4 wks
15 Oct 64 **THE TIMES THEY ARE A-CHANGIN'**
Warner Bros. WB 142 ....44 2 wks
17 Jan 70 ● **LEAVIN' ON A JET PLANE** *Warner Bros. WB 7340* ....2 16 wks

PETERS and LEE *UK, male/female vocal duo* **57 wks**

26 May 73 ★ **WELCOME HOME** *Philips 6006 307* ....1 24 wks
3 Nov 73 **BY YOUR SIDE** *Philips 6006 339* ....39 4 wks
20 Apr 74 ● **DON'T STAY AWAY TOO LONG** *Philips 6006 388* ....3 15 wks
17 Aug 74 **RAINBOW** *Philips 6006 406* ....17 7 wks
6 Mar 76 **HEY MR. MUSIC MAN** *Philips 6006 502* ....16 7 wks

Ray PETERSON *US, male vocalist* **9 wks**

4 Sep 59 **THE WONDER OF YOU** *RCA 1131* ....23 1 wk
24 Mar 60 **ANSWER ME** *RCA 1175* ....47 1 wk
19 Jan 61 **CORRINE, CORRINA** *London HLX 9246* ....48 1 wk
2 Feb 61 **CORRINE, CORRINA (re-entry)** *London HLX 9246* ....41 6 wks

Tom PETTY and the HEARTBREAKERS **39 wks**
US, male vocal/instrumental group

25 Jun 77 **ANYTHING THAT'S ROCK 'N' ROLL**
Shelter WIP 6396 ....36 3 wks
13 Aug 77 **AMERICAN GIRL** *Shelter WIP 6403* ....40 5 wks
15 Aug 81 **STOP DRAGGIN' MY HEART AROUND**
WEA K 79231 * ....50 4 wks
13 Apr 85 **DON'T COME AROUND HERE NO MORE**
MCA MCA 926 ....50 4 wks
13 May 89 **I WON'T BACK DOWN** *MCA MCA 1334* ** ....28 10 wks
12 Aug 89 **RUNNIN' DOWN A DREAM** *MCA MCA 1359* ** ....55 4 wks
25 Nov 89 **FREE FALLIN'** *MCA MCA 1381* ** ....64 2 wks
29 Jun 91 **LEARNING TO FLY** *MCA MCS 1555* ....46 4 wks
4 Apr 92 **TOO GOOD TO BE TRUE** *MCA MCS 1616* ....34 3 wks

* Stevie Nicks with Tom Petty and the Heartbreakers ** Tom Petty

PHANTOMS – *See Johnny BRANDON*

PHARAOHS – *See SAM THE SHAM and the PHARAOHS*

PhD *UK, male vocal/instrumental duo* **14 wks**

3 Apr 82 ● **I WON'T LET YOU DOWN** *WEA K 79209* ....3 14 wks

PHILADELPHIA INTERNATIONAL ALL-STARS US, amalgamation of various acts   **8 wks**

13 Aug 77	**LET'S CLEAN UP THE GHETTO** *Philadelphia International PIR 5451* **34**	8 wks

PHILHARMONIA ORCHESTRA, conductor Lorin MAAZEL UK, orchestra, US, male conductor   **7 wks**

30 Jul 69	**THUS SPAKE ZARATHUSTRA** *Columbia DB 8607* **33**	7 wks

Esther PHILLIPS US, female vocalist   **8 wks**

4 Oct 75 ●	**WHAT A DIFFERENCE A DAY MADE** *Kudu 925* **6**	8 wks

Paul PHOENIX UK, male vocalist   **4 wks**

3 Nov 79	**NUNC DIMITTIS** *Different HAVE 20* **56**	4 wks

Full artist credit on hit as follows: Paul Phoenix (treble) with Instrumental Ensemble - James Watson (trumpet), John Scott (organ), conducted by Barry Rose.

PHOTOS UK, male/female vocal/instrumental group   **4 wks**

17 May 80	**IRENE** *Epic EPC 8517* **56**	4 wks

PHUTURE ASSASSINS UK, male instrumental/ production group   **1 wk**

6 Jun 92	**FUTURE SOUND (EP)** *Suburban Base SUBBASE 010* **64**	1 wk

Tracks on Future Sound (EP): *Future Sound/African Sanctus/Rydim Come Foward/Freedom Sound.*

PIA – *See Pia ZADORA*

Edith PIAF France, female vocalist   **15 wks**

12 May 60	**MILORD** *Columbia DC 754* **41**	4 wks
3 Nov 60	**MILORD (re-entry)** *Columbia DC 754* **24**	11 wks

Bobby 'Boris' PICKETT and the CRYPT-KICKERS US, male vocalist, male vocal/instrumental backing group   **13 wks**

1 Sep 73 ●	**MONSTER MASH** *London HL 10320* **3**	13 wks

Wilson PICKETT US, male vocalist   **61 wks**

23 Sep 65	**IN THE MIDNIGHT HOUR** *Atlantic AT 4036* **12**	11 wks
25 Nov 65	**DON'T FIGHT IT** *Atlantic AT 4052* **29**	8 wks
10 Mar 66	**634-5789** *Atlantic AT 4072* **36**	5 wks
1 Sep 66	**LAND OF 1000 DANCES** *Atlantic 584-039* **22**	9 wks
15 Dec 66	**MUSTANG SALLY** *Atlantic 584-066* **28**	7 wks
27 Sep 67	**FUNKY BROADWAY** *Atlantic 584-130* **43**	3 wks
11 Sep 68	**I'M A MIDNIGHT MOVER** *Atlantic 584-203* **38**	6 wks
8 Jan 69	**HEY JUDE** *Atlantic 584-236* **16**	9 wks
21 Nov 87	**IN THE MIDNIGHT HOUR** *Motown ZB 41583* **62**	3 wks

In The Midnight Hour *on Motown is a re-recording.*

PICKETTYWITCH UK, male/female vocal/ instrumental group   **34 wks**

28 Feb 70 ●	**THAT SAME OLD FEELING** *Pye 7N 17887* **5**	14 wks
4 Jul 70	**(IT'S LIKE A) SAD OLD KINDA MOVIE** *Pye 7N 17951* **16**	10 wks

7 Nov 70	**BABY I WON'T LET YOU DOWN** *Pye 7N 45002* **27**	10 wks

PIGBAG UK, male instrumental group   **20 wks**

7 Nov 81	**SUNNY DAY** *Y Records Y 12* **53**	3 wks
27 Feb 82	**GETTING UP** *Y Records Y 16* **61**	3 wks
3 Apr 82 ●	**PAPA'S GOT A BRAND NEW PIGBAG** *Y Records Y 10* **3**	11 wks
10 Jul 82	**THE BIG BEAN** *Y Records Y 24* **40**	3 wks

Nelson PIGFORD – *See De Etta LITTLE and Nelson PIGFORD*

PIGLETS UK, female vocal group   **12 wks**

6 Nov 71 ●	**JOHNNY REGGAE** *Bell 1180* **3**	12 wks

Dick PIKE – *See Ruby WRIGHT*

P.I.L. – *See PUBLIC IMAGE LTD.*

PILOT UK, male vocal/instrumental group   **29 wks**

2 Nov 74	**MAGIC** *EMI 2217* **11**	11 wks
18 Jan 75 ★	**JANUARY** *EMI 2255* **1**	10 wks
19 Apr 75	**CALL ME ROUND** *EMI 2287* **34**	4 wks
27 Sep 75	**JUST A SMILE** *EMI 2338* **31**	4 wks

PILTDOWN MEN US, male instrumental group   **36 wks**

8 Sep 60	**MACDONALD'S CAVE** *Capitol CL 15149* **14**	18 wks
12 Jan 61	**PILTDOWN RIDES AGAIN** *Capitol CL 15175* **14**	10 wks
9 Mar 61	**GOODNIGHT MRS. FLINTSTONE** *Capitol CL 15186* **18**	8 wks

Courtney PINE UK, male instrumentalist - saxophone   **6 wks**

30 Jul 88	**LIKE DREAMERS DO** *Fourth & Broadway BRW 108* * **26**	5 wks
7 Jul 90	**I'M STILL WAITING** *Mango MNG 749* ** **66**	1 wk

* *Mica Paris featuring Courtney Pine* ** *Courtney Pine featuring Carroll Thompson*
See also Movement 98 featuring Carroll Thompson.

PING PING and Al VERLAINE   **4 wks**
Belgium, male vocal duo

28 Sep 61	**SUCU SUCU** *Oriole CB 1589* **41**	4 wks

PINK FLOYD UK, male vocal/instrumental group   **48 wks**

30 Mar 67	**ARNOLD LAYNE** *Columbia DB 8156* **20**	8 wks
22 Jun 67 ●	**SEE EMILY PLAY** *Columbia DB 8214* **6**	12 wks
1 Dec 79 ★	**ANOTHER BRICK IN THE WALL** (PART 2) *Harvest HAR 5194* **1**	12 wks
7 Aug 82	**WHEN THE TIGERS BROKE FREE** *Harvest HAR 5222* **39**	5 wks
7 May 83	**NOT NOW JOHN** *Harvest HAR 5224* **30**	4 wks
19 Dec 87	**ON THE TURNING AWAY** *EMI EM 34* **55**	4 wks
25 Jun 88	**ONE SLIP** *EMI EM 52* **50**	3 wks

PINKEES UK, male vocal/instrumental group   **9 wks**

18 Sep 82 ●	**DANGER GAMES** *Creole CR 39* **8**	9 wks

PINKERTON'S ASSORTED COLOURS   **12 wks**
UK, male vocal/instrumental group

13 Jan 66 ●	**MIRROR MIRROR** *Decca F 12307* **9**	11 wks
21 Apr 66	**DON'T STOP LOVIN' ME BABY** *Decca F 12377* **50**	1 wk

PIONEERS Jamaica, male vocal/instrumental group — 34 wks

18 Oct 69		LONG SHOT KICK DE BUCKET Trojan TR 672	21	10 wks
10 Jan 70		LONG SHOT KICK DE BUCKET (re-entry) Trojan TR 672	40	1 wk
31 Jul 71	●	LET YOUR YEAH BE YEAH Trojan TR 7825	5	12 wks
15 Jan 72		GIVE AND TAKE Trojan TR 7846	35	6 wks
29 Mar 80		LONG SHOT KICK DE BUCKET (re-issue) Trojan TRO 9063	42	5 wks

Re-issue of Long Shot Kick De Bucket coupled with re-issue of Liquidator by Harry J. All Stars.

PIPKINS UK, male vocal duo — 10 wks

28 Mar 70	●	GIMME DAT DING Columbia DB 8662	6	10 wks

PIPS – See Gladys KNIGHT and the PIPS

PIRANHAS UK, male vocal/instrumental group — 21 wks

2 Aug 80	●	TOM HARK Sire SIR 4044	6	12 wks
16 Oct 82		ZAMBESI Dakota DAK 6 *	17	9 wks

* Piranhas featuring Boring Bob Grover

PIRATES – See Johnny KIDD and the PIRATES

Gene PITNEY US, male vocalist — 212 wks

23 Mar 61		I WANNA LOVE MY LIFE AWAY London HL 9270	26	11 wks
8 Mar 62		TOWN WITHOUT PITY HMV POP 952	32	6 wks
5 Dec 63	●	TWENTY FOUR HOURS FROM TULSA United Artists UP 1035	5	19 wks
5 Mar 64	●	THAT GIRL BELONGS TO YESTERDAY United Artists UP 1045	7	12 wks
15 Oct 64		IT HURTS TO BE IN LOVE United Artists UP 1063	36	4 wks
12 Nov 64	●	I'M GONNA BE STRONG Stateside SS 358	2	14 wks
18 Feb 65	●	I MUST BE SEEING THINGS Stateside SS 390	6	10 wks
10 Jun 65	●	LOOKING THROUGH THE EYES OF LOVE Stateside SS 420	3	12 wks
4 Nov 65	●	PRINCESS IN RAGS Stateside SS 471	9	12 wks
17 Feb 66	●	BACKSTAGE Stateside SS 490	4	10 wks
9 Jun 66	●	NOBODY NEEDS YOUR LOVE Stateside SS 518	2	13 wks
10 Nov 66	●	JUST ONE SMILE Stateside SS 558	8	12 wks
23 Feb 67		COLD LIGHT OF DAY Stateside SS 597	38	6 wks
15 Nov 67	●	SOMETHING'S GOTTEN HOLD OF MY HEART Stateside SS 2060	5	13 wks
3 Apr 68		SOMEWHERE IN THE COUNTRY Stateside SS 2103	19	9 wks
27 Nov 68		YOURS UNTIL TOMORROW Stateside SS 2131	34	7 wks
5 Mar 69		MARIA ELENA Stateside SS 2142	25	6 wks
14 Mar 70		A STREET CALLED HOPE Stateside SS 2164	37	5 wks
3 Oct 70		SHADY LADY Stateside SS 2177	29	8 wks
28 Apr 73		24 SYCAMORE Pye International 7N 25606	34	7 wks
2 Nov 74		BLUE ANGEL Bronze BRO 11	49	1 wk
16 Nov 74		BLUE ANGEL (re-entry) Bronze BRO 11	39	3 wks
14 Jan 89	★	SOMETHING'S GOTTEN HOLD OF MY HEART Parlophone R 6201 *	1	12 wks

* Marc Almond featuring special guest star Gene Pitney

PIXIES US, male/female vocal/instrumental group — 11 wks

1 Apr 89		MONKEY GONE TO HEAVEN 4AD AD 904	60	3 wks
1 Jul 89		HERE COMES YOUR MAN 4AD AD 909	54	1 wk
28 Jul 90		VELOURIA 4AD AD 0009	28	3 wks
10 Nov 90		DIG FOR FIRE 4AD AD 0014	62	1 wk
8 Jun 91		PLANET OF SOUND 4AD AD 1008	27	3 wks

Joe PIZZULO – See Sergio MENDES

PJ HARVEY – See PJ HARVEY

PJB featuring HANNAH and her SISTERS — 8 wks
Germany/US, male/female vocal/instrumental group

14 Sep 91		BRIDGE OVER TROUBLED WATER Dance Pool 6565467	21	8 wks

PKA UK, male producer – Phil Kelsey — 2 wks

20 Apr 91		TEMPERATURE RISING Stress SS 4	68	1 wk
7 Mar 92		POWERGEN (ONLY YOUR LOVE) Stress PKA 1	70	1 wk

PLANET PATROL US, male vocal/instrumental group — 3 wks

17 Sep 83		CHEAP THRILLS Polydor POSP 639	64	3 wks

PLANETS UK, male vocal/instrumental group — 8 wks

18 Aug 79		LINES Rialto TREB 104	36	6 wks
25 Oct 80		DON'T LOOK DOWN Rialto TREB 116	66	2 wks

Robert PLANT UK, male vocalist — 19 wks

9 Oct 82		BURNING DOWN ONE SIDE Swansong SSK 19429	73	1 wk
16 Jul 83		BIG LOG WEA B 9848	11	10 wks
30 Jan 88		HEAVEN KNOWS Es Paranza A 9373	33	5 wks
28 Apr 90		HURTING KIND (I'VE GOT MY EYES ON YOU) Es Paranza A 8985	45	3 wks

PLASMATICS US, female/male vocal/instrumental group — 4 wks

26 Jul 80		BUTCHER BABY Stiff BUY 76	55	4 wks

PLASTIC BERTRAND Belgium, male vocalist — 17 wks

13 May 78	●	CA PLANE POUR MOI Sire 6078 616	8	12 wks
5 Aug 78		SHA LA LA LA LEE Vertigo 6059 209	39	5 wks

PLASTIC JAM – See BUG KANN and PLASTIC JAM featuring Patti LOW and DOOGIE

PLASTIC ONO BAND – See John LENNON

PLASTIC PENNY UK, male vocal/instrumental group — 10 wks

3 Jan 68	●	EVERYTHING I AM Page One POF 051	6	10 wks

PLASTIC POPULATION – See YAZZ

PLATINUM HOOK US, male vocal/instrumental group — 1 wk

2 Sep 78		STANDING ON THE VERGE (OF GETTING IT ON) Motown TMG 1115	72	1 wk

PLATTERS US, male/female vocal group — 91 wks

7 Sep 56	●	THE GREAT PRETENDER/ONLY YOU Mercury MT 117	5	12 wks
2 Nov 56	●	MY PRAYER Mercury MT 120	4	10 wks
7 Dec 56		THE GREAT PRETENDER/ONLY YOU (re-entry) Mercury MT 117	21	1 wk
18 Jan 57		MY PRAYER (re-entry) Mercury MT 120	28	2 wks
25 Jan 57		YOU'LL NEVER NEVER KNOW/IT ISN'T RIGHT Mercury MT 130	23	1 wk

8 Feb 57	**YOU'LL NEVER NEVER KNOW/IT ISN'T**		
	RIGHT (re-entry) *Mercury MT 130*	**29**	1 wk
29 Mar 57	**MY PRAYER (2nd re-entry)** *Mercury MT 120*	**22**	1 wk
29 Mar 57	**ONLY YOU (2nd re-entry)** *Mercury MT 117*	**18**	3 wks
12 Apr 57	**YOU'LL NEVER NEVER KNOW/IT ISN'T**		
	RIGHT (2nd re-entry) *Mercury MT 130*	**29**	1 wk
17 May 57	**I'M SORRY** *Mercury MT 145*	**18**	6 wks
5 Jul 57	**I'M SORRY (re-entry)** *Mercury MT 145*	**23**	1 wk
19 Jul 57	**I'M SORRY (2nd re-entry)** *Mercury MT 145*	**22**	1 wk
16 May 58 ●	**TWILIGHT TIME** *Mercury MT 214*	**3**	18 wks
16 Jan 59 ★	**SMOKE GETS IN YOUR EYES** *Mercury AMT 1016*	**1**	20 wks
28 Aug 59	**REMEMBER WHEN** *Mercury AMT 1053*	**25**	2 wks
29 Jan 60	**HARBOUR LIGHTS** *Mercury AMT 1081*	**11**	11 wks

PLAYBOY BAND – *See John FRED and the PLAYBOY BAND*

PLAYBOYS – *See Gary LEWIS and the PLAYBOYS*

PLAYER *US/UK, male vocal/instrumental group*   **7 wks**

25 Feb 78	**BABY COME BACK** *RSO 2090 254*	**32**	7 wks

PLAYERS ASSOCIATION   **17 wks**
US, male/female vocal/instrumental group

10 Mar 79 ●	**TURN THE MUSIC UP** *Vanguard VS 5011*	**8**	9 wks
5 May 79	**RIDE THE GROOVE** *Vanguard VS 5012*	**42**	5 wks
9 Feb 80	**WE GOT THE GROOVE** *Vanguard VS 5016*	**61**	3 wks

PLUS ONE featuring SIRRON   **4 wks**
UK, male/female vocal/instrumental group

19 May 90	**IT'S HAPPENIN'** *MCA MCA 1405*	**40**	4 wks

PLUTO – *See Pluto SHERVINGTON*

PM DAWN *US, male vocal/instrumental duo*   **25 wks**

8 Jun 91	**A WATCHER'S POINT OF VIEW** *Gee Street GEE 32*	**36**	5 wks
17 Aug 91 ●	**SET ADRIFT ON MEMORY BLISS** *Gee Street GEE 33*	**3**	8 wks
19 Oct 91	**PAPER DOLL** *Gee Street GEE 35*	**49**	3 wks
22 Feb 92	**REALITY USED TO BE A FRIEND OF MINE**		
	Gee Street GEE 37	**29**	4 wks
7 Nov 92	**I'D DIE WITHOUT YOU** *Gee Street GEE 39*	**30**	5 wks

POETS *UK, male vocal/instrumental group*   **5 wks**

29 Oct 64	**NOW WE'RE THRU** *Decca F 11995*	**31**	5 wks

POGUES *Ireland, male/female vocal/instrumental group*   **63 wks**

6 Apr 85	**A PAIR OF BROWN EYES** *Stiff BUY 220*	**72**	2 wks
22 Jun 85	**SALLY MACLENNANE** *Stiff BUY 224*	**51**	4 wks
14 Sep 85	**DIRTY OLD TOWN** *Stiff BUY 229*	**62**	3 wks
8 Mar 86	**POGUETRY IN MOTION EP** *Stiff BUY 243*	**29**	6 wks
30 Aug 86	**HAUNTED** *MCA MCA 1084*	**42**	4 wks
28 Mar 87 ●	**THE IRISH ROVER** *Stiff BUY 258 **	**8**	8 wks
5 Dec 87 ●	**FAIRYTALE OF NEW YORK** *Pogue Mahone NY 7 ***	**2**	9 wks
5 Mar 88	**IF I SHOULD FALL FROM GRACE WITH GOD**		
	Pogue Mahone PG 1	**58**	3 wks
16 Jul 88	**FIESTA** *Pogue Mahone PG 2*	**24**	5 wks
17 Dec 88	**YEAH YEAH YEAH YEAH YEAH**		
	Pogue Mahone YZ 355	**43**	4 wks
8 Jul 89	**MISTY MORNING, ALBERT BRIDGE**		
	Pogue Mahone YZ 407	**41**	3 wks
16 Jun 90	**JACK'S HEROES/WHISKEY IN THE JAR**		
	*Pogue Mahone YZ 500 **	**63**	2 wks
15 Sep 90	**SUMMER IN SIAM** *Pogue Mahone YZ 519*	**64**	2 wks
21 Sep 91	**A RAINY NIGHT IN SOHO** *PM YZ 603*	**67**	1 wk
14 Dec 91	**FAIRYTALE OF NEW YORK (re-issue)**		
	*PM YZ 628 ***	**36**	5 wks
30 May 92	**HONKY TONK WOMEN** *PM YZ 673*	**56**	2 wks

* *Pogues and the Dubliners* ** *Pogues featuring Kirsty MacColl*

Tracks on Poguetry In Motion EP: London Girl/The Body of an American/A Rainy Night in Soho/Planxty Noel Hill.

POINTER SISTERS *US, female vocal group*   **87 wks**

3 Feb 79	**EVERYBODY IS A STAR** *Planet K 12324*	**61**	3 wks
17 Mar 79	**FIRE** *Planet K 12339*	**34**	8 wks
22 Aug 81 ●	**SLOWHAND** *Planet K 12530*	**10**	11 wks
5 Dec 81	**SHOULD I DO IT?** *Reprise K 12578*	**50**	5 wks
14 Apr 84 ●	**AUTOMATIC** *Planet RPS 105*	**2**	15 wks
23 Jun 84 ●	**JUMP (FOR MY LOVE)** *Planet RPS 106*	**6**	10 wks
11 Aug 84	**I NEED YOU** *Planet RPS 107*	**25**	9 wks
27 Oct 84	**I'M SO EXCITED** *Planet RPS 108*	**11**	11 wks
12 Jan 85	**NEUTRON DANCE** *Planet RPS 109*	**31**	7 wks
20 Jul 85	**DARE ME** *RCA PB 49957*	**17**	8 wks

POISON *US, male vocal/instrumental group*   **37 wks**

23 May 87	**TALK DIRTY TO ME** *Music For Nations KUT 125*	**67**	1 wk
7 May 88	**NOTHIN' BUT A GOOD TIME** *Capitol CL 486*	**35**	3 wks
5 Nov 88	**FALLEN ANGEL** *Capitol CL 500*	**59**	1 wk
11 Feb 89	**EVERY ROSE HAS ITS THORN** *Capitol CL 520*	**13**	9 wks
29 Apr 89	**YOUR MAMA DON'T DANCE** *Capitol CL 523*	**13**	4 wks
23 Sep 89	**NOTHIN' BUT A GOOD TIME** *Capitol CL 539*	**48**	3 wks
30 Jun 90	**UNSKINNY BOP** *Capitol CL 582*	**15**	7 wks
27 Oct 90	**SOMETHING TO BELIEVE IN** *Enigma CL 594*	**35**	4 wks
23 Nov 91	**SO TELL ME WHY** *Capitol CL 640*	**25**	2 wks

POLECATS *UK, male vocal/instrumental group*   **18 wks**

7 Mar 81	**JOHN I'M ONLY DANCING/BIG GREEN CAR**		
	Mercury POLE 1	**35**	8 wks
16 May 81	**ROCKABILLY GUY** *Mercury POLE 2*	**35**	6 wks
22 Aug 81	**JEEPSTER/MARIE CELESTE** *Mercury POLE 3*	**53**	4 wks

POLICE *UK/US, male vocal/instrumental group*   **142 wks**

7 Oct 78	**CAN'T STAND LOSING YOU** *A & M AMS 7381*	**42**	5 wks
28 Apr 79	**ROXANNE** *A & M AMS 7348*	**12**	9 wks
7 Jul 79 ●	**CAN'T STAND LOSING YOU (re-entry)**		
	A & M AMS 7381	**2**	11 wks
22 Sep 79 ★	**MESSAGE IN A BOTTLE** *A & M AMS 7474*	**1**	11 wks
17 Nov 79	**FALL OUT** *Illegal IL 001*	**47**	4 wks
1 Dec 79 ★	**WALKING ON THE MOON** *A & M AMS 7494*	**1**	10 wks
16 Feb 80 ●	**SO LONELY** *A & M AMS 7402*	**6**	10 wks
14 Jun 80	**SIX PACK** *A & M AMPP 6001*	**17**	4 wks
27 Sep 80 ★	**DON'T STAND SO CLOSE TO ME** *A & M AMS 7564*	**1**	10 wks
13 Dec 80 ●	**DE DO DO DO, DE DA DA DA** *A & M AMS 7578*	**5**	8 wks
26 Sep 81 ●	**INVISIBLE SUN** *A & M AMS 8164*	**2**	8 wks
24 Oct 81 ★	**EVERY LITTLE THING SHE DOES IS MAGIC**		
	A & M AMS 8174	**1**	13 wks
12 Dec 81	**SPIRITS IN THE MATERIAL WORLD**		
	A & M AMS 8194	**12**	8 wks
28 May 83 ★	**EVERY BREATH YOU TAKE** *A & M AM 117*	**1**	11 wks
23 Jul 83 ●	**WRAPPED AROUND YOUR FINGER** *A & M AM 127*	**7**	7 wks
5 Nov 83	**SYNCHRONICITY II** *A & M AM 153*	**17**	4 wks
14 Jan 84	**KING OF PAIN** *A & M AM 176*	**17**	5 wks

| 11 Oct 86 | DON'T STAND SO CLOSE TO ME '86 (re-mix) | | |
| | A & M AM 354 ....24 | | 4 wks |

Six Pack *consists of six separate Police singles as follows: The Bed's Too Big Without You/Roxanne/Message In A Bottle/Walking On The Moon/So Lonely/Can't Stand Losing You. The last five titles were re-issues.*

Su POLLARD UK, female vocalist — 11 wks

| 5 Oct 85 | COME TO ME (I AM WOMAN) Rainbow RBR 1 ....71 | 1 wk |
| 1 Feb 86 ● | STARTING TOGETHER Rainbow RBR 4 ....2 | 10 wks |

Jimi POLO US, male producer — 4 wks

| 9 Nov 91 | NEVER GOIN' DOWN MCA MCS 1578 * ....51 | 2 wks |
| 1 Aug 92 | EXPRESS YOURSELF Perfecto 74321101827 ....59 | 2 wks |

* Adamski featuring Jimi Polo
The listed flip side of Never Goin' Down was Born To Be Alive by Adamski featuring Soho.

PONI-TAILS US, female vocal group — 14 wks

| 19 Sep 58 ● | BORN TOO LATE HMV POP 516 ....5 | 11 wks |
| 10 Apr 59 | EARLY TO BED HMV POP 596 ....26 | 3 wks |

Brian POOLE and the TREMELOES — 90 wks
UK, male vocalist, male vocal/instrumental backing group

4 Jul 63 ●	TWIST AND SHOUT Decca F 11694 4	14 wks
12 Sep 63 ★	DO YOU LOVE ME Decca F 11739 1	14 wks
28 Nov 63	I CAN DANCE Decca F 11771 31	8 wks
30 Jan 64 ●	CANDY MAN Decca F 11823 6	13 wks
7 May 64 ●	SOMEONE SOMEONE Decca F 11893 2	17 wks
20 Aug 64	TWELVE STEPS TO LOVE Decca F 11951 32	7 wks
7 Jan 65	THREE BELLS Decca F 12037 17	9 wks
22 Jul 65	I WANT CANDY Decca F 12197 25	8 wks

See also Tremeloes.

Glyn POOLE UK, male vocalist — 8 wks

| 20 Oct 73 | MILLY MOLLY MANDY York SYK 565 ....35 | 8 wks |

Iggy POP US, male vocalist — 20 wks

13 Dec 86 ●	REAL WILD CHILD (WILD ONE) A & M AM 368 10	11 wks
10 Feb 90	LIVIN' ON THE EDGE OF THE NIGHT	
	Virgin America VUS 18 51	4 wks
13 Oct 90	CANDY Virgin America VUS 29 67	1 wk
5 Jan 91	WELL DID YOU EVAH! Chrysalis CHS 3646 * 42	4 wks

* Deborah Harry and Iggy Pop

POP TOPS Spain, male vocal group — 6 wks

| 9 Oct 71 | MAMY BLUE A & M AMS 859 ....34 | 6 wks |

POP WILL EAT ITSELF — 33 wks
UK, male vocal/instrumental group

30 Jan 88	THERE IS NO LOVE BETWEEN US ANYMORE	
	Chapter 22 CHAP 20 66	1 wk
23 Jul 88	DEF. CON ONE Chapter 22 PWE 001 63	4 wks
11 Feb 89	CAN U DIG IT RCA PB 42621 38	4 wks
22 Apr 89	WISE UP! SUCKER RCA PB 42761 41	3 wks
2 Sep 89	VERY METAL NOISE POLLUTION EP	
	RCA PB 42883 45	3 wks
9 Jun 90	TOUCHED BY THE HAND OF CICCIOLINA	
	RCA PB 43735 28	4 wks

13 Oct 90	DANCE OF THE MAD RCA PB 44023 32	2 wks
12 Jan 91	X Y & ZEE RCA PB 44243 15	4 wks
1 Jun 91	92 DEGREES RCA PB 44555 23	3 wks
6 Jun 92	KARMADROME/EAT ME DRINK ME LOVE ME	
	RCA PB 45467 17	2 wks
29 Aug 92	BULLETPROOF! RCA 74321110137 24	3 wks

Tracks on Very Metal Noise Pollution EP: Def Con. 1989 AD including the Twilight Zone/Preaching To The Perverted/P.W.E.I.-zation/92⁰F.

POPPY FAMILY — 14 wks
Canada, male/female vocal/instrumental group

| 15 Aug 70 ● | WHICH WAY YOU GOIN' BILLY Decca F 22976 ....7 | 14 wks |

Gary PORTNOY US, male vocalist — 3 wks

| 25 Feb 84 | THEME FROM 'CHEERS' Starblend CHEER 1 ....58 | 3 wks |

PORTSMOUTH SINFONIA UK, orchestra — 4 wks

| 12 Sep 81 | CLASSICAL MUDDLEY Island WIP 6736 ....38 | 4 wks |

Sandy POSEY US, female vocalist — 32 wks

15 Sep 66	BORN A WOMAN MGM 1321 24	11 wks
5 Jan 67	SINGLE GIRL MGM 1330 15	13 wks
13 Apr 67	WHAT A WOMAN IN LOVE WON'T DO MGM 1335 48	3 wks
6 Sep 75	SINGLE GIRL MGM 2006 533 35	5 wks

POSITIVE FORCE US, female vocal duo — 9 wks

| 22 Dec 79 | WE GOT THE FUNK Sugarhill SHL 102 ....18 | 9 wks |

Mike POST US, orchestra — 18 wks

9 Aug 75	AFTERNOON OF THE RHINO	
	Warner Bros. K 16588 * 48	1 wk
23 Aug 75	AFTERNOON OF THE RHINO (re-entry)	
	Warner Bros. K 16588 * 47	1 wk
16 Jan 82	THEME FROM 'HILL STREET BLUES'	
	Elektron K 12576 ** 25	11 wks
29 Sep 84	THE A TEAM RCA 443 45	5 wks

* Mike Post Coalition ** Mike Post featuring Larry Carlton

POTTERS UK, male vocal group — 2 wks

| 1 Apr 72 | WE'LL BE WITH YOU Pye JT 100 ....34 | 2 wks |

Cozy POWELL UK, male instrumentalist - drums — 35 wks

8 Dec 73 ●	DANCE WITH THE DEVIL RAK 164 3	15 wks
25 May 74	THE MAN IN BLACK RAK 173 18	8 wks
10 Aug 74 ●	NA NA NA RAK 180 10	10 wks
10 Nov 79	THEME ONE Ariola ARO 189 62	2 wks

POWER OF DREAMS — 2 wks
Ireland, male vocal/instrumental group

| 19 Jan 91 | AMERICAN DREAM Polydor PO 117 ....74 | 1 wk |
| 11 Apr 92 | THERE I GO AGAIN Polydor PO 200 ....65 | 1 wk |

POWER STATION UK/US, male vocal/instrumental group — 16 wks

| 16 Mar 85 | SOME LIKE IT HOT Parlophone R 6091 ....14 | 8 wks |

| 11 May 85 | GET IT ON *Parlophone R 6096* | 22 | 7 wks |
| 9 Nov 85 | COMMUNICATION *Parlophone R 6114* | 75 | 1 wk |

POWERCUT featuring NUBIAN PRINZ — 4 wks
US, male vocal/instrumental group

| 22 Jun 91 | GIRLS *Eternal YZ 570* | 50 | 4 wks |

POWERPILL *UK, male instrumental/production group* — 3 wks

| 6 Jun 92 | PAC-MAN *Ffrreedom TABX 110* | 43 | 3 wks |

Will POWERS *US, female vocalist – Lyn Goldsmith* — 9 wks

| 1 Oct 83 | KISSING WITH CONFIDENCE *Island IS 134* | 17 | 9 wks |

Hit features uncredited vocals by Carly Simon.

Perez PRADO *Cuba, orchestra* — 33 wks

| 25 Mar 55 | ★ CHERRY PINK AND APPLE BLOSSOM WHITE *HMV B 10833 ** | 1 | 17 wks |
| 25 Jul 58 | ● PATRICIA *RCA 1067* | 8 | 16 wks |

* Perez 'Prez' Prado and his Orchestra, the King of the Mambo

PRAISE *UK, male/female vocal/instrumental group* — 7 wks

| 2 Feb 91 | ● ONLY YOU *Epic 6566117* | 4 | 7 wks |

PRATT and McCLAIN with BROTHERLOVE — 6 wks
US, male vocal duo with male instrumental group

| 1 Oct 77 | HAPPY DAYS *Reprise K 14435* | 31 | 6 wks |

PRAYING MANTIS *UK, male vocal/instrumental group* — 2 wks

| 31 Jan 81 | CHEATED *Arista ARIST 378* | 69 | 2 wks |

PREFAB SPROUT — 53 wks
UK, male/female vocal/instrumental group

28 Jan 84	DON'T SING *Kitchenware SK 9*	64	2 wks
20 Jul 85	FARON YOUNG *Kitchenware SK 22*	74	1 wk
9 Nov 85	WHEN LOVE BREAKS DOWN *Kitchenware SK 21*	25	10 wks
8 Feb 86	JOHNNY JOHNNY *Kitchenware SK 24*	64	2 wks
13 Feb 88	CARS AND GIRLS *Kitchenware SK 35*	44	5 wks
30 Apr 88	● THE KING OF ROCK 'N' ROLL *Kitchenware SK 37*	7	10 wks
23 Jul 88	HEY MANHATTAN! *Kitchenware SK 38*	72	2 wks
18 Aug 90	LOOKING FOR ATLANTIS *Kitchenware SK 47*	51	3 wks
20 Oct 90	WE LET THE STARS GO *Kitchenware SK 48*	50	3 wks
5 Jan 91	JORDAN: THE EP *Kitchenware SK 49*	35	4 wks
13 Jun 92	THE SOUND OF CRYING *Kitchenware SK 58*	23	5 wks
8 Aug 92	IF YOU DON'T LOVE ME *Kitchenware SK 60*	33	4 wks
3 Oct 92	ALL THE WORLD LOVES LOVERS *Kitchenware SK 62*	61	2 wks

Tracks on Jordan: The EP: *Carnival 2000/The Ice Maiden/One Of The Broken/Jordan: The Comeback.*

PRELUDE *UK, male/female vocal group* — 26 wks

26 Jan 74	AFTER THE GOLDRUSH *Dawn DNS 1052*	21	9 wks
26 Apr 80	PLATINUM BLONDE *EMI 5046*	45	7 wks
22 May 82	AFTER THE GOLDRUSH (re-issue) *After Hours AFT 02*	28	7 wks

| 31 Jul 82 | ONLY THE LONELY *After Hours AFT 06* | 55 | 3 wks |

AFT 02 was a re-recording of DNS 1052. Both songs are a capella.

Elvis PRESLEY *US, male vocalist* — 1145 wks

11 May 56	● HEARTBREAK HOTEL *HMV POP 182*	2	21 wks
25 May 56	● BLUE SUEDE SHOES *HMV POP 213*	9	8 wks
13 Jul 56	I WANT YOU I NEED YOU I LOVE YOU *HMV POP 235*	25	2 wks
3 Aug 56	I WANT YOU I NEED YOU I LOVE YOU (re-entry) *HMV POP 235*	14	9 wks
17 Aug 56	BLUE SUEDE SHOES (re-entry) *HMV POP 213*	26	2 wks
21 Sep 56	● HOUND DOG *HMV POP 249*	2	23 wks
26 Oct 56	HEARTBREAK HOTEL (re-entry) *HMV POP 182*	23	1 wk
16 Nov 56	● BLUE MOON *HMV POP 272*	9	11 wks
23 Nov 56	I DON'T CARE IF THE SUN DON'T SHINE *HMV POP 272*	29	1 wk
7 Dec 56	LOVE ME TENDER *HMV POP 253*	11	9 wks
21 Dec 56	I DON'T CARE IF THE SUN DON'T SHINE (re-entry) *HMV POP 272*	23	3 wks
15 Feb 57	MYSTERY TRAIN *HMV POP 295*	25	5 wks
8 Mar 57	RIP IT UP *HMV POP 305*	27	1 wk
10 May 57	● TOO MUCH *HMV POP 330*	6	8 wks
14 Jun 57	ALL SHOOK UP *HMV POP 359*	24	1 wk
28 Jun 57	★ ALL SHOOK UP (re-entry) *HMV POP 359*	1	20 wks
12 Jul 57	● TEDDY BEAR *RCA 1013*	3	19 wks
12 Jul 57	TOO MUCH (re-entry) *HMV POP 330*	26	1 wk
30 Aug 57	● PARALYSED *HMV POP 378*	8	10 wks
4 Oct 57	● PARTY *RCA 1020*	2	15 wks
18 Oct 57	GOT A LOT O' LIVIN' TO DO *RCA 1020*	17	4 wks
1 Nov 57	LOVING YOU *RCA 1013*	24	2 wks
1 Nov 57	TRYING TO GET TO YOU *HMV POP 408*	16	4 wks
8 Nov 57	LAWDY MISS CLAWDY *HMV POP 408*	15	5 wks
15 Nov 57	● SANTA BRING MY BABY BACK TO ME *RCA 1025*	7	8 wks
17 Jan 58	I'M LEFT YOU'RE RIGHT SHE'S GONE *HMV POP 428*	21	2 wks
24 Jan 58	★ JAILHOUSE ROCK *RCA 1028*	1	14 wks
31 Jan 58	JAILHOUSE ROCK EP *RCA RCX 106*	18	5 wks
7 Feb 58	I'M LEFT YOU'RE RIGHT SHE'S GONE (re-entry) *HMV POP 428*	29	1 wk
28 Feb 58	● DON'T *RCA 1043*	2	11 wks
2 May 58	● WEAR MY RING AROUND YOUR NECK *RCA 1058*	3	10 wks
25 Jul 58	● HARD HEADED WOMAN *RCA 1070*	2	11 wks
3 Oct 58	● KING CREOLE *RCA 1081*	2	15 wks
23 Jan 59	★ ONE NIGHT/I GOT STUNG *RCA 1100*	1	12 wks
24 Apr 59	★ A FOOL SUCH AS I/I NEED YOUR LOVE TONIGHT *RCA 1113*	1	15 wks
24 Jul 59	● A BIG HUNK O' LOVE *RCA 1136*	4	9 wks
12 Feb 60	STRICTLY ELVIS EP *RCA RCX 175*	26	1 wk
7 Apr 60	● STUCK ON YOU *RCA 1187*	3	14 wks
28 Jul 60	● A MESS OF BLUES *RCA 1194*	2	18 wks
3 Nov 60	★ IT'S NOW OR NEVER *RCA 1207*	1	19 wks
19 Jan 61	★ ARE YOU LONESOME TONIGHT *RCA 1216*	1	15 wks
9 Mar 61	★ WOODEN HEART *RCA 1226*	1	27 wks
25 May 61	★ SURRENDER *RCA 1227*	1	15 wks
7 Sep 61	● WILD IN THE COUNTRY/I FEEL SO BAD *RCA 1244*	4	12 wks
2 Nov 61	★ HIS LATEST FLAME/LITTLE SISTER *RCA 1258*	1	13 wks
1 Feb 62	★ ROCK A HULA BABY/CAN'T HELP FALLING IN LOVE *RCA 1270*	1	20 wks
10 May 62	★ GOOD LUCK CHARM *RCA 1280*	1	17 wks
21 Jun 62	FOLLOW THAT DREAM EP *RCA RCX 211*	34	2 wks
30 Aug 62	★ SHE'S NOT YOU *RCA 1303*	1	14 wks
29 Nov 62	★ RETURN TO SENDER *RCA 1320*	1	14 wks
28 Feb 63	ONE BROKEN HEART FOR SALE *RCA 1337*	12	9 wks
4 Jul 63	● DEVIL IN DISGUISE *RCA 1355*	1	12 wks
24 Oct 63	BOSSA NOVA BABY *RCA 1374*	13	8 wks
19 Dec 63	KISS ME QUICK *RCA 1375*	14	10 wks
12 Mar 64	VIVA LAS VEGAS *RCA 1390*	17	12 wks
25 Jun 64	● KISSIN' COUSINS *RCA 1404*	10	11 wks
20 Aug 64	SUCH A NIGHT *RCA 1411*	13	10 wks
29 Oct 64	AIN'T THAT LOVIN' YOU BABY *RCA 1422*	15	8 wks
3 Dec 64	BLUE CHRISTMAS *RCA 1430*	11	4 wks
11 Mar 65	DO THE CLAM *RCA 1443*	19	8 wks
27 May 65	★ CRYING IN THE CHAPEL *RCA 1455*	1	15 wks
11 Nov 65	TELL ME WHY *RCA 1489*	15	10 wks
24 Feb 66	BLUE RIVER *RCA 1504*	22	7 wks

Date	Title	Pos	Wks
7 Apr 66	FRANKIE AND JOHNNY *RCA 1509*	21	9 wks
7 Jul 66 ●	LOVE LETTERS *RCA 1526*	6	10 wks
13 Oct 66	ALL THAT I AM *RCA 1545*	18	8 wks
1 Dec 66	IF EVERY DAY WAS LIKE CHRISTMAS *RCA 1557*	13	7 wks
9 Feb 67	INDESCRIBABLY BLUE *RCA 1565*	21	5 wks
11 May 67	YOU GOTTA STOP/LOVE MACHINE *RCA 1593*	38	5 wks
16 Aug 67	LONG LEGGED GIRL *RCA RCA 1616*	49	2 wks
21 Feb 68	GUITAR MAN *RCA 1663*	19	9 wks
15 May 68	U. S. MALE *RCA 1688*	15	8 wks
17 Jul 68	YOUR TIME HASN'T COME YET BABY *RCA 1714*	22	11 wks
16 Oct 68	YOU'LL NEVER WALK ALONE *RCA 1747*	44	3 wks
26 Feb 69	IF I CAN DREAM *RCA 1795*	11	10 wks
11 Jun 69 ●	IN THE GHETTO *RCA 1869*	2	16 wks
6 Sep 69	CLEAN UP YOUR OWN BACK YARD *RCA 1869*	21	7 wks
18 Oct 69	IN THE GHETTO (re-entry) *RCA 1831*	50	1 wk
29 Nov 69 ●	SUSPICIOUS MINDS *RCA 1900*	2	14 wks
28 Feb 70 ●	DON'T CRY DADDY *RCA 1916*	8	11 wks
16 May 70	KENTUCKY RAIN *RCA 1949*	21	11 wks
11 Jul 70 ★	THE WONDER OF YOU *RCA 1974*	1	20 wks
8 Aug 70	KENTUCKY RAIN (re-entry) *RCA 1949*	46	1 wk
14 Nov 70 ●	I'VE LOST YOU *RCA 1999*	9	12 wks
9 Jan 71	YOU DON'T HAVE TO SAY YOU LOVE ME *RCA 2046*	9	7 wks
23 Jan 71	THE WONDER OF YOU (re-entry) *RCA 1974*	47	1 wk
6 Mar 71	YOU DON'T HAVE TO SAY YOU LOVE ME (re-entry) *RCA 2046*	35	3 wks
20 Mar 71 ●	THERE GOES MY EVERYTHING *RCA 2060*	6	11 wks
15 May 71 ●	RAGS TO RICHES *RCA 2084*	9	11 wks
17 Jul 71 ●	HEARTBREAK HOTEL/HOUND DOG (re-issue) *RCA Maximillion 2153*	10	12 wks
2 Oct 71	I'M LEAVIN' *RCA 2125*	23	9 wks
4 Dec 71 ●	I JUST CAN'T HELP BELIEVING *RCA 2158*	6	16 wks
11 Dec 71	JAILHOUSE ROCK (re-issue) *RCA Maximillion 2153*	42	5 wks
1 Apr 72 ●	UNTIL IT'S TIME FOR YOU TO GO *RCA 2188*	5	9 wks
17 Jun 72 ●	AMERICAN TRILOGY *RCA 2229*	8	11 wks
30 Sep 72 ●	BURNING LOVE *RCA 2267*	7	9 wks
16 Dec 72 ●	ALWAYS ON MY MIND *RCA 2304*	9	13 wks
26 May 73	POLK SALAD ANNIE *RCA 2359*	23	7 wks
11 Aug 73	FOOL *RCA 2393*	15	10 wks
24 Nov 73	RAISED ON ROCK *RCA 2435*	36	7 wks
16 Mar 74	I'VE GOT A THING ABOUT YOU BABY *RCA APBO 0196*	33	5 wks
13 Jul 74	IF YOU TALK IN YOUR SLEEP *RCA APBO 0280*	40	3 wks
16 Nov 74 ●	MY BOY *RCA 2458*	5	13 wks
18 Jan 75 ●	PROMISED LAND *RCA PB 10074*	9	8 wks
24 May 75	T. R. O. U. B. L. E. *RCA 2562*	31	4 wks
29 Nov 75	GREEN GREEN GRASS OF HOME *RCA 2635*	29	7 wks
1 May 76	HURT *RCA 2674*	37	5 wks
4 Sep 76 ●	GIRL OF MY BEST FRIEND *RCA 2729*	9	12 wks
25 Dec 76 ●	SUSPICION *RCA 2768*	9	12 wks
5 Mar 77 ●	MOODY BLUE *RCA PB 0857*	6	9 wks
13 Aug 77 ★	WAY DOWN *RCA PB 0998*	1	13 wks
3 Sep 77	ALL SHOOK UP (re-issue) *RCA PB 2694*	41	2 wks
3 Sep 77	ARE YOU LONESOME TONIGHT (re-issue) *RCA PB 2699*	46	1 wk
3 Sep 77	CRYING IN THE CHAPEL (re-issue) *RCA PB 2708*	43	2 wks
3 Sep 77	IT'S NOW OR NEVER (re-issue) *RCA PB 2698*	39	2 wks
3 Sep 77	JAILHOUSE ROCK (2nd re-issue) *RCA PB 2695*	44	2 wks
3 Sep 77	RETURN TO SENDER (re-issue) *RCA PB 2706*	42	3 wks
3 Sep 77	THE WONDER OF YOU (re-issue) *RCA PB 2709*	48	1 wk
3 Sep 77	WOODEN HEART (re-issue) *RCA PB 2700*	49	1 wk
10 Dec 77 ●	MY WAY *RCA PB 1165*	9	8 wks
24 Jun 78	DON'T BE CRUEL *RCA PB 9265*	24	12 wks
15 Dec 79	IT WON'T SEEM LIKE CHRISTMAS (WITHOUT YOU) *RCA PB 9464*	13	6 wks
30 Aug 80 ●	IT'S ONLY LOVE/BEYOND THE REEF *RCA 4*	3	10 wks
6 Dec 80	SANTA CLAUS IS BACK IN TOWN *RCA 16*	41	5 wks
14 Feb 81	GUITAR MAN *RCA 43*	43	4 wks
18 Apr 81	LOVING ARMS *RCA 48*	47	6 wks
13 Mar 82	ARE YOU LONESOME TONIGHT *RCA 196*	25	7 wks
26 Jun 82	THE SOUND OF YOUR CRY *RCA 232*	59	2 wks
5 Feb 83	JAILHOUSE ROCK (re-entry) *RCA 1028*	27	6 wks
7 May 83	BABY I DON'T CARE *RCA 332*	61	3 wks
3 Dec 83	I CAN HELP *RCA 369*	30	9 wks
10 Nov 84	THE LAST FAREWELL *RCA 459*	48	6 wks
19 Jan 85	THE ELVIS MEDLEY *RCA 476*	51	3 wks
10 Aug 85	ALWAYS ON MY MIND *RCA PB 49944*	59	4 wks
11 Apr 87	AIN'T THAT LOVIN' YOU BABY/BOSSA NOVA BABY *RCA ARON 1*	47	5 wks
22 Aug 87	LOVE ME TENDER/IF I CAN DREAM (re-issue) *RCA ARON 2*	56	3 wks
16 Jan 88	STUCK ON YOU (re-issue) *RCA PB 49595*	58	2 wks
17 Aug 91	ARE YOU LONESOME TONIGHT (LIVE) (re-issue) *RCA PB 49177*	68	2 wks
29 Aug 92	DON'T BE CRUEL (re-issue) *RCA 74321110777*	42	2 wks

Tracks on Jailhouse Rock (EP): Jailhouse Rock/Young And Beautiful/I Want To Be Free/Don't Leave Me Now/Baby I Don't Care. On Strictly Elvis (EP): Old Shep/Any Place Is Paradise/Paralysed/Is It So Strange. On Follow That Dream (EP): Follow That Dream/Angel/What A Wonderful Life/I'm Not The Marrying Kind. On 5 July 62 a note on the Top 50 for that week stated 'Due to difficulties in assessing returns of Follow That Dream EP, it has been decided not to include it in Britain's Top 50. It is of course No.1 in the EP charts'. Therefore this EP only had a 2 week run on the chart when its sales would certainly have justified a much longer one. Beyond The Reef listed only 30 Aug to 13 Sep 80. Are You Lonesome Tonight on RCA 196 is a live version. RCA PB 49177 is a re-issue of RCA 196. Can't Help Falling In Love credited from 1 Mar 62. Tracks on The Elvis Medley: Jailhouse Rock/Teddy Bear/Hound Dog/Don't Be Cruel/Burning Love/Suspicious Minds. Both sides of RCA ARON 1 are alternate versions to the original hits. RCA PB 49944 is also an alternate version.

Billy PRESTON *US, male vocalist/instrumentalist - keyboards* **51 wks**

Date	Title	Pos	Wks
23 Apr 69 ★	GET BACK *Apple R 5777* *	1	17 wks
2 Jul 69	THAT'S THE WAY GOD PLANNED IT *Apple 12*	11	10 wks
16 Sep 72	OUTA SPACE *A & M AMS 7007*	44	3 wks
3 Apr 76	GET BACK (re-entry) *Apple R 5777* *	28	5 wks
15 Dec 79 ●	WITH YOU I'M BORN AGAIN *Motown TMG 1159* **	2	11 wks
8 Mar 80	IT WILL COME IN TIME *Motown TMG 1175* **	47	4 wks
22 Apr 89	GET BACK (2nd re-entry) *Apple R 5777* *	74	1 wk

* Beatles with Billy Preston ** Billy Preston and Syreeta

See also Various Artists (LPs & EPs) - The Apple EP.

Johnny PRESTON *US, male vocalist* **45 wks**

Date	Title	Pos	Wks
12 Feb 60 ★	RUNNING BEAR *Mercury AMT 1079*	1	14 wks
21 Apr 60 ●	CRADLE OF LOVE *Mercury AMT 1092*	2	16 wks
2 Jun 60	RUNNING BEAR (re-entry) *Mercury AMT 1079*	41	1 wk
28 Jul 60	I'M STARTING TO GO STEADY *Mercury AMT 1104*	49	1 wk
11 Aug 60	FEEL SO FINE *Mercury AMT 1104*	18	10 wks
8 Dec 60	CHARMING BILLY *Mercury AMT 1114*	34	1 wk
22 Dec 60	CHARMING BILLY (re-entry) *Mercury AMT 1114*	42	2 wks

Mike PRESTON *UK, male vocalist* **33 wks**

Date	Title	Pos	Wks
30 Oct 59	MR. BLUE *Decca F 11167*	12	8 wks
25 Aug 60	I'D DO ANYTHING *Decca F 11255*	23	10 wks
22 Dec 60	TOGETHERNESS *Decca F 11287*	41	5 wks
9 Mar 61	MARRY ME *Decca F 11335*	14	10 wks

PRETENDERS *UK/US, male/female vocal/instrumental group* **110 wks**

Date	Title	Pos	Wks
10 Feb 79	STOP YOUR SOBBING *Real ARE 6*	34	9 wks
14 Jul 79	KID *Real ARE 9*	33	7 wks
17 Nov 79 ★	BRASS IN POCKET *Real ARE 11*	1	17 wks
5 Apr 80 ●	TALK OF THE TOWN *Real ARE 12*	8	8 wks
14 Feb 81	MESSAGE OF LOVE *Real ARE 15*	11	7 wks
12 Sep 81	DAY AFTER DAY *Real ARE 17*	45	4 wks
14 Nov 81 ●	I GO TO SLEEP *Real ARE 18*	7	10 wks
2 Oct 82	BACK ON THE CHAIN GANG *Real ARE 19*	17	9 wks
26 Nov 83	2000 MILES *Real ARE 20*	15	9 wks
9 Jun 84	THIN LINE BETWEEN LOVE AND HATE *Real ARE 22*	49	3 wks
11 Oct 86 ●	DON'T GET ME WRONG *Real YZ 85*	10	9 wks
13 Dec 86 ●	HYMN TO HER *Real YZ 93*	8	12 wks
15 Aug 87	IF THERE WAS A MAN *Real YZ 149* *	49	6 wks

* Pretenders For 007

PRETTY BOY FLOYD **1 wk**

US, male vocal/instrumental group

Date	Title	Pos	Wks
10 Mar 90	ROCK AND ROLL (IS GONNA SET THE NIGHT ON FIRE) *MCA MCA 1393*	75	1 wk

PRETTY THINGS UK, male vocal/instrumental group   41 wks

18 Jun 64	**ROSALYN** *Fontana TF 469* **41**	5 wks
22 Oct 64 ●	**DON'T BRING ME DOWN** *Fontana TF 503* **10**	11 wks
25 Feb 65	**HONEY I NEED** *Fontana TF 537* **13**	10 wks
15 Jul 65	**CRY TO ME** *Fontana TF 585* **28**	7 wks
20 Jan 66	**MIDNIGHT TO SIX MAN** *Fontana TF 647* **46**	1 wk
5 May 66	**COME SEE ME** *Fontana TF 688* **43**	5 wks
21 Jul 66	**A HOUSE IN THE COUNTRY** *Fontana TF 722* **50**	1 wk
4 Aug 66	**A HOUSE IN THE COUNTRY (re-entry)**	
	Fontana TF 722	
	....**50**	1 wk

Alan PRICE UK, male vocalist/instrumentalist - keyboards   88 wks

31 Mar 66 ●	**I PUT A SPELL ON YOU** *Decca F 12367* * **9**	10 wks
14 Jul 66	**HI LILI HI LO** *Decca F 12442* * **11**	12 wks
2 Mar 67 ●	**SIMON SMITH AND HIS AMAZING DANCING**	
	BEAR *Decca F 12570* * **4**	12 wks
2 Aug 67 ●	**THE HOUSE THAT JACK BUILT** *Decca F 12641* * **4**	10 wks
15 Nov 67	**SHAME** *Decca F 12691* * **45**	2 wks
31 Jan 68	**DON'T STOP THE CARNIVAL** *Decca F 12731* * **13**	8 wks
10 Apr 71	**ROSETTA** *CBS 7108* ** **11**	10 wks
25 May 74 ●	**JARROW SONG** *Warner Bros. K 16372* **6**	9 wks
29 Apr 78	**JUST FOR YOU** *Jet UP 36358* **43**	8 wks
17 Feb 79	**BABY OF MINE/JUST FOR YOU (re-issue)** *Jet 135* **32**	3 wks
30 Apr 88	**CHANGES** *Ariola 109911* **54**	4 wks

* Alan Price Set ** Fame and Price Together

Lloyd PRICE US, male vocalist   36 wks

13 Feb 59 ●	**STAGGER LEE** *HMV POP 580* **7**	14 wks
15 May 59	**WHERE WERE YOU** *HMV POP 598* **15**	6 wks
12 Jun 59 ●	**PERSONALITY** *HMV POP 626* **9**	8 wks
14 Aug 59	**PERSONALITY (re-entry)** *HMV POP 626* **25**	2 wks
11 Sep 59	**I'M GONNA GET MARRIED** *HMV POP 650* **23**	5 wks
21 Apr 60	**LADY LUCK** *HMV POP 712* **45**	1 wk

Dickie PRIDE UK, male vocalist   1 wk

30 Oct 59	**PRIMROSE LANE** *Columbia DB 4340* **28**	1 wk

Maxi PRIEST UK, male vocalist   84 wks

29 Mar 86	**STROLLIN' ON** *10 TEN 84* **32**	9 wks
12 Jul 86	**IN THE SPRINGTIME** *10 TEN 127* **54**	3 wks
8 Nov 86	**CRAZY LOVE** *10 TEN 135* **67**	5 wks
4 Apr 87	**LET ME KNOW** *10 TEN 156* **49**	4 wks
24 Oct 87	**SOME GUYS HAVE ALL THE LUCK** *10 TEN 198* **12**	12 wks
20 Feb 88	**HOW CAN WE EASE THE PAIN** *10 TEN 207* * **41**	6 wks
4 Jun 88 ●	**WILD WORLD** *10 TEN 221* **5**	9 wks
27 Aug 88	**GOODBYE TO LOVE AGAIN** *10 TEN 238* **57**	3 wks
9 Jun 90 ●	**CLOSE TO YOU** *10 TEN 294* **7**	10 wks
1 Sep 90	**PEACE THROUGHOUT THE WORLD**	
	10 TEN 317 ** **41**	4 wks
1 Dec 90	**HUMAN WORK OF ART** *10 TEN 328* **75**	1 wk
15 Dec 90	**HUMAN WORK OF ART (re-entry)** *10 TEN 328* **71**	3 wks
24 Aug 91	**HOUSECALL** *Epic 6573477* *** **31**	7 wks
5 Oct 91	**THE MAXI PRIEST EP** *Ten TEN 343* **62**	3 wks
26 Sep 92	**GROOVIN' IN THE MIDNIGHT** *Ten TEN 412* **50**	2 wks
28 Nov 92	**JUST WANNA KNOW/FE' REAL** *Ten TEN 416* **** ...**33**	3 wks

* Maxi Priest featuring Beres Hammond ** Maxi Priest featuring Jazzie B
*** Shabba Ranks featuring Maxi Priest **** Maxi Priest/Maxi Priest featuring
Apache Indian

Tracks on The Maxi Priest EP: *Just A Little Bit Longer/Best Of Me/Searching/Fever.*

Louis PRIMA US, male vocalist   1 wk

21 Feb 58	**BUONA SERA** *Capitol CL 14841* **25**	1 wk

British Hit Singles Part One: Alphabetically by Artist
Date of chart entry/Title & catalogue no./Peak position reached/Weeks on chart
★ Number one   ● Top Ten   † still on chart at 31 Dec 1992
* = credited to act billed in footnote

PRIMA DONNA UK, male/female vocal group   4 wks

26 Apr 80	**LOVE ENOUGH FOR TWO** *Ariola ARO 221* **48**	4 wks

PRIMAL SCREAM UK, male vocal/instrumental group   25 wks

3 Mar 90	**LOADED** *Creation CRE 070* **16**	9 wks
18 Aug 90	**COME TOGETHER** *Creation CRE 0778* **26**	6 wks
22 Jun 91	**HIGHER THAN THE SUN** *Creation CRE 096* **40**	2 wks
24 Aug 91	**DON'T FIGHT IT FEEL IT** *Creation CRE 110* * **41**	2 wks
8 Feb 92	**DIXIE-NARCO EP** *Creation CRE 117* **11**	6 wks

* Primal Scream featuring Denise Johnson

Tracks on Dixie-Narco EP: *Movin' On Up/Stone My Soul/Carry Me Home/Screamadelica.*

PRIME MOVERS US, male vocal/instrumental group   1 wk

8 Feb 86	**ON THE TRAIL** *Island IS 263* **74**	1 wk

PRIMITIVES UK, male/female vocal/instrumental group   27 wks

27 Feb 88 ●	**CRASH** *Lazy PB 41761* **5**	10 wks
30 Apr 88	**OUT OF REACH** *Lazy PB 42011* **25**	4 wks
3 Sep 88	**WAY BEHIND ME** *Lazy PB 42209* **36**	4 wks
29 Jul 89	**SICK OF IT** *Lazy PB 42947* **24**	4 wks
30 Sep 89	**SECRETS** *Lazy PB 43173* **49**	3 wks
3 Aug 91	**YOU ARE THE WAY** *RCA PB 44481* **58**	2 wks

PRINCE US, male vocalist   235 wks

19 Jan 80	**I WANNA BE YOUR LOVER** *Warner Bros. K 17537* **41**	3 wks
29 Jan 83	**1999** *Warner Bros. W 9896* **25**	7 wks
30 Apr 83	**LITTLE RED CORVETTE** *Warner Bros. W 9688* **35**	6 wks
26 Nov 83	**LITTLE RED CORVETTE (re-issue)**	
	Warner Bros. W 9436 ....**66**	2 wks
30 Jun 84 ●	**WHEN DOVES CRY** *Warner Bros. W 9286* **4**	15 wks
22 Sep 84 ●	**PURPLE RAIN** *Warner Bros. W 9174* * **8**	9 wks
8 Dec 84	**I WOULD DIE 4 U** *Warner Bros. W 9121* * **58**	6 wks
19 Jan 85 ●	**1999/LITTLE RED CORVETTE (re-issue)**	
	Warner Bros. W 1999 ....**2**	10 wks
23 Feb 85 ●	**LET'S GO CRAZY/TAKE ME WITH YOU**	
	Warner Bros. W 2000 * **7**	9 wks
25 May 85	**PAISLEY PARK** *WEA W 9052* * **18**	10 wks
27 Jul 85	**RASPBERRY BERET** *WEA W 8929* * **25**	8 wks
26 Oct 85	**POP LIFE** *Paisley Park W 8858* * **60**	2 wks
8 Mar 86 ●	**KISS** *Paisley Park W 8751* * **6**	9 wks
14 Jun 86	**MOUNTAINS** *Paisley Park W 8711* * **45**	4 wks
16 Aug 86	**GIRLS AND BOYS** *Paisley Park W 8586* * **11**	8 wks
1 Nov 86	**ANOTHERLOVERHOLENYOHEAD**	
	Paisley Park W 8521 * **36**	3 wks
14 Mar 87 ●	**SIGN 'O' THE TIMES** *Paisley Park W 8399* **10**	9 wks
20 Jun 87	**IF I WAS YOUR GIRLFRIEND** *Paisley Park W 8334* **20**	6 wks
15 Aug 87	**U GOT THE LOOK** *Paisley Park W 8289* **11**	9 wks
28 Nov 87	**I COULD NEVER TAKE THE PLACE OF YOUR**	
	MAN *Paisley Park W 8288* **29**	6 wks
7 May 88 ●	**ALPHABET STREET** *Paisley Park W 7900* **9**	6 wks
23 Jul 88	**GLAM SLAM** *Paisley Park W 7806* **29**	4 wks
5 Nov 88	**I WISH U HEAVEN** *Paisley Park W 7745* **24**	5 wks
24 Jun 89 ●	**BATDANCE** *Warner Bros. W 2924* **2**	12 wks
9 Sep 89	**PARTYMAN** *Warner Bros. W 2814* **14**	6 wks
18 Nov 89	**THE ARMS OF ORION** *Warner Bros. W 2757* ** **27**	5 wks
4 Aug 90 ●	**THIEVES IN THE TEMPLE** *Paisley Park W 9751* **7**	6 wks
10 Nov 90	**NEW POWER GENERATION** *Paisley Park W 9525* **26**	4 wks
31 Aug 91 ●	**GETT OFF** *Paisley Park W 0056* *** **4**	8 wks

ELVIS PRESLEY wears his Army uniform for the benefit of his parents, Vernon and Gladys.

Left: In a classic example of different national tastes, 'Stumblin', the only top ten hit SUZI QUATRO had back home in the USA, was not one of her five British top ten successes.

PM DAWN sampled Spandau Ballet's 'True' to achieve chart bliss.

21 Sep 91		CREAM *Paisley Park W 0061* ***	15	7 wks
7 Dec 91		DIAMONDS AND PEARLS *Paisley Park W 0075* ***	25	6 wks
28 Mar 92		MONEY DON'T MATTER 2 NIGHT *Paisley Park W 0091* ***	19	5 wks
27 Jun 92		THUNDER *Paisley Park W 01132P* ***	28	3 wks
18 Jul 92	●	SEXY MF/STROLLIN' *Paisley Park W 0123* ***	4	7 wks
10 Oct 92	●	MY NAME IS PRINCE *Paisley Park W 0132* ***	7	5 wks
14 Nov 92		MY NAME IS PRINCE (re-mix) *Paisley Park W 0142T* ***	51	1 wk
5 Dec 92		7 *Paisley Park W 0147* ***	27†	4 wks

* Prince and the Revolution ** Prince with Sheena Easton *** Prince and the New Power Generation

Although uncredited, Sheena Easton also vocalises on U Got The Look.

PRINCE BUSTER *Jamaica, male vocalist*   **13 wks**

| 23 Feb 67 | | AL CAPONE *Blue Beat BB 324* | 18 | 13 wks |

PRINCE CHARLES and the CITY BEAT BAND *US, male vocalist with male vocal/instrumental group*   **2 wks**

| 22 Feb 86 | | WE CAN MAKE IT HAPPEN *PRT 7P 348* | 56 | 2 wks |

PRINCESS *UK, female vocalist*   **44 wks**

3 Aug 85	●	SAY I'M YOU'RE NO. 1 *Supreme SUPE 101*	7	12 wks
9 Nov 85		AFTER THE LOVE HAS GONE *Supreme SUPE 103*	28	13 wks
19 Apr 86		I'LL KEEP ON LOVING YOU *Supreme SUPE 105*	16	8 wks
5 Jul 86		TELL ME TOMORROW *Supreme SUPE 106*	34	5 wks
25 Oct 86		IN THE HEAT OF A PASSIONATE MOMENT *Supreme SUPE 109*	74	1 wk
13 Jun 87		RED HOT *Polydor POSP 868*	58	5 wks

PRINCESS IVORI *US, female rapper*   **2 wks**

| 17 Mar 90 | | WANTED *Supreme SUPE 163* | 69 | 2 wks |

PRIVATE LIVES *UK, male vocal/instrumental duo*   **4 wks**

| 11 Feb 84 | | LIVING IN A WORLD (TURNED UPSIDE DOWN) *EMI PRIV 2* | 53 | 4 wks |

P.J. PROBY *US, male vocalist*   **89 wks**

28 May 64	●	HOLD ME *Decca F 11904*	3	15 wks
3 Sep 64	●	TOGETHER *Decca F 11967*	8	11 wks
10 Dec 64	●	SOMEWHERE *Liberty LIB 10182*	6	12 wks
25 Feb 65		I APOLOGISE *Liberty LIB 10188*	11	8 wks
8 Jul 65		LET THE WATER RUN DOWN *Liberty LIB 10206*	19	8 wks
30 Sep 65		THAT MEANS A LOT *Liberty LIB 10215*	30	6 wks
25 Nov 65	●	MARIA *Liberty LIB 10218*	8	9 wks
10 Feb 66		YOU'VE COME BACK *Liberty LIB 10223*	25	7 wks
16 Jun 66		TO MAKE A BIG MAN CRY *Liberty LIB 10236*	34	3 wks
27 Oct 66		I CAN'T MAKE IT ALONE *Liberty LIB 10250*	37	5 wks
6 Mar 68		IT'S YOUR DAY TODAY *Liberty LBF 15046*	32	5 wks

PROCLAIMERS *UK, male vocal/instrumental duo*   **41 wks**

14 Nov 87	●	LETTER FROM AMERICA *Chrysalis CHS 3178*	3	10 wks
5 Mar 88		MAKE MY HEART FLY *Chrysalis CLAIM 1*	63	3 wks
27 Aug 88		I'M GONNA BE *Chrysalis CLAIM 2*	11	11 wks
12 Nov 88		SUNSHINE ON LEITH *Chrysalis CLAIM 3*	41	5 wks
11 Feb 89		I'M ON MY WAY *Chrysalis CLAIM 4*	43	4 wks
24 Nov 90	●	KING OF THE ROAD (EP) *Chrysalis CLAIM 5*	9	8 wks

Tracks on King Of The Road (EP): King Of The Road/Long Black Veil/Lulu Selling Tea/Not Ever.

PROCOL HARUM *UK, male vocal/instrumental group*   **56 wks**

25 May 67	★	A WHITER SHADE OF PALE *Deram DM 126*	1	15 wks
4 Oct 67	●	HOMBURG *Regal Zonophone RZ 3003*	6	10 wks
24 Apr 68		QUITE RIGHTLY SO *Regal Zonophone RZ 3007*	50	1 wk
18 Jun 69		SALTY DOG *Regal Zonophone RZ 3019*	44	1 wk
2 Jul 69		SALTY DOG (re-entry) *Regal Zonophone RZ 3019*	44	1 wk
16 Jul 69		SALTY DOG (2nd re-entry) *Regal Zonophone RZ 3019*	44	1 wk
22 Apr 72		A WHITER SHADE OF PALE (re-issue) *Magnifly ECHO 10*	13	13 wks
5 Aug 72		CONQUISTADOR *Chrysalis CHS 2003*	22	7 wks
23 Aug 75		PANDORA'S BOX *Chrysalis CHS 2073*	16	7 wks

PRODIGY *UK, male producer - Liam Howlett and dancers*   **29 wks**

24 Aug 91	●	CHARLY *XL XLS 21*	3	10 wks
4 Jan 92	●	EVERYBODY IN THE PLACE (EP) *XL XLS 26*	2	9 wks
26 Sep 92		FIRE/JERICHO *XL XLS 30*	11	4 wks
21 Nov 92	●	OUT OF SPACE/RUFF IN THE JUNGLE BIZNESS *XL XLS 35*	5†	6 wks

Tracks on Everybody In The Place (EP): Everybody In The Place/Crazy Man/G-Force/Rip Up The Sound System. Ruff In The Jungle Bizness only listed 27 Nov and 5 Dec '92.

PROFESSIONALS *UK, male vocal/instrumental group*   **4 wks**

| 11 Oct 80 | | 1-2-3 *Virgin VS 376* | 43 | 4 wks |

PROGRAM 2 BELTRAM – *See BELTRAM*

PROJECT 1 *UK, male producer - Mark Williams*   **3 wks**

| 16 May 92 | | ROUGHNECK EP *Rising High RSN 22* | 49 | 2 wks |
| 29 Aug 92 | | DON CARGON COMIN' *Rising High RSN 35* | 64 | 1 wk |

Tracks on Roughneck EP: Come My Selector/Can't Take The Heartbreak/Live Vibe 4 (Summer Vibes).

PRONG *US, male vocal/instrumental group*   **1 wk**

| 25 Apr 92 | | WHOSE FIST IS THIS ANYWAY EP *Epic 6580026* | 58 | 1 wk |

Tracks on Whose Fist Is This Anyway EP: Prove You Wrong/Hell If I Could/(Get A) Grip (On Yourself)/Prove You Wrong (re-mix).

PROPAGANDA   **35 wks**
Germany, male/female vocal/instrumental group

17 Mar 84		DR MABUSE *ZTT ZTAS 2*	27	9 wks
4 May 85		DUEL *ZTT ZTAS 8*	21	12 wks
10 Aug 85		P MACHINERY *ZTT ZTAS 12*	50	11 wks
28 Apr 90		HEAVEN GIVE ME WORDS *Virgin VS 1245*	36	5 wks
8 Sep 90		ONLY ONE WORD *Virgin VS 1271*	71	4 wks

Brian PROTHEROE *UK, male vocalist*   **6 wks**

| 7 Sep 74 | | PINBALL *Chrysalis CHS 2043* | 22 | 6 wks |

Dorothy PROVINE *US, female vocalist*   **15 wks**

| 7 Dec 61 | | DON'T BRING LULU *Warner Bros. WB 53* | 17 | 12 wks |
| 28 Jun 62 | | CRAZY WORDS CRAZY TUNE *Warner Bros. WB 70* | 45 | 3 wks |

PSEUDO ECHO *Australia, male vocal/instrumental group*   **12 wks**

| 18 Jul 87 | ● | FUNKY TOWN *RCA PB 49705* | 8 | 12 wks |

QUEEN are shown on
the set of the video for
'I'm Going Slightly
Mad'.

PSYCHEDELIC FURS *UK, male vocal/instrumental group* **31 wks**

2 May 81	**DUMB WAITERS** *CBS 1166* **59**	2 wks
27 Jun 81	**PRETTY IN PINK** *CBS A 1327* **43**	5 wks
31 Jul 82	**LOVE MY WAY** *CBS A 2549* **42**	6 wks
31 Mar 84	**HEAVEN** *CBS A 4300* **29**	6 wks
16 Jun 84	**GHOST IN YOU** *CBS A 4470* **68**	2 wks
23 Aug 86	**PRETTY IN PINK** *CBS A 7242* **18**	9 wks
9 Jul 88	**ALL THAT MONEY WANTS** *CBS FURS 4* **75**	1 wk

A 7242 was a re-recording of A 1327.

PSYCHIC TV *UK, male/female vocal/instrumental group* **4 wks**

26 Apr 86	**GODSTAR** *Temple TOPY 009* * **67**	2 wks
20 Sep 86	**GOOD VIBRATIONS/ROMAN P.** *Temple TOPY 23*..........**65**	2 wks

* Psychic TV and the Angels of Light

PSYCHOTROPIC – *See FREEFALL featuring PSYCHOTROPIC; SALT-N-PEPA*

PUBLIC ANNOUNCEMENT – *See R KELLY and PUBLIC ANNOUNCEMENT*

PUBLIC ENEMY *US, male rap duo* **44 wks**

21 Nov 87	**REBEL WITHOUT A PAUSE** *Def Jam 651245 7* **37**	5 wks
2 Jan 88	**REBEL WITHOUT A PAUSE (re-entry)**	
	Def Jam 651245 7 ....**71**	2 wks
9 Jan 88	**BRING THE NOISE** *Def Jam 651335 7* **32**	5 wks
2 Jul 88	**DON'T BELIEVE THE HYPE** *Def Jam 652833 7* **18**	5 wks
15 Oct 88	**NIGHT OF THE LIVING BASEHEADS**	
	Def Jam 6530460 ....**63**	2 wks
24 Jun 89	**FIGHT THE POWER** *Motown ZB 42877*............................**29**	5 wks
20 Jan 90	**WELCOME TO THE TERRORDOME**	
	Def Jam 655476 0 ....**18**	4 wks
7 Apr 90	**911 IS A JOKE** *Def Jam 655830 7* **41**	3 wks
23 Jun 90	**BROTHERS GONNA WORK IT OUT**	
	Def Jam 656018 1 ....**46**	2 wks
3 Nov 90	**CAN'T DO NUTTIN' FOR YA MAN** *Def Jam 656385 7* **53**	2 wks
12 Oct 91	**CAN'T TRUSS IT** *Def Jam 6575307* **22**	4 wks
25 Jan 92	**SHUT 'EM DOWN** *Def Jam 6577617*................................**21**	3 wks
11 Apr 92	**NIGHTTRAIN** *Def Jam 6578647* **55**	2 wks

PUBLIC IMAGE LTD. **61 wks**

UK, male vocal/instrumental group

21 Oct 78	● **PUBLIC IMAGE** *Virgin VS 228* **9**	8 wks
7 Jul 79	**DEATH DISCO** (PARTS 1 & 2) *Virgin VS 274* **20**	7 wks
20 Oct 79	**MEMORIES** *Virgin VS 299* **60**	2 wks
4 Apr 81	**FLOWERS OF ROMANCE** *Virgin VS 397* **24**	7 wks
17 Sep 83	● **THIS IS NOT A LOVE SONG** *Virgin VS 529* **5**	10 wks
19 May 84	**BAD LIFE** *Virgin VS 675* **71**	2 wks
1 Feb 86	**RISE** *Virgin VS 841* **11**	8 wks
3 May 86	**HOME** *Virgin VS 855* **75**	1 wk
22 Aug 87	**SEATTLE** *Virgin VS 988* **47**	4 wks
6 May 89	**DISAPPOINTED** *Virgin VS 1181* **38**	5 wks
20 Oct 90	**DON'T ASK ME** *Virgin VS 1231* **22**	5 wks
22 Feb 92	**CRUEL** *Virgin VS 1390*..**49**	2 wks

Group often known as P.I.L.

Gary PUCKETT – *See UNION GAP featuring Gary PUCKETT*

James and Bobby PURIFY *US, male vocal duo* **16 wks**

24 Apr 76	**I'M YOUR PUPPET** *Mercury 6167 324* **12**	10 wks
7 Aug 76	**MORNING GLORY** *Mercury 6167 380* **27**	6 wks

PURPLE HEARTS *UK, male vocal/instrumental group* **5 wks**

22 Sep 79	**MILLIONS LIKE US** *Fiction FICS 003* **57**	3 wks
8 Mar 80	**JIMMY** *Fiction FICS 9* **60**	2 wks

PUSSYCAT *Holland, male/female vocal/instrumental group* **30 wks**

28 Aug 76	★ **MISSISSIPPI** *Sonet SON 2077* **1**	22 wks
25 Dec 76	**SMILE** *Sonet SON 2096* **24**	8 wks

PYRAMIDS *Jamaica, male vocal/instrumental group* **4 wks**

22 Nov 67	**TRAIN TOUR TO RAINBOW CITY** *President PT 161* **35**	4 wks

PYTHON LEE JACKSON **12 wks**

Australia, male vocal/instrumental group

30 Sep 72	● **IN A BROKEN DREAM** *Youngblood YB 1002* **3**	12 wks

Uncredited lead vocals by Rod Stewart.

Q

Q UNIQUE – *See C&C MUSIC FACTORY/CLIVILLES & COLE*

Q-BASS *UK, male production/instrumental group* **1 wk**

8 Feb 92	**HARDCORE WILL NEVER DIE**	
	Suburban Base SUBBASE 007 ....**64**	1 wk

Q-TEE – *See HISTORY featuring Q-TEE*

QUADROPHONIA **15 wks**

Belgium, male instrumental/production group

13 Apr 91	**QUADROPHONIA** *ARS 6567687*..**14**	9 wks
6 Jul 91	**THE WAVE OF THE FUTURE** *ARS 6569937* **40**	3 wks
21 Dec 91	**FIND THE TIME** (PART ONE) *ARS 6576260* **41**	3 wks

QUADS *UK, male vocal/instrumental group* **2 wks**

22 Sep 79	**THERE MUST BE THOUSANDS** *Big Bear BB 23* **66**	2 wks

QUANTUM JUMP *UK, male vocal/instrumental group* **10 wks**

2 Jun 79	● **THE LONE RANGER** *Electric WOT 33* **5**	10 wks

QUARTERFLASH **5 wks**

US, male/female vocal/instrumental group

27 Feb 82	**HARDEN MY HEART** *Geffen GEF A 1838* **49**	5 wks

QUARTZ *UK, male instrumental group* **19 wks**

17 Mar 90	**WE'RE COMIN' AT YA** *Mercury ITMR 2* * **65**	2 wks
2 Feb 91	● **IT'S TOO LATE** *Mercury ITM 3* ** **8**	14 wks
15 Jun 91	**NAKED LOVE (JUST SAY YOU WANT ME)**	
	Mercury ITM 4 *** **39**	3 wks

* Quartz featuring Stepz ** Quartz introducing Dina Carroll *** Quartz and Dina Carroll

Jackie QUARTZ *France, female vocalist* **3 wks**

11 Mar 89	**A LA VIE, A L'AMOUR** *PWL PWL 30*..................................**55**	3 wks

Suzi QUATRO US, female vocalist/instrumentalist - bass guitar   122 wks

19 May 73	★ CAN THE CAN RAK 150	1	14 wks
28 Jul 73	● 48 CRASH RAK 158	3	9 wks
27 Oct 73	DAYTONA DEMON RAK 161	14	13 wks
9 Feb 74	★ DEVIL GATE DRIVE RAK 167	1	11 wks
29 Jun 74	TOO BIG RAK 175	14	6 wks
9 Nov 74	THE WILD ONE RAK 185	7	10 wks
8 Feb 75	YOUR MAMA WON'T LIKE ME RAK 191	31	5 wks
5 Mar 77	TEAR ME APART RAK 248	27	6 wks
18 Mar 78	● IF YOU CAN'T GIVE ME LOVE RAK 271	4	13 wks
22 Jul 78	THE RACE IS ON RAK 278	43	5 wks
11 Nov 78	STUMBLIN' IN RAK 285 *	41	8 wks
20 Oct 79	SHE'S IN LOVE WITH YOU RAK 299	11	9 wks
19 Jan 80	MAMA'S BOY RAK 303	34	5 wks
5 Apr 80	I'VE NEVER BEEN IN LOVE RAK 307	56	3 wks
25 Oct 80	ROCK HARD Dreamland DLSP 6	68	2 wks
13 Nov 82	HEART OF STONE Polydor POSP 477	60	3 wks

* Suzi Quatro and Chris Norman

QUEEN UK, male vocal/instrumental group   345 wks

9 Mar 74	● SEVEN SEAS OF RHYE EMI 2121	10	10 wks
26 Oct 74	● KILLER QUEEN EMI 2229	2	12 wks
25 Jan 75	NOW I'M HERE EMI 2256	11	7 wks
8 Nov 75	★ BOHEMIAN RHAPSODY EMI 2375	1	17 wks
3 Jul 76	● YOU'RE MY BEST FRIEND EMI 2494	7	8 wks
27 Nov 76	● SOMEBODY TO LOVE EMI 2565	2	9 wks
19 Mar 77	TIE YOUR MOTHER DOWN EMI 2593	31	4 wks
4 Jun 77	QUEEN'S FIRST EP EMI 2623	17	10 wks
22 Oct 77	● WE ARE THE CHAMPIONS EMI 2708	2	11 wks
25 Feb 78	SPREAD YOUR WINGS EMI 2757	34	4 wks
28 Oct 78	BICYCLE RACE/FAT BOTTOMED GIRLS EMI 2870	11	12 wks
10 Feb 79	● DON'T STOP ME NOW EMI 2910	9	12 wks
14 Jul 79	LOVE OF MY LIFE EMI 2959	63	2 wks
20 Oct 79	● CRAZY LITTLE THING CALLED LOVE EMI 5001	2	14 wks
2 Feb 80	SAVE ME EMI 5022	11	6 wks
14 Jun 80	PLAY THE GAME EMI 5076	14	8 wks
6 Sep 80	● ANOTHER ONE BITES THE DUST EMI 5102	7	9 wks
6 Dec 80	● FLASH EMI 5126	10	13 wks
14 Nov 81	★ UNDER PRESSURE EMI 5250 *	1	11 wks
1 May 82	BODY LANGUAGE EMI 5293	25	6 wks
12 Jun 82	LAS PALABRAS DE AMOR EMI 5316	17	8 wks
21 Aug 82	BACKCHAT EMI 5325	40	4 wks
4 Feb 84	● RADIO GAGA EMI QUEEN 1	2	9 wks
14 Apr 84	I WANT TO BREAK FREE EMI QUEEN 2	3	15 wks
28 Jul 84	IT'S A HARD LIFE EMI QUEEN 3	6	9 wks
22 Sep 84	HAMMER TO FALL EMI QUEEN 4	13	7 wks
8 Dec 84	THANK GOD IT'S CHRISTMAS EMI QUEEN 5	21	6 wks
16 Nov 85	● ONE VISION EMI QUEEN 6	7	10 wks
29 Mar 86	● A KIND OF MAGIC EMI QUEEN 7	3	11 wks
21 Jun 86	FRIENDS WILL BE FRIENDS EMI QUEEN 8	14	8 wks
27 Sep 86	WHO WANTS TO LIVE FOREVER EMI QUEEN 9	24	5 wks
13 May 89	● I WANT IT ALL Parlophone QUEEN 10	3	7 wks
1 Jul 89	● BREAKTHRU' Parlophone QUEEN 11	7	7 wks
19 Aug 89	THE INVISIBLE MAN Parlophone QUEEN 12	12	6 wks
21 Oct 89	SCANDAL Parlophone QUEEN 14	25	4 wks
9 Dec 89	THE MIRACLE Parlophone QUEEN 15	21	5 wks
26 Jan 91	★ INNUENDO Parlophone QUEEN 16	1	5 wks
16 Mar 91	I'M GOING SLIGHTLY MAD Parlophone QUEEN 17	22	5 wks
25 May 91	HEADLONG Parlophone QUEEN 18	14	4 wks
26 Oct 91	THE SHOW MUST GO ON Parlophone QUEEN 19	16	5 wks
7 Dec 91	THE SHOW MUST GO ON (re-entry) Parlophone QUEEN 19	27	5 wks
21 Dec 91	★ BOHEMIAN RHAPSODY (re-issue)/THESE ARE THE DAYS OF OUR LIVES Parlophone QUEEN 20	1	14 wks

* Queen and David Bowie

Tracks on Queen's First EP: Good Old Fashioned Lover Boy/Death On Two Legs (Dedicated To...)/Tenement Funster/White Queen (As it Began).

QUEEN LATIFAH US, female rapper   10 wks

24 Mar 90	MAMA GAVE BIRTH TO THE SOUL CHILDREN Gee Street GEE 26 *	14	7 wks
26 May 90	FIND A WAY Ahead Of Our Time CCUT 8 **	52	2 wks
31 Aug 91	FLY GIRL Gee Street GEE 34	67	1 wk

* Queen Latifah De La Soul ** Coldcut featuring Queen Latifah

QUEENSRYCHE US, male vocal/instrumental group   16 wks

13 May 89	EYES OF A STRANGER EMI USA MT 65	59	1 wk
10 Nov 90	EMPIRE EMI USA MT 90	61	1 wk
20 Apr 91	SILENT LUCIDITY EMI USA MT 94	34	5 wks
6 Jul 91	BEST I CAN EMI USA MT 97	36	3 wks
7 Sep 91	JET CITY WOMAN EMI USA MT 98	39	2 wks
8 Aug 92	SILENT LUCIDITY (re-issue) EMI USA MT 104	18	4 wks

? (QUESTION MARK) and the MYSTERIANS US, male vocal/instrumental group   4 wks

17 Nov 66	96 TEARS Cameo Parkway C428	37	4 wks

QUESTIONS UK, male vocal/instrumental group   8 wks

23 Apr 83	PRICE YOU PAY Respond KOB 702	56	3 wks
17 Sep 83	TEAR SOUP Respond KOB 705	66	1 wk
10 Mar 84	TUESDAY SUNSHINE Respond KOB 707	46	4 wks

QUICK UK, male vocal/instrumental group   7 wks

15 May 82	RHYTHM OF THE JUNGLE Epic EPC A 2013	41	7 wks

Tommy QUICKLY UK, male vocalist   8 wks

22 Oct 64	WILD SIDE OF LIFE Pye 7N 15708	33	8 wks

QUIET FIVE UK, male vocal/instrumental group   3 wks

13 May 65	WHEN THE MORNING SUN DRIES THE DEW Parlophone R 5273	45	1 wk
21 Apr 66	HOMEWARD BOUND Parlophone R 5421	44	2 wks

QUIET RIOT US, male vocal/instrumental group   5 wks

3 Dec 83	METAL HEALTH/CUM ON FEEL THE NOIZE Epic A 3968	45	5 wks

Cum on Feel the Noize *only credited from 10 Dec 83.*

Paul QUINN and Edwyn COLLINS UK, male vocal duo   2 wks

11 Aug 84	PALE BLUE EYES Swamplands SWP 1	72	2 wks

QUIREBOYS UK, male vocal/instrumental group   24 wks

4 Nov 89	7 O'CLOCK Parlophone R 6230	36	4 wks
6 Jan 90	HEY YOU Parlophone R 6241	14	7 wks
7 Apr 90	I DON'T LOVE YOU ANYMORE Parlophone R 6248	24	6 wks
8 Sep 90	THERE SHE GOES AGAIN/MISLED Parlophone R 6267	37	4 wks
10 Oct 92	TRAMPS AND THIEVES Parlophone RS 6323	41	3 wks

QUIVER – *See SUTHERLAND BROTHERS and QUIVER*

R

Eddie RABBITT *US, male vocalist* — 14 wks

27 Jan 79	**EVERY WHICH WAY BUT LOOSE** *Elektra K 12331*	**41**	9 wks
28 Feb 81	**I LOVE A RAINY NIGHT** *Elektra K 12498*	**53**	5 wks

Steve RACE *UK, male instrumentalist – piano* — 9 wks

28 Feb 63	**PIED PIPER (THE BEEJE)** *Parlophone R 4981*	**29**	9 wks

RACEY *UK, male vocal/instrumental group* — 44 wks

25 Nov 78 ●	**LAY YOUR LOVE ON ME** *RAK 284*	**3**	14 wks
31 Mar 79 ●	**SOME GIRLS** *RAK 291*	**2**	11 wks
18 Aug 79	**BOY OH BOY** *RAK 297*	**22**	9 wks
20 Dec 80	**RUNAROUND SUE** *RAK 325*	**13**	10 wks

RACING CARS *UK, male vocal/instrumental group* — 7 wks

12 Feb 77	**THEY SHOOT HORSES DON'T THEY** *Chrysalis CHS 2129*	**14**	7 wks

RACKETEERS – *See Elbow BONES and the RACKETEERS*

Jimmy RADCLIFFE *US, male vocalist* — 2 wks

4 Feb 65	**LONG AFTER TONIGHT IS ALL OVER** *Stateside SS 374*	**40**	2 wks

RADHA KRISHNA TEMPLE — 17 wks
Oxford Street, male/female vocal/instrumental group

13 Sep 69	**HARE KRISHNA MANTRA** *Apple 15*	**12**	9 wks
28 Mar 70	**GOVINDA** *Apple 25*	**23**	8 wks

RADICAL ROB *UK, male producer – Rob McLuan* — 1 wk

11 Jan 92	**MONKEY WAH** *R&S RSUK 8*	**67**	1 wk

RADIO HEART – *See Gary NUMAN*

RADIO 1 DJ POSSE – *See Liz KERSHAW and Bruno BROOKES*

RADIO REVELLERS – *See Anthony STEEL and the RADIO REVELLERS*

RADIO STARS *UK, male vocal/instrumental group* — 3 wks

4 Feb 78	**NERVOUS WRECK** *Chiswick NS 23*	**39**	3 wks

Fonda RAE *US, female vocalist* — 4 wks

6 Oct 84	**TUCH ME** *Streetwave KHAN 28*	**49**	4 wks

Jesse RAE *UK, male vocalist* — 2 wks

11 May 85	**OVER THE SEA** *Scotland-Video YZ 36*	**65**	2 wks

RAF *Italy, male/female vocal/instrumental group* — 3 wks

14 Mar 92	**WE'VE GOT TO LIVE TOGETHER** *PWL Continental PWL 218*	**34**	3 wks

Gerry RAFFERTY *UK, male vocalist* — 47 wks

18 Feb 78 ●	**BAKER STREET** *United Artists UP 36346*	**3**	15 wks
26 May 79 ●	**NIGHT OWL** *United Artists UP 36512*	**5**	13 wks
18 Aug 79	**GET IT RIGHT NEXT TIME** *United Artists BP 301*	**30**	9 wks
22 Mar 80	**BRING IT ALL HOME** *United Artists BP 340*	**54**	4 wks
21 Jun 80	**ROYAL MILE** *United Artists BP 354*	**67**	2 wks
10 Mar 90	**BAKER STREET (re-mix)** *EMI EM 132*	**53**	4 wks

RAGE *UK, male vocal/instrumental group* — 9 wks

31 Oct 92 ●	**RUN TO YOU** *Pulse 8 LOSE 33*	**3†**	9 wks

RAGGA TWINS *UK, male vocal group* — 10 wks

10 Nov 90	**ILLEGAL GUNSHOT/SPLIFFHEAD** *Shut Up And Dance SUAD 7*	**51**	2 wks
6 Apr 91	**WIPE THE NEEDLE/JUGGLING** *Shut Up And Dance SUAD 12S*	**71**	2 wks
6 Jul 91	**HOOLIGAN 69** *Shut Up And Dance SUAD 16S*	**56**	2 wks
7 Mar 92	**MIXED TRUTH/BRING UP THE MIC SOME MORE** *Shut Up And Dance SUAD 27S*	**65**	2 wks
11 Jul 92	**SHINE EYE** *Shut Up And Dance SUAD 32S* *	**63**	2 wks

* Ragga Twins featuring Junior Reid

RAGTIMERS *UK, male instrumental group* — 8 wks

16 Mar 74	**THE STING** *Pye 7N 45323*	**46**	1 wk
30 Mar 74	**THE STING (re-entry)** *Pye 7N 45323*	**31**	7 wks

RAH BAND *UK, male/female vocal/instrumental group* — 50 wks

9 Jul 77 ●	**THE CRUNCH** *Good Earth GD 7*	**6**	12 wks
1 Nov 80	**FALCON** *DJM DJS 10954*	**35**	7 wks
7 Feb 81	**SLIDE** *DJM DJS 10964*	**50**	7 wks
1 May 82	**PERFUMED GARDEN** *KR KR 5*	**45**	7 wks
9 Jul 83	**MESSAGES FROM THE STARS** *TMT TMT 5*	**42**	5 wks
19 Jan 85	**ARE YOU SATISFIED? (FUNKA NOVA)** *RCA RCA 470*	**70**	2 wks
30 Mar 85 ●	**CLOUDS ACROSS THE MOON** *RCA PB 40025*	**6**	10 wks

RAILWAY CHILDREN — 13 wks
UK, male vocal/instrumental group

24 Mar 90	**EVERY BEAT OF THE HEART** *Virgin VS 1237*	**68**	2 wks
2 Jun 90	**MUSIC STOP** *Virgin VS 1255*	**66**	2 wks
20 Oct 90	**SO RIGHT** *Virgin VS 1289*	**68**	1 wk
2 Feb 91	**EVERY BEAT OF THE HEART (re-entry)** *Virgin VS 1237*	**24**	6 wks
20 Apr 91	**SOMETHING SO GOOD** *Virgin VS 1318*	**57**	2 wks

RAIN – *See Stephanie DE SYKES*

RAIN TREE CROW — 1 wk
UK, male vocal/instrumental group - Japan under an assumed name

30 Mar 91	**BLACKWATER** *Virgin VS 1340*	**62**	1 wk

Number one in the country with 'Just Walkin' in the Rain', JOHNNIE RAY celebrates on 8 December 1956 by drawing a pint at the Denmark pub in Kensington.

CLIFF RICHARD embraces fellow members of the cast of the musical *Time*.

GERRY RAFFERTY wrote and recorded the classic 'Baker Street' and had no kind words for its hit revival by Undercover.

RAINBOW UK, male vocal/instrumental group — 62 wks

17 Sep 77	KILL THE KING Polydor 2066 845	44	3 wks
8 Apr 78	LONG LIVE ROCK 'N' ROLL Polydor 2066 913	33	3 wks
30 Sep 78	L. A. CONNECTION Polydor 2066 968	40	4 wks
15 Sep 79 ●	SINCE YOU'VE BEEN GONE Polydor POSP 70	6	10 wks
16 Feb 80 ●	ALL NIGHT LONG Polydor POSP 104	5	11 wks
31 Jan 81 ●	I SURRENDER Polydor POSP 221	3	10 wks
20 Jun 81	CAN'T HAPPEN HERE Polydor POSP 251	20	8 wks
11 Jul 81	KILL THE KING (re-issue) Polydor POSP 274	41	4 wks
3 Apr 82	STONE COLD Polydor POSP 421	34	4 wks
27 Aug 83	STREET OF DREAMS Polydor POSP 631	52	3 wks
5 Nov 83	CAN'T LET YOU GO Polydor POSP 654	43	2 wks

RAINBOW COTTAGE UK, male vocal/instrumental group — 4 wks

| 6 Mar 76 | SEAGULL Penny Farthing PEN 906 | 33 | 4 wks |

RAINMAKERS US, male vocal/instrumental group — 11 wks

| 7 Mar 87 | LET MY PEOPLE GO-GO Mercury MER 238 | 18 | 11 wks |

Marvin RAINWATER US, male vocalist — 22 wks

| 7 Mar 58 ★ | WHOLE LOTTA WOMAN MGM 974 | 1 | 15 wks |
| 6 Jun 58 | I DIG YOU BABY MGM 980 | 19 | 7 wks |

Bonnie RAITT US, female vocalist — 4 wks

| 14 Dec 91 | I CAN'T MAKE YOU LOVE ME Capitol CL 639 | 50 | 4 wks |

Tony RALLO and the MIDNIGHT BAND — 8 wks
France/US, male vocal/instrumental group

| 23 Feb 80 | HOLDIN' ON Calibre CAB 150 | 34 | 8 wks |

Sheryl Lee RALPH US, female vocalist — 2 wks

| 26 Jan 85 | IN THE EVENING Arista ARIST 595 | 64 | 2 wks |

RAM JAM US, male vocal/instrumental group — 20 wks

| 10 Sep 77 ● | BLACK BETTY Epic EPC 5492 | 7 | 12 wks |
| 17 Feb 90 | BLACK BETTY (re-mix) Epic 655430 7 | 13 | 8 wks |

RAM JAM BAND – See Geno WASHINGTON and the RAM JAM BAND

RAMBLERS (from the Abbey Hey — 15 wks
Junior School) UK, children's choir

| 13 Oct 79 | THE SPARROW Decca F 13860 | 11 | 15 wks |

RAMONES US, male vocal/instrumental group — 32 wks

21 May 77	SHEENA IS A PUNK ROCKER Sire RAM 001	22	7 wks
6 Aug 77	SWALLOW MY PRIDE Sire 6078 607	36	3 wks
30 Sep 78	DON'T COME CLOSE Sire SRE 1031	39	5 wks
8 Sep 79	ROCK 'N' ROLL HIGH SCHOOL Sire SIR 4021	67	2 wks
26 Jan 80 ●	BABY I LOVE YOU Sire SIR 4031	8	9 wks
19 Apr 80	DO YOU REMEMBER ROCK 'N' ROLL RADIO Sire SIR 4037	54	3 wks

| 10 May 86 | SOMEBODY PUT SOMETHING IN MY DRINK/SOMETHING TO BELIEVE IN Beggars Banquet BEG 157 | 69 | 1 wk |
| 19 Dec 92 | POISON HEART Chrysalis CHS 3917 | 69† | 2 wks |

RAMRODS US, male/female instrumental group — 12 wks

| 23 Feb 61 ● | RIDERS IN THE SKY London HLU 9282 | 8 | 12 wks |

RANGE – See Bruce HORNSBY and the RANGE

RANKING ANN – See SCRITTI POLITTI

Shabba RANKS Jamaica, male vocalist — 28 wks

16 Mar 91	SHE'S A WOMAN Virgin VS 1333 *	20	7 wks
18 May 91	TRAILER LOAD A GIRLS Epic 6568747	63	2 wks
24 Aug 91	HOUSECALL Epic 6573477 **	31	7 wks
8 Aug 92	MR LOVERMAN Epic 6582517	23	7 wks
28 Nov 92	SLOW AND SEXY Epic 6587727 ***	17†	5 wks

* Scritti Politti featuring Shabba Ranks ** Shabba Ranks featuring Maxi Priest
*** Shabba Ranks featuring Johnny Gill

RAPINATION – See Kym MAZELLE

RARE BIRD UK, male vocal/instrumental group — 8 wks

| 14 Feb 70 | SYMPATHY Charisma CB 120 | 27 | 8 wks |

O. RASBURY – See Rahni HARRIS and F.L.O.

Roland RAT SUPERSTAR UK, male rat vocalist — 20 wks

19 Nov 83	RAT RAPPING Rodent RAT 1	14	12 wks
28 Apr 84	LOVE ME TENDER Rodent RAT 2	32	7 wks
2 Mar 85	NO. 1 RAT FAN Rodent RAT 4	72	1 wk

RATPACK UK, male instrumental/production duo — 3 wks

| 6 Jun 92 | SEARCHIN' FOR MY RIZLA Big Giant BIGT 02 | 58 | 3 wks |

RATTLES Germany, male vocal/instrumental group — 15 wks

| 3 Oct 70 ● | THE WITCH Decca F 23058 | 8 | 15 wks |

RAVESIGNAL III — 2 wks
Belgium, male producer - Raymond Bolland

| 14 Dec 91 | HORSEPOWER R&S RSUK 6 | 61 | 2 wks |

RAW SILK US, female vocal group — 12 wks

| 16 Oct 82 | DO IT TO THE MUSIC KR KR 14 | 18 | 9 wks |
| 10 Sep 83 | JUST IN TIME West End WEND 2 | 49 | 3 wks |

Lou RAWLS US, male vocalist — 10 wks

| 31 Jul 76 ● | YOU'LL NEVER FIND ANOTHER LOVE LIKE MINE Philadelphia International PIR 4372 | 10 | 10 wks |

Gene Anthony RAY – See KIDS FROM FAME

Johnnie RAY US, male vocalist — 152 wks

Date	Title	Pos	Wks
14 Nov 52	WALKING MY BABY BACK HOME *Columbia DB 3060*	12	1 wk
19 Dec 52 ●	FAITH CAN MOVE MOUNTAINS *Columbia DB 3154 **	7	2 wks
9 Jan 53 ●	FAITH CAN MOVE MOUNTAINS (re-entry) *Columbia DB 3154 **	9	1 wk
3 Apr 53	MA SAYS PA SAYS *Columbia DB 3242 ***	12	1 wk
10 Apr 53	SOMEBODY STOLE MY GAL *Philips PB 123*	6	1 wk
17 Apr 53	FULL TIME JOB *Columbia DB 3242 ***	11	1 wk
24 Apr 53 ●	SOMEBODY STOLE MY GAL (re-entry) *Philips PB 123*	6	4 wks
29 May 53	SOMEBODY STOLE MY GAL (2nd re-entry) *Philips PB 123*	12	1 wk
24 Jul 53 ●	LET'S WALK THAT-A-WAY *Philips PB 157 ***	4	14 wks
7 Aug 53	SOMEBODY STOLE MY GAL (3rd re-entry) *Philips PB 123*	11	1 wk
9 Apr 54 ★	SUCH A NIGHT *Philips PB 244*	1	18 wks
8 Apr 55	IF YOU BELIEVE *Philips PB 379*	15	1 wk
13 May 55 ●	IF YOU BELIEVE (re-entry) *Philips PB 379*	7	10 wks
20 May 55	PATHS OF PARADISE *Philips PB 441*	20	1 wk
7 Oct 55	HERNANDO'S HIDEAWAY *Philips PB 495*	11	5 wks
14 Oct 55 ●	HEY THERE *Philips PB 495*	5	9 wks
28 Oct 55 ●	SONG OF THE DREAMER *Philips PB 516*	10	5 wks
17 Feb 56	WHO'S SORRY NOW *Philips PB 546*	17	2 wks
20 Apr 56	AIN'T MISBEHAVIN' *Philips PB 580*	17	6 wks
8 Jun 56	AIN'T MISBEHAVIN' (re-entry) *Philips PB 580*	24	1 wk
12 Oct 56 ★	JUST WALKIN' IN THE RAIN *Philips PB 624*	1	19 wks
18 Jan 57	YOU DON'T OWE ME A THING *Philips PB 655*	12	15 wks
8 Feb 57 ●	LOOK HOMEWARD ANGEL *Philips PB 655*	7	16 wks
10 May 57 ★	YES TONIGHT JOSEPHINE *Philips PB 686*	1	16 wks
6 Sep 57	BUILD YOUR LOVE *Philips PB 721*	17	7 wks
4 Oct 57	GOOD EVENING FRIENDS/UP ABOVE MY HEAD *Philips PB 708 ****	25	4 wks
4 Dec 59	I'LL NEVER FALL IN LOVE AGAIN *Philips PB 952*	26	4 wks
8 Jan 60	I'LL NEVER FALL IN LOVE AGAIN (re-entry) *Philips PB 952*	26	1 wk
5 Feb 60	I'LL NEVER FALL IN LOVE AGAIN (2nd re-entry) *Philips PB 952*	28	1 wk

* Johnnie Ray and the Four Lads ** Doris Day and Johnnie Ray *** Frankie Laine and Johnnie Ray

The chart history of You Don't Owe Me A Thing/Look Homeward Angel *is complicated, as follows:* You Don't Owe Me A Thing *entered the chart by itself on 18 Jan 57. On 8 and 15 Feb 57* Look Homeward Angel *was coupled with* You Don't Owe Me A Thing *but from 22 Feb 57 the two sides went their individual ways on the chart and were listed separately,* You Don't Owe Me A Thing *for a further 10 weeks and* Look Homeward Angel *for a further 14.*

RAYDIO US, male/female vocal/instrumental group — 21 wks

Date	Title	Pos	Wks
8 Apr 78	JACK AND JILL *Arista 161*	11	12 wks
8 Jul 78	IS THIS A LOVE THING *Arista 193*	27	9 wks

RAZE US, male/female vocal/instrumental group — 45 wks

Date	Title	Pos	Wks
1 Nov 86	JACK THE GROOVE *Champion CHAMP 23*	57	7 wks
3 Jan 87	JACK THE GROOVE (re-entry) *Champion CHAMP 23*	20	8 wks
28 Feb 87	LET THE MUSIC MOVE U *Champion CHAMP 27*	57	3 wks
31 Dec 88	BREAK 4 LOVE *Champion CHAMP 67*	28	11 wks
15 Jul 89	LET IT ROLL *Atlantic A 8866 **	27	5 wks
2 Sep 89	BREAK 4 LOVE (re-entry) *Champion CHAMP 67*	59	5 wks
27 Jan 90	ALL 4 LOVE (BREAK 4 LOVE 1990) *Champion CHAMP 228 ***	30	5 wks
10 Feb 90	CAN YOU FEEL IT/CAN YOU FEEL IT *Champion CHAMP 227*	62	1 wk

* Raze presents Doug Lazy ** Raze featuring Lady J and Secretary of Entertainment

Can You Feel It *was listed with* Can You Feel It *by Champion Legend, a montage of six Raze tracks.*

Chris REA UK, male vocalist — 107 wks

Date	Title	Pos	Wks
7 Oct 78	FOOL (IF YOU THINK IT'S OVER) *Magnet MAG 111*	30	7 wks
21 Apr 79	DIAMONDS *Magnet MAG 144*	44	3 wks
27 Mar 82	LOVING YOU *Magnet MAG 215*	65	3 wks
1 Oct 83	I CAN HEAR YOUR HEARTBEAT *Magnet MAG 244*	60	2 wks
17 Mar 84	I DON'T KNOW WHAT IT IS BUT I LOVE IT *Magnet MAG 255*	65	2 wks
30 Mar 85	STAINSBY GIRLS *Magnet MAG 276*	27	10 wks
29 Jun 85	JOSEPHINE *Magnet MAG 280*	67	2 wks
29 Mar 86	IT'S ALL GONE *Magnet MAG 283*	69	1 wk
31 May 86	ON THE BEACH *Magnet MAG 294*	57	3 wks
28 Jun 86	ON THE BEACH (re-entry) *Magnet MAG 294*	75	1 wk
12 Jul 86	ON THE BEACH (2nd re-entry) *Magnet MAG 294*	66	4 wks
6 Jun 87	LET'S DANCE *Magnet MAG 299*	12	10 wks
29 Aug 87	LOVING YOU AGAIN *Magnet MAG 300*	47	4 wks
5 Dec 87	JOYS OF CHRISTMAS *Magnet MAG 314*	67	1 wk
13 Feb 88	QUE SERA *Magnet MAG 318*	73	2 wks
13 Aug 88	ON THE BEACH SUMMER '88 *WEA YZ 195*	12	6 wks
22 Oct 88	I CAN HEAR YOUR HEARTBEAT *WEA YZ 320*	74	2 wks
17 Dec 88	DRIVING HOME FOR CHRISTMAS EP *WEA YZ 325*	53	3 wks
18 Feb 89	WORKING ON IT *WEA YZ 50*	53	3 wks
14 Oct 89 ●	THE ROAD TO HELL (PART 2) *WEA YZ 431*	10	9 wks
10 Feb 90	TELL ME THERE'S A HEAVEN *East West YZ 455*	24	6 wks
5 May 90	TEXAS *East West YZ 468*	69	1 wk
16 Feb 91	AUBERGE *East West YZ 555*	16	6 wks
6 Apr 91	HEAVEN *East West YZ 566*	57	2 wks
29 Jun 91	LOOKING FOR THE SUMMER *East West YZ 584*	49	3 wks
9 Nov 91	WINTER SONG *East West YZ 629*	27	4 wks
24 Oct 92	NOTHING TO FEAR *East West YZ 699*	16	4 wks
28 Nov 92	GOD'S GREAT BANANA SKIN *East West YZ 706*	31	3 wks

Both On The Beach Summer '88 *and* I Can Hear Your Heartbeat *in 1988 are re-recordings. Tracks on* Driving Home For Christmas *EP: Driving Home For Christmas/Footsteps In The Snow/Joys Of Christmas/Smile.*

Eileen READ – *See CADETS*

READY FOR THE WORLD — 8 wks
US, male vocal/instrumental group

Date	Title	Pos	Wks
26 Oct 85	OH SHEILA *MCA MCA 1005*	50	5 wks
14 Mar 87	LOVE YOU DOWN *MCA MCA 1110*	60	3 wks

REAL PEOPLE UK, male vocal/instrumental group — 8 wks

Date	Title	Pos	Wks
16 Feb 91	OPEN UP YOUR MIND (LET ME IN) *CBS 6566127*	70	1 wk
20 Apr 91	THE TRUTH *Columbia 6567877*	73	1 wk
6 Jul 91	WINDOW PANE (EP) *Columbia 6569327*	60	1 wk
11 Jan 92	THE TRUTH (re-issue) *Columbia 6576987*	41	3 wks
23 May 92	BELIEVER *Columbia 6580067*	38	2 wks

Tracks on Window Pane (EP): Window Pane/See Through You/Everything Must Change.

REAL ROXANNE US, female vocalist — 10 wks

Date	Title	Pos	Wks
28 Jun 86	BANG ZOOM (LET'S GO GO) *Cooltempo COOL 124 **	11	9 wks
12 Nov 88	RESPECT *Cooltempo COOL 176*	71	1 wk

* Real Roxanne with Hitman Howie Tee

REAL THING UK, male vocal/instrumental group — 114 wks

Date	Title	Pos	Wks
5 Jun 76 ★	YOU TO ME ARE EVERYTHING *Pye International 7N 25709*	1	11 wks
4 Sep 76 ●	CAN'T GET BY WITHOUT YOU *Pye 7N 45618*	2	10 wks
12 Feb 77	YOU'LL NEVER KNOW WHAT YOU'RE MISSING *Pye 7N 45662*	16	9 wks
30 Jul 77	LOVE'S SUCH A WONDERFUL THING *Pye 7N 45701*	33	5 wks
4 Mar 78	WHENEVER YOU WANT MY LOVE *Pye 7N 46045*	18	9 wks
3 Jun 78	LET'S GO DISCO *Pye 7N 46078*	39	7 wks
12 Aug 78	RAININ' THROUGH MY SUNSHINE *Pye 7N 46113*	40	8 wks
17 Feb 79 ●	CAN YOU FEEL THE FORCE *Pye 7N 46147*	5	11 wks
21 Jul 79	BOOGIE DOWN (GET FUNKY NOW) *Pye 7P 109*	33	6 wks
22 Nov 80	SHE'S A GROOVY FREAK *Calibre CAB 105*	52	4 wks

8 Mar 86 ●	YOU TO ME ARE EVERYTHING (THE DECADE REMIX 76-86) PRT 7P 349	5	12 wks
24 May 86 ●	CAN'T GET BY WITHOUT YOU (THE SECOND DECADE REMIX) PRT 7P 352	6	13 wks
7 Jun 86	YOU TO ME ARE EVERYTHING (THE DECADE REMIX 76-86) (re-entry) PRT 7P 349	72	1 wk
2 Aug 86	CAN YOU FEEL THE FORCE ('86 REMIX) PRT 7P 358	24	6 wks
25 Oct 86	STRAIGHT TO THE HEART Jive JIVE 129	71	2 wks

REAL TO REEL US, male vocal/instrumental group　　2 wks

| 21 Apr 84 | LOVE ME LIKE THIS Arista ARIST 565 | 68 | 2 wks |

REBEL MC UK, male vocalist　　52 wks

27 May 89	JUST KEEP ROCKIN' Desire WANT 9 *	11	12 wks
7 Oct 89 ●	STREET TUFF Desire WANT 18 **	3	14 wks
31 Mar 90	BETTER WORLD Desire WANT 25	20	6 wks
2 Jun 90	REBEL MUSIC Desire WANT 31	53	2 wks
6 Apr 91	WICKEDEST SOUND Desire WANT 40 ***	43	6 wks
15 Jun 91	TRIBAL BASE Desire WANT 44 ****	20	6 wks
31 Aug 91	BLACK MEANING GOOD Desire WANT 47	73	1 wk
21 Mar 92	RICH AH GETTING RICHER Big Life BLR 70 *****	48	4 wks
8 Aug 92	HUMANITY Big Life BLR 78 ******	62	1 wk

* Double Trouble and the Rebel MC ** Rebel MC and Double Trouble
*** Rebel MC featuring Tenor Fly **** Rebel MC featuring Tenor Fly and
Barrington Levy ***** Rebel MC introducing Little T ****** Rebel MC
featuring Lincoln Thompson

REBEL ROUSERS – See Cliff BENNETT and the REBEL ROUSERS

REBELETTES – See Duane EDDY

REBELS – See Duane EDDY

Ezz RECO and the LAUNCHERS with Boysie GRANT Jamaica, male vocal/instrumental group　　4 wks

| 5 Mar 64 | KING OF KINGS Columbia DB 7217 | 44 | 4 wks |

RECOIL UK, male vocal/instrumental group　　1 wk

| 21 Mar 92 | FAITH HEALER Mute MUTE 110 | 60 | 1 wk |

RED BOX UK, male vocal/instrumental duo　　28 wks

24 Aug 85 ●	LEAN ON ME (AH-LI-AYO) Sire W 8926	3	14 wks
25 Oct 86 ●	FOR AMERICA Sire YZ 84	10	12 wks
31 Jan 87	HEART OF THE SUN Sire YZ 100	71	2 wks

RED CAR AND THE BLUE CAR
UK, male vocal/instrumental group　　4 wks

| 14 Dec 91 | HOME FOR CHRISTMAS DAY Virgin VS 1394 | 44 | 4 wks |

RED HOT CHILI PEPPERS
US, male vocal/instrumental group　　16 wks

10 Feb 90	HIGHER GROUND EMI-USA MT 75	55	3 wks
23 Jun 90	TASTE THE PAIN EMI-USA MT 85	29	3 wks
8 Sep 90	HIGHER GROUND (re-issue) EMI-USA MT 88	54	3 wks
14 Mar 92	UNDER THE BRIDGE Warner Bros. W 0084	26	4 wks
15 Aug 92	BREAKING THE GIRL Warner Bros. W 0126	41	3 wks

REDBONE US, male vocal/instrumental group　　12 wks

| 25 Sep 71 ● | WITCH QUEEN OF NEW ORLEANS Epic EPC 7351 | 2 | 12 wks |

Sharon REDD US, female vocalist　　32 wks

28 Feb 81	CAN YOU HANDLE IT Epic EPC 9572	31	8 wks
2 Oct 82	NEVER GIVE YOU UP Prelude PRL A2755	20	9 wks
15 Jan 83	IN THE NAME OF LOVE Prelude PRL A2905	31	5 wks
22 Oct 83	LOVE HOW YOU FEEL Prelude A3868	39	5 wks
1 Feb 92	CAN YOU HANDLE IT EMI EM 219 *	17	5 wks

* DNA featuring Sharon Redd

Otis REDDING US, male vocalist　　124 wks

25 Nov 65	MY GIRL Atlantic AT 4050	11	16 wks
7 Apr 66	SATISFACTION Atlantic AT 4080	33	4 wks
14 Jul 66	MY LOVER'S PRAYER Atlantic 584 019	37	6 wks
25 Aug 66	I CAN'T TURN YOU LOOSE Atlantic 584 030	29	8 wks
24 Nov 66	FA FA FA FA FA (SAD SONG) Atlantic 584 049	23	9 wks
26 Jan 67	TRY A LITTLE TENDERNESS Atlantic 584 070	46	4 wks
23 Mar 67	DAY TRIPPER Stax 601 005	43	6 wks
4 May 67	LET ME COME ON HOME Stax 601 007	48	1 wk
15 Jun 67	SHAKE Stax 601 011	28	10 wks
19 Jul 67	TRAMP Stax 601 012 *	18	11 wks
11 Oct 67	KNOCK ON WOOD Stax 601 021 *	35	5 wks
14 Feb 68	MY GIRL (re-issue) Atlantic 584 092	36	9 wks
21 Feb 68 ●	(SITTIN' ON) THE DOCK OF THE BAY Stax 601 031	3	15 wks
29 May 68	HAPPY SONG Stax 601 040	24	5 wks
31 Jul 68	HARD TO HANDLE Atlantic 584 199	15	12 wks
9 Jul 69	LOVE MAN Atco 226 001	43	3 wks

* Otis Redding and Carla Thomas

Helen REDDY Australia, female vocalist　　18 wks

| 18 Jan 75 ● | ANGIE BABY Capitol CL 15799 | 5 | 10 wks |
| 28 Nov 81 | I CAN'T SAY GOODBYE TO YOU MCA 744 | 43 | 8 wks |

REDHEAD KINGPIN and the FBI　　11 wks
US, male vocalist

| 22 Jul 89 | DO THE RIGHT THING 10 TEN 271 | 13 | 10 wks |
| 2 Dec 89 | SUPERBAD SUPERSLICK 10 TEN 286 | 68 | 1 wk |

REDSKINS UK, male vocal/instrumental duo　　12 wks

10 Nov 84	KEEP ON KEEPIN' ON Decca F 1	43	5 wks
22 Jun 85	BRING IT DOWN (THIS INSANE THING) Decca F 2	33	5 wks
22 Feb 86	THE POWER IS YOURS Decca F 3	59	2 wks

Jimmy REED US, male vocalist　　2 wks

| 10 Sep 64 | SHAME SHAME SHAME Stateside SS 330 | 45 | 2 wks |

Lou REED US, male vocalist　　19 wks

| 12 May 73 ● | WALK ON THE WILD SIDE RCA 2303 | 10 | 9 wks |
| 17 Jan 87 | SOUL MAN A & M AM 364 * | 30 | 10 wks |

* Sam Moore and Lou Reed

Michael REED ORCHESTRA – See Richard HARTLEY/Michael REED
ORCHESTRA

Dan REED NETWORK　　16 wks
US, male vocal/instrumental group

20 Jan 90	**COME BACK BABY** *Mercury DRN 2*	51	3 wks
17 Mar 90	**RAINBOW CHILD** *Mercury DRN 3*	60	3 wks
21 Jul 90	**STARDATE 1990/RAINBOW CHILD (re-issue)** *Mercury DRN 4*	39	4 wks
8 Sep 90	**LOVER/MONEY** *Mercury DRN 5*	45	3 wks
13 Jul 91	**MIX IT UP** *Mercury MER 345*	49	2 wks
21 Sep 91	**BABY NOW I** *Mercury MER 352*	65	1 wk

Tony REES and the COTTAGERS　　1 wk
UK, male vocal group

10 May 75	**VIVA EL FULHAM** *Sonet SON 2059*	46	1 wk

REESE PROJECT *US, male producer - Kevin Saunderson*　　3 wks

8 Aug 92	**THE COLOUR OF LOVE** *Network NWK 51*	52	2 wks
12 Dec 92	**I BELIEVE** *Network NWKT 63*	74	1 wk

Jim REEVES *US, male vocalist*　　322 wks

24 Mar 60	**HE'LL HAVE TO GO** *RCA 1168*	36	1 wk
7 Apr 60	**HE'LL HAVE TO GO (re-entry)** *RCA 1168*	12	30 wks
16 Mar 61	**WHISPERING HOPE** *RCA 1223*	50	1 wk
23 Nov 61	**YOU'RE THE ONLY GOOD THING** *RCA 1261*	17	19 wks
28 Jun 62	**ADIOS AMIGO** *RCA 1293*	23	21 wks
22 Nov 62	**I'M GONNA CHANGE EVERYTHING** *RCA 1317*	42	2 wks
13 Jun 63 ●	**WELCOME TO MY WORLD** *RCA 1342*	6	15 wks
17 Oct 63	**GUILTY** *RCA 1364*	29	7 wks
20 Feb 64 ●	**I LOVE YOU BECAUSE** *RCA 1385*	5	39 wks
18 Jun 64 ●	**I WON'T FORGET YOU** *RCA 1400*	3	25 wks
5 Nov 64 ●	**THERE'S A HEARTACHE FOLLOWING ME** *RCA 1423*	6	13 wks
7 Jan 65	**I WON'T FORGET YOU (re-entry)** *RCA 1400*	47	1 wk
4 Feb 65 ●	**IT HURTS SO MUCH** *RCA 1437*	8	10 wks
15 Apr 65	**NOT UNTIL THE NEXT TIME** *RCA 1446*	13	12 wks
6 May 65	**HOW LONG HAS IT BEEN** *RCA 1445*	45	5 wks
15 Jul 65	**THIS WORLD IS NOT MY HOME** *RCA 1412*	22	9 wks
11 Nov 65	**IS IT REALLY OVER** *RCA 1488*	17	9 wks
18 Aug 66 ★	**DISTANT DRUMS** *RCA 1537*	1	25 wks
2 Feb 67	**I WON'T COME IN WHILE HE'S THERE** *RCA 1563*	12	11 wks
26 Jul 67	**TRYING TO FORGET** *RCA 1611*	33	5 wks
22 Nov 67	**I HEARD A HEART BREAK LAST NIGHT** *RCA 1643*	38	6 wks
27 Mar 68	**PRETTY BROWN EYES** *RCA 1672*	33	5 wks
25 Jun 69	**WHEN TWO WORLDS COLLIDE** *RCA 1830*	17	17 wks
6 Dec 69	**BUT YOU LOVE ME DADDY** *RCA 1899*	15	16 wks
21 Mar 70	**NOBODY'S FOOL** *RCA 1915*	32	5 wks
12 Sep 70	**ANGELS DON'T LIE** *RCA 1997*	44	1 wk
26 Sep 70	**ANGELS DON'T LIE (re-entry)** *RCA 1997*	32	2 wks
26 Jun 71	**I LOVE YOU BECAUSE/HE'LL HAVE TO GO/MOONLIGHT & ROSES (re-issues)** *RCA Maximillion 2092*	34	8 wks
19 Feb 72	**YOU'RE FREE TO GO (re-issue)** *RCA 2174*	48	2 wks

Martha REEVES and the VANDELLAS　　85 wks
US, female vocal group

29 Oct 64	**DANCING IN THE STREET** *Stateside SS 345* *	28	8 wks
1 Apr 65	**NOWHERE TO RUN** *Tamla Motown TMG 502* *	26	8 wks
1 Dec 66	**I'M READY FOR LOVE** *Tamla Motown TMG 582* *	29	8 wks
30 Mar 67	**JIMMY MACK** *Tamla Motown TMG 599* *	21	9 wks
17 Jan 68	**HONEY CHILE** *Tamla Motown TMG 636*	30	9 wks
15 Jan 69 ●	**DANCING IN THE STREET (re-issue)** *Tamla Motown TMG 684*	4	12 wks
16 Apr 69	**NOWHERE TO RUN (re-issue)** *Tamla Motown TMG 694*	42	3 wks
29 Aug 70	**JIMMY MACK (re-entry)** *Tamla Motown TMG 599*	21	12 wks
13 Feb 71	**FORGET ME NOT** *Tamla Motown TMG 762*	11	8 wks
8 Jan 72	**BLESS YOU** *Tamla Motown TMG 794*	33	5 wks
23 Jul 88	**NOWHERE TO RUN (2nd re-issue)** *A & M AM 444*	52	3 wks

* Martha and the Vandellas

The listed flip side of Nowhere To Run *in 1988 was* I Got You (I Feel Good) *by James Brown.*

Vic REEVES *UK, male vocalist*　　21 wks

27 Apr 91 ●	**BORN FREE** *Sense SIGH 710* *	6	6 wks
26 Oct 91 ★	**DIZZY** *Sense SIGH 712* **	1	12 wks
14 Dec 91	**ABIDE WITH ME** *Sense SIGH 713*	47	3 wks

* Vic Reeves and the Roman Numerals ** Vic Reeves and the Wonder Stuff

RE-FLEX *UK, male vocal/instrumental group*　　9 wks

28 Jan 84	**THE POLITICS OF DANCING** *EMI FLEX 2*	28	9 wks

Joan REGAN *UK, female vocalist*　　62 wks

11 Dec 53 ●	**RICOCHET** *Decca F 10193* *	8	1 wk
8 Jan 54 ●	**RICOCHET (re-entry)** *Decca F 10193* *	9	4 wks
14 May 54 ●	**SOMEONE ELSE'S ROSES** *Decca F 10257*	5	8 wks
1 Oct 54	**IF I GIVE MY HEART TO YOU** *Decca F 10373*	20	1 wk
29 Oct 54 ●	**IF I GIVE MY HEART TO YOU (re-entry)** *Decca F 10373*	3	10 wks
5 Nov 54	**WAIT FOR ME DARLING** *Decca F 10362* **	18	1 wk
25 Mar 55 ●	**PRIZE OF GOLD** *Decca F 10432*	6	8 wks
6 May 55	**OPEN UP YOUR HEART** *Decca F 10474*	19	1 wk
1 May 59 ●	**MAY YOU ALWAYS** *HMV POP 593*	9	16 wks
5 Feb 60	**HAPPY ANNIVERSARY** *Pye 7N 15238*	29	1 wk
19 Feb 60	**HAPPY ANNIVERSARY (re-entry)** *Pye 7N 15238*	29	1 wk
28 Jul 60	**PAPA LOVES MAMA** *Pye 7N 15278*	29	8 wks
24 Nov 60	**ONE OF THE LUCKY ONES** *Pye 7N 15310*	47	1 wk
5 Jan 61	**IT MUST BE SANTA** *Pye 7N 15303*	42	1 wk

* Joan Regan with the Squadronaires ** Joan Regan and the Johnston Brothers
See also Various Artists (EPs & LPs) - All Star Hit Parade.

REGENTS *UK, male/female vocal/instrumental group*　　14 wks

22 Dec 79	**7 TEEN** *Rialto TREB 111*	11	12 wks
7 Jun 80	**SEE YOU LATER** *Arista ARIST 350*	55	2 wks

REGGAE PHILHARMONIC ORCHESTRA　　11 wks
UK, male/female vocal/instrumental group

19 Nov 88	**MINNIE THE MOOCHER** *Mango IS 378*	35	9 wks
28 Jul 90	**LOVELY THING** *Mango MNG 742*	71	2 wks

REGINA *US, female vocalist*　　3 wks

1 Feb 86	**BABY LOVE** *Funkin' Marvellous MARV 01*	50	3 wks

REID *UK, male vocal group*　　12 wks

8 Oct 88	**ONE WAY OUT** *Syncopate SY 16*	66	2 wks

11 Feb 89	REAL EMOTION *Syncopate SY 24*	**65**	2 wks
15 Apr 89	GOOD TIMES *Syncopate SY 27*	**55**	6 wks
21 Oct 89	LOVIN' ON THE SIDE *Syncopate REID 1*	**71**	2 wks

Junior REID – *See COLDCUT; RAGGA TWINS; SOUPDRAGONS*

Mike REID *UK, male vocalist* — 8 wks

22 Mar 75 ●	THE UGLY DUCKLING *Pye 7N 45434*	**10**	8 wks

Neil REID *UK, male vocalist* — 26 wks

1 Jan 72 ●	MOTHER OF MINE *Decca F 13264*	**2**	20 wks
8 Apr 72	THAT'S WHAT I WANT TO BE *Decca F 13300*	**49**	1 wk
22 Apr 72	THAT'S WHAT I WANT TO BE (re-entry) *Decca F 13300*	**45**	5 wks

Maggie REILLY – *See Mike OLDFIELD*

Keith RELF *UK, male vocalist* — 1 wk

26 May 66	MR. ZERO *Columbia DB 7920*	**50**	1 wk

R.E.M. *US, male vocal/instrumental group* — 67 wks

28 Nov 87	THE ONE I LOVE *IRS IRM 46*	**51**	8 wks
30 Apr 88	FINEST WORKSONG *IRS IRM 161*	**50**	2 wks
4 Feb 89	STAND *Warner Bros. W 7577*	**51**	3 wks
3 Jun 89	ORANGE CRUSH *Warner Bros. W 2960*	**28**	5 wks
12 Aug 89	STAND (re-issue) *Warner Bros. W 2833*	**48**	2 wks
9 Mar 91	LOSING MY RELIGION *Warner Bros. W 0015*	**19**	9 wks
18 May 91 ●	SHINY HAPPY PEOPLE *Warner Bros. W 0027*	**6**	11 wks
17 Aug 91	NEAR WILD HEAVEN *Warner Bros. W 0055*	**27**	4 wks
21 Sep 91	THE ONE I LOVE (re-issue) *IRS IRM 178*	**16**	6 wks
16 Nov 91	RADIO SONG *Warner Bros. W 0072*	**28**	3 wks
14 Dec 91	IT'S THE END OF THE WORLD AS WE KNOW IT *IRS IRM 180*	**39**	4 wks
3 Oct 92	DRIVE *Warner Bros. W 0136*	**11**	5 wks
28 Nov 92	MAN ON THE MOON *Warner Bros. W 0143*	**18†**	5 wks

RENAISSANCE *UK, male/female vocal/instrumental group* — 11 wks

15 Jul 78 ●	NORTHERN LIGHTS *Warner Bros. K 17177*	**10**	11 wks

RENE and ANGELA *US, male/female vocal duo* — 15 wks

15 Jun 85	SAVE YOUR LOVE (FOR NUMBER 1) *Club JAB 14 **	**66**	2 wks
7 Sep 85	I'LL BE GOOD *Club JAB 18*	**22**	10 wks
2 Nov 85	SECRET RENDEZVOUS *Champion CHAMP 5*	**54**	3 wks

* Rene and Angela featuring Kuris Blow

RENE and YVETTE *UK, male/female vocal duo* — 4 wks

22 Nov 86	JE T'AIME (ALLO ALLO)/RENE D.M.C. (DEVASTATING MACHO CHARISMA) *Sedition EDIT 3319*	**57**	4 wks

RENEE and RENATO *UK/Italy, female/male vocal duo* — 22 wks

30 Oct 82 ★	SAVE YOUR LOVE *Hollywood HWD 003*	**1**	16 wks
12 Feb 83	JUST ONE MORE KISS *Hollywood HWD 006*	**48**	6 wks

RENEGADE SOUNDWAVE — 6 wks
UK, male vocal/instrumental group

3 Feb 90	PROBABLY A ROBBERY *Mute MUTE 102*	**38**	6 wks

REO SPEEDWAGON *US, male vocal/instrumental group* — 38 wks

11 Apr 81 ●	KEEP ON LOVING YOU *Epic EPC 9544*	**7**	14 wks
27 Jun 81	TAKE IT ON THE RUN *Epic EPC A 1207*	**19**	14 wks
16 Mar 85	CAN'T FIGHT THIS FEELING *Epic A 4880*	**16**	10 wks

REPARATA and the DELRONS — 12 wks
US, female vocal group

20 Mar 68	CAPTAIN OF YOUR SHIP *Bell 1002*	**13**	10 wks
18 Oct 75	SHOES *Dart 2066 562 **	**43**	2 wks

* Reparata

REUNION *US, male vocal group* — 4 wks

21 Sep 74	LIFE IS A ROCK (BUT THE RADIO ROLLED ME) *RCA PB 10056*	**33**	4 wks

REVILLOS – *See REZILLOS*

REVOLUTION – *See PRINCE*

Debbie REYNOLDS *US, female vocalist* — 17 wks

30 Aug 57 ●	TAMMY *Vogue-Coral Q 72274*	**2**	17 wks

Jody REYNOLDS *US, male vocalist* — 1 wk

14 Apr 79	ENDLESS SLEEP *Lightning LIG 9015*	**66**	1 wk

Endless Sleep *was coupled with* To Know Him Is To Love Him *by the Teddy Bears as a double A-side.*

L.J. REYNOLDS *US, male vocalist* — 3 wks

30 Jun 84	DON'T LET NOBODY HOLD YOU DOWN *Club JAB 5*	**53**	3 wks

REYNOLDS GIRLS *UK, female vocal duo* — 12 wks

25 Feb 89 ●	I'D RATHER JACK *PWL PWL 25*	**8**	12 wks

REZILLOS *UK, male/female vocal/instrumental group* — 21 wks

12 Aug 78	TOP OF THE POPS *Sire SIR 4001*	**17**	9 wks
25 Nov 78	DESTINATION VENUS *Sire SIR 4008*	**43**	4 wks
18 Aug 79	I WANNA BE YOUR MAN/I CAN'T STAND MY BABY *Sensible SAB 1*	**71**	1 wk
1 Sep 79	I WANNA BE YOUR MAN/I CAN'T STAND MY BABY (re-entry) *Sensible SAB 1*	**75**	1 wk
26 Jan 80	MOTORBIKE BEAT *Dindisc DIN 5 **	**45**	6 wks

* Revillos

RHC *Belgium, male/female vocal/instrumental duo* — 1 wk

11 Jan 92	FEVER CALLED LOVE *R&S RSUK 9*	**65**	1 wk

RHODA – *See SPECIALS*

RHYTHM ETERNITY — 1 wk
UK, male/female vocal/instrumental group

23 May 92	PINK CHAMPAGNE *Dead Dead Good GOOD 15T*	**72**	1 wk

RHYTHM IS RHYTHM US, male instrumental duo — 1 wk

11 Nov 89	STRINGS OF LIFE '89 *Kool Kat KOOL 509*	74	1 wk

RHYTHM-N-BASS UK, male rap group — 2 wks

19 Sep 92	ROSES *Epic 6582907*	56	2 wks

RHYTHM QUEST UK, male producer – Mark Hadfield — 2 wks

20 Jun 92	CLOSER TO ALL YOUR DREAMS *Network NWK 40*	45	2 wks

RHYTHM SECTION UK, male vocal/instrumental group — 1 wk

18 Jul 92	MIDSUMMER MADNESS EP *Rhythm Section RSEC 006*	66	1 wk

Tracks on Midsummer Madness EP: *Dreamworld/Burnin' Up/Perfect Love 2am/Perfect Love 8am.*

RHYTHMATIC UK, male instrumental group — 3 wks

12 May 90	TAKE ME BACK *Network NWK 8*	74	1 wk
26 May 90	TAKE ME BACK (re-entry) *Network NWK 8*	71	1 wk
3 Nov 90	FREQUENCY *Network NWK 13*	62	1 wk

Charlie RICH US, male vocalist — 29 wks

16 Feb 74 ●	THE MOST BEAUTIFUL GIRL *CBS 1897*	2	14 wks
13 Apr 74	BEHIND CLOSED DOORS *Epic EPC 1539*	16	10 wks
1 Feb 75	WE LOVE EACH OTHER *Epic EPC 2868*	37	5 wks

Richie RICH UK, male vocalist — 15 wks

16 Jul 88	TURN IT UP *Club JAB 68*	48	3 wks
22 Oct 88	I'LL HOUSE YOU *Gee Street GEE 003* *	22	5 wks
10 Dec 88	MY DJ (PUMP IT UP SOME) *Gee Street GEE 7*	74	1 wk
2 Sep 89	SALSA HOUSE *ffrr F 113*	50	3 wks
9 Mar 91	YOU USED TO SALSA *ffrr F 156* **	52	3 wks

* Richie Rich meets the Jungle Brothers ** Richie Rich's Salsa House featuring Ralphi Rosario

RICH KIDS UK, male vocal/instrumental group — 5 wks

28 Jan 78	RICH KIDS *EMI 2738*	24	5 wks

Cliff RICHARD UK, male vocalist — 1077 wks

12 Sep 58 ●	MOVE IT *Columbia DB 4178*	2	17 wks
21 Nov 58 ●	HIGH CLASS BABY *Columbia DB 4203*	7	10 wks
30 Jan 59	LIVIN' LOVIN' DOLL *Columbia DB 4249*	20	6 wks
8 May 59 ●	MEAN STREAK *Columbia DB 4290*	10	9 wks
15 May 59	NEVER MIND *Columbia DB 4290*	21	9 wks
10 Jul 59 ★	LIVING DOLL *Columbia DB 4306*	1	21 wks
9 Oct 59 ★	TRAVELLIN' LIGHT *Columbia DB 4351*	1	17 wks
9 Oct 59	DYNAMITE *Columbia DB 4351*	16	2 wks
30 Oct 59	DYNAMITE (re-entry) *Columbia DB 4351*	21	2 wks
11 Dec 59	LIVING DOLL (re-entry) *Columbia DB 4306*	26	1 wk
1 Jan 60	LIVING DOLL (2nd re-entry) *Columbia DB 4306*	28	1 wk
15 Jan 60	EXPRESSO BONGO EP *Columbia SEG 7971*	14	7 wks
22 Jan 60 ●	VOICE IN THE WILDERNESS *Columbia DB 4398*	2	13 wks
24 Mar 60 ●	FALL IN LOVE WITH YOU *Columbia DB 4431*	2	15 wks
5 May 60	VOICE IN THE WILDERNESS (re-entry) *Columbia DB 4398*	36	2 wks
30 Jun 60 ★	PLEASE DON'T TEASE *Columbia DB 4479*	1	18 wks
22 Sep 60 ●	NINE TIMES OUT OF TEN *Columbia DB 4506*	3	12 wks
1 Dec 60 ★	I LOVE YOU *Columbia DB 4547*	1	16 wks
2 Mar 61 ●	THEME FOR A DREAM *Columbia DB 4593*	3	14 wks
30 Mar 61 ●	GEE WHIZ IT'S YOU *Columbia DC 756*	4	14 wks
22 Jun 61 ●	A GIRL LIKE YOU *Columbia DB 4667*	3	14 wks
19 Oct 61 ●	WHEN THE GIRL IN YOUR ARMS IS THE GIRL IN YOUR HEART *Columbia DB 4716*	3	15 wks
11 Jan 62 ★	THE YOUNG ONES *Columbia DB 4761*	1	21 wks
10 May 62 ●	I'M LOOKING OUT THE WINDOW/DO YOU WANNA DANCE *Columbia DB 4828*	2	17 wks
6 Sep 62 ●	IT'LL BE ME *Columbia DB 4886*	2	12 wks
6 Dec 62 ★	THE NEXT TIME/BACHELOR BOY *Columbia DB 4950*	1	18 wks
21 Feb 63 ★	SUMMER HOLIDAY *Columbia DB 4977*	1	18 wks
9 May 63 ●	LUCKY LIPS *Columbia DB 7034*	4	15 wks
22 Aug 63 ●	IT'S ALL IN THE GAME *Columbia DB 7089*	2	13 wks
7 Nov 63 ●	DON'T TALK TO HIM *Columbia DB 7150*	2	13 wks
6 Feb 64 ●	I'M THE LONELY ONE *Columbia DB 7203*	8	10 wks
13 Feb 64	DON'T TALK TO HIM (re-entry) *Columbia DB 7150*	50	1 wk
30 Apr 64 ●	CONSTANTLY *Columbia DB 7272*	4	13 wks
2 Jul 64 ●	ON THE BEACH *Columbia DB 7305*	7	13 wks
8 Oct 64 ●	THE TWELFTH OF NEVER *Columbia DB 7372*	8	11 wks
10 Dec 64 ●	I COULD EASILY FALL *Columbia DB 7420*	9	11 wks
11 Mar 65 ★	THE MINUTE YOU'RE GONE *Columbia DB 7496*	1	14 wks
10 Jun 65	ON MY WORD *Columbia DB 7596*	12	10 wks
19 Aug 65	THE TIME IN BETWEEN *Columbia DB 7660*	22	8 wks
4 Nov 65 ●	WIND ME UP (LET ME GO) *Columbia DB 7745*	2	16 wks
24 Mar 66	BLUE TURNS TO GREY *Columbia DB 7866*	15	9 wks
21 Jul 66	VISIONS *Columbia DB 7968*	7	12 wks
13 Oct 66	TIME DRAGS BY *Columbia DB 8017*	10	12 wks
15 Dec 66 ●	IN THE COUNTRY *Columbia DB 8094*	6	10 wks
16 Mar 67 ●	IT'S ALL OVER *Columbia DB 8150*	9	10 wks
8 Jun 67	I'LL COME RUNNING *Columbia DB 8210*	26	8 wks
16 Aug 67	THE DAY I MET MARIE *Columbia DB 8245*	10	14 wks
15 Nov 67 ●	ALL MY LOVE *Columbia DB 8293*	6	12 wks
20 Mar 68 ★	CONGRATULATIONS *Columbia DB 8376*	1	13 wks
26 Jun 68	I'LL LOVE YOU FOREVER TODAY *Columbia DB 8437*	27	6 wks
25 Sep 68	MARIANNE *Columbia DB 8476*	22	8 wks
27 Nov 68	DON'T FORGET TO CATCH ME *Columbia DB 8503*	21	10 wks
26 Feb 69	GOOD TIMES (BETTER TIMES) *Columbia DB 8548*	12	11 wks
28 May 69 ●	BIG SHIP *Columbia DB 8581*	8	10 wks
13 Sep 69 ●	THROW DOWN A LINE *Columbia DB 8615* *	7	9 wks
6 Dec 69	WITH THE EYES OF A CHILD *Columbia DB 8641*	20	11 wks
21 Feb 70	JOY OF LIVING *Columbia DB 8657* *	25	8 wks
6 Jun 70 ●	GOODBYE SAM HELLO SAMANTHA *Columbia DB 8685*	6	15 wks
5 Sep 70	I AIN'T GOT TIME ANYMORE *Columbia DB 8708*	21	7 wks
23 Jan 71	SUNNY HONEY GIRL *Columbia DB 8747*	19	8 wks
10 Apr 71	SILVERY RAIN *Columbia DB 8774*	27	6 wks
17 Jul 71	FLYING MACHINE *Columbia DB 8797*	37	7 wks
13 Nov 71	SING A SONG OF FREEDOM *Columbia DB 8836*	13	12 wks
11 Mar 72	JESUS *Columbia DB 8864*	35	3 wks
26 Aug 72	LIVING IN HARMONY *Columbia DB 8917*	12	10 wks
17 Mar 73 ●	POWER TO ALL OUR FRIENDS *EMI 2012*	4	12 wks
12 May 73	HELP IT ALONG/TOMORROW RISING *EMI 2022*	29	6 wks
1 Dec 73	TAKE ME HIGH *EMI 2088*	27	12 wks
18 May 74	(YOU KEEP ME) HANGIN' ON *EMI 2150*	13	8 wks
7 Feb 76	MISS YOU NIGHTS *EMI 2376*	15	10 wks
8 May 76 ●	DEVIL WOMAN *EMI 2458*	9	8 wks
21 Aug 76	I CAN'T ASK FOR ANYMORE THAN YOU *EMI 2499*	17	8 wks
4 Dec 76	HEY MR. DREAM MAKER *EMI 2559*	31	5 wks
5 Mar 77	MY KINDA LIFE *EMI 2584*	15	8 wks
16 Jul 77	WHEN TWO WORLDS DRIFT APART *EMI 2633*	46	3 wks
31 Mar 79	GREEN LIGHT *EMI 2920*	57	3 wks
21 Jul 79 ★	WE DON'T TALK ANYMORE *EMI 2975*	1	14 wks
3 Nov 79	HOT SHOT *EMI 5003*	46	5 wks
2 Feb 80 ●	CARRIE *EMI 5006*	4	10 wks
16 Aug 80 ●	DREAMIN' *EMI 5095*	8	10 wks
25 Oct 80	SUDDENLY *Jet 7002* **	15	7 wks
24 Jan 81	A LITTLE IN LOVE *EMI 5123*	15	8 wks
29 Aug 81 ●	WIRED FOR SOUND *EMI 5221*	4	9 wks
21 Nov 81 ●	DADDY'S HOME *EMI 5251*	2	12 wks
17 Jul 82 ●	THE ONLY WAY OUT *EMI 5318*	10	9 wks
25 Sep 82	WHERE DO WE GO FROM HERE *EMI 5341*	60	3 wks
4 Dec 82	LITTLE TOWN *EMI 5348*	11	7 wks
19 Feb 83 ●	SHE MEANS NOTHING TO ME *Capitol CL 276* ***	9	9 wks
16 Apr 83	TRUE LOVE WAYS *EMI 5385* ****	8	8 wks
4 Jun 83	DRIFTING *DJM SHEIL 1* *****	64	2 wks
3 Sep 83	NEVER SAY DIE (GIVE A LITTLE BIT MORE) *EMI 5415*	15	7 wks

243

26 Nov 83 ●	**PLEASE DON'T FALL IN LOVE** *EMI 5437*	7	9 wks
31 Mar 84	**BABY YOU'RE DYNAMITE/OCEAN DEEP** *EMI 5457*	27	6 wks
19 May 84	**OCEAN DEEP/BABY YOU'RE DYNAMITE** (re-entry) *EMI 5457*	72	1 wk
3 Nov 84	**SHOOTING FROM THE HEART** *EMI RICH 1*	51	4 wks
9 Feb 85	**HEART USER** *EMI RICH 2*	46	3 wks
14 Sep 85	**SHE'S SO BEAUTIFUL** *EMI 5531*	17	9 wks
7 Dec 85	**IT'S IN EVERY ONE OF US** *EMI 5537*	45	6 wks
22 Mar 86 ★	**LIVING DOLL** *WEA YZ 65* ******	1	11 wks
4 Oct 86 ●	**ALL I ASK OF YOU** *Polydor POSP 802* *******	3	16 wks
29 Nov 86	**SLOW RIVERS** *Rocket EJS 13* ********	44	8 wks
20 Jun 87 ●	**MY PRETTY ONE** *EMI EM 4*	6	10 wks
29 Aug 87 ●	**SOME PEOPLE** *EMI EM 18*	3	10 wks
31 Oct 87	**REMEMBER ME** *EMI EM 31*	35	4 wks
13 Feb 88	**TWO HEARTS** *EMI EM 42*	34	4 wks
3 Dec 88 ★	**MISTLETOE AND WINE** *EMI EM 78*	1	8 wks
10 Jun 89 ●	**THE BEST OF ME** *EMI EM 78*	2	7 wks
26 Aug 89 ●	**I JUST DON'T HAVE THE HEART** *EMI EM 101*	3	8 wks
14 Oct 89	**LEAN ON YOU** *EMI EM 105*	17	6 wks
9 Dec 89	**WHENEVER GOD SHINES HIS LIGHT** *Polydor VANS 2* *********	20	6 wks
24 Feb 90	**STRONGER THAN THAT** *EMI EM 129*	14	5 wks
25 Aug 90 ●	**SILHOUETTES** *EMI EM 152*	10	7 wks
13 Oct 90	**FROM A DISTANCE** *EMI EM 155*	11	6 wks
8 Dec 90 ★	**SAVIOUR'S DAY** *EMI XMAS 90*	1	7 wks
14 Sep 91	**MORE TO LIFE** *EMI EM 205*	23	5 wks
7 Dec 91 ●	**WE SHOULD BE TOGETHER** *EMI XMAS 91*	10	6 wks
11 Jan 92	**THIS NEW YEAR** *EMI EMS 216*	30	2 wks
5 Dec 92 ●	**I STILL BELIEVE IN YOU** *EMI EM 255*	7†	4 wks

* Cliff and Hank ** Olivia Newton-John and Cliff Richard *** Phil Everly and Cliff Richard **** Cliff Richard with the London Philharmonic Orchestra ***** Sheila Walsh and Cliff Richard ****** Cliff Richard and the Young Ones featuring Hank B. Marvin ******* Cliff Richard and Sarah Brightman ******** Elton John and Cliff Richard ********* Van Morrison with Cliff Richard

The Shadows appear on all Cliff's hits from Move It *to* A Girl Like You. *After that they are on the following hits:* The Young Ones, Do You Wanna Dance, It'll Be Me, The Next Time, Bachelor Boy, Summer Holiday, Lucky Lips, Don't Talk To Him, I'm The Lonely One, On The Beach, I Could Easily Fall, The Time In Between, Blue Turns To Grey, Time Drags By, In The Country *and* Don't Forget To Catch Me. *Tracks on the* Expresso Bongo *EP:* Love/A Voice in The Wilderness/The Shrine On The Second Floor/Bongo Blues. Bongo Blues *features only the Shadows. The Shadows were the Drifters on Cliff's hits before* Living Doll. Bachelor Boy *was only listed with* The Next Time *from 10 Jan 63.* Ocean Deep *listed from 28 Apr 84 onwards.*

Wendy RICHARD – See Mike SARNE

Lionel RICHIE *US, male vocalist*   **159 wks**

12 Sep 81 ●	**ENDLESS LOVE** *Motown TMG 1240* *	7	12 wks
20 Nov 82 ●	**TRULY** *Motown TMG 1284*	6	11 wks
29 Jan 83	**YOU ARE** *Motown TMG 1290*	43	7 wks
7 May 83	**MY LOVE** *Motown TMG 1300*	70	3 wks
1 Oct 83 ●	**ALL NIGHT LONG (ALL NIGHT)** *Motown TMG 1319*	2	16 wks
3 Dec 83 ●	**RUNNING WITH THE NIGHT** *Motown TMG 1324*	9	12 wks
10 Mar 84 ★	**HELLO** *Motown TMG 1330*	1	15 wks
23 Jun 84	**STUCK ON YOU** *Motown TMG 1341*	12	12 wks
20 Oct 84	**PENNY LOVER** *Motown TMG 1356*	18	7 wks
16 Nov 85 ●	**SAY YOU, SAY ME** *Motown ZB 40421*	8	11 wks
26 Jul 86 ●	**DANCING ON THE CEILING** *Motown L10 1*	7	11 wks
11 Oct 86	**LOVE WILL CONQUER ALL** *Motown L10 2*	45	5 wks
20 Dec 86	**BALLERINA GIRL/DEEP RIVER WOMAN** *Motown L10 3*	17	8 wks
28 Mar 87	**SELA** *Motown L10 4*	43	6 wks
9 May 92	**DO IT TO ME** *Motown TMG 1407*	33	6 wks
22 Aug 92 ●	**MY DESTINY** *Motown TMG 1408*	7	13 wks
28 Nov 92	**LOVE OH LOVE** *Motown TMG 1413*	52	3 wks
26 Dec 92	**LOVE OH LOVE** (re-entry) *Motown TMG 1413*	73†	1 wk

* Diana Ross and Lionel Richie

Jonathan RICHMAN and the MODERN LOVERS *US, male vocal/instrumental group*   **27 wks**

16 Jul 77	**ROADRUNNER** *Beserkley BZZ 1*	11	9 wks
29 Oct 77 ●	**EGYPTIAN REGGAE** *Beserkley BZZ 2*	5	14 wks
21 Jan 78	**MORNING OF OUR LIVES** *Beserkley BZZ 7* *	29	4 wks

* Modern Lovers

RICO – See SPECIALS

RIDE *UK, male vocal/instrumental group*   **17 wks**

27 Jan 90	**RIDE EP** *Creation CRE 07T2*	71	2 wks
14 Apr 90	**PLAY EP** *Creation CRE 075T*	32	3 wks
29 Oct 90	**FALL EP** *Creation CRE 087T*	34	3 wks
16 Mar 91	**TODAY FOREVER** *Creation CRE 100T*	14	4 wks
15 Feb 92 ●	**LEAVE THEM ALL BEHIND** *Creation CRE 123T*	9	3 wks
25 Apr 92	**TWISTERELLA** *Creation CRE 150T*	36	2 wks

Tracks on Ride EP: *Chelsea Girl/Drive Blind/All I See/Close My Eyes. Tracks on* Play EP: *Like A Daydream/Silver/Furthest Sense/ Perfect Time. Tracks on* Fall EP: *Dreams Burn Down/Taste/ Hear And Now/Nowhere.*

Andrew RIDGELEY *UK, male vocalist*   **3 wks**

31 Mar 90	**SHAKE** *Epic AJR 1*	58	3 wks

Stan RIDGWAY *US, male vocalist*   **12 wks**

5 Jul 86 ●	**CAMOUFLAGE** *IRS IRM 114*	4	12 wks

RIGHEIRA *Spain, male vocal duo*   **3 wks**

24 Sep 83	**VAMOS A LA PLAYA** *A & M AM 137*	53	3 wks

RIGHT SAID FRED *UK, male vocal/instrumental group*   **46 wks**

27 Jul 91 ●	**I'M TOO SEXY** *Tug SNOG 1*	2	16 wks
7 Dec 91 ●	**DON'T TALK JUST KISS** *Tug SNOG 2* *	3	11 wks
21 Mar 92 ★	**DEEPLY DIPPY** *Tug SNOG 3*	1	14 wks
1 Aug 92	**THOSE SIMPLE THINGS/DAYDREAM** *Tug SNOG 4*	29	5 wks

* Right Said Fred, guest vocals: Jocelyn Brown

RIGHTEOUS BROTHERS *US, male vocal duo*   **86 wks**

14 Jan 65 ★	**YOU'VE LOST THAT LOVIN' FEELIN'** *London HLU 9943*	1	10 wks
12 Aug 65	**UNCHAINED MELODY** *London HL 9975*	14	12 wks
13 Jan 66	**EBB TIDE** *London HL 10011*	48	2 wks
14 Apr 66	**(YOU'RE MY) SOUL AND INSPIRATION** *Verve VS 535*	15	10 wks
10 Nov 66	**WHITE CLIFFS OF DOVER** *London HL 10086*	21	9 wks
22 Dec 66	**ISLAND IN THE SUN** *Verve VS 547*	36	5 wks
12 Feb 69	**YOU'VE LOST THAT LOVIN' FEELIN'** (re-issue) *London HL 10241*	10	11 wks
19 Nov 77	**YOU'VE LOST THAT LOVIN' FEELIN'** (2nd re-issue) *Phil Spector International 2010 022*	42	4 wks
27 Oct 90 ★	**UNCHAINED MELODY** (re-issue) *Verve/Polydor PO 101*	1	14 wks
15 Dec 90 ●	**YOU'VE LOST THAT LOVIN' FEELIN'** (3rd re-issue)/ **EBB TIDE** *Verve/Polydor PO 116*	3	9 wks

Cheryl Pepsii RILEY *US, female vocalist*   **1 wk**

28 Jan 89	**THANKS FOR MY CHILD** *CBS 653153 7*	75	1 wk

Jeannie C. RILEY *US, female vocalist*   **15 wks**

16 Oct 68	**HARPER VALLEY P. T. A.** *Polydor 56748*	12	15 wks

Teddy RILEY featuring Tammy LUCAS
2 wks
US, male/female vocal/instrumental duo

21 Mar 92   **IS IT GOOD TO YOU** *MCA MCS 1611* ....**53**   2 wks

RIMSHOTS *US, male instrumental/vocal group*
5 wks

19 Jul 75   **7-6-5-4-3-2-1 (BLOW YOUR WHISTLE)**
All Platinum 6146 304 ....**26**   5 wks

Miguel RIOS *Spain, male vocalist*
12 wks

11 Jul 70   **SONG OF JOY** *A & M AMS 790* ....**16**   12 wks

Waldo de los RIOS *Argentina, orchestra*
16 wks

10 Apr 71 ● **MOZART SYMPHONY NO. 40 IN G MINOR K550
1ST MOVEMENT (ALLEGRO MOLTO)**
A & M AMS 836 ....**5**   16 wks

Minnie RIPERTON *US, female vocalist*
10 wks

12 Apr 75 ● **LOVING YOU** *Epic EPC 3121* ....**2**   10 wks

RITCHIE FAMILY *US, female vocal group*
19 wks

23 Aug 75   **BRAZIL** *Polydor 2058 625* ....**41**   4 wks
18 Sep 76 ● **THE BEST DISCO IN TOWN** *Polydor 2058 777* ...**10**   9 wks
17 Feb 79   **AMERICAN GENERATION** *Mercury 6007 199* ...**49**   6 wks

Tex RITTER *US, male vocalist*
14 wks

22 Jun 56 ● **WAYWARD WIND** *Capitol CL 14581* ....**8**   14 wks

RIVER CITY PEOPLE *UK, male/female vocal/instrumental group*
27 wks

12 Aug 89   **(WHAT'S WRONG WITH) DREAMING** *EMI EM 95* ...**70**   3 wks
3 Mar 90   **WALKING ON ICE** *EMI EM 130* ....**62**   2 wks
30 Jun 90   **CARRY THE BLAME/CALIFORNIA DREAMIN'**
EMI EM 145 ....**13**   10 wks
22 Sep 90   **(WHAT'S WRONG WITH) DREAMING (re-issue)**
EMI EM 156 ....**40**   3 wks
2 Mar 91   **WHEN I WAS YOUNG** *EMI EM 176* ....**62**   2 wks
28 Sep 91   **SPECIAL WAY** *EMI EM 207* ....**44**   3 wks
22 Feb 92   **STANDING IN THE NEED OF LOVE** *EMI EM 216* ...**36**   4 wks

RIVER DETECTIVES *UK, male vocal/instrumental duo*
4 wks

29 Jul 89   **CHAINS** *WEA YZ 383* ....**51**   4 wks

Danny RIVERS *UK, male vocalist*
3 wks

12 Jan 61   **CAN'T YOU HEAR MY HEART** *Decca F 11294* ...**36**   3 wks

ROACHFORD *UK, male vocalist*
32 wks

18 Jun 88   **CUDDLY TOY** *CBS ROA 2* ....**61**   4 wks
14 Jan 89 ● **CUDDLY TOY (re-issue)** *CBS ROA 4* ....**4**   9 wks
18 Mar 89   **FAMILY MAN** *CBS ROA 5* ....**25**   6 wks
1 Jul 89   **KATHLEEN** *CBS ROA 6* ....**43**   5 wks
13 Apr 91   **GET READY!** *Columbia 6567057* ....**22**   8 wks

---

British Hit Singles Part One: Alphabetically by Artist
Date of chart entry/Title & catalogue no./Peak position reached/Weeks on chart
★ Number one   ● Top Ten   † still on chart at 31 Dec 1992
* = credited to act billed in footnote

ROB 'N' RAZ featuring Leila K
17 wks
Sweden, male production duo with female vocalist

25 Nov 89 ● **GOT TO GET** *Arista 112696* ....**8**   14 wks
17 Mar 90   **ROK THE NATION** *Arista 112971* ....**41**   3 wks

Kate ROBBINS and BEYOND
10 wks
UK, female/male vocal/instrumental group

30 May 81 ● **MORE THAN IN LOVE** *RCA 69* ....**2**   10 wks

Marty ROBBINS *US, male vocalist*
32 wks

29 Jan 60   **EL PASO** *Fontana H 233* ....**19**   7 wks
7 Apr 60   **EL PASO (re-entry)** *Fontana H 233* ....**44**   11 wks
26 May 60   **BIG IRON** *Fontana H 229* ....**48**   1 wk
27 Sep 62 ● **DEVIL WOMAN** *CBS AAG 114* ....**5**   17 wks
17 Jan 63   **RUBY ANN** *CBS AAG 128* ....**24**   6 wks

Al ROBERTS – *See* FOUR ACES

Austin ROBERTS *US, male vocalist*
7 wks

25 Oct 75   **ROCKY** *Private Stock PVT 33* ....**22**   7 wks

Malcolm ROBERTS *UK, male vocalist*
29 wks

11 May 67   **TIME ALONE WILL TELL** *RCA 1578* ....**45**   2 wks
30 Oct 68 ● **MAY I HAVE THE NEXT DREAM WITH YOU**
Major Minor MM 581 ....**8**   14 wks
12 Feb 69   **MAY I HAVE THE NEXT DREAM WITH
YOU (re-entry)** *Major Minor MM 581* ....**45**   1 wk
22 Nov 69   **LOVE IS ALL** *Major Minor MM 637* ....**12**   12 wks

B.A. ROBERTSON *UK, male vocalist*
60 wks

28 Jul 79 ● **BANG BANG** *Asylum K 13152* ....**2**   12 wks
27 Oct 79 ● **KNOCKED IT OFF** *Asylum K 12396* ....**8**   12 wks
1 Mar 80   **KOOL IN THE KAFTAN** *Asylum K 12427* ....**17**   12 wks
31 May 80 ● **TO BE OR NOT TO BE** *Asylum K 12449* ....**9**   11 wks
17 Oct 81   **HOLD ME** *Swansong BAM 1* * ....**11**   8 wks
17 Dec 83   **TIME** *Epic A 3983* ** ....**45**   5 wks

* B.A. Robertson and Maggie Bell   ** Frida and B.A. Robertson

Don ROBERTSON
9 wks
US, male instrumentalist - piano and whistler

11 May 56 ● **THE HAPPY WHISTLER** *Capitol CL 14575* ....**8**   9 wks

Robbie ROBERTSON *Canada, male vocalist*
10 wks

23 Jul 88   **SOMEWHERE DOWN THE CRAZY RIVER**
Geffen GEF 40 ....**15**   10 wks

Ivo ROBIC *Yugoslavia, male vocalist*
1 wk

6 Nov 59   **MORGEN** *Polydor 23923* ....**23**   1 wk

Floyd ROBINSON US, male vocalist — 9 wks

16 Oct 59 ●	**MAKIN' LOVE** RCA 1146	9	9 wks

Smokey ROBINSON US, male vocalist — 41 wks

23 Feb 74	**JUST MY SOUL RESPONDING** *Tamla Motown TMG 883* **35**		6 wks
24 Feb 79	**POPS WE LOVE YOU** *Motown TMG 1136 ** **66**		5 wks
9 May 81 ★	**BEING WITH YOU** *Motown TMG 1223*.................................**1**		13 wks
13 Mar 82	**TELL ME TOMORROW** *Motown TMG 1255* **51**		4 wks
28 Mar 87	**JUST TO SEE HER** *Motown ZB 41147* **52**		6 wks
25 Feb 89	**INDESTRUCTIBLE** *Arista 112074 ** * **30**		7 wks

* Diana Ross, Marvin Gaye, Smokey Robinson and Stevie Wonder ** Four Tops featuring Smokey Robinson

See also Smokey Robinson and the Miracles.

Smokey ROBINSON and the MIRACLES — 71 wks
US, male vocal group

24 Feb 66	**GOING TO A GO-GO** *Tamla Motown TMG 547* **44**		5 wks
22 Dec 66	**(COME 'ROUND HERE) I'M THE ONE YOU NEED** *Tamla Motown TMG 584* **45**		2 wks
27 Dec 67	**I SECOND THAT EMOTION** *Tamla Motown TMG 631* **27**		11 wks
3 Apr 68	**IF YOU CAN WANT** *Tamla Motown TMG 648* **50**		1 wk
7 May 69 ●	**TRACKS OF MY TEARS** *Tamla Motown TMG 696*.................**9**		13 wks
1 Aug 70 ★	**TEARS OF A CLOWN** *Tamla Motown TMG 745* **1**		14 wks
30 Jan 71	**(COME 'ROUND HERE) I'M THE ONE YOU NEED (re-issue)** *Tamla Motown TMG 761* **13**		9 wks
5 Jun 71	**I DON'T BLAME YOU AT ALL** *Tamla Motown TMG 774* **11**		10 wks
2 Oct 76	**TEARS OF A CLOWN (re-issue)** *Tamla Motown TMG 1048* **34**		6 wks

See also Miracles; Smokey Robinson.

Tom ROBINSON UK, male vocalist — 41 wks

22 Oct 77 ●	**2-4-6-8 MOTORWAY** *EMI 2715 ** **5**		9 wks
18 Feb 78	**DON'T TAKE NO FOR AN ANSWER** *EMI 2749 ** **18**		6 wks
13 May 78	**UP AGAINST THE WALL** *EMI 2787 ** **33**		6 wks
17 Mar 79	**BULLY FOR YOU** *EMI 2916 ** **68**		2 wks
25 Jun 83 ●	**WAR BABY** *Panic NIC 2* **6**		9 wks
12 Nov 83	**LISTEN TO THE RADIO: ATMOSPHERICS** *Panic NIC 3* **39**		6 wks
15 Sep 84	**RIKKI DON'T LOSE THAT NUMBER** *Castaway TR 2* **58**		3 wks

* Tom Robinson Band

John ROCCA – *See FREEEZ*

ROCHELLE US, female vocalist — 6 wks

1 Feb 86	**MY MAGIC MAN** *Warner Bros. W 8838* **27**		6 wks

ROCK AID ARMENIA — 5 wks
UK, male vocal/instrumental charity ensemble

16 Dec 89	**SMOKE ON THE WATER** *Life Aid Armenia ARMEN 001* **39**		5 wks

ROCK CANDY UK, male vocal/instrumental group — 6 wks

11 Sep 71	**REMEMBER** *MCA MK 5069* **32**		6 wks

Chubb ROCK US, male rapper — 1 wk

19 Jan 91	**TREAT 'EM RIGHT** *Champion CHAMP 272* **67**		1 wk

ROCK GODDESS UK, female vocal/instrumental group — 5 wks

5 Mar 83	**MY ANGEL** *A & M AMS 8311* **64**		2 wks
24 Mar 84	**I DIDN'T KNOW I LOVED YOU (TILL I SAW YOU ROCK 'N' ROLL)** *A & M AMS 185* **57**		3 wks

Sir Monti ROCK III – *See DISCO TEX and the SEX-O-LETTES*

ROCKER'S REVENGE — 20 wks
US, male/female vocal/instrumental group

14 Aug 82 ●	**WALKING ON SUNSHINE** *London LON 11 ** **4**		13 wks
29 Jan 83	**THE HARDER THEY COME** *London LON 18* **30**		7 wks

* Rocker's Revenge featuring Donnie Calvin

ROCKETS – *See Tony CROMBIE and his ROCKETS*

ROCKIN' BERRIES UK, male vocal/instrumental group — 41 wks

1 Oct 64	**I DIDN'T MEAN TO HURT YOU** *Piccadilly 7N 35197*.......**43**		1 wk
15 Oct 64 ●	**HE'S IN TOWN** *Piccadilly 7N 35203* **3**		13 wks
21 Jan 65	**WHAT IN THE WORLD'S COME OVER YOU** *Piccadilly 7N 35217* **23**		7 wks
13 May 65 ●	**POOR MAN'S SON** *Piccadilly 7N 35236* **5**		11 wks
26 Aug 65	**YOU'RE MY GIRL** *Piccadilly 7N 35254* **40**		7 wks
6 Jan 66	**THE WATER IS OVER MY HEAD** *Piccadilly 7N 35270* **43**		1 wk
20 Jan 66	**THE WATER IS OVER MY HEAD (re-entry)** *Piccadilly 7N 35270* **50**		1 wk

Lord ROCKINGHAM'S XI — 20 wks
UK, male instrumental group

24 Oct 58 ★	**HOOTS MON** *Decca F 11059* **1**		17 wks
6 Feb 59	**WEE TOM** *Decca F 11104* **16**		3 wks

Both of the group's hits contain a little spoken Scottish.

ROCKNEY – *See CHAS and DAVE*

ROCKSTEADY CREW US, male/female vocal group — 16 wks

1 Oct 83 ●	**(HEY YOU) THE ROCKSTEADY CREW** *Charisma/Virgin RSC 1* **6**		12 wks
5 May 84	**UPROCK** *Charisma/Virgin RSC 2* **64**		4 wks

ROCKWELL US, male vocalist — 11 wks

4 Feb 84 ●	**SOMEBODY'S WATCHING ME** *Motown TMG 1331* **6**		11 wks

ROCKY V – *See Joey B ELLIS*

ROCOCO UK/Italy, male/female vocal/instrumental group — 5 wks

16 Dec 89	**ITALO HOUSE MIX** *Mercury MER 314* **54**		5 wks

Clodagh RODGERS Ireland, female vocalist — 59 wks

26 Mar 69 ●	**COME BACK AND SHAKE ME** *RCA 1792* **3**		14 wks
9 Jul 69 ●	**GOODNIGHT MIDNIGHT** *RCA 1852* **4**		11 wks
4 Oct 69	**GOODNIGHT MIDNIGHT (re-entry)** *RCA 1852* **48**		1 wk
8 Nov 69	**BILJO** *RCA 1891* **22**		9 wks
4 Apr 70	**EVERYBODY GO HOME THE PARTY'S OVER** *RCA 1930* **47**		2 wks
20 Mar 71 ●	**JACK IN THE BOX** *RCA 2066* **4**		10 wks
9 Oct 71	**LADY LOVE BUG** *RCA 2117*...**28**		12 wks

Jimmie RODGERS US, male vocalist — 37 wks

1 Nov 57	**HONEYCOMB** *Columbia DB 3986* **30**		1 wk
20 Dec 57 ●	**KISSES SWEETER THAN WINE** *Columbia DB 4052* **7**		11 wks

28 Mar 58		OH OH, I'M FALLING IN LOVE AGAIN		
		Columbia DB 4078	..18	6 wks
19 Dec 58		WOMAN FROM LIBERIA Columbia DB 4206	..18	6 wks
14 Jun 62	●	ENGLISH COUNTRY GARDEN Columbia DB 4847	..5	13 wks

RODS – *See EDDIE and the HOT RODS*

Tommy ROE *US, male vocalist*   **74 wks**

6 Sep 62	●	SHEILA HMV POP 1060	..3	14 wks
6 Dec 62		SUSIE DARLIN' HMV POP 1092	..37	5 wks
21 Mar 63	●	THE FOLK SINGER HMV POP 1138	..4	13 wks
26 Sep 63		EVERYBODY HMV POP 1207	..9	11 wks
19 Dec 63		EVERYBODY (re-entry) HMV POP 1207	..49	3 wks
16 Apr 69	★	DIZZY Stateside SS 2143	..1	19 wks
23 Jul 69		HEATHER HONEY Stateside SS 2152	..24	9 wks

ROFO *UK, male instrumental/production duo*   **3 wks**

| 1 Aug 92 | ROFO'S THEME PWL Continental PWLT 236 | ..44 | 3 wks |

ROGER *US, male vocalist*   **7 wks**

| 17 Oct 87 | I WANT TO BE YOUR MAN Reprise W 8229 | ..61 | 4 wks |
| 12 Nov 88 | BOOM! THERE SHE WAS Virgin VS 1143 * | ..55 | 3 wks |

* Scritti Politti featuring Roger

Julie ROGERS *UK, female vocalist*   **38 wks**

13 Aug 64	●	THE WEDDING Mercury MF 820	..3	23 wks
10 Dec 64		LIKE A CHILD Mercury MF 838	..21	9 wks
25 Mar 65		HAWAIIAN WEDDING SONG Mercury MF 849	..31	6 wks

Kenny ROGERS *US, male vocalist*   **109 wks**

18 Oct 69	●	RUBY DON'T TAKE YOUR LOVE TO TOWN		
		Reprise RS 20829 *	..2	23 wks
7 Feb 70	●	SOMETHING'S BURNING Reprise RS 20888 *	..8	14 wks
30 Apr 77	★	LUCILLE United Artists UP 36242	..1	14 wks
17 Sep 77		DAYTIME FRIENDS United Artists UP 36289	..39	4 wks
2 Jun 79		SHE BELIEVES IN ME United Artists UP 36533	..42	7 wks
26 Jan 80	★	COWARD OF THE COUNTY United Artists UP 614	..1	12 wks
15 Nov 80		LADY United Artists UP 635	..12	12 wks
12 Feb 83		WE'VE GOT TONIGHT Liberty UP 658 **	..28	7 wks
22 Oct 83		EYES THAT SEE IN THE DARK RCA 358	..61	1 wk
12 Nov 83	●	ISLANDS IN THE STREAM RCA 378 ***	..7	15 wks

* Kenny Rogers and the First Edition ** Kenny Rogers and Sheena Easton
*** Kenny Rogers and Dolly Parton

ROKOTTO *UK, male vocal/instrumental group*   **10 wks**

| 22 Oct 77 | BOOGIE ON UP State STAT 62 | ..40 | 4 wks |
| 10 Jun 78 | FUNK THEORY State STAT 80 | ..49 | 6 wks |

ROLLING STONES *UK, male vocal/instrumental group*   **340 wks**

25 Jul 63		COME ON Decca F 11675	..21	14 wks
14 Nov 63		I WANNA BE YOUR MAN Decca F 11764	..12	16 wks
27 Feb 64	●	NOT FADE AWAY Decca F 11845	..3	15 wks
2 Jul 64	★	IT'S ALL OVER NOW Decca F 11934	..1	15 wks
19 Nov 64	★	LITTLE RED ROOSTER Decca F 12014	..1	12 wks
4 Mar 65	★	THE LAST TIME Decca F 12104	..1	13 wks
26 Aug 65	★	(I CAN'T GET NO) SATISFACTION Decca F 12220	..1	12 wks
28 Oct 65	★	GET OFF OF MY CLOUD Decca F 12263	..1	12 wks
10 Feb 66	●	NINETEENTH NERVOUS BREAKDOWN		
		Decca F 12331	..2	8 wks
19 May 66	★	PAINT IT, BLACK Decca F 12395	..1	10 wks
29 Sep 66	●	HAVE YOU SEEN YOUR MOTHER BABY		
		STANDING IN THE SHADOW Decca F 12497	..5	8 wks
19 Jan 67	●	LET'S SPEND THE NIGHT TOGETHER/RUBY		
		TUESDAY Decca F 12546	..3	10 wks
23 Aug 67	●	WE LOVE YOU/DANDELION Decca F 12654	..8	8 wks
29 May 68	★	JUMPING JACK FLASH Decca F 12782	..1	11 wks
9 Jul 69	★	HONKY TONK WOMEN Decca F 12952	..1	17 wks
24 Apr 71	●	BROWN SUGAR/BITCH/LET IT ROCK		
		Rolling Stones RS 19100	..2	13 wks
3 Jul 71		STREET FIGHTING MAN Decca F 13195	..21	8 wks
29 Apr 72	●	TUMBLING DICE Rolling Stones RS 19103	..5	8 wks
1 Sep 73	●	ANGIE Rolling Stones RS 19105	..5	10 wks
3 Aug 74	●	IT'S ONLY ROCK AND ROLL Rolling Stones RS 19114	..10	7 wks
20 Sep 75		OUT OF TIME Decca F 13597	..45	2 wks
1 May 76	●	FOOL TO CRY Rolling Stones RS 19121	..6	10 wks
3 Jun 78	●	MISS YOU/FAR AWAY EYES Rolling Stones EMI 2802	..3	13 wks
30 Sep 78		RESPECTABLE Rolling Stones EMI 2861	..23	9 wks
5 Jul 80	●	EMOTIONAL RESCUE Rolling Stones RSR 105	..9	8 wks
4 Oct 80		SHE'S SO COLD Rolling Stones RSR 106	..33	6 wks
29 Aug 81	●	START ME UP Rolling Stones RSR 108	..7	9 wks
12 Dec 81		WAITING ON A FRIEND Rolling Stones RSR 109	..50	6 wks
12 Jun 82		GOING TO A GO GO Rolling Stones RSR 110	..26	6 wks
2 Oct 82		TIME IS ON MY SIDE Rolling Stones RSR 111	..62	2 wks
12 Nov 83		UNDERCOVER OF THE NIGHT		
		Rolling Stones RSR 113	..11	9 wks
11 Feb 84		SHE WAS HOT Rolling Stones RSR 114	..42	4 wks
21 Jul 84		BROWN SUGAR (re-issue) Rolling Stones SUGAR 1	..58	2 wks
15 Mar 86		HARLEM SHUFFLE Rolling Stones A 6864	..13	7 wks
2 Sep 89		MIXED EMOTIONS Rolling Stones 655193 7	..36	5 wks
2 Dec 89		ROCK AND A HARD PLACE Rolling Stones 655422 7	..63	1 wk
23 Jun 90		PAINT IT, BLACK (re-issue) London LON 264	..61	3 wks
30 Jun 90		ALMOST HEAR YOU SIGH Rolling Stones 656065 7	..31	5 wks
30 May 91		HIGHWIRE Rolling Stones 6567567	..29	4 wks
1 Jun 91		RUBY TUESDAY (LIVE) Rolling Stones 6568927	..59	2 wks

Far Away Eyes *credited from 15 Jul 78.*

ROLLINS BAND *US, male vocalist - Henry Rollins*   **2 wks**

| 12 Sep 92 | TEARING Imago 72787250187 | ..54 | 2 wks |

ROMAN HOLLIDAY *UK, male vocal/instrumental group*   **19 wks**

2 Apr 83	STAND BY Jive JIVE 31	..61	3 wks
2 Jul 83	DON'T TRY TO STOP IT Jive JIVE 39	..14	9 wks
24 Sep 83	MOTORMANIA Jive JIVE 49	..40	7 wks

ROMAN NUMERALS – *See Vic REEVES*

ROMANTICS – *See RUBY and the ROMANTICS*

Max ROMEO *Jamaica, male vocalist*   **25 wks**

| 28 May 69 | ● | WET DREAM Unity UN 503 | ..10 | 24 wks |
| 29 Nov 69 | | WET DREAM (re-entry) Unity UN 503 | ..50 | 1 wk |

RONDO VENEZIANA *Italy, orchestra*   **3 wks**

| 22 Oct 83 | LA SERENISSIMA (THEME FROM 'VENICE IN | | |
| | PERIL') Ferroway 7 RON 1 | ..58 | 3 wks |

RONETTES *US, female vocal group*   **34 wks**

17 Oct 63	●	BE MY BABY London HLU 9793	..4	13 wks
9 Jan 64		BABY I LOVE YOU London HLU 9826	..11	14 wks
27 Aug 64		BEST PART OF BREAKING UP London HLU 9905	..43	3 wks
8 Oct 64		DO I LOVE YOU London HLU 9922	..35	4 wks

RONNETTE – *See FIDELFATTI featuring RONNETTE*

Linda RONSTADT *US, female vocalist*   **34 wks**

8 May 76		TRACKS OF MY TEARS Asylum K 13034	..42	3 wks
28 Jan 78		BLUE BAYOU Asylum K 13106	..35	4 wks
26 May 79		ALISON Asylum K 13149	..66	2 wks
11 Jul 87	●	SOMEWHERE OUT THERE MCA MCA 1132 *	..8	13 wks

11 Nov 89 ● DON'T KNOW MUCH *Elektra EKR 100* ....**2** 12 wks

* Linda Ronstadt and James Ingram

Don't Know Much *features the uncredited vocals of Aaron Neville.*

ROOFTOP SINGERS *US, male/female vocal group*　　　　**12 wks**

31 Jan 63 ● WALK RIGHT IN *Fontana TF 271700* ....**10** 12 wks

Ralphi ROSARIO – *See Richie RICH*

ROSE MARIE *UK, female vocalist*　　　　**5 wks**

19 Nov 83　WHEN I LEAVE MY WORLD BEHIND *A1 284* ....**75**　1 wk
3 Dec 83　WHEN I LEAVE MY WORLD BEHIND (re-entry)
　　　　　A1 284 ....**63**　2 wks
24 Dec 83　WHEN I LEAVE MY WORLD BEHIND
　　　　　(2nd re-entry) *A1 284* ....**66**　2 wks

ROSE OF ROMANCE ORCHESTRA　　　　**1 wk**
UK, orchestra

9 Jan 82　TARA'S THEME FROM 'GONE WITH THE WIND'
　　　　　BBC RESL 108 ....**71**　1 wk

ROSE ROYCE *US, male/female vocal/instrumental group*　　**110 wks**

25 Dec 76 ● CAR WASH *MCA 267* ....**9** 12 wks
22 Jan 77　PUT YOUR MONEY WHERE YOUR MOUTH IS
　　　　　MCA 259 ....**44**　5 wks
2 Apr 77　I WANNA GET NEXT TO YOU *MCA 278* ....**14**　8 wks
24 Sep 77　DO YOUR DANCE *Whitfield K 17006* ....**30**　6 wks
14 Jan 78 ● WISHING ON A STAR *Warner Bros. K 17060* ....**3** 14 wks
6 May 78　IT MAKES YOU FEEL LIKE DANCIN'
　　　　　Warner Bros. K 17148 ....**16** 10 wks
16 Sep 78 ● LOVE DON'T LIVE HERE ANYMORE
　　　　　Whitfield K 17236 ....**2** 10 wks
3 Feb 79　I'M IN LOVE (AND I LOVE THE FEELING)
　　　　　Whitfield K 17291 ....**51**　4 wks
17 Nov 79　IS IT LOVE YOU'RE AFTER *Whitfield K 17456* ....**13** 13 wks
8 Mar 80　OOH BOY *Whitfield K 17575* ....**46**　7 wks
21 Nov 81　ROSE ROYCE EXPRESS *Warner Bros. K 17875* ....**52**　3 wks
1 Sep 84　MAGIC TOUCH *Streetwave KHAN 21* ....**43**　8 wks
6 Apr 85　LOVE ME RIGHT NOW *Streetwave KHAN 39* ....**60**　3 wks
11 Jun 88　CAR WASH/IS IT LOVE YOU'RE AFTER (re-issues)
　　　　　MCA MCA 1253 ....**20**　7 wks

ROSE TATTOO *Australia, male vocal/instrumental group*　　**4 wks**

11 Jul 81　ROCK 'N' ROLL OUTLAW *Carrere CAR 200* ....**60**　4 wks

Jimmy ROSELLI *US, male vocalist*　　　　**8 wks**

5 Mar 83　WHEN YOUR OLD WEDDING RING WAS NEW
　　　　　A1 282 ....**51**　5 wks
20 Jun 87　WHEN YOUR OLD WEDDING RING WAS NEW
　　　　　(re-issue) *First Night SCORE 9* ....**52**　3 wks

Diana ROSS *US, female vocalist*　　　　**386 wks**

18 Jul 70　REACH OUT AND TOUCH *Tamla Motown TMG 743* ....**33**　5 wks
12 Sep 70 ● AIN'T NO MOUNTAIN HIGH ENOUGH
　　　　　Tamla Motown TMG 751 ....**6** 12 wks
3 Apr 71 ● REMEMBER ME *Tamla Motown TMG 768* ....**7** 12 wks
31 Jul 71 ★ I'M STILL WAITING *Tamla Motown TMG 781* ....**1** 14 wks
30 Oct 71 ● SURRENDER *Tamla Motown TMG 792* ....**10** 11 wks
13 May 72　DOOBEDOOD'NDOOBE DOOBEDOOD'NDOOBE
　　　　　Tamla Motown TMG 812 ....**12**　9 wks

14 Jul 73 ● TOUCH ME IN THE MORNING
　　　　　Tamla Motown TMG 861 ....**9** 12 wks
13 Oct 73　TOUCH ME IN THE MORNING (re-entry)
　　　　　Tamla Motown TMG 861 ....**50**　1 wk
5 Jan 74 ● ALL OF MY LIFE *Tamla Motown TMG 880* ....**9** 13 wks
23 Mar 74 ● YOU ARE EVERYTHING *Tamla Motown TMG 890* * ....**5** 12 wks
4 May 74　LAST TIME I SAW HIM *Tamla Motown TMG 893* ....**35**　4 wks
20 Jul 74　STOP LOOK LISTEN (TO YOUR HEART)
　　　　　Tamla Motown TMG 906 * ....**25**　8 wks
28 Sep 74　LOVE ME *Tamla Motown TMG 917* ....**38**　5 wks
29 Mar 75　SORRY DOESN'T ALWAYS MAKE IT RIGHT
　　　　　Tamla Motown TMG 941 ....**23**　9 wks
3 Apr 76 ● THEME FROM MAHOGANY (DO YOU KNOW
　　　　　WHERE YOU'RE GOING TO)
　　　　　Tamla Motown TMG 1010 ....**5**　8 wks
24 Apr 76 ● LOVE HANGOVER *Tamla Motown TMG 1024* ....**10** 10 wks
10 Jul 76　I THOUGHT IT TOOK A LITTLE TIME
　　　　　Tamla Motown TMG 1032 ....**32**　5 wks
16 Oct 76　I'M STILL WAITING (re-issue)
　　　　　Tamla Motown TMG 1041 ....**41**　4 wks
19 Nov 77　GETTIN' READY FOR LOVE *Motown TMG 1090* ....**23**　7 wks
22 Jul 78　LOVIN' LIVIN' AND GIVIN' *Motown TMG 1112* ....**54**　6 wks
18 Nov 78　EASE ON DOWN THE ROAD *MCA 396* ** ....**45**　4 wks
24 Feb 79　POPS WE LOVE YOU *Motown TMG 1136* *** ....**66**　6 wks
21 Jul 79　THE BOSS *Motown TMG 1150* ....**40**　7 wks
6 Oct 79　NO ONE GETS THE PRIZE *Motown TMG 1160* ....**59**　3 wks
24 Nov 79　IT'S MY HOUSE *Motown TMG 1169* ....**32** 10 wks
19 Jul 80 ● UPSIDE DOWN *Motown TMG 1195* ....**2** 12 wks
20 Sep 80 ● MY OLD PIANO *Motown TMG 1202* ....**5**　9 wks
15 Nov 80　I'M COMING OUT *Motown TMG 1210* ....**13** 10 wks
17 Jan 81　IT'S MY TURN *Motown TMG 1217* ....**16**　8 wks
28 Mar 81　ONE MORE CHANCE *Motown TMG 1227* ....**49**　5 wks
13 Jun 81　CRYIN' MY HEART OUT FOR YOU
　　　　　Motown TMG 1233 ....**58**　3 wks
12 Sep 81 ● ENDLESS LOVE *Motown TMG 1240* **** ....**7** 12 wks
7 Nov 81 ● WHY DO FOOLS FALL IN LOVE *Capitol CL 226* ....**4** 12 wks
23 Jan 82　TENDERNESS *Motown TMG 1248* ....**73**　1 wk
30 Jan 82　MIRROR MIRROR *Capitol CL 234* ....**36**　5 wks
6 Feb 82　TENDERNESS (re-entry) *Motown TMG 1248* ....**75**　1 wk
29 May 82 ● WORK THAT BODY *Capitol CL 241* ....**7** 11 wks
7 Aug 82　IT'S NEVER TOO LATE *Capitol CL 256* ....**41**　4 wks
23 Oct 82　MUSCLES *Capitol CL 268* ....**15**　9 wks
15 Jan 83　SO CLOSE *Capitol CL 277* ....**43**　4 wks
23 Jul 83　PIECES OF ICE *Capitol CL 298* ....**46**　3 wks
7 Jul 84　ALL OF YOU *CBS A 4522* ***** ....**43** 11 wks
15 Sep 84　TOUCH BY TOUCH *Capitol CL 337* ....**47**　6 wks
28 Sep 85　EATEN ALIVE *Capitol CL 372* ....**71**　1 wk
25 Jan 86 ★ CHAIN REACTION *Capitol CL 386* ....**1** 17 wks
3 May 86　EXPERIENCE *Capitol CL 400* ....**47**　3 wks
13 Jun 87　DIRTY LOOKS *EMI EM 2* ....**49**　3 wks
8 Oct 88　MR. LEE *EMI EM 73* ....**58**　2 wks
26 Nov 88　LOVE HANGOVER (re-mix) *Motown ZB 42307* ......**75**　1 wk
6 May 89　WORKIN' OVERTIME *EMI EM 91* ....**32**　5 wks
29 Jul 89　PARADISE *EMI EM 94* ....**61**　2 wks
7 Jul 90　I'M STILL WAITING (re-mix) *Motown ZB 43781* .....**21**　6 wks
30 Nov 91 ● WHEN YOU TELL ME THAT YOU LOVE ME
　　　　　EMI EM 217 ....**2** 11 wks
15 Feb 92　THE FORCE BEHIND THE POWER *EMI EM 221* .....**27**　3 wks
20 Jun 92 ● ONE SHINING MOMENT *EMI EM 239* ....**10**　8 wks
28 Nov 92　IF WE HOLD ON TOGETHER *EMI EM 257* ....**12†**　5 wks

* Diana Ross and Marvin Gaye ** Diana Ross and Michael Jackson *** Diana
Ross, Marvin Gaye, Smokey Robinson and Stevie Wonder **** Diana Ross and
Lionel Richie ***** Julio Iglesias and Diana Ross

See also Supremes.

Francis ROSSI and Bernard FROST　　　　**4 wks**
UK, male vocal/instrumental duo

11 May 85　MODERN ROMANCE (I WANT TO FALL IN LOVE
　　　　　AGAIN) *Vertigo FROS 1* ....**54**　4 wks

Laurent ROSSI – *See BIMBO JET*

Nini ROSSO *Italy, male instrumentalist - trumpet*　　**14 wks**

26 Aug 65 ● IL SILENZIO *Durium DRS 54000* ....**8** 14 wks

TOMMY ROE should have been pleased his 1969 number one 'Dizzy' was taken to the top 22 years later by Vic Reeves and the Wonder Stuff – he co-wrote the song with Freddy Weller.

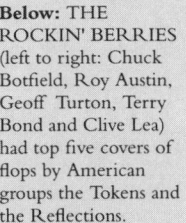

Below: THE ROCKIN' BERRIES (left to right: Chuck Botfield, Roy Austin, Geoff Turton, Terry Bond and Clive Lea) had top five covers of flops by American groups the Tokens and the Reflections.

JEANNIE C. RILEY was famous for 15 weeks relating how her mama socked it to the 'Harper Valley P.T.A.'.

RIGHT SAID FRED enjoyed delayed gratification when 'I'm Too Sexy', held at number two for six weeks by Bryan Adams, went to number one in America. They are shown here with Jocelyn Brown, guest vocalist on 'Don't Talk Just Kiss'.

David Lee ROTH US, male vocalist — **13 wks**

Date	Title	Pos	Wks
23 Feb 85	CALIFORNIA GIRLS *Warner Bros. W 9102*	68	2 wks
5 Mar 88	JUST LIKE PARADISE *Warner Bros. W 8119*	27	7 wks
3 Sep 88	DAMN GOOD/STAND UP *Warner Bros. W 7753*	72	1 wk
12 Jan 91	A LIL' AIN'T ENOUGH *Warner Bros. W 0002*	32	3 wks

ROTTERDAM TERMINATION SOURCE — **4 wks**
Holland, male instrumental duo

Date	Title	Pos	Wks
7 Nov 92	POING *SEP EDGE 74*	27	4 wks

ROULETTES – See Adam FAITH

Robert ROUNSEVILLE – See VARIOUS ARTISTS (EPs & LPs) - Carousel Soundtrack

Demis ROUSSOS Greece, male vocalist — **44 wks**

Date	Title	Pos	Wks
22 Nov 75 ●	HAPPY TO BE ON AN ISLAND IN THE SUN *Philips 6042 033*	5	10 wks
28 Feb 76	CAN'T SAY HOW MUCH I LOVE YOU *Philips 6042 114*	35	5 wks
26 Jun 76 ★	THE ROUSSOS PHENOMENON EP *Philips DEMIS 001*	1	12 wks
2 Oct 76 ●	WHEN FOREVER HAS GONE *Philips 6042 186*	2	10 wks
19 Mar 77	BECAUSE *Philips 6042 245*	39	4 wks
18 Jun 77	KYRILA (EP) *Philips Demis 002*	33	3 wks

Tracks on The Roussos Phenomenon EP: Forever And Ever/Sing An Ode To Love/So Dreamy/My Friend The Wind. Tracks on Kyrila (EP): Kyrila/I'm Gonna Fall In Love/I Dig You/Sister Emilyne.

ROUTERS US, male instrumental group — **7 wks**

Date	Title	Pos	Wks
27 Dec 62	LET'S GO *Warner Bros. WB 77*	32	7 wks

Kevin ROWLAND – See DEXY'S MIDNIGHT RUNNERS

John ROWLES New Zealand, male vocalist — **28 wks**

Date	Title	Pos	Wks
13 Mar 68 ●	IF I ONLY HAD TIME *MCA MU 1000*	3	18 wks
19 Jun 68	HUSH NOT A WORD TO MARY *MCA MU 1023*	12	10 wks

ROXETTE Sweden, male/female vocal/instrumental duo — **89 wks**

Date	Title	Pos	Wks
22 Apr 89 ●	THE LOOK *EMI EM 87*	7	10 wks
15 Jul 89	DRESSED FOR SUCCESS *EMI EM 96*	48	5 wks
28 Oct 89	LISTEN TO YOUR HEART *EMI EM 108*	62	3 wks
2 Jun 90 ●	IT MUST HAVE BEEN LOVE *EMI EM 141*	3	14 wks
11 Aug 90 ●	LISTEN TO YOUR HEART (re-issue)/DANGEROUS *EMI EM 149*	6	9 wks
27 Oct 90	DRESSED FOR SUCCESS (re-issue) *EMI EM 162*	18	7 wks
9 Mar 91 ●	JOYRIDE *EMI EM 177*	4	10 wks
11 May 91	FADING LIKE A FLOWER *EMI EM 190*	12	6 wks
7 Sep 91	THE BIG L *EMI EM 204*	21	6 wks
23 Nov 91	SPENDING MY TIME *EMI EM 215*	22	4 wks
28 Mar 92	CHURCH OF YOUR HEART *EMI EM 227*	21	4 wks
1 Aug 92	HOW DO YOU DO! *EMI EM 241*	13	7 wks
7 Nov 92	QUEEN OF RAIN *EMI EM 253*	28	4 wks

ROXY MUSIC UK, male vocal/instrumental group — **153 wks**

Date	Title	Pos	Wks
19 Aug 72 ●	VIRGINIA PLAIN *Island WIP 6144*	4	12 wks
10 Mar 73 ●	PYJAMARAMA *Island WIP 6159*	10	12 wks
17 Nov 73 ●	STREET LIFE *Island WIP 6173*	9	12 wks
12 Oct 74	ALL I WANT IS YOU *Island WIP 6208*	12	8 wks
11 Oct 75 ●	LOVE IS THE DRUG *Island WIP 6248*	2	10 wks
27 Dec 75	BOTH ENDS BURNING *Island WIP 6262*	25	7 wks
22 Oct 77	VIRGINIA PLAIN (re-issue) *Polydor 2001 739*	11	6 wks
3 Mar 79	TRASH *Polydor POSP 32*	40	6 wks
28 Apr 79 ●	DANCE AWAY *Polydor POSP 44*	2	14 wks
11 Aug 79 ●	ANGEL EYES *Polydor POSP 67*	4	11 wks
17 May 80 ●	OVER YOU *Polydor POSP 93*	5	9 wks
2 Aug 80 ●	OH YEAH (ON THE RADIO) *Polydor 2001 972*	5	8 wks
8 Nov 80	THE SAME OLD SCENE *Polydor ROXY 1*	12	7 wks
21 Feb 81 ★	JEALOUS GUY *EG ROXY 2*	1	11 wks
3 Apr 82 ●	MORE THAN THIS *EG ROXY 3*	6	8 wks
19 Jun 82	AVALON *EG ROXY 4*	13	6 wks
25 Sep 82	TAKE A CHANCE WITH ME *EG ROXY 5*	26	6 wks

Billy Joe ROYAL US, male vocalist — **4 wks**

Date	Title	Pos	Wks
7 Oct 65	DOWN IN THE BOONDOCKS *CBS 201802*	38	4 wks

The Central Band of the ROYAL AIR FORCE, Conductor W/Cdr. A.E. SIMS O.B.E. — **1 wk**
UK, military band

Date	Title	Pos	Wks
21 Oct 55	THE DAMBUSTERS MARCH *HMV B 10877*	18	1 wk

ROYAL GUARDSMEN — **17 wks**
US, male vocal/instrumental group

Date	Title	Pos	Wks
19 Jan 67 ●	SNOOPY VS. THE RED BARON *Stateside SS 574*	8	13 wks
6 Apr 67	RETURN OF THE RED BARON *Stateside SS 2010*	37	4 wks

ROYAL HOUSE US, male/female vocal/instrumental group — **18 wks**

Date	Title	Pos	Wks
10 Sep 88	CAN YOU PARTY *Champion CHAMP 79*	14	14 wks
7 Jan 89	YEAH! BUDDY *Champion CHAMP 91*	35	4 wks

ROYAL PHILHARMONIC ORCHESTRA arranged and conducted by Louis CLARK — **19 wks**
UK, orchestra and conductor

Date	Title	Pos	Wks
25 Jul 81 ●	HOOKED ON CLASSICS *RCA 109*	2	11 wks
24 Oct 81	HOOKED ON CAN-CAN *RCA 151*	47	3 wks
10 Jul 82	BBC WORLD CUP GRANDSTAND *BBC RESL 116*	61	3 wks
7 Aug 82	IF YOU KNEW SOUSA (AND FRIENDS) *RCA 256*	71	2 wks

See also Elvis Costello. Louis Clark did not conduct the third hit.

The Pipes and Drums and Military Band of the ROYAL SCOTS DRAGOON GUARDS — **43 wks**
UK, military band

Date	Title	Pos	Wks
1 Apr 72 ★	AMAZING GRACE *RCA 2191*	1	24 wks
19 Aug 72	HEYKENS SERENADE/THE DAY IS OVER *RCA 2251*	30	7 wks
2 Dec 72	LITTLE DRUMMER BOY *RCA 2301*	13	9 wks
23 Dec 72	AMAZING GRACE (re-entry) *RCA 2191*	42	3 wks

ROYALLE DELITE US, female vocal group — **6 wks**

Date	Title	Pos	Wks
14 Sep 85	(I'LL BE A) FREAK FOR YOU *Streetwave KHAN 51*	45	6 wks

Lita ROZA UK, female vocalist — **18 wks**

Date	Title	Pos	Wks
13 Mar 53 ★	(HOW MUCH IS) THAT DOGGIE IN THE WINDOW *Decca F 10070*	1	11 wks

7 Oct 55	**HEY THERE** *Decca F 10611*	..17	2 wks
23 Mar 56	**JIMMY UNKNOWN** *Decca F 10679*	..15	5 wks

See also Various Artists (EPs & LPs) - All Star Hit Parade.

ROZALLA *Zimbabwe, female vocalist*   **29 wks**

27 Apr 91	**FAITH (IN THE POWER OF LOVE)** *Pulse 8 LOSE 7*	..65	2 wks
7 Sep 91 ●	**EVERYBODY'S FREE (TO FEEL GOOD)** *Pulse 8 LOSE 13*	..6	11 wks
16 Nov 91	**FAITH (IN THE POWER OF LOVE)** (re-issue) *Pulse 8 LOSE 15*	..11	6 wks
22 Feb 92	**ARE YOU READY TO FLY** *Pulse 8 LOSE 21*	..14	6 wks
9 May 92	**LOVE BREAKDOWN** *Pulse 8 LOSE 25*	..65	2 wks
15 Aug 92	**IN 4 CHOONS LATER** *Pulse 8 LOSE 29*	..50	2 wks

RUBETTES *UK, male vocal/instrumental group*   **68 wks**

4 May 74 ★	**SUGAR BABY LOVE** *Polydor 2058 442*	..1	10 wks
13 Jul 74	**TONIGHT** *Polydor 2058 499*	..12	9 wks
16 Nov 74 ●	**JUKE BOX JIVE** *Polydor 2058 529*	..3	12 wks
8 Mar 75 ●	**I CAN DO IT** *State STAT 1*	..7	9 wks
21 Jun 75	**FOE-DEE-O-DEE** *State STAT 7*	..15	6 wks
22 Nov 75	**LITTLE DARLING** *State STAT 13*	..30	5 wks
1 May 76	**YOU'RE THE REASON WHY** *State STAT 20*	..28	4 wks
25 Sep 76	**UNDER ONE ROOF** *State STAT 27*	..40	3 wks
12 Feb 77 ●	**BABY I KNOW** *State STAT 37*	..10	10 wks

RUBY and the ROMANTICS   **6 wks**
US, female/male vocal group

28 Mar 63	**OUR DAY WILL COME** *London HLR 9679*	..38	6 wks

RUDE BOY OF HOUSE – *See HOUSEMASTER BOYZ and the RUDE BOY OF HOUSE*

RUDIES – *See Freddie NOTES and the RUDIES*

Bruce RUFFIN *Jamaica, male vocalist*   **23 wks**

1 May 71	**RAIN** *Trojan TR 7814*	..19	11 wks
24 Jun 72 ●	**MAD ABOUT YOU** *Rhino RNO 101*	..9	12 wks

David RUFFIN *US, male vocalist*   **10 wks**

17 Jan 76 ●	**WALK AWAY FROM LOVE** *Tamla Motown TMG 1017*	..10	8 wks
21 Sep 85	**A NIGHT AT THE APOLLO LIVE!** *RCA PB 49935* *	..58	2 wks

* *Hall and Oates featuring David Ruffin and Eddie Kendrick*

Jimmy RUFFIN *US, male vocalist*   **106 wks**

27 Oct 66 ●	**WHAT BECOMES OF THE BROKENHEARTED** *Tamla Motown TMG 577*	..10	15 wks
9 Feb 67	**I'VE PASSED THIS WAY BEFORE** *Tamla Motown TMG 593*	..29	7 wks
20 Apr 67	**GONNA GIVE HER ALL THE LOVE I'VE GOT** *Tamla Motown TMG 603*	..26	6 wks
9 Aug 69	**I'VE PASSED THIS WAY BEFORE** (re-issue) *Tamla Motown TMG 703*	..33	6 wks
28 Feb 70 ●	**FAREWELL IS A LONELY SOUND** *Tamla Motown TMG 726*	..8	16 wks
4 Jul 70 ●	**I'LL SAY FOREVER MY LOVE** *Tamla Motown TMG 740*	..7	12 wks
17 Oct 70 ●	**IT'S WONDERFUL** *Tamla Motown TMG 753*	..6	14 wks
27 Jul 74 ●	**WHAT BECOMES OF THE BROKENHEARTED** (re-issue) *Tamla Motown TMG 911*	..4	12 wks
2 Nov 74	**FAREWELL IS A LONELY SOUND** (re-issue) *Tamla Motown TMG 922*	..30	5 wks

16 Nov 74	**TELL ME WHAT YOU WANT** *Polydor 2058 433*	..39	4 wks
3 May 80 ●	**HOLD ON TO MY LOVE** *RSO 57*	..7	8 wks
26 Jan 85	**THERE WILL NEVER BE ANOTHER YOU** *EMI 5541*	..68	1 wk

RUFUS – *See Chaka KHAN*

Barbara RUICK – *See VARIOUS ARTISTS (EPs & LPs) - Carousel Soundtrack*

RUMOUR – *See Graham PARKER and the RUMOUR*

RUMPLE-STILTS-SKIN   **4 wks**
US, male/female vocal/instrumental group

24 Sep 83	**I THINK I WANT TO DANCE WITH YOU** *Polydor POSP 649*	..51	4 wks

RUN D.M.C. *US, male rap group*   **36 wks**

19 Jul 86	**MY ADIDAS/PETER PIPER** *London LON 101*	..62	2 wks
6 Sep 86 ●	**WALK THIS WAY** *London LON 104*	..8	10 wks
7 Feb 87	**YOU BE ILLIN'** *Profile LON 118*	..42	4 wks
30 May 87	**IT'S TRICKY** *Profile LON 130*	..16	7 wks
12 Dec 87	**CHRISTMAS IN HOLLIS** *Profile LON 163*	..56	4 wks
21 May 88	**RUN'S HOUSE** *London LON 177*	..37	4 wks
2 Sep 89	**GHOSTBUSTERS** *MCA Profile MCA 1360*	..65	2 wks
1 Dec 90	**WHAT'S IT ALL ABOUT** *Profile PROF 315*	..48	3 wks

RUN TINGS *UK, male instrumental/production duo*   **1 wk**

16 May 92	**FIRES BURNING** *Suburban Base SUBBASE 009*	..58	1 wk

Todd RUNDGREN *US, male vocalist*   **8 wks**

30 Jun 73	**I SAW THE LIGHT** *Bearsville K 15506*	..36	6 wks
14 Dec 85	**LOVING YOU'S A DIRTY JOB BUT SOMEBODY'S GOTTA DO IT** *CBS A 6662* *	..73	2 wks

* *Bonnie Tyler, guest vocals Todd Rundgren*

RUNRIG *UK, male vocal/instrumental group*   **8 wks**

29 Sep 90	**CAPTURE THE HEART EP** *Chrysalis CHS 3594*	..49	2 wks
7 Sep 91	**HEARTHAMMER (EP)** *Chrysalis CHS 3754*	..25	4 wks
9 Nov 91	**FLOWER OF THE WEST** *Chrysalis CHS 3805*	..43	2 wks

Tracks on Capture The Heart EP: *Stepping Down The Glory Road/Satellite Flood/Harvest Moon/The Apple Came Down. Tracks on* Hearthammer (EP): *Hearthammer/Pride Of The Summer (Live)/Loch Lomond (Live)/Solus Na Madainn.*

RUSH *Canada, male vocal/instrumental group*   **43 wks**

11 Feb 78	**CLOSER TO THE HEART** *Mercury RUSH 7*	..36	3 wks
15 Mar 80	**SPIRIT OF RADIO** *Mercury RADIO 7*	..13	7 wks
28 Mar 81	**VITAL SIGNS/A PASSAGE TO BANGKOK** *Mercury VITAL 7*	..41	4 wks
31 Oct 81	**TOM SAWYER** *Exit EXIT 7*	..25	6 wks
4 Sep 82	**NEW WORLD MAN** *Mercury RUSH 8*	..42	3 wks
30 Oct 82	**SUBDIVISIONS** *Mercury RUSH 9*	..53	2 wks
7 May 83	**COUNTDOWN/NEW WORLD MAN** *Mercury RUSH 10*	..36	5 wks
26 May 84	**THE BODY ELECTRIC** *Vertigo RUSH 11*	..56	3 wks
12 Oct 85	**THE BIG MONEY** *Vertigo RUSH 12*	..46	3 wks
31 Oct 87	**TIME STAND STILL** *Vertigo RUSH 13* *	..42	3 wks
23 Apr 88	**PRIME MOVER** *Vertigo RUSH 14*	..43	3 wks
7 Mar 92	**ROLL THE BONES** *Atlantic A 7524*	..49	1 wk

* *Rush with Aimee Mann*
New World Man *on* RUSH 10 *is a live version of* RUSH 8.

Donell RUSH US, male vocalist **1 wk**

| 5 Dec 92 | SYMPHONY *ID 6587977* ....66 | 1 wk |

Jennifer RUSH US, female vocalist **58 wks**

29 Jun 85 ★	THE POWER OF LOVE *CBS A 5003* 1	32 wks
14 Dec 85	RING OF ICE *CBS A 4745* 14	10 wks
20 Dec 86	THE POWER OF LOVE (re-entry) *CBS A 5003* 55	4 wks
20 Jun 87	FLAMES OF PARADISE *CBS 650865 7* * 59	3 wks
27 May 89 ●	TILL I LOVED YOU *CBS 654843 7* ** 24	9 wks

*Jennifer Rush and Elton John **Placido Domingo and Jennifer Rush

Patrice RUSHEN US, female vocalist **25 wks**

1 Mar 80	HAVEN'T YOU HEARD *Elektra K 12414* 62	3 wks
24 Jan 81	NEVER GONNA GIVE YOU UP (WON'T LET YOU BE) *Elektra K 12494* 66	3 wks
24 Apr 82 ●	FORGET ME NOTS *Elektra K 13173* 8	11 wks
10 Jul 82	I WAS TIRED OF BEING ALONE *Elektra K 13184* ...39	5 wks
9 Jun 84	FEELS SO REAL (WON'T LET GO) *Elektra E 9742* ...51	3 wks

Brenda RUSSELL US, female vocalist **17 wks**

| 19 Apr 80 | SO GOOD SO RIGHT/IN THE THICK OF IT *A & M AM 7515* ....51 | 5 wks |
| 12 Mar 88 | PIANO IN THE DARK *Breakout USA 623* ......23 | 12 wks |

Paul RUTHERFORD UK, male vocalist **6 wks**

| 8 Oct 88 | GET REAL *Fourth & Broadway BRW 113* ......47 | 3 wks |
| 19 Aug 89 | OH WORLD *Fourth & Broadway BRW 136* ......61 | 3 wks |

RUTHLESS RAP ASSASSINS UK, male rappers **2 wks**

| 9 Jun 90 | JUST MELLOW *Syncopate SY 35* ....75 | 1 wk |
| 1 Sep 90 | AND IT WASN'T A DREAM *Syncopate SY 38* ......75 | 1 wk |

RUTLES UK, male vocal group **4 wks**

| 15 Apr 78 | I MUST BE IN LOVE *Warner Bros. K 17125* ......39 | 3 wks |
| 13 May 78 | I MUST BE IN LOVE (re-entry) *Warner Bros. K 17125* ......64 | 1 wk |

RUTS UK, male vocal/instrumental group **28 wks**

16 Jun 79 ●	BABYLON'S BURNING *Virgin VS 271* 7	11 wks
8 Sep 79	SOMETHING THAT I SAID *Virgin VS 285* 29	5 wks
19 Apr 80	STARING AT THE RUDE BOYS *Virgin VS 327* 22	8 wks
30 Aug 80	WEST ONE (SHINE ON ME) *Virgin VS 370* 43	4 wks

Barry RYAN UK, male vocalist **33 wks**

23 Oct 68 ●	ELOISE *MGM 1442* 2	12 wks
19 Feb 69	LOVE IS LOVE *MGM 1464* 25	4 wks
4 Sep 69	HUNT *Polydor 56 348* 34	5 wks
21 Feb 70	MAGICAL SPIEL *Polydor 56 370* 49	1 wk
16 May 70	KITSCH *Polydor 2001 035* 37	6 wks
15 Jan 72	CAN'T LET YOU GO *Polydor 2001 256* 32	5 wks

See also Paul and Barry Ryan.

Marion RYAN UK, female vocalist **11 wks**

| 24 Jan 58 ● | LOVE ME FOREVER *Pye Nixa N 15121* ......5 | 11 wks |

Paul and Barry RYAN UK, male vocal duo **43 wks**

11 Nov 65	DON'T BRING ME YOUR HEARTACHES *Decca F 12260* 13	9 wks
3 Feb 66	HAVE PITY ON THE BOY *Decca F 12319* 18	6 wks
12 May 66	I LOVE HER *Decca F 12391* 17	8 wks
14 Jul 66	I LOVE HOW YOU LOVE ME *Decca F 12445* 21	7 wks
29 Sep 66	HAVE YOU EVER LOVED SOMEBODY *Decca F 12494* 49	1 wk
8 Dec 66	MISSY MISSY *Decca F 12520* 43	4 wks
2 Mar 67	KEEP IT OUT OF SIGHT *Decca F 12567* 30	6 wks
29 Jun 67	CLAIRE *Decca F 12633* 47	2 wks

See also Barry Ryan.

Bobby RYDELL US, male vocalist **60 wks**

10 Mar 60 ●	WILD ONE *Columbia DB 4429* 7	14 wks
23 Jun 60	WILD ONE (re-entry) *Columbia DB 4429* 47	1 wk
30 Jun 60	SWINGING SCHOOL *Columbia DB 4471* 44	1 wk
1 Sep 60	VOLARE *Columbia DB 4495* 46	1 wk
15 Sep 60	VOLARE (re-entry) *Columbia DB 4495* 22	5 wks
15 Dec 60	SWAY *Columbia DB 4545* 12	13 wks
23 Mar 61	GOOD TIME BABY *Columbia DB 4600* 42	7 wks
19 Apr 62	TEACH ME TO TWIST *Columbia DB 4802* * 45	1 wk
20 Dec 62	JINGLE BELL ROCK *Cameo-Parkway C 205* * 40	3 wks
23 May 63	FORGET HIM *Cameo Parkway C 108* 13	14 wks

* Chubby Checker and Bobby Rydell

Mitch RYDER and the DETROIT WHEELS **5 wks**
US, male vocalist, male vocal/instrumental backing group

| 10 Feb 66 | JENNY TAKE A RIDE *Stateside SS 481* ......44 | 1 wk |
| 24 Feb 66 | JENNY TAKE A RIDE (re-entry) *Stateside SS 481* ......33 | 4 wks |

RYTHM SYNDICATE US, male vocal/instrumental group **5 wks**

| 27 Jul 91 | P.A.S.S.I.O.N. *Impact American EM 197* ......58 | 5 wks |

S EXPRESS UK, male/female vocal/instrumental group **46 wks**

16 Apr 88 ★	THEME FROM S-EXPRESS *Rhythm King LEFT 21* 1	13 wks
23 Jul 88 ●	SUPERFLY GUY *Rhythm King LEFT 28* 5	9 wks
18 Feb 89 ●	HEY MUSIC LOVER *Rhythm King LEFT 30* * 6	10 wks
16 Sep 89	MANTRA FOR A STATE OF MIND *Rhythm King LEFT 35* 21	8 wks
15 Sep 90	NOTHING TO LOSE *Rhythm King SEXY 01* 32	4 wks
30 May 92	FIND 'EM, FOOL 'EM, FORGET 'EM *Rhythm King 6580137* 43	2 wks

* S Express featuring Eric & Billy

SABRES – *See Denny SEYTON and the SABRES*

SABRINA Italy, female vocalist **22 wks**

6 Feb 88	BOYS (SUMMERTIME LOVE) *IBIZA IBIZ 1* 60	3 wks
11 Jun 88 ●	BOYS (SUMMERTIME LOVE) (re-entry) *IBIZA IBIZ 1* 3	11 wks
1 Oct 88	ALL OF ME *PWL PWL 19* 25	7 wks
1 Jul 89	LIKE A YO-YO *Videogram DCUP 1* 72	1 wk

SAD CAFE UK, male vocal/instrumental group   44 wks

22 Sep 79 ●	EVERY DAY HURTS *RCA PB 5180*	**3**	12 wks
19 Jan 80	STRANGE LITTLE GIRL *RCA PB 5202*	**32**	5 wks
15 Mar 80	MY OH MY *RCA SAD 3*	**14**	11 wks
21 Jun 80	NOTHING LEFT TOULOUSE *RCA SAD 4*	**62**	4 wks
27 Sep 80	LA-DI-DA *RCA SAD 5*	**41**	6 wks
20 Dec 80	I'M IN LOVE AGAIN *RCA SAD 6*	**40**	6 wks

SADE UK, female/male vocal/instrumental group   50 wks

25 Feb 84 ●	YOUR LOVE IS KING *Epic A 4137*	**6**	11 wks
19 May 84	YOUR LOVE IS KING (re-entry) *Epic A 4137*	**75**	1 wk
26 May 84	WHEN AM I GONNA MAKE A LIVING *Epic A 4437*	**36**	5 wks
15 Sep 84	SMOOTH OPERATOR *Epic A 4655*	**19**	10 wks
12 Oct 85	THE SWEETEST TABOO *Epic A 6609*	**31**	5 wks
11 Jan 86	IS IT A CRIME *Epic A 6742*	**49**	3 wks
2 Apr 88	LOVE IS STRONGER THAN PRIDE *Epic SADE 1*	**44**	3 wks
4 Jun 88	PARADISE *Epic SADE 2*	**29**	7 wks
10 Oct 92	NO ORDINARY LOVE *Epic 6583567*	**26**	3 wks
28 Nov 92	FEEL NO PAIN *Epic 6588297*	**56**	2 wks

Staff Sergeant Barry SADLER US, male vocalist   8 wks

24 Mar 66	BALLAD OF THE GREEN BERETS *RCA 1506*	**24**	8 wks

SAFFRONS – *See CINDY and the SAFFRONS*

Mike SAGAR UK, male vocalist   5 wks

8 Dec 60	DEEP FEELING *HMV POP 819*	**44**	5 wks

Carole Bayer SAGER US, female vocalist   9 wks

28 May 77 ●	YOU'RE MOVING OUT TODAY *Elektra K 12257*	**6**	9 wks

SAILOR UK, male vocal/instrumental group   24 wks

6 Dec 75 ●	GLASS OF CHAMPAGNE *Epic EPC 3770*	**2**	12 wks
27 Mar 76 ●	GIRLS GIRLS GIRLS *Epic EPC 3858*	**7**	8 wks
19 Feb 77	ONE DRINK TOO MANY *Epic EPC 4804*	**35**	4 wks

General SAINT – *See Clint EASTWOOD and General SAINT*

ST. ANDREWS CHORALE UK, church choir   5 wks

14 Feb 76	CLOUD 99 *Decca F 13617*	**31**	5 wks

ST. CECILIA UK, male vocal/instrumental group   17 wks

19 Jun 71	LEAP UP AND DOWN (WAVE YOUR KNICKERS IN THE AIR) *Polydor 2058 104*	**12**	17 wks

SAINT ETIENNE UK, male/female vocal/instrumental group 12 wks

18 May 91	NOTHING CAN STOP US/SPEEDWELL *Heavenly HVN 009*	**54**	3 wks
7 Sep 91	ONLY LOVE CAN BREAK YOUR HEART/FILTHY *Heavenly HVN 12*	**39**	4 wks
16 May 92	JOIN OUR CLUB/PEOPLE GET REAL *Heavenly HVN 15*	**21**	3 wks
17 Oct 92	AVENUE *Heavenly HVN 2312*	**40**	2 wks

See also Various Artists (EPs & LPs) - The Fred EP.

Barry ST. JOHN UK, female vocalist   1 wk

9 Dec 65	COME AWAY MELINDA *Columbia DB 7783*	**47**	1 wk

ST. JOHN'S COLLEGE SCHOOL CHOIR and the Band of the GRENADIER GUARDS   3 wks
UK, school choir and military band

3 May 86	THE QUEEN'S BIRTHDAY SONG *Columbia Q1*	**40**	3 wks

ST. LOUIS UNION UK, male vocal/instrumental group   10 wks

13 Jan 66	GIRL *Decca F 12318*	**11**	10 wks

Crispian ST. PETERS UK, male vocalist   31 wks

6 Jan 66 ●	YOU WERE ON MY MIND *Decca F 12287*	**2**	14 wks
31 Mar 66 ●	PIED PIPER *Decca F 12359*	**5**	13 wks
15 Sep 66	CHANGES *Decca F 12480*	**49**	1 wk
29 Sep 66	CHANGES (re-entry) *Decca F 12480*	**47**	3 wks

ST. PHILIPS CHOIR UK, choir   4 wks

12 Dec 87	SING FOR EVER *BBC RESL 222*	**49**	4 wks

ST. THOMAS MORE SCHOOL CHOIR – *See Scott FITZGERALD*

ST. WINIFRED'S SCHOOL CHOIR   11 wks
UK, school choir

22 Nov 80 ★	THERE'S NO ONE QUITE LIKE GRANDMA *MFP FP 900*	**1**	11 wks

Buffy SAINTE-MARIE Canada, female vocalist   29 wks

17 Jul 71 ●	SOLDIER BLUE *RCA 2081*	**7**	18 wks
18 Mar 72	I'M GONNA BE A COUNTRY GIRL AGAIN *Vanguard VRS 35143*	**34**	5 wks
8 Feb 92	THE BIG ONES GET AWAY *Ensign ENY 650*	**39**	5 wks
4 Jul 92	FALLEN ANGELS *Ensign ENY 655*	**57**	1 wk

SAINTS Australia, male vocal/instrumental group   4 wks

16 Jul 77	THIS PERFECT DAY *Harvest HAR 5130*	**34**	4 wks

Kyu SAKAMOTO Japan, male vocalist   13 wks

27 Jun 63 ●	SUKIYAKI *HMV POP 1171*	**6**	13 wks

Riuichi SAKAMOTO – *See David SYLVIAN*

SAKKARIN – *See Jonathan KING*

SALFORD JETS UK, male vocal/instrumental group   2 wks

31 May 80	WHO YOU LOOKING AT *RCA PB 5239*	**72**	2 wks

SALSOUL ORCHESTRA – *See CHARO and the SALSOUL ORCHESTRA*

SALT-N-PEPA US, female rap duo — **85 wks**

Date	Title	Pos	Wks
26 Mar 88	PUSH IT/I AM DOWN *ffrr FFR 2*	41	6 wks
25 Jun 88 ●	PUSH IT/TRAMP *Champion CHAMP 51/ ffrr FFR 2*	2	13 wks
3 Sep 88	SHAKE YOUR THANG (IT'S YOUR THING) *ffrr FFR 11 **	22	8 wks
12 Nov 88 ●	TWIST AND SHOUT *ffrr FFR 16*	4	9 wks
14 Apr 90	EXPRESSION *ffrr F 127*	40	6 wks
25 May 91	DO YOU WANT ME *ffrr F 151*	5	12 wks
31 Aug 91 ●	LET'S TALK ABOUT SEX *ffrr F 162* **	2	13 wks
30 Nov 91	YOU SHOWED ME *ffrr F 174*	15	9 wks
28 Mar 92	EXPRESSION (re-issue) *ffrr F 182*	23	6 wks
3 Oct 92	START ME UP *ffrr F 196*	39	3 wks

* Salt-N-Pepa featuring E.U. ** Salt-N-Pepa featuring Psychotropic
I Am Down *only listed from 2 April 88. The disc re-entered on 25 June when it was made available on Champion with a different flip side. Sales for both discs were amalgamated.*

SAM and DAVE US, male vocal duo — **39 wks**

Date	Title	Pos	Wks
16 Mar 67	SOOTHE ME *Stax 601 004*	48	2 wks
13 Apr 67	SOOTHE ME (re-entry) *Stax 601 004*	35	6 wks
1 Nov 67	SOUL MAN *Stax 601 023*	24	14 wks
13 Mar 68	I THANK YOU *Stax 601 030*	34	9 wks
29 Jan 69	SOUL SISTER BROWN SUGAR *Atlantic 584 237*	15	8 wks

See also Lou Reed

SAM THE SHAM and the PHARAOHS — **18 wks**
US, male vocal/instrumental group

Date	Title	Pos	Wks
24 Jun 65	WOOLY BULLY *MGM 1269*	11	15 wks
4 Aug 66	LIL' RED RIDING HOOD *MGM 1315*	48	1 wk
18 Aug 66	LIL' RED RIDING HOOD (re-entry) *MGM 1315*	46	2 wks

Richie SAMBORA US, male vocalist/instrumentalist - bass — **1 wk**

Date	Title	Pos	Wks
7 Sep 91	BALLAD OF YOUTH *Mercury MER 350*	59	1 wk

Mike SAMMES SINGERS UK, male/female vocal group — **38 wks**

Date	Title	Pos	Wks
15 Sep 66	SOMEWHERE MY LOVE *HMV POP 1546*	22	19 wks
12 Jul 67	SOMEWHERE MY LOVE (re-entry) *HMV POP 1546*	14	19 wks

Dave SAMPSON UK, male vocalist — **6 wks**

Date	Title	Pos	Wks
19 May 60	SWEET DREAMS *Columbia DB 4449*	48	1 wk
2 Jun 60	SWEET DREAMS (re-entry) *Columbia DB 4449*	29	5 wks

SAMSON UK, male vocal/instrumental group — **6 wks**

Date	Title	Pos	Wks
4 Jul 81	RIDING WITH THE ANGELS *RCA 67*	55	3 wks
24 Jul 82	LOSING MY GRIP *Polydor POSP 471*	63	2 wks
5 Mar 83	RED SKIES *Polydor POSP 554*	65	1 wk

SAN JOSE featuring Rodriguez ARGENTINA UK, male instrumental group — **8 wks**

Date	Title	Pos	Wks
17 Jun 78	ARGENTINE MELODY (CANCION DE ARGENTINA) *MCA 369*	14	8 wks

Rodriguez Argentina is Rod Argent. See also Argent; Silsoe.

SAN REMO STRINGS US, orchestra — **8 wks**

Date	Title	Pos	Wks
18 Dec 71	FESTIVAL TIME *Tamla Motown TMG 795*	39	8 wks

Chris SANDFORD UK, male vocalist — **9 wks**

Date	Title	Pos	Wks
12 Dec 63	NOT TOO LITTLE NOT TOO MUCH *Decca F 11778*	17	9 wks

SANDPIPERS US, male vocal group — **33 wks**

Date	Title	Pos	Wks
15 Sep 66 ●	GUANTANAMERA *Pye International 7N 25380*	7	17 wks
5 Jun 68	QUANDO M'INNAMORO (A MAN WITHOUT LOVE) *A & M AMS 723*	33	6 wks
26 Mar 69	KUMBAYA *A & M AMS 744*	39	1 wk
9 Apr 69	KUMBAYA (re-entry) *A & M AMS 744*	49	1 wk
27 Nov 76	HANG ON SLOOPY *Satril SAT 114*	32	8 wks

SANDRA Germany, female vocalist — **8 wks**

Date	Title	Pos	Wks
17 Dec 88	EVERLASTING LOVE *Siren SRN 85*	45	8 wks

Jodie SANDS US, female vocalist — **10 wks**

Date	Title	Pos	Wks
17 Oct 58	SOMEDAY *HMV POP 533*	14	10 wks

Tommy SANDS US, male vocalist — **7 wks**

Date	Title	Pos	Wks
4 Aug 60	OLD OAKEN BUCKET *Capitol CL 15143*	25	7 wks

Samantha SANG Australia, female vocalist — **13 wks**

Date	Title	Pos	Wks
4 Feb 78	EMOTION *Private Stock PVT 128*	11	13 wks

SANTA CLAUS and the CHRISTMAS TREES — **10 wks**
UK, male vocal/instrumental group

Date	Title	Pos	Wks
11 Dec 82	SINGALONG-A-SANTA *Polydor IVY 1*	19	5 wks
10 Dec 83	SINGALONG-A-SANTA AGAIN *Polydor IVY 2*	39	5 wks

SANTA ESMERALDA and Leroy GOMEZ — **5 wks**
US/France, male/female vocal/instrumental group

Date	Title	Pos	Wks
12 Nov 77	DON'T LET ME BE MISUNDERSTOOD *Philips 6042 325*	41	5 wks

SANTANA US, male vocal/instrumental group — **25 wks**

Date	Title	Pos	Wks
28 Sep 74	SAMBA PA TI *CBS 2561*	27	7 wks
15 Oct 77	SHE'S NOT THERE *CBS 5671*	11	12 wks
25 Nov 78	WELL ALL RIGHT *CBS 6755*	53	3 wks
22 Mar 80	ALL I EVER WANTED *CBS 8160*	57	3 wks

SANTO and JOHNNY — **5 wks**
US, male instrumental duo - steel and electric guitars

Date	Title	Pos	Wks
16 Oct 59	SLEEP WALK *Pye International 7N 25037*	22	4 wks
31 Mar 60	TEARDROP *Parlophone R 4619*	50	1 wk

Mike SARNE UK, male vocalist — **43 wks**

Date	Title	Pos	Wks
10 May 62 ★	COME OUTSIDE *Parlophone R 4902* *	1	19 wks
30 Aug 62	WILL I WHAT *Parlophone R 4932* **	18	10 wks
10 Jan 63	JUST FOR KICKS *Parlophone R 4974*	22	7 wks
28 Mar 63	CODE OF LOVE *Parlophone R 5010*	29	7 wks

* Mike Sarne with Wendy Richard ** Mike Sarne with Billie Davis

Joy SARNEY *UK, female vocalist* — 6 wks

7 May 77	NAUGHTY NAUGHTY NAUGHTY *Alaska ALA 2005*	26	6 wks

SARR BAND *Italy/UK/France, male/female vocal/instrumental group* — 1 wk

16 Sep 78	MAGIC MANDRAKE *Calendar Day 111*	68	1 wk

Peter SARSTEDT *UK, male vocalist* — 25 wks

5 Feb 69	★ WHERE DO YOU GO TO MY LOVELY *United Artists UP 2262*	1	16 wks
4 Jun 69	● FROZEN ORANGE JUICE *United Artists UP 35021*	10	9 wks

Robin SARSTEDT *UK, male vocalist* — 9 wks

8 May 76	● MY RESISTANCE IS LOW *Decca F 13624*	3	9 wks

SATURDAY NIGHT BAND *US, male vocal/instrumental group* — 9 wks

1 Jul 78	COME ON DANCE DANCE *CBS 6367*	16	9 wks

Kevin SAUNDERSON – *See INNER CITY*

Edna SAVAGE *UK, female vocalist* — 1 wk

13 Jan 56	ARRIVEDERCI DARLING *Parlophone R 4097*	19	1 wk

Telly SAVALAS *US, male vocalist* — 12 wks

22 Feb 75	★ IF *MCA 174*	1	9 wks
31 May 75	YOU'VE LOST THAT LOVIN' FEELING *MCA 189*	47	3 wks

SAVANNA *US, male vocalist/instrumentalist - guitar* — 4 wks

10 Oct 81	I CAN'T TURN AWAY *R & B RBS 203*	61	4 wks

SAVUKA – *See Johnny CLEGG and SAVUKA*

SAXON *UK, male vocal/instrumental group* — 61 wks

22 Mar 80	WHEELS OF STEEL *Carrere CAR 143*	20	11 wks
21 Jun 80	747 (STRANGERS IN THE NIGHT) *Carrere CAR 151*	13	9 wks
28 Jun 80	BACKS TO THE WALL *Carrere HM 6*	64	2 wks
28 Jun 80	BIG TEASER/RAINBOW THEME *Carrere HM 5*	66	2 wks
29 Nov 80	STRONG ARM OF THE LAW *Carrere CAR 170*	63	3 wks
11 Apr 81	AND THE BANDS PLAYED ON *Carrere CAR 180*	12	8 wks
18 Jul 81	NEVER SURRENDER *Carrere CAR 204*	18	6 wks
31 Oct 81	PRINCESS OF THE NIGHT *Carrere CAR 208*	57	3 wks
23 Apr 83	POWER AND THE GLORY *RCA SAXON 1*	32	5 wks
30 Jul 83	NIGHTMARE *Carrere CAR 284*	50	3 wks
31 Aug 85	BACK ON THE STREETS *Parlophone R 6103*	75	1 wk
29 Mar 86	ROCK 'N' ROLL GYPSY *Parlophone R 6112*	71	1 wk
30 Aug 86	WAITING FOR THE NIGHT *EMI EMI 5575*	66	3 wks
5 Mar 88	RIDE LIKE THE WIND *EMI EM 43*	52	4 wks
30 Apr 88	I CAN'T WAIT ANYMORE *EMI EM 54*	71	1 wk

Al SAXON *UK, male vocalist* — 10 wks

16 Jan 59	YOU'RE THE TOP CHA *Fontana H 164*	17	4 wks
28 Aug 59	ONLY SIXTEEN *Fontana H 205*	24	3 wks
22 Dec 60	BLUE-EYED BOY *Fontana H 278*	39	2 wks
7 Sep 61	THERE I'VE SAID IT AGAIN *Piccadilly 7N 35011*	48	1 wk

British Hit Singles Part One: Alphabetically by Artist
Date of chart entry/Title & catalogue no./Peak position reached/Weeks on chart
★ Number one   ● Top Ten   † still on chart at 31 Dec 1992
* = credited to act billed in footnote

Leo SAYER *UK, male vocalist* — 146 wks

15 Dec 73	● THE SHOW MUST GO ON *Chrysalis CHS 2023*	2	13 wks
15 Jun 74	● ONE MAN BAND *Chrysalis CHS 2045*	6	9 wks
14 Sep 74	● LONG TALL GLASSES *Chrysalis CHS 2052*	4	9 wks
30 Aug 75	● MOONLIGHTING *Chrysalis CHS 2076*	2	8 wks
30 Oct 76	● YOU MAKE ME FEEL LIKE DANCING *Chrysalis CHS 2119*	2	12 wks
29 Jan 77	★ WHEN I NEED YOU *Chrysalis CHS 2127*	1	13 wks
9 Apr 77	● HOW MUCH LOVE *Chrysalis CHS 2140*	10	8 wks
10 Sep 77	THUNDER IN MY HEART *Chrysalis CHS 2163*	22	8 wks
16 Sep 78	● I CAN'T STOP LOVIN' YOU (THOUGH I TRY) *Chrysalis CHS 2240*	6	11 wks
25 Nov 78	RAINING IN MY HEART *Chrysalis CHS 2277*	21	10 wks
5 Jul 80	● MORE THAN I CAN SAY *Chrysalis CHS 2442*	2	11 wks
13 Mar 82	● HAVE YOU EVER BEEN IN LOVE *Chrysalis CHS 2596*	10	9 wks
19 Jun 82	HEART (STOP BEATING IN TIME) *Chrysalis CHS 2616*	22	10 wks
12 Mar 83	ORCHARD ROAD *Chrysalis CHS 2677*	16	8 wks
15 Oct 83	TILL YOU COME BACK TO ME *Chrysalis LEO 01*	51	3 wks
8 Feb 86	UNCHAINED MELODY *Chrysalis LEO 3*	54	4 wks

Alexei SAYLE *UK, male vocalist* — 8 wks

25 Feb 84	'ULLO JOHN GOT A NEW MOTOR? *Island IS 162*	15	8 wks

SCAFFOLD *UK, male vocal group* — 62 wks

22 Nov 67	● THANK U VERY MUCH *Parlophone R 5643*	4	12 wks
27 Mar 68	DO YOU REMEMBER *Parlophone R 5679*	34	5 wks
6 Nov 68	★ LILY THE PINK *Parlophone R 5734*	1	24 wks
1 Nov 69	GIN GAN GOOLIE *Parlophone R 5812*	38	11 wks
24 Jan 70	GIN GAN GOOLIE (re-entry) *Parlophone R 5812*	50	1 wk
1 Jun 74	● LIVERPOOL LOU *Warner Bros. K 16400*	7	9 wks

Boz SCAGGS *US, male vocalist* — 31 wks

30 Oct 76	LOWDOWN *CBS 4563*	28	4 wks
22 Jan 77	● WHAT CAN I SAY *CBS 4869*	10	10 wks
14 May 77	LIDO SHUFFLE *CBS 5136*	13	9 wks
10 Dec 77	HOLLYWOOD *CBS 5836*	33	8 wks

SCARLET FANTASTIC *UK, male/female vocal/instrumental group* — 12 wks

3 Oct 87	NO MEMORY *Arista RIS 36*	24	10 wks
23 Jan 88	PLUG ME IN (TO THE CENTRAL LOVE LINE) *Arista 109693*	67	2 wks

SCARLET PARTY *UK, male vocal/instrumental group* — 5 wks

16 Oct 82	101 DAM-NATIONS *Parlophone R 6058*	44	5 wks

Michael SCHENKER GROUP *Germany/UK, male vocal/instrumental group* — 9 wks

13 Sep 80	ARMED AND READY *Chrysalis CHS 2455*	53	3 wks
8 Nov 80	CRY FOR THE NATIONS *Chrysalis CHS 2471*	56	3 wks
11 Sep 82	DANCER *Chrysalis CHS 2636*	52	3 wks

Lalo SCHIFRIN US, orchestra — 9 wks

| 9 Oct 76 | JAWS CTI CTSP 005 | 14 | 9 wks |

Peter SCHILLING Germany, male vocalist — 6 wks

| 5 May 84 | MAJOR TOM (COMING HOME) PSP/WEA X 9438 | 42 | 5 wks |
| 16 Jun 84 | MAJOR TOM (COMING HOME) (re-entry) PSP/WEA X 9438 | 73 | 1 wk |

Philip SCHOFIELD UK, male vocalist — 4 wks

| 5 Dec 92 | CLOSE EVERY DOOR Really Useful RUR 11 | 27† | 4 wks |

SCIENTIST UK, male instrumentalist — 13 wks

6 Oct 90	THE EXORCIST Kickin KICK 1	62	3 wks
1 Dec 90	THE EXORCIST (re-mix) Kickin KICK 1TR	46	3 wks
15 Dec 90	THE BEE Kickin KICK 3S	52	3 wks
28 Jan 91	THE BEE (re-entry) Kickin KICK 3S	47	3 wks
11 May 91	SPIRAL SYMPHONY Kickin KICK 5	74	1 wk

SCORPIONS Germany, male vocal/instrumental group — 35 wks

26 May 79	IS THERE ANYBODY THERE/ANOTHER PIECE OF MEAT Harvest HAR 5185	39	4 wks
25 Aug 79	LOVEDRIVE Harvest HAR 5188	69	2 wks
31 May 80	MAKE IT REAL Harvest HAR 5206	72	2 wks
20 Sep 80	THE ZOO Harvest HAR 5212	75	1 wk
3 Apr 82	NO ONE LIKE YOU Harvest HAR 5219	65	3 wks
1 May 82	NO ONE LIKE YOU (re-entry) Harvest HAR 5219	64	1 wk
17 Jul 82	CAN'T LIVE WITHOUT YOU Harvest HAR 5221	63	2 wks
4 Jun 88	RHYTHM OF LOVE Harvest HAR 5240	59	2 wks
18 Feb 89	PASSION RULES THE GAME Harvest 5242	74	1 wk
1 Jun 91	WIND OF CHANGE Vertigo VER 54	53	3 wks
28 Sep 91 ●	WIND OF CHANGE (re-issue) Vertigo VER 58	2	9 wks
30 Nov 91	SEND ME AN ANGEL Vertigo VER 60	27	3 wks
28 Dec 91	SEND ME AN ANGEL (re-entry) Vertigo VER 60	68	2 wks

SCOTLAND WORLD CUP SQUAD — 22 wks
UK, male football team vocalists

22 Jun 74	EASY EASY Polydor 2058 452	20	4 wks
27 May 78 ●	OLE OLA (MULHER BRASILEIRA) Riva 15 *	4	6 wks
1 May 82 ●	WE HAVE A DREAM WEA K 19145	5	9 wks
9 Jun 90	SAY IT WITH PRIDE RCA PB 43791	45	3 wks

* Rod Stewart featuring the Scottish World Cup Football Squad

Jack SCOTT Canada, male vocalist — 28 wks

10 Oct 58 ●	MY TRUE LOVE London HLU 8626	9	10 wks
25 Sep 59	THE WAY I WALK London HLL 8912	30	1 wk
10 Mar 60	WHAT IN THE WORLD'S COME OVER YOU Top Rank JAR 280	11	15 wks
2 Jun 60	BURNING BRIDGES Top Rank JAR 375	32	2 wks

Linda SCOTT US, female vocalist — 14 wks

| 18 May 61 ● | I'VE TOLD EVERY LITTLE STAR Columbia DB 4638 | 7 | 13 wks |
| 14 Sep 61 | DON'T BET MONEY HONEY Columbia DB 4692 | 50 | 1 wk |

Millie SCOTT US, female vocalist — 11 wks

12 Apr 86	PRISONER OF LOVE Fourth & Broadway BRW 45	52	4 wks
23 Aug 86	AUTOMATIC Fourth & Broadway BRW 51	56	3 wks
21 Feb 87	EV'RY LITTLE BIT Fourth & Broadway BRW 58	63	4 wks

Simon SCOTT UK, male vocalist — 8 wks

| 13 Aug 64 | MOVE IT BABY Parlophone R 5164 | 37 | 8 wks |

Tony SCOTT US, male vocalist — 6 wks

| 15 Apr 89 | THAT'S HOW I'M LIVING/THE CHIEF Champion CHAMP 97 | 48 | 4 wks |
| 10 Feb 90 | GET INTO IT/THAT'S HOW I'M LIVING (re-issue) Champion CHAMP 232 | 63 | 2 wks |

The Chief only listed from 6 May 89.

SCOTTISH RUGBY TEAM with Ronnie BROWNE UK, male rugby team vocalists — 1 wk

| 2 Jun 90 | FLOWER OF SCOTLAND Greentrax STRAX 1001 | 73 | 1 wk |

SCREAMING BLUE MESSIAHS — 6 wks
UK, male vocal/instrumental group

| 16 Jan 88 | I WANNA BE A FLINTSTONE WEA YZ 166 | 28 | 6 wks |

SCRITTI POLITTI UK, male vocal/instrumental group — 77 wks

21 Nov 81	THE SWEETEST GIRL Rough Trade RT 091	64	3 wks
22 May 82	FAITHLESS Rough Trade RT 101	56	4 wks
7 Aug 82	ASYLUMS IN JERUSALEM/JACQUES DERRIDA Rough Trade RT 111	43	5 wks
10 Mar 84 ●	WOOD BEEZ (PRAY LIKE ARETHA FRANKLIN) Virgin VS 657	10	12 wks
9 Jun 84	ABSOLUTE Virgin VS 680	17	9 wks
17 Nov 84	HYPNOTIZE Virgin VS 725	68	2 wks
11 May 85 ●	THE WORD GIRL Virgin VS 747 *	6	12 wks
7 Sep 85	PERFECT WAY Virgin VS 780	48	5 wks
7 May 88	OH PATTI (DON'T FEEL SORRY FOR LOVERBOY) Virgin VS 1006	13	9 wks
27 Aug 88	FIRST BOY IN THIS TOWN (LOVE SICK) Virgin VS 1082	63	3 wks
12 Nov 88	BOOM! THERE SHE WAS Virgin VS 1143 **	55	3 wks
16 Mar 91	SHE'S A WOMAN Virgin VS 1333 ***	20	7 wks
3 Aug 91	TAKE ME IN YOUR ARMS AND LOVE ME Virgin VS 1346	47	3 wks

* Scritti Politti featuring Ranking Ann ** Scritti Politti featuring Roger *** Scritti Politti featuring Shabba Ranks

Sweetie Irie is credited on the sleeve only of Take Me In Your Arms And Love Me.

Earl SCRUGGS – See Lester FLATT and Earl SCRUGGS

SEA LEVEL US, male instrumental group — 4 wks

| 17 Feb 79 | FIFTY-FOUR Capricorn POSP 28 | 63 | 4 wks |

SEAL UK, male vocalist — 37 wks

8 Dec 90 ●	CRAZY ZTT ZANG 8	2	15 wks
4 May 91	FUTURE LOVE EP ZTT ZANG 11	12	6 wks
20 Jul 91	THE BEGINNING ZTT ZANG 21	24	6 wks
16 Nov 91 ●	KILLER (EP) ZTT ZANG 23	8	8 wks
29 Feb 92	VIOLET ZTT ZANG 27	39	2 wks

Tracks on Future Love EP: Future Love Paradise/A Minor Groove/Violet. Tracks on Killer (EP): Killer/Hey Joe/Come See What Love Has Done. See also Adamski.

SEARCHERS UK, male vocal/instrumental group — 128 wks

| 27 Jun 63 ★ | SWEETS FOR MY SWEET Pye 7N 15533 | 1 | 16 wks |
| 10 Oct 63 | SWEET NOTHINS Philips BF 1274 | 48 | 2 wks |

24 Oct 63	● SUGAR AND SPICE Pye 7N 15566	2	13 wks
16 Jan 64	★ NEEDLES AND PINS Pye 7N 15594	1	15 wks
16 Apr 64	★ DON'T THROW YOUR LOVE AWAY Pye 7N 15630	1	11 wks
16 Jul 64	SOMEDAY WE'RE GONNA LOVE AGAIN Pye 7N 15670	11	8 wks
17 Sep 64	● WHEN YOU WALK IN THE ROOM Pye 7N 15694	3	12 wks
3 Dec 64	WHAT HAVE THEY DONE TO THE RAIN Pye 7N 15739	13	11 wks
4 Mar 65	● GOODBYE MY LOVE Pye 7N 15794	4	11 wks
8 Jul 65	HE'S GOT NO LOVE Pye 7N 15878	12	10 wks
14 Oct 65	WHEN I GET HOME Pye 7N 15950	35	3 wks
16 Dec 65	TAKE ME FOR WHAT I'M WORTH Pye 7N 15992	20	8 wks
21 Apr 66	TAKE IT OR LEAVE IT Pye 7N 17094	31	6 wks
13 Oct 66	HAVE YOU EVER LOVED SOMEBODY Pye 7N 17170	48	2 wks

SEASHELLS UK, female vocal group — 5 wks

9 Sep 72	MAYBE I KNOW CBS 8218	32	5 wks

Jon SECADA US, male vocalist — 19 wks

18 Jul 92	● JUST ANOTHER DAY SBK SBK 35	5	15 wks
31 Oct 92	DO YOU BELIEVE IN US SBK SBK 37	30	4 wks

SECCHI featuring Orlando JOHNSON — 3 wks
Italy/US, male vocal/instrumental duo

4 May 91	I SAY YEAH Epic 6568467	46	3 wks

Harry SECOMBE UK, male vocalist — 35 wks

9 Dec 55	ON WITH THE MOTLEY Philips PB 523	16	3 wks
3 Oct 63	IF I RULED THE WORLD Philips BF 1261	44	2 wks
21 Nov 63	IF I RULED THE WORLD (re-entry) Philips BF 1261	18	15 wks
23 Feb 67	● THIS IS MY SONG Philips BF 1539	2	15 wks

SECOND CITY SOUND UK, male instrumental group — 8 wks

20 Jan 66	TCHAIKOVSKY ONE Decca F 12310	22	7 wks
2 Apr 69	DREAM OF OLWEN Major Minor MM 600	43	1 wk

SECOND IMAGE UK, male vocal/instrumental group — 11 wks

24 Jul 82	STAR Polydor POSP 457	60	2 wks
2 Apr 83	BETTER TAKE TIME Polydor POSP 565	67	2 wks
26 Nov 83	DON'T YOU MCA 848	68	2 wks
11 Aug 84	SING AND SHOUT MCA MCA 882	53	3 wks
2 Feb 85	STARTING AGAIN MCA 936	65	2 wks

SECOND PHASE US, male producer - Joey Beltram — 2 wks

21 Sep 91	MENTASM R&S RSUK 2	48	2 wks

SECRET AFFAIR UK, male vocal/instrumental group — 34 wks

1 Sep 79	TIME FOR ACTION I-Spy SEE 1	13	10 wks
10 Nov 79	LET YOUR HEART DANCE I-Spy SEE 3	32	6 wks
8 Mar 80	MY WORLD I-Spy SEE 5	16	9 wks
23 Aug 80	SOUND OF CONFUSION I-Spy SEE 8	45	4 wks
17 Oct 81	DO YOU KNOW I-Spy SEE 10	57	4 wks

SECRET LIFE UK, male vocal group — 3 wks

12 Dec 92	AS ALWAYS Cowboy 7RODEO 9	45†	3 wks

SECRETARY OF ENTERTAINMENT – See RAZE

Neil SEDAKA US, male vocalist — 190 wks

24 Apr 59	● I GO APE RCA 1115	9	13 wks
13 Nov 59	● OH CAROL RCA 1152	3	17 wks
14 Apr 60	● STAIRWAY TO HEAVEN RCA 1178	8	15 wks
1 Sep 60	YOU MEAN EVERYTHING TO ME RCA 1198	45	3 wks
2 Feb 61	● CALENDAR GIRL RCA 1220	8	14 wks
18 May 61	● LITTLE DEVIL RCA 1236	9	12 wks
21 Dec 61	● HAPPY BIRTHDAY SWEET SIXTEEN RCA 1266	3	18 wks
19 Apr 62	KING OF CLOWNS RCA 1282	23	11 wks
19 Jul 62	● BREAKING UP IS HARD TO DO RCA 1298	7	16 wks
22 Nov 62	NEXT DOOR TO AN ANGEL RCA 1319	29	4 wks
30 May 63	LET'S GO STEADY AGAIN RCA 1343	42	1 wk
13 Jun 63	LET'S GO STEADY AGAIN (re-entry) RCA 1343	43	2 wks
7 Oct 72	OH CAROL/BREAKING UP IS HARD TO DO/LITTLE DEVIL (re-issue) RCA Maximillion 2259	19	14 wks
4 Nov 72	BEAUTIFUL YOU RCA 2269	43	3 wks
24 Feb 73	THAT'S WHEN THE MUSIC TAKES ME RCA 2310	18	10 wks
2 Jun 73	STANDING ON THE INSIDE MGM 2006 267	26	9 wks
25 Aug 73	OUR LAST SONG TOGETHER MGM 2006 307	31	8 wks
9 Feb 74	A LITTLE LOVIN' Polydor 2058 434	34	6 wks
22 Jun 74	LAUGHTER IN THE RAIN Polydor 2058 494	15	9 wks
22 Mar 75	THE QUEEN OF 1964 Polydor 2058 546	35	5 wks

SEDUCTION US, female vocal group — 1 wk

21 Apr 90	HEARTBEAT Breakout USA 685	75	1 wk

SEEKERS Australia/Sri Lanka, male/female vocal group — 120 wks

7 Jan 65	★ I'LL NEVER FIND ANOTHER YOU Columbia DB 7431	1	23 wks
15 Apr 65	● A WORLD OF OUR OWN Columbia DB 7532	3	18 wks
28 Oct 65	★ THE CARNIVAL IS OVER Columbia DB 7711	1	17 wks
24 Mar 66	SOMEDAY ONE DAY Columbia DB 7867	11	11 wks
8 Sep 66	● WALK WITH ME Columbia DB 8000	10	12 wks
24 Nov 66	MORNINGTOWN RIDE Columbia DB 8060	2	15 wks
23 Feb 67	● GEORGY GIRL Columbia DB 8134	3	11 wks
20 Sep 67	WHEN WILL THE GOOD APPLES FALL Columbia DB 8273	11	12 wks
13 Dec 67	EMERALD CITY Columbia DB 8313	50	1 wk

Bob SEGER and the SILVER BULLET BAND US, male vocal/instrumental group — 21 wks

30 Sep 78	HOLLYWOOD NIGHTS Capitol CL 16004	42	6 wks
3 Feb 79	WE'VE GOT TONITE Capitol CL 16028	41	6 wks
24 Oct 81	HOLLYWOOD NIGHTS Capitol CL 223	49	3 wks
6 Feb 82	WE'VE GOT TONITE Capitol CL 235	60	4 wks
9 Apr 83	EVEN NOW Capitol CL 284	73	2 wks

Capitol CL 223 and CL 235 were live versions of earlier studio hits.

SEIKO and Donnie WAHLBERG — 5 wks
Japan/US, female/male vocal duo

18 Aug 90	THE RIGHT COMBINATION Epic 656203 7	44	5 wks

SELECTER UK, male/female vocal/instrumental group — 28 wks

13 Oct 79	● ON MY RADIO 2 Tone CHSTT 4	8	9 wks
2 Feb 80	THREE MINUTE HERO 2 Tone CHS TT 8	16	6 wks
29 Mar 80	MISSING WORDS 2 Tone CHS TT 10	23	8 wks
23 Aug 80	THE WHISPER Chrysalis CHSS 1	36	5 wks

Peter SELLERS UK, male vocalist — 37 wks

2 Aug 57	ANY OLD IRON Parlophone R 4337	21	3 wks
6 Sep 57	ANY OLD IRON (re-entry) Parlophone R 4337	17	8 wks

10 Nov 60 ●	GOODNESS GRACIOUS ME *Parlophone R 4702* *	4	14 wks
12 Jan 61	BANGERS AND MASH *Parlophone R 4724* *	22	5 wks
23 Dec 65	A HARD DAY'S NIGHT *Parlophone R 5393*	14	7 wks

* Peter Sellers and Sophia Loren

Michael SEMBELLO *US, male vocalist*   **6 wks**

20 Aug 83	MANIAC *Casablanca CAN 1017*	43	6 wks

SEMPRINI *UK, orchestra*   **8 wks**

16 Mar 61	THEME FROM 'EXODUS' *HMV POP 842*	25	8 wks

SENSELESS THINGS *UK, male vocal/instrumental group*   **14 wks**

22 Jun 91	EVERYBODY'S GONE *Epic 6569807*	73	1 wk
28 Sep 91	GOT IT AT THE DELMAR *Epic 6574497*	50	3 wks
11 Jan 92	EASY TO SMILE *Epic 6576957*	18	4 wks
11 Apr 92	HOLD IT DOWN *Epic 6579267*	19	4 wks
5 Dec 92	HOMOPHOBIC ASSHOLE *Epic 6588337*	52	2 wks

SERIOUS INTENTION   **6 wks**
US, male vocal/instrumental group

16 Nov 85	YOU DON'T KNOW (OH-OH-OH) *Important TAN 8*	75	1 wk
5 Apr 86	SERIOUS *Pow Wow LON 93*	51	5 wks

SET THE TONE *UK, male vocal/instrumental group*   **4 wks**

22 Jan 83	DANCE SUCKER *Island WIP 6836*	62	2 wks
26 Mar 83	RAP YOUR LOVE *Island IS 110*	67	2 wks

SETTLERS *UK, male/female vocal/instrumental group*   **5 wks**

16 Oct 71	THE LIGHTNING TREE *York SYK 505*	36	5 wks

Taja SEVELLE *US, female vocalist*   **13 wks**

20 Feb 88 ●	LOVE IS CONTAGIOUS *Paisley Park W 8257*	7	9 wks
14 May 88	WOULDN'T YOU LOVE TO LOVE ME *Paisley Park W 8127*	59	4 wks

7TH HEAVEN *UK, male vocal group*   **5 wks**

14 Sep 85	HOT FUN *Mercury MER 199*	47	5 wks

SEVERINE *France, female vocalist*   **11 wks**

24 Apr 71 ●	UN BANC, UN ARBRE, UNE RUE *Philips 6009 135*	9	11 wks

David SEVILLE *US, male vocalist*   **6 wks**

23 May 58	WITCH DOCTOR *London HLU 8619*	11	6 wks

See also Chipmunks; Alfi and Harry.

Janette SEWELL – *See DOUBLE TROUBLE*

SEX PISTOLS *UK, male vocal/instrumental group*   **85 wks**

18 Dec 76	ANARCHY IN THE U.K. *EMI 2566*	38	4 wks
4 Jun 77 ●	GOD SAVE THE QUEEN *Virgin VS 181*	2	9 wks
9 Jul 77 ●	PRETTY VACANT *Virgin VS 184*	6	8 wks
22 Oct 77 ●	HOLIDAYS IN THE SUN *Virgin VS 191*	8	6 wks
8 Jul 78 ●	NO ONE IS INNOCENT/MY WAY *Virgin VS 220* *	7	10 wks
3 Mar 79 ●	SOMETHING ELSE/FRIGGIN' IN THE RIGGIN' *Virgin VS 240*	3	12 wks
7 Apr 79 ●	SILLY THING *Virgin VS 256*	6	8 wks
30 Jun 79 ●	C'MON EVERYBODY *Virgin VS 272*	3	9 wks
13 Oct 79	THE GREAT ROCK 'N' ROLL SWINDLE *Virgin VS 290*	21	6 wks
14 Jun 80	(I'M NOT YOUR) STEPPING STONE *Virgin VS 339*	21	8 wks
3 Oct 92	ANARCHY IN THE UK (re-issue) *Virgin VS 1431*	33	3 wks
5 Dec 92	PRETTY VACANT (re-issue) *Virgin VS 1448*	56	2 wks

* Sex Pistols, punk prayer by Ronald Biggs

The listed flip side of Silly Thing *was* Who Killed Bambi *by Ten Pole Tudor. The listed flip side of* The Great Rock 'n' Roll Swindle *was* Rock Around The Clock, *also by Ten Pole Tudor.*

SEX-O-LETTES – *See DISCO TEX and the SEX-O-LETTES*

Denny SEYTON and the SABRES   **1 wk**
UK, male vocal/instrumental group

17 Sep 64	THE WAY YOU LOOK TONIGHT *Mercury MF 824*	48	1 wk

SHADES OF RHYTHM   **19 wks**
UK, male instrumental/production group

2 Feb 91	HOMICIDE/EXORCIST *ZTT ZANG 13*	53	3 wks
13 Apr 91	SWEET SENSATION *ZTT ZANG 18*	54	4 wks
20 Jul 91	THE SOUND OF EDEN *ZTT ZANG 22*	35	5 wks
30 Nov 91	EXTACY *ZTT ZANG 24*	16	7 wks

SHADOWS *UK, male instrumental/vocal group*   **359 wks**

21 Jul 60 ★	APACHE *Columbia DB 4484*	1	21 wks
10 Nov 60 ●	MAN OF MYSTERY/THE STRANGER *Columbia DB 4530*	5	15 wks
9 Feb 61 ●	F. B. I. *Columbia DB 4580*	6	19 wks
11 May 61 ●	FRIGHTENED CITY *Columbia DB 4637*	3	20 wks
7 Sep 61 ★	KON-TIKI *Columbia DB 4698*	1	10 wks
16 Nov 61 ●	THE SAVAGE *Columbia DB 4726*	10	8 wks
23 Nov 61	KON-TIKI (re-entry) *Columbia DB 4698*	37	2 wks
1 Mar 62 ★	WONDERFUL LAND *Columbia DB 4790*	1	19 wks
2 Aug 62 ●	GUITAR TANGO *Columbia DB 4870*	4	15 wks
13 Dec 62 ★	DANCE ON *Columbia DB 4948*	1	15 wks
7 Mar 63 ★	FOOT TAPPER *Columbia DB 4984*	1	16 wks
6 Jun 63 ●	ATLANTIS *Columbia DB 7047*	2	17 wks
19 Sep 63 ●	SHINDIG *Columbia DB 7106*	6	12 wks
5 Dec 63	GERONIMO *Columbia DB 7163*	11	12 wks
5 Mar 64	THEME FOR YOUNG LOVERS *Columbia DB 7231*	12	10 wks
7 May 64 ●	THE RISE AND FALL OF FLINGEL BUNT *Columbia DB 7261*	5	14 wks
3 Sep 64	RHYTHM AND GREENS *Columbia DB 7342*	22	7 wks
3 Dec 64	GENIE WITH THE LIGHT BROWN LAMP *Columbia DB 7416*	17	10 wks
11 Feb 65	MARY ANNE *Columbia DB 7476*	17	10 wks
10 Jun 65	STINGRAY *Columbia DB 7588*	19	7 wks
5 Aug 65 ●	DON'T MAKE MY BABY BLUE *Columbia DB 7650*	10	10 wks
25 Nov 65	WAR LORD *Columbia DB 7769*	18	9 wks
17 Mar 66	I MET A GIRL *Columbia DB 7853*	22	5 wks
7 Jul 66	A PLACE IN THE SUN *Columbia DB 7952*	24	6 wks
3 Nov 66	THE DREAMS I DREAM *Columbia DB 8034*	42	6 wks
13 Apr 67	MAROC 7 *Columbia DB 8170*	24	8 wks
8 Mar 75	LET ME BE THE ONE *EMI 2269*	12	9 wks
16 Dec 78 ●	DON'T CRY FOR ME ARGENTINA *EMI 2890*	5	14 wks
28 Apr 79 ●	THEME FROM THE DEER HUNTER (CAVATINA) *EMI 2939*	9	14 wks
26 Jan 80	RIDERS IN THE SKY *EMI 5027*	12	12 wks
23 Aug 80	EQUINOXE (PART V) *Polydor POSP 148*	50	3 wks
2 May 81	THE THIRD MAN *Polydor POSP 255*	44	4 wks

All the above hits were instrumentals except for Mary Anne, Don't Make My Baby Blue, I Met A Girl, The Dream I Dream *and* Let Me Be The One. *See also Cliff Richard.*

...k "nasties" who shocked
...rs with their filthy language
...a fresh barrage of belches
...last night.
...old members of the Sex Pistols
...ed by the criticism of their per...
...nes TV's teatime programme.

Manager McLaren

My boys were goaded says Sex Pistols' boss

"We do not need Rolls Royces and houses in the country. We can see all through that bulls---."

Steve Jones refused to move nearer to Rotten for a photograph.

"He has got really smelly armpits," he said.

The centre of Britain's notorious new pop cult is a boutique called "Sex" in trendy King's Road, Chelsea.

Its owner, Vivienne Westwood is the girl-friend of the Sex Pistols manager Malcolm McLaren. They have lived together for ten years and have a nine-year-old son.

"There's nothing wrong with being nasty or rude," said 35-year-old Miss Westwood.

"Young people are trying to control their lives and the younger you are the less chance you have of being f------ up."

She said viewers who complained about the Sex Pistols' TV performance were "hypocrites."

Amazed

"I was amazed that people can get so up-tight about a word that is used constantly."

Leslie Hill, the managing director of EMI Records, who have backed the Sex Pistols with £40,000, also sprang to the group's defence.

"We deplore this type of incident but feel that in many cases it is deliberately provoked by the media," he said.

● DID YOU KNOW?

WHEN rock star Elvis Presley first became famous, sponsors of TV shows in America refused to have him shown below the waist because the considered his act—below the waist anyway—was obscene.

THE SHOCKERS: punk rockers Steve Jones (left), Paul Cook, Johnny Rotten and Glen Matlock. Their filthy language on television outraged vie...

YOBS! Tough-talking Grundy hits at the punk rock kings

Bleeps and the blame

THE SEX PISTOLS shocked Fleet Street, if not the nation, with their language on the December 1976 *Today* programme on Thames TV.

Right: SAM AND DAVE are given a gold disc for 'Soul Man' by Stax Vice-President Al Bell. Holding Sam's arm is Atlantic Records Executive Vice-President Jerry Wexler and standing alongside Bell is Atlantic President Ahmet Ertegun.

Left: SHAKESPEARS SISTER had the longest run at number one during 1992, eight weeks, with 'Stay'.

British Hit Singles Part One: Alphabetically by Artist
Date of chart entry/Title & catalogue no./Peak position reached/Weeks on chart
★ Number one   ● Top Ten   † still on chart at 31 Dec 1992
* = credited to act billed in footnote

SHAFT *UK, male instrumental/production duo* — 9 wks

| 21 Dec 91 ● | ROOBARB AND CUSTARD *Ffrreedom TAB 100* | 7 | 8 wks |
| 25 Jul 92 | MONKEY *Ffrreedom TAB 114* | 61 | 1 wk |

SHAG – *See Jonathan KING*

SHAI *US, male vocal group* — 2 wks

| 19 Dec 92 | IF I EVER FALL IN LOVE *MCA MCS 1727* | 41† | 2 wks |

SHAKATAK *UK, male/female vocal/instrumental group* — 85 wks

8 Nov 80	FEELS LIKE THE RIGHT TIME *Polydor POSP 188*	41	5 wks
7 Mar 81	LIVING IN THE U.K. *Polydor POSP 230*	52	4 wks
25 Jul 81	BRAZILIAN DAWN *Polydor POSP 282*	48	3 wks
21 Nov 81	EASIER SAID THAN DONE *Polydor POSP 375*	12	17 wks
3 Apr 82 ●	NIGHT BIRDS *Polydor POSP 407*	9	8 wks
19 Jun 82	STREETWALKIN' *Polydor POSP 452*	38	6 wks
4 Sep 82	INVITATIONS *Polydor POSP 502*	24	7 wks
6 Nov 82	STRANGER *Polydor POSP 530*	43	3 wks
4 Jun 83	DARK IS THE NIGHT *Polydor POSP 595*	15	8 wks
27 Aug 83	IF YOU COULD SEE ME NOW *Polydor POSP 635*	49	4 wks
7 Jul 84 ●	DOWN ON THE STREET *Polydor POSP 688*	9	11 wks
15 Sep 84	DON'T BLAME IT ON LOVE *Polydor POSP 699*	55	3 wks
16 Nov 85	DAY BY DAY *Polydor POSP 770* *	53	3 wks
24 Oct 87	MR. MANIC AND SISTER COOL *Polydor MANIC 1*	56	3 wks

* Shakatak with Al Jarreau

SHAKESPEARS SISTER — 48 wks
UK/US, female vocal/instrumental duo

29 Jul 89 ●	YOU'RE HISTORY *ffrr F 112*	7	9 wks
14 Oct 89	RUN SILENT *ffrr F 119*	54	3 wks
10 Mar 90	DIRTY MIND *ffrr F 128*	71	1 wk
12 Oct 91	GOODBYE CRUEL WORLD *London LON 309*	59	2 wks
25 Jan 92 ★	STAY *London LON 314*	1	16 wks
16 May 92 ●	I DON'T CARE *London LON 318*	7	7 wks
18 Jul 92	GOODBYE CRUEL WORLD (re-issue) *London LON 322*	32	4 wks
7 Nov 92	HELLO (TURN YOUR RADIO ON) *London LON 330*	14	6 wks

SHAKY and BONNIE – *See Shakin' STEVENS; Bonnie TYLER*

SHALAMAR *US, male/female vocal group* — 134 wks

14 May 77	UPTOWN FESTIVAL *Soul Train FB 0885*	30	5 wks
9 Dec 78	TAKE THAT TO THE BANK *RCA FB 1379*	20	12 wks
24 Nov 79	THE SECOND TIME AROUND *Solar FB 1709*	45	9 wks
9 Feb 80	RIGHT IN THE SOCKET *Solar SO2*	44	6 wks
30 Aug 80	I OWE YOU ONE *Solar SO 11*	13	10 wks
28 Mar 81	MAKE THAT MOVE *Solar SO 17*	30	10 wks
27 Mar 82 ●	I CAN MAKE YOU FEEL GOOD *Solar K 12599*	7	11 wks
12 Jun 82 ●	A NIGHT TO REMEMBER *Solar K 13162*	5	12 wks
4 Sep 82 ●	THERE IT IS *Solar K 13194*	5	10 wks
27 Nov 82	FRIENDS *Solar CHUM 1*	12	10 wks
11 Jun 83 ●	DEAD GIVEAWAY *Solar E 9819*	8	10 wks
13 Aug 83	DISAPPEARING ACT *Solar E 9807*	18	8 wks
15 Oct 83	OVER AND OVER *Solar E 9792*	23	6 wks
24 Mar 84	DANCING IN THE SHEETS *CBS A 4171*	41	3 wks
31 Mar 84	DEADLINE USA *MCA MCA 866*	52	3 wks

---

24 Nov 84	AMNESIA *Solar/MCA SHAL 1*	61	2 wks
2 Feb 85	MY GIRL LOVES ME *MCA SHAL 2*	45	3 wks
26 Apr 86	A NIGHT TO REMEMBER (re-mix) *MCA SHAL 3*	52	4 wks

SHAM 69 *UK, male vocal/instrumental group* — 53 wks

13 May 78	ANGELS WITH DIRTY FACES *Polydor 2059 023*	19	10 wks
29 Jul 78 ●	IF THE KIDS ARE UNITED *Polydor 2059 050*	9	9 wks
14 Oct 78 ●	HURRY UP HARRY *Polydor POSP 7*	10	8 wks
24 Mar 79	QUESTIONS AND ANSWERS *Polydor POSP 27*	18	9 wks
4 Aug 79 ●	HERSHAM BOYS *Polydor POSP 64*	6	9 wks
27 Oct 79	YOU'RE A BETTER MAN THAN I *Polydor POSP 82*	49	5 wks
12 Apr 80	TELL THE CHILDREN *Polydor POSP 136*	45	3 wks

SHAMEN *UK, male/female vocal/instrumental group* — 52 wks

7 Apr 90	PRO-GEN *One Little Indian 36 TP7*	55	4 wks
22 Sep 90	MAKE IT MINE *One Little Indian 46 TP7*	42	5 wks
8 Apr 91	HYPERREAL *One Little Indian 48 TP7*	29	5 wks
27 Jul 91 ●	MOVE ANY MOUNTAIN (re-mix) *One Little Indian 52 TP7*	4	10 wks
18 Jul 92 ●	LSI *One Little Indian 68 TP7*	6	8 wks
5 Sep 92 ★	EBENEEZER GOODE *One Little Indian 78 TP7*	1	10 wks
7 Nov 92 ●	BOSS DRUM *One Little Indian 88 TP7*	4	7 wks
7 Nov 92	BOSS DRUM (re-mix) *One Little Indian 88 TP12*	58	1 wk
19 Dec 92 ●	PHOREVER PEOPLE *One Little Indian 98 TP7*	5†	2 wks

Move Any Mountain is a re-mix of Pro-Gen. Group were male only duo for first four hits.

Jimmy SHAND *UK, male dance band* — 2 wks

| 23 Dec 55 | BLUEBELL POLKA *Parlophone F 3436* | 20 | 2 wks |

Paul SHANE and the YELLOWCOATS — 5 wks
UK, male vocalist with male/female vocal group

| 16 May 81 | HI DE HI (HOLIDAY ROCK) *EMI 5180* | 36 | 5 wks |

SHANGRI-LAS *US, female vocal group* — 48 wks

8 Oct 64	REMEMBER (WALKIN' IN THE SAND) *Red Bird RB 10008*	14	13 wks
14 Jan 65	LEADER OF THE PACK *Red Bird RB 10014*	11	9 wks
14 Oct 72 ●	LEADER OF THE PACK (re-issue) *Kama Sutra 2013 024*	3	14 wks
5 Jun 76 ●	LEADER OF THE PACK (2nd re-issue) *Charly CS 1009*	7	11 wks
12 Jun 76 ●	LEADER OF THE PACK (3rd re-issue) *Contempo CS 9032*	7	10 wks

From 19 Jun 76 until 14 Aug 76, the last week of the disc's chart run, the Charly and Contempo releases of Leader Of The Pack *were bracketed together on the chart.*

SHANICE *US, female vocalist* — 15 wks

23 Nov 91	I LOVE YOUR SMILE *Motown ZB 44907*	55	4 wks
22 Feb 92 ●	I LOVE YOUR SMILE (re-mix) *Motown TMG 1401*	2	10 wks
14 Nov 92	LOVIN' YOU *Motown TMG 1409*	54	1 wk

SHANNON *US, female vocalist* — 36 wks

19 Nov 83	LET THE MUSIC PLAY *Club LET 1*	51	3 wks
28 Jan 84	LET THE MUSIC PLAY (re-entry) *Club LET 1*	14	12 wks
7 Apr 84	GIVE ME TONIGHT *Club JAB 1*	24	7 wks
30 Jun 84	SWEET SOMEBODY *Club JAB 3*	25	8 wks
20 Jul 85	STRONGER TOGETHER *Club JAB 15*	46	6 wks

Del SHANNON *US, male vocalist* — 147 wks

| 27 Apr 61 ★ | RUNAWAY *London HLX 9317* | 1 | 22 wks |

14 Sep 61 ●	**HATS OFF TO LARRY** *London HLX 9402*	6	12 wks
7 Dec 61 ●	**SO LONG BABY** *London HLX 9462*	10	11 wks
15 Mar 62 ●	**HEY LITTLE GIRL** *London HLX 9515*	2	15 wks
6 Sep 62	**CRY MYSELF TO SLEEP** *London HLX 9587*	29	6 wks
11 Oct 62 ●	**SWISS MAID** *London HLX 9609*	2	17 wks
17 Jan 63 ●	**LITTLE TOWN FLIRT** *London HLX 9653*	4	13 wks
25 Apr 63 ●	**TWO KINDS OF TEARDROPS** *London HLX 9710*	5	13 wks
22 Aug 63	**TWO SILHOUETTES** *London HLX 9761*	23	8 wks
24 Oct 63	**SUE'S GOTTA BE MINE** *London HLU 9800*	21	8 wks
12 Mar 64	**MARY JANE** *Stateside SS 269*	35	5 wks
30 Jul 64	**HANDY MAN** *Stateside SS 317*	36	4 wks
14 Jan 65 ●	**KEEP SEARCHIN' (WE'LL FOLLOW THE SUN)** *Stateside SS 368*	3	11 wks
18 Mar 65	**STRANGER IN TOWN** *Stateside SS 395*	40	2 wks

Roxanne SHANTE US, *female rapper*　　10 wks

1 Aug 87	**HAVE A NICE DAY** *Breakout USA 612*	58	3 wks
4 Jun 88	**GO ON GIRL** *Breakout USA 633*	55	3 wks
29 Oct 88	**SHARP AS A KNIFE** *Club JAB 73* *	45	3 wks
14 Apr 90	**GO ON GIRL (re-mix)** *Breakout USA 689*	74	1 wk

* Brandon Cooke featuring Roxanne Shante

Helen SHAPIRO UK, *female vocalist*　　119 wks

23 Mar 61 ●	**DON'T TREAT ME LIKE A CHILD** *Columbia DB 4589*	3	20 wks
29 Jun 61 ★	**YOU DON'T KNOW** *Columbia DB 4670*	1	23 wks
28 Sep 61 ★	**WALKIN' BACK TO HAPPINESS** *Columbia DB 4715*	1	19 wks
15 Feb 62 ●	**TELL ME WHAT HE SAID** *Columbia DB 4782*	2	15 wks
3 May 62	**LET'S TALK ABOUT LOVE** *Columbia DB 4824*	23	7 wks
12 Jul 62 ●	**LITTLE MISS LONELY** *Columbia DB 4869*	8	11 wks
18 Oct 62	**KEEP AWAY FROM OTHER GIRLS** *Columbia DB 4908*	40	6 wks
7 Feb 63	**QUEEN FOR TONIGHT** *Columbia DB 4966*	33	5 wks
25 Apr 63	**WOE IS ME** *Columbia DB 7026*	35	6 wks
24 Oct 63	**LOOK WHO IT IS** *Columbia DB 7130*	47	3 wks
23 Jan 64	**FEVER** *Columbia DB 7190*	38	4 wks

Feargal SHARKEY UK, *male vocalist*　　58 wks

13 Oct 84	**LISTEN TO YOUR FATHER** *Zarjazz JAZZ 1*	23	7 wks
29 Jun 85	**LOVING YOU** *Virgin VS 770*	26	10 wks
12 Oct 85 ★	**A GOOD HEART** *Virgin VS 808*	1	16 wks
4 Jan 86 ●	**YOU LITTLE THIEF** *Virgin VS 840*	5	9 wks
5 Apr 86	**SOMEONE TO SOMEBODY** *Virgin VS 828*	64	3 wks
16 Jan 88	**MORE LOVE** *Virgin VS 922*	44	5 wks
16 Mar 91	**I'VE GOT NEWS FOR YOU** *Virgin VS 1294*	12	8 wks

SHARONETTES UK, *female vocal group*　　8 wks

26 Apr 75	**PAPA OOM MOW MOW** *Black Magic BM 102*	26	5 wks
12 Jul 75	**GOING TO A GO-GO** *Black Magic BM 104*	46	3 wks

Debbie SHARP – *See DREAM FREQUENCY*

Dee Dee SHARP US, *female vocalist*　　2 wks

25 Apr 63	**DO THE BIRD** *Cameo Parkway C 244*	46	2 wks

Barrie K. SHARPE – *See Diana BROWN and Barrie K. SHARPE*

SHARPE and NUMAN – *See Gary NUMAN*

Rocky SHARPE and the REPLAYS　　41 wks
UK, *male/female vocal group*

16 Dec 78	**RAMA LAMA DING DONG** *Chiswick CHIS 104*	17	10 wks
24 Mar 79	**IMAGINATION** *Chiswick CHIS 110*	39	6 wks

25 Aug 79	**LOVE WILL MAKE YOU FAIL IN SCHOOL** *Chiswick CHIS 114* *	60	4 wks
9 Feb 80	**MARTIAN HOP** *Chiswick CHIS 121* *	55	4 wks
17 Apr 82	**SHOUT SHOUT (KNOCK YOURSELF OUT)** *Chiswick DICE 3*	19	9 wks
7 Aug 82	**CLAP YOUR HANDS** *RAK 345*	54	3 wks
26 Feb 83	**IF YOU WANNA BE HAPPY** *Polydor POSP 560*	46	5 wks

* Rocky Sharpe and the Replays featuring the Top Liners

Mark SHAW UK, *male vocalist/instrumentalist*　　1 wk

17 Nov 90	**LOVE SO BRIGHT** *EMI EM 161*	54	1 wk

Sandie SHAW UK, *female vocalist*　　163 wks

8 Oct 64 ★	**(THERE'S) ALWAYS SOMETHING THERE TO REMIND ME** *Pye 7N 15704*	1	11 wks
10 Dec 64 ●	**GIRL DON'T COME** *Pye 7N 15743*	3	12 wks
18 Feb 65 ●	**I'LL STOP AT NOTHING** *Pye 7N 15783*	4	11 wks
13 May 65 ★	**LONG LIVE LOVE** *Pye 7N 15841*	1	14 wks
23 Sep 65 ●	**MESSAGE UNDERSTOOD** *Pye 7N 15940*	6	10 wks
18 Nov 65	**HOW CAN YOU TELL** *Pye 7N 15987*	21	9 wks
27 Jan 66	**TOMORROW** *Pye 7N 17036*	9	9 wks
19 May 66	**NOTHING COMES EASY** *Pye 7N 17086*	14	9 wks
8 Sep 66	**RUN** *Pye 7N 17163*	32	5 wks
24 Nov 66	**THINK SOMETIMES ABOUT ME** *Pye 7N 17212*	32	4 wks
19 Jan 67	**I DON'T NEED ANYTHING** *Pye 7N 17239*	50	1 wk
16 Mar 67 ★	**PUPPET ON A STRING** *Pye 7N 17272*	1	18 wks
12 Jul 67	**TONIGHT IN TOKYO** *Pye 7N 17346*	21	6 wks
4 Oct 67	**YOU'VE NOT CHANGED** *Pye 7N 17378*	18	12 wks
7 Feb 68	**TODAY** *Pye 7N 17441*	27	7 wks
12 Feb 69 ●	**MONSIEUR DUPONT** *Pye 7N 17675*	6	15 wks
14 May 69	**THINK IT ALL OVER** *Pye 7N 17726*	42	4 wks
21 Apr 84	**HAND IN GLOVE** *Rough Trade RT 130*	27	5 wks
14 Jun 86	**ARE YOU READY TO BE HEARTBROKEN** *Polydor POSP 793*	68	1 wk

Winifred SHAW US, *female vocalist*　　4 wks

14 Aug 76	**LULLABY OF BROADWAY** *United Artists UP 36131*	42	4 wks

SHE ROCKERS UK, *female vocal duo*　　2 wks

13 Jan 90	**JAM IT JAM** *Jive JIVE 233*	58	2 wks

George SHEARING UK, *male instrumentalist - piano*　　15 wks

19 Jul 62	**LET THERE BE LOVE** *Capitol CL 15257* *	11	14 wks
4 Oct 62	**BAUBLES BANGLES AND BEADS** *Capitol CL 15269*	49	1 wk

* Nat 'King' Cole with George Shearing

Gary SHEARSTON Australia, *male vocalist*　　8 wks

5 Oct 74 ●	**I GET A KICK OUT OF YOU** *Charisma CB 234*	7	8 wks

SHEER ELEGANCE UK, *male vocal group*　　23 wks

20 Dec 75	**MILKY WAY** *Pye International 7N 25697*	18	10 wks
3 Apr 76 ●	**LIFE IS TOO SHORT GIRL** *Pye International 7N 25703*	9	9 wks
24 Jul 76	**IT'S TEMPTATION** *Pye International 7N 25715*	41	4 wks

SHEILA and B. DEVOTION – *See Sheila B. DEVOTION*

Doug SHELDON UK, *male vocalist*　　15 wks

9 Nov 61	**RUNAROUND SUE** *Decca F 11398*	36	3 wks

4 Jan 62	**YOUR MA SAID YOU CRIED IN YOUR SLEEP**		
	LAST NIGHT *Decca F 11416*	29	6 wks
7 Feb 63	**I SAW LINDA YESTERDAY** *Decca F 11564*	36	6 wks

Pete SHELLEY *UK, male vocalist* — 1 wk

12 Mar 83	**TELEPHONE OPERATOR** *Genetic XX1*	66	1 wk

Peter SHELLEY *UK, male vocalist* — 20 wks

14 Sep 74	● **GEE BABY** *Magnet MAG 12*	4	10 wks
22 Mar 75	● **LOVE ME LOVE MY DOG** *Magnet MAG 22*	3	10 wks

Anne SHELTON *UK, female vocalist* — 31 wks

16 Dec 55	**ARRIVEDERCI DARLING** *HMV POP 146*	17	4 wks
13 Apr 56	**SEVEN DAYS** *Philips PB 567*	20	4 wks
24 Aug 56	★ **LAY DOWN YOUR ARMS** *Philips PB 616*	1	14 wks
20 Nov 59	**VILLAGE OF ST. BERNADETTE** *Philips PB 969*	27	1 wk
26 Jan 61	● **SAILOR** *Philips PB 1096*	10	8 wks

SHEPHERD SISTERS *US, female vocal group* — 6 wks

15 Nov 57	**ALONE** *HMV POP 411*	14	5 wks
3 Jan 58	**ALONE (re-entry)** *HMV POP 411*	22	1 wk

SHERBET *Australia, male vocal/instrumental group* — 10 wks

25 Sep 76	● **HOWZAT** *Epic EPC 4574*	4	10 wks

Tony SHERIDAN – *See BEATLES*

Allan SHERMAN *US, male vocalist* — 10 wks

12 Sep 63	**HELLO MUDDAH HELLO FADDAH**		
	Warner Bros. WB 106	14	10 wks

Bobby SHERMAN *US, male vocalist* — 4 wks

31 Oct 70	**JULIE DO YA LOVE ME** *CBS 5144*	28	4 wks

SHERRICK *US, male vocalist* — 10 wks

1 Aug 87	**JUST CALL** *Warner Bros. W 8380*	23	8 wks
21 Nov 87	**LET'S BE LOVERS TONIGHT** *Warner Bros. W 8146*	63	2 wks

Pluto SHERVINGTON *Jamaica, male vocalist* — 20 wks

7 Feb 76	● **DAT** *Opal PAL 5*	6	8 wks
10 Apr 76	**RAM GOAT LIVER** *Trojan TR 7978*	43	4 wks
6 Mar 82	**YOUR HONOUR** *KR KR 4 ***	19	8 wks

* Pluto

Holly SHERWOOD *US, female vocalist* — 7 wks

5 Feb 72	**DAY BY DAY** *Bell 1182*	29	7 wks

Tony SHEVETON *UK, male vocalist* — 1 wk

13 Feb 64	**MILLION DRUMS** *Oriole CB 1895*	49	1 wk

SHIRELLES *US, female vocal group* — 29 wks

9 Feb 61	● **WILL YOU LOVE ME TOMORROW**		
	Top Rank JAR 540	4	15 wks
31 May 62	**SOLDIER BOY** *HMV POP 1019*	23	9 wks
23 May 63	**FOOLISH LITTLE GIRL** *Stateside SS 181*	38	5 wks

SHIRLEY and COMPANY — 9 wks
US, female vocalist and male vocal/instrumental backing group

8 Feb 75	● **SHAME SHAME SHAME** *All Platinum 6146 301*	6	9 wks

SHO NUFF *US, male vocal/instrumental group* — 4 wks

24 May 80	**IT'S ALRIGHT** *Ensign ENY 37*	53	4 wks

Michelle SHOCKED *US, female vocalist* — 10 wks

8 Oct 88	**ANCHORAGE** *Cooking Vinyl LON 193*	60	4 wks
14 Jan 89	**IF LOVE WAS A TRAIN** *Cooking Vinyl LON 212*	63	3 wks
11 Mar 89	**WHEN I GROW UP** *Cooking Vinyl LON 219*	67	3 wks

SHOCKING BLUE — 14 wks
Holland, male/female vocal/instrumental group

17 Jan 70	● **VENUS** *Penny Farthing PEN 702*	8	11 wks
25 Apr 70	**MIGHTY JOE** *Penny Farthing PEN 713*	43	3 wks

Troy SHONDELL *US, male vocalist* — 11 wks

2 Nov 61	**THIS TIME** *London HLG 9432*	22	11 wks

SHONDELLS – *See Tommy JAMES and the SHONDELLS*

SHOOTING PARTY *UK, male vocal duo* — 2 wks

31 Mar 90	**LET'S HANG ON** *Lisson DOLE 15*	66	2 wks

SHOWADDYWADDY *UK, male vocal/instrumental group* — 209 wks

18 May 74	● **HEY ROCK AND ROLL** *Bell 1357*	2	14 wks
17 Aug 74	**ROCK 'N' ROLL LADY** *Bell 1374*	15	9 wks
30 Nov 74	**HEY MR. CHRISTMAS** *Bell 1387*	13	8 wks
22 Feb 75	**SWEET MUSIC** *Bell 1403*	14	9 wks
17 May 75	● **THREE STEPS TO HEAVEN** *Bell 1426*	2	11 wks
6 Sep 75	● **HEARTBEAT** *Bell 1450*	7	7 wks
15 Nov 75	**HEAVENLY** *Bell 1460*	34	6 wks
29 May 76	**TROCADERO** *Bell 1476*	32	3 wks
6 Nov 76	★ **UNDER THE MOON OF LOVE** *Bell 1495*	1	15 wks
5 Mar 77	● **WHEN** *Arista 91*	3	11 wks
23 Jul 77	● **YOU GOT WHAT IT TAKES** *Arista 126*	2	10 wks
5 Nov 77	● **DANCIN' PARTY** *Arista 149*	4	11 wks
25 Mar 78	● **I WONDER WHY** *Arista 174*	2	11 wks
24 Jun 78	● **A LITTLE BIT OF SOAP** *Arista 191*	5	12 wks
4 Nov 78	● **PRETTY LITTLE ANGEL EYES** *Arista ARIST 222*	5	12 wks
31 Mar 79	**REMEMBER THEN** *Arista 247*	17	8 wks
28 Jul 79	**SWEET LITTLE ROCK 'N' ROLLER** *Arista 278*	15	9 wks
10 Nov 79	**A NIGHT AT DADDY GEE'S** *Arista 314*	39	5 wks
27 Sep 80	**WHY DO LOVERS BREAK EACH OTHER'S**		
	HEARTS *Arista ARIST 359*	22	10 wks
29 Nov 80	**BLUE MOON** *Arista ARIST 379*	32	9 wks
13 Jun 81	**MULTIPLICATION** *Arista ARIST 416*	39	4 wks
28 Nov 81	**FOOTSTEPS** *Bell BELL 1499*	31	9 wks
28 Aug 82	**WHO PUT THE BOMP (IN THE**		
	BOMP-A-BOMP-A-BOMP) *RCA 236*	37	6 wks

SHOWDOWN US, male vocal/instrumental group — 3 wks

17 Dec 77	KEEP DOIN' IT State STAT 63	41	3 wks

SHOWSTOPPERS US, male vocal group — 25 wks

13 Mar 68	AIN'T NOTHING BUT A HOUSEPARTY Beacon 3-100	11	15 wks
13 Nov 68	EENY MEENY MGM 1436	33	7 wks
30 Jan 71	AIN'T NOTHING BUT A HOUSEPARTY (re-issue) Beacon BEA 100	43	1 wk
13 Feb 71	AIN'T NOTHING BUT A HOUSEPARTY (re-entry of re-issue) Beacon BEA 100	33	1 wk
27 Feb 71	AIN'T NOTHING BUT A HOUSEPARTY (2nd re-entry of re-issue) Beacon BEA 100	36	1 wk

SHRIEKBACK UK, male vocal/instrumental group — 4 wks

28 Jul 84	HAND ON MY HEART Arista SHRK 1	52	4 wks

SHUT UP AND DANCE — 10 wks
UK, male vocal/production group

21 Apr 90	£20 TO GET IN Shut Up And Dance SUAD 3	56	3 wks
28 Jul 90	LAMBORGHINI Shut Up And Dance SUAD 4	55	2 wks
8 Feb 92	AUTOBIOGRAPHY OF A CRACKHEAD/THE GREEN MAN Shut Up And Dance SUAD 21	43	2 wks
30 May 92 ●	RAVING I'M RAVING Shut Up And Dance SUAD 30S *	2	2 wks
15 Aug 92	THE ART OF MOVING BUTTS Shut Up And Dance SUAD 34S **	69	1 wk

* Shut Up And Dance featuring Peter Bouncer ** Shut Up And Dance featuring Erin

SHY UK, male vocal/instrumental group — 3 wks

19 Apr 80	GIRL (IT'S ALL I HAVE) Gallery GA 1	60	3 wks

Labi SIFFRE UK, male vocalist — 44 wks

27 Nov 71	IT MUST BE LOVE Pye International 7N 25572	14	12 wks
25 Mar 72	CRYING LAUGHING LOVING LYING Pye International 7N 25576	11	9 wks
29 Jul 72	WATCH ME Pye International 7N 25586	29	6 wks
4 Apr 87 ●	(SOMETHING INSIDE) SO STRONG China WOK 12	4	13 wks
21 Nov 87	NOTHIN'S GONNA CHANGE China WOK 16	52	4 wks

SIGUE SIGUE SPUTNIK — 20 wks
UK, male vocal/instrumental group

1 Mar 86 ●	LOVE MISSILE F1-11 Parlophone SSS 1	3	9 wks
7 Jun 86	TWENTY-FIRST CENTURY BOY Parlophone SSS 2	20	5 wks
19 Nov 88	SUCCESS Parlophone SSS 3	31	3 wks
1 Apr 89	DANCERAMA Parlophone SSS 5	50	2 wks
20 May 89	ALBINONI VS STAR WARS Parlophone SSS 4	75	1 wk

SILENCERS UK, male vocal/instrumental group — 6 wks

25 Jun 88	PAINTED MOON RCA HUSH 1	57	4 wks
27 May 89	SCOTTISH RAIN RCA PB 42701	71	2 wks

SILENT UNDERDOG — 1 wk
UK, male instrumentalist - Paul Hardcastle

16 Feb 85	PAPA'S GOT A BRAND NEW PIGBAG Kaz KAZ 50	73	1 wk

SILJE Norway, female vocalist — 6 wks

15 Dec 90	TELL ME WHERE YOU'RE GOING EMI EM 159	55	6 wks

SILKIE UK, male/female vocal/instrumental group — 6 wks

23 Sep 65	YOU'VE GOT TO HIDE YOUR LOVE AWAY Fontana TF 603	28	6 wks

SILSOE UK, male instrumentalist - keyboards — 4 wks

21 Jun 86	AZTEC GOLD CBS A 7231	48	4 wks

Aztec Gold was the ITV theme to the 1986 World Cup Finals and was performed by Rod Argent under the title Silsoe. See also Argent; San Jose featuring Rodriquez Argentina.

SILVER BULLET UK, male vocal/instrumental duo — 20 wks

2 Sep 89	BRING FORTH THE GUILLOTINE Tam Tam TTT 013	70	1 wk
9 Dec 89	20 SECONDS TO COMPLY Tam Tam 7TTT 019	11	10 wks
3 Mar 90	BRING FORTH THE GUILLOTINE (re-entry) Tam Tam TTT 013	45	5 wks
13 Apr 91	UNDERCOVER ANARCHIST Parlophone R 6284	33	4 wks

SILVER BULLET BAND – See Bob SEGER and the SILVER BULLET BAND

SILVER CONVENTION — 35 wks
Germany/US, female vocal group

5 Apr 75	SAVE ME Magnet MAG 26	30	7 wks
15 Nov 75	FLY ROBIN FLY Magnet MAG 43	28	8 wks
3 Apr 76 ●	GET UP AND BOOGIE Magnet MAG 55	7	11 wks
19 Jun 76	TIGER BABY/NO NO JOE Magnet MAG 69	41	4 wks
29 Jan 77	EVERYBODY'S TALKIN' 'BOUT LOVE Magnet MAG 81	25	5 wks

Dooley SILVERSPOON US, male vocalist — 3 wks

31 Jan 76	LET ME BE THE NUMBER ONE Seville SEV 1020	44	3 wks

Harry SIMEONE CHORALE US, choir — 14 wks

13 Feb 59	LITTLE DRUMMER BOY Top Rank JAR 101	13	7 wks
22 Dec 60	ONWARD CHRISTIAN SOLDIERS Ember EMBS 118	35	1 wk
5 Jan 61	ONWARD CHRISTIAN SOLDIERS (re-entry) Ember EMBS 118	38	1 wk
21 Dec 61	ONWARD CHRISTIAN SOLDIERS (2nd re-entry) Ember EMBS 118	36	3 wks
20 Dec 62	ONWARD CHRISTIAN SOLDIERS (re-issue) Ember EMBS 144	38	2 wks

Gene SIMMONS US, male vocalist — 4 wks

27 Jan 79	RADIOACTIVE Casablanca CAN 134	41	4 wks

Carly SIMON US, female vocalist — 76 wks

16 Dec 72 ●	YOU'RE SO VAIN Elektra K 12077	3	15 wks
31 Mar 73	THE RIGHT THING TO DO Elektra K 12095	17	9 wks
16 Mar 74	MOCKINGBIRD Elektra K 12134 *	34	5 wks
6 Aug 77 ●	NOBODY DOES IT BETTER Elektra K 12261	7	12 wks
21 Aug 82 ●	WHY WEA K 79300	10	13 wks
24 Jan 87 ●	COMING AROUND AGAIN Arista ARIST 687	10	12 wks
10 Jun 89	WHY (re-issue) WEA U 7501	56	5 wks
20 Apr 91	YOU'RE SO VAIN (re-issue) Elektra EKR 123	41	5 wks

* Carly Simon and James Taylor
See also Will Powers.

Mick Hucknall of
SIMPLY RED was
chosen Songwriter of
the Year in the 1992
Ivor Novello Awards.

Joe SIMON US, male vocalist — 10 wks

16 Jun 73	**STEP BY STEP** Mojo 2093 030	14	10 wks

Paul SIMON US, male vocalist — 83 wks

19 Feb 72 ●	**MOTHER AND CHILD REUNION** CBS 7793	5	12 wks
29 Apr 72	**ME AND JULIO DOWN BY THE SCHOOLYARD** CBS 7964	15	9 wks
16 Jun 73 ●	**TAKE ME TO THE MARDI GRAS** CBS 1578	7	11 wks
22 Sep 73	**LOVES ME LIKE A ROCK** CBS 1700	39	5 wks
10 Jan 76	**50 WAYS TO LEAVE YOUR LOVER** CBS 3887	23	6 wks
3 Dec 77	**SLIP SLIDIN' AWAY** CBS 5770	36	5 wks
6 Sep 80	**LATE IN THE EVENING** Warner Bros. K 17666	58	4 wks
13 Sep 86 ●	**YOU CAN CALL ME AL** Warner Bros. W 8667	4	13 wks
13 Dec 86	**THE BOY IN THE BUBBLE** Warner Bros. W 8509	26	8 wks
6 Oct 90	**THE OBVIOUS CHILD** Warner Bros W 9549	15	10 wks

See also Simon and Garfunkel.

Tito SIMON Jamaica, male vocalist — 4 wks

8 Feb 75	**THIS MONDAY MORNING FEELING** Horse HOSS 57	45	4 wks

SIMON and GARFUNKEL US, male vocal duo — 87 wks

24 Mar 66 ●	**HOMEWARD BOUND** CBS 202045	9	12 wks
16 Jun 66	**I AM A ROCK** CBS 202303	17	10 wks
10 Jul 68 ●	**MRS. ROBINSON** CBS 3443	4	12 wks
8 Jan 69 ●	**MRS. ROBINSON (EP)** CBS EP 6400	9	5 wks
30 Apr 69 ●	**THE BOXER** CBS 4162	6	14 wks
21 Feb 70 ★	**BRIDGE OVER TROUBLED WATER** CBS 4790	1	19 wks
15 Aug 70	**BRIDGE OVER TROUBLED WATER (re-entry)** CBS 4790	45	1 wk
7 Oct 72	**AMERICA** CBS 8336	25	7 wks
7 Dec 91	**A HAZY SHADE OF WINTER/SILENT NIGHT - SEVEN O'CLOCK NEWS** Columbia 6576537	30	6 wks
15 Feb 92	**THE BOXER (re-issue)** Columbia 6578067	75	1 wk

Titles on Mrs. Robinson (EP): Mrs. Robinson/Scarborough Fair - Canticle/Sounds of Silence/April Come She Will. This EP would have stayed more than 5 weeks on chart had a decision to exclude EPs from chart in Feb 69 not been taken. See also Paul Simon; Art Garfunkel.

SIMONE US, female vocalist — 1 wk

23 Nov 91	**MY FAMILY DEPENDS ON ME** Strictly Rhythm A 8678	75	1 wk

Nina SIMONE US, female vocalist — 43 wks

5 Aug 65	**I PUT A SPELL ON YOU** Philips BF 1415	49	1 wk
16 Oct 68 ●	**AIN'T GOT NO - I GOT LIFE/DO WHAT YOU GOTTA DO** RCA 1743	2	18 wks
15 Jan 69 ●	**TO LOVE SOMEBODY** RCA 1779	5	9 wks
15 Jan 69	**I PUT A SPELL ON YOU (re-issue)** Philips BF 1736	28	4 wks
31 Oct 87 ●	**MY BABY JUST CARES FOR ME** Charly CYZ 7112	5	11 wks

Do What You Gotta Do was only listed for the first 8 weeks of the record's chart run.

SIMPLE MINDS UK, male vocal/instrumental group — 174 wks

12 May 79	**LIFE IN A DAY** Zoom ZUM 10	62	2 wks
23 May 81	**THE AMERICAN** Virgin VS 410	59	3 wks
15 Aug 81	**LOVE SONG** Virgin VS 434	47	4 wks
7 Nov 81	**SWEAT IN BULLET** Virgin VS 451	52	3 wks
10 Apr 82	**PROMISED YOU A MIRACLE** Virgin VS 488	13	11 wks
28 Aug 82	**GLITTERING PRIZE** Virgin VS 511	16	11 wks
13 Nov 82	**SOMEONE SOMEWHERE (IN SUMMERTIME)** Virgin VS 538	36	5 wks
26 Nov 83	**WATERFRONT** Virgin VS 636	13	10 wks

British Hit Singles Part One: Alphabetically by Artist
Date of chart entry/Title & catalogue no./Peak position reached/Weeks on chart

★ Number one   ● Top Ten   † still on chart at 31 Dec 1992

* = credited to act billed in footnote

28 Jan 84	**SPEED YOUR LOVE TO ME** Virgin VS 649	20	4 wks
24 Mar 84	**UP ON THE CATWALK** Virgin VS 661	27	5 wks
20 Apr 85 ●	**DON'T YOU (FORGET ABOUT ME)** Virgin VS 749	7	11 wks
17 Aug 85	**DON'T YOU (FORGET ABOUT ME) (re-entry)** Virgin VS 749	61	8 wks
12 Oct 85 ●	**ALIVE AND KICKING** Virgin VS 817	7	9 wks
28 Dec 85	**DON'T YOU (FORGET ABOUT ME) (2nd re-entry)** Virgin VS 749	74	1 wk
4 Jan 86	**ALIVE AND KICKING (re-entry)** Virgin VS 817	60	2 wks
1 Feb 86 ●	**SANCTIFY YOURSELF** Virgin SM 1	10	7 wks
15 Feb 86	**DON'T YOU (FORGET ABOUT ME) (3rd re-entry)** Virgin VS 779	62	3 wks
15 Mar 86	**DON'T YOU (FORGET ABOUT ME) (4th re-entry)** Virgin VS 779	68	1 wk
12 Apr 86 ●	**ALL THE THINGS SHE SAID** Virgin VS 860	9	8 wks
14 Jun 86	**ALL THE THINGS SHE SAID (re-entry)** Virgin VS 860	73	1 wk
15 Nov 86	**GHOSTDANCING** Virgin VS 907	13	6 wks
3 Jan 87	**GHOSTDANCING (re-entry)** Virgin VS 907	68	2 wks
20 Jun 87	**PROMISED YOU A MIRACLE** Virgin SM 2	19	7 wks
18 Feb 89 ★	**BELFAST CHILD** Virgin SMX 3	1	11 wks
22 Apr 89	**THIS IS YOUR LAND** Virgin SMX4	13	4 wks
29 Jul 89	**KICK IT IN** Virgin SM 5	15	5 wks
9 Dec 89	**THE AMSTERDAM EP** Virgin SMX 6	18	6 wks
23 Mar 91 ●	**LET THERE BE LOVE** Virgin VS 1332	6	7 wks
25 May 91	**SEE THE LIGHTS** Virgin VS 1343	20	4 wks
31 Aug 91	**STAND BY LOVE** Virgin VS 1358	13	4 wks
28 Oct 91	**REAL LIFE** Virgin VS 1382	34	3 wks
10 Oct 92 ●	**LOVE SONG/ALIVE AND KICKING (re-issues)** Virgin VS 1440	6	6 wks

The 1987 version of Promised You A Miracle was a live recording. Tracks on The Amsterdam EP: Let It All Come Down/Jerusalem/Sign Of The Times.

SIMPLICIOUS US, male vocal group — 9 wks

29 Sep 84	**LET HER FEEL IT** Fourth & Broadway BRW 13	65	3 wks
2 Feb 85	**LET HER FEEL IT (re-issue)** Fourth & Broadway BRW 18	34	6 wks

The re-issue of Let Her Feel It was listed with Personality by Eugene Wilde.

SIMPLY RED UK, male vocal/instrumental group — 135 wks

15 Jun 85	**MONEY'S TOO TIGHT (TO MENTION)** Elektra EKR 9	13	12 wks
21 Sep 85	**COME TO MY AID** Elektra EKR 19	66	2 wks
16 Nov 85	**HOLDING BACK THE YEARS** Elektra EKR 29	51	4 wks
8 Mar 86	**JERICHO** WEA YZ 63	53	3 wks
17 May 86 ●	**HOLDING BACK THE YEARS (re-issue)** WEA YZ 70	2	13 wks
9 Aug 86	**OPEN UP THE RED BOX** WEA YZ 75	61	4 wks
14 Feb 87	**THE RIGHT THING** WEA YZ 103	11	10 wks
23 May 87	**INFIDELITY** Elektra YZ 114	31	5 wks
28 Nov 87	**EV'RY TIME WE SAY GOODBYE** Elektra YZ 161	11	9 wks
13 Mar 88	**I WON'T FEEL BAD** Elektra YZ 172	68	3 wks
28 Jan 89	**IT'S ONLY LOVE** Elektra YZ 349	13	8 wks
8 Apr 89 ●	**IF YOU DON'T KNOW ME BY NOW** Elektra YZ 377	2	10 wks
8 Jul 89	**A NEW FLAME** WEA YZ 404	17	8 wks
28 Oct 89	**YOU'VE GOT IT** Elektra YZ 424	46	3 wks
21 Sep 91	**SOMETHING GOT ME STARTED** East West YZ 614	11	8 wks
30 Nov 91 ●	**STARS** East West YZ 626	8	10 wks
8 Feb 92 ●	**FOR YOUR BABIES** East West YZ 642	9	8 wks
2 May 92	**THRILL ME** East West YZ 671	33	5 wks
25 Jul 92	**YOUR MIRROR** East West YZ 689	17	4 wks
21 Nov 92	**MONTREUX EP** East West YZ 716	11†	6 wks

Tracks on Montreux EP: Drowning In My Own Tears/Granma's Hands/lady Godiva's Room/Love For Sale.

Paul SIMPSON – *See ADEVA*

SIMPSONS *US, male/female cartoon group*   **19 wks**

26 Jan 91 ★	**DO THE BARTMAN** *Geffen GEF 87* **1**	12 wks
6 Apr 91 ●	**DEEP DEEP TROUBLE** *Geffen GEF 88* * **7**	7 wks

* Simpsons featuring Bart and Homer

W/Cdr. A.E. SIMS – *See Central Band of the ROYAL AIR FORCE, conductor W/Cdr. A.E. SIMS, O.B.E*

Joyce SIMS *US, female vocalist*   **35 wks**

19 Apr 86	**ALL AND ALL** *London LON 94* **16**	10 wks
13 Jun 87	**LIFETIME LOVE** *London LON 137* **34**	6 wks
9 Jan 88 ●●	**COME INTO MY LIFE** *London LON 161* **7**	9 wks
23 Apr 88	**WALK AWAY** *London LON 176* **24**	6 wks
17 Jun 89	**LOOKING FOR A LOVE** *FFRR F 109* **39**	4 wks

Kym SIMS *US, female vocalist*   **22 wks**

7 Dec 91 ●	**TOO BLIND TO SEE IT** *Atco B 8667* **5**	12 wks
28 Mar 92	**TAKE MY ADVICE** *Atco B 8591* **13**	7 wks
27 Jun 92	**A LITTLE BIT MORE** *Atco B 8528* **30**	3 wks

Frank SINATRA *US, male vocalist*   **428 wks**

9 Jul 54	**YOUNG AT HEART** *Capitol CL 14064* **12**	1 wk
16 Jul 54 ★	**THREE COINS IN THE FOUNTAIN** *Capitol CL 14120* **1**	19 wks
10 Jun 55	**YOU MY LOVE** *Capitol CL 14240* **13**	3 wks
22 Jul 55	**YOU MY LOVE (re-entry)** *Capitol CL 14240* **17**	2 wks
5 Aug 55 ●	**LEARNIN' THE BLUES** *Capitol CL 14296* **2**	13 wks
12 Aug 55	**YOU MY LOVE (2nd re-entry)** *Capitol CL 14240* **17**	1 wk
2 Sep 55	**NOT AS A STRANGER** *Capitol CL 14326* **18**	1 wk
13 Jan 56 ●	**LOVE AND MARRIAGE** *Capitol CL 14503* **3**	8 wks
20 Jan 56 ●	**THE TENDER TRAP** *Capitol CL 14511* **2**	9 wks
15 Jun 56	**SONGS FOR SWINGING LOVERS** (LP) *Capitol LCT 6106* **12**	8 wks
22 Nov 57	**ALL THE WAY** *Capitol CL 14800* **29**	1 wk
29 Nov 57	**CHICAGO** *Capitol CL 14800* **25**	1 wk
6 Dec 57	**ALL THE WAY (re-entry)/CHICAGO** *Capitol CL 14800* **21**	1 wk
13 Dec 57 ●	**ALL THE WAY (2nd re-entry)** *Capitol CL 14800* **3**	17 wks
7 Feb 58	**WITCHCRAFT** *Capitol CL 14819* **12**	8 wks
14 Nov 58	**MR. SUCCESS** *Capitol CL 14956* **29**	1 wk
12 Dec 58	**MR. SUCCESS (re-entry)** *Capitol CL 14956* **25**	2 wks
2 Jan 59	**MR. SUCCESS (2nd re-entry)** *Capitol CL 14956* **26**	1 wk
10 Apr 59	**FRENCH FOREIGN LEGION** *Capitol CL 14997* **18**	5 wks
15 May 59	**COME DANCE WITH ME** (LP) *Capitol LCT 6179* **30**	1 wk
28 Aug 59	**HIGH HOPES** *Capitol CL 15052* **28**	1 wk
11 Sep 59 ●	**HIGH HOPES (re-entry)** *Capitol CL 15052* **6**	13 wks
10 Mar 60	**HIGH HOPES (2nd re-entry)** *Capitol CL 15052* **42**	1 wk
7 Apr 60	**IT'S NICE TO GO TRAV'LING** *Capitol CL 15116* **48**	2 wks
16 Jun 60	**RIVER STAY 'WAY FROM MY DOOR** *Capitol CL 15135* **18**	9 wks
8 Sep 60	**NICE 'N EASY** *Capitol CL 15150* **15**	12 wks
24 Nov 60	**OL' MACDONALD** *Capitol CL 15168* **11**	8 wks
20 Apr 61	**MY BLUE HEAVEN** *Capitol CL 15193* **33**	7 wks
28 Sep 61	**GRANADA** *Reprise R 20010* **15**	8 wks
23 Nov 61	**THE COFFEE SONG** *Reprise R 20035* **39**	3 wks
5 Apr 62	**EVERYBODY'S TWISTING** *Reprise R 20063* **22**	12 wks
13 Dec 62	**ME AND MY SHADOW** *Reprise R 20128* * **20**	7 wks
7 Feb 63	**ME AND MY SHADOW (re-entry)** *Reprise R 20128* * **47**	2 wks
7 Mar 63	**MY KIND OF GIRL** *Reprise R 20148* ** **35**	6 wks
24 Sep 64	**HELLO DOLLY** *Reprise R 20351* ** **47**	1 wk
12 May 66 ★	**STRANGERS IN THE NIGHT** *Reprise R 23052* **1**	20 wks
29 Sep 66	**SUMMER WIND** *Reprise RS 20509* **36**	5 wks
15 Dec 66	**THAT'S LIFE** *Reprise RS 20531* **46**	5 wks
23 Mar 67 ★	**SOMETHIN' STUPID** *Reprise RS 23166* *** **1**	18 wks
23 Aug 67	**THE WORLD WE KNEW** *Reprise RS 20610* **33**	11 wks
2 Apr 69 ●	**MY WAY** *Reprise RS 20817* **5**	42 wks
4 Oct 69 ●	**LOVE'S BEEN GOOD TO ME** *Reprise RS 20852* **8**	18 wks
31 Jan 70	**MY WAY (re-entry)** *Reprise RS 20817* **49**	1 wk
28 Feb 70	**MY WAY (2nd re-entry)** *Reprise RS 20817* **30**	5 wks
11 Apr 70	**MY WAY (3rd re-entry)** *Reprise RS 20817* **33**	9 wks
27 Jun 70	**MY WAY (4th re-entry)** *Reprise RS 20817* **28**	21 wks
28 Nov 70	**MY WAY (5th re-entry)** *Reprise RS 20817* **18**	16 wks
6 Mar 71	**I WILL DRINK THE WINE** *Reprise RS 23487* **16**	12 wks
27 Mar 71	**MY WAY (6th re-entry)** *Reprise RS 20817* **22**	19 wks
4 Sep 71	**MY WAY (7th re-entry)** *Reprise RS 20817* **39**	8 wks
1 Jan 72	**MY WAY (8th re-entry)** *Reprise RS 20817* **50**	1 wk
20 Dec 75	**I BELIEVE I'M GONNA LOVE YOU** *Reprise K 14400* **34**	7 wks
9 Aug 80	**THEME FROM NEW YORK, NEW YORK** *Reprise K 14502* **59**	4 wks
22 Feb 86 ●	**THEME FROM NEW YORK, NEW YORK (re-entry)** *Reprise K 14502* **4**	10 wks

* Frank Sinatra and Sammy Davis Jr ** Frank Sinatra with Count Basie
*** Nancy Sinatra and Frank Sinatra

Tracks on Songs For Swinging Lovers *LP:* You Make Me Feel So Young/It Happened In Monterey/You're Getting To Be A Habit With Me/You Brought A New Kind Of Love To Me/Too Marvellous For Words/Old Devil Moon/Pennies From Heaven/Love Is Here To Stay/I've Got You Under My Skin/I Thought About You/We'll Be Together Again/Making Whoopee/Swingin' Down The Lane/Anything Goes/How About You. *On* Come Dance With Me *LP:* Something's Gotta Give/Just In Time/Dancing In The Dark/Too Close For Comfort/I Could Have Danced All Night/Saturday Night Is The Loneliest Night Of The Week/Day In Day Out/Cheek To Cheek/Baubles Bangles And Beads/The Song Is You/The Last Dance. All The Way *and* Chicago, Capitol CL 14800, *were at first billed separately, then together for one week, then* All The Way *on its own.*

Nancy SINATRA *US, female vocalist*   **99 wks**

27 Jan 66 ★	**THESE BOOTS ARE MADE FOR WALKING** *Reprise R 20432* **1**	14 wks
28 Apr 66	**HOW DOES THAT GRAB YOU DARLIN'** *Reprise R 20461* **19**	8 wks
19 Jan 67 ●	**SUGAR TOWN** *Reprise RS 20527* **8**	10 wks
23 Mar 67 ★	**SOMETHIN' STUPID** *Reprise RS 23166* * **1**	18 wks
5 Jul 67	**YOU ONLY LIVE TWICE/JACKSON** *Reprise RS 20595* ** **11**	19 wks
8 Nov 67	**LADYBIRD** *Reprise RS 20629* *** **47**	1 wk
29 Nov 69	**HIGHWAY SONG** *Reprise RS 20869* **21**	10 wks
21 Aug 71 ●	**DID YOU EVER** *Reprise K 14093* **** **2**	19 wks

* Nancy Sinatra and Frank Sinatra ** Nancy Sinatra/Nancy Sinatra and Lee Hazlewood *** Nancy Sinatra and Lee Hazlewood **** Nancy and Lee
Jackson *listed with* You Only Live Twice *from 12 Jul 67.*

SINE *US, disco aggregation*   **9 wks**

10 Jun 78	**JUST LET ME DO MY THING** *CBS 6351* **33**	9 wks

SINFONIA OF LONDON – *See Peter AUTY and the SINFONIA OF LONDON*

SINGING CORNER – *See DONOVAN*

SINGING DOGS *Denmark, canine vocal group*   **4 wks**

25 Nov 55	**THE SINGING DOGS** (MEDLEY) *Nixa N 15009* **13**	4 wks

Medley *songs:* Pat-a-cake/Three Blind Mice/Jingle Bells/Oh Susanna.

SINGING NUN (Soeur Sourire)   **14 wks**
Belgium, female vocalist

5 Dec 63 ●	**DOMINIQUE** *Philips BF 1293* **7**	14 wks

SINGING SHEEP *UK, computerized sheep noises*   **5 wks**

18 Dec 82	**BAA BAA BLACK SHEEP** *Sheep BAA 1* **42**	5 wks

Maxine SINGLETON *US, female vocalist*   **3 wks**

2 Apr 83	**YOU CAN'T RUN FROM LOVE** *Creole CR 50* **57**	3 wks

SINITTA US, female vocalist | 102 wks

8 Mar 86	SO MACHO/CRUISING Fanfare FAN 7	47	11 wks
28 Jun 86 ●	SO MACHO/CRUISING (re-entry) Fanfare FAN 7	2	17 wks
11 Oct 86	FEELS LIKE THE FIRST TIME Fanfare FAN 8	45	5 wks
25 Jul 87 ●	TOY BOY Fanfare FAN 12	4	14 wks
12 Dec 87	G.T.O Fanfare FAN 14	15	9 wks
19 Mar 88 ●	CROSS MY BROKEN HEART Fanfare FAN 15	6	9 wks
24 Sep 88	I DON'T BELIEVE IN MIRACLES Fanfare FAN 16	22	8 wks
3 Jun 89 ●	RIGHT BACK WHERE WE STARTED FROM Fanfare FAN 18	4	10 wks
7 Oct 89	LOVE ON A MOUNTAIN TOP Fanfare FAN 21	20	6 wks
21 Apr 90	HITCHIN' A RIDE Fanfare FAN 24	24	6 wks
22 Sep 90	LOVE AND AFFECTION Fanfare FAN 31	62	3 wks
4 Jul 92	SHAME SHAME SHAME Arista 74321100327	28	4 wks

SIOUXSIE and the BANSHEES | 144 wks
UK, female/male vocal/instrumental group

26 Aug 78 ●	HONG KONG GARDEN Polydor 2059 052	7	10 wks
31 Mar 79	THE STAIRCASE (MYSTERY) Polydor POSP 9	24	8 wks
7 Jul 79	PLAYGROUND TWIST Polydor POSP 59	28	6 wks
29 Sep 79	MITTAGEISEN (METAL POSTCARD) Polydor 2059 151	47	3 wks
15 Mar 80	HAPPY HOUSE Polydor POSP 117	17	8 wks
7 Jun 80	CHRISTINE Polydor 2059 249	24	8 wks
6 Dec 80	ISRAEL Polydor POSP 205	41	8 wks
30 May 81	SPELLBOUND Polydor POSP 273	22	8 wks
1 Aug 81	ARABIAN KNIGHTS Polydor POSP 309	32	7 wks
29 May 82	FIRE WORKS Polydor POSPG 450	22	6 wks
9 Oct 82	SLOWDIVE Polydor POSP 510	41	4 wks
4 Dec 82	MELT/IL EST NE LE DIVIN ENFANT Polydor POSP 539	49	5 wks
1 Oct 83 ●	DEAR PRUDENCE Wonderland SHE 4	3	8 wks
24 Mar 84	SWIMMING HORSES Wonderland SHE 6	28	4 wks
2 Jun 84	DAZZLE Wonderland SHE 7	33	3 wks
27 Oct 84	THE THORN EP Wonderland SHEEP 8	47	3 wks
26 Oct 85	CITIES IN DUST Wonderland SHE 9	21	6 wks
8 Mar 86	CANDYMAN Wonderland SHE 10	34	5 wks
17 Jan 87	THIS WHEEL'S ON FIRE Wonderland SHE 11	14	6 wks
28 Mar 87	THE PASSENGER Wonderland SHE 12	41	6 wks
25 Jul 87	SONG FROM THE EDGE OF THE WORLD Wonderland SHE 13	59	3 wks
30 Jul 88	PEEK-A-BOO Wonderland SHE 14	16	6 wks
8 Oct 88	THE KILLING JAR Wonderland SHE 15	41	3 wks
3 Dec 88	THE LAST BEAT OF MY HEART Wonderland SHE 16	44	1 wk
25 May 91	KISS THEM FOR ME Wonderland SHE 19	32	4 wks
13 Jul 91	SHADOWTIME Wonderland SHE 20	57	1 wk
25 Jul 92	FACE TO FACE Wonderland SHE 21	21	4 wks

Tracks on The Thorn EP: Overground/Voices/Placebo Effect/Red Over White.

SIR DOUGLAS QUINTET US, male vocal/ instrumental group | 10 wks

17 Jun 65	SHE'S ABOUT A MOVER London HLU 9964	15	10 wks

SIR MIX-A-LOT US, male rapper | 2 wks

8 Aug 92	BABY GOT BACK Def American DEFA 20	56	2 wks

SIRRON – See PLUS ONE featuring SIRRON

SISTER SLEDGE US, female vocal group | 94 wks

21 Jun 75	MAMA NEVER TOLD ME Atlantic K 10619	20	6 wks
17 Mar 79 ●	HE'S THE GREATEST DANCER Atlantic/Cotillion K 11257	6	11 wks
26 May 79 ●	WE ARE FAMILY Atlantic/Cotillion K 11293	8	10 wks
11 Aug 79	LOST IN MUSIC Atlantic/Cotillion K 11337	17	10 wks
19 Jan 80	GOT TO LOVE SOMEBODY Atlantic/Cotillion K 11404	34	4 wks
28 Feb 81	ALL AMERICAN GIRLS Atlantic K 11656	41	5 wks

26 May 84	THINKING OF YOU Cotillion/Atlantic B 9744	11	13 wks
8 Sep 84 ●	LOST IN MUSIC (re-mix) Cotillion/Atlantic B 9718	4	12 wks
17 Nov 84	WE ARE FAMILY (re-mix) Cotillion/Atlantic B 9692	33	4 wks
1 Jun 85 ★	FRANKIE Atlantic A 9547	1	16 wks
31 Aug 85	DANCING ON THE JAGGED EDGE Atlantic A 9520	50	3 wks

SISTERS OF MERCY | 37 wks
UK, male/female vocal/instrumental duo

16 Jun 84	BODY AND SOUL/TRAIN Merciful Release MR 029	46	3 wks
20 Oct 84	WALK AWAY Merciful Release MR 033	45	3 wks
9 Mar 85	NO TIME TO CRY Merciful Release MR 035	63	2 wks
3 Oct 87 ●	THIS CORROSION Merciful Release MR 39	7	6 wks
27 Feb 88	DOMINION Merciful Release MR 43	13	6 wks
18 Jun 88	LUCRETIA MY REFLECTION Merciful Release MR 45	20	4 wks
13 Oct 90	MORE Merciful Release MR 47	14	4 wks
22 Dec 90	DOCTOR JEEP Merciful Release MR 51	37	4 wks
2 May 92 ●	TEMPLE OF LOVE Merciful Release MR 53	3	5 wks

SIVUCA Brazil, male vocalist | 3 wks

28 Jul 84	AIN'T NO SUNSHINE London LON 51	56	3 wks

SKATALITES Jamaica, male instrumental group | 6 wks

20 Apr 67	GUNS OF NAVARONE Island WI 168	36	6 wks

Peter SKELLERN UK, male vocalist | 24 wks

23 Sep 72 ●	YOU'RE A LADY Decca F 13333	3	11 wks
29 Mar 75	HOLD ON TO LOVE Decca F 13568	14	9 wks
28 Oct 78	LOVE IS THE SWEETEST THING Mercury 6008 603 *	60	4 wks

* Peter Skellern featuring Grimethorpe Colliery Band

SKID ROW US, male/female vocal/instrumental group | 25 wks

18 Nov 89	YOUTH GONE WILD Atlantic A 8935	42	3 wks
3 Feb 90	18 AND LIFE Atlantic A 8883	12	6 wks
31 May 90	I REMEMBER YOU East West A 8836	36	4 wks
15 Jun 91	MONKEY BUSINESS Atlantic A 7673	19	3 wks
14 Sep 91	SLAVE TO THE GRIND Atlantic A 7603	43	2 wks
23 Nov 91	WASTED TIME Atlantic A 7570	20	3 wks
29 Aug 92	YOUTH GONE WILD (re-issue)/DELIVERING THE GOODS Atlantic A 7444	22	4 wks

SKIDS UK, male vocal/instrumental group | 60 wks

23 Sep 78	SWEET SUBURBIA Virgin VS 227	70	1 wk
7 Oct 78	SWEET SUBURBIA (re-entry) Virgin VS 227	71	2 wks
4 Nov 78	THE SAINTS ARE COMING Virgin VS 232	48	3 wks
17 Feb 79 ●	INTO THE VALLEY Virgin VS 241	10	11 wks
26 May 79	MASQUERADE Virgin VS 262	14	9 wks
29 Sep 79	CHARADE Virgin VS 288	31	6 wks
24 Nov 79	WORKING FOR THE YANKEE DOLLAR Virgin VS 306	20	11 wks
1 Mar 80	ANIMATION Virgin VS 323	56	3 wks
16 Aug 80	CIRCUS GAMES Virgin VS 359	32	7 wks
18 Oct 80	GOODBYE CIVILIAN Virgin VS 373	52	4 wks
6 Dec 80	WOMEN IN WINTER Virgin VSK 101	49	3 wks

SKIN UP UK, male producer | 9 wks

7 Sep 91	IVORY Love EVOL 4	48	3 wks
14 Mar 92	A JUICY RED APPLE Love EVOL 11	32	4 wks
18 Jul 92	ACCELERATE Love EVOL 17	45	2 wks

SKIPWORTH and TURNER US, male vocal duo — 12 wks

27 Apr 85	**THINKING ABOUT YOUR LOVE** *Fourth & Broadway BRW 23*......**24**	10 wks
21 Jan 89	**MAKE IT LAST** *Fourth & Broadway BRW 118* **60**	2 wks

SKY UK/Australia, male instrumental group — 11 wks

5 Apr 80 ●	**TOCCATA** *Ariola ARO 300* **5**	11 wks

SKYHOOKS Australia, male vocal/instrumental group — 1 wk

9 Jun 79	**WOMEN IN UNIFORM** *United Artists UP 36508*........**73**	1 wk

SLADE UK, male vocal/instrumental group — 276 wks

19 Jun 71	**GET DOWN AND GET WITH IT** *Polydor 2058 112* **16**	14 wks
30 Oct 71 ★	**COZ I LUV YOU** *Polydor 2058 155* **1**	15 wks
5 Feb 72 ●	**LOOK WOT YOU DUN** *Polydor 2058 195* **4**	10 wks
3 Jun 72 ★	**TAKE ME BAK 'OME** *Polydor 2058 231* **1**	13 wks
2 Sep 72 ★	**MAMA WEER ALL CRAZEE NOW** *Polydor 2058 274*..........**1**	10 wks
25 Nov 72 ●	**GUDBUY T'JANE** *Polydor 2058 312* **2**	13 wks
3 Mar 73 ★	**CUM ON FEEL THE NOIZE** *Polydor 2058 339* **1**	12 wks
30 Jun 73 ★	**SKWEEZE ME PLEEZE ME** *Polydor 2058 377* **1**	10 wks
6 Oct 73 ●	**MY FREND STAN** *Polydor 2058 407* **2**	8 wks
15 Dec 73 ★	**MERRY XMAS EVERYBODY** *Polydor 2058 422* **1**	9 wks
6 Apr 74 ●	**EVERYDAY** *Polydor 2058 453* **3**	7 wks
6 Jul 74 ●	**BANGIN' MAN** *Polydor 2058 492* **3**	7 wks
19 Oct 74 ●	**FAR FAR AWAY** *Polydor 2058 522* **2**	6 wks
15 Feb 75	**HOW DOES IT FEEL** *Polydor 2058 547* **15**	7 wks
17 May 75 ●	**THANKS FOR THE MEMORY (WHAM BAM THANK YOU MAM)** *Polydor 2058 585* **7**	7 wks
22 Nov 75	**IN FOR A PENNY** *Polydor 2058 663* **11**	8 wks
7 Feb 76	**LET'S CALL IT QUITS** *Polydor 2058 690* **11**	7 wks
5 Feb 77	**GYPSY ROAD HOG** *Barn 2014 105* **48**	2 wks
29 Oct 77	**MY BABY LEFT ME - THAT'S ALL RIGHT (MEDLEY)** *Barn 2014 114* **32**	4 wks
18 Oct 80	**SLADE ALIVE AT READING '80 EP** *Cheapskate CHEAP 5* **44**	5 wks
27 Dec 80	**MERRY XMAS EVERYBODY** *Cheapskate CHEAP 11* * **70**	2 wks
31 Jan 81 ●	**WE'LL BRING THE HOUSE DOWN** *Cheapskate CHEAP 16* **10**	9 wks
4 Apr 81	**WHEELS AIN'T COMING DOWN** *Cheapskate CHEAP 21* **60**	3 wks
19 Sep 81	**LOCK UP YOUR DAUGHTERS** *RCA 124*..........**29**	8 wks
19 Dec 81	**MERRY XMAS EVERYBODY (re-entry)** *Polydor 2058 422* **32**	4 wks
27 Mar 82	**RUBY RED** *RCA 191*..........**51**	3 wks
27 Nov 82	**(AND NOW - THE WALTZ) C'EST LA VIE** *RCA 291* **50**	6 wks
25 Dec 82	**MERRY XMAS EVERYBODY (2nd re-entry)** *Polydor 2058 422* **67**	3 wks
19 Nov 83 ●	**MY OH MY** *RCA 373* **2**	11 wks
10 Dec 83	**MERRY XMAS EVERYBODY (3rd re-entry)** *Polydor 2058 422* **20**	5 wks
4 Feb 84 ●	**RUN RUN AWAY** *RCA 385*..........**7**	10 wks
17 Nov 84	**ALL JOIN HANDS** *RCA 455*..........**15**	9 wks
15 Dec 84	**MERRY XMAS EVERYBODY (4th re-entry)** *Polydor 2058 422* **47**	4 wks
26 Jan 85	**7 YEAR BITCH** *RCA 475*..........**60**	1 wk
23 Mar 85	**MYZSTERIOUS MIZTER JONES** *RCA PB 40027*..........**50**	5 wks
30 Nov 85	**DO YOU BELIEVE IN MIRACLES** *RCA PB 40449* **54**	6 wks
21 Dec 85	**MERRY XMAS EVERYBODY (re-issue)** *Polydor POSP 780* **48**	3 wks
27 Dec 86	**MERRY XMAS EVERYBODY (re-entry of re-issue)** *Polydor POSP 780* **71**	1 wk
21 Feb 87	**STILL THE SAME** *RCA PB 41137*..........**73**	2 wks
19 Oct 91	**RADIO WALL OF SOUND** *Polydor PO 180*..........**21**	5 wks

* Slade and the Reading Choir

Tracks on Slade Live At Reading EP: When I'm Dancin' I Ain't Fightin'/Born To Be Wild/Somethin' Else/Pistol Packin' Mama/Keep A Rollin'.

SLAUGHTER US, male vocal/instrumental group — 2 wks

29 Sep 90	**UP ALL NIGHT** *Chrysalis CHS 3556* **62**	1 wk
2 Feb 91	**FLY TO THE ANGELS** *Chrysalis CHS 3634*..........**55**	1 wk

SLAVE US, male vocal/instrumental group — 3 wks

8 Mar 80	**JUST A TOUCH OF LOVE** *Atlantic/Cotillion K 11442*..........**64**	3 wks

SLAYER US, male vocal/instrumental group — 2 wks

13 Jun 87	**CRIMINALLY INSANE** *Def Jam LON 133* **64**	1 wk
26 Oct 91	**SEASONS IN THE ABYSS** *Def American DEFA 9*..........**51**	1 wk

Kathy SLEDGE US, female vocalist — 2 wks

16 May 92	**TAKE ME BACK TO LOVE AGAIN** *Epic 6579837* **62**	2 wks

Percy SLEDGE US, male vocalist — 34 wks

12 May 66 ●	**WHEN A MAN LOVES A WOMAN** *Atlantic 584 001*..........**4**	17 wks
4 Aug 66	**WARM AND TENDER LOVE** *Atlantic 584 034*..........**34**	7 wks
14 Feb 87 ●	**WHEN A MAN LOVES A WOMAN (re-issue)** *Atlantic YZ 96* **2**	10 wks

SLICK US, male/female vocal/instrumental group — 15 wks

16 Jun 79	**SPACE BASS** *Fantasy FTC 176* **16**	10 wks
15 Sep 79	**SEXY CREAM** *Fantasy FTC 182* **47**	5 wks

Grace SLICK US, female vocalist — 4 wks

24 May 80	**DREAMS** *RCA PB 9534*..........**50**	4 wks

SLIK UK, male vocal/instrumental group — 18 wks

17 Jan 76 ★	**FOREVER AND EVER** *Bell 1464* **1**	9 wks
8 May 76	**REQUIEM** *Bell 1478* **24**	9 wks

SLIM CHANCE – *See Ronnie LANE and SLIM CHANCE*

SLIPSTREEM UK, male vocal group — 2 wks

19 Dec 92	**WE ARE RAVING - THE ANTHEM** *Boogie Food 7BF 1* ... **22**†	2 wks

SLITS UK, female vocal/instrumental group — 3 wks

13 Oct 79	**TYPICAL GIRLS/I HEARD IT THROUGH THE GRAPEVINE** *Island WIP 6505*..........**60**	3 wks

P.F. SLOAN US, male vocalist — 3 wks

4 Nov 65	**SINS OF THE FAMILY** *RCA 1482*..........**38**	3 wks

SLOWDIVE UK, male/female vocal/instrumental group — 1 wk

15 Jun 91	**CATCH THE BREEZE/SHINE** *Creation CRE 112*..........**52**	1 wk

SL2 UK, male instrumental/production duo — 19 wks

2 Nov 91	**DJS TAKE CONTROL/WAY IN MY BRAIN** *XL XLS 24* **11**	5 wks

Siouxsie's a punk shocker

59

ex Pistols are sent packing

handle orders for the disc, Anarchy in the UK.

As the fury grew, the group's planned concert tour was hit by a spate of cancellations.

Bookings made for Bournemouth, Preston, Lancaster and Newcastle were scrubbed by anxious organisers.

A spokesman for Rank Leisure Services, who had arranged the Bournemouth show said: "It is not the type of presentation with which we wish to be associated."

Preston entertainments chief Mike Smith said: "If anything like the TV programme happened here parents would be up in arms."

ill Grundy anned for fortnight TV chiefs

SIOUXSIE AND THE BANSHEES get their first tabloid newspaper front page.

4 Jan 92	DJS TAKE CONTROL/WAY IN MY BRAIN (re-entry) XL XLS 24	71	1 wk
18 Apr 92 ●	ON A RAGGA TIP XL XLS 29	2	11 wks
19 Dec 92	WAY IN MY BRAIN (re-issue)/DRUMBEATS XL XLS 36	26†	2 wks

SLY and the FAMILY STONE   42 wks
US, male/female vocal/instrumental group

10 Jul 68 ●	DANCE TO THE MUSIC Direction 58 3568	7	14 wks
2 Oct 68	M'LADY Direction 58 3707	32	7 wks
19 Mar 69	EVERYDAY PEOPLE Direction 58 3938	36	1 wk
9 Apr 69	EVERYDAY PEOPLE (re-entry) Direction 58 3938	37	4 wks
8 Jan 72	FAMILY AFFAIR Epic EPC 7632	15	8 wks
15 Apr 72	RUNNIN' AWAY Epic EPC 7810	17	8 wks

SLY FOX US, male vocal/instrumental duo   16 wks

| 31 May 86 ● | LET'S GO ALL THE WAY Capitol CL 403 | 3 | 16 wks |

SLY and ROBBIE Jamaica, male vocal/instrumental duo   15 wks

| 4 Apr 87 | BOOPS (HERE TO GO) Fourth & Broadway BRW 61 | 12 | 11 wks |
| 25 Jul 87 | FIRE Fourth & Broadway BRW 71 | 60 | 4 wks |

SMALL ADS UK, male vocal/instrumental group   3 wks

| 18 Apr 81 | SMALL ADS Bronze BRO 115 | 63 | 3 wks |

SMALL FACES UK, male vocal/instrumental group   137 wks

2 Sep 65	WHATCHA GONNA DO ABOUT IT? Decca F 12208	14	12 wks
10 Feb 66 ●	SHA LA LA LA LEE Decca F 12317	3	11 wks
12 May 66 ●	HEY GIRL Decca F 12393	10	9 wks
11 Aug 66 ★	ALL OR NOTHING Decca F 12470	1	12 wks
17 Nov 66 ●	MY MIND'S EYE Decca F 12500	4	11 wks
9 Mar 67	I CAN'T MAKE IT Decca F 12565	26	7 wks
8 Jun 67	HERE COME THE NICE Immediate IM 050	12	10 wks
9 Aug 67 ●	ITCHYCOO PARK Immediate IM 057	3	14 wks
6 Dec 67 ●	TIN SOLDIER Immediate IM 062	9	12 wks
17 Apr 68 ●	LAZY SUNDAY Immediate IM 064	2	11 wks
10 Jul 68	UNIVERSAL Immediate IM 069	16	11 wks
19 Mar 69	AFTERGLOW OF YOUR LOVE Immediate IM 077	36	1 wk
13 Dec 75 ●	ITCHYCOO PARK (re-issue) Immediate IMS 102	9	11 wks
20 Mar 76	LAZY SUNDAY (re-issue) Immediate IMS 106	39	5 wks

Heather SMALL – See M PEOPLE

SMART E'S UK, male instrumental/production group   9 wks

| 11 Jul 92 ● | SESAME'S TREET Suburban Base SUBBASE 12S | 2 | 9 wks |

SMASHING PUMPKINS   1 wk
US, male vocal/instrumental duo

| 5 Sep 92 | I AM ONE Hut HUTT 18 | 73 | 1 wk |

SMEAR CAMPAIGN – See MR. BEAN and SMEAR CAMPAIGN featuring Bruce DICKINSON

'Fast' Eddie SMITH – See DJ 'FAST' EDDIE

Hurricane SMITH UK, male vocalist   35 wks

12 Jun 71 ●	DON'T LET IT DIE Columbia DB 8785	2	12 wks
29 Apr 72 ●	OH BABE WHAT WOULD YOU SAY? Columbia DB 8878	4	16 wks
2 Sep 72	WHO WAS IT Columbia DB 8916	23	7 wks

Jimmy SMITH US, male instrumentalist – organ   3 wks

| 28 Apr 66 | GOT MY MOJO WORKING Verve VS 536 | 48 | 2 wks |
| 19 May 66 | GOT MY MOJO WORKING (re-entry) Verve VS 536 | 48 | 1 wk |

Keely SMITH US, female vocalist   10 wks

| 18 Mar 65 | YOU'RE BREAKIN' MY HEART Reprise R 20346 | 14 | 10 wks |

Mandy SMITH UK, female vocalist   2 wks

| 20 May 89 | DON'T YOU WANT ME BABY PWL PWL 37 | 59 | 2 wks |

Mel SMITH UK, male vocalist   10 wks

| 5 Dec 87 ● | ROCKIN' AROUND THE CHRISTMAS TREE 10 TEN 2 * | 3 | 7 wks |
| 21 Dec 91 | ANOTHER BLOOMING CHRISTMAS Epic 6576877 | 59 | 3 wks |

* Mel and Kim

Muriel SMITH UK, female vocalist   17 wks

| 15 May 53 ● | HOLD ME THRILL ME KISS ME Philips PB 122 | 3 | 17 wks |

O.C. SMITH US, male vocalist   23 wks

| 29 May 68 ● | SON OF HICKORY HOLLER'S TRAMP CBS 3343 | 2 | 15 wks |
| 26 Mar 77 | TOGETHER Caribou CRB 4910 | 25 | 8 wks |

Patti SMITH GROUP   16 wks
US, female vocalist, male instrumental backing group

29 Apr 78 ●	BECAUSE THE NIGHT Arista 181	5	12 wks
19 Aug 78	PRIVILEGE (SET ME FREE) Arista 197	72	1 wk
2 Jun 79	FREDERICK Arista 264	63	3 wks

Rex SMITH – See Rachel SWEET

Richard Jon SMITH South Africa, male vocalist   2 wks

| 16 Jul 83 | SHE'S THE MASTER OF THE GAME Jive JIVE 38 | 63 | 2 wks |

Whistling Jack SMITH UK, male whistler   12 wks

| 2 Mar 67 ● | I WAS KAISER BILL'S BATMAN Deram DM 112 | 5 | 12 wks |

SMITHS UK, male vocal/instrumental group   104 wks

12 Nov 83	THIS CHARMING MAN Rough Trade RT 136	25	12 wks
28 Jan 84	WHAT DIFFERENCE DOES IT MAKE Rough Trade RT 146	12	9 wks
2 Jun 84 ●	HEAVEN KNOWS I'M MISERABLE NOW Rough Trade RT 156	10	8 wks

1 Sep 84	**WILLIAM, IT WAS REALLY NOTHING**		
	Rough Trade RT 166	**17**	6 wks
9 Feb 85	**HOW SOON IS NOW?** *Rough Trade RT 176*	**24**	6 wks
30 Mar 85	**SHAKESPEARE'S SISTER** *Rough Trade RT 181*	**26**	4 wks
13 Jul 85	**THAT JOKE ISN'T FUNNY ANYMORE**		
	Rough Trade RT 186	**49**	3 wks
5 Oct 85	**THE BOY WITH THE THORN IN HIS SIDE**		
	Rough Trade RT 191	**23**	5 wks
31 May 86	**BIG MOUTH STRIKES AGAIN** *Rough Trade RT 192*	**26**	4 wks
2 Aug 86	**PANIC** *Rough Trade RT 193*	**11**	8 wks
1 Nov 86	**ASK** *Rough Trade RT 194*	**14**	5 wks
7 Feb 87	**SHOPLIFTERS OF THE WORLD UNITE**		
	Rough Trade RT 195	**12**	4 wks
25 Apr 87 ●	**SHEILA TAKE A BOW** *Rough Trade RT 196*	**10**	5 wks
22 Aug 87	**GIRLFRIEND IN A COMA** *Rough Trade RT 197*	**13**	5 wks
14 Nov 87	**I STARTED SOMETHING I COULDN'T FINISH**		
	Rough Trade RT 198	**23**	4 wks
19 Dec 87	**LAST NIGHT I DREAMT THAT SOMEBODY**		
	LOVED ME *Rough Trade RT 200*	**30**	4 wks
15 Aug 92 ●	**THIS CHARMING MAN (re-issue)** *WEA YZ 0001*	**8**	5 wks
12 Sep 92	**HOW SOON IS NOW (re-issue)** *WEA YZ 0002*	**16**	4 wks
24 Oct 92	**THERE IS A LIGHT THAT NEVER GOES OUT**		
	WEA YZ 0003	**25**	3 wks

SMOKE *UK, male vocal/instrumental group* **3 wks**

9 Mar 67	**MY FRIEND JACK** *Columbia DB 8115*	**45**	3 wks

SMOKIE *UK, male vocal/instrumental group* **106 wks**

19 Jul 75 ●	**IF YOU THINK YOU KNOW HOW TO LOVE ME**		
	*RAK 206 **	**3**	9 wks
4 Oct 75 ●	**DON'T PLAY YOUR ROCK 'N ROLL TO ME**		
	*RAK 217 **	**8**	7 wks
31 Jan 76	**SOMETHING'S BEEN MAKING ME BLUE** *RAK 227*	**17**	8 wks
25 Sep 76	**I'LL MEET YOU AT MIDNIGHT** *RAK 241*	**11**	9 wks
4 Dec 76 ●	**LIVING NEXT DOOR TO ALICE** *RAK 244*	**5**	11 wks
19 Mar 77	**LAY BACK IN THE ARMS OF SOMEONE** *RAK 251*	**12**	9 wks
16 Jul 77 ●	**IT'S YOUR LIFE** *RAK 260*	**5**	9 wks
15 Oct 77 ●	**NEEDLES AND PINS** *RAK 263*	**10**	9 wks
28 Jan 78	**FOR A FEW DOLLARS MORE** *RAK 267*	**17**	6 wks
20 May 78 ●	**OH CAROL** *RAK 276*	**5**	13 wks
23 Sep 78	**MEXICAN GIRL** *RAK 283*	**19**	9 wks
19 Apr 80	**TAKE GOOD CARE OF MY BABY** *RAK 309*	**34**	7 wks

* Smokey

Joe SMOOTH *US, male vocalist* **4 wks**

4 Feb 89	**PROMISED LAND** *DJ International DJIN 6*	**56**	4 wks

SMURFS – See FATHER ABRAHAM and the SMURFS

Patty SMYTH – See Don HENLEY

SNAP *US/Germany, male/female vocal/instrumental duo* **72 wks**

24 Mar 90 ★	**THE POWER** *Arista 113133*	**1**	15 wks
16 Jun 90 ●	**OOOPS UP** *Arista 113296*	**5**	12 wks
22 Sep 90 ●	**CULT OF SNAP** *Arista 113596*	**8**	7 wks
8 Dec 90 ●	**MARY HAD A LITTLE BOY** *Arista 113831*	**8**	10 wks
30 Mar 91 ●	**SNAP MEGAMIX** *Arista 114169*	**10**	6 wks
21 Dec 91	**THE COLOUR OF LOVE** *Arista 114678*	**54**	3 wks
4 Jul 92 ★	**RHYTHM IS A DANCER** *Arista 115309*	**1**	19 wks

SNIFF 'N' THE TEARS **5 wks**
UK, male vocal/instrumental group

23 Jun 79	**DRIVER'S SEAT** *Chiswick CHIS 105*	**42**	5 wks

Phoebe SNOW *US, female vocalist* **7 wks**

6 Jan 79	**EVERY NIGHT** *CBS 6842*	**37**	7 wks

SNOWMAN – See Peter AUTY

SNOWMEN *UK, male vocal/instrumental group* **12 wks**

12 Dec 81	**HOKEY COKEY** *Stiff ODB 1*	**18**	8 wks
18 Dec 82	**XMAS PARTY** *Solid STOP 006*	**44**	4 wks

SO *UK, male vocal/instrumental group* **3 wks**

13 Feb 88	**ARE YOU SURE** *Parlophone R 6173*	**62**	3 wks

Gino SOCCIO *Canada, male instrumentalist - keyboards* **5 wks**

28 Apr 79	**DANCER** *Warner Bros. K 17357*	**46**	5 wks

SOEUR SOURIRE – See SINGING NUN

SOFT CELL *UK, male vocal/instrumental duo* **107 wks**

1 Aug 81 ★	**TAINTED LOVE** *Some Bizzare BZS 2*	**1**	16 wks
14 Nov 81	**BED SITTER** *Some Bizzare BZS 6*	**4**	12 wks
9 Jan 82	**TAINTED LOVE (re-entry)** *Some Bizzare BZS 2*	**43**	10 wks
6 Feb 82 ●	**SAY HELLO WAVE GOODBYE** *Some Bizzare BZS 7*	**3**	9 wks
29 May 82 ●	**TORCH** *Some Bizzare BZS 9*	**2**	9 wks
24 Jul 82	**TAINTED LOVE (2nd re-entry)** *Some Bizzare BZS 2*	**50**	4 wks
21 Aug 82 ●	**WHAT** *Some Bizzare BZS 11*	**3**	8 wks
4 Dec 82	**WHERE THE HEART IS** *Some Bizzare BZS 16*	**21**	7 wks
5 Mar 83	**NUMBERS/BARRIERS** *Some Bizzare BZS 17*	**25**	4 wks
24 Sep 83	**SOUL INSIDE** *Some Bizzare BZS 20*	**16**	5 wks
25 Feb 84	**DOWN IN THE SUBWAY** *Some Bizzare BZS 22*	**24**	6 wks
9 Feb 85	**TAINTED LOVE (3rd re-entry)** *Some Bizzare BZS 2*	**43**	6 wks
23 Mar 91	**SAY HELLO WAVE GOODBYE** *Mercury SOFT 1*	**38**	3 wks
18 May 91 ●	**TAINTED LOVE (re-recording)** *Mercury SOFT 2 **	**5**	8 wks

* Soft Cell/Marc Almond

SOHO *UK, male/female vocal/instrumental group* **11 wks**

5 May 90	**HIPPY CHICK** *Savage 7SAV 106*	**67**	1 wk
19 Jan 91 ●	**HIPPY CHICK (re-entry)** *Savage 7SAV 106*	**8**	8 wks
9 Nov 91	**BORN TO BE ALIVE** *MCA MCS 1578 **	**51**	2 wks

* Adamski featuring Soho
The listed flip side of Born To Be Alive was Never Goin' Down by Adamski featuring Jimi Polo.

SOLO *UK, male producer - Stuart Crichton* **3 wks**

20 Jul 91	**RAINBOW (SAMPLE FREE)** *Reverb RVBT 003*	**59**	2 wks
18 Jan 92	**COME ON!** *Reverb RVBT 008*	**75**	1 wk

Sal SOLO *UK, male vocalist* **13 wks**

15 Dec 84	**SAN DAMIANO (HEART AND SOUL)**		
	MCA MCA 930	**15**	10 wks
6 Apr 85	**MUSIC AND YOU** *MCA MCA 946 **	**52**	3 wks

* Sal Solo with the London Community Gospel Choir

Belouis SOME *UK, male vocalist* **26 wks**

27 Apr 85	**IMAGINATION** *Parlophone R 6097*	**50**	7 wks
18 Jan 86	**IMAGINATION (re-issue)** *Parlophone R 1986*	**17**	10 wks

12 Apr 86	**SOME PEOPLE** *Parlophone R 6130*	33	7 wks
16 May 87	**LET IT BE WITH YOU** *Parlophone R 6154*	53	2 wks

Jimmy SOMERVILLE *UK, male vocalist*   36 wks

11 Nov 89	**COMMENT TE DIRE ADIEU** *London LON 241* *	14	9 wks
13 Jan 90 ●	**YOU MAKE ME FEEL (MIGHTY REAL)** *London LON 249*	5	8 wks
17 Mar 90	**READ MY LIPS (ENOUGH IS ENOUGH)** *London LON 254*	26	6 wks
3 Nov 90 ●	**TO LOVE SOMEBODY** *London LON 281*	8	11 wks
10 Aug 91	**RUN FROM LOVE** *London LON 301*	52	2 wks

*Jimmy Somerville featuring June Miles-Kingston

See also Bronski Beat.

SONIA *UK, female vocalist*   70 wks

24 Jun 89 ★	**YOU'LL NEVER STOP ME LOVING YOU** *Chrysalis CHS 3385*	1	13 wks
7 Oct 89	**CAN'T FORGET YOU** *Chrysalis CHS 3419*	17	6 wks
9 Dec 89 ●	**LISTEN TO YOUR HEART** *Chrysalis CHS 3465*	10	10 wks
7 Apr 90	**COUNTING EVERY MINUTE** *Chrysalis CHS 3492*	16	7 wks
23 Jun 90	**YOU'VE GOT A FRIEND** *Jive CHILD 90* *	14	6 wks
25 Aug 90	**END OF THE WORLD** *Chrysalis/PWL CHS 357*	18	7 wks
1 Jun 91 ●	**ONLY FOOLS (NEVER FALL IN LOVE)** *IQ ZB 44613*	10	8 wks
31 Aug 91	**BE YOUNG BE FOOLISH BE HAPPY** *IQ ZB 44935*	22	5 wks
16 Nov 91	**YOU TO ME ARE EVERYTHING** *IQ ZB 45121*	13	5 wks
12 Sep 92	**BOOGIE NIGHTS** *Arista 74321113467*	30	3 wks

*Big Fun and Sonia

SONIC SOLUTION   1 wk
UK, male/producer Steve Cop

4 Apr 92	**BEATSTIME** *R&S RSUK 11*	59	1 wk

SONIC THE HEDGEHOG – *See HWA featuring SONIC THE HEDGEHOG*

SONIC YOUTH *US, male/female vocal/instrumental group*   6 wks

11 Jul 92	**100%** *DGC DGCS 11*	28	4 wks
7 Nov 92	**YOUTH AGAINST FASCISM** *Geffen GFS 26*	52	2 wks

SONNY *US, male vocalist*   11 wks

19 Aug 65 ●	**LAUGH AT ME** *Atlantic AT 4038*	9	11 wks

See also Sonny and Cher.

SONNY and CHER *US, male/female vocal duo*   77 wks

12 Aug 65 ★	**I GOT YOU BABE** *Atlantic AT 4035*	1	12 wks
16 Sep 65	**BABY DON'T GO** *Reprise R 20309*	11	9 wks
21 Oct 65	**BUT YOU'RE MINE** *Atlantic AT 4047*	17	8 wks
17 Feb 66	**WHAT NOW MY LOVE** *Atlantic AT 4069*	13	11 wks
30 Jun 66	**HAVE I STAYED TOO LONG** *Atlantic 584 018*	42	3 wks
8 Sep 66 ●	**LITTLE MAN** *Atlantic 584 040*	4	10 wks
17 Nov 66	**LIVING FOR YOU** *Atlantic 584 057*	44	4 wks
2 Feb 67	**THE BEAT GOES ON** *Atlantic 584 078*	29	8 wks
15 Jan 72 ●	**ALL I EVER NEED IS YOU** *MCA MU 1145*	8	12 wks

See also Sonny; Cher.

SON'Z OF A LOOP DA LOOP ERA   4 wks
UK, male producer - Danny Breaks

15 Feb 92	**FAR OUT** *Suburban Base SUBBASE 008*	36	3 wks
17 Oct 92	**PEACE + LOVEISM** *Suburban Base SUBBASE 14*	60	1 wk

SORROWS *UK, male vocal/instrumental group*   8 wks

16 Sep 65	**TAKE A HEART** *Piccadilly 7N 35260*	21	8 wks

S.O.S. BAND *US, male/female vocal/instrumental group*   46 wks

19 Jul 80	**TAKE YOUR TIME (DO IT RIGHT) PART 1** *Tabu TBU 8564*	51	4 wks
26 Feb 83	**GROOVIN' (THAT'S WHAT WE'RE DOIN')** *Tabu TBU A3120*	72	1 wk
7 Apr 84	**JUST BE GOOD TO ME** *Tabu A 3626*	13	11 wks
4 Aug 84	**JUST THE WAY YOU LIKE IT** *Tabu A 4621*	32	7 wks
13 Oct 84	**WEEKEND GIRL** *Tabu A 4785*	51	5 wks
29 Mar 86	**THE FINEST** *Tabu A 6997*	17	10 wks
5 Jul 86	**BORROWED LOVE** *Tabu A 7241*	50	5 wks
2 May 87	**NO LIES** *Tabu 650444 7*	64	3 wks

David SOUL *US, male vocalist*   56 wks

18 Dec 76 ★	**DON'T GIVE UP ON US** *Private Stock PVT 84*	1	16 wks
26 Mar 77 ●	**GOING IN WITH MY EYES OPEN** *Private Stock PVT 99*	2	8 wks
27 Aug 77 ★	**SILVER LADY** *Private Stock PVT 115*	1	14 wks
17 Dec 77 ●	**LET'S HAVE A QUIET NIGHT IN** *Private Stock PVT 130*	8	9 wks
27 May 78	**IT SURE BRINGS OUT THE LOVE IN YOUR EYES** *Private Stock PVT 137*	12	9 wks

Jimmy SOUL *US, male vocalist*   5 wks

11 Jul 63	**IF YOU WANNA BE HAPPY** *Stateside SS 178*	39	2 wks
15 Jun 91	**IF YOU WANNA BE HAPPY (re-issue)** *Epic 6569647*	68	3 wks

SOUL BROTHERS *UK, male vocal/instrumental group*   3 wks

22 Apr 65	**I KEEP RINGING MY BABY** *Decca F 12116*	42	3 wks

SOUL CITY SYMPHONY – *See Van McCOY*

SOUL FAMILY SENSATION   4 wks
UK, male/female vocal/instrumental group

11 May 91	**I DON'T EVEN KNOW IF I SHOULD CALL YOU BABY** *One Little Indian 47 TP7*	49	4 wks

SOUL SONIC FORCE – *See Afrika BAMBAATAA*

SOUL II SOUL *UK, male producer - Jazzie B*   70 wks

21 May 88	**FAIRPLAY** *10 TEN 228* *	63	3 wks
17 Sep 88	**FEEL FREE** *10 TEN 236* **	64	2 wks
18 Mar 89 ●	**KEEP ON MOVING** *10 TEN 263* ***	5	12 wks
10 Jun 89 ★	**BACK TO LIFE (HOWEVER DO YOU WANT ME)** *10 TEN 265* ***	1	14 wks
9 Dec 89 ●	**GET A LIFE** *10 TEN 284*	3	13 wks
5 May 90 ●	**A DREAM'S A DREAM** *10 TEN 300*	6	6 wks
24 Nov 90	**MISSING YOU** *10 TEN 345* ****	22	7 wks
4 Apr 92 ●	**JOY** *Ten TEN 350*	4	7 wks
13 Jun 92	**MOVE ME NO MOUNTAIN** *Ten TEN 400* *****	31	4 wks
26 Sep 92	**JUST RIGHT** *Ten TEN 410*	38	2 wks

* Soul II Soul featuring Rose Windross ** Soul II Soul featuring Do'reen
*** Soul II Soul featuring Caron Wheeler **** Soul II Soul featuring Kym Mazelle ***** Soul II Soul, lead vocals Kofi

SOULED OUT   1 wk
Italy/US/UK, male/female vocal/instrumental group

9 May 92	**IN MY LIFE** *Columbia 6578367*	75	1 wk

SOUND 9418 – *See Jonathan KING*

SOUNDGARDEN *US, male vocal/instrumental group* **5 wks**

11 Apr 92	**JESUS CHRIST POSE** *A & M AM 862*	30	3 wks
20 Jun 92	**RUSTY CAGE** *A & M AM 874*	41	1 wk
21 Nov 92	**OUTSHINED** *A & M AM 0102*	50	1 wk

SOUNDS INCORPORATED **11 wks**
UK, male instrumental group

23 Apr 64	**THE SPARTANS** *Columbia DB 7239*	30	6 wks
30 Jul 64	**SPANISH HARLEM** *Columbia DB 7321*	35	5 wks

SOUNDS NICE *UK, male instrumental group* **11 wks**

6 Sep 69	**LOVE AT FIRST SIGHT (JE T'AIME ... MOI NON PLUS)** *Parlophone R 5797*	18	11 wks

Has credit: Tim Mycroft on organ.

SOUNDS OF BLACKNESS **11 wks**
US, male/female gospel choir

22 Jun 91	**OPTIMISTIC** *Perspective PERSS 786*	45	4 wks
28 Sep 91	**THE PRESSURE PART 1** *Perspective PERSS 816*	71	1 wk
15 Feb 92	**OPTIMISTIC (re-issue)** *Perspective PERSS 849*	28	4 wks
25 Apr 92	**THE PRESSURE PART 1 (re-issue)** *Perspective PERSS 867*	49	2 wks

SOUNDS ORCHESTRAL *UK, orchestra* **18 wks**

3 Dec 64 ●	**CAST YOUR FATE TO THE WIND** *Piccadilly 7N 35206*	5	16 wks
8 Jul 65	**MOONGLOW** *Piccadilly 7N 35248*	43	2 wks

SOUNDSOURCE **1 wk**
Sweden/UK, male instrumental/production group

11 Jan 92	**TAKE ME UP** *ffrr FX 177*	62	1 wk

SOUP DRAGONS *UK, male vocal/instrumental group* **23 wks**

20 Jun 87	**CAN'T TAKE NO MORE** *Raw TV RTV 3*	65	1 wk
5 Sep 87	**SOFT AS YOUR FACE** *Raw TV RTV 4*	66	2 wks
14 Jul 90 ●	**I'M FREE** *Raw TV RTV 9 **	5	12 wks
20 Oct 90	**MOTHER UNIVERSE** *Big Life BLR 30*	26	5 wks
11 Apr 92	**DIVINE THING** *Big Life BLR 68*	53	3 wks

* Soup Dragons featuring Junior Reid

SOURCE *UK, male producer – John Truelove* **12 wks**

2 Feb 91 ●	**YOU GOT THE LOVE** *Truelove TLOVE 7001 **	4	11 wks
26 Dec 92	**ROCK THE HOUSE** *React 12REACT 12 ***	63†	1 wk

* Source featuring Candi Staton ** Source featuring Nicole

Joe SOUTH *US, male vocalist* **11 wks**

5 Mar 69 ●	**GAMES PEOPLE PLAY** *Capitol CL 15579*	6	11 wks

Jeri SOUTHERN *US, female vocalist* **3 wks**

21 Jun 57	**FIRE DOWN BELOW** *Brunswick 05665*	22	3 wks

SOUTHLANDERS *UK, male vocal group* **10 wks**

22 Nov 57	**ALONE** *Decca F 10946*	17	10 wks

SOVEREIGN COLLECTION *UK, orchestra* **6 wks**

3 Apr 71	**MOZART 40** *Capitol CL 15676*	27	6 wks

Red SOVINE *US, male vocalist* **8 wks**

13 Jun 81 ●	**TEDDY BEAR** *Starday SD 142*	4	8 wks

Bob B SOXX and the BLUE JEANS **2 wks**
US, male/female vocal group

31 Jan 63	**ZIP-A-DEE-DOO-DAH** *London HLU 9646*	45	2 wks

SPACE *France, male instrumental group* **12 wks**

13 Aug 77 ●	**MAGIC FLY** *Pye International 7N 25746*	2	12 wks

SPACE MONKEY *UK, male producer – Paul Goodchild* **4 wks**

8 Oct 83	**CAN'T STOP RUNNING** *Innervision A 3742*	53	4 wks

SPAGNA *Italy, female vocalist* **23 wks**

25 Jul 87 ●	**CALL ME** *CBS 650279 7*	2	12 wks
17 Oct 87	**EASY LADY** *CBS 651169 7*	62	3 wks
20 Aug 88	**EVERY GIRL AND BOY** *CBS SPAG 1*	23	8 wks

SPANDAU BALLET *UK, male vocal/instrumental group* **159 wks**

15 Nov 80 ●	**TO CUT A LONG STORY SHORT** *Reformation CHS 2473*	5	11 wks
24 Jan 81	**THE FREEZE** *Reformation CHS 2486*	17	8 wks
4 Apr 81 ●	**MUSCLEBOUND/GLOW** *Reformation CHS 2509*	10	10 wks
18 Jul 81 ●	**CHANT NO. 1 (I DON'T NEED THIS PRESSURE ON)** *Reformation CHS 2528*	3	10 wks
14 Nov 81	**PAINT ME DOWN** *Reformation CHS 2560*	30	5 wks
30 Jan 82	**SHE LOVED LIKE DIAMOND** *Chrysalis CHS 2585*	49	4 wks
10 Apr 82 ●	**INSTINCTION** *Chrysalis CHS 2602*	10	11 wks
2 Oct 82 ●	**LIFELINE** *Chrysalis CHS 2642*	7	9 wks
12 Feb 83	**COMMUNICATION** *Reformation CHS 2662*	12	10 wks
23 Apr 83 ★	**TRUE** *Reformation SPAN 1*	1	12 wks
13 Aug 83 ●	**GOLD** *Reformation SPAN 2*	2	9 wks
9 Jun 84 ●	**ONLY WHEN YOU LEAVE** *Reformation SPAN 3*	3	9 wks
18 Aug 84	**ONLY WHEN YOU LEAVE (re-entry)** *Reformation SPAN 3*	74	1 wk
25 Aug 84 ●	**I'LL FLY FOR YOU** *Reformation SPAN 4*	9	9 wks
20 Oct 84	**HIGHLY STRUNG** *Reformation SPAN 5*	15	5 wks
8 Dec 84	**ROUND AND ROUND** *Reformation SPAN 6*	18	8 wks
26 Jul 86	**FIGHT FOR OURSELVES** *Reformation A 7264*	15	7 wks
8 Nov 86 ●	**THROUGH THE BARRICADES** *Reformation SPANS 1*	6	10 wks
14 Feb 87	**HOW MANY LIES** *Reformation SPANS 2*	34	4 wks
3 Sep 88	**RAW** *CBS SPANS 3*	47	3 wks
26 Aug 89	**BE FREE WITH YOUR LOVE** *CBS SPANS 4*	42	4 wks

SPARKS *US/UK, male vocal/instrumental group* **70 wks**

4 May 74 ●	**THIS TOWN AIN'T BIG ENOUGH FOR BOTH OF US** *Island WIP 6193*	2	10 wks
20 Jul 74 ●	**AMATEUR HOUR** *Island WIP 6203*	7	9 wks
19 Oct 74	**NEVER TURN YOUR BACK ON MOTHER EARTH** *Island WIP 6211*	13	7 wks

18 Jan 75	SOMETHING FOR THE GIRL WITH EVERYTHING *Island WIP 6221*	17	7 wks
19 Jul 75	GET IN THE SWING *Island WIP 6236*	27	7 wks
4 Oct 75	LOOKS LOOKS LOOKS *Island WIP 6249*	26	4 wks
21 Apr 79	THE NUMBER ONE SONG IN HEAVEN *Virgin VS 244*	14	12 wks
21 Jul 79 ●	BEAT THE CLOCK *Virgin VS 270*	10	9 wks
27 Oct 79	TRYOUTS FOR THE HUMAN RACE *Virgin VS 289*	45	5 wks

SPEAR OF DESTINY UK, *male vocal/instrumental group*   43 wks

21 May 83	THE WHEEL *Epic A 3372*	59	5 wks
21 Jan 84	PRISONER OF LOVE *CBS A 4068*	59	3 wks
14 Apr 84	LIBERATOR *Epic A 4310*	67	3 wks
15 Jun 85	ALL MY LOVE (ASK NOTHING) *Epic A 6333*	61	3 wks
10 Aug 85	COME BACK *Epic 6445*	53	3 wks
7 Feb 87	STRANGERS IN OUR TOWN *10 TEN 148*	49	4 wks
4 Apr 87	NEVER TAKE ME ALIVE *10 TEN 162*	14	11 wks
25 Jul 87	WAS THAT YOU *10 TEN 173*	55	4 wks
3 Oct 87	THE TRAVELLER *10 TEN 189*	44	3 wks
24 Sep 88	SO IN LOVE WITH YOU *Virgin VS 1123*	36	5 wks

Billie Jo SPEARS US, *female vocalist*   40 wks

12 Jul 75 ●	BLANKET ON THE GROUND *United Artists UP 35805*	6	13 wks
17 Jul 76 ●	WHAT I'VE GOT IN MIND *United Artists UP 36118*	4	13 wks
11 Dec 76	SING ME AN OLD FASHIONED SONG *United Artists UP 36179*	34	9 wks
21 Jul 79	I WILL SURVIVE *United Artists UP 601*	47	5 wks

SPECIALS UK, *male vocal/instrumental group*   100 wks

28 Jul 79 ●	GANGSTERS *2 Tone CHS TT 1* *	6	12 wks
27 Oct 79 ●	A MESSAGE TO YOU RUDY/NITE CLUB *2 Tone CHS TT 5* **	10	14 wks
26 Jan 80 ★	THE SPECIAL A.K.A. LIVE! EP *2 Tone CHS TT 7* *	1	10 wks
24 May 80 ●	RAT RACE/RUDE BOYS OUTA JAIL *2 Tone CHS TT 11*	5	9 wks
20 Sep 80 ●	STEREOTYPE/INTERNATIONAL JET SET *2 Tone CHS TT 13*	6	8 wks
13 Dec 80 ●	DO NOTHING/MAGGIE'S FARM *2 Tone CHS TT 16*	4	11 wks
20 Jun 81 ★	GHOST TOWN *2 Tone CHS TT 17*	1	14 wks
23 Jan 82	THE BOILER *2 Tone CHS TT 18* ***	35	5 wks
3 Sep 83	RACIST FRIEND *2 Tone CHS TT 25* *	60	3 wks
17 Mar 84 ●	NELSON MANDELA *2 Tone CHS TT 26* *	9	10 wks
8 Sep 84	WHAT I LIKE MOST ABOUT YOU IS YOUR GIRLFRIEND *2 Tone CHS TT 27* *	51	4 wks

* Special A.K.A. ** Specials (featuring Rico +) *** Rhoda with the Special A.K.A.

Tracks on The Special A.K.A. Live! EP: *Too Much Too Young/Guns Of Navarone/Long Shot Kick De Bucket/Liquidator/Skinhead Moonstomp. Maggie's Farm only listed with Do Nothing from 10 Jan 81. Group were male/female for last four hits.*

SPECTRUM UK, *male instrumental/production group*   1 wk

| 26 Sep 92 | TRUE LOVE WILL FIND YOU IN THE END *Silvertone ORE 44* | 70 | 1 wk |

Chris SPEDDING UK, *male vocalist/instrumentalist - guitar*   8 wks

| 23 Aug 75 | MOTOR BIKING *RAK 210* | 14 | 8 wks |

Johnny SPENCE UK, *orchestra*   15 wks

| 1 Mar 62 | THEME FROM DR. KILDARE *Parlophone R 4872* | 15 | 15 wks |

Don SPENCER UK, *male vocalist*   12 wks

| 21 Mar 63 | FIREBALL XL5 *HMV POP 1087* | 32 | 11 wks |
| 13 Jun 63 | FIREBALL XL5 (re-entry) *HMV POP 1087* | 49 | 1 wk |

Tracie SPENCER US, *female vocalist*   2 wks

| 4 May 91 | THIS HOUSE *Capitol CL 612* | 65 | 2 wks |

SPIDER UK, *male vocal/instrumental group*   5 wks

| 5 Mar 83 | WHY D'YA LIE TO ME *RCA 313* | 65 | 2 wks |
| 10 Mar 84 | HERE WE GO ROCK 'N' ROLL *A & M AM 180* | 57 | 3 wks |

SPINAL TAP US/UK, *male vocal/instrumental group*   3 wks

| 28 Mar 92 | BITCH SCHOOL *MCA MCS 1624* | 35 | 2 wks |
| 2 May 92 | THE MAJESTY OF ROCK *MCA MCS 1629* | 61 | 1 wk |

SPINNERS – *See* DETROIT SPINNERS

SPIRAL TRIBE UK, *male/female vocal/instrumental group*   2 wks

| 29 Aug 92 | BREACH THE PEACE (EP) *Butterfly BLRT 79* | 66 | 1 wk |
| 21 Nov 92 | FORWARD THE REVOLUTION *Butterfly BLRT 85* | 70 | 1 wk |

Tracks on Breach The Peace (EP): *Breach The Peace/Do Et/Seven/25 Minute Warning.*

SPIRITUAL COWBOYS – *See* David A. STEWART

SPIRITUALIZED UK, *male vocal/instrumental group*   3 wks

30 Jun 90	ANYWAY YOU WANT ME/STEP INTO THE BREEZE *Dedicated ZB 43783*	75	1 wk
17 Aug 91	RUN *Dedicated SPIRIT 002*	59	1 wk
25 Jul 92	MEDICATION *Dedicated SPIRIT 005T*	55	1 wk

SPITTING IMAGE UK, *male/female puppets*   18 wks

10 May 86 ★	THE CHICKEN SONG *Virgin SPIT 1*	1	10 wks
26 Jul 86	THE CHICKEN SONG (re-entry) *Virgin SPIT 1*	67	1 wk
6 Dec 86	SANTA CLAUS IS ON THE DOLE/FIRST ATHEIST TABERNACLE CHOIR *Virgin VS 921*	22	7 wks

SPLINTER UK, *male vocal/instrumental duo*   10 wks

| 2 Nov 74 | COSTAFINE TOWN *Dark Horse AMS 7135* | 17 | 10 wks |

SPLIT ENZ New Zealand/UK, *male vocal/instrumental group*   15 wks

| 16 Aug 80 | I GOT YOU *A & M AMS 7546* | 12 | 11 wks |
| 23 May 81 | HISTORY NEVER REPEATS *A & M AMS 8128* | 63 | 4 wks |

A SPLIT SECOND   1 wk
Belgium/Italy, male instrumental/production group

| 14 Dec 91 | FLESH *ffrr FX 178* | 68 | 1 wk |

SPLODGENESSABOUNDS   17 wks
UK, male vocal/instrumental group

14 Jun 80 ●	SIMON TEMPLAR/TWO PINTS OF LAGER AND A PACKET OF CRISPS PLEASE *Deram BUM 1*	7	8 wks
6 Sep 80	TWO LITTLE BOYS/HORSE *Deram ROLF 1*	26	7 wks
13 Jun 81	COWPUNK MEDLUM *Deram BUM 3*	69	2 wks

SPOTNICKS Sweden, *male instrumental group*   37 wks

| 14 Jun 62 | ORANGE BLOSSOM SPECIAL *Oriole CB 1724* | 29 | 10 wks |

6 Sep 62	ROCKET MAN *Oriole CB 1755*	38	9 wks
31 Jan 63	HAVA NAGILA *Oriole CB 1790*	13	12 wks
25 Apr 63	JUST LISTEN TO MY HEART *Oriole CB 1818*	36	6 wks

British Hit Singles Part One: Alphabetically by Artist

Date of chart entry/Title & catalogue no./Peak position reached/Weeks on chart

★ Number one   ● Top Ten   † still on chart at 31 Dec 1992

* = credited to act billed in footnote

Dusty SPRINGFIELD *UK, female vocalist*   **206 wks**

21 Nov 63	●	I ONLY WANT TO BE WITH YOU *Philips BF 1292*	4	18 wks
20 Feb 64		STAY AWHILE *Philips BF 1313*	13	10 wks
2 Jul 64	●	I JUST DON'T KNOW WHAT TO DO WITH MYSELF *Philips BF 1348*	3	12 wks
22 Oct 64	●	LOSING YOU *Philips BF 1369*	9	13 wks
18 Feb 65		YOUR HURTIN' KIND OF LOVE *Philips BF 1396*	37	4 wks
1 Jul 65	●	IN THE MIDDLE OF NOWHERE *Philips BF 1418*	8	10 wks
16 Sep 65	●	SOME OF YOUR LOVIN' *Philips BF 1430*	8	9 wks
27 Jan 66		LITTLE BY LITTLE *Philips BF 1466*	17	9 wks
31 Mar 66	★	YOU DON'T HAVE TO SAY YOU LOVE ME *Philips BF 1482*	1	13 wks
7 Jul 66	●	GOING BACK *Philips BF 1502*	10	10 wks
15 Sep 66	●	ALL I SEE IS YOU *Philips BF 1510*	9	12 wks
23 Feb 67		I'LL TRY ANYTHING *Philips BF 1553*	13	9 wks
25 May 67		GIVE ME TIME *Philips BF 1577*	24	6 wks
10 Jul 68	●	I CLOSE MY EYES AND COUNT TO TEN *Philips BF 1682*	4	12 wks
4 Dec 68	●	SON OF A PREACHER MAN *Philips BF 1730*	9	9 wks
20 Sep 69		AM I THE SAME GIRL *Philips BF 1811*	43	3 wks
18 Oct 69		AM I THE SAME GIRL (re-entry) *Philips BF 1811*	46	1 wk
19 Sep 70		HOW CAN I BE SURE *Philips 6006 045*	36	4 wks
20 Oct 79		BABY BLUE *Mercury DUSTY 4*	61	5 wks
22 Aug 87	●	WHAT HAVE I DONE TO DESERVE THIS *Parlophone R 6163 **	2	9 wks
25 Feb 89		NOTHING HAS BEEN PROVED *Parlophone R 6207*	16	7 wks
2 Dec 89		IN PRIVATE *Parlophone R 6234*	14	10 wks
26 May 90		REPUTATION *Parlophone R 6253*	38	6 wks
24 Nov 90		ARRESTED BY YOU *Parlophone R 6266*	70	2 wks

* Pet Shop Boys and Dusty Springfield

See also Springfields.

Rick SPRINGFIELD *Australia, male vocalist*   **13 wks**

| 14 Jan 84 | HUMAN TOUCH *RCA RICK 1* | 23 | 7 wks |
| 24 Mar 84 | JESSIE'S GIRL *RCA RICK 2* | 43 | 6 wks |

SPRINGFIELDS *UK, male/female vocal/instrumental group*   **66 wks**

31 Aug 61		BREAKAWAY *Philips BF 1168*	31	8 wks
16 Nov 61		BAMBINO *Philips BF 1178*	16	11 wks
13 Dec 62	●	ISLAND OF DREAMS *Philips 326557 BF*	5	26 wks
28 Mar 63	●	SAY I WON'T BE THERE *Philips 326577 BF*	5	15 wks
25 Jul 63		COME ON HOME *Philips BF 1263*	31	6 wks

Bruce SPRINGSTEEN *US, male vocalist*   **117 wks**

22 Nov 80		HUNGRY HEART *CBS 9309*	44	4 wks
13 Jun 81		THE RIVER *CBS A 1179*	35	6 wks
26 May 84		DANCING IN THE DARK *CBS A 4436*	28	7 wks
6 Oct 84		COVER ME *CBS 4662*	38	5 wks
12 Jan 85	●	DANCING IN THE DARK (re-entry) *CBS A 4436*	4	16 wks
23 Mar 85		COVER ME (re-entry) *CBS A 4662*	16	8 wks
15 Jun 85	●	I'M ON FIRE/BORN IN THE USA *CBS A 6342*	5	12 wks
3 Aug 85		GLORY DAYS *CBS A 6375*	17	6 wks
14 Dec 85	●	SANTA CLAUS IS COMIN' TO TOWN/MY HOMETOWN *CBS A 6773*	9	5 wks
29 Nov 86		WAR *CBS 650193 7*	18	7 wks
7 Feb 87		FIRE *CBS 650381 7*	54	2 wks
23 May 87		BORN TO RUN *CBS BRUCE 2*	16	4 wks
3 Oct 87		BRILLIANT DISGUISE *CBS 651141 7*	20	5 wks
12 Dec 87		TUNNEL OF LOVE *CBS 651295 7*	45	4 wks
18 Jun 88		TOUGHER THAN THE REST *CBS BRUCE 3*	13	8 wks
24 Sep 88		SPARE PARTS *CBS BRUCE 4*	32	3 wks
21 Mar 92		HUMAN TOUCH *Columbia 6578727*	11	5 wks
23 May 92		BETTER DAYS *Columbia 6578907*	34	3 wks
25 Jul 92		57 CHANNELS (AND NOTHIN' ON) *Columbia 6581387*	32	4 wks
24 Oct 92		LEAP OF FAITH *Columbia 6583697*	46	3 wks

SPRINGWATER *UK, male instrumentalist – Phil Cordell*   **12 wks**

| 23 Oct 71 | ● | I WILL RETURN *Polydor 2058 141* | 5 | 12 wks |

SPYRO GYRA *US, male instrumental group*   **10 wks**

| 21 Jul 79 | MORNING DANCE *Infinity INF 111* | 17 | 10 wks |

SQUADRONAIRES – *See Joan REGAN*

SQUEEZE *UK, male vocal/instrumental group*   **110 wks**

8 Apr 78		TAKE ME I'M YOURS *A & M AMS 7335*	19	9 wks
10 Jun 78		BANG BANG *A & M AMS 7360*	49	5 wks
18 Nov 78		GOODBYE GIRL *A & M AMS 7398*	63	2 wks
24 Mar 79	●	COOL FOR CATS *A & M AMS 7426*	2	11 wks
2 Jun 79	●	UP THE JUNCTION *A & M AMS 7444*	2	11 wks
8 Sep 79		SLAP AND TICKLE *A & M AMS 7466*	24	8 wks
1 Mar 80		ANOTHER NAIL IN MY HEART *A & M AMS 7507*	17	9 wks
10 May 80		PULLING MUSSELS (FROM THE SHELL) *A & M AMS 7523*	44	6 wks
16 May 81		IS THAT LOVE *A & M AMS 8129*	35	8 wks
25 Jul 81		TEMPTED *A & M AMS 8147*	41	5 wks
10 Oct 81	●	LABELLED WITH LOVE *A & M AMS 8166*	4	10 wks
24 Apr 82		BLACK COFFEE IN BED *A & M AMS 8219*	51	4 wks
23 Oct 82		ANNIE GET YOUR GUN *A & M AMS 8259*	43	4 wks
15 Jun 85		LAST TIME FOREVER *A & M AM 255*	45	5 wks
8 Aug 87		HOURGLASS *A & M AM 400*	16	10 wks
17 Oct 87		TRUST ME TO OPEN MY MOUTH *A & M AM 412*	72	1 wk
25 Apr 92		COOL FOR CATS (re-issue) *A & M AM 860*	62	2 wks

Billy SQUIER *US, male vocalist*   **3 wks**

| 3 Oct 81 | THE STROKE *Capitol CL 214* | 52 | 3 wks |

Dorothy SQUIRES *UK, female vocalist*   **56 wks**

5 Jun 53	I'M WALKING BEHIND YOU *Polygon P 1068*	12	1 wk
24 Aug 61	SAY IT WITH FLOWERS *Columbia DB 4665 **	23	10 wks
20 Sep 69	FOR ONCE IN MY LIFE *President PT 267*	24	10 wks
20 Dec 69	FOR ONCE IN MY LIFE (re-entry) *President PT 267*	48	1 wk
21 Feb 70	TILL *President PT 281*	25	10 wks
9 May 70	TILL (re-entry) *President PT 281*	48	1 wk
8 Aug 70	MY WAY *President PT 305*	25	5 wks
19 Sep 70	MY WAY (re-entry) *President PT 305*	34	8 wks
28 Nov 70	MY WAY (2nd re-entry) *President PT 305*	25	10 wks

* Dorothy Squires and Russ Conway

Jim STAFFORD *US, male vocalist*   **16 wks**

| 27 Apr 74 | SPIDERS AND SNAKES *MGM 2006 374* | 14 | 8 wks |
| 6 Jul 74 | MY GIRL BILL *MGM 2006 423* | 20 | 8 wks |

Jo STAFFORD *US, female vocalist*   **28 wks**

14 Nov 52	★	YOU BELONG TO ME *Columbia DB 3152*	1	19 wks
19 Dec 52		JAMBALAYA *Columbia DB 3169*	11	2 wks
7 May 54	●	MAKE LOVE TO ME *Philips PB 233*	8	1 wk
9 Dec 55		SUDDENLY THERE'S A VALLEY *Philips PB 509*	12	5 wks
3 Feb 56		SUDDENLY THERE'S A VALLEY (re-entry) *Philips PB 509*	19	1 wk

Eunice Wayman found
fame as NINA
SIMONE.

Right: The only
British hit by
BOBBY SHERMAN
was the last of his four
American top ten suc-
cesses.

FRANK SINATRA
AND SAMMY DAVIS
JR. (left and centre),
chart partners in 1962-
63, are joined by
famous friends (left to
right: Dean Martin,
Peter Lawford and Joey
Bishop).

Cartoonist Matt
Groening's creations
THE SIMPSONS are
shown at the 1990
Hollywood Christmas
parade.

Terry STAFFORD US, male vocalist — 9 wks

7 May 64	SUSPICION London HLU 9871	31	9 wks

STAIFFI and his MUSTAFAS
France, male vocal/instrumental group — 1 wk

28 Jul 60	MUSTAFA Pye International 7N 25057	43	1 wk

Frank STALLONE US, male vocalist — 2 wks

22 Oct 83	FAR FROM OVER RSO 95	68	2 wks

STAMFORD BRIDGE UK, male vocal group — 1 wk

16 May 70	CHELSEA Penny Farthing PEN 715	47	1 wk

Lisa STANSFIELD UK, female vocalst — 70 wks

25 Mar 89	PEOPLE HOLD ON Ahead Of Our Time CCUT 5 *	11	9 wks
12 Aug 89	THIS IS THE RIGHT TIME Arista 112512	13	8 wks
28 Oct 89 ★	ALL AROUND THE WORLD Arista 112693	1	14 wks
10 Feb 90 ●	LIVE TOGETHER Arista 112914	10	6 wks
12 May 90	WHAT DID I DO TO YOU (EP) Arista 113168	25	4 wks
19 Oct 91 ●	CHANGE Arista 114820	10	7 wks
21 Dec 91	ALL WOMAN Arista 115000	20	8 wks
14 Mar 92	TIME TO MAKE YOU MINE Arista 115113	14	8 wks
6 Jun 92	SET YOUR LOVING FREE Arista 74321100587	28	4 wks
19 Dec 92	SOMEDAY (I'M COMING BACK) Arista 74321123567	11†	2 wks

* Coldcut featuring Lisa Stansfield

Tracks on What Did I Do To You (EP): What Did I Do To You/My Apple Heart/Lay Me Down/Something's Happenin'.

STAPLE SINGERS US, male/female vocal group — 14 wks

10 Jun 72	I'LL TAKE YOU THERE Stax 2025 110	30	8 wks
8 Jun 74	IF YOU'RE READY (COME GO WITH ME) Stax 2025 224	34	6 wks

Cyril STAPLETON UK, orchestra — 27 wks

27 May 55	ELEPHANT TANGO Decca F 10488	20	2 wks
1 Jul 55	ELEPHANT TANGO (re-entry) Decca F 10488	20	1 wk
22 Jul 55	ELEPHANT TANGO (2nd re-entry) Decca F 10488	19	1 wk
23 Sep 55 ●	BLUE STAR (THE MEDIC THEME) Decca F 10559 *	2	12 wks
6 Apr 56	THE ITALIAN THEME Decca F 10703	18	2 wks
1 Jun 56	THE HAPPY WHISTLER Decca F 10735 **	22	4 wks
19 Jul 57	FORGOTTEN DREAMS Decca F 10912	27	5 wks

* Cyril Stapleton Orchestra featuring Julie Dawn ** Cyril Stapleton Orchestra featuring Desmond Lane, penny whistle

STARDUST Sweden, male/female vocal/instrumental group — 3 wks

8 Oct 77	ARIANA Satril SAT 120	42	3 wks

Alvin STARDUST UK, male vocalist — 119 wks

3 Nov 73 ●	MY COO-CA-CHOO Magnet MAG 1	2	21 wks
16 Feb 74 ★	JEALOUS MIND Magnet MAG 5	1	11 wks
4 May 74 ●	RED DRESS Magnet MAG 8	7	8 wks
31 Aug 74 ●	YOU YOU YOU Magnet MAG 13	6	10 wks
30 Nov 74 ●	TELL ME WHY Magnet MAG 19	16	10 wks
1 Feb 75	GOOD LOVE CAN NEVER DIE Magnet MAG 21	11	9 wks
12 Jul 75	SWEET CHEATIN' RITA Magnet MAG 32	37	4 wks
5 Sep 81 ●	PRETEND Stiff BUY 124	4	10 wks
21 Nov 81	A WONDERFUL TIME UP THERE Stiff BUY 132	56	8 wks
5 May 84 ●	I FEEL LIKE BUDDY HOLLY Chrysalis CHS 2784	7	11 wks
27 Oct 84 ●	I WON'T RUN AWAY Chrysalis CHS 2829	7	13 wks
15 Dec 84	SO NEAR TO CHRISTMAS Chrysalis CHS 2835	29	4 wks
23 Mar 85	GOT A LITTLE HEARTACHE Chrysalis CHS 2856	55	2 wks

Alvin started his career as Shane Fenton. See also Shane Fenton and the Fentones.

STARGARD US, female vocal group — 14 wks

28 Jan 78	THEME FROM 'WHICH WAY IS UP' MCA 346	19	7 wks
15 Apr 78	LOVE IS SO EASY MCA 354	45	1 wk
9 Sep 78	WHAT YOU WAITING FOR MCA 382	39	6 wks

STARGAZERS UK, male vocal/instrumental group — 50 wks

13 Feb 53	BROKEN WINGS Decca F 10047	11	1 wk
27 Feb 53 ★	BROKEN WINGS (re-entry) Decca F 10047	1	11 wks
19 Feb 54 ★	I SEE THE MOON Decca F 10213	1	15 wks
9 Apr 54	HAPPY WANDERER Decca F 10259	12	1 wk
4 Mar 55	SOMEBODY Decca F 10437	20	1 wk
3 Jun 55	CRAZY OTTO RAG Decca F 10523	18	3 wks
9 Sep 55 ●	CLOSE THE DOOR Decca F 10594	6	9 wks
11 Nov 55 ●	TWENTY TINY FINGERS Decca F 10626	4	11 wks
22 Jun 56	HOT DIGGITY Decca F 10731	28	1 wk

See also Dickie Valentine.

STARGAZERS UK, male vocal/instrumental group — 3 wks

6 Feb 82	GROOVE BABY GROOVE (EP) Epic EPC A 1924	56	3 wks

Tracks on Groove Baby Groove EP: Groove Baby Groove/Jump Around/La Rock 'N' Roll (Quelques Uns A La Lune)/Red Light Green Light.

STARJETS UK, male vocal/instrumental group — 5 wks

8 Sep 79	WAR STORIES Epic EPC 7770	51	5 wks

STARLAND VOCAL BAND
US, male/female vocal group — 10 wks

7 Aug 76	AFTERNOON DELIGHT RCA 2716	18	10 wks

STARLIGHT Italy, male instrumental/production group — 11 wks

19 Aug 89 ●	NUMERO UNO Citybeat CBE 742	9	11 wks

STARLITERS – See Joey DEE and the STARLITERS

Edwin STARR US, male vocalist — 68 wks

12 May 66	STOP HER ON SIGHT (SOS) Polydor BM 56 702	35	8 wks
18 Aug 66	HEADLINE NEWS Polydor 56 717	39	3 wks
11 Dec 68	STOP HER ON SIGHT (SOS)/HEADLINE NEWS (re-issues) Polydor 56 753	11	11 wks
13 Sep 69	25 MILES Tamla Motown TMG 672	36	6 wks
24 Oct 70 ●	WAR Tamla Motown TMG 754	3	12 wks
20 Feb 71	STOP THE WAR NOW Tamla Motown TMG 764	33	1 wk
27 Jan 79 ●	CONTACT 20th Century BTC 2396	6	12 wks
26 May 79 ●	H.A.P.P.Y. RADIO RCA TC 2408	9	11 wks
1 Jun 85	IT AIN'T FAIR Hippodrome HIP 101	56	4 wks

Headline News not listed with SOS from 22 Jan 69 to 19 Feb 69.

Freddie STARR UK, male vocalist — 14 wks

23 Feb 74 ●	IT'S YOU Tiffany 6121 501	9	10 wks
20 Dec 75	WHITE CHRISTMAS Thunderbird THE 102	41	4 wks

Kay STARR US, female vocalist — 58 wks

5 Dec 52	★	COMES A-LONG A-LOVE Capitol CL 13808	1	16 wks
24 Apr 53	●	SIDE BY SIDE Capitol CL 13871	7	4 wks
19 Mar 54	●	CHANGING PARTNERS Capitol CL 14050	4	14 wks
15 Oct 54		AM I A TOY OR A TREASURE Capitol CL 14151	17	3 wks
12 Nov 54		AM I A TOY OR A TREASURE (re-entry) Capitol CL 14151	20	1 wk
17 Feb 56	★	ROCK AND ROLL WALTZ HMV POP 168	1	20 wks

Ringo STARR UK, male vocalist — 56 wks

17 Apr 71	●	IT DON'T COME EASY Apple R 5898	4	11 wks
1 Apr 72	●	BACK OFF BOOGALOO Apple R 5944	2	10 wks
27 Oct 73	●	PHOTOGRAPH Apple R 5992	8	13 wks
23 Feb 74	●	YOU'RE SIXTEEN Apple R 5995	4	10 wks
30 Nov 74		ONLY YOU Apple R 6000	28	11 wks
6 Jun 92		WEIGHT OF THE WORLD Private Music 115392	74	1 wk

STARSHIP US, female/male vocal/instrumental group — 41 wks

26 Jan 80		JANE Grunt FB 1750 *	21	9 wks
16 Nov 85		WE BUILT THIS CITY RCA PB 49929	12	12 wks
8 Feb 86		SARA RCA PB 49893	66	3 wks
11 Apr 87	★	NOTHING'S GONNA STOP US NOW Grunt FB 49757	1	17 wks

* Jefferson Starship

STARSOUND — 37 wks
Holland, producer Jaap Eggermont with male/female session singers

18 Apr 81	●	STARS ON 45 CBS A 1102	2	14 wks
4 Jul 81	●	STARS ON 45 VOL.2 CBS A 1407	2	10 wks
19 Sep 81		STARS ON 45 VOL.3 CBS A 1521	17	6 wks
27 Feb 82		STARS ON STEVIE CBS A 2041	14	7 wks

STARTRAX UK, male/female session group — 8 wks

1 Aug 81		STARTRAX CLUB DISCO Picksy KSY 1001	18	8 wks

STARTURN ON 45 (PINTS) UK, male vocal group — 9 wks

24 Oct 81		STARTURN ON 45 (PINTS) V Tone V TONE 003	45	4 wks
30 Apr 88		PUMP UP THE BITTER Pacific DRINK 1	12	5 wks

STARVATION — 6 wks
Multi-national, male/female vocal/instrumental charity assembly

9 Mar 85		STARVATION/TAM-TAM POUR L'ETHIOPE Zarjazz JAZZ 3	33	6 wks

STATLER BROTHERS US, male vocal group — 4 wks

24 Feb 66		FLOWERS ON THE WALL CBS 201976	38	4 wks

Candi STATON US, female vocalist — 58 wks

29 May 76	●	YOUNG HEARTS RUN FREE Warner Bros. K 16730	2	13 wks
18 Sep 76		DESTINY Warner Bros. K 16806	41	4 wks
23 Jul 77	●	NIGHTS ON BROADWAY Warner Bros. K 16972	6	12 wks
3 Jun 78		HONEST I DO LOVE YOU Warner Bros. K 17164	48	5 wks
24 Apr 82		SUSPICIOUS MINDS Sugarhill SH 112	31	9 wks
31 May 86		YOUNG HEARTS RUN FREE (re-mix) Warner Bros. W 8680	47	5 wks
2 Feb 91	●	YOU GOT THE LOVE Truelove TLOVE 7001 *	4	11 wks

* Source featuring Candi Staton

STATUS IV US, male vocal group — 3 wks

9 Jul 83		YOU AIN'T REALLY DOWN TMT TMT 4	56	3 wks

STATUS QUO UK, male vocal/instrumental group — 394 wks

24 Jan 68	●	PICTURES OF MATCHSTICK MEN Pye 7N 17449	7	12 wks
21 Aug 68	●	ICE IN THE SUN Pye 7N 17581	8	12 wks
28 May 69		ARE YOU GROWING TIRED OF MY LOVE Pye 7N 17728	46	2 wks
18 Jun 69		ARE YOU GROWING TIRED OF MY LOVE (re-entry) Pye 7N 17728	50	1 wk
2 May 70		DOWN THE DUSTPIPE Pye 7N 17907	12	17 wks
7 Nov 70		IN MY CHAIR Pye 7N 17998	21	14 wks
13 Jan 73	●	PAPER PLANE Vertigo 6059 071	8	11 wks
14 Apr 73		MEAN GIRL Pye 7N 45229	20	11 wks
8 Sep 73	●	CAROLINE Vertigo 6059 085	5	13 wks
4 May 74	●	BREAK THE RULES Vertigo 6059 101	8	8 wks
7 Dec 74	★	DOWN DOWN Vertigo 6059 114	1	11 wks
17 May 75	●	ROLL OVER LAY DOWN Vertigo QUO 13	9	8 wks
14 Feb 76	●	RAIN Vertigo 6059 133	7	7 wks
10 Jul 76		MYSTERY SONG Vertigo 6059 146	11	9 wks
11 Dec 76	●	WILD SIDE OF LIFE Vertigo 6059 153	9	12 wks
8 Oct 77	●	ROCKIN' ALL OVER THE WORLD Vertigo 6059 184	3	16 wks
2 Sep 78		AGAIN AND AGAIN Vertigo QUO 1	13	9 wks
25 Nov 78		ACCIDENT PRONE Vertigo QUO 2	36	8 wks
22 Sep 79		WHATEVER YOU WANT Vertigo 6059 242	4	9 wks
24 Nov 79		LIVING ON AN ISLAND Vertigo 6059 248	16	10 wks
11 Oct 80	●	WHAT YOU'RE PROPOSING Vertigo QUO 3	2	11 wks
6 Dec 80		LIES/DON'T DRIVE MY CAR Vertigo QUO 4	11	10 wks
28 Feb 81	●	SOMETHING 'BOUT YOU BABY I LIKE Vertigo QUO 5	9	7 wks
28 Nov 81	●	ROCK 'N' ROLL Vertigo QUO 6	8	11 wks
27 Mar 82		DEAR JOHN Vertigo QUO 7	10	8 wks
12 Jun 82		SHE DON'T FOOL ME Vertigo QUO 8	36	5 wks
30 Oct 82		CAROLINE (LIVE AT THE N.E.C.) Vertigo QUO 10	13	7 wks
10 Sep 83	●	OL' RAG BLUES Vertigo QUO 11	9	8 wks
5 Nov 83		A MESS OF THE BLUES Vertigo QUO 12	15	6 wks
10 Dec 83	●	MARGUERITA TIME Vertigo QUO 14	3	11 wks
19 May 84		GOING DOWN TOWN TONIGHT Vertigo QUO 15	20	6 wks
27 Oct 84	●	THE WANDERER Vertigo QUO 16	7	11 wks
17 May 86	●	ROLLIN' HOME Vertigo QUO 18	9	6 wks
26 Jul 86		RED SKY Vertigo QUO 19	19	8 wks
4 Oct 86	●	IN THE ARMY NOW Vertigo QUO 20	2	14 wks
6 Dec 86		DREAMIN' Vertigo QUO 21	15	8 wks
26 Mar 88		AIN'T COMPLAINING Vertigo QUO 22	19	6 wks
21 May 88		WHO GETS THE LOVE Vertigo QUO 23	34	4 wks
20 Aug 88		RUNNING ALL OVER THE WORLD Vertigo QUAID 1	17	6 wks
3 Dec 88	●	BURNING BRIDGES (ON AND OFF AND ON AGAIN) Vertigo QUO 25	5	10 wks
28 Oct 89		NOT AT ALL Vertigo QUO 26	50	2 wks
29 Sep 90	●	THE ANNIVERSARY WALTZ - PART 1 Vertigo QUO 28	2	9 wks
15 Dec 90		THE ANNIVERSARY WALTZ - PART 2 Vertigo QUO 29	16	10 wks
7 Sep 91		CAN'T GIVE YOU MORE Vertigo QUO 30	37	3 wks
18 Jan 92		ROCK 'TIL YOU DROP Vertigo QUO 32	38	3 wks
10 Oct 92		ROADHOUSE MEDLEY (ANNIVERSARY WALTZ PART 25) Polydor QUO 33	21	4 wks

Don't Drive My Car listed from 20 Dec 80 only. Running All Over The World is a re-recorded version of Rockin' All Over The World, with a slightly changed lyric, released to promote the Race Against Time of 28 Aug 88.

STEALER'S WHEEL UK, male vocal/instrumental group — 22 wks

26 May 73	●	STUCK IN THE MIDDLE WITH YOU A & M AMS 7036	8	10 wks

| 1 Sep 73 | **EVERYTHING'L TURN OUT FINE** *A & M AMS 7079* ....**33** | 6 wks |
| 26 Jan 74 | **STAR** *A & M AMS 7094* ....**25** | 6 wks |

STEAM US, *male vocal/instrumental group*   **14 wks**

| 31 Jan 70 ● | **NA NA HEY HEY KISS HIM GOODBYE** *Fontana TF 1058* ....**9** | 14 wks |

Anthony STEEL and the RADIO REVELLERS UK, *male vocalist/male instrumental group*   **6 wks**

| 10 Sep 54 | **WEST OF ZANZIBAR** *Polygon P 1114* ....**11** | 6 wks |

STEEL PULSE UK, *male vocal/instrumental group*   **12 wks**

1 Apr 78	**KU KLUX KLAN** *Island WIP 6428* **41**	4 wks
8 Jul 78	**PRODIGAL SON** *Island WIP 6449* **35**	6 wks
23 Jun 79	**SOUND SYSTEM** *Island WIP 6490* **71**	2 wks

Tommy STEELE UK, *male vocalist*   **145 wks**

26 Oct 56	**ROCK WITH THE CAVEMAN** *Decca F 10795* **13**	4 wks
30 Nov 56	**ROCK WITH THE CAVEMAN (re-entry)** *Decca F 10795* **23**	1 wk
14 Dec 56 ★	**SINGING THE BLUES** *Decca F 10819* **1**	13 wks
15 Feb 57	**KNEE DEEP IN THE BLUES** *Decca F 10849* ...**15**	9 wks
19 Apr 57	**SINGING THE BLUES (re-entry)** *Decca F 10819* ..**24**	1 wk
3 May 57	**BUTTERFINGERS** *Decca F 10877* **25**	1 wk
17 May 57 ●	**BUTTERFINGERS (re-entry)** *Decca F 10877* **8**	17 wks
17 May 57	**SINGING THE BLUES (2nd re-entry)** *Decca F 10849* ...**29**	1 wk
16 Aug 57	**WATER WATER/HANDFUL OF SONGS** *Decca F 10923* **5**	16 wks
30 Aug 57	**SHIRALEE** *Decca F 10896* **11**	4 wks
22 Nov 57	**HEY YOU** *Decca F 10941* **28**	1 wk
13 Dec 57	**WATER WATER/HANDFUL OF SONGS (re-entry)** *Decca F 10923* **28**	1 wk
7 Mar 58 ●	**NAIROBI** *Decca F 10991* **3**	11 wks
25 Apr 58	**HAPPY GUITAR** *Decca F 10976* **20**	5 wks
18 Jul 58	**THE ONLY MAN ON THE ISLAND** *Decca F 11041* ...**16**	8 wks
14 Nov 58 ●	**COME ON LET'S GO** *Decca F 11072* **10**	13 wks
14 Aug 59	**TALLAHASSEE LASSIE** *Decca F 11152* **16**	4 wks
28 Aug 59	**GIVE GIVE GIVE** *Decca F 11152* **28**	5 wks
25 Sep 59	**TALLAHASSEE LASSIE (re-entry)** *Decca F 11152* ..**25**	1 wk
4 Dec 59 ●	**LITTLE WHITE BULL** *Decca F 11177* **6**	12 wks
10 Mar 60	**LITTLE WHITE BULL (re-entry)** *Decca F 11177* ...**30**	5 wks
23 Jun 60 ●	**WHAT A MOUTH** *Decca F 11245* **5**	11 wks
29 Dec 60	**MUST BE SANTA** *Decca F 11299* **40**	1 wk
17 Aug 61	**WRITING ON THE WALL** *Decca F 11372* **30**	5 wks

Handful Of Songs *listed together with* Water Water *from week of 23 Aug 57. See also Various Artists (EPs & LPs) - All Star Hit Parade No.2.*

STEELEYE SPAN UK, *male/female vocal/instrumental group*   **18 wks**

| 8 Dec 73 | **GAUDETE** *Chrysalis CHS 2007* ....**14** | 9 wks |
| 15 Nov 75 ● | **ALL AROUND MY HAT** *Chrysalis CHS 2078* ......**5** | 9 wks |

STEELY DAN US, *male vocal/instrumental group*   **21 wks**

30 Aug 75	**DO IT AGAIN** *ABC 4075* **39**	4 wks
11 Dec 76	**HAITIAN DIVORCE** *ABC 4152* **17**	9 wks
29 Jul 78	**FM (NO STATIC AT ALL)** *MCA 374* **49**	4 wks
2 Sep 78	**FM (NO STATIC AT ALL) (re-entry)** *MCA 374* **75**	1 wk
10 Mar 79	**RIKKI DON'T LOSE THAT NUMBER** *ABC 4241* ...**58**	3 wks

Jim STEINMAN US, *male vocalist*   **9 wks**

| 4 Jul 81 | **ROCK 'N' ROLL DREAMS COME THROUGH** *Epic EPC A 1236* * ....**52** | 7 wks |

| 23 Jun 84 | **TONIGHT IS WHAT IT MEANS TO BE YOUNG** *MCA MCA 889* * * ....**67** | 2 wks |

* Jim Steinman, vocals by Rory Dodd * * Jim Steinman and Fire Inc.

STEINSKI and MASS MEDIA   **2 wks**
US, *male producer and rapper*

| 31 Jan 87 | **WE'LL BE RIGHT BACK** *Fourth & Broadway BRW 59* ....**63** | 2 wks |

Mike STEIPHENSON – *See BURUNDI STEIPHENSON BLACK*

Doreen STEPHENS – *See Billy COTTON and his BAND*

Martin STEPHENSON and the DAINTEES   **7 wks**
UK, *male vocal/instrumental group*

8 Nov 86	**BOAT TO BOLIVIA** *Kitchenware SL 27* **70**	2 wks
17 Jan 87	**TROUBLE TOWN** *Kitchenware SK 13* * **58**	3 wks
27 Jun 92	**BIG SKY NEW LIGHT** *Kitchenware SK 57* **71**	2 wks

* Daintees

STEPPENWOLF US/Canada, *male vocal/instrumental group*   **9 wks**

| 11 Jun 69 | **BORN TO BE WILD** *Stateside SS 8017* ....**30** | 7 wks |
| 9 Aug 69 | **BORN TO BE WILD (re-entry)** *Stateside SS 8017* ...**50** | 2 wks |

STEREO MC'S UK, *male rap group*   **14 wks**

29 Sep 90	**ELEVATE MY MIND** *Fourth & Broadway BRW 186* ...**74**	1 wk
9 Mar 91	**LOST IN MUSIC** *Fourth & Broadway BRW 198* **46**	3 wks
26 Sep 92	**CONNECTED** *Fourth & Broadway BRW 262* **18**	6 wks
5 Dec 92	**STEP IT UP** *Fourth & Broadway BRW 266* ....**12**†	4 wks

STETASONIC US, *male rap group*   **2 wks**

| 24 Sep 88 | **TALKIN' ALL THAT JAZZ** *Breakout USA 640* ...**73** | 2 wks |

STEVE and EYDIE – *See Steve LAWRENCE; Eydie GORMÉ*

April STEVENS – *See Nino TEMPO and April STEVENS*

Cat STEVENS UK, *male vocalist*   **96 wks**

20 Oct 66	**I LOVE MY DOG** *Deram DM 102* **28**	7 wks
12 Jan 67 ●	**MATTHEW AND SON** *Deram DM 110* **2**	10 wks
30 Mar 67 ●	**I'M GONNA GET ME A GUN** *Deram DM 118* **6**	10 wks
2 Aug 67	**A BAD NIGHT** *Deram DM 140* **20**	8 wks
20 Dec 67	**KITTY** *Deram DM 156* **47**	1 wk
27 Jun 70 ●	**LADY D'ARBANVILLE** *Island WIP 6086* **8**	13 wks
28 Aug 71	**MOON SHADOW** *Island WIP 6092* **22**	11 wks
1 Jan 72 ●	**MORNING HAS BROKEN** *Island WIP 6121* **9**	13 wks
9 Dec 72	**CAN'T KEEP IT IN** *Island WIP 6152* **13**	12 wks
24 Aug 74	**ANOTHER SATURDAY NIGHT** *Island WIP 6206* ...**19**	8 wks
2 Jul 77	**(REMEMBER THE DAYS OF THE) OLD SCHOOL YARD** *Island WIP 6387* **44**	3 wks

Connie STEVENS US, *female vocalist*   **20 wks**

5 May 60 ●	**SIXTEEN REASONS** *Warner Bros. WB 3* **9**	11 wks
5 May 60	**KOOKIE KOOKIE (LEND ME YOUR COMB)** *Warner Bros. WB 5* * **27**	8 wks
4 Aug 60	**SIXTEEN REASONS (re-entry)** *Warner Bros. WB 3* ...**45**	1 wk

* Edward Byrnes and Connie Stevens

Ray STEVENS US, male vocalist — **64 wks**

16 May 70 ●	EVERYTHING IS BEAUTIFUL CBS 4953	6	16 wks
13 Mar 71 ●	BRIDGET THE MIDGET (THE QUEEN OF THE BLUES) CBS 7070	2	14 wks
25 Mar 72	TURN YOUR RADIO ON CBS 7634	33	4 wks
25 May 74 ★	THE STREAK Janus 6146 201	1	12 wks
21 Jun 75 ●	MISTY Janus 6146 204	2	10 wks
27 Sep 75	INDIAN LOVE CALL Janus 6146 205	34	4 wks
5 Mar 77	IN THE MOOD Warner Bros. K 16875	31	4 wks

In The Mood features Ray Stevens not as a conventional vocalist, but as a group of chickens.

Ricky STEVENS UK, male vocalist — **7 wks**

14 Dec 61	I CRIED FOR YOU Columbia DB 4739	34	7 wks

Shakin' STEVENS UK, male vocalist — **277 wks**

16 Feb 80	HOT DOG Epic EPC 8090	24	9 wks
16 Aug 80	MARIE MARIE Epic EPC 8725	19	10 wks
28 Feb 81 ★	THIS OLE HOUSE Epic EPC 9555	1	17 wks
2 May 81 ●	YOU DRIVE ME CRAZY Epic A 1165	2	12 wks
25 Jul 81 ★	GREEN DOOR Epic A 1354	1	12 wks
10 Oct 81 ●	IT'S RAINING Epic A 1643	10	9 wks
16 Jan 82 ★	OH JULIE Epic EPC A 1742	1	10 wks
24 Apr 82 ●	SHIRLEY Epic EPC A 2087	6	6 wks
21 Aug 82	GIVE ME YOUR HEART TONIGHT Epic EPC A 2656	11	10 wks
16 Oct 82 ●	I'LL BE SATISFIED Epic EPC A 2846	10	8 wks
11 Dec 82 ●	THE SHAKIN' STEVENS EP Epic SHAKY 1	2	7 wks
23 Jul 83	IT'S LATE Epic A 3565	11	7 wks
5 Nov 83 ●	CRY JUST A LITTLE BIT Epic A 3774	3	12 wks
7 Jan 84 ●	A ROCKIN' GOOD WAY Epic A 4071 *	5	9 wks
24 Mar 84 ●	A LOVE WORTH WAITING FOR Epic A 4291	2	10 wks
15 Sep 84 ●	A LETTER TO YOU Epic A 4677	10	8 wks
24 Nov 84 ●	TEARDROPS Epic A 4882	5	9 wks
2 Mar 85	BREAKING UP MY HEART Epic A 6072	14	7 wks
12 Oct 85	LIPSTICK POWDER AND PAINT Epic A 6610	11	9 wks
7 Dec 85 ★	MERRY CHRISTMAS EVERYONE Epic A 6769	1	8 wks
8 Feb 86	TURNING AWAY Epic A 6819	15	7 wks
1 Nov 86	BECAUSE I LOVE YOU Epic SHAKY 2	14	10 wks
20 Dec 86	MERRY CHRISTMAS EVERYONE (re-entry) Epic A 6769	58	3 wks
27 Jun 87	A LITTLE BOOGIE WOOGIE (IN THE BACK OF MY MIND) Epic SHAKY 3	12	10 wks
19 Sep 87	COME SEE ABOUT ME Epic SHAKY 4	24	6 wks
28 Nov 87 ●	WHAT DO YOU WANT TO MAKE THOSE EYES AT ME FOR Epic SHAKY 5	5	8 wks
23 Jul 88	FEEL THE NEED IN ME Epic SHAKY 6	26	5 wks
15 Oct 88	HOW MANY TEARS CAN YOU HIDE Epic SHAKY 7	47	4 wks
10 Dec 88	TRUE LOVE Epic SHAKY 8	23	6 wks
18 Feb 89	JEZEBEL Epic SHAKY 9	58	2 wks
13 May 89	LOVE ATTACK Epic SHAKY 10	28	4 wks
24 Feb 90	I MIGHT Epic SHAKY 11	18	6 wks
12 May 90	YES I DO Epic SHAKY 12	60	2 wks
18 Aug 90	PINK CHAMPAGNE Epic SHAKY 13	59	2 wks
13 Oct 90	MY CUTIE CUTIE Epic SHAKY 14	75	1 wk
15 Dec 90	THE BEST CHRISTMAS OF THEM ALL Epic SHAKY 15	19	4 wks
7 Dec 91	I'LL BE HOME THIS CHRISTMAS Epic 6576507	34	5 wks
10 Oct 92	RADIO Epic 6584367 **	37	3 wks

** Shaky and Bonnie ** Shaky featuring Roger Taylor*
Tracks on The Shakin' Stevens EP: Blue Christmas/Que Sera Sera/Josephine/Lawdy Miss Clawdy.

STEVENSON'S ROCKET — **5 wks**
UK, male vocal/instrumental group

29 Nov 75	ALRIGHT BABY Magnet MAG 47	37	2 wks
20 Dec 75	ALRIGHT BABY (re-entry) Magnet MAG 47	45	3 wks

Al STEWART UK, male vocalist — **6 wks**

29 Jan 77	YEAR OF THE CAT RCA 2771	31	6 wks

Amii STEWART US, female vocalist — **61 wks**

7 Apr 79 ●	KNOCK ON WOOD Atlantic/Hansa K 11214	6	12 wks
16 Jun 79 ●	LIGHT MY FIRE/137 DISCO HEAVEN (MEDLEY) Atlantic/Hansa K 11278	5	11 wks
3 Nov 79	JEALOUSY Atlantic/Hansa K 11386	58	3 wks
19 Jan 80	THE LETTER/PARADISE BIRD Atlantic/Hansa K 11424	39	4 wks
19 Jul 80	MY GUY - MY GIRL (MEDLEY) Atlantic/Hansa K 11550 *	39	5 wks
29 Dec 84	FRIENDS RCA 471	12	11 wks
17 Aug 85 ●	KNOCK ON WOOD/LIGHT MY FIRE (re-mix) Sedition EDIT 3303	7	12 wks
25 Jan 86	MY GUY - MY GIRL (MEDLEY) Sedition EDIT 3310 **	63	3 wks

** Amii Stewart and Johnny Bristol ** Amii Stewart and Deon Estus*

Andy STEWART UK, male vocalist — **67 wks**

15 Dec 60	DONALD WHERE'S YOUR TROOSERS Top Rank JAR 427	37	1 wk
12 Jan 61	A SCOTTISH SOLDIER Top Rank JAR 512	19	38 wks
1 Jun 61	THE BATTLE'S O'ER Top Rank JAR 565	28	13 wks
12 Oct 61	A SCOTTISH SOLDIER (re-entry) Top Rank JAR 512	43	2 wks
12 Aug 65	DR. FINLAY HMV POP 1454	50	1 wk
26 Aug 65	DR. FINLAY (re-entry) HMV POP 1454	43	4 wks
9 Dec 89 ●	DONALD WHERE'S YOUR TROOSERS (re-issue) Stone SON 2353	4	8 wks

Billy STEWART US, male vocalist — **2 wks**

8 Sep 66	SUMMERTIME Chess CRS 8040	39	2 wks

Dave STEWART UK, male instrumentalist - keyboards — **30 wks**

14 Mar 81	WHAT BECOMES OF THE BROKEN HEARTED Stiff BROKEN 1 *	13	10 wks
19 Sep 81 ★	IT'S MY PARTY Broken BROKEN 2 **	1	13 wks
13 Aug 83	BUSY DOING NOTHING Broken BROKEN 5 **	49	4 wks
14 Jun 86	THE LOCOMOTION Broken BROKEN 8 **	70	3 wks

** Dave Stewart, guest vocals Colin Blunstone ** Dave Stewart with Barbara Gaskin*

David A. STEWART — **14 wks**
UK, male vocalist/instrumentalist - guitar

24 Feb 90 ●	LILY WAS HERE RCA ZB 43045 *	6	12 wks
18 Aug 90	JACK TALKING RCA PB 43907 **	69	2 wks

** David A. Stewart featuring Candy Dulfer ** Dave Stewart and the Spiritual Cowboys*

Jermaine STEWART US, male vocalist — **42 wks**

9 Aug 86 ●	WE DON'T HAVE TO... 10 TEN 96	2	14 wks
1 Nov 86	JODY 10 TEN 143	50	4 wks
16 Jan 88 ●	SAY IT AGAIN 10 TEN 188	7	12 wks
2 Apr 88	GET LUCKY Siren SRN 82	13	9 wks
24 Sep 88	DON'T TALK DIRTY TO ME Siren SRN 86	61	3 wks

John STEWART US, male vocalist — **6 wks**

30 Jun 79	GOLD RSO 35	43	6 wks

Rod STEWART UK, male vocalist — 393 wks

Date	Title	Peak	Wks
4 Sep 71	REASON TO BELIEVE Mercury 6052 097	19	2 wks
18 Sep 71 ★	MAGGIE MAY Mercury 6052 097	1	19 wks
12 Aug 72 ★	YOU WEAR IT WELL Mercury 6052 171	1	12 wks
18 Nov 72 ●	ANGEL /WHAT MADE MILWAUKEE FAMOUS (HAS MADE A LOSER OUT OF ME) Mercury 6052 198	4	11 wks
5 May 73	I'VE BEEN DRINKING RAK RR 4 *	27	6 wks
8 Sep 73 ●	OH NO NOT MY BABY Mercury 6052 371	6	9 wks
5 Oct 74 ●	FAREWELL — BRING IT ON HOME TO ME/YOU SEND ME Mercury 6167 033	7	7 wks
16 Aug 75 ★	SAILING Warner Bros. K 16600	1	11 wks
15 Nov 75 ●	THIS OLD HEART OF MINE Riva 1	4	9 wks
5 Jun 76 ●	TONIGHT'S THE NIGHT Riva 3	5	9 wks
21 Aug 76 ●	THE KILLING OF GEORGIE Riva 4	2	10 wks
4 Sep 76 ●	SAILING (re-entry) Warner Bros. K 16600	3	20 wks
20 Nov 76	GET BACK Riva 6	11	9 wks
4 Dec 76	MAGGIE MAY (re-entry) Mercury 6160 006	31	7 wks
23 Apr 77 ★	I DON'T WANT TO TALK ABOUT IT/FIRST CUT IS THE DEEPEST Riva 7	1	13 wks
15 Oct 77 ●	YOU'RE IN MY HEART Riva 11	3	10 wks
28 Jan 78 ●	HOTLEGS/I WAS ONLY JOKING Riva 10	5	8 wks
27 May 78 ●	OLE OLA (MULHER BRASILEIRA) Riva 15 **	4	6 wks
18 Nov 78 ★	DA YA THINK I'M SEXY? Riva 17	1	13 wks
3 Feb 79	AIN'T LOVE A BITCH Riva 18	11	8 wks
5 May 79	BLONDES (HAVE MORE FUN) Riva 19	63	3 wks
31 May 80	IF LOVING YOU IS WRONG (I DON'T WANT TO BE RIGHT) Riva 23	23	9 wks
8 Nov 80	PASSION Riva 26	17	10 wks
20 Dec 80	MY GIRL Riva 28	32	7 wks
17 Oct 81 ●	TONIGHT I'M YOURS (DON'T HURT ME) Riva 33	8	13 wks
12 Dec 81	YOUNG TURKS Riva 34	11	9 wks
27 Feb 82	HOW LONG Riva 35	41	4 wks
4 Jun 83 ★	BABY JANE Warner Bros. W 9608	1	14 wks
27 Aug 83 ●	WHAT AM I GONNA DO Warner Bros. W 9564	3	8 wks
10 Dec 83	SWEET SURRENDER Warner Bros. W 9440	23	7 wks
26 May 84	INFATUATION Warner Bros. W 9256	27	7 wks
28 Jul 84	SOME GUYS HAVE ALL THE LUCK Warner Bros. W 9204	15	10 wks
24 May 86	LOVE TOUCH Warner Bros. W 8668	27	5 wks
5 Jul 86	LOVE TOUCH (re-entry) Warner Bros. W 8668	69	3 wks
12 Jul 86 ●	EVERY BEAT OF MY HEART Warner Bros. W 8625	2	9 wks
20 Sep 86	ANOTHER HEARTACHE Warner Bros. W 8631	54	2 wks
28 Mar 87	SAILING (2nd re-entry) Warner Bros. K 16600	41	3 wks
28 May 88	LOST IN YOU Warner Bros. W 7927	21	6 wks
13 Aug 88	FOREVER YOUNG Warner Bros. W 7796	57	3 wks
6 May 89	MY HEART CAN'T TELL YOU NO Warner Bros. W 7729	49	4 wks
11 Nov 89	THIS OLD HEART OF MINE Warner Bros. W 2686 ***	51	3 wks
13 Jan 90 ●	DOWNTOWN TRAIN Warner Bros. W 2647	10	12 wks
24 Nov 90 ●	IT TAKES TWO Warner Bros. ROD 1 ****	5	8 wks
16 Mar 91 ●	RHYTHM OF MY HEART Warner Bros. W 0017	3	11 wks
15 Jun 91 ●	THE MOTOWN SONG Warner Bros. W 0030	10	8 wks
7 Sep 91	BROKEN ARROW Warner Bros. W 0059	54	3 wks
7 Mar 92	PEOPLE GET READY Epic 6577567 *	49	3 wks
18 Apr 92	YOUR SONG/BROKEN ARROW (re-issue) Warner Bros. W 0104	41	4 wks
5 Dec 92 ●	TOM TRAUBERT'S BLUES (WALTZING MATILDA) Warner Bros. W 0144	6†	4 wks

* Jeff Beck and Rod Stewart ** Rod Stewart featuring the Scottish World Cup Football Squad *** Rod Stewart featuring Ronald Isley **** Rod Stewart and Tina Turner

See also Faces; Glass Tiger; Python Lee Jackson.

STEX UK, male vocal group — 2 wks

Date	Title	Peak	Wks
19 Jan 91	STILL FEEL THE RAIN Some Bizzare SBZ 7002	63	2 wks

STIFF LITTLE FINGERS — 39 wks
UK, male vocal/instrumental group

Date	Title	Peak	Wks
29 Sep 79	STRAW DOGS Chrysalis CHS 2368	44	4 wks
16 Feb 80	AT THE EDGE Chrysalis CHS 2406	15	9 wks
24 May 80	NOBODY'S HERO/TIN SOLDIERS Chrysalis CHS 2424	36	5 wks
2 Aug 80	BACK TO FRONT Chrysalis CHS 2447	49	4 wks
28 Mar 81	JUST FADE AWAY Chrysalis CHS 2510	47	6 wks
30 May 81	SILVER LINING Chrysalis CHS 2517	68	3 wks
23 Jan 82	LISTEN EP Chrysalis CHS 2580	33	6 wks
18 Sep 82	BITS OF KIDS Chrysalis CHS 2637	73	2 wks

Tracks on Listen EP: That's When Your Blood Bumps/Two Guitars Clash/Listen/Sad-Eyed People.

Curtis STIGERS US, male vocalist — 30 wks

Date	Title	Peak	Wks
18 Jan 92 ●	I WONDER WHY Arista 114716	5	10 wks
28 Mar 92 ●	YOU'RE ALL THAT MATTERS TO ME Arista 115273	6	12 wks
11 Jul 92	SLEEPING WITH THE LIGHTS ON Arista 74321102307	53	4 wks
17 Oct 92	NEVER SAW A MIRACLE Arista 74321117257	34	4 wks

Stephen STILLS US, male vocalist — 4 wks

Date	Title	Peak	Wks
13 Mar 71	LOVE THE ONE YOU'RE WITH Atlantic 2091 046	37	4 wks

See also Crosby Stills Nash and Young.

STING UK, male vocalist — 67 wks

Date	Title	Peak	Wks
14 Aug 82	SPREAD A LITTLE HAPPINESS A & M AMS 8217	16	8 wks
8 Jun 85	IF YOU LOVE SOMEBODY SET THEM FREE A & M AM 258	26	7 wks
24 Aug 85	LOVE IS THE SEVENTH WAVE A & M AM 272	41	5 wks
19 Oct 85	FORTRESS AROUND YOUR HEART A & M AM 286	49	3 wks
7 Dec 85	RUSSIANS A & M AM 292	12	11 wks
15 Feb 86	MOON OVER BOURBON STREET A & M AM 305	44	4 wks
1 Mar 86	RUSSIANS (re-entry) A & M AM 292	71	1 wk
7 Nov 87	WE'LL BE TOGETHER A & M AM 410	41	4 wks
20 Feb 88	ENGLISHMAN IN NEW YORK A & M AM 431	51	3 wks
9 Apr 88	FRAGILE A & M AM 439	70	2 wks
11 Aug 90	ENGLISHMAN IN NEW YORK (re-mix) A & M AM 580	15	7 wks
12 Jan 91	ALL THIS TIME A & M AM 713	22	4 wks
9 Mar 91	MAD ABOUT YOU A & M AM 721	56	2 wks
4 May 91	THE SOUL CAGES A & M AM 759	57	1 wk
29 Aug 92	IT'S PROBABLY ME A & M AM 883 *	30	5 wks

* Sting with Eric Clapton

STINGERS – See B. BUMBLE and the STINGERS

Catherine STOCK UK, female vocalist — 6 wks

Date	Title	Peak	Wks
18 Oct 86	TO HAVE AND TO HOLD Sierra FED 29	17	6 wks

STOCK AITKEN WATERMAN UK, male producers — 36 wks

Date	Title	Peak	Wks
25 Jul 87	ROADBLOCK Breakout USA 611	13	9 wks
24 Oct 87 ●	MR. SLEAZE London NANA 14	3	10 wks
12 Dec 87	PACKJAMMED (WITH THE PARTY POSSE) Breakout USA 620	41	6 wks
21 May 88	ALL THE WAY MCA GOAL 1 *	64	1 wk
3 Dec 88	SS PAPARAZZI PWL PWL 22	68	2 wks
20 May 89 ★	FERRY 'CROSS THE MERSEY PWL PWL 41 **	1	7 wks

* England Football Team with the 'sound' of Stock Aitken and Waterman
** Christians, Holly Johnson, Paul McCartney, Gerry Marsden and Stock Aitken Waterman

The listed flip side of Mr. Sleaze was Love In The First Degree by Bananarama.

ROD STEWART
stands behind only
Elvis and Cliff for Most
Number One Hits by a
male soloist.

Left: SNAP sampled
Jocelyn Brown for the
title hook of 'The
Power' but didn't need
to borrow for their sec-
ond number one.

LISA STANSFIELD is
shown singing 'I Want
to Break Free' at the
Freddie Mercury
Tribute Concert at
Wembley in 1992.

Rhet STOLLER UK, male instrumentalist – guitar   8 wks

| 12 Jan 61 | CHARIOT Decca F 11302 | 26 | 8 wks |

Morris STOLOFF US, orchestra   11 wks

| 1 Jun 56 ● | MOONGLOW/THEME FROM PICNIC Brunswick 05553 | 7 | 11 wks |

R & J STONE UK/US, male/female vocal duo   9 wks

| 10 Jan 76 ● | WE DO IT RCA 2616 | 5 | 9 wks |

STONE ROSES UK, male vocal/instrumental group   57 wks

29 Jul 89	SHE BANGS THE DRUMS Silvertone ORE 6	36	3 wks
25 Nov 89 ●	WHAT THE WORLD IS WAITING FOR/FOOL'S GOLD Silvertone ORE 13	8	14 wks
6 Jan 90	SALLY CINNAMON Revolver REV 36	75	1 wk
20 Jan 90	SALLY CINNAMON (re-entry) Revolver REV 36	46	4 wks
3 Mar 90 ●	ELEPHANT STONE Silvertone ORE 1	8	6 wks
17 Mar 90	MADE OF STONE Silvertone ORE 2	4	4 wks
31 Mar 90	SHE BANGS THE DRUMS (re-entry) Silvertone ORE 6	34	3 wks
14 Jul 90 ●	ONE LOVE Silvertone ORE 17	4	7 wks
15 Sep 90	WHAT THE WORLD IS WAITING FOR/FOOL'S GOLD (re-entry) Silvertone ORE 13	22	5 wks
14 Sep 91	I WANNA BE ADORED Silvertone ORE 31	20	3 wks
11 Jan 92	WATERFALL Silvertone ORE 35	27	4 wks
11 Apr 92	I AM THE RESURRECTION Silvertone ORE 40	33	2 wks
30 May 92	FOOL'S GOLD (re-mix) Silvertone ORET 13	73	1 wk

STONEBRIDGE McGUINNESS
UK, male vocal/instrumental duo   2 wks

| 14 Jul 79 | OO-EEH BABY RCA PB 5163 | 54 | 2 wks |

STONEFREE UK, male vocalist   1 wk

| 23 May 87 | CAN'T SAY GOODBYE Ensign ENY 607 | 73 | 1 wk |

STONKERS – See HALE and PACE and the STONKERS

STOP THE VIOLENCE
US, male/female rap charity ensemble   1 wk

| 18 Feb 89 | SELF DESTRUCTION Jive BDPST 1 | 75 | 1 wk |

Axel STORDAHL – See June HUTTON and Axel STORDAHL

STORM UK, male/female vocal/instrumental group   10 wks

| 17 Nov 79 | IT'S MY HOUSE Scope SC 10 | 36 | 10 wks |

Danny STORM UK, male vocalist   4 wks

| 12 Apr 62 | HONEST I DO Piccadilly 7N 35025 | 42 | 4 wks |

Rebecca STORM UK, female vocalist   13 wks

| 13 Jul 85 | THE SHOW (THEME FROM 'CONNIE') Towerbell TVP 3 | 22 | 13 wks |

STORYVILLE JAZZ BAND – See Bob WALLIS and his STORYVILLE JAZZ BAND

Izzy STRADLIN' US, male vocalist/instrumentalist – guitar   2 wks

| 26 Sep 92 | PRESSURE DROP Geffen GFS 25 | 45 | 2 wks |

Nick STRAKER BAND   15 wks
UK, male vocal/instrumental group

| 2 Aug 80 | A WALK IN THE PARK CBS 8525 | 20 | 12 wks |
| 15 Nov 80 | LEAVING ON THE MIDNIGHT TRAIN CBS 9088 | 61 | 3 wks |

Peter STRAKER and the HANDS OF DR. TELENY UK, male vocalist and male vocal/instrumental group   4 wks

| 19 Feb 72 | THE SPIRIT IS WILLING RCA 2163 | 40 | 4 wks |

STRANGE BEHAVIOUR – See Jane KENNAWAY and STRANGE BEHAVIOUR

STRANGLERS UK, male vocal/instrumental group   194 wks

19 Feb 77	(GET A) GRIP (ON YOURSELF) United Artists UP 36211	44	4 wks
21 May 77 ●	PEACHES/GO BUDDY GO United Artists UP 36248	8	14 wks
30 Jul 77 ●	SOMETHING BETTER CHANGE/STRAIGHTEN OUT United Artists UP 36277	9	8 wks
24 Sep 77 ●	NO MORE HEROES United Artists UP 36300	8	9 wks
4 Feb 78	FIVE MINUTES United Artists UP 36350	11	9 wks
6 May 78	NICE 'N SLEAZY United Artists UP 36379	18	8 wks
12 Aug 78	WALK ON BY United Artists UP 36429	21	8 wks
18 Aug 79	DUCHESS United Artists BP 308	14	9 wks
20 Oct 79	NUCLEAR DEVICE (THE WIZARD OF AUS) United Artists BP 318	36	4 wks
1 Dec 79	DON'T BRING HARRY (EP) United Artists STR 1	41	3 wks
22 Mar 80	BEAR CAGE United Artists BP 344	36	5 wks
7 Jun 80	WHO WANTS THE WORLD United Artists BPX 355	39	4 wks
31 Jan 81	THROWN AWAY Liberty BP 383	42	4 wks
14 Nov 81	LET ME INTRODUCE YOU TO THE FAMILY United Artists BP 405	42	3 wks
9 Jan 82 ●	GOLDEN BROWN Liberty BP 407	2	12 wks
24 Apr 82	LA FOLIE Liberty BP 410	47	3 wks
24 Jul 82 ●	STRANGE LITTLE GIRL Liberty BP 412	7	9 wks
8 Jan 83 ●	EUROPEAN FEMALE Epic EPC A 2893	9	6 wks
26 Feb 83	MIDNIGHT SUMMER DREAM Epic EPC A 3167	35	4 wks
6 Aug 83	PARADISE Epic A 3387	48	3 wks
6 Oct 84	SKIN DEEP Epic A 4738	15	7 wks
1 Dec 84	NO MERCY Epic A 4921	37	7 wks
16 Feb 85	LET ME DOWN EASY Epic A 6045	48	4 wks
23 Aug 86	NICE IN NICE Epic 650057	30	5 wks
18 Oct 86	ALWAYS THE SUN Epic SOLAR 1	30	5 wks
13 Dec 86	BIG IN AMERICA Epic HUGE 1	48	6 wks
7 Mar 87	SHAKIN' LIKE A LEAF Epic SHEIK 1	58	4 wks
9 Jan 88 ●	ALL DAY AND ALL OF THE NIGHT Epic VICE 1	7	7 wks
28 Jan 89	GRIP '89 (GET A) GRIP (ON YOURSELF) (re-mix) EMI EM 84	33	3 wks
17 Feb 90	96 TEARS Epic TEARS 1	17	6 wks
21 Apr 90	SWEET SMELL OF SUCCESS Epic TEARS 2	65	2 wks
5 Jan 91	ALWAYS THE SUN (re-mix) Epic 6564307	29	5 wks
30 Mar 91	GOLDEN BROWN (re-mix) Epic 6567617	68	2 wks
22 Aug 92	HEAVEN OR HELL Psycho WOK 2025	46	2 wks

Go Buddy Go credited with Peaches from 11 Jun 77. Straighten Out credited with Something Better Change from 13 Aug 77. Tracks on Don't Bring Harry (EP): Don't Bring Harry/ Wired/Crabs (Live)/In The Shadows (Live).

STRAWBERRY SWITCHBLADE   26 wks
UK, female vocal duo

17 Nov 84 ●	SINCE YESTERDAY Korova KOW 38	5	17 wks
23 Mar 85	LET HER GO Korova KOW 39	59	5 wks
21 Sep 85	JOLENE Korova KOW 42	53	4 wks

STRAWBS UK, male vocal/instrumental group — 27 wks

28 Oct 72		LAY DOWN A & M AMS 7035 12	13 wks
27 Jan 73	●	PART OF THE UNION A & M AMS 7047 2	11 wks
6 Oct 73		SHINE ON SILVER SUN A & M AMS 7082 34	3 wks

STRAY CATS US, male vocal/instrumental group — 49 wks

29 Nov 80	●	RUNAWAY BOYS Arista SCAT 1 9	10 wks
7 Feb 81	●	ROCK THIS TOWN Arista SCAT 2 9	8 wks
25 Apr 81		STRAY CAT STRUT Arista SCAT 3 11	10 wks
20 Jun 81		THE RACE IS ON Swansong SSK 19425 * 34	6 wks
7 Nov 81		YOU DON'T BELIEVE ME Arista SCAT 4 57	1 wk
6 Aug 83		(SHE'S) SEXY AND 17 Arista SCAT 6 29	9 wks
4 Mar 89		BRING IT BACK AGAIN EMI USA MT 62 64	3 wks

* Dave Edmunds and the Stray Cats

STRAY MOB – See MC SKAT KAT and the STRAY MOB

STREETBAND UK, male vocal/instrumental group — 6 wks

4 Nov 78	TOAST/HOLD ON Logo GO 325 18	6 wks

Barbra STREISAND US, female vocalist — 121 wks

20 Jan 66		SECOND HAND ROSE CBS 202025 14	13 wks
30 Jan 71		STONEY END CBS 5321 46	1 wk
13 Feb 71		STONEY END (re-entry) CBS 5321 27	10 wks
30 Mar 74		THE WAY WE WERE CBS 1915 31	4 wks
9 Apr 77	●	LOVE THEME FROM 'A STAR IS BORN' (EVERGREEN) CBS 4855 3	19 wks
25 Nov 78	●	YOU DON'T BRING ME FLOWERS CBS 6803 * 5	12 wks
3 Nov 79	●	NO MORE TEARS (ENOUGH IS ENOUGH) Casablanca CAN 174/ CBS 8000 ** 3	13 wks
4 Oct 80	★	WOMAN IN LOVE CBS 8966 1	16 wks
6 Dec 80		GUILTY CBS 9315 *** 34	10 wks
30 Jan 82		COMIN' IN AND OUT OF YOUR LIFE CBS A 1789 66	3 wks
20 Mar 82		MEMORY CBS A 1903 34	6 wks
5 Nov 88		TILL I LOVED YOU (LOVE THEME FROM 'GOYA') CBS BARB 2 **** 16	7 wks
7 Mar 92		PLACES THAT BELONG TO YOU Columbia 6577947 17	5 wks

* Barbra and Neil ** Donna Summer and Barbra Streisand *** Barbra Streisand and Barry Gibb **** Barbra Streisand and Don Johnson

No More Tears (Enough Is Enough) was released simultaneously on two different labels, a 7 inch single on Casablanca and a 12 inch on CBS.

STRESS UK, male vocal/instrumental group — 1 wk

13 Oct 90	BEAUTIFUL PEOPLE Eternal YZ 495 74	1 wk

STRETCH UK, male vocal/instrumental group — 9 wks

8 Nov 75	WHY DID YOU DO IT Anchor ANC 1021 16	9 wks

STRIKERS US, male vocal/instrumental group — 5 wks

6 Jun 81	BODY MUSIC Epic EPC A 1290 45	5 wks

STRING-A-LONGS US, male instrumental group — 16 wks

23 Feb 61	●	WHEELS London HLU 9278 8	16 wks

STRINGS OF LOVE
Italy, male/female vocal/instrumental group — 2 wks

3 Mar 90	NOTHING HAS BEEN PROVED Breakout USA 688 59	2 wks

Joe STRUMMER UK, male vocalist — 1 wk

2 Aug 86	LOVE KILLS CBS A 7244 69	1 wk

Chad STUART and Jeremy CLYDE — 7 wks
UK, male vocal duo

28 Nov 63	YESTERDAY'S GONE Ember EMB S 180 37	7 wks

STUMP UK, male vocal/instrumental group — 1 wk

13 Aug 88	CHARLTON HESTON Ensign ENY 614 72	1 wk

STUTZ BEARCATS and the Denis KING ORCHESTRA UK, male/female vocal group with orchestra — 6 wks

24 Apr 82	THE SONG THAT I SING (THEME FROM 'WE'LL MEET AGAIN') Multi-Media Tapes MMT 6 36	6 wks

STYLE COUNCIL UK, male vocal/instrumental duo — 103 wks

19 Mar 83	●	SPEAK LIKE A CHILD Polydor TSC 1 4	8 wks
28 May 83		MONEY GO ROUND (PART 1) Polydor TSC 2 11	6 wks
13 Aug 83		LONG HOT SUMMER/PARIS MATCH Polydor TSC 3 3	9 wks
20 Aug 83		MONEY GO ROUND (PART 1) (re-entry) Polydor TSC 2 74	1 wk
19 Nov 83		SOLID BOND IN YOUR HEART Polydor TSC 4 11	8 wks
18 Feb 84	●	MY EVER CHANGING MOODS Polydor TSC 5 5	7 wks
26 May 84	●	GROOVIN' (YOU'RE THE BEST THING)/BIG BOSS GROOVE Polydor TSC 6 5	8 wks
13 Oct 84		SHOUT TO THE TOP Polydor TSC 7 7	8 wks
11 May 85	●	WALLS COME TUMBLING DOWN! Polydor TSC 8 6	7 wks
6 Jul 85		COME TO MILTON KEYNES Polydor TSC 9 23	5 wks
28 Sep 85		THE LODGERS Polydor TSC 10 13	6 wks
5 Apr 86		HAVE YOU EVER HAD IT BLUE Polydor CINE 1 14	6 wks
17 Jan 87	●	IT DIDN'T MATTER Polydor TSC 12 9	5 wks
14 Mar 87		WAITING Polydor TSC 13 52	3 wks
31 Oct 87		WANTED Polydor TSC 14 20	4 wks
28 May 88		LIFE AT A TOP PEOPLE'S HEALTH FARM Polydor TSC 15 28	3 wks
23 Jul 88		HOW SHE THREW IT ALL AWAY (EP) Polydor TSC 16 41	2 wks
18 Feb 89		PROMISED LAND Polydor TSC 17 27	5 wks
27 May 89		LONG HOT SUMMER 89 (re-mix) Polydor LHS 1 48	2 wks

Paris Match was listed with Long Hot Summer from 3 Sep 83. Tracks on How She Threw It All Away EP: How She Threw It All Away/Love The First Time/Long Hot Summer/I Do Like To Be B-Side The A-Side. The version of Long Hot Summer on the EP is a re-recording of their third hit.

STYLISTICS US, male vocal group — 143 wks

24 Jun 72		BETCHA BY GOLLY WOW Avco 6105 011 13	12 wks
4 Nov 72	●	I'M STONE IN LOVE WITH YOU Avco 6105 015 9	10 wks
17 Mar 73		BREAK UP TO MAKE UP Avco 6105 020 34	5 wks
30 Jun 73		PEEK-A-BOO Avco 6105 023 35	6 wks
19 Jan 74	●	ROCKIN' ROLL BABY Avco 6105 026 6	9 wks
13 Jul 74	●	YOU MAKE ME FEEL BRAND NEW Avco 6105 028 2	14 wks
19 Oct 74	●	LET'S PUT IT ALL TOGETHER Avco 6105 032 9	9 wks
25 Jan 75		STAR ON A TV SHOW Avco 6105 035 12	8 wks
10 May 75	●	SING BABY SING Avco 6105 036 3	10 wks
26 Jul 75	★	CAN'T GIVE YOU ANYTHING (BUT MY LOVE) Avco 6105 039 1	11 wks
15 Nov 75	●	NA NA IS THE SADDEST WORD Avco 6105 041 5	10 wks
14 Feb 76	●	FUNKY WEEKEND Avco 6105 044 10	7 wks
24 Apr 76	●	CAN'T HELP FALLING IN LOVE Avco 6105 050 4	7 wks
7 Aug 76	●	16 BARS H & L 6105 059 7	9 wks
27 Nov 76		YOU'LL NEVER GET TO HEAVEN EP H & L STYL 001 24	9 wks
26 Mar 77		7000 DOLLARS AND YOU H & L 6105 073 24	7 wks

Tracks on You'll Never Get To Heaven EP: You'll Never Get To Heaven/Country Living/You Are Beautiful/The Miracle.

285

STYX US, male vocal/instrumental group — 18 wks

5 Jan 80 ●	BABE A & M AMS 7489	6	10 wks
24 Jan 81	THE BEST OF TIMES A & M AMS 8102	42	5 wks
18 Jun 83	DON'T LET IT END A & M AM 120	56	3 wks

SUBSONIC 2 UK, male rap duo — 3 wks

13 Jul 91	THE UNSUNG HEROES OF HIP HOP Unity 6577947	63	3 wks

SUEDE UK, male vocal/instrumental group — 5 wks

23 May 92	THE DROWNERS/TO THE BIRDS Nude NUD 1S	49	2 wks
26 Sep 92	METAL MICKEY Nude NUD 3S	17	3 wks

SUENO LATINO featuring Carolina DAMAS Italy, male production duo and female vocalist — 5 wks

23 Sep 89	SUENO LATINO BCM BCM 323	47	5 wks

SUGAR UK, male vocal/instrumental group — 1 wk

31 Oct 92	A GOOD IDEA Creation CRE 143	65	1 wk

SUGAR CANE US, male/female vocal group — 5 wks

30 Sep 78	MONTEGO BAY Ariola Hansa AHA 524	54	5 wks

SUGARCUBES Iceland, male/female vocal/instrumental group — 22 wks

14 Nov 87	BIRTHDAY One Little Indian TP 7	65	3 wks
30 Jan 88	COLD SWEAT One Little Indian 7TP 9	56	4 wks
16 Apr 88	DEUS One Little Indian 7TP 10	51	3 wks
3 Sep 88	BIRTHDAY One Little Indian 7TP 11	65	3 wks
16 Sep 89	REGINA One Little Indian 26TP7	55	2 wks
11 Jan 92	HIT One Little Indian 62 TP7	17	6 wks
3 Oct 92	BIRTHDAY (re-mix) One Little Indian 104 TP12	64	1 wk

7TP 11 is a re-recording of their first hit.

SUGARHILL GANG US, male rap group — 16 wks

1 Dec 79 ●	RAPPER'S DELIGHT Sugarhill SHL 101	3	11 wks
11 Sep 82	THE LOVER IN YOU Sugarhill SH 116	54	3 wks
25 Nov 89	RAPPER'S DELIGHT (re-mix) Sugarhill SHRD 0007	58	2 wks

SULTANS OF PING FC Ireland, male vocal/instrumental group — 4 wks

8 Feb 92	WHERE'S ME JUMPER Divine ATHY 01	67	2 wks
9 May 92	STUPID KID Divine ATHY 02	67	1 wk
10 Oct 92	VERONICA Divine ATHY 03	69	1 wk

Donna SUMMER US, female vocalist — 284 wks

17 Jan 76 ●	LOVE TO LOVE YOU BABY GTO GT 17	4	9 wks
29 May 76	COULD IT BE MAGIC GTO GT 60	40	7 wks
25 Dec 76	WINTER MELODY GTO GT 76	27	6 wks
9 Jul 77 ★	I FEEL LOVE GTO GT 100	1	11 wks
20 Aug 77 ●	DEEP DOWN INSIDE (THEME FROM 'THE DEEP') Casablanca CAN 111	5	10 wks
24 Sep 77	I REMEMBER YESTERDAY GTO GT 107	14	7 wks
3 Dec 77 ●	LOVE'S UNKIND GTO GT 113	3	13 wks
10 Dec 77 ●	I LOVE YOU Casablanca CAN 114	10	9 wks
25 Feb 78	RUMOUR HAS IT Casablanca CAN 122	19	8 wks
22 Apr 78	BACK IN LOVE AGAIN GTO GT 117	29	7 wks
10 Jun 78	LAST DANCE Casablanca TGIF 2	70	1 wk
24 Jun 78	LAST DANCE (re-entry) Casablanca TGIF 2	51	8 wks
14 Oct 78 ●	MACARTHUR PARK Casablanca CAN 131	5	10 wks
17 Feb 79	HEAVEN KNOWS Casablanca CAN 141	34	8 wks
12 May 79	HOT STUFF Casablanca CAN 151	11	10 wks
7 Jul 79	BAD GIRLS Casablanca CAN 155	14	10 wks
1 Sep 79	DIM ALL THE LIGHTS Casablanca CAN 162	29	9 wks
3 Nov 79 ●	NO MORE TEARS (ENOUGH IS ENOUGH) Casablanca CAN 174/ CBS 8000 *	3	13 wks
16 Feb 80	ON THE RADIO Casablanca NB 2236	32	6 wks
21 Jun 80	SUNSET PEOPLE Casablanca CAN 198	46	5 wks
27 Sep 80	THE WANDERER Warner Bros./Geffen K 79810	48	6 wks
17 Jan 81	COLD LOVE Geffen K 79183	44	3 wks
10 Jul 82	LOVE IS IN CONTROL (FINGER ON THE TRIGGER) Warner Bros. K 79302	18	11 wks
6 Nov 82	STATE OF INDEPENDENCE Warner Bros. K 79344	14	11 wks
4 Dec 82	I FEEL LOVE (re-mix) Casablanca FEEL 7	21	10 wks
5 Mar 83	THE WOMAN IN ME Warner Bros. W 9983	62	2 wks
18 Jun 83	SHE WORKS HARD FOR THE MONEY Mercury DONNA 1	25	8 wks
24 Sep 83	UNCONDITIONAL LOVE Mercury DONNA 2	14	12 wks
21 Jan 84	STOP LOOK AND LISTEN Mercury DONNA 3	57	2 wks
24 Oct 87	DINNER WITH GERSHWIN Warner Bros. U 8237	13	11 wks
23 Jan 88	ALL SYSTEMS GO WEA U 8122	54	3 wks
25 Feb 89 ●	THIS TIME I KNOW IT'S FOR REAL Warner Bros. U 7780	3	14 wks
27 May 89 ●	I DON'T WANNA GET HURT Warner Bros. U 7567	7	9 wks
26 Aug 89	LOVE'S ABOUT TO CHANGE MY HEART Warner Bros. U 7494	20	6 wks
25 Nov 89	WHEN LOVE TAKES OVER YOU WEA U 7361	72	1 wk
17 Nov 90	STATE OF INDEPENDENCE (re-issue) Warner Bros. U 2857	45	3 wks
12 Jan 91	BREAKAWAY Warner Bros. U 3308	49	4 wks
30 Nov 91	WORK THAT MAGIC Warner Bros. U 5937	74	1 wk

*Donna Summer and Barbra Streisand

No More Tears (Enough Is Enough) *was released simultaneously on two different labels, a 7 inch single on Casablanca and 12 inch on CBS. Unconditional Love features the additional vocals of Musical Youth.*

Mark SUMMERS UK, male producer — 6 wks

26 Jan 91	SUMMER'S MAGIC 4th + B'way BRW 205	27	6 wks

SUNDANCE – See DJ 'FAST' EDDIE

SUNDAYS UK, male/female vocal/instrumental group — 7 wks

11 Feb 89	CAN'T BE SURE Rough Trade RT 218	45	5 wks
3 Oct 92	GOODBYE Parlophone R 6319	27	2 wks

SUNDRAGON UK, male vocal/instrumental duo — 1 wk

21 Feb 68	GREEN TAMBOURINE MGM 1380	50	1 wk

SUNFIRE US, male vocal/instrumental group — 11 wks

12 Mar 83	YOUNG, FREE AND SINGLE Warner Bros. W 9897	20	11 wks

SUNNY UK, female vocalist — 10 wks

30 Mar 74 ●	DOCTOR'S ORDERS CBS 2068	7	10 wks

SUNSCREEM UK, male/female vocal/instrumental group — 13 wks

29 Feb 92	PRESSURE Sony S2 6578017	60	2 wks
18 Jul 92	LOVE U MORE Sony S2 6581727	23	6 wks
17 Oct 92	PERFECT MOTION Sony S2 6584057	18	5 wks

SUNSHINE BAND – See KC and the SUNSHINE BAND

AL B SURE! (real name Al Brown) was sure about his fiancée Carole Gist.

The SUPREMES line-up that recorded 'Someday We'll Be Together' was (left to right) Diana Ross, Cindy Birdsong and Mary Wilson.

EDWIN STARR (right) congratulates Carmen Marks, who has just been judged beauty queen of Gary, Indiana and crowned by Mayor Richard Hatcher (left).

Below: STEPHEN STILLS changed partners often in his album career but only had one solo hit single.

SUPERCAT *Jamaica, male/female vocal duo* **1 wk**

1 Aug 92	**IT FE DONE** *Columbia 6582737* 66	1 wk

SUPERTRAMP *UK/US, male vocal/instrumental group* **52 wks**

15 Feb 75	**DREAMER** *A & M AMS 7132* 13	10 wks
25 Jun 77	**GIVE A LITTLE BIT** *A & M AMS 7293* 29	7 wks
31 Mar 79	**THE LOGICAL SONG** *A & M AMS 7427* 7	11 wks
30 Jun 79 ●	**BREAKFAST IN AMERICA** *A & M AMS 7451* 9	10 wks
27 Oct 79	**GOODBYE STRANGER** *A & M AMS 7481* 57	3 wks
30 Oct 82	**IT'S RAINING AGAIN** *A & M AMS 8255* * 26	11 wks

* Supertramp featuring vocals by Roger Hodgson

SUPREMES *US, female vocal group* **306 wks**

3 Sep 64 ●	**WHERE DID OUR LOVE GO** *Stateside SS 327* 3	14 wks
22 Oct 64 ★	**BABY LOVE** *Stateside SS 350* 1	15 wks
21 Jan 65	**COME SEE ABOUT ME** *Stateside SS 376* 27	6 wks
25 Mar 65 ●	**STOP IN THE NAME OF LOVE** *Tamla Motown TMG 501* 7	12 wks
10 Jun 65	**BACK IN MY ARMS AGAIN** *Tamla Motown TMG 516*........40	5 wks
9 Dec 65	**I HEAR A SYMPHONY** *Tamla Motown TMG 543* 50	1 wk
23 Dec 65	**I HEAR A SYMPHONY (re-entry)** *Tamla Motown TMG 543* 39	4 wks
8 Sep 66 ●	**YOU CAN'T HURRY LOVE** *Tamla Motown TMG 575* 3	12 wks
1 Dec 66 ●	**YOU KEEP ME HANGIN' ON** *Tamla Motown TMG 585* 8	10 wks
2 Mar 67	**LOVE IS HERE AND NOW YOU'RE GONE** *Tamla Motown TMG 597* 17	10 wks
11 May 67 ●	**THE HAPPENING** *Tamla Motown TMG 607* 6	12 wks
30 Aug 67 ●	**REFLECTIONS** *Tamla Motown TMG 616* * 5	14 wks
29 Nov 67	**IN AND OUT OF LOVE** *Tamla Motown TMG 632* * 13	13 wks
10 Apr 68	**FOREVER CAME TODAY** *Tamla Motown TMG 650* * 28	8 wks
3 Jul 68	**SOME THINGS YOU NEVER GET USED TO** *Tamla Motown TMG 662* * 34	6 wks
20 Nov 68	**LOVE CHILD** *Tamla Motown TMG 677* * 15	14 wks
29 Jan 69 ●	**I'M GONNA MAKE YOU LOVE ME** *Tamla Motown TMG 685* ** 3	11 wks
23 Apr 69	**I'M GONNA MAKE YOU LOVE ME (re-entry)** *Tamla Motown TMG 685* ** 49	1 wk
23 Apr 69	**I'M LIVING IN SHAME** *Tamla Motown TMG 695* * 14	9 wks
2 Jul 69	**I'M LIVING IN SHAME (re-entry)** *Tamla Motown TMG 695* * 50	1 wk
16 Jul 69	**NO MATTER WHAT SIGN YOU ARE** *Tamla Motown TMG 704* * 37	7 wks
20 Sep 69	**I SECOND THAT EMOTION** *Tamla Motown TMG 709* * 18	8 wks
13 Dec 69	**SOMEDAY WE'LL BE TOGETHER** *Tamla Motown TMG 721* * 13	13 wks
21 Mar 70	**WHY (MUST WE FALL IN LOVE)** *Tamla Motown TMG 730* ** 31	7 wks
2 May 70 ●	**UP THE LADDER TO THE ROOF** *Tamla Motown TMG 735* 6	15 wks
16 Jan 71 ●	**STONED LOVE** *Tamla Motown TMG 760* 3	13 wks
26 Jun 71	**RIVER DEEP MOUNTAIN HIGH** *Tamla Motown TMG 777* *** 11	10 wks
21 Aug 71 ●	**NATHAN JONES** *Tamla Motown TMG 782*..........5	11 wks
20 Nov 71	**YOU GOTTA HAVE LOVE IN YOUR HEART** *Tamla Motown TMG 793* *** 25	10 wks
4 Mar 72 ●	**FLOY JOY** *Tamla Motown TMG 804* 9	10 wks
15 Jul 72 ●	**AUTOMATICALLY SUNSHINE** *Tamla Motown TMG 821* 10	9 wks
21 Apr 73	**BAD WEATHER** *Tamla Motown TMG 847* 37	4 wks
24 Aug 74	**BABY LOVE (re-issue)** *Tamla Motown TMG 915* * 12	10 wks
18 Feb 89	**STOP! IN THE NAME OF LOVE (re-issue)** *Motown ZB 41963* * 62	1 wk

* Diana Ross and the Supremes ** Diana Ross and the Supremes and the
Temptations *** Supremes and the Four Tops

Al B. SURE! *US, male vocalist* **11 wks**

16 Apr 88	**NITE AND DAY** *Uptown W 8192* 44	5 wks
30 Jul 88	**OFF ON YOUR OWN (GIRL)** *Uptown W 7870* 70	2 wks

10 Jun 89	**IF I'M NOT YOUR LOVER** *Warner Bros. W 2908* 54	3 wks
31 Mar 90	**SECRET GARDEN** *Qwest W 9992* * 67	1 wk

* Quincy Jones featuring Al B. Sure!, James Ingram, El DeBarge and Barry White

SURFACE *US, male vocal/instrumental duo* **14 wks**

23 Jul 83	**FALLING IN LOVE** *Salsoul SAL 104* 67	3 wks
23 Jun 84	**WHEN YOUR 'EX' WANTS YOU BACK** *Salsoul SAL 106* 52	4 wks
28 Feb 87	**HAPPY** *CBS 650393 7* 56	5 wks
12 Jan 91	**THE FIRST TIME** *Columbia 6564767* 60	2 wks

SURFACE NOISE *UK, male instrumental group* **11 wks**

31 May 80	**THE SCRATCH** *WEA K 18291* 26	8 wks
30 Aug 80	**DANCIN' ON A WIRE** *Groove GP102* 59	3 wks

SURFARIS *US, male instrumental group* **14 wks**

25 Jul 63 ●	**WIPE OUT** *London HLD 9751* 5	14 wks

SURPRISE SISTERS *UK, female vocal group* **3 wks**

13 Mar 76	**LA BOOGA ROOGA** *Good Earth GD 1* 38	3 wks

SURVIVOR *US, male vocal/instrumental group* **26 wks**

31 Jul 82 ★	**EYE OF THE TIGER** *Scotti Brothers SCT A 2411*....................1	15 wks
1 Feb 86 ●	**BURNING HEART** *Scotti Brothers A 6708* 5	11 wks

SUTHERLAND BROTHERS and QUIVER **20 wks**
UK, male vocal/instrumental group

3 Apr 76 ●	**ARMS OF MARY** *CBS 4001*........................5	12 wks
20 Nov 76	**SECRETS** *CBS 4668* 35	4 wks
2 Jun 79	**EASY COME EASY GO** *CBS 7121* * 50	4 wks

* Sutherland Brothers

Pat SUZUKI *US, female vocalist* **1 wk**

14 Apr 60	**I ENJOY BEING A GIRL** *RCA 1171* 49	1 wk

Billy SWAN *US, male vocalist* **13 wks**

14 Dec 74 ●	**I CAN HELP** *Monument MNT 2752* 6	9 wks
24 May 75	**DON'T BE CRUEL** *Monument MNT 3244* 42	4 wks

SWAN LAKE *US, male vocalist/multi-instrumentalist* **4 wks**

17 Sep 88	**IN THE NAME OF LOVE** *Champion CHAMP 86*............53	4 wks

SWANS WAY *UK, male/female vocal/instrumental group* **12 wks**

4 Feb 84	**SOUL TRAIN** *Exit EXT 3* 20	7 wks
26 May 84	**ILLUMINATIONS** *Balgier PH 5* 57	5 wks

Patrick SWAYZE featuring Wendy FRASER
US, male/female vocal duo   **11 wks**

26 Mar 88	SHE'S LIKE THE WIND *RCA PB 49565*	**17**	11 wks

Keith SWEAT *US, male vocalist*   **13 wks**

20 Feb 88	I WANT HER *Vintertainment EKR 68*	**26**	10 wks
14 May 88	SOMETHING JUST AIN'T RIGHT *Vintertainment EKR 72*	**55**	3 wks

SWEET *UK, male vocal/instrumental group*   **159 wks**

13 Mar 71		FUNNY FUNNY *RCA 2051*	**13**	14 wks
12 Jun 71	●	CO-CO *RCA 2087*	**2**	15 wks
16 Oct 71		ALEXANDER GRAHAM BELL *RCA 2121*	**33**	5 wks
5 Feb 72		POPPA JOE *RCA 2164*	**11**	12 wks
10 Jun 72	●	LITTLE WILLY *RCA 2225*	**4**	14 wks
9 Sep 72		WIG-WAM BAM *RCA 2260*	**4**	13 wks
13 Jan 73	★	BLOCKBUSTER *RCA 2305*	**1**	15 wks
5 May 73	●	HELL RAISER *RCA 2357*	**2**	11 wks
22 Sep 73	●	BALLROOM BLITZ *RCA 2403*	**2**	9 wks
19 Jan 74	●	TEENAGE RAMPAGE *RCA LPBO 5004*	**2**	8 wks
13 Jul 74	●	THE SIX TEENS *RCA LPBO 5037*	**9**	7 wks
9 Nov 74		TURN IT DOWN *RCA 2480*	**41**	2 wks
15 Mar 75	●	FOX ON THE RUN *RCA 2524*	**2**	10 wks
12 Jul 75		ACTION *RCA 2578*	**15**	6 wks
24 Jan 76		LIES IN YOUR EYES *RCA 2641*	**35**	4 wks
28 Jan 78	●	LOVE IS LIKE OXYGEN *Polydor POSP 1*	**9**	9 wks
26 Jan 85		IT'S IT'S THE SWEET MIX *Anagram ANA 28*	**45**	5 wks

It's It's The Sweet Mix *is a medley of the following songs: Blockbuster/Fox On The Run/Teenage Rampage/Hell Raiser/Ballroom Blitz.*

Rachel SWEET *US, female vocalist*   **15 wks**

9 Dec 78	B-A-B-Y *Stiff BUY 39*	**35**	8 wks
22 Aug 81	EVERLASTING LOVE *CBS A 1405* *	**35**	7 wks

* Rex Smith and Rachel Sweet

SWEET DREAMS *UK, male/female vocal duo*   **12 wks**

20 Jul 74	●	HONEY HONEY *Bradley's BRAD 7408*	**10**	12 wks

SWEET DREAMS *UK, male/female vocal group*   **7 wks**

9 Apr 83	I'M NEVER GIVING UP *Ariola ARO 333*	**21**	7 wks

SWEET PEOPLE *France, male vocal/instrumental group*   **10 wks**

4 Oct 80	●	ET LES OISEAUX CHANTAIENT (AND THE BIRDS WERE SINGING) *Polydor POSP 179*	**4**	8 wks
29 Aug 87		ET LES OISEAUX CHANTAIENT (AND THE BIRDS WERE SINGING) (re-entry) *Polydor POSP 179*	**73**	2 wks

SWEET SENSATION *UK, male vocal group*   **17 wks**

14 Sep 74	★	SAD SWEET DREAMER *Pye 7N 45385*	**1**	10 wks
18 Jan 75		PURELY BY COINCIDENCE *Pye 7N 45421*	**11**	7 wks

SWEET TEE *US, female rapper*   **6 wks**

16 Jan 88	IT'S LIKE THAT Y'ALL/I GOT DA FEELIN' *Cooltempo COOL 160*	**31**	6 wks

Sally SWEETLAND – *See Eddie FISHER*

SWERVEDRIVER *UK, male vocal/instrumental group*   **2 wks**

10 Aug 91	SANDBLASTED EP *Creation CRE 102*	**67**	1 wk
30 May 92	NEVER LOSE THAT FEELING *Creation CRE 120*	**62**	1 wk

Tracks on Sandblasted EP: *Sandblaster/Flawed/Out/Laze It Up.*

SWIMMING WITH SHARKS
Germany, female vocal duo   **3 wks**

7 May 88	CARELESS LOVE *WEA YZ 173*	**63**	3 wks

SWING OUT SISTER   **53 wks**
UK, male/female vocal/instrumental group

25 Oct 86	●	BREAKOUT *Mercury SWING 2*	**4**	14 wks
10 Jan 87	●	SURRENDER *Mercury SWING 3*	**7**	8 wks
18 Apr 87		TWILIGHT WORLD *Mercury SWING 4*	**32**	6 wks
11 Jul 87		FOOLED BY A SMILE *Mercury SWING 5*	**43**	4 wks
8 Apr 89		YOU ON MY MIND *Fontana SWING 6*	**28**	9 wks
8 Jul 89		WHERE IN THE WORLD *Fontana SWING 7*	**47**	4 wks
11 Apr 92		AM I THE SAME GIRL *Fontana SWING 9*	**21**	6 wks
20 Jun 92		NOTGONNACHANGE *Fontana SWING 10*	**49**	2 wks

SWINGING BLUE JEANS   **57 wks**
UK, male vocal/instrumental group

20 Jun 63		IT'S TOO LATE NOW *HMV POP 1170*	**30**	6 wks
8 Aug 63		IT'S TOO LATE NOW (re-entry) *HMV POP 1170*	**46**	3 wks
12 Dec 63	●	HIPPY HIPPY SHAKE *HMV POP 1242*	**2**	17 wks
19 Mar 64		GOOD GOLLY MISS MOLLY *HMV POP 1273*	**11**	10 wks
4 Jun 64	●	YOU'RE NO GOOD *HMV POP 1304*	**3**	13 wks
20 Jan 66		DON'T MAKE ME OVER *HMV POP 1501*	**31**	8 wks

SWITCH *US, male vocal/instrumental group*   **5 wks**

10 Nov 84	KEEPING SECRETS *Total Experience RCA XE 502*	**41**	5 wks

SYBIL *US, female vocalist*   **35 wks**

1 Nov 86		FALLING IN LOVE *Champion CHAMP 22*	**68**	3 wks
25 Apr 87		LET YOURSELF GO *Champion CHAMP 42*	**32**	6 wks
29 Aug 87		MY LOVE IS GUARANTEED *Champion CHAMP 55*	**42**	5 wks
22 Jul 89		DON'T MAKE ME OVER *Champion CHAMP 213*	**59**	5 wks
14 Oct 89		DON'T MAKE ME OVER (re-entry) *Champion CHAMP 213*	**19**	6 wks
27 Jan 90	●	WALK ON BY *PWL PWL 48*	**6**	9 wks
21 Apr 90		CRAZY FOR YOU *PWL PWL 53*	**71**	1 wk

SYLVESTER *US, male vocalist*   **45 wks**

19 Aug 78	●	YOU MAKE ME FEEL (MIGHTY REAL) *Fantasy FTC 160*	**8**	15 wks
18 Nov 78		DANCE (DISCO HEAT) *Fantasy FTC 163*	**29**	12 wks
31 Mar 79		I (WHO HAVE NOTHING) *Fantasy FTC 171*	**46**	5 wks
7 Jul 79		STARS *Fantasy FTC 177*	**47**	3 wks
11 Sep 82		DO YOU WANNA FUNK *London LON 13* *	**32**	8 wks
3 Sep 83		BAND OF GOLD *London LON 33*	**67**	2 wks

* Sylvester with Patrick Cowley

SYLVIA *US, female vocalist*   **11 wks**

23 Jun 73	PILLOW TALK *London HL 10415*	**14**	11 wks

SYLVIA *Sweden, female vocalist*   **33 wks**

10 Aug 74	●	Y VIVA ESPANA *Sonet SON 2037*	**4**	19 wks

4 Jan 75	**Y VIVA ESPANA (re-entry)** Sonet SON 2037	35	9 wks
26 Apr 75	**HASTA LA VISTA** Sonet SON 2055	38	5 wks

David SYLVIAN UK, male vocalist — 32 wks

7 Aug 82	**BAMBOO HOUSES/BAMBOO MUSIC** Virgin VS 510 *	30	4 wks
2 Jul 83	**FORBIDDEN COLOURS** Virgin VS 601 **	16	8 wks
2 Jun 84	**RED GUITAR** Virgin VS 633	17	5 wks
18 Aug 84	**THE INK IN THE WELL** Virgin VS 700	36	3 wks
3 Nov 84	**PULLING PUNCHES** Virgin VS 717	56	2 wks
14 Dec 85	**WORDS WITH THE SHAMAN** Virgin VS 835	72	1 wk
9 Aug 86	**TAKING THE VEIL** Virgin VS 815	53	3 wks
17 Jan 87	**BUOY** Virgin VS 910 ***	63	2 wks
10 Oct 87	**LET THE HAPPINESS IN** Virgin VS 1001	66	1 wk
13 Jun 92	**HEARTBEAT (TAINAI KAIKI II) RETURNING TO THE WOMB** Virgin America VUS 57 ****	58	3 wks

* Sylvian Sakamoto ** David Sylvian and Riuichi Sakamoto *** Mick Karn featuring David Sylvian **** David Sylvian and Riuichi Sakamoto featuring Ingrid Chavez

SYMARIP UK, male vocal/instrumental group — 3 wks

2 Feb 80	**SKINHEAD MOONSTOMP** Trojan TRO 9062	54	3 wks

SYMBOLS UK, male vocal/instrumental group — 15 wks

2 Aug 67	**BYE BYE BABY** President PT 144	44	3 wks
3 Jan 68	**BEST PART OF BREAKING UP** President PT 173	25	12 wks

SYREETA US, female vocalist — 30 wks

21 Sep 74	**SPINNIN' AND SPINNIN'** Tamla Motown TMG 912	49	3 wks
1 Feb 75	**YOUR KISS IS SWEET** Tamla Motown TMG 933	12	8 wks
12 Jul 75	**HARMOUR LOVE** Tamla Motown TMG 954	32	4 wks
15 Dec 79 ●	**WITH YOU I'M BORN AGAIN** Motown TMG 1159 *	2	11 wks
8 Mar 80	**IT WILL COME IN TIME** Motown TMG 1175 *	47	4 wks

* Billy Preston and Syreeta

SYSTEM US, male vocal/instrumental duo — 2 wks

9 Jun 84	**I WANNA MAKE YOU FEEL GOOD** Polydor POSP 685	73	2 wks

T

TACK HEAD US, male rapper — 3 wks

30 Jun 90	**DANGEROUS SEX** SBK SBK 7014	48	3 wks

TAFFY UK, female vocalist — 14 wks

10 Jan 87 ●	**I LOVE MY RADIO (MY DEE JAY'S RADIO)** Transglobal TYPE 1	6	10 wks
18 Jul 87	**STEP BY STEP** Transglobal TYPE 5	59	4 wks

TAKE THAT UK, male vocal group — 31 wks

23 Nov 91	**PROMISES** RCA PB 45085	38	2 wks
8 Feb 92	**ONCE YOU'VE TASTED LOVE** RCA PB 45257	47	3 wks
6 Jun 92 ●	**IT ONLY TAKES A MINUTE** RCA 74321101007	7	8 wks
15 Aug 92	**I FOUND HEAVEN** RCA 74321108137	15	6 wks
10 Oct 92 ●	**A MILLION LOVE SONGS** RCA 74321116307	7	9 wks
12 Dec 92 ●	**COULD IT BE MAGIC** RCA 74321123137	4†	3 wks

TALK TALK UK, male vocal/instrumental group — 73 wks

24 Apr 82	**TALK TALK** EMI 5284	52	4 wks
24 Jul 82	**TODAY** EMI 5314	14	13 wks
13 Nov 82	**TALK TALK (re-mix)** EMI 5352	23	10 wks
19 Mar 83	**MY FOOLISH FRIEND** EMI 5373	57	3 wks
14 Jan 84	**IT'S MY LIFE** EMI 5443	46	5 wks
7 Apr 84	**SUCH A SHAME** EMI 5433	49	6 wks
11 Aug 84	**DUM DUM GIRL** EMI 5480	74	1 wk
18 Jan 86	**LIFE'S WHAT YOU MAKE IT** EMI EMI 5540	16	9 wks
15 Mar 86	**LIVING IN ANOTHER WORLD** EMI EMI 5551	48	4 wks
17 May 86	**GIVE IT UP** Parlophone R 6131	59	3 wks
19 May 90	**IT'S MY LIFE (re-issue)** Parlophone R 6254	13	9 wks
1 Sep 90	**LIFE'S WHAT YOU MAKE IT (re-issue)** Parlophone R 6264	23	6 wks

TALKING HEADS — 54 wks
US/UK, male/female vocal/instrumental group

7 Feb 81	**ONCE IN A LIFETIME** Sire SIR 4048	14	10 wks
9 May 81	**HOUSES IN MOTION** Sire SIR 4050	50	3 wks
21 Jan 84	**THIS MUST BE THE PLACE** Sire W 9451	51	3 wks
3 Nov 84	**SLIPPERY PEOPLE** EMI 5504	68	2 wks
12 Oct 85 ●	**ROAD TO NOWHERE** EMI EMI 5530	6	16 wks
8 Feb 86	**AND SHE WAS** EMI EMI 5543	17	4 wks
6 Sep 86	**WILD WILD LIFE** EMI EMI 5567	43	4 wks
16 May 87	**RADIO HEAD** EMI EM 1	52	2 wks
13 Aug 88	**BLIND** EMI EM 68	59	3 wks
10 Oct 92	**LIFETIME PILING UP** EMI EM 250	50	3 wks

TAMS US, male vocal group — 31 wks

14 Feb 70	**BE YOUNG BE FOOLISH BE HAPPY** Stateside SS 2123	32	7 wks
31 Jul 71 ★	**HEY GIRL DON'T BOTHER ME** Probe PRO 532	1	17 wks
21 Nov 87	**THERE AIN'T NOTHING LIKE SHAGGIN'** Virgin VS 1029	21	7 wks

Norma TANEGA US, female vocalist — 8 wks

7 Apr 66	**WALKING MY CAT NAMED DOG** Stateside SS 496	22	8 wks

The Children of TANSLEY SCHOOL — 4 wks
UK, children's choir

28 Mar 81	**MY MUM IS ONE IN A MILLION** EMI 5151	27	4 wks

Jimmy TARBUCK UK, male vocalist — 2 wks

16 Nov 85	**AGAIN** Safari SAFE 68	74	1 wk
30 Nov 85	**AGAIN (re-entry)** Safari SAFE 68	68	1 wk

TARRIERS US, male vocal/instrumental group — 6 wks

14 Dec 56	**CINDY OH CINDY** London HLN 8340 *	26	1 wk
1 Mar 57	**BANANA BOAT SONG** Columbia DB 3891	15	5 wks

* Vince Martin and the Tarriers

A TASTE OF HONEY US, female vocal duo — 19 wks

17 Jun 78 ●	**BOOGIE OOGIE OOGIE** Capitol CL 15988	3	16 wks
18 May 85	**BOOGIE OOGIE OOGIE (re-mix)** Capitol CL 357	59	3 wks

TAVARES US, male vocal group — 77 wks

Date	Title	Pos	Wks
10 Jul 76 ●	HEAVEN MUST BE MISSING AN ANGEL Capitol CL 15876	4	11 wks
9 Oct 76 ●	DON'T TAKE AWAY THE MUSIC Capitol CL 15886	4	10 wks
5 Feb 77	MIGHTY POWER OF LOVE Capitol CL 15905	25	6 wks
9 Apr 77 ●	WHODUNIT Capitol CL 15914	5	10 wks
2 Jul 77	ONE STEP AWAY Capitol CL 15930	16	7 wks
18 Mar 78	THE GHOST OF LOVE Capitol CL 15968	29	6 wks
6 May 78 ●	MORE THAN A WOMAN Capitol CL 15977	7	11 wks
12 Aug 78	SLOW TRAIN TO PARADISE Capitol CL 15996	62	3 wks
22 Feb 86	HEAVEN MUST BE MISSING AN ANGEL (re-issue) Capitol TAV 1	12	9 wks
3 May 86	IT ONLY TAKES A MINUTE Capitol TAV 2	46	4 wks

TAXMAN – See KICKING BACK with TAXMAN

Andy TAYLOR UK, male vocalist — 2 wks

Date	Title	Pos	Wks
20 Oct 90	LOLA A & M AM 596	60	2 wks

Dina TAYLOR – See BBG

Felice TAYLOR US, female vocalist — 13 wks

Date	Title	Pos	Wks
25 Oct 67	I FEEL LOVE COMIN' ON President PT 155	11	13 wks

James TAYLOR US, male vocalist — 23 wks

Date	Title	Pos	Wks
21 Nov 70	FIRE AND RAIN Warner Bros. WB 6104	42	3 wks
28 Aug 71 ●	YOU'VE GOT A FRIEND Warner Bros. WB 16085	4	15 wks
16 Mar 74	MOCKINGBIRD Elektra K 12134 *	34	5 wks

* Carly Simon and James Taylor

John TAYLOR UK, male vocalist — 4 wks

Date	Title	Pos	Wks
15 Mar 86	I DO WHAT I DO…THEME FOR '9 ½ WEEKS' Parlophone R 6125	42	4 wks

Johnnie TAYLOR US, male vocalist — 7 wks

Date	Title	Pos	Wks
24 Apr 76	DISCO LADY CBS 4044	25	7 wks

J.T. TAYLOR US, male vocalist — 5 wks

Date	Title	Pos	Wks
24 Aug 91	LONG HOT SUMMER NIGHT MCA MCS 1567	63	2 wks
30 Nov 91	FEEL THE NEED MCA MCS 1592	57	1 wk
18 Apr 92	FOLLOW ME MCA MCS 1617	59	2 wks

R. Dean TAYLOR Canada, male vocalist — 48 wks

Date	Title	Pos	Wks
19 Jun 68	GOTTA SEE JANE Tamla Motown TMG 656	17	12 wks
3 Apr 71 ●	INDIANA WANTS ME Tamla Motown TMG 763	2	15 wks
11 May 74 ●	THERE'S A GHOST IN MY HOUSE Tamla Motown TMG 896	3	12 wks
31 Aug 74	WINDOW SHOPPING Polydor 2058 502	36	5 wks
21 Sep 74	GOTTA SEE JANE (re-issue) Tamla Motown TMG 918	41	4 wks

Roger TAYLOR UK, male vocalist — 9 wks

Date	Title	Pos	Wks
18 Apr 81	FUTURE MANAGEMENT EMI 5157	49	4 wks
16 Jun 84	MAN ON FIRE EMI 5478	66	2 wks
10 Oct 92	RADIO Epic 6584367 *	37	3 wks

* Shaky featuring Roger Taylor

TC 1991/TC 1992 Italy, male instrumental/production duo — 3 wks

Date	Title	Pos	Wks
14 Mar 92	BERRY Union City UCRT 1 *	73	1 wk
21 Nov 92	FUNKY GUITAR Union City UCRT 13 **	40	2 wks

* TC 1991 ** TC 1992

T-CONNECTION US, male vocal/instrumental group — 27 wks

Date	Title	Pos	Wks
18 Jun 77	DO WHAT YOU WANNA DO TK XC 9109	11	8 wks
14 Jan 78	ON FIRE TK TKR 6006	16	5 wks
10 Jun 78	LET YOURSELF GO TK TKR 6024	52	3 wks
24 Feb 79	AT MIDNIGHT TK TKR 7517	53	5 wks
5 May 79	SATURDAY NIGHT TK TKR 7536	41	6 wks

T-COY – See VARIOUS ARTISTS (EPs & LPs) - The Further Adventures Of North EP

Kiri TE KANAWA New Zealand, female vocalist — 11 wks

Date	Title	Pos	Wks
28 Sep 91 ●	WORLD IN UNION Columbia 6574817	4	11 wks

TEACH-IN Holland, male/female vocal/instrumental group — 7 wks

Date	Title	Pos	Wks
12 Apr 75	DING-A-DONG Polydor 2058 570	13	7 wks

TEAM UK, male vocal/instrumental group — 5 wks

Date	Title	Pos	Wks
1 Jun 85	WICKI WACKY HOUSE PARTY EMI 5519	55	5 wks

TEARDROP EXPLODES
UK, male vocal/instrumental group — 50 wks

Date	Title	Pos	Wks
27 Sep 80	WHEN I DREAM Mercury TEAR 1	47	6 wks
31 Jan 81 ●	REWARD Vertigo TEAR 2	6	13 wks
2 May 81	TREASON (IT'S JUST A STORY) Mercury TEAR 3	18	8 wks
29 Aug 81	PASSIONATE FRIEND Zoo TEAR 5	25	10 wks
21 Nov 81	COLOURS FLY AWAY Mercury TEAR 6	54	3 wks
19 Jun 82	TINY CHILDREN Mercury TEAR 7	44	7 wks
19 Mar 83	YOU DISAPPEAR FROM VIEW Mercury TEAR 8	41	3 wks

TEARS FOR FEARS UK, male vocal/instrumental duo — 133 wks

Date	Title	Pos	Wks
2 Oct 82 ●	MAD WORLD Mercury IDEA 3	3	16 wks
5 Feb 83 ●	CHANGE Mercury IDEA 4	4	9 wks
30 Apr 83 ●	PALE SHELTER Mercury IDEA 5	5	8 wks
3 Dec 83	THE WAY YOU ARE Mercury IDEA 6	24	8 wks
18 Aug 84	MOTHER'S TALK Mercury IDEA 7	14	8 wks
1 Dec 84 ●	SHOUT Mercury IDEA 8	4	16 wks
30 Mar 85 ●	EVERYBODY WANTS TO RULE THE WORLD Mercury IDEA 9	2	14 wks
22 Jun 85	HEAD OVER HEELS Mercury IDEA 10	12	9 wks
31 Aug 85	SUFFER THE CHILDREN Mercury IDEA 1	52	4 wks
7 Sep 85	PALE SHELTER (re-issue) Mercury IDEA 2	73	2 wks
12 Oct 85	I BELIEVE (A SOULFUL RE-RECORDING) Mercury IDEA 11	23	4 wks
22 Feb 86	EVERYBODY WANTS TO RULE THE WORLD (re-entry) Mercury IDEA 9	73	1 wk
31 May 86 ●	EVERYBODY WANTS TO RUN THE WORLD Mercury RACE 1	5	6 wks
19 Jul 86	EVERYBODY WANTS TO RUN THE WORLD (re-entry) Mercury RACE 1	73	1 wk
2 Sep 89 ●	SOWING THE SEEDS OF LOVE Fontana IDEA 12	5	9 wks
18 Nov 89	WOMAN IN CHAINS Fontana IDEA 13	26	8 wks
3 Mar 90	ADVICE FOR THE YOUNG AT HEART Fontana IDEA 14	36	4 wks

22 Feb 92	**LAID SO LOW (TEARS ROLL DOWN)** *Fontana IDEA 17*	**17**	5 wks
25 Apr 92	**WOMAN IN CHAINS (re-issue)** *Fontana IDEA 16* *	**57**	1 wk

* Tears For Fears featuring Oleta Adams

Mercury RACE 1 was a slightly changed version of Mercury IDEA 9, released to promote the Race Against Time of 15 May 1986. Oleta Adams is given no label credit on the original release of Woman In Chains.

TECHNICIAN 2 *UK, male instrumental/production group*   **1 wk**

14 Nov 92	**PLAYING WITH THE BOY** *MCA MCS 1710*	**70**	1 wk

---

TECHNO TWINS *UK, male/female vocal duo*   **2 wks**

16 Jan 82	**FALLING IN LOVE AGAIN** *PRT 7P 224*	**75**	1 wk
30 Jan 82	**FALLING IN LOVE AGAIN (re-entry)** *PRT 7P 224*	**70**	1 wk

---

TECHNOTRONIC *Belgium, male producer – Jo Bogaert*   **64 wks**

2 Sep 89	● **PUMP UP THE JAM** *Swanyard SYR 4* *	**2**	15 wks
3 Feb 90	● **GET UP (BEFORE THE NIGHT IS OVER)** *Swanyard SYR 8* **	**2**	10 wks
7 Apr 90	**THIS BEAT IS TECHNOTRONIC** *Swanyard SYR 9* ***	**14**	7 wks
14 Jul 90	● **ROCKIN' OVER THE BEAT** *Swanyard SYR 14* **	**9**	9 wks
6 Oct 90	● **MEGAMIX** *Swanyard SYR 19*	**6**	8 wks
15 Dec 90	**TURN IT UP** *Swanyard SYD 9* ****	**42**	4 wks
25 May 91	**MOVE THAT BODY** *ARS 6568377* *****	**12**	7 wks
3 Aug 91	**WORK** *ARS 6573317* *****	**40**	4 wks

* Technotronic featuring Felly ** Technotronic featuring Ya Kid K *** Technotronic featuring MC Eric **** Technotronic featuring Melissa and Einstein ***** Technotronic featuring Reggie

See also Hi-Tek 3 featuring Ya Kid K.

TEDDY BEARS *US, male/female vocal group*   **17 wks**

19 Dec 58	● **TO KNOW HIM IS TO LOVE HIM** *London HLN 8733*	**2**	16 wks
14 Apr 79	**TO KNOW HIM IS TO LOVE HIM (re-issue)** *Lightning LIG 9015*	**66**	1 wk

To Know Him Is To Love Him re-issue was coupled with Endless Sleep by Jody Reynolds as a double A-side.

TEENAGE FANCLUB *UK, male vocal/instrumental group*   **5 wks**

24 Aug 91	**STAR SIGN** *Creation CRE 105*	**44**	2 wks
2 Nov 91	**THE CONCEPT** *Creation CRE 111*	**51**	1 wk
8 Feb 92	**WHAT YOU DO TO ME (EP)** *Creation CRE 115*	**31**	2 wks

Tracks on What You Do To Me (EP): What You Do To Me/B-Side/Life's A Gas/Filler.

TEENAGERS – *See Frankie LYMON and the TEENAGERS*

TEKNO TOO *UK, male instrumental/production duo*   **2 wks**

13 Jul 91	**JET-STAR** *D-Zone DANCE 012*	**56**	2 wks

TELEVISION *US, male vocal/instrumental group*   **10 wks**

16 Apr 77	**MARQUEE MOON** *Elektra K 12252*	**30**	4 wks
30 Jul 77	**PROVE IT** *Elektra K 12262*	**25**	4 wks
22 Apr 78	**FOXHOLE** *Elektra K 12287*	**36**	2 wks

TELEX *Belgium, male vocal/instrumental duo*   **7 wks**

21 Jul 79	**ROCK AROUND THE CLOCK** *Sire SIR 4020*	**34**	7 wks

---

Sylvia TELLA – *See BLOW MONKEYS*

TEMPERANCE SEVEN   **45 wks**
UK, male vocal/instrumental band

30 Mar 61	★ **YOU'RE DRIVING ME CRAZY** *Parlophone R 4757*	**1**	16 wks
15 Jun 61	● **PASADENA** *Parlophone R 4781*	**4**	17 wks
28 Sep 61	**HARD HEARTED HANNAH/CHILI BOM BOM** *Parlophone R 4823*	**28**	4 wks
7 Dec 61	**CHARLESTON** *Parlophone R 4851*	**22**	8 wks

Chili Bom Bom only listed with Hard Hearted Hannah for the weeks of 12 and 19 Oct 61.

TEMPLE OF THE DOG   **2 wks**
US, male vocal/instrumental group

24 Oct 92	**HUNGER STRIKE** *A & M AM 0091*	**51**	2 wks

Nino TEMPO and April STEVENS   **19 wks**
US, male/female vocal duo

7 Nov 63	**DEEP PURPLE** *London HLK 9782*	**17**	11 wks
16 Jan 64	**WHISPERING** *London HLK 9829*	**20**	8 wks

TEMPTATIONS *US, male vocal group*   **203 wks**

18 Mar 65	**MY GIRL** *Stateside SS 378*	**43**	1 wk
1 Apr 65	**IT'S GROWING** *Tamla Motown TMG 504*	**49**	1 wk
15 Apr 65	**IT'S GROWING (re-entry)** *Tamla Motown TMG 504*	**45**	1 wk
14 Jul 66	**AIN'T TOO PROUD TO BEG** *Tamla Motown TMG 565*	**21**	11 wks
6 Oct 66	**BEAUTY IS ONLY SKIN DEEP** *Tamla Motown TMG 578*	**18**	10 wks
15 Dec 66	**(I KNOW) I'M LOSING YOU** *Tamla Motown TMG 587*	**19**	9 wks
6 Sep 67	**YOU'RE MY EVERYTHING** *Tamla Motown TMG 620*	**26**	15 wks
6 Mar 68	**I WISH IT WOULD RAIN** *Tamla Motown TMG 641*	**45**	1 wk
12 Jun 68	**I COULD NEVER LOVE ANOTHER** *Tamla Motown TMG 658*	**47**	1 wk
29 Jan 69	● **I'M GONNA MAKE YOU LOVE ME** *Tamla Motown TMG 685* *	**3**	11 wks
5 Mar 69	● **GET READY** *Tamla Motown TMG 688*	**10**	9 wks
23 Apr 69	**I'M GONNA MAKE YOU LOVE ME (re-entry)** *Tamla Motown TMG 685* *	**49**	1 wk
23 Aug 69	**CLOUD NINE** *Tamla Motown TMG 707*	**15**	10 wks
20 Sep 69	**I SECOND THAT EMOTION** *Tamla Motown TMG 709* *	**18**	8 wks
17 Jan 70	**I CAN'T GET NEXT TO YOU** *Tamla Motown TMG 722*	**13**	9 wks
21 Mar 70	**WHY (MUST WE FALL IN LOVE)** *Tamla Motown TMG 730* *	**31**	7 wks
13 Jun 70	**PSYCHEDELIC SHACK** *Tamla Motown TMG 741*	**33**	7 wks
19 Sep 70	● **BALL OF CONFUSION** *Tamla Motown TMG 749*	**7**	12 wks
19 Dec 70	**BALL OF CONFUSION (re-entry)** *Tamla Motown TMG 749*	**48**	3 wks
22 May 71	● **JUST MY IMAGINATION (RUNNING AWAY WITH ME)** *Tamla Motown TMG 773*	**8**	16 wks
5 Feb 72	**SUPERSTAR (REMEMBER HOW YOU GOT WHERE YOU ARE)** *Tamla Motown TMG 800*	**32**	5 wks
15 Apr 72	**TAKE A LOOK AROUND** *Tamla Motown TMG 808*	**13**	10 wks
13 Jan 73	**PAPA WAS A ROLLIN' STONE** *Tamla Motown TMG 839*	**14**	8 wks
29 Sep 73	**LAW OF THE LAND** *Tamla Motown TMG 866*	**41**	4 wks
12 Jun 82	**STANDING ON THE TOP (PART 1)** *Motown TMG 1263* **	**53**	3 wks

17 Nov 84	TREAT HER LIKE A LADY *Motown TMG 1365*	12	10 wks
15 Aug 87	PAPA WAS A ROLLIN' STONE (re-mix) *Motown ZB 41431*	31	6 wks
6 Feb 88	LOOK WHAT YOU STARTED *Motown ZB 41733*	63	2 wks
21 Oct 89	ALL I WANT FROM YOU *Motown ZB 43233*	71	1 wk
15 Feb 92 ●	MY GIRL (re-issue) *Epic 6576767*	2	10 wks
22 Feb 92	THE JONES' *Motown TMG 1403*	69	1 wk

* Diana Ross and the Supremes and the Temptations ** Temptations featuring Rick James

10 C. C. *UK, male vocal/instrumental group* — 131 wks

23 Sep 72 ●	DONNA *UK 6*	2	13 wks
19 May 73 ★	RUBBER BULLETS *UK 36*	1	15 wks
25 Aug 73 ●	THE DEAN AND I *UK 48*	10	8 wks
15 Jun 74 ●	WALL STREET SHUFFLE *UK 69*	10	10 wks
14 Sep 74	SILLY LOVE *UK 77*	24	7 wks
5 Apr 75 ●	LIFE IS A MINESTRONE *Mercury 6008 010*	7	8 wks
31 May 75 ★	I'M NOT IN LOVE *Mercury 6008 014*	1	11 wks
29 Nov 75 ●	ART FOR ART'S SAKE *Mercury 6008 017*	5	10 wks
20 Mar 76 ●	I'M MANDY FLY ME *Mercury 6008 019*	6	9 wks
11 Dec 76 ●	THINGS WE DO FOR LOVE *Mercury 6008 022*	6	11 wks
16 Apr 77 ●	GOOD MORNING JUDGE *Mercury 6008 025*	5	12 wks
12 Aug 78 ★	DREADLOCK HOLIDAY *Mercury 6008 035*	1	13 wks
7 Aug 82	RUN AWAY *Mercury MER 113*	50	4 wks

From Things We Do For Love *10 C.C. were a male vocal/instrumental duo.*

TEN CITY *US, male vocal/instrumental group* — 19 wks

21 Jan 89 ●	THAT'S THE WAY LOVE IS *Atlantic A 8963*	8	10 wks
8 Apr 89	DEVOTION *Atlantic A 8916*	29	4 wks
22 Jul 89	WHERE DO WE GO *Atlantic A 8864*	60	1 wk
27 Oct 90	WHATEVER MAKES YOU HAPPY *Atlantic A 7819*	60	2 wks
15 Aug 92	ONLY TIME WILL TELL/MY PEACE OF HEAVEN *East West America A 8516*	63	2 wks

TEN POLE TUDOR *UK, male vocal/instrumental group* — 40 wks

7 Apr 79 ●	WHO KILLED BAMBI *Virgin VS 256*	6	8 wks
13 Oct 79	ROCK AROUND THE CLOCK *Virgin VS 290*	21	6 wks
25 Apr 81 ●	SWORDS OF A THOUSAND MEN *Stiff BUY 109*	6	12 wks
1 Aug 81	WUNDERBAR *Stiff BUY 120*	16	9 wks
14 Nov 81	THROWING MY BABY OUT WITH THE BATHWATER *Stiff BUY 129*	49	5 wks

The listed flip side of Who Killed Bambi *was* Silly Thing *by the Sex Pistols. The listed flip side of* Rock Around The Clock *was* The Great Rock 'n' Roll Swindle *also by the Sex Pistols.*

TEN SHARP *Holland, male vocal/instrumental duo* — 15 wks

21 Mar 92 ●	YOU *Columbia 6566647*	10	13 wks
20 Jun 92	AIN'T MY BEATING HEART *Columbia 6580947*	63	2 wks

10,000 MANIACS *US, male/female vocal/instrumental group* — 3 wks

12 Sep 92	THESE ARE DAYS *Elektra EKR 156*	58	3 wks

TEN YEARS AFTER *UK, male vocal/instrumental group* — 18 wks

6 Jun 70 ●	LOVE LIKE A MAN *Deram DM 299*	10	18 wks

TENNESSEE THREE – *See Johnny CASH*

TERMINATERS – *See ARNEE and the TERMINATERS*

Tammi TERRELL – *See Marvin GAYE*

TERRORIZE *UK, male producer - Shaun Imrei* — 6 wks

2 May 92	IT'S JUST A FEELING *Hamster STER 1*	52	3 wks

22 Aug 92	FEEL THE RHYTHM *Hamster 12STER 2*	69	1 wk
14 Nov 92	IT'S JUST A FEELING (re-issue) *Hamster STER 8*	47	2 wks

Helen TERRY *UK, female vocalist* — 6 wks

12 May 84	LOVE LIES LOST *Virgin VS 678*	34	6 wks

Todd TERRY PROJECT *US, male producer* — 3 wks

12 Nov 88	WEEKEND *Sleeping Bag SBUK 1T*	56	3 wks

Tony TERRY *US, male vocalist* — 6 wks

27 Feb 88	LOVEY DOVEY *Epic TONY 2*	44	6 wks

TESLA *US, male vocal/instrumental group* — 1 wk

27 Apr 91	SIGNS *Geffen GFS 3*	70	1 wk

Joe TEX *US, male vocalist* — 11 wks

23 Apr 77 ●	AIN'T GONNA BUMP NO MORE (WITH NO BIG FAT WOMAN) *Epic EPC 5035*	2	11 wks

TEXAS *UK, male/female vocal/instrumental group* — 32 wks

4 Feb 89 ●	I DON'T WANT A LOVER *Mercury TEX 1*	8	11 wks
6 May 89	THRILL HAS GONE *Mercury TEX 2*	60	3 wks
5 Aug 89	EVERYDAY NOW *Mercury TEX 3*	44	5 wks
2 Dec 89	PRAYER FOR YOU *Mercury TEX 4*	73	1 wk
7 Sep 91	WHY BELIEVE IN YOU *Mercury TEX 5*	66	1 wk
26 Oct 91	IN MY HEART *Mercury TEX 6*	74	1 wk
8 Feb 92	ALONE WITH YOU *Mercury TEX 7*	32	4 wks
25 Apr 92	TIRED OF BEING ALONE *Mercury TEX 8*	19	6 wks

THAT PETROL EMOTION — 24 wks
UK, male vocal/instrumental group

11 Apr 87	BIG DECISION *Polydor TPE 1*	43	7 wks
11 Jul 87	DANCE *Polydor TPE 2*	64	2 wks
17 Oct 87	GENIUS MOVE *Virgin VS 1002*	65	2 wks
31 Mar 90	ABANDON *Virgin VS 1242*	73	1 wk
1 Sep 90	HEY VENUS *Virgin VS 1290*	49	4 wks
9 Feb 91	TINGLE *Virgin VS 1312*	49	4 wks
27 Apr 91	SENSITIZE *Virgin VS 1261*	55	4 wks

THE THE — 36 wks
UK, male vocalist/multi-instrumentalist - Matt Johnson

4 Dec 82	UNCERTAIN SMILE *Epic EPC A 2787*	68	3 wks
17 Sep 83	THIS IS THE DAY *Epic A 3710*	71	3 wks
9 Aug 86	HEARTLAND *Some Bizzare TRUTH 2*	29	10 wks
25 Oct 86	INFECTED *Some Bizzare TRUTH 3*	48	5 wks
24 Jan 87	SLOW TRAIN TO DAWN *Some Bizzare TENSE 1*	64	2 wks
23 May 87	SWEET BIRD OF TRUTH *Epic TENSE 2*	55	2 wks
1 Apr 89	THE BEAT(EN) GENERATION *Epic EMU 8*	18	5 wks
22 Jul 89	GRAVITATE TO ME *Epic EMU 9*	63	3 wks
7 Oct 89	ARMAGEDDON DAYS ARE HERE (AGAIN) *Epic EMU 10*	70	2 wks
2 Mar 91	SHADES OF BLUE EP *Epic 6557968*	54	1 wk

Tracks on Shades Of Blue EP: *Jealous Of Youth/Another Boy Drowning (Live)/Solitude/Dolphins.*

THEATRE OF HATE *UK, male vocal/instrumental group* — 9 wks

23 Jan 82	DO YOU BELIEVE IN THE WESTWORLD *Burning Rome BRR 2*	40	7 wks

29 May 82   **THE HOP** *Burning Rome BRR 3*.....................................**70**   2 wks

---

THEM *UK, male vocal/instrumental group*   **23 wks**

7 Jan 65 ●	**BABY PLEASE DON'T GO** *Decca F 12018* **10**	9 wks
25 Mar 65 ●	**HERE COMES THE NIGHT** *Decca F 12094*....................**2**	12 wks
9 Feb 91	**BABY PLEASE DON'T GO (re-issue)**	
	London LON 292 ....**65**	2 wks

THEN JERICHO *UK, male vocal/instrumental group*   **36 wks**

31 Jan 87	**LET HER FALL** *London LON 97* **65**	3 wks
25 Jul 87	**THE MOTIVE (LIVING WITHOUT YOU)**	
	London LON 145 ....**18**	12 wks
24 Oct 87	**MUSCLE DEEP** *London LON 156* **48**	4 wks
28 Jan 89	**BIG AREA** *London LON 204* **13**	7 wks
8 Apr 89	**WHAT DOES IT TAKE** *London LON 223* **33**	4 wks
12 Aug 89	**SUGAR BOX** *London LON 235* **22**	6 wks

---

THERAPY? *UK, male vocal/instrumental group*   **2 wks**

31 Oct 92   **TEETHGRINDER** *A & M AM 0097*......................**30**   2 wks

---

THEY MIGHT BE GIANTS   **13 wks**
US, male vocal/instrumental duo

3 Mar 90 ●	**BIRDHOUSE IN YOUR SOUL** *Elektra EKR 104* **6**	11 wks
2 Jun 90	**ISTANBUL (NOT CONSTANTINOPLE)**	
	Elektra EKR 110 ....**61**	2 wks

THIN LIZZY *Ireland, male vocal/instrumental group*   **128 wks**

20 Jan 73 ●	**WHISKEY IN THE JAR** *Decca F 13355* **6**	12 wks
29 May 76 ●	**THE BOYS ARE BACK IN TOWN** *Vertigo 6059 139*...........**8**	10 wks
14 Aug 76	**JAILBREAK** *Vertigo 6059 150*.........................**31**	4 wks
15 Jan 77	**DON'T BELIEVE A WORD** *Vertigo Lizzy 001* **12**	7 wks
13 Aug 77	**DANCIN' IN THE MOONLIGHT (IT'S CAUGHT**	
	ME IN THE SPOTLIGHT) *Vertigo 6059 177* **14**	8 wks
13 May 78	**ROSALIE - COWGIRLS' SONG (MEDLEY)**	
	Vertigo LIZZY 2 ....**20**	13 wks
3 Mar 79 ●	**WAITING FOR AN ALIBI** *Vertigo LIZZY 003* **9**	8 wks
16 Jun 79	**DO ANYTHING YOU WANT TO** *Vertigo LIZZY 004*......**14**	9 wks
20 Oct 79	**SARAH** *Vertigo LIZZY 5* **24**	13 wks
24 May 80	**CHINATOWN** *Vertigo LIZZY 6* **21**	9 wks
27 Sep 80 ●	**KILLER ON THE LOOSE** *Vertigo LIZZY 7* **10**	7 wks
2 May 81	**KILLERS LIVE EP** *Vertigo LIZZY 8* **19**	7 wks
8 Aug 81	**TROUBLE BOYS** *Vertigo LIZZY 9* **53**	4 wks
6 Mar 82	**HOLLYWOOD (DOWN ON YOUR LUCK)**	
	Vertigo LIZZY 10 ....**53**	3 wks
12 Feb 83	**COLD SWEAT** *Vertigo LIZZY 11* **27**	5 wks
7 May 83	**THUNDER AND LIGHTNING** *Vertigo LIZZY 12* **39**	2 wks
6 Aug 83	**THE SUN GOES DOWN** *Vertigo LIZZY 13* **52**	3 wks
26 Jan 91	**DEDICATION** *Vertigo LIZZY 14* **35**	3 wks
23 Mar 91	**THE BOYS ARE BACK IN TOWN (re-issue)**	
	Vertigo LIZZY 15...**63**	1 wk

Tracks on Killers Live EP: *Bad Reputation/Are You Ready/Dear Miss Lonely Hearts.*

3RD BASS *US, male rap group*   **5 wks**

10 Feb 90	**THE GAS FACE** *Def Jam 655627 0*....................**71**	1 wk
7 Apr 90	**BROOKLYN-QUEENS** *Def Jam 655830 7*........**61**	2 wks
22 Jun 91	**POP GOES THE WEASEL** *Def Jam 6569547* ...**64**	2 wks

---

THIRD WORLD *Jamaica, male vocal/instrumental group*   **53 wks**

23 Sep 78 ●	**NOW THAT WE'VE FOUND LOVE** *Island WIP 6457*........**10**	9 wks
6 Jan 79	**COOL MEDITATION** *Island WIP 6469* **17**	10 wks
16 Jun 79	**TALK TO ME** *Island WIP 6496* **56**	5 wks

---

6 Jun 81 ●	**DANCING ON THE FLOOR (HOOKED ON LOVE)**	
	CBS A 1214 ....**10**	15 wks
17 Apr 82	**TRY JAH LOVE** *CBS A 2063* **47**	6 wks
9 Mar 85	**NOW THAT WE'VE FOUND LOVE**	
	(re-issue) *Island IS 219* **22**	8 wks

---

THIRST *UK, male vocal/instrumental group*   **2 wks**

6 Jul 91   **THE ENEMY WITHIN** *Ten TEN 379*...................**61**   2 wks

---

THIS ISLAND EARTH   **5 wks**
UK, male/female vocal/instrumental group

5 Jan 85   **SEE THAT GLOW** *Magnet MAG 266* ....**47**   5 wks

---

THIS MORTAL COIL   **3 wks**
UK, male/female vocal/instrumental group

| 22 Oct 83 | **SONG TO THE SIREN** *4AD AD 310* ....**66** | 2 wks |
| 12 Nov 83 | **SONG TO THE SIREN (re-entry)** *4AD AD 310* ....**75** | 1 wk |

THIS WAY UP *UK, male vocal/instrumental duo*   **2 wks**

22 Aug 87   **TELL ME WHY** *Virgin VS 954*.........................**72**   2 wks

---

THIS YEAR'S BLONDE   **8 wks**
UK, male/female vocal/instrumental group

| 10 Oct 81 | **PLATINUM POP** *Creole CR 19* ....**46** | 5 wks |
| 14 Nov 87 | **WHO'S THAT MIX** *Debut DEBT 3034* ....**62** | 3 wks |

B. J. THOMAS *US, male vocalist*   **4 wks**

21 Feb 70	**RAINDROPS KEEP FALLING ON MY HEAD**	
	Wand WN1 ....**38**	3 wks
2 May 70	**RAINDROPS KEEP FALLING ON MY**	
	HEAD (re-entry) *Wand WN1* **49**	1 wk

Carla THOMAS – *See Otis REDDING*

Evelyn THOMAS *US, female vocalist*   **29 wks**

24 Jan 76	**WEAK SPOT** *20th Century BTC 1014* **26**	7 wks
17 Apr 76	**DOOMSDAY** *20th Century BTC 1017* **41**	1 wk
1 May 76	**DOOMSDAY (re-entry)** *20th Century BTC 1017*...............**45**	1 wk
21 Apr 84 ●	**HIGH ENERGY** *Record Shack SOHO 18* **5**	17 wks
25 Aug 84	**MASQUERADE** *Record Shack SOHO 25* **60**	3 wks

---

Jamo THOMAS *US, male vocalist*   **2 wks**

| 26 Feb 69 | **I SPY FOR THE FBI** *Polydor 56755* ....**48** | 1 wk |
| 12 Mar 69 | **I SPY FOR THE FBI (re-entry)** *Polydor 56755* ....**44** | 1 wk |

Kenny THOMAS *UK, male vocalist*   **36 wks**

26 Jan 91	**OUTSTANDING** *Cooltempo COOL 227* **12**	10 wks
1 Jun 91 ●	**THINKING ABOUT YOUR LOVE**	
	Cooltempo COOL 235 ....**4**	13 wks
5 Oct 91	**BEST OF YOU** *Cooltempo COOL 243* **11**	7 wks
30 Nov 91	**TENDER LOVE** *Cooltempo COOL 247* **26**	6 wks

---

Lillo THOMAS *US, male vocalist*   **10 wks**

27 Apr 85   **SETTLE DOWN** *Capitol CL 356*.........................**66**   2 wks

| 21 Mar 87 | **SEXY GIRL** Capitol CL 445 | **23** | 5 wks |
| 30 May 87 | **I'M IN LOVE** Capitol CL 450 | **54** | 3 wks |

Mickey THOMAS – *See Elvin BISHOP*

Nicky THOMAS *Jamaica, male vocalist* — **14 wks**

| 13 Jun 70 | ● **LOVE OF THE COMMON PEOPLE** Trojan TR 7750 | **9** | 14 wks |

Rufus THOMAS *US, male vocalist* — **12 wks**

| 11 Apr 70 | **DO THE FUNKY CHICKEN** Stax 144 | **18** | 12 wks |

Tasha THOMAS *US, female vocalist* — **3 wks**

| 20 Jan 79 | **SHOOT ME (WITH YOUR LOVE)** Atlantic LV 4 | **59** | 3 wks |

Timmy THOMAS *US, male vocalist* — **20 wks**

14 Feb 73	**WHY CAN'T WE LIVE TOGETHER** Mojo 2027 012	**12**	11 wks
28 Dec 85	**NEW YORK EYES** Portrait A 6805 *	**41**	7 wks
14 Jul 90	**WHY CAN'T WE LIVE TOGETHER (re-mix)** TK TKR 1	**54**	2 wks

* Nicole with Timmy Thomas

THOMAS and TAYLOR *US, male/female vocal duo* — **5 wks**

| 17 May 86 | **YOU CAN'T BLAME LOVE** Cooltempo COOL 123 | **53** | 5 wks |

Carroll THOMPSON – *See MOVEMENT 98 featuring Carroll THOMPSON; Courtney PINE*

Chris THOMPSON *UK, male vocalist* — **5 wks**

| 27 Oct 79 | **IF YOU REMEMBER ME** Planet K 12389 | **42** | 5 wks |

Sue THOMPSON *US, female vocalist* — **9 wks**

2 Nov 61	**SAD MOVIES** Polydor NH 66967	**46**	1 wk
16 Nov 61	**SAD MOVIES (re-entry)** Polydor NH 66967	**48**	1 wk
21 Jan 65	**PAPER TIGER** Hickory 1284	**50**	1 wk
11 Feb 65	**PAPER TIGER (re-entry)** Hickory 1284	**30**	6 wks

THOMPSON TWINS *UK/New Zealand, male/female vocal/instrumental group* — **108 wks**

6 Nov 82	**LIES** Arista ARIST 486	**67**	3 wks
29 Jan 83	● **LOVE ON YOUR SIDE** Arista ARIST 504	**9**	12 wks
16 Apr 83	● **WE ARE DETECTIVE** Arista ARIST 526	**7**	9 wks
16 Jul 83	**WATCHING** Arista TWINS 1	**33**	6 wks
19 Nov 83	● **HOLD ME NOW** Arista TWINS 2	**4**	15 wks
4 Feb 84	● **DOCTOR DOCTOR** Arista TWINS 3	**3**	10 wks
31 Mar 84	● **YOU TAKE ME UP** Arista TWINS 4	**2**	9 wks
7 Jul 84	**SISTER OF MERCY** Arista TWINS 5	**11**	8 wks
8 Sep 84	**SISTER OF MERCY (re-entry)** Arista TWINS 5	**66**	1 wk
8 Dec 84	**LAY YOUR HANDS ON ME** Arista TWINS 6	**13**	9 wks
31 Aug 85	**DON'T MESS WITH DOCTOR DREAM** Arista TWINS 9	**15**	6 wks
19 Oct 85	**KING FOR A DAY** Arista TWINS 7	**22**	6 wks
7 Dec 85	**REVOLUTION** Arista TWINS 10	**56**	3 wks
4 Jan 86	**REVOLUTION (re-entry)** Arista TWINS 10	**75**	1 wk
11 Apr 87	**GET THAT LOVE** Arista TWINS 12	**66**	1 wk
15 Oct 88	**IN THE NAME OF LOVE '88** Arista 111808	**46**	3 wks
28 Sep 91	**COME INSIDE** Warner Bros. W 0058	**56**	4 wks
25 Jan 92	**THE SAINT** Warner Bros. W 0080	**53**	2 wks

David THORNE *US, male vocalist* — **8 wks**

| 24 Jan 63 | **ALLEY CAT SONG** Stateside SS 141 | **21** | 8 wks |

Ken THORNE *UK, orchestra* — **15 wks**

| 18 Jul 63 | ● **THEME FROM THE FILM 'THE LEGION'S LAST PATROL'** HMV POP 1176 | **4** | 15 wks |

THOUSAND YARD STARE *UK, male vocal/instrumental group* — **4 wks**

26 Oct 91	**SEASONSTREAM EP** Stifled Aardvark AARD 5T	**65**	1 wk
8 Feb 92	**COMEUPPANCE** Stifled Aardvark AARD 007	**37**	2 wks
11 Jul 92	**SPINDRIFT EP** Stifled Aardvark AARDT 010	**58**	1 wk

Tracks on Seasonstream EP: O-O AET/Village End/Keepsake/Worse For Wear. Tracks on Spindrift EP: Wideshire Two/Hand, Son/Happenstance/Mocca Pune.

THRASHING DOVES *UK, male vocal/instrumental group* — **3 wks**

| 24 Jan 87 | **BEAUTIFUL IMBALANCE** A & M TDOVE 1 | **50** | 3 wks |

THREE DEGREES *US, female vocal group* — **111 wks**

13 Apr 74	**YEAR OF DECISION** Philadelphia International PIR 2073	**13**	10 wks
27 Apr 74	**TSOP (THE SOUND OF PHILADELPHIA)** Philadelphia International PIR 2289 *	**22**	9 wks
13 Jul 74	★ **WHEN WILL I SEE YOU AGAIN** Philadelphia International PIR 2155	**1**	16 wks
2 Nov 74	**GET YOUR LOVE BACK** Philadelphia International PIR 2737	**34**	4 wks
12 Apr 75	● **TAKE GOOD CARE OF YOURSELF** Philadelphia International PIR 3177	**9**	9 wks
5 Jul 75	**LONG LOST LOVER** Philadelphia International PIR 3352	**40**	4 wks
1 May 76	**TOAST OF LOVE** Epic EPC 4215	**36**	4 wks
7 Oct 78	**GIVIN' UP GIVIN' IN** Ariola ARO 130	**12**	10 wks
13 Jan 79	● **WOMAN IN LOVE** Ariola ARO 141	**3**	11 wks
24 Mar 79	● **THE RUNNER** Ariola ARO 154	**10**	10 wks
23 Jun 79	**THE GOLDEN LADY** Ariola ARO 170	**56**	3 wks
29 Sep 79	**JUMP THE GUN** Ariola ARO 183	**48**	5 wks
24 Nov 79	● **MY SIMPLE HEART** Ariola ARO 202	**9**	11 wks
5 Oct 85	**THE HEAVEN I NEED** Supreme SUPE 102	**42**	5 wks

* MFSB featuring the Three Degrees

THREE DOG NIGHT *US, male vocal/instrumental group* — **23 wks**

| 8 Aug 70 | ● **MAMA TOLD ME NOT TO COME** Stateside SS 8052 | **3** | 14 wks |
| 29 May 71 | **JOY TO THE WORLD** Probe PRO 523 | **24** | 9 wks |

THREE GOOD REASONS *UK, male vocal/instrumental group* — **3 wks**

| 10 Mar 66 | **NOWHERE MAN** Mercury MF 899 | **47** | 3 wks |

THREE KAYES – *See KAYE SISTERS*

THREE TONS OF JOY – *See Johnny OTIS SHOW*

THROWING MUSES *US, male/female vocal/instrumental group* — **3 wks**

| 9 Feb 91 | **COUNTING BACKWARDS** 4AD AD 1001 | **70** | 2 wks |
| 1 Aug 92 | **FIREPILE (EP)** 4AD BAD 2012 | **46** | 1 wk |

Tracks on Firepile (EP): Firepile/Manic Depression/Snailhead/City Of The Dead.

THS - THE HORN SECTION
US, male/female vocal/instrumental group **3 wks**

18 Aug 84	LADY SHINE (SHINE ON) *Fourth & Broadway BRW 10*	54	3 wks

Harry THUMANN
Germany, male instrumentalist - keyboards **6 wks**

21 Feb 81	UNDERWATER *Decca F 13901*	41	6 wks

THUNDER *UK/US, male vocal/instrumental group* **27 wks**

17 Feb 90	DIRTY LOVE *EMI EM 126*	32	4 wks
12 May 90	BACKSTREET SYMPHONY *EMI EM 137*	25	4 wks
14 Jul 90	GIMME SOME LOVIN' *EMI EM 148*	36	3 wks
29 Sep 90	SHE'S SO FINE *EMI EM 158*	34	3 wks
23 Feb 91	LOVE WALKED IN *EMI EM 175*	21	4 wks
15 Aug 92	LOW LIFE IN HIGH PLACES *EMI EM 242*	22	5 wks
10 Oct 92	EVERYBODY WANTS HER *EMI EM 249*	36	4 wks

THUNDERBIRDS – *See Chris FARLOWE*

THUNDERCLAP NEWMAN
UK, male vocal/instrumental group **13 wks**

11 Jun 69	★ SOMETHING IN THE AIR *Track 604-031*	1	12 wks
27 Jun 70	ACCIDENTS *Track 2094 001*	46	1 wk

THUNDERTHIGHS *UK, female vocal group* **5 wks**

22 Jun 74	CENTRAL PARK ARREST *Philips 6006 386*	30	5 wks

Bobby THURSTON *US, male vocalist* **10 wks**

29 Mar 80	● CHECK OUT THE GROOVE *Epic EPC 8348*	10	10 wks

TIFFANY *US, female vocalist* **45 wks**

16 Jan 88	★ I THINK WE'RE ALONE NOW *MCA MCA 1211*	1	13 wks
19 Mar 88	● COULD'VE BEEN *MCA TIFF 2*	4	9 wks
4 Jun 88	● I SAW HIM STANDING THERE *MCA TIFF 3*	8	7 wks
6 Aug 88	FEELINGS OF FOREVER *MCA TIFF 4*	52	2 wks
12 Nov 88	RADIO ROMANCE *MCA TIFF 5*	13	11 wks
11 Feb 89	ALL THIS TIME *MCA TIFF 6*	47	3 wks

TIGERTAILZ *US, male vocal/instrumental group* **2 wks**

24 Jun 89	LOVE BOMB BABY *Music For Nations KUT 132*	75	1 wk
16 Feb 91	HEAVEN *Music For Nations KUT 137*	71	1 wk

TIGHT FIT *UK, male/female vocal group* **49 wks**

18 Jul 81	● BACK TO THE SIXTIES *Jive JIVE 002*	4	11 wks
26 Sep 81	BACK TO THE SIXTIES PART 2 *Jive JIVE 005*	33	5 wks
23 Jan 82	★ THE LION SLEEPS TONIGHT *Jive JIVE 9*	1	15 wks
1 May 82	● FANTASY ISLAND *Jive JIVE 13*	5	12 wks
31 Jul 82	SECRET HEART *Jive JIVE 20*	41	6 wks

TIJUANA BRASS – *See Herb ALPERT*

TIK and TOK *UK, male vocal duo* **2 wks**

8 Oct 83	COOL RUNNING *Survival SUR 016*	69	2 wks

Tanita TIKARAM *UK, female vocalist* **27 wks**

30 Jul 88	● GOOD TRADITION *WEA YZ 196*	10	10 wks
22 Oct 88	TWIST IN MY SOBRIETY *WEA YZ 321*	22	8 wks
14 Jan 89	CATHEDRAL SONG *WEA YZ 331*	48	3 wks
18 Mar 89	WORLD OUTSIDE YOUR WINDOW *WEA YZ 363*	58	2 wks
13 Jan 90	WE ALMOST GOT IT TOGETHER *WEA YZ 443*	52	3 wks
9 Feb 91	ONLY THE ONES WE LOVE *East West YZ 558*	69	1 wk

Johnny TILLOTSON *US, male vocalist* **50 wks**

1 Dec 60	★ POETRY IN MOTION *London HLA 9231*	1	15 wks
2 Feb 61	JIMMY'S GIRL *London HLA 9275*	50	1 wk
16 Feb 61	JIMMY'S GIRL (re-entry) *London HLA 9275*	43	1 wk
12 Jul 62	IT KEEPS RIGHT ON A HURTIN' *London HLA 9550*	31	10 wks
4 Oct 62	SEND ME THE PILLOW YOU DREAM ON *London HLA 9598*	21	10 wks
27 Dec 62	I CAN'T HELP IT *London HLA 9642*	42	1 wk
10 Jan 63	I CAN'T HELP IT (re-entry) *London HLA 9642*	47	1 wk
24 Jan 63	I CAN'T HELP IT (2nd re-entry) *London HLA 9642*	41	4 wks
9 May 63	OUT OF MY MIND *London HLA 9695*	34	5 wks
14 Apr 79	POETRY IN MOTION (re-issue)/PRINCESS PRINCESS *Lightning LIG 9016*	67	2 wks

TIMBUK 3 *US, male/female vocal/instrumental duo* **7 wks**

31 Jan 87	FUTURE'S SO BRIGHT I GOTTA WEAR SHADES *IRS IRM 126*	21	7 wks

TIME FREQUENCY
UK, male instrumental/production group **1 wk**

6 Jun 92	REAL LOVE *Jive JIVET 307*	60	1 wk

TIME UK *UK, male vocal/instrumental group* **3 wks**

8 Oct 83	THE CABARET *Red Bus/Arcadia TIM 123*	63	3 wks

TIME ZONE *UK/US, male vocal/instrumental duo* **9 wks**

19 Jan 85	WORLD DESTRUCTION *Virgin VS 743*	44	9 wks

TIMEBOX *UK, male vocal/instrumental group* **4 wks**

24 Jul 68	BEGGIN' *Deram DM 194*	38	4 wks

TIMELORDS *UK, male/female instrumental group* **9 wks**

4 Jun 88	★ DOCTORIN' THE TARDIS *KLF KLF 003*	1	9 wks

TIMEX SOCIAL CLUB
US, male vocal/instrumental group **9 wks**

13 Sep 86	RUMORS *Cooltempo COOL 133*	13	9 wks

TIN MACHINE *US/UK, male vocal/instrumental group* **10 wks**

1 Jul 89	UNDER THE GOD *EMI-USA MT 68*	51	2 wks
9 Sep 89	TIN MACHINE/MAGGIE'S FARM (LIVE) *EMI-USA MT 73*	48	2 wks
24 Aug 91	YOU BELONG IN ROCK 'N' ROLL *London LON 305*	33	3 wks
2 Nov 91	BABY UNIVERSAL *London LON 310*	48	3 wks

TINGO TANGO *UK, male instrumental group* **2 wks**

21 Jul 90	IT IS JAZZ *Champion CHAMP 250*	68	2 wks

TINY TIM US, male vocalist · 1 wk

5 Feb 69	GREAT BALLS OF FIRE Reprise RS 20802	45	1 wk

TITANIC Norway/UK, male instrumental group · 12 wks

25 Sep 71 ●	SULTANA CBS 5365	5	12 wks

TITIYO Sweden, female vocalist · 4 wks

3 Mar 90	AFTER THE RAIN Arista 112722	60	3 wks
6 Oct 90	FLOWERS Arista 113212	71	1 wk

Cara TIVEY – See Billy BRAGG

TLC US, female vocal group · 10 wks

20 Jun 92	AIN'T 2 PROUD 2 BEG Arista 115265	13	5 wks
22 Aug 92	BABY-BABY-BABY LaFace 74321111297	55	3 wks
24 Oct 92	WHAT ABOUT YOUR FRIENDS LaFace 74321118177	59	2 wks

T99 Belgium, male instrumental/production group · 10 wks

11 May 91	ANASTHASIA XL XLS 19	14	6 wks
19 Oct 91	NOCTURNE Emphasis 6574097	33	4 wks

TOADS – See Stan FREBERG

Art and Dotty TODD US, male/female vocal duo · 7 wks

13 Feb 53 ●	BROKEN WINGS HMV B 10399	6	7 wks

TOGETHER UK, male vocal/instrumental group · 8 wks

4 Aug 90	HARDCORE UPROAR ffrr F 143	12	8 wks

TOKENS US, male vocal group · 12 wks

21 Dec 61	THE LION SLEEPS TONIGHT RCA 1263	11	12 wks

TOL and TOL Holland, male vocal/instrumental duo · 2 wks

14 Apr 90	ELENI Dover ROJ 5	73	2 wks

TOM TOM CLUB US, female/male vocal/instrumental group · 20 wks

20 Jun 81 ●	WORDY RAPPINGHOOD Island WIP 6694	7	9 wks
10 Oct 81	GENIUS OF LOVE Island WIP 6735	65	2 wks
7 Aug 82	UNDER THE BOARDWALK Island WIP 6762	22	9 wks

Satoshi TOMIIE – See Frankie KNUCKLES

TONGUE 'N' CHEEK
UK, male/female vocal/instrumental group · 28 wks

27 Feb 88	NOBODY (CAN LOVE ME) Criminal BUS 6 *	59	6 wks
25 Nov 89	ENCORE Syncopate SY 33	41	4 wks
14 Apr 90	TOMORROW Syncopate SY 34	20	7 wks
4 Aug 90	NOBODY Syncopate SY 37	37	5 wks
19 Jan 91	FORGET ME NOTS Syncopate SY 39	26	6 wks

* Tongue In Cheek

British Hit Singles Part One: Alphabetically by Artist
Date of chart entry/Title & catalogue no./Peak position reached/Weeks on chart
★ Number one ● Top Ten † still on chart at 31 Dec 1992
* = credited to act billed in footnote

TONIGHT UK, male vocal/instrumental group · 10 wks

28 Jan 78	DRUMMER MAN Target TDS 1	14	8 wks
20 May 78	MONEY THAT'S YOUR PROBLEM Target TDS 2	66	2 wks

TONY! TONI! TONÉ! US, male vocal group · 7 wks

30 Jun 90	OAKLAND STROKE Wing WING 7	50	5 wks
9 Mar 91	IT NEVER RAINS (IN SOUTHERN CALIFORNIA) Wing WING 10	69	2 wks

TOO TOUGH TEE – See DYNAMIX featuring TOO TOUGH TEE

TOP UK, male vocal/instrumental group · 2 wks

20 Jul 91	NUMBER ONE DOMINATOR Island IS 496	67	2 wks

TOP LINERS – See Rocky SHARPE and the REPLAYS

TOPOL Israel, male vocalist · 20 wks

20 Apr 67 ●	IF I WERE A RICH MAN CBS 202651	9	20 wks

Mel TORMÉ US, male vocalist · 32 wks

27 Apr 56	MOUNTAIN GREENERY Vogue/Coral Q 72150	15	11 wks
27 Jul 56 ●	MOUNTAIN GREENERY (re-entry) Vogue/Coral Q 72150	4	13 wks
3 Jan 63	COMING HOME BABY London HLK 9643	13	8 wks

TORNADOS UK, male instrumental group · 59 wks

30 Aug 62 ★	TELSTAR Decca F 11494	1	25 wks
10 Jan 63 ●	GLOBETROTTER Decca F 11562	5	11 wks
21 Mar 63	ROBOT Decca F 11606	17	12 wks
6 Jun 63	THE ICE CREAM MAN Decca F 11662	18	9 wks
10 Oct 63	DRAGONFLY Decca F 11745	41	2 wks

Mitchell TOROK US, male vocalist · 19 wks

28 Sep 56 ●	WHEN MEXICO GAVE UP THE RUMBA Brunswick 05586	6	17 wks
11 Jan 57	RED LIGHT GREEN LIGHT Brunswick 05626	29	1 wk
1 Feb 57	WHEN MEXICO GAVE UP THE RUMBA (re-entry) Brunswick 05586	30	1 wk

Peter TOSH Jamaica, male vocalist · 12 wks

21 Oct 78	(YOU GOTTA WALK) DON'T LOOK BACK Rolling Stones 2859	43	7 wks
2 Apr 83	JOHNNY B. GOODE EMI RIC 115	48	5 wks

TOTAL CONTRAST UK, male vocal/instrumental duo · 22 wks

3 Aug 85	TAKES A LITTLE TIME London LON 71	17	10 wks
19 Oct 85	HIT AND RUN London LON 76	41	5 wks
1 Mar 86	THE RIVER London LON 83	44	3 wks
10 May 86	WHAT YOU GONNA DO ABOUT IT London LON 95	63	4 wks

TOTO US, male vocal/instrumental group — 34 wks

Date	Title	Pos	Wks
10 Feb 79	**HOLD THE LINE** CBS 6784	14	11 wks
5 Feb 83 ●	**AFRICA** CBS A 2510	3	10 wks
9 Apr 83	**ROSANNA** CBS A 2079	12	8 wks
18 Jun 83	**I WON'T HOLD YOU BACK** CBS A 3392	37	5 wks

TOTO COELO UK, female vocal group — 14 wks

Date	Title	Pos	Wks
7 Aug 82 ●	**I EAT CANNIBALS** PART 1 Radialchoice TIC 10	8	10 wks
13 Nov 82	**DRACULA'S TANGO/MUCHO MACHO** Radialchoice TIC 11	54	4 wks

TOTTENHAM HOTSPUR F.A. CUP FINAL SQUAD UK, male football team vocalists — 23 wks

Date	Title	Pos	Wks
9 May 81 ●	**OSSIE'S DREAM (SPURS ARE ON THEIR WAY TO WEMBLEY)** Rockney SHELF 1	5	8 wks
1 May 82	**TOTTENHAM TOTTENHAM** Rockney SHELF 2	19	7 wks
9 May 87	**HOT SHOT TOTTENHAM!** Rainbow RBR 16	18	5 wks
11 May 91	**WHEN THE YEAR ENDS IN 1** A1 A 1324	44	3 wks

All hits feature the vocal and instrumental talents of Chas and Dave.

TOUCH OF SOUL — 3 wks
UK, male/female vocal/instrumental group

Date	Title	Pos	Wks
19 May 90	**WE GOT THE LOVE** Cooltempo COOL 204	46	3 wks

TOURISTS UK, male/female vocal/instrumental group — 40 wks

Date	Title	Pos	Wks
9 Jun 79	**BLIND AMONG THE FLOWERS** Logo GO 350	52	5 wks
8 Sep 79	**THE LONELIEST MAN IN THE WORLD** Logo GO 360	32	7 wks
10 Nov 79 ●	**I ONLY WANT TO BE WITH YOU** Logo GO 370	4	14 wks
9 Feb 80 ●	**SO GOOD TO BE BACK HOME AGAIN** Logo TOUR 1	8	9 wks
18 Oct 80	**DON'T SAY I TOLD YOU SO** RCA TOUR 2	40	5 wks

Carol Lynn TOWNES US, female vocalist — 7 wks

Date	Title	Pos	Wks
4 Aug 84	**99 ½** Polydor POSP 693	47	4 wks
19 Jan 85	**BELIEVE IN THE BEAT** Polydor POSP 720	56	3 wks

Pete TOWNSHEND UK, male vocalist — 17 wks

Date	Title	Pos	Wks
5 Apr 80	**ROUGH BOYS** Atco K 11460	39	6 wks
21 Jun 80	**LET MY LOVE OPEN YOUR DOOR** Atco K 11486	46	6 wks
21 Aug 82	**UNIFORMS (CORPS D'ESPRIT)** Atco K 11751	48	5 wks

TOXIC TWO US, male instrumental/production duo — 6 wks

Date	Title	Pos	Wks
7 Mar 92	**RAVE GENERATOR** PWL International PWL 223	13	6 wks

TOY DOLLS UK, male vocal/instrumental group — 12 wks

Date	Title	Pos	Wks
1 Dec 84 ●	**NELLIE THE ELEPHANT** Volume VOL 11	4	12 wks

TOYAH UK, female vocalist — 87 wks

Date	Title	Pos	Wks
14 Feb 81 ●	**FOUR FROM TOYAH EP** Safari TOY 1	4	14 wks
16 May 81 ●	**I WANT TO BE FREE** Safari SAFE 34	8	11 wks
3 Oct 81 ●	**THUNDER IN THE MOUNTAINS** Safari SAFE 38	4	9 wks
28 Nov 81 ●	**FOUR MORE FROM TOYAH EP** Safari TOY 2	14	9 wks
22 May 82	**BRAVE NEW WORLD** Safari SAFE 45	21	8 wks
17 Jul 82	**IEYA** Safari SAFE 28	48	5 wks
9 Oct 82	**BE LOUD BE PROUD (BE HEARD)** Safari SAFE 52	30	7 wks
24 Sep 83	**REBEL RUN** Safari SAFE 56	24	5 wks
19 Nov 83	**THE VOW** Safari SAFE 58	50	5 wks
27 Apr 85	**DON'T FALL IN LOVE (I SAID)** Portrait A 6160	22	6 wks
29 Jun 85	**SOUL PASSING THROUGH SOUL** Portrait A 6359	57	3 wks
25 Apr 87	**ECHO BEACH** EG EGO 31	54	5 wks

Tracks on Four From Toyah EP: It's A Mystery/Revelations/War Boys/Angels And Demons.
Tracks on Four More From Toyah EP: Good Morning Universe/Urban Tribesman/In The Fairground/The Furious Futures.

TOYS US, female vocal group — 17 wks

Date	Title	Pos	Wks
4 Nov 65 ●	**A LOVER'S CONCERTO** Stateside SS 460	5	13 wks
27 Jan 66	**ATTACK** Stateside SS 483	36	4 wks

T'PAU UK, male/female vocal/instrumental group — 76 wks

Date	Title	Pos	Wks
8 Aug 87 ●	**HEART AND SOUL** Siren SRN 41	4	13 wks
24 Oct 87 ★	**CHINA IN YOUR HAND** Siren SRN 64	1	15 wks
30 Jan 88 ●	**VALENTINE** Siren SRN 69	9	8 wks
2 Apr 88	**SEX TALK (LIVE)** Siren SRN 80	23	7 wks
25 Jun 88	**I WILL BE WITH YOU** Siren SRN 87	14	6 wks
1 Oct 88	**SECRET GARDEN** Siren SRN 93	18	7 wks
3 Dec 88	**ROAD TO OUR DREAM** Siren SRN 100	42	6 wks
25 Mar 89	**ONLY THE LONELY** Siren SRN 107	28	6 wks
18 May 91	**WHENEVER YOU NEED ME** Siren SRN 140	16	6 wks
27 Jul 91	**WALK ON AIR** Siren SRN 142	52	2 wks

TRACIE UK, female vocalist — 24 wks

Date	Title	Pos	Wks
26 Mar 83 ●	**THE HOUSE THAT JACK BUILT** Respond KOB 701	9	8 wks
16 Jul 83	**GIVE IT SOME EMOTION** Respond KOB 704	24	9 wks
14 Apr 84	**SOUL'S ON FIRE** Respond KOB 708	73	2 wks
9 Jun 84	**(I LOVE YOU) WHEN YOU SLEEP** Respond KOB 710	59	3 wks
17 Aug 85	**I CAN'T LEAVE YOU ALONE** Respond SBS 1 *	60	2 wks

* Tracie Young

TRACY – *See MASSIVO featuring TRACY*

TRAFFIC UK, male vocal/instrumental group — 40 wks

Date	Title	Pos	Wks
1 Jun 67 ●	**PAPER SUN** Island WIP 6002	5	10 wks
6 Sep 67 ●	**HOLE IN MY SHOE** Island WIP 6017	2	14 wks
29 Nov 67 ●	**HERE WE GO ROUND THE MULBERRY BUSH** Island WIP 6025	8	12 wks
6 Mar 68	**NO FACE, NO NAME, NO NUMBER** Island WIP 6030	40	4 wks

TRAMAINE US, female vocalist — 2 wks

Date	Title	Pos	Wks
5 Oct 85	**FALL DOWN (SPIRIT OF LOVE)** A & M AM 281	60	2 wks

TRAMMPS US, male vocal group — 53 wks

Date	Title	Pos	Wks
23 Nov 74	**ZING WENT THE STRINGS OF MY HEART** Buddah BDS 405	29	10 wks
1 Feb 75	**SIXTY MINUTE MAN** Buddah BDS 415	40	4 wks
11 Oct 75 ●	**HOLD BACK THE NIGHT** Buddah BDS 437	5	8 wks
13 Mar 76	**THAT'S WHERE THE HAPPY PEOPLE GO** Atlantic K 10703	35	8 wks
24 Jul 76	**SOUL SEARCHIN' TIME** Atlantic K 10797	42	5 wks
14 May 77	**DISCO INFERNO** Atlantic K 10914	16	7 wks
24 Jun 78	**DISCO INFERNO (re-issue)** Atlantic K 11135	47	10 wks
12 Dec 92	**HOLD BACK THE NIGHT** Network NWK 65 *	30†	3 wks

* KWS features guest vocals from the Trammps

TRANSVISION VAMP — 59 wks
UK, male/female vocal/instrumantal group

Date	Title	Pos	Wks
16 Apr 88	**TELL THAT GIRL TO SHUT UP** MCA TVV 2	45	3 wks
25 Jun 88 ●	**I WANT YOUR LOVE** MCA TVV 3	5	13 wks

Although *The Joshua Tree* is their most famous album, U2 have had more top ten singles from *Rattle And Hum*.

Left: The concerto by THE TOYS was adapted from Bach's 'Minuet in G'.

Dutch duo 2 UNLIMITED got ready for success in 1991.

17 Sep 88		REVOLUTION BABY *MCA TVV 4*	30	5 wks
19 Nov 88		SISTER MOON *MCA TVV 5*	41	5 wks
1 Apr 89	●	BABY I DON'T CARE *MCA TVV 6*	3	11 wks
10 Jun 89		THE ONLY ONE *MCA TVV 7*	15	6 wks
5 Aug 89		LANDSLIDE OF LOVE *MCA TVV 8*	14	5 wks
4 Nov 89		BORN TO BE SOLD *MCA TVV 9*	22	4 wks
13 Apr 91		(I JUST WANNA) B WITH U *MCA TVV 10*	30	4 wks
22 Jun 91		IF LOOKS COULD KILL *MCA TVV 11*	41	3 wks

TRANS-X *Canada, female/male vocal/instrumental group*   **9 wks**

13 Jul 85	●	LIVING ON VIDEO *Boiling Point POSP 650*	9	9 wks

TRASH *UK, male vocal/instrumental group*   **3 wks**

25 Oct 69	GOLDEN SLUMBERS/CARRY THAT WEIGHT *Apple 17*	35	3 wks

TRAVELING WILBURYS   **19 wks**
UK/US, male vocal/instrumental group

29 Oct 88	HANDLE WITH CARE *Wilbury W 7732*	21	13 wks
11 Mar 89	END OF THE LINE *Wilbury W 7637*	52	4 wks
30 Jun 90	NOBODY'S CHILD *Wilbury W 9773*	44	2 wks

Randy TRAVIS *US, male vocalist*   **6 wks**

21 May 88	FOREVER AND EVER, AMEN *Warner Bros. W 8384*	55	6 wks

John TRAVOLTA *US, male vocalist*   **81 wks**

20 May 78	★	YOU'RE THE ONE THAT I WANT *RSO 006* *	1	26 wks
16 Sep 78	★	SUMMER NIGHTS *RSO 18* *	1	19 wks
7 Oct 78	●	SANDY *Polydor POSP 6*	2	15 wks
2 Dec 78		GREASED LIGHTNIN' *Polydor POSP 14*	11	9 wks
22 Dec 90	●	GREASE MEGAMIX *Polydor PO 114* *	3	10 wks
23 Mar 91		GREASE - THE DREAM MIX *PWL/Polydor PO 136* *	47	2 wks

* John Travolta and Olivia Newton-John

TREMELOES *UK, male vocal/instrumental group*   **131 wks**

2 Feb 67	●	HERE COMES MY BABY *CBS 202519*	4	11 wks
27 Apr 67	★	SILENCE IS GOLDEN *CBS 2723*	1	15 wks
2 Aug 67	●	EVEN THE BAD TIMES ARE GOOD *CBS 2930*	4	13 wks
8 Nov 67		BE MINE *CBS 3043*	39	2 wks
17 Jan 68	●	SUDDENLY YOU LOVE ME *CBS 3234*	6	11 wks
8 May 68		HELULE HELULE *CBS 2889*	14	9 wks
18 Sep 68	●	MY LITTLE LADY *CBS 3480*	6	12 wks
11 Dec 68		I SHALL BE RELEASED *CBS 3873*	29	5 wks
19 Mar 69		HELLO WORLD *CBS 4065*	14	8 wks
1 Nov 69	●	(CALL ME) NUMBER ONE *CBS 4582*	2	14 wks
21 Mar 70		BY THE WAY *CBS 4815*	35	6 wks
12 Sep 70	●	ME AND MY LIFE *CBS 5139*	4	18 wks
10 Jul 71		HELLO BUDDY *CBS 7294*	32	7 wks

See also Brian Poole and the Tremeloes.

Jackie TRENT *UK, female vocalist*   **17 wks**

22 Apr 65	★	WHERE ARE YOU NOW (MY LOVE) *Pye 7N 15776*	1	11 wks
1 Jul 65		WHEN THE SUMMERTIME IS OVER *Pye 7N 15865*	39	2 wks
2 Apr 69		I'LL BE THERE *Pye 7N 17693*	38	4 wks

Ralph TRESVANT *US, male vocalist*   **21 wks**

12 Jan 91	SENSITIVITY *MCA MCS 1462*	18	8 wks

15 Aug 92	●	THE BEST THINGS IN LIFE ARE FREE *Perspective PERSS 7400* *	2	13 wks

* Luther Vandross and Janet Jackson with special guests BBD and Ralph Tresvant

T. REX *UK, male vocal/instrumental group*   **235 wks**

8 May 68		DEBORA *Regal Zonophone RZ 3008* *	34	7 wks
4 Sep 68		ONE INCH ROCK *Regal Zonophone RZ 3011* *	28	7 wks
9 Aug 69		KING OF THE RUMBLING SPIRES *Regal Zonophone RZ 3022* *	44	1 wk
24 Oct 70	●	RIDE A WHITE SWAN *Fly BUG 1*	2	20 wks
27 Feb 71	●	HOT LOVE *Fly BUG 6*	1	17 wks
10 Jul 71	★	GET IT ON *Fly BUG 10*	1	13 wks
13 Nov 71	●	JEEPSTER *Fly BUG 16*	2	15 wks
29 Jan 72	★	TELEGRAM SAM *T. Rex 101*	1	12 wks
1 Apr 72	●	DEBORA/ONE INCH ROCK (re-issue) *Magnifly Echo 102* *	7	10 wks
13 May 72	★	METAL GURU *EMI MARC 1*	1	14 wks
16 Sep 72	●	CHILDREN OF THE REVOLUTION *EMI MARC 2*	2	10 wks
9 Dec 72	●	SOLID GOLD EASY ACTION *EMI MARC 3*	2	11 wks
10 Mar 73	●	20TH CENTURY BOY *EMI MARC 4*	3	9 wks
16 Jun 73	●	THE GROOVER *EMI MARC 5*	4	9 wks
24 Nov 73		TRUCK ON (TYKE) *EMI MARC 6*	12	11 wks
9 Feb 74		TEENAGE DREAM *EMI MARC 7* **	13	5 wks
13 Jul 74		LIGHT OF LOVE *EMI MARC 8*	22	5 wks
16 Nov 74		ZIP GUN BOOGIE *EMI MARC 9*	41	3 wks
12 Jul 75		NEW YORK CITY *EMI MARC 10*	15	8 wks
11 Oct 75		DREAMY LADY *EMI MARC 11* ***	30	5 wks
6 Mar 76		LONDON BOYS *EMI MARC 13*	40	3 wks
19 Jun 76		I LOVE TO BOOGIE *EMI MARC 14*	13	9 wks
2 Oct 76		LASER LOVE *EMI MARC 15*	41	4 wks
2 Apr 77		THE SOUL OF MY SUIT *EMI MARC 16*	42	3 wks
9 May 81		RETURN OF THE ELECTRIC WARRIOR EP *Rarn MBSF 001* ****	50	4 wks
19 Sep 81		YOU SCARE ME TO DEATH *Cherry Red CHERRY 29* ****	51	4 wks
27 Mar 82		TELEGRAM SAM (re-entry) *T. Rex 101*	69	2 wks
18 May 85		MEGAREX *Marc On Wax TANX 1* **	72	2 wks
9 May 87		GET IT ON (re-mix) *Marc On Wax MARC 10* **	54	4 wks
24 Aug 91		20TH CENTURY BOY (re-issue) *Marc On Wax MARC 501* **	13	8 wks

* Tyrannosaurus Rex ** Marc Bolan and T. Rex *** T. Rex Disco Party
**** Marc Bolan

Tracks on Return Of The Electric Warrior EP: *Sing Me A Song/Endless Sleep/The Lilac Hand Of Menihol Dan.* Megarex *is a medley of extracts from the following T. Rex hits: Truck On (Tyke)/The Groover/Telegram Sam/Shock Rock/Metal Guru/20th Century Boy/Children Of The Revolution/Hot Love.*

TRIBAL HOUSE *US, male vocal/instrumental group*   **2 wks**

3 Feb 90	MOTHERLAND-A-FRI-CA *Cooltempo COOL 198*	57	2 wks

Tony TRIBE *Jamaica, male vocalist*   **2 wks**

16 Jul 69	RED RED WINE *Downtown DT 419*	50	1 wk
9 Aug 69	RED RED WINE (re-entry) *Downtown DT 419*	46	1 wk

A TRIBE CALLED QUEST *US, male rap group*   **10 wks**

18 Aug 90	BONITA APPLEBUM *Jive JIVE 256*	47	3 wks
19 Jan 91	CAN I KICK IT *Jive JIVE 265*	15	7 wks

TRIBE OF TOFFS *UK, male vocal/instrumental group*   **5 wks**

24 Dec 88	JOHN KETTLEY (IS A WEATHERMAN) *Completely Different DAFT 1*	21	5 wks

TRICKY DISCO *UK, male vocal/instrumental group*   **10 wks**

28 Jul 90	TRICKY DISCO *Warp WAP 7*	14	8 wks
20 Apr 91	HOUSE FLY *Warp 7WAP 11*	55	2 wks

TRIFFIDS *New Zealand, male vocal/instrumental group* **1 wk**

6 Feb 88 **A TRICK OF THE LIGHT** *Island IS 350* ....**73** 1 wk

TRINIDAD OIL COMPANY **5 wks**
Trinidad, male/female vocal/instrumental group

21 May 77 **THE CALENDAR SONG** *Harvest HAR 5122* ....**34** 5 wks

TRINITY – *See Julie DRISCOLL, Brian AUGER and the TRINITY*

TRIO *Germany, male vocal/instrumental group* **10 wks**

3 Jul 82 ● **DA DA DA** *Mobile Suit Corporation CORP 5* ....**2** 10 wks

TRIUMPH *Canada, male vocal/instrumental group* **2 wks**

22 Nov 80 **I LIVE FOR THE WEEKEND** *RCA 13* ....**59** 2 wks

TROGGS *UK, male vocal/instrumental group* **85 wks**

5 May 66 ● **WILD THING** *Fontana TF 689* ....**2** 12 wks
14 Jul 66 ★ **WITH A GIRL LIKE YOU** *Fontana TF 717*.............**1** 12 wks
29 Sep 66 ● **I CAN'T CONTROL MYSELF** *Page One POF 001* .....**2** 14 wks
15 Dec 66 ● **ANY WAY THAT YOU WANT ME** *Page One POF 010*.......**8** 10 wks
16 Feb 67 **GIVE IT TO ME** *Page One POF 015* ....**12** 10 wks
1 Jun 67 **NIGHT OF THE LONG GRASS** *Page One POF 022*...........**17** 6 wks
26 Jul 67 **HI HI HAZEL** *Page One POF 030* ....**42** 3 wks
18 Oct 67 ● **LOVE IS ALL AROUND** *Page One POF 040* ....**5** 14 wks
28 Feb 68 **LITTLE GIRL** *Page One POF 056* ....**37** 4 wks

TRONIKHOUSE *US, male producer - Kevin Saunderson* **1 wk**

14 Mar 92 **UP TEMPO** *KMS UK KMSUK 1* ....**68** 1 wk

TROUBADOURS DU ROI BAUDOUIN **11 wks**
Zaire, male/female vocal group

19 Mar 69 **SANCTUS (MISSA LUBA)** *Philips BF 1732* ....**28** 6 wks
7 May 69 **SANCTUS (MISSA LUBA) (re-entry)** *Philips BF 1732* ....**37** 5 wks

TROUBLE FUNK *US, male vocal/instrumental group* **3 wks**

27 Jun 87 **WOMAN OF PRINCIPLE** *Fourth & Broadway BRW 70*.......**65** 3 wks

Doris TROY *US, female vocalist* **12 wks**

19 Nov 64 **WHATCHA GONNA DO ABOUT IT** *Atlantic AT 4011* ....**37** 7 wks
21 Jan 65 **WHATCHA GONNA DO ABOUT IT (re-entry)**
Atlantic AT 4011 ....**38** 5 wks

TRUCKIN' CO. – *See Garnet MIMMS and TRUCKIN' CO.*

Andrea TRUE CONNECTION **16 wks**
US, female vocalist, male instrumental backing group

17 Apr 76 ● **MORE MORE MORE** *Buddah BDS 442*.......................**5** 10 wks
4 Mar 78 **WHAT'S YOUR NAME WHAT'S YOUR NUMBER**
Buddah BDS 467 ....**34** 6 wks

TRUE FAITH with FINAL CUT **4 wks**
US, male/female vocal/instrumental group

2 Mar 91 **TAKE ME AWAY** *Network NWK 20* ....**51** 4 wks

TRUE IMAGE – *See Monie LOVE*

TRUSSEL *US, male vocal/instrumental group* **4 wks**

8 Mar 80 **LOVE INJECTION** *Elektra K 12412* ....**43** 4 wks

TRUTH *UK, male vocal duo* **6 wks**

3 Feb 66 **GIRL** *Pye 7N 17035*.................................**27** 6 wks

TRUTH *UK, male vocal/instrumental group* **16 wks**

11 Jun 83 **CONFUSION (HITS US EVERY TIME)**
Formation TRUTH 1 ....**22** 7 wks
27 Aug 83 **A STEP IN THE RIGHT DIRECTION**
Formation TRUTH 2 ....**32** 7 wks
4 Feb 84 **NO STONE UNTURNED** *Formation TRUTH 3* ....**66** 2 wks

TUBES *US, male vocal/instrumental group* **18 wks**

19 Nov 77 **WHITE PUNKS ON DOPE** *A & M AMS 7323*....................**28** 4 wks
28 Apr 79 **PRIME TIME** *A & M AMS 7423* ....**34** 10 wks
12 Sep 81 **DON'T WANT TO WAIT ANYMORE** *Capitol CL 208* ......**60** 4 wks

TUBEWAY ARMY – *See Gary NUMAN*

Junior TUCKER *UK, male vocalist* **2 wks**

2 Jun 90 **DON'T TEST** *10 TEN 299* ....**54** 2 wks

Louise TUCKER *Holland, female vocalist* **5 wks**

9 Apr 83 **MIDNIGHT BLUE** *Ariola ARO 289* ....**59** 5 wks

Tommy TUCKER *US, male vocalist* **10 wks**

26 Mar 64 **HI-HEEL SNEAKERS** *Pye 7N 25238*....................**23** 10 wks

Claramae TURNER – *See VARIOUS ARTISTS (EPs & LPs) - Carousel Soundtrack*

Ike and Tina TURNER **44 wks**
US, male/female vocal instrumental duo

9 Jun 66 ● **RIVER DEEP MOUNTAIN HIGH** *London HL 10046*...........**3** 13 wks
28 Jul 66 **TELL HER I'M NOT HOME** *Warner Bros. WB 5753*...........**48** 1 wk
27 Oct 66 **A LOVE LIKE YOURS** *London HL 10083* ....**16** 10 wks
12 Feb 69 **RIVER DEEP MOUNTAIN HIGH (re-issue)**
London HLU 10242 ....**33** 7 wks
8 Sep 73 ● **NUTBUSH CITY LIMITS** *United Artists UP 35582* ....**4** 13 wks
See also Tina Turner.

Ruby TURNER *UK, female vocalist* **27 wks**

25 Jan 86 **IF YOU'RE READY (COME GO WITH ME)**
Jive JIVE 109 * ....**30** 7 wks
29 Mar 86 **I'M IN LOVE** *Jive JIVE 118* ....**61** 4 wks
13 Sep 86 **BYE BABY** *Jive JIVE 126* ....**52** 3 wks
14 Mar 87 **I'D RATHER GO BLIND** *Jive RTS 1* ....**24** 8 wks
16 May 87 **I'M IN LOVE** *Jive RTS 2* ....**57** 2 wks
13 Jan 90 **IT'S GONNA BE ALRIGHT** *Jive RTS 7* ....**57** 3 wks
* *Ruby Turner featuring Jonathan Butler*

Sammy TURNER *US, male vocalist* **2 wks**

13 Nov 59 **ALWAYS** *London HLX 8963*.................................**26** 2 wks

Tina TURNER *US, female vocalist* **164 wks**

19 Nov 83 ● **LET'S STAY TOGETHER** *Capitol CL 316* .....**6** 13 wks
25 Feb 84 **HELP** *Capitol CL 325*.................................**40** 6 wks

16 Jun 84 ●	WHAT'S LOVE GOT TO DO WITH IT		
	Capitol CL 334	3	16 wks
15 Sep 84	BETTER BE GOOD TO ME Capitol CL 338	45	5 wks
17 Nov 84	PRIVATE DANCER Capitol CL 343	26	9 wks
2 Mar 85	I CAN'T STAND THE RAIN Capitol CL 352	57	3 wks
20 Jul 85 ●	WE DON'T NEED ANOTHER HERO (THUNDERDOME) Capitol CL 364	3	12 wks
12 Oct 85	ONE OF THE LIVING Capitol CL 376	55	2 wks
2 Nov 85	IT'S ONLY LOVE A & M AM 285 *	29	6 wks
23 Aug 86	TYPICAL MALE Capitol CL 419	33	6 wks
8 Nov 86	TWO PEOPLE Capitol CL 430	43	4 wks
14 Mar 87	WHAT YOU GET IS WHAT YOU SEE Capitol CL 439	30	7 wks
13 Jun 87	BREAK EVERY RULE Capitol CL 452	43	3 wks
20 Jun 87	TEARING US APART Duck W 8299 **	56	3 wks
19 Mar 88	ADDICTED TO LOVE (LIVE) Capitol CL 484	71	2 wks
2 Sep 89 ●	THE BEST Capitol CL 543	5	12 wks
18 Nov 89 ●	I DON'T WANNA LOSE YOU Capitol CL 553	8	11 wks
17 Feb 90	STEAMY WINDOWS Capitol CL 560	13	6 wks
11 Aug 90	LOOK ME IN THE HEART Capitol CL 584	31	6 wks
13 Oct 90	BE TENDER WITH ME BABY Capitol CL 593	28	4 wks
24 Nov 90 ●	IT TAKES TWO Warner Bros. ROD 1 ***	5	8 wks
21 Sep 91	NUTBUSH CITY LIMITS Capitol CL 630	23	5 wks
23 Nov 91	WAY OF THE WORLD Capitol CL 637	13	7 wks
15 Feb 92	LOVE THING Capitol CL 644	29	4 wks
6 Jun 92	I WANT YOU NEAR ME Capitol CL 659	22	4 wks

* Bryan Adams and Tina Turner ** Eric Clapton and Tina Turner *** Rod Stewart and Tina Turner

See also Ike and Tina Turner.

TURNTABLE ORCHESTRA   4 wks
US, male vocal/instrumental duo

21 Jan 89	YOU'RE GONNA MISS ME Republic LIC 012	52	4 wks

TURTLES   *US, male vocal/instrumental group*   39 wks

23 Mar 67	HAPPY TOGETHER London HL 10115	12	12 wks
15 Jun 67 ●	SHE'D RATHER BE WITH ME London HLU 10135	4	15 wks
30 Oct 68 ●	ELENORE London HL 10223	7	12 wks

TUXEDOS – *See Bobby ANGELO and the TUXEDOS*

TWEETS   *UK, male instrumental group*   34 wks

12 Sep 81 ●	THE BIRDIE SONG (BIRDIE DANCE) PRT 7P 219	2	23 wks
5 Dec 81	LET'S ALL SING LIKE THE BIRDIES SING PRT 7P 226	44	6 wks
18 Dec 82	THE BIRDIE SONG (BIRDIE DANCE) (re-entry) PRT 7P 219	46	5 wks

TWENTY 4 SEVEN featuring CAPTAIN HOLLYWOOD   20 wks
US/Holland/Germany/Italy, male/female vocal/instrumental group

22 Sep 90 ●	I CAN'T STAND IT BCM BCMR 395	7	10 wks
24 Nov 90	ARE YOU DREAMING BCM BCM 07504	17	10 wks

TWICE AS MUCH   *UK, male vocal duo*   9 wks

16 Jun 66	SITTIN' ON A FENCE Immediate IM 033	25	9 wks

TWIGGY   *UK, female vocalist*   10 wks

14 Aug 76	HERE I GO AGAIN Mercury 6007 100	17	10 wks

TWIN HYPE   *US, male rap duo*   2 wks

15 Jul 89	DO IT TO THE CROWD Profile PROF 255	65	2 wks

TWINKLE   *UK, female vocalist*   20 wks

26 Nov 64 ●	TERRY Decca F 12013	4	15 wks
25 Feb 65	GOLDEN LIGHTS Decca F 12076	21	5 wks

TWISTED SISTER   *US, male vocal/instrumental group*   28 wks

26 Mar 83	I AM (I'M ME) Atlantic A 9854	18	9 wks
28 May 83	THE KIDS ARE BACK Atlantic A 9827	32	6 wks
20 Aug 83	YOU CAN'T STOP ROCK 'N' ROLL Atlantic A 9792	43	4 wks
2 Jun 84	WE'RE NOT GONNA TAKE IT Atlantic A 9657	58	4 wks
18 Jan 86	LEADER OF THE PACK Atlantic A 9478	47	3 wks

Conway TWITTY   *US, male vocalist*   36 wks

14 Nov 58 ★	IT'S ONLY MAKE BELIEVE MGM 992	1	15 wks
27 Mar 59	STORY OF MY LOVE MGM 1003	30	1 wk
21 Aug 59 ●	MONA LISA MGM 1029	5	14 wks
21 Jul 60	IS A BLUE BIRD BLUE MGM 1082	43	3 wks
23 Feb 61	C'EST SI BON MGM 1118	40	3 wks

2 BAD MICE   *UK, male instrumental/production group*   3 wks

15 Feb 92	HOLD IT DOWN Moving Shadow SHADOW 14	70	1 wk
8 Aug 92	HOLD IT DOWN (re-entry) Moving Shadow SHADOW 14	48	2 wks

2 FOR JOY   *UK, male instrumental/production duo*   3 wks

1 Dec 90	IN A STATE Mercury MER 333	61	1 wk
9 Nov 91	LET THE BASS KICK All Around The World GLOBE 102	67	2 wks

2 HOUSE   *US, male instrumental/production duo*   1 wk

21 Mar 92	GO TECHNO Atlantic A 7519	65	1 wk

2 IN A ROOM   *US, male vocal duo*   11 wks

18 Nov 89	SOMEBODY IN THE HOUSE SAY YEAH! Big Life BLR 12	66	1 wk
26 Jan 91 ●	WIGGLE IT SBK SBK 19	3	8 wks
6 Apr 91	SHE'S GOT ME GOING CRAZY SBK SBK 23	54	2 wks

2 MAD   *UK, male vocal/instrumental duo*   4 wks

9 Feb 91	THINKING ABOUT YOUR BODY Big Life BLR 37	43	4 wks

TWO MAN SOUND   7 wks
Belgium, male vocal/instrumental group

20 Jan 79	QUE TAL AMERICA Miracle M 1	46	7 wks

TWO MEN, A DRUM MACHINE AND A TRUMPET   17 wks
UK, male instrumental duo

9 Jan 88	I'M TIRED OF GETTING PUSHED AROUND London LON 141	18	8 wks
25 Jun 88	HEAT IT UP Jive JIVE 174 *	21	9 wks

* Wee Papa Girl Rappers featuring Two Men and a Drum Machine

TWO NATIONS   *UK, male vocal/instrumental group*   1 wk

20 Jun 87	THAT'S THE WAY IT FEELS 10 TEN 168	74	1 wk

TWO PEOPLE UK, male vocal/instrumental group — 2 wks

31 Jan 87		HEAVEN *Polydor POSP 844*	63	2 wks

2 UNLIMITED Holland, male/female vocal duo — 39 wks

5 Oct 91	●	GET READY FOR THIS *PWL Continental PWL 206*	2	15 wks
25 Jan 92	●	TWILIGHT ZONE *PWL Continental PWL 211*	2	10 wks
2 May 92	●	WORKAHOLIC *PWL Continental PWL 228*	4	7 wks
15 Aug 92		THE MAGIC FRIEND *PWL Continental PWL 240*	11	7 wks

TYGERS OF PAN TANG — 15 wks
UK, male vocal/instrumental group

14 Feb 81		HELLBOUND *MCA 672*	48	3 wks
27 Mar 82		LOVE POTION NO. 9 *MCA 769*	45	6 wks
10 Jul 82		RENDEZVOUS *MCA 777*	49	4 wks
11 Sep 82		PARIS BY AIR *MCA 790*	63	2 wks

Bonnie TYLER UK, female vocalist — 79 wks

30 Oct 76	●	LOST IN FRANCE *RCA 2734*	9	10 wks
19 Mar 77		MORE THAN A LOVER *RCA PB 5008*	27	6 wks
3 Dec 77	●	IT'S A HEARTACHE *RCA PB 5057*	4	12 wks
30 Jun 79		MARRIED MEN *RCA PB 5164*	35	6 wks
19 Feb 83	★	TOTAL ECLIPSE OF THE HEART *CBS TYLER 1*	1	12 wks
7 May 83		FASTER THAN THE SPEED OF NIGHT *CBS A 3338*	43	4 wks
25 Jun 83		HAVE YOU EVER SEEN THE RAIN *CBS A 3517*	47	3 wks
7 Jan 84	●	A ROCKIN' GOOD WAY *Epic A 4071 **	5	9 wks
31 Aug 85	●	HOLDING OUT FOR A HERO *CBS A 4251*	2	13 wks
14 Dec 85		LOVING YOU'S A DIRTY JOB BUT SOMEBODY'S GOTTA DO IT *CBS A 6662 ***	73	2 wks
28 Dec 91		HOLDING OUT FOR A HERO (re-issue) *Total TYLER 10*	69	2 wks

* Shaky and Bonnie ** Bonnie Tyler, guest vocalist Todd Rundgren

TYMES US, male vocal group — 41 wks

25 Jul 63		SO MUCH IN LOVE *Cameo Parkway P 871*	21	8 wks
15 Jan 69		PEOPLE *Direction 58 3903*	16	10 wks
21 Sep 74		YOU LITTLE TRUST MAKER *RCA 2456*	18	9 wks
21 Dec 74	★	MS GRACE *RCA 2493*	1	11 wks
17 Jan 76		GOD'S GONNA PUNISH YOU *RCA 2626*	41	3 wks

TYPICALLY TROPICAL — 11 wks
UK, male vocal/instrumental duo

5 Jul 75	★	BARBADOS *Gull GULS 14*	1	11 wks

TYREE US, male producer — 10 wks

25 Feb 89		TURN UP THE BASS *ffrr FFR 24 **	12	7 wks
6 May 89		HARDCORE HIP HOUSE *DJ International DJIN 11*	70	2 wks
2 Dec 89		MOVE YOUR BODY *CBS 655470 7 ***	72	1 wk

* Tyree featuring Kool Rock Steady ** Tyree featuring J.M.D.

TYRREL CORPORATION — 4 wks
UK, male vocal/instrumental duo

14 Mar 92		THE BOTTLE *Volante TYR 1*	71	1 wk

15 Aug 92		GOING HOME *Volante TYR 2*	58	2 wks
10 Oct 92		WAKING WITH A STRANGER/ONE DAY *Volante TYRS 3*	59	1 wk

Judie TZUKE UK, female vocalist — 10 wks

14 Jul 79		STAY WITH ME TILL DAWN *Rocket XPRES 17*	16	10 wks

UB40 UK, male vocal/instrumental group — 264 wks

8 Mar 80	●	KING/FOOD FOR THOUGHT *Graduate GRAD 6*	4	13 wks
14 Jun 80	●	MY WAY OF THINKING/I THINK IT'S GOING TO RAIN *Graduate GRAD 8*	6	10 wks
1 Nov 80	●	THE EARTH DIES SCREAMING/DREAM A LIE *Graduate GRAD 10*	10	12 wks
23 May 81		DON'T LET IT PASS YOU BY/DON'T SLOW DOWN *DEP International DEP 1*	16	9 wks
8 Aug 81	●	ONE IN TEN *DEP International DEP 2*	7	10 wks
13 Feb 82		I WON'T CLOSE MY EYES *DEP International DEP 3*	32	8 wks
15 May 82		LOVE IS ALL IS ALRIGHT *DEP International DEP 4*	29	7 wks
28 Aug 82		SO HERE I AM *DEP International DEP 5*	25	9 wks
5 Feb 83		I'VE GOT MINE *DEP International 7 DEP 6*	45	4 wks
20 Aug 83	★	RED RED WINE *DEP International 7 DEP 7*	1	14 wks
15 Oct 83	●	PLEASE DON'T MAKE ME CRY *DEP International 7 DEP 8*	10	8 wks
10 Dec 83		MANY RIVERS TO CROSS *DEP International 7 DEP 9*	16	8 wks
17 Mar 84		CHERRY OH BABY *DEP International 7 DEP 10*	12	8 wks
22 Sep 84	●	IF IT HAPPENS AGAIN *DEP International DEP 11*	9	8 wks
1 Dec 84		RIDDLE ME *DEP International DEP 15*	59	2 wks
3 Aug 85	★	I GOT YOU BABE *DEP International DEP 20 **	1	13 wks
26 Oct 85	●	DON'T BREAK MY HEART *DEP International DEP 22 **	3	13 wks
12 Jul 86	●	SING OUR OWN SONG *DEP International DEP 23*	5	9 wks
27 Sep 86		ALL I WANT TO DO *DEP International DEP 24*	41	4 wks
17 Jan 87		RAT IN MI KITCHEN *DEP International DEP 25*	12	7 wks
9 May 87		WATCHDOGS *DEP International DEP 26*	39	4 wks
10 Oct 87		MAYBE TOMORROW *DEP International DEP 27*	14	8 wks
27 Feb 88		RECKLESS *EMI EM 41 ***	17	8 wks
18 Jun 88	●	BREAKFAST IN BED *DEP International DEP 29 **	6	11 wks
20 Aug 88		WHERE DID I GO WRONG *DEP International DEP 30*	26	6 wks
17 Jun 89		I WOULD DO FOR YOU *DEP International DEP 32*	45	4 wks
18 Nov 89	●	HOMELY GIRL *DEP International DEP 33*	6	10 wks
27 Jan 90		HERE I AM (COME AND TAKE ME) *DEP International DEP 34*	46	3 wks
31 Mar 90	●	KINGSTON TOWN *DEP International DEP 35*	4	12 wks
28 Jul 90		WEAR YOU TO THE BALL *DEP International DEP 36*	35	6 wks
3 Nov 90	●	I'LL BE YOUR BABY TONIGHT *EMI EM 167 ****	6	10 wks
1 Dec 90		IMPOSSIBLE LOVE *DEP International DEP 37*	47	2 wks
2 Feb 91		THE WAY YOU DO THE THINGS YOU DO *DEP International DEP 38*	49	3 wks
12 Dec 92		ONE IN TEN *ZTT ZANG 39 *****	17†	3 wks

* UB40 featuring Chrissie Hynde ** Afrika Bambaataa with UB40 and Family
*** Robert Palmer and UB40 **** 808 State vs UB40

UFO UK, male vocal/instrumental group — 31 wks

5 Aug 78		ONLY YOU CAN ROCK ME *Chrysalis CHS 2241*	50	4 wks
27 Jan 79		DOCTOR DOCTOR *Chrysalis CHS 2287*	35	6 wks
31 Mar 79		SHOOT SHOOT *Chrysalis CHS 2318*	48	5 wks
12 Jan 80		YOUNG BLOOD *Chrysalis CHS 2399*	36	5 wks
17 Jan 81		LONELY HEART *Chrysalis CHS 2482*	41	5 wks
30 Jan 82		LET IT RAIN *Chrysalis CHS 2576*	62	3 wks
19 Mar 83		WHEN IT'S TIME TO ROCK *Chrysalis CHS 2672*	70	3 wks

UGLY KID JOE US, male vocal/instrumental group — 15 wks

16 May 92	●	EVERYTHING ABOUT YOU *Mercury MER 367*	3	9 wks

UGLY KID JOE
(singer Whitfield Crane
shown) had an instant
hit when 'Everything
About You' was used in
the film *Wayne's
World*.

VANITY FARE model
1969 fashions.

| 22 Aug 92 | NEIGHBOR *Mercury MER 374* | .... | **28** | 4 wks |
| 31 Oct 92 | SO DAMN COOL *Mercury MER 383* | .... | **44** | 2 wks |

UHF *US, male instrumental/production group*   **4 wks**

| 14 Dec 91 | UHF/EVERYTHING *XL XLS 25* | .... | **46** | 4 wks |

U. K. *UK, male vocal/instrumental group*   **2 wks**

| 30 Jun 79 | NOTHING TO LOSE *Polydor POSP 55* | .... | **67** | 2 wks |

U.K. MIXMASTERS *UK, male producer – Nigel Wright*   **15 wks**

2 Feb 91	THE NIGHT FEVER MEGAMIX *IQ ZB 44339* *	....	**23**	5 wks
27 Jul 91	LUCKY 7 MEGAMIX *IQ ZB 44731*	....	**43**	3 wks
14 Dec 91	BARE NECESSITIES MEGAMIX *Connect ZB 35135*	....	**14**	7 wks

* Mixmasters

U.K. PLAYERS *UK, male vocal/instrumental group*   **3 wks**

| 14 May 83 | LOVE'S GONNA GET YOU *RCA 326* | .... | **52** | 3 wks |

U.K. SUBS *UK, male vocal/instrumental group*   **39 wks**

23 Jun 79	STRANGLEHOLD *Gem GEMS 5*	....	**26**	8 wks
8 Sep 79	TOMORROW'S GIRLS *Gem GEMS 10*	....	**28**	6 wks
1 Dec 79	SHE'S NOT THERE/KICKS EP *Gem GEMS 14*	....	**36**	7 wks
8 Mar 80	WARHEAD *Gem GEMS 23*	....	**30**	4 wks
17 May 80	TEENAGE *Gem GEMS 30*	....	**32**	5 wks
25 Oct 80	PARTY IN PARIS *Gem GEMS 42*	....	**37**	4 wks
18 Apr 81	KEEP ON RUNNIN' (TILL YOU BURN) *Gem GEMS 45*	....	**41**	5 wks

Tracks on She's Not There/Kicks EP: *She's Not There/Kicks/Victim/The Same Thing.*

Tracey ULLMAN *UK, female vocalist*   **49 wks**

19 Mar 83	● BREAKAWAY *Stiff BUY 168*	....	**4**	11 wks
24 Sep 83	● THEY DON'T KNOW *Stiff BUY 180*	....	**2**	11 wks
3 Dec 83	● MOVE OVER DARLING *Stiff BUY 195*	....	**8**	9 wks
3 Mar 84	MY GUY *Stiff BUY 197*	....	**23**	6 wks
28 Jul 84	SUNGLASSES *Stiff BUY 205*	....	**18**	9 wks
27 Oct 84	HELPLESS *Stiff BUY 211*	....	**61**	3 wks

ULTRACYNIC *UK, male/female vocal/instrumental group*   **2 wks**

| 29 Aug 92 | NOTHING IS FOREVER *380 PEW 2* | .... | **50** | 2 wks |

ULTRAVOX *UK/Canada, male vocal/instrumental group*   **138 wks**

5 Jul 80	SLEEPWALK *Chrysalis CHS 2441*	....	**29**	11 wks
18 Oct 80	PASSING STRANGERS *Chrysalis CHS 2457*	....	**57**	4 wks
17 Jan 81	● VIENNA *Chrysalis CHS 2481*	....	**2**	14 wks
28 Mar 81	SLOW MOTION *Island WIP 6691*	....	**33**	4 wks
6 Jun 81	● ALL STOOD STILL *Chrysalis CHS 2522*	....	**8**	10 wks
22 Aug 81	THE THIN WALL *Chrysalis CHS 2540*	....	**14**	8 wks
7 Nov 81	THE VOICE *Chrysalis CHS 2559*	....	**16**	12 wks
25 Sep 82	REAP THE WILD WIND *Chrysalis CHS 2639*	....	**12**	9 wks
27 Nov 82	HYMN *Chrysalis CHS 2657*	....	**11**	11 wks
19 Mar 83	VISIONS IN BLUE *Chrysalis CHS 2676*	....	**15**	9 wks
4 Jun 83	WE CAME TO DANCE *Chrysalis VOX 1*	....	**18**	7 wks
11 Feb 84	ONE SMALL DAY *Chrysalis VOX 2*	....	**27**	6 wks
19 May 84	● DANCING WITH TEARS IN MY EYES *Chrysalis UV 1*	....	**3**	10 wks
7 Jul 84	LAMENT *Chrysalis UV 2*	....	**22**	6 wks
4 Aug 84	DANCING WITH TEARS IN MY EYES (re-entry) *Chrysalis UV 1*	....	**74**	1 wk

25 Aug 84	LAMENT (re-entry) *Chrysalis UV 2*	....	**73**	1 wk
20 Oct 84	LOVE'S GREAT ADVENTURE *Chrysalis UV 3*	....	**12**	9 wks
27 Sep 86	SAME OLD STORY *Chrysalis UV 4*	....	**31**	4 wks
22 Nov 86	ALL FALL DOWN *Chrysalis UV 5*	....	**30**	5 wks

Piero UMILIANI *Italy, orchestra and chorus*   **8 wks**

| 30 Apr 77 | ● MAH NA MAH NA *EMI International INT 530* | .... | **8** | 8 wks |

UNCANNY ALLIANCE   **2 wks**
US, male/female vocal/instrumental duo

| 19 Dec 92 | I GOT MY EDUCATION *A & M AM 0128* | .... | **39**† | 2 wks |

UNDERCOVER *UK, male vocal/instrumental group*   **21 wks**

| 15 Aug 92 | ● BAKER STREET *PWL Int PWL 239* | .... | **2** | 14 wks |
| 14 Nov 92 | ● NEVER LET HER SLIP AWAY *PWL Int PWL 255* | .... | **5**† | 7 wks |

UNDERTAKERS *UK, male vocal/instrumental group*   **1 wk**

| 9 Apr 64 | JUST A LITTLE BIT *Pye 7N 15607* | .... | **49** | 1 wk |

UNDERTONES *UK, male vocal/instrumental group*   **67 wks**

21 Oct 78	TEENAGE KICKS *Sire SIR 4007*	....	**31**	6 wks
3 Feb 79	GET OVER YOU *Sire SIR 4010*	....	**57**	4 wks
28 Apr 79	JIMMY JIMMY *Sire SIR 4015*	....	**16**	10 wks
21 Jul 79	HERE COMES THE SUMMER *Sire SIR 4022*	....	**34**	6 wks
20 Oct 79	YOU'VE GOT MY NUMBER (WHY DON'T YOU USE IT?) *Sire SIR 4024*	....	**32**	6 wks
5 Apr 80	● MY PERFECT COUSIN *Sire SIR 4038*	....	**9**	10 wks
5 Jul 80	WEDNESDAY WEEK *Sire SIR 4042*	....	**11**	9 wks
2 May 81	IT'S GOING TO HAPPEN! *Ardeck AROS 8*	....	**18**	9 wks
25 Jul 81	JULIE OCEAN *Ardeck ARDS 9*	....	**41**	5 wks
9 Jul 83	TEENAGE KICKS (re-issue) *Ardeck ARDS 1*	....	**60**	2 wks

UNDISPUTED TRUTH   **4 wks**
US, male/female vocal/instrumental group

| 22 Jan 77 | YOU + ME = LOVE *Warner Bros. K 16804* | .... | **43** | 4 wks |

U96 *Germany, male producer – Alex Christiansen*   **5 wks**

| 29 Aug 92 | DAS BOOT *M&G MAGS 28* | .... | **18** | 5 wks |

UNION featuring the ENGLAND WORLD CUP SQUAD   **7 wks**
UK/Holland, male instrumental group with UK rugby team vocalists

| 12 Oct 91 | SWING LOW (RUN WITH THE BALL) *Columbia 6575317* | .... | **16** | 7 wks |

UNION GAP featuring Gary PUCKETT   **47 wks**
US, male vocal/instrumental group

17 Apr 68	★ YOUNG GIRL *CBS 3365*	....	**1**	17 wks
7 Aug 68	● LADY WILLPOWER *CBS 3551*	....	**5**	16 wks
28 Aug 68	WOMAN WOMAN *CBS 3110* *	....	**48**	1 wk
15 Jun 74	● YOUNG GIRL *CBS 8202* *	....	**6**	13 wks

* Gary Puckett and the Union Gap

UNIQUE US, male/female vocal/instrumental group — 7 wks

10 Sep 83	**WHAT I GOT IS WHAT YOU NEED** *Prelude A 3707*	27	7 wks

UNIQUE 3 UK, male rap/scratch group — 12 wks

4 Nov 89	**THE THEME** *10 TEN 285*	61	3 wks
14 Apr 90	**MUSICAL MELODY/WEIGHT FOR THE BASS** *10 TEN 298*	29	5 wks
10 Nov 90	**RHYTHM TAKES CONTROL** *10 TEN 327 *	41	3 wks
16 Nov 91	**NO MORE** *10 TEN 387*	74	1 wk

* Unique 3 featuring Karin

UNIT FOUR PLUS TWO UK, male vocal/instrumental group — 29 wks

13 Feb 64	**GREEN FIELDS** *Decca F 11821*	48	2 wks
25 Feb 65 ★	**CONCRETE AND CLAY** *Decca F 12071*	1	15 wks
13 May 65	**YOU'VE NEVER BEEN IN LOVE LIKE THIS BEFORE** *Decca F 12144*	14	11 wks
17 Mar 66	**BABY NEVER SAY GOODBYE** *Decca F 12333*	49	1 wk

UNITED KINGDOM SYMPHONY ORCHESTRA UK, orchestra — 4 wks

27 Jul 85	**SHADES (THEME FROM THE CROWN PAINT TELEVISION COMMERCIAL)** *Food For Thought YUM 108*	68	4 wks

UNITONE – *See Laurel AITKEN and the UNITONE*

UNITY UK, male/female vocal/instrumental group — 2 wks

31 Aug 91	**UNITY** *Cardiac CNY 6*	64	2 wks

UNTOUCHABLES US, male vocal/instrumental group — 16 wks

6 Apr 85	**FREE YOURSELF** *Stiff BUY 221*	26	11 wks
27 Jul 85	**I SPY FOR THE FBI** *Stiff BUY 227*	59	5 wks

Phil UPCHURCH COMBO
US, male instrumental group, Phil Upchurch bass guitar — 2 wks

5 May 66	**YOU CAN'T SIT DOWN** *Sue WI 4005*	39	2 wks

UPSETTERS Jamaica, male instrumental group — 15 wks

4 Oct 69 ●	**RETURN OF DJANGO/DOLLAR IN THE TEETH** *Upsetter US 301*	5	15 wks

URBAN ALL STARS UK, male/female vocal/instrumental group — 2 wks

27 Aug 88	**IT BEGAN IN AFRICA** *Urban URB 23*	64	2 wks

URBAN HYPE UK, male production/instrumental group — 9 wks

11 Jul 92 ●	**A TRIP TO TRUMPTON** *Faze 2 FAZE 5*	6	8 wks
17 Oct 92	**THE FEELING** *Faze 2 FAZE 10*	67	1 wk

URBAN SHAKEDOWN featuring Micky FINN UK/Italy, male vocal/instrumental group — 7 wks

27 Jun 92	**SOME JUSTICE** *Urban Shakedown URBST 1*	23	5 wks
12 Sep 92	**BASS SHAKE** *Urban Shakedown URBST 2*	59	2 wks

URBAN SOUL US, male producer - Roland Clarke — 10 wks

30 Mar 91	**ALRIGHT** *Cooltempo COOL 231*	60	4 wks
21 Sep 91	**ALRIGHT (re-mix)** *Cooltempo COOL 244*	43	3 wks
28 Mar 92	**ALWAYS** *Cooltempo COOL 251*	41	3 wks

Midge URE UK, male vocalist — 55 wks

12 Jun 82 ●	**NO REGRETS** *Chrysalis CHS 2618*	9	10 wks
9 Jul 83	**AFTER A FASHION** *Musicfest FEST 1 *	39	4 wks
14 Sep 85 ★	**IF I WAS** *Chrysalis URE 1*	1	11 wks
16 Nov 85	**THAT CERTAIN SMILE** *Chrysalis URE 2*	28	4 wks
8 Feb 86	**WASTELANDS** *Chrysalis URE 3*	46	3 wks
7 Jun 86	**CALL OF THE WILD** *Chrysalis URE 4*	27	8 wks
20 Aug 88	**ANSWERS TO NOTHING** *Chrysalis URE 5*	49	4 wks
19 Nov 88	**DEAR GOD** *Chrysalis URE 6*	55	4 wks
17 Aug 91	**COLD COLD HEART** *Arista 114555*	17	7 wks

* Midge Ure and Mick Karn

USA FOR AFRICA US, male/female vocal group — 9 wks

13 Apr 85 ★	**WE ARE THE WORLD** *CBS USAID 1*	1	9 wks

UTAH SAINTS UK, male instrumental/production duo — 20 wks

24 Aug 91 ●	**WHAT CAN YOU DO FOR ME** *ffrr F 164*	10	11 wks
6 Jun 92 ●	**SOMETHING GOOD** *ffrr F 187*	4	9 wks

U2 Ireland, male vocal/instrumental group — 140 wks

8 Aug 81	**FIRE** *Island WIP 6679*	35	6 wks
17 Oct 81	**GLORIA** *Island WIP 6733*	55	4 wks
3 Apr 82	**A CELEBRATION** *Island WIP 6770*	47	4 wks
22 Jan 83 ●	**NEW YEARS DAY** *Island UWIP 6848*	10	8 wks
2 Apr 83	**TWO HEARTS BEAT AS ONE** *Island IS 109*	18	5 wks
15 Sep 84 ●	**PRIDE (IN THE NAME OF LOVE)** *Island IS 202*	3	11 wks
4 May 85 ●	**THE UNFORGETTABLE FIRE** *Island IS 220*	6	6 wks
28 Mar 87 ●	**WITH OR WITHOUT YOU** *Island IS 319*	4	11 wks
6 Jun 87 ●	**I STILL HAVEN'T FOUND WHAT I'M LOOKING FOR** *Island IS 328*	6	11 wks
12 Sep 87 ●	**WHERE THE STREETS HAVE NO NAME** *Island IS 340*	4	6 wks
26 Dec 87	**IN GOD'S COUNTRY** (IMPORT) *Island 7-99385*	48	4 wks
1 Oct 88 ★	**DESIRE** *Island IS 400*	1	8 wks
17 Dec 88 ●	**ANGEL OF HARLEM** *Island IS 402*	9	6 wks
15 Apr 89 ●	**WHEN LOVE COMES TO TOWN** *Island IS 411 *	6	7 wks
24 Jun 89 ●	**ALL I WANT IS YOU** *Island IS 422*	4	6 wks
2 Nov 91 ★	**THE FLY** *Island IS 500*	1	5 wks
14 Dec 91	**MYSTERIOUS WAYS** *Island IS 509*	13	7 wks
4 Jan 92	**THE FLY (re-entry)** *Island IS 500*	62	1 wk
7 Mar 92 ●	**ONE** *Island IS 515*	7	6 wks
20 Jun 92	**EVEN BETTER THAN THE REAL THING** *Island IS 525*	12	7 wks
11 Jul 92 ●	**EVEN BETTER THAN THE REAL THING (re-mix)** *Island Real U2*	8	7 wks
5 Dec 92	**WHO'S GONNA RIDE YOUR WILD HORSES** *Island IS 550*	14†	4 wks

* U2 featuring B.B. King

VAGABONDS – *See Jimmy JAMES and the VAGABONDS*

Ricky VALANCE UK, male vocalist — 16 wks

25 Aug 60 ★	**TELL LAURA I LOVE HER** *Columbia DB 4493*	1	16 wks

Ritchie VALENS US, male vocalist — 5 wks

6 Mar 59	DONNA *London HL 8803*	29	1 wk
1 Aug 87	LA BAMBA *RCA PB 41435*	49	4 wks

Caterina VALENTE France, female vocalist — 14 wks

19 Aug 55 ●	THE BREEZE AND I *Polydor BM 6002*	5	14 wks

Dickie VALENTINE UK, male vocalist — 92 wks

20 Feb 53	BROKEN WINGS *Decca F 9954*	12	1 wk
13 Mar 53 ●	ALL THE TIME AND EVERYWHERE *Decca F 10038*	9	3 wks
5 Jun 53 ●	IN A GOLDEN COACH *Decca F 10098*	7	1 wk
5 Nov 54	ENDLESS *Decca F 10346*	19	1 wk
17 Dec 54 ●	MR. SANDMAN *Decca F 10415*	5	12 wks
17 Dec 54 ★	FINGER OF SUSPICION *Decca F 10394 *	1	15 wks
18 Feb 55 ●	A BLOSSOM FELL *Decca F 10430*	9	9 wks
29 Apr 55	A BLOSSOM FELL (re-entry) *Decca F 10430*	18	1 wk
3 Jun 55 ●	I WONDER *Decca F 10493*	4	15 wks
25 Nov 55 ★	CHRISTMAS ALPHABET *Decca F 10628*	1	7 wks
16 Dec 55	OLD PIANNA RAG *Decca F 10645*	15	5 wks
7 Dec 56 ●	CHRISTMAS ISLAND *Decca F 10798*	8	5 wks
27 Dec 57	SNOWBOUND FOR CHRISTMAS *Decca F 10950*	28	1 wk
13 Mar 59	VENUS *Pye Nixa 7N 15192*	28	1 wk
3 Apr 59	VENUS (re-entry) *Pye Nixa 7N 15192*	25	1 wk
17 Apr 59	VENUS (2nd re-entry) *Pye Nixa 7N 15192*	20	4 wks
22 May 59	VENUS (3rd re-entry) *Pye Nixa 7N 15192*	25	1 wk
19 Jun 59	VENUS (4th re-entry) *Pye Nixa 7N 15192*	28	1 wk
23 Oct 59	ONE MORE SUNRISE (MORGEN) *Pye 7N 15221*	14	8 wks

* Dickie Valentine with the Stargazers

See also Stargazers; Various Artists (EPs & LPs) - All Star Hit Parade.

VALENTINE BROTHERS US, male vocal duo — 1 wk

23 Apr 83	MONEY'S TOO TIGHT (TO MENTION) *Energy NRG 1*	73	1 wk

Joe VALINO US, male vocalist — 2 wks

18 Jan 57	GARDEN OF EDEN *HMV POP 283*	23	2 wks

Frankie VALLI US, male vocalist — 50 wks

12 Dec 70	YOU'RE READY NOW *Philips 320226*	11	13 wks
1 Feb 75 ●	MY EYES ADORED YOU *Private Stock PVT 1*	5	11 wks
21 Jun 75	SWEARIN' TO GOD *Private Stock PVT 21*	31	5 wks
17 Apr 76	FALLEN ANGEL *Private Stock PVT 51*	11	7 wks
26 Aug 78 ●	GREASE *RSO 012*	3	14 wks

See also Four Seasons.

David VAN DAY UK, male vocalist — 3 wks

14 May 83	YOUNG AMERICANS TALKING *WEA DAY 1*	43	3 wks

George VAN DUSEN UK, male vocalist — 4 wks

17 Dec 88	IT'S PARTY TIME AGAIN *Bri-Tone 7BT 001*	43	4 wks

Leroy VAN DYKE US, male vocalist — 20 wks

4 Jan 62 ●	WALK ON BY *Mercury AMT 1166*	5	17 wks
26 Apr 62	BIG MAN IN A BIG HOUSE *Mercury AMT 1173*	34	3 wks

VAN HALEN US/Holland, male vocal/instrumental group — 44 wks

28 Jun 80	RUNNIN' WITH THE DEVIL *Warner Bros. HM 10*	52	3 wks
4 Feb 84 ●	JUMP *Warner Bros. W 9384*	7	13 wks
19 May 84	PANAMA *Warner Bros. W 9273*	61	2 wks
5 Apr 86 ●	WHY CAN'T THIS BE LOVE *Warner Bros. W 8740*	8	14 wks
12 Jul 86	DREAMS *Warner Bros. W 8642*	62	2 wks
6 Aug 88	WHEN IT'S LOVE *Warner Bros. W 7816*	28	7 wks
1 Apr 89	FEELS SO GOOD *Warner Bros. W 7565*	63	1 wk
22 Jun 91	POUNDCAKE *Warner Bros. W 0045*	74	1 wk
10 Oct 91	TOP OF THE WORLD *Warner Bros. W 0066*	63	1 wk

VAN TWIST — 2 wks
Zaire/Belgium, male/female vocal/instrumental group

16 Feb 85	SHAFT *Polydor POSP 729*	57	2 wks

VANDELLAS – *See Martha REEVES and the VANDELLAS*

Luther VANDROSS US, male vocalist — 92 wks

19 Feb 83	NEVER TOO MUCH *Epic EPC A 3101*	44	6 wks
26 Jul 86	GIVE ME THE REASON *Epic A 7288*	60	3 wks
21 Feb 87	GIVE ME THE REASON (re-issue) *Epic 650216 7*	71	2 wks
28 Mar 87	SEE ME *Epic LUTH 1*	60	4 wks
11 Jul 87	I REALLY DIDN'T MEAN IT *Epic LUTH 3*	16	10 wks
5 Sep 87	STOP TO LOVE *Epic LUTH 2*	24	7 wks
7 Nov 87	SO AMAZING *Epic LUTH 4*	33	6 wks
23 Jan 88	GIVE ME THE REASON (2nd re-issue) *Epic LUTH 5*	26	6 wks
16 Apr 88	I GAVE IT UP (WHEN I FELL IN LOVE) *Epic LUTH 6*	28	5 wks
9 Jul 88	THERE'S NOTHING BETTER THAN LOVE *Epic LUTH 7 *	72	1 wk
8 Oct 88	ANY LOVE *Epic LUTH 8*	31	4 wks
4 Feb 89	SHE WON'T TALK TO ME *Epic LUTH 9*	34	4 wks
22 Apr 89	COME BACK *Epic LUTH 10*	53	3 wks
28 Oct 89	NEVER TOO MUCH (re-mix) *Epic LUTH 12*	13	7 wks
6 Jan 90	HERE AND NOW *Epic LUTH 13*	43	3 wks
27 Apr 91	POWER OF LOVE - LOVE POWER *Epic 6568227*	46	5 wks
18 Jan 92	THE RUSH *Epic 6577237*	53	3 wks
15 Aug 92 ●	THE BEST THINGS IN LIFE ARE FREE *Perspective PERSS 7400 **	2	13 wks

* Luther Vandross, duet with Gregory Hines ** Janet Jackson and Luther Vandross with special guests BBD and Ralph Tresvant

VANGELIS Greece, male instrumentalist - keyboards — 25 wks

9 May 81	CHARIOTS OF FIRE - TITLES *Polydor POSP 246*	12	10 wks
11 Jul 81	HEAVEN AND HELL, THIRD MOVEMENT (THEME FROM THE BBC-TV SERIES, THE COSMOS) *BBC 1*	48	6 wks
24 Apr 82	CHARIOTS OF FIRE - TITLES (re-entry) *Polydor POSP 246*	41	7 wks
31 Oct 92	CONQUEST OF PARADISE *East West YZ 704*	60	2 wks

See also Jon and Vangelis.

VANILLA FUDGE US, male vocal/instrumental group — 11 wks

9 Aug 67	YOU KEEP ME HANGIN' ON *Atlantic 584 123*	18	11 wks

VANILLA ICE US, male rapper — 32 wks

24 Nov 90 ★	ICE ICE BABY *SBK SBK 18*	1	13 wks
2 Feb 91 ●	PLAY THAT FUNKY MUSIC *SBK SBK 20*	10	6 wks
29 Jun 91	ROLLIN' IN MY 5.0 *SBK SBK 27*	27	4 wks
30 Mar 91	I LOVE YOU *SBK SBK 22*	45	5 wks
10 Aug 91	SATISFACTION *SBK SBK 29*	22	4 wks

VANITY FARE *UK, male vocal/instrumental group* — **34 wks**

28 Aug 68	I LIVE FOR THE SUN *Page One POF 075* 20	9 wks
23 Jul 69 ●	EARLY IN THE MORNING *Page One POF 142* 8	12 wks
27 Dec 69	HITCHIN' A RIDE *Page One POF 158* 16	13 wks

Randy VANWARMER *US, male vocalist* — **11 wks**

4 Aug 79 ●	JUST WHEN I NEEDED YOU MOST	
	Bearsville WIP 6516 8	11 wks

VAPORS *UK, male vocal/instrumental group* — **23 wks**

9 Feb 80 ●	TURNING JAPANESE *United Artists BP 334* 3	13 wks
5 Jul 80	NEWS AT TEN *United Artists BP 345*.................44	4 wks
11 Jul 81	JIMMIE JONES *Liberty BP 401*.................44	6 wks

VARDIS *UK, male vocal/instrumental group* — **4 wks**

27 Sep 80	LET'S GO *Logo VAR 1* 59	4 wks

VARIOUS ARTISTS (EPs and LPs) — **27 wks**

15 Jun 56	CAROUSEL - ORIGINAL SOUNDTRACK (LP)	
	Capitol LCT 6105 27	1 wk
29 Jun 56 ●	ALL STAR HIT PARADE *Decca F 10752* 2	9 wks
6 Jul 56	CAROUSEL - ORIGINAL SOUNDTRACK	
	(LP) (re-entry) *Capitol LCT 6105* 26	1 wk
26 Jul 57	ALL STAR HIT PARADE NO. 2 *Decca F 10915* 15	7 wks
9 Dec 89	THE FOOD CHRISTMAS EP *Food FOOD 23* 63	1 wk
20 Jan 90	THE FURTHER ADVENTURES OF NORTH EP	
	Deconstruction PT 43372 64	2 wks
2 Nov 91	THE APPLE EP *Apple APP 1* 60	1 wk
11 Jul 92	FOURPLAY EP *XL XLFP 1* 45	2 wks
7 Nov 92	THE FRED EP *Heavenly HVN 19* 26	3 wks

Tracks and artists on Carousel *are as follows: Carousel Waltz - Orchestra conducted by Alfred Newman; You're A Queer One Julie Jordan - Barbara Ruick and Shirley Jones; Mister Snow - Barbara Ruick; If I Loved You - Shirley Jones and Gordon MacRae; June Is Busting Out All Over - Claramae Turner; Soliloquy - Gordon MacRae; Blow High Blow Low - Cameron Mitchell; When The Children Are Asleep - Robert Rounseville and Barbara Ruick; This Was A Real Nice Clambake - Barbara Ruick, Claramae Turner, Robert Rounseville and Cameron Mitchell; Stonecutters Cut It On Stone (There's Nothing So Bad For A Woman) - Cameron Mitchell; What's The Use Of Wonderin' - Shirley Jones; You'll Never Walk Alone - Claramae Turner; If I Loved You - Gordon MacRae; You'll Never Walk Alone - Shirley Jones. Tracks on* All Star Hit Parade: *Theme From The Threepenny Opera - Winifred Atwell; No Other Love - Dave King; My September Love - Joan Regan; A Tear Fell - Lita Roza; It's Almost Tomorrow - David Whitfield. Tracks on* All Star Hit Parade No. 2: *Around The World - Johnston Brothers; Puttin' On The Style - Billy Cotton; When I Fall In Love - Jimmy Young; A White Sport Coat - Max Bygraves; Freight Train - Beverley Sisters; Butterfly - Tommy Steele. Tracks on* The Food Christmas EP: *Like Princes Do - Crazyhead; I Don't Want That Kind Of Love - Jesus Jones; Info Freako - Diesel Park West. Tracks on* The Further Adventures Of North EP: *Dream 17 - Annette; Carino 90 - T-Coy; The Way I Feel - Frequency 9; Stop This Thing - Dynasty Of Two featuring Rowetta. Tracks on* The Apple EP: *Those Were The Days - Mary Hopkin; That's The Way God Planned It - Billy Preston; Sour Milk Sea - Jackie Lomax; Come And Get It - Badfinger. Tracks on* Fourplay EP: *DJs Unite - DJs Unite; Alright - Glide; Be Free - Noise Factory; True Devotion - EQ. Tracks on* The Fred EP: *Deeply Dippy - Rockingbirds; Don't Talk Just Kiss - Flowered Up; I'm Too Sexy - Saint Etienne.*

VARIOUS ARTISTS (MONTAGES) — **31 wks**

17 May 80	CALIBRE CUTS *Calibre CAB 502* 75	2 wks
25 Nov 89	DEEP HEAT '89 *Deep Heat DEEP 10* 12	11 wks
3 Mar 90 ●	THE BRITS 1990 *RCA PB 43565* 2	7 wks
28 Apr 90	THE SIXTH SENSE *Deep Heat DEEP 12* 49	2 wks
10 Nov 90	TIME TO MAKE THE FLOOR BURN	
	Megabass MEGAX 1 16	9 wks

The following tracks are sampled:
Calibre Cuts: *Big Apples Rock - Black Ivory; Don't Hold Back - Chanson; The River Drive - Jupiter Beyond; Dancing In The Disco - LAX; Mellow Mellow Right On - Lowrell; Pata Pata - Osibisa; I Like It - Players Association; We Got The Funk - Positive Force; Holdin' On - Tony*

Rallo and the Midnight Band; Can You Feel The Force - Real Thing; Miami Heatwave - Seventh Avenue; Rappers Delight - Sugarhill Gang; Que Tal America - Two Man Sound; Remakes by session musicians: Ain't No Stoppin' Us Now, Bad Girls, We Are Family
Deep Heat '89 (credited to Latino Rave): *Pump Up The Jam - Technotronic; Stakker Humanoid - Humanoid; A Day In The Life - Black Riot; Work It To The Bone - LNR; I Can Make U Dance - DJ 'Fast' Eddie; Voodoo Ray - A Guy Called Gerald; Numero Uno - Starlight; Bango (To The Batmobile) - Todd Terry; Break 4 Love - Raze; Don't Scandalize Mine - Sugar Bear*
The Brits 1990: *Street Tuff - Double Trouble and the Rebel MC; Voodoo Ray - A Guy Called Gerald; Theme From S Express - S Express; Hey DJ I Can't Dance To That Music You're Playing - Beatmasters; Eve Of The War - Jeff Wayne; Pacific State - 808 State; We Call It Acieed - D Mob; Got To Keep On - Cookie Crew*
The Sixth Sense (credited to Latino Rave): *Get Up - Technotronic; The Magic Number - De La Soul; G'Ding G'Ding (Do You Wanna Wanna) - Anna G; Show 'M The Bass - MC Miker G; Turn It Out (Go Base) - Rob Base; Eve Of The War (War Of The Worlds) - Project D; Moments In Love - 2 To The Power*
Time To Make The Floor Burn (credited to Megabass): *Do This My Way - Kid 'N' Play; Street Tuff - Double Trouble and the Rebel MC; Sex 4 Daze - Lake Eerie; Ride On Time - Black Box; Make My Body Rock - Jomanda; Don't Miss The Partyline - Bizz Nizz; Pump Pump It Up - Hypnotek; Big Fun - Inner City; Pump That Body - Mr Lee; Pump Up The Jam - Technotronic; This Beat Is Technotronic - Technotronic; Get Busy - Mr Lee; Touch Me - 49ers; Thunderbirds Are Go - FAB*

Elaine VASSELL – *See BEATMASTERS*

Frankie VAUGHAN *UK, male vocalist* — **232 wks**

29 Jan 54	ISTANBUL *HMV B 10599* 11	1 wk
28 Jan 55	HAPPY DAYS AND LONELY NIGHTS	
	HMV B 10783 12	3 wks
22 Apr 55	TWEEDLE DEE *Philips PB 423* 17	1 wk
2 Dec 55	SEVENTEEN *Philips PB 511* 18	3 wks
3 Feb 56	MY BOY FLAT TOP *Philips PB 544* 20	2 wks
9 Nov 56 ●	GREEN DOOR *Philips PB 640* 2	15 wks
11 Jan 57 ★	GARDEN OF EDEN *Philips PB 660* 1	13 wks
4 Oct 57 ●	MAN ON FIRE /WANDERIN' EYES *Philips PB 729* 6	12 wks
1 Nov 57 ●	GOTTA HAVE SOMETHING IN THE BANK	
	FRANK *Philips PB 751* * 8	11 wks
20 Dec 57 ●	KISSES SWEETER THAN WINE *Philips PB 775* 8	11 wks
7 Mar 58	CAN'T GET ALONG WITHOUT YOU/WE ARE	
	NOT ALONE *Philips PB 793* 11	6 wks
9 May 58 ●	KEWPIE DOLL *Philips PB 825* 10	12 wks
1 Aug 58	WONDERFUL THINGS *Philips PB 834* 22	3 wks
12 Sep 58	WONDERFUL THINGS (re-entry) *Philips PB 834* 27	3 wks
10 Oct 58	AM I WASTING MY TIME ON YOU *Philips PB 865* 25	2 wks
9 Jan 59	AM I WASTING MY TIME ON YOU (re-entry)	
	Philips PB 865 27	2 wks
30 Jan 59	THAT'S MY DOLL *Philips PB 895* 28	2 wks
1 May 59 ●	COME SOFTLY TO ME *Philips PB 913* * 9	9 wks
24 Jul 59 ●	THE HEART OF A MAN *Philips PB 930* 5	14 wks
18 Sep 59	WALKIN' TALL *Philips PB 931* 28	1 wk
2 Oct 59	WALKIN' TALL (re-entry) *Philips PB 931* 29	1 wk
29 Jan 60	WHAT MORE DO YOU WANT *Philips PB 985* 25	2 wks
22 Sep 60	KOOKIE LITTLE PARADISE *Philips PB 1054* 31	5 wks
27 Oct 60	MILORD *Philips PB 1066* 34	6 wks
9 Nov 61 ★	TOWER OF STRENGTH *Philips PB 1195* 1	13 wks
1 Feb 62	DON'T STOP TWIST *Philips 1219* 22	7 wks
27 Sep 62	HERCULES *Philips 326542 BF* 42	4 wks
24 Jan 63 ●	LOOP-DE-LOOP *Philips 326566 BF* 5	12 wks
20 Jun 63	HEY MAMA *Philips BF 1254* 21	9 wks
4 Jun 64	HELLO DOLLY *Philips BF 1339* 18	11 wks
11 Mar 65	SOMEONE MUST HAVE HURT YOU A LOT	
	Philips BF 1394 46	1 wk
23 Aug 67 ●	THERE MUST BE A WAY *Columbia DB 8248* 7	21 wks
15 Nov 67	SO TIRED *Columbia DB 8298* 21	9 wks
28 Feb 68	NEVERTHELESS *Columbia DB 8354* 29	5 wks

* Frankie Vaughan and the Kaye Sisters

Malcolm VAUGHAN *UK, male vocalist* — **106 wks**

1 Jul 55 ●	EVERY DAY OF MY LIFE *HMV B 10874* 5	16 wks
27 Jan 56	WITH YOUR LOVE *HMV POP 130* 20	1 wk
10 Feb 56	WITH YOUR LOVE (re-entry) *HMV POP 130* 18	1 wk
2 Mar 56	WITH YOUR LOVE (2nd re-entry) *HMV POP 130* 20	1 wk
26 Oct 56	ST. THERESE OF THE ROSES *HMV POP 250* 27	1 wk

16 Nov 56	● ST. THERESE OF THE ROSES (re-entry)		
	HMV POP 250	3	19 wks
12 Apr 57	THE WORLD IS MINE HMV POP 303	30	1 wk
3 May 57	THE WORLD IS MINE (re-entry) HMV POP 303	29	2 wks
10 May 57	CHAPEL OF THE ROSES HMV POP 325	13	8 wks
31 May 57	THE WORLD IS MINE (2nd re-entry) HMV POP 303	26	1 wk
29 Nov 57	● MY SPECIAL ANGEL HMV POP 419	3	14 wks
21 Mar 58	TO BE LOVED HMV POP 459 *	14	12 wks
17 Oct 58	● MORE THAN EVER (COME PRIMA)		
	HMV POP 538 *	5	14 wks
27 Feb 59	WAIT FOR ME/WILLINGLY HMV POP 590	28	1 wk
13 Mar 59	WAIT FOR ME (re-entry) HMV POP 590	13	14 wks

* Malcolm Vaughan with the Michael Sammes Singers

Norman VAUGHAN UK, male vocalist — 5 wks

17 May 62	SWINGING IN THE RAIN Pye 7N 15438	34	5 wks

Sarah VAUGHAN US, female vocalist — 34 wks

27 Sep 57	PASSING STRANGERS Mercury MT 164 *	22	2 wks
11 Sep 59	● BROKEN HEARTED MELODY Mercury AMT 1057	7	13 wks
29 Dec 60	LET'S/SERENATA Columbia DB 4542	37	3 wks
2 Feb 61	LET'S/SERENATA (re-entry) Columbia DB 4542	47	1 wk
12 Mar 69	PASSING STRANGERS (re-issue) Mercury MF 1082 *	20	15 wks

* Billy Eckstine and Sarah Vaughan

Billy VAUGHN US, orchestra and chorus — 8 wks

27 Jan 56	SHIFTING WHISPERING SANDS		
	London HLD 8205 *	20	1 wk
23 Mar 56	THEME FROM THE 'THREEPENNY OPERA'		
	London HLD 8238	12	7 wks

* Billy Vaughn Orchestra and Chorus, narration by Ken Nordene

Bobby VEE US, male vocalist — 134 wks

19 Jan 61	● RUBBER BALL London HLG 9255	4	11 wks
13 Apr 61	● MORE THAN I CAN SAY/STAYING IN		
	London HLG 9316	4	16 wks
3 Aug 61	● HOW MANY TEARS London HLG 9389	10	13 wks
26 Oct 61	● TAKE GOOD CARE OF MY BABY London HLG 9438	3	16 wks
21 Dec 61	● RUN TO HIM London HLG 9470	6	15 wks
8 Mar 62	PLEASE DON'T ASK ABOUT BARBARA		
	Liberty LIB 55419	29	9 wks
7 Jun 62	● SHARING YOU Liberty LIB 55451	10	13 wks
27 Sep 62	A FOREVER KIND OF LOVE Liberty LIB 10046	13	19 wks
7 Feb 63	● THE NIGHT HAS A THOUSAND EYES		
	Liberty LIB 10069	3	12 wks
20 Jun 63	BOBBY TOMORROW Liberty LIB 55530	21	10 wks

Staying In listed with More Than I Can Say from 13 Apr to 4 May 61.

Louie VEGA and Marc ANTHONY
US, male vocal/instrumental duo — 2 wks

5 Oct 91	RIDE ON THE RHYTHM Atlantic A 7602 *	71	1 wk
23 May 92	RIDE ON THE RHYTHM (re-issue) Atlantic A 7486	70	1 wk

* Little Louie Vega and Marc Anthony

Suzanne VEGA US, female vocalist — 49 wks

18 Jan 86	SMALL BLUE THING A & M AM 294	65	3 wks
22 Mar 86	MARLENE ON THE WALL A & M AM 309	21	9 wks
7 Jun 86	LEFT OF CENTER A & M AM 320 *	32	9 wks
23 May 87	LUKA A & M VEGA 1	23	8 wks
18 Jul 87	TOM'S DINER A & M VEGA 2	58	3 wks
19 May 90	BOOK OF DREAMS A & M AM 559	66	1 wk

British Hit Singles Part One: Alphabetically by Artist

Date of chart entry/Title & catalogue no./Peak position reached/Weeks on chart

★ Number one ● Top Ten † still on chart at 31 Dec 1992

* = credited to act billed in footnote

28 Jul 90	● TOM'S DINER A & M AM 592 **	2	10 wks
22 Aug 92	IN LIVERPOOL A & M AM 0029	52	2 wks
24 Oct 92	99.9 °F A & M AM 0085	46	2 wks
19 Dec 92	BLOOD MAKES NOISE A & M AM 0112	60†	2 wks

* Suzanne Vega featuring Joe Jackson ** DNA featuring Suzanne Vega

Tata VEGA US, female vocalist — 4 wks

26 May 79	GET IT UP FOR LOVE/I JUST KEEP THINKING		
	ABOUT YOU BABY Motown TMG 1140	52	4 wks

VEGAS UK, male vocal/instrumental duo — 8 wks

19 Sep 92	POSSESSED RCA 74321110437	32	4 wks
28 Nov 92	SHE RCA 74321124657	43	4 wks

Rosie VELA US, female vocalist — 7 wks

17 Jan 87	MAGIC SMILE A & M AM 369	27	7 wks

VELVELETTES US, female vocal group — 7 wks

31 Jul 71	THESE THINGS WILL KEEP ME LOVING YOU		
	Tamla Motown TMG 780	34	7 wks

VELVETS US, male vocal group — 2 wks

11 May 61	THAT LUCKY OLD SUN London HLU 9328	46	1 wk
17 Aug 61	TONIGHT (COULD BE THE NIGHT)		
	London HLU 9372	50	1 wk

VENTURES US, male instrumental group — 31 wks

8 Sep 60	● WALK DON'T RUN Top Rank JAR 417	8	13 wks
1 Dec 60	● PERFIDIA London HLG 9232	4	13 wks
9 Mar 61	RAM-BUNK-SHUSH London HLG 9292	45	1 wk
11 May 61	LULLABY OF THE LEAVES London HLG 9344	43	4 wks

Al VERLAINE – See PING PING and Al VERLAINE

VERNONS GIRLS UK, female vocal group — 31 wks

17 May 62	LOVER PLEASE Decca F 11450	16	9 wks
23 Aug 62	LOVER PLEASE/YOU KNOW WHAT I		
	MEAN (re-entry) Decca F 11450	39	7 wks
6 Sep 62	LOCO-MOTION Decca F 11495	47	1 wk
18 Oct 62	YOU KNOW WHAT I MEAN (2nd re-entry)		
	Decca F 11450	37	3 wks
15 Nov 62	YOU KNOW WHAT I MEAN (3rd re-entry)		
	Decca F 11450	50	1 wk
3 Jan 63	FUNNY ALL OVER Decca F 11549	31	8 wks
18 Apr 63	DO THE BIRD Decca F 11629	50	1 wk
2 May 63	DO THE BIRD (re-entry) Decca F 11629	44	1 wk

You Know What I Mean was not coupled with Lover Please on the chart of 23 Aug 62, but both sides of this record were listed for the following 6 weeks.

VERVE UK, male vocal/instrumental group — 1 wk

4 Jul 92	SHE'S A SUPERSTAR Hut HUT 16	66	1 wk

VIBRATIONS – See Tony JACKSON and the VIBRATIONS

'Blue Velvet' by BOBBY VINTON succeeded in the UK 27 years after it was an American number one. It had been the title song of a David Lynch film and the music in a skin cream TV commerical.

CRYSTAL WATERS sits in the make-up department preparing to perform.

When Tina Turner charted with 'Steamy Windows' in 1990, it gave TONY JOE WHITE hit compositions in four consecutive decades.

VIBRATORS UK, male vocal/instrumental group — **8 wks**

18 Mar 78	**AUTOMATIC LOVER** Epic EPC 6137	35	5 wks
17 Jun 78	**JUDY SAYS (KNOCK YOU IN THE HEAD)** Epic EPC 6393	70	3 wks

VICE SQUAD UK, male/female vocal/instrumental group — **1 wk**

13 Feb 82	**OUT OF REACH** Zonophone Z 26	68	1 wk

VICIOUS PINK UK, male/female vocal/instrumental duo — **4 wks**

15 Sep 84	**CCCAN'T YOU SEE** Parlophone R 6074	67	4 wks

Mike VICKERS – See Kenny EVERETT

Maria VIDAL US, female vocalist — **13 wks**

24 Aug 85	**BODY ROCK** EMI America EA 189	11	13 wks

VIDEO KIDS Holland, male/female vocal duo — **1 wk**

5 Oct 85	**WOODPECKERS FROM SPACE** Epic A 6504	72	1 wk

VIDEO SYMPHONIC UK, orchestra — **3 wks**

24 Oct 81	**THE FLAME TREES OF THIKA** EMI EMI 5222	42	3 wks

VIENNA PHILHARMONIC ORCHESTRA — **14 wks**
Austria, orchestra

18 Dec 71	**THEME FROM 'THE ONEDIN LINE'** Decca F 13259	15	14 wks

VIEW FROM THE HILL — **6 wks**
UK, male/female vocal/instrumental group

19 Jul 86	**NO CONVERSATION** EMI EMI 5565	58	3 wks
21 Feb 87	**I'M NO REBEL** EMI EM 5580	59	3 wks

VIKKI UK, female vocalist — **3 wks**

4 May 85	**LOVE IS...** PRT 7P 326	49	3 wks

VILLAGE PEOPLE US, male vocal/instrumental group — **54 wks**

3 Dec 77	**SAN FRANCISCO (YOU'VE GOT ME)** DJM DJS 10817	45	5 wks
25 Nov 78	★ **Y.M.C.A.** Mercury 6007 192	1	16 wks
17 Mar 79	● **IN THE NAVY** Mercury 6007 209	2	9 wks
16 Jun 79	**GO WEST** Mercury 6007 221	15	8 wks
9 Aug 80	**CAN'T STOP THE MUSIC** Mercury MER 16	11	11 wks
9 Feb 85	**SEX OVER THE PHONE** Record Shack SOHO 34	59	5 wks

VIM UK, male instrumental/production group — **1 wk**

26 Jan 91	**MAGGIE'S LAST PARTY** F2 BOZ 1	68	1 wk

Gene VINCENT US, male vocalist — **51 wks**

13 Jul 56	**BE BOP A LULA** Capitol CL 14599	30	2 wks
24 Aug 56	**BE BOP A LULA (re-entry)** Capitol CL 14599	16	3 wks
28 Sep 56	**BE BOP A LULA (2nd re-entry)** Capitol CL 14599	23	2 wks
12 Oct 56	**RACE WITH THE DEVIL** Capitol CL 14628	28	1 wk
19 Oct 56	**BLUE JEAN BOP** Capitol CL 14637	16	5 wks
8 Jan 60	**WILD CAT** Capitol CL 15099	21	3 wks
10 Mar 60	**MY HEART** Capitol CL 15115	16	6 wks
10 Mar 60	**WILD CAT (re-entry)** Capitol CL 15099	39	3 wks
28 Apr 60	**MY HEART (re-entry)** Capitol CL 15115	47	1 wk
19 May 60	**MY HEART (2nd re-entry)** Capitol CL 15115	36	1 wk
16 Jun 60	**PISTOL PACKIN' MAMA** Capitol CL 15136	15	9 wks
1 Jun 61	**SHE SHE LITTLE SHEILA** Capitol CL 15202	22	10 wks
17 Aug 61	**SHE SHE LITTLE SHEILA (re-entry)** Capitol CL 15202	44	1 wk
31 Aug 61	**I'M GOING HOME** Capitol CL 15215	36	4 wks

VINDALOO SUMMER SPECIAL — **3 wks**
UK, male/female vocal/instrumental group

19 Jul 86	**ROCKIN' WITH RITA (HEAD TO TOE)** Vindaloo UGH 13	56	3 wks

Bobby VINTON US, male vocalist — **29 wks**

2 Aug 62	**ROSES ARE RED** Columbia DB 4878	15	8 wks
19 Dec 63	**THERE I'VE SAID IT AGAIN** Columbia DB 7179	34	10 wks
29 Sep 90	● **BLUE VELVET** Epic 6505240	2	10 wks
17 Nov 90	**ROSES ARE RED (MY LOVE) (re-issue)** Epic 6564677	71	1 wk

VIOLINSKI UK, male instrumental group — **9 wks**

17 Feb 79	**CLOG DANCE** Jet 136	17	9 wks

VIPERS SKIFFLE GROUP — **18 wks**
UK, male vocal/instrumental group

25 Jan 57	● **DON'T YOU ROCK ME DADDY-O** Parlophone R 4261	10	9 wks
22 Mar 57	● **CUMBERLAND GAP** Parlophone R 4289	10	6 wks
31 May 57	**STREAMLINE TRAIN** Parlophone R 4308	23	3 wks

V.I.P's UK, male vocal/instrumental group — **4 wks**

6 Sep 80	**THE QUARTER MOON** Gem GEMS 39	55	4 wks

VISAGE UK, male vocal/instrumental group — **54 wks**

20 Dec 80	● **FADE TO GREY** Polydor POSP 194	8	15 wks
14 Mar 81	**MIND OF A TOY** Polydor POSP 236	13	8 wks
11 Jul 81	**VISAGE** Polydor POSP 293	21	7 wks
13 Mar 82	**DAMNED DON'T CRY** Polydor POSP 390	11	8 wks
26 Jun 82	**NIGHT TRAIN** Polydor POSP 441	12	10 wks
13 Nov 82	**PLEASURE BOYS** Polydor POSP 523	44	3 wks
1 Sep 84	**LOVE GLOVE** Polydor POSP 691	54	3 wks

VISCOUNTS UK, male vocal group — **18 wks**

13 Oct 60	**SHORT'NIN' BREAD** Pye 7N 15287	16	8 wks
14 Sep 61	**WHO PUT THE BOMP** Pye 7N 15379	21	10 wks

VISION UK, male vocal/instrumental group — **1 wk**

9 Jul 83	**LOVE DANCE** MVM MVM 2886	74	1 wk

VISIONMASTERS – See Kylie MINOGUE

VIXEN US, female vocal/instrumental group — **21 wks**

3 Sep 88	**EDGE OF A BROKEN HEART** Manhattan MT 48	51	4 wks
4 Mar 89	**CRYIN'** EMI Manhattan MT 60	27	4 wks

3 Jun 89	LOVE MADE ME *EMI-USA MT 66*	36	4 wks
2 Sep 89	EDGE OF A BROKEN HEART (re-entry) *EMI-USA MT 48*	59	2 wks
28 Jul 90	HOW MUCH LOVE *EMI-USA MT 87*	35	3 wks
20 Oct 90	LOVE IS A KILLER *EMI-USA MT 91*	41	2 wks
16 Mar 91	NOT A MINUTE TOO SOON *EMI America MT 93*	37	2 wks

VOGGUE *Canada, female vocal duo* — **6 wks**

| 18 Jul 81 | DANCIN' THE NIGHT AWAY *Mercury MER 76* | 39 | 6 wks |

VOICE OF THE BEEHIVE — **51 wks**
US/UK, male/female vocal/instrumental group

14 Nov 87	I SAY NOTHING *London LON 151*	45	5 wks
5 Mar 88	I WALK THE EARTH *London LON 169*	42	4 wks
14 May 88	DON'T CALL ME BABY *London LON 175*	15	10 wks
23 Jul 88	I SAY NOTHING (re-issue) *London LON 190*	22	6 wks
22 Oct 88	I WALK THE EARTH (re-issue) *London LON 206*	46	4 wks
13 Jul 91	MONSTERS AND ANGELS *London LON 302*	17	10 wks
28 Sep 91	I THINK I LOVE YOU *London LON 308*	25	6 wks
11 Jan 92	PERFECT PLACE *London LON 312*	37	6 wks

Sterling VOID *UK, male vocalist* — **3 wks**

| 4 Feb 89 | RUNAWAY GIRL/IT'S ALRIGHT *ffrr FFR 21* | 53 | 3 wks |

VOYAGE *UK/France, disco aggregation* — **27 wks**

17 Jun 78	FROM EAST TO WEST/SCOTS MACHINE *GTO GT 224*	13	13 wks
25 Nov 78	SOUVENIRS *GTO GT 241*	56	7 wks
24 Mar 79	LET'S FLY AWAY *GTO GT 245*	38	7 wks

Scots Machine *credited from 24 Jun 78 until end of record's chart run.*

VOYAGER *UK, male vocal/instrumental group* — **8 wks**

| 26 May 79 | HALFWAY HOTEL *Mountain VOY 001* | 33 | 8 wks |

Adam WADE *US, male vocalist* — **6 wks**

| 8 Jun 61 | TAKE GOOD CARE OF HER *HMV POP 843* | 38 | 1 wk |
| 22 Jun 61 | TAKE GOOD CARE OF HER (re-entry) *HMV POP 843* | 38 | 5 wks |

WAG YA TAIL *UK, male vocal/instrumental group* — **1 wk**

| 3 Oct 92 | XPAND YA MIND (EXPANSIONS) *PWL Int PWL 238* | 49 | 1 wk |

WAH! *UK, male vocal/instrumental group* — **26 wks**

25 Dec 82	● THE STORY OF THE BLUES *Eternal JF 1*	3	12 wks
19 Mar 83	HOPE (I WISH YOU'D BELIEVE ME) *WEA X 9880*	37	5 wks
30 Jun 84	COME BACK *Beggars Banquet BEG 111* *	20	9 wks

* Mighty Wah

Donnie WAHLBERG – *See SEIKO and Donnie WAHLBERG*

WAIKIKIS *Belgium, male instrumental group* — **2 wks**

| 11 Mar 65 | HAWAII TATTOO *Pye International 7N 25286* | 41 | 2 wks |

WAILERS – *See Bob MARLEY and the WAILERS*

John WAITE *UK, male vocalist* — **11 wks**

| 29 Sep 84 | ● MISSING YOU *EMI America EA 182* | 9 | 11 wks |

WAITRESSES *UK, female vocal group* — **4 wks**

| 18 Dec 82 | CHRISTMAS WRAPPING *Ze/Island WIP 6821* | 45 | 4 wks |

Johnny WAKELIN *UK, male vocalist* — **20 wks**

| 18 Jan 75 | ● BLACK SUPERMAN (MUHAMMAD ALI) *Pye 7N 45420* * | 7 | 10 wks |
| 24 Jul 76 | ● IN ZAIRE *Pye 7N 45595* | 4 | 10 wks |

* Johnny Wakelin and the Kinshasa Band

Narada Michael WALDEN *US, male vocalist/producer* — **28 wks**

23 Feb 80	TONIGHT I'M ALL RIGHT *Atlantic K 11437*	34	9 wks
26 Apr 80	● I SHOULDA LOVED YA *Atlantic K 11413*	8	9 wks
23 Apr 88	● DIVINE EMOTIONS *Reprise W 7967* *	8	10 wks

* Narada

Gary WALKER *US, male vocalist* — **12 wks**

| 24 Feb 66 | YOU DON'T LOVE ME *CBS 202036* | 26 | 6 wks |
| 26 May 66 | TWINKIE LEE *CBS 202081* | 26 | 6 wks |

See also Walker Brothers.

John WALKER *US, male vocalist* — **6 wks**

| 5 Jul 67 | ANNABELLA *Philips BF 1593* | 48 | 1 wk |
| 19 Jul 67 | ANNABELLA (re-entry) *Philips BF 1593* | 24 | 5 wks |

See also Walker Brothers.

Junior WALKER and the ALL-STARS — **59 wks**
US, male instrumental/vocal group

18 Aug 66	HOW SWEET IT IS *Tamla Motown TMG 571*	22	10 wks
2 Apr 69	(I'M A) ROAD RUNNER *Tamla Motown TMG 691*	12	12 wks
18 Oct 69	WHAT DOES IT TAKE (TO WIN YOUR LOVE) *Tamla Motown TMG 712*	13	12 wks
26 Aug 72	WALK IN THE NIGHT *Tamla Motown TMG 824*	16	11 wks
27 Jan 73	TAKE ME GIRL I'M READY *Tamla Motown TMG 840*	16	9 wks
30 Jun 73	WAY BACK HOME *Tamla Motown TMG 857*	35	5 wks

Scott WALKER *US, male vocalist* — **30 wks**

6 Dec 67	JACKIE *Philips BF 1628*	22	9 wks
1 May 68	● JOANNA *Philips BF 1662*	7	11 wks
11 Jun 69	LIGHTS OF CINCINATTI *Philips BF 1793*	13	10 wks

See also Walker Brothers.

WALKER BROTHERS *US, male vocal group* — **93 wks**

| 29 Apr 65 | LOVE HER *Philips BF 1409* | 20 | 13 wks |
| 19 Aug 65 | ★ MAKE IT EASY ON YOURSELF *Philips BF 1428* | 1 | 14 wks |

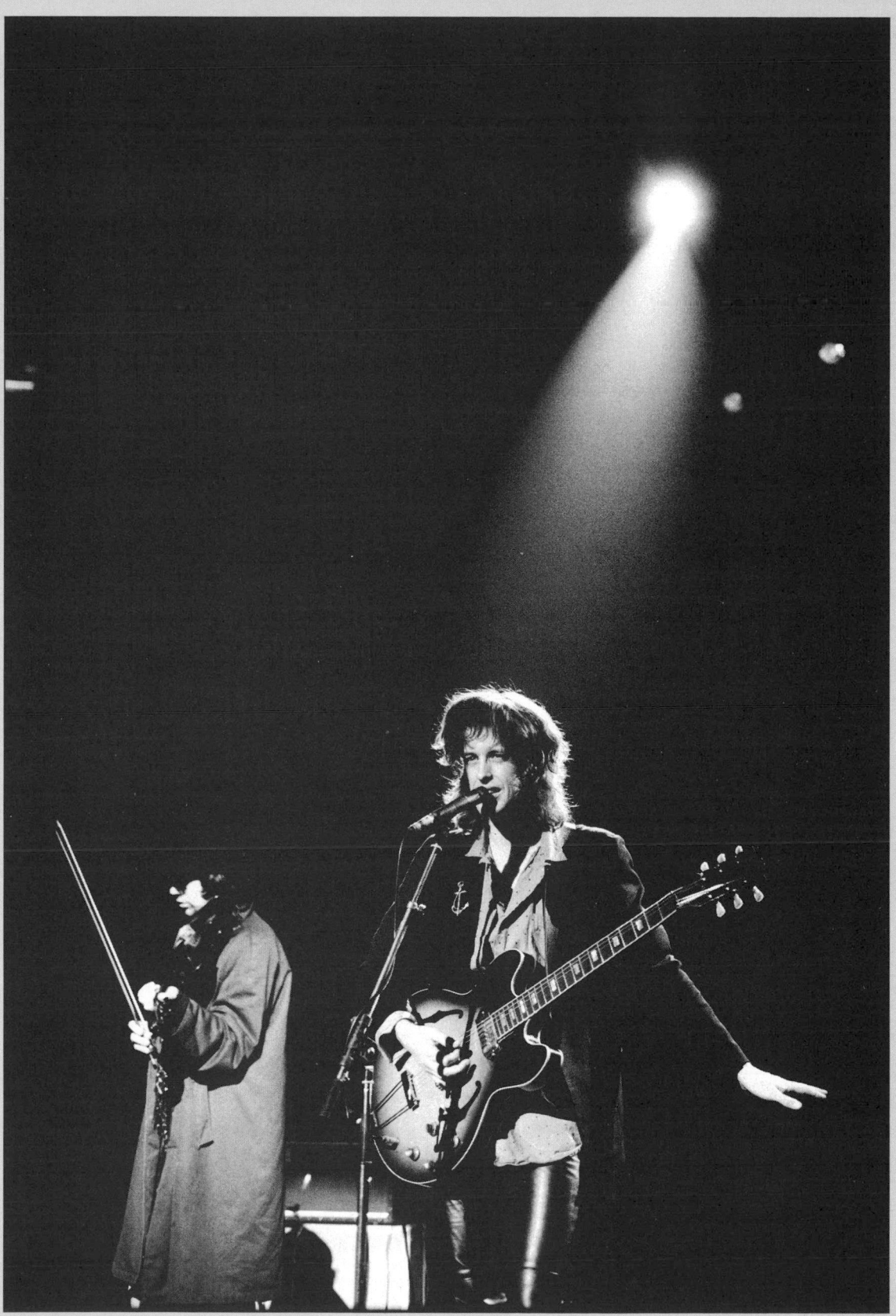

THE WATERBOYS had their greatest success with a re-issue that won composer Mike Scott (right) an Ivor Novello award.

2 Dec 65 ●	MY SHIP IS COMING IN *Philips BF 1454*	3	12 wks
3 Mar 66 ★	THE SUN AIN'T GONNA SHINE ANYMORE		
	Philips BF 1473	1	11 wks
14 Jul 66	(BABY) YOU DON'T HAVE TO TELL ME		
	Philips BF 1497	13	8 wks
22 Sep 66	ANOTHER TEAR FALLS *Philips BF 1514*	12	8 wks
15 Dec 66	DEADLIER THAN THE MALE *Philips BF 1537*	34	6 wks
9 Feb 67	STAY WITH ME BABY *Philips BF 1548*	26	6 wks
18 May 67	WALKING IN THE RAIN *Philips BF 1576*	26	6 wks
17 Jan 76 ●	NO REGRETS *GTO GT 42*	7	9 wks

See also Gary Walker; John Walker; Scott Walker.

WALL OF VOODOO US, *male vocal/instrumental group* 3 wks

19 Mar 83	MEXICAN RADIO *Illegal ILS 36*	64	3 wks

Jerry WALLACE US, *male vocalist* 1 wk

23 Jun 60	YOU'RE SINGING OUR LOVE SONG TO		
	SOMEBODY ELSE *London HLH 9110*	46	1 wk

Bob WALLIS and his STORYVILLE JAZZ BAND 7 wks

UK, male jazz band, Bob Wallis vocalist/instrumentalist - trumpet

6 Jul 61	I'M SHY MARY ELLEN I'M SHY *Pye Jazz 7NJ 2043*	44	2 wks
4 Jan 62	COME ALONG PLEASE *Pye Jazz 7NJ 2048*	33	5 wks

Joe WALSH US, *male vocalist* 15 wks

16 Jul 77	ROCKY MOUNTAIN WAY EP *ABC ABE 12002*	39	4 wks
8 Jul 78	LIFE'S BEEN GOOD *Asylum K 13129*	14	11 wks

Tracks on Rocky Mountain Way EP: *Rocky Mountain Way/Turn To Stone/Meadows/Walk Away.*

Maureen WALSH – *See Maureen*

Sheila WALSH – *See Cliff RICHARD*

Steve WALSH UK, *male vocalist* 18 wks

18 Jul 87	I FOUND LOVIN' *A1 A1 299*	74	1 wk
29 Aug 87 ●	I FOUND LOVIN' (re-entry) *A1 A1 299*	9	12 wks
12 Dec 87	LET'S GET TOGETHER TONITE *A1 A1 303*	74	1 wk
30 Jul 88	AIN'T NO STOPPING US NOW (PARTY FOR THE		
	WORLD) *A1 A1 304*	44	4 wks

Trevor WALTERS UK, *male vocalist* 22 wks

24 Oct 81	LOVE ME TONIGHT *Magnet MAG 198*	27	8 wks
21 Jul 84 ●	STUCK ON YOU *Sanity IS 002*	9	12 wks
1 Dec 84	NEVER LET HER SLIP AWAY *Polydor POSP 716*	73	2 wks

WANG CHUNG UK, *male vocal/instrumental group* 12 wks

28 Jan 84	DANCE HALL DAYS *Geffen A 3837*	21	12 wks

Dexter WANSELL US, *male instrumentalist - keyboards* 3 wks

20 May 78	ALL NIGHT LONG *Philadelphia International PIR 6255*	59	3 wks

WAR US/Canada/Denmark, *male vocal/instrumental group* 32 wks

24 Jan 76	LOW RIDER *Island WIP 6267*	12	7 wks
26 Jun 76	ME AND BABY BROTHER *Island WIP 6303*	21	7 wks

14 Jan 78	GALAXY *MCA 339*	14	7 wks
15 Apr 78	HEY SENORITA *MCA 359*	40	2 wks
10 Apr 82	YOU GOT THE POWER *RCA 201*	58	4 wks
6 Apr 85	GROOVIN' *Bluebird BR 16*	43	5 wks

Anita WARD US, *female vocalist* 11 wks

2 Jun 79 ★	RING MY BELL *TK TKR 7543*	1	11 wks

Billy WARD US, *male vocalist* 13 wks

13 Sep 57	STARDUST *London HLU 8465*	13	11 wks
29 Nov 57	DEEP PURPLE *London HLU 8502*	30	1 wk
3 Jan 58	STARDUST (re-entry) *London HLU 8465*	26	1 wk

Clifford T. WARD UK, *male vocalist* 16 wks

30 Jun 73 ●	GAYE *Charisma CB 205*	8	11 wks
26 Jan 74	SCULLERY *Charisma CB 221*	37	5 wks

Michael WARD UK, *male vocalist* 13 wks

29 Sep 73	LET THERE BE PEACE ON EARTH (LET IT		
	BEGIN WITH ME) *Philips 6006 340*	15	10 wks
15 Dec 73	LET THERE BE PEACE ON EARTH (LET IT		
	BEGIN WITH ME) (re-entry) *Philips 6006 340*	50	3 wks

WARD BROTHERS UK, *male vocal/instrumental group* 8 wks

10 Jan 87	CROSS THAT BRIDGE *Siren SIREN 37*	32	8 wks

WARM SOUNDS UK, *male vocal duo* 6 wks

4 May 67	BIRDS AND BEES *Deram DM 120*	27	6 wks

Toni WARNE UK, *female vocalist* 4 wks

25 Apr 87	BEN *Mute CHEW 110*	50	4 wks

Jennifer WARNES US, *female vocalist* 37 wks

15 Jan 83 ●	UP WHERE WE BELONG *Island WIP 6831* *	7	13 wks
25 Jul 87	FIRST WE TAKE MANHATTAN *Cypress PB 49709*	74	1 wk
31 Oct 87 ●	(I'VE HAD) THE TIME OF MY LIFE		
	RCA PB 49625 **	6	12 wks
15 Dec 90 ●	(I'VE HAD) THE TIME OF MY LIFE (re-entry)		
	RCA PB 49625 **	8	11 wks

* Joe Cocker and Jennifer Warnes ** Bill Medley and Jennifer Warnes

WARRANT US, *male vocal/instrumental group* 7 wks

17 Nov 90	CHERRY PIE *CBS 6562587*	59	2 wks
9 Mar 91	CHERRY PIE (re-issue) *Columbia 6566867*	35	5 wks

Ann WARREN – *See Ruby MURRAY*

Dionne WARWICK US, *female vocalist* 101 wks

13 Feb 64	ANYONE WHO HAD A HEART		
	Pye International 7N 25234	42	3 wks
16 Apr 64 ●	WALK ON BY *Pye International 7N 25241*	9	14 wks
30 Jul 64	YOU'LL NEVER GET TO HEAVEN		
	Pye International 7N 25256	20	8 wks

British Hit Singles Part One: Alphabetically by Artist
Date of chart entry/Title & catalogue no./Peak position reached/Weeks on chart
★ Number one ● Top Ten † still on chart at 31 Dec 1992
* = credited to act billed in footnote

8 Oct 64	**REACH OUT FOR ME** Pye International 7N 25265	.23	7 wks
1 Apr 65	**YOU CAN HAVE HIM** Pye International 7N 25290	.37	5 wks
13 Mar 68	**VALLEY OF THE DOLLS** Pye International 7N 25445	.28	8 wks
15 May 68 ●	**DO YOU KNOW THE WAY TO SAN JOSÉ** Pye International 7N 25457	.8	10 wks
19 Oct 74	**THEN CAME YOU** Atlantic K 10495 *	.29	6 wks
23 Oct 82 ●	**HEARTBREAKER** Arista ARIST 496	.2	13 wks
11 Dec 82 ●	**ALL THE LOVE IN THE WORLD** Arista ARIST 507	.10	10 wks
26 Feb 83	**YOURS** Arista ARIST 518	.66	2 wks
28 May 83	**I'LL NEVER LOVE THIS WAY AGAIN** Arista ARIST 530	.62	3 wks
9 Nov 85	**THAT'S WHAT FRIENDS ARE FOR** Arista ARIST 638 **	.16	9 wks
15 Aug 87	**LOVE POWER** Arista RIS 27 ***	.63	3 wks

* Dionne Warwick and the Detroit Spinners ** Dionne Warwick and Friends featuring Elton John, Stevie Wonder and Gladys Knight *** Dionne Warwick and Jeffrey Osborne

WAS (NOT WAS) US, male vocal/instrumental duo — 58 wks

3 Mar 84	**OUT COME THE FREAKS** Ze/Geffen A 4178	.41	5 wks
18 Jul 87	**SPY IN THE HOUSE OF LOVE** Fontana WAS 2	.51	7 wks
3 Oct 87 ●	**WALK THE DINOSAUR** Fontana WAS 3	.10	10 wks
6 Feb 88	**SPY IN THE HOUSE OF LOVE (re-entry)** Fontana WAS 2	.21	8 wks
7 May 88	**OUT COME THE FREAKS (AGAIN)** Fontana WAS 4	.44	3 wks
16 Jul 88	**ANYTHING CAN HAPPEN** Fontana WAS 5	.67	3 wks
26 May 90	**PAPA WAS A ROLLING STONE** Fontana WAS 7	.12	7 wks
11 Aug 90	**HOW THE HEART BEHAVES** Fontana WAS 8	.53	3 wks
23 May 92	**LISTEN LIKE THIEVES** Fontana WAS 10	.58	2 wks
11 Jul 92 ●	**SHAKE YOUR HEAD** Fontana WAS 11	.4	9 wks
26 Sep 92	**SOMEWHERE IN AMERICA (THERE'S A STREET NAMED AFTER MY DAD)** Fontana WAS 12	.57	1 wk

Fontana WAS 4 was a re-recorded version of their first hit. Shake Your Head features uncredited vocals by Ozzy Osbourne and Kim Basinger. See also Ozzy Osbourne.

Martha WASH US, female vocalist — 1 wk

28 Nov 92	**CARRY ON** RCA 74321125457	.74	1 wk

Dinah WASHINGTON US, female vocalist — 8 wks

30 Nov 61	**SEPTEMBER IN THE RAIN** Mercury AMT 1162	.35	3 wks
18 Jan 62	**SEPTEMBER IN THE RAIN (re-entry)** Mercury AMT 1162	.49	1 wk
4 Apr 92	**MAD ABOUT THE BOY** Mercury DINAH 1	.41	4 wks

Geno WASHINGTON and the RAM JAM BAND UK, male vocalist, male instrumental backing group — 20 wks

19 May 66	**WATER** Piccadilly 7N 35312	.39	8 wks
21 Jul 66	**HI HI HAZEL** Piccadilly 7N 35329	.45	3 wks
25 Aug 66	**HI HI HAZEL (re-entry)** Piccadilly 7N 35329	.48	1 wk
6 Oct 66	**QUE SERA SERA** Piccadilly 7N 35346	.43	3 wks
2 Feb 67	**MICHAEL** Piccadilly 7N 35359	.39	5 wks

Grover WASHINGTON Jr.
US, male instrumentalist - saxophone — 7 wks

16 May 81	**JUST THE TWO OF US** Elektra K 12514	.34	7 wks

Although uncredited, Bill Withers vocalises on Just The Two Of Us.

Keith WASHINGTON – See Kylie MINOGUE

W.A.S.P. US, male vocal/instrumental group — 36 wks

31 May 86	**WILD CHILD** Capitol CL 388	.71	2 wks
11 Oct 86	**95 - NASTY** Capitol CL 432	.70	1 wk
29 Aug 87	**SCREAM UNTIL YOU LIKE IT** Capitol CL 458	.32	5 wks
31 Oct 87	**I DON'T NEED NO DOCTOR (LIVE)** Capitol CL 469	.31	5 wks
20 Feb 88	**LIVE ANIMAL (F ** K LIKE A BEAST)** Music For Nations KUT 109	.61	3 wks
4 Mar 89	**MEAN MAN** Capitol CL 521	.21	5 wks
27 May 89	**THE REAL ME** Capitol CL 534	.23	5 wks
9 Sep 89	**FOREVER FREE** Capitol CL 546	.25	5 wks
4 Apr 92	**CHAINSAW CHARLIE (MURDERS IN THE NEW MORGUE)** Parlophone RS 6308	.17	2 wks
6 Jun 92	**THE IDOL** Parlophone RPD 6314	.41	2 wks
31 Oct 92	**I AM ONE** Parlophone 10RG 6324	.56	1 wk

WATERBOYS UK/Ireland, male vocal/instrumental group — 27 wks

2 Nov 85	**THE WHOLE OF THE MOON** Ensign ENY 520	.26	7 wks
14 Jan 89	**FISHERMAN'S BLUES** Ensign ENY 621	.32	6 wks
1 Jul 89	**AND A BANG ON THE EAR** Ensign ENY 624	.51	4 wks
6 Apr 91 ●	**THE WHOLE OF THE MOON (re-issue)** Ensign ENY 642	.3	9 wks
8 Jun 91	**FISHERMAN'S BLUES (re-issue)** Ensign ENY 645	.75	1 wk

WATERFRONT UK, male vocal/instrumental duo — 19 wks

15 Apr 89	**BROKEN ARROW** Polydor WON 3	.63	2 wks
27 May 89	**CRY** Polydor WON 1	.17	13 wks
9 Sep 89	**NATURE OF LOVE** Polydor WON 2	.63	4 wks

Dennis WATERMAN UK, male vocalist — 17 wks

25 Oct 80 ●	**I COULD BE SO GOOD FOR YOU** EMI 5009 *	.3	12 wks
17 Dec 83	**WHAT ARE WE GONNA GET 'ER INDOORS** EMI MIN 101 **	.21	5 wks

* Dennis Waterman with the Dennis Waterman Band ** Dennis Waterman and George Cole

Crystal WATERS US, female vocalist — 21 wks

18 May 91 ●	**GYPSY WOMAN (LA DA DEE)** A & M AM 772	.2	10 wks
7 Sep 91	**MAKIN' HAPPY** A & M AM 790	.18	6 wks
11 Jan 92	**MEGAMIX** A & M AM 843	.39	3 wks
3 Oct 92	**GYPSY WOMAN (re-mix)** Epic 6584377	.35	2 wks

The listed flip side of Gypsy Woman (re-mix) was Peace (re-mix) by Sabrina Johnston.

Muddy WATERS US, male vocalist/instrumentalist - guitar — 6 wks

16 Jul 88	**MANNISH BOY** Epic MUD 1	.51	6 wks

Roger WATERS UK, male vocalist/instrumentalist — 8 wks

30 May 87	**RADIO WAVES** Harvest EM 6	.74	1 wk
26 Dec 87	**THE TIDE IS TURNING (AFTER LIVE AID)** Harvest EM 37	.54	4 wks
5 Sep 92	**WHAT GOD WANTS PART 1** Columbia 6581390	.35	3 wks

Jody WATLEY US, female vocalist — 32 wks

9 May 87	**LOOKING FOR A NEW LOVE** MCA MCA 1107	.13	11 wks
17 Oct 87	**DON'T YOU WANT ME** MCA MCA 1198	.55	3 wks
8 Apr 89	**REAL LOVE** MCA MCA 1324	.31	7 wks
12 Aug 89	**FRIENDS** MCA MCA 1352 *	.21	6 wks
10 Feb 90	**EVERYTHING** MCA MCA 1395	.74	2 wks
11 Apr 92	**I'M THE ONE YOU NEED** MCA MCS 1608	.50	3 wks

* Jody Watley with Eric B. and Rakim

Johnny 'Guitar' WATSON
US, male vocalist, instrumentalist - guitar   **8 wks**

| 28 Aug 76 | I NEED IT *DJM DJS 10694* | 35 | 5 wks |
| 23 Apr 77 | A REAL MOTHER FOR YA *DJM DJT 10762* | 44 | 3 wks |

WAVELENGTH *UK, male vocal group*   **12 wks**

| 10 Jul 82 | HURRY HOME *Ariola ARO 281* | 17 | 12 wks |

WAX *US/UK, male vocal/instrumental duo*   **16 wks**

| 12 Apr 86 | RIGHT BETWEEN THE EYES *RCA PB 40509* | 60 | 5 wks |
| 1 Aug 87 | BRIDGE TO YOUR HEART *RCA PB 41405* | 12 | 11 wks |

A WAY OF LIFE *US, male/female vocal/instrumental group*   **3 wks**

| 21 Apr 90 | TRIPPIN' ON YOUR LOVE *Eternal YZ 464* | 55 | 3 wks |

WAY OF THE WEST *UK, male vocal/instrumental group*   **5 wks**

| 25 Apr 81 | DON'T SAY THAT'S JUST FOR WHITE BOYS *Mercury MER 66* | 54 | 5 wks |

Jeff WAYNE *US, orchestra*   **3 wks**

| 10 Jul 82 | MATADOR *CBS A 2493* | 57 | 3 wks |

See also Jeff Wayne's War Of The Worlds.

Jeff WAYNE'S WAR OF THE WORLDS   **18 wks**
US/UK, male/female vocal/instrumental cast

| 9 Sep 78 | EVE OF THE WAR *CBS 6496* | 36 | 8 wks |
| 25 Nov 89 ● | EVE OF THE WAR (re-mix) *CBS 6551267* | 3 | 10 wks |

See also Jeff Wayne.

WEATHER GIRLS *US, female vocal duo*   **14 wks**

| 27 Aug 83 | IT'S RAINING MEN *CBS A 2924* | 73 | 3 wks |
| 3 Mar 84 ● | IT'S RAINING MEN (re-entry) *CBS A 2924* | 2 | 11 wks |

WEATHER PROPHETS
UK, male vocal/instrumental group   **2 wks**

| 28 Mar 87 | SHE COMES FROM THE RAIN *Elevation ACID 1* | 62 | 2 wks |

WEATHERMEN – *See Jonathan KING*

Marti WEBB *UK, female vocalist*   **42 wks**

9 Feb 80 ●	TAKE THAT LOOK OFF YOUR FACE *Polydor POSP 100*	3	12 wks
19 Apr 80	TELL ME ON A SUNDAY *Polydor POSP 111*	67	2 wks
20 Sep 80	YOUR EARS SHOULD BE BURNING NOW *Polydor POSP 166*	61	4 wks
8 Jun 85 ●	BEN *Starblend STAR 6*	5	11 wks
20 Sep 86	ALWAYS THERE *BBC RESL 190*	13	12 wks
6 Jun 87	I CAN'T LET GO *Rainbow RBR 12*	65	1 wk

Always There features the Simon May Orchestra. See also Simon May.

Joan WEBER *US, female vocalist*   **1 wk**

| 18 Feb 55 | LET ME GO LOVER *Philips PB 389* | 16 | 1 wk |

WEDDING PRESENT *UK, male vocal/instrumental group*   **33 wks**

5 Mar 88	NOBODY'S TWISTING YOUR ARM *Reception REC 009*	46	2 wks
1 Oct 88	WHY ARE YOU BEING SO REASONABLE NOW *Reception REC 011*	42	2 wks
7 Oct 89	KENNEDY *RCA PB 43117*	33	3 wks
17 Feb 90	BRASSNECK *RCA PB 43403*	24	3 wks
29 Sep 90	3 SONGS EP *RCA PB 44021*	25	4 wks
11 May 91	DALLIANCE *RCA PB 44495*	29	3 wks
27 Jul 91	LOVENEST *RCA PT 44750*	58	1 wk
18 Jan 92	BLUE EYES *RCA PB 45185*	26	2 wks
15 Feb 92	GO-GO DANCER *RCA PB 45183*	20	1 wk
14 Mar 92	THREE *RCA PB 45181*	14	2 wks
18 Apr 92	SILVER SHORTS *RCA PB 45311*	14	1 wk
16 May 92 ●	COME PLAY WITH ME *RCA PB 45313*	10	2 wks
13 Jun 92	CALIFORNIA *RCA PB 45315*	16	1 wk
18 Jul 92	FLYING SAUCER *RCA 74321101157*	22	1 wk
15 Aug 92	BOING! *RCA 74321101177*	19	1 wk
19 Sep 92	LOVE SLAVE *RCA 743211101167*	17	1 wk
17 Oct 92	STICKY *RCA 74321116917*	17	1 wk
14 Nov 92	THE QUEEN OF OUTER SPACE *RCA 74321116927*	23	1 wk
19 Dec 92	NO CHRISTMAS *RCA 74321116937*	25	1 wk

Tracks on 3 Songs EP: Corduroy/Crawl/Make Me Smile (Come Up And See Me).

Fred WEDLOCK *UK, male vocalist*   **10 wks**

| 31 Jan 81 ● | OLDEST SWINGER IN TOWN *Rocket XPRES 46* | 6 | 10 wks |

WEE PAPA GIRL RAPPERS *UK, female vocal duo*   **27 wks**

12 Mar 88	FAITH *Jive JIVE 164*	60	4 wks
25 Jun 88	HEAT IT UP *Jive JIVE 174* *	21	9 wks
1 Oct 88 ●	WEE RULE *Jive JIVE 185*	6	9 wks
24 Dec 88	SOULMATE *Jive JIVE 193*	45	4 wks
25 Mar 89	BLOW THE HOUSE DOWN *Jive JIVE 197*	65	1 wk

* *Wee Papa Girl Rappers featuring Two Men And A Drum Machine*

Bert WEEDON *UK, male instrumentalist - guitar*   **38 wks**

15 May 59 ●	GUITAR BOOGIE SHUFFLE *Top Rank JAR 117*	10	9 wks
20 Nov 59	NASHVILLE BOOGIE *Top Rank JAR 221*	29	2 wks
10 Mar 60	BIG BEAT BOOGIE *Top Rank JAR 300*	37	3 wks
7 Apr 60	BIG BEAT BOOGIE (re-entry) *Top Rank JAR 300*	49	1 wk
9 Jun 60	TWELFTH STREET RAG *Top Rank JAR 360*	47	2 wks
28 Jul 60	APACHE *Top Rank JAR 415*	44	1 wk
11 Aug 60	APACHE (re-entry) *Top Rank JAR 415*	24	3 wks
27 Oct 60	SORRY ROBBIE *Top Rank JAR 517*	28	11 wks
2 Feb 61	GINCHY *Top Rank JAR 537*	35	5 wks
4 May 61	MR. GUITAR *Top Rank JAR 559*	47	1 wk

WEEKEND   **5 wks**
Multi-national, male/female vocal/instrumental group

| 14 Dec 85 | CHRISTMAS MEDLEY/AULD LANG SYNE *Lifestyle XY 1* | 47 | 5 wks |

Frank WEIR *UK, orchestra*   **4 wks**

| 15 Sep 60 | CARIBBEAN HONEYMOON *Oriole CB 1559* | 42 | 4 wks |

See also Vera Lynn.

Eric WEISSBERG – *See 'DELIVERANCE' SOUNDTRACK*

Paul WELLER *UK, male vocalist*   **10 wks**

| 18 May 91 | INTO TOMORROW *Freedom High FHP 1* * | 36 | 3 wks |

| 15 Aug 92 | **UH HUH OH YEH** Go! Discs GOD 86 | **18** | 5 wks |
| 10 Oct 92 | **ABOVE THE CLOUDS** Go! Discs GOD 91 | **47** | 2 wks |

*Paul Weller Movement

Brandi WELLS US, female vocalist **1 wk**

| 20 Feb 82 | **WATCH OUT** Virgin VS 479 | **74** | 1 wk |

Houston WELLS UK, male vocalist **10 wks**

| 1 Aug 63 | **ONLY THE HEARTACHES** Parlophone R 5031 | **22** | 10 wks |

Mary WELLS US, female vocalist **25 wks**

21 May 64 ●	**MY GUY** Stateside SS 288	**5**	14 wks
30 Jul 64	**ONCE UPON A TIME** Stateside SS 316 *	**50**	1 wk
8 Jul 72	**MY GUY (re-issue)** Tamla Motown TMG 820	**14**	10 wks

* Marvin Gaye and Mary Wells

Terri WELLS US, female vocalist **9 wks**

| 2 Jul 83 | **YOU MAKE IT HEAVEN** Phillyworld PWS 111 | **53** | 2 wks |
| 5 May 84 | **I'LL BE AROUND** Phillyworld LON 48 | **17** | 7 wks |

Alex WELSH UK, male instrumentalist - trumpet **4 wks**

| 10 Aug 61 | **TANSY** Columbia DB 4686 | **45** | 4 wks |

WENDY and LISA US, female vocal duo **31 wks**

5 Sep 87	**WATERFALL** Virgin VS 999	**66**	4 wks
16 Jan 88	**SIDE SHOW** Virgin VS 1012	**49**	5 wks
18 Feb 89	**ARE YOU MY BABY** Virgin VS 1156	**70**	3 wks
29 Apr 89	**LOLLY LOLLY** Virgin VS 1175	**64**	3 wks
8 Jul 89	**SATISFACTION** Virgin VS 1194	**27**	8 wks
18 Nov 89	**WATERFALL (re-mix)** Virgin VS 1223	**69**	2 wks
30 Jun 90	**STRUNG OUT** Virgin VS 1272	**44**	5 wks
10 Nov 90	**RAINBOW LAKE** Virgin VS 1280	**70**	1 wk

Dodie WEST UK, female vocalist **4 wks**

| 14 Jan 65 | **GOING OUT OF MY HEAD** Decca F 12046 | **39** | 4 wks |

Keith WEST UK, male vocalist **18 wks**

| 9 Aug 67 ● | **EXCERPT FROM A TEENAGE OPERA** Parlophone R 5623 | **2** | 15 wks |
| 22 Nov 67 | **SAM** Parlophone R 5651 | **38** | 3 wks |

Kit WEST – See DEGREES OF MOTION featuring BITI

WEST HAM UNITED CUP SQUAD **2 wks**
UK, male football team vocalists

| 10 May 75 | **I'M FOREVER BLOWING BUBBLES** Pye 7N 45470 | **31** | 2 wks |

WEST STREET MOB US, male vocal group **3 wks**

| 8 Oct 83 | **BREAK DANCIN'-ELECTRIC BOOGIE** Sugarhill SH 128 | **71** | 1 wk |
| 22 Oct 83 | **BREAK DANCIN'-ELECTRIC BOOGIE (re-entry)** Sugarhill SH 128 | **64** | 2 wks |

Kim WESTON – See Marvin GAYE

WESTWORLD UK/US, male/female vocal/instrumental group **23 wks**

21 Feb 87	**SONIC BOOM BOY** RCA BOOM 1	**11**	7 wks
2 May 87	**BA-NA-NA-BAM-BOO** RCA BOOM 2	**37**	5 wks
25 Jul 87	**WHERE THE ACTION IS** RCA BOOM 3	**54**	4 wks
17 Oct 87	**SILVERMAC** RCA BOOM 4	**42**	5 wks
15 Oct 88	**EVERYTHING GOOD IS BAD** RCA PB 42243	**72**	2 wks

WET WET WET UK, male vocal/instrumental group **106 wks**

11 Apr 87 ●	**WISHING I WAS LUCKY** Precious JEWEL 3	**6**	14 wks
25 Jul 87 ●	**SWEET LITTLE MYSTERY** Precious JEWEL 4	**5**	12 wks
5 Dec 87 ●	**ANGEL EYES (HOME AND AWAY)** Precious JEWEL 6	**5**	12 wks
19 Mar 88	**TEMPTATION** Precious JEWEL 7	**12**	8 wks
14 May 88 ★	**WITH A LITTLE HELP FROM MY FRIENDS** Childline CHILD 1	**1**	11 wks
30 Sep 89 ●	**SWEET SURRENDER** Precious JEWEL 9	**6**	8 wks
9 Dec 89	**BROKE AWAY** Precious JEWEL 10	**19**	7 wks
10 Mar 90	**HOLD BACK THE RIVER** Precious JEWEL 11	**31**	4 wks
11 Aug 90	**STAY WITH ME HEARTACHE/I FEEL FINE** Precious JEWEL 13	**30**	4 wks
14 Sep 91	**MAKE IT TONIGHT** Precious JEWEL 15	**37**	3 wks
2 Nov 91	**PUT THE LIGHT ON** Precious JEWEL 16	**56**	2 wks
4 Jan 92 ★	**GOODNIGHT GIRL** Precious JEWEL 17	**1**	11 wks
21 Mar 92	**MORE THAN LOVE** Precious JEWEL 18	**19**	5 wks
11 Jul 92	**LIP SERVICE (EP)** Precious JEWEL 19	**15**	5 wks

The listed A-side with With A Little Help From My Friends *was* She's Leaving Home *by Billy Bragg with Cara Tivey. Tracks on* Lip Service (EP): Lip Service/High On The Happy Side/Lip Service (Live)/More Than Love (Live).

WE'VE GOT A FUZZBOX AND WE'RE GONNA USE IT UK, female vocal/instrumental group **39 wks**

26 Apr 86	**XX SEX/RULES AND REGULATIONS** Vindaloo UGH 11	**41**	7 wks
15 Nov 86	**LOVE IS THE SLUG** Vindaloo UGH 14	**31**	4 wks
7 Feb 87	**WHAT'S THE POINT** Vindaloo YZ 101	**51**	2 wks
25 Feb 89	**INTERNATIONAL RESCUE** WEA YZ 347	**11**	10 wks
20 May 89	**PINK SUNSHINE** WEA YZ 401	**14**	10 wks
5 Aug 89	**SELF!** WEA YZ 408	**24**	6 wks

WHALERS – See Hal PAGE and the WHALERS

WHAM! UK, male vocal duo **137 wks**

16 Oct 82 ●	**YOUNG GUNS (GO FOR IT)** Innervision IVL A2766	**3**	17 wks
15 Jan 83 ●	**WHAM RAP** Innervision IVL A2442	**8**	11 wks
14 May 83 ●	**BAD BOYS** Innervision A 3143	**2**	14 wks
30 Jul 83 ●	**CLUB TROPICANA** Innervision A 3613	**4**	11 wks
3 Dec 83	**CLUB FANTASTIC MEGAMIX** Innervision A 3586	**15**	8 wks
26 May 84 ★	**WAKE ME UP BEFORE YOU GO GO** Epic A 4440	**1**	16 wks
13 Oct 84 ★	**FREEDOM** Epic A 4743	**1**	14 wks
15 Dec 84	**LAST CHRISTMAS/EVERYTHING SHE WANTS** Epic A 4949	**2**	13 wks
23 Nov 85 ★	**I'M YOUR MAN** Epic A 6716	**1**	12 wks
14 Dec 85	**LAST CHRISTMAS (re-issue)** Epic WHAM 1	**6**	7 wks
21 Jun 86 ★	**THE EDGE OF HEAVEN/WHERE DID YOUR HEART GO** Epic FIN 1	**1**	10 wks
20 Dec 86	**LAST CHRISTMAS (2nd re-issue)** Epic 650269 7	**45**	4 wks

Where Did Your Heart Go *only listed from 2 August '86.*

WHATNAUTS – See MOMENTS

Caron WHEELER UK, female vocalist **41 wks**

| 18 Mar 89 ● | **KEEP ON MOVING** 10 TEN 263 * | **5** | 12 wks |
| 10 Jun 89 ★ | **BACK TO LIFE (HOWEVER DO YOU WANT ME)** 10 TEN 265 * | **1** | 14 wks |

JACKIE WILSON is shown in 1969, the year his 1967 American hit '(Your Love Keeps Lifting Me) Higher and Higher' finally charted in Britain.

BOBBY WOMACK is shown in the advertisement for his first US solo hit in 1968. He waited sixteen more years for his first UK solo hit.

VANESSA WILLIAMS (right) is joined at the 1992 Soul Train awards by 'Fresh Prince' Will Smith, Patti Labelle and Luther Vandross.

Date	Title	Pos	Weeks
8 Sep 90	LIVIN' IN THE LIGHT *RCA PB 43939*	14	6 wks
10 Nov 90	UK BLAK *RCA PB 43719*	40	4 wks
8 Feb 91	DON'T QUIT *RCA PB 44259*	53	3 wks
7 Nov 92	I ADORE YOU *Perspective PERSS 7407*	59	2 wks

* Soul II Soul featuring Caron Wheeler

WHEN IN ROME UK, male vocal/instrumental group   3 wks

Date	Title	Pos	Weeks
28 Jan 89	THE PROMISE *10 TEN 244*	58	3 wks

Nancy WHISKEY – See Charles McDEVITT SKIFFLE GROUP featuring Nancy WHISKEY

WHISPERS US, male vocal group   52 wks

Date	Title	Pos	Weeks
2 Feb 80 ●	AND THE BEAT GOES ON *Solar SO 1*	2	12 wks
10 May 80	LADY *Solar SO 4*	55	3 wks
12 Jul 80	MY GIRL *Solar SO 8*	26	6 wks
14 Mar 81 ●	IT'S A LOVE THING *Solar SO 16*	9	11 wks
13 Jun 81	I CAN MAKE IT BETTER *Solar SO 19*	44	5 wks
19 Jan 85	CONTAGIOUS *MCA MCA 937*	56	3 wks
28 Mar 87	AND THE BEAT GOES ON (re-issue) *Solar MCA 1126*	45	4 wks
23 May 87	ROCK STEADY *Solar MCA 1152*	38	6 wks
15 Aug 87	SPECIAL F/X *Solar MCA 1178*	69	2 wks

WHISTLE US, male rap group   8 wks

Date	Title	Pos	Weeks
1 Mar 86 ●	(NOTHIN' SERIOUS) JUST BUGGIN' *Champion CHAMP 12*	7	8 wks

Barry WHITE US, male vocalist   127 wks

Date	Title	Pos	Weeks
9 Jun 73	I'M GONNA LOVE YOU JUST A LITTLE BIT MORE BABY *Pye International 7N 25610*	23	7 wks
26 Jan 74	NEVER NEVER GONNA GIVE YA UP *Pye International 7N 25633*	14	11 wks
17 Aug 74 ●	CAN'T GET ENOUGH OF YOUR LOVE BABE *Pye International 7N 25661*	8	12 wks
2 Nov 74 ★	YOU'RE THE FIRST THE LAST MY EVERYTHING *20th Century BTC 2133*	1	14 wks
8 Mar 75 ●	WHAT AM I GONNA DO WITH YOU *20th Century BTC 2177*	5	8 wks
24 May 75	I'LL DO ANYTHING YOU WANT ME TO *20th Century BTC 2208*	20	6 wks
27 Dec 75 ●	LET THE MUSIC PLAY *20th Century BTC 2265*	9	8 wks
6 Mar 76 ●	YOU SEE THE TROUBLE WITH ME *20th Century BTC 2277*	2	10 wks
21 Aug 76	BABY WE BETTER TRY AND GET IT TOGETHER *20th Century BTC 2298*	15	7 wks
13 Nov 76	DON'T MAKE ME WAIT TOO LONG *20th Century BTC 2309*	17	8 wks
5 Mar 77	I'M QUALIFIED TO SATISFY *20th Century BTC 2328*	37	5 wks
15 Oct 77	IT'S ECSTASY WHEN YOU LAY DOWN NEXT TO ME *20th Century BTC 2350*	40	3 wks
16 Dec 78	JUST THE WAY YOU ARE *20th Century BTC 2380*	12	12 wks
24 Mar 79	SHA LA LA MEANS I LOVE YOU *20th Century BTC 1041*	55	6 wks
7 Nov 87	SHO' YOU RIGHT *Breakout USA 614*	14	7 wks
16 Jan 88	NEVER NEVER GONNA GIVE YOU UP (re-mix) *Club JAB 59*	63	2 wks
31 Mar 90	SECRET GARDEN *Qwest W 9992* *	67	1 wk

* Quincy Jones featuring Al B. Sure!, James Ingram, El DeBarge and Barry White

Chris WHITE UK, male vocalist   4 wks

Date	Title	Pos	Weeks
20 Mar 76	SPANISH WINE *Charisma CB 272*	37	4 wks

Karyn WHITE US, female vocalist   37 wks

Date	Title	Pos	Weeks
5 Nov 88	THE WAY YOU LOVE ME *Warner Bros. W 7773*	42	5 wks
18 Feb 89	SECRET RENDEZVOUS *Warner Bros. W 7562*	52	3 wks
10 Jun 89	SUPERWOMAN *Warner Bros. W 2920*	11	13 wks
9 Sep 89	SECRET RENDEZVOUS (re-issue) *Warner Bros. W 2855*	22	9 wks
17 Aug 91	ROMANTIC *Warner Bros. W 0028*	23	5 wks
18 Jan 92	THE WAY I FEEL ABOUT YOU *Warner Bros. W 0073*	65	2 wks

Snowy WHITE UK, male vocalist/instrumentalist - guitar   12 wks

Date	Title	Pos	Weeks
24 Dec 83 ●	BIRD OF PARADISE *Towerbell TOW 42*	6	10 wks
28 Dec 85	FOR YOU *R4 FOR 3*	65	1 wk
18 Jan 86	FOR YOU (re-entry) *R4 FOR 3*	72	1 wk

Tam WHITE UK, male vocalist   4 wks

Date	Title	Pos	Weeks
15 Mar 75	WHAT IN THE WORLD'S COME OVER YOU *RAK 193*	36	4 wks

Tony Joe WHITE US, male vocalist   10 wks

Date	Title	Pos	Weeks
6 Jun 70	GROUPIE GIRL *Monument MON 1043*	22	10 wks

WHITE and TORCH UK, male vocal/instrumental duo   4 wks

Date	Title	Pos	Weeks
2 Oct 82	PARADE *Chrysalis CHS 2641*	54	4 wks

WHITE PLAINS UK, male vocal group   56 wks

Date	Title	Pos	Weeks
7 Feb 70 ●	MY BABY LOVES LOVIN' *Deram DM 280*	9	11 wks
18 Apr 70	I'VE GOT YOU ON MY MIND *Deram DM 291*	17	11 wks
24 Oct 70	JULIE DO YA LOVE ME *Deram DM 315*	8	14 wks
12 Jun 71	WHEN YOU ARE A KING *Deram DM 333*	13	11 wks
17 Feb 73	STEP INTO A DREAM *Deram DM 371*	21	9 wks

WHITESNAKE UK, male vocal/instrumental group   107 wks

Date	Title	Pos	Weeks
24 Jun 78	SNAKE BITE EP *EMI International INEP 751* *	61	3 wks
10 Nov 79	LONG WAY FROM HOME *United Artists BP 324* *	55	2 wks
26 Apr 80	FOOL FOR YOUR LOVING *United Artists BP 352*	13	9 wks
12 Jul 80	READY AN' WILLING (SWEET SATISFACTION) *United Artists BP 363*	43	4 wks
22 Nov 80	AIN'T NO LOVE IN THE HEART OF THE CITY *Sunburst/Liberty BP 381*	51	4 wks
11 Apr 81	DON'T BREAK MY HEART AGAIN *Liberty BP 395*	17	9 wks
6 Jun 81	WOULD I LIE TO YOU *Liberty BP 399*	37	6 wks
6 Nov 82	HERE I GO AGAIN/BLOODY LUXURY *Liberty BP 416*	34	10 wks
13 Aug 83	GUILTY OF LOVE *Liberty BP 420*	31	5 wks
14 Jan 84	GIVE ME MORE TIME *Liberty BP 422*	29	4 wks
28 Apr 84	STANDING IN THE SHADOW *Liberty BP 423*	62	2 wks
9 Feb 85	LOVE AIN'T NO STRANGER *Liberty BP 424*	44	4 wks
28 Mar 87	STILL OF THE NIGHT *EMI EMI 5606*	16	8 wks
6 Jun 87	IS THIS LOVE *EMI EM 3*	9	11 wks
31 Oct 87 ●	HERE I GO AGAIN (re-mix) *EMI EM 35*	9	11 wks
6 Feb 88	GIVE ME ALL YOUR LOVE *EMI EM 23*	18	6 wks
2 Dec 89	FOOL FOR YOUR LOVING *EMI EM 123*	43	2 wks
10 Mar 90	THE DEEPER THE LOVE *EMI EM 128*	35	3 wks
25 Aug 90	NOW YOU'RE GONE *EMI EM 150*	31	4 wks

* David Coverdale's Whitesnake

Tracks on Snake Bite EP: Bloody Mary/Steal Away/Ain't No Love In The Heart Of The City/Come On. EM 123 is a re-recording of their third hit.

David WHITFIELD UK, male vocalist   181 wks

Date	Title	Pos	Weeks
2 Oct 53 ●	BRIDGE OF SIGHS *Decca F 10129*	9	1 wk
16 Oct 53 ★	ANSWER ME *Decca F 10192*	1	13 wks
11 Dec 53	RAGS TO RICHES *Decca F 10207*	12	1 wk
8 Jan 54 ●	RAGS TO RICHES (re-entry) *Decca F 10207*	3	10 wks
29 Jan 54	ANSWER ME (re-entry) *Decca F 10192*	12	1 wk

19 Feb 54	● THE BOOK *Decca F 10242*	5	12 wks
28 May 54	● THE BOOK (re-entry) *Decca F 10242*	10	3 wks
18 Jun 54	★ CARA MIA *Decca F 10327 **	1	25 wks
12 Nov 54	● SANTO NATALE *Decca F 10399*	2	10 wks
11 Feb 55	● BEYOND THE STARS *Decca F 10458 **	8	9 wks
27 May 55	MAMA *Decca F 10515*	20	1 wk
24 Jun 55	MAMA (re-entry) *Decca F 10515*	19	2 wks
8 Jul 55	● EV'RYWHERE *Decca F 10515*	3	20 wks
29 Jul 55	MAMA (2nd re-entry) *Decca F 10515*	12	8 wks
25 Nov 55	● WHEN YOU LOSE THE ONE YOU LOVE *Decca F 10627 **	7	11 wks
2 Mar 56	MY SEPTEMBER LOVE *Decca F 10690*	19	2 wks
23 Mar 56	MY SEPTEMBER LOVE (re-entry) *Decca F 10690*	18	1 wk
6 Apr 56	● MY SEPTEMBER LOVE (2nd re-entry) *Decca F 10690*	3	20 wks
24 Aug 56	MY SON JOHN *Decca F 10769*	22	4 wks
31 Aug 56	MY UNFINISHED SYMPHONY *Decca F 10769*	29	1 wk
7 Sep 56	MY SEPTEMBER LOVE (3rd re-entry) *Decca F 10690*	25	1 wk
25 Jan 57	● ADORATION WALTZ *Decca F 10833*	9	11 wks
5 Apr 57	I'LL FIND YOU *Decca F 10864*	28	2 wks
7 Jun 57	I'LL FIND YOU (re-entry) *Decca F 10864*	27	2 wks
14 Feb 58	CRY MY HEART *Decca F 10978*	22	3 wks
16 May 58	ON THE STREET WHERE YOU LIVE *Decca F 11018*	16	14 wks
8 Aug 58	THE RIGHT TO LOVE *Decca F 11039*	30	1 wk
24 Nov 60	I BELIEVE *Decca F 11289*	49	1 wk

* David Whitfield with chorus and Mantovani and his orchestra
See also Various Artists (EPs & LPs) - All-Star Hit Parade; Mantovani.

Slim WHITMAN US, *male vocalist*   **75 wks**

15 Jul 55	★ ROSE MARIE *London HL 8061*	1	19 wks
29 Jul 55	● INDIAN LOVE CALL *London L 1149*	7	12 wks
23 Sep 55	CHINA DOLL *London L 1149*	15	2 wks
9 Mar 56	TUMBLING TUMBLEWEEDS *London HLU 8230*	19	2 wks
13 Apr 56	I'M A FOOL *London HLU 8252*	16	3 wks
11 May 56	I'M A FOOL (re-entry) *London HLU 8252*	29	1 wk
22 Jun 56	SERENADE *London HLU 8287*	24	3 wks
27 Jul 56	● SERENADE (re-entry) *London HLU 8287*	8	12 wks
12 Apr 57	● I'LL TAKE YOU HOME AGAIN KATHLEEN *London HLP 8403*	7	13 wks
5 Oct 74	HAPPY ANNIVERSARY *United Artists UP 35728*	14	10 wks

Roger WHITTAKER Kenya, *male vocalist*   **85 wks**

8 Nov 69	DURHAM TOWN (THE LEAVIN') *Columbia DB 8613*	12	18 wks
11 Apr 70	● I DON'T BELIEVE IN IF ANYMORE *Columbia DB 8664*	8	18 wks
10 Oct 70	NEW WORLD IN THE MORNING *Columbia DB 8718*	17	14 wks
3 Apr 71	WHY *Columbia DB 8752*	47	1 wk
2 Oct 71	MAMMY BLUE *Columbia DB 8822*	31	1 wk
26 Jul 75	● THE LAST FAREWELL *EMI 2294*	2	14 wks
8 Nov 86	● THE SKYE BOAT SONG *Tembo TML 119 **	10	10 wks

* Roger Whittaker and Des O'Connor

WHO UK, *male vocal/instrumental group*   **245 wks**

18 Feb 65	● I CAN'T EXPLAIN *Brunswick 05926*	8	13 wks
27 May 65	● ANYWAY ANYHOW ANYWHERE *Brunswick 05935*	10	12 wks
4 Nov 65	● MY GENERATION *Brunswick 05944*	2	13 wks
10 Mar 66	● SUBSTITUTE *Reaction 591 001*	5	13 wks
24 Mar 66	A LEGAL MATTER *Brunswick 05956*	32	6 wks
1 Sep 66	● I'M A BOY *Reaction 591 004*	2	13 wks
1 Sep 66	THE KIDS ARE ALRIGHT *Brunswick 05965*	41	2 wks
22 Sep 66	THE KIDS ARE ALRIGHT (re-entry) *Brunswick 05965*	48	1 wk
15 Dec 66	● HAPPY JACK *Reaction 591 010*	3	11 wks
27 Apr 67	● PICTURES OF LILY *Track 604 002*	4	10 wks
26 Jul 67	THE LAST TIME/UNDER MY THUMB *Track 604 006*	44	3 wks
18 Oct 67	● I CAN SEE FOR MILES *Track 604 011*	10	12 wks
19 Jun 68	DOGS *Track 604 023*	25	5 wks
23 Oct 68	MAGIC BUS *Track 604 024*	26	6 wks
19 Mar 69	● PINBALL WIZARD *Track 604 027*	4	13 wks
4 Apr 70	THE SEEKER *Track 604 036*	19	11 wks
8 Aug 70	SUMMERTIME BLUES *Track 2094 002*	38	4 wks

10 Jul 71	● WON'T GET FOOLED AGAIN *Track 2094 009*	9	12 wks
23 Oct 71	LET'S SEE ACTION *Track 2094 012*	16	12 wks
24 Jun 72	● JOIN TOGETHER *Track 2094 102*	9	9 wks
13 Jan 73	RELAY *Track 2094 106*	21	5 wks
13 Oct 73	5:15 *Track 2094 115*	20	6 wks
24 Jan 76	● SQUEEZE BOX *Polydor 2121 275*	10	9 wks
30 Oct 76	● SUBSTITUTE (re-issue) *Polydor 2058 803*	7	7 wks
22 Jul 78	● WHO ARE YOU *Polydor WHO 1*	18	12 wks
28 Apr 79	LONG LIVE ROCK *Polydor WHO 2*	48	5 wks
7 Mar 81	● YOU BETTER YOU BET *Polydor WHO 004*	9	8 wks
9 May 81	DON'T LET GO THE COAT *Polydor WHO 005*	47	4 wks
2 Oct 82	ATHENA *Polydor WHO 6*	40	4 wks
26 Nov 83	READY STEADY WHO (EP) *Polydor WHO 7*	58	2 wks
20 Feb 88	MY GENERATION (re-issue) *Polydor POSP 907*	68	2 wks

Tracks on Ready Steady Who EP: Disguises/Circles/Batman/Bucket 'T'/Barbara Ann. See also High Numbers.

WHODINI US, *male rap/scratch duo*   **10 wks**

25 Dec 82	MAGIC'S WAND *Jive JIVE 28*	47	6 wks
17 Mar 84	MAGIC'S WAND (THE WHODINI ELECTRIC EP) *Jive JIVE 61*	63	4 wks

Tracks on The Whodini Electric EP: Jive Magic Wand/Nasty Lady/Rap Machine/The Haunted House of Rock.

Jane WIEDLIN US, *female vocalist*   **14 wks**

6 Aug 88	RUSH HOUR *Manhattan MT 36*	12	11 wks
29 Oct 88	INSIDE A DREAM *Manhattan MT 55*	64	3 wks

WIGAN'S CHOSEN FEW   **11 wks**
US, *instrumental track plus UK crowd vocal*

18 Jan 75	● FOOTSEE *Pye Disco Demand DDS 111*	9	11 wks

WIGAN'S OVATION UK, *male vocal/instrumental group* **19 wks**

15 Mar 75	SKIING IN THE SNOW *Spark SRL 1122*	12	10 wks
28 Jun 75	PER-SO-NAL-LY *Spark SRL 1129*	38	6 wks
29 Nov 75	SUPER LOVE *Spark SRL 1133*	41	3 wks

Jack WILD UK, *male vocalist*   **2 wks**

2 May 70	SOME BEAUTIFUL *Capitol CL 15635*	46	2 wks

WILD CHERRY US, *male vocal/instrumental group*   **11 wks**

9 Oct 76	● PLAY THAT FUNKY MUSIC *Epic EPC 4593*	7	11 wks

WILD PAIR – *See Paula ABDUL*

WILD WEEKEND UK, *male vocal/instrumental group*   **2 wks**

29 Apr 89	BREAKIN' UP *Parlophone R 6204*	74	1 wk
5 May 90	WHO'S AFRAID OF THE BIG BAD LOVE *Parlophone R 6249*	70	1 wk

Eugene WILDE US, *male vocalist*   **15 wks**

13 Oct 84	GOTTA GET YOU HOME TONIGHT *Fourth & Broadway BRW 15*	18	9 wks
2 Feb 85	PERSONALITY *Fourth & Broadway BRW 18*	34	6 wks

Personality was coupled with Let Her Feel It by Simplicious.

Kim WILDE UK, *female vocalist*   **182 wks**

21 Feb 81	● KIDS IN AMERICA *RAK 327*	2	13 wks

9 May 81 ●	CHEQUERED LOVE *RAK 330*	4	9 wks
1 Aug 81	WATER ON GLASS/BOYS *RAK 334*	11	8 wks
14 Nov 81	CAMBODIA *RAK 336*	12	12 wks
17 Apr 82	VIEW FROM A BRIDGE *RAK 342*	16	7 wks
16 Oct 82	CHILD COME AWAY *RAK 352*	43	4 wks
30 Jul 83	LOVE BLONDE *RAK 360*	23	8 wks
12 Nov 83	DANCING IN THE DARK *RAK 365*	67	2 wks
13 Oct 84	THE SECOND TIME *MCA KIM 1*	29	6 wks
8 Dec 84	THE TOUCH *MCA KIM 2*	56	3 wks
27 Apr 85	RAGE TO LOVE *MCA KIM 3*	19	8 wks
25 Oct 86 ●	YOU KEEP ME HANGIN' ON *MCA KIM 4*	2	14 wks
4 Apr 87 ●	ANOTHER STEP CLOSER TO YOU *MCA KIM 5* *	6	11 wks
8 Aug 87	SAY YOU REALLY WANT ME *MCA KIM 6*	29	5 wks
5 Dec 87 ●	ROCKIN' AROUND THE CHRISTMAS TREE *10 TEN 2* **	3	7 wks
14 May 88	HEY MISTER HEARTACHE *MCA KIM 7*	31	5 wks
16 Jul 88 ●	YOU CAME *MCA KIM 8*	3	11 wks
1 Oct 88 ●	NEVER TRUST A STRANGER *MCA KIM 9*	7	9 wks
3 Dec 88 ●	FOUR LETTER WORD *MCA KIM 10*	6	12 wks
4 Mar 89	LOVE IN THE NATURAL WAY *MCA KIM 11*	32	6 wks
14 Apr 90	IT'S HERE *MCA KIM 12*	42	4 wks
16 Jun 90	TIME *MCA KIM 13*	71	3 wks
15 Dec 90	I CAN'T SAY GOODBYE *MCA KIM 14*	51	3 wks
2 May 92	LOVE IS HOLY *MCA KIM 15*	16	6 wks
27 Jun 92	HEART OVER MIND *MCA KIM 16*	34	3 wks
12 Sep 92	WHO DO YOU THINK YOU ARE *MCA KIM 17*	49	3 wks

* Kim Wilde and Junior ** Mel and Kim
Mel was Mel Smith.

Marty WILDE *UK, male vocalist* **117 wks**

11 Jul 58 ●	ENDLESS SLEEP *Philips PB 835*	4	14 wks
6 Mar 59 ●	DONNA *Philips PB 902*	3	16 wks
5 Jun 59 ●	A TEENAGER IN LOVE *Philips PB 926*	2	17 wks
3 Jul 59	DONNA (re-entry) *Philips PB 902*	25	2 wks
25 Sep 59 ●	SEA OF LOVE *Philips PB 959*	3	12 wks
11 Dec 59 ●	BAD BOY *Philips PB 972*	7	8 wks
10 Mar 60	JOHNNY ROCCO *Philips PB 1002*	30	4 wks
19 May 60	THE FIGHT *Philips PB 1022*	47	1 wk
22 Dec 60	LITTLE GIRL *Philips PB 1078*	16	9 wks
26 Jan 61 ●	RUBBER BALL *Philips PB 1101*	9	9 wks
27 Jul 61	HIDE AND SEEK *Philips PB 1161*	47	2 wks
9 Nov 61	TOMORROW'S CLOWN *Philips PB 1191*	33	5 wks
24 May 62	JEZEBEL *Philips PB 1240*	19	11 wks
25 Oct 62	EVER SINCE YOU SAID GOODBYE *Philips 326546 BF*	31	7 wks

Matthew WILDER *US, male vocalist* **11 wks**

21 Jan 84 ●	BREAK MY STRIDE *Epic A 3908*	4	11 wks

Sue WILKINSON *UK, female vocalist* **8 wks**

2 Aug 80	YOU GOTTA BE A HUSTLER IF YOU WANNA GET ON *Cheapskate CHEAP 2*	25	8 wks

WILL TO POWER *US, male/female vocal/instrumental duo* **18 wks**

7 Jan 89 ●	BABY I LOVE YOUR WAY - FREEBIRD *Epic 653094 7*	6	9 wks
22 Dec 90	I'M NOT IN LOVE *Epic 6565377*	29	9 wks

Alyson WILLIAMS *US, female vocalist* **28 wks**

4 Mar 89	SLEEP TALK *Def Jam 654656 7*	17	9 wks
6 May 89	MY LOVE IS SO RAW *Def Jam 654898 7* *	34	5 wks
19 Aug 89 ●	I NEED YOUR LOVIN' *Def Jam 655143 7*	8	11 wks
18 Nov 89	I SECOND THAT EMOTION *Def Jam 655456 7*	44	3 wks

* Alyson Williams featuring Nikki D

Andy WILLIAMS *US, male vocalist* **228 wks**

19 Apr 57 ★	BUTTERFLY *London HLA 8399*	1	15 wks
21 Jun 57	I LIKE YOUR KIND OF LOVE *London HLA 8437*	16	10 wks
30 Aug 57	BUTTERFLY (re-entry) *London HLA 8399*	29	1 wk
14 Jun 62	STRANGER ON THE SHORE *CBS AAG 103*	30	10 wks
21 Mar 63 ●	CAN'T GET USED TO LOSING YOU *CBS AAG 138*	2	18 wks
27 Feb 64	A FOOL NEVER LEARNS *CBS AAG 182*	40	4 wks
16 Sep 65 ●	ALMOST THERE *CBS 201813*	2	17 wks
24 Feb 66	MAY EACH DAY *CBS 202042*	19	8 wks
22 Sep 66	IN THE ARMS OF LOVE *CBS 202300*	33	7 wks
4 May 67	MUSIC TO WATCH GIRLS BY *CBS 2675*	33	6 wks
2 Aug 67	MORE AND MORE *CBS 2886*	45	1 wk
13 Mar 68 ●	CAN'T TAKE MY EYES OFF YOU *CBS 3298*	5	18 wks
7 May 69	HAPPY HEART *CBS 4062*	47	1 wk
21 May 69	HAPPY HEART (re-entry) *CBS 4062*	19	9 wks
14 Mar 70 ●	CAN'T HELP FALLING IN LOVE *CBS 4818*	3	17 wks
1 Aug 70	IT'S SO EASY *CBS 5113*	13	13 wks
7 Nov 70	IT'S SO EASY (re-entry) *CBS 5113*	49	1 wk
21 Nov 70	HOME LOVIN' MAN *CBS 5267*	7	12 wks
20 Mar 71 ●	(WHERE DO I BEGIN) LOVE STORY *CBS 7020*	4	17 wks
24 Jul 71	(WHERE DO I BEGIN) LOVE STORY (re-entry) *CBS 7020*	49	1 wk
5 Aug 72	LOVE THEME FROM THE GODFATHER *CBS 8166*	50	1 wk
2 Sep 72	LOVE THEME FROM THE GODFATHER (re-entry) *CBS 8166*	44	3 wks
30 Sep 72	LOVE THEME FROM THE GODFATHER (2nd re-entry) *CBS 8166*	42	5 wks
8 Dec 73 ●	SOLITAIRE *CBS 1824*	4	18 wks
18 May 74	GETTING OVER YOU *CBS 2181*	35	4 wks
31 May 75	YOU LAY SO EASY ON MY MIND *CBS 3167*	32	7 wks
6 Mar 76	THE OTHER SIDE OF ME *CBS 3903*	42	3 wks

Andy and David WILLIAMS *US, male vocal duo* **5 wks**

24 Mar 73	I DON'T KNOW WHY *MCA MUS 1183*	37	5 wks

Do not see Andy Williams. This Andy is the nephew of the other Andy.

Billy WILLIAMS *US, male vocalist* **9 wks**

2 Aug 57	I'M GONNA SIT RIGHT DOWN AND WRITE MYSELF A LETTER *Vogue Coral Q 72266*	22	8 wks
18 Oct 57	I'M GONNA SIT RIGHT DOWN AND WRITE MYSELF A LETTER (re-entry) *Vogue Coral Q 72266*	28	1 wk

Danny WILLIAMS *UK, male vocalist* **74 wks**

25 May 61	WE WILL NEVER BE AS YOUNG AS THIS AGAIN *HMV POP 839*	44	3 wks
6 Jul 61	THE MIRACLE OF YOU *HMV POP 885*	41	8 wks
2 Nov 61 ★	MOON RIVER *HMV POP 932*	1	19 wks
18 Jan 62	JEANNIE *HMV POP 968*	14	14 wks
12 Apr 62 ●	WONDERFUL WORLD OF THE YOUNG *HMV POP 1002*	8	13 wks
5 Jul 62	TEARS *HMV POP 1035*	22	7 wks
28 Feb 63	MY OWN TRUE LOVE *HMV POP 1112*	45	3 wks
30 Jul 77	DANCIN' EASY *Ensign ENY 3*	30	7 wks

Deniece WILLIAMS *US, female vocalist* **59 wks**

2 Apr 77 ★	FREE *CBS 4978*	1	10 wks
30 Jul 77 ●	THAT'S WHAT FRIENDS ARE FOR *CBS 5432*	8	11 wks
12 Nov 77	BABY BABY MY LOVE'S ALL FOR YOU *CBS 5779*	32	5 wks
25 Mar 78 ●	TOO MUCH TOO LITTLE TOO LATE *CBS 6164* *	3	14 wks
29 Jul 78	YOU'RE ALL I NEED TO GET BY *CBS 6483* *	45	6 wks
5 May 84 ●	LET'S HEAR IT FOR THE BOY *CBS A 4319*	2	12 wks
4 Aug 84	LET'S HEAR IT FOR THE BOY (re-entry) *CBS A 4319*	75	1 wk

* Johnny Mathis and Deniece Williams

Diana WILLIAMS *US, female vocalist* **3 wks**

25 Jul 81	TEDDY BEAR'S LAST RIDE *Capitol CL 207*	54	3 wks

Don WILLIAMS US, male vocalist — 16 wks

19 Jun 76	**I RECALL A GYPSY WOMAN** ABC 4098	**13**	10 wks
23 Oct 76	**YOU'RE MY BEST FRIEND** ABC 4144	**35**	6 wks

Freedom WILLIAMS – See C & C MUSIC FACTORY/CLIVILLES & COLE

Geoffrey WILLIAMS UK, male vocalist — 5 wks

11 Apr 92	**IT'S NOT A LOVE THING** EMI EM 228	**63**	2 wks
22 Aug 92	**SUMMER BREEZE** EMI EM 245	**56**	3 wks

Iris WILLIAMS UK, female vocalist — 8 wks

27 Oct 79	**HE WAS BEAUTIFUL (CAVATINA) (THE THEME FROM 'THE DEER HUNTER')** Columbia DB 9070	**18**	8 wks

John WILLIAMS UK, male instrumentalist - guitar — 11 wks

19 May 79	**CAVATINA** Cube BUG 80	**13**	11 wks

John WILLIAMS US, orchestra leader with US, orchestra — 10 wks

18 Dec 82	**THEME FROM 'E.T.' (THE EXTRA-TERRESTRIAL)** MCA 800	**17**	10 wks

Kenny WILLIAMS US, male vocalist — 7 wks

19 Nov 77	**(YOU'RE) FABULOUS BABE** Decca FR 13731	**35**	7 wks

Larry WILLIAMS US, male vocalist — 18 wks

20 Sep 57	**SHORT FAT FANNY** London HLN 8472	**21**	8 wks
17 Jan 58	**BONY MORONIE** London HLU 8532	**11**	10 wks

Lenny WILLIAMS US, male vocalist — 7 wks

5 Nov 77	**SHOO DOO FU FU OOH** ABC 4194	**38**	4 wks
16 Sep 78	**YOU GOT ME BURNING** ABC 4228	**67**	3 wks

Mark WILLIAMS – See Karen BODDINGTON and Mark WILLIAMS

Mason WILLIAMS US, male instrumentalist - guitar — 13 wks

28 Aug 68	● **CLASSICAL GAS** Warner Bros. WB 7190	**9**	13 wks

Maurice WILLIAMS and the ZODIACS
US, male vocal group — 9 wks

5 Jan 61	**STAY** Top Rank JAR 526	**14**	9 wks

Vanessa WILLIAMS US, female vocalist — 16 wks

20 Aug 88	**THE RIGHT STUFF** Wing WING 3	**71**	1 wk
25 Mar 89	**DREAMIN'** Wing WING 4	**74**	2 wks
19 Aug 89	**THE RIGHT STUFF (re-mix)** Wing WINR 3	**62**	2 wks
21 Mar 92	● **SAVE THE BEST FOR LAST** Polydor PO 192	**3**	11 wks

Vesta WILLIAMS US, female vocalist — 13 wks

20 Dec 86	**ONCE BITTEN TWICE SHY** A & M AM 362	**14**	13 wks

---

British Hit Singles Part One: Alphabetically by Artist
Date of chart entry/Title & catalogue no./Peak position reached/Weeks on chart
★ Number one ● Top Ten † still on chart at 31 Dec 1992
* = credited to act billed in footnote

Wendell WILLIAMS US, male rapper — 6 wks

6 Oct 90	**EVERYBODY (RAP)** Deconstruction PB 44701 *	**30**	4 wks
18 May 91	**SO GROOVY** Deconstruction PB 44567	**74**	2 wks

* Criminal Element Orchestra and Wendell Williams

WILLING SINNERS – See Marc ALMOND

Bruce WILLIS US, male vocalist — 30 wks

7 Mar 87	● **RESPECT YOURSELF** Motown ZB 41117	**7**	10 wks
30 May 87	● **UNDER THE BOARDWALK** Motown ZB 41349	**2**	15 wks
12 Sep 87	**SECRET AGENT MAN - JAMES BOND IS BACK** Motown ZB 41437	**43**	4 wks
23 Jan 88	**COMIN' RIGHT UP** Motown ZB 41453	**73**	1 wk

Chill WILLS – See LAUREL and HARDY with the AVALON BOYS featuring Chill WILLS

Viola WILLS US, female vocalist — 16 wks

6 Oct 79	● **GONNA GET ALONG WITHOUT YOU NOW** Ariola/Hansa AHA 546	**8**	10 wks
15 Mar 86	**BOTH SIDES NOW/DARE TO DREAM** Streetwave KHAN 66	**35**	6 wks

Al WILSON US, male vocalist — 5 wks

23 Aug 75	**THE SNAKE** Bell 1436	**41**	5 wks

Dooley WILSON US, male vocalist — 9 wks

3 Dec 77	**AS TIME GOES BY** United Artists UP 36331	**15**	9 wks

Disc has credit 'with the voices of Humphrey Bogart and Ingrid Bergman'.

Jackie WILSON US, male vocalist — 97 wks

15 Nov 57	● **REET PETITE** Coral Q 72290	**6**	14 wks
14 Mar 58	**TO BE LOVED** Coral Q 72306	**27**	1 wk
28 Mar 58	**TO BE LOVED (re-entry)** Coral Q 72306	**23**	6 wks
16 May 58	**TO BE LOVED (2nd re-entry)** Coral Q 72306	**23**	1 wk
15 Sep 60	**ALL MY LOVE** Coral Q 72407	**33**	6 wks
3 Nov 60	**ALL MY LOVE (re-entry)** Coral Q 72407	**47**	1 wk
22 Dec 60	**ALONE AT LAST** Coral Q 72412	**50**	1 wk
14 May 69	**(YOUR LOVE KEEPS LIFTING ME) HIGHER AND HIGHER** MCA BAG 2	**11**	11 wks
29 Jul 72	● **I GET THE SWEETEST FEELING** MCA MU 1160	**9**	13 wks
3 May 75	**I GET THE SWEETEST FEELING/HIGHER AND HIGHER (re-issues)** Brunswick BR 18	**25**	8 wks
29 Nov 86	★ **REET PETITE (re-issue)** SMP SKM 3	**1**	17 wks
28 Feb 87	● **I GET THE SWEETEST FEELING (2nd re-issue)** SMP SKM 1	**3**	11 wks
4 Jul 87	**HIGHER AND HIGHER (2nd re-issue)** SMP SKM 10	**15**	7 wks

Higher and Higher was not listed together with I Get The Sweetest Feeling on Brunswick until 17 May 75.

Mari WILSON UK, female vocalist — 34 wks

6 Mar 82	**BEAT THE BEAT** Compact PINK 2	**59**	3 wks
8 May 82	**BABY IT'S TRUE** Compact PINK 3	**42**	6 wks

11 Sep 82	●	**JUST WHAT I ALWAYS WANTED** *Compact PINK 4*	**8**	10 wks
13 Nov 82		**(BEWARE) BOYFRIEND** *Compact PINK 5*	**51**	4 wks
19 Mar 83		**CRY ME A RIVER** *Compact PINK 6*	**27**	7 wks
11 Jun 83		**WONDERFUL** *Compact PINK 7*	**47**	4 wks

Meri WILSON *US, female vocalist* — **10 wks**

27 Aug 77	●	**TELEPHONE MAN** *Pye International 7N 25747*	**6**	10 wks

Mike 'Hitman' WILSON *US, male producer* — **1 wk**

22 Sep 90		**ANOTHER SLEEPLESS NIGHT** *Arista 113506*	**74**	1 wk

Precious WILSON – *See ERUPTION; MESSIAH*

WILSON PHILLIPS *US, female vocal group* — **33 wks**

26 May 90	●	**HOLD ON** *SBK SBK 6*	**6**	12 wks
18 Aug 90		**RELEASE ME** *SBK SBK 11*	**36**	5 wks
10 Nov 90		**IMPULSIVE** *SBK SBK 16*	**42**	3 wks
11 May 91		**YOU'RE IN LOVE** *SBK SBK 25*	**29**	5 wks
23 May 92		**YOU WON'T SEE ME CRY** *SBK SBK 34*	**18**	5 wks
22 Aug 92		**GIVE IT UP** *SBK SBK 36*	**36**	3 wks

Chris WILTSHIRE – *See CLASS ACTION featuring Chris WILTSHIRE*

WIN *UK, male vocal/instrumental group* — **3 wks**

4 Apr 87		**SUPER POPOID GROOVE** *Swamplands LON 128*	**63**	3 wks

WINANS *US, male vocal group* — **1 wk**

30 Nov 85		**LET MY PEOPLE GO (PART 1)** *Qwest W 8874*	**71**	1 wk

WINDJAMMER *US, male vocal/instrumental group* — **12 wks**

30 Jun 84		**TOSSING AND TURNING** *MCA MCA 897*	**18**	12 wks

Rose WINDROSS – *See SOUL II SOUL*

WING AND A PRAYER FIFE AND DRUM CORPS *US, male/female vocal/instrumental group* — **7 wks**

24 Jan 76		**BABY FACE** *Atlantic K 10705*	**12**	7 wks

WINGER *US, male vocal/instrumental group* — **3 wks**

19 Jan 91		**MILES AWAY** *Atlantic A 7802*	**56**	3 wks

Pete WINGFIELD *UK, male vocalist* — **7 wks**

28 Jun 75	●	**EIGHTEEN WITH A BULLET** *Island WIP 6231*	**7**	7 wks

WINGS – *See Paul McCARTNEY*

Edgar WINTER GROUP *US, male instrumental group* — **9 wks**

26 May 73		**FRANKENSTEIN** *Epic EPC 1440*	**18**	9 wks

Ruby WINTERS *US, female vocalist* — **35 wks**

5 Nov 77	●	**I WILL** *Creole CR 141*	**4**	13 wks
29 Apr 78		**COME TO ME** *Creole CR 153*	**11**	12 wks

26 Aug 78		**I WON'T MENTION IT AGAIN** *Creole CR 160*	**45**	5 wks
16 Jun 79		**BABY LAY DOWN** *Creole CR 171*	**43**	5 wks

Steve WINWOOD *UK, male vocalist* — **33 wks**

17 Jan 81		**WHILE YOU SEE A CHANCE** *Island WIP 6655*	**45**	5 wks
9 Oct 82		**VALERIE** *Island WIP 6818*	**51**	4 wks
28 Jun 86		**HIGHER LOVE** *Island IS 288*	**13**	9 wks
13 Sep 86		**FREEDOM OVERSPILL** *Island IS 294*	**69**	1 wk
24 Jan 87		**BACK IN THE HIGH LIFE AGAIN** *Island IS 303*	**53**	2 wks
19 Sep 87		**VALERIE (re-issue)** *Island IS 336*	**19**	8 wks
11 Jun 88		**ROLL WITH IT** *Virgin VS 1085*	**53**	4 wks

WIRE *UK, male vocal/instrumental group* — **4 wks**

27 Jan 79		**OUTDOOR MINER** *Harvest HAR 5172*	**51**	3 wks
13 May 89		**EARDRUM BUZZ** *Mute MUTE 87*	**68**	1 wk

Norman WISDOM *UK, male vocalist* — **20 wks**

19 Feb 54	●	**DON'T LAUGH AT ME** *Columbia DB 3133*	**3**	15 wks
15 Mar 57		**WISDOM OF A FOOL** *Columbia DB 3903*	**13**	5 wks

Bill WITHERS *US, male vocalist* — **29 wks**

12 Aug 72		**LEAN ON ME** *A & M AMS 7004*	**18**	9 wks
14 Jan 78	●	**LOVELY DAY** *CBS 5773*	**7**	8 wks
25 May 85		**OH YEAH!** *CBS A 6154*	**60**	3 wks
10 Sep 88	●	**LOVELY DAY (re-mix)** *CBS 653001 7*	**4**	9 wks

See also Grover Washington Jr.

WIZZARD *UK, male vocal/instrumental group* — **77 wks**

9 Dec 72	●	**BALL PARK INCIDENT** *Harvest HAR 5062*	**6**	12 wks
21 Apr 73	★	**SEE MY BABY JIVE** *Harvest HAR 5070*	**1**	17 wks
1 Sep 73	★	**ANGEL FINGERS** *Harvest HAR 5076*	**1**	10 wks
8 Dec 73		**I WISH IT COULD BE CHRISTMAS EVERYDAY** *Harvest HAR 5079 **	**4**	9 wks
27 Apr 74	●	**ROCK 'N' ROLL WINTER** *Warner Bros. K 16357*	**6**	7 wks
10 Aug 74		**THIS IS THE STORY OF MY LOVE (BABY)** *Warner Bros. K 16434*	**34**	4 wks
21 Dec 74	●	**ARE YOU READY TO ROCK** *Warner Bros. K 16497*	**8**	10 wks
19 Dec 81		**I WISH IT COULD BE CHRISTMAS EVERYDAY (re-issue)** *Harvest HAR 5173 **	**41**	4 wks
15 Dec 84		**I WISH IT COULD BE CHRISTMAS EVERYDAY (re-entry of re-issue)** *Harvest HAR 5173 **	**23**	4 wks

Wizzard featuring vocal backing by the Suedettes plus the Stockland Green Bilateral School First Year Choir with additional noises by Miss Snob and Class 3C

Jah WOBBLE'S INVADERS OF THE HEART *UK, male vocalist/multi-instrumentalist* — **5 wks**

1 Feb 92		**VISIONS OF YOU** *Oval OVAL 103*	**35**	5 wks

Hit features the uncredited vocals of Sinead O'Connor.

Terry WOGAN *Ireland, male vocalist* — **5 wks**

7 Jan 78		**FLORAL DANCE** *Philips 6006 592*	**21**	5 wks

WOLFSBANE *US, male vocal/instrumental group* — **1 wk**

5 Oct 91		**EZY** *Def American DEFA 11*	**68**	1 wk

Bobby WOMACK *US, male vocalist* — **15 wks**

16 Jun 84		**TELL ME WHY** *Motown TMG 1339*	**60**	3 wks
5 Oct 85		**I WISH HE DIDN'T TRUST ME SO MUCH** *MCA MCA 994*	**64**	2 wks

| 26 Sep 87 | SO THE STORY GOES Chrysalis LIB 3 * | 34 | 8 wks |
| 7 Nov 87 | LIVING IN A BOX MCA MCA 1210 | 70 | 2 wks |

* Living In A Box featuring Bobby Womack

See also Wilton Felder.

WOMACK and WOMACK US, male/female vocal duo   48 wks

28 Apr 84	LOVE WARS Elektra E 9799	14	10 wks
30 Jun 84	BABY I'M SCARED OF YOU Elektra E 9733	72	2 wks
6 Dec 86	SOUL LOVE - SOUL MAN Manhattan MT 16	58	6 wks
6 Aug 88 ●	TEARDROPS Fourth & Broadway BRW 101	3	17 wks
12 Nov 88	LIFE'S JUST A BALLGAME Fourth & Broadway BRW 116	32	5 wks
25 Feb 89	CELEBRATE THE WORLD Fourth & Broadway BRW 125	19	8 wks

WOMBLES   87 wks

UK, male vocalist, arranger and producer - Mike Batt

26 Jan 74 ●	THE WOMBLING SONG CBS 1794	4	23 wks
6 Apr 74 ●	REMEMBER YOU'RE A WOMBLE CBS 2241	3	16 wks
22 Jun 74 ●	BANANA ROCK CBS 2465	9	13 wks
12 Oct 74	MINUETTO ALLEGRETTO CBS 2710	16	9 wks
7 Dec 74 ●	WOMBLING MERRY CHRISTMAS CBS 2842	2	8 wks
10 May 75	WOMBLING WHITE TIE AND TAILS CBS 3266	22	7 wks
9 Aug 75	SUPER WOMBLE CBS 3480	20	6 wks
13 Dec 75	LET'S WOMBLE TO THE PARTY TONIGHT CBS 3794	34	5 wks

Stevie WONDER US, male vocalist/multi-instrumentalist   404 wks

3 Feb 66	UPTIGHT Tamla Motown TMG 545	14	10 wks
18 Aug 66	BLOWIN' IN THE WIND Tamla Motown TMG 570	36	5 wks
5 Jan 67	A PLACE IN THE SUN Tamla Motown TMG 588	20	5 wks
26 Jul 67 ●	I WAS MADE TO LOVE HER Tamla Motown TMG 613	5	15 wks
25 Oct 67	I'M WONDERING Tamla Motown TMG 626	22	8 wks
8 May 68	SHOO BE DOO BE DOO DA DAY Tamla Motown TMG 653	46	4 wks
18 Dec 68 ●	FOR ONCE IN MY LIFE Tamla Motown TMG 679	3	13 wks
19 Mar 69	I DON'T KNOW WHY Tamla Motown TMG 690	14	10 wks
9 Jul 69	I DON'T KNOW WHY (re-entry) Tamla Motown TMG 690	43	1 wk
16 Jul 69 ●	MY CHERIE AMOUR Tamla Motown TMG 690	4	15 wks
15 Nov 69 ●	YESTER-ME YESTER-YOU YESTERDAY Tamla Motown TMG 717	2	13 wks
28 Mar 70 ●	NEVER HAD A DREAM COME TRUE Tamla Motown TMG 731	6	12 wks
18 Jul 70	SIGNED SEALED DELIVERED I'M YOURS Tamla Motown TMG 744	15	9 wks
26 Sep 70	SIGNED SEALED DELIVERED I'M YOURS (re-entry) Tamla Motown TMG 744	49	1 wk
21 Nov 70	HEAVEN HELP US ALL Tamla Motown TMG 757	29	11 wks
15 May 71	WE CAN WORK IT OUT Tamla Motown TMG 772	27	7 wks
22 Jan 72	IF YOU REALLY LOVE ME Tamla Motown TMG 798	20	7 wks
3 Feb 73	SUPERSTITION Tamla Motown TMG 841	11	9 wks
19 May 73 ●	YOU ARE THE SUNSHINE OF MY LIFE Tamla Motown TMG 852	7	11 wks
13 Oct 73	HIGHER GROUND Tamla Motown TMG 869	29	5 wks
12 Jan 74	LIVING FOR THE CITY Tamla Motown TMG 881	15	9 wks
13 Apr 74	HE'S MISSTRA KNOW IT ALL Tamla Motown TMG 892	10	9 wks
19 Oct 74	YOU HAVEN'T DONE NOTHIN' Tamla Motown TMG 921	30	5 wks
11 Jan 75	BOOGIE ON REGGAE WOMAN Tamla Motown TMG 928	12	8 wks
18 Dec 76 ●	I WISH Tamla Motown TMG 1054	5	10 wks
9 Apr 77 ●	SIR DUKE Motown TMG 1068	2	9 wks
10 Sep 77	ANOTHER STAR Motown TMG 1083	29	5 wks
24 Feb 79	POPS WE LOVE YOU Motown TMG 1136 *	66	5 wks
24 Nov 79	SEND ONE YOUR LOVE Motown TMG 1149	52	3 wks
26 Jan 80	BLACK ORCHID Motown TMG 1173	63	3 wks
29 Mar 80	OUTSIDE MY WINDOW Motown TMG 1179	52	4 wks
13 Sep 80 ●	MASTERBLASTER (JAMMIN') Motown TMG 1204	2	10 wks
27 Dec 80 ●	I AIN'T GONNA STAND FOR IT Motown TMG 1215	10	10 wks
7 Mar 81 ●	LATELY Motown TMG 1226	3	13 wks
25 Jul 81 ●	HAPPY BIRTHDAY Motown TMG 1235	2	11 wks
23 Jan 82	THAT GIRL Motown TMG 1254	39	6 wks
10 Apr 82 ★	EBONY AND IVORY Parlophone R 6054 **	1	10 wks
5 Jun 82 ●	DO I DO Motown TMG 1269	10	7 wks
25 Sep 82	RIBBON IN THE SKY Motown TMG 1280	45	4 wks
25 Aug 84 ★	I JUST CALLED TO SAY I LOVE YOU Motown TMG 1349	1	24 wks
1 Dec 84	LOVE LIGHT IN FLIGHT Motown TMG 1364	44	5 wks
29 Dec 84	DON'T DRIVE DRUNK Motown TMG 1372	71	1 wk
12 Jan 85	DON'T DRIVE DRUNK (re-entry) Motown TMG 1372	62	2 wks
7 Sep 85	PART-TIME LOVER Motown ZB 40351	3	12 wks
9 Nov 85	THAT'S WHAT FRIENDS ARE FOR Arista ARIST 638 ***	16	9 wks
23 Nov 85	GO HOME Motown ZB 40501	67	2 wks
28 Dec 85	I JUST CALLED TO SAY I LOVE YOU (re-entry) Motown TMG 1349	64	2 wks
8 Mar 86	OVERJOYED Motown ZB 40567	17	8 wks
17 Jan 87	STRANGER ON THE SHORE OF LOVE Motown WOND 2	55	3 wks
31 Oct 87	SKELETONS Motown ZB 41439	59	3 wks
28 May 88	GET IT Motown ZB 41883 ****	37	4 wks
6 Aug 88 ●	MY LOVE CBS JULIO 2 *****	5	11 wks
20 May 89	FREE Motown ZB 42855	49	5 wks
12 Oct 91	FUN DAY Motown ZB 44957	63	1 wk

* Diana Ross, Marvin Gaye, Smokey Robinson and Stevie Wonder ** Paul McCartney with Stevie Wonder *** Dionne Warwick and Friends featuring Elton John, Gladys Knight and Stevie Wonder **** Stevie Wonder and Michael Jackson ***** Julio Iglesias featuring Stevie Wonder

WONDER DOGS UK, canine vocal group   7 wks

| 21 Aug 82 | RUFF MIX Flip FLIP 001 | 31 | 7 wks |

WONDER STUFF UK, male vocal/instrumental group   53 wks

30 Apr 88	GIVE GIVE GIVE ME MORE MORE MORE Polydor GONE 3	72	2 wks
16 Jul 88	A WISH AWAY Polydor GONE 4	43	5 wks
24 Sep 88	IT'S YER MONEY I'M AFTER BABY Polydor GONE 5	40	3 wks
11 Mar 89	WHO WANTS TO BE THE DISCO KING Far Out GONE 6	28	3 wks
23 Sep 89	DON'T LET ME DOWN GENTLY Polydor GONE 7	19	4 wks
11 Nov 89	GOLDEN GREEN/GET TOGETHER Polydor GONE 8	33	3 wks
12 May 90	CIRCLESQUARE Polydor GONE 10	20	4 wks
13 Apr 91 ●	THE SIZE OF A COW Polydor GONE 11	5	7 wks
25 May 91	CAUGHT IN MY SHADOW Polydor GONE 12	18	3 wks
7 Sep 91	SLEEP ALONE Polydor GONE 13	43	2 wks
26 Oct 91 ★	DIZZY Sense SIGH 712 *	1	12 wks
25 Jan 92 ●	WELCOME TO THE CHEAP SEATS (EP) Polydor GONE 14	8	5 wks

* Vic Reeves and the Wonder Stuff

Tracks on Welcome To The Cheap Seats (EP): *Welcome To The Cheap Seats/Me, My Mom, My Dad And My Brother/Will The Circle Be Unbroken/That's Entertainment.*

WONDRESS – See MANTRONIX

Brenton WOOD US, male vocalist   14 wks

| 27 Dec 67 ● | GIMME LITTLE SIGN Liberty LBF 15021 | 8 | 14 wks |

Roy WOOD UK, male vocalist/multi-instrumentalist   39 wks

11 Aug 73	DEAR ELAINE Harvest HAR 5074	18	8 wks
1 Dec 73 ●	FOREVER Harvest HAR 5078	8	13 wks
15 Jun 74	GOING DOWN THE ROAD Harvest HAR 5083	13	7 wks
31 May 75	OH WHAT A SHAME Jet 754	13	7 wks
22 Nov 86	WATERLOO IRS IRM 125 *	45	4 wks

* Doctor and the Medics featuring Roy Wood

WOODENTOPS UK, male vocal/instrumental group — 1 wk

11 Oct 86	**EVERYDAY LIVING** Rough Trade RT 178	72	1 wk

Edward WOODWARD UK, male vocalist — 2 wks

16 Jan 71	**THE WAY YOU LOOK TONIGHT** DJM DJS 232	50	1 wk
30 Jan 71	**THE WAY YOU LOOK TONIGHT (re-entry)** DJM DJS 232	42	1 wk

Sheb WOOLEY US, male vocalist — 8 wks

20 Jun 58	**PURPLE PEOPLE EATER** MGM 981	12	8 wks

WORKING WEEK
UK, male/female vocal/instrumental group — 2 wks

9 Jun 84	**VENCEREMOS - WE WILL WIN** Virgin VS 684	64	2 wks

WORLD – See LIL' LOUIS

WORLD OF TWIST UK, male vocal/instrumental group — 12 wks

24 Nov 90	**THE STORM** Circa YR 55	42	3 wks
24 Nov 90	**THE STORM (re-entry)** Circa YR 55	74	2 wks
23 Mar 91	**SONS OF THE STAGE** Circa YR 62	47	3 wks
12 Oct 91	**SWEETS** Circa YR 72	58	2 wks
22 Feb 92	**SHE'S A RAINBOW** Circa YR 82	62	2 wks

WORLD PARTY Ireland/UK, male vocal/instrumental group — 15 wks

14 Feb 87	**SHIP OF FOOLS** Ensign ENY 606	42	6 wks
16 Jun 90	**MESSAGE IN THE BOX** Ensign ENY 631	39	6 wks
15 Sep 90	**WAY DOWN NOW** Ensign ENY 634	66	2 wks
18 May 91	**THANK YOU WORLD** Ensign ENY 643	68	1 wk

WORLD PREMIERE US, male vocal/instrumental group — 4 wks

28 Jan 84	**SHARE THE NIGHT** Epic A 4133	64	4 wks

WORLD'S FAMOUS SUPREME TEAM — 18 wks
US, male vocal/scratch group

4 Dec 82 ●	**BUFFALO GALS** Charisma MALC 1 *	9	12 wks
25 Feb 84	**HEY DJ** Charisma TEAM 1	52	5 wks
8 Dec 90	**OPERAA HOUSE** Virgin VS 1273 **	75	1 wk

* Malcolm McLaren and the World's Famous Supreme Team ** World's Famous Supreme Team Show

WRECKX-N-EFFECT US, male vocal group — 11 wks

13 Jan 90	**JUICY** Motown ZB 43295 *	29	7 wks
5 Dec 92	**RUMP SHAKER** MCA MCS 1725	24†	4 wks

* Wrecks-N-Effect

Betty WRIGHT US, female vocalist — 23 wks

25 Jan 75	**SHOORAH SHOORAH** RCA 2491	27	7 wks
19 Apr 75	**WHERE IS THE LOVE** RCA 2548	25	7 wks
8 Feb 86	**PAIN** Cooltempo COOL 117	42	6 wks
9 Sep 89	**KEEP LOVE NEW** Sure Delight SD 11	71	3 wks

Ruby WRIGHT UK, female vocalist — 15 wks

16 Apr 54 ●	**BIMBO** Parlophone R 3816	7	4 wks
21 May 54	**BIMBO (re-entry)** Parlophone R 3816	12	1 wk
22 May 59	**THREE STARS** Parlophone R 4556	19	10 wks

Three Stars is narrated by Dick Pike.

Steve WRIGHT UK, male vocalist — 10 wks

27 Nov 82	**I'M ALRIGHT** RCA 296 *	40	6 wks
15 Oct 83	**GET SOME THERAPY** RCA RCA 362 **	75	1 wk
1 Dec 84	**THE GAY CAVALIEROS (THE STORY SO FAR)** MCA 925	61	3 wks

* Young Steve and the Afternoon Boys ** Steve Wright and the Sisters of Soul

WURZELS UK, male vocal/instrumental group — 28 wks

2 Feb 67	**DRINK UP THY ZIDER** Columbia DB 8081 *	45	1 wk
15 May 76 ★	**COMBINE HARVESTER (BRAND NEW KEY)** EMI 2450	1	13 wks
11 Sep 76 ●	**I AM A CIDER DRINKER (PALOMA BLANCA)** EMI 2520	3	9 wks
25 Jun 77	**FARMER BILL'S COWMAN (I WAS KAISER BILL'S BATMAN)** EMI 2637	32	5 wks

* Adge Cutler and the Wurzels.

WWF SUPERSTARS US/UK, male wrestling vocalists — 3 wks

12 Dec 92 ●	**SLAM JAM** Arista 74321124887	4†	3 wks

Robert WYATT UK, male vocalist — 11 wks

28 Sep 74	**I'M A BELIEVER** Virgin VS 114	29	5 wks
7 May 83	**SHIPBUILDING** Rough Trade RT 115	35	6 wks

Michael WYCOFF US, male vocalist — 2 wks

23 Jul 83	**(DO YOU REALLY LOVE ME) TELL ME LOVE** RCA 348	60	2 wks

Pete WYLIE UK, male vocalist — 18 wks

3 May 86	**SINFUL** Eternal MDM 7	13	10 wks
13 Sep 86	**DIAMOND GIRL** Eternal MDM 12	57	3 wks
13 Apr 91	**SINFUL!** Siren SRN 138 *	28	5 wks

* Pete Wylie with the Farm

Bill WYMAN UK, male vocalist — 13 wks

25 Jul 81	**(SI SI) JE SUIS UN ROCK STAR** A & M AMS 8144	14	9 wks
20 Mar 82	**A NEW FASHION** A & M AMS 8209	37	4 wks

Jane WYMAN – See Bing CROSBY

Tammy WYNETTE US, female vocalist — 35 wks

26 Apr 75 ★	**STAND BY YOUR MAN** Epic EPC 7137	1	12 wks
28 Jun 75	**D. I. V. O. R. C. E.** Epic EPC 3361	12	7 wks
12 Jun 76	**I DON'T WANNA PLAY HOUSE** Epic EPC 4091	37	4 wks
7 Dec 91 ●	**JUSTIFIED AND ANCIENT** KLF Communications KLF 099 *	2	12 wks

* KLF, guest vocals: Tammy Wynette

Above and right:
BETTY WRIGHT is
shown before and after
her haircut.

Most unusually,
'Nobody's Child' by
KAREN YOUNG
went back up the chart
four times during its
top 20 run.

TAMMY WYNETTE
is shown in 1969, the
year 'Stand By Your
Man' became a top 20
hit in America.

Mark WYNTER UK, male vocalist   80 wks

25 Aug 60	**IMAGE OF A GIRL** Decca F 11263 .... **11**	10 wks
10 Nov 60	**KICKING UP THE LEAVES** Decca F 11279 .... **24**	10 wks
9 Mar 61	**DREAM GIRL** Decca F 11323 .... **27**	5 wks
8 Jun 61	**EXCLUSIVELY YOURS** Decca F 11354 .... **32**	7 wks
4 Oct 62 ●	**VENUS IN BLUE JEANS** Pye 7N 15466 .... **4**	15 wks
13 Dec 62 ●	**GO AWAY LITTLE GIRL** Pye 7N 15492 .... **6**	11 wks
6 Jun 63	**SHY GIRL** Pye 7N 15525 .... **28**	6 wks
14 Nov 63	**IT'S ALMOST TOMORROW** Pye 7N 15577 .... **12**	12 wks
9 Apr 64	**ONLY YOU** Pye 7N 15626 .... **38**	4 wks

Malcolm X US, male orator   4 wks

7 Apr 84	**NO SELL OUT** Tommy Boy IS 165 .... **60**	4 wks

Hit features credit: 'Music by Keith Le Blanc'.

Miss X UK, female vocalist - Joyce Blair   6 wks

1 Aug 63	**CHRISTINE** Ember S 175 .... **37**	6 wks

XAVIER US, male vocal/instrumental group   3 wks

20 Mar 82	**WORK THAT SUCKER TO DEATH** Liberty UP 651 .... **53**	3 wks

XPANSIONS UK, male producer - Ritchie Malone   16 wks

6 Oct 90	**ELEVATION** Optimism 113683 .... **49**	5 wks
23 Feb 91 ●	**MOVE YOUR BODY** Arista 113 683 .... **7**	9 wks
15 Jun 91	**WHAT YOU WANT** Arista 114 246 * **55**	2 wks

* Xpansions featuring Dale Joyner

X-RAY SPEX UK, male/female vocal/instrumental group   32 wks

29 Apr 78	**THE DAY THE WORLD TURNED DAY-GLO** EMI International INT 553 .... **23**	7 wks
22 Jul 78	**IDENTITY** EMI International INT 563 .... **24**	10 wks
4 Nov 78	**GERM FREE ADOLESCENCE** EMI International INT 573 .... **19**	11 wks
21 Apr 79	**HIGHLY INFLAMMABLE** EMI International INT 583 .... **45**	4 wks

XTC UK, male vocal/instrumental group   70 wks

12 May 79	**LIFE BEGINS AT THE HOP** Virgin VS 259 .... **54**	4 wks
22 Sep 79	**MAKING PLANS FOR NIGEL** Virgin VS 282 ...... **17**	11 wks
6 Sep 80	**GENERALS AND MAJORS/DON'T LOSE YOUR TEMPER** Virgin VS 365 .... **32**	8 wks
18 Oct 80	**TOWERS OF LONDON** Virgin VS 372 .... **31**	5 wks
24 Jan 81	**SGT ROCK (IS GOING TO HELP ME)** Virgin VS 384 ...... **16**	9 wks
23 Jan 82 ●	**SENSES WORKING OVERTIME** Virgin VS 462 .... **10**	9 wks
27 Mar 82	**BALL AND CHAIN** Virgin VS 482 .... **58**	4 wks
15 Oct 83	**LOVE ON A FARMBOY'S WAGES** Virgin VS 613 ...... **50**	5 wks
29 Sep 84	**ALL YOU PRETTY GIRLS** Virgin VS 709 .... **55**	5 wks
28 Jan 89	**MAYOR OF SIMPLETON** Virgin VS 1158 .... **46**	5 wks
4 Apr 92	**THE DISAPPOINTED** Virgin VS 1404 .... **33**	5 wks
13 Jun 92	**THE BALLAD OF PETER PUMPKINHEAD** Virgin VS 1415 .... **71**	1 wk

Y & T US, male vocal/instrumental group   4 wks

13 Aug 83	**MEAN STREAK** A & M AM 135 .... **41**	4 wks

YA KID K – *See HI-TEK 3 featuring YA KID K; TECHNOTRONIC*

Weird Al YANKOVIC US, male vocalist   8 wks

7 Apr 84	**EAT IT** Scotti Bros./Epic A 4257 .... **36**	7 wks
4 Jul 92	**SMELLS LIKE NIRVANA** Scotti Bros PO 219 ...... **58**	1 wk

YARBROUGH and PEOPLES   20 wks
US, male/female vocal/instrumental duo

27 Dec 80 ●	**DON'T STOP THE MUSIC** Mercury MER 53 .... **7**	12 wks
5 May 84	**DON'T WASTE YOUR TIME** Total Experience XE 501 ...... **60**	3 wks
11 Jan 86	**GUILTY** Total Experience FB 49905 .... **53**	3 wks
5 Jul 86	**I WOULDN'T LIE** Total Experience FB 49841 .... **61**	2 wks

YARDBIRDS UK, male vocal/instrumental group   62 wks

12 Nov 64	**GOOD MORNING LITTLE SCHOOLGIRL** Columbia DB 7391 .... **44**	4 wks
18 Mar 65 ●	**FOR YOUR LOVE** Columbia DB 7499 .... **3**	12 wks
17 Jun 65 ●	**HEART FULL OF SOUL** Columbia DB 7594 .... **2**	13 wks
14 Oct 65 ●	**EVIL HEARTED YOU/STILL I'M SAD** Columbia DB 7706 .... **3**	10 wks
3 Mar 66 ●	**SHAPES OF THINGS** Columbia DB 7848 .... **3**	9 wks
2 Jun 66 ●	**OVER UNDER SIDEWAYS DOWN** Columbia DB 7928 .... **10**	9 wks
27 Oct 66	**HAPPENINGS TEN YEARS TIME AGO** Columbia DB 8024 .... **43**	5 wks

YAZOO UK, female/male vocal/instrumental duo   53 wks

17 Apr 82 ●	**ONLY YOU** Mute MUTE 020 .... **2**	14 wks
17 Jul 82 ●	**DON'T GO** Mute YAZ 001 .... **3**	11 wks
20 Nov 82	**THE OTHER SIDE OF LOVE** Mute YAZ 002 .... **13**	9 wks
21 May 83 ●	**NOBODY'S DIARY** Mute YAZ 003 .... **3**	11 wks
8 Dec 90	**SITUATION** Mute YAZ 4 .... **14**	8 wks

YAZZ UK, female vocalist   57 wks

20 Feb 88 ●	**DOCTORIN' THE HOUSE** Ahead Of Our Time CCUT 27 * **6**	9 wks
23 Jul 88 ★	**THE ONLY WAY IS UP** Big Life BLR 4 * * **1**	15 wks
29 Oct 88 ●	**STAND UP FOR YOUR LOVE RIGHTS** Big Life BLR 5 .... **2**	12 wks
4 Feb 89	**FINE TIME** Big Life BLR 6 .... **9**	8 wks
29 Apr 89	**WHERE HAS ALL THE LOVE GONE** Big Life BLR 8 ...... **16**	6 wks
23 Jun 90	**TREAT ME GOOD** Big Life BLR 24 .... **20**	5 wks
28 Mar 92	**ONE TRUE WOMAN** Polydor PO 198 .... **60**	2 wks

* Coldcut featuring Yazz and the Plastic Population * * Yazz and the Plastic Population

YELL! UK, male vocal duo   8 wks

20 Jan 90 ●	**INSTANT REPLAY** Fanfare FAN 22 .... **10**	8 wks

YELLO Switzerland, male vocal/instrumental duo   41 wks

25 Jun 83	**I LOVE YOU** Stiff BUY 176 .... **41**	4 wks
26 Nov 83	**LOST AGAIN** Stiff BUY 191 .... **73**	1 wk

9 Aug 86		GOLDRUSH Mercury MER 218	54	3 wks
22 Aug 87		THE RHYTHM DIVINE Mercury MER 253 *	54	2 wks
27 Aug 88	●	THE RACE Mercury YELLO 1	7	11 wks
17 Dec 88		TIED UP Mercury YELLO 2	60	5 wks
25 Mar 89		OF COURSE I'M LYING Mercury YELLO 3	23	8 wks
22 Jul 89		BLAZING SADDLES Mercury YELLO 4	47	2 wks
8 Jun 91		RUBBERBANDMAN Mercury YELLO 5	58	2 wks
5 Sep 92		JUNGLE BILL Mercury MER 376	61	2 wks
7 Nov 92		THE RACE (re-issue)/BOSTICH Mercury MER 382	55	1 wk

* Yello featuring Shirley Bassey

YELLOW DOG US/UK, male vocal/instrumental group   13 wks

| 4 Feb 78 | ● | JUST ONE MORE NIGHT Virgin VS 195 | 8 | 9 wks |
| 22 Jul 78 | | WAIT UNTIL MIDNIGHT Virgin VS 217 | 54 | 4 wks |

YELLOW MAGIC ORCHESTRA   11 wks

Japan, male instrumental group

| 14 Jun 80 | | COMPUTER GAME (THEME FROM 'THE ') A & M AMS 7502 | 17 | 11 wks |

YELLOWCOATS – *See Paul SHANE and the YELLOWCOATS*

YES UK/South Africa, male vocal/instrumental group   31 wks

17 Sep 77	●	WONDEROUS STORIES Atlantic K 10999	7	9 wks
26 Nov 77		GOING FOR THE ONE Atlantic K 11047	24	4 wks
9 Sep 78		DON'T KILL THE WHALE Atlantic K 11184	36	4 wks
12 Nov 83		OWNER OF A LONELY HEART Acto B 9817	28	9 wks
31 Mar 84		LEAVE IT Acto B 9787	56	4 wks
3 Oct 87		LOVE WILL FIND A WAY Atco A 9449	73	1 wk

Group were UK only for first three hits.

Melissa YIANNAKOU – *See DESIYA featuring Melissa YIANNAKOU*

YIN and YAN UK, male vocal duo   5 wks

| 29 Mar 75 | | IF EMI 2282 | 25 | 5 wks |

YOTHU YINDI Australia, male vocal/instrumental group   1 wk

| 15 Feb 92 | | TREATY Hollywood HWD 116 | 72 | 1 wk |

Faron YOUNG US, male vocalist   23 wks

| 15 Jul 72 | ● | IT'S FOUR IN THE MORNING Mercury 6052 140 | 3 | 23 wks |

Jimmy YOUNG UK, male vocalist   88 wks

9 Jan 53		FAITH CAN MOVE MOUNTAINS Decca F 9986	11	1 wk
21 Aug 53	●	ETERNALLY Decca F 10130	8	9 wks
6 May 55	★	UNCHAINED MELODY Decca F 10502	1	19 wks
16 Sep 55	★	THE MAN FROM LARAMIE Decca F 10597	1	12 wks
23 Dec 55		SOMEONE ON YOUR MIND Decca F 10640	13	5 wks
16 Mar 56	●	CHAIN GANG Decca F 10694	9	6 wks
8 Jun 56		WAYWARD WIND Decca F 10736	27	1 wk
22 Jun 56		RICH MAN POOR MAN Decca F 10736	25	1 wk
28 Sep 56	●	MORE Decca F 10774	4	17 wks

3 May 57		ROUND AND ROUND Decca F 10875	30	1 wk
10 Oct 63		MISS YOU Columbia DB 7119	15	13 wks
26 Mar 64		UNCHAINED MELODY Columbia DB 7234	43	3 wks

The versions of Unchained Melody on Decca and on Columbia are different recordings of the same song. Round and Round is with the Michael Sammes Singers. See also Various Artists (EPs & LPs) - All Star Hit Parade No.2.

John Paul YOUNG Australia, male vocalist   16 wks

| 29 Apr 78 | ● | LOVE IS IN THE AIR Ariola ARO 117 | 5 | 13 wks |
| 14 Nov 92 | | LOVE IS IN THE AIR (re-mix) Columbia 6587697 | 49 | 3 wks |

Karen YOUNG UK, female vocalist   21 wks

| 6 Sep 69 | ● | NOBODY'S CHILD Major Minor MM 625 | 6 | 21 wks |

Karen YOUNG US, female vocalist   8 wks

| 19 Aug 78 | | HOT SHOT Atlantic K 11180 | 34 | 7 wks |
| 24 Feb 79 | | HOT SHOT (re-issue) Atlantic LV 8 | 75 | 1 wk |

Leon YOUNG STRING CHORALE – *See Mr Acker BILK*

Neil YOUNG Canada, male vocalist   15 wks

| 11 Mar 72 | ● | HEART OF GOLD Reprise K 14140 | 10 | 11 wks |
| 6 Jan 79 | | FOUR STRONG WINDS Reprise K 14493 | 57 | 4 wks |

See also Crosby, Stills, Nash and Young.

Paul YOUNG UK, male vocalist   118 wks

18 Jun 83	★	WHEREVER I LAY MY HAT (THAT'S MY HOME) CBS A 3371	1	15 wks
10 Sep 83	●	COME BACK AND STAY CBS A 3636	4	9 wks
19 Nov 83	●	LOVE OF THE COMMON PEOPLE CBS A 3585	2	13 wks
13 Oct 84	●	I'M GONNA TEAR YOUR PLAYHOUSE DOWN CBS A 4786	9	7 wks
8 Dec 84	●	EVERYTHING MUST CHANGE CBS A 4972	9	11 wks
9 Mar 85	●	EVERY TIME YOU GO AWAY CBS A 6300	4	11 wks
22 Jun 85		TOMB OF MEMORIES CBS A 6321	16	7 wks
17 Aug 85		TOMB OF MEMORIES (re-entry) CBS A 6321	74	1 wk
4 Oct 86		WONDERLAND CBS YOUNG 1	24	5 wks
29 Nov 86		SOME PEOPLE CBS YOUNG 2	56	3 wks
7 Feb 87		WHY DOES A MAN HAVE TO BE STRONG CBS YOUNG 3	63	2 wks
12 May 90		SOFTLY WHISPERING I LOVE YOU CBS YOUNG 4	21	6 wks
7 Jul 90		OH GIRL CBS YOUNG 5	25	6 wks
6 Oct 90		HEAVEN CAN WAIT CBS YOUNG 6	71	2 wks
12 Jan 91		CALLING YOU CBS YOUNG 7	57	2 wks
30 Mar 91	●	SENZA UNA DONNA (WITHOUT A WOMAN) London LON 294 *	4	12 wks
10 Aug 91		BOTH SIDES NOW MCA MCS 1546 **	74	1 wk
26 Oct 91		DON'T DREAM IT'S OVER Columbia 6574117	20	5 wks

* Zucchero and Paul Young ** Clannad and Paul Young

Retta YOUNG US, female vocalist   7 wks

| 24 May 75 | | SENDING OUT AN S. O. S. All Platinum 6146 305 | 28 | 7 wks |

Tracie YOUNG – *See TRACIE*

YOUNG and COMPANY   12 wks

US, male/female vocal/instrumental group

| 1 Nov 80 | | I LIKE (WHAT YOU'RE DOING TO ME) Excalibur EXC 501 | 20 | 12 wks |

YOUNG AND MOODY BAND   4 wks
UK, male vocal/instrumental group

| 10 Oct 81 | **DON'T DO THAT** Bronze BRO 130 ....63 | 4 wks |

YOUNG DISCIPLES *UK, male vocal/instrumental group*   17 wks

13 Oct 90	**GET YOURSELF TOGETHER** Talkin Loud TLK 2 68	1 wk
23 Feb 91	**APPARENTLY NOTHIN'** Talkin Loud TLK 5 46	4 wks
3 Aug 91	**APPARENTLY NOTHIN'** (re-entry)	
	Talkin Loud TLK 5 13	7 wks
5 Oct 91	**GET YOURSELF TOGETHER** (re-issue)	
	Talkin Loud TLK 15 65	2 wks
5 Sep 92	**YOUNG DISCIPLES EP** Talkin Loud TLK 18 48	3 wks

Tracks on Young Disciples EP: Move On/Freedom/All I Have In Me/Move On (re mix).

YOUNG IDEA *UK, male vocal duo*   6 wks

| 29 Jun 67 | ● **WITH A LITTLE HELP FROM MY FRIENDS** | |
| | Columbia DB 8205..................................10 | 6 wks |

YOUNG MC *US, male rapper*   7 wks

15 Jul 89	**BUST A MOVE** Delicious Vinyl BRW 137 73	2 wks
17 Feb 90	**PRINCIPAL'S OFFICE** Delicious Vinyl BRW 161 54	3 wks
17 Aug 91	**THAT'S THE WAY LOVE GOES** Capitol CL 623.........65	2 wks

YOUNG ONES – *See Cliff RICHARD*

YOUNG RASCALS *US, male vocal/instrumental group*   17 wks

| 25 May 67 | ● **GROOVIN'** Atlantic 584 111 ....8 | 13 wks |
| 16 Aug 67 | **A GIRL LIKE YOU** Atlantic 584 128 ....37 | 4 wks |

Sydney YOUNGBLOOD *US, male vocalist*   29 wks

26 Aug 89	● **IF ONLY I COULD** Circa YR 34 3	14 wks
9 Dec 89	**SIT AND WAIT** Circa YR 40 16	8 wks
31 Mar 90	**I'D RATHER GO BLIND** Circa YR 43 44	5 wks
29 Jun 91	**HOOKED ON YOU** Circa YR 65 72	2 wks

Z

Helmut ZACHARIAS *Germany, orchestra*   11 wks

| 29 Oct 64 | ● **TOKYO MELODY** Polydor YNH 52341 ....9 | 11 wks |

Pia ZADORA *US, female vocalist*   6 wks

27 Oct 84	**WHEN THE RAIN BEGINS TO FALL**	
	Arista ARIST 584 * 68	2 wks
12 Nov 88	**DANCE OUT OF MY HEAD** Epic 652886 1 ** 65	4 wks

* Jermaine Jackson and Pia Zadora ** Pia

Michael ZAGER BAND   12 wks
US, male/female vocal/instrumental group

| 1 Apr 78 | ● **LET'S ALL CHANT** Private Stock PVT 143 ....8 | 12 wks |

ZAGER and EVANS *US, male vocal duo*   13 wks

| 9 Aug 69 | ★ **IN THE YEAR 2525 (EXORDIUM AND** | |
| | **TERMINUS)** RCA 1860 ....1 | 13 wks |

Georghe ZAMFIR *Romania, male instrumentalist - pipes* 9 wks

| 21 Aug 76 | ● **(LIGHT OF EXPERIENCE) DOINA DE JALE** | |
| | Epic EPC 4310 ....4 | 9 wks |

Tommy ZANG *US, male vocalist*   1 wk

| 16 Feb 61 | **HEY GOOD LOOKING** Polydor NH 66957 ....45 | 1 wk |

ZAPP *US, male/female vocal/instrumental group*   6 wks

| 25 Jan 86 | **IT DOESN'T REALLY MATTER** Warner Bros. W 8879 .....57 | 3 wks |
| 24 May 86 | **COMPUTER LOVE (PART 1)** Warner Bros. W 8805 ....64 | 3 wks |

Francesco ZAPPALA *Italy, male producer*   3 wks

| 10 Aug 91 | **WE GOTTA DO IT** 4th + B'way BRW 225 * ....57 | 2 wks |
| 2 May 92 | **NO WAY OUT** PWL Continental PWL 230 ....69 | 1 wk |

* DJ Professor featuring Francesco Zappala

Lena ZAVARONI *UK, female vocalist*   14 wks

| 9 Feb 74 | ● **MA HE'S MAKING EYES AT ME** Philips 6006 367 ....10 | 11 wks |
| 1 Jun 74 | **PERSONALITY** Philips 6006 391 ....33 | 3 wks |

ZEPHYRS *UK, male vocal/instrumental group*   1 wk

| 18 Mar 65 | **SHE'S LOST YOU** Columbia DB 7481 ....48 | 1 wk |

ZERO B *UK, male instrumentalist - keyboards*   4 wks

| 22 Feb 92 | **THE EP** Ffrreedom TAB 102.............................32 | 4 wks |

Tracks on The EP: Lock Up/Spinning Wheel/Module/Eclipse.

ZERO ZERO *UK, male instrumental/production duo*   1 wk

| 10 Aug 91 | **ZEROXED** Kickin KICK 9...............................71 | 1 wk |

ZIGZAG JIVE FLUTES – *See ELIAS and his ZIGZAG JIVE FLUTES*

ZODIACS – *See Maurice WILLIAMS and the ZODIACS*

ZOE *UK, female vocalist*   22 wks

10 Nov 90	**SUNSHINE ON A RAINY DAY** M&G MAGS 6 53	5 wks
24 Aug 91	● **SUNSHINE ON A RAINY DAY** (re-mix)	
	M&G MAGS 14 4	11 wks
2 Nov 91	**LIGHTNING** M&G MAGS 18 37	4 wks
29 Feb 92	**HOLY DAYS** M&G MAGS 21 72	2 wks

ZOMBIES *UK, male vocal/instrumental group*   16 wks

| 13 Aug 64 | **SHE'S NOT THERE** Decca F 11940 ....12 | 11 wks |
| 11 Feb 65 | **TELL HER NO** Decca F 12072 ....42 | 5 wks |

ZOO EXPERIENCE featuring DESTRY
1 wk

UK/US, male/female vocal/instrumental group

22 Aug 92	LOVE'S GOTTA HOLD ON ME		
	Cooltempo COOL 261	66	1 wk

ZUCCHERO
24 wks

Italy, male vocalist/instrumentalist - guitar, Adelmo Fornaciari

30 Mar 91 ●	SENZA UNA DONNA (WITHOUT A WOMAN)		
	London LON 294 *	4	12 wks
18 Jan 92	DIAMANTE *London LON 313* **	44	7 wks
24 Oct 92	MISERERE *London LON 329* ***	15	5 wks

* Zucchero and Paul Young ** Zucchero with Randy Crawford *** Zucchero with Luciano Pavarotti

ZZ TOP *US, male vocal/instrumental group*
87 wks

3 Sep 83	GIMME ALL YOUR LOVIN' *Warner Bros. W 9693*	61	3 wks
26 Nov 83	SHARP DRESSED MAN *Warner Bros. W 9576*	53	3 wks
31 Mar 84	TV DINNERS *Warner Bros. W 9334*	67	3 wks
6 Oct 84 ●	GIMME ALL YOUR LOVIN' (re-entry) *Warner Bros. W 9693*	10	15 wks
15 Dec 84	SHARP DRESSED MAN (re-entry) *Warner Bros. W 9576*	22	10 wks
23 Feb 85	LEGS *Warner Bros. W 9272*	16	7 wks
13 Jul 85	SUMMER HOLIDAY EP *Warner, Bros. W 8946*	51	5 wks
19 Oct 85	SLEEPING BAG *Warner Bros. W 2001*	27	5 wks
15 Feb 86	STAGES *Warner Bros. W 2002*	43	3 wks
19 Apr 86	ROUGH BOY *Warner Bros. W 2003*	23	9 wks
4 Oct 86	VELCRO FLY *Warner Bros. W 8650*	54	3 wks
21 Jul 90	DOUBLEBACK *Warner Bros. W 9812*	29	6 wks
13 Apr 91	MY HEAD'S IN MISSISSIPPI *Warner Bros. W 0009*	37	5 wks
11 Apr 92 ●	VIVA LAS VEGAS *Warner Bros. W 0098*	10	7 wks
20 Jun 92	ROUGH BOY (re-issue) *Warner Bros. W 0111*	49	3 wks

Tracks on Summer Holiday *EP: Tush/Got Me Under Pressure/Beer Drinkers and Hell Raisers/I'm Bad, I'm Nationwide.*

A minor 1990 hit became a major 1991 success for the last solo artist in this book, ZOE.

Different songs/tunes with the same title (e.g. 'Zoom' which has been a hit title for both the Commodores and Fat Larry's Band) are indicated by [A], [B] etc. Where there is no letter in brackets after the title, all hit recordings are of just one song. Individual titles of songs or tunes on EP, LP, medley or megamix singles which made the chart are not included here, with the obvious exception of titles that are actually part of the overall title of the hit in question.

The recording act named alongside each song title is the act that is billed on the record, but is not necessarily the act under whose name all the information about the

indicating the fact that it was a duet with Jane Wyman. We have also simplified some act names in Part Two in the interests of saving space. For example 'Happy Xmas (War Is Over)' is credited here to John Lennon, but if you look up John Lennon in Part One, you will discover the actual credit for that hit was 'John and Yoko, the Plastic Ono Band with the Harlem Community Choir'.

The year of chart entry column contains the year in which each disc made its very first appearance on the chart. Subsequent appearances are only listed here if they signify a period of success *totally* separate from the

2 BRITISH HIT SINGLES ALPHABETICALLY BY TITLE

title can be found in Part One. So, for example 'Zing A Little Zong' is credited correctly in Part Two to Bing Crosby and Jane Wyman, but in Part One is to be found in the list of Bing Crosby hits, with a footnote

disc's first impact. So, for example, 'Bohemian Rhapsody' by Queen is listed as having been a hit in '75 and '91, but Cliff Richard's original version of 'Living Doll', which re-entered the charts for one brief week in 1960 after topping the charts in 1959, is shown only as a hit in 1959.

REM spent more weeks on chart during 1991 than any other act.

332

341

344

345

370

3 BRITISH HIT SINGLES

FACTS AND FEATS

All the chart achievements you need to know about are here. Which record took over from 'Baby Come Back' at the top of the chart? Who has had more consecutive top ten hits than Cliff Richard? From which chart position did 'Dancing Queen' leap to the top? How long did 'Tainted Love' stay on the chart? Did anybody spend more time on the charts in 1992 than Michael Jackson? Who has produced the most number one hits? What is the longest title (excluding brackets) ever to hit the charts? How long did Leeds United F.C. have to wait between their two hit records?

The answer to all these questions and a host of others can be found in this section. Nothing here proves that anybody produces better or worse music than anybody else, or that any particular record is more enjoyable to listen to than any other. All we are doing is listing the facts: we leave the opinions to you.

Monthly limited edition single releases of album tracks gave the WEDDING PRESENT twelve hits in 1992.

Most Weeks on Chart

This table lists the 244 recording acts that have spent 100 weeks or more on the British singles charts from 14 November 1952 up to the end of December 1992. It is of course possible for an act to be credited with two chart weeks in the same week if that act had two or more records on the chart at once. Double-sided hits, EPs and double singles only count as one hit each week, as do the handful of albums which have hit the singles chart over the years.

	Wks
ELVIS PRESLEY	1145
CLIFF RICHARD (includes 16 with Sarah Brightman, 11 with Young Ones, 9 with Phil Everly, 8 with Elton John, 7 with Olivia Newton-John, 6 with Van Morrison, 2 with Sheila Walsh)	1077
ELTON JOHN (includes 14 with Kiki Dee, 10 with George Michael, 9 with Dionne Warwick and Friends, 8 with Cliff Richard, 5 with Millie Jackson, 4 with Eric Clapton, 4 with John Lennon, 3 with Aretha Franklin, 3 with Jennifer Rush)	464
BEATLES (includes 23 with Billy Preston, 1 with Tony Sheridan)	434
FRANK SINATRA (includes 18 with Nancy Sinatra, 9 with Sammy Davis Jr)	428
DAVID BOWIE (includes 12 with Mick Jagger, 11 with Queen, 8 with Bing Crosby, 7 with Pat Metheny)	405
STEVIE WONDER (includes 11 with Julio Iglesias, 10 with Paul McCartney, 9 with Dionne Warwick and Friends, 5 with Diana Ross, Smokey Robinson and Marvin Gaye, 4 with Michael Jackson)	404
STATUS QUO	394
ROD STEWART (includes 9 with Jeff Beck, 8 with Tina Turner. + 46 with Faces)	393
PAUL McCARTNEY/WINGS (includes 25 with Michael Jackson, 10 with Stevie Wonder, 7 with Christians, Holly Johnson, Paul McCartney, Gerry Marsden and Stock Aitken Waterman)	388
DIANA ROSS (includes 20 with Marvin Gaye, 12 with Lionel Richie, 8 with Julio Iglesias, 5 with Marvin Gaye, Smokey Robinson and Stevie Wonder, 4 with Michael Jackson + 197 as a Supreme, 27 with Supremes and Temptations)	386
SHADOWS (+ 404 backing Cliff Richard)	359
MICHAEL JACKSON (includes 25 with Paul McCartney, 4 with Diana Ross, 4 with Stevie Wonder. +235 as a Jackson)	349
QUEEN (includes 11 with David Bowie)	345

	Wks
TOM JONES (includes 7 with Art Of Noise)	343
ROY ORBISON (includes 6 with k.d. lang)	343
ROLLING STONES	340
EVERLY BROTHERS (Phil Everly 6 more solo, 9 with Cliff Richard)	337
MADONNA	334
JIM REEVES	322
LONNIE DONEGAN	321
FOUR TOPS (includes 20 with Supremes)	318
HOLLIES	316
SHIRLEY BASSEY (includes 2 with Yello)	315
SUPREMES (includes 27 with Temptations, 20 with Four Tops)	306
BEE GEES	299
PAT BOONE	296
PERRY COMO	294
DONNA SUMMER (includes 13 with Barbra Streisand)	284
BILLY FURY	281
FRANKIE LAINE (includes 16 with Jimmy Boyd, 16 with Four Lads, 8 with Doris Day, 4 with Johnnie Ray)	281
BEACH BOYS (includes 12 with Fat Boys)	277
SHAKIN' STEVENS (includes 9 with Bonnie Tyler)	277
SLADE	276
HOT CHOCOLATE	267
UB40 (includes 8 with Afrika Bambaataa and Family, 9 with Robert Palmer, 3 with 808 State)	264
MADNESS	256
ELECTRIC LIGHT ORCHESTRA (includes 11 with Olivia Newton-John)	255
ABBA	252
ADAM FAITH	251
PETULA CLARK	247
WHO (+ 4 as High Numbers)	245
CONNIE FRANCIS	241
ENGELBERT HUMPERDINCK	235
JACKSON FIVE/JACKSONS (113 as Jackson Five, 122 as Jacksons)	235
PRINCE (includes 5 with Sheena Easton)	235
T. REX (includes 8 billed as Marc Bolan)	235
NAT 'KING' COLE	234
KEN DODD	233
FRANKIE VAUGHAN (includes 20 with Kaye Sisters)	232
ANDY WILLIAMS	228
FLEETWOOD MAC	223
OLIVIA NEWTON-JOHN (includes 57 with John Travolta, 11 with Electric Light Orchestra, 7 with Cliff Richard)	221
MANFRED MANN (includes 41 as Manfred Mann's Earth Band)	217
KINKS	213
GENE PITNEY (includes 12 with Marc Almond)	212
HERMAN'S HERMITS	211
BRENDA LEE	210
SHOWADDYWADDY	209
KOOL AND THE GANG	207

	Wks
DUSTY SPRINGFIELD (includes 9 with Pet Shop Boys. + 66 as a Springfield)	206
JAM	203
TEMPTATIONS (includes 27 with Supremes. +15 with Bruce Willis)	203
BILL HALEY AND HIS COMETS	199
MARVIN GAYE (includes 61 with Tammi Terrell, 20 with Diana Ross, 11 with Kim Weston, 5 with Diana Ross, Stevie Wonder and Smokey Robinson, 1 with Mary Wells)	199
BANANARAMA (includes 10 with Fun Boy Three, 9 with La Na Nee Nee Noo Noo)	198
EURYTHMICS (includes 11 with Aretha Franklin)	198
DUANE EDDY (includes 9 with Art of Noise)	196
DAVID ESSEX	196
STRANGLERS	194
CILLA BLACK	192
BUDDY HOLLY (+ 47 as a Cricket)	190
NEIL SEDAKA	190
DEPECHE MODE	189
ADAM AND THE ANTS/ADAM ANT	188
PHIL COLLINS (includes 13 with Marilyn Martin, 12 with Philip Bailey)	188
BACHELORS	187
DURAN DURAN	187
GLADYS KNIGHT AND THE PIPS (includes 2 with Johnny Mathis, 9 with Dionne Warwick and Friends)	187
JOHN LENNON/PLASTIC ONO BAND (includes 4 with Elton John)	184
ORCHESTRAL MANOEUVRES IN THE DARK	182
KIM WILDE (includes 11 with Junior, 7 with Mel Smith [Mel and Kim])	182
DAVID WHITFIELD (+ 9 as one of the artists on All Star Hit Parade)	181
GENESIS	180
RUSS CONWAY (includes 10 with Dorothy Squires)	178
DRIFTERS	176
KYLIE MINOGUE (includes 14 with Jason Donovan, 7 with Keith Washington, 1 with Visionmasters)	174
SIMPLE MINDS	174
MR. ACKER BILK	171
DAVE CLARK FIVE	171
CARPENTERS	169
ERASURE	169
GARY GLITTER	168
LEVEL 42	168
TINA TURNER (includes 8 with Rod Stewart, 6 with Bryan Adams, 3 with Eric Clapton. +44 with Ike And Tina Turner)	164
ARETHA FRANKLIN (includes 11 with Eurythmics, 9 with George Michael, 5 with Whitney Houston, 3 with George Benson, 3 with Elton John)	163
GUY MITCHELL	163
SANDIE SHAW	163

ROLLING STONES – 340 weeks on chart.

JONATHAN KING – 128 weeks on chart in many guises.

THOMPSON TWINS spent 108 weeks on chart.

MONKEES		101	

MONKEES	101
DIONNE WARWICK (includes 9 with Friends, 6 with Detroit Spinners and 3 with Jeffrey Osborne)	101
DONOVAN (includes 9 with Jeff Beck Group, 1 with Singing Corner Meets Donovan)	100
MIKE OLDFIELD	100
SPECIALS (includes 5 with Rhoda)	100

Also worth mentioning are:

TERRY HALL (1 solo, 78 with Specials, 50 with Funboy Three, 20 with Bananarama, 18 with Colourfield, 7 with Vegas)	174
PAUL SIMON (83 solo, 87 with Simon And Garfunkel)	170
ALAN PRICE (78 solo, 78 as an Animal, 10 with Fame And Price Together)	166
EDDY GRANT (94 solo, 69 as an Equal)	163
JIMMY SOMERVILLE (36 solo, 76 with Communards, 38 with Bronski Beat and 12 with Bronski Beat and Marc Almond)	162
MIDGE URE (51 solo, 4 with Mick Karn, 54 as part of Visage, 18 as part of Slik, 5 as a Rich Kid and 20 as a leader of Band Aid. This does not include his 138 weeks with Ultravox listed above)	152
ALISON MOYET (92 solo, 53 with Yazoo)	145
STEVE WINWOOD (33 solo, 71 with Spencer Davis Group, 40 with Traffic)	144
FEARGAL SHARKEY (58 solo, 67 with Undertones, 10 with Assembly)	135
ART GARFUNKEL (37 solo, 87 with Simon And Garfunkel)	124
SCOTT WALKER (30 solo, 93 with Walker Brothers)	123
BOBBY BROWN (80 solo, 9 with Glenn Medeiros, 28 with New Edition)	117
BILL MEDLEY (6 solo, 23 with Jennifer Warnes and 86 as a Righteous Brother)	115
DAVID SYLVIAN (15 solo, 81 with Japan, 15 with Sylvian Sakamoto, 2 with Mick Karn and 1 with Rain Tree Crow)	114
SMOKEY ROBINSON (29 solo, 71 with Miracles, 7 with Four Tops, 5 with Diana Ross, Marvin Gaye and Stevie Wonder)	112
B.E.F. (Ian Craig Marsh and Martin Ware have been on the charts for 5 weeks as B.E.F. featuring Lalah Hathaway, 79 weeks as part of Heaven 17 and 25 weeks as part of Human League)	109
DAVE EDMUNDS (87 solo, 14 with Love Sculpture, 6 with Stray Cats)	107
GARY WALKER (12 solo, 93 as a Walker Brother)	105
DAVID GRANT (38 solo, 45 with Linx, 21 with Jaki Graham)	104
LUTHER VANDROSS (79 Solo, 13 with Janet Jackson and 10 with Change)	102
DICKIE VALENTINE (92 solo, 9 with All Star Hit Parade)	101

CHUBBY CHECKER (includes 4 with Bobby Rydell, 11 with Fat Boys)	112
CRAIG DOUGLAS	112
BAD MANNERS	111
THREE DEGREES (includes 9 with MFSB)	111
ALMA COGAN	110
MOVE	110
RUBY MURRAY	110
PRETENDERS	110
ROSE ROYCE	110
SQUEEZE	110
DAVID CASSIDY (+ 53 with Partridge Family)	109
DAWN (Tony Orlando + 11 solo)	109
FATS DOMINO	109
JANET JACKSON (includes 13 with Luther Vandross. + 7 with Herb Alpert)	109
KENNY ROGERS (includes 37 with First Edition, 15 with Dolly Parton and 7 with Sheena Easton)	109
ISLEY BROTHERS	108
LITTLE RICHARD	108
THOMPSON TWINS	108

CHRIS REA	107
SOFT CELL	107
WHITESNAKE	107
HERB ALPERT	106
JOHNNY NASH	106
JIMMY RUFFIN	106
SMOKIE	106
MALCOLM VAUGHAN	106
WET WET WET	106
BRYAN ADAMS (includes 6 with Tina Turner)	105
EDDIE FISHER	105
IMAGINATION	105
DR. HOOK	104
KC AND THE SUNSHINE BAND	104
SMITHS	104
CULTURE CLUB	103
SHEENA EASTON (includes 7 with Kenny Rogers, and 5 with Prince)	103
HOWARD JONES	103
STYLE COUNCIL	103
SINITTA	102
BILLY IDOL	101

Most Weeks on Chart – 1991

36	**R.E.M.**
35	**KENNY THOMAS**
34	**BRYAN ADAMS**
32	**CHER**
30	**C&C MUSIC FACTORY**
30	**DANNII MINOGUE**
30	**SALT-N-PEPA**
30	**SEAL**
29	**MADONNA**
29	**ORCHESTRAL MANOEUVRES IN THE DARK**

In 1991, for the second year running, an American male band took the UK singles chart title. However, apart from nationality and gender, 1991's champs R.E.M. could hardly be more different from their predecessors, the teen heroes New Kids On The Block.

R.E.M. took the title for Most Weeks On Chart with the lowest ever score in a complete year, just 36 weeks. The previous low was 41 weeks, set by Madonna in 1987. Madonna herself was the only act from 1990's top ten to stay amongst the elite in 1991. This was her third consecutive year in the top ten, and her sixth in all. Dannii Minogue just crept into the leader list ahead of big sister Kylie (28 weeks in 1991), making them the first pair of sisters to feature among any year's most-charted acts.

Only Bryan Adams and Cher, of the top acts, enjoyed a number one hit during the year.

Most Weeks on Chart – 1992

38	**MICHAEL JACKSON**
33	**SHAKESPEARS SISTER**
30	**CURTIS STIGERS**
29	**CE CE PENISTON**
29	**TAKE THAT**
29	**U2**
28	**SHAMEN**
28	**SIMPLY RED**
27	**ERASURE**
27	**PRINCE & THE NEW POWER GENERATION**

Michael Jackson, by repeating his triumph of 1983, became only the fourth person to be the UK weeks-on-chart champion more than once, joining Elvis Presley, Madonna and Frankie Laine among the elite. No British act has ever won the annual title more than once. For the first time since 1985, none of the top ten acts of the previous year reappeared among the leaders twelve months later. The biggest-selling singles of the year were by acts which did not make the leader board (Whitney Houston and Snap!), but the longest running chart-topper of the year was by Shakespears Sister, who were the second most successful act of the year, largely due to the extended success of *Stay*.

Right:
MICHAEL JACKSON
Left:
CURTIS STIGERS

Most Weeks on Chart in Each Year

The acts who spent the most time on the charts in each year are as follows:

Year	Act	Weeks
1952	Vera Lynn	10
1953	Frankie Laine	84
1954	Frankie Laine	67
1955	Ruby Murray	80
1956	Bill Haley and his Comets	110
1957	Elvis Presley	108
1958	Elvis Presley	70
1959	Russ Conway	79
1960	Cliff Richard	78
1961	Elvis Presley	88
1962	Chubby Checker	73
1963	Beatles	68
1964	Jim Reeves	73
1965	Seekers	51
1966	Dave Dee, Dozy, Beaky, Mick and Tich	50
1967	Engelbert Humperdinck	97
1968	Tom Jones	58
1969	Marvin Gaye	60
1970	Elvis Presley	59
1971	Elvis Presley	66
1972	T. Rex	58
1973	David Bowie	55
1974	Wombles	65
1975	Mud	45
1976	Rod Stewart	48
1977	Elvis Presley	51
1978	John Travolta	60
1979	Donna Summer	46
1980	Madness	46
1981	Adam and the Ants	91
1982	Soft Cell	49
1983	Michael Jackson	60
1984	Frankie Goes To Hollywood	68
1985	Madonna	84
1986	Madonna	59
1987	Madonna	41
1988	Kylie Minogue	54
1989	Bobby Brown	52
1990	New Kids On The Block	56
1991	R.E.M.	36
1992	Michael Jackson	38

(Frankie Laine's 1953 total includes 16 weeks in duet with Jimmy Boyd and 2 with Doris Day. Chubby Checker's 1962 total includes 3 weeks in duet with Bobby Rydell. The Beatles' 1963 total includes 1 week backing Tony Sheridan. Marvin Gaye's 1969 total includes 29 weeks in duet with Tammi Terrell. John Travolta's 1978 total includes 42 weeks in duet with Olivia Newton-John. Donna Summer's 1979 total includes 9 weeks in duet with Barbra Streisand. Michael Jackson's 1983 total includes 14 weeks in duet with Paul McCartney. Kylie Minogue's 1988 total includes 4 weeks in duet with Jason Donovan).

DAVE DEE, DOZY, BEAKY, MICK AND TICH

Elvis Presley has been chart champion six times, over a span of 21 years. 1986 was the first year since the King's chart debut in 1956 in which he did not hit the British singles chart at all. Two other people, Frankie Laine and Michael Jackson, have been chart champions twice, and Madonna has been chart queen in three – consecutive – years, a feat that not even Elvis has achieved.

Vera Lynn has scored the fewest chart weeks in total of any year's champion – only 46 in her entire chart career.

The other chart champions who have not scored a total of 100 weeks are John Travolta (81 weeks), New Kids On The Block (85 weeks), Wombles (87 weeks), Bobby Brown (89 weeks) and 1991's winner, R.E.M., who have so far only clocked up 67 weeks of chart action in total. R.E.M.'s total of 36 weeks in 1991 was the lowest needed to take the title in a complete year.

Russ Conway (1959) is the only instrumentalist to have been chart champion.

ENGELBERT HUMPERDINCK, weeks champion, 1967.

Most Weeks on Chart in One Year

110	Bill Haley and his Comets	1956
108	Elvis Presley	1957
97	Engelbert Humperdinck	1967
91	Adam and the Ants	1981
88	Elvis Presley	1961
84	Frankie Laine	1953
84	Pat Boone	1957
84	Madonna	1985
80	Ruby Murray	1955
79	Russ Conway	1959
78	Cliff Richard	1960
77	Adam Faith	1960
73	Chubby Checker	1962
73	Jim Reeves	1964
72	Beatles	1964
71	Mr. Acker Bilk	1962
70	Bachelors	1964
70	Elvis Presley	1958

Frankie Laine's 1953 total includes 16 weeks in duet with Jimmy Boyd and 2 weeks in duet with Doris Day. Chubby Checker's 1962 total includes 3 weeks in duet with Bobby Rydell.

Most Hits

Double-sided hits, double singles, EPs and albums only count as one hit each time. Re-issues and re-entries do not count as new hits, nor do re-mixes, if the same vocal track is used. We follow the philosophy that if the named act on the label has not gone into the studio to make a new record, then there is no new hit. Re-recordings of the same song by the same act *do* count as two hits.

A record is a hit if it makes the charts, even if for only one week at number 75.

110	**CLIFF RICHARD** (includes 1 with Olivia Newton-John, 1 with Phil Everly, 1 with Sheila Walsh, 1 with Young Ones, 1 with Elton John, 1 with Van Morrison and 1 with Sarah Brightman)
109	**ELVIS PRESLEY**
60	**ELTON JOHN** (includes 1 with Kiki Dee, 1 with Millie Jackson, 1 with John Lennon, 1 with Cliff Richard, 1 with Aretha Franklin, 1 with George Michael, 1 with Eric Clapton, 1 with Dionne Warwick and Friends and 1 with Jennifer Rush)
51	**DIANA ROSS** (includes 2 with Marvin Gaye, 1 with Michael Jackson, 1 with Marvin Gaye, Smokey Robinson and Stevie Wonder, 1 with Lionel Richie and 1 with Julio Iglesias. + 18 with Supremes, 2 with Supremes & Temptations)
49	**DAVID BOWIE** (includes 1 with Queen, 1 with Bing Crosby, 1 with Pat Metheny and 1 with Mick Jagger. + 4 as part of Tin Machine)
49	**STEVIE WONDER** (includes 1 with Paul McCartney, 1 with Diana Ross, Marvin Gaye and Smokey Robinson, 1 with Michael Jackson, 1 with Dionne Warwick and Friends and 1 with Julio Iglesias)
45	**STATUS QUO**
45	**PAUL McCARTNEY/WINGS** (includes 21 as Wings, 2 with Michael Jackson, 1 with Stevie Wonder and 1 with Christians, Holly Johnson, Gerry Marsden and Stock Aitken Waterman)
44	**ROD STEWART** (includes 2 with Jeff Beck, 1 with Tina Turner. + 5 with Faces, 1 with Python Lee Jackson, 1 with Glass Tiger)
41	**QUEEN** (includes 1 with David Bowie)
38	**MICHAEL JACKSON** (includes 2 with Paul McCartney, 1 with Diana Ross, 1 with Stevie Wonder. + 25 as a Jackson)
38	**ROLLING STONES**
37	**SHAKIN' STEVENS** (includes 1 with Shaky and Bonnie)
35	**FRANK SINATRA** (includes 1 with Sammy Davis Jr. and 1 with Nancy Sinatra)
35	**DONNA SUMMER** (includes 1 with Barbra Streisand)

34	**PRINCE** (includes 1 with Sheena Easton)
34	**SLADE**
34	**UB40** (includes 1 with Afrika Bambaataa and Family, 1 with 808 State, 1 with Robert Palmer)
33	**ROY ORBISON** (includes 1 with k.d. lang)
32	**TOM JONES** (includes 1 with Art Of Noise)
32	**GARY NUMAN** (includes 3 with Sharpe and Numan, 2 with Radio Heart)
31	**SHADOWS** (+ 30 with Cliff Richard)
31	**STRANGLERS**
31	**FRANKIE VAUGHAN** (includes 2 with Kaye Sisters)
30	**BEE GEES**
30	**LONNIE DONEGAN**
30	**HOT CHOCOLATE**
29	**BEACH BOYS** (includes 1 with Fat Boys)
29	**BEATLES** (includes 1 with Tony Sheridan, 1 with Billy Preston)
29	**NAT 'KING' COLE** (includes 1 with George Shearing)
29	**ELVIS COSTELLO** (includes 2 as the Imposter)
29	**ELECTRIC LIGHT ORCHESTRA** (includes 1 with Olivia Newton-John)
29	**EVERLY BROTHERS** (Phil Everly + 1 solo and 1 with Cliff Richard)
29	**FOUR TOPS** (includes 2 with Supremes)
29	**BILLY FURY**
29	**HOLLIES**
29	**MADONNA**
29	**SUPREMES** (includes 3 with Temptations, 2 with Four Tops)
28	**WHO** (+ 1 as High Numbers)
27	**SHIRLEY BASSEY** (includes one with Yello)
27	**PETULA CLARK**
27	**FRANKIE LAINE** (includes 1 with Jimmy Boyd, 1 with Doris Day and 1 with Johnnie Ray)
27	**SIOUXSIE AND THE BANSHEES** (Siouxsie and Budgie + 3 as the Creatures)
26	**PAT BOONE**
26	**DEPECHE MODE**
26	**JACKSON FIVE/JACKSONS** (11 as Jackson Five, 15 as Jacksons)
26	**LEVEL 42**
26	**CHRIS REA**
26	**JIM REEVES**
26	**TEMPTATIONS** (includes 3 with Supremes)
26	**T. REX** (includes 2 credited to Marc Bolan)
26	**KIM WILDE** (includes 1 with Junior, 1 with Mel Smith [Mel and Kim])
25	**ABBA**
25	**BANANARAMA** (includes 2 with Funboy Three, 1 with La Na Nee Nee Noo Noo)
25	**ARETHA FRANKLIN** (includes 1 with George Benson, 1 with Eurythmics, 1 with George Michael, 1 with Elton John, 1 with Whitney Houston)
25	**MADNESS**

25	**TINA TURNER** (includes 1 with Rod Stewart, 1 with Bryan Adams and 1 with Eric Clapton. + 4 with Ike Turner)
24	**DAVID ESSEX**
24	**EURYTHMICS** (includes 1 with Aretha Franklin)
24	**ADAM FAITH**
24	**FLEETWOOD MAC**
24	**IRON MAIDEN**
24	**GLADYS KNIGHT AND THE PIPS** (includes 1 with Johnny Mathis, 1 with Dionne Warwick and Friends)
24	**ORCHESTRAL MANOEUVRES IN THE DARK**
24	**SIMPLE MINDS**
23	**PERRY COMO**
23	**CONNIE FRANCIS**
23	**OLIVIA NEWTON-JOHN** (includes 4 with John Travolta, 1 with Electric Light Orchestra and 1 with Cliff Richard)
23	**SHOWADDYWADDY**
23	**DUSTY SPRINGFIELD** (includes 1 with Pet Shop Boys. + 5 as a Springfield)
22	**AC/DC**
22	**DAVE CLARK FIVE**
22	**CURE**
22	**DURAN DURAN**
22	**DUANE EDDY** (includes 1 with Art Of Noise)
22	**MARVIN GAYE** (includes 6 with Tammi Terrell, 2 with Diana Ross, 1 with Kim Weston, 1 with Mary Wells and 1 with Diana Ross, Smokey Robinson and Stevie Wonder)
22	**KINKS**
22	**BRENDA LEE**
22	**MANFRED MANN** (17 as Manfred Mann, 5 as Manfred Mann's Earth Band)
22	**GENE PITNEY** (includes 1 with Marc Almond)
21	**GEORGE BENSON** (includes 1 with Aretha Franklin, 1 with Patti Austin)
21	**KATE BUSH** (includes 1 with Peter Gabriel)
21	**FIVE STAR**
21	**GARY GLITTER**
21	**KOOL AND THE GANG**
21	**ANDY WILLIAMS**
20	**ADAM AND THE ANTS/ADAM ANT**
20	**MARC ALMOND** (includes 1 as Marc & the Mambas, 1 with Bronski Beat, 1 with Gene Pitney, and 1 as Soft Cell/Marc Almond. + 9 with Soft Cell)
20	**BUCKS FIZZ**
20	**PHIL COLLINS** (includes 1 with Marilyn Martin, 1 with Philip Bailey)
20	**RUSS CONWAY** (includes 1 with Dorothy Squires)
20	**FATS DOMINO**
20	**GENESIS**
20	**HERMAN'S HERMITS**

TOM JONES – 32 chart hits.

20	**KYLIE MINOGUE** (includes 1 with Jason Donovan, 1 with Keith Washington, 1 with Visionmasters with Tony King)
20	**ROBERT PALMER** (includes 1 with UB40)
20	**SPANDAU BALLET**
20	**U2** (includes 1 with B.B. King)

Other acts that have clocked up 20 hits under more than one name are:

37	**MIDGE URE** (8 solo, 17 with Ultravox, 7 with Visage, 2 as part of Slik, 1 as a Rich Kid, 1 with Mick Karn. + 1 as a leader of Band Aid)
33	**BRYAN FERRY** (17 solo, 16 with Roxy Music)
31	**MORRISSEY** (14 solo, 17 as a Smith)
31	**LIONEL RICHIE** (16 solo, 13 with the Commodores, 1 with Diana Ross and 1 as a leader of USA For Africa)
29	**STING** (12 solo, 1 with Eric Clapton, 16 with Police)
28	**CHER** (18 solo, 9 with Sonny, 1 uncredited with Meatloaf)
28	**ERIC CLAPTON** (14 solo, 7 with Cream, 2 with the Yardbirds, 1 with Elton John, 1 with Sting, 1 as Derek & the Dominoes, 1 with Delaney & Bonnie & Friends and 1 with Tina Turner)
27	**GEORGE MICHAEL** (14 solo, 10 with Wham!, 1 with Elton John, 1 with Aretha Franklin and 1 with Boogie Box High)
25	**DONNY OSMOND** (11 solo, 10 as an Osmond, 4 as half of Donny & Marie)
24	**ROY WOOD** (4 solo, 10 with Move, 7 with Wizzard, 1 with Electric Light Orchestra, 1 with Doctor and the Medics, and 1 with Jive Bunny)
23	**BOY GEORGE** (9 solo, 10 with Culture Club, 4 as Jesus Loves You)
22	**BUDDY HOLLY** (18 solo, 4 as a Cricket)
22	**PHIL LYNOTT** (3 solo, 18 with Thin Lizzy, 1 with Gary Moore)
22	**GARY MOORE** (17 solo, 1 with Phil Lynott, 1 with B B King, and at least three with Thin Lizzy)
22	**DAVID SYLVIAN** (6 solo, 12 with Japan, 3 with Sylvian Sakamoto, 1 with Mick Karn)
22	**FRANKIE VALLI** (5 solo, 17 with Four Seasons)
22	**JODY WATLEY** (5 solo, 17 with Shalamar)
21	**NEW ORDER** (18 as New Order, 1 as part of Englandneworder, and 2 as Joy Division, more or less)
21	**TREMELOES** (13 as a group, plus 8 backing Brian Poole)
20	**STEVE WINWOOD** (6 solo, 10 with the Spencer Davis Group and 4 with Traffic)

Most Hits in One Calendar Year

During 1992, **The Wedding Present** released 12 singles, all of which hit the top 30, and 8 of which made the top 20. Only one, their May release *Come Play With Me*, hit the top ten, and none of them spent more than two weeks on the chart. Five of their singles were top 20 hits which spent only one week on the chart. No other act has ever had more than ten *new* hit singles in one calendar year.

In 1957, **Elvis Presley** actually charted with 16 different titles, but these involved only ten new hit singles during the year. Four titles were on the chart in the first week of the year, having hit the chart originally during 1956. Two of these titles were either side of the same record, *Blue Moon* at number 22 and *I Don't Care If The Sun Don't Shine* at number 30, both on HMV POP 272. Of the ten new hits he enjoyed in 1957, two were double-sided hits giving the King twelve more chart placings during the year.

In 1983, **Jam** enjoyed 14 chart entries, but these included one hit hanging over from 1982 and 13 re-issues of old hits. Nine of the re-entries came in the same chart, for the week ending 22 January 1983, which is a record for chart entries in one week. On 3 September 1977, **Elvis Presley** scored eight simultaneous chart entries, all re-issues. He had a further three new hits that year, giving him a total of 11 hits.

ELVIS PRESLEY

Most Top Ten Hits

The same rules apply as for the MOST HITS list, except that a disc must have made the top ten for at least one week to qualify.

BEACH BOYS - 13 top ten hits.

62	**CLIFF RICHARD** (includes 1 with Phil Everly, 1 with Young Ones and 1 with Sarah Brightman)
55	**ELVIS PRESLEY**
28	**MADONNA**
27	**MICHAEL JACKSON** (includes 2 with Paul McCartney. + 11 as a Jackson)
25	**BEATLES**
24	**PAUL McCARTNEY/WINGS** (includes 12 as Wings, and 2 with Michael Jackson, 1 with Stevie Wonder and 1 with Christians, Holly Johnson, Gerry Marsden and Stock Aitken Waterman)
23	**ROD STEWART** (includes 1 with Tina Turner. + 3 with Faces and 1 with Python Lee Jackson)
22	**DAVID BOWIE** (includes 1 with Queen, 1 with Bing Crosby and 1 with Mick Jagger)
22	**STATUS QUO**
21	**ROLLING STONES**
20	**ELTON JOHN** (includes 1 with Kiki Dee, 1 with George Michael)
20	**QUEEN** (includes 1 with David Bowie)
19	**ABBA**
19	**FRANKIE LAINE** (includes 1 with Jimmy Boyd and 1 with Doris Day)
18	**STEVIE WONDER** (includes 1 with Paul McCartney and 1 with Julio Iglesias)
17	**LONNIE DONEGAN**
17	**HOLLIES**
17	**DIANA ROSS** (includes 1 with Marvin Gaye and 1 with Lionel Richie. + 7 with Supremes, 1 with Supremes and Temptations)
16	**BEE GEES**
16	**MANFRED MANN** (includes 3 as Manfred Mann's Earth Band)
16	**SHADOWS** (+ 25 backing Cliff Richard)
16	**SLADE**
15	**ELECTRIC LIGHT ORCHESTRA** (includes 1 with Olivia Newton-John)
15	**TOM JONES** (includes 1 with Art Of Noise)
15	**MADNESS**
15	**KYLIE MINOGUE** (includes 1 with Jason Donovan)
15	**SHAKIN' STEVENS** (includes 1 with Bonnie Tyler)
14	**UB40** (includes 1 with Robert Palmer)
13	**BEACH BOYS** (includes 1 with Fat Boys)
13	**NAT 'KING' COLE**

13	**PERRY COMO**
13	**ERASURE**
13	**EVERLY BROTHERS** (Phil Everly + 1 with Cliff Richard)
13	**KINKS**
13	**SUPREMES** (includes 1 with Temptations)
13	**U2**
13	**WHO**
12	**SHIRLEY BASSEY**
12	**DURAN DURAN**
12	**GARY GLITTER** (+ 1 with the Timelords)
12	**HOT CHOCOLATE**
12	**GUY MITCHELL**
12	**ROY ORBISON**
12	**PET SHOP BOYS** (includes 1 with Dusty Springfield)
12	**PRINCE**
11	**WINIFRED ATWELL** (+ 1 as part of All Star Hit Parade)
11	**CILLA BLACK**
11	**PAT BOONE**
11	**PETULA CLARK**
11	**ADAM FAITH**
11	**FOUR TOPS**
11	**BILLY FURY**
11	**JACKSON FIVE/JACKSONS** (6 as Jackson Five, 5 as Jacksons)
11	**MUD**
11	**GENE PITNEY** (includes 1 with Marc Almond)
11	**FRANK SINATRA** (includes 1 with Nancy Sinatra)
11	**DUSTY SPRINGFIELD** (includes 1 with Pet Shop Boys. + 2 with Springfields)
11	**T. REX**
11	**10.C.C.** (+ 1 as Hotlegs, more or less)
11	**FRANKIE VAUGHAN** (includes 2 with the Kaye Sisters)
11	**DAVID WHITFIELD** (+ 1 as part of All Star Hit Parade)
10	**ADAM AND THE ANTS/ADAM ANT**

10	**BANANARAMA** (includes 1 with Funboy Three and 1 with La Na Nee Nee Noo Noo)
10	**BAY CITY ROLLERS**
10	**BLONDIE**
10	**BONEY M**
10	**DORIS DAY** (includes 2 with Frankie Laine and 1 with Johnnie Ray)
10	**JASON DONOVAN** (includes 1 with Kylie Minogue)
10	**DAVID ESSEX**
10	**CONNIE FRANCIS**
10	**HERMAN'S HERMITS**
10	**OLIVIA NEWTON-JOHN** (includes 3 with John Travolta, 1 with ELO)
10	**POLICE**
10	**JOHNNIE RAY** (includes 1 with Doris Day)
10	**ROXY MUSIC**
10	**LEO SAYER**
10	**SHOWADDYWADDY**
10	**SPANDAU BALLET**
10	**STYLISTICS**
10	**SWEET**

Also strongly represented on top ten hits are:

19	**GEORGE MICHAEL** (7 solo, 9 as part of Wham!, 1 with Aretha Franklin, 1 with Elton John and 1 as part of Boogie Box High)
18	**PHIL COLLINS** (8 solo, 8 as part of Genesis, 1 with Marilyn Martin and 1 with Philip Bailey)
15	**ROY WOOD** (1 solo, 7 with Move, 6 with Wizzard and 1 with Electric Light Orchestra)
13	**ANNIE LENNOX** (2 solo, 9 as part of Eurythmics, and 2 as a Tourist)
13	**DONNY OSMOND** (6 solo, 5 as one of the Osmonds and 2 with Marie Osmond)
12	**DAVE STEWART** (1 with Candy Dulfer, 9 as part of the Eurythmics, 2 as a Tourist)
12	**LIONEL RICHIE** (7 solo, 4 as a Commodore and 1 with Diana Ross)
11	**CHER** (7 solo, 3 with Sonny & Cher and one with Meatloaf)

Most Consecutive Top Ten Hits

27	**MADONNA**
26	**CLIFF RICHARD** (with the Shadows for 11 consecutive)
24	**BEATLES** (first 24 releases)
23	**ELVIS PRESLEY** (first 23 RCA releases)
19	**ROLLING STONES**
18	**ABBA**
15	**KYLIE MINOGUE** (first 13 hits, including 1 with Jason Donovan)
12	**SHADOWS** (first 12 hits), **SLADE**
11	**GARY GLITTER** (first 11 hits), **FRANKIE LAINE**, **GUY MITCHELL** (first 11 hits), **T. REX**
10	**BAY CITY ROLLERS** (first 10 hits), **DURAN DURAN**, **PET SHOP BOYS** (including 1 with Dusty Springfield), **DAVID WHITFIELD**

CLIFF RICHARD

At the start of Elvis Presley's run of 23 consecutive top ten hits, three old HMV releases appeared on the chart, one of which, *Paralysed*, reached the top ten. Three EPs by Elvis also hit the charts without reaching the top ten during the five-and-a-half years in which every Elvis single hit the top ten, with 20 of the 23 reaching the top three.

Holiday by Madonna reappeared in the top ten twice during her run of 27 top ten hits with consecutive releases. As it was first a top ten hit before the release of *Lucky Star*, her only single to fail to hit the upper reaches, it does not count as one of her consecutive top ten hits. Her remixed version of *Crazy For You*, which also hit the top ten, does not count as an extra hit.

Kylie Minogue's record of 13 consecutive top ten hits with her first 13 releases (including one in duet with Jason Donovan) represents the best start to a chart career by any act ever, beating even the Beatles whose first single reached the top ten only as a re-issue.

Between May 1959 and December 1963, the Shadows released 30 singles, either solo or backing Cliff Richard, all of which hit the top ten.

The Rolling Stones' run of 19 consecutive top ten hits began on 12 March 1964, with *Not Fade Away*, and finished on July 21 1978 when *Miss You/Far Away Eyes* dropped out of the top ten. This is the longest time span for a run of top ten hits with consecutive releases, none of which were re-mixes or re-issues.

Least Successful Chart Act

Since 13 May 1978, when the top 75 was first published, 19 acts have clocked up a chart career consisting of only one week at number 75. They are:

ADICTS	Bad Boy	14 May 83
ANGELWITCH	Sweet Danger	7 Jun 80
APPLES	Eye Wonder	23 Mar 91
BABY JUNE	Hey! What's Your Name	15 Aug 92
D'BORA	Dream About You	14 Sep 91
DAYTON	The Sound Of Music	10 Dec 83
DTOX	Shattered Glass	21 Nov 92
THULI DUMAKUDE	The Funeral	2 Jan 88
GEORGE FENTON and JONAS GWANGWA	Cry Freedom	2 Jan 88
GRAND PRIX	Keep On Believing	27 Feb 82
ANTHONY HOPKINS	Distant Star	27 Dec 86
LOST	Techno Funk	22 Jun 91
MICHAEL LOVESMITH	Ain't Nothing Like It	5 Oct 85
MC DUKE	I'm Riffin' (English Rasta)	11 Mar 89
PRETTY BOY FLOYD	Rock And Roll (Is Gonna Set The Night On Fire)	10 Mar 90
CHERYL PEPSII RILEY	Thanks For My Child	28 Jan 89
SEDUCTION	Heartbeat	21 Apr 89
SIMONE	My Family Depends On Me	23 Nov 91
SOULED OUT	In My Life	9 May 92

Adicts and **Grand Prix** have also hit the album charts, with marginally more success. **Thuli Dumakude**'s hit was the flip side of the **George Fenton and Jonas Gwangwa** record, both tracks from the soundtrack of the film, *Cry Freedom*.

The **Ruthless Rap Assassins** are the only act to the end of 1992 whose chart career has consisted of two singles, both of which peaked at number 75 for one week. **Five Thirty** began their chart career with two hits reaching number 75 for one week, but have since gone on to (slightly) greater chart things. **Robert Owens**' only chart hit, *I'll Be Your Friend*, peaked at number 75 for two weeks in December 1991.

From 10 March 1960 to 6 May 1978, when only a Top 50 was published, nine acts managed a chart career that consisted of only one week at number 50. They were **Angels**, **Chaquito**, **Jimmy Clanton**, **Cookies**, **Tim Hardin**, **Tony Hatch**, **Moontrekkers**, **Hal Page and the Whalers** and **Sundragon**.

Marvin Gaye and **Mary Wells** as a duo also spent only one week at number 50, but they both had much bigger solo successes. **Keith Relf**, lead vocalist of the hitmaking Yardbirds, also spent just one week at number 50 as a soloist.

There are seven other acts who have spent only one week at number 75 in this particular combination, but they have had hits under other guises.

PRETTY BOY FLOYD

JOHNNY CLEGG and SAVUKA	Scatterlings Of Africa	16 May 87
(Clegg also hit as part of Juluka)		
NIKKI D	Daddy's Little Girl	30 Mar 91
(has hit with Alyson Williams)		
DEJA	Serious	29 Aug 87
(Deja were Starlena Young and Curt Jones, who had hits as members of both Aurra and Slave)		
FISH and TONY BANKS	Shortcut To Somewhere	18 Oct 86
(both have had solo hits, as well as with Marillion and Genesis respectively)		
TERRY HALL	Missing	11 Nov 89
(has also hit as a member of Specials, Funboy Three, Colourfield and Vegas)		
MELISSA MANCHESTER and AL JARREAU	The Music Of Goodbye	5 Apr 86
(Jarreau has had 5 solo hits)		
STOP THE VIOLENCE	Self Destruction	18 Feb 89
(charity ensemble consisting of several chart acts)		

Most Hits Without a Top Ten Hit

This list is rapidly growing as more and more records make the top 75 for a shorter and shorter time, which means, statistically, that the average chart peak must be getting lower. The full list of those acts that have had at least ten hits without ever reaching the top ten is:

ACT	HITS	HIGHEST PLACING
AC/DC	22	12 Heatseeker, 1988
ALARM	16	17 68 Guns, 1983
SAXON	15	12 And The Bands Played On, 1981
MISSION	14	11 Wasteland, 1987
CULT	13	11 Lil' Devil, 1987
STING	13	12 Russians, 1986
LLOYD COLE	12	17 Lost Weekend, 1985
JULIAN COPE	12	19 World Shut Your Mouth, 1986
JUDAS PRIEST	12	12 Living After Midnight, 1980
		12 Breaking The Law, 1980
LOOSE ENDS	12	13 Hangin' On A String (Contemplating), 1985
		13 Don't Be A Fool, 1990
NEW MODEL ARMY	12	28 No Rest, 1985
PUBLIC ENEMY	12	18 Don't Believe The Hype, 1988
		18 Welcome To The Terrordome, 1990
RUSH	12	13 Spirit Of Radio, 1980
KILLING JOKE	11	16 Love Like Blood, 1985
POP WILL EAT ITSELF	11	15 XY And Zee, 1991
WASP	11	17 Chainsaw Charlie (Murders In The New Morgue), 1992
INSPIRAL CARPETS	10	12 Dragging Me Down, 1992
SPEAR OF DESTINY	10	14 Never Take Me Alive, 1987
The THE	10	18 The Beat(en) Generation, 1989

Sting and **Julian Cope** have, of course, been involved in top ten hits as members of Police and The Teardrop Explodes respectively. **Pop Will Eat Itself** hit the top ten with their 12th hit, in January 1993.

Clash had 19 hits without hitting the top ten before the re-release of their 16th hit, *Should I Stay Or Should I Go*, went all the way to number one. **Chris Rea**'s 18th hit was his first, and to date only, top ten hit. **Fats Domino** had 18 hits after his only top ten hit. **Elvis Costello** has charted 18 times since his last top ten hit at the end of 1981, 16 times under his own name and twice as **The Imposter**. Since **Gary Numan**'s last top ten appearance in June '82, he has clocked up 23 more hits – 18 solo hits (excluding the re-mix of *Cars*), three hits with Bill Sharpe and two with

Radio Heart. The highest position any of these hits reached was 17 (*Change Your Mind*).
Luther Vandross has had 14 solo hits without ever straying above position 13, but he reached no. 2 in duet with Janet Jackson in 1992 with *The Best Things In Life Are Free*.

That Petrol Emotion currently holds the record for most hits without reaching the top 40. They have had seven chart hits, but their highest position is number 43, which was the peak of their first chart hit, *Big Decision*, in 1987.

Longest Gap Between Chart Hits

This table shows which acts had to wait for the longest time between chart hits. The definition of a 'hit' is the same as in other lists in this section, i.e. re-issues and re-entries do not count as new hits. For that reason the Righteous Brothers, for example, do not feature in this list. The gap is calculated between the last day of one chart run and the first day of the chart run of the next hit.

Thirty-two acts have waited patiently for over 15 years between hits as follows:

Act	Gap	Dates
DINAH WASHINGTON	30 years 71 days	(24 Jan 62 to 4 Apr 92)
EARTHA KITT	28 years 170 days	(16 Jun 55 to 3 Dec 83)
RITCHIE VALENS	28 years 142 days	(12 Mar 59 to 1 Aug 87)
JOHN LEE HOOKER	28 years 66 days	(19 Aug 64 to 24 Oct 92)
PATSY CLINE	27 years 340 days	(2 Jan 63 to 8 Dec 90)
BOBBY VINTON	26 years 215 days	(27 Feb 64 to 29 Sep 90)
FRANK IFIELD	24 years 288 days	(22 Feb 67 to 7 Dec 91)
GLENN MILLER	21 years 312 days	(18 Mar 54 to 24 Jan 76)
LEEDS UNITED FC	19 years 293 days	(7 Jul 72 to 25 Apr 92)
BUFFY SAINTE-MARIE	19 years 293 days	(21 Apr 72 to 8 Feb 92)
GARY U.S. BONDS	19 years 223 days	(18 Oct 61 to 30 May 81)
ROY ORBISON	19 years 19 days	(26 Dec 69 to 14 Jan 89)
SIMON & GARFUNKEL	19 years 13 days	(24 Nov 72 to 7 Dec 91)
NINA SIMONE	18 years 262 days	(11 Feb 69 to 31 Oct 87)
WILSON PICKETT	18 years 255 days	(11 Mar 69 to 21 Nov 87)
PAUL EVANS	18 years 254 days	(6 Apr 60 to 16 Dec 78)
KENNY LYNCH	18 years 16 days	(4 Aug 65 to 20 Aug 83)
BING CROSBY	17 years 338 days	(5 Sep 57 to 9 Aug 75)
WILLIAM BELL	17 years 284 days	(16 Jul 68 to 26 Apr 86)
RINGO STARR	17 years 113 days	(14 Feb 75 to 6 Jun 92)
MONKEES	17 years 109 days	(1 Jul 69 to 18 Oct 86)
JOE COCKER	17 years 92 days	(14 Aug 70 to 14 Nov 87)
SLIM WHITMAN	17 years 86 days	(11 Jul 57 to 5 Oct 74)
MIKE BERRY	17 years 73 days	(22 May 63 to 2 Aug 80)
DOROTHY SQUIRES	16 years 101 days	(11 Jun 53 to 20 Sep 69)
EVERLY BROTHERS	16 years 96 days	(18 Jun 68 to 22 Sep 84)
BORIS GARDINER	16 years 87 days	(1 May 70 to 26 Jul 86)
DEE CLARK	16 years 3 days	(8 Oct 59 to 11 Oct 75)
TAMS	15 years 360 days	(26 Nov 71 to 21 Nov 87)
BILLY FURY	15 years 349 days	(21 Sep 66 to 4 Sep 82)
MAX BYGRAVES	15 years 325 days	(18 Jan to 9 Dec 89)
JOHNNY TILLOTSON	15 years 306 days	(12 Jun 63 to 14 Apr 79)

(**William Bell** hit the charts with Judy Clay in late 1968 and early 69. **Dorothy Squires** had a hit with Russ Conway in 1961. In 1983 both **Phil Everly** and **Joe Cocker** had top ten hits, with Cliff Richard and Jennifer Warnes respectively. **Roy Orbison** charted as a member of the Traveling Wilburys in 1988. **Glenn Miller** and **Johnny Tillotson**'s reappearances were both as a result of a re-issue of a hit, coupled with tracks that had not previously hit the chart, thus counting the re-issue as a new hit.)

Of these acts, the top five to come back with newly recorded material are Eartha Kitt, John Lee Hooker, Leeds United FC, Buffy Sainte-Marie and Gary 'US' Bonds.

There was an aching gap of 33 years and 87 days between appearances of the **Chipmunks**' name in the charts, but their comeback hit was not only with Billy Ray Cyrus, it came over 20 years after the death of the creator of the Chipmunks, Ross Bagdasarian, better known as David Seville.

The 1992 Chipmunks are the creation of Seville's son, Ross Bagdasarian Jr. There was a gap of 28 years 339 days between **Nat 'King' Cole**'s consecutive new hits *Dear Lonely Hearts* and *The Christmas Song*, but the re-issue of *When I Fall In Love* had given him a hit four years before *The Christmas Song* charted, thus disqualifying him from this table. After 25 years and 329 days off the chart, **Karl Denver** reappeared in June 1990 with Happy Mondays.

Donovan made his comeback with Singing Corner on 1 December 1990, 21 years and 307 days since his final solo chart hit, and 21 years and 83 days since his duet with Jeff Beck lapsed into chart oblivion. **Ray Charles** charted as vocalist with Quincy Jones 21 years and 261 days after his final solo hit dropped off the chart. For **P.P. Arnold** there was a chart hiatus of exactly 20 years between her last solo hit and her appearance on the Beatmasters hit, *Burn It Up* in 1988. **Crosby**

Stills and Nash spent 19 years and 269 days in the chart wilderness before Crosby Stills Nash and Young had their first UK chart hit in January 1989. **Jeff Beck** and **Rod Stewart** had consecutive hits as a duet 18 years and 266 days apart, but both partners hit the charts in the interim. There was a gap of 15 years 304 days between **Des O'Connor**'s last solo appearance and his re-emergence late in 1986 in partnership with Roger Whittaker. **Tammy Wynette**

enjoyed her final solo chart hit 15 years and 151 days before re-emerging on KLF's *Justified And Ancient* at the end of 1991.

38 other acts have been off the chart for over 10 years between hits. They are:

Sandie SHAW (14 yrs 315 days), Trini LOPEZ (14/223), Danny WILLIAMS (14/132), Dionne WARWICK (14/92), Mick JAGGER (14/60), Robin GIBB (13/349), CHER (13/271), Mr. Acker BILK (13/167), INNER CIRCLE (13/152), Frankie MILLER (13/28), DION (13/27), CHAIRMEN OF THE BOARD (13/20), LITTLE RICHARD (12/345), Murray HEAD (12/280), Donny OSMOND (12/253), Marianne FAITHFULL (12/247), EXCITERS (12/219), Billy PRESTON (12/105), Duncan BROWNE (12/84), PINK FLOYD (12/79), DOORS (12/70), Paul ANKA (12/37), Tony OSBORNE (11/339), Henry MANCINI (11/314), Johnny MATHIS (11/290), ENGLAND WORLD CUP SQUAD (11/232), Duane EDDY (11/185), Millie JACKSON (11/107), Robert JOHN (11/61), Gene CHANDLER (10/216), INCOGNITO (10/206), Dobie GRAY (10/

166), Linda RONSTADT (10/158), Betty WRIGHT (10/146), CHAKACHAS (10/130), BOOKER T & THE M.G.'s (10/80), Wayne GIBSON (10/68) and Charlie DRAKE (10/12).

Dionne Warwick, Mick Jagger, Robin Gibb, Billy Preston, Donny Osmond and Linda Ronstadt all appeared on the charts as part of groups during their solo absences.)

Barry Blue was absent from the charts for 14 years and 278 days before re-appearing under the guise of Cry Sisco! **The Trammps** disappeared for 14 years and 96 days before re-emerging in partnership with KWS in 1992. **Gene Pitney** missed 14 years and 39 days of chart action before hitting again with Marc Almond in 1989. **Shirley Bassey** had been absent from the chart for 14 years 33 days when she re-appeared with Yello. **Al Green**'s chart duet with Annie Lennox came 13 years 215 days after his last hit fell off the chart. **Timmy Thomas** disappeared from the charts for 12 years 231 days between his last solo hit and his duet with Nicole. **Lindisfarne** spent 12 years and 7 days out of chart sight before coming back with Gazza on 10 November 1990. **Pete Waterman** hit the charts as 14–18 11 years

DINAH WASHINGTON

239 days before he became one third of Stock Aitken Waterman and hit the charts again. **Scott Fitzgerald**'s solo chart debut came 10 years 44 days after his hit duet with Yvonne Keeley. **Roger Whittaker** had a gap of 11 years 9 days between his last solo chart appearance and his hit with Des O'Connor. **Duane Eddy** not only had a gap of 11 years 185 days between solo chart hits, he then had to wait a further 10 years 310

days after his last solo hit before re-emerging with Art Of Noise and a re-make of his first top ten hit, *Peter Gunn Theme*. **Roy Wood**'s name was out of the chart for 11 years and 127 days before his comeback with Dr. and the Medics, although he had a re-issued hit as leader of Wizzard in the interim. There was a gap of 11 years 59 days between **Shane Fenton**'s final day on the charts and **Alvin Stardust**'s first appearance.

Name and Number

Hit records are not usually dedicated to just one person. The most commonly used title for hit songs is *Tonight*, rather than *Yes Tonight Josephine*, a name which limits the song's use a bit if you are trying to impress somebody called Ann or Mary. The most successful songs, the ones that get to number one, use names quite rarely. *Ebeneezer Goode*, the Shamen's chart-topper of September 1992, was the first with a name in the title since *Rock Me Amadeus* in May 1986.

However, this has not stopped the songwriters from using names in their songs, and in the spirit of never-ending research which drives us on, we have compiled a list of the most frequently used names in hit song titles.

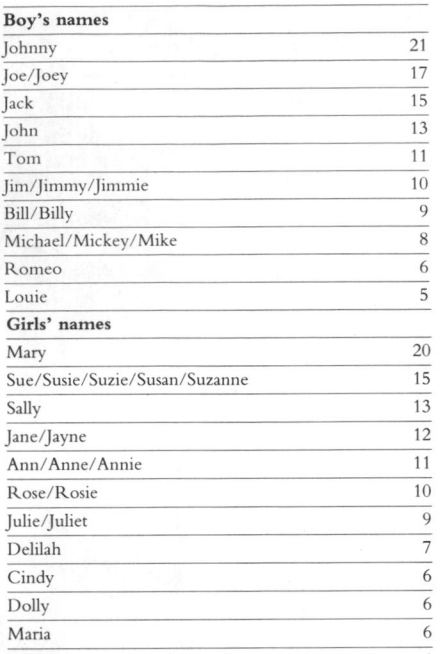

Boy's names	
Johnny	21
Joe/Joey	17
Jack	15
John	13
Tom	11
Jim/Jimmy/Jimmie	10
Bill/Billy	9
Michael/Mickey/Mike	8
Romeo	6
Louie	5
Girls' names	
Mary	20
Sue/Susie/Suzie/Susan/Suzanne	15
Sally	13
Jane/Jayne	12
Ann/Anne/Annie	11
Rose/Rosie	10
Julie/Juliet	9
Delilah	7
Cindy	6
Dolly	6
Maria	6
Marie	6

Although 49 first names have been used in number one hit titles, no name has been used twice except Mary, which crops up at number one in both chart-topping versions of the same song, *Mary's Boy Child*. Five of the 21 boys' names which have hit the top end in the letter 'O' (Hernando, Fernando, Figaro, Angelo and Geno), whereas all but five of the 28 number one hit girls' names end in either 'A', 'E' or 'Y'.

Among the many obscure names in hit titles are Almaz, Clyde, Cyril, Evangeline, Fergus, Jesamine, Norman, Pandora, Pepe, Rhonda, Rosetta, Valentino, and Ziggy.

The most commonly used surname for hit performers is still **Williams**. No fewer than 23 different Williams have hit the charts, including two called Andy and two called John. The only surnames used by ten or more hitmaking acts are:

Williams	23
Alyson, Andy, Andy and David, Billy, Danny, Deniece, Diana, Don, Freedom, Geoffrey, Iris, John, John, Kenny, Larry, Lenny, Mark, Mason, Maurice, Vanessa, Vesta and Wendell.	

Brown	18
Angie, Arthur, Bobby, Carl, Dennis, Diana, Errol, Gloria D., James, Joanne, Jocelyn, Joe, Miquel, Peter, Polly, Sam, Sharon and the Browns.	

Johnson	16
Bryan, Carey, Denise, Don, General, Holly, Howard, Johnny, Kevin, Laurie, L.J., Lou, Marv, Orlando, Paul and Teddy.	

Jones	16
Aled, Barbara, Catherine Zeta, Grace, Howard, Janie, Jimmy, Juggy, Mick, Oran 'Juice', Paul, Quincy, Rickie Lee, Shirley, Tammy, and Tom.	

Jackson	14
Chad, Dee D., Freddie, Janet, Jermaine, Joe, Michael, Mick, Millie, Stonewall, Tony, Wanda, the Jacksons/ Jackson Five and the Jackson Sisters.	

King	13
Albert, B.B., Ben E., Carole, Dave, Denis, Evelyn 'Champagne', Jonathan, Nosmo, Paul, Solomon, Tony and The King Brothers.	

Smith	13
Fast Eddie, Hurricane, Jimmy, Keely, Mandy, Mel, Muriel, O.C., Patti, Rex, Richard Jon, Whistling Jack and the Smiths.	

Harris	12
Anita, Emmylou, Jet, Keith, Major, Max, Rahni, Richard, Rolf, Ronnie, Sam and Simon.	

Thomas	12
B.J., Carla, Evelyn, Jamo, Kenny, Lillo, Mickey, Nicky, Rufus, Tasha, Timmy and Thomas and Taylor.	

Miller	10
Frankie, Gary, Glenn, Jody, Leza, Mitch, Ned, Roger, Suzi and Steve.	

Young	10
Faron, Jimmy, John Paul, Karen, Karen, Leon, Neil, Paul, Retta and Tracie.	

DANNY WILLIAMS shares his surname with 22 other chart acts.

The Top Twenty Chart Acts of All Time

Twelve of the top twenty acts, listed according to the number of weeks they have spent on the UK singles chart, featured on the charts of 1992, and really only the Shadows, the Everly Brothers and Jim Reeves can be described as hitmakers of the past. Cliff Richard is closing the gap on Elvis Presley at the very top, having already overtaken the King in terms of the number of hits and the number of top ten hits achieved. Elton John has overtaken the

ELTON JOHN – third in the top twenty chart acts.

Beatles, while David Bowie, Stevie Wonder, Status Quo, Rod Stewart, Paul McCartney and Diana Ross are within 19 weeks of each other all with continuing chart careers.

Michael Jackson and Madonna have made the biggest advances over the past two years, with Madonna in a class of her own in terms of the percentage of top ten hits. Only one of her UK releases (*Lucky Star*) has missed the top ten, giving her a 96.6% success rate, ahead even of the Beatles.

There is no completely satisfactory way of ranking chart careers, and this table which gives precedence to the number of weeks spent on the chart has attracted criticism, especially from Abba and Police fans. However, we feel that longevity is a major achievement in popular music, and the feature of Status Quo's career, for example, which puts them apart from other bands is that they just keep on going.

FRANK SINATRA
If you don't want to put Frank Sinatra on a higher pedestal than the Bee Gees, you can always refer to the Most Number One Hits table.

Act/Country	Chart Span	Wks	Hits	Top 10 Hits	No. 1s	Ave Wks/Hit	% of Top 10 Hits
Elvis Presley USA	56–92	1145	109	55	17	10.5	50.5%
Cliff Richard UK	58–92	1077	110	62	13	9.8	56.4%
Elton John UK	71–92	464	60	20	3	7.7	33.3%
Beatles UK	62–92	434	29	25	17	15.0	86.2%
Frank Sinatra USA	54–86	428	35	11	3	12.2	31.4%
David Bowie UK	69–92	405	49	22	5	8.3	44.9%
Stevie Wonder USA	66–91	404	49	18	2	8.2	36.7%
Status Quo UK	68–92	394	45	22	1	8.8	48.9%
Rod Stewart UK	71–92	393	44	23	6	8.9	52.3%
Paul McCartney UK	71–91	388	45	24	3	8.6	53.3%
Diana Ross USA	70–92	386	51	17	2	7.6	33.3%
Shadows UK	60–81	359	31	16	5	11.6	51.6%
Michael Jackson USA	72–92	349	38	27	4	9.2	71.1%
Queen UK	74–91	345	41	20	4	8.4	48.8%
Tom Jones UK	65–92	343	32	15	2	10.7	46.9%
Roy Orbison USA	60–92	343	33	12	3	10.4	36.4%
Rolling Stones UK	63–91	340	38	21	8	8.9	55.3%
Everly Brothers USA	57–84	337	29	13	4	11.6	44.8%
Madonna USA	84–92	334	29	28	7	11.5	96.6%
Jim Reeves USA	60–72	322	26	6	1	12.4	23.1%

By category, and again ranking the acts according to the number of weeks they have spent on the singles charts, the top acts are:

1. Male Vocalists

	OVERALL		UK		USA
1.	Elvis Presley	1.	Cliff Richard	1.	Elvis Presley
2.	Cliff Richard	2.	Elton John	2.	Frank Sinatra
3.	Elton John	3.	David Bowie	3.	Stevie Wonder
4.	Frank Sinatra	4.	Rod Stewart	4.	Michael Jackson
5.	David Bowie	5.	Paul McCartney	5.	Roy Orbison

2. Female Vocalists

	OVERALL		UK		USA
1.	Diana Ross	1.	Shirley Bassey	1.	Diana Ross
2.	Madonna	2.	Petula Clark	2.	Madonna
3.	Shirley Bassey	3.	Olivia Newton-John	3.	Donna Summer
4.	Donna Summer	4.	Dusty Springfield	4.	Connie Francis
5.	Petula Clark	5.	Cilla Black	5.	Brenda Lee

3. Groups

	OVERALL		UK		USA
1.	Beatles	1.	Beatles	1.	Everly Brothers
2.	Status Quo	2.	Status Quo	2.	Four Tops
3.	Shadows	3.	Shadows	3.	Supremes
4.	Queen	4.	Queen	4.	Beach Boys
5.	Rolling Stones	5.	Rolling Stones	5.	Jackson 5/Jacksons

4. Instrumentalists

	OVERALL		UK		USA
1.	Shadows	1.	Shadows	1.	Duane Eddy
2.	Duane Eddy	2.	Russ Conway	2.	Herb Alpert
3.	Russ Conway	3.	Acker Bilk	3.	Johnny & the Hurricanes
4.	Acker Bilk	4.	Kenny Ball	4.	Booker T & MGs
5.	Kenny Ball	5.	Winifred Atwell	5.	Sandy Nelson

5. Other Nationalities

1.	Abba	From these charts, it can be seen that America supplies the successful women and Britain the successful groups. After Duane Eddy and Herb Alpert, hitmaking American instrumentalists are few and far between. In climbing so quickly to second place behind Abba among chart heroes from other parts of the world, Kylie Minogue has proved stronger than her critics.
2.	Kylie Minogue	
3.	Boney M	
4.	U2	
5.	Bob Marley	

THE NUMBER ONE HITS

Date disc hit the top	❉ = Christmas Number One Title/Artist/Label	Number of weeks at No. 1

1 9 5 2

(Top Twelve – N.M.E. Chart)

14 Nov	HERE IN MY HEART Al Martino (Capitol) ❉	9

1 9 5 3

16 Jan	YOU BELONG TO ME Jo Stafford (Columbia)	1
23 Jan	COMES A-LONG A-LOVE Kay Starr (Capitol)	1
30 Jan	OUTSIDE OF HEAVEN Eddie Fisher (HMV)	1
6 Feb	DON'T LET THE STARS GET IN YOUR EYES Perry Como (HMV)	5
13 Mar	SHE WEARS RED FEATHERS Guy Mitchell (Columbia)	4
10 Apr	BROKEN WINGS Stargazers (Decca)	1
17 Apr	(HOW MUCH IS) THAT DOGGIE IN THE WINDOW Lita Roza (Decca)	1
24 Apr	I BELIEVE Frankie Laine (Philips)	9
26 Jun	I'M WALKING BEHIND YOU Eddie Fisher (HMV)	1
3 Jul	I BELIEVE Frankie Laine (Philips)	6
14 Aug	MOULIN ROUGE Mantovani (Decca)	1
21 Aug	I BELIEVE Frankie Laine (Philips)	3
11 Sep	LOOK AT THAT GIRL Guy Mitchell (Philips)	6
23 Oct	HEY JOE Frankie Laine (Philips)	2
6 Nov	ANSWER ME David Whitfield (Decca)	1
13 Nov	ANSWER ME Frankie Laine (Philips) ❉	8
	(ANSWER ME by David Whitfield returned to number one for one week to share the top spot with Frankie Laine's version on 11 Dec 1953)	

1 9 5 4

8 Jan	OH MEIN PAPA Eddie Calvert (Columbia)	9
12 Mar	I SEE THE MOON Stargazers (Decca)	5
16 Apr	SECRET LOVE Doris Day (Philips)	1
23 Apr	I SEE THE MOON Stargazers (Decca)	1
30 Apr	SUCH A NIGHT Johnnie Ray (Philips)	1
7 May	SECRET LOVE Doris Day (Philips)	8
2 Jul	CARA MIA David Whitfield with chorus and Mantovani and his orchestra (Decca)	10
10 Sep	LITTLE THINGS MEAN A LOT Kitty Kallen (Brunswick)	1
17 Sep	THREE COINS IN THE FOUNTAIN Frank Sinatra (Capitol)	3

Top Twenty began 1 Oct 1954.

8 Oct	HOLD MY HAND Don Cornell (Vogue)	4

5 Nov	MY SON MY SON Vera Lynn (Decca)	2
19 Nov	HOLD MY HAND Don Cornell (Vogue)	1
26 Nov	THIS OLE HOUSE Rosemary Clooney (Philips)	1
3 Dec	LET'S HAVE ANOTHER PARTY Winifred Atwell (Philips) ❉	5

1 9 5 5

7 Jan	FINGER OF SUSPICION Dickie Valentine (Decca)	1
14 Jan	MAMBO ITALIANO Rosemary Clooney (Philips)	1
21 Jan	FINGER OF SUSPICION Dickie Valentine (Decca)	2
4 Feb	MAMBO ITALIANO Rosemary Clooney (Philips)	2
18 Feb	SOFTLY SOFTLY Ruby Murray (Columbia)	3
11 Mar	GIVE ME YOUR WORD Tennessee Ernie Ford (Capitol)	7
29 Apr	CHERRY PINK AND APPLE BLOSSOM WHITE Perez Prado (HMV)	2
13 May	STRANGER IN PARADISE Tony Bennett (Philips)	2
27 May	CHERRY PINK AND APPLE BLOSSOM WHITE Eddie Calvert (Columbia)	4
24 Jun	UNCHAINED MELODY Jimmy Young (Decca)	3
15 Jul	DREAMBOAT Alma Cogan (HMV)	2
29 Jul	ROSE MARIE Slim Whitman (London)	11
14 Oct	THE MAN FROM LARAMIE Jimmy Young (Decca)	4
11 Nov	HERNANDO'S HIDEAWAY Johnston Brothers (Decca)	2
25 Nov	ROCK AROUND THE CLOCK Bill Haley and his Comets (Brunswick)	3
16 Dec	THE CHRISTMAS ALPHABET Dickie Valentine (Decca) ❉	3

On 30 Dec 1955 the chart was extended to 25 records for one week only.

1 9 5 6

6 Jan	ROCK AROUND THE CLOCK Bill Haley and his Comets (Brunswick)	2
20 Jan	SIXTEEN TONS Tennessee Ernie Ford (Capitol)	4
17 Feb	MEMORIES ARE MADE OF THIS Dean Martin (Capitol)	4
16 Mar	IT'S ALMOST TOMORROW Dreamweavers (Brunswick)	2
30 Mar	ROCK AND ROLL WALTZ Kay Starr (HMV)	1
6 Apr	IT'S ALMOST TOMORROW Dreamweavers (Brunswick)	1

Top Thirty began 13 Apr 1956.

13 Apr	POOR PEOPLE OF PARIS Winifred Atwell (Decca)	3
4 May	NO OTHER LOVE Ronnie Hilton (HMV)	6
15 Jun	I'LL BE HOME Pat Boone (London)	5
20 Jul	WHY DO FOOLS FALL IN LOVE Teenagers featuring Frankie Lymon (Columbia)	3
10 Aug	WHATEVER WILL BE WILL BE Doris Day (Philips)	6
21 Sep	LAY DOWN YOUR ARMS Anne Shelton (Philips)	4
19 Oct	A WOMAN IN LOVE Frankie Laine (Philips)	4
16 Nov	JUST WALKIN' IN THE RAIN Johnnie Ray (Philips) ❉	7

1 9 5 7

4 Jan	SINGING THE BLUES Guy Mitchell (Philips)	1
11 Jan	SINGING THE BLUES Tommy Steele (Decca)	1
18 Jan	SINGING THE BLUES Guy Mitchell (Philips)	1
25 Jan	GARDEN OF EDEN Frankie Vaughan (Philips)	4

(SINGING THE BLUES by Guy Mitchell returned to number one for one week to share the top spot with GARDEN OF EDEN by Frankie Vaughan on 1 Feb 1957)

22 Feb	YOUNG LOVE Tab Hunter (London)	7
12 Apr	CUMBERLAND GAP Lonnie Donegan (Pye Nixa)	5
17 May	ROCK-A-BILLY Guy Mitchell (Philips)	1
24 May	BUTTERFLY Andy Williams (London)	2
7 Jun	YES TONIGHT JOSEPHINE Johnnie Ray (Philips)	3
28 Jun	GAMBLIN' MAN/PUTTING ON THE STYLE Lonnie Donegan (Pye Nixa)	2
12 Jul	ALL SHOOK UP Elvis Presley (HMV)	7
30 Aug	DIANA Paul Anka (Columbia)	9
1 Nov	THAT'LL BE THE DAY Crickets (Vogue-Coral)	3
22 Nov	MARY'S BOY CHILD Harry Belafonte (RCA) ❋	7

1 9 5 8

10 Jan	GREAT BALLS OF FIRE Jerry Lee Lewis (London)	2
24 Jan	JAILHOUSE ROCK Elvis Presley (RCA)	3
14 Feb	THE STORY OF MY LIFE Michael Holliday (Columbia)	2
28 Feb	MAGIC MOMENTS Perry Como (RCA)	8
25 Apr	WHOLE LOTTA WOMAN Marvin Rainwater (MGM)	3
16 May	WHO'S SORRY NOW Connie Francis (MGM)	6
27 Jun	ON THE STREET WHERE YOU LIVE Vic Damone (Philips)	2

(On 4 Jul 1958 ON THE STREET WHERE YOU LIVE by Vic Damone and ALL I HAVE TO DO IS DREAM/CLAUDETTE by the Everly Brothers shared the top spot)

4 Jul	ALL I HAVE TO DO IS DREAM/CLAUDETTE Everly Brothers (London)	7
22 Aug	WHEN Kalin Twins (Brunswick)	5
26 Sep	CAROLINA MOON/STUPID CUPID Connie Francis (MGM)	6
7 Nov	IT'S ALL IN THE GAME Tommy Edwards (MGM)	3
28 Nov	HOOTS MON Lord Rockingham's XI (Decca)	3
19 Dec	IT'S ONLY MAKE BELIEVE Conway Twitty (MGM) ❋	5

1 9 5 9

23 Jan	THE DAY THE RAINS CAME Jane Morgan (London)	1
30 Jan	ONE NIGHT/I GOT STUNG Elvis Presley (RCA)	3
20 Feb	AS I LOVE YOU Shirley Bassey (Philips)	4
20 Mar	SMOKE GETS IN YOUR EYES Platters (Mercury)	1
27 Mar	SIDE SADDLE Russ Conway (Columbia)	4
24 Apr	IT DOESN'T MATTER ANYMORE Buddy Holly (Coral)	3
15 May	A FOOL SUCH AS I/I NEED YOUR LOVE TONIGHT Elvis Presley (RCA)	5
19 Jun	ROULETTE Russ Conway (Columbia)	2
3 Jul	DREAM LOVER Bobby Darin (London)	4
31 Jul	LIVING DOLL Cliff Richard and the Drifters (Columbia)	6
11 Sep	ONLY SIXTEEN Craig Douglas (Top Rank)	4
9 Oct	HERE COMES SUMMER Jerry Keller (London)	1
16 Oct	MACK THE KNIFE Bobby Darin (London)	2

30 Oct	TRAVELLIN' LIGHT Cliff Richard and the Shadows (Columbia)	5
4 Dec	WHAT DO YOU WANT Adam Faith (Parlophone)	3

(On 18 Dec 1959 WHAT DO YOU WANT by Adam Faith and WHAT DO YOU WANT TO MAKE THOSE EYES AT ME FOR by Emile Ford and the Checkmates shared the top spot)

18 Dec	WHAT DO YOU WANT TO MAKE THOSE EYES AT ME FOR Emile Ford and the Checkmates (Pye Nixa) ❋	6

1 9 6 0

29 Jan	STARRY EYED Michael Holliday (Columbia)	1
5 Feb	WHY Anthony Newley (Decca)	4

Record Retailer, now *Music Week*, **began publication of a Top Fifty on 10 Mar 1960. From this point on their charts are used. The final** *New Musical Express* **chart used is that of 26 Feb 1960, as the chart published in** *Record Retailer* **on 10 Mar 1960 was dated 5 Mar and clearly corresponded with the** *NME* **chart of 4 Mar 1960.**

10 Mar	POOR ME Adam Faith (Parlophone)	1
17 Mar	RUNNING BEAR Johnny Preston (Mercury)	2
31 Mar	MY OLD MAN'S A DUSTMAN Lonnie Donegan (Pye)	4
28 Apr	DO YOU MIND Anthony Newley (Decca)	1
5 May	CATHY'S CLOWN Everly Brothers (Warner Brothers)	7
23 Jun	THREE STEPS TO HEAVEN Eddie Cochran (London)	2
7 Jul	GOOD TIMIN' Jimmy Jones (MGM)	3
28 Jul	PLEASE DON'T TEASE Cliff Richard and the Shadows (Columbia)	2
4 Aug	SHAKIN' ALL OVER Johnny Kidd and the Pirates (HMV)	1
11 Aug	PLEASE DON'T TEASE Cliff Richard and the Shadows (Columbia)	5
25 Aug	APACHE Shadows (Columbia)	5
29 Sep	TELL LAURA I LOVE HER Ricky Valance (Columbia)	3
20 Oct	ONLY THE LONELY Roy Orbison (London)	2
3 Nov	IT'S NOW OR NEVER Elvis Presley (RCA)	8
29 Dec	I LOVE YOU Cliff Richard and the Shadows (Columbia) ❋	2

1 9 6 1

12 Jan	POETRY IN MOTION Johnny Tillotson (London)	2
26 Jan	ARE YOU LONESOME TONIGHT Elvis Presley (RCA)	4
23 Feb	SAILOR Petula Clark (Pye)	1
2 Mar	WALK RIGHT BACK/EBONY EYES Everly Brothers (Warner Brothers)	3
23 Mar	WOODEN HEART Elvis Presley (RCA)	6
4 May	BLUE MOON Marcels (Pye International)	2
18 May	ON THE REBOUND Floyd Cramer (RCA)	1
25 May	YOU'RE DRIVING ME CRAZY Temperance Seven (Parlophone)	1
1 Jun	SURRENDER Elvis Presley (RCA)	4
29 Jun	RUNAWAY Del Shannon (London)	3
20 Jul	TEMPTATION Everly Brothers (Warner Brothers)	2
3 Aug	WELL I ASK YOU Eden Kane (Decca)	1
10 Aug	YOU DON'T KNOW Helen Shapiro (Columbia)	3
31 Aug	JOHNNY REMEMBER ME John Leyton (Top Rank)	3
21 Sep	REACH FOR THE STARS/CLIMB EV'RY MOUNTAIN Shirley Bassey (Columbia)	1
28 Sep	JOHNNY REMEMBER ME John Leyton (Top Rank)	1
5 Oct	KON-TIKI Shadows (Columbia)	1
12 Oct	MICHAEL Highwaymen (HMV)	1
19 Oct	WALKIN' BACK TO HAPPINESS Helen Shapiro (Columbia)	3
9 Nov	LITTLE SISTER/HIS LATEST FLAME Elvis Presley (RCA)	4
7 Dec	TOWER OF STRENGTH Frankie Vaughan (Philips)	3
28 Dec	MOON RIVER Danny Williams (HMV) ❋	2

1962

11 Jan	THE YOUNG ONES Cliff Richard and the Shadows (Columbia)	6
22 Feb	ROCK-A-HULA BABY/CAN'T HELP FALLING IN LOVE Elvis Presley (RCA)	4
22 Mar	WONDERFUL LAND Shadows (Columbia)	8
17 May	NUT ROCKER B. Bumble and the Stingers (Top Rank)	1
24 May	GOOD LUCK CHARM Elvis Presley (RCA)	5
28 Jun	COME OUTSIDE Mike Sarne with Wendy Richard (Parlophone)	2
12 Jul	I CAN'T STOP LOVING YOU Ray Charles (HMV)	2
26 Jul	I REMEMBER YOU Frank Ifield (Columbia)	7
13 Sep	SHE'S NOT YOU Elvis Presley (RCA)	3
4 Oct	TELSTAR Tornados (Decca)	5
8 Nov	LOVESICK BLUES Frank Ifield (Columbia)	5
13 Dec	RETURN TO SENDER Elvis Presley (RCA) ✽	3

1963

3 Jan	THE NEXT TIME/BACHELOR BOY Cliff Richard and the Shadows (Columbia) (BACHELOR BOY listed from 10 Jan 63 only)	3
24 Jan	DANCE ON Shadows (Columbia)	1
31 Jan	DIAMONDS Jet Harris and Tony Meehan (Decca)	3
21 Feb	WAYWARD WIND Frank Ifield (Columbia)	3
14 Mar	SUMMER HOLIDAY Cliff Richard and the Shadows (Columbia)	2
28 Mar	FOOT TAPPER Shadows (Columbia)	1
4 Apr	SUMMER HOLIDAY Cliff Richard and the Shadows (Columbia)	1
11 Apr	HOW DO YOU DO IT Gerry and the Pacemakers (Columbia)	3
2 May	FROM ME TO YOU Beatles (Parlophone)	7
20 Jun	I LIKE IT Gerry and the Pacemakers (Columbia)	4
18 Jul	CONFESSIN' Frank Ifield (Columbia)	2
1 Aug	(YOU'RE THE) DEVIL IN DISGUISE Elvis Presley (RCA)	1
8 Aug	SWEETS FOR MY SWEET Searchers (Pye)	2
22 Aug	BAD TO ME Billy J. Kramer and the Dakotas (Parlophone)	3
12 Sep	SHE LOVES YOU Beatles (Parlophone)	4
10 Oct	DO YOU LOVE ME Brian Poole and the Tremeloes (Decca)	3
31 Oct	YOU'LL NEVER WALK ALONE Gerry and the Pacemakers (Columbia)	4
28 Nov	SHE LOVES YOU Beatles (Parlophone)	2
12 Dec	I WANT TO HOLD YOUR HAND Beatles (Parlophone) ✽	5

1964

16 Jan	GLAD ALL OVER Dave Clark Five (Columbia)	2
30 Jan	NEEDLES AND PINS Searchers (Pye)	3
20 Feb	DIANE Bachelors (Decca)	1
27 Feb	ANYONE WHO HAD A HEART Cilla Black (Parlophone)	3
19 Mar	LITTLE CHILDREN Billy J. Kramer and the Dakotas (Parlophone)	2
2 Apr	CAN'T BUY ME LOVE Beatles (Parlophone)	3
23 Apr	WORLD WITHOUT LOVE Peter and Gordon (Columbia)	2
7 May	DON'T THROW YOUR LOVE AWAY Searchers (Pye)	2
21 May	JULIET Four Pennies (Philips)	1
28 May	YOU'RE MY WORLD Cilla Black (Parlophone)	4
25 Jun	IT'S OVER Roy Orbison (London)	2
9 Jul	HOUSE OF THE RISING SUN Animals (Columbia)	1
16 Jul	IT'S ALL OVER NOW Rolling Stones (Decca)	1
23 Jul	A HARD DAY'S NIGHT Beatles (Parlophone)	3
13 Aug	DO WAH DIDDY DIDDY Manfred Mann (HMV)	2

27 Aug	HAVE I THE RIGHT Honeycombs (Pye)	2
10 Sep	YOU REALLY GOT ME Kinks (Pye)	2
24 Sep	I'M INTO SOMETHING GOOD Herman's Hermits (Columbia)	2
8 Oct	OH PRETTY WOMAN Roy Orbison (London)	2
22 Oct	(THERE'S) ALWAYS SOMETHING THERE TO REMIND ME Sandie Shaw (Pye)	3
12 Nov	OH PRETTY WOMAN Roy Orbison (London)	1
19 Nov	BABY LOVE Supremes (Stateside)	2
3 Dec	LITTLE RED ROOSTER Rolling Stones (Decca)	1
10 Dec	I FEEL FINE Beatles (Parlophone) ✽	5

1965

14 Jan	YEH YEH Georgie Fame and the Blue Flames (Columbia)	2
28 Jan	GO NOW Moody Blues (Decca)	1
4 Feb	YOU'VE LOST THAT LOVIN' FEELIN' Righteous Brothers (London)	2
18 Feb	TIRED OF WAITING FOR YOU Kinks (Pye)	1
25 Feb	I'LL NEVER FIND ANOTHER YOU Seekers (Columbia)	2
11 Mar	IT'S NOT UNUSUAL Tom Jones (Decca)	1
18 Mar	THE LAST TIME Rolling Stones (Decca)	3
8 Apr	CONCRETE AND CLAY Unit Four Plus Two (Decca)	1
15 Apr	THE MINUTE YOU'RE GONE Cliff Richard (Columbia)	1
22 Apr	TICKET TO RIDE Beatles (Parlophone)	3
13 May	KING OF THE ROAD Roger Miller (Philips)	1
20 May	WHERE ARE YOU NOW (MY LOVE) Jackie Trent (Pye)	1
27 May	LONG LIVE LOVE Sandie Shaw (Pye)	3
17 Jun	CRYING IN THE CHAPEL Elvis Presley (RCA)	1
24 Jun	I'M ALIVE Hollies (Parlophone)	1
1 Jul	CRYING IN THE CHAPEL Elvis Presley (RCA)	1
8 Jul	I'M ALIVE Hollies (Parlophone)	2
22 Jul	MR. TAMBOURINE MAN Byrds (CBS)	2
5 Aug	HELP! Beatles (Parlophone)	3
26 Aug	I GOT YOU BABE Sonny and Cher (Atlantic)	2
9 Sep	(I CAN'T GET NO) SATISFACTION Rolling Stones (Decca)	2
23 Sep	MAKE IT EASY ON YOURSELF Walker Brothers (Philips)	1
30 Sep	TEARS Ken Dodd (Columbia)	5
4 Nov	GET OFF OF MY CLOUD Rolling Stones (Decca)	3
25 Nov	THE CARNIVAL IS OVER Seekers (Columbia)	3
16 Dec	DAY TRIPPER/WE CAN WORK IT OUT Beatles (Parlophone) ✽	5

1966

20 Jan	KEEP ON RUNNING Spencer Davis Group (Fontana)	1
27 Jan	MICHELLE Overlanders (Pye)	3
17 Feb	THESE BOOTS ARE MADE FOR WALKIN' Nancy Sinatra (Reprise)	4
17 Mar	THE SUN AIN'T GONNA SHINE ANYMORE Walker Brothers (Philips)	4
14 Apr	SOMEBODY HELP ME Spencer Davis Group (Fontana)	2
28 Apr	YOU DON'T HAVE TO SAY YOU LOVE ME Dusty Springfield (Philips)	1
5 May	PRETTY FLAMINGO Manfred Mann (HMV)	3
26 May	PAINT IT, BLACK Rolling Stones (Decca)	1
2 Jun	STRANGERS IN THE NIGHT Frank Sinatra (Reprise)	3
23 Jun	PAPERBACK WRITER Beatles (Parlophone)	2
7 Jul	SUNNY AFTERNOON Kinks (Pye)	2
21 Jul	GET AWAY Georgie Fame and the Blue Flames (Columbia)	1
28 Jul	OUT OF TIME Chris Farlowe and the Thunderbirds (Immediate)	1
4 Aug	WITH A GIRL LIKE YOU Troggs (Fontana)	2
18 Aug	YELLOW SUBMARINE/ELEANOR RIGBY Beatles (Parlophone)	4

15 Sep	ALL OR NOTHING Small Faces (Decca)	1
22 Sep	DISTANT DRUMS Jim Reeves (RCA)	5
27 Oct	REACH OUT I'LL BE THERE Four Tops (Tamla Motown)	3
17 Nov	GOOD VIBRATIONS Beach Boys (Capitol)	2
1 Dec	GREEN GREEN GRASS OF HOME Tom Jones (Decca) ✳	7

1 9 6 7

19 Jan	I'M A BELIEVER Monkees (RCA)	4
16 Feb	THIS IS MY SONG Petula Clark (Pye)	2
2 Mar	RELEASE ME Engelbert Humperdinck (Decca)	6
13 Apr	SOMETHIN' STUPID Nancy Sinatra and Frank Sinatra (Reprise)	2
27 Apr	PUPPET ON A STRING Sandie Shaw (Pye)	3
18 May	SILENCE IS GOLDEN Tremeloes (CBS)	3
8 Jun	A WHITER SHADE OF PALE Procol Harum (Deram)	6
19 Jul	ALL YOU NEED IS LOVE Beatles (Parlophone)	3
9 Aug	SAN FRANCISCO (BE SURE TO WEAR SOME FLOWERS IN YOUR HAIR) Scott McKenzie (CBS)	4
6 Sep	THE LAST WALTZ Engelbert Humperdinck (Decca)	5
11 Oct	MASSACHUSETTS Bee Gees (Polydor)	4
8 Nov	BABY NOW THAT I'VE FOUND YOU Foundations (Pye)	2
22 Nov	LET THE HEARTACHES BEGIN Long John Baldry (Pye)	2
6 Dec	HELLO GOODBYE Beatles (Parlophone) ✳	7

1 9 6 8

24 Jan	THE BALLAD OF BONNIE AND CLYDE Georgie Fame (CBS)	1
31 Jan	EVERLASTING LOVE Love Affair (CBS)	2
14 Feb	MIGHTY QUINN Manfred Mann (Fontana)	2
28 Feb	CINDERELLA ROCKEFELLA Esther and Abi Ofarim (Philips)	3
20 Mar	THE LEGEND OF XANADU Dave Dee, Dozy, Beaky, Mick and Tich (Fontana)	1
27 Mar	LADY MADONNA Beatles (Parlophone)	2
10 Apr	CONGRATULATIONS Cliff Richard (Columbia)	2
24 Apr	WHAT A WONDERFUL WORLD/CABARET Louis Armstrong (HMV)	4
22 May	YOUNG GIRL Union Gap featuring Gary Puckett (CBS)	4
19 Jun	JUMPIN' JACK FLASH Rolling Stones (Decca)	2
3 Jul	BABY COME BACK Equals (President)	3
24 Jul	I PRETEND Des O'Connor (Columbia)	1
31 Jul	MONY MONY Tommy James and the Shondells (Major Minor)	2
14 Aug	FIRE Crazy World of Arthur Brown (Track)	1
21 Aug	MONY MONY Tommy James and the Shondells (Major Minor)	1
28 Aug	DO IT AGAIN Beach Boys (Capitol)	1
4 Sep	I'VE GOTTA GET A MESSAGE TO YOU Bee Gees (Polydor)	1
11 Sep	HEY JUDE Beatles (Apple)	2
25 Sep	THOSE WERE THE DAYS Mary Hopkin (Apple)	6
6 Nov	WITH A LITTLE HELP FROM MY FRIENDS Joe Cocker (Regal-Zonophone)	1
13 Nov	THE GOOD THE BAD AND THE UGLY Hugo Montenegro and his Orchestra and Chorus (RCA)	4
11 Dec	LILY THE PINK Scaffold (Parlophone) ✳	3

1 9 6 9

1 Jan	OB-LA-DI OB-LA-DA Marmalade (CBS)	1
8 Jan	LILY THE PINK Scaffold (Parlophone)	1
15 Jan	OB-LA-DI OB-LA-DA Marmalade (CBS)	2
29 Jan	ALBATROSS Fleetwood Mac (Blue Horizon)	1
5 Feb	BLACKBERRY WAY Move (Regal-Zonophone)	1
12 Feb	(IF PARADISE IS) HALF AS NICE Amen Corner (Immediate)	2
26 Feb	WHERE DO YOU GO TO MY LOVE Peter Sarstedt (United Artists)	4
26 Mar	I HEARD IT THROUGH THE GRAPEVINE Marvin Gaye (Tamla Motown)	3
16 Apr	THE ISRAELITES Desmond Dekker and the Aces (Pyramid)	1
23 Apr	GET BACK Beatles (Apple)	6
4 Jun	DIZZY Tommy Roe (Stateside)	1
11 Jun	THE BALLAD OF JOHN AND YOKO Beatles (Apple)	3
2 Jul	SOMETHING IN THE AIR Thunderclap Newman (Track)	3
23 Jul	HONKY TONK WOMEN Rolling Stones (Decca)	5
30 Aug	IN THE YEAR 2525 (EXORDIUM AND TERMINUS) Zager and Evans (RCA)	3
20 Sep	BAD MOON RISING Creedence Clearwater Revival (Liberty)	3
11 Oct	JE T'AIME...MOI NON PLUS Jane Birkin and Serge Gainsbourg (Major Minor)	1
18 Oct	I'LL NEVER FALL IN LOVE AGAIN Bobbie Gentry (Capitol)	1
25 Oct	SUGAR SUGAR Archies (RCA)	8
20 Dec	TWO LITTLE BOYS Rolf Harris (Columbia) ✳	6

1 9 7 0

31 Jan	LOVE GROWS (WHERE MY ROSEMARY GOES) Edison Lighthouse (Bell)	5
7 Mar	WAND'RIN' STAR Lee Marvin (Paramount)	3
28 Mar	BRIDGE OVER TROUBLED WATER Simon and Garfunkel (CBS)	3
18 Apr	ALL KINDS OF EVERYTHING Dana (Rex)	2
2 May	SPIRIT IN THE SKY Norman Greenbaum (Reprise)	2
16 May	BACK HOME England World Cup Squad (Pye)	3
6 Jun	YELLOW RIVER Christie (CBS)	1
13 Jun	IN THE SUMMER TIME Mungo Jerry (Dawn)	7
1 Aug	THE WONDER OF YOU Elvis Presley (RCA)	6
12 Sep	TEARS OF A CLOWN Smokey Robinson and the Miracles (Tamla Motown)	1
19 Sep	BAND OF GOLD Freda Payne (Invictus)	6
31 Oct	WOODSTOCK Matthews' Southern Comfort (Uni)	3
21 Nov	VOODOO CHILE Jimi Hendrix Experience (Track)	1
28 Nov	I HEAR YOU KNOCKIN' Dave Edmunds (MAM) ✳	6

1 9 7 1

9 Jan	GRANDAD Clive Dunn (Columbia)	3
30 Jan	MY SWEET LORD George Harrison (Apple)	5
6 Mar	BABY JUMP Mungo Jerry (Dawn)	2
20 Mar	HOT LOVE T. Rex (Fly)	6
1 May	DOUBLE BARREL Dave and Ansil Collins (Technique)	2
15 May	KNOCK THREE TIMES Dawn (Bell)	5
19 Jun	CHIRPY CHIRPY CHEEP CHEEP Middle Of The Road (RCA)	5
24 Jul	GET IT ON T. Rex (Fly)	4
21 Aug	I'M STILL WAITING Diana Ross (Tamla Motown)	4
18 Sep	HEY GIRL DON'T BOTHER ME Tams (Probe)	3
9 Oct	MAGGIE MAY Rod Stewart (Mercury)	5
13 Nov	COZ I LUV YOU Slade (Polydor)	4
11 Dec	ERNIE (THE FASTEST MILKMAN IN THE WEST) Benny Hill (Columbia) ✳	4

1 9 7 2

Date	Title	Weeks
8 Jan	I'D LIKE TO TEACH THE WORLD TO SING (IN PERFECT HARMONY) New Seekers (Polydor)	4
5 Feb	TELEGRAM SAM T. Rex (T. Rex)	2
19 Feb	SON OF MY FATHER Chicory Tip (CBS)	3
11 Mar	WITHOUT YOU Nilsson (RCA)	5
15 Apr	AMAZING GRACE Pipes and Drums and Military Band of the Royal Scots Dragoon Guards (RCA)	5
20 May	METAL GURU T. Rex (EMI)	4
17 Jun	VINCENT Don McLean (United Artists)	2
1 Jul	TAKE ME BAK 'OME Slade (Polydor)	1
8 Jul	PUPPY LOVE Donny Osmond (MGM)	5
12 Aug	SCHOOL'S OUT Alice Cooper (Warner Brothers)	3
2 Sep	YOU WEAR IT WELL Rod Stewart (Mercury)	1
9 Sep	MAMA WEER ALL CRAZEE NOW Slade (Polydor)	3
30 Sep	HOW CAN I BE SURE David Cassidy (Bell)	2
14 Oct	MOULDY OLD DOUGH Lieutenant Pigeon (Decca)	4
11 Nov	CLAIR Gilbert O'Sullivan (MAM)	2
25 Nov	MY DING-A-LING Chuck Berry (Chess)	4
23 Dec	LONG HAIRED LOVER FROM LIVERPOOL Little Jimmy Osmond (MGM) ❋	5

1 9 7 3

Date	Title	Weeks
27 Jan	BLOCKBUSTER Sweet (RCA)	5
3 Mar	CUM ON FEEL THE NOIZE Slade (Polydor)	4
31 Mar	THE TWELFTH OF NEVER Donny Osmond (MGM)	1
7 Apr	GET DOWN Gilbert O'Sullivan (MAM)	2
21 Apr	TIE A YELLOW RIBBON ROUND THE OLD OAK TREE Dawn featuring Tony Orlando (Bell)	4
19 May	SEE MY BABY JIVE Wizzard (Harvest)	4
16 Jun	CAN THE CAN Suzi Quatro (RAK)	1
23 Jun	RUBBER BULLETS 10 C.C. (UK)	1
30 Jun	SKWEEZE ME PLEEZE ME Slade (Polydor)	3
21 Jul	WELCOME HOME Peters and Lee (Philips)	1
28 Jul	I'M THE LEADER OF THE GANG (I AM) Gary Glitter (Bell)	4
25 Aug	YOUNG LOVE Donny Osmond (MGM)	4
22 Sep	ANGEL FINGERS Wizzard (Harvest)	1
29 Sep	EYE LEVEL Simon Park Orchestra (Columbia)	4
27 Oct	DAYDREAMER/THE PUPPY SONG David Cassidy (Bell)	3
17 Nov	I LOVE YOU LOVE ME LOVE Gary Glitter (Bell)	4
15 Dec	MERRY XMAS EVERYBODY Slade (Polydor) ❋	5

1 9 7 4

Date	Title	Weeks
19 Jan	YOU WON'T FIND ANOTHER FOOL LIKE ME New Seekers (Polydor)	1
26 Jan	TIGER FEET Mud (RAK)	4
23 Feb	DEVIL GATE DRIVE Suzi Quatro (RAK)	2
9 Mar	JEALOUS MIND Alvin Stardust (Magnet)	1
16 Mar	BILLY DON'T BE A HERO Paper Lace (Bus Stop)	3
6 Apr	SEASONS IN THE SUN Terry Jacks (Bell)	4
4 May	WATERLOO Abba (Epic)	2
18 May	SUGAR BABY LOVE Rubettes (Polydor)	4
15 Jun	THE STREAK Ray Stevens (Janus)	1

Date	Title	Weeks
22 Jun	ALWAYS YOURS Gary Glitter (Bell)	1
29 Jun	SHE Charles Aznavour (Barclay)	4
27 Jul	ROCK YOUR BABY George McCrae (Jayboy)	3
17 Aug	WHEN WILL I SEE YOU AGAIN Three Degrees (Philadelphia International)	2
31 Aug	LOVE ME FOR A REASON Osmonds (MGM)	3
21 Sep	KUNG FU FIGHTING Carl Douglas (Pye)	3
12 Oct	ANNIE'S SONG John Denver (RCA)	1
19 Oct	SAD SWEET DREAMER Sweet Sensation (Pye)	1
26 Oct	EVERYTHING I OWN Ken Boothe (Trojan)	3
16 Nov	GONNA MAKE YOU A STAR David Essex (CBS)	3
7 Dec	YOU'RE THE FIRST THE LAST MY EVERYTHING Barry White (20th Century)	2
21 Dec	LONELY THIS CHRISTMAS Mud (RAK) ❋	4

1 9 7 5

Date	Title	Weeks
18 Jan	DOWN DOWN Status Quo (Vertigo)	1
25 Jan	MS. GRACE Tymes (RCA)	1
1 Feb	JANUARY Pilot (EMI)	3
22 Feb	MAKE ME SMILE (COME UP AND SEE ME) Steve Harley and Cockney Rebel (EMI)	2
8 Mar	IF Telly Savalas (MCA)	2
22 Mar	BYE BYE BABY Bay City Rollers (Bell)	6
3 May	OH BOY Mud (RAK)	2
17 May	STAND BY YOUR MAN Tammy Wynette (Epic)	3
7 Jun	WHISPERING GRASS Windsor Davies and Don Estelle (EMI)	3
28 Jun	I'M NOT IN LOVE 10 C.C. (Mercury)	2
12 Jul	TEARS ON MY PILLOW Johnny Nash (CBS)	1
19 Jul	GIVE A LITTLE LOVE Bay City Rollers (Bell)	3
9 Aug	BARBADOS Typically Tropical (Gull)	1
16 Aug	I CAN'T GIVE YOU ANYTHING (BUT MY LOVE) Stylistics (Avco)	3
6 Sep	SAILING Rod Stewart (Warner Brothers)	4
4 Oct	HOLD ME CLOSE David Essex (CBS)	3
25 Oct	I ONLY HAVE EYES FOR YOU Art Garfunkel (CBS)	2
8 Nov	SPACE ODDITY David Bowie (RCA)	2
22 Nov	D.I.V.O.R.C.E. Billy Connolly (Polydor)	1
29 Nov	BOHEMIAN RHAPSODY Queen (EMI) ❋	9

1 9 7 6

Date	Title	Weeks
31 Jan	MAMMA MIA Abba (Epic)	2
14 Feb	FOREVER AND EVER Slik (Bell)	1
21 Feb	DECEMBER '63 (OH WHAT A NIGHT) Four Seasons (Warner Brothers)	2
6 Mar	I LOVE TO LOVE (BUT MY BABY LOVES TO DANCE) Tina Charles (CBS)	3
27 Mar	SAVE YOUR KISSES FOR ME Brotherhood Of Man (Pye)	6
8 May	FERNANDO Abba (Epic)	4
5 Jun	NO CHARGE J.J. Barrie (Power Exchange)	1
12 Jun	COMBINE HARVESTER (BRAND NEW KEY) Wurzels (EMI)	2
26 Jun	YOU TO ME ARE EVERYTHING Real Thing (Pye International)	3
17 Jul	THE ROUSSOS PHENOMENON (EP) Demis Roussos (Philips)	1
24 Jul	DON'T GO BREAKING MY HEART Elton John and Kiki Dee (Rocket)	6
4 Sep	DANCING QUEEN Abba (Epic)	6
16 Oct	MISSISSIPPI Pussycat (Sonet)	1
13 Nov	IF YOU LEAVE ME NOW Chicago (CBS)	3

4 Dec	UNDER THE MOON OF LOVE Showaddywaddy (Bell)	3
25 Dec	WHEN A CHILD IS BORN (SOLEADO) Johnny Mathis (CBS) ✽	3

1 9 7 7

15 Jan	DON'T GIVE UP ON US David Soul (Private Stock)	4
12 Feb	DON'T CRY FOR ME ARGENTINA Julie Covington (MCA)	1
19 Feb	WHEN I NEED YOU Leo Sayer (Chrysalis)	3
12 Mar	CHANSON D'AMOUR Manhattan Transfer (Atlantic)	3
2 Apr	KNOWING ME KNOWING YOU Abba (Epic)	5
7 May	FREE Deniece Williams (CBS)	2
21 May	I DON'T WANT TO TALK ABOUT IT/FIRST CUT IS THE DEEPEST Rod Stewart (Riva)	4
18 Jun	LUCILLE Kenny Rogers (United Artists)	1
25 Jun	SHOW YOU THE WAY TO GO Jacksons (Epic)	1
2 Jul	SO YOU WIN AGAIN Hot Chocolate (RAK)	3
23 Jul	I FEEL LOVE Donna Summer (GTO)	4
20 Aug	ANGELO Brotherhood Of Man (Pye)	1
27 Aug	FLOAT ON Floaters (ABC)	1
3 Sep	WAY DOWN Elvis Presley (RCA)	5
8 Oct	SILVER LADY David Soul (Private Stock)	3
29 Oct	YES SIR I CAN BOOGIE Baccara (RCA)	1
5 Nov	NAME OF THE GAME Abba (Epic)	4
3 Dec	MULL OF KINTYRE/GIRLS' SCHOOL Wings (Capitol) ✽	9

1 9 7 8

4 Feb	UP TOWN TOP RANKING Althia and Donna (Lightning)	1
11 Feb	FIGARO Brotherhood Of Man (Pye)	1
18 Feb	TAKE A CHANCE ON ME Abba (Epic)	3
11 Mar	WUTHERING HEIGHTS Kate Bush (EMI)	4
8 Apr	MATCHSTALK MEN AND MATCHSTALK CATS AND DOGS Brian and Michael (Pye)	3
29 Apr	NIGHT FEVER Bee Gees (RSO)	2

Top 75 began 6 May 1978.

13 May	RIVERS OF BABYLON Boney M (Atlantic/Hansa)	5
17 Jun	YOU'RE THE ONE THAT I WANT John Travolta and Olivia Newton-John (RSO)	9
19 Aug	THREE TIMES A LADY Commodores (Motown)	5
23 Sep	DREADLOCK HOLIDAY 10 C.C. (Mercury)	1
30 Sep	SUMMER NIGHTS John Travolta and Olivia Newton-John (RSO)	7
18 Nov	RAT TRAP Boomtown Rats (Ensign)	2
2 Dec	DA YA THINK I'M SEXY Rod Stewart (Riva)	1
9 Dec	MARY'S BOY CHILD – OH MY LORD Boney M (Atlantic/Hansa) ✽	4

1 9 7 9

6 Jan	Y.M.C.A. Village People (Mercury)	3
27 Jan	HIT ME WITH YOUR RHYTHM STICK Ian and the Blockheads (Stiff)	1
3 Feb	HEART OF GLASS Blondie (Chrysalis)	4
3 Mar	TRAGEDY Bee Gees (RSO)	2
17 Mar	I WILL SURVIVE Gloria Gaynor (Polydor)	4
14 Apr	BRIGHT EYES Art Garfunkel (CBS)	6
26 May	SUNDAY GIRL Blondie (Chrysalis)	3

16 Jun	RING MY BELL Anita Ward (TK)	2
30 Jun	ARE 'FRIENDS' ELECTRIC Tubeway Army (Beggars Banquet)	4
28 Jul	I DON'T LIKE MONDAYS Boomtown Rats (Ensign)	4
25 Aug	WE DON'T TALK ANYMORE Cliff Richard (EMI)	4
22 Sep	CARS Gary Numan (Beggars Banquet)	1
29 Sep	MESSAGE IN A BOTTLE Police (A&M)	3
20 Oct	VIDEO KILLED THE RADIO STAR Buggles (Island)	1
27 Oct	ONE DAY AT A TIME Lena Martell (Pye)	3
17 Nov	WHEN YOU'RE IN LOVE WITH A BEAUTIFUL WOMAN Dr. Hook (Capitol)	3
8 Dec	WALKING ON THE MOON Police (A&M)	1
15 Dec	ANOTHER BRICK IN THE WALL (PART II) Pink Floyd (Harvest) ✽	5

1 9 8 0

19 Jan	BRASS IN POCKET Pretenders (Real)	2
2 Feb	THE SPECIAL A.K.A. LIVE! (EP) Specials (2 Tone)	2
16 Feb	COWARD OF THE COUNTY Kenny Rogers (United Artists)	2
1 Mar	ATOMIC (Blondie (Chrysalis)	2
15 Mar	TOGETHER WE ARE BEAUTIFUL Fern Kinney (WEA)	1
22 Mar	GOING UNDERGROUND/DREAMS OF CHILDREN Jam (Polydor)	3
12 Apr	WORKING MY WAY BACK TO YOU Detroit Spinners (Atlantic)	2
26 Apr	CALL ME Blondie (Chrysalis)	1
3 May	GENO Dexy's Midnight Runners (Parlophone)	2
17 May	WHAT'S ANOTHER YEAR Johnny Logan (Epic)	2
31 May	THEME FROM M*A*S*H (SUICIDE IS PAINLESS) Mash (CBS)	3
21 Jun	CRYING Don McLean (EMI)	3
12 Jul	XANADU Olivia Newton-John and Electric Light Orchestra (Jet)	2
26 Jul	USE IT UP AND WEAR IT OUT Odyssey (RCA)	2
9 Aug	THE WINNER TAKES IT ALL Abba (Epic)	2
23 Aug	ASHES TO ASHES David Bowie (RCA)	2
6 Sep	START Jam (Polydor)	1
13 Sep	FEELS LIKE I'M IN LOVE Kelly Marie (Calibre)	2
27 Sep	DON'T STAND SO CLOSE TO ME Police (A&M)	4
25 Oct	WOMAN IN LOVE Barbra Streisand (CBS)	3
15 Nov	THE TIDE IS HIGH Blondie (Chrysalis)	2
29 Nov	SUPER TROUPER Abba (Epic)	3
20 Dec	(JUST LIKE) STARTING OVER John Lennon (Geffen)	1
27 Dec	THERE'S NO ONE QUITE LIKE GRANDMA St Winifred's School Choir (MFP) ✽	2

1 9 8 1

10 Jan	IMAGINE John Lennon (Parlophone)	4
7 Feb	WOMAN John Lennon (Geffen)	2
21 Feb	SHADDAP YOU FACE Joe Dolce Music Theatre (Epic)	3
14 Mar	JEALOUS GUY Roxy Music (EG)	2
28 Mar	THIS OLE HOUSE Shakin' Stevens (Epic)	3
18 Apr	MAKING YOUR MIND UP Bucks Fizz (RCA)	3
9 May	STAND AND DELIVER Adam and the Ants (CBS)	5
13 Jun	BEING WITH YOU Smokey Robinson (Motown)	2
27 Jun	ONE DAY IN YOUR LIFE Michael Jackson (Motown)	2
11 Jul	GHOST TOWN Specials (2 Tone)	3
1 Aug	GREEN DOOR Shakin' Stevens (Epic)	4
29 Aug	JAPANESE BOY Aneka (Hansa/Ariola)	1
5 Sep	TAINTED LOVE Soft Cell (Some Bizzare)	2
19 Sep	PRINCE CHARMING Adam and the Ants (CBS)	4
17 Oct	IT'S MY PARTY Dave Stewart with Barbara Gaskin (Broken)	4

Date	Title	Weeks
14 Nov	EVERY LITTLE THING SHE DOES IS MAGIC Police (A&M)	1
21 Nov	UNDER PRESSURE Queen and David Bowie (EMI)	2
5 Dec	BEGIN THE BEGUINE (VOLVER A EMPEZAR) Julio Iglesias (CBS)	1
12 Dec	DON'T YOU WANT ME Human League (Virgin) ✳	5

1 9 8 2

Date	Title	Weeks
16 Jan	THE LAND OF MAKE BELIEVE Bucks Fizz (RCA)	2
30 Jan	OH JULIE Shakin' Stevens (Epic)	1
6 Feb	THE MODEL/COMPUTER LOVE Kraftwerk (EMI)	1
13 Feb	A TOWN CALLED MALICE/PRECIOUS Jam (Polydor)	3
6 Mar	THE LION SLEEPS TONIGHT Tight Fit (Jive)	3
27 Mar	SEVEN TEARS Goombay Dance Band (Epic)	3
17 Apr	MY CAMERA NEVER LIES Bucks Fizz (RCA)	1
24 Apr	EBONY AND IVORY	
	Paul McCartney with Stevie Wonder (Parlophone)	3
15 May	A LITTLE PEACE Nicole (CBS)	2
29 May	HOUSE OF FUN Madness (Stiff)	2
12 Jun	GOODY TWO SHOES Adam Ant (CBS)	2
26 Jun	I'VE NEVER BEEN TO ME Charlene (Motown)	1
3 Jul	HAPPY TALK Captain Sensible (A&M)	2
17 Jul	FAME Irene Cara (RSO)	3
7 Aug	COME ON EILEEN	
	Dexy's Midnight Runners and the Emerald Express (Mercury)	4
4 Sep	EYE OF THE TIGER Survivor (Scotti Brothers)	4
2 Oct	PASS THE DUTCHIE Musical Youth (MCA)	3
23 Oct	DO YOU REALLY WANT TO HURT ME Culture Club (Virgin)	3
13 Nov	I DON'T WANNA DANCE Eddy Grant (Ice)	3
4 Dec	BEAT SURRENDER Jam (Polydor)	2
18 Dec	SAVE YOUR LOVE Renee and Renato (Hollywood) ✳	4

1 9 8 3

Date	Title	Weeks
15 Jan	YOU CAN'T HURRY LOVE Phil Collins (Virgin)	2
29 Jan	DOWN UNDER Men At Work (Epic)	3
19 Feb	TOO SHY Kajagoogoo (EMI)	2
5 Mar	BILLIE JEAN Michael Jackson (Epic)	1
12 Mar	TOTAL ECLIPSE OF THE HEART Bonnie Tyler (CBS)	2
26 Mar	IS THERE SOMETHING I SHOULD KNOW Duran Duran (EMI)	2
9 Apr	LET'S DANCE David Bowie (EMI America)	3
30 Apr	TRUE Spandau Ballet (Reformation)	4
28 May	CANDY GIRL New Edition (London)	1
4 Jun	EVERY BREATH YOU TAKE Police (A&M)	4
2 Jul	BABY JANE Rod Stewart (Warner Bros)	3
23 Jul	WHEREVER I LAY MY HAT (THAT'S MY HOME)	
	Paul Young (CBS)	3
13 Aug	GIVE IT UP KC And The Sunshine Band (Epic)	3
3 Sep	RED RED WINE UB40 (DEP International)	3
24 Sep	KARMA CHAMELEON Culture Club (Virgin)	6
5 Nov	UPTOWN GIRL Billy Joel (CBS)	5
10 Dec	ONLY YOU Flying Pickets (10) ✳	5

1 9 8 4

Date	Title	Weeks
14 Jan	PIPES OF PEACE Paul McCartney (Parlophone)	2
28 Jan	RELAX Frankie Goes To Hollywood (ZTT)	5
3 Mar	99 RED BALLOONS Nena (Epic)	3

Date	Title	Weeks
24 Mar	HELLO Lionel Richie (Motown)	6
5 May	THE REFLEX Duran Duran (EMI)	4
2 Jun	WAKE ME UP BEFORE YOU GO GO Wham! (Epic)	2
16 Jun	TWO TRIBES Frankie Goes To Hollywood (ZTT)	9
18 Aug	CARELESS WHISPER George Michael (Epic)	3
8 Sep	I JUST CALLED TO SAY I LOVE YOU Stevie Wonder (Motown)	6
20 Oct	FREEDOM Wham! (Epic)	3
10 Nov	I FEEL FOR YOU Chaka Khan (Warner Bros)	3
1 Dec	I SHOULD HAVE KNOWN BETTER Jim Diamond (A&M)	1
8 Dec	THE POWER OF LOVE Frankie Goes To Hollywood (ZTT)	1
15 Dec	DO THEY KNOW IT'S CHRISTMAS Band Aid (Mercury) ✳	5

1 9 8 5

Date	Title	Weeks
19 Jan	I WANT TO KNOW WHAT LOVE IS Foreigner (Atlantic)	3
9 Feb	I KNOW HIM SO WELL Elaine Paige and Barbara Dickson (RCA)	4
9 Mar	YOU SPIN ME ROUND (LIKE A RECORD) Dead Or Alive (Epic)	2
23 Mar	EASY LOVER Philip Bailey (duet with Phil Collins) (CBS)	4
20 Apr	WE ARE THE WORLD USA For Africa (CBS)	2
4 May	MOVE CLOSER Phyllis Nelson (Carrere)	1
11 May	19 Paul Hardcastle (Chrysalis)	5
15 Jun	YOU'LL NEVER WALK ALONE The Crowd (Spartan)	2
29 Jun	FRANKIE Sister Sledge (Atlantic)	4
27 Jul	THERE MUST BE AN ANGEL (PLAYING WITH MY HEART)	
	Eurythmics (RCA)	1
3 Aug	INTO THE GROOVE Madonna (Sire)	4
31 Aug	I GOT YOU BABE	
	UB40, guest vocals Chrissie Hynde (DEP International)	1
7 Sep	DANCING IN THE STREET	
	David Bowie and Mick Jagger (EMI America)	4
5 Oct	IF I WAS Midge Ure (Chrysalis)	1
12 Oct	THE POWER OF LOVE Jennifer Rush (CBS)	5
16 Nov	A GOOD HEART Feargal Sharkey (Virgin)	2
30 Nov	I'M YOUR MAN Wham! (Epic)	2
14 Dec	SAVING ALL MY LOVE FOR YOU Whitney Houston (Arista)	2
28 Dec	MERRY CHRISTMAS EVERYONE Shakin' Stevens (Epic) ✳	2

1 9 8 6

Date	Title	Weeks
11 Jan	WEST END GIRLS Pet Shop Boys (Parlophone)	2
25 Jan	THE SUN ALWAYS SHINES ON TV A-ha (Warner Bros)	2
8 Feb	WHEN THE GOING GETS TOUGH, THE TOUGH GET GOING	
	Billy Ocean (Jive)	4
8 Mar	CHAIN REACTION Diana Ross (Capitol)	3
29 Mar	LIVING DOLL Cliff Richard and The Young Ones (WEA)	3
19 Apr	A DIFFERENT CORNER George Michael (Epic)	3
10 May	ROCK ME AMADEUS Falco (A&M)	1
17 May	THE CHICKEN SONG Spitting Image (Virgin)	3
7 Jun	SPIRIT IN THE SKY Doctor and The Medics (IRS)	3
28 Jun	THE EDGE OF HEAVEN Wham! (Epic)	2
12 Jul	PAPA DON'T PREACH Madonna (Sire)	3
2 Aug	LADY IN RED Chris de Burgh (A&M)	3
23 Aug	I WANT TO WAKE UP WITH YOU Boris Gardiner (Revue)	3
13 Sep	DON'T LEAVE ME THIS WAY Communards (London)	4
11 Oct	TRUE BLUE Madonna (Sire)	1
18 Oct	EVERY LOSER WINS Nick Berry (BBC)	3
8 Nov	TAKE MY BREATH AWAY Berlin (CBS)	4
6 Dec	THE FINAL COUNTDOWN Europe (Epic)	2
20 Dec	CARAVAN OF LOVE Housemartins (Go! Discs)	1

27 Dec REET PETITE Jackie Wilson (SMP) ❄ 4

1 9 8 7

24 Jan JACK YOUR BODY Steve 'Silk' Hurley (DJ International) 2
7 Feb I KNEW YOU WERE WAITING (FOR ME)
       Aretha Franklin and George Michael (Epic) 2
21 Feb STAND BY ME Ben E. King (Atlantic) 3
14 Mar EVERYTHING I OWN Boy George (Virgin) 2
28 Mar RESPECTABLE Mel and Kim (Supreme) 1
4 Mar LET IT BE Ferry Aid (Sun) 3
25 Apr LA ISLA BONITA Madonna (Sire) 2
9 May NOTHING'S GONNA STOP US NOW Starship (Grunt) 4
6 Jun I WANNA DANCE WITH SOMEBODY (WHO LOVES ME)
       Whitney Houston (Arista) 2
20 Jun STAR TREKKIN' Firm (Bark) 2
4 Jul IT'S A SIN Pet Shop Boys (Parlophone) 3
25 Jul WHO'S THAT GIRL Madonna (Sire) 1
1 Aug LA BAMBA Los Lobos (Slash) 2
15 Aug I JUST CAN'T STOP LOVING YOU
       Michael Jackson with Siedah Garrett (Epic) 2
29 Aug NEVER GONNA GIVE YOU UP Rick Astley (RCA) 5
3 Oct PUMP UP THE VOLUME ANITINA (THE FIRST TIME I SEE
       SHE DANCE) M/A/R/R/S (4AD) 2
17 Oct YOU WIN AGAIN Bee Gees (Warner Bros) 4
14 Nov CHINA IN YOUR HAND T'Pau (Siren) 5
19 Dec ALWAYS ON MY MIND Pet Shop Boys (Parlophone) ❄ 4

1 9 8 8

16 Jan HEAVEN IS A PLACE ON EARTH Belinda Carlisle (Virgin) 2
30 Jan I THINK WE'RE ALONE NOW Tiffany (MCA) 3
20 Feb I SHOULD BE SO LUCKY Kylie Minogue (PWL) 5
26 Mar DON'T TURN AROUND Aswad (Mango) 2
9 Apr HEART Pet Shop Boys (Parlophone) 3
30 Apr THEME FROM S EXPRESS S Express (Rhythm King) 2
14 May PERFECT Fairground Attraction (RCA) 1
21 May WITH A LITTLE HELP FROM MY FRIENDS/SHE'S LEAVING
       HOME Wet Wet Wet/Billy Bragg and Cara Tivey (Childline) 4
18 Jun DOCTORIN' THE TARDIS Timelords (KLF) 1
25 Jun I OWE YOU NOTHING Bros (CBS) 2
9 Jul NOTHING'S GONNA CHANGE MY LOVE FOR YOU
       Glenn Medeiros (London) 4
6 Aug THE ONLY WAY IS UP Yazz and the Plastic Population (Big Life) 5
10 Sep A GROOVY KIND OF LOVE Phil Collins (Virgin) 2
24 Sep HE AIN'T HEAVY, HE'S MY BROTHER Hollies (EMI) 2
8 Oct DESIRE U2 (Island) 1
15 Oct ONE MOMENT IN TIME Whitney Houston (Arista) 2
29 Oct ORINOCO FLOW Enya (WEA) 3
19 Nov FIRST TIME Robin Beck (Mercury) 3
10 Dec MISTLETOE AND WINE Cliff Richard (EMI) ❄ 4

1 9 8 9

7 Jan ESPECIALLY FOR YOU Kylie Minogue and Jason Donovan (PWL) 3
28 Jan SOMETHING'S GOTTEN HOLD OF MY HEART
       Marc Almond with Gene Pitney (Parlophone) 4
25 Feb BELFAST CHILD Simple Minds (Virgin) 2

11 Mar TOO MANY BROKEN HEARTS Jason Donovan (PWL) 2
25 Mar LIKE A PRAYER Madonna (Sire) 3
15 Apr ETERNAL FLAME Bangles (CBS) 4
13 May HAND ON YOUR HEART Kylie Minogue (PWL) 1
20 May FERRY CROSS THE MERSEY
       Christians, Holly Johnson, Paul McCartney, Gerry Marsden and Stock
       Aitken Waterman (PWL) 3
10 Jun SEALED WITH A KISS Jason Donovan (PWL) 2
24 Jun BACK TO LIFE (HOWEVER DO YOU WANT ME)
       Soul II Soul featuring Caron Wheeler (10) 4
22 Jul YOU'LL NEVER STOP ME LOVING YOU Sonia (Chrysalis) 2
5 Aug SWING THE MOOD
       Jive Bunny and the Mastermixers (Music Factory Dance) 5
9 Sep RIDE ON TIME Black Box (deConstruction) 6
21 Oct THAT'S WHAT I LIKE
       Jive Bunny and the Mastermixers (Music Factory Dance) 3
11 Nov ALL AROUND THE WORLD Lisa Stansfield (Arista) 2
25 Nov YOU GOT IT (THE RIGHT STUFF)
       New Kids On The Block (CBS) 3
16 Dec LET'S PARTY Jive Bunny and the Mastermixers (Music Factory Dance) 1
23 Dec DO THEY KNOW IT'S CHRISTMAS? Band Aid II (PWL/Polydor) ❄ 3

1 9 9 0

13 Jan HANGIN' TOUGH New Kids On The Block (CBS) 2
27 Jan TEARS ON MY PILLOW Kylie Minogue (PWL) 1
3 Feb NOTHING COMPARES 2 U Sinead O'Connor (Ensign) 4
3 Mar DUB BE GOOD TO ME Beats International (Go Beat) 4
31 Mar THE POWER Snap (Arista) 2
14 Apr VOGUE Madonna (Sire) 4
12 May KILLER Adamski (MCA) 4
9 Jun WORLD IN MOTION Englandneworder (Factory) 2
23 Jun SACRIFICE/HEALING HANDS Elton John (Rocket) 5
28 Jul TURTLE POWER Partners In Kryme (SBK) 4
25 Aug ITSY BITSY TEENY WEENY YELLOW POLKA DOT BIKINI
       Bombalurina (Carpet) 3
15 Sep THE JOKER Steve Miller Band (Capitol) 2
29 Sep SHOW ME HEAVEN Maria McKee (Epic) 4
27 Oct A LITTLE TIME The Beautiful South (Go! Discs) 1
3 Nov UNCHAINED MELODY Righteous Brothers (Verve) 4
1 Dec ICE ICE BABY Vanilla Ice (SBK) 4
29 Dec SAVIOUR'S DAY Cliff Richard (EMI) ❄ 1

1 9 9 1

5 Jan BRING YOUR DAUGHTER...TO THE SLAUGHTER
       Iron Maiden (EMI) 2
19 Jan SADNESS PART 1 Enigma (Virgin) 1
26 Jan INNUENDO Queen (Parlophone) 1
2 Feb 3AM ETERNAL
       KLF featuring Children of the Revolution (KLF Communications) 2
16 Feb DO THE BARTMAN Simpsons (Geffen) 3
9 Mar SHOULD I STAY OR SHOULD I GO? Clash (Columbia) 2
23 Mar THE STONK Hale and Pace and the Stonkers (London) 1
30 Mar THE ONE AND ONLY Chesney Hawkes (Chrysalis) 5
4 May SHOOP SHOOP SONG (IT'S IN HIS KISS) Cher (Epic) 5
8 Jun I WANNA SEX YOU UP Color Me Badd (Giant) 3
29 Jun ANY DREAM WILL DO Jason Donovan (Really Useful) 2
13 Jul (EVERYTHING I DO) I DO IT FOR YOU Bryan Adams (A&M) 16

1 9 9 2

BEATLES – a total of 17 number ones.

Most Number One Hits

After 684 number one hits in a few weeks over 40 years, only 13 acts have achieved as many as five number one hits. Another 15 have topped the charts four times, and 24 have enjoyed three number ones. Between them, these 52 acts have accounted for 240 number one hits.

17	**BEATLES** (*including 1 with Billy Preston*)
	ELVIS PRESLEY
13	**CLIFF RICHARD** (*including 1 with Young Ones*)
9	**ABBA**
8	**ROLLING STONES**
7	**MADONNA**
6	**SLADE**
	ROD STEWART
5	**BEE GEES**
	BLONDIE
	DAVID BOWIE (*including 1 with Queen and 1 with Mick Jagger*)
	POLICE
	SHADOWS (+ 7 with Cliff Richard)
4	**JASON DONOVAN** (*including 1 with Kylie Minogue*)
	EVERLY BROTHERS
	WHITNEY HOUSTON
	FRANK IFIELD
	MICHAEL JACKSON (+ 1 with Jacksons)
	JAM
	FRANKIE LAINE
	GEORGE MICHAEL (*including 1 with Aretha Franklin and 1 with Elton John*)
	KYLIE MINOGUE (*including 1 with Jason Donovan*)
	GUY MITCHELL
	PET SHOP BOYS
	QUEEN (*including 1 with David Bowie*)
	SHAKIN' STEVENS
	T. REX
	WHAM!
3	**ADAM AND THE ANTS/ADAM ANT**
	BROTHERHOOD OF MAN
	BUCKS FIZZ
	PHIL COLLINS (*including 1 with Philip Bailey*)
	LONNIE DONEGAN
	GEORGIE FAME
	FRANKIE GOES TO HOLLYWOOD
	GERRY AND THE PACEMAKERS
	GARY GLITTER
	JIVE BUNNY AND THE MASTERMIXERS
	ELTON JOHN (*including 1 with Kiki Dee and 1 with George Michael*)
	KINKS
	JOHN LENNON
	PAUL McCARTNEY (*including 1 with Stevie Wonder and 1 with Christians, Holly Johnson, Gerry Marsden and Stock Aitken Waterman*)
	MANFRED MANN
	MUD
	OLIVIA NEWTON-JOHN (*2 with John Travolta and 1 with ELO*)
	ROY ORBISON
	DONNY OSMOND (+ 1 with Osmonds)
	JOHNNIE RAY
	SANDIE SHAW
	SEARCHERS
	FRANK SINATRA (*including 1 with Nancy Sinatra*)
	10 C.C.

Apart from those listed above, **Art Garfunkel** has had two solo number ones, and one more with Simon and Garfunkel. **Diana Ross** has had two solo number ones and one more with the Supremes. **Boy George** has headed the charts twice as lead singer with Culture Club, and once more as a soloist. **Midge Ure** first topped the charts as a member of Slik, and went on to co-write, produce and perform with Band Aid, before finally topping the charts as a soloist in 1985.

Most Weeks at Number One

1. By Artist

73	**ELVIS PRESLEY**
69	**BEATLES**
43	**CLIFF RICHARD** (*including 3 weeks with Young Ones*)
32	**FRANKIE LAINE** (*1 week top equal*)
31	**ABBA**
20	**SLADE**
19	**EVERLY BROTHERS** (*1 week top equal*)
18	**MADONNA**
18	**ROLLING STONES** (*Mick Jagger 4 more with David Bowie, total 22 weeks*)
18	**ROD STEWART**
17	**FRANK IFIELD**
17	**PAUL McCARTNEY** (*2 solo, 9 with Wings, 3 with Stevie Wonder, and 3 with Christians, Holly Johnson, Gerry Marsden and Stock Aitken Waterman*)
17	**QUEEN** (*including 2 weeks with David Bowie*)
16	**BRYAN ADAMS**
16	**SHADOWS** (+ 28 weeks backing Cliff Richard, total 44 weeks. Hank Marvin 3 more weeks with Cliff and the Young Ones, total 47 weeks)
16	**T. REX**
16	**JOHN TRAVOLTA AND OLIVIA NEWTON-JOHN** (*Olivia Newton-John 2 more weeks with Electric Light Orchestra, total 18 weeks*)
15	**DORIS DAY**
15	**FRANKIE GOES TO HOLLYWOOD** (*Holly Johnson 3 more weeks with Christians, Gerry Marsden, Paul McCartney and Stock Aitken Waterman, total 18 weeks*)
14	**GUY MITCHELL** (*1 week top equal*)
13	**BEE GEES**
13	**DAVID BOWIE** (*including 4 weeks with Mick Jagger and 2 weeks with Queen*)
13	**EDDIE CALVERT**
13	**PERRY COMO**
13	**ELTON JOHN** (*including 5 weeks with Kiki Dee and 2 weeks with George Michael*)
13	**POLICE**
12	**BLONDIE**
12	**CONNIE FRANCIS**
12	**PET SHOP BOYS**
12	**DAVID WHITFIELD** (*1 week top equal*)
11	**ADAM AND THE ANTS/ADAM ANT**
11	**LONNIE DONEGAN**
11	**TENNESSEE ERNIE FORD**
11	**GERRY AND THE PACEMAKERS** (*Gerry Marsden 3 more weeks with Christians, Holly Johnson, Paul McCartney and Stock Aitken Waterman and 2 more weeks as lead vocalist with Crowd, total 16 weeks*)
11	**ENGELBERT HUMPERDINCK**
11	**JOHNNIE RAY**
11	**SLIM WHITMAN**
10	**WHITNEY HOUSTON**
10	**GEORGE MICHAEL** (*including 2 weeks with Aretha Franklin and 2 weeks with Elton John*)
10	**KYLIE MINOGUE** (*including 3 weeks with Jason Donovan*)
10	**MUD**
10	**DONNY OSMOND** (+ 3 weeks with Osmonds, total 13 weeks)
10	**SHAKIN' STEVENS**

Art Garfunkel has been number one for eight weeks, plus five weeks with Simon and Garfunkel. **Mantovani** has been number one for one week, plus ten more backing David Whitfield. **Lionel Richie** has had six weeks at number one, plus five more as one of the Commodores. **Boy George** has also been at the top for 11 weeks, two solo and nine with Culture Club.

Most Weeks at Number One

2. By an artist in one calendar year

27	FRANKIE LAINE (*1 week top equal*)	1953
18	ELVIS PRESLEY	1961
16	BRYAN ADAMS	1991
16	BEATLES	1963
16	JOHN TRAVOLTA & OLIVIA NEWTON-JOHN	1978
15	ELVIS PRESLEY	1962
15	FRANKIE GOES TO HOLLYWOOD	1984
12	CONNIE FRANCIS	1958
12	FRANK IFIELD	1962
12	BEATLES	1964
12	ABBA	1976

Most Weeks at Number One

3. By one disc, in total

18	I BELIEVE – Frankie Laine	1953
16	(EVERYTHING I DO) I DO IT FOR YOU – Bryan Adams	1991
14	BOHEMIAN RHAPSODY – Queen	1975/6 and 1991/2
11	ROSE MARIE – Slim Whitman	1955
10	CARA MIA – David Whitfield	1954
9	HERE IN MY HEART – Al Martino	1952/3
9	OH MEIN PAPA – Eddie Calvert	1954
9	SECRET LOVE – Doris Day	1954
9	DIANA – Paul Anka	1957
9	MULL OF KINTYRE/GIRLS' SCHOOL – Wings	1977/8
9	YOU'RE THE ONE THAT I WANT – John Travolta and Olivia Newton-John	1978
9	TWO TRIBES – Frankie Goes To Hollywood	1984

4. By one disc – consecutive weeks

16	(EVERYTHING I DO) I DO IT FOR YOU – Bryan Adams	1991
11	ROSE MARIE – Slim Whitman	1955
10	CARA MIA – David Whitfield	1954
9	HERE IN MY HEART – Al Martino	1952/3
9	I BELIEVE – Frankie Laine	1953
9	OH MEIN PAPA – Eddie Calvert	1954

9	DIANA – Paul Anka	1957
9	BOHEMIAN RHAPSODY – Queen	1975/6
9	MULL OF KINTYRE/GIRLS' SCHOOL – Wings	1977/8
9	YOU'RE THE ONE THAT I WANT – John Travolta and Olivia Newton-John	1978
9	TWO TRIBES – Frankie Goes To Hollywood	1984
8	ANSWER ME – Frankie Laine (*1 week top equal*)	1953/4
8	SECRET LOVE – Doris Day	1954
8	MAGIC MOMENTS – Perry Como	1958
8	IT'S NOW OR NEVER – Elvis Presley	1960
8	WONDERFUL LAND – Shadows	1962
8	SUGAR SUGAR – Archies	1969
8	STAY – Shakespears Sister	1992

Between Stevie Wonder's *I Just Called To Say I Love You* in 1984, and the 1989 Black Box number one, *Ride On Time*, there were 93 chart-toppers, none of which lasted for more than five weeks at the top of the charts.

5. By one song

18 weeks	I BELIEVE	one version
16 weeks	(EVERYTHING I DO) I DO IT FOR YOU	one version
14 weeks	BOHEMIAN RHAPSODY	one version
11 weeks	MARY'S BOY CHILD	two versions
11 weeks	ROSE MARIE	one version
11 weeks	YOUNG LOVE	two versions
10 weeks	ANSWER ME	two versions

Whitney Houston's *I Will Always Love You*, which had spent four weeks at the top by the end of 1992, the cut-off date for this edition, went on to complete 10 weeks at number one, the most by a female artist.

Consecutive Number One Hits

11 in a row:	BEATLES (from *From Me To You* through to *Yellow Submarine/Eleanor Rigby*, 1963 to 1966)
6 in a row:	BEATLES (from *All You Need Is Love* through to *The Ballad Of John And Yoko*, 1967 to 1969)
5 in a row:	ELVIS PRESLEY (from *Little Sister/His Latest Flame* through to *Return To Sender*, 1961 to 1962)
5 in a row:	ROLLING STONES (from *It's All Over Now* through to *Get Off Of My Cloud*, 1964 to 1965)

4 in a row:	ELVIS PRESLEY (from *It's Now Or Never* through to *Surrender*, 1960 to 1961). The first number one hat-trick.
4 in a row:	T. REX (from *Hot Love* through to *Metal Guru*, 1971 to 1972)
3 in a row:	FRANK IFIELD (*I Remember You*, *Lovesick Blues* and *Wayward Wind*, 1962 to 1963). The first hat-trick by a British artist.
3 in a row:	GERRY AND THE PACEMAKERS (*How Do You Do It*, *I Like It* and *You'll Never Walk Alone*, 1963)
3 in a row:	ABBA (*Mamma Mia*, *Fernando* and *Dancing Queen*, 1975 to 1976)
3 in a row:	ABBA (*Knowing Me Knowing You*, *The Name Of The Game* and *Take A Chance On Me*, 1977 to 1978)
3 in a row:	POLICE (*Message in A Bottle*, *Walking On The Moon* and *Don't Stand So Close To Me*, 1979 to 1980)
3 in a row:	BLONDIE (*Atomic*, *Call Me* and *The Tide Is High*, 1980)
3 in a row:	JOHN LENNON (*Imagine*, (*Just Like*) *Starting Over* and *Woman*, 1980). Both the fastest and slowest hat-trick depending on whether it started when *Imagine* first entered the chart in November 1975, or when (*Just Like*) *Starting Over* came in late in 1980.
3 in a row:	FRANKIE GOES TO HOLLYWOOD (*Relax!*, *Two Tribes* and *The Power Of Love*, 1984)
3 in a row:	JIVE BUNNY AND THE MASTERMIXERS (*Swing The Mood*, *That's What I Like* and *Let's Party*, 1989).

Successive releases for the purpose of this table are successive official single releases. The Beatles' two runs of number ones were each interrupted by irregular releases. An old single with Tony Sheridan reached number 29 in the midst of their 11 number ones, and their double EP *Magical Mystery Tour* made number two while *Hello Goodbye* was becoming the second of their six chart toppers on the trot. An album track, *Jeepster*, and an old recording, *Debora/One Inch Rock* were released during T. Rex's run of number ones while the group were changing labels. An EP by Elvis Presley, *Follow That Dream*, pottered about the lower reaches of the charts during his run of five consecutive number ones. During Police's hat trick, one single on another label, one old single re-issued and a six-pack of singles hit the chart in an attempt to distract the compilers of this table. John Lennon's *Imagine* was the first of the three singles of his hat-trick (his last single for five years) but the second of the three to reach the top. During his hat-trick, a flood of old Lennon hits swarmed back on to the chart.

The third hit of the hat-tricks by both Police and Jive Bunny and the Mastermixers came on to the chart at number one.

Most Number One Hits in a Year

Four number ones in one year has been achieved twice, by **Elvis Presley** in 1961 and 1962. His chart-toppers in 1961 were *Are You Lonesome Tonight* (Jan/Feb), *Wooden Heart* (Mar/Apr), *Surrender* (June) and *Little Sister/His Latest Flame* (Nov/Dec). In 1962 they were *Rock-A-Hula Baby/Can't Help Falling In Love* (Feb/Mar), *Good Luck Charm* (May/Jun), *She's Not You* (Sept) and *Return To Sender* (Dec).

Three number ones in a year has been accomplished 12 times, as follows:

1953	Frankie Laine (*I Believe, Hey Joe, Answer Me*)
1963	Gerry and the Pacemakers (*How Do You Do It, I Like It, You'll Never Walk Alone*)
1963	Beatles (*From Me To You, She Loves You, I Want To Hold Your Hand*)
1964	Beatles (*Can't Buy Me Love, A Hard Day's Night, I Feel Fine*)
1965	Beatles (*Ticket To Ride, Help!, Day Tripper/We Can Work It Out*)
1965	Rolling Stones (*The Last Time, (I Can't Get No) Satisfaction, Get Off Of My Cloud*)
1973	Slade (*Cum On Feel The Noize, Skweeze Me Pleeze Me, Merry Xmas Everybody*)
1976	Abba (*Mamma Mia, Fernando, Dancing Queen*)
1980	Blondie (*Atomic, Call Me, The Tide Is High*)
1984	Frankie Goes To Hollywood (*Relax, Two Tribes, The Power Of Love*)
1989	Jason Donovan (*Especially For You, Too Many Broken Hearts, Sealed With A Kiss*)
1989	Jive Bunny and the Mastermixers (*Swing The Mood, That's What I Like, Let's Party*)

The most number one hits in total in any year is 24 in 1980. The longest-lived chart-topper of the year was *Don't Stand So Close To Me* by the Police, which only lasted four weeks at the top.

The fewest new number one hits in a complete year is 11 in 1954. Three number ones that year each spent at least nine weeks at the top. There were only 12 new number ones in 1962 and 1992. In 1962 only eight different acts topped the charts.

First Three Hits at Number One

Three acts have now achieved the feat of taking their first three hits to number one. They are **Gerry and the Pacemakers** in 1963, **Frankie Goes To Hollywood** in 1984 and **Jive Bunny and the Mastermixers** in 1989. All three are British, and all three are male vocal/instrumental outfits, although this loose description barely fits the production team behind Jive Bunny.

Gerry and the Pacemakers and Frankie Goes To Hollywood both came from Liverpool, both chose as their third single a pseudo-religious song, (*You'll Never Walk Alone* and *The Power Of Love* respectively) and both took their fourth release to number two. Jive Bunny's fourth single peaked at number four.

Gerry Marsden and Holly Johnson, the lead singers of Gerry and the Pacemakers and Frankie Goes To Hollywood subsequently combined with fellow Liverpudlians the Christians and Paul McCartney to create, along with ace producers Stock Aitken Waterman, yet another number one, *Ferry 'Cross The Mersey*.

GERRY AND THE PACEMAKERS

First Two Hits at Number One

Only 15 acts in the 40-year history of the chart have hit the top with each of their first two chart hits.

EDDIE CALVERT Oh Mein Papa, Cherry Pink and Apple Blossom White		1954, 55
ADAM FAITH What Do You Want, Poor Me		1959, 60
TENNESSEE ERNIE FORD Give Me Your Word, Sixteen Tons		1955, 56
FRANKIE GOES TO HOLLYWOOD Relax!, Two Tribes		1984
ART GARFUNKEL I Only Have Eyes For You, Bright Eyes		1975, 79
GERRY AND THE PACEMAKERS How Do You Do It, I Like It		1963
JIVE BUNNY AND THE MASTERMIXERS Swing The Mood, That's What I Like		1989
GEORGE MICHAEL Careless Whisper, A Different Corner		1984, 86
MUNGO JERRY In The Summertime, Baby Jump		1970, 71
GARY NUMAN/TUBEWAY ARMY Are "Friends" Electric?, Cars		1979
NEW KIDS ON THE BLOCK You Got It (The Right Stuff), Hangin' Tough		1989, 90
RIGHTEOUS BROTHERS You've Lost That Lovin' Feelin', Unchained Melody		1965, 90
STARGAZERS Broken Wings, I See The Moon		1953, 54
ROD STEWART Maggie May, You Wear It Well		1971, 72
JOHN TRAVOLTA AND OLIVIA NEWTON-JOHN You're The One That I Want, Summer Nights		1978

Of these acts only Frankie Goes To Hollywood, Gerry and the Pacemakers, Jive Bunny, George Michael, Mungo Jerry, New Kids On The Block and John Travolta and Olivia Newton-John hit the top with their first two UK releases. For both the Righteous Brothers and New Kids On The Block, it took a re-issue to push one of their hits to the top.

Band Aid and Band Aid II both hit number one with their only releases – the African famine relief singles, *Do They Know It's Christmas.*

GEORGE MICHAEL

ROLF HARRIS

Last Hit at Number One

Chart history shows that once an act has scored its first number one, it is far more likely to hit the top again than to have no more hits at all. Disappearing without trace otherwise, after a number one hit, is fairly rare, and apart from the one-hit wonders, listed separately, only 11 acts have failed to follow up a number one. They are:

CHARLES AZNAVOUR
FIRM
ROLF HARRIS
BENNY HILL
JAM
TOMMY JAMES AND THE SHONDELLS
STEVE MILLER BAND
QUEEN
KAY STARR
STARSHIP
WHAM!

Rolf Harris hit again in 1993 after 23 years off the chart. Both halves of Wham! have charted separately since the duo broke up, as have all three members of Jam since their demise. Paul Weller led Style Council to many hits, Bruce Foxton had three solo hits and Rick Buckler's Time UK nudged the charts once. Steve Miller's final UK hit was a re-issue of a track originally recorded before any of his other three UK hits, but it did not chart until 1990. Queen's final hit was a double-sided single, one side of which had been a hit before. Kay Starr uniquely holds the unlikely record of hitting number one with both her first and last British hit singles.

Whitney Houston and Snap! did not release a follow-up to their chart-topping hits in 1992, but both made their way back into the charts during early 1993.

The One Hit Wonders

Qualification: one number one hit, and nothing else – ever. Thirty-five immortal acts now make up the list.

1954	**KITTY KALLEN**	Little Things Mean A Lot
1956	**DREAMWEAVERS**	It's Almost Tomorrow
1958	**KALIN TWINS**	When
1959	**JERRY KELLER**	Here Comes Summer
1960	**RICKY VALANCE**	Tell Laura I Love Her
1962	**B. BUMBLE AND THE STINGERS**	Nut Rocker
1966	**OVERLANDERS**	Michelle
1968	**CRAZY WORLD OF ARTHUR BROWN**	Fire
1969	**ZAGER AND EVANS**	In The Year 2525
	JANE BIRKIN AND SERGE GAINSBOURG	Je T'Aime...Moi Non Plus
	ARCHIES	Sugar Sugar
1970	**LEE MARVIN**	Wand'rin Star
	NORMAN GREENBAUM	Spirit In The Sky
	MATTHEWS SOUTHERN COMFORT	Woodstock
1971	**CLIVE DUNN**	Grandad
1973	**SIMON PARK ORCHESTRA**	Eye Level
1975	**TYPICALLY TROPICAL**	Barbados
1976	**J.J. BARRIE**	No Charge
1977	**FLOATERS**	Float On
1978	**ALTHIA AND DONNA**	Up Town Top Ranking
	BRIAN AND MICHAEL	Matchstalk Men And Matchstalk Cats And Dogs
1979	**ANITA WARD**	Ring My Bell
	LENA MARTELL	One Day At A Time
1980	**FERN KINNEY**	Together We Are Beautiful
	MASH	Theme From M*A*S*H
	ST WINIFRED'S SCHOOL CHOIR	There's No One Quite Like Grandma
1981	**JOE DOLCE MUSIC THEATRE**	Shaddup You Face
1982	**CHARLENE**	I've Never Been To Me
1985	**PHYLLIS NELSON**	Move Closer
1987	**M/A/R/R/S**	Pump Up The Volume
1988	**ROBIN BECK**	First Time
1990	**PARTNERS IN KRYME**	Turtle Power
1991	**HALE & PACE and the STONKERS**	The Stonk
1992	**TASMIN ARCHER***	Sleeping Satellite
	CHARLES AND EDDIE*	Would I Lie To You

★ = charted again in '93.

Apart from these acts, 22 other one hit wonders exist, made up of acts who have had hits in other guises, as follows:

1967	**NANCY SINATRA AND FRANK SINATRA**	Somethin' Stupid (*both have had solo number one hits*)
1974	**JOHN DENVER**	Annie's Song (*has also hit with Placido Domingo*)
1976	**ELTON JOHN AND KIKI DEE**	Don't Go Breaking My Heart (*both have had solo hits*)
1980	**OLIVIA NEWTON-JOHN AND ELECTRIC LIGHT ORCHESTRA**	Xanadu (*both have had solo hits*)
1981	**QUEEN AND DAVID BOWIE**	Under Pressure (*both have had solo number one hits*)
1982	**PAUL McCARTNEY WITH STEVIE WONDER**	Ebony And Ivory (*both have had solo number one hits*)

KALIN TWINS

1984	**BAND AID**	Do They Know It's Christmas (*a conglomeration of hit makers*)
1985	**ELAINE PAIGE AND BARBARA DICKSON**	I Know Him So Well (*both have had solo hits*)
	USA FOR AFRICA	We Are The World (*another conglomeration of hitmakers*)
	CROWD	You'll Never Walk Alone (*and another conglomeration*)
	DAVID BOWIE AND MICK JAGGER	Dancing In The Street (*both have had solo hits*)
1986	**CLIFF RICHARD AND THE YOUNG ONES WITH HANK MARVIN**	Living Doll (*Cliff and the Young Ones [a.k.a. Bad News] have both had solo hits, as has Hank Marvin*)
1987	**STEVE 'SILK' HURLEY**	Jack Your Body (*Steve is one half of the duo J.M. Silk*)
	ARETHA FRANKLIN AND GEORGE MICHAEL	I Knew You Were Waiting For Me (*both have had solo hits*)
	FERRY AID	Let It Be (*yet another conglomeration*)
1988	**TIMELORDS**	Doctorin' The Tardis (*subsequently hit as The KLF*)
1989	**KYLIE MINOGUE AND JASON DONOVAN**	Especially For You (*both have had solo number one hits*)
	CHRISTIANS, HOLLY JOHNSON, PAUL McCARTNEY, GERRY MARSDEN AND STOCK AITKEN WATERMAN	Ferry Cross The Mersey (*charity disc for the Hillsborough Disaster Fund*)
	BAND AID II	Do They Know It's Christmas? (*The first case of two one-hit wonders reaching the top with the same song. Only Keren Woodward and Sarah Dallin of Bananarama appeared on both discs*)
1990	**ENGLANDNEWORDER**	World In Motion... (*a combination of New Order and the England World Cup Squad*)
1991	**VIC REEVES AND THE WONDER STUFF**	Dizzy (*both acts have had separate hits*)
	GEORGE MICHAEL AND ELTON JOHN	Don't Let The Sun Go Down On Me (*both have had solo number one hits, and number ones in other duets*)

Gap Between Number One Hits

Of all the acts that have enjoyed two or more number one hits, only eight acts have suffered through a gap of more than seven years between number ones, although two of them have, incredibly, done so twice. The Beatles crammed all of their 17 chart-toppers into a period of six years and 54 days.

25 years 259 days	**RIGHTEOUS BROTHERS**	(17 Feb 65 to 3 Nov 90)
23 years 65 days	**HOLLIES**	(21 Jul 65 to 24 Sep 88)
14 years 363 days	**QUEEN**	(24 Jan 76 to 20 Jan 91)
14 years 172 days	**DIANA ROSS**	(17 Sep 71 to 8 Mar 86)
11 years 238 days	**FRANK SINATRA**	(7 Oct 54 to 2 Jun 66)
11 years 124 days	**CLIFF RICHARD**	(23 Apr 68 to 25 Aug 79)
9 years 231 days	**BEE GEES**	(10 Sep 68 to 29 Apr 78)
9 years 80 days	**CLIFF RICHARD**	(21 Sep 79 to 10 Dec 88)
8 years 215 days	**BEE GEES**	(16 Mar 79 to 17 Oct 87)
7 years 357 days	**DON McLEAN**	(30 Jun 72 to 21 Jun 80)

During **Cliff**'s second hiatus, he took the top slot in March 1986 in association with the **Young Ones**. **Queen** hit the top with **David Bowie** in 1981, five years into their wait for a second chart-topper on their own.

Cher waited for 25 years 239 days between dropping from number one in duet with her then husband Sonny in 1965 and reaching the top again on her own in 1992. There was a gap of 21 years 200 days between 27 November 1963, the last day that **Gerry and the Pacemakers**' *You'll Never Walk Alone* was at number one, and 15 June 1985, when the same song, with Gerry Marsden again on lead vocals, hit number one, this time by **the Crowd**.

Twenty years and 4 days after *Back Home* by the **England World Cup Squad** dropped from number one, *World In Motion...* by **Englandneworder** knocked Adamski off the top. None of the artists who appeared on the England World Cup Squad disc in 1970 survived the selectors' axe to be playing still for England on the football field and in the recording studio in 1990.

Sixteen years and 9 days elapsed between the last day of the final **Rolling Stones** number one, and **Mick Jagger**'s reappearance at the top with David Bowie.

There was a gap of 14 years and 113 days between **Eddy Grant**'s last day at number one as one of the **Equals** and his first day on top as a soloist.

Elton John's first solo number one hit, *Sacrifice/Healing Hands*, happened 13 years 293 days after he and Kiki Dee dropped from number one with *Don't Go Breaking my Heart*.

Tears Of A Clown by **Smokey Robinson and the Miracles** dropped from number one ten years and 268 days before **Smokey Robinson**'s solo hit 'Being With You' reached the summit.

DIANA ROSS

Longest Span of Number One Hits

Only five acts have scored number one hits over a period of more than 20 years. They are:

31 years 153 days	**CLIFF RICHARD** (1959 to 1990)
25 years 286 days	**RIGHTEOUS BROTHERS** (1965 to 1990)
23 years 105 days	**HOLLIES** (1965 to 1988)
20 years 87 days	**ELVIS PRESLEY** (1957 to 1977)
20 years 34 days	**BEE GEES** (1967 to 1987)

Cher first hit number one as half of Sonny and Cher in August 1965, and dropped from the top after her solo number one in June 1991, almost 26 years later. **Diana Ross** first hit number one as lead singer for the Supremes in 1964 and dropped off the top for the final time as a soloist in 1986, over 21 years later.

Cliff Richard is the only act to have number one hits in *five* decades. In the 1950s he hit number one twice, in the 1960s seven times, in the 1970s once, in the 1980s once solo and once more with the Young Ones and Hank Marvin, and so far once in the 1990s. This record is unlikely ever to be equalled.

The only acts, apart from Cliff Richard, to have hit number one in three different decades are **Elvis Presley** (50s, 60s and 70s) and the **Bee Gees** (60s, 70s and 80s). **Queen** have hit number one in the 70s and 90s, and topped the charts in 1981 by teaming up with David Bowie.

Eight other acts (**Abba, Blondie, David Bowie, Don McLean, Police, Kenny Rogers, Diana Ross** and **Rod Stewart**) hit the top in the 70s and 80s, and so have a chance in the 90s to equal Cliff, Elvis and the Gibb brothers.

Nine acts topped the charts in both the 50s and the 60s (**Shirley Bassey, Lonnie Donegan, Everly Brothers, Adam Faith, Michael Holliday, Elvis Presley, Cliff Richard, Frank Sinatra** and **Frankie Vaughan**), but only three managed chart-toppers in the 60s and 70s – Elvis, Cliff and the Bee Gees.

The **Hollies** hit the top in the 60s and 80s, and the **Righteous Brothers** hit number one in the 60s and 90s.

Jason Donovan, Whitney Houston, Michael Jackson, Madonna, Kylie Minogue, New Kids On The Block, Snap! and **Wet Wet Wet** have already duplicated Cliff's feat of hitting number one in the 80s and 90s.

Cliff Richard's first week at the top came after 45 weeks on lower rungs. His final week at number one was his 1057th week on the chart, a span of 1012 chart weeks. **Elvis Presley**'s first week at number one came after he had already clocked up 103 weeks on the British charts. His final week at number one 20 years later was his 1034th of chart action, a span of a mere 931 chart weeks. No other act comes anywhere near these two in chart longevity.

Straight In At Number One

Thirty records, to the end of 1992, have hit the charts at number one. They are:

14 Nov 52	**HERE IN MY HEART** *Al Martino*
24 Jan 58	**JAILHOUSE ROCK** *Elvis Presley*
3 Nov 60	**IT'S NOW OR NEVER** *Elvis Presley*
11 Jan 62	**THE YOUNG ONES** *Cliff Richard*
23 Apr 69	**GET BACK** *Beatles*
3 Mar 73	**CUM ON FEEL THE NOIZE** *Slade*
30 Jun 73	**SKWEEZE ME PLEEZE ME** *Slade*
17 Nov 73	**I LOVE YOU LOVE ME LOVE** *Gary Glitter*
15 Dec 73	**MERRY XMAS EVERYBODY** *Slade*

22 Mar 80	**GOING UNDERGROUND/ DREAMS OF CHILDREN** *Jam*
27 Sep 80	**DON'T STAND SO CLOSE TO ME** *Police*
9 May 81	**STAND AND DELIVER** *Adam and the Ants*
13 Feb 82	**A TOWN CALLED MALICE/ PRECIOUS** *Jam*
4 Dec 82	**BEAT SURRENDER** *Jam*
26 Mar 83	**IS THERE SOMETHING I SHOULD KNOW?** *Duran Duran*
16 Jun 84	**TWO TRIBES** *Frankie Goes To Hollywood*
15 Dec 84	**DO THEY KNOW IT'S CHRISTMAS?** *Band Aid*
7 Sep 85	**DANCING IN THE STREET** *David Bowie and Mick Jagger*
4 Apr 87	**LET IT BE** *Ferry Aid*

20 May 89	**FERRY 'CROSS THE MERSEY** *Christians, Holly Johnson, Paul McCartney, Gerry Marsden and Stock Aitken Waterman*
10 Jun 89	**SEALED WITH A KISS** *Jason Donovan*
16 Dec 89	**LET'S PARTY** *Jive Bunny and the Mastermixers*
23 Dec 89	**DO THEY KNOW IT'S CHRISTMAS?** *Band Aid II*
5 Jan 91	**BRING YOUR DAUGHTER ... TO THE SLAUGHTER** *Iron Maiden*
26 Jan 91	**INNUENDO** *Queen*
2 Nov 91	**THE FLY** *U2*
23 Nov 91	**BLACK OR WHITE** *Michael Jackson*
7 Dec 91	**DON'T LET SUN GO DOWN ON ME** *George Michael & Elton John*
21 Dec 91	**BOHEMIAN RHAPSODY/THESE ARE THE DAYS OF OUR LIVES** *Queen*
13 Jun 92	**ABBA-ESQUE** (EP) *Erasure*

SLADE notched up two straight-in-at-number-one hits.

Slade remain the only act to enter the chart at number one with consecutive releases.

In 1991, *Black Or White*, *Don't Let The Sun Go Down On Me* and *Bohemian Rhapsody/These Are The Days Of Our Lives* were consecutive number ones, the only time that three chart-toppers in a row have entered the charts at number one. The six instant number ones in 1991 easily beat the previous record of four in a year, set in 1973 and equalled in 1989.

Gary Glitter's *I Love You Love Me Love* and **Slade**'s *Merry Xmas Everybody* in 1973 were consecutive number ones, as were *Ferry 'Cross The Mersey* and *Sealed With A Kiss* in May and June 1989.

In December 1989, for the first time ever, new hits crashed in at number one in consecutive weeks.

Both **Police** and **Jive Bunny & the Mastermixers** completed a hat-trick of number ones by going straight to the top.

Do They Know It's Christmas is, of course, the only song to have gone straight to number one in two different versions.

413

Biggest Jump to Number One

CAPTAIN SENSIBLE

There have been 31 records, apart from those that came on to the chart at number one which are listed separately, which have jumped from outside the top ten straight to the top spot.

33 to 1	HAPPY TALK Captain Sensible	3 Jul 82
27 to 1	SURRENDER Elvis Presley	1 Jun 61
26 to 1	PASS THE DUTCHIE Musical Youth	2 Oct 82
22 to 1	GREEN DOOR Shakin Stevens	1 Aug 81
21 to 1	HEY JUDE Beatles	11 Sep 68
21 to 1	(JUST LIKE) STARTING OVER John Lennon	20 Dec 80
19 to 1	ARE YOU LONESOME TONIGHT? Elvis Presley	26 Jan 61
19 to 1	(IF PARADISE IS) HALF AS NICE Amen Corner	12 Feb 69
19 to 1	LOVE ME FOR A REASON Osmonds	31 Aug 74
19 to 1	STAND BY ME Ben E. King	21 Feb 87
17 to 1	GET OFF OF MY CLOUD Rolling Stones	4 Nov 65
16 to 1	I HEAR YOU KNOCKIN' Dave Edmunds	28 Nov 70
16 to 1	CHIRPY CHIRPY CHEEP CHEEP Middle Of The Road	19 Jun 71
16 to 1	YOUNG LOVE Donny Osmond	25 Aug 73
16 to 1	DANCING QUEEN Abba	4 Sep 76
15 to 1	I DON'T LIKE MONDAYS Boomtown Rats	28 Jul 79
15 to 1	THE SPECIAL AKA LIVE EP Specials	2 Feb 80
14 to 1	EYE LEVEL Simon Park Orchestra	29 Sep 73
13 to 1	IN THE SUMMERTIME Mungo Jerry	13 Jun 70
13 to 1	STAR TREKKIN' Firm	20 Jun 87
12 to 1	LOVE GROWS (WHERE MY ROSEMARY GOES) Edison Lighthouse	31 Jan 70
12 to 1	THE POWER Snap	31 Mar 90
11 to 1	(THERE'S) ALWAYS SOMETHING THERE TO REMIND ME Sandie Shaw	22 Oct 64
11 to 1	TICKET TO RIDE Beatles	22 Apr 65
11 to 1	MICHELLE Overlanders	27 Jan 66
11 to 1	LADY MADONNA Beatles	20 Mar 68
11 to 1	SUGAR SUGAR Archies	25 Oct 69
11 to 1	SHE Charles Aznavour	29 Jun 74
11 to 1	SUMMER NIGHTS John Travolta and Olivia Newton-John	30 Sep 78
11 to 1	THE CHICKEN SONG Spitting Image	17 May 86
11 to 1	NOTHING'S GONNA CHANGE MY LOVE FOR YOU Glen Medeiros	9 Jul 88

The biggest jump within the chart is a leap of 62 places from 66 to 4 on 11 Oct 86 by **Nick Berry**'s *Every Loser Wins*. Two other number one hits have climbed over 50 places in one week on their way to the top – the **Firm**'s *Star Trekkin'* which leapt from 74 to 13 to 1, a leap of 61 places followed by a leap of 12 places, and the **Flying Pickets**' *Only You*, which jumped 51 places on 3 Dec 83. The lowest initial entry by a record that went on to hit the top is 74 by *Star Trekkin'*, on 6 Jun 87, beating the previous record-holder, **Charlene**'s *I've Never Been To Me* by one place. Charlene entered the chart at number 73 on 15 May 82.

Biggest Falls From Number One

Only 24 records have fallen out of the top five directly from the very top, as follows:

1 to 12	MARY'S BOY CHILD Harry Belafonte	10 Jan 58
1 to 10	ONLY YOU Flying Pickets	14 Jan 84
1 to 9	CHRISTMAS ALPHABET Dickie Valentine	6 Jan 56
1 to 9	YOU'RE DRIVING ME CRAZY Temperance Seven	1 Jun 61
1 to 9	THESE BOOTS ARE MADE FOR WALKIN' Nancy Sinatra	17 Mar 66
1 to 9	BRING YOUR DAUGHTER ... TO THE SLAUGHTER Iron Maiden	19 Jan 91
1 to 8	HELLO GOODBYE Beatles	24 Jan 68
1 to 8	LONELY THIS CHRISTMAS Mud	18 Jan 75
1 to 7	WAYWARD WIND Frank Ifield	14 Mar 63
1 to 7	YOUNG LOVE Donny Osmond	22 Sep 73
1 to 7	KNOWING ME KNOWING YOU Abba	7 May 77
1 to 6	HERE IN MY HEART Al Martino	16 Jan 53
1 to 6	ROCK AROUND THE CLOCK Bill Haley and his Comets	20 Jan 56
1 to 6	CATHY'S CLOWN Everly Brothers	23 Jun 60
1 to 6	SUMMER HOLIDAY Cliff Richard and the Shadows	11 Apr 63
1 to 6	SUGAR BABY LOVE Rubettes	15 Jun 74
1 to 6	YOU TO ME ARE EVERYTHING Real Thing	17 Jul 76
1 to 6	BRIGHT EYES Art Garfunkel	26 May 79
1 to 6	THERE'S NO ONE QUITE LIKE GRANDMA St Winifreds School Choir	10 Jan 81
1 to 6	IT'S MY PARTY Dave Stewart with Barbara Gaskin	14 Nov 81
1 to 6	LET'S DANCE David Bowie	30 Apr 83
1 to 6	YOU SPIN ME ROUND (LIKE A RECORD) Dead Or Alive	23 Mar 85
1 to 6	A DIFFERENT CORNER George Michael	10 May 86
1 to 6	BELFAST CHILD Simple Minds	11 Mar 89

At the end of 1988, three consecutive chart-toppers dropped from number one to number five. They were *Orinoco Flow* by **Enya** on 19 November, *First Time* by **Robin Beck** on 10 December, and *Mistletoe And Wine* by **Cliff Richard** on 7 January 1989.

Queen's second number one, *Innuendo*, is the only record ever to top the charts, but spend only two weeks in the Top Ten. It entered the chart at number one, then fell to number two and then to number 11.

On 30 May 1992 **Shut Up And Dance** hit the chart at number two with a rave version of Marc Cohn's *Walking In Memphis*, under the title *Raving I'm Raving*. The next week it fell to number 15, and a week later it had disappeared completely.

HARRY BELAFONTE

Most Successful Producers

In the early days of hit singles, a record producer was a rather poorly paid employee of the record company, whose job was to ensure that the artist's recorded version of a song sounded pretty close to the live performance version. It was not until producers like Mitch Miller, and a little later, the likes of Joe Meek, Norrie Paramor and George Martin, began to create original studio sounds that the producer became a credited part of the hitmaking team.

The most successful producers of no. 1 hit singles since 1952 are:

27	George Martin
	Norrie Paramor
17	Mitch Miller
15	Steve Sholes
13	Stock Aitken Waterman
11	Chet Atkins
10	Benny Andersson
	Johnny Franz
	Bjorn Ulvaeus
9	Mike Chapman
8	Dick Rowe
7	Tony Hatch
	Madonna
	George Michael
	Norman Newell
6	Chas Chandler
	Barry Gibb
	Andrew Loog Oldham
	Mike Smith
5	Nicky Chinn
	Mike Curb
	Trevor Horn
	Brian May
	Police (Stewart Copeland, Sting, Andy Summers)
	Walter Ridley
	Wesley Rose
	Tony Visconti

The record for most number one hits with different acts is ten, by Mike Stock, Matt Aitken and Pete Waterman. The ten SAW acts to hit the very top are: Rick Astley, Band Aid II, Christians Holly Johnson Paul McCartney Gerry Marsden and Stock Aitken Waterman, Dead Or Alive, Jason Donovan, Ferry Aid, Mel and Kim, Kylie Minogue, Kylie Minogue and Jason Donovan, and Sonia.

Norrie Paramor has had number ones with nine different acts, and Johnny Franz and Mitch Miller with eight each.

GEORGE MARTIN (right), most succesful producer, with Beatles manager Brian Epstein

Slowest Number One

If an artist is ever going to have a number one hit, it usually happens within a year or two of that artist's first hit. About half of all the acts who have hit the very top did so with their first chart hit. There are 19 acts whose first number one came more than ten years after their chart debut, as follows:

29 years 42 days	**JACKIE WILSON**	(15 Nov 57 to 27 Dec 86)
26 years 19 days	**BEN E. KING**	(2 Feb 61 to 21 Feb 87)
25 years 259 days	**CHER**	(19 Aug 65 to 4 May 91)
19 years 151 days	**ELTON JOHN**	(23 Jan 71 to 23 Jun 90)
18 years 218 days	**STEVIE WONDER**	(3 Feb 66 to 8 Sep 84)
18 years 216 days	**JOHNNY MATHIS**	(23 May 58 to 25 Dec 76)
16 years 218 days	**BORIS GARDINER**	(17 Jan 70 to 23 Aug 86)
15 years 157 days	**CHUCK BERRY**	(21 Jun 57 to 25 Nov 72)
15 years 127 days	**LOUIS ARMSTRONG**	(19 Dec 52 to 24 Apr 68)
14 years 279 days	**BARBRA STREISAND**	(20 Jan 66 to 25 Oct 80)
13 years 341 days	**CLASH**	(2 Apr 77 to 9 Mar 91)
13 years 327 days	**STEVE MILLER BAND**	(23 Oct 76 to 15 Sep 90)
13 years 140 days	**FOUR SEASONS**	(4 Oct 62 to 21 Feb 76)
12 years 321 days	**PAUL McCARTNEY**	(27 Feb 71 to 14 Jan 84)
12 years 260 days	**PINK FLOYD**	(30 Mar 67 to 15 Dec 79)
11 years 164 days	**JOHN LENNON**	(9 Jul 69 to 20 Dec 80)
10 years 314 days	**IRON MAIDEN**	(23 Feb 80 to 5 Jan 91)
10 years 298 days	**BENNY HILL**	(16 Feb 61 to 11 Dec 71)
10 years 8 days	**SISTER SLEDGE**	(21 Jun 75 to 29 Jun 85)

Of these acts, **Cher**, **Elton John**, **Stevie Wonder**, **Paul McCartney** and **John Lennon** had featured on number ones before their solo successes. John Lennon is the only act on this list to achieve more than one solo number one. His first number one was the first of a hat-trick. Stevie Wonder's first week at number one was his 301st of solo chart action, but Elton John's was his 371st week, the longest wait in chart terms for a number one. It was a re-issue of his 45th and 46th solo hits, the most hits ever achieved by any act before their first number one. Cher, who hit number one in duet with her then husband Sonny in only their third week of chart action, had less luck as a soloist. Hers is the longest wait of all those who finally hit the top with a newly-recorded song. The number one hits by Jackie Wilson, Ben E. King, Clash and the Steve Miller Band were re-issues of old recordings.

Before **Louis Armstrong** became the first act to take more than ten years to hit the top, in 1968, the slowest ascent of the charts was by **Petula Clark**, who took six years 257 days from her chart debut on 11 June 1954 until she first topped the charts on 23 February 1962.

Gene Pitney has never had a solo number one, but there was a gap of 27 years and 311 days from his first week on the charts on 23 March 1961 until he topped the charts with Marc Almond on 28 January 1989.

Twelve recordings have taken longer than 200 days to hit the top after their first appearance on the chart:

29 years	42 days	REET PETITE – Jackie Wilson	(15 Nov 57 to 27 Dec 86)
25 years	244 days	STAND BY ME – Ben E. King	(22 Jun 61 to 21 Feb 87)
25 years	83 days	UNCHAINED MELODY – Righteous Brothers	(12 Aug 65 to 3 Nov 90)
18 years	356 days	HE AIN'T HEAVY, HE'S MY BROTHER – Hollies	(4 Oct 69 to 24 Sep 88)
8 years	166 days	SHOULD I STAY OR SHOULD I GO – Clash	(25 Sep 82 to 9 Mar 91)
6 years	63 days	SPACE ODDITY – David Bowie	(6 Sep 69 to 8 Nov 75)
5 years	70 days	IMAGINE – John Lennon	(1 Nov 75 to 10 Jan 81)
	322 days	ROCK AROUND THE CLOCK – Bill Haley and his Comets	(7 Jan 55 to 25 Nov 55)
	308 days	EYE LEVEL – Simon Park Orchestra	(25 Nov 72 to 29 Sep 73)
	301 days	HEALING HANDS – Elton John	(26 Aug 89 to 23 Jun 90)
	231 days	SACRIFICE – Elton John	(4 Nov 89 to 23 Jun 90)
	210 days	THE MODEL/COMPUTER LOVE – Kraftwerk	(11 Jul 81 to 6 Feb 82)

All these records dropped off the charts between their original chart entry and their chart-topping reappearances. The slowest climb to number one by any record that stayed on the chart all the time is 16 weeks (112 days) by *The Power of Love* by **Jennifer Rush**, from 29 Jun 85 to 12 Oct 85. The previous record of 14 weeks (98 days) had been set only seven months earlier by **Dead Or Alive**'s *You Spin Me Round (Like A Record)*, which took from 1 Dec 84 to 9 Mar 85 to climb to number one.

BARBRA STREISAND

Fastest Number One

At the other end of the scale from Cher, these are the acts who moved from chart debut to the number one slot in the shortest time, starting with Al Martino's entry in the very first chart:

0 days	**AL MARTINO**	(14 Nov 52)
7 days	**EDISON LIGHTHOUSE**	(24 to 31 Jan 70)
7 days	**MUNGO JERRY**	(6 to 13 Jun 70)
7 days	**DAVE EDMUNDS**	(21 to 28 Nov 70)
7 days	**NICOLE**	(8 to 15 May 82)
7 days	**MUSICAL YOUTH**	(25 Sep to 3 Oct 82)
7 days	**SPITTING IMAGE**	(10 to 17 May 86)
7 days	**SNAP**	(24 to 31 Mar 90)
7 days	**PARTNERS IN KRYME**	(21 to 28 Jul 90)
7 days	**VANILLA ICE**	(24 Nov to 1 Dec 90)

Other first-time chart acts who had already been in the charts under some other name have also had rapid climbs to the top:

0 days	**BAND AID** (1984)
0 days	**DAVID BOWIE AND MICK JAGGER** (1985)
0 days	**FERRY AID** (1987)
0 days	**CHRISTIANS, HOLLY JOHNSON, PAUL McCARTNEY, GERRY MARSDEN AND STOCK AITKEN WATERMAN** (1989)
0 days	**BAND AID II** (1989)
0 days	**GEORGE MICHAEL AND ELTON JOHN** (1991)
7 days	**GEORGE HARRISON** (1971)
7 days	**QUEEN AND DAVID BOWIE** (1981)
7 days	**CAPTAIN SENSIBLE** (1982)
7 days	**USA FOR AFRICA** (1985)
7 days	**CLIFF RICHARD AND THE YOUNG ONES** (1986)
7 days	**ARETHA FRANKLIN AND GEORGE MICHAEL** (1987)
7 days	**BOY GEORGE** (1987)
7 days	**ENGLANDNEWORDER** (1990)

Highest New Entry

Vanilla Ice made his chart debut at number three in November 1990, the highest position achieved by a totally new chart act since the first week of the charts 38 years earlier. This record was matched in May 1991 by **Crystal Waters**, and in July 1992 by **Smart E's**. Apart from the top five acts in the first chart of all (Al Martino, Jo Stafford, Nat 'King' Cole, Bing Crosby and Guy Mitchell) the only acts to have spent their first week of chart action in the top five are:

BOY GEORGE

Date	Act	Title	Debut Position
2 Jul 54	**KITTY KALLEN**	Little Things Mean A Lot	5
14 Jul 84	**neil**	Hole In My Shoe	5
20 Feb 88	**BOMB THE BASS**	Beat Dis	5
21 Jul 90	**PARTNERS IN KRYME**	Turtle Power	4
24 Nov 90	**VANILLA ICE**	Ice Ice Baby	3
18 May 91	**CRYSTAL WATERS**	Gypsy Woman (La Da Dee)	3
30 May 92	**KRIS KROSS**	Jump	4
11 Jul 92	**SMART E'S**	Sesame's Treet	4
12 Dec 92	**WWF SUPERSTARS**	Slam Jam	4

There have been nine records by combinations of previous chart acts which have also crashed straight into the top five. They are the six discs which hit number one on their first week, listed in the Highest New Entry section on the previous page, and:

Date	Act / Title	
22 Mar 86	**CLIFF RICHARD AND THE YOUNG ONES** featuring **HANK MARVIN** Living Doll	4
10 Dec 88	**KYLIE MINOGUE AND JASON DONOVAN** Especially For You	2
2 Jun 90	**ENGLANDNEWORDER** World In Motion . . .	2

For 30 years after the chart became a top 50 in 1960 until the end of 1990, only four other new acts spent their first week of chart action in the top ten. They were the **Cars** in 1978 (number 10 first week), **Nicole** in 1982 (number 8 first week), **Style Council** in 1983 (number 6 first week) and **Sigue Sigue Sputnik** in 1986 (number 7 first week). Style Council was led by ex-Jam hitmaker Paul Weller.

In 1991 five more acts joined this list: **Hale and Pace and the Stonkers** (number 10 first week), **Prodigy** (number 9 first week), **Bassheads** (number 8 first week), **East Side Beat** (number 6 first week), and **Nirvana** (number 9 first week). East Side Beat and Nirvana made their chart debuts in the same week, 30 November 1991.

In 1992, **Opus III** (number 10 first week) and **Rage** (also number 10 first week) became the tenth and eleventh brand new acts to spend their first week of chart action between positions 6 and 10.

Four ex-members of chart bands have hit the lower half of the top ten in their first week of solo action (**George Harrison**, **Boy George**, **Morrissey** and **Annie Lennox**) as have six combinations of chart acts (**Queen and David Bowie**, **USA For Africa**, **Pet Shop Boys and Dusty Springfield**, **Various – Brits 1990**, **Vic Reeves and the Wonder Stuff** and **Luther Vandross and Janet Jackson**).

STYLE COUNCIL

Fewest Weeks on Chart by a Number One

In the past few years, the record for the shortest chart life of a number one hit has been rewritten several times. Of the 18 records which have topped the charts despite spending eight weeks or less on the chart, ten have done so since April 1987. The shortest-lived number ones of all time are:

5 wks	**BRING YOUR DAUGHTER... TO THE SLAUGHTER**	Iron Maiden
6 wks	**LET'S PARTY** Jive Bunny & the Mastermixers	
6 wks	**DO THEY KNOW IT'S CHRISTMAS** Band Aid II	
6 wks	**INNUENDO**	Queen
6 wks	**THE FLY**	U2
7 wks	**CHRISTMAS ALPHABET**	Dickie Valentine
7 wks	**LET IT BE**	Ferry Aid
7 wks	**FERRY CROSS THE MERSEY** Christians, Holly Johnson, Paul McCartney, Gerry Marsden and Stock Aitken Waterman	
7 wks	**THE STONK**	Hale and Pace and the Stonkers
8 wks	**HEY JOE**	Frankie Laine
8 wks	**LET'S HAVE ANOTHER PARTY** Winifred Atwell	
8 wks	**LADY MADONNA**	Beatles
8 wks	**MARY'S BOY CHILD – OH MY LORD** Boney M	
8 wks	**WHAT'S ANOTHER YEAR**	Johnny Logan
8 wks	**MY CAMERA NEVER LIES**	Bucks Fizz
8 wks	**HAPPY TALK**	Captain Sensible
8 wks	**DESIRE**	U2
8 wks	**TEARS ON MY PILLOW**	Kylie Minogue

Most Weeks on Chart Without a Number One Hit

Twenty-three of the 115 acts that have been on the charts for 150 weeks or more have never had a number one hit. They are:

Wks	
281	BILLY FURY
245	WHO
235	PRINCE
234	NAT 'KING' COLE
218	TEMPTATIONS
210	BRENDA LEE
207	KOOL AND THE GANG
198	BANANARAMA
196	DUANE EDDY
194	STRANGLERS
190	NEIL SEDAKA
189	DEPECHE MODE
187	GLADYS KNIGHT AND THE PIPS
182	ORCHESTRAL MANOEUVRES IN THE DARK
182	KIM WILDE
180	GENESIS
176	DRIFTERS
171	MR. ACKER BILK
169	CARPENTERS
168	LEVEL 42
164	TINA TURNER
161	ELVIS COSTELLO
154	DEAN MARTIN

BILLY FURY

BANANARAMA

Most Top Ten Hits Without a Number One

There are very few acts that have hit the top ten ten times without enjoying even one brief week at the very top.

13	NAT 'KING' COLE *(who has spent nine weeks at number two)*
13	WHO *(who had two number two hits)*
12	PRINCE *(who has had two number two hits, and has written two chart-toppers)*
11	BILLY FURY *(who had only one number two hit, the aptly titled 'Jealousy')*
10	BANANARAMA *(who have had three number three hits, and an American number one)*

The Stranglers, with 31 hits, have had more hits than any act never to top the charts, but only seven of those hits reached the top ten.

Most 'Unsuccessful' Number Twos

There have now been a total of 548 records which have reached number two but failed to make that all-important final climb to the very top. The 500th number two was *Step By Step*, by **New Kids On The Block**, which came straight on to the chart at number two on 16 June 1990, but failed to climb any higher. Over the past four years, many more records have stopped at number two than have hit the very top, an indication that the number one single very often outsells all the other records on the chart by a considerable distance. Being number one is becoming more and more important.

The acts whose chart climb has most often peaked at number two are:

10	CLIFF RICHARD
9	ELVIS PRESLEY
6	MADONNA
6	KYLIE MINOGUE
5	TOM JONES
5	PAUL McCARTNEY/WINGS *(+1 with Michael Jackson)*
5	QUEEN
5	SWEET
4	BEATLES, PAT BOONE, DAVID BOWIE, BROS, EVERLY BROTHERS, GARY GLITTER, HOLLIES, DEAN MARTIN, LEO SAYER, SHOWADDYWADDY, SLADE, T. REX, STEVIE WONDER
3	NAT 'KING' COLE, PHIL COLLINS, DARTS, DURAN DURAN, KINKS, FRANKIE LAINE, GUY MITCHELL, STATUS QUO, SHAKIN' STEVENS

The Beach Boys have had two number twos of their own and one with the Fat Boys.

Most Weeks at Number Two by an Act that has Never Reached Number One

The record for being so near and yet so far is held by:

NAT 'KING' COLE	9 wks
FRANK CHACKSFIELD	8 wks
DRIFTERS	7 wks
FATHER ABRAHAM AND THE SMURFS	6 wks
ALLISONS	6 wks
BRIGHOUSE AND RASTRICK BAND	6 wks
FREE	5 wks
JOHNNY OTIS SHOW	5 wks
OBERNKIRCHEN CHILDREN'S CHOIR	5 wks
SALT-N-PEPA	5 wks
SIMPLY RED	5 wks

Frank Chacksfield's 1953 recording of the theme from Charlie Chaplin's film *Limelight* spent a total of eight weeks at number two, between June and September of that year. However, the record was never at number two for more than three consecutive weeks. The most consecutive weeks at number two without hitting the top is six, a record jointly held by *The Floral Dance* by the Brighouse and Rastrick Brass Band (1977/78), *The Smurf Song* by Father Abraham and the Smurfs (1978) and *I'm Too Sexy* by Right Said Fred (1991). Johnny Ray's *Such A Night* spent eight consecutive weeks at number two from 7 May 1954, after spending one week at the very top. Jo Stafford's *You Belong To Me* spent seven consecutive weeks at number two, and eight weeks in all, before taking over from Al Martino's *Here In My Heart* as the second number one at the beginning of 1953.

Two recordings have reached number two on two totally separate occasions. 'Honey' by Bobby Goldsboro reached number two on 29 May 1968 for one week. It returned to number two as a re-issue on 26 April 1975, almost 7 years later. Madonna's *Crazy For You* hit number two for one week on 29 June 1985, and then a remixed version of the same record climbed back to the runner-up position for two weeks from 2 March 1991. Fleetwood Mac's *Albatross*, a number one hit when originally released, climbed to number two as a re-issue.

We Are Family

The charts are now 40 years old, and dynasties of hitmakers are beginning to emerge. It is, however, proving difficult for chartbusters to hand down their skills from one generation to the next.

The Crowd included **Zac Starkey**, son of **Ringo Starr**. Zac and Ringo thus became the first father and son ever to have topped the charts, separately or together, but of course they have both only done so as members of groups. **Karel Fialka** and his son Matthew both featured on Karel's 1987 top ten hit, *Hey Matthew*, which is the only top ten hit to feature a father and son double act. **Chip Hawkes**, a member of the chart-topping Tremeloes, is the father of solo number one hitmaker **Chesney Hawkes**, giving the Hawkes family a slight edge on the Starkeys. **John Lennon** and **Julian Lennon** are the nearest yet to a father and son topping the charts as soloists. Julian Lennon's biggest hits so far have reached number six.

Frank Sinatra and **Nancy Sinatra** became the first instance of a father and daughter topping the charts, and they have achieved this feat both separately and together. Father/daughter combinations are by far the most successful family connections, with **Nat 'King' Cole** and **Natalie Cole** both reaching number two, as did **Marty Wilde** and **Kim Wilde**.

The Woodwards, Hilda and Rob, both of **Lieutenant Pigeon**, are the only instance of a mother and son reaching number one. **Marion Ryan** with a number five hit and son **Barry Ryan** with a number two hit are the closest to a mother and son separately climbing to the very top.

No mother and daughter have yet both hit the very top of the British singles chart. The closest instance of this is by **Vicki Brown**, who sang on J.J. Barrie's one hit wonder chart-topper *No Charge*, and her daughter **Sam Brown**, whose highest chart placing to date is number 4. Dad **Joe Brown** also enjoyed three top ten hits, one reaching number two.

Pictured – JULIAN LENNON

Most Consecutive Number Twos

The hat-trick has been performed four times as follows:

TOM JONES	I'll Never Fall In Love Again, I'm Coming Home, Delilah	1967 to 1968
SWEET	Hell Raiser, Ballroom Blitz, Teenage Rampage	1973 to 1974
DARTS	Come Back My Love, Boy From New York City, It's Raining *(Darts never had a number one hit)*	1978
KYLIE MINOGUE	Got To Be Certain, The Loco-Motion, Je Ne Sais Pas Pourquoi	1988

Cliff Richard, who has never managed a hat-trick of number ones, and who has stopped more often at number two than any other act, has also achieved the rare distinction of a hat-trick of number three hits. The three singles were *Theme For A Dream, A Girl Like You* and *When The Girl In Your Arms Is The Girl In Your Heart*. An imported single, *Gee Whiz It's You*, which was never officially released by EMI in Britain, peaked at number four during this odd run. **Madonna** equalled Cliff's strange achievement in 1992, when *Erotica* followed *Rescue Me* and *This Used To Be My Playground* as a number three hit. Like Cliff, Miss Ciccone had another hit, the re-issue of *Holiday*, peaking at number 4 during her hat-trick of number threes. **Electric Light Orchestra** achieved three consecutive number 6 hits in 1978, and **Craig Douglas** peaked at number 9 with four consecutive hits, although these were not consecutive single releases. **Adeva**, in 1989, achieved the bizarre distinction of peaking at number 17 with each of her first three hits. No other hat-tricks of any size of hit have been achieved, although **Marillion** had four consecutive hits peaking at 34, 34, 33 and 34 during 1990 and 1991. The number 33 hit was *No One Can*, which was reissued a year later and climbed to no. 26. **Cinderella** also came close to a lower-rung hat-trick, beginning their chart career with three hits peaking at 54, 55 and 55.

Elvis Presley and **Lonnie Donegan** are the only people to have had hits peaking at every position from 1 to 10. Elvis has had hits peaking at every chart position from 1 to 19, but has never had a record which stopped at number 20. None of Cliff Richard's 62 top ten hits have peaked at number 5.

Silly Games

To the end of 1992, there have been 106 hit singles with a sporting connection. Of these 106 hits, 47 have been connected with football, and 59 with other sports. The chart ranking of all sports, by number of hits, is:

Sport	No. of hits	No. 1 hits	Top 10 hits	Weeks on chart
FOOTBALL	47	4	16	280
BOXING	8	0	5	76
BASEBALL	7	0	4	50
CRICKET	6	1	3	55
OLYMPICS	5	1	3	52
TENNIS	4	0	0	21
SNOOKER/POOL	3	0	2	34
BULLFIGHTING	3	0	2	32
ATHLETICS	3	0	2	29
PINBALL	3	0	1	21
RUGBY FOOTBALL	3	0	1	19
CHESS	2	1	1	29
MARTIAL ARTS	2	1	1	18
CYCLING	2	0	0	31
HORSERACING	2	0	0	6
STOCK CAR RACING	1	1	1	16
BASKETBALL	1	1	1	12
MOTORCYCLING	1	0	1	11
ICE DANCING	1	0	1	10
SKIING	1	0	0	10
AMERICAN FOOTBALL	1	0	0	4

Hits like *Run To You* by Rage, or any by the Crickets or Sultans Of Ping FC have not been included, as there is no real sporting connection there. Tunes that have been turned into football crowd chants, like *Let's Go* or *Banana Splits*, are also excluded. However, hits from films and stage shows about sport (*One Night In Bangkok* from *Chess*, or *Whatever Lola Wants* from *Damn Yankees*) and theme tunes of TV sports programmes are included, as are hits which mention sports in passing.

The ten number one hits with sporting connections are:	
FOOTBALL:	Ferry 'Cross the Mersey (Christians, Holly Johnson, Paul McCartney, Gerry Marsden and Stock Aitken Waterman)
	You'll Never Walk Alone (The Crowd)
	Back Home (England World Cup Squad)
	World In Motion (Englandneworder)
CRICKET:	Dreadlock Holiday (10 CC)
OLYMPICS:	One Moment In Time (Whitney Houston)
CHESS:	I Know Him So Well (Elaine Paige and Barbara Dickson)
MARTIAL ARTS:	Kung Fu Fighting (Carl Douglas)
STOCK CAR RACING:	Tell Laura I Love Her (Ricky Valance)
BASKETBALL:	The Streak (Ray Stevens)

Two duos have had hits featuring two different sports. Simon and Garfunkel have sung about baseball (*Mrs. Robinson*) and boxing (*The Boxer*), while Chas and Dave have helped Tottenham Hotspur F.C. out on most of their hits, as well as combining with the Matchroom Mob to bring us *Snooker Loopy*.

The Football League Table

NICE ONE CYRIL KNOWLES

Of the 47 football chart hits, nine are hits not related to any particular club, five TV theme tunes, two soccer disaster charity discs, Don Fardon's ode to George Best, (Belfast Boy), and the Piglets' (Johnny Reggae), which features the lyric, 'He's crazy about football and he looks me in the eye when he shoots'. Four more are by professional footballers, two by Paul 'Gazza' Gascoigne, one by Kevin Keegan and one by Glenn and Chris (Hoddle and Waddle).

Fourteen football clubs have had a total of 33 chart hits between them. Twelve are English league clubs and the others are the England and Scotland national squads. The clear football song champions are England, followed by Scotland, but Tottenham Hotspur win the title as the most successful League club in chart terms. If we added in Gazza's two hits and Glenn and Chris' hit, all of which were made while the players were on Tottenham's books, then Spurs are the runaway chart leaders.

TEAM	No. of hits	No. 1 hits	Top 10 hits	Weeks on chart
England	5	2	3	45
Scotland	5	0	3	30
Tottenham Hotspur	5	0	1	35
Liverpool	4	0	1	16
Leeds United	3	0	1	15
Manchester United	3	0	1	11
Chelsea	2	0	1	13
Arsenal	1	0	0	7
Nottingham Forest	1	0	0	6
West Ham United	1	0	0	2
Crystal Palace	1	0	0	2
Coventry City	1	0	0	2
Brighton & Hove Albion	1	0	0	2
Fulham	1	0	0	1

The ten biggest league club hits are:

	Title	Peak pos'n	Wks	Year
Liverpool	Anfield Rap	3	6	1988
Chelsea	Blue Is The Colour	5	12	1972
Tottenham Hotspur	Ossie's Dream	5	8	1981
Leeds United	Leeds United	10	10	1972
Manchester United	We All Follow Man United	10	5	1985
Manchester United	Glory Glory Man United	13	5	1983
Tottenham H.	Nice One Cyril *(by the Cockerel Chorus)*	14	12	1973
Liverpool	We Can Do It	15	4	1977
Arsenal	Good Old Arsenal	16	7	1971
Tottenham H.	Hot Shot Tottenham	18	5	1987

Most Weeks On Chart

By Recording

Total weeks on chart, regardless of the number of re-issues or re-entries. This list shows which recording has appeared on the singles charts for the most weeks. Re-recordings of the same song by the same artist do not count but re-mixes of the same track do.

Wks.	Chart Runs	
122	9	**MY WAY** Frank Sinatra
67	8	**AMAZING GRACE** Judy Collins
57	8	**ROCK AROUND THE CLOCK★** Bill Haley and his Comets
56	1	**RELEASE ME★** Engelbert Humperdinck
55	1	**STRANGER ON THE SHORE** Mr Acker Bilk
52	2	**RELAX!★** Frankie Goes To Hollywood
49	4	**BLUE MONDAY** New Order
47	2	**I LOVE YOU BECAUSE** Jim Reeves
44	5	**ALL RIGHT NOW** Free
44	5	**LET'S TWIST AGAIN** Chubby Checker
43	5	**WHITE LINES (DON'T DON'T DO IT)** Grandmaster Flash and Melle Mel
41	5	**DECK OF CARDS** Wink Martindale
40	1	**RIVERS OF BABYLON/BROWN GIRL IN THE RING★** Boney M
40	2	**TIE A YELLOW RIBBON ROUND THE OLD OAK TREE★** Dawn
40	2	**A SCOTTISH SOLDIER** Andy Stewart
39	3	**HE'LL HAVE TO GO** Jim Reeves
38	2	**SOMEWHERE MY LOVE** Mike Sammes Singers
36	1	**I BELIEVE★** Frankie Laine
36	1	**I PRETEND★** Des O'Connor
36	2	**THE POWER OF LOVE★** Jennifer Rush
36	3	**SHE LOVES YOU★** Beatles
36	4	**TAINTED LOVE★** Soft Cell
35	2	**AND I LOVE YOU SO** Perry Como
35	2	**ALBATROSS★** Fleetwood Mac
35	2	**HOUND DOG** Elvis Presley
35	4	**LEADER OF THE PACK** Shangri-Las
34	1	**CHIRPY CHIRPY CHEEP CHEEP★** Middle Of The Road
34	2	**WHAT A WONDERFUL WORLD★** Louis Armstrong
34	3	**HEARTBREAK HOTEL** Elvis Presley
34	3	**JE T'AIME . . . MOI NON PLUS★** Jane Birkin and Serge Gainsbourg
34	3	**NIGHTS IN WHITE SATIN** Moody Blues
34	3	**SAILING★** Rod Stewart
34	4	**YOU'VE LOST THAT LOVIN' FEELIN'★** Righteous Brothers
32	2	**LET'S DANCE** Chris Montez
32	3	**I GET THE SWEETEST FEELING** Jackie Wilson
32	5	**JAILHOUSE ROCK★** Elvis Presley
31	1	**GHOSTBUSTERS** Ray Parker Jr
31	2	**BOHEMIAN RHAPSODY★** Queen
31	2	**REET PETITE★** Jackie Wilson
31	5	**HAPPY CHRISTMAS (WAR IS OVER)** John Lennon
30	1	**AS LONG AS HE NEEDS ME** Shirley Bassey
30	1	**AGADOO** Black Lace
30	1	**SIDE SADDLE★** Russ Conway
30	1	**THEME FROM 'A SUMMER PLACE'** Percy Faith
30	1	**JUST LOVING YOU** Anita Harris
30	2	**PARANOID** Black Sabbath
30	2	**TRUE LOVE** Bing Crosby and Grace Kelly
30	2	**BREAKING UP IS HARD TO DO** Neil Sedaka
30	2	**OH CAROL** Neil Sedaka
30	2	**YOUNG GIRL★** Union Gap featuring Gary Puckett
30	3	**TAKE MY BREATH AWAY★** Berlin

Only 22 of the 51 records that have spent 30 or more weeks on the chart have reached number one (marked by an asterisk ★). Five of the records, those by **Wink Martindale, Mike Sammes Singers, Jane Birkin and Serve Gainsbourg, Percy Faith** and **Bing Crosby and Grace Kelly**, were the only hits by those artists.

Leader Of The Pack by the **Shangri-Las** holds the unique distinction of having been a hit on four different labels, Red Bird, Kama Sutra, Charly and Contempo.

SOFT CELL

Most consecutive weeks on chart:

56	**RELEASE ME** Engelbert Humperdinck
55	**STRANGER ON THE SHORE** Mr Acker Bilk
48	**RELAX!** Frankie Goes To Hollywood
42	**MY WAY** Frank Sinatra
40	**RIVERS OF BABYLON/BROWN GIRL IN THE RING** Boney M
39	**TIE A YELLOW RIBBON ROUND THE OLD OAK TREE** Dawn
39	**I LOVE YOU BECAUSE** Jim Reeves
38	**WHITE LINES (DON'T DON'T DO IT)** Grandmaster Flash & Melle Mel
38	**A SCOTTISH SOLDIER** Andy Stewart
36	**I BELIEVE** Frankie Laine
36	**I PRETEND** Des OConnor
34	**CHIRPY CHIRPY CHEEP CHEEP** Middle Of The Road
32	**THE POWER OF LOVE** Jennifer Rush
32	**AMAZING GRACE** Judy Collins
31	**SHE LOVES YOU** Beatles
31	**AND I LOVE YOU SO** Perry Como
31	**GHOSTBUSTERS** Ray Parker Jr
30	**AS LONG AS HE NEEDS ME** Shirley Bassey
30	**AGADOO** Black Lace
30	**SIDE SADDLE** Russ Conway
30	**THEME FROM 'A SUMMER PLACE'** Percy Faith
30	**JUST LOVING YOU** Anita Harris

Most Weeks on Chart by a Song in all its Recorded Versions

Weeks		Chart Versions
163	**MY WAY**	4, all vocal
94	**AMAZING GRACE**	2, one vocal, one instrumental
79	**UNCHAINED MELODY**	7, 6 vocal, 1 instrumental
70	**ROCK AROUND THE CLOCK**	3, all vocal
65	**STRANGER ON THE SHORE**	2, one vocal, one instrumental
62	**THEME FROM 'THE THREEPENNY OPERA'/MACK THE KNIFE**	6, all vocal
62	**ONLY YOU**	5, all vocal
58	**JE T'AIME . . . MOI NON PLUS/LOVE AT FIRST SIGHT**	4, 3 vocal, 1 instrumental
56	**DECK OF CARDS**	2, both vocal
56	**RELEASE ME**	1, vocal
54	**I BELIEVE**	3, all vocal
52	**CAN'T HELP FALLING IN LOVE**	4, all vocal
52	**RELAX!**	1, vocal
51	**IT'S ONLY MAKE BELIEVE**	4, all vocal
50	**LET'S TWIST AGAIN**	2, both vocal
	WHEN I FALL IN LOVE	3, all vocal

This list shows the most successful *songs* chartwise from 1952 to 1990. Only complete recordings of the song count – parts of songs in medley discs are not included.

Blue Monday has spent 49 weeks on the chart by New Order, while the derivative 1992 hit, *How Does It Feel* by Electroset, spent a further 3 weeks on the chart. *My Girl*, written by Smokey Robinson, has spent 43 weeks on the chart in three different versions, and a further 8 weeks on the chart in two versions of a medley with another Robinson song, *My Guy*. It also earned two weeks of chart action in a medley with *The Way You Do The Things You Do*, under the title *A Night At The Apollo Live!* by Hall and Oates, featuring David Ruffin and Eddie Kendrick.

It's Only Make Believe, written by Conway Twitty and Jack Nance, and *Unchained Melody*, written by Alex North and Hy Zaret, are the only songs in British chart history to have been top ten hits in 4 different versions.

White Christmas, written by Irving Berlin, has been a hit in 8 different versions – by Pat Boone, Max Bygraves, Bing Crosby, Darts, Jim Davidson, Keith Harris and Orville, Mantovani and Freddie Starr. *Unchained Melody* has been a hit in seven different versions.

Stranger in Paradise (written by Robert Wright and George Forrest, based on a theme by Aleksandr Borodin) and *Theme From The Threepenny Opera (Mack The Knife)* (written by Kurt Weill and Bertholt Brecht, English lyrics by Marc Blitzstein) have hit the charts in six versions each. A further instrumental version of the *Theme From The Threepenny Opera*, by Winifred Atwell, hit the chart as one track on the All Star Hit Parade in 1956.

The most commonly used title for a hit single is *Tonight*. There have been ten different hit songs called *Tonight*, by Shirley Bassey, Boomtown Rats, David Bowie, Zaine Griff, Steve Harvey, Kool And The Gang, Modettes, Move, New Kids On The Block and the Rubettes. The biggest hit version was by Kool and the Gang, who took it to number two. New Kids On The Block are the only other act to take this title into the Top Ten, climbing to number three in 1990.

MR ACKER BILK

NEW ORDER

SHIRLEY BASSEY

Number One in Two Different Versions

Fifteen songs have been taken to number one in two different versions, as follows:

ANSWER ME
David Whitfield	6 Nov 53 for 1 wk
	and 11 Dec for 1 wk
Frankie Laine	13 Nov 53 for 8 wks

(on 11 Dec 53, these two versions were placed top equal)

CHERRY PINK AND APPLE BLOSSOM WHITE
Perez Prado	29 Apr 55 for 2 wks
Eddie Calvert	27 May 55 for 4 wks

DIZZY
Tommy Roe	4 Jun 69 for 1 wk
Vic Reeves and the Wonder Stuff	9 Nov 91 for 2 wks

DO THEY KNOW IT'S CHRISTMAS
Band Aid	15 Dec 84 for 5 wks
Band Aid II	23 Dec 89 for 3 wks

EVERYTHING I OWN
Ken Boothe	26 Oct 74 for 3 wks
Boy George	14 Mar 87 for 2 wks

I GOT YOU BABE
Sonny and Cher	26 Aug 65 for 2 wks
UB40 with Chrissie Hynde	31 Aug 85 for 1 wk

LIVING DOLL
Cliff Richard and the Drifters	31 Jul 59 for 6 wks
Cliff Richard and the Young Ones	29 Mar 86 for 3 wks

MARY'S BOY CHILD
Harry Belafonte	22 Nov 57 for 7 wks
Boney M	9 Dec 78 for 4 wks

(Boney Ms version was in a medley with Oh My Lord*)*

SINGING THE BLUES
Guy Mitchell	4 Jan 57 for 1 wk, 18 Jan 57 for 1 wk
	and 1 Feb 57 for 1 wk
Tommy Steele	11 Jan 57 for 1 wk

SPIRIT IN THE SKY
Norman Greenbaum	2 May 70 for 2 wks
Doctor and the Medics	7 Jun 86 for 3 wks

THIS OLE HOUSE
Rosemary Clooney	26 Nov 54 for 1 wk
Shakin Stevens	28 Nov 81 for 3 wks

UNCHAINED MELODY
Jimmy Young	24 Jun 55 for 3 wks
Righteous Brothers	3 Nov 90 for 4 wks

WITH A LITTLE HELP FROM MY FRIENDS
Joe Cocker	6 Nov 68 for 1 wk
Wet Wet Wet	21 May 88 for 4 wks

YOU'LL NEVER WALK ALONE
Gerry and the Pacemakers	31 Oct 63 for 4 wks
Crowd	15 Jun 85 for 2 wks

YOUNG LOVE
Tab Hunter	22 Feb 57 for 7 wks
Donny Osmond	25 Aug 73 for 4 wks

JOE COCKER

DEMIS ROUSSOS

Four titles have been used twice for different songs at number one – **FOREVER AND EVER** (Slik and Demis Roussos, both 1976), **THE POWER OF LOVE** (Frankie Goes To Hollywood in 1984 and Jennifer Rush in 1985), **TEARS ON MY PILLOW** (Johnny Nash in 1975 and Kylie Minogue in 1990), and **WOMAN IN LOVE** (Frankie Laine in 1956 and Barbara Streisand in 1980).

Vanilla Ice's **ICE ICE BABY**, a 1990 number one, sampled heavily from Queen and David Bowie's 1981 number one, **UNDER PRESSURE**. Jive Bunny's three number ones were mixes featuring brief extracts of several chart-toppers.

Queen's **BOHEMIAN RHAPSODY** became the first recording to hit number one on two completely different occasions, when it topped the charts from 21 Dec 1991 for five weeks, 15 years and 325 days after it had dropped from number one after an earlier stay of nine weeks.

WET WET WET

Longest Titles of Number One Hits

The ten longest titled songs to hit the top are:

45 letters	**SAN FRANCISCO (BE SURE TO WEAR SOME FLOWERS IN YOUR HAIR)** (Scott McKenzie, 1967)	
43 letters	**I'D LIKE TO TEACH THE WORLD TO SING (IN PERFECT HARMONY)** (New Seekers, 1972)	
39 letters	**ITSY BITSY TEENY WEENY YELLOW POLKA DOT BIKINI** (Bombalurina, 1990)	
37 letters	**MATCHSTALK MEN AND MATCHSTALK CATS AND DOGS** (Brian and Michael, 1978)	
37 letters	**WHEN THE GOING GETS TOUGH THE TOUGH GET GOING** (Billy Ocean, 1986)	
36 letters	**(THERE'S) ALWAYS SOMETHING THERE TO REMIND ME** (Sandie Shaw, 1964)	
36 letters	**THERE MUST BE AN ANGEL (PLAYING WITH MY HEART)** (Eurythmics, 1985)	
35 letters	**WHAT DO YOU WANT TO MAKE THOSE EYES AT ME FOR?** (Emile Ford and the Checkmates, 1959)	
34 letters	**TIE A YELLOW RIBBON ROUND THE OLD OAK TREE** (Dawn featuring Tony Orlando, 1973)	
34 letters	**WHEN YOU'RE IN LOVE WITH A BEAUTIFUL WOMAN** (Dr Hook, 1979)	
33 letters	**I WANNA DANCE WITH SOMEBODY (WHO LOVES ME)** (Whitney Houston, 1987)	

Queen's double sided 1991 chart-topper **BOHEMIAN RHAPSODY/THESE ARE THE DAYS OF OUR LIVES** is 41 letters long.

The longest title ever used for a hit single in Britain is the 20 word, 77 letter mega-title of the Pet Shop Boys' March 1991 top 10 hit, **WHERE THE STREETS HAVE NO NAME – CAN'T TAKE MY EYES OFF YOU/HOW DO YOU EXPECT TO BE TAKEN SERIOUSLY**. This, however, was three titles rolled into one double A side, rather than a single song title.

The longest single song title to hit the charts is still the Carpenters' 1977 single which reached number 9, **CALLING OCCUPANTS OF INTERPLANETARY CRAFT (THE RECOGNISED ANTHEM OF WORLD CONTACT DAY)**. This contains 73 letters. It took over as the longest title from Winifred Atwell's 1954 instrumental, **RACHMANINOFF'S EIGHTEENTH VARIATION ON A THEME BY PAGANINI (THE STORY OF THREE LOVES)** which only runs to 70 letters.

The longest hit title which is not a medley and which contains no brackets is the 60 letter 1981 hit for the Freshies, **I'M IN LOVE WITH THE GIRL ON A CERTAIN MANCHESTER MEGASTORE CHECKOUT DESK**.

SCOTT McKENZIE

IF I SAID YOU HAVE A BEAUTIFUL BODY WOULD YOU HOLD IT AGAINST ME, a 51-letter hit for the Bellamy Brothers in 1979, contains more words (14) in its title than any other unbracketed non-medley hit.

Shortest Titles for Hit Singles

There has not yet been a one-letter hit title, the nearest being Ben E. King's US hit song which Shirley Bassey, Tom Jones and Sylvester covered, **I (WHO HAVE NOTHING)**, which has only one letter outside the brackets.

The shortest title for a number one hit, and the equal shortest title for any hit, is the David Gates song **IF**, a number one for Telly Savalas and a smaller hit for the comedy duo Yin and Yan.

There are, of course, several titles that contain no letters at all, only numbers, like the Who's *5.15*, Prince's *7* or Keith's *98.6*, four different hits called *1-2-3*, Wilson Pickett's *634-5789* and Desmond Dekker's *007*.

There are five other 2 letter hit titles:

D.J. (David Bowie, 1979)

FX (A Guy Called Gerald, 1989)

GO (Scott Fitzgerald, 1988)

OK? (Julie Covington, Rula Lenska, Charlotte Cornwell and Sue Jones-Davies, 1977)

T.V. (Flying Lizards 1980)

The longest word used in a hit single is Prince's original effort of 1986, **ANOTHERLOVERHOLENYOHEAD**, a 23 letter word. This beats Tom Browne's 1982 word **BEBOPAFUNKADISCOLYPSO** by two letters.

DAVID BOWIE

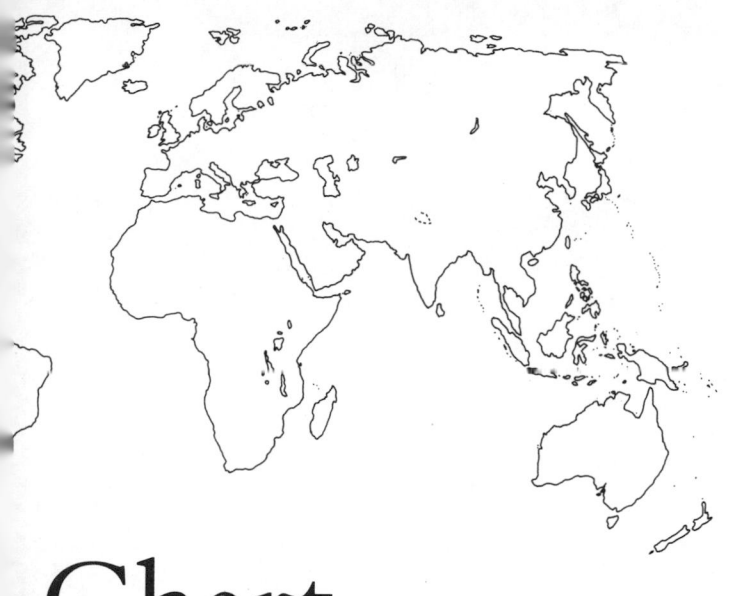

Country	Artists	Total Weeks?	Hits	Top 10 Hits	No.1 Hits	% Share	Weeks per mln pop'n
1 UK	2198	62025	8919	2475	391	52.5	1080.4
2 USA	1818	44491	5973	1641	248	37.7	178.0
3 Ireland	67	1728	244	75	13	1.5	493.3
4 Australia	60	1470	189	70	16	1.2	86.0
5 Jamaica	70	1391	168	53	9	1.2	574.8
6 Canada	57	1070	153	34	4	0.9	40.3
7 France	53	762	90	26	2	0.6	13.5
8 Germany	50	678	116	25	7	0.6	8.5
9 Italy	60	647	102	25	2	0.5	11.2
10 Netherlands	35	607	75	32	3	0.5	40.6
11 Sweden	17	538	70	27	10	0.5	62.9
12 Norway	7	413	49	28	10	0.3	97.4
13 South Africa	11	300	33	20	3	0.3	8.5
14 Belgium	25	220	42	7	0	0.2	22.0
15 New Zealand	8	217	31	7	0	0.2	64.9
16 Spain	16	201	23	9	2	0.2	5.2
17 Guyana	3	168	20	7	2	0.1	208.5
18 Greece	8	166	20	7	1	0.1	16.4
19 Japan	8	164	21	6	0	0.1	1.3
20 Sri Lanka	1	120	9	6	2	0.1	7.1
21 Denmark	6	101	20	3	0	0.1	19.6
22 Kenya	3	90	8	3	0	0.1	3.7
23 Switzerland	6	74	17	4	0	0.1	11.0
24 Israel	5	65	6	3	1	0.1	14.0
25 Austria	4	59	7	3	1	0.1	7.7
Rest Of The World	40	318	46	13	1	0.3	0.1

Chart Geography

Just for fun, we have taken a look at where our best-selling music has originated from. Over the years, there have been hits from places as far apart as Japan and Jamaica, Poland and Peru and Britain and Brazil. Inevitably, over the years it is the English-speaking countries that have provided most of our hits, with Britain and the United States way out in front, accounting for over 90% of all British hit singles. The right language is the most obvious ingredient for a hit single, but if artists are determined to sing in some indecipherable foreign tongue, then the closer their home country is to Britain, the more likely they are to provide us with hits. Our closest neighbour – France – is the most successful non-English speaking country, and of all the non-English speaking countries outside Europe, only Japan features among the top 25 most successful nations in our charts.

We have ranked the nations in order of most weeks spent on our charts, but it should be noted that if a group is made up of more than one nationality, the weeks and hits are credited to both countries. Thus, for example, hits by Police have been credited both to the UK and the USA, and the combination of Paul Young and Zucchero to both the UK and Italy.

The 'percentage share' merely shows each country's share of the total number of weeks, while the 'weeks per million population' divides the number of weeks each nation has spent on our charts by the population, in millions, to give an idea of which countries are having more than their fair share of hits. This shows that after Britain, the most successful countries per head of population are Jamaica, Ireland and Guyana, with the United States only in fifth place.

HIT MUSIC MAGAZINE

For the true fan of the UK music charts comes *Hit Music Magazine!*

The definitive companion to the weekly music charts
— from the publishers of The Chart Book —

Designed as the perfect compliment for the UK music charts, *Hit Music* offers a level of detail and analysis for the charts not available anywhere before. Not only are the top 100 Singles and Albums listed each week but much, much more!

Detailed analysis of all new entries in the Singles and Albums charts: producer, publisher, writer, line-up, first/last/biggest hit, album, contact number, background facts & information about each artist.

- The highest climbers in both charts.

- The potential UK hits of tomorrow.

- The American charts:
  Including R & B and Dance Single and Dance Album charts.
  The top performing UK acts in the US charts.

- No.1 singles from around the world.

- Full UK format charts:
  Artist Albums, Compilation Albums.

- Weekly genre charts:
  Kiss FM, Rock Singles.

- Plus other format/genre no. 1s each week:
  7", Cassette, CD, 12", Dance, Club, Indie, Metal.

- The best-selling singles and albums of the year to date.

Delivery is impressive. Less than 24 hours after the new chart is announced, the latest copy of *Hit Music* is distributed to all subscribers. All for less than £2 an issue (not including postage). Annual UK price is £99 (plus p+p). Total cost is £110.

For further information and subscription details on this magazine contact:
Phil Matcham, ERA, Spotlight Publications Ltd., Ludgate House,
245 Blackfriars Road, London SE1 9UR Telephone: 071-334 7333 Fax: 071-921 5942

THE GUINNESS BOOK OF BRITISH HIT SINGLES COMES TO LIFE

The Golden Oldies Club of Great Britain and Old Gold Records Ltd. are delighted to offer you over 3000 hits on 7 inch singles, 12 inch singles and CD singles, together with compilations on CD, LP and cassette.

Now you can buy thousands of the classic Golden Oldies of yesterday that span the pages of our historical archive – to build or rebuild your record collection.

For full details of this exciting service and a FREE Golden Oldies catalogue – photocopy and complete the coupon and send together with two second-class stamps to cover the return postage.

Also from Guinness Publishing:

The Guinness Book of Top 40 Charts presents popular music's life line through the years. The 700 plus pages feature every chart for every week dating back to 10 March 1960, plus a detailed year-by-year breakdown of the smaller charts from the 1950s.

If you ever wanted to know what the hits were on your birthday, *The Guinness Book of Top 40 Charts* will reveal all and there is so much more to discover:

What single was at the top of the charts the week the Beatles first hit the Top 40?

Was the summer of '67 all legend has made it out to be?

Who were the artists the Sex Pistols were shaking up when they first poked their gobs into the Top 40 in late 1976?

These questions and a host of others are answered in *The Guinness Book of Top 40 Charts*.

ISBN 0-85112-541-7

The Guinness Book of British Hit Albums is now in its fifth edition and lists every recording to have made the album chart since it began in 1958.

Illustrated with 100 photographs and running to 400 plus fact-filled pages, the latest edition is bigger and offers more value for money than ever.

ISBN 0-85112-967-6

The Guinness Hits Quiz 2 contains brain-busting quizzes, anagrams and acrostics covering the whole of the popular music scene. Ideal for journeys and get togethers - and indispensible for the pub quiz, *The Guinness Hits Quiz 2* was described by *Q* magazine as a book where '*the compilers really know their stuff and, as a result, there is something for everyone*'.

ISBN 0-85112-527-1

The Guinness UK Top 1000 Singles, now in its second edition lists the top 1000 releases since 1955. Paul Gambaccini, Tim Rice and Jonathan Rice give their ranking of the biggest UK hits of the rock era based on highest chart positions reached and sustained.

ISBN 0-85112-712-6

Guinness Publishing also publish the Billboard US chart statistics books, **The Guinness Book of Hits of the 80s** and **The Guinness Encyclopedia of Popular Music** (in four volumes).

A full listing of all Guinness Publishing titles is contained in a catalogue available from

The Marketing Department, Guinness Publishing, 33 London Road, Enfield, Middlesex, EN2 6DJ.

THE AUTHORS

PAUL GAMBACCINI

TIM RICE • JONATHAN RICE

Jonathan Rice is a consultant, lecturer, broadcaster, statistician, author, husband, father, brother, son, uncle, village cricketer, Fulham FC fan, Japanese speaker and dog walker. He has almost completed his collection of number one hit singles, very much helped by finding Rolf Harris' *Two Little Boys* and Jim Reeves' *Distant Drums* in good condition for 10p each at a local jumble sale. His latest book on cricket, *Curiosities Of Cricket* (Pavilion Books, £12.99), which features a portrait of the author as a teapot, has recently hit the bookstalls.

Paul Gambaccini has been recently associated with Classic FM, Radio 1 FM and *Television's Greatest Hits*. Over his shoulder he notices *Rolling Stone* and TV-am fading further into the past, while up ahead he sees – but that would be telling.

Tim Rice has co-written two number one hits since the eighth edition of British Hit Singles, one in Britain and one in the United States. His British number one was toppled by a song from Kevin Costner's *Robin Hood – Prince of Thieves* which went on to become the longest running number one in Britain for almost 40 years, but his Oscar winning American number one returned the compliment by displacing a song from Costner's *The Bodyguard*, which had by then become the biggest selling US single for almost 40 years. He awaits with interest to find out which Costner film song will compete with his next project, a Walt Disney animated feature called *The Lion King*, for which he has written the songs with Elton John.